Criminal Legislation in Ireland

Criminal Legislation in Ireland

Lynn O'Sullivan
Barrister at Law

Bloomsbury Professional

Published by
Bloomsbury Professional
Maxwelton House
41–43 Boltro Road
Haywards Heath
West Sussex
RH16 1BJ

Bloomsbury Professional
The Fitzwilliam Business Centre
26 Upper Pembroke Street
Dublin 2

© Bloomsbury Professional, an imprint of Bloomsbury Publishing Plc
ISBN 978 1 84766 718 2

British Library Cataloguing-in-Publication Data
A catalogue record for this book is available from the British Library

Typeset by Marlex Editorial Services Ltd., Dublin, Ireland
Printed and bound in Great Britain by
CPI Antony Rowe, Chippenham, Wiltshire

Foreword

Whether you practice criminal law in Dublin or in Leitrim, in the District Court or in the Central Criminal Court, one sight with which all practitioners are familiar is that of the fretful barrister (or sweating devil) frantically photocopying or downloading copy Acts of the Oireachtas for use in a trial that is about to begin.

Many statutes are now only available either online or in an unwieldy hardback edition of annual statutes along with a hundred other statutes, none of which will be relevant (unless the trial goes off the rails in wholly unanticipated ways). Each statute must be sought out individually and copied or printed off for use in court. It is a long time since any attempt was made to compile a complete collection of criminal statutes in one volume. Some of the most sweeping changes to the criminal law have been introduced in recent years with extensive new legislation in relation to many offences, including misuse of drugs and firearms offences, and new provisions affecting the right to silence, the right to bail and child offenders. Along with this recent legislation of course, there remains the huge body of statute law which has not been repealed or which has been amended but must still be considered in order to interpret an amending statute. Some frequently used provisions date back to the 19th century and many are not yet readily available online.

Finally, this collection is available so that you can bring one volume to court, you can consult one volume in an office or at home, and you can rest assured that if there's a problem with the jury, an issue with detention or an application to read a witness's statement into evidence, the relevant statute is right in front of you. For every lawyer who expects to appear in the criminal courts, this book is an excellent investment. For the circuit practitioner and for those travelling to various district courts in Dublin and elsewhere, it is essential.

Mary Rose Gearty SC
The Law Library,
Four Courts,
Dublin 7

17 February 2011

Mary Rose Gearty is a practising barrister. She spends most of the working week at trial in Dublin and, until now, photocopying. She taught Criminal Law in the Honorable Society of the King's Inns from 1997 until 2005.

Introduction

Irish criminal law is an area of law governed by a vast array of legislation, which is continuously amended, repealed, extended and updated. The creation of new criminal offences with corresponding penalties and the repeal and/or amendment of certain offences and penalties alike have been and continue to be regulated by legislation. This collection of Irish criminal statutes aims to provide an up-to-date reference guide for practitioners and students alike.

Unfortunately, due to space constraints, it has not been possible to include all Irish criminal legislation. However, major relevant legislation has been selected and all appropriate amendments and repeals have been included. Likewise, space limitations also required the exclusion of repealed sections and irrelevant sections of certain pieces of legislation.

The materials were taken from the Irish Statute Book where possible and the permission of the Attorney General's Office to reproduce the materials is acknowledged.

I am sincerely grateful to Bart Daly, Therese Carrick, Amy Hayes and Sandra Mulvey for all their assistance with this compilation and to Mary Rose Gearty SC for her assistance in general with all matters related to criminal law.

Lynn O'Sullivan BL
February 2011

Contents

Foreword v
Introduction vii
Contents ix
Contents (in alphabetical order) xiii

Primary Legislation

Petty Sessions (Ireland) Act 1851 1
Summary Jurisdiction Act 1857 33
Offences Against the Persons Act 1861 39
Explosives Act 1875 49
Explosive Substances Act 1883 121
Probation of Offenders Act 1907 125
Criminal Justice Administration Act 1914 131
Criminal Justice (Administration) Act 1924 159
Firearms Act 1925 175
Offences Against the State Act 1939 217
Criminal Justice Act 1951 259
Criminal Justice Act 1960 271
Courts (Supplemental Provisions) Act 1961 279
Criminal Justice (Legal Aid) Act 1962 297
Criminal Justice Act 1964 309
Firearms Act 1964 311
Extradition Act 1965 329
Criminal Procedure Act 1967 357
Criminal Law Act 1976 379
Juries Act 1976 389
Misuse of Drugs Act 1977 405
Criminal Law (Rape) Act 1981 449
Criminal Justice (Community Service) Act 1983 459
Misuse of Drugs Act 1984 467
Criminal Justice Act 1984 477
Courts (No 3) Act 1986 503
Firearms and Offensive Weapons Act 1990 507
Criminal Justice Act 1990 523
Criminal Law (Rape) (Amendment) Act 1990 531
Criminal Justice (Forensic Evidence) Act 1990 539

Courts Act 1991 547
Criminal Damage Act 1991 553
Criminal Evidence Act 1992.. 561
Criminal Justice Act 1993.. 579
Criminal Law (Sexual Offences) Act 1993...................................... 591
Criminal Law (Suicide) Act 1993 599
Criminal Procedure Act 1993 601
Criminal Justice (Public Order) Act 1994.. 609
Criminal Justice Act 1994.. 633
Criminal Law (Incest Proceedings) Act 1995.................................. 689
Domestic Violence Act 1996 693
Criminal Justice (Drug Trafficking) Act 1996.................................. 711
Proceeds of Crime Act 1996 723
Criminal Assets Bureau Act 1996.. 741
Criminal Justice (Miscellaneous Provisions) Act 1997 761
Criminal Law Act 1997.. 773
Bail Act 1997 791
Non-Fatal Offences Against the Person Act 1997 811
Child Trafficking And Pornography Act 1998 825
Criminal Justice Act 1999.. 833
Sex Offenders Act 2001 849
Children Act 2001 871
Criminal Justice (Theft And Fraud Offences) Act 2001.................. 1007
European Convention on Human Rights Act 2003........................... 1063
European Arrest Warrant Act 2003 1089
Immigration Act 2004.. 1149
Criminal Law (Insanity) Act 2006... 1163
Criminal Law (Sexual Offences) Act 2006 1191
Criminal Justice Act 2006 1197
Criminal Law (Sexual Offences) (Amendment) Act 2007 1297
Prisons Act 2007 1301
Criminal Justice Act 2007 1309
Criminal Law (Human Trafficking) Act 2008 1347
Criminal Justice (Surveillance) Act 2009 1355
Criminal Justice (Miscellaneous Provisions) Act 2009 1371
Criminal Justice (Amendment) Act 2009 1389
Courts and Court Officers Act 2009 1399
Criminal Justice (Money Laundering and Terrorist
     Financing) Act 2010.. 1409

Fines Act 2010 1425

Criminal Justice (Psychoactive Substances) Act 2010.. 1445

Criminal Procedure Act 2010 1465

Secondary Legislation

Criminal Justice Act 1984 (Treatment of Persons in Custody
  in Garda Síochána Stations) Regulations 1987.. 1493

Rules of the Superior Courts (Criminal Justice Act 1999) 2005........................... 1509

Contents (in alphabetical order)

Bail Act 1997.. 791
Child Trafficking And Pornography Act 1998....................... 825
Children Act 2001 871
Courts (No 3) Act 1986 503
Courts (Supplemental Provisions) Act 1961 279
Courts Act 1991.. 547
Courts and Court Officers Act 2009 1399
Criminal Assets Bureau Act 1996....................................... 741
Criminal Damage Act 1991.. 553
Criminal Evidence Act 1992 561
Criminal Justice (Administration) Act 1924 159
Criminal Justice (Amendment) Act 2009 1389
Criminal Justice (Community Service) Act 1983 459
Criminal Justice (Drug Trafficking) Act 1996 711
Criminal Justice (Forensic Evidence) Act 1990.................... 539
Criminal Justice (Legal Aid) Act 1962 297
Criminal Justice (Miscellaneous Provisions) Act 1997.......... 761
Criminal Justice (Miscellaneous Provisions) Act 2009 1371
Criminal Justice (Money Laundering and Terrorist
    Financing) Act 2010 1409
Criminal Justice (Psychoactive Substances) Act 2010........... 1445
Criminal Justice (Public Order) Act 1994 609
Criminal Justice (Surveillance) Act 2009 1355
Criminal Justice (Theft And Fraud Offences) Act 2001 1007
Criminal Justice Act 1951 259
Criminal Justice Act 1960 271
Criminal Justice Act 1964 309
Criminal Justice Act 1984 (Treatment of Persons in Custody
    in Garda Síochána Stations) Regulations 1987................. 1493
Criminal Justice Act 1984 477
Criminal Justice Act 1990 523
Criminal Justice Act 1993 579
Criminal Justice Act 1994 633
Criminal Justice Act 1999 833
Criminal Justice Act 2006 1197
Criminal Justice Act 2007 1309

Criminal Justice Administration Act 1914.. 131
Criminal Law (Human Trafficking) Act 2008 1347
Criminal Law (Incest Proceedings) Act 1995... 689
Criminal Law (Insanity) Act 2006 1163
Criminal Law (Rape) (Amendment) Act 1990 531
Criminal Law (Rape) Act 1981... 449
Criminal Law (Sexual Offences) (Amendment) Act 2007 1297
Criminal Law (Sexual Offences) Act 1993... 591
Criminal Law (Sexual Offences) Act 2006 1191
Criminal Law (Suicide) Act 1993 599
Criminal Law Act 1976... 379
Criminal Law Act 1997... 773
Criminal Procedure Act 1967 357
Criminal Procedure Act 1993 601
Criminal Procedure Act 2010 1465
Domestic Violence Act 1996 693
European Arrest Warrant Act 2003 1089
European Convention on Human Rights Act 2003................................ 1063
Explosive Substances Act 1883 121
Explosives Act 1875 49
Extradition Act 1965... 329
Fines Act 2010 1425
Firearms Act 1925... 175
Firearms Act 1964... 311
Firearms and Offensive Weapons Act 1990 507
Immigration Act 2004.. 1149
Juries Act 1976.. 389
Misuse of Drugs Act 1977 405
Misuse of Drugs Act 1984 467
Non-Fatal Offences Against the Person Act 1997.................................. 811
Offences Against the Persons Act 1861... 39
Offences Against the State Act 1939 217
Petty Sessions (Ireland) Act 1851 1
Prisons Act 2007 1301
Probation of Offenders Act 1907 125
Proceeds of Crime Act 1996 723
Rules of the Superior Courts (Criminal Justice Act 1999) 2005 1509
Sex Offenders Act 2001 849
Summary Jurisdiction Act 1857.. 33

Petty Sessions (Ireland) Act 1851

(14 & 15 Vict) C A P XCIII

An Act to consolidate and amend the Acts regulating the Proceedings at Petty Sessions, and the Duties of Justices of the Peace out of Quarter Sessions, in Ireland.

WHEREAS it is expedient to consolidate and amend the Acts regulating the Proceedings at Petty Sessions, and the Duties of Justices of the Peace out of Quarter Sessions, in Ireland: Be it therefore enacted by the Queen's most Excellent Majesty, by and with the Advice and Consent of the Lords Spiritual and Temporal, and Commons, in this present Parliament assembled, and by the Authority of the same, That—

I   **Existing Districts, &c. confirmed where they require no Alteration; but where they do, Justices at Quarter Sessions may revise them, proceeding as follows:**

The several Petty Sessions Districts into which any County or Riding of a County in Ireland is now divided, and the Places and Times at which Petty Sessions are now appointed to be held therein, shall, until altered in the Manner herein-after provided, be the several Districts, Places, and Times in such County or Riding for the Purposes of this Act: But whenever it shall appear to the Justices at Quarter Sessions that any of the said Districts, Places, and Times now fixed (or which shall hereafter be fixed) in any County or Riding require Alteration, or whenever they shall be called upon so to do either by the Lord Lieutenant or by a Requisition signed by any Seven or more of the Justices of any County or Riding, they shall proceed at the next Quarter Sessions which shall be held for such County or Riding, or at any Adjournment of the same for that Purpose, to revise the said Districts, Places, and Times, subject to the following Provisions:

TO DIVIDE THE COUNTY INTO PETTY SESSIONS DISTRICTS:

Parts of an adjoining County may be included:

1. They shall divide such County or Riding into convenient Petty Sessions Districts for the Purposes of this Act, and shall declare the several Parishes or Townlands of which each of such Districts shall consist; and in so doing it shall be lawful for them, with the Concurrence of the Justices of any adjoining County assembled at any like Quarter Sessions, or at any Adjournment of the same, to include in any of such Districts any Townlands of such adjoining County, where it shall be conducive to the Public Convenience, and where no Part of such Townlands shall be at a greater Distance than Seven Miles from the Place where Petty Sessions shall be held for the District to which same shall be annexed:

To fix Place for holding Petty Sessions:

2. They shall also fix some One convenient Place within each District at which Petty Sessions shall be held for the same:

To fix Times for holding Petty Sessions:

3. They shall also fix the Times when Petty Sessions shall be regularly held in each District; but it shall be lawful for the Justices of each District afterwards to fix the particular Days in each Week upon which such Petty Sessions shall be held:

And whenever any of the said Districts, Places, and Times shall have been so fixed or altered, the Clerk of the Peace shall forthwith enter all Particulars as to the same in the Crown Book, and shall transmit a certified Copy of such Entries to the Secretary of the Grand Jury, to be laid before such Grand Jury at the then next ensuing Assizes, (and in the County of Dublin at the then next ensuing Presentment Term,) and the same shall be printed with the Presentments: Provided always, that when it shall appear to such Justices at Quarter Sessions that such Alteration is required, or whenever a Requisition for the Consideration of an Alteration shall be received from the Lord Lieutenant, or from Seven or more Justices as aforesaid, the Clerk of the Peace of the County shall transmit a Notice in Writing of the intended Consideration of such Alteration to every Justice of the County or Riding, as the Case may be, and such Notice, stating the Time and Place appointed for the Consideration of such Alteration, shall be transmitted at least One Month before the Time so appointed.

II Appointment of Clerk

Justices to appoint a Clerk. Security by Recognizance.

It shall be lawful for the Justices of each Petty Sessions upon the passing of this Act, or whenever afterwards any Vacancy shall occur by reason of the Death, Resignation, or Dismissal of any Clerk, to appoint some One fit Person to act as Clerk of such Petty Sessions; but previous to entering upon the Duties of the said Office the said Clerk shall enter into a Recognizance (Form C.), before some Justice of the County, conditioned for the due Discharge of the several Duties required of him under the Provisions of this Act, with One or more Sureties, and in such Amount as the Lord Lieutenant shall direct.

III The Clerk to be entitled to certain Fees

The said Clerk of Petty Sessions shall be entitled to demand and receive, from the Persons at whose Instance the several Proceedings by or before any Justice or Justices shall be taken, the following Fees in respect to the same:

	s d
Drawing each Information, Deposition, or solemn Declaration (not being a Declaration as to the Loss of Pawnbrokers Duplicates, or as to the Admission of Paupers into Poorhouses)	1 0
Copy of any written Information or Complaint in Summary Proceedings	0 6
Drawing any Notice required by Law in Proceedings by or before Justices (when required by the Party)	0 6
Summons, and Copy	0 6
Warrant (except in any Case of a Committal for an Offence in which the Justices may see fit to remit the Fee)	0 6
Entry of each Order	0 6
Certificate of Order	1 0

	s d
Recognizance (when required by the Party or by the Justices to prepare the same, and when not at foot of a Deposition or Information)	1 0
Appeal (including the Recognizance to prosecute)	2 0

Clerk to keep an Account of Fees.
Justices may apply Surplus to Court Requisites.
List of Fees to be posted in Court House.
Clerk to hold subject to the following Provisions:

But the Clerk shall not be entitled to demand or receive a greater Amount of Fees for any Set of Informations, or for any Set of Summonses, or for any Set of any other Documents of the same Kind in the same Case than Two Shillings in the whole for each Set, unless the Justices shall specially authorize a greater Amount, but not in any Case exceeding the above Fees; nor shall he be entitled to demand or receive any of such Fees in any Case in which the Justices shall see fit to remit the same; nor shall he be entitled to receive any of such Fees in any Case of an Offence prosecuted by the Constabulary or by any public Officer on behalf of the Crown, unless where Costs shall be awarded to the Prosecutor and recovered by him, in which Case such Clerk shall be entitled to demand and receive from such Prosecutor the legal Fees to an Amount not exceeding the Amount of such Costs; and the said Clerk shall keep an Account of all Fees received by him under this Act in such Form and Manner as the Justices shall direct; and in case the said Fees shall amount to a greater Sum than the Justices shall deem an adequate Remuneration for such Clerk they way appropriate the Surplus to the Payment of Postage or to the Purchase of Stationery or other Court Requisites for their Use at Petty Sessions; and a printed List of Fees which the Clerk shall be entitled to receive under this Act shall be posted in a conspicuous Part of the Court House or Place in which the Petty Sessions shall be held in such Manner as the Justices shall direct.

IV   The said Clerk shall hold the said Office of Clerk of Petty Sessions subject to the following Provisions:

*To follow no Occupation inconsistent with his Duties, and forfeit Office
if he engages in certain Employments*

1. He shall not, during the Time that he shall hold such Office, practise as an Attorney or Solicitor in any Case either at such Petty Sessions or at the Quarter Sessions of the Division of the County in which such Petty Sessions shall be situated, nor shall he act as the Clerk of any Attorney or Solicitor so practising, or as the Clerk of a Poor Law Union, or as a Collector of any Public Tax, or as a Pound Keeper, or as the Keeper or Partner in keeping any Inn or Public House, nor shall he engage in any other Business or Occupation which shall appear to the Lord Lieutenant or to the Justices to be inconsistent with his Duties as Petty Sessions Clerk; or if he shall so act or engage, he shall ipso facto cease to hold such Office of Petty Sessions Clerk, and shall also be liable to the Penalties herein-after provided:

To hold Office at the Pleasure of the Justices, and be dismissed by Lord Lieutenant:

2. He shall hold his Office during the Pleasure of the Justices of the District:

3. He shall be subject to be dismissed by the Lord Lieutenant for Neglect, Misconduct, or Incompetency in the Discharge of his Duties as Petty Sessions Clerk:

And the said Clerk shall perform the Duties of his Office in Person, and not by Deputy, except in case of his Sickness, unavoidable Absence, or other Emergency, when the Justices at Petty Sessions may appoint some other Person to act as Clerk at such Petty Sessions for the Time being, who shall, if required by the Justices, enter into Security in like Manner as herein-before provided as to any Clerk.

V   Duties of Clerk

The Clerk of Petty Sessions shall perform the following Duties:

To make Minutes and Entries in Books:

1. He shall make, when required by any of the Justices, a Minute of all special Proceedings, taken either in or out of Petty Sessions, in a Book to be kept for that Purpose, to be called the 'Minute Book,' and shall also make such Entries in the 'Order Book' (Form D.) herein-after mentioned, as the Justices shall direct:

To have Custody of Books

2. He shall also have the Care and Custody of such Books, subject to their being kept at the Court House or Place where the Petty Sessions shall be held, or otherwise as the Justices shall direct, and also subject to their being at all Times open to the Inspection of the Justices and of any other Person or Persons whom the Lord Lieutenant may at any Time appoint to examine the same:

To prepare all Forms, &c.:

3. He shall also prepare, under the Directions of the Justices, all Informations, Summonses, Examinations, Warrants, Recognizances, and other documentary Forms of Proceeding:

To copy in a Book all Orders, Circulars, and Opinions of Law Officers
of the Crown, &c.

4. He shall retain, or (if so directed by the Justices) shall copy or cause to be copied into a Book to be kept for the Purpose, all Orders or Circulars, or Opinions of the Law Officers or Advisers of the Crown, addressed or transmitted to the Justices, and shall also make Copies of all Informations, Depositions, or Examinations, when so directed by the Justices, and shall also retain Copies of all Abstracts or Schedules of Documents transmitted to the Clerks of the Crown and Peace as herein-after provided:

To enter Cases in consecutive Order:

5. He shall enter all Cases in the Order in which the Summonses shall be issued at Petty Sessions, or if issued out of Petty Sessions, then in the Order in which the Application shall be made to him by the Complainant or his Agent to enter the same:

To enter and account for all Fines, &c. under Fines Act:

6. He shall enter a true Account of all Sums paid into Court under any Orders of the Justices, and of all Warrants issued for the Execution of any such Orders, and of all Sums levied under the same and paid over to him, (whether the said Sums shall be in the Nature of Penalties for Offences, or Sums awarded in Cases of a Civil Nature,) and shall otherwise account and act as to the same as required by the Provisions of 'The Fines Act, Ireland, 1851,' as to any Penal Sums:

To make Returns, and to observe general Regulations:

7. He shall also make such Returns of the Proceedings at Petty Sessions as the Chief or Under Secretary of the Lord Lieutenant shall from Time to Time require, and shall observe

such general Regulations in respect to the Discharge of his several Duties as the Lord Lieutenant shall from Time to Time prescribe:

And when required by the Clerks of the Crown or Peace, as the Case may be, the Clerk of Petty Sessions shall attend the Assizes or Quarter Sessions to which any Informations, Examinations, or Recognizances shall be returned by him, or to which any Informations, Examinations, or Recognizances prepared by him shall be returned, and as to which any Complaint shall have been made against him for Neglect, to answer such Inquiries respecting the same as shall be made by the Court; and in case it shall appear that such Clerk shall have committed any wilful Default or Neglect in preparing or in transmitting the same, or shall have improperly divulged the Contents of such Informations or Examinations, it shall be lawful for the Judge of Assize or for the Justices at Quarter Sessions, as the Case may be, for every such Offence to impose a Penalty not exceeding Twenty Pounds on the said Clerk, and in default of Payment of the same to commit him to Gaol for any Term not exceeding Three Months.

VI   **On Death, Suspension, or Dismissal of Clerk, Sub-Inspector to take charge of all Books, &c.**

Justice may grant Search Warrant for Books, &c. if detained

Whenever a Vacancy shall occur by reason of the Death, Resignation, Suspension, or Dismissal of any Clerk of Petty Sessions, the Sub-Inspector of Constabulary, or the Head Constable of the District, or such other Person as the Justices shall authorize, shall take charge of all Books, Papers, and other Effects belonging to the said Petty Sessions, and shall retain them in his Care and Custody until a Successor shall be appointed to such Clerk; and it shall be lawful for any Justice, upon being satisfied upon Oath that any such Books, Papers, or other Effects as aforesaid are or are suspected to be in the Possession of any Person who shall refuse to deliver up the same to such Sub-Inspector, Head Constable, or other Person so authorized, to issue a Warrant to any Sub-Inspector, Head or other Constable, to search the House of such Person for the same, and to seize and detain the same, if discovered therein; and such Sub-Inspector, Head or other Constable, so authorized by any such Warrant, may, upon the Refusal of such Person to open his Door for that Purpose, break it open.

VII   **Local Jurisdiction**

The Powers of Justices and others to act in and for different Localities shall be subject to the following Provisions:

Justice may act in adjoining County;

1. A Justice for any County may act as such in all Matters arising within such County, although he may at the Time happen to be in an adjoining County, provided he shall be also a Justice for such adjoining County:

or adjoining County of a City, though not a Justice of same; but not as to Matters arising in such County of a City, &c.

2. A Justice for any County may in like Manner act as such in all Matters arising within such County, although he may at the Time happen to be in any City, Town, or Place, being a County of itself, situated within or adjoining to such first-mentioned County, whether he shall be a Justice of such City, Town, or Place, or not; but nothing herein contained shall extend to empower any Justice for any County, not being also Justice for any such City,

Town, or Place as aforesaid, or any Person acting under him, to act or intermeddle in any Matters arising within any such City, Town, or Place:

Inspector General of Constabulary may act wherever he may be.

3. The Inspector General, or either of the Deputy Inspectors General of Constabulary, being a Justice of any County, may act in all Matters arising within such County, wherever he may happen to be at the Time;

Justices for One County may act for annexed Townlands of another.

4. Whenever any Townland belonging to One County shall be included in any Petty Sessions District of the adjoining County under the Provisions of this Act, any Justice having Jurisdiction in such Petty Sessions District shall have the like Jurisdiction in such Townland, although he may not be a Justice of the County to which such Townland belongs; and any Committal to any Gaol or Bridewell of such last-mentioned County, or any other magisterial Act done by any such Justice, in any Case in which the Offence or Cause of Complaint shall have arisen in such Townland, shall have the like Force and Effect as if such Justice was also a Justice of such last-mentioned County:

And all Constables or other Persons apprehending any Person whom they lawfully may and ought to apprehend by virtue of their Office or otherwise in any such County or Place as aforesaid, may lawfully convey such Person before any Justice for such County or Place whilst such Justice shall be in such adjoining County or Place as aforesaid, and such Constables or other Persons are hereby authorized and required in all such Cases to act in all things as if such Justice were within the County or Place for which he shall so act.

VIII   Place of Hearing

The Places where Justices shall sit in the Discharge of their Duties shall be subject to the following Provisions:

Petty Sessions to be held in Court House.

Where no Court House, Grand Jury may present Rent of Justice Room.

Summary Complaints to be determined in Petty Sessions, except, &c.; Two Justices may act where Offender cannot find Bail.

1. Whenever a public Court House shall be maintained by County Presentment at any Place fixed for the holding of Petty Sessions the Petty Sessions shall be held therein, if not inconvenient to the Public; but whenever no such public Court House shall be so maintained, or the holding of Petty Sessions therein would be inconvenient to the Public, it shall be lawful for the Grand Jury of the County to present an annual Sum not exceeding Ten Pounds for the Rent of a public Justice Room in which the Petty Sessions shall be held, and of a Lock-up; provided that such Room shall not be in a House where spirituous or fermented Liquors are sold, or in a Constabulary Barrack, or in any Building maintained in the whole or in part at the Public Expense, and that it shall be proved to the Satisfaction of the County Presentment Sessions where Application shall be made for such Rent that at least Four Meetings of Justices shall have been held in such Room during the Four Months next preceding such Application:

2. It shall not be lawful for any Justice or Justices to hear and determine any Cases of Summary Jurisdiction out of Petty Sessions, except Cases of Drunkenness or Vagrancy, or Fraud in the Sale of Goods, or Disputes as to Sales in Fairs or Markets; but it shall be lawful for Two Justices, if they shall see fit, to hear and determine out of Petty Sessions any

Complaint as to any Offence when the Offender shall be unable to give Bail for his Appearance at Petty Sessions:

Proviso.
Publicity of Proceedings.

Provided always, that nothing herein contained shall be construed to prevent any Justice or Justices acting out of Petty Sessions from making any Order (not being in the Nature of a Conviction, or of an Adjudication upon a Complaint,) which a Justice or Justices may be authorized or required by Law to make.

IX   Place in which Justices sit to hear Summary Proceedings to be deemed an open Court

The Right of the Public to have Access to the Place in which Justices shall sit shall be subject to the following Provisions:

Parties to be allowed to plead by Counsel, &c.

1. In all Cases of Summary Proceedings the Place in which any Justice or Justices shall sit to hear and determine any Complaint shall be deemed an open Court, to which the Public generally may have Access, so far as the same can conveniently contain them; and the Parties by and against whom any Complaint or Information shall there be beard shall be admitted to conduct or make their full Answer and Defence thereto respectively, and to have the Witnesses examined and cross-examined by themselves or by Counsel or Attorney on their Behalf:

[...]¹

And if any Person shall wilfully insult any Justice or Justices sitting in any such Court or Place, or shall commit any other Contempt of any such Court, it shall be lawful for such Justice or Justices by any verbal Order either to direct such Person to be removed from such Court or Place, or to be taken into Custody, and at any Time before the Rising of such Court by Warrant to commit such Person to Gaol for any Period not exceeding Seven Days, or to fine such Person in any Sum not exceeding Forty Shillings.

Amendments

1   Paragraph 2 repealed by Criminal Procedure Act 1967, s 3 and Sch.

X   Informations and Complaints.

JUSTICE MAY RECEIVE INFORMATION OR COMPLAINT:
AS TO OFFENCES WITHIN HIS JURISDICTION, AND OUT OF HIS JURISDICTION:
AS TO CIVIL CASES:

Whenever Information shall be given to any Justice that any Person has committed or is suspected to have committed any Treason, Felony, Misdemeanor, or other Offence, within the Limits of the Jurisdiction of such Justice, for which such Person shall be punishable either by Indictment or upon a Summary Conviction; or that any at any Person has committed or is suspected to have committed any such Crime or Offence elsewhere out of the Jurisdiction of such Justice, either in Great Britain or Ireland, or in the Isles of Man, Jersey, Guernsey

Alderney, or Sark, and such Person is residing or being, or is suspected to reside or be, within the Limits of the Jurisdiction of such Justice; or that any Person has committed or is suspected to have committed any Crime or Offence whatsoever on the High Seas, or in any Creek, Harbour, Haven, or other Place in which the Admiralty of England or Ireland have or claim to have Jurisdiction, or on Land beyond the Seas, for which an Indictment can be legally preferred in any Place in the United Kingdom of England and Ireland, and such Person is residing or being, or is suspected to reside or be, within the Limits of the Jurisdiction of such Justice; or whenever a Complaint shall be made to any Justice as to any other Matter arising within the Limits of his Jurisdiction, upon which he shall have Power to make a Summary Order, it shall be lawful for such Justice to receive such Information or Complaint, and to proceed in respect to the same, subject to the following Provisions:

It may be verbal, and without Oath, in certain Cases

1. Whenever it is intended that a Summons only shall issue to require the Attendance of any Person, the Information or Complaint may be made either with or without Oath, and either in Writing or not, according as the Justice shall see fit:

It must be in Writing, and on Oath, in certain other Cases

2. But whenever it is intended that a Warrant shall issue for the Arrest or Committal of any Person, the Information or Complaint shall be in Writing, and on the Oath of the Complainant or of some Person or Persons on his Behalf:

Binding the Informant to prosecute

3. Whenever any such Information shall have been taken on Oath and in Writing that any Person has committed or is suspected to have committed any Indictable Crime or Offence, (or any Offence for which such Person shall be punishable upon Summary Conviction, and for whose Arrest the Justice shall issue a Warrant,) it shall be lawful for the Justice, if he shall see fit, to bind the Informant or Complainant by Recognizance (A a.*) or (C.) to appear at the Court or Place where the Defendant is to be tried or the Complaint is to be heard to prosecute or give Evidence, as the Case may be, against such Person:

Complaints must be made for Poor Rate, &c. at any Time after the Date of the Warrant; for Wages, &c. within a Year; for Trespass, Two Months; in other Cases, Six Months.

4. In all Cases of Summary Jurisdiction the Complaint shall be made, [when it shall relate to the Non-payment of any Poor Rate, County Rate, or other public Tax, at any Time after the Date of the Warrant authorizing the Collection of the same, and when it shall relate to the Non-payment of Money for Wages, Hire, or Tuition, within One Year from the Termination of the Term or Period in respect of which it shall be payable, and when it shall relate to any Trespass, within Two Months from the Time when the Trespass shall have occurred, and in any other Case]¹ within Six Months from the Time when the Cause of Complaint shall have arisen, but not otherwise:

And in all Cases of Summary Jurisdiction any Person against whom any such Information or Complaint shall have been made in Writing shall, upon being amenable or appearing in Person or by Counsel or Attorney, be entitled to receive from the Clerk of Petty Sessions a Copy of such Information or Complaint, on Payment of the Sum of Sixpence to such Clerk; and such Clerk shall in no Case allow the original Information or Complaint to be taken out of his Possession.

Amendments

1 Paragraph 4 repealed by Statute of Limitations 1957, s 9 and Sch 2 save in so far as it relates to summary proceedings of a criminal nature in the District Court. Criminal Justice Act 2006, s 177 which amends Criminal Justice Act 1951, s 7 restricts para (4) – see the amended 1951 Act.

XI   Process to enforce Appearance

The Manner in which Persons against whom any such Informations or Complaints as aforesaid shall have been received by any Justice shall be made to appear to answer to the same shall be subject to the following Provisions:

In Cases of Indictable Offences Warrant to issue in the first instance; but in certain Cases a Summons may issue

If Party appears or is arrested Justice to proceed under subsequent Provisions.

1. In all Cases of Indictable Crimes and Offences (where an Information that any Person has committed the same shall have been taken in Writing and on Oath) the Justice shall issue a Warrant (B b.) to arrest and bring such Person before him, or some other Justice of the same County, to answer to the Complaint made in the Information (and which Warrant may be issued or executed on a Sunday as well as on any other Day); or if he shall think that the Ends of Justice would be thereby sufficiently answered, it shall be lawful for him, instead of issuing such Warrant, to issue a Summons in the first instance to such Person, requiring him to appear and answer to the said Complaint; but nothing herein contained shall prevent any Justice from issuing a Warrant for the Arrest of such Person at any Time before or after the Time mentioned in such Summons for his Appearance; and whenever such Person shall afterwards appear or be brought before any such Justice he shall proceed according to the Provisions herein-after contained as to taking the Evidence against such Person, and committing such Person for Trial:

In Summary Proceedings Summons to issue in the first instance; but in certain Cases a Warrant may issue.

If Party is arrested Justice may commit or discharge on Recognizance.

2. In all Cases of Summary Jurisdiction the Justice may issue his Summons (B a.) directed to such Person, requiring him to appear and answer to the Complaint, and it shall not be necessary that such Justice shall be the Justice or One of the Justices by whom the Complaint shall be afterwards heard and determined; and in all Cases of Offences where such Person shall not appear at the required Time and Place, and it shall be proved on Oath either that he was personally served with such Summons or that he is keeping out of the Way of such Service, (the Complaint being in Writing and on Oath,) the Justice may issue a Warrant to arrest and bring such Person before him or some other Justice of the same County, to answer to the said Complaint; and when such Person shall afterwards be arrested under such Warrant, the Justice before whom he shall be brought may either by Warrant (E b.) commit him to Gaol, until the Hearing of the Complaint, or may discharge him upon his entering into a Recognizance (C.), with or without Sureties, at the Discretion of the Justice, conditioned for his Appearance at such Hearing:

Summons or Warrant may run into an adjoining County

And each Summons or Warrant shall be signed by the Justice or One of the Justices issuing the same, and it shall state shortly the Cause of Complaint, and no Summons or Warrant shall be signed in Blank; and in every Case where the Offence shall have occurred, or the Cause of Complaint shall have arisen within the Petty Sessions District for which the Justice issuing any such Summons or Warrant shall act, but the Party or Witness to whom such Summons shall be directed or against whom such Warrant shall be issued shall reside in an adjoining County, it shall be lawful for such Justice to compel the Appearance of such Party or Witness at the Hearing of the Charge or Complaint within such District, in like Manner as if such Party or Witness resided in such District, although such Justice may not be a Justice of such adjoining County.

XII   Service of Summonses

The Manner in which Summonses shall be served shall be subject to the following Provisions:

Justices to appoint a Summons Server

1. It shall be lawful for the Justices of each Petty Sessions to appoint some One or more Persons, who shall be able to read and write, to act as Summons Server or Servers of the District during the Pleasure of such Justices; and any such Summons Server shall be entitled to be paid by the Complainant or Person for whom he may be employed such Sum not exceeding the Sum of Sixpence for the Service of each Summons upon each Party or Witness (or upon any Number of Parties or Witnesses in the same Case who shall be served in the same House) as the Justices shall fix:

By whom Summons to be served

2. In Cases of Offences prosecuted by the Constabulary the Summons shall be served by a Head or other Constable, but in all other Cases it may be served by the Summons Server of the District, or (if the Justice issuing the same shall so direct or permit) by any other Person whom the Complainant shall employ, and who shall be able to read and write, but in no Case by the Complainant himself:

What shall be due Service

Proof of Service

3. Every Summons shall be served upon the Person to whom it is directed by delivering to him a Copy of such Summons, or if he cannot be conveniently met with, by leaving such Copy for him at his last or most usual Place of Abode, or at his Office, Warehouse, Counting-house, Shop, Factory, or Place of Business, with some Inmate of the House not being under Sixteen Years of Age, a reasonable Time before the Hearing of the Complaint; and such last-mentioned Service shall be deemed sufficient Service of such Summons in every Case except where Personal Service shall be specially required by this Act; and in every Case the Person who shall serve such Summons shall endorse on the same the Time and Place where it was served, and shall attend with the same at the Hearing of the Complaint to depose, if necessary, to such Service:

Provided always, that nothing herein contained shall be construed to affect the Provisions of any Act authorizing the Substitution of Service in particular Cases.

XIII   Witnesses.—Justice may force Witnesses to attend and give Evidence

Whenever it shall be made to appear to any Justice that any Person is able to give material Evidence […][1] in Cases of Indictable Offences, or for the Complainant or Defendant in Cases of Summary Jurisdiction, and will not voluntarily appear for the Purpose of being examined as a Witness, such Justice may proceed as follows:

Issue of Summons

In Cases of Indictable Offences Warrant may issue in the first instance

1. He may issue a Summons (B a.) to such Person, requiring him to appear at a Time and Place mentioned in such Summons, to testify what he may know concerning the Matter of the Information or Complaint, and (if the Justice shall see fit) to bring with him and produce for Examination such Accounts, Papers, or other Documents as shall be in his Possession or Power, and as shall be deemed necessary by such Justice; but in any Case of an Indictable Crime or Offence, whenever the Justice shall be satisfied by Proof upon Oath that it is probable that such Person will not attend to give Evidence without being compelled so to do, then, (the Information or Complaint being in Writing and on Oath,) instead of issuing such Summons as aforesaid, he may issue a Warrant (B b.) in the first instance for the Arrest of such Person:

If Summons be not obeyed, Justices may issue Warrant to arrest Witness.

2. And in any Case when any Person to whom a Summons shall be issued in the first instance shall neglect or refuse to appear at the Time and Place appointed by such Summons, and no just Excuse shall be offered for such Neglect or Refusal, then, (the Information or Complaint being in Writing and on Oath,) after Proof upon Oath that such Summons was personally served upon such Person, or that such Person is keeping out of the Way of such Service, and that he is able to give material Evidence in the Case, the Justice before whom such Person should have appeared may issue a Warrant (B b.) to arrest such Person, and to bring him at the Time and Place appointed for the Hearing of the Case, to testify and to produce such Accounts, Papers, and Documents as may be required as aforesaid:

What Persons shall be competent Witnesses: Prosecutors and Complainants in all Cases: Defendants in Wages Cases.

3. In all Cases of Prosecutions for Offences the Evidence of the Informer or Party aggrieved shall be admissible in proof of the Offence; and in all Cases of Complaints on which a Justice can make an Order for the Payment of Money, or otherwise, the Evidence of the Complainant shall be admissible in proof of his Complaint; and in Cases of Wages, Hire, or Tuition the Evidence of the Master or Employer may, in the Discretion of the Justices, be admitted in proof against the Complaint:

Witnesses to be examined on Oath

4. All Witnesses shall be examined upon Oath, and any Justice before whom any such Witness shall appear for the Purpose of being so examined shall have full Authority to administer to every such Witness the usual Oath:

Witnesses refusing to be examined may be committed from Time to Time till they consent to be examined.

Witnesses.

Not to prevent Case being disposed of on other sufficient Evidence.

5. Whenever any Person shall appear as a Witness, either in obedience to a Summons or by virtue of a Warrant, (or shall be present, and shall be verbally required by the Justice or

Justices to give Evidence,) and he shall refuse to be examined upon Oath concerning the Matter of the Information or Complaint, or shall refuse to take such Oath, or having taken such Oath shall refuse to answer such Questions concerning the said Matter as shall then be put to him, or shall refuse or neglect to produce any such Accounts, Papers, or Documents as aforesaid, (without offering any just Excuse for such Refusal,) the Justice or Justices then present may adjourn the Proceedings for any Period not exceeding Eight clear Days, and may in the meantime by Warrant (E b.) commit the said Witness to Gaol, unless he shall sooner consent to be sworn or to testify as aforesaid, or to produce such Accounts, Papers, or Documents, as the Case may be; and if such Witness, upon being brought up upon such adjourned Hearing, shall again refuse to be sworn, or to testify as aforesaid, or to produce such Accounts, Papers, or Documents, as the Case may be, the said Justices, if they shall see fit, may again adjourn the Proceedings, and commit the Witness for the like Period, and so again from Time to Time until he shall consent to be sworn, or to testify as aforesaid, or to produce such Accounts, Papers, or Documents, as the Case may be (provided that no such Imprisonment shall in any case of Summary Jurisdiction exceed One Month in the whole); but nothing herein contained shall be deemed to prevent the Justice or Justices from sending any such Case for Trial, or otherwise disposing of the same in the meantime, according to any other sufficient Evidence which shall have been received by him or them:

In Cases of Indictable Offences Witnesses may be bound to give Evidence, and on Refusal may be committed; but if Party is not committed or bailed Witness to be liberated.

6. [...]²

Justices may order Payment to Witnesses in Civil Cases, not exceeding 2 s. 6 d.

7. In all Cases of Summary Jurisdiction it shall be lawful for the Justices by whom any Order for Payment of Money, not being in the Nature of a Penalty for an Offence, shall be made, to order the Party at whose Instance any Witness shall have been summoned to pay to such Witness such Sum, not exceeding Two Shillings and Sixpence, as to such Justices shall seem fit, for his Expenses or Loss of Time for each Day of attending to give Evidence, and in default of Payment thereof at such Time as such Justice shall appoint, then to issue a Warrant to levy the Amount thereof by Distress of the Goods of such Party:

And no Person who shall be summoned to attend before any Court of Petty Sessions, or before any Justice out of Petty Sessions, as a Witness, shall be liable to Arrest for Debt whilst at such Court, or at the Place where such Justice shall sit, or whilst proceeding to or returning from the same, provided he shall proceed and return by the most direct Road without unnecessary Delay; and it shall be lawful for the Court out of which the Writ or Process shall have issued to order the Discharge of any Person who shall be so arrested.

Amendments

1   Words deleted by Criminal Procedure Act 1967, Sch.

2   Paragraph 6 repealed by Criminal Procedure Act 1967, Sch.

XIV–XVII   [...][1]

Amendments

1   Sections 14 to 17 repealed by Criminal Procedure Act 1967, Sch.

XVIII   **Warrant to arrest a Party against whom an Indictment is found**

Party so arrested to be committed for Trial or bailed.
If Party indicted be in Prison for some other Offence, Justice to order his Detention.
But not to interfere with Bench Warrants, &c.

Whenever an Indictment shall have been found by the Grand Jury in any Court of Oyer and Terminer or General Gaol Delivery, or at any General or Quarter Sessions of the Peace in Ireland, against any Person who shall then be at large, and who shall not already have appeared and pleaded to such Indictment, (and whether such Person shall have been bound by Recognizance to answer to the same or not,) the Person who shall act as Clerk of the Crown at such Court, or as Clerk of the Peace at such Sessions, shall, at any Time after the End of the Assizes or Sessions at which such Indictment shall have been found, upon Application of the Prosecutor or of some Person on his Behalf, and free from Charge, grant unto such Prosecutor or Person a Certificate (I b.) of such Indictment having been found; and upon Production of such Certificate to any Justice for the County in which the Offence shall be alleged in such Indictment to have been committed, or in which the Person thereby indicted shall reside or be, or be suspected to reside or be, such Justice shall issue his Warrant to arrest such Person, and to cause him to be brought before him, or some other Justice for the same County, to be dealt with according to Law; and upon such Person being so brought before such Justice, and upon its being proved on Oath that the Person so arrested is the same Person who is charged and named in such Indictment, such Justice shall, without further Inquiry, either commit him for Trial or admit him to Bail, in manner aforesaid; and in any such Case as last aforesaid, if the Person so indicted shall at the Time be confined in any Gaol for any other Offence than that charged in such Indictment, such Justice shall, upon like Proof on Oath that the Person so confined is the same Person who is so charged in such Indictment, issue his Warrant (E b.) to the Keeper of such Gaol, commanding him to detain such Person in his Custody until he shall be discharged therefrom by due Course of Law; but nothing herein contained shall be deemed to prevent any Clerk of the Crown or Peace or other Officer from issuing any Warrant in any such Case for the Arrest of any such Person which he might otherwise by Law issue.

XIX   **Disposal of the Informations, &c. Indictable Offences**

[...][1]

Amendments

1   Section 19 repealed by Criminal Procedure Act 1967, Sch.

XX   Hearing the Case.—Summary Jurisdiction

In all Cases of Summary Jurisdiction the Proceedings upon the Hearing of the Complaint shall be subject to the following Provisions:

Where both Parties appear, Case to be heard on both Sides.

Right of Reply.

Proof of a Negative.

1. Whenever the Defendant or his Agent shall be present the Substance of the Complaint shall be stated to him, and if he thereupon admit the Truth of the Complaint, then the Justices shall, if they shall see no sufficient Reason to the contrary, convict or make an Order against him accordingly, but if he do not admit the Truth of the Complaint, then the Justices shall proceed to hear such Evidence as may be adduced in support of the Complaint, and also to hear the Defence, and such Evidence as may be adduced on behalf of the Defence, and also such Evidence as the Complainant may adduce in reply, if such Defendant shall have given any Evidence other than as to his the Defendant's general Character; but the Complainant or his Agent shall not be entitled to make any Observations in reply upon the Evidence given by the Defendant, nor shall the Defendant or his Agent be entitled to make any Observations in reply upon the Evidence given by the Compalinant in reply; and if the Information or Complaint shall negative any Exemption, Exception, Proviso, or Condition in the Statute on which the same shall be framed, it shall not be necessary for the Complainant to prove such Negative, but the Defendant may prove the Affirmative thereof, if he will have Advantage of the same:

Where Defendant does not appear Hearing may be ex parte.

2. Whenever the Defendant or his Agent shall not appear at the Time and Place mentioned in the Summons, and it shall appear to the Justices on Oath that the Summons was duly served a reasonable Time before the Time therein appointed for appearing, and no sufficient Grounds shall be shown for an Adjournment, the Justices may either proceed ex parte to hear and determine the Complaint, or may adjourn the Hearing to a future Day:

Where Complainant does not appear, Case to be dismissed or adjourned.

3. Whenever the Defendant or his Agent shall appear at the Time and Place appointed in the Summons, or shall be brought before the Justice by virtue of any Warrant, then, if the Complainant (having in the Case of a Warrant had due Notice of the Defendant's Arrest) do not appear by himself or his Agent, the Justices may either dismiss such Complaint, or may adjourn the Hearing to a future Day:

Justices to take down Evidence in Offence Cases in Writing, if required by Party.

[…]¹

And whenever all the Cases shall not have been heard and determined on any Court Day, the Justices then present may adjourn the remaining, cases either to the next Court Day or to such other Day as they shall see fit; and whenever, either before or during the Hearing of any Complaint, it shall appear advisable, the Justices present may, in their Discretion, adjourn the Hearing of the same to a certain Time or Place to be then appointed and stated in the Presence and Hearing of the Party or Parties or their Agents; and all Persons whose Attendance shall have been required by any Summons in any of the Cases so adjourned shall take notice of such Adjournment, and shall be obliged to attend on the Day to which such Adjournment shall take place, without the Issue or Service of any further Summons; and in all Cases of such Adjournments the said Justices may suffer the Defendant to go at large, or, in

Prosecutions for Offences (where there shall be an Information in Writing and on Oath that the Defendant is guilty of the Offence,) may commit him to Gaol by Warrant (E b.), or may discharge him upon his entering into a Recognizance (C.), with or without Sureties, at the Discretion of the Justices, con ditioned for his Appearance at the Time and Place to which such Hearing or further Hearing shall be adjourned.

Amendments

1   Paragraph 4 repealed by Civil Law (Miscellaneous Provisions) Act 2008, s 1(2) and 25.

XXI   Adjudication of Case.—Summary Jurisdiction

[…]¹

Amendments

1   Section 21 repealed by Criminal Justice Act 1951, s 26 and Sch 2.

XXII   General Powers in adjudicating

In all Cases of Summary Jurisdiction it shall be lawful for the Justices in adjudicating thereon to exercise the following general Powers, whether the same shall be authorized by the Act under which the Complaint shall be made or not:

Justices may in all Cases fix the Time and Manner of Payment

1. In every Case where the Justices shall be authorized to award any Penal or other Sum, they may order that the same shall be paid either forthwith or at such Time as they shall see fit to fix for that Purpose, and, in Cases of a Civil Nature, that such Sum may be paid either at once or by Instalments:

In all Cases Distress may be ordered on Non-payment.

2. In every Case where the Justices shall award any Penal or other Sum to be paid, they may order that, in default of the said Sum being paid at the Time and in the Manner directed by their Order, the Goods of the Person against whom the said Order shall be made shall be distrained for such Sum, or for so much of such Sum as shall remain unpaid at the Time fixed, and also for the Costs of such Distress:

In Offence Cases Imprisonment may be ordered in default of Distress, according to Scale;

3. In every Case of an Offence where they shall order that a Distress shall be made in default of Payment of any Penal Sum, they may order that in default of the said Sum being paid as directed the said Person shall be imprisoned for any Term not exceeding the Period specified in the following Scale:

For any Sum	The Imprisonment not to exceed
Not exceeding 5 s.	One Week.
Exceeding the last, but not exceeding 10 s.	Two Weeks.
Exceeding the last, but not exceeding 2 l.	One Month.
Exceeding the last, but not exceeding 5 l.	Two Months.
Exceeding the last, but not exceeding 10 l.	Three Months.
Exceeding the last, but not exceeding 30 l.	Four Months.
Exceeding the last, but not exceeding 50 l.	Six Months.
Exceeding the last	One Year;

So also in like Cases in the first instance where no Goods, &c.

And any such Imprisonment shall be determinable upon Payment of the said Sum and Costs and any Costs of the Distress, where a Distress shall have been made; and such Imprisonment may be directed in the same Warrant as such Distress; but if the said Person shall admit, or if it shall be otherwise proved on Oath, that he has no Goods, or that a Distress would be ruinous to him or his Family, they may order that such Person shall be imprisoned in the first instance for the like Period for which he might be imprisoned in default of Distress:

In Offence Cases Justices at Petty Sessions may substitute Distress for Committal, and vice versa on Failure of First Warrant.

4. In every Case of an Offence, where the Order shall only have directed Distress in default of Payment of a Penal Sum, and it shall afterwards be found impossible to execute a Warrant of Distress, it shall be lawful for the Justices at Petty Sessions to order a Warrant to issue to commit the Person against whom such Order shall have been made to Gaol for such Period as might have been directed by the original Order; and in like Manner where the Order shall have only directed Imprisonment, and it shall be found impossible to execute a Warrant of Committal, it shall be lawful for the Justices at Petty Sessions to order a Warrant to issue to levy by Distress of the Goods of such Person such Penal Sum as might have been awarded by the original Order; and in all such Cases a Note of such Proceeding shall be made by the Justices in the Order Book: [1]

Power to award Hard Labour in Offence Cases

5. In every Case of an Offence, where the Act shall authorize the Justices to order Imprisonment, they may adjudge by their Order that the said Imprisonment shall be either with or without Hard Labour, according as they shall see fit:

Imprisonment may commence at Expiration of Imprisonment under previous Conviction

6. [...] [2]

Any Compensation awarded shall be paid to Party aggrieved, except in certain Cases

7. In every Case where any Sum shall be awarded under the Provisions of any Act as Compensation for Damage, or as the Value of any Article, or as the Amount of any Injury done, such Sum shall be paid to the Party or Public Body aggrieved; but where the Party aggrieved is unknown, such Sum shall be applied in like Manner as any Penalties awarded to the Crown; and where several Persons join in an Offence, and are severally punished each in

the Amount of the Injury done, no more than One of such Sums shall be paid to the Party aggrieved, and the rest shall be applied as other Penalties awarded to the Crown:

Appropriation of Fines and Penalties

8. In every Case where the Act under which any Penal Sum shall be ordered to be paid as a Penalty for an Offence (and no Sum shall be awarded to the Complainant as Compensation for Damage), it shall be lawful for the Justices to award any Sum not exceeding One Third of such Penal Sum to the Prosecutor or Informer, and the Remainder of such Sum and all other Penal Sums shall be awarded to the Crown, any Act or Acts to the contrary notwithstanding:

Power to award Costs in all Cases to either Party

9. [...]³

Amendments

1   Paragraphs 2 to 4 of section 22, in so far as they apply to criminal proceedings, repealed by Courts (No 2) Act 1986, Sch 2.

2   Paragraph 6 repealed by Criminal Justice Administration Act 1914, s 44 and Sch 4.

3   Paragraph 9 repealed by Courts (No 2) Act 1986, s 9 and Sch 2.

XXIII   Enforcement of Orders.— Summary Jurisdiction — In Offence Cases Warrant to issue peremptorily

In Civil Cases Warrants to issue on Application of Party;
but no Execution of Order pending an Appeal;
except in certain Cases:
or if Warrant issued, not to be executed, or if executed, Party to be discharged or Distress to be returned.

In all Cases of Summary Jurisdiction, whenever an Order shall be made upon the Conviction of any Person for an Offence, the Justices shall issue the proper Warrant for its Execution forthwith, when the Imprisonment is to take place immediately, or at the Time fixed by the Order for the Imprisonment to take place where it is not to be immediate, or directly upon the Non-payment of any Penal Sum or the Non-performance of any Condition at the Time and in the Manner fixed by the Order for that Purpose, or at furthest upon the next Court Day after the Expiration of the Time so fixed for the Imprisonment, Payment, or Performance of a Condition, as the Case may be, unless the Imprisonment or Penal Sum shall have been remitted by the Crown or other competent Authority in the Interval; and whenever an Order shall be made in any Case of a Civil Nature, and the same shall not be obeyed, the Justice shall issue the proper Warrant for its Execution at any Time after the Time fixed for Compliance with its Directions, where required so to do, by the Person in whose Favour such Order shall have been made or by some Person on his Behalf, and it shall not be necessary that the Justice by whom any such Warrant shall be issued shall be the Justice or One of the Justices by whom the Order shall have been made: Provided always, that in every Case where the Party being entitled to appeal against any such Order shall have duly given Notice thereof, and entered into a Recognizance to prosecute the same in the Manner herein-after provided, it shall not be lawful for any Justice to issue any Warrant to execute the said Order until such Appeal shall have been decided, or until the Appellant shall have failed to perform the Condition of such Recognizance, as the Case may be, (except where any Act shall expressly authorize or direct the Levy of any Sum to be made notwithstanding the Appeal); and in any Case where any Person shall be in Custody, or shall have been committed to Gaol, or any Warrant of Distress shall have been issued or executed, under any such Order, the Justice by whom the Warrant shall have been issued, or any other Justice of the same County, shall, upon an Application being made to him in that Behalf, forthwith order the Discharge of such Person from Custody or from Gaol, or that such Warrant of Distress shall not be executed, or that if executed the Distress shall be returned to the Owner, as the Case may be.

XXIV   Appeals.—Summary Jurisdiction.—In what Cases Appeals shall be permitted

Appeal only to next Quarter Sessions of the Division.

In any Case of Summary Jurisdiction, where an Order shall be made by the Justices for Payment of any Penal or other Sum exceeding Twenty Shillings, or for any Term of Imprisonment exceeding One Month, or for the doing of anything at a greater Expense than Forty Shillings, or for the estreating of any Recognizance to a greater Amount than Twenty Shillings, (but in no other Case,) either Party (whether he shall be the Complainant or the Defendant) in Cases of a Civil Nature, or the Party against whom the Order shall have been made in other Cases, shall be entitled to appeal to the next Quarter Sessions to be held in the same Division of the County when the Order shall have been made by any Justice or Justices of any Petty Sessions District, (or to the Recorder of any Corporate or Borough Town at his next Sessions when the Order shall have been made by any Justice or Justices of such Corporate or Borough Town,) (unless when any such Sessions shall commence within Seven Days from the Date of the Order, in which Case the Appeal may be made to the next succeeding Sessions of such Division or Town); and such Appeal shall be subject to the following Provisions:

Notice to be given within Three Days

1. The Appellant shall serve Notice in Writing of his Intention to appeal upon the Clerk of Petty Sessions, within Three Days from the Date of the Order against which the Appeal shall be made:

Recognizance to prosecute Appeal
Amount of Recognizance

2. He shall also within Three Days after such Notice as aforesaid enter into a Recognizance, according to the Form (C.), with Two solvent Sureties, conditioned to prosecute such Appeal, and the Amount of such Recognizance shall be double the Amount of the Sum and Costs ordered to be paid, where Payment only is ordered, or of such reasonable Amount as the Justices shall see fit, where Imprisonment is ordered:

[2A

    (a)   A recognisance to which paragraph 2 applies may be taken by—

        (i)   any judge of the District Court,

       (ii)   any District Court clerk,

     (iii)   a peace commissioner designated for that purpose by order of the Minister for Justice, Equality and Law Reform,

     (iv)   the governor of a prison, or

(v)   a prison officer designated for that purpose by the governor of a prison.

(b)   in this paragraph 'prison' has the same meaning as it has in the Prisons Act 2007.]¹

Form of Appeal

3. Whenever the Appellant shall have given such Notice and entered into such Recognizance there shall be delivered to him the Form of Appeal (H.), containing a Certificate of the Order against which he shall appeal (signed by the Justice who shall have made the same, or by any other Justice of the same Petty Sessions); and it shall also be therein certified by the Clerk of Petty Sessions that the said Notice was duly given, and that the said Recognizance was duly entered into, if the Fact shall be so:

Recognizance to appeal to be transmitted to Clerk of Peace

4. In every Case where an Appeal shall be so made, the Clerk of Petty Sessions shall transmit the Recognizance entered into to prosecute such Appeal and all other Proceedings in such Case to the Clerk of the Peace of the County or to the proper Officer of the Recorder's Court, at least Seven Days before the Commencement of the Sessions to which the Appeal shall be made, or as soon afterwards as may be practicable, in the same Manner as is herein-before provided for the Transmission of Informations as to Indictable Offences:

Appellant to give Notice to opposite Party

[…]²

Quarter Sessions (or Recorder) may decide Appeal, and give Costs not exceeding 40 s.

Clerk of Peace or Officer of Recorder's Court to certify Decision; or certify upon and return Recognizance if Appeal is not prosecuted.

6. Whenever an Appeal shall have been so made, and such last-mentioned Notice shall have been duly given, it shall be lawful for the said Court of Quarter Sessions (or Recorder, as the Case may be) to entertain the same, and to confirm, vary, or reverse the Order made by the Justices (as so certified in such Form of Appeal), and to award to either Party any Sum not exceeding Forty Shillings for the Costs of such Appeal; and whenever the said Court of Appeal shall have decided any such Appeal, the Clerk of the Peace or proper Officer of the Recorder's Court, as the Case may be, shall certify such Decision at Foot of the Form of Appeal, and return the same and the said Proceedings to the Justices of the Petty Sessions at which the Order shall have been made, within Seven Days after such Appeal shall have been decided; and whenever any such Appeal shall not have been duly prosecuted, the Clerk of the Peace or proper Officer of the Recorder's Court, as the Case may be, shall so certify upon such Recognizance and return the same to the Justices of the Petty Sessions from which the same shall have been transmitted (in the same Manner and subject to the same Provisions as are herein-before contained as to the Transmission of Informations for Indictable Offences,) within Seven Days after the Termination of the Sessions at which such Appeal ought to have been prosecuted, and which Certificate shall be free from any Charge:

If Order is not varied on Appeal Justice shall issue Warrant for Execution of same; but where Order is varied, Warrant to issue for Execution of Quarter Sessions Order.

Costs of Appeal how recovered.

Where Party has been imprisoned, he is only to be imprisoned for Remainder of Period.

7. And whenever it shall appear from such Certificate that such Appeal has not been duly prosecuted, or that the original Order has been confirmed upon Appeal, the Justices who shall have made the original Order, or any other Justice of the same Petty Sessions, shall issue the proper Warrant for the Execution of the same, as if no such Appeal had been

brought; and in every Case in which it shall appear from such Certificate that the Court of Appeal shall have varied the original Order, the said Justices shall forthwith issue the proper Warrant for the Execution of the Order so made by the Court of Appeal, in like Manner as they might have issued a Warrant for the Execution of the original Order in case no Appeal had been prosecuted; and if upon any such Appeal either Party shall be ordered to pay Costs, it shall be lawful for such Justices to enforce Payment of the same in like Manner as any Costs awarded by the original Order; and in any Case where any Order by which any Person shall be adjudged to be imprisoned shall be confirmed on Appeal, such Person shall be liable to be imprisoned for the Period adjudged by the original Order, where he shall not have been apprehended under the original Order, or where he shall have so been apprehended and discharged, then for such Period as, together with the Time during which he shall so have been in Custody, shall be equal to the Period adjudged by the original Order:

Provided always, that whenever the Party bound by Recognizance to prosecute an Appeal against an Order to imprison shall have absconded, or when the Party bound to prosecute an Appeal against an Order for Payment of any Penal or other Sum shall have no Goods whereon to levy same by Distress, it shall be lawful for the Justices at the Petty Sessions where the original Order was made, and after like Proof of Notice to the Parties as in estreating other Recognizances in Summary Proceedings, to make an Order for estreating the Recognizance in any such Case to such Amount as they shall see fit, and for paying out of such Amount such Sum as shall have been directed to be paid to any Party by such original Order, and thereupon to issue a Warrant (E a.) for the Levy of the same upon the Goods of the several Persons bound thereby.

Amendments

1   Section 2A inserted by Courts and Court Officers Act 2009, s 26.
2   Paragraph 5 repealed by Courts of Justice Act 1928, s 22 and Sch.

XXV   Addressing Warrants

The Persons to whom Warrants shall be addressed for Execution shall be as follows:

To whom to be addressed: in Offence Cases;

[1. All warrants (except as otherwise provided by law) in proceedings in respect of offences punishable either on indictment or summarily issued by the District Court shall be addressed to the superintendent or an inspector of the Garda Síochána of the Garda Síochána district within which the place where the warrant is issued is situated or the person named in the warrant resides:][1]

in other Cases.

2. All Warrants in other Cases shall be addressed either to the Sub-Inspector or Head Constable of Constabulary in manner aforesaid, or to such other Person or Persons (not being the Complainant or a Party interested), as the Justices issuing the same shall see fit:

Gaoler to produce Prisoner at Adjournments or Remands

And it shall not be necessary to address any Warrant of Committal to the Keeper of the Gaol, but upon the Delivery of any such Warrant by the Person charged with its Execution to the

Keeper of the Gaol to which the Committal shall be made, such Keeper shall receive and detain the Person named therein, (or shall detain him if already in his Custody,) for such Period and in such Manner as it shall appear from the Warrant that the said Person is to be imprisoned; and in Cases of Adjournments or Remands such Keeper shall bring the said Person at the Time and Place fixed by the Warrant for that Purpose before such Justices as shall be there.

Amendments

1   Section XXV substituted by Criminal Justice Act 2006, s 193.

XXVI   By whom Warrants may be executed

The Execution of Warrants so addressed to the Sub-Inspector or Head Constable of Constabulary shall be subject to the following Provisions:

Executing Constabulary Warrants in the District

1. Whenever the Person against whom any Warrant so addressed shall have been issued shall be to be found in case of Committal, or shall have Goods in case of Distress, in any Place for which such Sub-Inspector or Head Constable shall act, it shall be lawful for the Sub-Inspector or Head Constable who shall act for the Time being for such Place, or for any Head or other Constable to be appointed by him, to execute the same:

Certifying to some other District of same County

2. Whenever it shall appear that the said Person or his Goods, as the Case may be, are not to be found in any Place for which such Sub-Inspector shall act, but that they are to be found elsewhere in the same County, the said Sub-Inspector or Head Constable shall certify on the Warrant, according to the Form (G b.) the Place where he believes that the said Person or his Goods are to be found, and also (having first satisfied himself as to the Fact) that he believes the Signature to the Warrant to be genuine, and shall forthwith transmit the said Warrant to the Sub-Inspector or Head Constable who shall act for such last-mentioned Place, and the same shall be executed in like Manner as any Warrant addressed to him in the first instance:

Certifying out of the County

3. Whenever it shall appear that the said Person or his Goods, as the Case may be, are not to be found in the County to which such Sub-Inspector or Head Constable shall belong, but that such Person or his Goods, as the Case may be, are to be found elsewhere out of the said County, the said Sub-Inspector or Head Constable shall, as before, certify on the Warrant, according to the Form (G b.), and forthwith transmit the same to the Inspector General of the Constabulary Force, to be backed as herein-after mentioned:

Provided always, that in any Case which shall appear to the Justice by whom any Warrant shall be issued, to be a Case of Emergency, he may address such Warrant to any Constable of the County; and it shall be lawful for such Constable to execute such Warrant at any Place within the County in which the Justice issuing such Warrant shall have Jurisdiction, or, in case of fresh Pursuit of an Offender, at any Place in the next adjoining County; but the Constable to whom any such Warrant shall be so addressed, shall, if the Time will permit, show or deliver the same to the Sub-Inspector or Head Constable under whose Command the said Constable shall be, who shall proceed in respect to the same according to the Acts regulating the Constabulary Force.

XXVII   Backing Warrants. Constabulary Warrants

Whenever any Warrant addressed to the Sub-Inspector of Constabulary, or to any Head or other Constable, shall be so certified and transmitted to the said Inspector General, the Manner in which it shall be backed for Execution elsewhere shall be as follows:

To any Constabulary District in Ireland:

1. Whenever it shall appear that the said Person or his Goods are to be found in any Place in Ireland (not being within the Police District of Dublin Metropolis), it shall be lawful for the said Inspector General or for either of the Deputy Inspectors General of Constabulary to indorse the said Warrant according to the Form (G c.), and to transmit the same to the Sub-Inspector who shall act for such Place, and the same shall be executed in like Manner as any Warrant addressed to him in the first instance:

To the Police District of Dublin Metropolis:

2. Whenever it shall appear that the said Person or his Goods are to be found in the Police District of Dublin Metropolis, it shall be lawful for the said Inspector General, or for either of the said Deputy Inspectors General, to indorse the said Warrant according to the Form (G c.), and to transmit the same to the Commissioners of Metropolitan Police, and the same shall be executed in like Manner as any Warrant addressed to them in the first instance:

3. [...][1]

And the said Provisions shall also apply to Cases in which the Sub-Inspector shall only certify that the Signature of the Warrant is genuine, but in which the Place where the said Person or his Goods are to be found shall appear by other Means than the said Certificate.

Amendments

1   Paragraph 3 repealed by Extradition Act 1965, Sch.

XXVIII   Warrants addressed to other Persons than the Constabulary

Whenever a Warrant shall be addressed to any other Person or Persons than the Constabulary, and it shall appear that the Person against whom the same shall have been issued or his Goods, as the Case may be, are not to be found within the County in which the Justice issuing the same shall have Jurisdiction, but in some other Place in Ireland, or in any of the Places out of Ireland herein-before mentioned, it shall be lawful for any Justice or other such Officer as aforesaid of such Place, upon Proof on Oath of the Handwriting of the Justice who shall have signed the Warrant, to indorse the same for Execution in such Place in like Manner as is herein-before provided as to any Warrant indorsed by the Inspector General of Constabulary.

XXIX   Backing Warrants from England, &c. into Ireland

[...][1]

Amendments

1   Section XXIX repealed by Extradition Act 1965, Sch.

XXX   The above Provisions to apply also to Judges Warrants

The aforesaid Provisions as to the Indorsement of Warrants shall equally apply to any Warrants for the Arrest of any Person charged with any Indictable Crime or Offence for which he is punishable by Law, whether the same shall be signed or indorsed or issued by a Justice of the Peace, or by a Judge of Her Majesty's Court of Queen's Bench, or Justices of Oyer and Terminer and General Gaol Delivery, in England or Ireland, or by the Lord Justice General, Lord Justice Clerk, or any of the Lords Commissioners of Justiciary, or by any Sheriff or Steward Depute or Substitute, in Scotland, or by the Chief or Under Secretary to the Lord Lieutenant.

XXXI   Warrants so backed to be valid for Execution;

but if the Prosecutor or Witnesses be on the Spot, Examinations may be taken.

Whenever any Warrant, addressed either to the Constabulary or to any other Person, shall be so indorsed by the said Inspector General or by either of the said Deputies Inspector General, or by any Justice or other such Officer as aforesaid, it shall be a sufficient Authority to the Person bringing such Warrant, and also to all Constables or Peace Officers of the County or Place where such Warrant shall be so indorsed, to execute the same by Arrest, Committal, or Levy, as the Case may be, within the Jurisdiction of the said Justice or Officer, and in case of a Warrant to arrest any Person, to convey him when arrested before the Justice or Officer by whom the same was issued, or before some other Justice or Officer of the same County or Place, to be dealt with according to Law: Provided always, that if the Prosecutor, or any of the Witnesses for the Prosecution, in Cases of Indictable Offences, shall then be in the County or Place where any Person shall have been arrested under any Warrant so backed as aforesaid, the Constable or other Person who shall have arrested such Person shall, if so directed by the Justice who shall have indorsed the Warrant, bring the Person so arrested before him or some other Justice of the same County or Place, who may thereupon take the Examinations of such Prosecutor or Witnesses, and proceed in every respect as herein-before directed with respect to Persons charged before a Justice with an Indictable Crime or Offence alleged to have been committed in any other County or Place than that in which such Person shall have been arrested.

XXXII   Execution of Warrants

The Manner in which Distresses and Committals under Warrants shall be made shall be as follows:

When addressed to Constabulary;

when addressed to other Persons.

1. Whenever any Warrant to levy any Penal or other Sum by Distress shall be addressed to the Constabulary, the Sums levied under it shall be accounted for, under the Provisions of the 'Fines Act, Ireland, 1851;' but whenever any such Warrant shall be addressed to any other

Person than the Constabulary, such Person shall pay over the Sum levied under it to the Person who shall appear by such Warrant to be entitled to the same, or in such other Manner, and subject to such Account of the same, as the Justices shall direct:

Distress may be sold in a certain Time

2. In every Case where a Distress shall be made under any such Warrant it shall be lawful for the Person charged with its Execution to sell the said Distress within such Period as shall be specially fixed by the said Warrant, or if no Period shall be so fixed, then within the Period of Three Days from the making of the Distress, unless the Sum for which the Warrant was issued, and also the reasonable Charges of taking and keeping the said Distress, shall be sooner paid; and in every Case where he shall sell any such Distress he shall render to the Owner the Overplus, if any, after retaining the Amount of the said Sums and Charges:

On Payment of Penalty, &c. Distress not to be levied

3. In every Case where any Person against whom any such Warrant shall be issued shall pay or tender to the Person having the Execution of the same the Sum in such Warrant mentioned, or shall produce the Receipt of the Officer of the Court for the same, and shall also pay the Amount of the Expenses of such Distress up to the Time of such Payment or Tender, such Person shall refrain from executing the same:

Distress may be sold by Auction without Licence

4. In every Case where any Sub-Inspector or Member of the Metropolitan Police Force shall be empowered to distrain any Goods under such Warrant, he may and is hereby authorized to sell or cause the same to be sold by Auction by any Head Constable of the said Constabulary Force, or by any Member of the said Metropolitan Police Force, as the Case may be, without procuring any Licence to act as an Auctioneer, and may deduct out of the Amount of such Sale all reasonable Costs and Charges actually incurred in effecting the same:

If Sum paid after Committal, Prisoner to be discharged

5. In every Case where any Person who shall be apprehended under any such Warrant shall pay or cause to be paid to the Keeper of the Gaol in which he shall be imprisoned the Sum in the Warrant mentioned, the said Keeper shall receive the same, and shall thereupon discharge such Person if he be in his Custody for no other Matter:

Gaoler to give Receipt for Prisoners

6. Whenever the Warrant shall be to commit any Prisoner to Gaol, the Head or other Constable or other Person whose Duty it shall be to convey such Prisoner to Gaol shall deliver over the said Warrant and the said Prisoner to the Keeper of the Gaol, who shall thereupon give to such Head or other Constable or other Person a Receipt for such Prisoner (Form F.), setting forth the State and Condition in which he shall have been delivered into the Custody of such Keeper:

To what Prisons Offenders shall be committed in Summary Proceedings.

7. In any Case of Summary Jurisdiction in which a Justice shall order any Person to be committed to Gaol for any Period, either in default of Payment of any Sum, or in default of Distress, or as a Punishment for any Offence, such Committal shall be to the County Gaol, District Bridewell, or House of Correction of the County in which the Party shall be arrested, unless where such Arrest shall be made in any County adjoining to that in which the Warrant shall have been issued, in which Case the Committal shall be to any of the said Prisons of such last-mentioned County; and whenever any Justices shall order any Person to be committed on account of any Adjournment of the Hearing, or until the Return of a Warrant

of Distress, or for any like temporary Purpose, such Committal shall be either to the Gaol or House of Correction, District Bridewell, or to any Bridewell or Lock-up of the County built or supported by County Presentment, according as shall appear to the Justices most convenient for that Purpose.

XXXIII   Return of unexecuted Warrants

Whenever the Person to whom any Warrant shall be so addressed, transmitted, or endorsed for Execution shall be unable to find the Person against whom such Warrant shall have been issued, or his Goods, as the Case may be, or to discover where such Person or his Goods are to be found, he shall return such Warrant to the Justices by whom the same shall have been issued within such Time as shall have been fixed by such Warrant (or within a reasonable Time where no Time shall have been so fixed), and together with it a Certificate (G a.) of the Reasons why the same shall not have been executed; and it shall be lawful for such Justice to examine such Person on Oath touching the Non-execution of such Warrant, and to re-issue the said Warrant again, or to issue any other Warrant for the same Purpose from Time to Time as shall seem expedient.

XXXIV   Recognizances. Mode of binding by Recognizance.

Whenever any Person shall be bound to appear, or to keep the Peace, it shall be done by a separate Recognizance (C.); but whenever any Person shall be bound to prosecute or to give Evidence as a Witness, it may be done either by Recognizance at Foot of his Deposition (A b.), or by a separate Recognizance at the Discretion of the Justice; and the taking of every Recognizance shall be subject to the following Provisions:

Amount of Recognizance:

1. It shall be in such Amount as the Justice shall, in his Discretion, think expedient, except in Cases of Appeal, in which the Amount shall be as herein-before provided:

To contain particular Description of Parties bound

2. It shall particularly specify the Profession, Trade, or Occupation of every Person entering into the same, together with his Christian and Surname, and the Name of the Parish and Townland or Town in which he resides, and if he resides in a Town the Name of the Street, and the Number (if any) of the House in which he resides, and whether he is Owner or Tenant thereof, or a Lodger therein:

To be in Form in Schedule

3. Every Recognizance so taken according to the Form in the Schedule to this Act, or to the like Effect, either at Foot of the Deposition or by a separate Form, shall have the like Force and Effect in binding the Lands, Tenements, Goods, and Chattels of the Persons acknowledging the same, and in all other respects, which any Recognizance now by Law has:

Recognizances to appear before Justices, or to keep the Peace, &c. to be deposited with Clerk of Petty Sessions;
and may be estreated by Justices;
after Proof on Oath of Notice to Parties.

And whenever the Condition of any such Recognizance shall be to appear at Assizes or Quarter Sessions, or at any Place other than before any Justice or Justices, or to perform the Duties of Petty Sessions Clerk, it shall be forwarded to the Clerk of the Crown or Peace as herein-before provided, and shall be liable, upon any Breach of the Condition thereof, to be estreated in the same Manner as any forfeited Recognizance to appear is now by Law liable to be estreated by the Court before which the principal Party thereto shall have been bound to appear: But whenever the Condition of such Recognizance shall be to keep the Peace, or to appear before any Justice out of Quarter Sessions, or to perform the Duties of a Pound Keeper, it shall be deposited with the Clerk of Petty Sessions of the District by the Justice by whom it shall have been taken, and upon Non-performance of the Condition thereof any Justice who may then be there present may certify on the Recognizance the Non-performance of the said Condition, and it shall thereupon be lawful for the Justices sitting at the Petty Sessions of the District, and in open Court, upon Proof of the Non-performance of the said Condition, to make an Order to estreat such Recognizance to such Amount as they shall see fit, and thereupon to issue a Warrant (E a.) to levy such Amount by Distress and Sale of the Goods of the Parties who shall have acknowledged the same: Provided always, that in every Case where any Justices shall order any such Recognizance to be estreated, Proof shall be first made on Oath that Notice in Writing (stating the general Grounds on which it is intended to sustain the Application), was left at the usual Place of Abode of the Party, or of each of the Parties if more than One, against whom it is sought to put such Recognizance in force, at least Seven Days before the Day on which the Application to estreat such Recognizance shall be made.

XXXV   Offences against this Act

Any of the Officers or Persons herein-after mentioned who shall commit any of the Offence or Neglects herein-after mentioned, and who shall be convicted thereof before any Two Justices of the County sitting at Petty Sessions, shall be liable to forfeit for every such Offence or Neglect the Penalties herein-after mentioned; (that is to say,)

Any Clerk of Petty Sessions who shall neglect or refuse to enter any Summons in the Order required under the Provisions of this Act shall be liable to a Penalty not exceeding Forty Shillings:

Any Clerk of Petty Sessions who shall demand or receive any other or different Fees, or any greater Amount of Fees, as to any Proceedings in any Case, than he can legally demand or receive under this Act, shall be liable to a Penalty not exceeding Five Pounds:

Any Person who whilst he shall hold the Office of Petty Sessions Clerk shall practise as an Attorney or Solicitor in any Case at such Petty Sessions or at the Quarter Sessions of the Division of the County in which such Petty Sessions shall be situated, or who shall act as the Clerk of any Attorney or Solicitor so practising, or as the Clerk of a Poor Law Union, or as a Collector of any Public Tax, or as a Pound Keeper, or as the Keeper or Partner in keeping any Inn or Public House, or who shall engage in any other Business or Occupation which the Justices or the Lord Lieutenant shall have forbidden as inconsistent with his Duties as Petty Sessions Clerk, shall be liable to a Penalty not exceeding Twenty Pounds:

Any Summons Server or other Person who shall make any wilful Default in serving any Summons shall be liable to a Penalty not exceeding Forty Shillings:

Any Sub-Inspector, Head or other Constable, or other Person who shall wilfully neglect to return any unexecuted Warrant at the Time required by the Justices, or who shall commit any wilful Default in respect to the Execution of the same, shall be liable to a Penalty not exceeding Five Pounds:

Any Person in whose Possession any Books, Papers, or other Effects belonging to the Justices at Petty Sessions, or relating to such Court, shall be, upon or after the Death, Resignation, Suspension, or Dismissal of any Petty Sessions Clerk, and who shall refuse to deliver up the same to the Sub-Inspector or Head Constable or other Person directed by the Justices under the Provisions of this Act to demand the same, shall be liable to a Penalty not exceeding Ten Pounds:

Any Person who shall oppose or hinder any Search under any Warrant issued by the Justices for the Discovery of any such Books, Papers, or other Effects shall be liable to a Penalty not exceeding Five Pounds:

Any Person having any other Duty to perform under the Provisions of this Act, and who shall wilfully neglect to perform the same, shall be liable to a Penalty not exceeding Five Pounds:

And it shall be lawful for the said Justices to award the said Penalties; and if the same shall be imposed upon any Member of the Constabulary Force, the Amount shall be deducted from his Pay; but if imposed on any other Person, then in default of Payment thereof forthwith, or at such Time as the Justices shall fix, such Person may be committed to Prison for the like Period, in proportion to the Amount of the Penalty imposed, for which the Justices are authorized to commit any Offender in default of Distress for any other Penalty under the Provisions of this Act.

FORMS OF PROCEDURE.

XXXVI   Forms in the Schedule to be deemed valid, and the proper Forms in all Proceedings;
but Informality not to vitiate any Proceeding.
Form of Order Book may be extended.
Warrants, &c. need not be sealed.

In all Proceedings under this Act the several Forms in the Schedule to this Act contained, or Forms to the like Effect, shall be deemed good, valid, and sufficient in Law, and shall be the proper Forms to be used, even in Cases in which other and different special Forms shall be or shall have been provided by the particular Act or Acts under which the Information or Complaint shall be made; but no Departure from any of the said first-mentioned Forms, or Omission of any of the Particulars required thereby, or Use of any other Words than those indicated in such Forms, shall vitiate or make void the Proceeding or Matter to which the same shall relate, if the Form used be otherwise sufficient in Substance and Effect, and the Words used clearly express the Intention of the Person who shall use the same; and it shall be sufficient in any of the Forms provided by this Act to state Sums of Money either in Words or Figures, according as the Person using the same shall see fit: Provided always, that it shall be lawful for the Lord Lieutenant, from Time to Time, with the Advice and Consent of the Privy Council, to extend the said Form of Order Book (D.) so far as to adapt it to any like Proceedings either new or not provided for therein: Provided also, that the Sealing of any Warrant or other Form of Procedure under this Act shall not be necessary in addition to the Signature of the Justice by whom the same shall be signed.

XXXVII   General Terms to be used in the Forms of Procedure

And with a view to simplify Forms, the Prosecutor or Party at whose Instance the Proceeding shall take place may be termed in such Forms the 'Complainant,' whether he shall be an Informant or Prosecutor or otherwise; and the Matter of the Proceeding may be termed the 'Complaint,' whether founded on an Information or otherwise; and in Summary Proceedings the Decision of the Justices may be termed their 'Order,' whether the same shall be a Conviction or otherwise.

XXXVIII Description of the Property of Partners, &c.

> **of the Property of Counties;**
> **of the Property in Goods provided for the Poor;**
> **of the Property in Materials for Roads;**
> **of the Property in Materials for Turnpike Roads, &c.**
> **of the Property of Commissioners, &c.**

It shall be sufficient, in any Information or Complaint, or the Proceedings thereon, to describe the Property belonging to or in the Possession of Partners, Joint Tenants, Parceners, or Tenants in Common, as the Property of any One of such Persons who shall be named, and of another or others, without naming them, as the Case may be; and any Work or Building made, maintained, or repaired at the Expense of any County or Place, or any Materials for the making, altering, or repairing of the same, as the Property of the Inhabitants of such County or Place respectively; and any Goods provided by Guardians of the Poor or their Officers respectively for the Use of the Poor, as the Goods of the Guardians of the Poor of the Union to which the same belong, without naming any of them; and any Materials and Tools provided for the Repair of Highways at the Expense of Baronies or other Districts in which such Highways may be situate as the Property of the County Surveyor or Surveyors respectively, without naming him or them; and any Materials or Tools provided for making or repairing any Turnpike Road, and any Buildings, Gates, Lamps, Boards, Stones, Posts, Fences, or other Things erected or provided for the Purpose of any such Turnpike Road, as the Property of the Commissioners or Trustees of such Turnpike Road, without naming them; and any Property of any Persons described in any Act of Parliament, or in any Charter or Letters of Incorporation, as Commissioners, Directors, Trustees, or by any other general Designation whatsoever, as the Property of such Commissioners, Directors, Trustees, or Persons described by such other general Designation, without naming them; and whenever it may be necessary to mention any of such Persons or Parties in any Suit, Information, or Complaint, it shall be sufficient to describe them in manner aforesaid.

XXXIX   No Objection allowed for Variance between Information and Evidence as to Time or Place of committing Offence, if Information be in Time, &c.; nor for Defect of Substance or Form in Warrant, or for Variance between it and Evidence;
but if Party charged is deceived by such Variation, &c. he may be committed or discharged upon Recognizance.

In Cases of Summary Proceedings no Variance between the Information or Complaint and the Evidence adduced in support thereof, as to the Time at which the Offence or Cause of Complaint shall be alleged to have been committed or to have arisen, shall be deemed material, if it be proved that such Information or Complaint was in fact laid or made within the Time limited by Law for laying or making the same; and any Variance between such Information or Complaint and the Evidence adduced in support thereof, as to the Place in which the same shall be alleged to have been committed or to have arisen, shall not be deemed material, provided that the said Offence or Cause be proved to have been committed or to have arisen within the Jurisdiction of the Justice or Justices by whom such Information or Compliant shall be heard and determined; and no Objection shall be taken or allowed in any Proceedings to any Information, Complaint, Summons, Warrant, or other Form of Procedure under this Act, for any alleged Defect therein in Substance or in Form, or for any

Variance between any Information, Complaint, or Summons and the Evidence adduced on the Part of the Complainant or Prosecutor at the Hearing of the Case in Summary Proceedings, or at the Examination of the Witnesses by a Justice or Justices in Proceedings for Indictable Offences: Provided always, that if any such Variance or Defect shall appear to the Justice or Justices at the Hearing to be such that the Defendant has been thereby deceived or misled, it shall be lawful for such Justice or Justices, upon such Terms as he or they shall think fit, to adjourn the Hearing of the Case to some future Day, and in the meantime, in Cases of Proceedings for Offences, to commit the said Defendant to Gaol, or to discharge him, upon his entering into a Recognizance conditioned for his Appearance at the Time and Place to which such Hearing shall be so adjourned.

XL   Miscellaneous. No Stamps on Receipts

[…]¹

Amendments

1   Section 40 repealed by Finance Act 1998, s 125 and Sch 8.

XLI   Act not to extend to Police District of Dublin Metropolis

Nothing in this Act shall extend to the Police District of Dublin Metropolis, or alter or affect in any Manner whatsoever any of the Provisions or Enactments contained in any Act regulating the Powers and Duties of Justices of the Peace or of the Police of the District of Dublin Metropolis, or be deemed applicable in any way to the same, save so far as relates to the backing or executing of any Warrants, or to alter the Provisions of any Act or Acts whereby any Part of any County is annexed for the Purpose of Criminal Proceedings to any other County, or whereby any Offences committed in One County are authorized to be tried in any other County.

XLII   Act shall not extend to Revenue, &c. Cases

[…]¹

Amendments

1   Section XLII repleaced by Finance Act 1991, s 125 and Sch 4.

XLIII   Repeal of following Statutes from 1st Nov. 1851.

> 7 & 8 G. 4. c. 67.
> 6 & 7 W. 4. c. 34.
> 12 & 13 Vict. c. 70.
> 12 & 13 Vict. c. 69.

The following Acts and Parts of Acts, so far as the same relate to Ireland, shall, from and after the First Day of November One thousand eight hundred and fifty-one, be and the same are hereby repealed; that is to say, an Act passed in the Seventh and Eighth Years of the Reign of King George the Fourth, intituled Fourth, intituled An Act for the better Administration of Justice at the holding of Petty Sessions by Justices of the Peace in Ireland, so far as relates to any Proceedings by Justices in or out of Petty Sessions; and an Act passed in the Sixth and Seventh Years of King William the Fourth, intituled An Act to amend an Act passed in the Seventh and Eighth Years of the Reign of His Majesty King George the Fourth, for the better Administration of Justice at the holding of Petty Sessions by Justices of the Peace in Ireland, so far as relates to any Proceedings by Justices in or out of Petty Sessions; and an Act passed in the Twelfth and Thirteenth Years of the Reign of Her present Majesty, intituled An Act to facilitate the Performance of the Duties of Justices of the Peace out of Quarter Sessions in Ireland, with respect to Persons charged with Indictable Offences; and an Act passed in the Twelfth and Thirteenth Years of the Reign of Her present Majesty, intituled An Act to facilitate the Performance of the Duties of Justices of the Peace out of Quarter Sessions in Ireland, with respect to Summary Convictions and Orders; and all other Act or Acts or Parts of Acts which are inconsistent with the Provisions of this Act, except as to Proceedings now pending to which the same or any of them are applicable.

XLIV   Interpretation of Terms

In the Interpretation of this Act and of the Schedules thereto annexed, save where there is anything in the Subject or Context repugnant to such Construction, the Word 'County' shall be deemed to include 'County of a City,' 'County of a Town,' or 'Riding of a County,' as the Case may be; the Expression 'Summary Jurisdiction' shall be deemed to mean any Case as to which a Summary Conviction or Order may be made by a Justice or Justices out of Quarter Sessions; and 'Summary Proceedings' shall mean any Proceedings in respect to such Case; the Word 'Complaint' shall include 'Information,' and 'Complainant' shall include 'Informant' or 'Prosecutor;' the Word 'Order' shall include 'Conviction;' the Words 'Lord Lieutenant' shall include any other 'Chief Governor or Governors of Ireland;' the Word 'Quarter Sessions' shall include any General Sessions of the Peace for the County; the Word 'Justice' shall mean 'Justice of the Peace,' and shall include the 'Chief Magistrate' for the Time being or the 'Borough Justices' of any Corporate Town; the Word 'Constabulary' shall mean the Constabulary Force of Ireland; the Words 'proper Officer of the Recorder's Court' shall mean the Town Clerk where there shall be a Town Clerk, and where there shall be no Town Clerk, the Person whose Duty it shall be to make Entries of the Proceedings; the Word 'Month' shall mean 'Calendar Month;' the Word 'Gaol' shall include any 'House of Correction' or 'Bridewell,' or other 'Place' of Imprisonment of the County; the Word 'Keeper of the Gaol' shall include 'Bridewell Keeper,' or the Keeper or Governor of any other Prison; the Word 'Goods' shall include 'Chattels;' and the Word 'Oath' shall include, 'Affirmation' or 'solemn Declaration,' as the Case may be; and the References in this Act by Letters to the Forms to be used shall be to the Forms in the Schedule to this Act annexed.

XLV   Short Title of Act

In citing this Act in other Acts of Parliament, or in any legal or other Instruments or Proceedings, it shall be sufficient to use the Expression 'The Petty Sessions (Ireland) Act, 1851.'

XLVI   Commencement of Act

The First and Second Sections of this Act shall commence and take effect upon the passing of the Act, and the other Sections of the Act shall commence and take effect upon the First Day of November One thousand eight hundred and fifty-one.

XLVII   Act to extend to Ireland only, and not to affect Queen's Bench Jurisdiction

This Act shall extend and be construed to extend to Ireland only, save and except the several Provisions herein-before contained respecting the backing and Execution of Warrants and the taking of Examinations; and nothing in this Act shall be deemed to alter or affect the Jurisdiction or Practice of the Court of Queen's Bench in Ireland.

XLVIII

Schedule to be Part of Act

The Schedule to this Act annexed shall be deemed to be Part of this Act.

SCHEDULE

Forms; (A.)—Proofs.

(A a.) Information.

(A b.) Deposition of a Witness.

(A c.) Statement of the Accused.

(A d.) Solemn Declaration.

Forms (B.)—Process to enforce Appearance.

(B a.) Summons.

(B b.) Warrant to arrest.

Form (C.) Recognizance (to appear, &c.)

Form (D.)—Order Book.

Forms (E.)—Warrants.

(E a.) Warrant of Execution (Summary Jurisdiction).

(E b.) Warrant to commit (or detain) for Trial, &c.

(E c.) Warrant to convey before a Justice of another County.

(E d.) Warrant to discharge from Gaol.

(E e.) Warrant to search.

Form (F.)—Receipt for Prisoner.

Forms (G.)—Indorsements on Warrants.

Form (H.)—Appeal.

Forms (I.)—Certificates.

(I a) Certificate of Order.

(I b) Of Indictment being found.

(I c) Of Consent to Bail.

Summary Jurisdiction Act 1857

C A P XLIII

An Act to improve the Administration of the Law so far as respects summary Proceedings before Justices of the Peace. [17th August 1857.]

WHEREAS it is expedient that Provision should be made for obtaining the Opinion of a Superior Court on Questions of Law which arise in the Exercise of Summary Jurisdiction by Justices of the Peace: Be it enacted by the Queen's most Excellent Majesty, by and with the Advice and Consent of the Lords Spiritual and Temporal, and Commons, in this present Parliament assembled, and by the Authority of the same, as follows:

I   Interpretation of Terms

In the Interpretation and for the Purposes of this Act, the following Words shall have the Meaning herein-after assigned to them; that is to say,

> "Superior Courts of Law" shall for England mean the Supreme Courts of Law at Westminster, and for Ireland the Supreme Courts at Law at Dublin
>
> "Court of Queen's Bench" shall mean for England the Court of Queen's Bench at Westminster, and for Ireland the Court of Queen's Bench at Dublin.

II   Justices on Application of a Party aggrieved to state a Case for the Opinion of Superior Court.

After the Hearing and Determination by a Justice or Justices of the Peace of any Information or Complaint which he or they have Power to determine in a summary Way, by any Law now in force or hereafter to be made, either Party to the Proceeding before the said Justice or Justices may, if dissatisfied with the said Determination as being erroneous in point of Law, apply in Writing within [fourteen days][1] after the same to the said Justice or Justices, to state and sign a Case setting forth the Facts and the Grounds of such Determination, for the Opinion thereon of One of the Superior Courts of Law to be named by the Party applying; and such Party, herein-after called "the Appellant," shall, within [fourteen days][1] after receiving such Case [or such longer period as may be provided for by Rules of Court][2], transmit the same to the Court named in his Application, first giving Notice in Writing of such Appeal, with a Copy of the Case so stated and signed, to the other Party to the Proceeding in which the Determination was given, herein-after called "the Respondent."

Amendments

1   Section 2 extended by the Courts (Supplemental Provisions) Act 1961, s 51 which provides as follows:

> '(1) Section 2 of the Summary Jurisdiction Act, 1857, is hereby extended so as to enable any party to any proceedings whatsoever heard and determined by a justice of the District Court (other than proceedings relating to an indictable offence which was not dealt with summarily by the court) if dissatisfied with such determination as being erroneous on a point of law, to apply in writing within fourteen days after such determination to the said justice to state and sign a case setting forth the facts and the grounds of such determination for the opinion thereon of the High Court.

(2) Upon the making of an application under section 2 of the Summary Jurisdiction Act, 1857, as extended by subsection (1) of this section, for a case stated, the determination in respect of which the application is made shall be suspended—

(a)   where the justice of the District Court to whom the application is made grants the application, until the case stated has been heard and determined, and

(b)   where he refuses to grant the application, until he so refuses.

(3) The references in sections 6, 8, 9, 10 and, 14 of the Summary Jurisdiction Act, 1857, to that Act shall be construed as references to that Act as extended by subsection (1) of this section.

(4) In section 2 of the Summary Jurisdiction Act, 1857, and in this section, "party" means any person who was, entitled to be heard and was heard in the proceedings in which the determination in respect of which an application for a case stated is made was given.'

2   Words "or such longer period as may be provided for by Rules of Court" inserted by Criminal Justice (Miscellaneous) Provisions Act 2009, s 45.

2A   (1) Notice in writing of an appeal and a copy of the case stated and signed, required by section 2 (as extended by section 51 of the Courts (Supplemental Provisions) Act 1961 and amended by section 45 of the Criminal Justice (Miscellaneous Provisions) Act 2009) of this Act to be given to any other party to the proceedings may, subject to subsection (2), be so given—

(a)   by delivering it to him or her or to his or her solicitor,

(b)   by addressing it to him or her and leaving it at his or her usual or last known residence or place of business or by addressing it to his or her solicitor and leaving it at the solicitor's office,

(c)   by sending it by registered post to him or her at his or her usual or last known residence or place of business or to his or her solicitor at the solicitor's office, or

(d)   in the case of a body corporate, by delivering it, or sending it by registered post, to the secretary or any other officer of the body at its registered or principal office.

(2) Notice in writing of an appeal and a copy of the case stated and signed, required by section 2 (as so extended and amended) of this Act to be given to any other party to the proceeding shall, if that party is not represented by a solicitor be given personally to him or her.

(3) For the purposes of subsections (1) and (2) the solicitor retained to appear on behalf of any party at the hearing and determination of the information or complaint shall be deemed to continue to be retained on his or her behalf unless the Court has otherwise been advised.

Amendments

1   Section 2A inserted by Criminal Justice (Miscellaneous Provisions) Act 2009, s 46.

III   Security and Notice to be given by the Appellant

The Appellant, at the Time of making such Application, and before a Case shall be stated and delivered to him by the Justice or Justices, shall in every Instance enter into a Recognizance, before such Justice or Justices, or any One or more of them, or any other Justice exercising the same Jurisdiction, with or without Surety or Sureties, and in such Sum as to the Justice or Justices shall seem meet, conditioned to prosecute without Delay such Appeal, and to submit to the Judgment of the Superior Court, and pay such Costs as may be awarded by the same; and the Appellant shall at the same Time, and before he shall be entitled to have the Case delivered to him, pay to the Clerk to the said Justice or Justices his Fees for and in respect of the Case and Recognizances, and any other Fees to which such Clerk shall be entitled, [...]¹; and the Appellant, if then in Custody, shall be liberated upon the Recognizance being further conditioned for his Appearance before the same Justice or Justices, or, if that is impracticable, before some other Justice or Justices exercising the same Jurisdiction who shall be then sitting, within Ten Days after the Judgment of the Superior Court shall have been given, to abide such Judgment, unless the Determination appealed against be reversed.

Amendments

1   Words repealed by Criminal Justice Administration Act 1914, s 44 and Sch 4.

IV   Justices may refuse a Case where they think the Application frivolous

If the Justice or Justices be of opinion that the Application is merely frivolous, but not otherwise, he or they may refuse to state a Case, and shall, on the Request of the Appellant, sign and deliver to him a Certificate of such Refusal; provided, that the Justice or Justices shall not refuse to state a Case where Application for that Purpose is made to them by or under the Direction of Her Majesty's Attorney General for England or Ireland, as the Case may be.

V   Where the Justices refuse, the Court of Queen's Bench may by Rule order a Case to be stated

Where the Justice or Justices shall refuse to state a Case as aforesaid, it shall be lawful for the Appellant to apply to the Court of Queen's Bench upon an Affidavit of the Facts for a Rule calling upon such Justice or Justices, and also upon the Respondent, to show Cause why such Case should not be stated; and the said Court may make the same absolute or discharge it, with or without Payment of Costs, as to the Court shall seem meet, and the Justice or Justices upon being served with such Rule Absolute, shall state a Case accordingly, upon the Appellant entering into such Recognizance as is herein-before provided.

VI   Superior Court to determine the Questions on the Case

Its Decisions to be final

The Court to which a Case is transmitted under this Act shall hear and determine the Question or Questions of Law arising thereon, and shall thereupon reverse, affirm, or amend the Determination in respect of which the Case has been stated, or remit the Matter to the Justice or Justices, with the Opinion of the Court thereon, or may make such other Order in relation to the Matter, and may make such Orders as to Costs, as to the Court may seem fit; and all such Orders shall be final and conclusive on all Parties: Provided always, that no Justice or Justices of the Peace who shall state and deliver a Case in pursuance of this Act shall be liable to any Costs in respect or by reason of such Appeal against his or their Determination.

VII   Case may be sent back for Amendment

The Court for the Opinion of which a Case is stated shall Case may e have Power, if they think fit, to cause the Case to be sent back for Amendment, and thereupon the same shall be amended accordingly, and Judgment shall be delivered after it shall have been amended.

VIII   Powers of Superior Court may be exercised by a Judge at Chambers

The Authority and Jurisdiction hereby vested in a Superior Court for the Opinion of which a Case is stated under this Act shall and may (subject to any Rules and Orders of such Court in relation thereto) be exercised by a Judge of such Court sitting in Chambers, and as well in Vacation as in Term Time.

IX   After the Decision of Superior Court, Justices may issue Warrants

After the Decision of the Superior Court in relation to any Case stated for their Opinion under this Act, the Justice or Justices in relation to whose Determination the Case has been stated, or any other Justice or Justices of the Peace exercising the same Jurisdiction, shall have the same Authority to enforce any Conviction or Order, which may have been affirmed, amended, or made by such Superior Court, as the Justice or Justices who originally decided the Case would have had to enforce his or their Determination if the same had not been appealed against; and no Action or Proceeding whatsoever shall be commenced or had against the Justice or Justices for enforcing such Conviction or Order, by reason of any Defect in the same respectively.

X   Certiorari not to be required for Proceedings under this Act

No Writ of Certiorari or other Writ shall be required for the Removal of any Conviction, Order, or other Determination in relation to which a Case is stated under this Act, or otherwise, for obtaining the Judgment or Determination of the Superior Court on such Case under this Act.

XI   Superior Courts may make Rules for Proceedings.

The Superior Courts of Law may from Time to Time, and as often as they shall see Occasion, make and alter Rules and Orders to regulate the Practice and Proceedings in reference to the Cases herein-before mentioned.

XII   "Justices" to include a Stipendiary Magistrate

The Words "Justice or Justices" in this Act shall include a Magistrate of the Police Courts of the Metropolis and any Stipendiary Magistrate.

XIII   Recognizances how to be enforced

In all Cases where the Conditions, or any of them, in the said Recognizance mentioned, shall not have been complied with, the Justice or Justices who shall have taken the same, or any other Justice or Justices, shall certify upon the Back of the Recognizance

36

in what respect the Conditions thereof have not been observed, and transmit the same to the Clerk of the Peace of the County, Riding, Division, Liberty, City, Borough, or Place within which such Recognizance shall have been taken, to be proceeded upon in like Manner as other Recognizances forfeited at Quarter Sessions may now by Law be enforced, and such Certificate shall be deemed sufficient *prima facie* Evidence of the said Recognizance haying been forfeited: Provided, that where any such Recognizances shall have been taken in *England* before a Magistrate of the Police Courts of the Metropolis, or by any Stipendiary Magistrate, all Sums of Money in which any Person or Persons shall be therein bound may, if the said Magistrate shall think fit, be levied, upon such Recognizance being forfeited, and on Nonpayment thereof, together with the Costs of the Proceedings to enforce such Payment, in the same Manner as a, Police Magistrate of the Metropolis is now empowered to recover any Penalty, Forfeiture, or Sum of Money, by Section Forty-five of an Act passed in the Second and Third Years of the Reign of Her present Majesty, intituled An Act for regulating the Police Courts in the Metropolis, and that all and every the Provisions and Enactments contained in the said Section Forty-five shall extend to and be applicable to this Act, in as ample a Manner as if they had been herein reenacted and made Part of the same.

XIV   Appellants under this Act not allowed to appeal to the Quarter Sessions

Any Person who shall appeal under the Provisions of this Act against any Determination of a Justice or Justices of the Peace to from which he is by Law entitled, to appeal to the Quarter Sessions shall be taken to have abandoned such last-mentioned Right of Appeal, finally and conclusively, and to all Intents and Purposes.

XV   Extent of Act

This Act shall not extend to Scotland,

SCHEDULE (A.)
FEES TO BE TAKEN BY CLERKS TO JUSTICES

Amendments

1   Sch A repealed by Criminal Justice Administration Act 1914, s 44 and Sch 4.

Offences Against the Persons Act 1861

C A P C

An Act to consolidate and amend the Statute Law of England and Ireland relating to Offences against the Person [6th August 1861.]

WHEREAS it is expedient to consolidate and amend the Statute Law of England and Ireland relating to Offences against the Person: Be it enacted by the Queen's most Excellent Majesty, by and with the Advice and Consent of the Lords Spiritual and Temporal, and Commons, in this present Parliament assembled, and by the Authority of the same, as follows:

HOMICIDE

1   [...]¹

Amendments

1   Section 1 repealed by Criminal Justice Act 1990, s 9 and Sch 2. Repeal of s 1 shall not affect the operation of ss 64 to 68 of this Act.

---

2   [...]¹

Amendments

1   Section 2 repealed by Criminal Justice Act 1990, s 9 and Sch 2.

---

3   [...]¹

Amendments

1   Section 3 repealed by Criminal Justice Act 1990, s 9 and Sch 2.

---

4   **Conspiring or soliciting to commit Murder**

All Persons who shall conspire, confederate, and agree to murder any Person, whether, he be a Subject of Her Majesty or not, and whether he be within the Queen's Dominions or not, and whosoever shall solicit, encourage, persuade, or endeavour to persuade, or shall propose to any Person, to murder any other Person, whether he be a Subject of Her Majesty or not, and whether he be within the Queen's Dominions or not, shall be guilty of a Misdemeanor, and being convicted thereof shall be liable, at the Discretion of the Court, to be kept in Penal

Servitude for any Term not more than Ten and not less than Three Years, or to be imprisoned for any Term not exceeding Two Years, with or without Hard Labour.

5   Manslaughter

Whosoever shall be convicted of Manslaughter shall be liable, at the Discretion of the Court, to be kept in Penal Servitude for Life or for any Term not less than Three Years,—or to be imprisoned for any Term not exceeding Two Years, with or without Hard Labour, or to pay such Fine as the Court shall award, in addition to or without any such other discretionary Punishment as aforesaid.

6   [...]¹

Amendments

1   Section 6 repealed by Criminal Justice (Administration) Act 1924, s 16 and Sch 2.

7   [...]¹

Amendments

1   Section 7 repealed by Criminal Law Act 1997, s 16 and Sch 3.

8   [...]¹

Amendments

1   Section 8 repealed by Criminal Law Act 1997, s 16 and Sch 3.

9   Murder or Manslaughter abroad

Where any Murder or Manslaughter shall be committed on Land out of the United Kingdom, whether within the Queen's Dominions or without, and whether the Person killed were a Subject of Her Majesty or not, every Offence committed by any Subject of Her Majesty, in respect of any such Case, whether the same shall amount to the Offence of Murder or of Manslaughter, [...]¹, may be dealt with, inquired of, tried, determined, and punished in any County or Place in England or Ireland in which such Person shall be apprehended or be in Custody, in the same Manner in all respects as if such Offence had been actually committed in that County or Place; provided that nothing herein contained shall prevent any Person from being tried in any Place out of England or Ireland for any Murder or Manslaughter committed out of England or Ireland, in the same Manner as such Person might have been tried before the passing of this Act.

Amendments

1   Words repealed by Criminal Law Act 1997, s 16 and Sch 3.

10   Provision for the Trial of Murder and Manslaughter where the Death or Cause of Death only happens in England or Ireland

Where any Person, being feloniously stricken, poisoned, or otherwise hurt upon the Sea, or at any Place out of England or Ireland, shall die of such Stroke, Poisoning, or Hurt in England or Ireland, or, being feloniously stricken, poisoned, or otherwise hurt at any Place in England or Ireland, shall die of such Stroke, Poisoning, or Hurt upon the Sea, or at any Place out of England or Ireland, every Offence committed in respect of any such Case, whether the same shall amount to the Offence of Murder or of Manslaughter, [...],[1] may be dealt with, inquired of, tried, determined, and punished in the County or Place in England or Ireland in which such Death, Stroke, Poisoning, or Hurt shall happen, in the same Manner in all respects as if such Offence had been wholly committed in that County or Place.

Amendments

1   Words repealed by Criminal Law Act 1997, s 16 and Sch 3.

ATTEMPTS TO MURDER

11–15   [...][1]

Amendments

1   Sections 11 to 15 repealed by Criminal Law Act 1997, s 16 and Sch 3.

LETTERS THREATENING TO MURDER

16–34   [...][1]

Amendments

1   Sections 16 to 26 repealed by Non-Fatal Offences Against the Person Act 1997, s 31 and Sch 3.

Section 27 repealed by Children Act 2001, Sch 2.

Sections 28 to 34 repealed by Non-Fatal Offences Against the Person Act 1997, Sch 3.

35   Drivers of Carriages injuring Persons by Furious Driving

Whosoever, having the Charge of any Carriage or Vehicle, shall, by wanton or furious Driving or Racing, or other wilful Misconduct, or by wilful Neglect, do or cause to be done any bodily Harm to any Person whatsoever, shall be guilty of a Misdemeanor, and being convicted thereof shall be liable, at the Discretion of the Court, to be imprisoned for any Term not exceeding Two Years, with or without Hard Labour.

ASSAULTS

36–40   […]¹

Amendments

1   Sections 36 and 37 repealed by Non-Fatal Offences Against the Person Act 1997, Sch 3.

Section 38 repealed by Criminal Justice (Public Order) Act 1994.

Sections 39 and 40 repealed by Non-Fatal Offences Against the Person Act 1997, Sch 3.

41   Assaults arising from Combination

Whosoever, in pursuance of any unlawful Combination or Conspiracy to raise the Rate of Wages, or of any unlawful Combination or Conspiracy respecting any Trade, Business, or Manufacture, or respecting any Person concerned or employed therein, shall unlawfully assault any Person, shall be guilty of a Misdemeanor, and being convicted thereof shall be liable, at the Discretion of the Court, to be imprisoned for any Term not exceeding Two Years, with or without Hard Labour.

42–47   […]¹

Amendments

1   Section 42 repealed by Non-Fatal Offences Against the Person Act 1997, Sch 3.

Sections 43 to 45 repealed by Criminal Justice Act 1951, Sch 2.

Sections 46 and 47 repealed by Non-Fatal Offences Against the Person Act 1997, Sch 3.

RAPE, ABDUCTION, AND DEFILEMENT OF WOMEN

48   Rape

Whosoever shall be convicted of the Crime of Rape shall guilty of Felony, and being convicted thereof shall be liable, at the Discretion of the Court, to be kept in Penal Servitude for Life or for any Term not less than Three Years, or to be imprisoned for any Term not exceeding Two Years, with or without Hard Labour.

49 Procuring the Defilement of Girl under Age

Whosoever shall, by false Pretences, false Representations, or other fraudulent Means, procure any Woman or Girl under the Age of Twenty-one Years to have illicit carnal Connexion with any Man, shall be guilty of a Misdemeanor, and being convicted thereof shall be liable, at the Discretion of the Court, to be imprisoned for any Term not exceeding Two Years, with or without Hard Labour.

50 Carnally knowing a Girl under Ten Years of Age

Whosoever shall unlawfully and carnally know and abuse any Girl under the Age of Ten Years shall be guilty of Felony, and being convicted thereof shall be liable, at the Discretion of the Court, to be kept in Penal Servitude for Life or for any Term not less than Three Years,—or to be imprisoned for any Term not exceeding Two Years, with or without Hard Labour.

51 Carnally knowing a Girl between the Ages of Ten and Twelve.

Whosoever shall unlawfully and carnally know and abuse any Girl being above the Age of Ten Years and under the Age of 10 and Twelve Years shall be guilty of a Misdemeanor, and being convicted thereof shall be liable, at the Discretion of the Court, to be kept in Penal Servitude for the Term of Three Years, or to be imprisoned for any Term not exceeding Two Years, with or without Hard Labour.

52 [...][1]

Amendments

1 Section 52 repealed by Criminal Law (Amendment) Act 1935 and again by Criminal Law (Rape) Act 1981.

53–56 [...][1]

Amendments

1 Section 53 to 56 repealed by Non-Fatal Offences Against the Person Act 1997, Sch 3.

BIGAMY

57 Bigamy. Offence may be dealt with where Offender shall be apprehended Not to extend to Second Marriages, &c. herein stated.

Whosoever, being married, shall marry any other Person during the Life of the former Husband or Wife, whether the Second Marriage shall have taken place in England or Ireland or elsewhere, shall be guilty of Felony, and being convicted thereof shall be liable, at the

Discretion of the Court, to be kept in Penal Servitude for any Term not exceeding Seven Years and not less than Three Years,—or to be imprisoned for any Term not exceeding Two Years, with or without Hard Labour; and any such Offence may be dealt with, inquired of, tried, determined, and punished in any County or Place in England or Ireland where the Offender shall be apprehended or be in Custody, in the same Manner in all respects as if the Offence had been actually committed in that County or Place: Provided that nothing in this Section contained shall extend to any Second Marriage contracted elsewhere than in England and Ireland by any other than a Subject of Her Majesty, or to any Person marrying a Second Time whose Husband or Wife shall have been continually absent from such Person for the Space of Seven Years then last past, and shall not have been known by such Person to be living within that Time, or shall extend to any Person who, at the Time of such Second Marriage, shall have been divorced from the Bond of the First Marriage, or to any Person whose former Marriage shall have been declared void by the Sentence of any Court of Competent Jurisdiction.

ATTEMPTS TO PROCURE ABORTION

58   Administering Drugs or using Instruments to procure Abortion.

Every Woman, being with Child, who, with Intent to procure her own Miscarriage, shall unlawfully administer to herself any Poison or other noxious Thing, or shall unlawfully use any Instrument or other Means whatsoever with the like Intent, and whosoever, with Intent to procure the Miscarriage of any Woman, whether she be or be not with Child, shall unlawfully administer to her or cause to be taken by her any Poison or other noxious Thing, or shall unlawfully use any Instrument or other Means whatsoever with the like Intent, shall be guilty of Felony, and being convicted thereof shall be liable, at the Discretion of the Court, to be kept in Penal Servitude for Life or for any Term not less than Three Years, or to be imprisoned for any Term not exceeding Two Years, with or without Hard Labour, and with or without Solitary Confinement.

59   Procuring Drugs, &c. to cause Abortion

Whosoever shall unlawfully supply or procure any Poison or other noxious Thing, or any Instrument or Thing whatsoever, knowing that the same is intended to be unlawfully used or employed with Intent to procure the Miscarriage of any Woman, whether she be or be not with Child, shall be guilty of a Misdemeanor, and being convicted thereof shall be liable, at the Discretion of the Court, to be kept in Penal Servitude for the Term of Three Years, or to be imprisoned for any Term not exceeding Two Years, with or without Hard Labour.

CONCEALING THE BIRTH OF A CHILD

60   Concealing the Birth of a Child

If any Woman shall be delivered of a Child, every Person who shall, by any secret Disposition of the dead Body of the said Child, whether such Child died before, at, or after its Birth, endeavour to conceal the Birth thereof, shall be guilty of a Misdemeanor, and being convicted thereof shall be liable, at the Discretion of the Court, to be imprisoned for any Term not exceeding Two Years, with or without Hard Labour: Provided that if any Person tried for the Murder of any Child shall be acquitted thereof, it shall be lawful for the Jury by whose Verdict such Person shall be acquitted to find, in case it shall so appear in Evidence, that the Child had recently been born, and that such Person did, by some secret Disposition of the dead Body of such Child, endeavour to conceal the Birth thereof, and thereupon the Court may pass such Sentence as if such Person had been convicted upon an Indictment for the Concealment of the Birth.

Note

Infanticide Act 1949, s 1(4) provides that "Section 60 of the Offences Against the Person Act 1861, shall have effect as if the reference therein to the murder of any child included a reference to infanticide."

UNNATURAL OFFENCES

61   Sodomy and Bestiality

Whosoever shall be convicted of the abominable Crime of Buggery, committed either with Mankind or with any Animal, shall be liable, at the Discretion of the Court, to be kept in Penal Servitude for Life or for any Term not less than Ten Years.[1]

Amendments

1   Section 61 repealed by Criminal Law (Sexual Offences) Act 1993 (save in so far as it applies to buggery or attempted buggery with animals).

62   Attempt to commit an infamous Crime

Whosoever shall attempt to commit the said abominable Crime, or shall be guilty of any Assault with Intent to commit the same, [...][1], shall be guilty of a Misdemeanor, and being convicted thereof shall be liable, at the Discretion of the Court, to be kept in Penal Servitude for any Term not exceeding Ten Years and not less than Three Years, or to be imprisoned for any Term not exceeding Two Years, with or without Hard Labour.[2]

Amendments

1   Words repealed by Criminal Law (Rape) (Amendment) Act 1990, s 21 and Sch.
2   Section 62 repealed by Criminal Law (Sexual Offences) Act 1993 (save in so far as it applies to buggery or attempted buggery with animals).

63   Carnal Knowledge defined

Whenever, upon the Trial for any Offence punishable under this Act, it may be necessary to prove carnal Knowledge, it shall not be necessary to prove the actual Emission of Seed in order to constitute a carnal Knowledge, but the carnal Knowledge shall be deemed complete upon Proof of Penetration only.

64–65   [...]¹

Amendments

1   Section 64 to 65 repealed by Non-Fatal Offences Against the Person Act 1997.

66–67   [...]¹

Amendments

1   Sections 66 and 67 repealed by Criminal Law Act 1997, Sch 3.

68   Offences committed within the Jurisdiction of the Admiralty

All indictable Offences mentioned in this Act which shall be committed within the Jurisdiction of the Admiralty of England or Ireland shall be [...]¹ liable to the same Punishments as if they had been committed upon the Land in England or Ireland, and may be dealt with, inquired of, tried, and determined in any County or Place in England or Ireland in which the Offender shall be apprehended or be in Custody, in the same Manner in all respects as if they had been actually committed in that County or Place; and in any Indictment for any such Offence, or for being an Accessory to such an Offence, the Venue in the Margin shall be the same as if the Offence had been committed in such County or Place, and the Offence shall be averred to have been committed "on the High Seas:" Provided that nothing herein contained shall alter or affect any of the Laws relating to the Government of Her Majesty's Land or Naval Forces.

Amendments

1   Words repealed by Criminal Law Act 1997, Sch 3.

69   Hard Labour in Gaol or House of Correction

Whenever Imprisonment, with or without Hard Labour, may be awarded for any indictable Offence under this Act, the Court boar may sentence the Offender to be imprisoned, or to be imprisoned kept to Hard Labour, in the Common Gaol or House of Correction.

70   [...]¹

Amendments

1   Section 70 repealed by Criminal Law Act 1997, Sch 3.

---

71   Fine, and Sureties for keeping the Peace; in what Cases.

Whenever any Person shall be convicted of any indictable Misdemeanor punishable under this Act, the Court may, if it shall think fit, in addition to or in lieu of any Punishment by this Act authorized, [...]¹, and require him to enter into his own Recognizances, and to find Sureties, both or either, for keeping the Peace and being of good Behaviour; [...]¹; provided that no Person shall be imprisoned for not finding Sureties under this Clause for any Period exceeding One Year.

Amendments

1   Words repealed by Criminal Law Act 1997, Sch 3.

---

72   No Certiorari, &c.

No summary Conviction under this Act shall be quashed for Want of Form, or be removed by Certiorari into any of Her Majesty's Superior Courts of Record; and no Warrant of Commitment shall be held void by reason of any Defect therein, provided it be therein alleged that the Party has been convicted, and there be a good and valid Conviction to sustain the same.

73   [...]¹

Amendments

1   Section 73 repealed by Non-Fatal Offences Against the Person Act 1997, Sch 3.

74–75   [...]¹

Amendments

1   Sections 74 and 75 repealed by Criminal Law Act 1997.

---

76 **Summary Proceedings in England may be under the 11 & 12 Vict. c. 43., and in Ireland under the 14 & 15 Vict. c. 93**

Except in London and the Metropolitan Police District

Every Offence hereby made punishable on summary Conviction may be prosecuted in England in the Manner directed by the Act of the Session holden in the Eleventh and Twelfth Years of Queen Victoria, Chapter Forty-three, and may be prosecuted in Ireland before Two or more Justices of the Peace, or One Metropolitan or Stipendiary Magistrate, in the Manner directed by the Act of the Session holden in the Fourteenth and Fifteenth Years of Queen Victoria, Chapter Ninety-three, or in such other Manner as may be directed by any Act that may be passed for like Purposes; and all Provisions contained in the said Acts shall be applicable to such Prosecutions in the same Manner as if they were incorporated in this Act: Provided that nothing in this Act contained shall in any Manner alter or affect any Enactment now in force relating to Procedure, in the Case of any Offence punishable on summary Conviction, within the City of London or the Metropolitan Police District, or the Recovery or Application of any Penalty or Forfeiture for any such Offence.

77 [...]¹

Amendments

1 Section 77 repealed by Criminal Law Act 1997.

---

78 **Act not to extend to Scotland.**

Nothing in this Act contained shall extend to Scotland, except as herein-before otherwise expressly provided.

79 **Commencement of Act**

This Act shall commence and take effect on the First Day of November One thousand eight hundred and sixty-one.

Explosives Act 1875

c 17 38_and_39_Vict

ARRANGEMENTS OF CLAUSES

Clause

PRELIMINARY

1. Short title.

2. Commencement of Act.

3. Substances to which this Act applies.

PART I
LAW RELATING TO GUNPOWDER

GENERAL LAW AS TO MANUFACTURE AND KEEPING OF GUNPOWDER.

4. Gunpowder to be manufactured only at factory lawfully existing or licensed under this Act.

5. Gunpowder (except for private use) to be kept only in existing or new magazine or store, or in registered premises.

LICENSING OF FACTORIES AND MAGAZINES FOR GUNPOWDER.

6. Application for license for new factory or magazine.

7. Application for assent of local authority to site of new factory or magazine.

8. Grant and confirmation of license.

REGULATION OF FACTORIES AND MAGAZINES FOR GUNPOWDER.

9. Regulation of factories and magazines for gunpowder.

10. General rules for factories and magazines.

11. Special rules, for regulation of workmen in factory or magazine.

SUPPLEMENTAL AS TO FACTORIES AND MAGAZINES FOR GUNPOWDER.

12. Alteration of terms of license and enlargement of factory or magazine.

13. Devolution and determination of license.

APPLICATION OF ACT TO EXISTING FACTORIES AND MAGAZINES FOR GUNPOWDER.

14. Continuing certificate for existing factories and magazines.

CONSUMERS STORES FOR GUNPOWDER.

LICENSING AND REGULATION OF STORES.

15. Store license to be obtained from local authority.

16. Order in Council prescribing situation and construction of stores.

17. General rules for stores.

18. Non-transferability, renewal, and forms of store licenses.

19. Special rules for regulation of workmen in stores.

APPLICATION OF ACT TO EXISTING STORES FOR. GUNPOWDER.

20. Definition of and continuing certificate for existing stores which are to be subject to this Act.

RETAIL DEALING WITH GUNPOWDER.
REGISTRATION AND REGULATION OF REGISTERED PREMISES.

21. Registration of premises with local authority.

22. General rules for registered premises.

SUPPLEMENTAL PROVISIONS.

23. Precautions against fire or explosion to be taken by occupier.

24. Explanation as to quantities of gunpowder allowed in buildings.

25. Regulations as to arbitration.

26. Fees for licenses.

27. Adjoining places occupied together to be one place.

28. Register of store licenses and registered premises to be kept by local authority.

29. Provision in case of death, &c. of occupier of store or registered premises.

SALE OF GUNPOWDER.

30. Restriction on sale of gunpowder in highways, &c.

31. Penalty for sale of gunpowder to children.

32. Sale of gunpowder to be in closed packages labelled.

CONVEYANCE OF GUNPOWDER

33. General rules as to, packing of gunpowder for conveyance.

34. Byelaws by harbour authority as to conveyance, loading, &c. A.D. 1875. of gunpowder.

35. Byelaws by railway and canal company as to conveyance, loading, &c. of gunpowder.

36. Byelaws as to wharves in which gunpowder is loaded, or unloaded.

37. Byelaws as to conveyance by road or otherwise, or loading of gunpowder.

38. Confirmation and publication of byelaw's.

PART II
LAW RELATING TO OTHER EXPLOSIVES

APPLICATION OF PART I. TO OTHER EXPLOSIVES

39. Part I. relating to gunpowder applied to other explosives.

40. Modification of Part I. as applied to explosives other than gunpowder.

41. Exemption of making and carrying safety cartridges for private use.

42. Extension of 18 & 19 Vict. c. 119. s. 29. and 36 & 37 Vict. c. 85. ss. 23-27. to all explosives.

SPECIALLY DANGEROUS EXPLOSIVES

43. Power to prohibit manufacture, importation, storage, and carriage of specially dangerous explosives.

PROVISIONS IN FAVOUR OF CERTAIN MANUFACTURERS AND DEALERS

44.   Provision in favour of makers, &c. of blasting cartridges.

45.   Provision in favour of makers of new explosive for experiment.

46.   Provision in favour of gunmakers, &c. making cartridges.

47.   Provision in favour of owners of mines and quarries as to making charges, &c. for blasting.

48:   Provision in favour of small firework manufacturer who may obtain a license from the local authority.

49.   Licensing by local authority and regulation of small firework factories.

50. Keeping without a license and conveyance of percussion caps, &c.

EXISTING FACTORIES, MAGAZINES, AND STORES

51.   Application of Part I. of the Act to existing factories and magazines.

52.   Continuing certificate not required for factory, magazine, importation license expiring within 12 months, or for stores licensed under Nitro-glycerine Act, 1869.

PART III
ADMINISTRATION OF LAW

GOVERNMENT SUPERVISION, INSPECTION

53.   Appointment of Government inspectors.

54.   Disqualification of persons as inspectors.

55.   Powers of Government inspectors.

56.   Notice by Government inspector to remedy dangerous practices, &c., and penalty for non-compliance.

57.   Annual report of Government inspectors proceedings.

58.   Inspection by railway inspectors or inspectors of Board of Trade.

59.   Application of 35 & 36 Vict. c. 76. and c. 77. to magazines used for mines.

60.   License and special rules certified by. Government inspector to be evidence.

61.   Keeping and carriage of samples by Government inspector.

62.   Salaries of Government inspectors and expenses of Act.

ACCIDENTS

63.   Notice to be given of accidents connected with explosive.

64.   Reconstruction of buildings destroyed by accident.

65.   Provisions as to coroners inquests on deaths from accidents connected with explosives.

66.   Inquiry into accidents and formal investigation in serious cases.

LOCAL SUPERVISION. DEFINITION AND POWERS OF LOCAL AUTHORITY

67.   Definition of local authority.

68.   Power of certain local bodies to become a 'local authority.

69.   Duty of local authority and power of officer.

70. Expenses of local authority. Power of Local Authority to provide Carriages and Magazines.

71. Undertaking of carriage by harbour authority and canal company.

72. Provision of magazines. by local authority. General Power of Search.

73. Search for explosive when in place in contravention of this Act, or offence being committed with respect to it.

74. Seizure and detention of explosives liable to forfeiture.

75. Inspection of wharf, carriage, boat, &c. with explosives in transitu.

76. Payment for samples of explosives.

PART IV
SUPPLEMENTAL PROVISIONS, LEGAL PROCEEDINGS, EXEMPTIONS, AND DEFINITIONS

SUPPLEMENTAL PROVISIONS

77. Penalty on and removal of trespassers.

78. Arrest without warrant, of persons committing dangerous offences.

79. Imprisonment for wilful act or neglect endangering life or limb.

80. Penalty for throwing fireworks in thoroughfare.

81. Forgery and falsification of documents.

82. Punishment for defacing notices.

83. Provisions as to Orders in Council and orders of Secretary of State.

84. Publication of byelaws, notices, &c.

85. Requisitions, notices, &c. to be in writing, &c., and how to be served.

86. Construction of enactments referring to powers of searching for gunpowder. Legal Proceedings.

87. Exemption of occupier from penalty upon proof of another being real offender.

88. Exemption of carrier and owner and master of ship where consignee, &c. in fault.

89. Supplemental provisions as to forfeiture of explosive.

90. Jurisdiction in tidal waters or on boundaries.

91. Prosecution of offences either summarily or on indictment.

92. Power of offender in certain cases to elect to be tried 'on indictment, and. not by summary jurisdiction.

93. Appeal to quarter sessions.

94. Constitution of court.

95. Distress of ship.

96. Application of penalties and disposal of forfeitures.

EXEMPTIONS AND SAVINGS

97. Exemption of Government factories, &c. from the Act.

98. Saving for rocket and fog stations.

99. Exemption of magazines in the Mersey.

100. Saving for master of ship and carrier in case of emergency.

101. Saving for rockets, gunpowder, &c. on board ship in compliance with 17 & 18 Vict. c. 104.

102. Saving clause as to liability.

103. Powers of Act cumulative, with power to make provisional order for repealing local Acts.

DEFINITIONS

104. Extension of definition of explosive to other explosive substances.

105. Persons carrying on certain processes to be deemed manufacturers.

106. Definition and classification of explosives by Order ii Council.

107. Definition of "chief officer of police" and "police district."

108. General definitions. Application of Act to Scotland.

109. Definitions.

110. Local authority.

111. Expenses of local authority.

112. Secretary of State empowered to declare police commissioners the local authority in certain cases.

113. Local authority to have certain powers to take land otherwise than by agreement.

114. Provision for making and enforcing byelaws, &c.

115. Board of Trade empowered to make byelaws for the lower estuary of the Clyde: Secretary of State to define the authority for enforcing such byelaws. Application of Act to Ireland.

116. Definition of local authority.

117. Power of certain local bodies to become a local authority.

118. Expenses of local authority.

119. Form of registers of store licenses and registered premises, and amount of fees, to be approved by Secretary of State.

120. Definitions.

121. Application of penalties in Ireland. Repeal of Acts.

122. Repeal of certain Acts and part of Act in 4th and 5th schedules.

SCHEDULES

An Act to amend the Law with respect to manufacturing, keeping, selling, carrying, and importing Gunpowder, Nitro-glycerine, and other Explosive Substances. [14th June 1875]

Note

1   SI 273/1986, art 4 declares potassium nitrate and sodium nitrate to be explosives within this Act.

PRELIMINARY

1   Short title

This Act may be cited as "The Explosives Act 1875."

2   Commencement of Act

This Act shall come into operation on the first day of January one thousand eight hundred and seventy-six, in this Act referred to as the commencement of this Act; but any Order in Council, order, general rules, and byelaws, and any appointment to an office, may be made under this Act at any time after the passing thereof, but shall not take effect until the commencement of this Act.

3   Substances to which this Act applies

This Act shall apply to gunpowder and other explosives as defined by this section. The term "explosive" in this Act—

> (1) Means gunpowder, nitro–glycerine, dynamite, gun–cotton, blasting powders, fulminate of mercury or of other metals, coloured fires, and every other substance, whether similar to those above–mentioned or not, used or manufactured with a view to produce a practical effect by explosion or a pyrotechnic effect; and

> (2) Includes fog–signals, fireworks, fuzes, rockets, percussion caps, detonators, cartridges, ammunition of all descriptions, and every adaptation or preparation of an explosive as above defined.

PART I

LAW RELATING TO GUNPOWDER

General Law as to Manufacture and Keeping of Gunpowder

4   Gunpowder to be manufactured only at factory lawfully existing or licensed under this Act

The manufacture of gunpowder shall not, nor shall any process of such manufacture, be carried on except at a factory for gunpowder either lawfully existing or licensed for the same under this Act.

Provided that nothing in this section shall apply to the making of a small quantity of gunpowder for the Purpose of chemical experiment and not for practical use or for sale.

If any person manufactures gunpowder or carries on any process of such manufacture at any place at which he is not allowed by this section so to do, he shall be deemed to manufacture gunpowder at an unauthorised place.

Where gunpowder is manufactured at an unauthorised place—

1. All or any part of the gunpowder or the ingredients of gunpowder which may be found either in or about such place or in the possession or under the control of any person convicted under this section, may be forfeited; and

2. The person so manufacturing shall be liable[, on summary conviction, to a fine not exceeding €5,000 or, on conviction on indictment, to a fine not exceeding €10,000.]¹

Amendments

1   Words substituted by Criminal Justice Act 2006, s 69 and Sch 2.

5   Gunpowder (except for private use) to be kept only in existing or new magazine or store, or in registered premises

Gunpowder shall not be kept at any place except as follows; that is to say,

(1.) Except in the factory (either lawfully existing or licensed for the same under this Act) in which it is manufactured; or

(2.) Except in a magazine or store for gunpowder either lawfully existing or licensed under this Act for keeping gunpowder; or

(3.) Except in premises registered under this Act for keeping gunpowder.

Provided that this section shall not apply—

(1) To a person keeping for his private use and not for sale gunpowder to an amount not exceeding on the same premises thirty pounds; or

(2) To the keeping of any gunpowder by a carrier or other person for the purpose of conveyance, when the same is being conveyed or kept in accordance with the provisions of this Act with respect to the conveyance of gunpowder.

Any gunpowder kept in any place other than as above in this section mentioned shall be deemed to be kept in an unauthorised place.

Where any gunpowder is kept in an unauthorised place—

(1) All or any part of the gunpowder found in such place may be forfeited; and

(2) The occupier of such place, and also the owner of, or other person guilty of keeping the gunpowder, shall each be liable[, on summary conviction, to a fine not exceeding €5,000 or, on conviction on indictment, to a fine not exceeding €10,000]¹.

Amendments

1   Words substituted by Criminal Justice Act 2006, s 69 and Sch 2.

Licensing of Factories and Magazines for Gunpowder.

6   Application for license for new factory or magazine

An applicant for such a license shall submit to the Secretary of magazine. State the draft of a license accompanied by a plan (drawn to scale) of the proposed factory or magazine, and the site thereof (which plan shall be deemed to form part of and to be in this Act included in the expression "the license").

The draft license shall contain the terms which the applicant proposes to have inserted in the license, and shall specify such of the following matters as are applicable; namely,

(a) The boundaries of the land forming the site of the factory. or magazine and either any belt of land surrounding the site which is to be kept clear, and the buildings and works from which it is to be kept clear, or the distances to be maintained between the factory or magazine, or any part thereof, and other buildings and works; and

(b) The situation, character, and construction of all the mounds, buildings, and works on or connected with the factory or magazine, and the distances thereof from each other; and

(c) The nature of the processes to be carried on in the factory and in each part thereof, and the place at which each process of the manufacture, and each description of work connected with the factory or magazine, is to be carried on, and the places in the factory or magazine at which gunpowder and any ingredients of gunpowder, and any articles liable to spontaneous ignition, or inflammable or otherwise dangerous, are to be kept; and

(d) The amount of gunpowder and of ingredients thereof wholly or partly mixed to be allowed at the same time in any building or machine or any process of the manufacture or within a limited distance from such building or machine, having regard to the situation and construction of such building, and to the distance thereof from any other building or any works; and

(e) The situation, in the case of a factory, of each factory magazine, and in the case of another magazine, of each building forming part of such magazine in which gunpowder is to be kept, and the maximum amount of gunpowder to be kept in each factory magazine, and in each such building as aforesaid; and

(f) The maximum number of persons to be employed in each building in the factory; and

(g) Any special terms which the applicant may propose by reason of any special circumstances arising from the locality, the situation or construction of any buildings or works, or the nature of any process, or otherwise.

The Secretary of State, after examination of the proposal, may reject the application altogether or may approve of the draft license, with or without modification or addition, and grant to the applicant permission to apply to the local authority for their assent to the establishment of the factory or magazine on the proposed site.

7   Application for assent of local authority to site of new factory or magazine

The local authority, upon application being made for their assent to the establishment of a new factory or magazine on the proposed site, shall cause notice to be published by the applicant in manner directed by this Act of the application and of the time and place at which they will be prepared to hear the applicant, and any persons objecting to such establishment who have not less than seven clear days before the day of hearing sent to the clerk of the local authority and to the applicant notice of their intention to appear and object, with their name, address, and calling, and a short statement of the grounds of their objection.

Upon the hearing of the application, or any adjournment thereof, the local authority may dissent altogether from the establishment of such new factory or magazine on the proposed site, or assent thereto, either absolutely or on any conditions requiring additional restrictions or precautions.

Where the site of the proposed factory or magazine is situate within or within one mile of the limits of the jurisdiction of any urban sanitary authority, or of any harbour authority, the applicant shall serve on such authority, if they are not the heal authority, notice of the application and of the time and place of hearing fixed by the local authority.

The said notices shall be published and served by the applicant not less than one month before the hearing.

The local authority shall fix the time and place of hearing as soon as practicable after application made to them, and the time so fixed shall be as soon as practicable after the expiration of the said month from the publication and service of the notices by the applicant, and their final decision shall be given as soon as practicable after the expiration of the said month.

The place so fixed shall be situate within the jurisdiction of the local authority, or within a convenient distance of the limits of that jurisdiction.

The costs of any objections which the local authority may deem to be frivolous shall be ascertained by an order made by the local authority, and shall be a debt due from the objector to the applicant, of which such order shall be conclusive evidence.

Where the site of the proposed factory or magazine is situate partly within the jurisdiction of one local authority and partly within the jurisdiction of another, the assent of both local authorities shall be applied for in manner provided by this Act.

8   Grant and confirmation of license

If on the hearing of the application for the establishment of a factory or magazine the local authority assent thereto either absolutely or on conditions submitted to by the applicant, the applicant shall be entitled to the license applied for in accordance with the draft approved by the Secretary of State, with the addition (if the assent was on conditions) of the additional restrictions and precautions required by those conditions.

If the local authority assent on any conditions not submitted to by the applicant, or dissent, the applicant may appeal to the Secretary of State, giving notice of such appeal to the local authority, and requiring them to state in writing their reasons for such conditions or dissent; and the Secretary of State, after considering the reasons (if any) so stated, and after such inquiry, local or other, as he may think necessary, may if the local authority dissented, refuse the license, or may in either case grant the license applied for in accordance with the draft license either as previously approved by him, or with such modifications and additions as he may consider required to meet the reasons (if any) so stated by the local authority.

The Secretary of State, when satisfied that the factory or magazine is sufficiently completed according to the license to justify the use thereof, shall confirm the license, but until so confirmed the license shall not come into force.

The land forming the site bounded as described in the license shall, with every mound, building, and work thereon for whatever purpose, be deemed, for the purposes of this Act, to be the factory or magazine referred to in the license.

Regulation of Factories and Magazines for Gunpowder

9   Regulation of factories and magazines for gunpowder

In every gunpowder factory and magazine—

(1) The factory or magazine, or any part thereof, shall not be used for any purpose not in accordance with the license; and

(2) The terms of the license shall be duly observed, and the manufacture or keeping or any process in or work connected with the manufacture or keeping of gunpowder shall not be carried on except in accordance with those terms; and

(3) The factory or magazine and every part thereof shall be maintained in accordance with the license; and any material alteration in the factory or magazine by enlarging or adding to the site, or by externally enlarging or adding to any building, or by altering any mound otherwise than by enlargement, or by making any new work, shall not be made except in pursuance of an amending license granted under this Act.

In the event of any breach (by any act or default) of this section in any factory or magazine,

(a) All or any part of the gunpowder or ingredients thereof in respect to which, or being in any building or machine in respect to which, the offence was committed, may be forfeited; and

(b) The occupier shall be liable[on summary conviction, to a fine not exceeding €5,000 or, on conviction on indictment, to a fine not exceeding €10,000.]¹

The occupier of a factory shall not be deemed guilty of a breach of this section for using in a case of emergency, or temporarily, one building or part of a building in which any process of the manufacture is, under the terms of the license, carried on, for another process of the manufacture, if he do not carry on in such building or part more than one process at the same time, and if the quantity of gunpowder or ingredients thereof in such building or part do not exceed the quantity allowed to be therein, or any less quantity allowed to be in the building or part of a building in which such other process is usually carried on; and if upon such use being continued after the lapse of twenty-eight days from the first beginning of such use he send notice of such use to a Government inspector, and the Government inspector do not require the discontinuance of such use.

Amendments

1   Words substituted by Criminal Justice Act 2006, s 69 and Sch 2.

10   General rules for factories and magazines

In every gunpowder factory and magazine the following general rules shall be observed:

(1) In a factory every factory magazine, and in any other magazine every building in which gunpowder is kept, shall be factories used only for the keeping of

gunpowder, and receptacles for or tools or implements for work connected with the keeping of such gunpowder; and

(2) The interior of every building in which any process of the manufacture is carried on or in which gunpowder or any ingredients thereof, either mixed or partially mixed, are kept, or in the course of manufacture are liable to be (in this Act referred to as a danger building), and the benches, shelves, and fittings in such building (other than machinery), shall be so constructed or so lined or covered as to prevent the exposure of any iron or steel in such manner, and the detaching of any grit, iron, steel, or similar substance in such manner, as to come into contact with the gunpowder or ingredients thereof in such building, and such interior, benches, shelves, and fittings shall, so far as is reasonably practicable, be kept free from grit and otherwise clean; and

(3) Every factory magazine and expense magazine in a factory, and every danger building in a magazine, shall have attached thereto a sufficient lightning conductor, unless, by reason of the construction by excavation or the position of such magazine or building, or otherwise, the Secretary of State considers a conductor unnecessary, and every danger building in a factory shall, if so required by the Secretary of State, have attached thereto a sufficient lightning conductor; and

(4) Charcoal, whether ground or otherwise, and oiled cotton, oiled rags, and oiled waste, and any articles whatever liable to spontaneous ignition, shall not be taken into any danger building, except for the purpose of immediate supply and work or immediate use in such building, and upon the cessation of such work or use shall be forthwith removed; and

(5) Before repairs are done to or in any room in or other part of a danger building, that room or part shall, so far as practicable, be cleaned by the removal of all gunpowder, and wholly or partly mixed ingredients thereof, and the thorough washing out of such room or part; and such room or part of the building after being so cleaned shall not be deemed to be a danger building within the meaning of these rules until gunpowder or the wholly or partly mixed ingredients thereof are again taken into it; and

(6) There shall be constantly kept affixed in every danger building, either outside or inside, in such manner as to be easily read, a statement of the quantities of gunpowder or ingredients allowed to be in the building, and a copy of these rules, and of any other part of this Act required by the Secretary of State to be affixed, and of such part of the license and special rules made under this Act as apply to the building; and with the addition in a factory of the name of the building, or words indicating the purpose for which it is used; and

(7) All tools and implements used in any repairs to or in a danger building shall be made only of wood or copper or brass or some soft metal or material, or shall be covered with some safe and suitable material; and

(8) Due provision shall be made, by the use of suitable working clothes without pockets, suitable shoes, searching, and otherwise, or by some of such means, for preventing the introduction into any danger building of fire, lucifer matches, or any substance or article likely to cause explosion or fire, and for preventing the introduction of any iron, steel, or grit into any part of a danger building where it would be likely to come into contact with gunpowder or the wholly or partly mixed

ingredients thereof; but this rule shall not prevent the introduction of an artificial light of such construction, position, or character as not to cause any danger of fire or explosion; and

(9) No person shall smoke in' any part of the factory or magazine, except in such part (if any) as may be allowed by the special rules; and

(10) Any carriage, boat, or other receptacle in which gunpowder, or the wholly or partly mixed ingredients thereof, are conveyed from one building to another in a factory or magazine, or from any such building to any place outside of such factory or magazine, shall be constructed without any exposed iron or steel in the interior thereof, and shall contain only the gunpowder and ingredients, and shall be closed or otherwise properly covered over; and the gunpowder and ingredients shall be so conveyed with all due diligence, and with such precautions and in such manner as will sufficiently guard against any accidental ignition; and

(11) A person under the age of sixteen years shall not be employed in or enter any danger building, except in the presence and under the supervision of some grown-up person; and

(12) In a factory the ingredients in course of manufacture into gunpowder shall be removed with all due diligence from each working building so soon as the process connected with those ingredients which. is carried on in such building is completed, and all finished gunpowder shall with all due diligence either be removed to a factory magazine or sent away immediately from the factory, and such ingredients and gunpowder shall be loaded and unloaded with all due diligence; and

(13) In a factory all ingredients to be made or mixed into gunpowder shall, before being so made or mixed, be carefully sifted, for the purpose of removing therefrom, so far as practicable, all dangerous foreign matter.

The Secretary of State may, from time to time, by order, make, and when made rescind and alter, such modifications in the foregoing general rules as may appear to him to be necessary for adapting the same to floating magazines, and such modifications shall have effect as if they were contained in this section.

In the event of any breach (by any act or default) of the general rules in any factory or magazine,—

(a) All or any part of the gunpowder or ingredients thereof in respect to which, or being in any building or machine in respect to which, the offence was committed, may be forfeited; and

(b) The occupier shall be liable[, on summary conviction, to a fine not exceeding €5,000 or, on conviction on indictment, to a fine not exceeding €10,000.][1]

Amendments

1   Words substituted by Criminal Justice Act 2006, s 69 and Sch 2.

---

11   Special rules for regulation of workmen in factory or magazine

Every occupier of a gunpowder factory or magazine shall, with the sanction of the Secretary of State, make special rules for the regulation of the persons managing or employed in or about such workmen in factory or magazine, with a view to secure the observance of this factory or Act therein, and the safety and proper discipline of the said persons magazine. and the safety of the public.

There may be annexed to any breach of special rules made in pursuance of this section such penalties, not exceeding [€100]¹ for each offence, as may be deemed just.

The occupier may, and if required by the Secretary of State shall, with the sanction of the Secretary of State, repeal, alter, or add to any special rules made in pursuance of this section.

If an occupier is required by the Secretary of State to make, repeal, alter, or add to any rules under this section, and fail within three months after such requisition to comply therewith to the satisfaction of the Secretary of State, the Secretary of State may make, repeal, alter, or add to the special rules, and anything so done by the Secretary of State shall have effect as if done by the occupier with the sanction of the Secretary of State.

If the occupier feel aggrieved by any such requisition, or by anything so done by the Secretary of State, he may, after receiving such requisition or notice of the same being so done, require the matter to be referred to arbitration in manner provided by this Act.

Amendments

1   Words substituted by Criminal Justice Act 2006, s 69 and Sch 2.

Supplemental as to Factories and Magazines for Gunpowder

12   Alteration of terms of license and enlargement of factory or magazine

Where the occupier of any gunpowder factory or magazine desires that any alteration should be made in the terms of his license, or any' material alteration made in the factory or magazine by enlarging or adding to the site or by externally enlarging or adding to any building, or by altering any mound otherwise than by enlargement, or by making any new work, he may apply for an amending license. or by making any new work, he may apply for an amending license.

If he satisfy the Secretary of State that the alteration may be properly permitted, having regard to the safety of the persons employed in the factory or magazine, and will not materially either increase the danger to the public from fire or explosion, or diminish the distance of any danger building in the factory or magazine from any building or work outside and in the neighbourhood of the factory or magazine, or increase the amount of gunpowder allowed to be kept in the factory magazine, or in any building in the magazine, the Secretary of State may grant the amending license of his own authority, but, save as aforesaid, the provisions of this Act with respect to the application for and grant of a new license shall apply to such amending license.

13   Devolution and determination of license

A gunpowder factory or magazine license shall not be avoided by any change in the occupier of the factory or magazine; but notice of the name, address, and calling of the new occupier shall be sent to the Secretary of State within three months after the change, and in default such new occupier shall be liable to a penalty not exceeding [€50]¹ for every week during which such default continues.

A factory or magazine license shall be determined by a discontinuance of the business carried on in pursuance of any such license if such discontinuance continues for a period of two years or more, or if the factory or magazine is used for any purpose not authorised by the license:

Provided that if the occupier sends to the Secretary of State, and publishes in manner directed by the Secretary of State, a notice to the effect that the right to the factory or magazine license is not intended to be surrendered, the license shall not be determined until after the expiration of five years after the first discontinuance of the business, whether the factory or magazine has or has not been used for any purpose not authorised by the license.

Amendments

1   Words substituted by Criminal Justice Act 2006, s 69 and Sch 2.

Application of Act to existing Factories and Magazines for Gunpowder

14   Continuing certificate for existing factories and magazines

A factory or magazine for gunpowder used at the time of the passing of this Act shall not be deemed to be a lawfully existing factory or magazine within the meaning of this Act unless the occupier thereof apply for and obtain in manner provided by this Act a certificate (in this Act referred to as a continuing certificate) in respect of such factory or magazine.

The occupier desirous of obtaining such certificate shall, before the expiration of three months after the commencement of this Act, send to the Secretary of State an application for such certificate, stating his name, address, and calling, and the situation of his factory or magazine, and accompanied with such particulars respecting the factory or magazine and the site thereof, and the mounds, buildings, and works thereon or connected therewith, and such copies of any plans in the possession of the occupier, as the Secretary of State may deem necessary for enabling him to make out the certificate.

The Secretary of State upon receiving such application shall grant the continuing certificate for the factory or magazine to which the application relates, and shall insert therein, by reference to a plan (which shall be deemed part of the certificate) or otherwise, such particulars as he may consider sufficient to identify the factory or magazine and indicate the site and all the existing mounds, buildings, and works thereon or connected therewith: the plan so referred to may be either the plan sent by the occupier or such other plan as the Secretary of State may cause to be made for the purpose.

The continuing certificate shall specify the maximum amount of gunpowder to be, kept if the certificate is for a factory in each factory magazine, or in all the factory magazines of the factory, and if for a magazine in each building in the magazine, or in all the buildings of the magazine, and the amount so specified, where the maximum amount so to be kept is at the passing of this Act limited by any Act or by license or otherwise, shall be that amount, and where there is no such limitation, shall be the maximum amount which the factory magazine, or all the factory magazines of the factory, or the building or all the buildings of the magazine, was or were capable of holding on the first day of January one thousand eight hundred and seventy-five.

The regulations in Part One of the first schedule to this Act shall be deemed to form part of the terms of a continuing certificate for a factory.

The land forming the site bounded as described in the certificate shall, with every mound, building, and work thereon, for whatever purpose, be deemed, for the purpose of this Act, to be the factory or magazine referred to in the certificate.

Where a license has been obtained before the twenty-fifth day of February one thousand eight hundred and seventy-five, for a factory or magazine for gunpowder, and such factory or magazine has not been completed before the passing of this Act, such factory or magazine shall be deemed to be, for the purposes of this section, a factory or magazine for gunpowder used at the time of the passing of this Act:

Provided that—

(1) The particulars to be stated in the continuing certificate shall, as regards such mounds, buildings, and works as are not completed at the date of the certificate, relate to the same as designed on the commencement of the construction of the factory or magazine; and

(2) The maximum amount of gunpowder to be specified in the continuing certificate as being allowed to be kept in any building shall, subject to the provisions of any Act or license, be the maximum amount which such building was designed on the commencement of the building thereof to hold, or such less amount as it is completed for holding at the time of the passing of this Act.

For the purposes of this Act, a continuing certificate shall (save as otherwise expressly provided) be deemed to be a license, and the factory or magazine, as the case may be, mentioned therein to be a factory or magazine licensed under this Act, and the provisions of this Act shall be construed accordingly.

Provided that—

(1) It shall not be necessary in any case to apply for the assent of the local authority to an amending license for an alteration in the terms of such certificate, or for an alteration in the factory or magazine; and

(2) Such factory or magazine, if the certificate is determined by the discontinuance of the business carried on therein, shall cease to be deemed an existing factory or magazine.

The occupier of any lawfully existing factory or magazine may, until the expiration of the time within which he is required by this section to send to the Secretary of State an application for a continuing certificate, and if he has sent such an application as is required by this section, may, until he obtains such certificate, carry on his business in such factory or magazine in like manner as if this Act had not passed.

Consumers Stores for Gunpowder Licensing and Regulation of Stores

15   Store license to be obtained from local authority

Any person may apply for a license for a gunpowder store to the local authority at the time and place appointed by such authority, stating his name, address, and calling, the proposed site and construction of the store and the amount of gunpowder he proposes to store therein; and the local authority shall, as soon as practicable, if the proposed site, construction of the store, and amount of gunpowder are in accordance with the Order in Council herein-after mentioned, grant to the applicant, on payment of such fee, not exceeding five shillings, as may be fixed by that authority, the license applied for.

16   Order in Council prescribing situation and construction of stores

Her Majesty may from time to time, by Order in Council made on the recommendation of the Secretary of State—

(1) Regulate the construction and materials and fittings of gunpowder stores; and

(2) Prescribe the buildings and works from which gunpowder stores are to be separated and the distances by which they are to be separated; and

(3) Prescribe the maximum amount of gunpowder, not exceeding two tons, to be kept in stores, graduated according to their construction and situation and their distance from the said buildings and works.

Provided that an Order under this section shall not require the removal of any building lawfully in use at the date of the making of such Order.

17   General rules for stores

In every gunpowder store the following general rules shall be observed; that is to say,

(1) The provisions of an Order in Council relating to stores, so far as they apply to such store, shall be duly observed:

(2) There shall not be at the same time in the store an amount of gunpowder exceeding the amount specified in the license; and

(3) The store shall be used only for the keeping of gunpowder, and receptacles for or tools or implements for work connected with the keeping of such gunpowder; and

(4) The interior of the store, and the benches, shelves, and fittings therein, shall be so constructed or so lined or covered as to prevent the exposure of any iron or steel and the detaching of any grit, iron, steel, or similar substance, in such manner as to come into contact with the gunpowder, and such interior, benches, shelves, and fittings shall, so far as is reasonably practicable, be kept free from grit, and otherwise clean; and

(5) The store shall have attached thereto a sufficient lightning conductor, unless it is made by excavation or is licensed for less than one thousand pounds of gunpowder; and

(6) Before repairs are done to or in any part of a store, the store shall, as far as practicable, be cleaned by the removal of all gunpowder and the thorough washing out of the store; and after such cleaning, these rules shall cease to apply to the store until gunpowder is again taken there; and

(7) Except after such cleaning, all tools and implements used in or in any repairs to the store shall be made only of wood, copper, or brass, or some soft metal or material, or shall be covered with some safe and suitable material; and

(8) Due provision shall be made, by the use of suitable working clothes without pockets, suitable shoes, searching, and otherwise, or by some of such means, for preventing the introduction into the store of fire, lucifer matches, or any substance or article likely to cause explosion or fire, or any iron, steel, or grit; but this rule shall not prevent the introduction of an artificial light of such construction, position, or character as not to cause any danger of fire or explosion; and

(9) No person shall smoke in any part of the store; and

(10) A person under the age of sixteen years shall not be employed in or enter the store, except in the presence and under the supervision of some grown-up person.

In the event of any breach (by any act or default) of the general rules in any store,—

(a) All or any part of the gunpowder in respect to which or being in the store when the offence was committed may be forfeited; and

(b) The occupier shall be liable[, on summary conviction, to a fine not exceeding €5,000 or, on conviction on indictment, to a fine not exceeding €10,000.]¹

Amendments

1   Words substituted by Criminal Justice Act 2006, s 69 and Sch 2.

---

18   Non-transferability, renewal, and forms of store licenses

A store license shall be valid only for the person named in it, and shall annually, unless the circumstances have so changed that the grant of a new license would not be authorised by this Act, on application by post or otherwise, and payment of such fee, not exceeding one shilling, as may be from time to time fixed by the local authority, be renewed by that authority, by endorsement or otherwise, for that year, and unless so renewed shall expire.

Store licenses shall be in the form from time to time directed by the Secretary of State.

19   Special rules for regulation of workmen in stores

Every occupier of a gunpowder store may, with the sanction of the Secretary of State, make, and when made, may, with the like sanction, repeal, alter, or add to, special rules for the, regulation of the persons managing or employed in or about such store, with a view to secure the observance of this Act therein, and the safety and proper discipline of the said persons and the safety of the public.

There may be annexed to any breach of special rules made in pursuance of this section such penalties, not exceeding [€100]¹ for each offence, as may be deemed just.

Amendments

1   Words substituted by Criminal Justice Act 2006, s 69 and Sch 2.

Application of Act to existing Stores for Gunpowder

20   Definition of and continuing certificate for existing stores which are to be subject to this Act

Any magazine established without a license from a local authority in pursuance of the Gunpowder Act, 1860, or of any enactment repealed by that Act, for the use of any mine, quarry, colliery, or factory of safety-fuzes, and in use at the passing of this Act, is in this Act referred to as an existing gunpowder store.

An existing gunpowder store shall not require a continuing certificate as a magazine from the Secretary of State, but shall require a continuing certificate from the local authority, and if such certificate is not applied for and obtained in manner provided by this Act, shall not be deemed to be a lawfully existing store.

The occupier of the store desirous of obtaining a continuing certificate shall, before the expiration of three months after the commencement of this Act, send an application for such certificate to the local authority, stating his name, address, and calling, and the situation and construction of the store, and accompanied by such particulars respecting the store as may be necessary to enable the local authority to make out the certificate.

The local authority upon receiving such application shall, as soon as practicable, on payment of such fee, not exceeding half-a-crown, as may be fixed by that authority, grant the continuing certificate, inserting therein such particulars as appear to them to be sufficient to identify the store, and inserting the maximum amount of gunpowder which the store is to be limited to hold, and such amount shall be the maximum amount which the store was capable of holding on the first day of January one thousand eight hundred and seventy-five, or such less amount as is limited by the regulations below in this section mentioned.

The regulations in Part Two of the first schedule to this Act shall apply to every store to which a continuing certificate is granted, as if they were contained in an Order in Council under this Act relating to stores.

For the purposes of this Act a continuing certificate for a store shall, save as otherwise expressly provided, be deemed to be a license, and the store a store licensed under this Act, and the provisions of this Act shall be construed accordingly.

Provided that—

(1)   The store shall not be enlarged, or added to, or so altered as to be of a less secure construction, and any breach of this proviso shall be deemed to be a breach of the general rules relating to stores; and

(2)   The continuing certificate shall not be limited in duration, but if the business carried on in the store is discontinued and either such discontinuance continues for a period of twelve months or more, or the store is used for another purpose, such store shall cease to be deemed an existing gunpowder store.

Nothing in this section shall prevent the obtaining for any existing gunpowder store of a license from the local authority under this Act, as in the case of a new store, and a store for which such license is obtained shall, whether a continuing certificate has or has not been previously obtained for the same, cease to be deemed an existing gunpowder store.

The occupier of an existing gunpowder store may, until the expiration of the time within which he is required by this section to send to the local authority an application for a continuing certificate, and if he has sent such an application as is required by this section may, until the expiration of six months after the expiration of the said time, or any earlier date at which he obtains such certificate, carry on his business in such store in like manner as if this Act had not passed.

Retail Dealing with Gunpowder Registration and Regulation of Registered Premises

21   Registration of premises with local authority

A person desirous of registering with the local authority any premises for the keeping of gunpowder shall register his name and calling, and the said premises (in this Act referred to as his registered premises) in such manner and on payment of such fee, not exceeding one shilling, as may be directed by the local authority.

Such registration shall be valid only for the person registered, and shall be annually renewed by sending by post or otherwise notice of such renewal to the local authority, together with such fee, not exceeding one shilling, as may be fixed by that authority.

22   General rules for registered premises

The following general rules shall be observed with respect to registered premises:

(1) The gunpowder shall be kept in a house or building, or in a fire-proof safe, such safe, if not within a house or building, to be at a safe distance from any highway, street, public thoroughfare, or public place; and

(2) The amount of gunpowder on the same registered premises shall not—

(a) If it is kept in a substantially constructed building exclusively appropriated for the purpose and detached from a dwelling-house, or in a fire-proof safe outside a dwelling-house, and detached therefrom, and at a safe distance from any highway, street, public thoroughfare, or public place, exceed two hundred pounds; and

(b) If it is kept inside a dwelling-house, or in any building other than as last aforesaid, exceed fifty pounds, unless it is kept in a fire-proof safe within such house or building, in which case the amount shall not exceed one hundred pounds; and

(3) An article or substance of an explosive or highly inflammable nature shall not be kept in a fire-proof safe with the gunpowder, and in every case shall be kept at a safe distance from the gunpowder or the safe containing the same; and

(4) Neither the building exclusively appropriated for the purpose of keeping the gunpowder nor the fire-proof safe shall have any exposed iron or steel in the interior thereof; and

(5) All gunpowder exceeding one pound in amount shall be kept in a substantial case, bag, canister, or other receptacle made and closed so as to prevent the gunpowder from escaping.

In the event of any breach (by any act or default) of such general rules in any registered premises,—

   (a) All or any part of the gunpowder in respect to which, or being in any house, building, place, safe, or receptacle in respect to which, the offence was committed may be forfeited; and

   (b) The occupier shall be liable[,on summary conviction, to a fine not exceeding €5,000 or, on conviction on indictment, to a fine not exceeding €10,000.]¹

Amendments

1   Words substituted by Criminal Justice Act 2006, s 69 and Sch 2.

Supplemental Provisions

23   Precautions against fire or explosion to be taken by occupier

The occupier of every factory, magazine, store, and registered premises for gunpowder, and every person employed in or about the same, shall take all due precaution for the prevention of accidents by fire or explosion in the same, and for preventing unauthorised persons having access to the factory, magazine, or store, or to the gunpowder therein or in the registered premises, and shall abstain from any act whatever which tends to cause fire or explosion and is not reasonably necessary for the purpose of the work in such factory, magazine, store, or premises.

Any breach (by any act or default) of this section in any factory, magazine, store, or registered premises shall be deemed to be a breach of the general rules applying thereto.

24   Explanation as to quantities of gunpowder allowed in buildings

Where any provision of this Act limits the quantity of gunpowder or ingredients of gunpowder to be allowed in any building at any one time, all gunpowder and ingredients within the radius of twenty yards from the building and in course either of removal from the building, or of removal to the building for the supply and work thereof, shall be deemed to be in the building:

Provided that, if while the gunpowder or ingredients so in course of removal are within the radius, every machine and manufacturing process in the building is wholly stopped, there may, in addition to the quantity so allowed as aforesaid to be in the building, be within the radius a further quantity of gunpowder and ingredients so in course of removal as aforesaid, not exceeding the quantity specified in that behalf in the license, or in the case of an existing building in a lawfully existing factory for gunpowder ten hundredweight, or any less quantity so allowed as aforesaid to be in the building.

Where any provision of this Act limits the quantity of gunpowder or ingredients of gunpowder to be allowed in any machine at any one time, but does not limit the quantity to be in the building containing such machine, the foregoing provisions of this section shall apply, so far as circumstances admit, as if such machine were a building.

Where the quantity allowed to be in any building is -limited to what is required for the immediate supply and work of such building, or by words not specifying the exact quantity, a

Government inspector who considers that the quantity in any such building is in excess, may, after hearing the explanation of the occupier, require the occupier to diminish such quantity to the maximum named in the requisition.

The occupier, if he feel aggrieved by such requisition, may require the matter to be referred to arbitration in manner provided by this Act.

The exact quantity to be allowed in such building shall be determined by the requisition, or if the matter is referred to arbitration, by the award.

25   Regulations as to arbitration

An occupier authorised by this Act to require any matter to be referred to arbitration may, within one month after receiving the requisition, notice, or document relating to the matter to be so referred, send an objection thereto to the Secretary of State; and if the cause of such objection is not, within one month after such objection is received by the Secretary of State, removed by the Secretary of State waiving or varying the said requisition, notice, document, or matter, or otherwise (which the Secretary of State is hereby authorised to do), such occupier may, by notice sent within seven days after the expiration of the said month to the Secretary of State, require the matter to be referred to arbitration, and the date of the receipt by the Secretary of State of the last-mentioned notice shall be deemed to be the date of the reference.

Arbitrations under this Act shall be conducted in manner provided by the second schedule to this Act.

26   Fees for licenses

There shall be payable in respect of licenses and continuing Fees for certificates granted by the Secretary of State such fees as may be licenses. from time to time fixed by him with the consent of the Treasury, not exceeding the fees in the third schedule to this Act, and if no fee is fixed the fees mentioned in the said schedule.

Such fees shall be taken and paid into the receipt of Her Majesty's Exchequer in such manner as the Treasury may from time to time direct, and shall be carried to the Consolidated Fund.

The Secretary of State may also require any applicant for a new license to pay such sum as the Secretary of State may think reasonable for expenses incurred upon any inquiry made by order of the Secretary of State with respect to the grant of such license.

When the local authority do not fix any fee which they are authorised by this Act to fix, the fee payable shall be the maximum fee which such authority are authorised to fix.

The fees payable to the local authority in respect of any license, certificate, or otherwise in pursuance of this Act, shall, where the clerk of the local authority is not wholly paid by fees, be carried to the credit of the local rate, or otherwise disposed of as such local, authority may direct, and where such clerk is wholly paid by fees, shall, unless the local authority otherwise direct, be paid to such clerk.

27   Adjoining places occupied together to be one place

For the purposes of the provisions of this Act with respect to the manufacture and keeping of gunpowder, all buildings and places adjoining each other and occupied together shall be deemed to be the same factory, magazine, store, or premises, and shall accordingly be included in one license or one registration.

28   Register of store licenses and registered premises to be kept by local authority

The local authority shall cause registers of all store licenses granted by and of all premises registered with them under this Act to be kept in such form and with such particulars as they may direct.

The local authority shall, when so required by the Secretary of State, send to him, within the time fixed by such requisition, a copy of such register or any part thereof, and in default the clerk of such authority, and also the authority if they are in fault, shall be liable to a penalty not exceeding one pound for every day during which such default continues.

A ratepayer within the area of the local authority, and a licensee or person registered under this Act, upon payment of a fee of one shilling, and a Government inspector, and an officer appointed by any local authority for the purposes of this Act, and an officer of police, without payment, shall be entitled at all reasonable times to inspect and take copies of or extracts from any register kept in pursuance of this section; and the clerk of the local authority and every other person who fails to allow such inspection or taking copies of or extracts from the same, or demands any unauthorised fee therefor, shall be liable to a penalty not exceeding one pound for each offence.

29   Provision in case of death, &c. of occupier of store or registered premises

If the occupier of a store or registered premises dies or becomes bankrupt, or has his affairs liquidated by arrangement, or becomes mentally incapable or otherwise disabled, the person carrying on the business of such occupier shall not be liable to any penalty or forfeiture under this Act for carrying on the business and acting under the license or registration during such reasonable time as may be necessary to allow him to obtain a store license from or to register with the local authority, so that he otherwise conform with the provisions of this Act.

Sale of Gunpowder

30   Restriction on sale of gunpowder in highways, &c

Gunpowder shall not be hawked, sold, or exposed for sale upon any highway, street, public thoroughfare, or public place.

If any gunpowder is hawked, sold, or exposed for sale in contravention of this section—

(1)   The person hawking, selling, or exposing for sale the same, Shall be liable to a penalty not exceeding, [, on summary conviction, to a fine not exceeding €2,500 or, on conviction on indictment, to a fine not exceeding €5,000.][1]

(2)   All or any part of the gunpowder which is so hawked or exposed for sale, or is found in the possession of any person convicted under this section, may be forfeited.

Amendments

1   Words substituted by Criminal Justice Act 2006, s 69 and Sch 2.

---

31   Penalty for sale of gunpowder to children

Gunpowder shall not be sold to any child apparently under the age of [18 years][1]; and any person selling gunpowder in contravention of this section shall be liable, on summary conviction, to a fine not exceeding €2,500 or, on conviction on indictment, to a fine not exceeding €5,000.][1]

Amendments

1   Words substituted by Criminal Justice Act 2006, s 69 and Sch 2.

32   Sale of gunpowder to be in closed packages labelled

All gunpowder exceeding one pound in weight, when publicly exposed for sale or sold, shall be in a substantial case, bag, canister, or other receptacle made and closed so as to prevent the gunpowder from escaping, and (except when the same is sold to any person employed by or on the property occupied by the vendor for immediate use in the service of the vendor or on such property,) the outermost receptacle containing such gunpowder shall have affixed the word "gunpowder" in conspicuous characters by means of a brand or securely attached label, or other mark.

If any gunpowder is sold or exposed for sale in contravention of this section—

1.   The person selling or exposing for sale the same shall be liable[,on summary conviction, to a fine not exceeding €2,500 or, on conviction on indictment, to a fine not exceeding €5,000][1]; and

2.   All or any part of the gunpowder so exposed for sale may be forfeited.

Amendments

1   Words substituted by Criminal Justice Act 2006, s 69 and Sch 2.

Conveyance of Gunpowder

33   General rules as to packing of gunpowder for conveyance

The following general rules shall be observed with respect to the packing of gunpowder for conveyance:

1.   The gunpowder, if not exceeding five pounds in amount, shall be contained in a substantial case, bag, canister, or other receptacle, made and closed so as to prevent the gunpowder from escaping; and

2.   The gunpowder, if exceeding five pounds in amount, shall be contained either in a single package or a double package. A single package shall be a box, barrel, or case of such strength, construction, and character as may be for the time being approved by the Government inspector as being of such strength, construction, and character that it will not be broken or accidentally opened, or become defective or insecure whilst being conveyed, and will not allow the gunpowder to escape. If the

gunpowder is packed in a double package the inner package shall be a substantial case, bag, canister: or other receptacle made and closed so as to prevent the gunpowder from escaping, and the outer package shall be a box, barrel, or case of wood or metal or other solid material, and shall be of such strength, construction, and character that it will not be broken or accidentally opened, or become defective or insecure whilst being conveyed, and will not allow the gunpowder to escape; and

3. The interior of every package, whether single or double, shall be kept free from grit and otherwise clean; and

4. Every package, whether single or double, when actually used for the package of gunpowder, shall not be used for any other purpose; and

5. There shall not be any iron or steel in the construction of any such single package or inner or outer package, unless the same is effectually covered with tin, zinc, or other material; and

6. The amount of gunpowder in any single package, or if there is a double package in any one outer package, shall not exceed one hundred pounds, except with the consent of and under conditions approved by a Government inspector; and

7. On the outermost package there shall be affixed the word "gunpowder" in conspicuous characters by means of a brand or securely attached label or other mark.

In the event of any breach (by any act or default) of any general rule in this section, the gunpowder in respect of which the breach is committed may be forfeited, and the person guilty of such breach shall be liable[on summary conviction, to a fine not exceeding €2,500 or, on conviction on indictment, to a fine not exceeding €5,000.][1]

The Secretary of State may from time to time make, and when made, repeal, alter, and add to, rules for the 'purpose of rescinding, altering, or adding to the general rules contained in this section, and the rules so made by the Secretary of State shall have the same effect as if they were enacted in this section.

Amendments

1 Words substituted by Criminal Justice Act 2006, s 69 and Sch 2.

34   Byelaws by harbour authority as to conveyance, loading, &c. of gunpowder

Every harbour authority shall, with the sanction of the Board of Trade, make byelaws for regulating the conveyance, loading, and unloading of gunpowder within the jurisdiction of the said authority, and in particular for declaring or regulating all or any of the following matters within the jurisdiction of the said authority; namely,

1. Determining the notice to be given by ships and boats conveying, loading, or unloading gunpowder as merchandise within the said jurisdiction; and

2. Regulating the navigation and place of mooring of such ships and boats; and

3. Regulating, subject to the general rules with respect to packing in this Act contained, the mode of stowing and keeping gunpowder on board any such ship or

boat, and of giving notice by brands, labels, or otherwise of the nature of the package containing the gunpowder; and

4. Regulating the description, construction, fitting up, and licensing of the ships, boats, or carriages to be used for the conveyance of gunpowder, and the licensing and dress of the persons having charge thereof; and

5. Prohibiting or subjecting to conditions and restrictions the conveyance of gunpowder with any explosive or any articles or substances, or in passenger ships, boats, trains, or carriages; and

6. Prohibiting in cases where the loading or unloading of gunpowder within the jurisdiction of such authority appears to be specially dangerous to the public such loading or unloading, and fixing the places and times at which the gunpowder is to be loaded or unloaded, and the quantity to be loaded or unloaded or conveyed at one time or in one ship, boat, or carriage; and

7. Regulating the mode of and the precautions to be observed in conveying any gunpowder, and in the loading or unloading any ship, boat, or carriage conveying gunpowder as merchandise, and the time during which gunpowder may be kept during such conveyance, loading, or unloading; and

8. Fixing the times at which lights or fires are to be allowed or not allowed on board such ships or boats, as before mentioned, or at which a constable or officer of the harbour authority is to be on board them; and

9. Providing for the publication and supply of copies of the byelaws; and

10. Enforcing the observance of this Act both by their own servants and agents and also by other persons when within the said jurisdiction; and

11. Generally for protecting, whether by means similar to those above mentioned or not, persons and property from danger.

The penalties to be annexed to any breach or attempt to commit any breach of any such byelaws may be all or any of the following penalties, and may be imposed on such persons and graduated in such manner as may be deemed just, according to the gravity of the offence, and according as it may be a first or second or other subsequent offence, that is to say, [on summary conviction, a fine not exceeding €5,000 or, on conviction on indictment, a fine not exceeding €10,000],[1] and forfeiture of all or any part of the gunpowder in respect of which, or found in the ship, boat, or carriage in respect of which, the breach of byelaw has taken place.

In the event of any breach of a byelaw under this section in the case of any ship, boat, carriage, or gunpowder, whether there has or has not been any conviction for such breach, it shall be lawful for the harbour-master, or other officer named in the byelaws, or any person acting under the orders of the harbour authority, to cause such ship, boat, carriage, or gunpowder, at the expense of the owner thereof, to be removed to such place or otherwise dealt with in such manner as may be in conformity with the byelaws, and all expenses incurred in such removal may be recovered in the same manner as a penalty under this section, and any person resisting such harbour-master or officer or other person in such removal shall be liable to the same penalties as a person is liable to for obstructing the harbour-master in the execution of his duty.

On any part of the coast of the United Kingdom or in any tidal water for which there is no harbour authority, the Board of Trade may, if they think it expedient, make byelaws under this section for that part or water as if it were a harbour and they were the harbour authority, and such byelaws shall be deemed to have been made by a harbour authority with the sanction of the Board of Trade; and they may by such byelaws define the area within which such byelaws are to be observed, and the authorities and officers by whom such byelaws are to be enforced and carried into effect within such area, and every such authority and officer shall for the purposes of this Act, other than making byelaws or assenting to a site for a new factory or magazine, have the same power within the said area as a harbour authority and an officer of a harbour authority have respectively under this Act in a harbour.

Amendments

1   Words substituted by Criminal Justice Act 2006, s 69 and Sch 2.

35   Byelaws by railway and canal company as to conveyance, loading, &c. of gunpowder

Every railway company and every canal company over whose railway or canal any gunpowder is carried, or intended to be carried, shall, with the sanction of the Board of Trade, make byelaws for regulating the conveyance, loading, and unloading of such gunpowder on the railway or canal of the company making the byelaws, and in particular for declaring and regulating all or any of the following matters in the case of such railway or canal; that is to say,

1. Determining the notice to be given of the intention to send gunpowder for conveyance as merchandise on the railway or canal; and

2. Regulating, subject to the general rules with respect to packing A.D. 1875. in this Act contained, the mode of stowing and keeping gunpowder for conveyance and of giving notice by brands, labels, or otherwise of the nature of the package containing the gunpowder; and

3. Regulating the description and construction of carriages, ships, or boats to be used in the conveyance of gunpowder; and

4. Prohibiting or subjecting to conditions and restrictions the conveyance of gunpowder with any explosive, or with any articles or substances, or in passenger trains, carriages, ships, or boats; and

5. Fixing the places and times at which the gunpowder is to be loaded or unloaded, and the quantity to be loaded or unloaded or conveyed at one time, or in one carriage, ship, or boat; and

6. Determining the precautions to be observed in conveying gunpowder, and in loading and unloading the carriages, ships, and boats used in such conveyance, and the time during which the gunpowder may be kept during such conveyance, loading and unloading; and

7. Providing for the publication and supply of copies of the byelaws; and

8. Enforcing the observance of this Act both by their servants and agents and also by other persons when on the canal or railway of such company; and

9. Generally for protecting, whether by means similar to those above mentioned or not, persons and property from danger.

Such byelaws, when confirmed by the Board of Trade, shall apply to the railway, canal, agents, and servants of the company making the same, and to the persons using such railway or canal, or the premises connected therewith and occupied by or under the control of such company.

The penalties to be annexed to any breach or attempt to commit any breach of any such byelaws may be all or any of the following penalties, and may be imposed on such persons and graduated in such manner as may be deemed just, according to the gravity of the offence, and according as it may be a first, second, or other subsequent offence, that is to say, [on summary conviction, a fine not exceeding €5,000 or, on conviction on indictment, a fine not exceeding €10,000],[1] and forfeiture of all or any part of the gunpowder in respect of which, or being in the carriage, ship, or boat or train of carriages, ships, or boats, in respect of which, the breach of byelaw has taken place.

Amendments

1 Words substituted by Criminal Justice Act 2006, s 69 and Sch 2.

36 Byelaws as to wharves, in which gunpowder is loaded, or unloaded

The occupier of every wharf or clock on or in which gunpowder is loaded or unloaded (if such loading or unloading is not otherwise subject to any byelaws under this Act) may, and if so required by the Secretary of State shall, from time to time, with the sanction of the Secretary of State, make byelaws for regulating the loading and unloading of gunpowder on or in such wharf or dock, and in particular for declaring or regulating all or any of the matters which can be declared or regulated in the case of any wharf or dock within the jurisdiction of a harbour authority by byelaws made by such authority in pursuance of this Act.

The penalties to be annexed to any breach, or attempt to commit any breach, of any such byelaws may be all or any of the following penalties, and may be imposed on such persons and graduated in such manner as may be deemed just, according to the gravity of the offence, and according as it may be a first or second or other subsequent offence, that is to say, [on summary conviction, a fine not exceeding €5,000 or, on conviction on indictment, a fine not exceeding €10,000,][1] and forfeiture of all or any part of the gunpowder in respect of which, or found on the wharf or in the dock or part of the wharf or dock in respect of which, the breach of byelaw has taken place.

Any byelaws made in pursuance of this section may, and if required by the Secretary of State shall, be rescinded, altered, or added to by byelaws made by the occupier, with the sanction of the Secretary of State.

If an occupier is required by the Secretary of State to make byelaws under this section for any matter, and fail within three months after such requisition to comply therewith to the satisfaction of the Secretary of State, the Secretary of State may make such byelaws, which shall have effect as if made by the occupier with the sanction of the Secretary of State.

Where by reason of a wharf being a public wharf or otherwise, there is no occupier thereof, or the occupier thereof is unknown, the Secretary of State may make byelaws with respect to such wharf in like manner as if the occupier had failed to comply with his requisition: Provided that where such wharf abuts on any harbour, canal, or railway, the harbour authority or canal or railway company shall have the same power, and, if so required by the Secretary of State, shall be under the same obligation to make byelaws under this section for such wharf as if they were the occupiers thereof.

Amendments

1   Words substituted by Criminal Justice Act 2006, s 69 and Sch 2.

---

37   Byelaws as to conveyance by road or. otherwise, or loading of gunpowder

The Secretary of State may from time to time make, and when made, rescind, alter, or add to, byelaws for regulating the conveyance, loading, and unloading of gunpowder in any case in which byelaws made under any other provision of this Act do not apply, and in particular for declaring or regulating all or any of the following matters; that is to say,

1. Regulating the description and construction of carriages to be used in the conveyance of gunpowder as merchandise; and

2. Prohibiting or subjecting to conditions and restrictions the conveyance of gunpowder with any explosive, or with any articles or substances, or in passenger carriages; and

3. Fixing the places and times at which the gunpowder is to be loaded or unloaded, and the quantity to be loaded or unloaded or conveyed at one time or in one carriage; and

4. Determining the precautions to be observed in conveying gunpowder, and in loading and unloading the carriages used in such conveyance, and the time during which the gunpowder may be kept during such conveyance, loading and unloading; and

5. Providing for the publication and supply of copies of the byelaws; and

6. Generally for protecting, whether by means similar to those above mentioned or not, persons or property from danger; and

7. Adapting on good cause being shown the byelaws in force under this section to the circumstances of any particular locality.

The penalties to be annexed to any breach, or attempt to commit any breach, of any such byelaws may be all or any of the following penalties, and may be imposed on such persons and graduated in such manner as may be deemed just, according to the gravity of the offence, and according as it may be a first, second, or other subsequent offence, that is to say, on summary conviction, a fine not exceeding €5,000 or, on conviction on indictment, a fine not exceeding €10,000,]¹ and forfeiture of all or any part of the gunpowder in respect of which, or being in the carriage in respect of which, the breach of byelaw has taken place. For the purpose of any mode of conveyance which is not a conveyance by land this section shall be construed as if ship and boat were included in the term carriage.

Amendments

1   Words substituted by Criminal Justice Act 2006, s 69 and Sch 2.

38   Confirmation and publication of byelaws

Any recommendation to Her Majesty in Council, any general rules with respect to packing, and any byelaws which is or are proposed to be made under this Act by a Secretary of State or the Board of Trade shall, before being so made, be published in such manner as the Secretary of State or the Board of Trade, as the case may be, may direct as being in his or their opinion sufficient forgiving information thereof to all local authorities, corporations, and persons interested.

The byelaws framed by any railway company, canal company, or harbour authority under this Act shall, before being sanctioned by the Board of Trade, be published in such manner as may be directed by the Board of Trade, with a notice of the intention of such company or authority to apply for the confirmation thereof, and may be sanctioned by the Board of Trade with or without any omission, addition, or alteration, or may be disallowed.

Every such byelaw may be from time to time added to, altered, or rescinded by a byelaw made in like manner and with the like sanction as the original byelaw.

The Secretary of State or the Board of Trade, as the case may be, shall receive and consider any objections or suggestions made by any local authority, corporation, or persons interested with respect to any recommendation, general rules, or byelaws published in pursuance of this section, and may, if it seem fit, amend such recommendation, general rules, or byelaws with a view of meeting such objections or suggestions without again publishing the same.

PART II
LAW RELATING TO OTHER EXPLOSIVES
Application of Part I to other Explosives

39   Part I. relating to gunpowder applied to other explosives

Subject to the provisions hereafter in this part of this Act relating to contained, Part One of this Act relating to gunpowder shall apply to every other description of explosive, in like manner as if those provisions were herein re-enacted with the substitution of that description of explosive for gunpowder.

40   Modification of Part I. as applied to explosives other than gunpowder

The following modifications and additions shall be made in and to Part One of this Act as applied to explosives other than gunpowder:

(1)   The draft license for a factory or magazine submitted by an applicant to the Secretary of State shall specify such particulars as the Secretary of State may require; and

(2)   The prescribed general rules shall be substituted for the general rules in Part One of this Act relating to factories, magazines, stores, and registered premises

respectively; but no such general rule shall require the removal of any building or work in use at the date of the Order in Council by which such rule is made;

(3) The Secretary of State may from time to time alter the general rules relating to packing contained in Part One of this Act for the purpose of adapting the same to the packing of any explosive other than gunpowder; and

(4) For the maximum amount limited by Part One of this Act to be kept for private use and not for sale, or in a store, and for the minimum amount limited by Part One of this Act to be exposed for sale or sold otherwise than in a substantial case, box, canister, or other receptacle as therein mentioned, there shall be substituted in the case of explosives other than gunpowder the following amounts; namely,

    (a) where such explosive consists of safety cartridges made with gunpowder, an amount containing not more than five times the maximum or minimum amount of gunpowder, as the case may be, above mentioned; and

    (b) In the case of any other explosive, the prescribed amount; and

(5) Two or more descriptions of explosives shall not be kept in the same store or registered premises, except such descriptions as may be described in that behalf; and, when so kept, shall be kept subject to the prescribed conditions and restrictions; and

(6) Where any explosive, other than gunpowder, is allowed to be kept in the same store or registered premises with gunpowder, the maximum amount of gunpowder to be kept therein shall be the prescribed amount in lieu of the amount fixed by Part One of this Act; and

(7) Where any explosive, other than gunpowder, is allowed to be kept in the same magazine, store, or registered premises with gunpowder, the prescribed general rules shall be observed instead of the general rules in Part One of this Act; and

(8) There shall be on the outermost package containing the explosive in lieu of the word "gunpowder" the name of the explosive, with the addition of the word "explosive," and if such name is materially false the person selling or exposing for sale such explosive, and also the owner of the explosive, shall be liable to a penalty not exceeding fifty pounds:

(9) With respect to the importation from any place out of the United Kingdom of either dynamite or gun-cotton, or any explosive (other than gunpowder, cartridges made with gunpowder, percussion caps, fireworks, and any prescribed explosive), the following provisions shall have effect; that is to say,

    (a) The owner and master of any ship having on board any such explosive shall not permit the same to does not hold a license to import the same (in this Act called an importation license) from the Secretary of State, and any transhipment shall for the purpose of this section be deemed to be delivery; and

    (b) The Secretary of State may grant an importation license for any such explosive, and may annex thereto any prohibitions and restrictions with respect to the composition and quality of the explosive, and the unloading, landing, delivery, and conveyance thereof, and such further provisions and restrictions as he may think fit, for the protection of the public from danger; and

(c) The license shall be of such duration as the Secretary of State may fix, and shall be available only for the person named in the license; and

(d) In the event of any breach by any act or default of the provisions of this section with respect to the importation of an explosive, or of the provisions of any importation license, all or any part of the explosive with respect to which such breach is committed, or being in any ship or boat in connexion with which such breach is committed, may be forfeited, and the owner and master of such ship or boat, and the licensee or person to whom the explosive is delivered, shall each be liable[, on summary conviction, to a fine not exceeding €5,000 or, on conviction on indictment, to a fine not exceeding €10,000][1]; and

(e) The Commissioners of Customs and their officers shall have the same power with respect to any such explosive, and the ship containing the same, as they have for the time being with respect to any article on the importation of which restrictions are for the time being imposed by the law relating to the Customs, and the ship containing the same, and the enactments for the time being in force relating to the Customs or any such article or ship shall apply accordingly.

Amendments

1 Words substituted by Criminal Justice Act 2006, s 69 and Sch 2.

41 Exemption of making and carrying safety cartridges for private use

Nothing in this Act shall apply to the filling or conveying, for private use and not for sale, of any safety cartridges to the amount allowed by this Act to be kept for private use.

42 Extension of 18 & 19 Vict. c. 119. s. 29. and 36 & 37 Vict. c. 85. ss. 23-27. to all explosives

Section twenty-nine of the Passengers Act, 1855, and sections twenty-three to twenty-seven, both inclusive, of the Merchant Shipping Act, 1873, shall apply to every explosive within the meaning of this Act in like manner as they apply to gunpowder.

Specially Dangerous Explosives

43 Power to prohibit manufacture, importation, storage, and carriage of specially dangerous explosives

Notwithstanding anything in this Act, Her Majesty from time to time, by Order in Council, may prohibit, either absolutely, or except in pursuance of a license of the Secretary of State under this Act, or may subject to conditions or restrictions the manufacture, keeping, importation from any place out of the United Kingdom, conveyance, and sale, or any of them, of any explosive which is of so dangerous a character that, in the judgment of Her Majesty, it is expedient for the public safety to make such Order:

Provided that such Order shall not absolutely prohibit anything which may be lawfully done in pursuance of any continuing certificate under this Act.

Any explosive manufactured or kept in contravention of any such Order shall be deemed to be manufactured or kept, as the case may be, in an unauthorised place.

Any explosive conveyed in contravention of any such Order shall be deemed to be conveyed in contravention of a byelaw made under this Act with respect to the conveyance of explosives.

If any explosive is imported or sold in contravention of any such Order,—

1. All or any part of such explosive may be forfeited; and

2. The owner or master of the ship in which it was imported shall be liable [on summary conviction, to a fine not exceeding €5,000 or, on conviction on indictment, to a fine not exceeding €10,000][1]; and

3. The person to whom it was delivered and the person selling the same shall be liable[, on summary conviction, to a fine not exceeding €5,000 or, on conviction on indictment, to a fine not exceeding €10,000][1].

The Commissioners of Customs and their officers shall have the same power with respect to any such explosive, and the ship containing the same, as they have for the time being with respect to any article prohibited to be imported by the law relating to the Customs, and the ship containing the same, and the enactments for the time being in force relating to the Customs and any such article or ship shall apply accordingly.

Amendments

1   Words substituted by Criminal Justice Act 2006, s 69 and Sch 2.

Provisions in favour of certain Manufacturers and Dealers

44   **Provision in favour of makers, &c. of blasting cartridges**

The occupier of a factory for any explosive shall not be required by this Act to take out a factory license for making up on such factory the explosive made thereon into cartridges or charges for cannon or blasting not containing within themselves their own means of ignition.

The occupier of any magazine, store, or registered premises for keeping any explosive may keep that explosive when made up into such cartridges or charges as above in this section mentioned, as if it were not so made up, and the provisions of this Act with respect to the keeping of any explosive shall apply to the keeping of that explosive when made up into the said cartridges or charges, in like manner as if the explosive were not so made up.

45   **Provision in favour of makers of new explosive for experiment**

The occupier of a factory for any explosive who manufactures a new explosive or new form of explosive similar to the one specified in his license, shall not be deemed to have manufactured the same in an unauthorised place if he manufactured the same on a small scale, and exclusively for the purpose of trial and not for sale, and he send notice of the same, as soon as he has manufactured it, to the Secretary of State, and if he observe the provisions of this Act, so far as they are applicable.

46 Provision in favour of gunmakers, &c. making cartridges

The occupier of a magazine, store, or registered premises for any explosive shall not be required by this Act to take out a factory license by reason that in connexion with such magazine, store, or premises he fills for sale or otherwise any cartridge for small arms with the said explosive, so that he observe the following regulations; namely,

(1) There shall not be in the room in which such filling is being carried on more than five pounds of gunpowder, or the prescribed amount of any other explosive, except it is made up into safety cartridges; and

(2) Any work unconnected with the making of the cartridges shall not be carried on in the room while such filling is being carried on; and

(3) There shall not be in the room while such filling is being carried on any fire nor any artificial light, except a light of such construction, position, or character as not to cause any danger of fire or explosion; and

(4) In the case of a magazine or store, the room in which the filling is carried on shall be detached from the magazine or store, but in the immediate neighbourhood thereof, and at such distance therefrom as may be specified in the case of a magazine by the license, and in the case of a store by an Order in Council relating to stores; and

(5) The occupier shall give notice in the case of a magazine to the Secretary of State, and in the case of a store or registered premises to the local authority, that he intends to carry on such filling of cartridges as is allowed by this section. Provided that this section shall not, except with the consent of the Secretary of State, apply to any magazine or store for which a continuing certificate has been obtained under this Act, which consent the Secretary of State, if satisfied that the filling of cartridges in accordance with this section ought (due regard being had to the safety of the public) to be allowed, may grant either absolutely or upon such conditions as he may, under the special circumstances of the case, think expedient to secure the safety of the public.

The regulations in this section and any conditions so made by the Secretary of State as last aforesaid, shall be deemed to be general rules under this Act relating to the magazine, store, and registered premises respectively, and the breach of them shall be punished accordingly.

47 Provision in favour of owners of mines and quarries, as to making charges, &c. for blasting

The occupier of any magazine or store for any explosive shall not be required by this Act to take out a factory license by reason that, in connexion with such magazine or store, he, by filling cartridges, making charges, drying, sifting, fitting, or otherwise, adapts or prepares the said explosive for use exclusively in his mine or quarry, or in some excavation or work carried on by him or under his control, so that he observe the following regulations; namely,

(1) There shall not be in the workshop in which such adaptation or preparation is carried on more than one hundred pounds of gunpowder or the prescribed amount of any other explosive; and

(2) Any work unconnected with such adaptation or preparation shall not be carried on in the said workshop while such adaptation or preparation is being carried on; and

(3) The said workshop shall be detached from the magazine or store, but in the immediate neighbourhood thereof, and at such distance therefrom as may be specified, in the case of a magazine by the license, and in the case of a store by an Order in Council. relating to stores; and

(4) An explosive of one description shall not be converted into an explosive of another description, and shall not be unmade or resolved into its ingredients; and

(5) The occupier shall give notice in the case of a magazine to the Secretary of State; and in the case of a store to the local authority, that he intends to carry on such adaptation or preparation as is allowed by this section.

Provided that this section shall not, except with the consent of the Secretary of State, apply to any magazine or store for which a continuing certificate has been obtained under this Act, which consent the Secretary of State, if satisfied that the adaptation or preparation in accordance with this section ought (due regard being had to the safety of the public) to be allowed, may grant either absolutely or upon such conditions as he may, under the special circumstances of the case, think expedient to secure the safety of the public.

The regulations in this section, and any conditions so made by the Secretary of State as last aforesaid, shall be deemed to be general rules under this Act relating to the magazine and store respectively, and the breach of them shall be punished accordingly.

The following general rules shall apply as if the said workshop were a danger building, that is to say, if the adaptation or preparation carried on is of gunpowder only, the general rules with respect to a factory in Part One of this Act, and in any other case the prescribed general rules; and the breach of such general rules shall be punished in like manner as the breach of general rules with respect to a factory.

48   Provision in favour of small firework manufacturer who may obtain a license from the local authority

A firework factory shall not be deemed to be a small firework factory for the purposes of this Act if there is upon the same factory at the same time—

(a) More than one hundred pounds of any explosive other than manufactured fireworks and coloured fires and stars; or

(b) More than five hundred pounds of manufactured fireworks, either finished or partly finished; or

(c) More than twenty-five pounds of coloured fires or stars, not made up into manufactured fireworks.

The occupier of a small firework factory shall not be required to obtain a license under Part One of this Act for such factory if he has obtained a license from the local authority under this part of this Act.

A person having such license from the local authority who manufactures an explosive (other than nitro-glycerine or any prescribed explosive) for the purpose only of the manufacture of coloured fires or a manufactured firework in accordance with this Act, and does not sell the same except in the form of coloured fires packed in the manner required by this Act, or of a manufactured firework, shall not be deemed to manufacture an explosive in an unauthorised place.

49   Licensing by local authority and regulation of small firework factories

Any person may apply for a small firework factory license to the local authority at the time and place appointed by such authority, stating his name, address, and calling, and the proposed site and construction of the factory, and the amount and description of explosive he proposes to have therein, and in any building therein; and the local authority shall, as soon as practicable, if the proposed site, construction of the factory, and amount of explosive is in accordance with the Order in Council regulating small firework factories, grant to the applicant, on payment of such fee, not exceeding five shillings, as may be fixed by that authority, the license applied for.

The powers of this Act of making Orders in Council with respect to stores and of prescribing general rules with respect to stores shall extend to making Orders in Council and prescribing general rules with respect to small firework factories and the buildings thereon; and any breach (by any act or default) of any such general rule shall involve the same penalties and forfeitures as a breach of a general rule relating to stores.

A small firework factory license shall be valid only for the person named in it, and the provisions of this Act with respect to the renewal, expiration, and form of store licenses, and fees for such renewal, and to special rules for the regulation of persons managing or employed in or about stores, shall apply in like manner as if they were herein enacted, and in terms made applicable to small firework factory licenses and small firework factories respectively.

50   Keeping without a license and conveyance of percussion caps, &c

A person shall not be required by this Act to take out a license or to register any premises for the keeping of percussion caps, or safety-fuzes for blasting, or fog-signals kept by any railway company for use on the railway of such company, or any prescribed explosive.

It shall not be obligatory on any harbour authority, railway company, canal company, or occupier of a wharf, to make any byelaws with respect to the conveyance, loading, or unloading of any explosives to which this section applies.

It shall be lawful for Her Majesty, by Order in Council, to exempt any explosive to which this section applies, or any description thereof, from any other of the provisions of this Act, or to declare that a license shall be required for the keeping of any explosive to which this section applies, or any description thereof, or that byelaws shall be made with respect to the loading, unloading, and conveyance thereof.

Existing Factories, Magazines, and Stores

51   Application of Part I. of the Act to existing factories and magazines

In any continuing certificate for a lawfully existing factory the Act to or magazine for any explosive other than gunpowder, the regulations set out in the first schedule to this Act shall not form part of the terms of such certificate, but in lieu thereof the Secretary of State shall insert in the certificate as the terms thereof,—

(1) If the factory or magazine is for dynamite or any substance having nitro-glycerine as one of its component parts or ingredients, the conditions contained in the existing license, with such modifications (if any) as the Secretary of State may think necessary in order to bring the same into conformity with this Act, and also any limitation of time for the expiration of the license contained in the existing

license, and also the existing power of the Secretary of State to revoke the license; and

(2) In any other case, such terms as the Secretary of State may think expedient, having regard to the conditions (if any) contained in the license under which the factory or magazine is established; and such terms shall include any limitation of time contained in such license, but shall not require the removal of any lawfully existing building or work.

If a new license under this Act is obtained for keeping in an existing gunpowder store any explosive other than gunpowder, the continuing certificate of such store shall be determined, and the store shall cease to be deemed to be an existing gunpowder store within the meaning of this Act.

52   Continuing certificate not required for factory, magazine, or importation license expiring within 12 months, or, for stores licensed under Nitro-glycerine Act, 1869

Where the license of a factory or magazine or any explosive other than gunpowder will expire within twelve months after the commencement of this Act, the occupier of such factory or magazine shall not require a continuing certificate under this Act, but until such license expires shall be entitled to use such factory or magazine in like manner as if this Act had not passed, without prejudice nevertheless to any, application by him for a license under this Act for such factory or magazine, but after a license under this Act is obtained for the same, or after the expiration of the old license, such factory or magazine shall not be deemed to be a lawfully existing factory or magazine within the meaning of this Act.

The occupier of any magazine licensed at the time of the passing of this Act by a general magazine license under the Nitro-glycerine Act, 1869, shall not require a continuing certificate under this Act, but until the expiration of six months after the commencement of this Act shall be entitled to use such magazine in like manner as if this Act had not passed, without prejudice nevertheless to a license under this Act being obtained for the same; but after a license under this Act is obtained for the same, or after the expiration of the said six months, such license shall determine, and such magazine shall not be deemed to be a lawfully existing magazine or store within the meaning of this Act.

The holder of any importation license under the Nitro-glycerine Act, 1869, shall, until the expiration of six months after the commencement of this Act, be entitled to act under such license in like manner as if this Act had not passed, without prejudice nevertheless to any application by him for an importation license under this Act; but after such license under this Act is obtained, or after the expiration of the said six months, such existing license shall determine.

PART III

ADMINISTRATION OF LAW

Government Supervision

Inspection

53   Appointment of Government inspectors

The Secretary of State may from time to time by order appoint any fit persons to be inspectors for the purposes of this Act, and assign them their duties, and award them such salaries as the Commissioners of Her Majesty's Treasury may approve, and remove such inspectors, and any such inspector is referred to in this Act as a Government inspector.

Every order appointing an inspector shall be published in the London Gazette.

54   Disqualification of persons as inspectors

Any person who practises or acts, or is a partner with any person who practises or acts, as a manufacturer, storer, carrier, importer or exporter of or trader or dealer in an explosive, or holds any patent connected with an explosive, or is otherwise directly or indirectly engaged or interested in any such manufacture, storage, conveyance, importation, exportation, trade, dealing, or patent, shall not act as an inspector under this Act.

55   Powers of Government Inspectors

A Government inspector shall have power to make such examination and inquiry as may be necessary to ascertain whether this Act is complied with, and for that purpose,—

(1)   He may enter, inspect, and examine any factory, magazine, or store of any explosive, and every part thereof, at all times by day and night, but so as not to unnecessarily impede or obstruct the work in such factory, magazine, or store, and may make inquiries as to the observance of this Act and all matters and things relating to the safety of the public or of the persons employed in or about such factory, magazine, or store; and

(2)   He may enter, inspect, and examine any premises registered under this Act, and every part thereof, in which any explosive is kept, or is reasonably supposed by him to be kept, at all reasonable times by day; and

(3)   He may require the occupier of any factory, magazine, store, or premises which he is entitled, under this section, to enter, or a person employed by such occupier therein, to give him samples of any explosive or ingredients of an explosive therein, or of any substance therein, the keeping of which is restricted or regulated by this Act, or of any substance therein which the inspector believes to be an explosive, or such ingredients or substance.

The occupier of every such factory, magazine, store, and registered premises, his agents and servants, shall furnish the means required by the inspector as necessary for every such entry, inspection, examination, and inquiry.

Any person who fails to permit a Government inspector to enter, inspect, examine, or make inquiries in pursuance of this section, or to comply with any requisition of such inspector in pursuance of this section, or who in any manner obstructs such inspector in the execution of his duties under this Act, shall be guilty of an offence and liable[, on summary conviction, to a fine not exceeding €1,000.][1]

Amendments

1   Words substituted by Criminal Justice Act 2006, s 69 and Sch 2.

---

56   **Notice by, Government inspector, to remedy 'dangerous practices, &c., and penalty for non-compliance**

If in any matter (which is not provided for by any express provision of this Act) an inspector find any factory, magazine, or store for an explosive, or any part thereof, or any thing or practice therein or connected therewith, to be unnecessarily dangerous or defective, so as in his opinion to tend to endanger the public safety or the bodily safety of any person, such inspector may require the occupier of such factory, magazine, or store to remedy the same.

Where the occupier objects to comply with the requisition he may require the matter to be referred to arbitration in manner provided by this Act.

No person shall be precluded by any contract from doing such acts as may be necessary to comply with a requisition or award under this section; and no person shall be liable under any contract to any penalty or forfeiture for doing those acts if he gave notice of such contract to the inspector at or before the time at which the inspector made the requisition or to the arbitrators before the award was made.

If the occupier fail to comply with the requisition or award within twenty days after the expiration of the time for requiring the matter to be referred to arbitration if there is no reference to arbitration, or if there is such a reference after the date of the award, he shall be liable[, on summary conviction, to a fine not exceeding €1,000].[1]

Provided that the court, if satisfied that the occupier has taken active measures for complying with the requisition or award, but has not, with reasonable diligence, been able to complete the works, may adjourn any proceedings taken before them for punishing such failure, and if the works are completed within a reasonable time in the opinion of the court, no penalty shall be inflicted.

Amendments

1   Words substituted by Criminal Justice Act 2006, s 69 and Sch 2.

57   **Annual Report of Government Inspectors Proceedings**

A report of the proceedings under this Act shall be made annually to the Secretary of State, by such inspectors and in such manner and form as may be directed by him, and shall be laid before both Houses of Parliament.

58   **Inspection by railway inspectors or inspectors of Board of Trade**

The Board of Trade may from time to time, by order, direct—

    (a) Any person acting under the Board as an inspector of railways to inquire into the observance of this Act by any railway company or canal company, and generally to act with respect to any railway or canal as an inspector under this Act; or

    (b) Any person acting under the Board as an inspector or otherwise for the purposes of the Merchant Shipping Act, 1854, or the Acts amending the same, to inquire into the observance of this Act in any harbour or in the case of any ship, and generally to act in such harbour and with respect to ships as an inspector under this Act.

The Board of Trade may revoke any such order; and each such inspector shall, while such order is in force, have for that purpose the same powers and authorities as he has under the Acts in pursuance of which he was originally appointed inspector, and also the powers and authorities of a Government inspector under this Act.

59   Application of 35 & 36 Vict. c. 76. and c. 77. to magazines used for mines

Where a magazine or store is established for the purpose of any mine subject to the Coal Mines Regulation Act, 1872, or the Metalliferous Mines Regulation Act, 1872, by the owner (as defined by such Act) of the mine, the Secretary of State may from time to time by order direct an inspector under either of those Acts to act with respect to such magazine or store as a Government inspector under this Act, and may revoke any such order; and such inspector shall, while such order is in force, have for that purpose the same powers and authorities as he has under the said Acts, and also the powers and authorities of a Government inspector under this Act.

60   License and special rules certified by Government inspector to be evidence

A copy of any license confirmed by the Secretary of State under this Act, and of any special rules under this Act, certified by a Government inspector, shall be evidence of such license and special rules respectively, and of the fact of such license having been duly granted and confirmed and such special rules duly established under this Act.

61   Keeping and carriage of samples by Government inspector

A Government inspector, and any other person authorised by him for the purpose, may keep and convey any sample taken for the purposes of this Act by or by authority of such inspector, so that the amount of it do cot exceed what is reasonably necessary for the purpose of enabling such inspector to perform his duties under this Act, and be kept and carried with all due precautions to prevent accident; and such inspector or person shall not be liable to any penalty, punishment, or forfeiture under this or any other Act for keeping or conveying such sample.

62   Salaries of Government inspectors and expenses of Act

The salaries of the Government inspectors, and the expenses incurred by the Secretary of State or the Government inspectors in carrying this Act into execution, shall be defrayed out of moneys provided by Parliament.

Accidents

63   Notice to be given of accidents connected with explosive

Whenever there occurs any accident by explosion or by fire in or about or in connexion with any factory, magazine, or store, or any accident by explosion or by fire causing loss of life or personal injury in or about or in connexion with any registered premises, the occupier of such factory, magazine, store, or premises shall forthwith send or cause to be sent notice of such accident and of the loss of life or personal injury (if any) occasioned thereby to the Secretary of State. A notice of any accident of which notice is sent in pursuance of this section to a Government inspector need not be sent to any inspector or sub-inspector of factories or any inspector of mines.

Where in, about, or in connexion with any carriage, ship, or boat, either conveying an explosive, or on or from which an explosive is being loaded or unloaded, there occurs any accident by explosion or by fire causing loss of life or personal injury, or if the amount of explosive conveyed or being so loaded or unloaded exceeds in the case of gunpowder half a ton, and in the case of any other explosive the prescribed amount, any accident by explosion or by fire, the owner or master of such carriage, ship, or boat, and the owner of the explosive conveyed therein or being loaded or unloaded therefrom, or one of them, shall forthwith send or cause to be sent notice of such accident, and of the loss of life or personal injury, if any, occasioned thereby, to the Secretary of State.

Every such occupier, owner, or master as aforesaid who fails to comply with this section shall be liable[, on summary conviction, to a fine not exceeding €5,000 or, on conviction on indictment, to a fine not exceeding €10,000.]¹

Amendments

1 Words substituted by Criminal Justice Act 2006, s 69 and Sch 2.

64 Reconstruction of buildings destroyed by accident

Where an accident by explosion or fire has occurred in, and wholly or partly destroyed a factory magazine, or any magazine or store, the factory magazine, magazine, or store shall not be reconstructed, and any further supply of an explosive shall not be put therein, except with the permission of the Secretary of State; and any explosive put therein in contravention of this section shall be deemed to be kept in an unauthorised place, and the offence may be punished accordingly:

Provided, that this enactment shall not prevent the reconstruction of a factory magazine in any lawfully existing factory upon such site in the factory, and with such precautions as may seem reasonable to the Secretary of State, due regard being had to the working of the factory as well as to the safety of the public and of the persons employed therein.

Where an accident by explosion or fire in a factory has wholly or partly destroyed any building of such factory as to which a Government inspector has previously to the accident sent to the occupier a notice that the building is unduly near to some building or work outside the factory, such building shall be reconstructed only upon such site in the factory and with such precautions as may seem reasonable to the Secretary of State, due regard being had to the working of the factory as well as to the safety of the public and of the persons employed therein.

Where an accident by explosion or by fire in a factory has wholly or partly destroyed two or more buildings in such factory, not more than one of such buildings shall be reconstructed except with the permission of the Secretary of State; provided that this enactment shall not apply to any buildings in a lawfully existing factory, if either both or all such buildings are incorporating mills, or if as regards any other buildings a Government inspector has not previously to the accident sent to the occupier a notice that such buildings are unduly near to each other.

Where a building is constructed on a different site in pursuance of this section, the Secretary of State shall cause the necessary alterations to be made in the license, and such alterations shall be deemed to be part of the license.

The reconstruction of any building in contravention of this section shall be deemed to be a breach of the terms of the license, and shall be punished accordingly.

65   Provisions as to coroners inquests on deaths from accidents connected with explosives

With respect to coroners inquests on the bodies of persons whose death may have been caused by the explosion of any explosive or by any accident in connexion with an explosive, the following provisions shall have effect:

(1)   Where a coroner holds an inquest upon a body of any person whose death may have been caused by any accident of which notice is required by this Act to be given to the Secretary of State, or by the explosion of any explosive, the coroner shall adjourn such inquest unless a Government inspector, or some person on behalf of the Secretary of State, is present to watch the proceedings:

(2)   The coroner, at least four days before holding the adjourned inquest, shall send to the Secretary of State notice in writing of the time and place of holding the adjourned inquest:

(3)   The coroner, before the adjournment, may take evidence to ° identify the body, and may order the interment thereof

(4)   If an explosion or accident has not occasioned the death of more than one person, and the coroner has sent to the Secretary of State notice of the time and place of holding the inquest not less than forty-eight hours before the time of holding the same, it shall not be imperative on him to adjourn such inquest in pursuance of this section, if the majority of the jury think it unnecessary so to adjourn:

(5)   A Government inspector or person employed on behalf of the Secretary of State shall be at liberty at any such inquest to examine any witness, subject nevertheless to the order of the coroner on points of law:

(6)   Where evidence is given at an inquest at which no Government inspector or person employed on behalf of the Secretary of State is present, of any neglect as having caused or contributed to the explosion or accident, or of any defect in or about or in connexion with any factory, magazine, store, or registered premises, or any carriage, ship, or boat carrying an explosive, appearing to the coroner or jury to require a remedy, the coroner shall send to the Secretary of State notice in writing of such neglect or defect.

66   Inquiry into accidents and formal investigation in serious cases

The Secretary of State may direct an inquiry to be made by a Government inspector into the cause of any accident which is caused by an explosion or fire either in connexion with any explosive, or of which notice is required by this Act to be given to the Secretary of State, and where it appears to the Secretary of State, either before or after the commencement of any such inquiry, that a more formal investigation of the accident, and of the causes thereof, and of the circumstances attending the same, is expedient, the Secretary of State may by order direct such investigation to be held, and with respect to such inquiry and investigation the following provisions, shall have effect:

(1)   The Secretary of State may, by the same or any subsequent order, appoint any person or persons possessing legal or special knowledge- to assist the Government inspector in holding the formal investigation, or may direct the county court judge,

stipendiary magistrate, metropolitan police magistrate, or other 'person or persons named in the same or any subsequent order, to hold the same with the assistance of a Government inspector or any other assessor or assessors named in the order:

(2) The persons holding any such formal investigation (in this section referred to as the court) shall hold the same in open court in such manner and under such conditions as they may think most effectual for ascertaining the causes and circumstances of the accident, and enabling them to make the report in this section mentioned:

(3) The court shall have for the purpose of such investigation all the powers of a court of summary jurisdiction when acting as a court in hearing informations for offences against this Act, and all the powers of a Government inspector under this Act, and in addition the following powers; namely,

(a) They may enter and inspect any place or building the entry or inspection whereof appears to them requisite for the said purpose:

(b) They may by summons under their hands require the attendance of all such persons as they think fit to call before them and examine for the said purpose, and may for such purpose require answers or returns to such inquiries as they think fit to make:

(c) They may require the production of all books, papers and documents which they consider important for the said purpose:

(d) They may administer an oath, and require any person examined to make and sign a declaration of the truth of the statements made by him in his examination:

(e) Persons attending as witnesses before the court shall be allowed such expenses as would be allowed to witnesses attending before a court of record; and in case of dispute as to the amount to be allowed, the same shall be referred by the court to a master of one of the superior courts, who, on request under the hands of the members of the court, shall ascertain and certify the proper amount of such expenses:

(4) The Government inspector making an inquiry into any accident and the court holding an investigation of any accident under this section shall make a report to the Secretary of State, stating the causes of the accident and all the circumstances attending the same, and any observations thereon or on the evidence or on any matters arising out of the inquiry or investigation which he or they think right to make to the Secretary of State, and the Secretary of State shall cause every such report to be made public in such manner as he thinks expedient:

(5) All expenses incurred in and about an inquiry or investigation under this section shall be deemed to be part of the expenses of the Secretary of State in carrying this Act into execution: and

(6) Any person who without reasonable excuse (proof whereof shall lie on him) either fails, after having had the expenses (if any) to which he is entitled tendered to him, to comply with any summons or requisition of a court holding an investigation under this Act, or prevents or impedes such court in the execution of their duty, is guilty of an offence and liable[, on summary conviction, to a fine not exceeding €5,000 or, on conviction on indictment, to a fine not exceeding €10,000.]¹

Amendments

1   Words substituted by Criminal Justice Act 2006, s 69 and Sch 2.

Local Supervision
Definition and Powers of Local Authority

67   Definition of local authority

The local authority, for the purposes of this Act, shall be—

(1)   In the city of London, except as hereafter in this section mentioned, the court of the Lord Mayor and aldermen of the said city; and

(2)   In the metropolis, (that is, in places for the time being within the jurisdiction of the Metropolitan Board of Works under the' Metropolis Management Act, 1855,) except the city of London, and except as hereafter in this section mentioned, the Metropolitan Board of Works; and

(3)   In any borough in England which is not assessed to the county rate of any county by the justices of such county, except as hereafter in this section mentioned, the mayor, aldermen, and burgesses acting by the council; and

(4)   In any harbour within the jurisdiction of a harbour authority, whether situate or not within the jurisdiction of any local authority before in this section mentioned, the harbour authority, to the exclusion of any other local authority; and

(5)   In any place in which there is no local authority as before in this section defined, the justices in petty sessions assembled.

68   Power of certain local bodies to become a local authority

The council of any borough which is assessed to the county rate of any county by the justices of such county and the commissioners of any improvement district may by order of a Secretary of State made upon the application of such council or commissioners, and published in the London Gazette, be declared to be a local authority for the purposes of this Act, and thereupon shall become a local authority accordingly for such part of their borough or district as is not included in any harbour, to the exclusion of the justices in petty sessions.

69   Duty of local authority and power of officer

It shall be the duty of every local authority to carry into effect within their jurisdiction the powers vested in them under this Act.

Any officer authorised by the local authority may, on producing, if demanded, either a copy of his authority purporting to be certified by the clerk or some member of the local authority, or some other sufficient evidence of his authority, require the occupier of any store (not being subject to the inspection under this Act of any inspector of mines) or any registered premises, or any small firework factory, to show him every or any place and all or any of the receptacles in which any explosive or ingredient of an explosive or any substance the keeping of which is restricted or regulated by this Act, that is in his possession is kept, and to give him samples of such explosive, ingredient, or substance, or of any substance which the officer believes to be an explosive or such ingredient or substance.

Any occupier of a store or registered premises or a small firework factory who refuses to comply with any such requisition of an officer of the local authority, or to give him such assistance as he may require for the purpose of this section, or who wilfully obstructs the local authority, or any officer of the local authority, in the execution of this Act, shall be liable[, on summary conviction, to a fine not exceeding €1,000.][1]

Amendments

1   Words substituted by Criminal Justice Act 2006, s 69 and Sch 2.

70   Expenses of local authority

All expenses incurred by any local authority in carrying into effect the execution of this Act, including the salary and expenses of any officer directed by them to act under this Act, shall be paid out of the local rate. The local rate shall for the purposes of this Act mean as follows; that is to say,

> In the city of London the consolidated rate;
>
> In the metropolis (exclusive of the city of London) the consolidated rate as levied in the metropolis exclusive of the city of London, and without any demand on such city;
>
> In a borough the borough fund or borough rate;
>
> In a harbour any moneys, fund, or rate applicable or leviable by the harbour authority for any harbour purposes;
>
> In any place where the justices in petty sessions are the local authority the county rate; and
>
> In an improvement district any fund, moneys, or rate applicable or leviable by the Improvement Commissioners for any purposes of improvement within their district;

And the local rate or any increase of the local rate may notwithstanding any limitation in any Act be levied for the purposes of this Act.

Power of Local Authority to provide Carriages and Magazines

71   Undertaking of carriage by harbour authority and canal company

Every harbour authority and canal company shall, in addition to any other powers they may have for the like purpose, have power to provide carriages, ships, and boats for the conveyance, loading, or unloading of an explosive within the jurisdiction of such authority or company, and may charge a reasonable sum fixed by a byelaw under this Act for the use of such carriage, ship, or boat.

72   Provision of magazines by local authority

Where any local authority other than justices in petty sessions satisfy the Secretary of State that the erection of a magazine by such authority, either within or without their jurisdiction, for the keeping of any explosive, would conduce to the safety of the public within their jurisdiction, and would not be injurious to any harbour or urban sanitary district out of their jurisdiction, the Secretary of State may grant a license under this Act for such magazine.

Where the magazine is without the jurisdiction of the local authority erecting the same, the assent of the local authority within whose jurisdiction the site is situate to such site shall be applied for in manner provided by this Act, and when the magazine is within the said jurisdiction notice of the application to the Secretary of State for the license shall be given in like manner as notice of the intention to apply for the assent of the local authority to a site is required by this Act to be given.

The local authority may, for the purpose of any such license, acquire any land or right over land, or appropriate any land or right belonging to them, and acquire or build a magazine, and may maintain and manage such magazine, and may charge for the use by persons of any such magazine such reasonable sums as they may from time to time, with the approval of the Secretary of State, fix.

Such sums shall be applied in aid of the local rate, and the expenses incurred for the purposes of this section may be defrayed out' of the local rate, and the local authority may borrow on the security of the local rate the amount required for the purpose of acquiring any land or right over land, or acquiring or building a magazine in pursuance of this section.

Any such loan shall be made with the approval, in the case of a council, of the Treasury, and in the case of Improvement Commissioners, of the Local Government Board, and in the case of a harbour authority, of the Board of Trade.

For the purpose of such borrowing the clauses of "The Commissioners Clauses Act, 1847," with respect to the mortgages to be executed by the Commissioners, shall be incorporated with this Act, and in the construction of those clauses for the purpose of this Act, this Act shall be deemed to be the special Act, and the local authority which is borrowing shall be deemed to be the Commissioners.

For the purpose of the purchase of any land or right over land for the purpose of this section "The Lands Clauses Consolidation Act, 1845," and the Acts amending the same (except so much as relates to the purchase of land otherwise than by agreement), shall be incorporated with this section, and in construing those Acts for the purposes of this section the special Act shall be construed to mean this Act, and the •promoters of the undertaking shall be construed to mean the local authority, and land shall be construed to include any right over land.

Where any offence under this Act is committed in or about any magazine erected in pursuance of this section, such offence may be prosecuted and tried and the penalty and forfeiture therefor recovered either in the county or place in which the magazine is situate, or in any adjoining county or place.

General Power of Search

73   Search for explosive when in place in contravention of this Act, or offence being committed with respect to it

Where any of the following officers, namely, any Government inspector, or any constable or any officer of the local authority, if such constable or officer is specially authorised either (a) by a warrant of a justice (which warrant such justice may grant upon reasonable ground being assigned on oath), or (b) (where it appears to a superintendent or other officer of police of equal or superior rank, or to a Government inspector, that the case is one of emergency and that the delay in obtaining a warrant would be likely to endanger life,) by a written order from such superintendent, officer, or inspector,—has reasonable cause to believe that any offence has been or is being committed with respect to an explosive in any place (whether a building or not, or a carriage, boat, or ship), or that any explosive is in any such place in contravention of this Act, or that the provisions of this Act are not duly observed in any such place, such officer may, on producing, if demanded, in the case of a Government inspector a copy of his appointment, and in the case of any other officer his authority, enter at any time, and if needs be by force, and as well on Sunday as on other days, the said place, and every part thereof, and examine the same, and search for explosives therein, and take samples of any explosive and ingredient of an explosive therein, and any substance reasonably supposed to be an explosive, or such ingredient which may be found therein.

Any person who, by himself or by others, fails to admit into any place occupied by or under the control of such person any officer demanding to enter in pursuance of this section, or in any way obstructs such officer in the execution of his duty under this section, shall be liable[, on summary conviction, to a fine not exceeding €1,000,][1] and shall also be liable to forfeit all explosives, and ingredients thereof, which are at the time of the offence in his possession or under his control at the said place.

Where a constable or officer of the local authority specially authorised by written authority other than a warrant of a justice of the peace, enters and searches as above provided, a special report in writing of every act done by such constable or officer in pursuance of that authority, and of the grounds on which it is done, shall be forthwith sent by the person by whom or under whose authority it was done to the Secretary of State.

Amendments

1   Words substituted by Criminal Justice Act 2006, s 69 and Sch 2.

74   Seizure and detention of explosives liable to forfeiture

Where any of the following officers, namely, any Government inspector, or any constable, or any officer of the local authority, has reasonable cause to believe that any explosive or ingredient of an explosive or substance found by him is liable to be forfeited under this Act, he may seize and detain the same until some court of summary jurisdiction has determined whether the same is or is not so liable to be forfeited, and with respect thereto the following provisions shall have effect:

(1)   The officer seizing may either require the occupier of the place in which it was seized (whether a building or not, or a carriage, boat, or ship) to detain the same in such place or in any place under the control of such occupier, or may remove it in such manner and to such place as will in his opinion least endanger the public safety, and there detain it, and may, where the matter appears to him to be urgent and fraught with serious public danger, and he is a Government inspector, or is authorised by an order from a Government inspector or a justice of the peace, or from a superintendent or other officer of police of equal or superior rank, cause the same to be destroyed or otherwise rendered harmless; but before destroying or rendering harmless the same he shall take and keep a sample thereof, and shall, if required, give a portion of the sample to the person owning the explosive, or having the same under his control at the time of the seizure; and any such occupier who, by himself or by others, fails to keep the same when he is required in pursuance of, this

section to detain it, and any such occupier or other person who, except with the authority of the officer seizing the same, or of a Government inspector, or in case of emergency for the purpose of preventing explosion or fire, removes, alters, or in any way tampers or deals with the same while so detained, shall be liable [, on summary conviction, to a fine not exceeding €5,000 or, on conviction on indictment, to a fine not exceeding €10,000][1], and shall also be liable to forfeit all explosives, and ingredients thereof, which are at the time of the offence in his possession or under his control at the said place:

(2) The proceedings before a court of summary jurisdiction for determining whether the same is or is not liable to forfeiture shall be commenced as soon as practicable after the seizure; and

(3) The receptacles containing the same may be seized, detained, and removed in like manner as the contents thereof; and

(4) The officer seizing the same may use for the purposes of the removal and detention thereof any ship, boat, or carriage in which the same was seized, and any tug, tender, engine, tackle, beasts, and accoutrements belonging to or drawing or provided for drawing such ship, boat, or carriage, and shall pay to the owner a reasonable compensation for such use, to be determined, in case of dispute, by a court of summary jurisdiction, and to be recovered in like manner as penalties under this Act; and

(5) The same shall, so far as practicable, be kept and conveyed in accordance with this Act, and with all due precaution to prevent accident, but the person seizing, removing, detaining, keeping, or conveying the same shall not be liable to any penalty, punishment, or forfeiture under this or any other Act, or to any damages, for keeping or conveying the same, so that he use all such due precautions as aforesaid; and

(6) The officer seizing the same, or dealing with the same in pursuance of this section, shall not be liable to damages or otherwise in respect of such seizure or dealing, or any act incidental to or consequential thereon, unless it is proved that he made such seizure without reasonable cause, or that he caused damage to the article seized by some wilful neglect or default.

Amendments

1 Words substituted by Criminal Justice Act 2006, s 69 and Sch 2.

75 Inspection of wharf, carriage, boat, &c. with explosives in transitu

Any of the following officers, namely, any Government inspector under this Act, any chief officer of police, and any superior officer appointed for the purposes of this Act where the justices in petty sessions are the local authority, by the court of quarter sessions to which such justices belong, and in the case of any other local authority by the local authority itself, may, for the purpose of ascertaining whether the provisions of this Act with respect to the conveyance, loading, unloading, and importation of an explosive are complied with, enter, inspect, and examine at any time, and as well on Sundays as on other days, the wharf, carriage, ship, or boat of any carrier or other person who conveys goods for hire, or of the occupier of any factory, magazine, or store, or of the importer of any explosive, on or in which wharf, carriage, ship, or boat he has reasonable cause to suppose an explosive to be for the purpose of or in course of conveyance, but so as not to unnecessarily obstruct the work or business of any such carrier, person, occupier, or importer.

Any such officer, if he find any offence being committed under this Act in any such wharf, carriage, ship, or boat, or on any public wharf, may seize and detain or remove the said carriage, ship, or boat, or the explosive, in such manner and with such precautions as appear to him to be necessary to remove any danger to the public, and may seize and detain the said explosive, as if it were liable to forfeiture.

Any officer above mentioned in this section, and any officer of police, or officer of the local authority who has reasonable cause to suppose that any offence against this Act is being committed in respect of any carriage (not being on a railway) or any boat conveying, loading, or unloading any explosive, and that the case is one of emergency, and that the delay in obtaining a warrant will be likely to endanger life, may stop, and enter, inspect, and _examine, such carriage or boat, and by detention or removal thereof or otherwise take such precautions as may be reasonably necessary for removing, such danger, in like manner as if such explosive were liable to forfeiture.

Every officer shall for the purpose of this section have the same powers and be in the same position as if he were authorised by a search warrant granted under this Act, and any person failing to admit or obstructing such officer shall be liable to the same penalty.

76 Payment for samples of explosives

When a Government inspector, constable, or officer of the local authority in pursuance of this Act takes samples of any explosive, or ingredient, or substance, he shall pay for or tender payment for the same to such amount as he considers to be the market value thereof, and the occupier of the place in which, or the owner of the bulk from which, the sample was taken, may recover any excess of the real value over the amount so paid or tendered, and any amount so tendered, from the inspector, constable, or officer taking the sample as a debt in the county court of the district within which the sample was taken.

PART IV

SUPPLEMENTAL PROVISIONS, LEGAL PROCEEDINGS, EXEMPTIONS, AND DEFINITIONS

Supplemental Provisions

77 Penalty on and removal of trespassers

Any person who enters without permission or otherwise trespasses upon any factory, magazine, or store, or the land immediately adjoining thereto which is occupied by the occupier of such factory, magazine, or store, or on any wharf for which byelaws are made by the occupier thereof under this Act, shall for every such offence, if not otherwise punishable, be liable[, on summary conviction, to a fine not exceeding €3,000 or, on conviction on indictment, to a fine not exceeding €5,000],¹ and may be forthwith removed from such factory, magazine, store, land, or wharf, by any constable, or by the occupier of such factory, magazine, store, or wharf, or any agent or servant of or other person authorised by such occupier.

Any person other than the occupier of or person employed in or about any factory, magazine, or store who is found committing any act which tends to cause explosion or fire in or about such factory, magazine, or store, shall be liable[, on summary conviction, to a fine not exceeding €5,000 or, on conviction on indictment, to a fine not exceeding €10,000.]¹

The occupier of any such factory, magazine, store, or wharf shall post up in some conspicuous place or places a notice or notices warning all persons of their liability to penalties under this section; but the absence of any such notice or notices shall not exempt a person from a penalty under this section.

Amendments

1   Words substituted by Criminal Justice Act 2006, s 69 and Sch 2.

78   Arrest without warrant of persons committing dangerous offences

Any person who is found committing any act for which he is liable to a penalty under this Act, and which tends to cause explosion or fire in or about any factory, magazine, store, railway, canal, harbour, or wharf, or any carriage, ship, or boat, may be apprehended without a warrant by a constable, or an officer of the local authority, or, by the occupier of or the agent or servant of or other person authorised by the occupier of such factory, magazine, store, or wharf, or by any agent or servant of or other person authorised by the railway or canal company or harbour authority, and be removed from the place at which he is arrested, and conveyed as soon as conveniently may be before a court of summary jurisdiction.

79   Imprisonment for wilful act or neglect endangering life or limb

Where any person is guilty of any offence which under this Act is punishable by a pecuniary penalty only, and which, in the opinion of the court that tries the case, was reasonably calculated to endanger the safety of or to cause serious personal injury to any of the public or the persons employed in or about any factory, magazine, store, or registered premises, or any harbour, railway, canal, wharf, ship, boat, carriage, or place where such offence is committed, or to cause a dangerous accident, and was committed wilfully by the personal act, personal default, or personal negligence of the person accused, such person shall be liable, if the court is of opinion that a pecuniary penalty will not meet the circumstances [of the case—

(a)   on summary conviction, to imprisonment for a term not exceeding 12 months or both the pecuniary penalty and such imprisonment, or

(b)   on conviction on indictment, to imprisonment for a term not exceeding 5 years or both the pecuniary penalty and such imprisonment.]¹

Amendments

1   Words substituted by Criminal Justice Act 2006, s 69 and Sch 2.

80 Penalty for throwing fireworks in thoroughfare

[(1) Any person who in any place—

    (a) ignites a firework or causes it to be ignited, or

    (b) throws, directs or propels an ignited firework at or towards a person or property,

is guilty of an offence.

(2) Any person—

    (a) who possesses a firework with intent to sell or otherwise to supply it to another, and

    (b) who does not hold a licence under this Act to import it,

is guilty of an offence.

(3) In any proceedings for an offence under subsection (2) it is not necessary for the prosecution to negative by evidence the existence of a licence to import the firework concerned, and accordingly the onus of proving the existence of any such licence is on the defendant.

(4) A member of the Garda Síochána who, with reasonable cause, suspects that a person possesses a firework in contravention of subsection (2) may—

    (a) request that the person give his or her name and address and that the information given by the person in response to the request be verified,

    (b) if not satisfied that the information so given is correct, request that the person accompany the member to a Garda Síochána station for the purpose of verifying the information,

    (c) without warrant—

        (i) search the person and, if the member considers it necessary for that purpose, detain the person for such time as is reasonably necessary to make the search,

        (ii) enter and search any vehicle, vessel or aircraft in which the member suspects that a firework may be found, and

        (iii) seize and detain anything found in the course of the search which the member reasonably believes to be evidence of, or relating to, an offence under this section.

(5) This section is without prejudice to any power to detain or search a person or to seize or detain property which may be exercised by a member of the Garda Síochána under any other enactment.

(6) A member of the Garda Síochána who suspects, with reasonable cause, that a person has committed an offence under this section may arrest the person without warrant.

(7) If a judge of the District Court is satisfied by information on oath of a member of the Garda Síochána not below the rank of sergeant that there are reasonable grounds for suspecting that evidence of, or relating to, the commission of an offence under this section is to be found in any place, the judge may issue a warrant for the search of that place and any persons found at that place.

(8) The search warrant shall be expressed, and shall operate, to authorise a named member of the Garda Síochána, accompanied by such other members of the Garda Síochána or other persons as the member thinks necessary—

(a) to enter the place named in the warrant at any time or times within one week of the date of issue of the warrant, on production if so requested of the warrant and if necessary by the use of reasonable force,

(b) to search it and any persons found at the place, and

(c) to seize anything found at the place, or anything found in the possession of any person present there at the time of the search that that member reasonably believes to be evidence of, or relating to, the commission of an offence under this section.

(9) A member of the Garda Síochána acting under the authority of a search warrant under this section may—

(a) require any person present at the place where the search is being carried out to give to the member his or her name and address, and

(b) arrest without warrant any person who—

(i) obstructs or attempts to obstruct the member in the carrying out of his or her duties,

(ii) fails to comply with a requirement under paragraph (a), or

(iii) gives a name or address which the member has reasonable cause for believing is false or misleading.

(10) A person who—

(a) does not give his or her name and address when requested to do so under subsection (4)(a) of this section or gives a name and address that is false or misleading, or

(b) does not comply with a request under subsection (4)(b) of this section,

is guilty of an offence and liable on summary conviction to a fine not exceeding €2,500 or imprisonment for a term not exceeding 6 months or both.

(11) A person who—

(a) obstructs or attempts to obstruct a member of the Garda Síochána acting under the authority of a search warrant under this section,

(b) does not comply with a requirement under subsection (9)(a) of this section, or

(c) gives a false or misleading name or address to such a member,

is guilty of an offence and liable on summary conviction to a fine not exceeding €2,500 or imprisonment for a term not exceeding 6 months or both.

(12) A person guilty of an offence under this section (except subsection (10) or (11)) is liable—

(a) on summary conviction, to a fine not exceeding €2,500 or imprisonment for a term not exceeding 6 months or both, or

(b) on conviction on indictment, to a fine not exceeding €10,000 or imprisonment for a term not exceeding 5 years or both.

(13) A court by which a person is convicted of an offence under subsection (1) or (2) may order anything shown to the satisfaction of the court to relate to the offence to be forfeited and either destroyed or dealt with in such other manner as the court thinks fit.

(14) In this section—

"banger" means a non-metallic case containing black powder, the principal purpose of which is to make a noise when ignited or initiated;

"black powder" means a powder consisting of a mixture of charcoal and sodium nitrate or potassium nitrate, with or without sulphur;

"firework"—

(a) means a device containing pyrotechnic material which, when functioning, burns or explodes to produce a visual or aural effect or movement or a gas, either separately or in any combination, as a direct form of entertainment, but

(b) except in subsection (1)(b) does not include—

(i) a low hazard firework (except a banger), or

(ii) a firework imported under licence in accordance with section 40(9) of this Act;

"low hazard firework" means a firework which presents a low hazard and is designed for indoor use;

"place" includes a dwelling;

"pyrotechnic material" means a substance or mixture of substances designed, when ignited, to produce an aural or visual effect or a gas either separately or in any combination.".

Amendments

1   Section 80 substituted by Criminal Justice Act 2006, s 68.

81   Forgery and falsification of documents

Every person who forges or counterfeits any license, certificate, document, or plan granted or required in pursuance or for the purposes of this Act, or gives or signs any such document or plan to his knowledge false in any material particular, or wilfully makes use of any such forged, counterfeit, or false license, certificate, document, or plan, shall be liable [on summary conviction, to a fine not exceeding €5,000 or imprisonment for a term not exceeding 12 months or both or, on conviction on indictment, to a fine not exceeding €10,000 or imprisonment for a term not exceeding five years or both.]¹

Amendments

1   Words substituted by Criminal Justice Act 2006, s 69 and Sch 2.

82   Punishment for defacing notices

Every person who, without due authority, pulls down, injures or defaces any notice, copy of rules, or document, when affixed in pursuance of this Act, or of the special rules, shall be liable to a penalty not exceeding [€100.]¹

Amendments

1   Words substituted by Criminal Justice Act 2006, s 69 and Sch 2.

83   Provisions as to Orders in Council and orders of Secretary of State

Her Majesty may from time to time make orders in Council for doing anything which is in this Act expressed to be authorised, directed, regulated, prescribed, or done by Order in Council.

Every Order in Council or order of the Secretary of State which purports to be made in pursuance of this Act shall be presumed to have been duly made and to be within the powers of this Act, and no objection to the legality thereof shall be entertained in any legal proceeding whatever.

Every Order in Council made in pursuance of this Act shall take effect as if it were enacted in this Act, and shall be published in the London Gazette, and Akan be laid before both Houses of Parliament within one month after it is made, if Parliament be then sitting, or if not, within one month after the commencement of the then next session of Parliament.

Her Majesty may by Order in Council, and a Secretary of State may by order, from time to time revoke, add to, or alter any previous Orders in Council or orders of the Secretary of State, as the case may be, under this Act.

84   Publication of byelaws, notices, &c

All byelaws, notices, and documents directed by this Act to be published or advertised shall, save as otherwise provided by this Act, be published in the place which such notices and documents affect, by advertisement in some newspapers circulating generally in such place, or by placards or handbills, or in such manner as the Secretary of State may from time to time direct as being in his opinion sufficient for giving information thereof to all persons interested.

85   Requisitions, notices, &c. to be in writing, &c., and how to be served

All orders, permissions, notices, and documents issued or given by the Secretary of State for the purposes of this, Act, and all notices under this Act, shall be in writing or print or partly in writing and partly in print, and all notices and documents required by this Act to be served, given, or sent by, on, or to a Government inspector or Secretary of State may be sent by post, by a prepaid letter, and if sent by post shall be deemed to have been served, given, and received respectively at the time when the letter containing the same would be delivered in the ordinary course of post; and in proving such service, giving, or sending, it shall be sufficient to prove that the letter containing the notice was properly addressed and prepaid and put into the post.

All notices and documents directed by or required for the purposes of this Act to be given or sent to the Secretary of State shall, if sent to a Government inspector under this Act, be deemed to have been sent to the Secretary of State.

All notices and documents directed by or required for the purposes of this Act to be given or sent to a local authority may be sent, by post or otherwise, to the Clerk or office of the local authority, or delivered to some person employed by them for the purposes of this Act.

86   Construction of enactments referring to powers of searching for gunpowder

Where any enactment refers to any power of searching for gunpowder, or to any provisions of an Act of the twelfth year of King George the Third, chapter sixty-one, or of any Act repealed by this Act relative to the search for gunpowder, such enactment shall be deemed to refer to the provisions of this Act with respect to the search for and seizure, detention, and removal of an explosive by a Government inspector.

Legal Proceedings

87 **Exemption of occupier from penalty upon proof of another being real offender**

Where any offence under this Act for which the occupier of any factory, magazine, store, or registered premises is liable to a penalty or forfeiture has in fact been committed by some other person, such other person shall be liable to a penalty not exceeding twenty pounds.

Where such occupier is charged with an offence so committed by some other person, the occupier shall be exempt from any penalty and forfeiture upon proving that he had supplied proper means and issued proper orders for the observance and used due diligence to enforce the observance of this Act, and that the offence in question was actually committed by some other person without his connivance, and if the actual offender be alive, that he has taken all practicable means in his power to prosecute such offender to conviction.

Where a Government inspector, or an officer of the local authority, or the local authority, is satisfied, before instituting a proceeding for any offence under this Act against an occupier, that such occupier, if such proceeding were instituted against him, would, under the foregoing provisions of this section, upon taking all practicable means in his power to prosecute the actual offender to conviction, be exempt from any penalty and forfeiture, and the occupier gives all facilities in his power for proceeding against and convicting the person whom the inspector, officer, or local authority believes actually to have committed the offence, the inspector, officer, or local authority shall proceed against that person in the first instance. without first proceeding against the occupier.

The occupier or other defendant, when charged in respect of any offence by another person, may, if he think fit, be sworn and examined as an ordinary witness in the case.

Where any offence under this Act for which any warehouseman, carrier, occupier of a wharf or dock, or owner or master of any ship, boat, or carriage, is liable to a penalty or forfeiture, has in fact been committed by some other person, this section shall apply in like manner as if the warehouseman, carrier, occupier of a wharf or dock, owner, or master were such an occupier as above in this section mentioned.

88 **Exemption of carrier and owner and master of ship where consignee, &c. in fault**

Where a carrier or owner or master of a ship or boat is prevented from complying with this Act by the wilful act, neglect, or default of the consignor or consignee of the explosive, or other person, or by the improper refusal of the consignee or other person to accept delivery of the explosive, such consignor, consignee, or other person who is guilty of such wilful act, neglect, default, or refusal shall be liable to the same penalty to which the carrier, owner, or master is liable for a breach of this Act, and his conviction shall exempt the carrier, owner, or master from any penalty or forfeiture under this Act.

89 **Supplemental provisions as to forfeiture of explosive**

Where a court before whom a person is convicted of an offence against this Act has power to forfeit any explosive owned by or found in the possession or under the control of such person, the court may, if it think it just and expedient, in lieu of forfeiting such explosive, impose upon such person, in addition to any other penalty or punishment, a penalty not exceeding such sum as appears to the court to be the value of the explosive so liable to be forfeited.

Where any explosive, or ingredient of an explosive, is alleged to be liable under this Act to be forfeited, any indictment, information, or complaint may be laid against the owner of such explosive or ingredient, for the purpose only of enforcing such forfeiture, and where the owner is unknown, or cannot be found, a court may cause a notice to be advertised, stating that unless cause is shown to the contrary at the time and place named in the notice, such explosive will be forfeited, and at such time and place the court, after hearing the owner or any person on his behalf (who may be present), may order all or any part of such explosive or ingredient to be forfeited.

90   Jurisdiction in tidal waters or on boundaries

For all the purposes of this Act—

(1)   Any harbour, tidal water, or inland water which runs between or abuts on or forms the boundary of the jurisdiction of two or more courts shall be deemed to be wholly within the jurisdiction of each of such courts; and

(2)   Any tidal water not included in the foregoing descriptions, and within the territorial jurisdiction of Her Majesty, and adjacent to or surrounding any part of the shore of the United Kingdom, and any pier, jetty, mole, or work extending into the same, shall be deemed to form part of the shore to which such water or part of the sea is adjacent, or which it surrounds.

91   Prosecution of offences either summarily or on indictment

Every offence under this Act may be prosecuted and every penalty under this Act may be recovered, and all explosives and ingredients liable to be forfeited under this Act may be forfeited either on indictment or before a court of summary jurisdiction, in manner directed by the Summary Jurisdiction Acts.

Provided that the penalty imposed by a court of summary jurisdiction shall not exceed one hundred pounds exclusive of costs, and exclusive of any forfeiture or penalty in lieu of forfeiture, and the term of imprisonment imposed by any such court shall not exceed one month.

All costs and money directed to be recovered as penalties may be recovered before a court of summary jurisdiction in mariner directed by the Summary Jurisdiction Acts.

A court of summary jurisdiction may by order prohibit a person from doing any act for doing which such person has twice been convicted under this Act, and may order any person disobeying such summary order to be imprisoned for any period not exceeding six months.

92   Power of offender in certain cases to elect to be tried on indictment, and. not by summary jurisdiction

Where a person is accused before a court of summary jurisdiction of any offence under this Act, the penalty for which offence as assigned by this Act, exclusive of forfeiture, exceeds one hundred pounds, the accused may, on appearing before the court of summary jurisdiction, declare that he objects to being tried for such offence by a court of summary jurisdiction, and thereupon the court of summary jurisdiction may deal with the case in all respects as if the accused were charged with an indictable offence and not an offence punishable on summary conviction, and the offence may be prosecuted on indictment accordingly.

93   Appeal to quarter sessions

If any party feels aggrieved by any summary order made by a court of summary jurisdiction under this Act, or by any order or conviction made by a court of summary jurisdiction in determining any complaint or information under this Act, by which order or conviction the sum adjudged to be paid, including costs, and including the value of any forfeiture, exceeds twenty pounds, -the party so aggrieved may appeal therefrom to quarter sessions, in manner provided with respect to an appeal to quarter sessions by section one hundred and ten of the Act of the session of the twenty-fourth and twenty-fifth years of the reign of Her present Majesty, chapter ninety-six.

94   Constitution of court

The court of summary jurisdiction, when hearing and Constitution determining an information or complaint, in respect of any offence of court under this Act, shall be constituted either of two or more justices of the peace in petty sessions sitting at a place appointed for holding petty sessions, or of some magistrate or officer sifting alone or with others at some court or other place appointed for the administration of justice, and for the time being empowered by law to do alone any act authorised to be done by more than one justice of the peace.

95   Distress of ship

Where the owner or master of a ship or boat is adjudged to pay a penalty for an offence committed with or in relation to such ship or boat, the court may, in addition to any other power they may have for the purpose of compelling payment of such penalty, direct the same to be levied by distress or arrestment and sale of the said ship or boat and her tackle.

96   Application of penalties and disposal of forfeitures

All penalties imposed in pursuance of this Act by a court of summary jurisdiction upon the prosecution of a Government inspector shall, notwithstanding anything in any other Act, be paid into the receipt of Her Majesty's Exchequer, in such manner as the Treasury may from time to time direct, and be carried to the Consolidated Fund.

Any explosive or ingredient forfeited in pursuance of this Act may be sold, destroyed, or otherwise disposed of in such manner as the court declaring the forfeiture, or the Secretary of State, may direct, and the proceeds of any such sale or disposal shall be paid, applied, and accounted for in like manner as penalties under this Act.

The receptacle containing any such explosive or ingredients may be forfeited, sold, destroyed, or otherwise disposed of, in like manner as the contents thereof.

The provisions of Part Three of this Act with respect to an explosive, or ingredient of an explosive, seized in pursuance of this Act, and to the officer seizing, 'removing, detaining, keeping, or conveying, or otherwise dealing with the same, shall apply to any explosive and ingredient declared by any court to be forfeited, and to the officer removing, detaining, keeping, conveying, selling, destroying, or otherwise disposing of the same.

The court declaring the forfeiture, or the Secretary of State directing the sale or other disposal of any forfeited explosive or ingredient, and the receptacles thereof, may require the owner of such explosive or ingredient to permit the use of any ship, boat, or carriage containing such explosive or ingredient for the purpose of such sale or disposal, upon payment of a reasonable compensation for the same, to be determined in case of dispute by a court of summary jurisdiction; and where the explosive or ingredient is directed to be destroyed, the owner and the person having possession of such explosive or ingredient, and the owner and master of the ship, boat, or carriage containing the same, or some or one of them, shall destroy the same accordingly, and if the court or Secretary of State so order, the ship, boat, or carriage may be detained until the same is so destroyed; and if the Secretary of State is satisfied that default has been made in complying with any such direction by him or by a court, and that the detention of the ship, boat, or carriage will not secure the safety of the public, and that it is impracticable, having regard to the safety of the public or of the persons employed in such destruction, to effect the same without using such ship, boat, or carriage, or otherwise dealing with such ship, boat, or carriage, in like manner as if it were a receptacle for an explosive forfeited under this Act, the Secretary of State may direct such ship, boat, and carriage, or any of them, to be, and the same may accordingly be, so used or dealt with.

Exemptions and Savings

97　　Exemption of Government factories, &c. from the Act

This Act shall not apply—

(1) To any factory, magazine, store, premises, wharf, place, or explosive under the control of a Secretary of State, the Commissioners of the Admiralty, or other department of the Government, or otherwise held for the service of the Crown, or to the manufacture, keeping, or importation of such explosive; or

(2) To any of Her Majesty's ships, boats, or carriages; or

(3) To the keeping or making up, or adapting for the use of any explosive issued by or by the authority of a Secretary of State for the use of any volunteer corps or administrative regiment, or by or by the authority of the Commissioners of the Admiralty for the use of any force under the control of those commissioners, so far as such explosive is kept, made up, and adapted for use in accordance with the regulations of the Secretary of State or the said commissioners, as the case may be; or

(4) To any storehouse appointed for receiving any such explosive as last above mentioned in pursuance of section twenty-six of the Volunteer Act, 1863, and any Act amending the same, or otherwise, if such storehouse is approved by the Secretary of State or the Commissioners of the Admiralty, as the case may be, as a fit place for the storing of such explosive, and is managed in accordance with the regulations of a Secretary of State or such commissioners for the management of such storehouses, or for the management of the like storehouses appointed for the use of Her Majesty's army or navy; or

(5) To the conveyance of any explosive under the control of a Secretary of State, the Commissioners of the Admiralty, or other department of the Government, or to the conveyance of any explosive otherwise held for the service of the Crown when the same is being conveyed in accordance with the regulations of a Secretary of State or the Commissioners of the Admiralty or other department of the Government:

Provided that every person who enters without permission or otherwise trespasses upon any factory, magazine, or storehouse above in this section mentioned or the land immediately adjoining thereto in the, occupation of the Crown or of a Secretary of State or the Commissioner of the Admiralty or other department of the Government or if it adjoin such a storehouse in the occupation of the officer or person in whom such storehouse is vested, and any person found committing any act tending to cause explosion or fire in or about such factory, magazine, or storehouse, shall be liable to the like penalty, and may be removed and arrested in like manner as if this section had not been enacted and this Act applied to such factory, magazine, or storehouse, as above in this section mentioned.

98   Saving for rocket and fog stations

This Act shall not apply—

(1)   To the keeping of any rockets for use in any apparatus for saving life, kept under the control of the Commissioners of the Admiralty or the Board of Trade; or

(2)   To the keeping of any explosive kept for the purpose of signalling at or near a station on the sea coast, under the control of any general lighthouse authority, as defined by the Merchant Shipping Act, 1854.

99   Exemption of magazines in the Mersey

Nothing in this Act with respect to the keeping of gunpowder shall apply to any vessel for the storage of gunpowder moored in the river Mersey at a place appointed either before or after the passing of this Act, in pursuance of the Act of the session of the fourteenth and fifteenth years of the reign of Her present Majesty, chapter sixty-seven, intituled An Act to repeal so much of an Act of the twelfth year of King George the Third relating to the making, keeping, and carriage of gunpowder, as exempts therefrom certain gunpowder magazines and stores near Liverpool, and to make certain temporary provisions with regard to the said magazines and stores; nor shall anything in this Act affect the powers of the Commissioners of the Admiralty, or a Secretary of State, or the Commissioners for the Conservancy of the River Mersey under the said Act:

Provided that any explosive other than, gunpowder shall not be kept in such vessel except in pursuance of a license under this Act.

100   Saving for master of ship and carrier in case of emergency

Nothing in this Act shall render liable to any penalty or forfeiture the owner or master of any ship or boat, or any carrier or warehouseman, or the person having charge of any carriage, for any act done in breach of this Act, if he proves that by reason of stress of weather, inevitable accident, or other emergency, the doing of such act was, under the circumstances, necessary and proper.

101   Saving for rockets, gunpowder, &c. on board ship in compliance with 17 & 18 Vict. c. 104

Where any gunpowder, rockets, or other explosive are on board any ship in pursuance of the provisions of the Merchant Shipping Act, 1854, and the Acts amending the same, or any order or regulation made under any of those Acts, nothing in this Act shall apply to such gunpowder, rockets, or explosive, except that the conveyance and keeping thereof on board the ship or elsewhere while the ship is in harbour shall be subject to the byelaws under this Act, and byelaws under this Act may be made for regulating such conveyance and keeping.

102   Saving clause as to liability

This Act shall not, save as is herein expressly provided, exempt any person from any action or suit in respect of any nuisance, tort, or otherwise, which might, but for the provisions of this Act, have been brought against him.

This Act shall not exempt any person from any indictment or other proceeding for a nuisance, or for an offence which is indictable at common law, or by any Act of Parliament other than this Act, so that no person be punished twice for the same offence.

When proceedings are taken before any court against any person in respect of any offence under this Act, which is also an offence indictable at common law or by some Act of Parliament other than this Act, the court may direct that, instead of such proceedings being continued, proceedings shall be taken for indicting such person at common law or under some Act of Parliament other, than this Act.

A continuing certificate granted under this Act shall not make lawful any factory, magazine, or store, or any part thereof, which immediately before the passing of this Act was unlawful.

103   Powers of Act cumulative, with power to make provisional order for repealing local Acts

All powers given by this Act shall be deemed to be in addition to and not in derogation of any other powers conferred on any local authority by Act of Parliament, but the Secretary of State may, on the application of any local authority, or of any council of a borough, or any urban sanitary authority, or on the application of any persons making, keeping, importing, exporting, or selling any explosive within the jurisdiction of any local authority, council, or urban sanitary authority, after notice to such authority, make an order for repealing, altering, or amending all or any of the provisions of any Act of Parliament, charter, or custom respecting the manufacture, keeping, conveyance, importation, exportation, or sale of an explosive, or the powers of such council or authority for regulating the same, or otherwise in relation to an explosive.

Notice of the draft of every such order shall be advertised not less than one month before the order is made, and the Secretary of State shall consider all objections to such draft order sent to him in writing during the said month, and shall, if it seem to him necessary, direct a local inquiry into the validity of any such objections.

Any such order shall be of no force unless confirmed by Parliament, but when so confirmed shall have effect with such modifications or alterations as may be therein made by Parliament.

If while a Bill confirming any such order is pending in either House of Parliament, a petition is presented against such order, the Bill, so far as it relates to such order, may be referred to a Select Committee, and the petitioner shall be allowed to appear and oppose the same as in the case of a Bill for a private Act.

An order under this section may also be made for revoking or altering an order under this section previously made and confirmed by Parliament.

Definitions

104   Extension of definition of explosive to other explosive substances

Her Majesty may, by Order in Council, declare that any substance which appears to Her Majesty to be specially dangerous to life or property by reason either of its explosive properties, or of any process in the manufacture thereof being liable to explosion, shall be deemed to be an explosive within the meaning of this Act, and the provisions of this Act (subject to such exceptions, limitations, and restrictions as may be specified in the order) shall accordingly extend to such substance in like manner as if it were included in the term explosive in this Act.

105 Persons carrying on certain processes to be deemed manufacturers

Any person who carries on any of the following processes, namely, the process of dividing into its component parts or otherwise breaking up or unmaking any explosive, or making fit for use any damaged explosive, or the process of remaking, altering, or repairing any explosive, shall be subject to the provisions of this Act as if he manufactured an explosive, and the expression "manufacture" shall in this Act be construed accordingly.

106 It shall be lawful for Her Majesty from time to time, by Order in Council, to define, for the purposes of this Act, the composition, quality, and character of any explosive, and to classify explosives.

Where the composition, quality, or character of any explosive has been defined by an Order in Council, any article alleged to be such explosive which differs from such definition in composition, quality, or character, whether by reason of deterioration or otherwise, shall not be deemed, for the purposes of this Act, to be the explosives so defined.

107 Definition of "chief officer of police" and "police district"

In this Act—

The expression "chief officer of police" means—

(1) In the city of London and the liberties thereof, the police commissioner of city police; and

(2) In the metropolitan police district, the commissioner or any assistant commissioner or any district superintendent of metropolitan police; and

(3) Elsewhere the chief constable, or head constable, or other officer, by whatever name called, having the chief command of the police in the police district in reference to which such expression occurs:

The expression "police district" means—

(1) The city of London and the liberties thereof; and

(2) The metropolitan police district; and

(3) Any county, or liberty of a county, borough, town, place, or union, or combination of places maintaining a separate police force; and all the police under one chief constable shall be deemed to constitute one force for the purposes of this section.

108 General definitions

In this Act, unless the context otherwise requires—

The expression "this Act" includes any license, certificate, byelaw, regulation, rule, and order granted or made in pursuance of this Act:

The expression "existing" means existing at the passing of this Act

The expression "person" includes a body corporate:

The expression "occupier" includes any number of persons and a body corporate; and in the case of any manufacture or trade, includes any person carrying on such manufacture or trade:

The expression "master" includes every person (except a pilot) having command or charge of a ship, and in reference to any boat belonging to a ship, means the master of the ship; and when used in reference to any other boat, includes every person having command or charge of such boat:

The expression "magazine" includes any ship or other vessel used for the purpose of keeping any explosive:

The expression "factory magazine" means a building for keeping the finished explosive made in the factory, and includes, if such explosive is not gunpowder, any building for keeping the partly manufactured explosive or the ingredients of such explosive which is mentioned in that behalf in the license:

The expression "store" means an existing gunpowder store as defined by this Act, or a place for keeping an explosive licensed by a license granted by a local authority under this Act:

The expression "Secretary of State" means one of Her Majesty's Principal Secretaries of State:

The expression "warehouseman" includes all persons owning or managing any warehouse, store, wharf, or other premises in which goods are deposited:

The expression "carrier" includes all persons carrying goods or passengers for hire by land or water:

The expression "harbour authority" means any person or body of persons, corporate or unincorporate, being or claiming to be proprietor or proprietors of or intrusted with the duty or invested with the power of improving, managing, maintaining, or regulating any harbour properly so called, whether natural or artificial, and any port, haven, and estuary, or intrusted with the duty of conserving, maintaining, or improving the navigation of any tidal water, and any such harbour, port, haven, estuary, tidal water, and any wharf, dock, pier, jetty, and work, and other area, whether land or water, over which the harbour authority as above defined have control or exercise powers, are in the other portions of this Act included in the expression "harbour".

The expression "canal company" means any person or body of persons, corporate or unincorporate, being owner or lessee or owners, or lessees of, or working, or entitled to charge tolls for the use of any canal in the United Kingdom, constructed or carried on under the powers of any Act of Parliament, or intrusted with the duty of conserving, maintaining, or improving the navigation of any inland water, and every such canal and inland water under the control of a canal company as above defined, and any wharf, dock, pier, jetty, and work in or at which barges do or can ship or unship goods or passengers, and other area, whether land or water, which belong to or are under the control of such canal company, are in the other portions of this Act included in the expression "canal":

The expression "tidal water" means any part of the sea or of a river within the ebb and flow of the tides at ordinary spring tides:

The expression "inland water" means any canal, river, navigation, lake, or water which is not tidal water:

The expression "railway company" means any person or body of persons, corporate or unincorporate, being the owner or lessee or owners or lessees of or working any railway worked by steam or otherwise than by animal power in the United Kingdom, constructed or carried on under the powers of any Act of Parliament and used for public traffic, and every building, station, wharf, dock, and place which belong to or are under the control of a railway company, are in the other portions of this Act included in the expression "railway":

The expression "wharf" includes any quay, landing-place, siding, or other place at which goods are landed, loaded, or unloaded:

The expression "carriage" includes any carriage, waggon, cart, truck, vehicle, or other means of conveying goods or passengers by land, in whatever manner the same may be propelled:

The expression "ship" includes every description of vessel used in sea navigation, whether propelled by oars or otherwise:

The expression "boat" means every vessel not a ship as above defined which is used in navigation in any inland water or any harbour, whether propelled by oars or otherwise:

The expression "prescribed" means prescribed by Order in Council:

The expression "borough" means any place for the time being subject to the Act of the session of the fifth and sixth years of the reign of King William the Fourth, chapter seventy-six, intituled "An Act to provide for the regulation of municipal corporations in England and Wales," and the Acts amending the same:

The expression "county" does not include a county of a city or a county of a town:

Every riding, division, liberty, or part of a county having a separate commission of the peace and separate court of quarter sessions is for the purposes of this Act to be deemed to be a county

The expressions "urban sanitary district" and "urban sanitary authority" mean the districts and authorities declared to be urban sanitary districts and authorities by the Public Health Act, 1872; and any urban sanitary district which is an Improvement Act district within the meaning of that Act, is in this Act referred to as an improvement district; and the expression "Improvement Commissioners" in this Act means the Commissioners who are the urban sanitary authority for such district:

The expression "safety cartridges" means cartridges for small arms of which the case can be extracted from the small arm after firing, and which are so closed as to prevent any explosion in one cartridge being communicated to other cartridges:

The expression "Gunpowder Act, 1860," means the Act of the session of the twenty-third and twenty-fourth years of the reign of Her present Majesty, chapter one hundred and thirty-nine, intituled "An Act to amend the law concerning the making, keeping, and carriage of gunpowder and compositions of an explosive nature, and concerning the manufacture, sale, and use of fireworks," and the Acts amending the same:

The expression "Summary Jurisdiction Acts" means the Act of the session of the eleventh and twelfth years of the reign of Her present Majesty, chapter forty-three, intituled "An Act to facilitate the performance of the duties of justices of the peace out of sessions within England and Wales with respect to summary convictions and orders," and any Acts amending the same:

The expression "court of summary jurisdiction" means any justice or justices of the peace, metropolitan police magistrate, stipendiary or other magistrate or officer, by whatever name called, to whom jurisdiction is given by the Summary Jurisdiction Acts or any Acts therein referred to:

The expression "quarter sessions" includes general sessions.

Application of Act to Scotland.

This Act shall apply to Scotland, with the following modifications; that is to say,

109   In this Act with respect to Scotland—

(1)   The expression "borough" means any royal burgh, and any burgh returning or contributing to return a member to Parliament:

(2)   The expression "a master of one of the superior courts" means the auditor of the Court of Session:

(3)   The expression "umpire" means oversman:

(4)   The expression "attending before a court of record" means attending on citation the Court of Justiciary:

(5)   The expression "stipendiary magistrate" means a sheriff or sheriff substitute:

(6)   The expression "defendant" means defender and includes respondent:

(7)   The expression "chief officer of police" means the chief constable, superintendent of police, or other officer, by whatever name called, having the chief command of the police in any district maintaining a separate police force:

(8)   The expression "chairman of quarter sessions" means the sheriff of the county:

(9)   The expression "misdemeanour" means a crime and offence:

(10)   The expression "the court of summary jurisdiction" means the sheriff of the county or any one of his substitutes:

(11)   This Act shall be read and construed as if for the expression "The Lands Clauses Consolidation Act, 1845," where-ever it occurs therein, the expression "The Lands Clauses Consolidation (Scotland) Act, 1845," were substituted.

110   Local authority

In Scotland, the local authority for the purposes of this Act shall be as follows:

1.   In any borough the magistrates and town council; and

2.   In any harbour within the jurisdiction of a harbour authority, whether situate or not within the jurisdiction of any local authority for a borough, the harbour authority, to the exclusion of any other local authority; and

3.   In any place other than a borough or harbour as aforesaid, the justices of the peace for the county in which such place is situated.

111   Expenses of local authority

In Scotland, the local rate for defraying the expenses of the local authorities under this Act shall be—

(a)   In any borough the police rate or assessment; and

(b)   In any harbour as aforesaid any moneys, fund, or rate applicable or leviable by the harbour authority for any harbour purpose; and

(c)   In any place other than a borough or harbour as aforesaid the county general assessment.

The rates or assessments in this sub-section mentioned, or any increase of any such rate or assessment, may, notwithstanding any limitation in any Act, be levied for the purposes of this Act.

112   Secretary of State empowered to declare police commissioners the local authority in certain cases

The police commissioners of any burgh in Scotland, not being a burgh as defined by this Act, may, by order of a Secretary of State made upon the application of such commissioners and published in the Edinburgh Gazette, be declared to be a local authority for the purposes of this Act, and thereupon shall become the local authority accordingly for such part of their burgh as is not included in any harbour to the exclusion of the justices of the peace for any county in which such burgh is situated:

Provided that—

(a)   On such police commissioners becoming such local authority, the local rate for defraying their expenses under this Act shall be the police rate or assessment of the burgh; and

(b)   Such rate or assessment, or any increase thereof, may, notwithstanding any limitation in any Act, be levied for the purposes of this Act.

113   Local authority to have certain powers to take land otherwise than by agreement

In Scotland, every local authority under this Act shall have and may exercise the same powers for the purchase and taking of lands otherwise than by agreement, for the purpose of erecting a gunpowder magazine thereon, that any local authority under "The Public Health (Scotland) Act, 1867," have and may exercise under the provisions of section ninety of the said last-mentioned Act.

114   Provision for making and enforcing byelaws, &c

In Scotland, the following provisions shall have effect:

(a)   Where an obligation is laid by this Act on any harbour authority, company, or local authority to make or enforce any byelaws or to grant any license or to do anything, the Court of Session may, upon summary application by any corporation, harbour authority, or local authority, or party interested, compel such harbour authority, company, or local authority to discharge such obligation:

(b)   Every offence under this Act shall be prosecuted, every penalty recovered, and every forfeiture or order made at the instance of the Lord Advocate or of the procurator fiscal of the sheriff court:

(c)   The proceedings may be on indictment in the Court of Justiciary in Edinburgh or on circuit, or in the sheriff court, or may be taken summarily in the sheriff court under the provisions of the Summary Procedure Act, 1864, as the Lord Advocate shall direct:

(d)   All costs and moneys directed to be recovered as penalties may be recovered in the sheriff court at the instance of the procurator fiscal of that court, under the provisions of the Summary Procedure Act, 1864:

(e)   In Scotland, all penalties imposed in pursuance of this Act shall be paid to the clerk of the court imposing them, and shall by him be accounted for and paid to the Queen's and Lord Treasurer's Remembrancer, and be carried to the Consolidated Fund; and the proceeds of any sales of explosives or of the ingredients of explosives, or of the receptacles of explosives or their ingredients, or of any ship, boat, or carriage, forfeited and directed to be sold, or directed to be sold and disposed of as if the same were forfeited under this Act, shall be paid, accounted for, and applied in like manner as penalties under this Act:

(f) In Scotland, every person found liable in any penalty or costs or to pay any money directed by. this Act to be recovered as a penalty, shall be liable, in default of immediate payment, to imprisonment for a term not exceeding six months, or until such penalty, costs, or money shall be sooner paid.

115　Board of Trade empowered to make byelaws for the lower estuary of the Clyde: Secretary of State to define the authority for enforcing such byelaws

Whereas upon that part of the estuary of the Clyde which lies below the jurisdiction of the Trustees of the Clyde Navigation (and which. part is in this section referred to as the lower estuary of the Clyde) doubts have arisen as to the limits of the several harbour authorities on that estuary, be it enacted, the Board of Trade may, if they think it expedient, make bye-laws under this Act for the lower estuary of the Clyde as if it were a harbour and they were the harbour authority, and such byelaws shall be deemed to have been made by a harbour authority with the sanction of the Board of Trade; and they may by such byelaws define the area within which such byelaws are to be observed, and the Secretary of State shall have power to define the authority or authorities and officers by whom such byelaws are to be enforced and carried into effect within such area; and such authority or authorities and officers shall, for the purposes of this Act, other than making byelaws or assenting to a site for a new factory or magazine, have the same power within the said area as a harbour authority and an officer of a harbour authority have respectively under this Act in a harbour.

Application of Act to Ireland.

This Act shall apply to Ireland, with the following modifications; that is to say,

116　Definition of local authority

The local authority for the purposes of this Act shall be—

(1) In the city of Dublin, the Lord Mayor, aldermen, and burgesses acting by the town council:

(2) In any urban sanitary district in which the powers, jurisdictions, and authorities of the grand jury of the county in which such district is situate are vested and exerciseable by the urban sanitary authority, except as hereafter in this section mentioned, the urban sanitary authority

(3) In any harbour within the jurisdiction of a harbour authority, whether situate or not within the jurisdiction of any local authority, before in this section mentioned, the harbour authority, to the exclusion of any other local authority:

(4) In any place in which there is no local authority as before in this section defined, the justices in petty sessions assembled.

The expressions "urban sanitary authority" and "urban sanitary district" have the same meanings respectively as in the Public Health, Ireland, Act, 1874.

117　Power of certain local bodies to become a local authority

The urban sanitary authority of any district in Ireland which is not constituted a local authority by this Act may, by order become a of a Secretary of State made upon the application of such authority and published in the Dublin Gazette, be declared to be a local authority for the purposes of this Act, and thereupon shall become a local authority accordingly for such part of their district as is not included in any harbour, to the exclusion of the justices in petty sessions.

118 All expenses incurred by any local authority in carrying into effect the execution of this Act in Ireland, including the salary and expenses of any officer directed by them to act under this Act, shall be paid out of the local rate. The local rate shall for the purposes of this Act mean as follows; that is to say,

In the city of Dublin, the borough fund or borough rate; In urban sanitary districts where the urban sanitary authority are the local authority, any fund, moneys, or rate applicable or leviable by such authority for any purposes of improvement within their district;

In harbours, any moneys, fund, or rate applicable or leviable by the harbour authority for any harbour purposes; and

In any place where the justices in petty sessions are the local authority, the poor rates:

And the local rate or any increase of the local rate may, notwithstanding any limitation in any Act, be levied for the purposes of this Act.

All expenses incurred in any petty sessions district which are by this Act payable out of poor rates shall be paid upon the written order of the local authority which shall have incurred the same by the treasurer of the poor law union, or the treasurers of the poor law unions within which such petty sessions district is situate, according to the terms of such order.

Where such petty sessions district is situate within two or more poor law unions, the local authority shall in making such order apportion the amount of such expenses fairly between such unions, according to the net annual value of the rateable property forming the parts of such petty sessions district situate within the same respectively.

All moneys by this Act made payable by the treasurer of any poor law union in respect of expenses incurred in any petty sessions district wholly or partly within such union by the local authority shall be paid by him out of the funds then lying in his hands to the credit of the guardians of such union, and such guardians shall in their account with the electoral divisions of such union, debit each electoral division wholly or partly within such petty sessions district with its proportion of the sum so paid by the treasurer according to the net annual value for the time being of the rateable property within such electoral division, and also within such petty sessions district.

119   Form of registers of store licenses and registered premises, and amount of fees, to be approved by Secretary of State

The register of store licenses and of registered premises to be kept by the local authorities in Ireland shall be kept in such form and manner, and the fees for entries to be made therein shall (subject to the limits as to fees prescribed by this Act) be such as the Secretary of State shall from time to time approve.

120   Definitions

In this Act with respect to Ireland—

The expression "police district" means—

    (1)   The police district of Dublin metropolis; and

    (2)   The town of Belfast; and

(3) Elsewhere in Ireland, any district, whether city, town, or part of a county, over which is appointed a sub-inspector of the Royal Irish Constabulary.

The expression "chief officer of police" means—

(1) In the police district of Dublin metropolis, the chief commissioner of police for the said district; and in his absence the assistant commissioner of police for the said district; and

(2) In the town of Belfast, the town inspector, and in his absence the sub-inspector of the Royal Irish Constabulary acting for him;, and

(3) Elsewhere in Ireland, the sub-inspector of the Royal Irish Constabulary, and in his absence the head constable of such force acting for him.

The expression "the county court judge" means the judge of the civil bill court.

The expression "borough" means any place for the time being subject to the Act of the session of the third and fourth years of

the reign of Her present Majesty, chapter one hundred and eight, intituled "An Act for the regulation of municipal corporations in Ireland."

The expression "Summary Jurisdiction Acts" means, as regards the police district of Dublin metropolis, the Acts regulating the powers and duties of justices of the peace for such district, and elsewhere in Ireland, the Act of the session of the fourteenth and fifteenth years of the reign of Her present Majesty, chapter ninety-three, intituled "An Act to consolidate and amend the Acts regulating the proceedings of petty sessions, and the duties of justices of the peace out of quarter sessions in Ireland," and any Acts amending the same.

The expression "court of summary jurisdiction" means any justice or justices of the peace, or other magistrate or officer, by whatever name called, to whom jurisdiction is given by the Summary Jurisdiction Acts or any Acts therein referred to.

121   Application of penalties in Ireland

Except as by this Act expressly provided, all penalties imposed under this Act in Ireland shall be applied in manner directed by the Fines (Ireland) Act, 1851, and any Acts amending the same.

122   Repeal of certain Acts and part of Act in 4th and 5th schedules

The Acts specified in the fourth schedule to this Act are hereby repealed from and after the commencement of this Act and the Act specified in the fifth schedule to this Act is hereby repealed from and after the commencement of this Act to the extent in the third column of that schedule mentioned.

Provided that—

(1) The enactments hereby repealed shall continue in force—

For the purpose of any business or thing which any person is authorised to carry on or do in like manner as if this Act had not passed, for the time during which such business or thing is authorised to be carried on or done; and

(2) Any rules made in pursuance of any enactment hereby repealed, for the purpose of regulating the conduct of servants and workmen employed in any mill, magazine, or place, shall continue in force, and the penalties under the said enactments for a breach of such rules may be enforced until the expiration of three months after the grant of a continuing certificate under this Act to the occupier of such mill,

magazine, or place, and such further period as the Secretary of State may by order direct, for the purpose of enabling such occupier to make special rules under this Act; and

(3) This repeal shall not affect—

(a) The past operation of any enactment hereby repealed, nor anything duly done or suffered under any enactment hereby repealed; or

(b) Any right, privilege, obligation, or liability acquired, accrued, or incurred under any enactment hereby repealed; or

(c) Any penalty, forfeiture, or punishment incurred in respect of any offence committed against any enactment hereby repealed; or

(d) Any investigation, legal proceeding, or remedy in respect of any such right, privilege, obligation, liability, penalty, forfeiture, or punishment as aforesaid; and any such investigation, legal proceeding, and remedy may be carried on as if this Act had not passed; and

(4) This repeal shall not revive any enactment, right, privilege, matter, or thing not in force or existing at the commencement of this Act.

SCHEDULES

FIRST SCHEDULE

Part One
Gunpowder Factories

Regulations which are to form part of the terms of every continuing certificate of a factory for gunpowder.

(1) The quantity of gunpowder or ingredients to be made into gunpowder to be at one time under any single pair of mill stones or rollers or runners shall not exceed fifty pounds as respects sporting and Government powder, and sixty pounds as respects all inferior powders; and every incorporating mill or group of incorporating mills shall be provided with a charge house for the store of mill charges, properly constructed of stone or brick, and situate at a safe and suitable distance from each incorporating mill or group of incorporating mills.

(2) The quantity of gunpowder to be subjected to pressure at one time in any press house shall not exceed ten hundredweight.

(3) The quantity of gunpowder to be corned or granulated at one time in any corning or granulating house shall not exceed twelve hundredweight.

(4) The quantity of gunpowder to be dried at one time in one stove or place used for the drying of gunpowder shall not exceed fifty hundredweight.

(5) The respective quantities to be at any one time in any press house or coming or granulating house shall not exceed twice the respective quantities hereby allowed to be subjected to pressure and to be corned or granulated at one time; and the quantity to be at any one time in any drying house or dusting house shall not be more than is necessary for the immediate supply and work of such house; and for the purposes of this provision any building used with any such press house, corning or granulating house, drying house or dusting house, shall be deemed part thereof, save only magazines constructed with stone or brick and situate forty yards at least

from every such press house or other house as aforesaid (herein-after distinguished as expense magazines), and save only the stove in which the powder which has been dried may be cooling.

(6) Every person keeping or using any mill for the making gunpowder shall have (in addition to the expense magazines) a good and sufficient factory magazine or magazines, situate (unless otherwise authorised by a certificate of the Secretary of State under the Gunpowder Act, 1860) at least one hundred and forty yards distant from the mill or mills and every press house and other house or place used for or in the making of gunpowder, such magazine or magazines to be well and substantially built with brick or stone, and situate in such place as may have been lawfully used or duly licensed by justices before the commencement of the Gunpowder Act, 1860, and not made unlawful by that Act, or may have been after the commencement of that Act duly licensed under the Gunpowder Act, 1860.

(7) No maker of gunpowder shall keep or permit to be kept any charcoal within twenty yards of any mill or other engine for making gunpowder, or of any press house, or drying, corning, or dusting house or other place used in or for the making of gunpowder, or any magazine or storehouse thereto belonging.

Part Two

Gunpowder Stores

Regulations which are to form part of the terms of every continuing, certificate for a gunpowder store.

(1) The store shall be exclusively for the use of a mine, quarry, colliery, or factory for safety fuzes:

(2) The amount of gunpowder in the store shall not exceed, if the store is well and substantially built of brick or stone, four thousand pounds, and in any other case three hundred pounds

(3) Where the amount of gunpowder in the store exceeds three hundred pounds, such store shall, unless otherwise authorised before the passing of this Act by a certificate of the Secretary of State, be within two hundred yards of the mine, quarry, colliery, or factory for safety fuzes, or one of the mines, quarries, collieries, or factories for safety fuzes for the use of which such gunpowder is kept, and not within two hundred yards of any inhabited house without the consent in writing of the occupier of such house:

(4) Where such certificate has been given, the conditions on which it was given shall be duly observed as if they were contained in this schedule:

(5) Where the amount of gunpowder does not exceed three hundred pounds, the store shall be within two hundred yards of the mine, quarry, colliery, or factory for the use of which it is erected, and unless it was erected and used for the said purpose before the passing of the Gunpowder Act, 1860, shall not be within two hundred yards from any inhabited house without the consent in writing of the occupier of such house:

(6) The store shall not be within the city of London or Westminster or within three miles of either of them, or within any borough or market town or one mile of the same, or within two miles of any palace or house of residence of Her Majesty, her heirs and successors, or within two miles of any gunpowder magazine belonging to the Crown, or within half a mile of any parish church.

SECOND SCHEDULE

ARBITRATION

Provisions as to arbitrations

With respect to arbitrations under this Act, the following provisions shall have effect:

(1) The parties to the arbitration are in this section deemed to be the occupier of the factory, magazine, or store on the one hand, and on the other the Government inspector (on behalf of the Secretary of State):

(2) Each of the parties to the arbitration may, within twenty-one days after the date of the reference, appoint an arbitrator:

(3) No person shall act as arbitrator or umpire under this Act who is employed in or in the management of or is directly or indirectly interested in the manufacture, trade, factory, magazine, store, business, or premises to which the arbitration relates, or is in any manner interested directly or indirectly in the matter to which the arbitration relates:

(4) The appointment of an arbitrator undo; this section shall be in writing, and notice of the appointment shall be forthwith sent to the other party to the arbitration, and shall not be revoked without the consent of such other party:

(5) The death, removal, or other change in any of the parties to the arbitration shall not affect the proceedings under this section:

(6) If within the said twenty-one days either of the parties fail to appoint an arbitrator, the arbitrator appointed by the other party may proceed to hear and determine the matter in difference, and in such case the award of the single arbitrator shall be final:

(7) If before an award has been made any arbitrator appointed by either party die or become incapable to act, or for fourteen days refuse or neglect to act, the party by whom such arbitrator was appointed may appoint some other person to act in his place; and if he fail to do so within fourteen days after notice in writing from the other party for that purpose, the remaining arbitrator may proceed to hear and determine the matters in difference, and in such case the award of such single arbitrator shall be final:

(8) In either of the foregoing cases where an arbitrator is empowered to act singly, upon one of the parties failing to appoint, the party so failing may, before the single arbitrator has actually proceeded in the arbitration, appoint an arbitrator, who shall then act as if no failure had been made:

(9) If the arbitrators fail to make their award within twenty-one days after the day on which the last of them was appointed, or within such extended time (if any) as may have been appointed for that purpose by both arbitrators under their hands, the matter in difference shall be determined, by the umpire appointed as herein-after mentioned:

(10) The arbitrators, before they enter upon the matters referred to them, shall appoint by writing under their hands an umpire to decide on points on which they may differ:

(11) If the umpire die or become incapable to act before he has made his award, or refuses to make his award within a reasonable time after the matter has been brought within his cognizance, the persons or person who appointed such umpire shall forthwith appoint another umpire in his place:

(12) If the arbitrators refuse or fail or for seven days after the request of either party neglect to appoint an umpire, then on the application of either party an umpire shall be appointed by the chairman of the quarter sessions of the peace within the jurisdiction of which the factory, magazine, or store is situate:

(13) The decision of every umpire on the matters referred to him shall be final:

(14) If a single arbitrator fail to make his award within twenty-one days after the day on which he was appointed, the party who appointed him may appoint another arbitrator to act in his place:

The arbitrator and their umpire or any of them may examine the parties and their witnesses on oath, they may also consult any counsel, engineer, or scientific person whom they may think it expedient to consult:

(15) The payment, if any, to be made to any arbitrator or umpire for his services shall be fixed by the Secretary of State, and together with the costs of the arbitration and award shall be paid by the parties, or one of them, according as the award may direct. Such costs may be taxed by a master of one of the superior courts, who, on the written application of either of the parties, shall ascertain and certify the proper amount of such costs. The amount, if any, payable by, the Secretary of State shall be paid as part of the expenses of inspectors under this Act. The amount, if any, payable by any other party may in the event of nonpayment be recovered in the same manner as penalties under this Act.

Third Schedule
Maximum Fees for Licenses Granted by the Secretary of State

Factory license, original	Ten pounds.
Do., amending	Five pounds.
Do., renewal when lost	Five shillings.
Magazine license, original	Ten pounds.
Do., amending	Five pounds.
Do.,. renewal when lost	Five shillings.
Inportation license, first grant	One pound.
Do., renewal	Ten shillings.
Continuing certificate	Forty shillings

FOURTH SCHEDULE

Session and Chapter	Title
23 & 24 Vict. c. 139	An Act to amend the law concerning the making, keeping, and carriage of gunpowder and compositions of an explosive nature, and concerning the manufacture, sale, and use of fireworks.
24 & 25 Vict. c. 130	An Act for amending an Act passed in the last session of Parliament to amend the law concerning the making, keeping, and carriage of gunpowder and compositions of an explosive nature, and concerning the manufacture, sale, and use of fireworks.
25 & 26 Vict. c. 98	An Act for the amendment of an Act of the session of the twenty-third and twenty-fourth years of the reign of Her present Majesty, chapter one hundred and thirtynine, intituled An Act to amend the law concerning the making, keeping, and carriage of gunpowder and compositions of an explosive nature, and concerning the manufacture, sale and use of fireworks and of an Act amending the last-mentioned Act.
29 & 30 Vict c. 69	An Act for the amendment of the law with respect to the carriage and deposit of dangerous goods.
32 & 33 Vict. c. 113	An Act to prohibit for a limited time the importation and to restrict and regulate the carriage of nitro-glycerine.

FIFTH SCHEDULE

Session and Chapter	Abbreviated Title	Extent of Repeal
26 & 27 Viet, c 65	The Volunteer Act, 1863	Section twenty-six from "all exemptions contained in the Gunpowder Act, 1860," inclusive, to the end of the section.

Explosive Substances Act 1883

46 Vict Ch 3

ARRANGEMENT OF SECTIONS

Section.

1. Short title.
2. Punishment for causing explosion likely to endanger life or property.
3. Punishment for attempt to cause explosion, or for making or keeping explosive with intent to endanger life or property.
4. Punishment for making or possession of explosive under suspicious circumstances.
5. Punishment of accessories.
6. Inquiry under order of Attorney General, and apprehension of absconding witnesses.
7. No prosecution except by leave of Attorney General. Procedure and saving.
8. Search for and seizure of explosive substances.
9. Definitions, and application to Scotland.

CHAPTER 3

An Act to amend the Law relating to Explosive Substances. [10th April 1883.]

Be it enacted by the Queen's most Excellent Majesty, by and with the advice and consent of the Lords Spiritual and Temporal, and Commons, in this present Parliament assembled, and by the authority of the same, as follows:

1   Short title

This Act may be cited as the Explosive Substances Act, 1883.

2   Punishment for causing explosion likely to endanger life-or property

[A person who in the State or (being an Irish citizen) outside the State unlawfully and maliciously causes by an explosive substance an explosion of a nature likely to endanger life, or cause serious injury to property, shall, whether any injury to person or property is actually caused or not, be guilty of an offence and, on conviction on indictment, shall be liable to imprisonment for life.][1]

Amendments

1 Section 2 substituted by Criminal Law (Jurisdiction) Act 1976, s 4.

---

3   Punishment for attempt to cause explosion, or for making or keeping explosive with intent to endanger. life or property

[A person who in the State or (being an Irish citizen) outside the State unlawfully and maliciously—

(a) does any act with intent to cause, or conspires to cause by an explosive substance an explosion of a nature likely to endanger life, or cause serious injury to property, whether in the State or elsewhere, or

(b) makes or has in his possession or under his control an explosive substance with intent by means thereof to endanger life, or cause serious injury to property, whether in the State or elsewhere, or to enable any other person so to do,

shall, whether any explosion does or does not take place, and whether any injury to person or property is actually caused or not, be guilty of an offence and, on conviction on indictment [shall be liable to a fine or imprisonment for life][2] and the explosive substance shall be forfeited.][1]

Amendments

1   Section 3 substituted by Criminal Law (Jurisdiction) Act 1976, s 4.

2   Words substituted by Criminal Justice Act 1999, s 36.

4   Punishment for making or possession of explosive under suspicious circumstances.

(1) Any person who makes or knowingly has in his possession or under his control any explosive substance, under such circumstances as to give rise to a reasonable suspicion that he is not making it or does not have it in his possession or under his control for a lawful object, shall, unless he can show that he made it or had it in his possession or under his control for a lawful object, be guilty of [an offence and shall be liable, on conviction on indictment, to a fine or imprisonment for a term not exceeding 14 years or both, and the explosive substance shall be forfeited.][1]

(2) ...[2]

Amendments

1   Words substituted by the Offences Against the State (Amendment) Act 1998, 15.

2   Subsection (2) repealed by Criminal Evidence Act 1992, s 3 and Sch.

5   Punishment of accessories

Any person who within or (being a subject of Her Majesty) without Her Majesty's dominions by the supply of or solicitation for money, the providing of premises, the supply of materials, or in any manner whatsoever, procures, counsels, aids, abets, or is accessory to, the commission of any crime under this Act, shall be guilty of, felony, and shall be liable to be tried and punished for that crime, as if he had been guilty as a principal.

6   Inquiry by Attorney General, and apprehension of absconding witnesses.

(1) Where the Attorney General has reasonable ground to believe that any crime under this Act has been committed, he may order an inquiry, under this section, and thereupon any

justice for the county, borough, or place in which the crime was committed or is suspected to have been committed, who is authorised in that behalf by the Attorney General, may, although no person may be charged before him with the commission of such crime, sit at a police court, or petty sessional or occasional court-house, or police station in the said county, borough, or place, and examine on oath concerning such crime any witness appearing before him, and may take the deposition of such witness, and, if he see cause, may bind such witness by recognizance to appear and give evidence at the next petty sessions, or when called upon within three months from the date of such recognizance; and the law relating to the compelling of the attendance of a witness before a justice, and to a witness attending before a justice and required to give evidence concerning the matter of an information or complaint, shall apply to compelling the attendance of a witness for examination and to a witness attending under this section.

(2) A witness examined under this section shall not be excised from answering any question' on the ground that the answer thereto may criminate, or tend to criminate, himself; but any statement made by any person in answer to any question put to him on any examination under this section shall not, except in the case of an indictment or other criminal proceeding for perjury, be admissible in evidence against him in any proceeding, civil or criminal.

(3) A justice who conducts the examination under this section of a person concerning any crime shall not take part in the committing for trial of such person for such crime.

(4) Whenever any person is bound by recognizance to give evidence before justices, or any criminal court, in respect of any crime under this Act, any justice, if he sees fit, upon information being made in writing, and on oath, that such person is about to abscond, or has absconded, may issue his warrant for the arrest of such person, and if such person. is arrested any justice, upon being satisfied that the ends of justice would otherwise be defeated, may commit such person to prison until the time at which he is bound by such recognizance to give evidence, unless in the meantime he produces sufficient sureties: Provided that any person so arrested shall be entitled on demand to receive a copy of the information upon which the warrant for his arrest was issued.

7   No prosecution except by leave of Attorney General. Procedure and saving

(1) If any person is charged before a justice with any crime under this Act, no further proceeding shall be taken against such person without the consent of the Attorney General, except such as the justice may think necessary by remand, or otherwise, to secure the safe custody of such person.

(2) [...]¹

(3) For all purposes of and incidental to arrest, trial, and punishment, a crime for which a person is liable to be punished under this Act, when committed out of the United Kingdom, shall be deemed to have been committed in the place in which such person, is apprehended or is in custody.

(4) This Act shall not exempt any person from any indictment or proceeding for a crime or offence which is punishable at common law, or by any Act of Parliament other than this Act, but no person shall be punished twice for the same criminal act.

Amendments

1   Subsection 2 repealed by Criminal Justice (Administration) Act 1924, s 16 and Sch 2.

8   Search for and seizure of explosive substances

(1) Sections seventy-three, seventy-four, seventy-five, eighty-nine, and ninety-six of the Explosives Act, 1875, (which sections relate to the search for, seizure, and detention of explosive substances, and the forfeiture thereof, and the disposal of explosive substances seized or forfeited), shall apply in like manner as if a crime or forfeiture under this Act were an offence or forfeiture under the Explosives Act, 1875.

(2) Where the master or owner of any vessel has reasonable cause to suspect that any dangerous goods or goods of a dangerous nature which, if found, he would be entitled to throw overboard in pursuance of the Merchant Shipping Act, 1873, are concealed. on board his vessel, he may search any part of such vessel for such goods, and for the purpose of such search may, if necessary, break open any box, package, parcel, or receptacle on board the vessel, and such master or owner, if he finds any such dangerous goods or goods of a dangerous nature shall be entitled to deal with the same in manner provided by the said Act, and if he do not find the same, he shall not be subject to any liability, civil or criminal, if it appears to the tribunal before which the question of his liability is raised that' he had reasonable cause to suspect that such goads were so concealed as aforesaid.

9   Definitions, and application to Scotland

(1) In this Act, unless the context otherwise requires,—

The expression "explosive substance" shall be deemed to include any materials for making any explosive substance; also any apparatus, machine, implement, or materials used, or intended to be used, or adapted for causing, or aiding in causing; any explosion in or with any explosive substance; also any part of any such apparatus, machine, or implement.

The expression "Attorney General" means Her Majesty's Attorney General for England or Ireland, as the case may be, and in case of his inability or o a vacancy-in the office, Her Majesty's Solicitor General for England or Ireland, as the case requires.

(2) In the application of this Act to Scotland the following modifications shall be made—

The expression "Attorney General" shall be deemed to mean the Lord Advocate, and in case of his inability or of a vacancy in the office, Her Majesty's Solicitor General for Scotland.

The expression "petty sessional court-house" shall be deemed to mean the sheriff court.

The expression "felony "shall be deemed to mean a high crime and offence.

The expression "recognizance" shall be juratory caution.

The expression "justice "shall include substitute.

Probation of Offenders Act 1907

7 Edw 7 Ch 17

ARRANGEMENT OF SECTIONS

Section.

1. Power of courts to permit conditional release of offenders.
2. Probation orders and conditions of recognizances.
3. Probation officers.
4. Duties of probation officers.
5. Power to vary conditions of release.
6. Provision in case of offender failing to observe conditions of release.
7. Power to make rules.
8. Application to Scotland.
9. Application to Ireland.
10. Short title and repeal.

SCHEDULE

CHAPTER 17

An Act to permit the Release on Probation of Offenders in certain cases, and for other matters incidental thereto. [21st August 1907]

Be it enacted by the King's most Excellent Majesty, by and with advice and consent of the Lords Spiritual and Temporal, and Commons, in this present Parliament assembled, and by the authority of the same, as follows:

1   Power of courts to permit conditional release of offenders

(1) Where any person is charged before a court of summary jurisdiction with an offence punishable by such Court and the court thinks that the charge is proved, but is of opinion that, having regard to the character, antecedents, age, health, or mental condition of the person charged, or to the trivial nature of the offence, or to the extenuating circumstances under which the offence was committed, it is inexpedient to inflict any punishment or any other than a nominal punishment, or that it is expedient to release the offender on probation, the court may, without proceeding to conviction, make an order either—

(i) dismissing the information or charge; or

(ii) discharging the offender conditionally on his entering into a recognizance, with or without sureties, to be of good behaviour and to appear for conviction and sentence when called on at any time during such period, not exceeding three years, as may be specified in the order.

(2) Where any person has been convicted on indictment of any offence punishable with imprisonment, and the court is of opinion that, having regard to the character, antecedents, age, health, or mental condition of the person charged, or to the trivial nature of the offence, or to the extenuating circumstances under which the offence was committed, it is inexpedient

to inflict any punishment or any other than a nominal punishment, or that it is expedient to release the offender on probation, the court may, in lieu of imposing a sentence of imprisonment, make an order discharging the offender conditionally on his entering into a recognizance, with or without sureties, to be of good behaviour and to appear for sentence when called on at any time during such period, not exceeding three years, as may be specified in the order.

(3) The court may, in addition to any such order, order the offender to pay such damages for injury or compensation for loss (not exceeding in the case of a court of summary jurisdiction ten pounds, or, if a higher limit is fixed by any enactment relating to the offence, that higher limit) and to pay such costs of the proceedings as the court thinks reasonable. ....][1].

(4) Where an order under this section is made by a court of summary jurisdiction, the order shall, for the purpose of revesting or restoring stolen property, and of enabling the court to make orders as to the restitution or delivery of property to the owner and as to the payment of money upon or in connexion with such restitution or delivery, have the like effect as a conviction.

Amendments

1   Words repealed by Children Act 1908, s 134.

---

2   Probation Orders and Conditions of recognizances

(1) A recognizance ordered to be entered into under this Act shall, if the court so order, contain a condition that the offender be under the supervision of such person as may be named in the order during the period specified in the order and such other for securing such supervision as may be specified in the order, and an order requiring the insertion of such conditions as aforesaid in the recognizance is in this Act referred to as a probation order.

(2) ...[1]

(3) The court by which a probation order is made shall furnish to the offender a notice in writing stating in simple terms the conditions he is required to observe.

Amendments

1   Subsection (2) repealed by Criminal Justice Administration Act 1914, s 44 and Sch 4.

---

3   Probation Officers

(1) There may be appointed as probation officer or officers for a petty sessional division such person or persons of either sex as the authority having power to appoint a clerk to the justices of that division may determine, and a probation officer when acting under a probation order shall be subject to the control of petty sessional courts for the division for which he is so appointed.

(2) There shall be appointed, where circumstances permit, special probation officers, to be called children's probation officers, who shall, in the absence of any reasons to the contrary, be named in a probation order made in the case of an offender under the age of sixteen.

(3) The person named in any probation order shall,—

    (a)   where the court, making the order is a court of summary jurisdiction, be selected from amongst the probation officers for the petty sessional division in or for which the court acts; or

    (b)   where the court making the order is a court of assize or a court of quarter sessions, be selected from amongst the probation officers for the petty sessional division from which the person charged was committed for trial:

Provided that the person so named may, if the court considers it expedient on account of the place of residence of the offender, or for any other special reason, be a probation officer for some other petty sessional division, and may, if the court considers that the special circumstances of the case render it desirable, be a person who has not been appointed to be probation officer for any petty sessional division.

(4) A probation order appointed for a petty sessional division may be paid such salary as the authority having the control of the fund out of which the salary of the clerk to the justices of that petty sessional division is paid may determine, and if not so paid by salary may receive such remuneration for acting under a probation order as the court making the order thinks fit, not exceeding such renumeration as may be allowed by the regulations of such authority as aforesaid, and may in either case be paid such out-of-pocket expenses as may be allowed under such regulations as aforesaid, and the salary or remuneration and expenses shall be paid by that authority by that authority out of the said funds.

(5) A person named in a probation order not being a probation officer for a petty sessional division may be paid such remuneration and out-of-pocket expenses out of such fund as the court making the probation order may direct, not exceeding such as may be allowed under the regulations of the authority having control of the fund out of which the remuneration is directed to be paid.

(6) The person named in a probation order may at any time be relieved of his duties, and in any such case or in case of the death of the person so named, another person may be substituted by the court before which the offender is bound by his recognizance to appear for conviction or sentence, or, if he be a probation and welfare officer for a petty sessional division, by a court to whose control that officer is subject.

(7) In the application of this Act to the City of London and the metropolitan police court district, the city and each division of that district shall be deemed to be a petty sessional division.

4   Duties of probation officers

It shall be the duty of a probation officer, subject to the directions of the court—

    (a)   to visit or receive reports from the person under supervision at such reasonable intervals as may be specified in the probation order or, subject thereto, as the probation officer may think fit;

    (b)   to see that he observes the conditions of his recognizance;

    (c)   to report to the court as to his behaviour;

(d) to advise, assist, and befriend him, and, when necessary, to endeavour to find him suitable employment.

5   Power to vary conditions of release

[...]¹

Amendments

1   Section 5 repealed by Criminal Justice Administration Act 1914, s 44 and Sch 4.

---

6   Provision in case of offenders failing to observe conditions of release

(1) If the court before which an offender is bound by his recognizance under this Act to appear for conviction or sentence, or any court of summary jurisdiction, is satisfied by information on oath that the offender has failed to observe any of the conditions of his recognizance, it may issue a warrant for his apprehension, or may, if it thinks fit, instead of issuing a warrant in the first instance, issue a summons to the offender and his sureties (if any) requiring him or them to attend at such court and at such time as may be specified in the summons.

(2) The offender, when apprehended, shall, if not brought forthwith before the court before which he is bound by his recognizance to appear for conviction or sentence, be brought before a court of summary jurisdiction.

(3) The court before which an offender on apprehension is brought, or before which he appears in pursuance of such summons as aforesaid, may, if it is not the court before which he is bound by his recognizance to appear for conviction or sentence, remand him to custody or on bail until he can be brought before the last-mentioned court.

(4) An offender so remanded to custody may be committed during remand to any prison to which the court having power to convict or sentence him has power to commit prisoners [...].¹

(5) A court before which a person is bound by his recognizance to appear for conviction and sentence, on being satisfied that he has failed to observe any condition of his recognizance, may forthwith, without further proof of his guilt, convict and sentence him for the original offence or, if the case was one in which the court in the first instance might, under section fifteen of the Industrial Schools Act, 1866, have ordered the offender to be sent to a certified industrial school, and the offender is still apparently under the age of twelve years, make such an order.

Amendments

1   Words repealed by Children Act 1908, s 134.

---

7   Power to make rules

The Secretary of State may make rules for carrying this Act into effect, and in particular for prescribing such matters incidental to the appointment, resignation, and removal of probation officers, and the performance of their duties, and the reports to be made by them, as may appear necessary.

8   Application to Scotland

This Act shall apply to Scotland, subject to the following modifications:-

(1)   There may be appointed as probation officers for a district being a royal, parliamentary, or police burgh, or a county outwith the police boundaries of any such burgh, such persons as the burgh magistrates may determine for the burgh and the sheriff for the county; and a probation officer when acting under a probation order shall be subject to the control of the burgh police court or sheriff court, as the case may be:

(2)   The immediately preceding subsection shall be substituted for subsection one of section three of this Act, and references in this Act to a petty sessional division shall be construed as references to a district:

(3)   The expression "court of summary jurisdiction" where occurring in section three of this Act shall include the sheriff sitting with a jury:

(4)   "Bond" shall be substituted for "recognizance", the "Secretary for Scotland" shall be substituted for "the Secretary of State" and "the High Court of Justiciary" shall be substituted for "a court of assize or a court of quarter sessions".

(5)   The authority having power to regulate the remuneration of probation officers shall be the town council in a burgh and the county council in a county, and such remuneration shall be paid out of the burgh general or police assessment or the county general assessment, as the case may be.

9   Application to Ireland

In the application of this Act to Ireland "Lord Lieutenant" shall be substituted for "Secretary of State," and each division of the police district of Dublin metropolis shall be deemed to a petty sessional division.

10   Short title and repeal

(1) This Act may be cited as the Probation of Offenders Act, 1907.

(2) The enactments mentioned in the schedule to this Act shall be repealed to the extent specified in the third column of that schedule.

(3) This Act shall come into operation on the first day of January one thousand nine hundred and eight.

SCHEDULE

Section 10

ENACTMENTS REPEALED

Session and Chapter	Short Title	Extent of Repeal
42 & 43 Vict. c. 49.	The Summary Jurisdiction Act, 1879	Section sixteen
50 & 51 Vict. c. 25.	The Probation of First Offenders Act, 1887	The whole Act
1. Edw. 7. c. 20	The Youthful Offenders Act, 1901	Section twelve

Criminal Justice Administration Act 1914

4 & 5 Geo 5 Ch 58

ARRANGEMENT OF SECTIONS

FINES, FEES, &E

Section.

1. Obligation to allow time for payment of fines.

2. Allowance of further time.

3. Reduction of imprisonment on part payment of sums adjudged to be paid.

4. Provisions for enforcement of payment of fines, &c.

5. Payment and allocation of fines and fees.

6. Uniform scale of court fees as respects all courts of summary jurisdiction.

PROBATION

7. Power to recognise and subsidise societies for care of youthful offenders on probation, &c.

8. Conditions of probation.

9. Variation of terms and conditions of probation.

COMMITTALS TO BORSTAL INSTITUTIONS

10. Power to send youthful delinquents to Borstal Institutions.

11. Amendment and application of Part I. of the Prevention of Crime Act, 1908.

NEW POWERS OF DEALING WITH OFFENDERS

12. Power to order detention for one day in precincts of the court.

13. Substitution of police custody for imprisonment in case of short sentences.

14. Provisions as to malicious damage to property.

15. Extension of powers to deal with cases summarily.

IMPRISONMENT

16. Hard labour and classification of prisoners.

17. Commitment and removal of prisoners.

18. Consecutive sentences of imprisonment.

19. Continuous bail.

20. Powers of remand.

21. Endorsement on warrants as to release on bail.

22. Release on bail of a person arrested without warrant.

23. Notice of right to apply for bail.

24. Declaration of law as to mode of entering into recognisance.

MISCELLANEOUS AND GENERAL

25.   Manner of enforcing payment of sums adjudged to be paid.

26.   Provisions with respect to holders of licences and persons under police supervision.

27.   Power to issue warrants of arrest in certain cases.

28.   Provisions as to evidence.

29.   Power of justices to order production of documents.

30.   Periodical payments ordered by courts of summary jurisdiction.

31.   Costs.

32.   Recovery of arrears on bastardy orders, &c.

33.   Amendment of the law with respect to the recovery of rates.

34.   Appointment and remuneration of and accounting by justices' clerks.

35.   Punishment for accusation, &c. of dead person with intent to extort.

36.   Corporal punishment.

37.   Right of appeal from decision of court of summary jurisdiction.

38.   One justice to be competent to exercise certain powers in respect of charges of drunkenness.

39.   Convictions on indictments.

40.   Rules.

41.   Definitions.

42.   Application to Scotland.

43.   Application to Ireland.

44.   Short title, commencement, and repeal.

SCHEDULES

CHAPTER 58

An Act to diminish the number of cases committed to prison, to amend the Law with respect to the treatment and punishment of young offenders, and otherwise to improve the Administration of Criminal Justice. [10th August 1914.]

Be it enacted by the King's most Excellent Majesty, by and with the advice and consent of the Lords Spiritual and Temporal, and Commons, in this present Parliament assembled, and by the authority of the same, as follows:

FINES, FEES, &C

1   Obligation to allow time for payment of fines

(1) A warrant committing a person to prison in respect of non-payment of a sum adjudged to be paid by a conviction of a court of summary jurisdiction shall not be issued forthwith unless the court which passed the sentence is satisfied that he is possessed of sufficient means to enable him to pay the sum forthwith, or unless, upon being asked by the court

whether he desires that time should be allowed for payment, he does not express any such desire, or fails to satisfy the court that he has a fixed abode within its jurisdiction, or unless the court for any other special reason expressly directs that no time shall be allowed.

(2) Where any such person desires to be allowed time for payment the court in deciding what time shall be allowed shall consider any representation made by him, but the time allowed shall not be less than seven clear days:

Provided that if before the expiration of the time allowed the person convicted surrenders himself to any court of summary jurisdiction having jurisdiction to issue a warrant of commitment in respect of the non-payment of such sum as aforesaid, and states that he prefers immediate committal to awaiting the expiration of the time allowed, that court may if it thinks fit forthwith issue a warrant committing him to prison.

(3) Where a person so allowed time for payment as aforesaid appears to the court to be not less than sixteen nor more than twenty-one years of age, the court may, if it thinks fit, and subject to any rules made under this Act, order that he be placed under the supervision of such person as may be appointed by the court until the sum adjudged to be paid is paid, and in such case before issuing a warrant committing the offender to prison in respect of non-payment of the sum a court of summary jurisdiction shall consider any report as to the conduct and means of the offender, which may be made by the person under whose supervision the offender has been placed.

(4) In all cases where time is not allowed for payment, the reasons of the court for the immediate committal shall be stated in the warrant of commitment.

2   Allowance of further time

Where time has been allowed for the payment of a sum adjudged to be paid by a conviction or order of a court of summary jurisdiction, further time may, subject to any rules made under this Act, on an application by or on behalf of the offender, be allowed by a court of summary jurisdiction having jurisdiction to issue a warrant of commitment in respect of the non-payment of such sum as aforesaid, or such court may, subject as aforesaid, direct payment by instalments of the sum so adjudged to be paid.

3   Reduction of imprisonment on part payment of sums adjudged to be paid

(1) Where a term of imprisonment is imposed by a court of summary jurisdiction in respect of the non-payment of any sum of money adjudged to be paid by a conviction or order of that or any other court of summary jurisdiction, that term shall, on payment of a part of such sum to any person authorised to receive it, be reduced by a number of days bearing as nearly as possible the same proportion to the total number of days in the term as the sum paid bears to the sum adjudged to be paid:

Provided that, in reckoning the number of days by which any term of imprisonment would be reduced under this section, the first day of imprisonment shall not be taken into account, and that, in reckoning the sum which will secure the reduction of a term of imprisonment, fractions of a penny shall be omitted.

(2) Provision may be made by rules under section twenty-nine of the Summary Jurisdiction Act, 1879, as to the application of sums paid under this section and for determining the persons authorised to receive such payments and the conditions under which such payments may be made.

4   Provisions for enforcement of payment of fines, &c

(1) Where a person has been adjudged to pay a sum by a conviction of a court of summary jurisdiction, or in proceedings in any such court for enforcing an order in any matter of bastardy, or an order under which weekly sums are made payable towards the maintenance of a wife, the court may order him to be searched and any money found on him on apprehension, or when so searched, or which may be found on him when taken to prison in default of payment of the sum so adjudged to be paid, may, unless the court otherwise directs, be applied towards the payment of the sum so adjudged to be paid, and the surplus,. if any, shall be returned to him.

Provided that the money shall not be so applied if the court is satisfied that the money does not belong to the person on whom it was found, or that the loss of the money will be more injurious to his family than his imprisonment.

(2) Where a warrant of distress is issued by a court of summary jurisdiction it shall authorise the person charged with the execution thereof to take any money as well as any goods of the person against whom the distress is levied, and any money so taken shall be treated as if it were the proceeds of sale of goods taken under the warrant, and the provisions of the Summary Jurisdiction Acts shall apply accordingly.

5   Payment and allocation of fines and fees

(1) A. court of summary jurisdiction in fixing the amount of any fine to be imposed on an offender shall take into consideration, amongst other things, the means of the offender so far as they appear or are known to the court; and where a fine is imposed the payment of the court fees and police fees payable in the case up to and including conviction shall not be taken into consideration in fixing the amount of the fine or be imposed in addition to the fine, but the amount of the fine, or of such part thereof as may be paid or recovered, shall be applied as follows:-

(a)   in the first place in the repayment to the informant or complainant of any court or police fees paid by him;

(b)   in the second place in the payment of any court fees not already paid by the informant or complainant which may be payable under the table of fees set out in the First Schedule to this Act;

(c)   in the third place in the payment of any police fees not already paid by the informant or complainant; and

(d)   the balance (if any) remaining after the aforesaid payments have been made shall be paid to the fund or person to which the fine is directed to be paid by the enactments relating to the offence in respect of which the fine was imposed, or, if there is no such fund or person, then to the fund into which the court fees are paid.

(2) In this section the expression "police fees" means all duly authorised fees payable to any constable in the execution of his duty.

6   Uniform scale of court fees as respects all courts of summary jurisdiction.

(1) The table of court fees set out in Part I. of the First Schedule to this Act shall have effect in all courts of summary courts jurisdiction, and shall be substituted for any table of fees in force at the commencement of this Act in any court of summary jurisdiction, and references

in any enactment to any fees for which fees in the said table are so substituted shall be construed as references to the fees so substituted.

(2) Notwithstanding any provisions in any other general or local Act or in any rules made under any such Act enabling fees to be charged by clerks to justices, the fees set out in Part I. of that schedule, and no other fees, may be charged by clerks to justices:

Provided that nothing in this section shall affect the fees chargeable in metropolitan police courts or the police courts of the City of London, or in respect of the matters specified in Part II. of that schedule.

(3) The Secretary of State may, in the event of new or additional duties being imposed on courts of summary jurisdiction or clerks to justices, or for other sufficient reason, by order make such variations in the said table of fees as may seem to him to be proper, and upon such order coming into operation the table shall have effect subject to the variations made by the order:

Provided that before any such order is made a draft of the proposed order shall be laid before each House of Parliament for a period of not less than thirty days during which the House is sitting, and if either of those Houses before the expiration of those thirty days presents an address to His Majesty against the draft order or any part thereof no further proceedings shall be taken thereon, without prejudice to the making of a new draft order.

PROBATION

7 **Power to recognise and subsidise societies for care of youthful offenders on probation, &c.**

(1) If a society is formed or is already in existence having as-its object or amongst its objects the care and control of persons under the age of twenty-one whilst on probation under the Probation of Offenders Act, 1907, or of persons whilst placed out on licence from a reformatory or industrial school or Borstal institution, or under supervision after the determination of the period of their detention in such a school or institution, or under supervision in pursuance of this Act, or some one or more of such objects the society may apply to the Secretary of State for recognition, and the Secretary of State, if he approves of the constitution of the society and is satisfied as to the means adopted by the society for securing such objects as aforesaid, may grant his recognition to the society.

(2) Where a probation order is made by a court of summary jurisdiction in respect of a person who appears to the court to be under the age of twenty-one, the court may appoint any person provided by a recognised society to act as probation officer in the case.

(3) Where a probation officer provided by a recognised society has been appointed to act in any case and it is subsequently found by the society expedient that some other officer provided by the society should be substituted for the officer originally appointed, the society may, subject to the approval of the court, appoint such other officer to act, and thereupon the probation order shall have effect as if such substituted officer had originally been appointed to act as probation officer.

(4) There may be paid to a recognised society out of moneys provided by Parliament towards the expenses incurred by the society such sums on such conditions as the Secretary of State, with the approval of the Treasury, may recommend.

8   Conditions of probation

(1) For subsection (2) of section two of the Probation of conditions of Offenders Act, 1907, which specifies the additional conditions which may be inserted in a recognisance under the Act, the following subsection shall be substituted:-

(2) A recognisance under this Act may contain such additional conditions with respect to residence, abstention from intoxicating liquor, and any other matters, as the court may, having regard to the particular circumstances of the case, consider necessary for preventing a repetition of the same offence or the commission of other offences.

9   Variation of terms and conditions of probation

The following section shall be substituted for section variation of five of the Probation of Offenders Act, 1907, which relates to the power of varying the conditions of recognisances

The court before which any person is bound by a recognisance under this Act to appear for conviction and sentence or for sentence—

   (a)   may at any time if it appears to it, upon the application of the probation officer, that it is expedient that the terms or conditions of the recognisance should be varied, summon the person bound by the recognisance to appear before it, and, if he fails to show cause why such variation should not be made, vary the terms of the recognisance by extending or diminishing the duration thereof (so, however, that it shall not exceed three years from the date of the original order), or by altering the conditions thereof, or by inserting additional conditions; or

   (b)   may on application being made by the probation officer, and on being satisfied that the conduct of the person bound by the recognisance has been such as to make it unnecessary that he any longer be under supervision, discharge the recognisance.

COMMITTALS TO BORSTAL INSTITUTIONS

10   Power to send youthful delinquents to Borstal Institutions

(1) Where a person is summarily convicted of any offence for which the court has power to impose a sentence of imprisonment for one month or upwards without the option of. a fine, and—

   (a)   it appears to the court that the offender is not less than sixteen nor more than twenty-one years of age; and

   (b)   it is proved that the offender has previously been convicted of any offence or, that having been previously discharged on probation, he failed to observe a condition of his recognizance; and

   (c)   it appears to the court that by reason of the offender's criminal habits or tendencies, or association with persons of bad character, it is expedient that he should be subject to detention fox such term and under such instruction and discipline as appears most conducive to his reformation and the repression of crime,

it shall be lawful for the court, in lieu of passing sentence, to commit the offender to prison until the next quarter sessions, and the court of quarter sessions shall inquire into the circumstances of the case, and, if it appears to the court that the offender is of such age as aforesaid and that for any such reason as aforesaid it is expedient that the offender should be subject to such detention as aforesaid, shall pass such sentence of detention in a Borstal institution as is authorised by Part I. of the Prevention of Crime Act, 1908, as amended by this Act; otherwise the court shall deal with the case in any way in which the court of summary jurisdiction might have dealt with it.

(2) A court of summary jurisdiction or court of quarter sessions, before dealing with any case under this section, shall consider any report or representations which may be made to it by or on behalf of the Prison Commissioners as to the suitability of the offender for such detention as aforesaid, and a court of summary jurisdiction shall, where necessary, adjourn the case for the purpose of giving an opportunity for such a report or representations being made.

(3) Where a person is committed to prison under this section his treatment in prison shall, so far as practicable, be similar to that in Borstal institutions, or he may, if the Secretary of State so directs, be transferred to a Borstal institution.

(4) The. Costs in Criminal Cases Act, 1908, shall apply in the case of a person committed to prison by a court of summary jurisdiction under this section as if that person were committed for trial for an indictable offence.

(5) A person sentenced by a court of quarter sessions under this section to detention in a Borstal institution may appeal against the sentence to the Court of Criminal Appeal as if he had been convicted on indictment, and the provisions of the Criminal Appeal Act, 1907, shall apply accordingly.

(6) This section shall come into operation on the first day of 8eptember nineteen hundred and fifteen.

11   Amendment and application of Part I. of the Prevention of Crime Act 1908

(1) The term for which a person or youthful offender may be sentenced to detention in a Borstal institution under section one or section two of the Prevention of Crime Act, 1908, shall not be less than two years, and accordingly "two years" of crime shall be substituted for "one year" in subsection (1) of section Act, 1908. one and in section two respectively of that Act.

(2) The period for which a person sentenced to detention in a Borstal institution is on the expiration of the term of his sentence to remain under the supervision of the Prison Commissioners shall be one year, and accordingly "one year" shall be substituted for "six months" in subsection (1) of section six of the same Act.

(3) The maximum period for which a person so under the supervision of the Prison Commissioners may on recall to a Borstal institution be detained in such an institution shall be one year, and he may be so detained notwithstanding that the period of supervision has expired, and accordingly "one year" shall be substituted for "three months" in subsection (2) of section six of that Act.

(4) The provisions of Part I of the Prevention of Crime Act, 1908, as so amended, shall apply to persons sentenced to detention in a Borstal institution under this Act in like manner as they apply to persons sentenced under that Part of that Act.

NEW POWERS OF DEALING WITH OFFENDERS

12   Power to order detention for one day in precincts of the court.

Where a court of summary jurisdiction has power to pass a sentence of imprisonment, the court, in lieu of passing a sentence of imprisonment, may order that the offender be detained within the precincts of the court, or at any police station, till such hour, not later than eight in the evening on the day on which he is convicted, as the court may direct:

Provided that a court of summary jurisdiction shall, before making an order of detention under this section, take into consideration the distance between the place of detention and the offender's abode (if his abode is known to, or ascertainable by, the court), and shall not make any such order of detention under this section as will deprive the offender of a reasonable opportunity of returning to his abode on the day on which such order of detention is made.

13   Substitution of police custody for imprisonment in case of short sentences

(1) No person shall be sentenced to imprisonment by a court of summary jurisdiction for a period of less than five days.

(2) Where a person is liable to be sentenced to imprisonment by a court of summary jurisdiction, the court may, if any suitable places provided and certified in manner hereinafter appearing are available for the purpose, order the person to be detained therein for such period not exceeding four days as the court thinks fit, and the order shall be delivered with the offender to the person in charge of the place where the offender is to be detained, and shall be a sufficient authority for his detention in that place in accordance with the tenour thereof.

(3) The expenses of the maintenance of persons detained under this section shall be defrayed in like manner as the expenses of the maintenance of prisoners in prisons to which the Prison Act, 1877, applies.

(4) The Secretary of State may, on the application of any police authority, certify any police cells, bridewells, or other similar places provided by the authority to be suitable places for the detention of persons sentenced to detention under this section, and may make regulations for the inspection of places so provided, the treatment of persons detained therein, and generally for carrying this section into effect:

Provided that no place so certified shall be used for the detention of females unless provision is made for their supervision by female officers.

(5) For the purposes of this section the expression "police authority" with respect to the City of London, means the Commissioner of City Police, and with respect to other places has the same meaning as in the Police Act, 1890.

14   Provisions as to malicious damage to property

(1) If any person wilfully or maliciously commits any damage to any real or personal property whatsoever, either of a public or private nature, and the amount of the damage does not, in the opinion of the court, exceed twenty pounds, he shall be liable on summary conviction—

(a) if the amount of the damage, in the opinion of the court, exceeds five pounds, to imprisonment for a term not exceeding three months or to a fine not exceeding twenty pounds; and

(b) if the amount of the damage is, in the opinion of the court, five pounds or less, to imprisonment for a term not exceeding two months or to a fine not exceeding five pounds;

and in either case to the payment of such further amount as appears to the court reasonable compensation for the damage so committed which last-mentioned amount shall be paid to the party aggrieved:

Provided that this provision shall not apply where the alleged offender acted under a fair and reasonable supposition that he had a right to do the act complained of.

(2) So much of section fifty-one of the Malicious Damage Act, 1861, as limits the cases which may be dealt with under that section to cases where the damage, injury or spoil exceeds five pounds, shall be repealed but a court of summary jurisdiction shall not commit any person for trial for an offence under that section unless it is of opinion that the damage, injury or spoil exceeds five pounds.

(3) Except so far as otherwise provided in the last foregoing subsection, nothing in this section shall be construed as preventing a court of summary jurisdiction from committing a person for trial for an offence notwithstanding that the offence is an offence which the court has power to deal with summarily under this section.

15   Extension of powers to deal with cases summarily

(1) "Twenty pounds" shall be substituted for "forty shillings" wherever those words occur in the second column of the First Schedule to the Summary Jurisdiction Act, 1879, or in the second column of the Schedule to the Summary Jurisdiction Act, 1899, in which columns are set forth the indictable offences for which an adult may, with his consent, be dealt with summarily.

In section twelve of the Summary Jurisdiction Act,1879, after the words "not exceeding twenty pounds" there shall be inserted the following words or, if the value of the property which was the subject of the offence, in the opinion of the court before which the charge is brought, exceeds forty shillings, to be imprisoned with or without hard labour for any term not exceeding six months or to pay a fine not exceeding fifty pounds.

(2) Section fourteen of the same Act (which imposes certain restrictions on the power to deal summarily with adults charged with indictable offences) is hereby repealed.

(3) Where a child is charged before a court of summary jurisdiction with a felony, and the court, in pursuance of the power conferred by section ten of the same Act, as amended by any subsequent enactment, deals with the case summarily, the court may, notwithstanding anything in that section, inflict a fine not exceeding forty shillings as a punishment.

IMPRISONMENT

16   Hard labour and classification of prisoners

[…][1]

Amendments

1   Section 16 repealed by Criminal Law Act 1997, s 16 and Sch 3.

---

17   Commitment and removal of prisoners

There shall be substituted for sections twenty-four, twenty-five, twenty-six, and twenty-seven of the Prison Act, 1877, the following provisions:-

(1) The Secretary of State may from time to time by any general or special rule under the Prison Acts, 1865 to 1902, appropriate, either wholly or partially, particular prisons within his jurisdiction to particular classes of prisoners:

(2) A. prisoner sentenced to imprisonment or committed to prison on remand, or pending trial, or otherwise, may be lawfully confined in any prison to which the Prison Acts, 1865 to 1902, apply:

(3) Prisoners shall be committed to such prisons as the Secretary of State may from time to time direct; and may on the like direction be removed therefrom during the term of their imprisonment to any other prison

(4) Where a prisoner is discharged from a prison situate beyond the limits of the county, borough, or place in which he was arrested, the cost of his return to the place in which he was at the time of his arrest or to the place where he was convicted, whichever is the nearest, shall be paid out of moneys provided by Parliament on account of prisons:

(5) A prisoner shall not in any case be liable to pay the costs of his conveyance to prison:

(6) The Secretary of State, on being satisfied that a prisoner is suffering from disease and cannot be properly treated in the prison, or that he should undergo and desires to undergo a surgical operation which cannot properly be performed in the prison, may order that the prisoner be taken to a hospital or other suitable place for the purpose of treatment or the operation, and while absent from the prison in pursuance of such an order the prisoner shall be deemed to be in legal custody.

18   Consecutive sentences of imprisonment

[...]¹

Amendments

1   Section 18 repealed by Criminal Justice Act 1951, s 26 and Sch 2.

BAIL AND REMAND

19–21   [...]¹

Amendments

1   Sections 19–21 repealed by Criminal Procedure Act 1967, s 3 and Sch.

---

22   Release on bail of a person arrested without warrant

For section thirty-eight of the Summary Jurisdiction Act, 1879, the following section shall be substituted:—

> 'On a person being taken into custody for an offence without a warrant, a superintendent or inspector of police, or other officer of police of equal or superior rank, or in charge of any police station, may in any case, and shall, if it will not be practicable to bring such person before a court of summary jurisdiction within twenty-four hours after he was so taken into custody, inquire into the case, and, unless the offence appears to such superintendent, inspector, or officer to be of a serious nature, discharge the person upon his entering into a recognisance with or without sureties for a reasonable amount to appear before some court of summary jurisdiction at the time and place named in the recognisance, but where such person is retained in custody he shall be brought before a court of summary jurisdiction as soon as practicable.'

23   Notice of right to apply for bail

Where a court of summary jurisdiction commits a person charged with any misdemeanour for trial and does not admit him to bail the court shall inform the person accused of his right to apply for bail to a judge of the High Court of Justice.

24   Declaration of law as to mode of entering into recognisance

For removing doubts it is hereby declared that where as a condition of the release of any person he is required to enter into a recognisance with sureties, the recognisances of the sureties may be taken separately and either before or after the recognisances of the principal, and if so taken the recognisances of the principal and sureties shall be as binding as if they had been taken together and at the same time.

MISCELLANEOUS AND GENERAL

25   Manner of enforcing payment of sums adjudged to be paid

(1) The following provision shall be substituted for subsection 31 of section twenty-one of the Summary Jurisdiction Act, 1879:-

> "Where a sum is adjudged to be paid by a conviction of a court of summary jurisdiction, or in the case of a sum not a civil debt by an order of such court, and on default of payment of such sum a warrant of distress is authorised to be issued, the court may, in any case in which it appears expedient to do so, instead of issuing a warrant of distress, issue a warrant of commitment:
>
> Provided that where time is not allowed for the payment of such sum, a warrant of commitment shall not be issued in the first instance unless it appears to the court that the offender has no goods or insufficient goods to satisfy the money payable or that the levy of distress will be more injurious to him or his family than imprisonment."

(2) Where a sum is adjudged to be paid by a conviction or order of a court of summary jurisdiction, and, by the statute authorising such conviction or order, a mode of enforcing the payment thereof is provided which does not authorise the issue of a warrant of distress for the purpose, a warrant of distress may nevertheless be issued in like manner in all respects and

with the like consequences as if no mode of enforcing the payment were provided in such statute.

26   Provisions with respect to holders of licences and persons under police supervision

[…]¹

Amendments

1   Section 26 repealed by Criminal Law Act 1997, s 16 and Sch 3.

---

27   Power to issue warrants of arrest in certain cases

It is hereby declared that where at common law or under any Act, whether passed before or after the commencement of this Act, there is power to arrest a person without warrant, a warrant for his arrest may be issued.

28   Provisions as to evidence

(1) The record or extract by which a conviction may be proved under section eighteen of the Prevention of Crimes Act, 1871, may in the case of a summary conviction consist of a copy of the minute or memorandum of the conviction entered is the register required to be kept under section twenty-two of the Summary Jurisdiction Act, 1879, purporting to be signed by the clerk of the court by whom the register is kept.

(2) […]¹.

(3) The wife or husband of a person charged with bigamy may be- called as a witness either for the prosecution or defence and without the consent of the person charged.

(4) In any proceedings. before a court of summary jurisdiction to enforce the payment of a sum of money adjudged by that or any other court of summary jurisdiction to be paid by one person to another person, then—

(a)   if the person to whom the sum is ordered to be paid was an officer of a court of summary jurisdiction, the production of a certificate purporting to be signed by that officer that the sum has not been paid to him; and

(b)   in any other case the production of a statutory declaration to a like effect purporting to be made by the person to whom the sum is ordered to be paid;

shall be evidence of the facts therein stated, unless the court requires such officer or other person to be called as a witness.

Amendments

1   Subsection (2) repealed by Criminal Evidence Act 1992, s 3 and Sch.

---

29 Power of justices to order production of documents

The provisions of section sixteen of the Indictable Offences Act, 1848, section seven of the Summary Jurisdiction Act, 1848, and section thirty-six of the Summary Jurisdiction Act, 1879, enabling a justice to issue a summons to any witness to attend to give evidence before a court of summary jurisdiction, shall be deemed to include the power to summon and require a witness to produce to such court books, plans, papers, documents, articles, goods, and things likely to be material evidence on the hearing of any charge, information, or complaint, and the provisions of those sections relating to the neglect or refusal of a witness, without just excuse, to attend to give evidence, or to be sworn, or to give evidence, shall apply accordingly.

30 Periodical payments ordered by courts of summary jurisdiction

(1) Where a court of summary jurisdiction orders money to be paid periodically by one person to another, the court may, if it thinks fit, order that the payment shall be made jurisdiction. through an officer of the court or any other person or officer specified in the order.

(2) Where a court of summary jurisdiction has either before or after the commencement of this Act ordered money to be paid periodically by one person to another, the court which made the order, or any other court of summary jurisdiction for the same petty sessional division, may, if it thinks fit, order that the payment shall be made through an officer of the court or any other person or officer specified in the order.

(3) Any order made either before or after the commencement of this Act by a court of summary jurisdiction for the periodical payment of money may, upon cause being shown upon fresh evidence to the satisfaction of the court, be revoked, revived, or varied by a subsequent order.

(4) Where a court of summary jurisdiction makes an order for the periodical payment of money through an officer of the court or other person or officer specified in the order, the authority having the control of the fund out of which the salary of the clerk of that court is paid may pay to that officer or person out of that fund, in manner provided by rules made by the Secretary of State, a sum not exceeding five pounds percentum on the money actually paid through him in pursuance of the order, as remuneration to him in respect of the work done and expenses incurred by him in respect of the order.

(5) Nothing in this section shall prejudice or affect the powers and duties of courts of summary jurisdiction under the Affiliation Orders Act, 1914.

31 Costs

A court of summary jurisdiction to which an application is made for an order for the periodical payment of money, or for the variation, revocation, revival, or enforcement of such an order, may make an order for the payment by the applicant or the defendant, or both of them, of the costs of the court and such reasonable costs of either of the parties as the court thinks fit.

32 Recovery of arrears on bastardy orders, &c

(1) It is hereby declared that, notwithstanding anything in section fifty-four of the Summary Jurisdiction Act, 1879, the provisions of section eleven of the Summary Jurisdiction Act, 1848 (which relate to the time within which summary proceedings are to be taken), do not

apply to proceedings for enforcing the payment of sums adjudged to be paid by an order in any matter of bastardy or by an order enforceable as an order of affiliation.

(2) Proceedings for the enforcement of an order in any matter of bastardy or of an order enforceable as an order of affiliation may be taken at any time after the expiration of fourteen clear days from the making of the order, and accordingly in section four of the Bastardy Laws Amendment Act, 1872, "after the expiration of fourteen clear days "shall be substituted for" after the expiration of one calendar month.

(3) Where in any proceedings for the enforcement of an order 'in any matter of bastardy or of an order enforceable as an order of affiliation the court commits the defendant to prison then; unless the court otherwise directs, no arrears shall accrue under the order during the time that the defendant is in prison.

33   Amendment of the law with respect to the recovery of rates

The provisions of the Summary Jurisdiction Acts Amendment of relating to the backing of warrants, and of section forty-one of the Summary Jurisdiction Act, 1879, relating to the proof of service of documents and of the handwriting and seal on documents, shall apply to proceedings in respect of the non-payment of, any rate.

34   Appointment and remuneration of and accounting by justices' clerks

(1) Clerks to justices shall continue to be appointed as heretofore, but no appointment made after the commencement of this Act shall be valid unless and until it is confirmed by the Secretary of State, and the Secretary of State shall, before confirming any such appointment, take into consideration any representations that may be made to him, in the case of the appointment of a clerk to borough justices by the council of the borough, and in the case of the appointment of a clerk to county justices by the standing joint committee of the county.

(2) Notwithstanding the provisions of any other general or local Act to the contrary, the salaries of clerks to justices shall be fixed and may from time to time be varied—

    (a) in the case of a clerk to borough justices, by the justices of the borough; and

    (b) in the case of a clerk to county justices, by the standing joint committee of the county:

Provided that—

    (i) in the case of the salary of a clerk to borough justices, the council of the borough; and

    (ii) in the case of the salary of a clerk to county justices, the county justices for whom the clerk acts; and

    (iii) in either case where the proposal is for a reduction of salary, the clerk to the justices may appeal to the Secretary of State against the decision of the justices or standing joint committee, as the case may be, and the amount of the salary shall thereupon be determined by the Secretary of State.

(3) If the justices for any petty sessional division make representations to the standing joint committee of the county with a view to the variation of the salary of their clerk, the standing joint committee shall at a meeting of which special notice has been given take into consideration the question of varying the salary.

(4) The authority by whom the salary of a clerk is fixed may allow him such special remuneration in addition to his salary as they may, subject to the approval of the Secretary of

State, determine, in respect of any duties which were not taken into account in fixing his salary.

(5) Nothing in the foregoing provisions of this section shall apply to clerks at metropolitan police courts nor to the clerks to the justices of the city of London nor, to the clerk to any stipendiary magistrate other than a stipendiary magistrate appointed under the Municipal Corporations Act, 1882.

(6) If any clerk to justices fails without sufficient reason to account for or pay over any sum within one month from the time when he was required to account for or pay over the sum under section six of the Justices' Clerks Act, 1877, he shall be deemed to have wilfully omitted to account for or pay over that sum within the meaning of that section, but no person shall sue for a sum recoverable under that section, as amended by this section, except the person or authority to whom the account or payment is required to be made.

35   Punishment for accusation, &c. of dead person with intent to extort

[…]¹

Amendments

1   Section 35 repealed as to England and Ireland by Larceny Act 1916, s 48 and Sch.

36   Corporal punishment

[…]¹

Amendments

1   Section 36 repealed by Criminal Law Act 1997, s 16 and Sch 3.

37   Right of appeal from decision of court of summary jurisdiction

(1) Any person aggrieved by any conviction of a court of summary jurisdiction in respect of any offence, who did not plead guilty or admit the truth of the information, may appeal from the conviction in manner provided by the Summary Jurisdiction Acts to a court of quarter sessions.

(2) An appeal shall lie to a court of quarter sessions in manner provided by the Summary Jurisdiction Acts from any order made by a court of summary jurisdiction under the enactments relating to bastardy, or from any refusal by a court of summary jurisdiction to make such an order, or from the revocation, revival, or variation by a court of summary jurisdiction of such an order.

38   One justice to be competent to exercise certain powers in respect of charges of drunkenness

Notwithstanding any enactment to the contrary, it shall be sufficient for a court of summary jurisdiction to consist of one justice only when hearing, trying, adjudging, and determining a charge or information against any person of having been found drunk in any highway or other public place, whether a building or not, or on any licensed premises, under section twelve of the Licensing Act, 1872.

39   Convictions on indictments

(1) [...][1]

(2) [...][2]

Amendments

1   Subsection (1) repealed by Criminal Justice (Verdicts) Act 1976, 1(4).

2   Subsection (2) repealed as to England and Ireland by Larceny Act 1916, s 48 and Sch.

---

40   Rules

(1) The power of the Lord Chancellor to make rules under section twenty-nine of the Summary Jurisdiction Act, 1879, shall extend to the making of rules—

(a)   for regulating the manner in which convictions and orders of courts of summary jurisdiction are to be drawn up, and in such cases as may be provided for by the rules, the transmission of such convictions and orders and any other documents therewith to the clerk of the peace and the filing of them by him, and

(b)   for annulling, altering, or adding to the forms contained in the schedule to the Indictable Offences Act, 1848, and

(c)   for regulating the procedure of courts of summary jurisdiction under this Act, and the procedure in any legal proceedings which under any Act, whether general or local, and whether passed before or after the commencement of this Act (other than the Summary Jurisdiction Acts), are to be taken before any police or stipendiary magistrate or other court of summary jurisdiction.

(2) His Majesty may, by Order in Council, make rules extending the operation of the Summary Jurisdiction (Process) Act, 1881, as amended by any subsequent enactment (which relates to the service and execution in Scotland of process issued by courts of summary jurisdiction in England, and in England of process issued by courts of summary jurisdiction and sheriff courts in Scotland, and to the jurisdiction of courts in England and Scotland respectively in bastardy proceedings), so as to make the provisions of that Act, subject to the. necessary adaptations, applicable as between any one part of the British Islands and any other part of the British Islands in like manner as it applies as between England and Scotland.

This subsection shall extend to the Isle of Man and the Channel Islands, and the Royal Courts of the Channel Islands shall register the same accordingly.

41   Definitions

For the purposes of this Act, unless the context otherwise requires,—

(1)   The expression "sentenced to imprisonment" shall include cases where imprisonment is imposed by a court on any person either with or without the option of a fine, or in respect of the non-payment of any sum of money, or for failing to do

or abstaining from doing any act or thing required to be done or left undone, and the expression "sentence of imprisonment" shall be construed. accordingly:

(2) The expressions "fine," "sum adjudged to be paid by a conviction," and "sum adjudged to be paid by an order," have the same meanings as in, the Summary Jurisdiction Act, 1879.

42   Application to Scotland

[...]¹

---

1   Text not reproduced here.

---

43   Application to Ireland

(1) The provisions of sections one to four inclusive, sections seven to twelve inclusive, sections [...]¹ twenty-one Ireland. inclusive, section twenty-four, subsection (2) of section twenty-five, sections [...]¹ and twenty-seven, subsections (2) and (4) of section twenty-eight, sections thirty-five, [...]¹, and thirty-nine, and subsection (1) of section forty-one of this Act shall apply to Ireland, subject to the following modifications, namely:-

(a)   references to the Lord Lieutenant shall be substituted for references to the Secretary of State, and references to the General Prisons Board for Ireland shall be substituted for references to the Prison Commissioners;

(b)   a reference to the Prisons (Ireland) Acts, 1826 to 1907, shall be substituted for any reference to the Prison Acts, 1865 to 1902, and a reference to sections thirty-six, thirty-seven, thirty-eight, and thirty-nine of the General Prisons (Ireland) Act, 1877, shall be substituted for the reference to sections twenty-four, twenty-five, twenty-six, and twenty-seven of the Prison Act, 1877.

(c)   references to the Court of Criminal Appeal, the Criminal Appeal Act, 1907, and the Costs in Criminal Cases Act, 1908, and the provision of section two of this Act relative to payment by instalments, shall not apply; and

(d)   [...]²

(2) A court of summary jurisdiction, in fixing the amount of any fine to be imposed on an offender, shall take into consideration, amongst other things, the means of the offender so far as they appear or are known to the court.³

(3) Proceedings for the recovery in a summary manner of a penalty for an offence under the Births and Deaths Registration Act (Ireland), 1880, may be commenced at any time within three years after the commission of the offence.

(4) Where upon summary conviction an offender is adjudged to pay a penalty exceeding five pounds, the offender in case of non-payment thereof may without any warrant of distress be committed to prison for any term not exceeding the period for which he might be committed to prison in default of distress: Provided that where time is not allowed for the payment of the penalty a warrant of commitment shall not be issued in the first instance unless it appears to the court that the offender has no goods or insufficient goods to satisfy the penalty, or that the levy of distress would be more injurious to him or his family than imprisonment.

(5) So much of section three of the Fines Act (Ireland), 1851, as requires that a warrant for the execution of an order of a divisional justice of the police district of Dublin metropolis for the imposition or levy of a penal sum shall be issued within one week from the making of the order, shall cease to have effect.

(6) Upon any information or complaint laid or made before a divisional justice of the police district of Dublin metropolis of an offence punishable on summary conviction, if the person charged resides within the limits of that district, the justice shall, notwithstanding that the offence has been or is alleged to have been committed outside those limits, have all the like powers, jurisdiction, and authority as he has upon an information or complaint laid or made of a similar offence committed or alleged to have been committed within those limits.

(7) So much of section twenty-two of the Petty Sessions (Ireland) Act, 1851, as relates to the liability of persons aiding, abetting, counselling, or procuring the commission of offences punishable on summary conviction shall, as amended by any subsequent enactment, extend to the police district of Dublin metropolis; and every person who aids, abets, counsels, or procures the commission of any such offence may be proceeded against and convicted in that district in any case where the principal offender may be convicted in that district, or where the offence of aiding, abetting, counselling, or procuring was committed in that district.

(8) [...]⁴, section six (which relates to divisions of prisoners), section eleven (which relates to orders for production of prisoners), and, so far as respects sentences of imprisonment passed after the commencement of this Act, section twelve (which relates to calculation of term of sentence) [...]¹, shall, as amended by this Act, extend to Ireland subject to the following modifications, namely:—

    (a) references to the Lord Lieutenant shall be substituted for references to the Secretary of State '

    (b) references to rules made by the General Prisons Board for Ireland with the approval of the Lord Lieutenant and Privy Council under the General Prisons (Ireland) Act, 1877, shall be substituted for any references to prison rules or special prison rules;

    (c) a reference to section forty-nine of the General Prisons (Ireland) Act, 1877, shall be substituted for the reference to sections forty and forty-one of the Prison Act, 1877, and references to provisions of the Prison Act, 1865, or the Criminal Procedure Act, 1853, shall not apply.

(9) [...]⁴

(10) The Lord Chancellor may make rules for the purposes of this Act regulating the procedure to be followed, and prescribing the forms to be used in summary proceedings and regulating and prescribing any other matter or thing which for the purposes aforesaid requires to be regulated or prescribed, and adapting to the requirements of this Act any forms relating to summary proceedings prescribed by or in pursuance of any other Act, and all rules so made shall be laid as soon as may be before both Houses of Parliament.

(11) An appeal under section twenty-seven of the Dublin Police Act, 1837, section twenty-three of the Summary Jurisdiction (Ireland) Act, 1851, or section twenty-four of the Petty Sessions (Ireland) Act, 1851, against a conviction of a court of summary jurisdiction in respect of an offence shall lie whatever may be the amount of the fine or the term of the imprisonment imposed.

(12) Where a person convicted of an offence by a court of summary jurisdiction is committed to prison by the court under section ten of this Act without sentence he may appeal under the

Summary Jurisdiction Acts against the conviction, and the provisions of those Acts with respect to appeals shall apply accordingly.

(13) Upon any information, summons, or complaint laid or made before a court of summary jurisdiction in Ireland wherein the defendant is called upon to show cause why such defendant should not be bound over to keep the peace or be of good behaviour, the defendant shall be entitled to call witnesses and tender evidence at the hearing of the information, summons, or complaint.

(14) Save as provided in this section, the foregoing provisions of this Act shall not extend to Ireland.

Amendments

1   Words deleted by Criminal Law Act 1997, s 16 and Sch 3.
2   Subsection (1)(d) repealed by Criminal Procedure Act 1967, Sch.
3   Subsection (2) repealed by Fines Act 2010, s 22 which has not yet come into operation (February 2011).
4   Subsection (8) repealed in part by Prisons (Visiting Committees) Act 1925, s 7 and Sch.
5   Subsection (9) repealed by Prisons (Visiting Committees) Act 1925, s 7 and Sch.

44   Short title, commencement, and repeal

(1) This Act may be cited as the Criminal Justice Administration Act, 1914, and shall, save as otherwise expressly provided, come into operation on the first day of December nineteen hundred and fourteen.

(2) The enactments mentioned in the Fourth Schedule to this Act are hereby repealed to the extent specified in the third column of that schedule.

SCHEDULES

FIRST SCHEDULE

Sections 5, 6.

PART I
TABLE OF COURT FEES TO BE TAKEN BY CLERKS TO JUSTICES OF THE PEACE

	£	s	d
INDICTABLE OFFENCES:			
For the performance of all the several duties in every case committed for trial to the assizes or sessions, without regard to the number of prisoners included in the same charge	1	5	0

	£	s	d
(This fee does not cover taking recognizances or giving notice to the accused and his sureties when admitted to bail; nor attending to take the deposition of a witness prevented by sickness or otherwise from appearing in court; nor supplying a copy of depositions. In cases of dismissal the separate fees for information, &c., are chargeable.)			
For the performance of all the several duties (including commitment) in respect of any indictable offence dealt with summarily without regard to the number of persons charged in each case, and whether there is a conviction or not	1	5	0
SUMMARY ADJUDICATIONS:			
For the performance of all the several duties up to and including conviction in respect of any charge for an offence (other than an indictable offence) punishable on summary conviction	0	4	0
ELEMENTARY EDUCATION ACTS:			
Proceedings under the Acts, in each case, including summons, order, and conviction	0	4	0
Distress warrants (if any)	0	1	–
Committal (if any)	0	1	0
For services not covered by the foregoing fees the following fees may be charged:—			
APPOINTMENT:			
Of parochial or other officers (except constables), to contain. the names of all the persons appointed at the same time to the same office in the parish, hamlet, or place, including notice and oath when necessary	0	5	0
Of any constable (other than special)	0	1	0
Of valuer, arbitrator, &c.	0	10	0
Of special constables, if less than 28, for each person, to include notice, oath, and certificate	0	1	0
If more than 28 are appointed on one occasion, for attending to summons, swear in, and make out appointments, and the business thereof, for each day	2	2	0
ARMY ACT, 1881 (44 & 45 VIcT. c. 58)			
Attestation of recruit (section 80(4)(d))	0	1	0
Descriptive return in relation to deserter (section 154(6))	0	2	0
Certificate of civil conviction or acquittal (section 164)	0	3	0
Warrant to provide carriages (section 112)	0	1	0
ATTENDANCE:			

	£	s	d
On a justice, to view deserted premises in order to affix notice or to give possession thereof, to view a highway, bridge, or nuisance, or to take an examination elsewhere than in court	0	6	8
If required to go more than one mile from the place of holding petty sessions, for each mile after the first (one way)	0	1	0
CASE FOR THE OPINION OF SUPERIOR COURT (20 & 21 VicT. c. 43, SECTION 3):			
Drawing case and copy, when the case does not exceed five folios of 90 words	0	10	0
For every additional folio beyond five	0	1	0
Taking recognizance as required by the Act	0	5	0
Every enlargement or renewal thereof	0	2	6
For certificate of refusal of case	0	2	0
CERTIFICATE:	0	2	0
Every certificate not otherwise charged	0	2	0
CERTIORARI:			
Return to and filing	0	13	4
CIVIL DEBT (not including Rates):			
Summons and copy	0	1	6
Complaint	0	1	0
Order and copy	0	3	0
Oath (each witness)	0	1	0
Judgment summons and copy, including hearing	0	3	0
Warrant of distress	0	2	0
Commitment. (See Warrant.)			
COMPLAINT:			
Every complaint not otherwise charged	0	1	0
CONVICTION:-			
Every conviction, including returning same to the court (to include all persons convicted on the same charge, except in cases where all persons convicted on the same charge cannot be included in the same conviction)	0	2	6
COPY:			
Of depositions for prosecutor on the trial, per folio of 90 words	0	0	4
Of depositions for prisoner, under 11 & 12 Vi ct. c. 42. s. 27, per folio of 90 words, not exceeding	0	0	1½

	£	s	d
Of any other document, per folio of 72 words	0	0	4
DUPLICATE:			
For the duplicate of any document	One-half the original fee.		
EXAMINATION. (See Information.)			
EXHIBIT:			
Each document annexed to or referred to in any affidavit or declaration and marked	0	1	0
EXPLOSIVES ACT, 1875 (38 VICT. C. 17):			
Store licence (s. 15), not exceeding	0	5	0
Store licence, renewal (s. 18), not exceeding	0	1	0
Registering premises (s. 21), not exceeding	0	1	0
Registering premises, renewal, not exceeding	0	1	0
Small firework factory (s. 49) licence, not exceeding	0	5	0
Small firework factory (s. 49) licence, renewal, not exceeding	0	1	0
EXTRADITION ACT, 1873 (36 & 37 VICT. C. 60. s. 5)			
For taking a deposition in pursuance of an order made by the Secretary of State	1	1	0
Each subsequent deposition taken in pursuance of the same order	0	5	0
HEARING:			
When no conviction or order is made	0	1	0
INFORMATION:			
Each information or examination (including oath)	0	1	0
JURY LISTS:			
For forwarding lists with schedule to the clerk of the peace (25 & 26 Vict. c. 107. s. 9)	0	2	6
Revision fee to be fixed by the local authority subject to approval of Secretary of State.			
LICENCES:			
For every licence, consent, or authority not otherwise provided for, to include registration when necessary	0	5	0
LIST:			
Every list not otherwise provided for which it is the duty of the clerk to the justices to make or transmit	0	2	6
NOTICE:			

	£	s	d
Every notice not otherwise provided for	0	1	0
OATH:			
Every oath, affirmation, or solemn declaration not otherwise charged	0	1	0
(Vide note at end of table.)			
ORDER:			
Order, certificate, or record of proceedings in case of deserted premises, or relating to a highway, bridge, or nuisance, or for protecting separate property of a married woman	0	5	0
Order as to the settlement, removal, or maintenance of a pauper or lunatic, or in case of fraudulent removal of goods	0	5	0
Order for payment of allowance to special constables (one order to include all the constables appointed)	0	2	0
Every order or minute thereof not otherwise charged	0	3	0
Order as to the affiliation of a bastard or under the Summary Jurisdiction (Married Women) Act, 1895	0	2	0
Variation, revocation, or revival of order	0	1	0
PRECEPT:			
Every precept	0	1	6
RATE:			
Amending a rate, each name	0	1	0
Taxing costs and order thereon	0	3	0
Order on appeal	0	5	0
Order for adjourning appeal, if required	0	1	0
Allowance of rate	0	2	0
Enforcement of any poor, general district, or other rate, to include complaint, summons, and all other proceedings for which separate fees are not provided hereunder	0	2	0
Order	0	2	0
Warrant of distress	0	2	0
Judgment summons (including hearing)	0	2	6
Summons (if any) in poor rate cases to show cause why defaulter should not be committed	0	2	0
Commitment	0	2	0
If more than one rate is included in the summons, for each rate after the first	0	0	6

	£	s	d
When the form of warrant provided for by 12 & 13 Vict. c. 14. s. 3. is used, for each name inserted in the schedule over and above eight	0	0	3
RECOGNIZANCE:			
Every recognizance	0	2	6
Notice to each person bound	0	0	6
SUMMONS			
Every summons (to include all the names included in the same charge or intended to be summoned as witnesses in the same case for the prosecution or defence if applied for at the same time	0	1	0
Every copy	0	0	6
Backing summons for service from outside jurisdiction-	0	1	0
WARRANT:			
Every warrant of distress when not otherwise provided for	0	2	0
To commit after conviction or order in which the conviction or order is set forth	0	2	0
Every other warrant	0	1	0
Return to warrant or endorsing warrant, including oath-	0	1	0
Backing warrant for execution from outside jurisdiction	0	1	0

NOTE.—Nothing herein contained shall be construed to authorise the demand of any fee for re-swearing any person to any examination, or for any oath, affirmation, or declaration to obtain pay, pension, or allowance from government or friendly society, or charitable fund, or for any declaration relating to lost duplicates of articles pledged where the amount advanced on such articles does not exceed 20s., or in any other case where an Act of Parliament directs that no fee shall be taken.

PART II

MATTERS TO WHICH PART I DOES NOT APPLY

1. Matters in respect of which fees are authorised to be charged by the Licensing (Consolidation) Act, 1910 (10 Edw. 7. and 1 Geo. 5. c. 24).

2. Billiard licences, under section ten of the Gaming Act, 1844 (8 & 9 Vict. c. 109).

3. Theatre licences, under section six of the Theatres Act, 1843 A.D. 1914. (6 & 7 Vict. c. 68).

4. The registration of music and dancing licences under section fifty-one of the Public Health Act, 1890 (53 & 54 Vict. c. 59).

5. Licences under the Cinematograph Act, 1909 (9 Edw. 7. c. 30).

6. Assessment appeals under the Valuation Metropolis Act, 1869 (32 & 33 Vict. c. 67).

7. Formal investigations into shipping casualties under section four hundred and seventy-nine of the Merchant Shipping Act, 1894 (57 & 58 Vict. c. 60).

8. Appeals from pilotage authority under section twenty-eight of the Pilotage Act, 1913 (2 & 3 Geo. 5. c. 31).

SECOND SCHEDULE

Section 42.

Sentence £   , fine payable within   days or days' imprisonment. In respect of which sentence the accused, having surrendered himself to the court and stated that he prefers immediate imprisonment to waiting the expiration of the time allowed, warrant is hereby granted to officers of law to convey the accused to the prison of [place] and for the detention of the accused therein until such fine is paid, but not exceeding days from the date of imprisonment.

THIRD SCHEDULE
AMENDMENT OF ENACTMENTS RELATING TO BLACKMAIL

[...]¹

Amendments

1   Sch 3 repealed as to England and Ireland by Larceny Act 1916, s 48 and Sch.

FOURTH SCHEDULE
ENACTMENTS REPEALED

Section 44

Session and Chapter	Title or Short Title	Extent of Repeal
3 Jas. 1. c. 10.	An Act for the rating and levying of the charges for conveying Malefactors and Offenders to the Gaole.	The whole Act so far as unrepealed.
15 Geo. 2. c. 24.	The Justices Commitment Act, 1741.	The whole Act.
26 Geo. 2. c. 14.	The Justices' Clerks' Fees Act, 1753.	The whole Act.
27 Geo. 2. c. 3.	The Offenders (Conveyance) Act, 1754.	The whole Act so far a unrepealeds
27 Geo. 2. c. 16.	The Justices' Clerks' Fees (Middlesex) Act, 1754.	Section four

Session and Chapter	Title or Short Title	Extent of Repeal
54 Geo. 3. c.170.	The Poor Relief Act, 1814	Section twelve from "and if sufficient distress" to the end of the section.
7 Geo. 4. c. 74.	The Prisons (Ireland) Act, 1826.	In section six, the words "hereinafter enumerated," and from "provision shall be made," to "vagrants," section one hundred and nine.
1 & 2 Will. 4. c. 44.	The Tumultuous Risings (Ireland) Act, 1831.	In sections two, three, four, five and six, the words "twice or thrice."
5 & 6 Will. 4. c. 50.	The Highway Act, 1835	Section one hundred and ten, so far as it relates to clerks to justices.
5 & 6 Vict. c. 28.	The Capital Punishment (Ireland) Act, 1842.	In section eight, the words "twice or thrice."
5 & 6 Vict. c. 51.	The Treason Act, 1842	In section two, the words "as often and" and "not exceeding thrice."
1.1 & 12 Vict. c. 42.	The Indictable Offences Act, 1848.	Section twenty-six from "Provided nevertheless" to the end of the section.
11 & 12 Vict. c. 43.	The Summary Jurisdiction Act, 1848.	In section fourteen the words from "and the conviction or order shall afterwards be drawn up" to "quarter sessions of the peace." Section twenty-one the words "and conveying of a defendant to prison." Section twenty-three from "and also the costs" to "think fit so to order." Section twenty-five from "and it shall be lawful" to the end of the section.
13 & 14 Vict. c. 101.	The Criminal Justice Administration Act, 1851.	Section-nine, except so far as that section relates to -clerks of the peace.
14 & 15 Vict. c. 93.	The Petty Sessions (Ireland) Act, 1851.	In section twenty-two, paragraph (6).

Session and Chapter	Title or Short Title	Extent of Repeal
20 & 21 Vict. c. 43.	The Summary Jurisdiction Act, 1857.	In section three the words from "which fees" to "section thirty," and Schedule A.
24 & 25 Vict. c. 97.	The Malicious Damage Act, 1861.	In section fifty-one the words "the damage, injury, or spoil" being to an amount exceeding "five pounds" and sections fifty-two and fifty-three, so far as those words and sections relate to England.
26 & 2 7 Vict. c. 44.	The Garrotters Act, 1863,	In section one, the words "twice or thrice."
39 & 40 Vict. c. 36.	The Customs Consolidation Act, 1876.	Section two hundred and forty-six and the table of fees therein referred to, so far as the same relate to England.
39 & 40 Vict. c. 61.	The Divided Parishes and Poor Law Amendment Act, 1876	Section thirty-two.
40 & 41 Vict. c. 21.	The Prison Act, 1877	Sections twenty-four, twenty-five, twenty-six, twenty-seven, and forty-one, and in section fifty-seven the words "in respect of his conveyance to prison or otherwise."
40 & 41 Vict. c. 43.	The Justices' Clerks Act 1877	Section eight.
40 & 41 Vict. c. 49.	The General Prisons (Ireland) Act, 1877.	Sections thirty-six, thirty-seven, thirty-eight, thirty-nine, and forty-eight, in section three, the words "in respect of his conveyance to prison or otherwise," in section twelve, from "no rule" to the end of the section.
42 & 43 Vict. c.49.	The Summary Jurisdiction Act, 1879.	Section five from "And such imprisonment" to the end of the section. Section fourteen. Section eighteen. Subsections (3) and (4) of section twenty-one.

Session and Chapter	Title or Short Title	Extent of Repeal
42 & 43 Vict. c.49. (contd)		Subsection (2) of section twenty-two from "but nothing in this section" to the end of that subsection. Paragraph (6) of section twenty seven.
61 & 62 Vict. c. 41.	The Prison Act, 1898	Subsection (4) of section six and section nine.
4 Edw. 7. c. 15.	The Prevention of Cruelty to Children Act, 1904.	Section fifteen.
7 Edw. 7. c. 17.	The Probation of Offenders Act, 1907.	Subsection (2) of section two, and section five.
8 Edw. 7. c. 59.	The Prevention of Crimes Act, 1908.	In subsection (2) of section six from "and at latest within three months" to the end of that subsection.

Criminal Justice (Administration) Act 1924

Number 44 of 1924

ARRANGEMENT OF SECTIONS

Section
1. Rules as to indictments.
2. Making of rules under this Act.
3. Rules which may be made under this Act.
4. General provisions as to indictments.
5. Joinder of charges in the same indictment.
6. Orders for amendment of indictment, separate trial, and postponement of trial.
7. Costs of defective or redundant indictments.
8. Provision as to Vexatious Indictments Act.
9. Prosecutions to be at suit of Attorney-General.
10. Form of oath on issue of competence to plead.
11. Form of oath where prisoner stands mute.
12. *Nolle prosequi* and form thereof.
13. Form of recognizance.
14. Form of juror's oath in criminal cases.
15. Savings and interpretation.
16. Repeal, extent, and short title.

FIRST SCHEDULE
RULES

SECOND SCHEDULE
ENACTMENTS REPEALED

AN ACT TO AMEND THE LAW RELATING TO INDICTMENTS IN CRIMINAL CASES AND MATTERS INCIDENTAL OR SIMILAR THERETO. [5th August, 1924.]

BE IT ENACTED BY THE OIREACHTAS OF SAORSTÁT EIREANN AS FOLLOWS:—

1   Rules as to indictments

The rules contained in the First Schedule to this Act with respect to indictments shall have effect as if enacted in this Act, but those rules may be added to, varied, or annulled by further rules made under this Act.

2   Making of rules under this Act

(1) Rules made under this Act shall be made by and with the concurrence of the same persons as those by whom and with whose concurrence the Rules of Court mentioned in

section 36 of the Courts of Justice Act, 1924 (No. 10 of 1924), are by that section authorised or required to be made.

(2) Section 101 of the Courts of Justice Act, 1924 (No. 10 of 1924), shall apply to all rules made under this Act.

3   Rules which may be made under this Act

(1) Rules may from time to time be made under this Act varying or annulling all or any of the rules contained in the First Schedule to this Act.

(2) In addition to the rules contained in the First Schedule to this Act, further rules may be made under this Act in respect of any of the matters dealt with in the said rules contained in the First Schedule to this Act.

(3) The rules contained in the First Schedule to this Act shall have effect subject to any modifications or additions made therein or thereto by rules made under this Act.

4   General provisions as to indictments

(1) Every indictment shall contain, and shall be sufficient if it contains, a statement of the specific offence or offences with which the accused person is charged, together with such particulars as may be necessary for giving reasonable information as to the nature of the charge.

(2) Notwithstanding any rule of law or practice, an indictment shall, subject to the provisions of this Act, not be open to objection in respect of its form or contents if it is framed in accordance with the rules under this Act.

5   Joinder of charges in the same indictment

Subject to the provisions of the rules under this Act, charges for more than one felony or for more than one misdemeanour, and charges for both felonies and misdemeanours, may be joined in the same indictment, but where a felony is tried together with any misdemeanour, the jury shall be sworn and the person accused shall have the same right of challenging jurors as if all the offences charged in the indictment were felonies.

6   Orders for amendment of indictment, separate trial, and postponement of trial

(1) Where, before trial, or at any stage of a trial, it appears to the court that the indictment is defective, the court shall make such order for the amendment of the indictment as the court thinks necessary to meet the circumstances of the case, unless the required amendments cannot in the opinion of the court be made without injustice, and may make such order as to the payment of any costs incurred owing to the necessity for amendment as the court thinks fit.

(2) Where an indictment is so amended, a note of the order for amendment shall be endorsed on the indictment, and the indictment shall be treated for the purposes of the trial and for the purposes of all proceedings in connection therewith as having been preferred to the jury in the amended form.

(3) Where, before trial, or at any stage of a trial, the court is of opinion that a person accused may be prejudiced or embarrassed in his defence by reason of being charged with more than one offence in the same indictment, or that for any other reason it is desirable to direct that the person should be tried separately for any one or more offences charged in an indictment, the court may order a separate trial of any count or counts of such indictment.

(4) Where, before trial, or at any stage of a trial, the court is of opinion that the postponement of the trial of a person accused is expedient as a consequence of the exercise of any power of the court under this Act to amend an indictment or to order a separate trial of a count, the court shall make such order as to the postponement of the trial as appears necessary.

(5) Where an order of the court is made under this section for a separate trial or for the postponement of a trial—

(a) if such an order is made during a trial the court may order that the jury are to be discharged from giving a verdict on the count or counts the trial of which is postponed or on the indictment, as the case may be; and

(b) the procedure on the separate trial of a count shall be the same in all respects as if the count had been preferred in a separate indictment, and the procedure on the postponed trial shall be the same in all respects (if the jury has been discharged) as if the trial had not commenced; and

(c) the court may make such order as to costs and as to admitting the accused person to bail, and as to the enlargement of recognizances and otherwise as the court thinks fit.

(6) Any power of the court under this section shall be in addition to and not in derogation of any other power of the court for the same or similar purposes.

7 Costs of defective or redundant indictments

Where it appears to the court that an indictment contains unnecessary matter, or is of unnecessary length, or is materially defective in any respect, the court may make such order as to the payment of that part of the costs of the prosecution which has been incurred by reason of the indictment so containing unnecessary matter, or being of unnecessary length, or being materially defective as the court thinks fit.

8 Provision as to Vexatious Indictments Act

Nothing in this Act shall prevent an indictment being open to objection if it contravenes or fails to comply with the Vexatious Indictments Act 1859.

9 Prosecutions to be at suit of Attorney-General

(1) All criminal charges prosecuted upon indictment in any court shall be prosecuted at the suit of the Attorney-General of Saorstát Eireann.

(2) Save where a criminal prosecution in a court of summary jurisdiction is prosecuted by a Minister, Department of State, or person (official or unofficial) authorised in that behalf by the law for the time being in force, all prosecutions in any court of summary jurisdiction shall be prosecuted at the suit of the Attorney-General of Saorstát Eireann.

10 Form of oath on issue of competence to plead

[…]¹

Amendments

1 Section 10 repealed by Juries Act 1927, s 70 and Sch 2.

---

11   **Form of oath where prisoner stands mute**

[...]¹

Amendments

1   Section 11 repealed by Juries Act 1927, s 70 and Sch 2.

---

12   *Nolle prosequi* **and form thereof**

At the trial of a prisoner on indictment at the prosecution of the Attorney-General of Saorstát Éireann a *nolle prosequi* may be entered at the instance of the Attorney-General of Saorstát Éireann at any time after the indictment is preferred to the jury and before a verdict is found thereon, and every such *nolle prosequi* shall be in the following form, that is to say:—

On the_____day of_____19_____, at the trial of A.B. on the prosecution of the Attorney-General of Saorstát Éireann on an indictment for_____ the said Attorney-General in his proper person (or by his counsel) stated to the court that he would not further prosecute the said A.B. on the said indictment, whereupon it was ordered by the court that the said A.B. be discharged of and from the indictment aforesaid.

13   **Form of recognizance**

Every recognizance entered into by way of bail before a District Justice or a Justice of the District Court or a Peace Commissioner shall be in the following form, or in such similar form as the circumstances may require:—

Be it remembered that on the _____ day of _____, in the year of our Lord_____, A. B., of_____ (labourer), C. D., of_____(grocer), and E. F., of_____(butcher), personally came before me the undersigned, a District Justice in Saorstát Éireann (*or* a Justice of the District Court of Saorstát Éireann *or* a Peace Commissioner) for the District of_____, and severally acknowledged themselves to owe to Saorstát Éireann the several sums following, that is to say, the said A. B. the sum of _____, and the said C. D. and E. F. the sum of _____ each, to be made and levied of their several goods and chattels, lands and tenements respectively, to the use of the Minister for Finance of Saorstát Eireann, if he the said A. B. fail in the condition endorsed. Taken and acknowledged the day and year first above mentioned, at _____ before me,_____

The condition of the within-written recognizance is such, that whereas the said A. B. was this day charged before me, the Justice *or* Peace Commissioner within mentioned for that (etc., as in the warrant); if, therefore, the said A. B. will appear at the next sitting of the District Court (*or* of the Circuit Court, *or* of the High Court *or* of the Central Criminal Court, as the case may be) to be holden in and for the District (*or* as the case may be) and there surrender himself into the custody of the keeper of the (common gaol) there, and plead to such charge or indictment as may be preferred against him, and take his trial upon the same, and not depart the said Court without leave, then the said recognizance to be void, or else to stand in full force and virtue.

14

Form of juror's oath in criminal cases

[...]¹

Amendments

1   Section 14 repealed by Juries Act 1927, s 70 and Sch 2.

---

15   Savings and interpretation

(1) Nothing in this Act or the rules thereunder shall affect the law or practice relating to the jurisdiction of a court or the place where an accused person can be tried, nor prejudice or diminish in any respect the obligation to establish by evidence according to law any acts, omissions, or intentions which are legally necessary to constitute the offence with which the person accused is charged, nor otherwise affect the laws of evidence in criminal cases.

(2) In this Act, unless the context otherwise requires, the expression "*the court*" means the court before which any indictable offence is tried or prosecuted.

(3) The provisions of this Act relating to indictments shall apply to criminal informations in the High Court and inquisitions, and also to any plea, replication, or other criminal pleading, with such modifications as may be made by rules made under this Act.

16   Repeal, extent, and short title

(1) The enactments specified in the Second Schedule to this Act are hereby repealed to the extent mentioned in the third column of that schedule.

(2) This Act may be cited as the Criminal Justice (Administration) Act, 1924.

(3) This Act shall come into force on such day as the Minister for Justice shall by order appoint.

FIRST SCHEDULE
RULES

Sections 1, 2(2).

1   Material, etc., for indictments.

(1) An indictment may be on parchment or durable paper, and may be either written or printed, or partly written and partly printed.

(2) Each sheet on which an indictment is set out shall be not more than 12 and not less than 6 inches in length, and not more than 14 and not less than 12 inches in width, and if more than one sheet is required, the sheets shall be fastened together in book form.

(3) A proper margin not less than 3 inches in width shall be kept on the left-hand side of each sheet.

(4) Figures and abbreviations may be used in an indictment for expressing anything which is commonly expressed thereby.

(5) An indictment shall not be open to objection by reason only of any failure to comply with this rule.

2   Commencement of the indictment.

The commencement of the indictment shall be in the following form:—

> The Attorney-General of Saorstát Éireann v. A.B.
> COURT OF TRIAL (e.g. Central Criminal Court, (or) Court of the High Court Circuit, (or) The Circuit Court of Justice in Saorstát Éireann, (or) The Court of the County Court Judge of Waterford, (or) The Court of the Recorder of Cork).

CHARGE PREFERRED TO THE JURY

A.B. is charged with the following offence (offences):—

3   Joining of charges in one indictment.

Charges for any offences, whether felonies or misdemeanours, may be joined in the same indictment if those charges are founded on the same facts, or form or are a part of a series of offences of the same or a similar character.

4   Mode in which offences are to be charged.

(1) A description of the offence charged in an indictment, or where more than one offence is charged in an indictment, of each offence so charged, shall be set out in the indictment in a separate paragraph called a count.

(2) A count of an indictment shall commence with a statement of the offence charged, called the statement of offence.

(3) The statement of offence shall describe the offence shortly in ordinary language, avoiding as far as possible the use of technical terms, and without necessarily stating all the essential elements of the offence, and if the offence charged is one created by statute, shall contain a reference to the section of the statute creating the offence.

(4) After the statement of the offence, particulars of such offence shall be set out in ordinary language, in which the use of technical terms shall not be necessary:

Provided that where any rule of law or any statute limits the particulars of an offence which are required to be given in an indictment, nothing in this rule shall require any more particulars to be given than those so required.

(5) The forms set out in the appendix to these rules or forms conforming thereto as nearly as may be shall be used in cases to which they are applicable, and in other cases forms to the like effect or conforming thereto as nearly as may be shall be used, the statement of offence and the particulars of offence being varied according to the circumstances in each case.

(6) Where an indictment contains more than one count, the counts shall be numbered consecutively.

5   Provisions as to statutory offences

(1) Where an enactment constituting an offence states the offence to be the doing or the omission to do any one of any different acts in the alternative, or the doing or the omission to do any act in any one of any different capacities, or with any one of any different intentions, or states any part of the offence in the alternative, the acts, omissions, capacities, or

intentions, or other matters stated in the alternative in the enactment, may be stated in the alternative in the count charging the offence.

(2) It shall not be necessary, in any count charging a statutory offence, to negative any exception or exemption from or qualification to the operation of the statute creating the offence.

6   Description of property

(1) The description of property in a count in an indictment shall be in ordinary language and such as to indicate with reasonable clearness the property referred to, and if the property is so described it shall not be necessary (except when required for the purpose of describing an offence depending on any special ownership of property or special value of property) to name the person to whom the property belongs or the value of the property.

(2) Where property is vested in more than one person, and the owners of the property are referred to in an indictment it shall be sufficient to describe the property as owned by one of those persons by name with others, and if the persons owning the property are a body of persons with a collective name, such as "Inhabitants," "Trustees," "Commissioners," or "Club" or other such name, it shall be sufficient to use the collective name without naming any individual.

7   Description of persons

The description or designation in an indictment of the accused person, or of any other person to whom reference is made therein, shall be such as is reasonably sufficient to identify him, without necessarily stating his correct name, or his abode, style, degree, or occupation; and if, owing to the name of the person not being known, or for any other reason, it is impracticable to give such a description or designation, such description or designation shall be given as is reasonably practicable in the circumstances, or such person may be described as "*a person unknown.*"

8   Description of document

Where it is necessary to refer to any document or instrument in an indictment, it shall be sufficient to describe it by any name or designation by which it is usually known, or by the purport thereof, without setting out any copy thereof.

9   General rule as to description

Subject to any other provisions of these rules, it shall be sufficient to describe any place, time, thing, matter, act, or omission whatsoever to which it is necessary to refer in any indictment, in ordinary language in such a manner as to indicate with reasonable clearness the place, time, thing, matter, act or omission referred to.

10   Statement of intent

It shall not be necessary in stating any intent to defraud, deceive or injure, to state an intent to defraud, deceive or injure any particular person where the statute creating the offence does not make an intent to defraud, deceive or injure a particular person an essential ingredient of the offence.

11   Charge of previous convictions, etc

Any charge of a previous conviction of an offence or of being a habitual criminal or a habitual drunkard shall be charged at the end of the indictment by means of a statement—in the case of a previous conviction that the person accused has been previously convicted of that offence at a certain time and place without stating the particulars of the offence, and in the case of a habitual criminal or habitual drunkard, that the offender is a habitual criminal or a habitual drunkard, as the case may be.

12   Saving for s. 32(4) of the Children Act 1908

Nothing in these rules or in any rules made under section two of this Act shall affect the provisions of sub-section (4) of section 32 of the Children Act, 1908.

13   Duty to furnish copy of indictment

(1) It shall be the duty of the registrar of the court to supply to the accused person, on request, a copy of the indictment free of charge.

(2) In the application of this rule to county courts, the clerk of the peace shall be substituted for the registrar of the court.

14   Interpretation

The Interpretation Act, 1923 (No. 46 of 1923) applies for the interpretation of these rules as it applies for the interpretation of an Act of the Oireachtas.

15   Short title

These rules may be cited as the Indictment Rules, 1924, and these rules, together with any rules made under this Act, may be cited together by such collective title as may be prescribed by the last-mentioned rules.

APPENDIX TO RULES
FORMS OF INDICTMENT

1. STATEMENT OF OFFENCE

Murder

Particulars of Offence

A.B., on the _____ day of _____, murdered J.S., in the County of _____

2. STATEMENT OF OFFENCE

Accessory after the fact to murder.

Particulars of Offence

A.B., well knowing that one H.C. did on the _____ day of _____ in the county of _____ murder C.C., did on the _____ day of _____ in the County of _____ and on other days thereafter receive, comfort, harbour, assist and maintain the said H.C

3. STATEMENT OF OFFENCE

Manslaughter.

Particulars of Offence

A.B., on the_____ day of _____, unlawfully killed J.S., in the County of_____

4. STATEMENT OF OFFENCE.

Rape.

Particulars of Offence

A.B., on the _____ day of _____, in the County of _____, had carnal knowledge of E.F without her consent.

5. STATEMENT OF OFFENCE.

First Count

Wounding with intent, contrary to section 18 of the Offences against the Person Act, 1861.

Particulars of Offence.

A.B., _____ on the day of _____,in the County of _____, wounded C.D., with intent to do him grievous bodily harm, or to maim, disfigure, or disable him, or to resist the lawful apprehension of him the said A.B.

STATEMENT OF OFFENCE

Second Count

Wounding, contrary to section 20 of the Offences against the Person Act, 1861

Particulars of Offence.

A.B., on the _____ day of _____, maliciously wounded C.D., in the County of _____

6. STATEMENT OF OFFENCE

Cruelty to a child, contrary to section 12 of the Children Act, 1908.

Particulars of Offence

A.B., between the _____ day of _____ and the _____ day of _____, in the County of _____, being a person over the age of sixteen years having the custody, charge, or care of C.D., a child, ill-treated or neglected the said child, or caused or procured the said child to be ill-treated or neglected in a manner likely to cause the said child unnecessary suffering or injury to its health.

7. STATEMENT OF OFFENCE

Larceny, contrary to section 17(1)(a) of the Larceny Act, 1916.

Particulars of Offence

A.B., _____ on the day of _____, in the County of _____, being clerk or servant to M.N., stole from the said M.N. ten yards of cloth.

8. STATEMENT OF OFFENCE

Robbery, with violence, contrary to section 23(1)(b) of the Larceny Act, 1916.

Particulars of Offence

A.B., _____ on the day of _____, in the County of _____ robbed C.D. of a watch, and at the time of or immediately before or immediately after such robbery did use personal violence to the said C.D.

9. STATEMENT OF OFFENCE

First Count

Larceny after a previous conviction.

Particulars of Offence

A.B., on the _____ day of _____, in the County of _____, stole a bag, the property of C.D. A.B. has been previously convicted of burglary on the _____ day of _____ at the Court sitting at Galway.

Statement of Offence

Second Count

Receiving stolen goods, contrary to section 33(1) of the Larceny Act, 1916.

Particulars of Offence

A.B., _____ on the day of _____, in the County of _____, did receive a bag, the property of C.D., knowing the same to have been stolen.

10. STATEMENT OF OFFENCE

Larceny, contrary to section 13 of the Larceny Act, 1916.

Particulars of Offence

A.B., in the night of the _____ day of _____, in the County of _____, did break and enter the dwelling-house of C.D. with intent to steal therein, and did steal therein one watch, the property of S.T., the said watch being of the value of ten pounds.

11. STATEMENT OF OFFENCE

Threatening to publish a libel, contrary to section 31 of the Larceny Act, 1916.

Particulars of Offence

A.B., on the _____ day of _____, in the County of _____, sent, delivered or uttered to or caused to be received by C.D., a letter accusing or threatening to accuse the said C.D. of an infamous crime with intent to extort money from the said C.D.

12. STATEMENT OF OFFENCE

Obtaining goods by false pretences, contrary to section 32(1) of the Larceny Act, 1916.

Particulars of Offence

A.B., _____ on the day of _____, in the County of _____, with intent to defraud, obtained from S.P. five yards of cloth by falsely pretending that he, the said A.B., was a servant to J.S., and that he, the said A.B., had been sent by the said J.S. to S.P. for the said cloth, and that he, the said A.B., was then authorised by the said J.S. to receive the said cloth on behalf of the said J.S.

13. STATEMENT OF OFFENCE

Conspiracy to defraud.

Particulars of Offence

A.B., and C.D., on the _____ day of _____ and on divers days between that day and the day of _____ in the County of _____, conspired together with indent to defraud by means of an advertisement inserted by them, the said A.B. and C.D., in the H.S. newspaper, falsely representing that A.B, and C.D. were then carrying on a genuine business as jewellers at _____, in the County of _____, and that they were then able to supply certain articles of jewellery to whomsoever would remit to them the sum of two pounds.

14·STATEMENT OF OFFENCE

First Count

Arson, contrary to section 2 of the Malicious Damage Act, 1861.

Particulars of Offence

A.B., _____ on the day of _____, in the County of _____, maliciously set fire to a dwelling house, one F.G. being therein.

Statement of Offence

Second Count

Arson, contrary to section 3 of the Malicious Damage Act, 1861.

Particulars of Offence

A.B., _____ on the day of _____, in the County of _____, maliciously set fire to a house with intent to injure or defraud.

15. STATEMENT OF OFFENCES

A.B., arson, contrary to section 3 of the Malicious Damage Act, 1861; C.D., accessory before the fact to same offence.

Particulars of Offences

A.B., on the _____ day of _____, in the County of _____, set fire to a house with intent to injure or defraud. C.D., on the same day, in the County of _____, did counsel, procure, and command the said A.B. to commit the said offence.

16. STATEMENT OF OFFENCE

First Count

Offence under section 35 of the Malicious Damage Act, 1861.

Particulars of Offence

A.B., on the _____ day of _____, in the County of _____, displaced a sleeper belonging to the Great Southern and Western Railway with intent to obstruct, upset, overthrow, injure, or destroy any engine, tender, carriage or truck using the said railway.

Statement of Offence

Second Count

Obstructing railway, contrary to section 36 of the Malicious Damage Act, 1861.

Particulars of Offence

A.B., on the _____ day of _____, in the County of _____, by unlawfully displacing a sleeper belonging to the Great Southern and Western Railway did obstruct or cause to be obstructed an engine or carriage using the said railway.

17. STATEMENT OF OFFENCE

Damaging trees, contrary to section 22 of the Malicious Damage Act, 1861.

Particulars of Offence

A.B., on the _____ day of _____, in the County of _____, maliciously damaged an oak tree there growing.

A.B. has been twice previously convicted of an offence under section 22 of the Malicious Damage Act, 1861, namely at _____ , on the day of _____, and at _____, on the day of _____.

18. STATEMENT OF OFFENCE

First Count

Forgery, contrary to section 2(1)(*a*) of the Forgery Act, 1913.

Particulars of Offence

A.B., on the _____ day of _____, in the County of _____, with intent to defraud, forged a certain will purporting to be the will of C.D.

Statement of Offence

Second Count

Uttering forged document, contrary to section 6 of the Forgery Act, 1913.

Particulars of Offence

A.B., on the _____ day of _____, in the County of _____, uttered a certain forged will purporting to be the will of C.D., knowing the same to be forged and with intent to defraud.

19. STATEMENT OF OFFENCE

Uttering counterfeit coin, contrary to section 9 of the Coinage Offences Act, 1861.

Particulars of Offence

A.B., on the _____ day of _____, at the shop kept by C.D. in the County of _____, uttered a counterfeit half-crown, knowing the same to be counterfeit.

20. STATEMENT OF OFFENCE

Uttering counterfeit coin, contrary to section 12 of the Coinage Offences Act, 1861.

Particulars of Offence

A.B., on the _____ day of _____, at the shop kept by C.D. in the County of _____, uttered a counterfeit sovereign, knowing the same to be counterfeit.

A B. has been previously convicted of a misdemeanour under section 9 of the Coinage Offences Act, 1861, on the _____ day of _____ at.

21. STATEMENT OF OFFENCE

Libel.

Particulars of Offence

A.B., on the _____ day of _____, in the County of _____, published a defamatory libel concerning E.F., in the form of a letter (book, pamphlet, picture, or as the case may be). (Innuendo should be stated where necessary).

22. STATEMENT OF OFFENCE

First Count

Publishing obscene libel.

Particulars of Offence

E.M., on the _____ day of _____, in the County of _____, sold, uttered, and published and caused or procured to be sold, uttered, and published an obscene libel the particulars of which are deposited with this indictment.

(Particulars to specify pages and lines complained of where necessary, as in a book.)

Statement of Offence

Second Count

Procuring obscene libel (or thing) with intent to sell or publish.

Particulars of Offence

E.M., on the _____ day of _____, in the County of _____, procured an obscene libel (or thing), the particulars of which are deposited with this indictment, with intent to sell, utter or publish such obscene libel (or thing).

23. STATEMENT OF OFFENCE

First Count

Falsification of accounts, contrary to section 1 of Falsification of Accounts Act, 1875.

Particulars of Offence

A.B., on the _____ day of _____, in the County of _____, being clerk or servant to C.D., with intent to defraud, made or concurred in making a false entry in a cash-book belonging to the said C.D., his employer, purporting to show that on the said day £100 had been paid to L.M.

Statement of Offence

Second Count

Same as first count.

Particulars of Offence

A.B., on the _____ day of _____, in the County of _____ being clerk or servant to C.D., with intent to defraud, omitted or concurred in omitting from or in a cash book belonging to the said C.D., his employer, a material particular, that is to say, the receipt on the said day of £50 from H.S.

24. STATEMENT OF OFFENCE

First Count.

Fraudulent conversion of property, contrary to section 20(1)(iv)(a) of Larceny Act, 1916.

Particulars of Offence

A.B., on the _____ day of _____, in the County of _____, fraudulently converted to his own use and benefit certain property, that is to say £100, entrusted to him by H.S., in order that he, the said A.B., might retain the same in safe custody.

Statement of Offence

Second Count

Fraudulent conversion of property, contrary to section 20(1)(iv)(b) of Larceny Act, 1916.

PARTICULARS OF OFFENCE.

A.B., on the _____ day of _____, in the County of _____, fraudulently converted to his own use and benefit certain property, that is to say, the sum of £200, received by him for and on account of L.M.

SECOND SCHEDULE

ENACTMENTS REPEALED

Session and Chapter	Short Title	Extent of Repeal
11 & 12 Vict. c. 12	The Treason Felony Act, 1848.	Section five.
11 & 12 Vict. c. 46.	The Criminal Procedure Act, 1848	The whole Act so far as unrepealed.
14 & 15 Vict. c. 100.	The Criminal Procedure Act, 1851.	Sections one, two, three, five, seven, twenty-three, twenty-four, and twenty-five.
24 & 25 Vict. c. 96.	The Larceny Act, 1861.	Section twenty-eight from "and in any indictment" to the end of the section, and section one hundred and sixteen from the beginning of the section to "offences; and."

Session and Chapter	Short Title	Extent of Repeal
24 & 25 Vict. c. 97.	The Malicious Damage Act, 1861.	Section sixty, down to "alleging an intent to injure or defraud any particular person; and."
24 & 25 Vict. c. 98.	The Forgery Act, 1861	Sections forty-two and forty-three, and section forty-four down to "any particular person; and."
24 & 25 Vict. c. 99.	The Coinage Offences Act, 1861.	Section thirty-seven, from "it shall be sufficient to conviction for the previous offence; and."
24 & 25 Vict. c. 100.	The Offences against the Person Act, 1861.	Section 6.
26 & 27 Vict. c. 29.	The Corrupt Practices Prevention Act, 1863.	Section six, down to "require; and."
38 & 39 Vict. c. 24.	The Falsification of Accounts Act, 1875.	Section two.
39 & 40 Vict. c. 36.	The Customs Consolidation Act, 1876.	Section twenty-nine, from "and in any information" to the end of the section.
46 & 47 Vict. c. 3	The Explosive Substances Act, 1883.	Sub-section (2) of section seven.
51 & 52 Vict. c. 64.	The Law of Libel Amendment Act, 1888.	Section seven.
61 & 62 Vict. c. 60.	The Inebriates Act, 1898.	In sub-section (2) of section one the words "in any indictment under this section, it shall be sufficient, after charging the offence, to state that the offender is a habitual drunkard."
8 Edw. VII., c. 48.	The Post Office Act, 1908.	Section seventy-three so far as respects indictments.
8 Edw. VII., c	The Prevention of Crime Act, 1908.	Sub-section (3) of section ten.

Firearms Act 1925

Number 17 of 1925

ARRANGEMENT OF SECTIONS

Section

1. Definitions and interpretation.
2. Restrictions on possession, use, and carriage of firearms.
2A Firearms training certificate.
2B Restricted firearms and ammunition.
2C Prohibited firearms and ammunition.
3. Applications for, and form and effect of, firearm certificates.
3A Issue of guidelines by Minister and Commissioner.
3B Payment of fees for prescribed firearm certificates.
3C Arrangement for payment of prescribed fees.
3D Restriction on licensing of short firearms.
3E
4. Conditions of grant of firearm certificate.
4A Authorisation of rifle or pistol clubs or shooting ranges.
4B Firearms range inspectors.
4C Prohibition of practical or dynamic shooting.
5. Revocation of firearm certificates.
5A
6. Sale of firearm when certificate refused or revoked.
7. Permit to bring firearm ashore.
8. Persons disentitled to hold a firearm certificate or a permit.
9. Register of firearms dealers to be kept.
9A Tax clearance.
10. Restrictions on manufacture and sale of firearms.
10A Reloading of ammunition
11. Removal of names from register of firearms dealers.
12. Register to be kept by firearms dealer.
13. Inspection of stock of firearms dealer.
14. Prohibition of manufacture and possession, etc., of weapons discharging noxious liquids.
15. Possession of firearms with intent to endanger life.
15A Appeal to District Court.
16. Restriction on export or removal of firearms or ammunition.

17. Restrictions on the import of firearms, prohibited weapons, and ammunition.

18. Powers of officers of customs and excise.

19. Powers and duties of officers of the Post Office.

20. Prohibition of taking firearms or ammunition in pawn.

21. Garda Síochána may search for and seize certain firearms, etc.

22. Powers of members of Garda Síochána.

23. Forfeiture of firearms, etc., in certain cases.

24. Search orders.

25. Punishments.

25A Surrender of firearms and offensive weapons

25B Surrender of firearm for ballistic testing

25C Delegation of Commissioner's functions

25D Liability of officers of bodies corporate

26. Savings.

27. Regulations.

27A Laying of orders or regulations before Houses of Oireachtas.

28. Partial continuance of Firearms (Temporary Provisions) Act, 1924.

29. Repeal.

30. Short title and commencement.

AN ACT TO PLACE RESTRICTIONS ON THE POSSESSION OF FIREARMS AND OTHER WEAPONS AND AMMUNITION, AND FOR THAT AND OTHER PURPOSES TO AMEND THE LAW RELATING TO FIREARMS AND OTHER WEAPONS AND AMMUNITION. [6th June, 1925.]

BE IT ENACTED BY THE OIREACHTAS OF SAORSTÁT ÉIREANN AS FOLLOWS:—

1   Definitions and interpretation

[(1) In this Act—

"ammunition" (except where used in relation to a prohibited weapon) means ammunition for a firearm and includes—

(a) grenades, bombs and other similar missiles, whether or not capable of being used with a firearm,

(b) any ingredient or component part of any such ammunition or missile, and

(c) restricted ammunition, unless the context otherwise requires;

"Commissioner" means the Commissioner of the Garda Síochána or a member of the Garda Síochána, or members of a particular rank in the Garda Síochána, not below the rank of superintendent appointed in writing by the Commissioner for the purpose of performing any of the Commissioner's functions under this Act;

"firearm" means—

(a) a lethal firearm or other lethal weapon of any description from which any shot, bullet or other missile can be discharged,

(b) an air gun (including an air rifle and air pistol) with a muzzle energy greater than one joule or any other weapon incorporating a barrel from which any projectile can be discharged with such a muzzle energy,

(c) a crossbow,

(d) any type of stun gun or other weapon for causing any shock or other disablement to a person by means of electricity or any other kind of energy emission,

(e) a prohibited weapon,

(f) any article which would be a firearm under any of the foregoing paragraphs [or paragraph (h)]² but for the fact that, owing to the lack of a necessary component part or parts, or to any other defect or condition, it is incapable of discharging a shot, bullet or other missile or projectile or of causing a shock or other disablement, as the case may be,

(g) except where the context otherwise requires, any component part of any article referred to in any of the foregoing paragraphs and, without prejudice to the generality of the foregoing, the following articles shall be deemed to be such component parts:

    (i) telescope sights with a light beam, or telescope sights with an electronic light amplification device or an infra-red device, designed to be fitted to a firearm specified in paragraph (a), (b), (c) or (e),

    (ii) a silencer designed to be fitted to a firearm specified in paragraph (a), (b) or (e), and

    (iii) any object—

        (I) manufactured for use as a component in connection with the operation of a firearm, and

        (II) without which it could not function as originally designed,

    and

(h) a device capable of discharging blank ammunition and to be used as a starting gun or blank firing gun,

and includes a restricted firearm, unless otherwise provided or the context otherwise requires;

"firearm certificate" means a firearm certificate granted under this Act and, unless the context otherwise requires, includes a restricted firearm certificate, a firearms training certificate and a firearm certificate granted under the Firearms (Firearm Certificates for Non-Residents) Act 2000;

"firearm dealer" means a person who, by way of trade or business, manufactures, sells, lets on hire, repairs, tests, proves, purchases, or otherwise deals in firearms or ammunition;

"firearms training certificate" has the meaning given to it by section 2A of this Act;

"issuing person", in relation to the grant or renewal of a firearm certificate, authorisation or licence, means, as the case may be, the Minister, the Commissioner or the superintendent of the Garda Síochána of the district where an applicant for or holder of the firearm certificate, authorisation or licence is residing;

"Minister" means the Minister for Justice, Equality and Law Reform;

"muzzle energy", in relation to a firearm, means the energy of a projectile discharged by it, measured at its muzzle in joules;

["prohibited ammunition" means ammunition that is declared by order under section 2C of this Act to be prohibited ammunition;

"prohibited firearm" means a firearm that is declared by order under section 2C of this Act to be a prohibited firearm.][3]

"prohibited weapon" means and includes any weapon of whatever description designed for the discharge of any noxious liquid, noxious gas or other noxious thing, and also any ammunition (whether for any such weapon or any other weapon) which contains or is designed or adapted to contain any noxious liquid, noxious gas or other noxious thing;

"place" includes a dwelling;

"prescribed" means prescribed by regulations made under this Act;

"registered firearms dealer" means a firearms dealer who is for the time being registered in the register of firearms dealers established in pursuance of this Act;

"restricted ammunition" means ammunition which is declared under section 2B(b) of this Act to be restricted ammunition;

"restricted firearm" means a firearm which is declared under section 2B(a) of this Act to be a restricted firearm;

"working mechanism", in relation to a firearm, includes the mechanism for loading, cocking and discharging it and ejecting spent ammunition.][1]

(2) In this Act the word "port" means any authorised place of entry into Saorstát Éireann, and the words "export" and "import" include respectively export and import over a land frontier as well as export and import over a sea frontier, and all cognate words shall be construed accordingly.

[(3) In this Act references to a Superintendent of the Garda Síochána include references to an Inspector of the Garda Síochána acting as a Superintendent.][4]

Amendments

1 Subsection (1) substituted by Criminal Justice Act 2006, s 26.
2 Words inserted by Criminal Justice (Miscellaneous Provisions) Act 2009, s 25(a).
3 Definitions inserted by Criminal Justice (Miscellaneous Provisions) Act 2009, s 25(b).
4 Subsection (3) inserted by Firearms Act 1964, s 14.

---

2   Restrictions on possession, use, and carriage of firearms

(1) Subject to the exceptions from this section hereinafter mentioned, it shall not be lawful for any person after the commencement of this Act to have in his possession, use, or carry any firearm or ammunition save in so far as such possession, use, or carriage is authorised by a firearm certificate granted under this Act and for the time being in force.

(2) Save in any of the cases hereinafter excepted from this section, every person who after the commencement of this Act has in his possession, uses, or carries any firearm without holding a firearm certificate therefor or otherwise than as authorised by such certificate, or

purchases, uses, has in his possession, or carries any ammunition without holding a firearm certificate therefor or in quantities in excess of those authorised by such certificate, or fails to comply with any condition subject to which a firearm certificate was granted to him, shall be guilty of an offence [under this section][1].

[(2A) A person who is guilty of an offence under this section is liable—

(a) in case the firearm is a restricted firearm or the ammunition is restricted ammunition—

    (i) on summary conviction, to a fine not exceeding €5,000 or imprisonment for a term not exceeding 12 months or both, and

    (ii) on conviction on indictment, to a fine not exceeding €20,000 or imprisonment for a term not exceeding 7 years or both,

and

(b) in any other case—

    (i) on summary conviction, to a fine not exceeding €2,500 or imprisonment for a term not exceeding 12 months or both, and

    (ii) on conviction on indictment, to a fine not exceeding €10,000 or imprisonment for a term not exceeding 5 years or both.

(2B)...][2]

(3) This section shall not apply to any of the following cases and such cases are accordingly excepted from this section, that is to say:—

(a) the possession or carriage of a firearm under and in accordance with a permit issued under this Act and for the time being in force;

(b) the possession, use, or carriage of a firearm or ammunition by a member of the Defence Forces of Saorstát Éireann or of a lawful police force in Saorstát Éireann in the performance of his duty as such member;

(c) the possession, use, or carriage of a firearm or ammunition by a registered firearms dealer in the ordinary course of his business as such dealer;

(d) the possession or carriage of a firearm or ammunition in the ordinary course of business by a person engaged in the business of carrying or of warehousing goods for reward;

(e) the possession of a firearm or ammunition on board a ship as part of the equipment of the ship;

(f) the carriage for sporting purposes only of a firearm or ammunition under instructions from and for the use of the holder of a firearm certificate for such firearm or ammunition;

(g) the possession, carriage, or use of a humane killer [or ammunition therefore][3] in the ordinary course of business by a butcher, slaughterman, knacker, or other person engaged in the business of the humane slaughter of animals.

[(4) This section shall not apply to any of the following cases and such cases are accordingly excepted from this section, that is to say:

(a) the possession, use or carriage of a firearm or ammunition by an employee of a registered firearms dealer in the ordinary course of business of the dealer as a firearms dealer,

(b) the possession or carriage of a firearm or ammunition by an employee of a person engaged in the business of carrying or of warehousing goods for reward in the ordinary course of such business,

(c) the possession or carriage of a firearm or ammunition for purposes of sale by an auctioneer who stands authorised under section 13 of [the Firearms Act 1964][1] or by an employee of such an auctioneer in the ordinary course of business as an auctioneer,][4]

[(d) the possession, use or carriage of a firearm or ammunition during a competition or target practice at a club, shooting range or any other place that stands authorised under this section or section 4A of this Act][5]

[(e) the possession, use or carriage of a firearm (other than a shot-gun) of a calibre not exceeding 23 inches or of ammunition by a person operating a range or shooting gallery in an amusement hall or at a fun fair, carnival or other like event for the purposes of the range or shooting gallery who stands authorised in that behalf under this section or by a person using such range or shooting gallery,

(f) the possession, use or carriage of a firearm or ammunition by a person taking part in a theatrical performance or rehearsal or in the production of a cinematograph film for the purpose of the performance, rehearsal or production, being a performance, rehearsal or production the person in charge of which stands authorised in that behalf under this section,][4]

[(g) the possession, use or carriage of a firearm, within the meaning of paragraph (h) of section 1, or of ammunition therefor for the purpose of being used as a starting gun or blank firing gun by a person who stands authorised in that behalf under this section,][6]

[(h) the possession, use or carriage of a firearm or blank ammunition provided by the Minister for Defence by a person taking part in a ceremony of any kind for the purposes of the ceremony, being a person who stands authorised in that behalf under this section.][4]

[(i) the possession, use, or carriage of a firearm or ammunition in the course of his duties by an officer of the Institute for Industrial Research and Standards charged with the operation of facilities for proofing firearms provided or procured by that Institute under the Firearms (Proofing) Act 1968.][7]

[(j) the possession or carriage of a firearm or ammunition by a person, or the employee of a person, authorised under section 10(4A) of this Act,

(k) the possession, use or carriage of a firearm or ammunition for the purpose of bird control at an airport by an employee or agent of the airport authority who stands authorised in that behalf under this section.][8]

[(5) (a) The Superintendent of any district may authorise in writing the possession, use or carriage of firearms or ammunition in that district in any of the circumstances specified in paragraphs (d), (e), (f), (g), [(h), (j) or k] of subsection (4) of this section [or of any component parts of a firearm] during such period, not exceeding one year, as may be specified in the authorisation.

(b) A Superintendent shall not grant an authorisation under this section unless he is satisfied having regard to all the circumstances (including the provision made or to be made for the storage of the firearms and ammunition to which the authorisation (if granted) would relate and the supervision of their use) that the possession, use or carriage, as the case may be, of firearms or ammunition in pursuance of the authorisation will not endanger the public safety or the peace.

(c) Where it is proposed to grant an authorisation under this section in respect of a [....] club or a range or other place referred to in paragraph (d) of subsection 4 of this section, the authorisation shall be granted to an officer of the club nominated by the club or to the person in charge of the range or other place as the case may be, and where there is a contravention of a condition imposed in relation to the grant of such an authorisation and the contravention is proved to have been committed with the consent or approval of or to have been facilitated by any neglect on the part of the person to whom the authorisation is granted, that person shall be guilty of an offence under this Act.

(d) A Superintendent may impose in relation to the grant of an authorisation under this section such conditions (if any) as he considers necessary to prevent danger to the public and, where a condition is imposed, it shall be specified in the authorisation.

(e) An authorisation under this section may be revoked at any time by the Superintendent of the district in which it is granted.

(f) A person who contravenes a condition imposed in relation to the grant of an authorisation under this section shall be guilty of an offence under this Act.][9]

[(6) In subsections (3)(g) and (4) (other than paragraphs [...],[11] (i) and (k)), references to a firearm or ammunition do not include references to a restricted firearm or restricted ammunition.][10]

[(7) The superintendent of any district may authorise the Board of the National Museum in writing to possess for a specified period a firearm that is a museum heritage object within the meaning of the National Cultural Institutions Act 1997.][12]

Amendments

1   Words substituted by Firearms Act 1971, s 3(a).

2   Subsection (2A) substituted and (2B) deleted by Criminal Justice Act 2006, s 27(a) and (b).

3   Words inserted by Firearms Act 1964, s 15(a) and amended by Criminal Justice Act 2007, s 34(a).

4   Subsection (4) inserted by Firearms Act 1964, s 15(b) and amended by Criminal Justice Act 2006, s 27(c).

5   Subsection (4)(d) substituted by Criminal Justice Act 2006, s 27(c)(ii).

6   Subsection (4)(g) inserted by Criminal Justice (Miscellaneous Provisions) Act 2009, s 26(a).

7   Subsection (4)(i) inserted by Firearms (Proofing) Act 1968, s 8.

8   Subsection (4)(j) and (k) inserted by Criminal Justice Act 2006, s 27(c)(iii).

9   Subsection (5) inserted by Firearms Act 1964, s 15(b), amended by Firearms Act 1971, s 3, Criminal Justice Act 2006, s 27(d) and further amended by Criminal Justice Act 2007, s 34(a).

10 Subsection (6) inserted by Criminal Justice Act 2006, s 27(f).

11 Words deleted by Criminal Justice (Miscellaneous Provisions) Act 2009, s 26(b).

12 Subsection (7) inserted by Criminal Justice Act 2007, s 34(b).

[2A   Firearms training certificate.

(1) The Commissioner, on application and payment of the prescribed fee (if any), may issue to a person over 14 years of age a certificate (in this Act referred to as a "firearms training certificate") authorising the person to possess a firearm and ammunition (except a restricted firearm and restricted ammunition) only while—

    (a) carrying and using the firearm for hunting or target shooting—

        (i) under the supervision of a specified person over 18 years of age who holds a firearm certificate in respect of it, and

        (ii) where the firearm is used for target shooting, on the premises of an authorised rifle or pistol club or at an authorised shooting range or other place that stands authorised under section 2(5) of this Act,

    and

    (b) complying with such other conditions (if any) as the Commissioner may impose in the interests of public safety and security.

(2) Where the applicant is under 16 years of age, the application for a firearms training certificate shall be accompanied by the written consent of the applicant's parent or guardian.

(3) The firearms training certificate shall be in the prescribed form.

(4) Where such an application is refused, the Commissioner shall inform the applicant in writing and give the reasons for the refusal.

(5) A firearms training certificate shall continue in force for a period of 3 years from the date on which it was granted, unless revoked.

(6) The Commissioner may revoke a firearms training certificate if of opinion that the holder is not complying, or has not complied, with the conditions subject to which the certificate was granted.

(7) A holder of a firearms training certificate who, without reasonable excuse, does not comply with the conditions subject to which the certificate was granted is guilty of an offence and liable on summary conviction—

    (a) for a first offence, to a fine not exceeding €500, and

    (b) for any subsequent offence, to a fine not exceeding €1,000.

(8) It is an offence under this Act for the holder of a firearm certificate in respect of the firearm to which the firearms training certificate relates to permit, without reasonable excuse, the holder of that certificate to carry or use the firearm while not under his or her supervision.]¹

Amendments

1   Section 2A inserted by Criminal Justice Act 2006, s 28.

[2B   Restricted firearms and ammunition The Minister may, in the interests of public safety and security, by order—

    (a) declare specified firearms to be restricted firearms for the purposes of this Act by reference to one or more than one of the following criteria:

     (i)   category;

    (ii)   calibre;

   (iii) working mechanism;

   (iv) muzzle energy;

    (v) description;

and

(b) declare specified ammunition to be restricted ammunition for the purposes of this Act by reference to one or more than one of the following criteria:

     (i)   category;

    (ii)   calibre;

   (iii) weight;

   (iv) kinetic energy;

    (v) ballistic co-efficient;

   (vi) design;

  (vii) composition;

(viii) description.][1]

Amendments

1   Section 2B inserted by Criminal Justice Act 2006, s 29.

[2C   Prohibited firearms and ammunition

(1) The Minister may, in the interests of public safety and security, by order—

(a) declare specified firearms to be prohibited firearms for the purposes of this Act by reference to one or more than one of the following criteria:

     (i)   category;

    (ii)   calibre;

   (iii) working mechanism;

   (iv) muzzle energy;

    (v) description;

and

(b) declare specified ammunition to be prohibited ammunition for the purposes of this Act by reference to one or more than one of the following criteria:

     (i)   category;

    (ii)   calibre;

   (iii) weight;

   (iv) kinetic energy;

    (v) ballistic co-efficient;

   (vi) design;

  (vii) composition;

(viii) description.

(2) Any person who—

   (a) possesses, uses or carries,

   (b) manufactures, sells or hires, or offers or exposes for sale or hire, or by way of business repairs or modifies,

   (c) puts on display, or lends or gives to any other person, or

   (d) imports in to the State,

a prohibited firearm or prohibited ammunition shall be guilty of an offence.

(3) A person who is guilty of an offence under this section is liable—

   (a) on summary conviction, to a fine not exceeding €5,000 or imprisonment for a term not exceeding 12 months or both, and

   (b) on conviction on indictment, to a fine not exceeding €20,000 or imprisonment for a term not exceeding 7 years or both.

(4) This section shall not apply to any firearm or ammunition possessed, used, carried, manufactured, sold, hired, offered or exposed for sale or hire, repaired or modified by way of business, possessed for the purpose of sale or hire or for the purpose of modification by way of business, put on display, lent or given to another or imported into the State under the authority of the Minister for Defence for use by the Defence Forces of the State or under the authority of the Minister for use by any lawful police force in the State.]¹

Amendments

1   Section 2C inserted by Criminal Justice (Miscellaneous Provisions) Act 2009, s 27.

3   **[Applications for, and form and effect of, firearm certificates.**

[(1) Application for a firearm certificate (other than a restricted firearm certificate) shall be made to the Superintendent of the Garda Síochána of the district in which the applicant resides.

(2) Application for a restricted firearm certificate shall be made to the Commissioner.

[(3) Pending the commencement of section 30 of the Criminal Justice Act 2006, the following provisions shall have effect for the purpose of continuing in force on a phased basis, for a maximum period of 12 months after the date of expiry of each certificate, all firearm certificates in force at the date of commencement of this subsection and that would otherwise expire on 31 July 2009 (" relevant firearm certificates "):

   (a) The Commissioner shall establish a prescribed number of groups of relevant firearm certificates.

   (b) Each group established shall be assigned a prescribed number of relevant firearm certificates selected randomly by the Commissioner in a prescribed manner.

   (c) Notwithstanding paragraph (b), those certificates relating to firearms that would be deemed to be restricted firearms in accordance with section 29 of the Criminal Justice Act 2006 shall be assigned to the first group established.

   (d) The firearm certificates in the first group shall continue in force until a prescribed date or dates in a prescribed month after July 2009.

   (e) The firearm certificates in each subsequent group shall continue in force until a prescribed date in each subsequent month after the firearm certificates in the first group expire, and not later than 31 July 2010, until all relevant firearm certificates have expired.

(f) The Commissioner shall notify each holder of a relevant firearm certificate of the new date of expiry for that certificate determined under this section and shall invite each such holder to apply in due course under this section (as substituted by section 30 of the Criminal Justice Act 2006) for a new 3 year firearm certificate within a prescribed timeframe before the new date of expiry.

(g) A notification under paragraph (f) shall constitute part of the relevant firearm certificate to which it relates and shall be evidence of the new date of expiry of that certificate determined under this section.]²

(4) The applicant shall supply in writing any further information that the Superintendent or the Commissioner may require in the performance of his or her functions under this section.

(5) A firearm certificate shall be in the prescribed form and, subject to subsection (6) of this section, shall authorise the person to whom it is granted—

(a) to possess, use and carry the firearm specified in the certificate,

(b) to purchase ammunition for use in the firearm, and

(c) at any one time to possess or carry not more than the amount of ammunition specified in the certificate.

(6) Where the firearm is a shot-gun, the firearm certificate may, subject to subsection (11) of this section, authorise it to be used only for killing animals or birds other than protected wild animals or protected wild birds within the meaning of the Wildlife Act 1976 by the holder of the certificate either (as may be expressed in the certificate)—

(a) on land occupied by the holder, or

(b) on land occupied by another person.

(7) A firearm certificate which is in force, other than a relevant firearm certificate continued in force under section 3(3) of this Act, as amended by section 28 of the Criminal Justice (Miscellaneous Provisions) Act 2009, shall continue in force for a period of 3 years from the date on which it was granted, unless revoked, and for any further such period for which it may be renewed.

(8) The holder of a firearm certificate may apply for renewal of the certificate within three months before it ceases to be in force.

(9) A decision on an application for a firearm certificate or its renewal shall be given within 3 months from the date on which the applicant submitted a completed application form.

(10) Where the application is refused, the applicant shall be informed in writing of the refusal and the reason for it.

(11) The following provisions have effect in relation to a certificate in the form referred to in subsection (6) of this section (in this subsection referred to as a " limited certificate "):

(a) a limited certificate relating to land occupied by a person other than the applicant for the certificate shall not be granted unless the occupier of the land has given the applicant a nomination in writing for holding the certificate;

(b) a limited certificate relating to any land shall not be granted in respect of any period if there is a limited certificate relating to the land already in force in respect of that period;

   (c) a limited certificate shall not be granted unless the whole of the land to which it would relate is occupied by the same person;

   (d) where a nomination referred to in paragraph (a) of this subsection is revoked, the limited certificate to which it related, if then in force, shall not be capable of being renewed.

(12) A firearm in respect of which a firearm certificate is granted shall be marked in the prescribed manner with a number or other prescribed identifying mark, and the number or mark shall be entered on the certificate.

(13) A person who—

   (a) knowingly gives false or misleading information to an issuing person in relation to an application for a firearm certificate or for its renewal,

   (b) forges a document purporting to be a firearm certificate or uses or knowingly possesses it, or

   (c) with intent to deceive, uses or alters a firearm certificate or uses a firearm certificate so altered, is guilty of an offence and liable—

      (i) on summary conviction, to a fine not exceeding €2,500 or imprisonment for a term not exceeding 6 months or both, or

      (ii on conviction on indictment, to a fine not exceeding €20,000 or imprisonment for a term not exceeding 5 years or both.

(14) Subsection (13) of this section is without prejudice to Part 4 of the Criminal Justice (Theft and Fraud Offences) Act 2001.

(15) Section 12 (limited use of shot-gun) of the Firearms Act 1964 is repealed.][1]

Amendments

1   Section 3 (originally substituted by Criminal Justice Act 2006, s 30) substituted by Criminal Justice (Miscellaneous Provisions) Act 2009, s 43.

2   Subsection (3) substituted by Criminal Justice (Miscellaneous Provisions) Act 2009, s 28.

[3A   Issue of guidelines by Minister and Commissioner

(1) The Minister, or the Commissioner with the consent of the Minister, may from time to time issue guidelines in relation to the practical application and operation of any provision of the Firearms Acts 1925 to 2009, or of any regulation made under any provision of those Acts.

(2) The Commissioner with the consent of the Minister may, in particular, issue guidelines in relation to applications for firearm certificates and authorisations under this Act and to the conditions which may be attached to those certificates and authorisations.][1]

Amendments

1   Section 3A (inserted by Criminal Justice Act 2006, s 31) substituted by Criminal Justice (Miscellaneous Provisions) Act 2009, s 29.

[3B   Payment of fees for prescribed firearm certificates

(1) A prescribed fee is payable on the grant or renewal of a prescribed firearm certificate.

(2) Any fee payable under subsection (1) shall be paid to a prescribed person at a prescribed place and be disposed of by the prescribed person for the benefit of the Exchequer in accordance with the directions of the Minister for Finance.

(3) Any notice issued by a prescribed person in relation to the grant or renewal of a prescribed firearm certificate or the payment of a prescribed fee under subsection (1) shall be in the prescribed form.

3C   Arrangement for payment of prescribed fees

The Minister may, with the consent of the Minister for Finance, make such arrangements, including contractual arrangements, as he or she considers appropriate with such person or persons (other than a member or members of the Garda Síochána) as he or she thinks fit in relation to accounting for prescribed fees received by them.

3D   Restriction on licensing of short firearms

(1) As and from the date of commencement of this section, no application for a firearm certificate in respect of a short firearm shall be considered by an issuing person other than for—

(a)   a device capable of discharging blank ammunition and to be used as a starting gun or blank firing gun;

(b)   a short firearm of a type specified at paragraph 4(2)(e) of the Fire-arms (Restricted Firearms and Ammunition) Order 2008 (S.I. No. 21 of 2008) and designed for use as so specified;

(c)   a short firearm for which the applicant for the firearm certificate held a firearm certificate on or before 19 November 2008.

(2) Any firearm certificate in respect of a short firearm, other than one to which paragraphs (a) to (c) of subsection (1) relates, granted between 19 November 2008 and the date of commencement of this section and in force shall stand revoked.

(3) For the purposes of this section, "short fire arm" means a firearm either with a barrel not longer than 30 centimetres or whose overall length (excluding the length of any detachable component) does not exceed 60 centimetres.][1]

Amendments

1   Sections 3B–3D inserted by Criminal Justice (Miscellaneous Provisions) Act 2009, s 30.

[3E   The Commissioner shall conduct an annual review of the operation of the Firearms Acts 1925 to 2009 and shall submit a report to the Minister specifying the number and classes of certificates and authorisations issued under the Acts. The Minister shall lay a copy of such report before each House of the Oireachtas.][1]

Amendments

1   Section 3E inserted by Criminal Justice (Miscellaneous Provisions) Act 2009, s 31.

4   Conditions of grant of firearm certificate

[(1) An issuing person shall not grant a firearm certificate unless he or she is satisfied that the applicant complies with the conditions referred to in subsection (2) and will continue to comply with them during the currency of the certificate.

(2) The conditions subject to which a firearm certificate may be granted are that, in the opinion of the issuing person, the applicant—

(a) has a good reason for requiring the firearm in respect of which the certificate is applied for,

(b) can be permitted to possess, use and carry the firearm and ammunition without danger to the public safety or security or the peace,

(c) is not a person declared by this Act to be disentitled to hold a firearm certificate,

(d) has provided secure accommodation for the firearm and ammunition at the place where it is to be kept,

(e) where the firearm is a rifle or pistol to be used for target shooting, is a member of an authorised rifle or pistol club,

(f) has complied with subsection (3),

(g) complies with such other conditions (if any) specified in the firearm certificate, including any such conditions to be complied with before a specified date as the issuing person considers necessary in the interests of public safety or security, and

(h) in case the application is for a restricted firearm certificate—

(i) has a good and sufficient reason for requiring such a firearm, and

(ii) has demonstrated that the firearm is the only type of weapon that is appropriate for the purpose for which it is required.

(3) An applicant for a firearm certificate shall supply to the issuing person the information requested in the application form and such further information as the issuing person may require in the performance of the person's functions under this Act, including, in particular—

(a) proof of identity,

(b) proof of competence in the use of the firearm concerned,

(c) written consent for any enquiries in relation to the applicant's medical history that may be made from a health professional by or on behalf of the issuing person, and

(d) names and addresses of two referees who may be contacted to attest to the applicant's character.

(4) A member of the Garda Síochána may inspect the accommodation for a firearm provided by an applicant for a firearm certificate or require the applicant to provide proof of its existence.

(5) The Minister, in consultation with the Commissioner, may by regulations provide for minimum standards to be complied with by holders of firearm certificates in relation to the provision of secure accommodation for their firearms.

(6) In this section "health professional" means doctor or psychiatrist registered under any enactments governing the profession concerned or a clinical psychologist.]¹

Amendments

1   Section 4 substituted by Criminal Justice Act 2006, s 32.

[4A   Authorisation of rifle or pistol clubs or shooting ranges

(1) A rifle or pistol club or the owner or operator of a rifle or pistol shooting range shall not allow any firearm or ammunition to be used or stored on the premises of or at the club or shooting range in connection with target shooting unless an authorisation under this section to do so is in force.

(2) An application for such an authorisation shall be made to the Commissioner in the prescribed form by an officer of the club authorised in that behalf or by the owner or operator of the shooting range.

(3) The application shall be accompanied by—

(a)   the prescribed fee, and

(b)   in the case of a shooting range, a firearms range certificate which is in force.

(4) The application form shall contain a copy of any regulations under subsection (13) or of the material part of them.

(5) The applicant shall supply in writing any further information that the Commissioner may need in the performance of his or her functions under this Act.

(6) The Commissioner shall grant an authorisation to the applicant for the use and storage of rifles, pistols and ammunition on the premises of the club or shooting range concerned, or on a specified part of those premises, for the purpose of target shooting only if satisfied—

(a)   that their use or storage will not endanger public safety or security or the peace,

(b)   that the club or shooting range is responsibly managed, and

(c)   in the case of a shooting range, that a firearms range certificate in respect of it is in force.

(7) A decision on the application shall be given within 3 months from the date on which a completed application form was submitted.

(8) The Commissioner may at any time by notice in writing—

(a)   attach to the authorisation such conditions as he or she thinks necessary for the purpose of securing that the operation of the club or shooting range and the use and storage of rifles, pistols and ammunition on the premises of or at the club or range concerned does not endanger public safety or security or the peace,

(b)   at any time for that purpose vary any of those conditions, and

(c)   require that some or all of them be complied with before a specified date.

(9) An authorisation which is in force shall continue in force for a period of 5 years from the date on which it was granted, unless revoked, and for any further such period or periods for which it may be renewed.

(10) A renewal of an authorisation may be applied for within 3 months before the authorisation ceases to be in force.

(11) The Commissioner may, if no longer satisfied in relation to any of the matters mentioned in paragraphs (a) to (c) of subsection (6), revoke the authorisation of the club or shooting range concerned by notice in writing addressed to the applicant or the person or persons for the time being responsible for its management.

(12) On receipt of such a notice the person or persons so notified shall forthwith surrender to the superintendent of the district in which the club or range is situated the authorisation and any rifles, pistols or ammunition stored on its premises.

(13) The Minister, in consultation with the Commissioner, may by regulations specify minimum standards to be complied with by a rifle or pistol club or shooting range before an authorisation under this section may be granted in respect of it.

(14) The minimum standards shall be determined—

    (a) in the case of a club, by reference to any or all of the following matters:

        (i) security of its premises;

        (ii) membership;

        (iii) management,

    (b) in the case of a shooting range, by reference to any or all of the following matters:

        (i) security of the range;

        (ii) membership;

        (iii) management;

        (iv) design, construction and maintenance;

        (v) types of firearms and ammunition to be used;

        (vi) level of competence of persons using the range.

(15) For the purpose of ascertaining whether conditions attached to an authorisation under this section are being complied with, a member of the Garda Síochána authorised in that behalf may, on production if required of the authorisation or a copy of it, enter any premises occupied or used by the club or shooting range concerned and inspect the premises and anything in them.

(16) Any person who by act or omission impedes or obstructs a member of the Garda Síochána in the exercise of the member's functions under subsection (15) of this section is guilty of an offence and liable on summary conviction to a fine of €1,000 and imprisonment for a term of 3 months or both.

(17) The Commissioner shall cause a register of clubs and shooting ranges for the time being authorised under this section to be established and maintained.

(18) It is an offence—

    (a) for a club or the owner or operator of a shooting range—

        (i) to contravene subsection (1) of this section, or

        (ii) without reasonable excuse, not to comply with any conditions attached to an authorisation under this section,

    (b) for a person not to comply with subsection (12) of this section, or

    (c) for a person, without reasonable excuse, to participate in the activities of such a club or shooting range for which an authorisation under this section is not in force.

(19) In proceedings against a person for an offence under subsection (18)(a)(i) of this section it is a defence to prove that the defendant took reasonable precautions and exercised due diligence to avoid committing the offence.

(20) A person guilty of an offence under subsection (18) of this section is liable—

(a) on summary conviction, to a fine not exceeding €2,500 or imprisonment for a term not exceeding 6 months or both, and

(b) on conviction on indictment, to a fine not exceeding €20,000 or imprisonment for a term not exceeding 7 years or both.

(21) In this section—

"firearms range certificate" means a certificate issued under section 4B(3)(a) of this Act;

"rifle or pistol club" means a club established for the purpose of promoting skill in the use of rifles and pistols for target shooting;

"shooting range" does not include a range or shooting gallery referred to in section 2(4)(e) of this Act.]¹

Amendments

1   Section 4A inserted by Criminal Justice Act 2006, s 33.

[4B   Firearms range inspectors

(1) The Minister may by warrant appoint such and so many persons as he or she thinks necessary to be firearms range inspectors and may revoke any such appointment.

(2) It shall be the duty of a firearms range inspector—

(a) to examine applications for the [certification]² of rifle and pistol shooting ranges, and

(b) to inspect rifle and pistol shooting ranges for the purpose of ensuring their compliance with the minimum standards provided for in regulations under section 4A(13) of this Act.

(3) After inspecting a rifle or pistol shooting range, an inspector may—

(a) if satisfied that the range complies with those minimum standards, issue a firearms range certificate in respect of it, and

(b) if not so satisfied, refuse to issue such a certificate or revoke any such certificate that is in force.

(4) An inspector who suspects, with reasonable cause, that any place is being used for rifle or pistol target shooting may enter and inspect it.

(5) The Minister shall issue to each inspector the warrant of appointment, or a copy of it, for production, on request, when an inspector is exercising any power conferred by this section.

(6) The terms and conditions of appointment of firearms range inspectors shall be determined by the Minister, with the consent of the Minister for Finance.]¹

Amendments

1   Section 4B inserted by Criminal Justice Act 2006, s 34.
2   Words substituted by Criminal Justice (Miscellaneous Provisions) Act 2009, s 32.

[4C   Prohibition of practical or dynamic shooting

(1) It is an offence for a person to facilitate or engage in the use of a firearm for the purposes of practical or dynamic shooting.

(2) Subsection (1) does not apply to the facilitation or engagement in the use of a firearm pursuant to an authorisation under section 2(5)(a) of this Act, where the muzzle energy of the firearm is less than 16 Joules.

(3) A person who is guilty of an offence under this section is liable—

(a)on summary conviction, to a fine not exceeding €5,000 or imprisonment for a term not exceeding 12 months or both, and

(b)   on conviction on indictment, to a fine not exceeding €20,000 or imprisonment for a term not exceeding 7 years or both.

(4) In this section "practical or dynamic shooting" means any form of activity in which firearms are used to simulate combat or combat training.]¹

Amendments

1   Section 4C inserted by Criminal Justice (Miscellaneous Provisions) Act 2009, s 33.

5   Revocation of firearm certificates

[(1) An issuing person may at any time revoke a firearm certificate granted by the person if satisfied that the holder of the certificate—

(a)   has not a good reason for requiring the firearm to which the certificate relates,

(b)   is a person who cannot, without danger to the public safety or security or the peace, be permitted to possess a firearm,

(c)   is a person who is declared by this Act to be disentitled to hold a firearm certificate,

(d)   where the firearm certificate limits the purposes for which the firearm to which it relates may be used, is using the firearm for purposes not authorised by the certificate,

(e)   has not complied with a condition attached to the grant of the certificate, or

(f)   where the firearm is authorised to be carried or used by a holder of a firearms training certificate, has, without reasonable excuse, permitted the holder of that certificate to carry or use the firearm while not under his or her supervision.

(2) The reason for revoking a firearm certificate shall be communicated in writing by the issuing person to the holder of the certificate.

(3) Where a firearm certificate is revoked or otherwise ceases to be in force, the issuing person may direct in writing that the holder surrender the firearm or ammunition concerned or both to the custody of the superintendent of the district where the holder resides or to a member of the Garda Síochána acting on the superintendent's behalf.]¹

Amendments

1   Section 5 substituted by Criminal Justice Act 2006, s 35.

[5A   (1) Where a firearm or ammunition is lost (whether by theft or otherwise) after the commencement of this section, the certificate holder to whom the firearm or ammunition relates, shall within three days of becoming aware of the loss, report the loss to the issuing person who granted the certificate.

(2) A person who fails, without reasonable excuse, to report the loss of a firearm or ammunition in accordance with this section shall be guilty of an offence.

(3) A person guilty of an offence under this section shall be liable—

(a)   in case the firearm is a restricted firearm or the ammunition is restricted ammunition—

(i)   on summary conviction, to a fine not exceeding €5,000 or imprisonment for a term not exceeding 12 months or both, or

(ii)   on conviction on indictment, to a fine not exceeding €20,000 or imprisonment not exceeding 5 years or both,

or

(b)   in any other case—

(i)   on summary conviction, to a fine not exceeding €2,500 or imprisonment for a term not exceeding 6 months or both, or

(ii)   on conviction on indictment, to a fine not exceeding €10,000 or imprisonment not exceeding 3 years or both.]¹

Amendments

1   Section 5A inserted by Criminal Justice (Miscellaneous Provisions) Act 2009, s 34 but is not yet in operation (February 2011).

6   Sale of firearm when certificate refused or revoked

[When a firearm certificate is revoked] and the person who is the holder of the certificate has a firearm, with or without ammunition, in his possession in the State at the time of such revocation or where a person has a firearm, with or without ammunition, in his possession in the State but is not the holder of a firearm certificate in respect thereof and such possession is not otherwise authorised under this Act—

(a)   the person shall forthwith deliver the firearm and ammunition (if any) to the Superintendent [of the district in which the person resides],

(b) the Superintendent shall forthwith cause the person to be informed by notice in writing of his right to dispose of the firearm and ammunition (if any) in any manner not contrary to law,

(c) upon such delivery, the person may dispose of the firearm and ammunition (if any) as aforesaid,

(d) if the person does not, within three months after the delivery of the firearm and ammunition (if any) to the Superintendent, arrange for its or their disposal in accordance with the provisions of this Act, inform the Superintendent of the arrangements and carry out the arrangements, the Superintendent may send to the person by post to his last known address a notice informing him that unless arrangements of the kind aforesaid are made, communicated to the Superintendent and carried out within one month after the date on which the notice is sent, the firearm and ammunition (if any) will be sold or destroyed,

(e) if within one month after the date on which the notice aforesaid is sent, arrangements of the kind aforesaid are not made, communicated to the Superintendent and carried out, the Superintendent may cause the firearm and ammunition (if any) to be sold and shall, as soon as may be, cause the proceeds of the sale to be paid to the person,

(f) the Superintendent may cause to be destroyed any firearm or ammunition that has been offered for sale under paragraph (e) of this section and has not been sold if, in the opinion of the Superintendent, the firearm or ammunition is unlikely to be sold if offered for sale again and shall send to the person by post to his last known address a notice informing him of such destruction,

(g) where the address of the person is unknown or the Superintendent is of opinion that notices as aforesaid would not be understood by the person, the Superintendent may, at his discretion, send the notices by post or otherwise give them to any member of the family of the person or to such other person, if any, as he may, in the particular circumstances, think appropriate.][1]

Amendments

1   Section 6 substituted by Firearms Act, 1964, s 8 and amended by Criminal Justice Act 2006, s 36.

7   Permit to bring firearm ashore

(1) Where a person has a firearm in his possession on board ship as part of the equipment of the ship, any superintendent of the Garda Síochána may, if he thinks fit so to do, and subject to the provisions of this Act, issue to such person a permit to bring such firearm ashore for repair and to have such firearm repaired at any specified place in Saorstát Éireann.

(2) Every permit issued under this section shall remain in force only for such period (not exceeding in any case one month) from the date of the issue thereof as shall be nominated by the person applying for the permit and approved by the superintendent issuing the same and specified by him in the permit.

8   Persons disentitled to hold a firearm certificate or a permit

(1) The following persons are hereby declared to be disentitled to hold a firearm certificate, that is to say:—

    (a) any person under the age of [sixteen years][1], and

    (b) any person of intemperate habits, and

    (c) any person of unsound mind, and

    [(d) any person who has been sentenced to imprisonment for—

        (i) an offence under the Firearms Acts 1925 to 2006, the Offences Against the State Acts 1939 to 1998 or the Criminal Justice (Terrorist Offences) Act 2005, or

        (ii) an offence under the law of another state involving the production or use of a firearm,

    and the sentence has not expired or it expired within the previous 5 years,

    (e) any person who is bound by a recognisance to keep the peace or be of good behaviour, a condition of which is that the person shall not possess, use or carry any firearm or ammunition, and

    (f) any person not ordinarily resident in the State (except a person who is temporarily so resident) for a period of 6 months before applying for a firearm certificate.][2]

(2) Any person who is by virtue of this section disentitled to hold a firearm certificate shall also be disentitled to hold a permit under this Act in relation to any firearm or ammunition.

Amendments

1   Words substituted by Firearms Act 1964, s 17(a).

2   Subsection (1)(d)–(f) substituted by Criminal Justice Act 2006, s 37.

---

9   Register of firearms dealers to be kept

(1) The Minister shall cause a register of firearms dealers to be established and kept.

(2) Every person, who, immediately before the expiration of the Firearms (Temporary Provisions) Act, 1924 (No. 9 of 1924), as continued by the Firearms (Temporary Provisions) (Continuance) Act, 1925, is registered in the register of firearms dealers kept in pursuance of regulations made under that Act shall be entitled at any time before the expiration of that Act to apply in accordance with the provisions of this section for registration in the register of firearms dealers to be established under this section, and every such person who so applies and pays the fee (if any) for the time being required by law shall be entitled to be registered in the last-mentioned register as on and from the commencement of this Act.

(3) Any person who, after the commencement of this Act, applies in accordance with the provisions of this section to be registered in the register of firearms dealers and pays the fee (if any) for the time being required by law and satisfies the Minister that he is immediately about to carry on business as a firearms dealer in Saorstát Éireann in premises suitable for that business, may be registered in such register, but when considering any such application

for registration the Minister shall have regard to the character of the applicant, [....]¹, and generally to the public safety and the preservation of the peace.

[(4) The registration of a person in the register of firearms dealers shall continue in force for a period of 3 years from the date of the registration, unless previously revoked and, if renewed, for a further period of 3 years from the expiration of that period or, as the case may be, of any subsequent such period for which the registration was renewed.]²

(5) Every registered firearms dealer shall be entitled to renew his registration in the register of firearms dealers at any time within one month before the expiration of his existing registration or renewal on application therefor in accordance with the provisions of this section and payment of the fee (if any) for the time being required by law.

(6) Every application for registration in the register of firearms dealers or for renewal of such registration shall be made to the Minister in the prescribed form and manner and shall contain the prescribed particulars.

(7) Every person registered in the register of firearms dealers shall be entitled on such registration and on every renewal thereof to obtain from the Minister a certificate in writing of such registration or renewal.

[(8) Registration (including registration in pursuance of a renewal of a previous registration) of a person in the register of firearms dealers may, at the discretion of the Minister, be made subject to the condition that the person shall not deal in firearms or deal in ammunition otherwise than by the sale and purchase of ammunition for shotguns, for unrifled airguns and for rifled firearms of a calibre not exceeding .22 inches, and a person whose registration in the register of firearms dealers is made subject to the condition aforesaid and who fails to comply with it shall, notwithstanding anything contained in section 10(1) of this Act, be guilty of an offence under this Act.

(9) In any proceedings a certificate under the seal of the Minister stating that the registration of a person in the register of firearms dealers was subject, on a specified day or during a specified period, to the condition referred to in subsection (8) of this section shall be evidence of that fact unless the contrary is proved.]³

[(10) The Minister, after consultation with the Commissioner, may by regulations specify minimum standards to be complied with in relation to premises in which a firearms dealer carries on business or proposes to do so.

(11) The minimum standards shall be determined by reference to—

    (a)   the security of the premises,

    (b)   their safety, and

    (c)   their standard of construction,

and having regard to their use for, as the case may be, the manufacture, repair, testing, proving or sale of firearms or ammunition.

(12) Applicants for renewal of registration shall satisfy the Minister that their premises comply with the minimum standards specified in any regulations under subsection (10) of this section.

(13) Without prejudice to subsection (3) of this section, the following persons are declared to be disentitled to be registered in the register of firearms dealers:

    (a)   a person under the age of 21 years;

    (b)   a person of unsound mind;

(c) a person who has been sentenced to imprisonment for an offence under the Firearms Acts 1925 to 2006, the Offences Against the State Acts 1939 to 1998 or the Criminal Justice (Terrorist Offences) Act 2005;

(d) a person who is bound by a recognisance to keep the peace or be of good behaviour, a condition of which is that the person shall not possess, use or carry a firearm or ammunition.][4]

Amendments

1 Words deleted by Firearms Act 1964, s 18.

2 Subsection (4) substituted by Criminal Justice Act 2006, s 38(a).

3 Subsection (8) and (9) inserted by Firearms Act 1971, s 6.

4 Subsection (10)–(13) substituted by Criminal Justice Act 2006, s 38(b).

[9A   Tax clearance

(1) In this section—

"Act of 1997" means the Taxes Consolidation Act 1997;

"Collector-General" means the Collector-General appointed under section 851 of the Act of 1997;

"tax clearance certificate" means a certificate under section 1095 (as substituted by section 127(b) of the Finance Act 2002) of the Act of 1997.

(2) The Minister shall refuse to register a person in the register of firearms dealers or renew any such registration in respect of that person if that person is a person in relation to whom a tax clearance certificate is not in force.

(3) The Minister may nevertheless register a person in the register of firearms dealers or renew any such registration in respect of that person if—

(a) the person has, at least four months before applying for such registration or renewal, applied for a tax clearance certificate and it has been refused and an appeal against the refusal has been made under section 1094(7) of the Act of 1997 but not determined, and

(b) the Minister would, but for subsection (2), have registered that person in the register of firearms dealers or renewed any such registration in respect of the person.

(4) Where an appeal referred to in subsection (3) is made but is not successful, any registration or renewal of registration under that subsection shall expire 7 days after the appeal is determined or, where appropriate, finally determined.

(5) The Collector-General shall notify the Minister of any appeal against a refusal of an application for a tax clearance certificate and of the determination or, as appropriate, final determination of any such appeal.][1]

Amendments

1   Section 9A inserted by Criminal Justice (Miscellaneous Provisions) Act 2009, s 35.

10   Restrictions on manufacture and sale of firearms

(1) On and after the commencement of this Act it shall not be lawful for any person to manufacture, sell, repair, test, or prove, or expose for sale, or have in his possession for sale, repair, test, or proof, by way of trade or business, any firearm or ammunition unless such person is registered in the register of firearms dealers.

(2) It shall not be lawful for [any person]¹ to sell to any person (other than a registered firearms or a person officially authorised) any firearm or ammunition, unless at the time of such sale the person to whom such firearm or ammunition is sold—

     (a)   produces a firearm certificate authorising him to purchase or hire (as the case may be) such firearm or ammunition, or

     (b)   proves to the satisfaction of [such person]¹ that he is by virtue of this Act entitled to have possession of such firearm or ammunition without having a firearm certificate therefor.

(3) It shall be the duty of every person who sells a firearm or ammunition to any person (other than a registered firearms dealer or a person officially authorised)—

     (a)   to comply with the instructions (if any) addressed to such seller contained in the firearm certificate produced at the time of such sale by the person to whom such firearm or ammunition is sold, and

     (b)   in the case of a sale of a firearm within forty-eight hours after such sale to send by registered post notice thereof to the superintendent of the Garda Síochána of the district in which the firearm certificate aforesaid was granted.

[(3A)(a) A person shall not sell, transfer or otherwise dispose of a firearm or ammunition for a firearm to a person who habitually resides, or to a body at an address, in a country that stands prescribed for the time being for the purposes of this section unless the superintendent of the Garda Síochána of the district in which the firearm or ammunition is kept, being satisfied that the transaction is authorised by the competent authorities of that country, also authorises it.

     (b)   This subsection is without prejudice to the other provisions of this section and to section 16 of this Act but subsection (4) of that section does not apply to a firearm or ammunition for a firearm carried by a person from the State for the purpose of transferring it permanently to such a country as aforesaid.

     (c)   In this subsection 'firearm' does not include a firearm specified in paragraph (c) or (d) (or in paragraph (f) or (g) so far as either of those paragraphs relates to the said paragraph (c) or (d)) of section 4(1) of the Firearms and Offensive Weapons Act, 1990.]²

[(4) It shall not be lawful for any registered firearms dealer to return to any person a firearm or ammunition given to the dealer for repair, test or proof unless the person—

(a) produces a firearm certificate authorising him to have possession of the firearm or ammunition, or

(b) proves to the satisfaction of the dealer that he is entitled to have possession of the firearm or ammunition without having a firearm certificate therefor, and.][3]

[(4A) It is an offence for—

(a) a registered firearms dealer (notwithstanding subsection (1) of this section),

(b) a person engaged in the business of carrying or warehousing goods for reward, or

(c) an auctioneer who stands authorised under section 13 of the Firearms Act 1964,

to possess, use, carry, sell or expose for sale a restricted firearm in the ordinary course of business, unless authorised to do so by an authorisation under this section which is in force.

(4B) Application for such an authorisation shall be made to the Minister in the prescribed form by a person mentioned in subsection (4A) and be accompanied by the prescribed fee (if any).

(4C) The applicant shall supply in writing any further information that the Minister may require in the performance of his or her functions under this section.

(4D) An application for renewal of an authorisation may be made within 3 months before it ceases to be in force.

(4E) An application for an authorisation or its renewal shall be refused if granting it would, in the opinion of the Minister, prejudice public safety or security.

(4F) A decision on an application for an authorisation or its renewal shall be given within 3 months from the date on which the applicant submitted a completed application form.

(4G) An authorisation under this section which is in force shall, unless earlier revoked, continue in force for a period of 3 years from the date on which it was granted and, if renewed, for a further period of 3 years from the expiration of that period or, as the case may be, of any subsequent such period for which the authorisation was renewed.][4]

(5) Every person who contravenes any of the provisions of this section shall be guilty of an offence under this Act and shall be punishable accordingly.

(6) In this section—

(a) the expression "a person officially authorised" means a person authorised by the Minister for Defence to effect the transaction in question for the purposes of the Defence Forces of Saorstát Éireann or authorised by the Minister to effect the transaction in question for the purposes of any lawful police force in Saorstát Éireann, and

(b) the word "sell" includes letting on hire[, giving][5] and lending and the word "purchase" includes hiring of[, receiving][5] and borrowing, and cognate words shall be construed accordingly.

[(7) The references in subsections (2) and (3) of this section to a registered firearms dealer shall, in relation to a sale of any firearm or ammunition, be construed as references to a registered firearms dealer for whom it is lawful to purchase that firearm or ammunition by way of trade or business.][6]

Amendments

1   Words inserted by Firearms Act 1964, s 19(a).

2   Subsection 3A inserted by Firearms and Offensive Weapons Act 1990, s 5.

3   Subsection (4) substituted by Firearms Act 1964, s 19(b).

4   Subsections (4A)–(4G) inserted by Criminal Justice Act 2006, s 39.

5   Words inserted by Firearms Act 1964, s 19(c).

6   Subsection (7) inserted by Firearms Act 1971, s 6(2).

[10A   Reloading of ammunition

(1) A person (except a registered firearms dealer or the holder of a licence under this section) who reloads ammunition is guilty of an offence.

(2) An application for a licence under this section shall be in the prescribed form, be accompanied by the prescribed fee (if any) and be made to the superintendent of the Garda Síochána of the district in which the applicant resides.

(3) A superintendent shall not grant a licence under this section unless satisfied that the following conditions are complied with:

(a)   the applicant holds a firearm certificate;

(b)   the reloading of ammunition will not, in the particular circumstances, endanger public safety or security or the peace;

(c)   the person has a special need which, in the opinion of the superintendent, is sufficient to justify granting the licence;

(d)   the applicant is competent to reload ammunition;

(e)   the premises where the reloading is to take place are sufficiently safe and secure for that purpose.

(4) The superintendent may at any time—

(a)   attach to the licence such further conditions as he or she considers necessary for the purpose of preventing danger to members of the public or the peace or for ensuring that ammunition is reloaded only to satisfy the special need of the applicant, and

(b)   for that purpose vary any of those conditions.

(5) The licence—

(a)   shall be in the prescribed form,

(b)   shall be granted for a specified period not exceeding 3 years, and

(c)   may be revoked by the superintendent if he or she is no longer satisfied that any condition mentioned in subsection (3) of this section is being or will be complied with.

(6) A person who, without reasonable excuse, does not comply with a condition mentioned in subsection (3) or (4) of this section is guilty of an offence and liable—

(a)   on summary conviction, to a fine not exceeding €5,000 or imprisonment for a term not exceeding one year or both, or

(b)   on conviction on indictment, to a fine or imprisonment for a term not exceeding 5 years or both.

(7) The Minister may by order specify the maximum quantity and type of component parts of ammunition that may be purchased, sold, stored or used to reload ammunition by an individual who holds a licence under this section or a registered firearms dealer.

(8) In this section "reloading ammunition" means making ammunition from spent ammunition, and cognate expressions shall be construed accordingly.][1]

Amendments

1   Section 10A inserted by Criminal Justice Act 2006, s 40.

---

11   Removal of names from register of firearms dealers

(1) The Minister may at the request of any person who is registered in the register of firearms dealers remove the name of such person from the register aforesaid.

(2) If and when the Minister is satisfied that any person who is registered in the register of firearms dealers—

    (a)   no longer carries on business as a firearms dealer, or

    (b)   no longer has a place of business as such firearms dealer in Saorstát Éireann, or

    (c)   cannot any longer be permitted to carry on such business without danger to the public safety or to the peace, or

    [(d)   has become a person who is declared under section 9(13) of this Act to be disentitled to be registered in the register of firearms dealers,][1]

the Minister may remove the name of such person from the register aforesaid.

[(2A) If and when the Minister is satisfied that any person who is registered in the register of firearms dealers and whose registration is subject to the condition referred to in section 9(8) of this Act has failed to comply with the condition, the Minister may remove the name of such person from the register aforesaid.][2]

[(3) A person whose name is removed under this section from the register of firearms dealers shall, on such removal, forthwith deliver up to the Minister—

    (a)   the person's certificate of registration or renewal, and

    (b)   the register kept by the person under subsection (1) of section 12 of this Act.

(4) A person who contravenes subsection (3) of this section is guilty of an offence and on summary conviction is liable to a fine not exceeding €3,000.][3]

Amendments

1   Paragraph (d) substituted by Criminal Justice Act 2006, s 41(a).

2   Subsection (2A) inserted by Firearms Act 1971, s 6(3).

3   Subsection (3) substituted and (4) inserted by Criminal Justice Act 2006, s 41(b).

---

12   Register to be kept by firearms dealer

(1) It shall be the duty of every registered firearms dealer to keep or cause to be kept a register of all purchases, hirings, sales, repairs, and other transactions of or in relation to firearms or ammunition made by him, and within twenty-four hours after every such

transaction to enter or cause to be entered in such register the prescribed particulars in respect of such transaction.

(2) Where the particulars required by this section to be entered in the register aforesaid in respect of any transaction are not known to the firearms dealer it shall be his duty at or before the completion of such transaction to demand such particulars from the person with whom the transaction takes place and it shall be the duty of such person on such demand to furnish such particulars accordingly.

(3) Every register kept in pursuance of this section may be inspected at all reasonable times by any member of the Garda Síochána or any officer of customs and excise for any purpose arising out of or in connection with this Act or any regulation made thereunder, and it shall be the duty of the firearms dealer by or for whom such register is kept to produce for the inspection of such member of the Garda Síochána or such officer of customs and excise on demand such register and also all invoices, consignment notes, receipts, and other documents (including copies thereof where the originals are not available) reasonably demanded by such member or officer for the purpose of verifying any entry in or explaining any omission from such register.

(4) If any registered firearms dealer—

    (a) fails to keep or cause to be kept such register as is required by this section, or

    (b) fails to make or cause to be made in such register within the time prescribed by this section any entry required by this section to be made therein, or

    (c) makes or permits to be made in such register any entry which is to his knowledge false or misleading in any material respect,

he shall be guilty of an offence under this section and shall be liable on summary conviction thereof to a fine not exceeding [€3,000][1].

(5) If any person required by this section to furnish any particulars to a registered firearms dealer refuses so to furnish such particulars or furnishes any such particulars which are to his knowledge false or misleading in any material respect, he shall be guilty of an offence under this section and shall be liable on summary conviction thereof to a fine not exceeding [€1,500.][1]

(6) For the purposes of this section—

    (a) inspection of a register or document shall include taking copies or extracts therefrom, and

    (b) a demand for inspection of a register or other document shall be deemed to have been duly made by a member of the Garda Síochána or an officer of customs and excise if such demand is made verbally on the premises on which such register or document is kept to the manager, secretary, book-keeper, or other member of the clerical staff of such premises, and

    (c) a refusal or failure to produce a register or other document for inspection if made or committed on any premises in which, the registered firearms dealer carries on business as such dealer by a person in his employment shall be deemed to have been committed by the registered firearms dealer.

Amendments

1   Words substituted by Criminal Justice Act 2006, s 64 and Sch 1.

13   Inspection of stock of firearms dealer

(1) Any member of the Garda Síochána may at all reasonable times enter the premises of any registered firearms dealer and there inspect any firearms and ammunition and any materials used in the manufacture, repair, test, or proof thereof found on such premises.

(2) Every person who shall obstruct or impede any member of the Garda Síochána in the exercise of any of the powers conferred on him by this section shall be guilty of an offence under this section and shall be liable on summary conviction thereof to a fine not exceeding [€1,000 or imprisonment for a term not exceeding 6 months or both.]¹

Amendments

1   Words substituted by Criminal Justice Act 2006, s 64 and Sch 1.

14   Prohibition of manufacture and possession, etc., of weapons discharging noxious liquids

[...]¹

Amendments

1   Section 14 was repealed by Firearms Act, 1964, s 28. However s 28(2) provides as follows: "Where, immediately before the passing of this Act, there was in force an authorisation under section 14 of the Principal Act there shall, upon such passing, be deemed to be in force a firearm certificate relating to the weapon to which the authorisation related granted by a Superintendent."

15   Possession of firearms with intent to endanger life

[(1) Any person who possesses or controls any firearm or ammunition—

(a)   with intent to endanger life or cause serious injury to property, or

(b)   with intent to enable any other person by means of the firearm or ammunition to endanger life or cause serious injury to property,

shall, whether any injury to person or property has or has not been caused thereby, be guilty of an offence.

(2) A person guilty of an offence under this section is liable on conviction on indictment—

(a) to imprisonment for life or such shorter term as the court may determine, subject to subsections (4) to (6) of this section or, where subsection (8) of this section applies, to that subsection, and

(b) at the court's discretion, to a fine of such amount as the court considers appropriate, and the firearm or ammunition concerned shall be forfeited.

(3) The court, in imposing sentence on a person for an offence under this section, may, in particular, have regard to whether the person has a previous conviction for an offence under the Firearms Acts 1925 to 2006, the Offences against the State Acts 1939 to 1998 or the Criminal Justice (Terrorist Offences) Act 2005.

(4) Where a person (except a person under the age of 18 years) is convicted of an offence under this section, the court shall, in imposing sentence, specify a term of imprisonment of not less than 10 years as the minimum term of imprisonment to be served by the person.

[(4A) The purpose of subsections (5) and (6) of this section is to provide that in view of the harm caused to society by the unlawful possession and use of firearms, a court, in imposing sentence on a person (except a person under the age of 18 years) for an offence under this section, shall specify as the minimum term of imprisonment to be served by the person a term of not less than 10 years, unless the court determines that by reason of exceptional and specific circumstances relating to the offence, or the person convicted of it, it would be unjust in all the circumstances to do so.]²

(5) Subsection (4) of this section does not apply where the court is satisfied that there are exceptional and specific circumstances relating to the offence, or the person convicted of it, which would make a sentence of imprisonment of not less than 10 years unjust in all the circumstances, and for this purpose the court may[, subject to subsection (6)]³ have regard to any matters it considers appropriate, including—

(a) whether the person pleaded guilty to the offence and, if so—

(i) the stage at which the intention to plead guilty was indicated,

(ii) the circumstances in which the indication was given,

and

(b) whether the person materially assisted in the investigation of the offence.

(6) The court, in considering for the purposes of subsection (5) of this section whether a sentence of not less than 10 years imprisonment is unjust in all the circumstances, may have regard, in particular, to—

(a) whether the person convicted of the offence has a previous conviction for an offence under the Firearms Acts 1925 to 2006, the Offences Against the State Acts 1939 to 1998 or the Criminal Justice (Terrorist Offences) Act 2005, and

(b) whether the public interest in preventing the unlawful possession or use of firearms would be served by the imposition of a lesser sentence.

(7) Subsections (4) to (6) of this section apply and have effect only in relation to a person convicted of a first offence under this section (other than a person who falls under subsection (8)(b) of this section), and accordingly references in those first-mentioned subsections to an offence under this section are to be construed as references to a first such offence.

(8) Where a person (except a person under the age of 18 years)—

(a) is convicted of a second or subsequent offence under this section,

(b) is convicted of a first offence under this section and has been convicted of an offence under section 26, 27, 27A or 27B of the Firearms Act 1964 or section 12A of the Firearms and Offensive Weapons Act 1990,

the court shall, in imposing sentence, specify a term of imprisonment of not less than 10 years as the minimum term of imprisonment to be served by the person.

(9) Section 27C of the Firearms Act 1964 applies in relation to proceedings for an offence under this section and to any minimum term of imprisonment imposed under subsection (4) or (8) of this section in those proceedings.][1]

Amendments

1 Section 15 substituted by Criminal Justice Act 2006, s 42.

2 Subsection (4A) inserted by Criminal Justice Act 2007, s 35(a).

3 Words inserted by Criminal Justice Act 2007, s 35(b).

[15A   Appeal to District Court

(1) An appeal may be made to the District Court by a person aggrieved by any of the following decisions made by an issuing person:

(a) to refuse to grant a firearms training certificate under section 2A of this Act;

(b) to refuse to grant or renew a firearm certificate under section 3 of this Act;

(c) to refuse to grant or renew an authorisation for a rifle or pistol club or shooting range under section 4A of this Act;

(d) to revoke a firearm certificate under section 5 of this Act;

(e) to refuse to register a person, or to renew a registration, in the register of firearms dealers under section 9 of this Act;

(f) to grant or renew an authorisation under section 10 of this Act;

(g) to remove the name of a person from the register of firearms dealers under section 11 of this Act;

(h) to refuse to grant a licence under section 10A of this Act;

(i) to refuse to grant an authorisation under section 16(1) of this Act;

(j) to refuse to grant a licence for the import of firearms or ammunition or a prohibited weapon under section 17 of this Act or to vary such a licence or conditions named in it;

(k) to refuse to renew a firearm certificate under section 9 of the Firearms Act 1964; or

(l) to refuse to grant a firearm certificate, or to revoke such a certificate, under section 2 of the Firearms (Firearm Certificate for Non-Residents) Act 2000.

(2) An appeal shall be made within 30 days of receipt of notice of the decision concerned.

(3) On the appeal the Court may—

   (a) confirm the decision,

   (b) adjourn the proceedings and direct the issuing person to reconsider the decision in the light of the appeal proceedings, or

   (c) allow the appeal.

(4) Where the appeal is allowed, the issuing person shall give effect to the Court's decision.

(5) For the purposes of this section—

   (a) an issuing person—

      (i) who is required under section 3(9), 4A(7) or 10(4F) to decide on an application within a specified period, and

      (ii) who does not so decide,

    is deemed to have decided to refuse to grant the application,

   (b) the applicant is deemed to have received notice of the decision on the expiration of that period, and

   (c) as the case may be, section 3(10) does not apply in relation to the application.

(6) The jurisdiction conferred on the District Court by this section shall be exercised by the judge of that Court assigned to the district in which the appellant resides or carries on business.][1]

Amendments

1   Section 15A inserted by Criminal Justice Act 2006, s 43.

---

16   Restriction on export or removal of firearms or ammunition

(1) It shall not be lawful for any person to consign—

   (a) for export from Saorstát Éireann, or

   (b) for removal from one place in Saorstát Éireann to another such place,

any firearm or ammunition, unless such export or removal is authorised in writing by the superintendent of the Garda Síochána of the district from which such firearm or ammunition is consigned for export or removal.

(2) Every person who consigns for export or removal as aforesaid any firearm or ammunition contrary to the provisions of this section shall be guilty of an offence under this Act and shall be punishable accordingly.

(3) Upon the conviction of any person of the offence of contravening the provisions of this section, the court may, where the person so convicted is the owner of any firearm or ammunition the subject of such offence, in addition to any other punishment awarded under this Act, make such order as to the forfeiture of such firearm or ammunition as the court thinks fit.

(4) The offence of contravening the provisions of this section shall not be deemed to have been committed by the holder of a firearm certificate carrying with him from or in Saorstát Éireann [or consigning for export][1] the firearm or any ammunition authorised by such certificate to be carried by the holder thereof.

206

(5) This section shall not apply to any consignment of any firearm or ammunition belonging to or purchased or intended for the use of the Defence Forces of Saorstát Éireann or any lawful police force in Saorstát Éireann.

Amendments

1 Words inserted by Firearms Act 1964, s 20.

---

17 Restrictions on the import of firearms, prohibited weapons and ammunition

(1) No person shall import into Saorstát Éireann any firearm, ammunition, or prohibited weapon unless such import is authorised by a continuing licence granted under this section and in force at the time, or by an occasional licence granted under this section and relating to the specific firearm, ammunition or prohibited weapon so imported.

(2) An occasional licence to import a prohibited weapon may be granted by the Minister for Defence to such person, upon such terms, and subject to such conditions as he shall think fit, and every such occasional licence shall operate and be expressed to authorise the importation into Saorstát Éireann of the prohibited weapon specified in such licence through the port, by the person, within the time, and subject to the conditions named in such licence.

(3) A continuing licence to import firearms or ammunition may on application in the prescribed manner be granted by the Minister if he thinks fit so to do to any registered firearms dealer, and every such continuing licence shall operate and be expressed to authorise the importation into Saorstát Éireann of firearms and ammunition generally or of any specified class or classes of firearms and ammunition through the port, by the registered dealer, during the period [...]¹, and subject to the conditions named in such licence.

(4) An occasional licence to import into Saorstát Éireann a firearm, with or without ammunition therefor, may, on application in the prescribed manner be granted by the Minister to any person who holds or could be granted a firearm certificate for the firearm and ammunition (if any) in respect of which the occasional licence is sought or is a registered firearms dealer and every such occasional licence shall operate and be expressed to authorise the importation into Saorstát Éireann of the firearm and the quantity of ammunition (if any) specified in such licence through the port, by the person, within the time [....],¹ and subject to the conditions named in such licence.

(5) Every continuing licence granted by the Minister under this section may be varied or revoked by the Minister at any time before its expiration.

(6) If any person imports into Saorstát Éireann a firearm or prohibited weapon or any ammunition without or otherwise than in accordance with a licence under this section authorising such importation or, in the case of ammunition, in quantities in excess of those so authorised, or fails to comply with any condition named in a licence granted to him under this section, he shall be guilty of an offence under this Act and shall be punishable accordingly.

(7) The possession of a licence granted under this section shall not relieve from the obligation to obtain or hold any certificate, permit, or authority required by any other provision of this Act.

(8) This section shall not apply to the importation into Saorstát Éireann of any firearms, ammunition or prohibited weapon which is so imported under the authority of the Minister for Defence for the use of the Defence Forces of Saorstát Éireann or under the authority of the Minister for the use of any lawful police force in Saorstát Éireann.

Amendments

1   Words deleted by Firearms Act 1964, s 21.

Note

Section 17 substituted by Criminal Justice (Miscellaneous Provisions) Act 2009, s 36 which is not yet in operation (February 2011). See the amending Act.

18   Powers of officers of customs and excise

Officers of customs and excise shall have the like powers in relation to any firearms and ammunition the import, export or removal of which is prohibited or restricted by this Act as such officers have by law in relation to other articles, the import or export of which is prohibited or restricted by law.

19   Powers and duties of officers of the Post Office

Any officer of [An Post][1] may detain and examine and if necessary open for that purpose any postal packet known to him to contain or suspected by him of containing a firearm or prohibited weapon or any ammunition, and if a postal packet so detained contains a firearm or prohibited weapon or any ammunition the officers of the said Minister shall make such inquiries in regard thereto as they think proper, and shall dispose of the packet and the contents thereof (including the firearm, prohibited weapon, or ammunition) in accordance with the instructions of the Minister for Justice, or any superintendent of the Garda Síochána, and may detain the said packet and contents pending the making of such inquiries and the receipt of such instructions.

Amendments

1   Words substituted by Postal and Telecommunications Services Act 1983, s 8(1) and Sch 4.

20   Prohibition of taking firearms or ammunition in pawn

[...][1]

Amendments

1   Section 20 repealed by Pawnbrokers Act 1964, s 6 and Sch 1.

21   Garda Síochána may search for and seize certain firearms, etc

(1) Any member of the Garda Síochána may at all reasonable times enter upon and have free access to the interior of—

(a)   any premises used for the manufacture, sale, repair, test, or proof of firearms or ammunition, or

(b)   the premises of any person engaged in the business of carrying goods for reward, or

(c)   any warehouse or other premises of any person engaged in the business of warehousing goods for reward, or

(d)   any pier, quay, wharf, jetty, dock, or dock premises, or

(e)   any ship, boat, railway waggon, motor, lorry, cart, or other vessel or vehicle used for the conveyance of goods.

(2) Any member of the Garda Síochána may inspect any firearms or ammunition, or any case, box or package found by him in any place entered by him under the authority of this section or upon or in any public place, and may open any such case, box, or package which he reasonably believes or suspects to contain firearms or ammunition, and may seize any firearms or ammunition found in any such place as aforesaid and which he reasonably believes or suspects are being imported into or exported from Saorstát Éireann or are being or have been removed from one place to another in Saorstát Éireann in contravention of the provisions of this Act [and may seize any firearms found in any such place to which a mark, being a mark mentioned in section 4(1)(a) or 4(1)(b) of the Firearms (Proofing) Act, 1968, has not been applied and in relation to which he reasonably believes or suspects that a breach of an order under the said section 4 has occurred.][1]

(3) It shall be the duty of every person having custody or control of any firearms or ammunition in any such place as is mentioned in sub-section (1) of this section or upon or in any public place on demand by a member of the Garda Síochána to afford such member all reasonable facilities for the inspection of such firearms and ammunition and to produce to such member on demand by him any documents in his possession relating to such firearms or ammunition.

(4) If any person—

(a)   obstructs or impedes any member of the Garda Síochána in the exercise of any of the powers conferred on him by this section, or

(b)   knowing the name or other particulars of the consignor, consignee, or owner of any firearms or ammunition or of any case, box, or package which such member is entitled to inspect under this section, refuses to give such name or other particulars to such member, or

(c)   wilfully or recklessly gives to such member any false or misleading name or other particular of any such consignor, consignee, or owner,

such person shall be guilty of an offence under this section and shall be liable on summary conviction to a fine not exceeding [€1,000 or imprisonment for a term not exceeding 6 months or both.][2]

(5) Where any firearms or ammunition are seized by a member of the Garda Síochána under this section it shall be the duty of such member to notify the owner or the consignor or consignee (if and so far as their names and addresses are known to or can reasonably be ascertained by him) of such seizure.

[(6) Where a firearm or ammunition is seized under this section or under section 22 of this Act and a prosecution for an offence under this Act in relation to the firearm or ammunition is not instituted, the firearm or ammunition shall be—

(a) returned to the person who is the owner, consignor or consignee thereof, as may be appropriate, or disposed of, subject to the provisions of this Act, in accordance with the directions of such person, or

(b) made the subject of an application to the District Court under the Police (Property) Act, 1897, and disposed of in accordance with the terms of the order made by the District Court under that Act in relation to the application.]³

Amendments

1   Words substituted by Firearms (Proofing) Act 1968, s 9.

2   Words substituted by Criminal Justice Act 2006, s 64 and Sch 1.

3   Words substituted by Firearms Act 1964, s 22.

22   Powers of members of Garda Síochána

(1) Any member of the Garda Síochána may demand from any person whom he observes or believes to be in possession of, using, or carrying a firearm or any ammunition, the production of his firearm certificate and if such person fails to produce and permit such member to read a firearm certificate authorising him to have possession of, use, or carry (as the case may require) such firearm or ammunition, such member of the Garda Síochána may unless such person shows that he is entitled by law to have possession of, use, or carry (as the case may require) at that time and in that place such firearm or ammunition without having a firearm certificate therefor demand from such person his name and address.

(2) If any person, on demand being made to him under this section by a member of the Garda Síochána, refuses to give to such member his name and address or gives a name or address which is false or misleading in any material particular, he shall be guilty of an offence under this section and shall be liable on summary conviction thereof to a fine not exceeding [€1,000.]¹

(3) Any member of the Garda Síochána may arrest without warrant any person who, on demand being made under this section, refuses to give his name and address or gives a name or address which the member of the Garda Síochána demanding the same knows or suspects to be false or misleading in any material particular.

(4) In addition to any other powers conferred on him under this Act or otherwise, any member of the Garda Síochána may stop and search and may also arrest without warrant any person whom he believes to be in possession of or to be using or carrying a firearm or ammunition in contravention of any of the provisions of this Act, and may search any such person, and, whether arresting him or not, may seize and detain any firearm or ammunition in his possession or used or carried by him.

Amendments

1   Words substituted by Criminal Justice Act 2006, s 64 and Sch 1.

23   Forfeiture of firearms, etc., in certain cases

(1) Where any person is convicted of an offence under this Act, or is convicted of any crime for which he is sentenced to penal servitude or imprisonment, or is ordered to be subject to police supervision, or is ordered to enter into a recognizance to keep the peace or to be of good behaviour, a condition of which is that the offender shall not possess, use, or carry a firearm, the court before whom such person is convicted or by whom the order is made may make such order as to the forfeiture or disposal of any firearm, prohibited weapon, or ammunition found in the possession of such person, or used or carried by him, as the court shall think fit and may cancel any firearm certificate held by such person.

(2) Where the court cancels a firearm certificate under this section, it shall cause notice of such cancellation to be sent forthwith to the superintendent of the Garda Síochána of the area in which the certificate was granted.

24   Search orders

(1) If any superintendent of the Garda Síochána is of opinion that there is reasonable ground for supposing that an offence under this Act has been, is being, or is about to be committed, he may issue an order in writing (in this Act called a search order) to any one or more members of the Garda Síochána under his command and named therein to search any place or premises named in such order.

(2) A search order issued under this section shall authorise the member of the Garda Síochána named therein to enter the place or premises to which the order relates at any time within [forty-eight hours]¹ after the issuing of such search order, and if need be by force, and to inspect the place or premises so entered, and to take the names and addresses of any persons found therein, and if the premises are premises of a firearms dealer, to seize any books and papers relating to the business of such firearms dealer.

(3) Any member of the Garda Síochána making a search under a search order may arrest without warrant any person found in the place or on the premises to which the order relates whom he has reason to believe to be guilty of an offence under this Act.

Amendments

1   Words substituted by Firearms Act 1964, s 23.

25   Punishments

[Any person who commits an offence under this Act in respect of which no other punishment is provided is liable in respect of each such offence—

(a) on summary conviction, to a fine not exceeding €5,000 or imprisonment for a term not exceeding 12 months or both, or

(b) on conviction on indictment, to a fine not exceeding €20,000 or imprisonment for a term not exceeding 5 years or both.]¹

Amendments

1 Section 25 substituted by Criminal Justice Act 2006, s 45.

[25A   Surrender of firearms and offensive weapons

(1) The Minister may by order appoint a specified period during which a person may surrender at any Garda station or at any other place approved for the purpose by a superintendent of the Garda Síochána any of the following weapons:

(a) a firearm;

(b) a flick-knife;

(c) a weapon of offence.

(2) When surrendering a weapon during the specified period, the person—

(a) shall give his or her name, address and proof of identity to a member of the Garda Síochána at the Garda Síochána station or place concerned, and

(b) shall be informed by the member that the weapon and any thing in which it was surrendered may be forensically examined or tested.

(3) Proceedings for an offence shall not be instituted against any person who surrenders a weapon under this section if—

(a) in the case of a firearm, the offence consists only in the possession, carrying and use (other than in the commission of another offence) of the firearm without being the holder of a firearm certificate, in contravention of section 2 of this Act, or

(b) in the case of a flick-knife or other weapon of offence, the offence is an offence under section 9(4) or 10(1)(b) of the Firearms and Offensive Weapons Act 1990.

(4) Any surrendered weapon or any substance or thing found on or in it or on or in any thing in which it was surrendered may be subjected to forensic examination or testing for the purpose of—

(a) determining whether any such weapon, substance or thing is in a safe and stable condition, or

(b) discovering information concerning an offence other than an offence referred to in subsection (3) of this section.

(5) In any proceedings, a surrendered weapon and any substance or thing referred to in subsection (4) of this section is admissible in evidence.

(6) A surrendered weapon may be disposed of in a manner deemed appropriate by the Commissioner.

(7) In this section—

"firearm" includes ammunition;

"flick-knife" has the meaning given to it in section 9(9) of the Firearms and Offensive Weapons Act 1990;

"weapon of offence" has the meaning given to it in section 10(2) of the said Act of 1990.]¹

Amendments

1   Section 25A inserted by Criminal Justice Act 2006, s 46.

[25B   Surrender of firearm for ballistic testing

(1) The Commissioner may by notice in writing require any person lawfully possessing a firearm to produce it at such time and place as may be specified in the notice for the purpose of having ballistic or other tests carried out on it and of establishing and recording its distinctive characteristics.

(2) A person who, without reasonable excuse, does not comply with such a notice is guilty of an offence under this Act.]¹

Amendments

1   Section 25B inserted by Criminal Justice Act 2006, s 47.

[25C   Delegation of Commissioner's functions

The Commissioner may appoint in writing a member of the Garda Síochána, or members of a particular rank in the Garda Síochána, not below the rank of superintendent to perform any of the Commissioner's functions under this Act.]¹

Amendments

1   Section 25C inserted by Criminal Justice Act 2006, s 48.

[25D   Liability of officers of bodies corporate

(1) Where—

(a) an offence under this Act is committed by a body corporate, and

(b) it is proved to have been committed with the consent, connivance or approval of, or to have been attributable to any neglect on the part of, a person who—

(i) was a director, manager, secretary or other officer of the body corporate, or

(ii) was a person purporting to act in any such capacity,

that person, as well as the body corporate, is guilty of an offence and liable to be proceeded against and punished as if the person were guilty of the first-mentioned offence.

(2) Where the affairs of a body corporate are managed by its members, subsection (1) of this section applies in relation to the acts and defaults of a member in connection with the member's functions of management as if the member were a director or manager of the body corporate.

(3) The foregoing provisions apply, with the necessary modifications, where the offence was committed by an unincorporated body.]¹

Amendments

1   Section 25D inserted by Criminal Justice Act 2006, s 49.

---

26   Savings

(1) Nothing in this Act relating to firearms shall apply to any antique firearm which is sold, bought, carried, or possessed as a curiosity or ornament.

(2) The provisions of this Act relating to ammunition shall be in addition to and not in derogation of any enactment relating to the keeping and sale of explosives.

27   Regulations.

[(1) The Minister may make regulations prescribing any matter referred to in this Act as prescribed or to be prescribed or to be the subject of regulations or for the purpose of enabling any of its provisions to have full effect.

(2) The regulations may contain such incidental, supplementary and consequential provisions as appear to the Minister to be necessary for the purposes of the regulations.

(3) Regulations prescribing fees shall be made with the consent of the Minister for Finance]¹.

Amendments

1   Section 27 substituted by Criminal Justice Act 2006, s 50.

[27A   Laying of orders or regulations before Houses of Oireachtas

An order or regulation under this Act shall be laid before each House of the Oireachtas as soon as may be after it is made and, if a resolution annulling it is passed by either such House within the next 21 days on which that House has sat after it has been laid before it, the order or regulation shall be annulled accordingly, but without prejudice to the validity of anything previously done under it.]¹

Amendments

1   Section 27A inserted by Criminal Justice Act 2006, s 51.

---

28   Partial continuance of Firearms (Temporary Provisions) Act, 1924

Notwithstanding anything to the contrary contained in the Firearms (Temporary Provisions) (Continuance) Act, 1925 (No. 10 of 1925), the Firearms (Temporary Provisions) Act, 1924 (No. 9 of 1924), and every regulation made thereunder which is in force on the 31st day of July, 1925, shall continue in force after that day so far as but no further than is necessary to authorise and enable persons charged before, on, or after the said 31st day of July, 1925, with having committed on or before that day any offence under the said Firearms (Temporary Provisions) Act, 1924, or any breach of any such regulation as aforesaid to be prosecuted and tried and, if found guilty, to be convicted and sentenced under the said Act and regulations after the said 31st day of July, 1925, and to authorise and enable any appeal (including an appeal by way of case stated) against any conviction and sentence (whether before, on, or after the said 31st day of July, 1925) for an offence under the said Act or breach of any such regulation to be brought, heard, and determined after the said 31st day of July, 1925.

29

Repeal

The Firearms Act, 1920, is hereby repealed.

30   Short title and commencement

(1) This Act may be cited as the Firearms Act, 1925.

(2) This Act shall come into operation on the 1st day of August, 1925.

Offences Against the State Act 1939

Number 13 of 1939

ARRANGEMENT OF SECTIONS

PART I
PRELIMINARY AND GENERAL

1   Short title.

2   Definitions.

3   Exercise of powers by superintendents of the Garda Síochána.

4   Expenses.

5   Repeals.

PART II
OFFENCES AGAINST THE STATE

6   Usurpation of functions of government.

7   Obstruction of government.

8   Obstruction of the President.

9   Interference with military or other employees of the State.

10 Prohibition of printing, etc, certain documents.

11 Foreign newspapers, etc, containing seditious or unlawful matter.

12 Possession of treasonable, seditious, or incriminating documents.

13 Provisions in respect of documents printed for reward.

14 Obligation to print printer's name and address on documents.

15 Unauthorised military exercises prohibited.

16 Secret societies in army or police.

17 Administering unlawful oaths.

PART III
UNLAWFUL ORGANISATION

18 Unlawful organisations.

19 Suppression orders.

20 Declaration of legality.

21 Prohibition of membership of an unlawful organisation.

21A Offence of providing assistance to an unlawful organisation.

22 Provisions consequent upon the making of a suppression order.

22A Definitions for, and operation of, sections 22B to 22I.

22B Interim order respecting specified property.

22C Disposal order respecting specified property.

22D Ancillary orders and provision in relation to certain profits or gains, etc.

22E   Evidence.

22F   Seizure of certain property.

22G   Compensation.

22H   Application of certain provisions of Act of 1996.

22I   Immunity from proceedings.

23   Provisions consequent upon the making of a declaration of legality.

24   Proof of membership of an unlawful organisation by possession of incriminating document.

25   Closing of buildings.

PART IV
MISCELLANEOUS

26   Evidence of publication of treasonable, seditious or incriminating document.

27   Prohibition of certain public meetings.

28   Prohibition of meetings in the vicinity of the Oireachtas.

29   Search warrants in relation to the commission of offences under this Act or to treason.

30   Arrest and detention of suspected persons.

30A

31   Offences by bodies corporate.

32   Re-capture of escaped prisoners.

33   Remission etc, in respect of convictions by a Special Criminal Court.

34   Forfeiture and disqualifications on certain convictions by a Special Criminal Court.

PART V
SPECIAL CRIMINAL COURTS

35   Commencement and cesser of this Part of this Act.

36   Schedule offences.

37   Attempting, etc, to commit a scheduled offence.

38   Establishment of Special Criminal Courts.

39   Constitution of Special Criminal Courts.

40   Verdicts of Special Criminal Courts.

41   Procedure of Special Criminal Courts.

42   Authentication of orders of Special Criminal Courts.

43   Jurisdiction of Special Criminal Courts.

44   Appeal to Court of Criminal Appeal.

45   Proceedings in the District Court in relation to scheduled offences.

46   Proceedings in the District Court in relation to non-scheduled offences.

47   Charge before Special Criminal Court in lieu of District Court.

48   Transfer of trials from ordinary Courts to a Special Criminal Court.

49   Selection of the Special Criminal Court by which a person is to be tried.

50   Orders and sentences of Special Criminal Courts.

51   Standing mute of malice and refusal to plead etc.

52   Examination of detained persons.

53   Immunities of members, etc, of Special Criminal Courts.

PART VI

POWERS OF INTERNMENT

54   Commencement and cesser of this Part of this Act.

55   Special powers of arrest and detention.

56   Powers of search, etc, of detained persons.

57   Release of detained persons.

58   Regulations in relation to places of detention.

59   Commission for inquiring into detention.

AN ACT TO MAKE PROVISION IN RELATION TO ACTIONS AND CONDUCT CALCULATED TO UNDERMINE PUBLIC ORDER AND THE AUTHORITY OF THE STATE, AND FOR THAT PURPOSE TO PROVIDE FOR THE PUNISHMENT OF PERSONS GUILTY OF OFFENCES AGAINST THE STATE, TO REGULATE AND CONTROL IN THE PUBLIC INTEREST THE FORMATION OF ASSOCIATIONS, TO ESTABLISH SPECIAL CRIMINAL COURTS IN ACCORDANCE WITH ARTICLE 38 OF THE CONSTITUTION AND PROVIDE FOR THE CONSTITUTION, POWERS, JURISDICTION, AND PROCEDURE OF SUCH COURTS, TO REPEAL CERTAIN ENACTMENTS AND TO MAKE PROVISION GENERALLY IN RELATION TO MATTERS CONNECTED WITH THE MATTERS AFORESAID. [14th June, 1939].

BE IT ENACTED BY THE OIREACHTAS AS FOLLOWS:—

PART I

PRELIMINARY AND GENERAL

1   Short title

This Act may be cited as the Offences against the State Act, 1939.

2   Definitions

In this Act—

the word "organisation" includes associations, societies, and other organisations or combinations of persons of whatsoever nature or kind, whether known or not known by a distinctive name;

the word "document" includes a book and also a newspaper, magazine, or other periodical publication, and also a pamphlet, leaflet, circular, or advertisement [and also—

(a)   any map, plan, graph or drawing,

(b)   any photograph,

219

(c) any disc, tape, sound track or other device in which sounds or other data (not being visual images) are embodied so as to be capable (with or without the aid of some other equipment) of being reproduced therefrom, and

(d) any film, microfilm, negative, tape or ether device in which one or more visual images are embodied (whether with or without sounds or other data) so as to be capable (as aforesaid) of being reproduced therefrom and a reproduction or still reproduction of the image or images embodied therein whether enlarged or not and whether with or without sounds or other data][1];

the expression "incriminating document" means a document of whatsoever date, or bearing no date, issued by or emanating from an unlawful organisation or appearing to be so issued or so to emanate or purporting or appearing to aid or abet any such organisation or calculated to promote the formation of an unlawful organisation;

the expression "treasonable document" includes a document which relates directly or indirectly to the commission of treason; the expression "seditious document" includes—

(a) a document consisting of or containing matter calculated or tending to undermine the public order or the authority of the State, and

(b) a document which alleges, implies, or suggests or is calculated to suggest that the government functioning under the Constitution is not the lawful government of the State or that there is in existence in the State any body or organisation not functioning under the Constitution which is entitled to be recognised as being the government of the country, and

(c) a document which alleges, implies, or suggests or is calculated to suggest that the military forces maintained under the Constitution are not the lawful military forces of the State, or that there is in existence in the State a body or organisation not established and maintained by virtue of the Constitution which is entitled to be recognised as a military force, and

(d) a document in which words, abbreviations, or symbols referable to a military body are used in referring to an unlawful organisation;

the word "offence" includes treason, felonies, misdemeanours, and statutory and other offences;

references to printing include every mode of representing or reproducing words in a visible form, and the word "print" and all cognate words shall be construed accordingly.

Amendments

1 Words inserted by Offences Against the State (Amendment) Act 1972, s 5.

---

3   **Exercise of powers by superintendents of the Garda Síochána**

Any power conferred by this Act on an officer of the Garda Síochána not below the rank- of chief superintendent may be exercised by any superintendent of the Garda Síochána who is authorised (in respect of any particular power or any particular case) in that behalf in writing by the Commissioner of the Garda Síochána.

4   Expenses

The expenses incurred by any Minister of State in the administration of this Act shall, to such extent as may be sanctioned by the Minister for Finance, be paid out of moneys provided by the Oireachtas.

5   Repeals

The Treasonable Offences Act, 1925 (No. 18 of 1925), and the Public Safety (Emergency Powers) Act, 1926 (No. 42 of 1926), are hereby repealed.

PART II
OFFENSES AGAINST THE STATE

6   Usurpation of functions of government

(1) Every person who usurps or unlawfully exercises any function of government, whether by setting up, maintaining or taking part in any way in a body of persons purporting to be a government or a legislature but not authorised in that behalf by or under the Constitution, or by setting up, maintaining, or taking part in any way in a purported court or other tribunal not lawfully established, or by forming, maintaining, or being a member of an armed force or a purported police force not so authorised, or by any other action or conduct whatsoever, shall be guilty of felony and shall be liable on conviction thereof [to imprisonment for a term not exceeding 20 years][1].

(2) Every person who shall attempt to do any thing the doing of which is a felony under the foregoing sub-section of this section or who aids or abets or conspires with another person to do or attempt to do any such thing or advocates or encourages the doing of any such thing shall be guilty of a misdemeanour and shall be liable on conviction thereof to [imprisonment for a term not exceeding 20 years][2].

Amendments

1   Words "to imprisonment for a term not exceeding 20 years" substituted for "to suffer penal servitude for a term not exceeding ten years or to imprisonment for a term not exceeding two years" by Criminal Law Act 1976, s 2(1).

2   Words "imprisonment for a term not exceeding 20 years" substituted for "imprisonment for a term not exceeding two years" by Criminal Law Act 1976, s 2(2).

7   Obstruction of government

(1) Every person who [(whether in or outside the State)][1] prevents or obstructs, or attempts or is concerned in an attempt to prevent or obstruct, by force of arms or other violent means or by any form of intimidation the carrying on of the government of the State or any branch (whether legislative, judicial, or executive) of the government of the State or the exercise or performance by any member of the legislature, the judiciary, or the executive or by any officer or employee (whether civil (including police) or military) of the State of any of his functions, powers, or duties shall be guilty of felony and shall be liable on conviction thereof [to imprisonment for a term not exceeding 20 years][2].

(2) Every person who [(whether in or outside the State)]³ aids or abets or conspires with another person to do any thing the doing of which is a felony under the foregoing sub-section of this section or advocates or encourages the doing of any such thing shall be guilty of a misdemeanour and shall be liable on conviction thereof to [imprisonment for a term not exceeding 20 years]⁴.

[(3) A person shall be guilty of an offence under this section for conduct that the person engages in outside the State only if—

    (a) the conduct takes place on board an Irish ship (within the meaning of section 9 of the Mercantile Marine Act 1955),

    (b) the conduct takes place on an aircraft registered in the State,

    (c) the person is an Irish citizen, or

    (d) the person is ordinarily resident in the State.

(4) A person who has his principal residence in the State for the 12 months immediately preceding the commission of an offence under subsection (1) or (2) of this section is, for the purposes of subsection (3)(d) of this section, ordinarily resident in the State on the date of the commission of the offence.]⁵

Amendments

1   Words inserted by Criminal Justice (Amendment) Act 2009, s 18(1)(a).

2   Words "to imprisonment for a term not exceeding 20 years" substituted for "to suffer penal servitude for a term not exceeding seven years or to imprisonment for a term not exceeding two years" by Criminal Law Act 1976, s 2(3).

3   Words inserted by Criminal Justice (Amendment) Act 2009, s 18(1)(b).

4   Words "imprisonment for a term not exceeding 20 years" substituted for "imprisonment for a term not exceeding two years" by Criminal Law Act 1976, s 2(4).

5   Subsections (3) and (4) inserted by Criminal Justice (Amendment) Act 2009, s 18(2).

8   Obstruction of the President

(1) Every person who prevents, or obstructs, or attempts or is concerned in an attempt to prevent or obstruct, by force of arms or other violent means or by any form of intimidation the exercise or performance by the President of any of his functions, powers, or duties shall be guilty of felony and shall be liable on conviction thereof to suffer penal servitude for a term not exceeding seven years or to imprisonment for a term not exceeding two years.

(2) Every person who aids or abets or conspires with another person to do any thing the doing of which is a felony under the foregoing sub-section of this section or advocates or encourages the doing of any such thing shall be guilty of a misdemeanour and shall be liable on, conviction thereof to imprisonment for a term not exceeding two years.

9   Interference with military or other employees of the State

(1) Every person who shall with intent to undermine public order or the authority of the State commit any act of violence against or of interference with a member of a lawfully established military or police force (whether such member is or is not on duty) or shall take away, injure,

or otherwise interfere with the arms or equipment, or any part of the arms or equipment, of any such member shall be guilty of a misdemeanour and shall be liable on conviction thereof to imprisonment for a term not exceeding two years.

(2) Every person who shall incite or encourage any person employed in any capacity by the State to refuse, neglect, or omit (in a manner or to an extent calculated to dislocate the public service or a branch thereof) to perform his duty or shall incite or encourage any person so employed to be negligent or insubordinate (in such manner or to such extent as aforesaid) in the performance of his duty shall be guilty of a misdemeanour and shall be liable on conviction thereof to imprisonment for a term not exceeding two years

(3) Every person who attempts to do anything the doing of which is a misdemeanour under either of the foregoing sub-sections of this section or who aids or abets or conspires with another person to do or attempt to do any such thing or advocates or encourages the doing of any such thing shall be guilty of a misdemeanour and shall be liable on conviction thereof to imprisonment for a term not exceeding twelve months.

10   Prohibition of printing, etc, certain documents

(1) It shall not be lawful to set up in type, print, publish, send through the post, distribute, sell, or offer for sale any document—

    (a)   which is or contains or includes an incriminating document, or

    (b)   which is or contains or includes a treasonable document, or

    (c)   which is or contains or includes a seditious document.

(2) In particular and without prejudice to the generality of the foregoing sub-section of this section, it shall not be lawful for any person to send or contribute to any newspaper or other periodical publication or for the proprietor of any newspaper or other periodical publication to publish in such newspaper or publication any letter, article, or communication which is sent or contributed or purports to be sent or contributed by or on behalf of an unlawful organisation or which is of such nature or character that the printing of it would be a contravention of the foregoing sub-section of this section.

(3) Every person who shall contravene either of the foregoing sub-sections of this section shall be guilty of an offence under this sub-section and shall be liable on summary conviction thereof to a fine not exceeding one hundred pounds, or, at the discretion of the Court, to imprisonment for a term not exceeding six months or to both such fine and such imprisonment and also (in any case), if the Court so directs, to forfeit every copy in his possession of the document, newspaper, or publication in relation to which the offence, was committed and also (where the act constituting the offence was the setting up in type or the printing of a document) to forfeit, if the Court so directs, so much of the printing machinery in his possession as is specified in that behalf by the Court.

(4) Every person who unlawfully has in his possession a document which was printed or published in contravention of this section or a newspaper or other periodical publication containing a letter, article, or other communication published therein in contravention of this section shall, when so requested by a member of the Garda, Síochána, deliver up to such member every copy in his possession of such document or of such newspaper or publication (as the case may be), and if he fails or refuses so to do he shall be guilty of an offence under this sub-section and shall be liable on summary conviction thereof to imprisonment for a term not exceeding three months and also, if the Court so directs, to forfeit every copy in his

possession of the document, newspaper or publication in relation to which the offence was committed.

(5) Nothing in this section shall render unlawful the setting tip in type, printing, publishing, sending through the post, distributing, selling, offering for sale, or having possession of a document or a copy of a document which is published at the request or by permission of the Government or is published in the course or as part of a fair report of the proceedings in either House of the Oireachtas or in a court of justice or before any other court or tribunal lawfully exercising jurisdiction.

11   Foreign newspapers, etc, containing seditious or unlawful matter

(1) Whenever the Minister for Justice is of opinion, in respect of a newspaper or other periodical publication ordinarily printed outside the State, that a particular issue of such publication either is seditious contains any matter the publication of which is a contravention of this Act, the said Minister may by order, if he considers that it is in the public interest so to do, do either or both of the, following things, that is to say:—

(a) authorise members of the Garda Síochána to seize and destroy all copies of the said issue of such publication wherever they may be found;

(b) prohibit the importation of any copy of any issue of such publication published within a specified period (not exceeding three months) after the publication of the said issue of such publication.

(2) The Minister for Justice may by order, whenever he thinks proper so to do, revoke or amend any order made by him under the foregoing sub-section of this section or any order (made 'by him under this sub-section) amending any such order.

(3) It shall not be lawful for any person to import any copy of an issue of a periodical publication the importation of which is prohibited by an order under this section [...][1]

Amendments

1   Words ", and all such copies shall be deemed to be included amongst the goods enumerated and described in the Table of Prohibitions and Restrictions Inwards annexed to section 42 of the Customs Consolidation Act, 1876, and the provisions of that Act (as amended or extended by subsequent Acts) relating to the importation of prohibited or restricted goods shall apply accordingly." repealed by Customs (Temporary Provisions) Act 1945, s 13 and Sch.

---

12   Possession of treasonable, seditious, or incriminating documents

(1) It shall not be lawful for any person to have any treasonable document, seditious document, or incriminating document in his possession or on any lands or premises owned or occupied by him or under his control.

(2) Every person who has a treasonable document, seditious document, or incriminating document in his possession or on any lands or premises owned or occupied by him or under his control shall be guilty of an offence under this sub-section and shall be liable on summary conviction thereof to a fine not exceeding fifty pounds or, at the discretion of the Court, to imprisonment for a term not exceeding three mouths or to both such fine and such imprisonment.

(3) Where a person is charged with an offence under this section, it shall be a good defence to such charge for Such person to prove—

(a) that he is an officer of the State and had possession or custody of the document in respect of which the offence is alleged to have been committed in the course of his duties as such officer, or

(b) that he did not know that the said document was in his possession or on any lands or premises owned or occupied by him or under his control, or

(c) that he did not know the nature or contents of the said document.

(4) Every person who has in his possession a treasonable document, seditious document, or incriminating document shall, when so requested by a member of the Garda Síochána, deliver up to such member the said document and every copy thereof in his possession, and if he fails or refuses so to do he shall be guilty of an offence under this sub-section and shall be liable on summary conviction thereof to imprisonment for a term not exceeding three months.

(5) Where the proprietor or the editor or other chief officer of a newspaper or other periodical publication receives a document which appears to him to be a treasonable document, a seditious document, or an incriminating document and such document is not published in such newspaper or periodical publication, the following provisions shall have effect, that is to say:—

(a) if such proprietor, editor, or chief officer is requested by a member of the Garda Síochána to deliver up such document to such member, such proprietor, editor, or chief officer may, in lieu of so delivering up such document, destroy such document and every (if any) copy thereof in his possession in the presence and to the satisfaction of such member;

(b) if such proprietor, editor, or chief officer destroys under the next preceding paragraph of this sub-section such document and every (if any) copy thereof in his possession or of his own motion destroys such document within twenty-four hours after receiving it and without having made any copy of it or permitted any such copy to be made, such destruction shall be a good defence to any charge against such proprietor, editor, or chief officer of an offence under any sub-section of this section in respect of such document and no civil or criminal action or other proceeding shall lie against such proprietor, editor, or chief officer on account of such destruction.

13   Provisions in respect of documents printed for reward

(1) Every person who shall print for reward any document shall do every of the following things, that is to say—

(a) at the time of or within twenty-four hours after printing such document, print or write on at least one copy of such document the name and address of the person for whom or on whose instructions such document was printed;

(b) retain, for six months from the date on which such document was printed, a copy of such document on which the said name and address is printed or written as aforesaid;

(c) on the request of a member of the Garda Síochána at any time during the said period of six months, produce for the inspection of such member the said copy of such document so retained as aforesaid.

(2) Every person who shall print for reward any document and shall fail to comply in any respect with the foregoing sub-section of this section shall be guilty of an offence under this section and shall be liable on summary conviction thereof, in the case of a first such offence, to a fine not exceeding twenty-five pounds and, in the case of a second or any subsequent such offence, to a fine not exceeding fifty pounds.

(3) This section does not apply to any newspaper, magazine or other periodical publication which is printed by the proprietor thereof on his own premises.

Note

Criminal Law Act 1976, s 14 provides: "In sections 13 and 14 of the Act of 1939, "document" does not include any of the things specified in the amendment of the definition of "document" made by section 5 of the Offences Against the State (Amendment) Act 1972."

14   Obligation to print printer's name and address on documents

(1) Every person who shall print for reward any document (other than a document to which this section does not apply) which he knows or has reason to believe is intended to be sold or distributed (whether to the public generally or to a restricted class or number of persons) or to be publicly or privately displayed shall, if such document consists only of one page or sheet printed on one side only, print his name and the address of his place of business on the front of such document and shall, in every other case, print the said name and address on the first or the last page of such document.

(2) Every person who shall contravene by act or omission the foregoing sub-section of this section shall be guilty of an offence under this section and shall be liable on summary conviction thereof, in the case of a first such offence, to a fine not exceeding twenty-five pounds and, in the case of a second or any subsequent such offence, to a fine not exceeding fifty pounds.

(3) This section does not apply to any of the following documents, that is to say:—

(a) currency notes, bank notes, bills of exchange, promissory notes, cheques, receipts and other financial or commercial documents,

(b) writs, orders, summonses, warrants, affidavits, and other documents for the purposes of or for use in any lawful court or tribunal,

(c) any document printed by order of the Government, either House of the Oireachtas, a Minister of State, or any officer of the State in the execution of his duties as such officer,

(d) any document which the Minister for Justice shall by order declare to be a document to which this section does not apply.

Note

Criminal Law Act 1976, s 14 provides: "In sections 13 and 14 of the Act of 1939, "document" does not include any of the things specified in the amendment of the definition of "document" made by section 5 of the Offences Against the State (Amendment) Act 1972."

15　　Unauthorised military exercises prohibited

(1) Save as authorised by a Minister of State under this section, and subject to the exceptions hereinafter mentioned, it shall not be lawful for any assembly of persons to practise or to train or drill themselves in or be trained or drilled in the use of arms or the performance of military exercises, evolutions, or manoeuvres nor for any persons to meet together or assemble for the purpose of so practising or training or drilling or being trained or drilled.

(2) A Minister of State may at his discretion by order, subject to such limitations, qualifications and conditions as he shall think fit to impose and shall express in the order, authorise the members of any organisation to meet together and do such one or more of the following things as shall be specified in such order, that is to say, to practise or train or drill themselves in or be trained or drilled in the use of arms or the performance of military exercises, evolutions, or manoeuvres.

(3) If any person is present at or takes part in or gives instruction to or trains or drills an assembly of persons who without or otherwise than in accordance with an authorisation, granted by a Minister of State under this section practise, or train or drill themselves in, or are trained or drilled in the use of arms or the performance of any military exercise, evolution, or manoeuvre or who without or otherwise than in accordance with such authorisation have assembled or met together for the purpose of so practising, or training or drilling or being trained or drilled, such person shall be guilty of a misdemeanour and shall be liable on conviction thereof to imprisonment for a term not exceeding [15 years][1].

(4) This section shall not apply to any assembly of members of any military or police force lawfully maintained by the Government.

(5) In any prosecution under this section the burden of proof that any act was authorised under this section shall lie on the person prosecuted.

Amendments

1　　"15 years" substituted for "two years" by Criminal Law Act 1976, s 2(5).

16　　Secret societies in army or police

(1) Every person who shall—

    (a)　form, organise, promote, or maintain any secret society amongst or consisting of or including members of any military or police force lawfully maintained by the Government, or

    (b)　attempt to form, organise, promote or maintain any such secret society, or

(c) take part, assist, or be concerned in any way in the formation, organisation, promotion, management, or maintenance of any such society, or

(d) induce, solicit, or assist any member of a military of police force lawfully maintained by the Government to join any secret society whatsoever,

shall be guilty of a misdemeanour and shall be liable on conviction thereof to suffer penal servitude for any term not exceeding five years or imprisonment for any term not exceeding two years.

(2) In this section the expression "secret society" means an association, society, or other body the members of which are required by the regulations thereof to take or enter into, or do in fact take or enter into, an oath, affirmation, declaration or agreement not to disclose the proceedings or some part of the proceedings of the association, society, or body.

17 Administering unlawful oaths

(1) Every person who shall administer or cause to be administered or take part in, be present at, or consent to the administering or taking in any form or manner of any oath, declaration, or engagement purporting or intended to bind the person taking the same to do all or any of the following things, that is to say:—

(a) to commit or to plan, contrive, promote, assist, or conceal the commission of any crime or any breach of the peace, or

(b) to join or become a member of or associated with any organisation having for its object or one of its objects the commission of any crime, or breach of the peace, or

(c) to abstain from disclosing or giving information of the existence or formation or proposed or intended formation of any such organisation, association, or other body as aforesaid or from informing or giving evidence against any member of or person concerned in the formation of any such organisation, association, or other body, or

(d) to abstain from disclosing or giving information of the Commission or intended or proposed commission of any crime, breach of the peace, or from informing or giving evidence against the person who committed such an act,

shall be guilty of a misdemeanour and shall be liable on conviction thereof to suffer imprisonment for any term not exceeding two years.

(2) Every person who shall take any such oath, declaration, or engagement as is mentioned in the foregoing sub-section shall be guilty of a misdemeanour and be liable on conviction thereof to suffer imprisonment for any term not exceeding two years unless he shall show—

(a) that he was compelled by force or duress to take such oath, declaration, or engagement (as the case may be), and

(b) that within four days after the taking, of such oath, declaration, or engagement, if not prevented by actual force or incapacitated by illness or other sufficient cause, or where so prevented or incapacitated then within four days after the cessor of the hindrance caused by such force, illness or other cause, he declared to an officer of the Garda Síochána the fact of his having taken such oath, declaration, or engagement, and all the circumstances connected therewith and the names and descriptions of all persons concerned in the administering thereof so far as such circumstances, names, and descriptions were known to him.

PART III

UNLAWFUL ORGANISATION

18   Unlawful organisations

In order to regulate and control in the public interest the exercise of the constitutional right of citizens to form associations, it is hereby declared that any organisation which—

(a) engages in, promotes, encourages, or advocates the commission of treason or any activity of a treasonable nature, or

(b) advocates, encourages, or attempts the procuring by force, violence, or other unconstitutional means of an alteration of the Constitution, or

(c) raises or maintains or attempts to raise or maintain a military or armed force in contravention of the Constitution or without constitutional authority, or.

(d) engages in, promotes, encourages, or advocates the commission of any criminal offence or the obstruction of or interference with the administration of justice or the enforcement of the law, or

(e) engages in, promotes, encourages, or advocates the attainment of any particular object, lawful or unlawful, by violent, criminal, or other unlawful means, or

(f) promotes, encourages, or advocates the non-payment of moneys payable to the Central Fund or any other public fund or the non-payment of local taxation,

shall be an unlawful organisation within the meaning and for the purposes of this Act, and this Act shall apply and have effect in relation to such organisation accordingly.

19   Suppression orders

(1) If and whenever the Government are of opinion that any particular organisation is an unlawful organisation, it shall be lawful for the Government by order (in this Act referred to as a suppression order) to declare that such organisation is an unlawful organisation and ought, in the public interest, to be suppressed.

(2) The Government may by order, whenever they so think proper, amend or revoke a suppression order.

(3) Every suppression order shall be published in the Iris Oifigiúil as soon as conveniently may be after the making thereof

(4) A suppression order shall be conclusive evidence for an purposes other than an application for a declaration of legality that the organisation to which it relates is an unlawful organisation within the meaning of this Act.

20   Declaration of legality

(1) Any person (in this section referred to as the applicant) who claims to be a member of an organisation in respect of which a suppression order has been made may, at any time within thirty days after the publication of such order in the Iris Oifigiúil, apply to the High Court in a summary manner on notice to the Attorney-General for a declaration (in this Act referred to as a declaration of legality) that such organisation is not an unlawful organisation.

(2) Where, on an application under the foregoing sub-section of this section, the High Court, after hearing such evidence as may be adduced by the applicant or by the Attorney-General, is satisfied that the organisation to which such application relates is not an unlawful

organisation, it shall be lawful for the High Court to make a declaration of legality in respect of such organisation.

(3) The High Court shall not make a declaration of legality unless the applicant for such declaration either—

(a) gives evidence in support of the application and submits himself to cross-examination by counsel for the Attorney-General, or

(b) satisfies the High Court that he is unable by reason of illness or other sufficient cause to give such evidence and adduces in support of the application the evidence of at least one person who submits himself to cross-examination by counsel for the Attorney-General.

(4) Whenever, on an application under this section, the High Court, or the Supreme Court on appeal from the High Court, makes a declaration of legality in respect of an organisation, the suppression order relating to such organisation shall forthwith become null and void, but without prejudice to the validity of anything previously done thereunder.

(5) Where the High Court makes a declaration of legality, it shall be lawful for that court, on the application of the Attorney-General, to suspend the operation of the next preceding sub-section of this section in respect of such declaration until the final determination of an appeal by the Attorney-General to the Supreme Court against such declaration, and if the High Court so suspends the said sub-section, the said sub-section shall only come into operation in respect of such declaration if and when the Supreme Court affirms the order of the High Court making such declaration.

(6) Whenever an application for a declaration of legality is made under this section and is refused by the High Court, or by the Supreme Court on appeal from the High Court, it shall not be lawful, in any prosecution of the applicant for the offence of being a member of the organisation to which such application relates, to give in evidence against the applicant any of the following matters, that is to say:—

(a) the fact that he made the said application, or

(b) any admission made by him or on his behalf for the purposes of or during the hearing of the said application, or

(c) any statement made in the oral evidence given by him or on his behalf (whether on examination in chief, cross examination, or re-examination) at the hearing of the said application, or

(d) any affidavit made by him or on his behalf for the purposes of the said application.

21   Prohibition of membership of an unlawful organisation

(1) It shall not be lawful for any person to be a member of an unlawful organisation.

(2) Every person who is a member of an unlawful organisation in contravention of this section shall be guilty of an offence under this section and shall—

(a) on summary conviction thereof, be liable to a fine not exceeding [€3,000][1] or, at the discretion of the court, to imprisonment for a term not exceeding [12 months][2] or to both such fine and such imprisonment, or

(b) on conviction thereof on indictment, be liable to [a fine or imprisonment for a term not exceeding 8 years or both][3].

(3) It shall be a good defence for a person charged with the offence under this section of being a member of an unlawful organisation, to show—

(a)   that he did not know that such organisation was an unlawful organisation, or

(b)   that, as soon as reasonably possible after he became aware of the real nature of such organisation or after the making of a suppression order in relation to such organisation, he ceased to be a member thereof and dissociated himself therefrom.

(4) Where an application has been made to the High Court for a declaration of legality in respect of an organisation no person who is, before the final determination of such application, charged with an offence under this section in relation to that organisation shall be brought to trial on such charge before such final determination, but a postponement of the said trial in pursuance of this sub-section shall not prevent the detention of such person in custody during the period of such postponement.

Amendments

1   "€3,000" substituted for "fifty pounds" by Criminal Justice (Terrorist Offences) Act 2005, s 48(a)(i).

2   "12 months" substituted for "three months" by Criminal Justice (Terrorist Offences) Act 2005, s 48(a)(ii).

3   Words "a fine or imprisonment for a term not exceeding 8 years or both" substituted for "imprisonment for a term not exceeding 7 years" by Criminal Justice (Terrorist Offences) Act 2005, s 48(b) – "7 years" having been substituted for "two years" by Criminal Law Act 1976, s 2(6).

[21A   Offence of providing assistance to an unlawful organisation

(1) A person who knowingly renders assistance (including financial assistance) to an unlawful organisation, whether directly or indirectly, in the performance or furtherance of an unlawful object is guilty of an offence.

(2) A person guilty of an offence under this section is liable—

(a)   on summary conviction, to a fine not exceeding €3,000 or imprisonment for a term not exceeding 12 months or both, or

(b)   on conviction on indictment, to a fine or imprisonment for a term not exceeding 8 years or both.][1]

Amendments

1   Section 21A inserted by Criminal Justice (Terrorist Offences) Act 2005, s 49.

22   Provisions consequent upon the making of a suppression order

Immediately upon the making of a suppression order, the following provisions shall have effect in respect of the organisation to which such order relates, that is to say:—

(a)   [all the property (including money and all other property, real or personal, heritable or moveable, including choses in action and other intangible or incorporeal property, including funds as defined in section 12 of the Criminal Justice (Terrorist Offences) Act 2005 of such organisation][1] shall become and be forfeited to and vested in the Minister for Justice;

(b) the said Minister shall take possession of all lands and premises which become forfeited to him under his section and the said Minister may cause all such things to be done by members of the Garda Síochána as appear to him to be necessary or expedient for the purpose of such taking possession;

(c) subject to the subsequent provisions of this section, it shall be lawful for the said Minister to sell or let, on such terms as he shall, with the sanction of the Minister for Finance, think proper, any lands or premises which become forfeited to him under this section or to use any such lands or premises for such government purposes as he shall, with the sanction aforesaid, think proper;

(d) the Minister for Justice shall take possession of, recover, and get in all personal property which becomes forfeited to him under this section and may take such legal proceedings and other steps as shall appear to him to be necessary or expedient for that purpose;

(e) subject to the subsequent provisions of this section, it shall be lawful for the said Minister to sell or otherwise realise, in such manner and upon such terms as he shall, with the sanction of the Minister for Finance, think proper, all personal property which becomes forfeited to him under this section;

(f) the Minister for Justice shall pay into or dispose of for the benefit of the Exchequer, in accordance with the directions of the Minister for Finance, all money which becomes forfeited to him under this section and the net proceeds of every sale, letting, realisation, or other disposal of any other property which becomes so forfeited;

(g) no property which becomes forfeited to the Minister for Justice under this section shall be sold, let, realised, or otherwise disposed of by him until the happening of whichever of the following events is applicable, that is to say:—

　(i) if no application is made under this Act for a declaration of legality in respect of the said organisation within the time limited by this Act for the making of such application, the expiration of the time so limited,

　(ii) if any such application is so made, the final determination of such application.

Amendments

1　Words "all the property (including money and all other property, real or personal, heritable or moveable, including choses in action and other intangible or incorporeal property, including funds as defined in section 12 of the Criminal Justice (Terrorist Offences) Act 2005 of such organisation" substituted for "all the property (whether real, chattel real, or personal and whether in possession or in action) of such organisation" by Criminal Justice (Terrorist Offences) Act 2005, s 50.

[22A   Definitions for, and operation of, sections 22B to 22I

(1) For the purposes of sections 22B to 22I—

"disposal order" means an order under section 22C;

"interim order" means an order made under section 22B;

"Minister" means Minister for Justice, Equality and Law Reform;

"property" does not include moneys held in a bank;

"respondent" means—

(a)   a person in respect of whom an application for an interim order has been made, or

(b)   a person in respect of whom an interim order has been made,

and includes a person who, but for this Act, would become entitled on the death of a person referred to in paragraph (*a*) or (*b*) to any property to which such an order relates (being an order that is in force and is in respect of that person).

(2) Sections 22B to 22I shall not be construed to limit the generality of section 22.]¹

Amendments

1   Section 22A inserted by Criminal Justice (Terrorist Offences) Act 2005, s 51.

[22B   Interim order respecting specified property

(1) The Minister may apply ex parte to the High Court for an interim order under subsection (2) in respect of specified property where the Minister is of the opinion that it—

(a)   is the property of an unlawful organisation, whether or not the property is in the possession or control of that organisation, and

(b)   is forfeited to and vested in the Minister by virtue of section 22.

(2) On application under subsection (1), the Court may issue an interim order prohibiting any of the following from disposing of or otherwise dealing with the property specified in the order or from diminishing its value:

(a)   any person in possession or control of the property;

(b)   any person having notice of the order;

(c   any other person specified in the order.

(3) An interim order—

(a)   may contain such provisions, conditions and restrictions as the Court considers necessary or expedient, and

(b)   shall provide for notice of the order to be given to—

(i)   any person named in the order, and

(ii)   any other person who is or appears to be affected by it, unless the Court is satisfied that it is not reasonably possible to ascertain the person's whereabouts.

(4) On application by the respondent or any other person claiming ownership of any property specified in an interim order that is in force under this section, the Court may discharge or

vary the order, as it considers appropriate, if it is shown to the Court's satisfaction that the property is not the property of an unlawful organisation.

(5) On application at any time by the Minister, the Court shall discharge an interim order.

(6) Subject to subsections (4) and (5), an interim order continues in force until the expiry of 12 months from the date of its making and then lapses, unless an application for a disposal order in respect of any property specified in the interim order is brought during that period.

(7) If an application for a disposal order is brought within the period allowed under subsection (6), the interim order lapses on—

(a) the determination of the application,

(b) the expiry of the ordinary time for bringing an appeal against the determination, or

(c) if such appeal is brought, the determination or abandonment of the appeal or any further appeal or the expiry of the time for bringing any further appeal,

whichever is the latest.

(8) Notice of an application under subsection (4) shall be given by the respondent or other person making the application to—

(a) the Minister, and

(b) any person to whom the Court directs that notice of the application be given.

(9) Notice of an application under subsection (5) shall be given by the Minister to—

(a) the respondent, unless the Court is satisfied that it is not reasonably possible to ascertain the respondent's whereabouts, and

(b) any person to whom the Court directs that notice of the application be given.]¹

Amendments

1   Section 22B inserted by Criminal Justice (Terrorist Offences) Act 2005, s 51.

[22C   Disposal order respecting specified property

(1) Subject to subsection (2), where an interim order has been in force for not less than 12 months in relation to specified property, the High Court may, on application by the Minister, make an order authorising the Minister to dispose of the property as he sees fit.

(2) Subject to subsection (4), the Court shall make a disposal order in relation to any property that is the subject of an application under subsection (1) unless it is satisfied that the property is not the property of an unlawful organisation.

(3) The Minister shall give notice of an application under this section to—

(*a*) the respondent unless the Court is satisfied that it is not reasonably possible to ascertain the respondent's whereabouts, and

(*b*) such other (if any) persons as the Court may direct.

(4) Before deciding whether to make a disposal order under subsection (1), the Court shall give any person claiming ownership of the specified property an opportunity to be heard by the Court and to show cause why the order should not be made.

(5) On application by the respondent or, if the respondent's whereabouts cannot be ascertained, on the Court's own initiative, the Court may, if it considers it appropriate to do so

in the interests of justice, adjourn the hearing of an application under subsection (1) for such period not exceeding 2 years as it considers reasonable.]¹

Amendments

1   Section 22C inserted by Criminal Justice (Terrorist Offences) Act 2005, s 51.

[22D   Ancillary orders and provision in relation to certain profits or gains, etc.

(1) At any time while an interim order is in force, the High Court may, on application by the Minister, make such orders as it considers necessary or expedient to enable the interim order to have full effect.

(2) The Minister shall give notice of an application under this section to—

    (a)   the respondent unless the Court is satisfied that it is not reasonably possible to ascertain the respondent's whereabouts, and

    (b)   such other (if any) persons as the Court may direct.

(3) An interim order or disposal order may be expressed to apply to—

    (a)   any profit, gain or interest,

    (b)   any dividend or other payment, or

    (c)   any other property,

payable or arising, after the making of the order, in connection with any other property to which the order relates.]¹

Amendments

1   Section 22D inserted by Criminal Justice (Terrorist Offences) Act 2005, s 51.

[22E   Evidence

(1) Production in court in any proceedings of a document signed by the Minister and stating that the property specified in the document would, but for the operation of section 22, have been the property of an unlawful organisation is evidence that the specified property would, but for the operation of that section, have been the property of an unlawful organisation, unless the contrary is shown.

(2) A document purporting to be a document of the Minister under subsection (1) and to be signed by the Minister shall be deemed for the purposes of this section to be such a document and to have been so signed, unless the contrary is shown.]¹

Amendments

1   Section 22E inserted by Criminal Justice (Terrorist Offences) Act 2005, s 51.

[22F   Seizure of certain property

(1) Where an interim order or a disposal order is in force, a member of the Garda Síochána or an officer of customs and excise may seize any property that is the subject of the order for the purpose of preventing the property being removed from the State.

(2) Property seized under this section shall be dealt with in accordance with the directions of the High Court.]¹

Amendments

1   Section 22F inserted by Criminal Justice (Terrorist Offences) Act 2005, s 51.

[22G   Compensation

(1) An application to the High Court for an order under this section may be made where—

    (a)   an interim order is discharged or lapses and a disposal order in relation to the matter is not made or, if made, is discharged, or

    (b)   an interim order or a disposal order is varied on appeal.

(2) On application under subsection (1) by a person who satisfies the Court that the person is the owner of any property to which—

    (a)   an interim order referred to in subsection (1)(a) related,

    (b)   an order referred to in subsection (1)(*b*) had related, but, by reason of its being varied by a court, has ceased to relate,

the Court may award the person such (if any) compensation payable by the Minister as it considers just in the circumstances in respect of any loss incurred by the person by reason of the order concerned.

(3) The Minister shall be given notice of, and be entitled to be heard in, any proceedings under this section.]¹

Amendments

1   Section 22G inserted by Criminal Justice (Terrorist Offences) Act 2005, s 51.

[22H   Application of certain provisions of Act of 1996

For the purposes of this Part, sections 6, 7 and 9 to 13 of the Act of 1996 apply with the following modifications and any other necessary modifications as if an interim order or a disposal order made under this Part, or an application for such order, had been made under the Act of 1996:

    (a)   a reference in any of the applicable provisions of the Act of 1996 to applicant or Minister shall be construed as referring to the Minister for Justice, Equality and Law Reform;

(b) a reference in any of the applicable provisions of the Act of 1996 to respondent shall be construed as defined in section 22A of this Act.]¹

Amendments

1   Section 22H inserted by Criminal Justice (Terrorist Offences) Act 2005, s 51.

[22I   Immunity from proceedings

No action or proceeding of any kind lies against a person in any court in respect of any act done or omission made in compliance with an order under any of sections 22B to 22D and 22H.]¹

Amendments

1   Section 22I inserted by Criminal Justice (Terrorist Offences) Act 2005, s 51.

23   Provisions consequent upon the making of a declaration of legality

(1) Whenever a declaration of legality is made, the following provisions shall have effect, that is to say:—

(a) every person who is detained in custody charged with the offence of being a member of the organisation to which such declaration of legality relates shall forthwith be released from such custody;

(b) all the property of the said organisation which became forfeited to the Minister for Justice by virtue of this Act on the making of the suppression order in respect of the said organisation shall become and be the property of the said organisation and shall be delivered to the said organisation by the said Minister on demand.

(2) Where the High Court makes a declaration of legality, it shall be lawful for that court, on the application of the Attorney-General, to suspend the operation of the foregoing sub-section of this section in respect of such declaration until the final determination of an appeal by the Attorney-General to the Supreme Court against such declaration, and if the High Court so suspends the said sub-section, the said sub-section shall only come into operation in respect of such declaration if and when the Supreme Court affirms the order of the High Court making such declaration.

24   Proof of membership of an unlawful organisation by possession of incriminating document

On the trial of a person charged with the offence of being a member of an unlawful organisation, Proof to the satisfaction of the court that an incriminating document relating to the said organisation was found on such person or in his possession or on lands or in premises owned or occupied by him or under his control shall, without more, be evidence until the contrary is proved that such person was a member of the said organisation at the time alleged in the said charge.

25   Closing of buildings

(1) Whenever an officer of the Garda Síochána not below the rank of chief superintendent is satisfied that a building is being used or has been used in any way for the purposes, direct or indirect, of an unlawful organisation, such officer may make an order (in this section referred to as a closing order) that such building be closed for the period of [12 months][1] from the date of such order.

(2) Whenever a closing order has been made an officer of the Garda Síochána not below the rank of chief superintendent may—

(a) extend the operation of such closing order for a farther period not exceeding [12 months][1] from the expiration of the period mentioned in such closing order;

(b) terminate the operation of such closing order.

(3) Whenever a closing order has been made or has been extended, any person having an estate or interest in the building to which such closing order relates may apply to the High Court, in a summary manner on notice to the Attorney-General, for such order as is hereinafter mentioned, and on such application the High Court, if it is satisfied that, having regard to all the circumstances of the case, the making or the extension (as the case may be) of such closing order was not reasonable, may make an order quashing such closing order or the said extension thereof, as the case may be.

(4) Whenever and so long as a closing order is in operation, the following provisions shall have effect, that is to say:—

(a) it shall not be lawful for any person to use or occupy the building to which such closing order relates or any part of such building;

(b) any member of the Garda Síochána not below the rank of inspector may take all such steps as he shall consider necessary or expedient to prevent such building or any part thereof being used or occupied in contravention of this sub-section;

(c) every person who uses or ʻoccupies such building or any part of such building in contravention of this sub-section shall be guilty of an offence under this section and shall be liable on summary conviction thereof to imprisonment for a term not exceeding three months.

(5) In this section the word "building" includes a part of a building and also all outhouses, yards, and gardens within the curtilage of the building.

[(6) Whenever a closing order has been extended, a member of the Garda Síochána not below the rank of chief superintendent may extend the operation of such closing order for a further period or periods each of which shall not exceed 12 months, but a closing order shall not be in operation for more than three years.][2]

Amendments

1   "12 months" substituted for "three months" by Criminal Law Act 1976, s 4(a).

2   Subsection (6) inserted by Criminal Law Act 1976, s 4(b).

PART IV

MISCELLANEOUS

26   Evidence of publication of treasonable, seditious or incriminating document

(1) Where in any criminal proceedings the question whether a particular treasonable document, seditious document, or incriminating document was or was not published by the accused (whether by himself or in concert with other persons or by arrangement between himself and other persons) is in issue and an officer of the Garda Síochána not below the rank of chief superintendent states on oath that he believes that such document was published (as the case may be) by the accused or by the accused in concert with other persons or by arrangement between the accused and other persons, such statement shall be evidence (until the accused denies on oath that he published such document either himself or in concert or by arrangement as aforesaid) that the accused published such document as alleged in the said statement on oath of such officer.

27   Prohibition of certain public meetings

(1) It shall not be lawful to hold a public meeting which is held or purports to be held by or on behalf of or by arrangement or in concert with an unlawful organisation or which is held or purports to be held for the purpose of supporting, aiding, abetting, or encouraging an unlawful organisation or of advocating the support of an unlawful organisation.

(2) Whenever an officer of the Garda Síochána not below the rank of chief superintendent is of opinion that the holding of a particular public meeting about to be or proposed to be held would be a contravention of the next preceding sub-section of this section, it shall be lawful for such officer by notice given to a person concerned in the holding or organisation of such meeting or published in a manner reasonably calculated to come to the knowledge of the persons so concerned, to prohibit the holding of such meeting, and thereupon the holding of such meeting shall become and be unlawful.

(3) Whenever an officer of the Garda, Síochána gives any such notice as is mentioned in the next preceding sub-section of this section, any person claiming to be aggrieved by such notice may apply to the High Court in a summary manner on notice to the Attorney General for such order as is hereinafter mentioned and, upon the hearing of such application, the High Court if it so thinks proper, may make an order annulling such notice.

(4) Every person who organises or holds or attempts to organise or hold a public meeting the holding of which is a contravention of this section or who takes part or is concerned in the organising or the holding of any such meeting shall be guilty of an offence under this section and shall be liable on summary conviction thereof to a fine not exceeding [£500][1] or, at the discretion of the court, to imprisonment for a term not exceeding [12 months][2] or to both such fine and such imprisonment.

(5) In this section the expression "public meeting" includes a procession and also includes (in addition to a meeting held in a public place or on unenclosed land) a meeting held in a building or on enclosed land to which the public are admitted, whether with or without payment.

Amendments

1   "£500" substituted for "fifty pounds" by Criminal Law Act 1976, s 2(7).

2   "12 months" substituted for "three months" by Criminal Law Act 1976, s 2(7).

28   Prohibition of meetings in the vicinity of the Oireachtas

(1) It shall not be lawful for any public meeting to be held in, or any procession to pass along or through, any public street or unenclosed place which or any part of which is situate within one-half of a mile from any building in which both Houses or either House of the Oireachtas are or is sitting or about to sit if either—

(a)   an officer of the Garda Síochána not below the rank of chief superintendent has, by notice given to a person concerned in the holding or organisation of such meeting or procession or published in a manner reasonably calculated to come to the knowledge of the persons so concerned, prohibited the holding of such meeting in or the passing of such procession along or through any such public street or unenclosed place as aforesaid, or

(b)   a member of the Garda Síochána calls on the persons taking part in such meeting or procession to disperse.

(2) Every person who—

(a)   shall organise, hold, or take part in or attempt to organise, hold or take part in a public meeting or a procession in any such public street or unenclosed place as is mentioned in the foregoing sub-section of this section after such meeting or procession has been prohibited by a notice under paragraph (a) of the said sub-section,

(b)   shall hold or take part in or attempt to hold or take part in a public meeting or a procession in any such Public street or unenclosed place as aforesaid after a member of the Garda Síochána has, under paragraph (b) of the said sub-section, called upon the persons taking part in such meeting or procession to disperse, or

(c)   shall remain in or enter into any such public street or unenclosed space after being called upon to disperse as aforesaid,

shall be guilty of an offence under this section and shall be liable on summary conviction thereof to a fine not exceeding fifty pounds or, at the discretion of the court, to imprisonment for a term not exceeding three months or to both such fine and such imprisonment.

29   Search warrants in relation to the commission of offences under this Act or to treason

[(1) Where a member of the Garda Síochána not below the rank of superintendent is satisfied that there is reasonable ground for believing that evidence of or relating to the commission or intended commission of an offence under this Act or the Criminal Law Act, 1976, or an offence which is for the time being a scheduled offence for the purposes of Part V of this Act, or evidence relating to the commission or intended commission of treason, is to be found in any building or part of a building or in any vehicle, vessel, aircraft or hovercraft or in any other place whatsoever, he may issue to a member of the Garda Síochána not below the rank of sergeant a search warrant under this section in relation to such place.

(2) A search warrant under this section shall operate to authorise the member of the Garda Síochána named in the warrant, accompanied by any members of the Garda Síochána or the Defence Forces, to enter, within one week from the date of the warrant, and if necessary by the use of force, any building or part of a building or any vehicle, vessel, aircraft or hovercraft or any other place named in the warrant, and to search it and any person found there, and to seize anything found there or on such person.

(3) A member of the Garda Síochána or the Defence Forces acting under the authority of a search warrant under this section may—

(a) demand the name and address of any person found where the search takes place, and

(b) arrest without warrant any such person who fails or refuses to give his name and address when demanded, or gives a name or address which is false or misleading or which the member with reasonable cause suspects to be false or misleading.

(4) Any person who obstructs or attempts to obstruct any member of the Garda Síochána or the Defence Forces acting under the authority of a search warrant under this section or who fails or refuses to give his name and address when demanded, or gives a name or address which is false or misleading, shall be guilty of an offence and shall be liable—

(a) on summary conviction, to a fine not exceeding £500 or to imprisonment for a term not exceeding 12 months, or to both, or

(b) on conviction on indictment, to imprisonment for a term not exceeding 5 years.

(5) Any reference in subsection (1) of this section to an offence includes a reference to attempting or conspiring to commit the offence.][1]

Amendments

1   Section 29 substituted by Criminal Law Act 1976, s 5.

30   Arrest and detention of suspected persons

(1) A member of the Garda Síochána (if he is not in uniform on production of 'his identification card if demanded) may without warrant stop, search, interrogate, and arrest any person, or do any one or more of those things in respect of any person, whom he suspects of having committed or being about to commit or being or having been concerned in the commission of an offence under any section or sub-section of this Act or an offence which is for the time being a scheduled offence for the purposes of Part V of this Act or whom he suspects of carrying a document relating to the commission or intended commission of any such offence as aforesaid or whom he suspects of being in possession of information relating to the commission or intended commission of any such offence as aforesaid.

(2) Any member of the Garda Síochána (if he is not in uniform on production of his identification card if demanded) may, for the purpose of the exercise of any of the powers conferred by the next preceding sub-section of this section, stop and search (if necessary by

force) any vehicle or any ship, boat, or other vessel which he suspects to contain a person whom he is empowered by the said sub-section to arrest without warrant.

(3) Whenever a person is arrested under this section, he may be removed to and detained in custody in a Garda Síochána station, a prison, or some other convenient place for a period of twenty-four hours from the time of his arrest and may, if an officer of the Garda Síochána not below the rank of Chief Superintendent so directs, be so detained for a further period of twenty-four hours.

[(3A) If at any time during the detention of a person pursuant to this section a member of the Garda Síochána, with reasonable cause, suspects that person of having committed an offence (the 'other offence') referred to in subsection (1) of this section, being an offence other than the offence to which the detention relates, and—

(a) the member of the Garda Síochána then in charge of the Garda Síochána station, or

(b) in case the person is being detained in a place of detention, other than a Garda Síochána station, an officer of the Garda Síochána not below the rank of inspector who is not investigating the offence to which the detention relates or the other offence,

has reasonable grounds for believing that the continued detention of the person is necessary for the proper investigation of the other offence, the person may continue to be detained in relation to the other offence as if that offence was the offence for which the person was originally detained, but nothing in this subsection authorises the detention of the person for a period that is longer than the period which is authorised by or under the other provisions of this section.]¹

[(4) An officer of the Garda Síochána not below the rank of superintendent may apply to a judge of the District Court for a warrant authorising the detention of a person detained pursuant to a direction under subsection (3) of this section for a further period not exceeding 24 hours if he has reasonable grounds for believing that such further detention is necessary for the proper investigation of the offence concerned.

(4A) On an application under subsection (4) of this section the judge concerned shall issue a warrant authorising the detention of the person to whom the application relates for a further period not exceeding 24 hours if, but only if, the judge is satisfied that such further detention is necessary for the proper investigation of the offence concerned and that the investigation is being conducted diligently and expeditiously.

(4B) On an application under subsection (4) of this section the person to whom the application relates shall be produced before the judge concerned and the judge shall hear any submissions made and consider any evidence adduced by or on behalf of the person and the officer of the Garda Síochána making the application.]²

[(4BA)

(a) Without prejudice to paragraph (*b*) of this subsection, where a judge hearing an application under subsection (4) of this section is satisfied, in order to avoid a risk of prejudice to the investigation concerned, that it is desirable to do so, he may—

(i) direct that the application be heard otherwise than in public, or

(ii) exclude from the Court during the hearing all persons except officers of the Court, persons directly concerned in the proceedings, bona fide representatives of the Press and such other persons as the Court may permit to remain.

(b) On the hearing of an application under subsection (4) of this section, the judge may, of his own motion or on application by the officer of the Garda Síochána making the application under that subsection (4), where it appears that—

    (i) particular evidence to be given by any member of the Garda Síochána during the hearing (including evidence by way of answer to a question asked of the member in cross-examination) concerns steps that have been, or may be, taken in the course of any inquiry or investigation being conducted by the Garda Síochána with respect to the suspected involvement of the person to whom the application relates, or any other person, in the commission of the offence to which the detention relates or any other offence, and

    (ii) the nature of those steps is such that the giving of that evidence concerning them could prejudice, in a material respect, the proper conducting of any foregoing inquiry or investigation,

direct that, in the public interest, the particular evidence shall be given in the absence of every person, including the person to whom the application relates and any legal representative (whether of that person or the applicant), other than—

    (I) the member or members whose attendance is necessary for the purpose of giving the evidence to the judge; and

    (II) if the judge deems it appropriate, such one or more of the clerks of the Court as the judge determines.

(c) If, having heard such evidence given in that manner, the judge considers the disclosure of the matters to which that evidence relates would not have the effect referred to in paragraph (b)(ii) of this subsection, the judge shall direct the evidence to be re-given in the presence of all the other persons (or, as the case may be, those of them not otherwise excluded from the Court under paragraph (a) of this subsection).

(d) No person shall publish or broadcast or cause to be published or broadcast any information about an application under subsection (4) of this section other than a statement of—

    (i) the fact that the application has been made by the Garda Síochána in relation to a particular investigation, and

    (ii) any decision resulting from the application.

(e) If any matter is published or broadcast in contravention of paragraph (d) of this subsection, the following persons, namely—

    (i) in the case of a publication in a newspaper or periodical, any proprietor, any editor and any publisher of the newspaper or periodical,

    (ii) in the case of any other publication, the person who publishes it, and

    (iii) in the case of a broadcast, any person who transmits or provides the programme in which the broadcast is made and any person having functions in relation to the programme corresponding to those of the editor of a newspaper,

shall be guilty of an offence and shall be liable—

    (I) on summary conviction to a fine not exceeding €5,000 or to imprisonment for a term not exceeding 12 months or to both, or

(II) on conviction on indictment, to a fine not exceeding €50,000 or to imprisonment for a term not exceeding 3 years or to both.

(f) In this subsection—

"broadcast" means the transmission, relaying or distribution by wireless telegraphy, cable or the internet of communications, sounds, signs, visual images or signals, intended for direct reception by the general public whether such communications, sounds, signs, visual images or signals are actually received or not;

"publish" means publish, other than by way of broadcast, to the public or a portion of the public.

(4BB) Save where any rule of law requires such an issue to be determined by the Court, in an application under subsection (4) of this section no issue as to the lawfulness of the arrest or detention of the person to whom the application relates may be raised.

(4BC)

(a) In an application under subsection (4) of this section it shall not be necessary for a member of the Garda Síochána, other than the officer making the application, to give oral evidence for the purposes of the application and the latter officer may testify in relation to any matter within the knowledge of another member of the Garda Síochána that is relevant to the application notwithstanding that it is not within the personal knowledge of the officer.

(b) However, the Court hearing such an application may, if it considers it to be in the interests of justice to do so, direct that another member of the Garda Síochána give oral evidence and the Court may adjourn the hearing of the application for the purpose of receiving such evidence.]³

[(4C) A person detained under this section may, at any time during such detention, be charged before the District Court or a Special Criminal Court with an offence or be released by direction of an officer of the Garda Síochána and shall, if not so charged or released, be released at the expiration of the period of detention authorised by or under subsection (3) of this section or, as the case may be, that subsection and subsection (4A) of this section.]⁴

[(4D) If—

(a) an application is to be made, or is made, under subsection (4) of this section for a warrant authorising the detention for a further period of a person detained pursuant to a direction under subsection (3) of this section, and

(b the period of detention under subsection (3) of this section has not expired at the time of the arrival of the person concerned at the court house for the purposes of the hearing of the application but would, but for this subsection, expire before, or during the hearing (including, if such should occur, any adjournment of the hearing),

it shall be deemed not to expire until the final determination of the application; and, for purposes of this subsection—

(i) a certificate signed by the court clerk in attendance at the court house concerned stating the time of the arrival of the person concerned at that court house shall be evidence, until the contrary is shown, of the time of that person's arrival there;

(ii) "court house" includes any venue at which the hearing of the application takes place.]⁵

(5) A member of the Garda Síochána may do all or any of the following things in respect of a person detained under this section, that is to say:—

    (a) demand of such person his name and address;

    (b) search such person or cause him to be searched;

    (c) photograph such person or cause him to be photographed;

    (d) take, or cause to be taken, the fingerprints of such person.

(6) Every person who shall obstruct or impede the exercise in respect of him by a member of the Garda Síochána of any of the powers conferred by the next preceding sub-section of this section or shall fail or refuse to give his name and address or shall give, in response to any such demand, a name or an address which is false or misleading shall be guilty of an offence under this section and shall be liable on summary conviction thereof to imprisonment for a term not exceeding six mouths.

Amendments

1   Subsection (3A) inserted by Criminal Justice (Amendment) Act 2009, s 21(1)(a).

2   Subsection (4) substituted and sub-ss (4A)–(4B) inserted by Offences Against the State (Amendment) Act 1998, s 10.

3   Subsections (4BA)–(4BC) inserted by Criminal Justice (Amendment) Act 2009, s 21(1)(b).

4   Subsection (4C) inserted by Offences Against the State (Amendment) Act 1998, s 10.

5   Subsection (4D) inserted by Criminal Justice Act 2006, s 187(a) and then substituted by Criminal Justice (Amendment) Act 2009, s 21(1)(c).

[30A   [(1) Where a person arrested on suspicion of having committed an offence is detained pursuant to section 30 of this Act and is released without any charge having been made against him, he shall not—

    (a) be arrested again in connection with the offence to which the detention related, or

    (b) be arrested for any other offence of which, at the time of the first arrest, the member of the Garda Síochána by whom he was arrested, suspected, or ought reasonably to have suspected, him of having committed,

except under the authority of a warrant issued by a judge of the District Court who is satisfied on information supplied on oath by a member of the Garda Síochána not below the rank of superintendent that either of the following cases apply, namely—

    (i) further information has come to the knowledge of the Garda Síochána since the person's release as to his suspected participation in the offence for which his arrest is sought,

    (ii) notwithstanding that the Garda Síochána had knowledge, prior to the person's release, of the person's suspected participation in the offence for which his arrest is sought, the questioning of the person in relation to that offence, prior to his release, would not have been in the interests of the proper investigation of the offence.

(1A) An application for a warrant under this section shall be heard otherwise than in public.]¹

(2) Section 30 of this Act, and, in particular, any powers conferred thereby, shall apply to or in respect of a person arrested in connection with an offence to which that section relates

under a warrant issued pursuant to subsection (1) of this section as it applies to or in respect of a person to whom that section applies, with the following and any other necessary modifications:

(a) the substitution of the following subsection for subsection (3):

' (3) Whenever a person is arrested under a warrant issued pursuant to section 30A(1) of this Act, he may be removed to and detained in custody in a Garda Síochána station, a prison or some other convenient place for a period of 24 hours from the time of his arrest.',

(b) the deletion of [subsections (4), (4A), [(4B), (4BA), (4BB), (4BC)]² and (4D)]³, and

(c) the addition of the following at the end of subsection (4C):

'or, in case the detention follows an arrest under a warrant issued pursuant to section 30A of this Act, by subsection (3) of this section as substituted by the said section 30A.'.

(3) Notwithstanding subsection (1) of this section, a person to whom that subsection relates may be arrested for any offence [for the purpose of charging him or her with that offence forthwith or bringing him or her before a Special Criminal Court as soon as practicable so that he or she may be charged with that offence before that Court]⁴.]⁵

Amendments

1 Subsection (1) substituted and sub-s (1A) inserted by Criminal Justice (Amendment) Act 2009, s 21(2).

2 "(4B), (4BA), (4BB), (4BC)" substituted for "(4B)" by Criminal Justice (Amendment) Act 2009, s 21(3).

3 "subsections (4), (4A), (4B) and (4D)" substituted for "subsections (4), (4A) and (4B)" by Criminal Justice Act 2006, s 187(b)(i).

4 "for the purpose of charging him or her with that offence forthwith or bringing him or her before a Special Criminal Court as soon as practicable so that he or she may be charged with that offence before that Court" substituted for "for the purpose of charging him with that offence forthwith" by Criminal Justice Act 2006, s 187(b)(ii).

5 Section 30A inserted by Offences Against the State (Amendment) Act 1998, s 11.

---

31   Offences by bodies corporate

Where an offence under any section or sub-section of this Act is committed by a body corporate and is proved to have been so committed with the consent or approval of or to have been facilitated by any neglect on the part of, any director, manager, secretary, or other officer of such body corporate, such director, manager, secretary, or other officer shall be deemed to be guilty of that offence and shall be liable to be proceeded against and punished accordingly, whether such body corporate has or has not been proceeded, against in respect of the said offence.

32   Re-capture of escaped prisoners

(1) Whenever any person detained under this Act shall have escaped from such detention, such person may be arrested without warrant by any member of the Garda Síochána and shall thereupon be returned in custody to the place from which he so escaped.

(2) Every person who shall aid or abet a person detained under this Act to escape from such detention or to avoid recapture after having so escaped shall be guilty of an offence under this section and shall be liable on summary conviction thereof to imprisonment for a term not exceeding three months.

33   Remission etc, in respect of convictions by a Special Criminal Court

(1) Except in capital cases, the Government may, at their absolute discretion, at any time remit in whole or in part or modify (by way of mitigation only) or defer any punishment imposed by a Special Criminal Court.

(2) Whenever the Government remits in whole or in part or defers a punishment imposed by a Special Criminal Court, the Government may attach to such remittal or deferment such conditions (if any) as they may think proper.

(3) Whenever the Government defers under the next preceding sub-section of this section the whole or any part of a sentence of imprisonment, the person on whom such sentence was imposed shall be bound to serve such deferred sentence, or part of a sentence, of imprisonment when the same comes into operation and may for that purpose be arrested without warrant.

34   Forfeiture and disqualifications on certain convictions by a Special Criminal Court

(1) Whenever a person who is convicted by a Special Criminal Court of an offence which is, at the time of such conviction, a scheduled offence for the purposes of Part V of this Act, holds at the time of such conviction an office or employment remunerated out of the Central Fund or moneys provided by the Oireachtas or moneys raised by local taxation, or in or under or as a paid member of a board or body established by or under statutory authority, such person shall immediately on such conviction forfeit such office, employment, place, or emolument and the same shall forthwith become and be vacant.

(2) Whenever a person who is convicted by a Special Criminal Court of an offence which is, at the time of such conviction, a scheduled offence for the purposes of Part V of this Act, is at the time of such conviction in receipt of a pension or superannuation allowance payable out of the Central Fund or moneys provided by the Oireachtas or moneys raised by local taxation, or the funds of a board or body established by or under statutory authority, such person shall immediately upon such conviction forfeit such pension or superannuation allowance and such pension or superannuation allowance shall forthwith cease to be payable.

(3) Every person who is convicted by a Special Criminal Court of an offence which is, at the time of such conviction, a scheduled offence for the purposes of Part V of this Act, shall be disqualified—

(a) for holding, within seven years after the date of such conviction, any office or employment remunerated out of the Central Fund or moneys provided by the Oireachtas or moneys raised by local taxation or in or under or as a paid member of a board or body established by or under statutory authority, and

(b) for being granted out of the Central Fund or any such moneys or the funds of any such board or body, at any time after the date of such conviction, any pension, superannuation allowance, or gratuity in respect wholly or partly of any service rendered or thing done by him before the date of such conviction, and

(c) for receiving at any time after such conviction any such pension, superannuation allowance, or gratuity as is mentioned in the next preceding paragraph of this section which was granted but not paid on or before the date of such conviction.

(4) Whenever a conviction which occasions by virtue of this section any forfeiture or disqualification is quashed or annulled or the convicted person is granted a free pardon such forfeiture or disqualification shall be annulled, in the case of a quashing or annulment, as from the date of the conviction and, in the case of a free pardon, as from the date of such pardon.

(5) The Government may, at their absolute discretion, remit, in whole or in part, any forfeiture or disqualification incurred under this section and restore or revive, in whole or in part, the subject of such forfeiture as from the date of such remission.

PART V
SPECIAL CRIMINAL COURTS

35   Commencement and cesser of this Part of this Act

(1) This Part of this Act shall not come into or be in force save as and when and for so long as is provided by the subsequent sub-sections of this section.

(2) If and whenever and so often as the Government is satisfied that the ordinary courts are inadequate to secure the effective administration of justice and the preservation of public peace and order and that it is therefore necessary that this Part of this Act should come into force, the Government may make and publish a proclamation declaring that the Government is satisfied as aforesaid and ordering that this Part of this Act shall come into force.

(3) Whenever the Government makes and publishes, under the next preceding sub-section of this section, such proclamation as is mentioned in that sub-section, this Part of this Act shall come into force forthwith.

(4) If at any time while this Part of this Act is in force the Government is satisfied that the ordinary courts are adequate to secure the effective administration of justice and the preservation of public peace and order, the Government shall make and publish a proclamation declaring that this Part of this Act shall cease to be in force, and thereupon this Part of this Act shall forthwith cease to be in force.

(5) It shall be lawful for Dáil Éireann, at any time while this Part of this Act is in force, to pass a resolution annulling the proclamation by virtue of which this Part of this Act is then in force, and thereupon such proclamation shall be annulled and this Part of this Act shall cease to be in force, but without prejudice to the validity of anything done under this Part of this Act after the making of such proclamation and before the passing of such resolution.

(6) A proclamation made by the Government under this section shall be published by publishing a copy thereof in the Iris Oifigiúil and may also be published in any other manner which the Government shall think proper.

36   Schedule offences

(1) Whenever while this Part of this Act is in force the Government is satisfied that the ordinary courts are inadequate to secure the effective administration of justice and the preservation of public peace and order in relation to offences of any particular class or kind or under any particular enactment, the Government may by order declare that offences of that particular class or kind or under that particular enactment shall be scheduled offences for the purposes of this Part of this Act.

(2) Whenever the Government has made under the foregoing sub-section of this section any such declaration as is authorised by that sub-section, every offence of the particular class or kind or under the particular enactment to which such declaration relates shall, until otherwise provided by an order under the next following sub-section of this section, be a scheduled offence for the purposes of this Part of this Act.

(3) Whenever the Government is satisfied that the effective administration of justice and the preservation of public peace and order in relation to offences of any particular class or kind or under any particular enactment which are for the time being scheduled offences for the purposes of this Part of this Act can be secured through the medium of the ordinary courts, the Government may by order declare that offences of that particular class or kind or under that particular enactment shall, upon the making of such order, cease to be scheduled offences for the purposes of this Part of this Act.

37   Attempting, etc, to commit a scheduled offence

In addition to the offences which are, by virtue of an order made under the next preceding section, for the time being scheduled offences for the purposes of this Part of this Act, each of the following acts, that is to say, attempting or conspiring or inciting to commit, or aiding or abetting the commission of, any such schedule offence shall itself be a scheduled offence for the said purposes.

38   Establishment of Special Criminal Courts

(1) As soon as may be after the coming into force of this Part of this Act, there shall be established for the purposes of this Part of this Act, a court which shall be styled and known and is in this Act referred to as a Special Criminal Court.

(2) The Government may, whenever they consider it necessary or desirable so to do, establish such additional number of courts for the purposes of this Part of this Act as they think fit, and each court so established shall also be styled and known and is in this Act referred to as a Special Criminal Court.

(3) Whenever two or more Special Criminal Courts are in existence under this Act, the Government may, if and so often as they so think fit, reduce the number of such Courts and for that purpose abolish such of those existing Courts as appear to the Government to be redundant.

[(4) For the purposes of this Act, a Special Criminal Court is in existence if it has been established under this section and has at the relevant time not fewer than 3 members appointed under section 39.][1]

Amendments

1   Subsection (4) inserted by Criminal Justice (Terrorist Offences) Act 2005, s 52.

39   Constitution of Special Criminal Courts

(1) Every Special Criminal Court established under this Part of this Act shall consist of such uneven number (not being less than three) of members as the Government shall, from time to time determine, and different numbers of members may be so fixed in respect of different Special Criminal Courts.

(2) Each member of a Special Criminal Court shall be appointed, and be removable at will, by the Government.

(3) No person shall be appointed to be a member of a Special Criminal Court unless he is a judge of the High Court or the Circuit Court, or a justice of the District Court, or a barrister of not less than seven years standing, or a solicitor of not less than seven years standing, or an officer of the Defence Forces not below the rank of commandant.

(4) The Minister for Finance may pay to every member of a Special Criminal Court such (if any) remuneration and allowances as the said Minister may think proper, and different rates of remuneration and allowances may be so paid to different members of any such Court, or to the members of different such Courts.

(5) The Government may appoint such registrars for the purposes of any Special Criminal Court as they think proper, and every such registrar shall hold his office on such terms and conditions and shall receive such (if any) remuneration as the Minister for Finance shall from time to time direct.

40   Verdicts of Special Criminal Courts

(1) The determination of every question before a Special Criminal Court shall be according to the opinion of the majority of the members of such Special Criminal Court present at and taking part in such determination, but no member or officer of such Court shall disclose whether any such determination was or was not unanimous or, where such determination was not unanimous, the opinion of any individual member of such Court.

(2) Every decision of a Special Criminal Court shall be pronounced by such one member of the Court as the Court shall determine, and no other member of the Court shall pronounce or indicate his concurrence in or dissent from such decision.

41   Procedure of Special Criminal Courts

(1) Every Special Criminal Court shall have power, in its absolute discretion, to appoint the times and places of its sittings, and shall have control of its own procedure in all respects and, shall for that purpose make, with the concurrence of the Minister for Justice, rules regulating its practice and procedure and may in particular provide by such rules for the issuing of summonses, the procedure for bringing (in custody or on bail) persons before it for trial, the admission or exclusion of the public to or from its sittings, the enforcing of the attendance of witnesses, and the production of documents.

(2) A Special Criminal Court sitting for the purpose of the trial of a person, the making of any order, or the exercise of any other jurisdiction or function shall consist of an uneven number (not less than three) of members of such Court present at and taking part in such sitting.

(3) Subject and without prejudice to the provisions of the next preceding sub-section of this section, a Special Criminal Court may exercise any power, jurisdiction, or function notwithstanding one or more vacancies in the membership of such court.

(4) Subject to the provisions of this Act, the practice and procedure applicable to the trial of a person on indictment in the Central Criminal Court shall, so far as practicable, apply to the trial of a person by a Special Criminal Court, and the rules of evidence applicable upon such trial in the Central Criminal Court shall apply to every trial by a Special Criminal Court.

42   Authentication of orders of Special Criminal Courts

(1) Every order or other act of a Special Criminal Court shall be authenticated by the signature of a registrar of that Court.

(2) Every document which purports to be an order or other act of a Special Criminal Court and to be authenticated by the signature of a registrar of that Court shall be received in evidence in all Courts and be deemed to be an order or other act (as the case may require) of such Special Criminal Court without proof of the signature by which such order or act purports to be authenticated or that the person whose signature such signature purports to be was a registrar of the said Special Criminal Court.

43   Jurisdiction of Special Criminal Courts

(1) A Special Criminal Court shall have jurisdiction to try and to convict or acquit any person lawfully brought before that Court for trial under this Act, and shall also have the following ancillary jurisdictions, that is to say:—

  (a) jurisdiction to sentence every person convicted by that Court of any offence to suffer the punishment provided by law in, respect of such offence;

  (b) jurisdiction, in lieu of or in addition to making any other order in respect of a person, to require such person to enter into a recognisance before such Special Criminal Court or before a justice of the District Court, in such amount and with or without sureties as such Special Criminal Court shall direct, to keep the peace and be of good behaviour for such period as that Court shall specify;

  (c) jurisdiction to order the detention of and to detain in civil or military custody, or to admit to bail in such amount and with or without sureties as that Court shall direct, pending trial by that Court and during and after such trial until conviction or acquittal, any person sent, sent forward, transferred, or otherwise brought for trial by that Court;

  (d) power to administer oaths to witnesses;

  (e) jurisdiction and power to punish, in the same manner and in the like cases as the High Court, all persons whom such Special Criminal Court finds guilty of contempt of that Court or any member thereof, whether such contempt is or is not committed in the presence of that Court;

  (f) power, in relation to recognisances and bail bonds entered into before such Special Criminal Court, to estreat such recognisances and bail bonds in the like manner and in the like cases as the District Court estreats recognisances and bail bonds entered into before it.

(2) The provisions of this Part of this Act in relation to the carrying out of sentences of imprisonment pronounced by Special Criminal Courts and the regulations made under those provisions shall apply and have effect in relation to the carrying out of orders made by Special Criminal Courts under the foregoing sub-section of this section for the detention of persons in custody, whether civil or military.

44   Appeal to Court of Criminal Appeal

[(1) A person convicted by a Special Criminal Court of any offence or sentenced by a Special Criminal Court to suffer any punishment may appeal to the Court of Criminal Appeal from such conviction or sentence.]¹

(2) Sections 28 to 30 and sections 32 to 35 of the Courts of Justice Act, 1924 (No. 10 of 1924), and sections 5, 6, and 7 of the Courts of Justice Act, 1928 (No. 15 of 1928), shall apply and have effect in relation to appeals under this section in like manner as they apply and have effect in relation to appeals under section 31 of the Courts of Justice Act, 1924.

Amendments

1   Subsection (1) substituted by Criminal Procedure Act 2010, s 32.

---

45   Proceedings in the District Court in relation to scheduled offences

(1) Whenever a person is brought before a justice of the District Court charged with a scheduled offence which such justice has jurisdiction to dispose of summarily, such justice shall, if the Attorney-General so requests; send such person (in custody or on bail) for trial by a Special Criminal Court on such charge.

(2) Whenever a person is brought before a justice of the District Court charged with a scheduled offence which is an indictable offence and such justice [...]¹ sends such person forward for trial on such charge, such justice shall (unless the Attorney-General otherwise directs) send such person forward in custody or, with the consent of the Attorney-General, at liberty on bail for trial by a Special Criminal Court on such charge.

(3) Where under this section a person is sent or sent forward in custody for trial by a Special Criminal Court, it shall be lawful for the High Court, on the application of such person, to allow him to be at liberty on such bail (with or without sureties) as the High Court shall fix for his due attendance before the proper Special Criminal Court for trial on the charge on which he was so sent forward.

Amendments

1   Words deleted by Criminal Justice Act 1999, s 11.

---

46   Proceedings in the District Court in relation to non-scheduled offences

(1) Whenever a person is brought before a justice of the District Court charged with an offence which is not a scheduled offence and which such justice has jurisdiction to dispose of summarily, such justice shall, if the Attorney-General so requests and certifies in writing that the ordinary courts are in his opinion inadequate to secure the effective administration of justice and the preservation of public peace and order in relation to the trial of such person on such charge, send such person (in custody or on bail) for trial by a Special Criminal Court on such charge.

(2) Whenever a person is brought before a justice of the District Court charged with an indictable offence which is not a scheduled offence and such justice [...][1] sends such person forward for trial on such charge, such justice shall, if an application in this behalf is made to him by or on behalf of the Attorney-General grounded on the certificate of the Attorney-General that the ordinary Courts are, in his opinion inadequate to secure the effective administration of justice and the preservation of public peace and order in relation to the trial of such person on such charge, send such person forward in custody or, with the consent of the Attorney-General, at liberty on bail for trial by a Special Criminal Court on such charge.

(3) Where under this section a person is sent or sent forward in custody for trial by a Special Criminal Court, it shall be lawful for the High Court, on the application of such person, to allow him to be at liberty on such bail (with or without sureties) as the High Court shall fix for his due attendance before the proper Special Criminal Court for trial on the charge on which he was so sent forward.

Amendments

1   Words deleted by Criminal Justice Act 1999, s 11.

47   Charge before Special Criminal Court in lieu of District Court

(1) Whenever it is intended to charge a person with a scheduled offence, the Attorney-General may, if he so thinks proper, direct that such person shall, in lieu of being, charged with such offence before a justice of the District Court, be brought before a Special Criminal Court and there charged with such offence and, upon such direction being so given, such person shall be brought before a Special Criminal Court and shall be charged before that Court with such offence and shall be tried by such Court on such charge.

(2) Whenever it is intended to charge a person with an offence which is not a scheduled offence and the Attorney-General certifies that the ordinary Courts are, in his opinion, inadequate to secure the effective administration of justice and the preservation of public peace and order in relation to the trial of such person on such charge, the foregoing sub-section of this section shall apply and have effect as if the offence with which such person is so intended to be charged were a scheduled offence.

(3) Whenever a person is required by this section to be brought before a Special Criminal Court and charged before that Court with such offence, it shall be lawful for such Special Criminal Court to issue a warrant for the arrest of such person and the bringing of him before

such Court and, upon the issue of such warrant, it shall be lawful for such person to be arrested thereunder and brought in custody before such Court.

48   Transfer of trials from ordinary Courts to a Special Criminal Court

Whenever a person charged with an offence has been sent forward by a justice of the District Court for trial by the Central Criminal Court or the Circuit Court on such charge, then and in every such case the following provisions shall have effect, that is to say:—

    (a) if the Attorney-General certifies that the ordinary Courts are, in his opinion, inadequate to secure the effective administration of justice and the preservation of public peace and order in relation to the trial of such person on such charge, the Attorney-General shall cause an application, grounded on his said certificate, to be made on his behalf to the High Court for the transfer of the trial of such person on such charge to a Special Criminal Court, and on the hearing of such application the High Court shall make the order applied for, and thereupon such person shall be deemed to have been sent forward to a Special Criminal Court for trial on such charge;

    (b) whenever the High Court has made, under the next preceding paragraph of this sub-section, such order as is mentioned in that Paragraph, the following provisions shall have effect, that is to say:—

        (i) a copy of such order shall be served on such person by a member of the Garda Síochána,

       (ii) a copy of such order shall be sent to the appropriate county registrar,

      (iii) such person shall be brought before a Special Criminal Court for trial at such time and place as that Court shall direct,

      (iv) if such person is in custody when such order is made, he may be detained in custody until brought before such Special Criminal Court for trial,

       (v) if such person is at liberty on bail when such order is made, such bail shall be deemed to be for his attendance before a Special Criminal Court for trial at such time and place as that Court shall direct and, if he fails so to attend before the said Court, he shall be deemed to have broken his bail and his bail bond shall be estreated accordingly.

49   Selection of the Special Criminal Court by which a person is to be tried

[(1)][1] Where a person is (in the case of an offence triable summarily) sent or (in the case of an indictable offence) sent forward by a justice of the District Court to a Special Criminal Court for trial or the trial of a person is transferred under this Act to a Special Criminal Court or a person is to be charged before and tried by a Special Criminal Court, such of the following, provisions as are applicable shall have effect, that is to say:—

    (a) where a person is so sent or sent forward, the justice shall not specify the particular Special Criminal Court to which he sends or sends forward such person for trial;

    (b) where the trial of a person is so transferred, the order effecting such transfer shall not specify the particular Special Criminal Court to which such trial is transferred;

    (c) if only one Special Criminal Court is in existence under this Act at the time of such sending or sending forward or such transfer (as the case may be), such sending, sending forward, or transfer shall be deemed to be to such one Special Criminal Court;

(d) if only one Special Criminal Court is in existence under this Act when such person is to be so charged and tried, such person shall be charged before and tried by that Special Criminal Court;

(e) if two or more Special Criminal Courts are in existence under this Act at the time of such sending or sending forward or such transfer or such charging (as the case may be), it shall be lawful for the Attorney General to cause an application to be made on his behalf to such Special Criminal Court as he shall think proper for an order that such person be tried by or charged before and tried by that Court and thereupon the said Court shall make the order so applied for;

(f) upon the making of the order mentioned in the next preceding paragraph of this section, whichever of the following provisions is applicable shall have effect, that is to say:—

    (i) such person shall be deemed to have been sent or sent forward for trial by the Special Criminal Court which made the said order and all persons concerned shall act accordingly, or

    (ii) the trial of such person shall be deemed to have been transferred to the said Special Criminal Court and all persons concerned shall act accordingly, or

    (iii) such person shall be charged before and tried by the said Special Criminal Court and all persons concerned shall act accordingly.

[(2) A trial that is to be heard before a Special Criminal Court may be transferred by the Court, on its own motion or on the application of a triable person or the Director of Public Prosecutions, to another Special Criminal Court, but only if the first Court decides that it would be in the interests of justice to do so.

(3) In deciding whether it is in the interests of justice to transfer a trial, the Special Criminal Court may consider any factors it thinks relevant, including—

(a) whether the transfer would be in the interests of the expeditious administration of justice, and

(b) whether the transfer would prejudice the triable person or persons or the prosecution.

(4) A trial may be transferred under this section notwithstanding that an order has been made under subsection (1)(e) in relation to the triable person or persons.

(5) Where 2 or more triable persons are to be tried jointly, the decision of the Special Criminal Court to transfer the trial applies in relation to all of them.

(6) Subsection (5) does not affect the right of a triable person to apply for a separate trial and, if the application is granted, then to apply for a transfer of that trial.

(7) The decision of a Special Criminal Court to transfer a trial is final and unappealable.

(8) In this section 'triable person' means a person sent or sent forward for trial to, or charged before or transferred under this Act to, a Special Criminal Court.][1]

Amendments

1   Section 49 renumbered as 49(1) and sub-ss (2)–(8) added by Criminal Justice (Terrorist Offences) Act 2005, s 53.

_₀ **Orders and sentences of Special Criminal Courts**

(1) Save as shall be otherwise provided by regulations made under this section, every order made or sentence pronounced by a Special Criminal Court shall be carried out by the authorities and officers by whom, and in the like manner as, a like order made or sentence pronounced by the Central Criminal Court is required by law to be carried out.

(2) Every order, conviction, and sentence made or pronounced by a Special Criminal Court shall have the like consequences in law as a like order, conviction, or sentence made or pronounced by the Central Criminal Court would have and, in particular, every order made and every sentence pronounced by a Special Criminal Court shall confer on the persons carrying out the same the like protections and immunities as are conferred by law on such persons when carrying out a like order made or a like sentence pronounced by the Central Criminal Court.

(3) The Minister for Justice may make regulations in relation to the carrying out of sentences of penal servitude or of imprisonment pronounced by Special Criminal Courts and the prisons and other places in which persons so sentenced shall be imprisoned and the maintenance and management of such places, and the said Minister may also, if he so thinks proper, make by writing under his hand such special provision as he shall think fit in relation to the carrying out of any such sentence in respect of any particular individual, including transferring to military custody any particular individual so sentenced.

(4) The Minister for Defence may make regulations in relation to the places and the manner generally in which persons transferred to military custody under the next preceding sub-section of this section shall be kept in such custody, and the said Minister may also, if he so thinks proper, make by writing under his hand such special provision as he shall think fit in respect of the custody of any particular such person.

51   **Standing mute of malice and refusal to plead etc**

Whenever a person brought before a Special Criminal Court for trial stands mute when called upon to plead to the charge made against him, that Court shall hear such evidence (if any) relevant to the issue as to whether such person stands mute of malice or by the visitation of God as may then and there be adduced before it, and

    (a)   if that Court is satisfied on such evidence that such person is mute by the visitation of God, all such consequences shall ensue as would have ensued if such person had been found to be so mute by a Judge sitting in the Central Criminal Court, and

    (b)   if that Court is not so satisfied or if no such evidence is adduced, that Court shall direct a plea of "not guilty" to be entered for that person.

(2) Whenever a person brought, before a Special Criminal Court for trial fails or refuses in any way, other than standing mute, to plead to the charge made against him when called upon to do so, that Court shall (without prejudice to its powers under the next following sub-section of this section) direct a plea of "not guilty" to be entered for such person.

(3) Whenever a person at any stage of his trial before a Special Criminal Court by any act or omission refuses to recognise the authority or jurisdiction of that Court, or does any act (other than lawfully objecting in due form of law to the jurisdiction of that Court to try him) which, in the opinion of that Court, is equivalent to a refusal to recognise that Court, or the authority or jurisdiction thereof, such person shall be guilty of contempt of that Court and may be punished by that Court accordingly.

52   Examination of detained persons

(1) Whenever a person is detained in custody under the provisions in that behalf contained in Part IV of this Act, any member of the Garda Síochána may demand of such person, at any time while he is so detained, a full account of such person's movements and actions during any specified period and all information in his possession in relation to the commission or intended commission by another person of any offence under any section or sub-section of this Act or any scheduled offence.

(2) If any person, of whom any such account or information as is mentioned in the foregoing sub-section of this section is demanded under that sub-section by a member of the Garda Síochána, fails or refuses to give to such member such account or any such information or gives to such member any account or information which is false or misleading, he shall be guilty of an offence under this section and shall be liable on summary conviction thereof to imprisonment for a term not exceeding six months.

53   Immunities of members, etc, of Special Criminal Courts

(1) No action, prosecution, or other proceeding, civil or criminal, shall lie against any member of a Special Criminal Court in respect of any order made, conviction or sentence pronounced, or other thing done by that Court or in respect of anything done by such member in the course of the performance of his duties or the exercise of his powers as a member of that Court or otherwise in his capacity as a member of that Court, whether such thing was or was not necessary to the performance of such duties or the exercise of such powers.

(2) No action or other proceeding for defamation shall lie against any person in respect of anything written or said by him in giving evidence, whether written or oral, before a Special Criminal Court or for use in proceedings before a Special Criminal Court.

(3) No action, prosecution, or other proceeding, civil or criminal, shall lie against any registrar, clerk, or servant of a Special Criminal Court in respect of anything done by him in the performance of his duties as such registrar, clerk, or servant, whether such thing was or was not necessary to the performance of such duties.

PART VI
POWERS OF INTERNMENT

[...]¹

Amendments

1   Part VI repealed by Offences Against the State (Amendment) Act 1940, s 2.

Criminal Justice Act 1951

Number 2 of 1951

ARRANGEMENT OF SECTIONS

1 Court.
2 Summary trial of indictable offences.
3 Procedure where accused pleads guilty in District Court to indictable offence.
4 Punishment on summary conviction for certain indictable offences.
5 Imposition of consecutive terms of imprisonment by District Court.
6 Inclusion of summary offences in indictment.
7 Restriction of section 10(4) of Petty Sessions (Ireland) Act, 1851.
8 Taking of other offences into consideration in awarding punishment.
9 Deposition as evidence at trial.
10 Obtaining by false pretences.
11 Amendment of section 42 of the Offences against the Person Act, 1861.
12 Amendment of sections 51 and 52 of the Malicious Damage Act, 1861.
13 Unlawful possession.
14 Release on bail in certain cases by members of Garda Síochána.
15 Proceedings on arrest.
16 Power of Circuit Court to release from recognisance.
17 Recognisances by Corporation.
18 Exemption of Minister of State, the Attorney General and members of the Garda, Síochána from liability to enter into recognisances.
19 Transfer of trials by Circuit Court from place to place.
20 Clearing of court and prohibition of reports of proceedings.
21 Evidence of decision in cases of summary jurisdiction.
22 Fiats etc, of Attorney General to be admissible in evidence.
23 Remission of punishment, forfeitures and disqualifications.
24 Right of appeal from order of committal to industrial or reformatory school or Borstal Institution or place of detention.
25 Disposal of property in possession of Garda Síochána.
26 Repeals.
27 Short Title.

FIRST SCHEDULE

SECOND SCHEDULE

AN ACT TO AMEND CRIMINAL LAW AND ADMINISTRATION. [21st February, 1951]

BE IT ENACTED BY THE OIREACHTAS AS FOLLOWS:—

1   Court

In this Act "Court" refers to any court exercising criminal jurisdiction, save where the context otherwise requires, but does not include courtmartial.

2   Summary trial of indictable offences

(1) (a)   In this Act, "scheduled offence" means—
  (i)   an offence specified in the First Schedule to this Act, or
  (ii) an indictable offence declared to be a scheduled offence by an order under paragraph (b) for the time being in force.
  (b)   The Minister for Justice may by order declare that any specified indictable offence shall be a scheduled offence.
  (c)   An order shall not come into force unless approved by resolution of each House of the Oireachtas but, upon being so approved, shall come into force forthwith.

[(2) The District Court may try summarily a person charged with a scheduled offence if—
  (a)   the Court is of opinion that the facts proved or alleged constitute a minor offence fit to be tried summarily,
  (b)   the accused, on being informed by the Court of his right to be tried with a jury, does not object to being tried summarily, and
  (c)   the Director of Public Prosecutions consents to the accused being tried summarily for such offence.][1]

(3) This section shall not prevent the Court from sending forward a person for trial for a scheduled offence.

Amendments

1   Subsection (2) substituted by Criminal Justice (Miscellaneous Provisions) Act 1997, s 8.

---

3   Procedure where accused pleads guilty in District Court to indictable offence

[...][1]

Amendments

1   Section 3 repealed by Criminal Procedure Act 1967, Sch.

---

4   Punishment on summary conviction for certain indictable offences

(1) On conviction by the District Court for a scheduled offence [...],[1] the accused shall be liable to a fine not exceeding [£1000][2] or, at the discretion of the Court, to imprisonment for a term not exceeding twelve months, or to both such fine and imprisonment.

(2) [...][3]

Amendments

1   Words deleted by Criminal Procedure Act 1967, Sch.

2   Amended by Criminal Justice Act 1984, s 17.

3   Subsection (2) repealed by Broadcasting and Wireless Telegraphy Act 1988, s 12(3).

5   Imposition of consecutive terms of imprisonment by District Court

Where a sentence of imprisonment is passed on any person by the District Court, the Court may order that the sentence shall commence at the expiration of any other term of imprisonment to which that person has been previously sentenced, so however that where two or more sentences passed by the District Court are ordered to run consecutively the aggregate term of imprisonment shall not exceed [two years].[1]

Amendments

1   Words inserted by Criminal Justice Act 1984, s 12.

Note

The amending provision states that in this section (s 5) imprisonment includes detention in Saint Patrick's Institution.

6   Inclusion of summary offences in indictment

Where a person is sent forward for trial for an indictable offence, the indictment may contain a count for having committed any offence triable summarily (in this section referred to as a summary offence) with which he has been charged and which arises out of the same set of facts and, if found guilty on that count, he may be sentenced to suffer any punishment which could be inflicted on a person summarily convicted of the summary offence.

7   Restriction of section 10(4) of Petty Sessions (Ireland) Act, 1851

[Paragraph 4 (which prescribes time limits for the making of complaints in cases of summary jurisdiction) of section 10 of the Petty Sessions (Ireland) Act 1851 shall not apply to a complaint in respect of:

(a)   a scheduled offence, or

(b)   an offence that is triable—

   (i)   at the election of the prosecution, either on indictment or summarily, or

   (ii)   either on indictment or, subject to certain conditions including the consent of the prosecution, summarily.][1]

Amendments

1   Section 7 substituted by Criminal Justice Act 2006, s 177.

8   Taking of other offences into consideration in awarding punishment

[(1) Where a person, on being convicted of an offence, admits himself guilty of any other offence and asks to have it taken into consideration in awarding punishment, the Court may, if the Director of Public Prosecutions consents, take it into consideration accordingly.]¹
(2) If the Court takes an offence into consideration, a note of that fact shall be made and filed with the record of the sentence, and the accused shall not be prosecuted for that offence, unless his conviction is reversed on appeal.

Amendments

1   Subsection (1) substituted by Criminal Justice (Miscellaneous Provisions) Act 1997, s 9.

9   Deposition as evidence at trial

[…]¹

Amendments

1   Section 9 repealed by Criminal Procedure Act 1967, Sch.

10   Obtaining by false pretences

[…]¹

Amendments

1   Section 10 repealed by Criminal Justice (Theft And Fraud Offences) Act 2001, Sch 1.

11   Amendment of section 42 of the Offences against the Person Act, 1861

[…]¹

Amendments

1   Section 11 repealed by Non-Fatal Offences Against The Person Act 1997, s 31 and Sch.

12   Amendment of sections 51 and 52 of the Malicious Damage Act, 1861

(1) Section 51 of the Malicious Damage Act, 1861, is hereby amended by the substitution of "fifty pounds" for "five pounds" and section 52 of the Act shall be construed accordingly.

(2) Where a person is convicted by the Court of an offence under section 52 of the Malicious Damage Act, 1861,—

(a)   he shall be liable to a fine not exceeding fifty pounds or, at the discretion of the Court, to imprisonment for a term not exceeding six months;

(b)   the compensation which he may, if fined, be required to pay under the section may be of an amount not exceeding fifty pounds.

(3) Section 135 of the Grand Jury (Ireland) Act, 1836, as extended by subsection (1) of section 5 of the Local Government (Ireland) Act, 1898, shall continue to have the like operation as it had before the passing of this Act.

13   Unlawful possession

[…]¹

Amendments

1   Section 13 repealed by Criminal Justice (Theft And Fraud Offences) Act 2001, Sch 1.

14   Release on bail in certain cases by members of Garda Síochána

[…]¹

Amendments

1   Section 14 repealed by Criminal Procedure Act 1967, Sch.

15   Proceedings on arrest

[(1) A person arrested pursuant to a warrant shall on arrest be brought, as soon as practicable, before a judge of the District Court having jurisdiction to deal with the offence concerned.

(2) A person arrested without warrant shall, on being charged with an offence, be brought, as soon as practicable, before a judge of the District Court having jurisdiction to deal with the offence concerned.

(3) Where a person is arrested pursuant to a warrant later than the hour of 5 o'clock on any evening or, having been arrested without warrant, is charged after that hour and a judge of the District Court is due to sit in the District Court District in which the person was arrested not later than noon on the following day, it shall be sufficient compliance with subsection (1) or (2) of this section, as the case may be, if he is brought before a judge of the District Court sitting in that District Court District at the commencement of the sitting.

(4) If the accused is remanded on bail and there and then finds bail, the case shall be remitted to the next sitting of the District Court.

(5) In any other event, the case shall be remitted to a sitting of the District Court at a named place to be held within a period not exceeding 8 days of the arrest.

(6) This section is without prejudice to the provisions of any enactment relating to proceedings after arrest or charge in particular cases.]¹

Amendments

1   Section 15 substituted by Criminal Justice (Miscellaneous Provisions) Act 1997, s 18.

16   Power of Circuit Court to release from recognisance

Whenever an order is made by the District Court binding a person to the peace or to good behaviour or to both the peace and good behaviour and requiring him to enter into a recognisance in that behalf, such person may, at any time within one month and on giving seven days' notice to the officer of the Garda Síochána in charge of the district in which such person resides, apply in a summary manner to the judge of the Circuit Court within whose circuit the courthouse in which such order was made is situate to be released from the obligations imposed on him by such order and such recognisance respectively (if he has entered into such recognisance) and on the hearing of such application such judge may, if he so thinks proper, release such person from such obligations or modify in such manner as such judge thinks proper all or any of such obligations, and may make such release or modification either absolutely or subject to conditions and, in particular, subject to such person entering in the District Court into a new recognisance in lieu of such first-mentioned recognisance.

17   Recognisances by Corporation

(1) Whenever a corporation (whether aggregate or sole) is required by law or by an order of a court to enter into a recognisance, the recognisance may be entered into by an agent for and on behalf of the corporation, if—

(a)   the agent is authorised by the corporation in writing under the seal of the corporation to enter into the recognisance on its behalf and he produces such authorisation when executing the recognisance, and

(b)   the recognisance is expressed to be entered into on behalf of the corporation and to bind the goods of the corporation and generally to bind the corporation by the conditions of the recognisance.

(2) Where the form of a recognisance is prescribed by statute or by rule of court or any statutory instrument and the recognisance is entered into on behalf of a corporation under this section, such modifications may be made in the form so prescribed as are needed to comply with this section.

(3) A recognisance entered into under this section on behalf of a corporation shall bind the corporation and its goods as fully and in like manner as a like recognisance entered into by an individual would bind the individual and his goods.

18   Exemption of Minister of State, the Attorney General and members of the Garda, Síochána from liability to enter into recognisances

To avoid doubt, it is hereby declared that, notwithstanding anything contained in any enactment, it shall not be necessary for a Minister of State, the Attorney General or a member of the Garda Síochána, in prosecuting any appeal (whether by way of case stated or otherwise), to enter into a recognisance.

19   Transfer of trials by Circuit Court from place to place

[...]¹

Amendments

1   Section 19 repealed by Courts (Supplemental Provisions) Act 1961, Sch 1.

---

20   Clearing of court and prohibition of reports of proceedings

(1) [...]¹

(2) [...]¹

(3) In any criminal proceedings for an offence which is, in the opinion of the Court, of an indecent or obscene nature, the Court may, subject to subsection (4), exclude from the Court during the hearing all persons except officers of the Court, persons directly concerned in the proceedings, bona fide representatives of the Press and such other persons as the Court may, in its discretion, permit to remain.

(4) In any criminal proceedings—

(a)   where the accused is a person under the age of twenty-one years, or

(b)   where the offence is of an indecent or obscene nature and the person with or against whom it is alleged to have been committed is under that age or is a female,

a parent or other relative or friend of that person shall be entitled to remain in Court during the whole of the hearing.

(5) A person who contravenes an order or direction of the Court under this section shall, without prejudice to his liability for any other offence of which he may be guilty, be guilty of an offence under this section and shall be liable on summary conviction thereof to a fine not exceeding one hundred pounds or, at the discretion of the Court, to imprisonment for a term not exceeding six months or to both such fine and imprisonment.

(6) The powers conferred by this section are in addition to any other power of the Court to do all or any of the things which this section authorises.

Amendments

1   Subsections (1) and (2) repealed by Criminal Procedure Act 1967, Sch.

---

21 Evidence of decision in cases of summary jurisdiction

[...]¹

Amendments

1 Section 21 repealed by Courts Act 1971, s 24.

22 Fiats etc, of Attorney General to be admissible in evidence

[...]¹

Amendments

1 Section 22 repealed by Prosecution of Offences Act 1974, s 11.

23 Remission of punishment, forfeitures and disqualifications

(1) [...]¹ The Government may commute or remit, in whole or in part, any punishment imposed by a Court exercising criminal jurisdiction, subject to such conditions as they may think proper.

(2) The Government may remit, in whole or in part, any forfeiture or disqualification imposed by a Court exercising criminal jurisdiction and restore or revive, in whole or in part, the subject of the forfeiture.

(3) ...²

(4) This section shall not affect any power conferred by law on other authorities.

(5) Where a disqualification for holding a driving licence under the Road Traffic Act, 1933 (No. 11 of 1933), is remitted, in whole or in part, under this section, notice of the remission shall be published as soon as may be in Iris Oifigiúil.

Amendments

1 Words "Except in capital cases," deleted by Criminal Justice Act 1990, s 9 and Sch 2.

2 Subsection (3) deleted by Criminal Justice (Miscellaneous Provisions) Act 1997, s 17(a).

23A (1) The Government, may by order, delegate to the Minister for Justice any power of the Government under section 23 of this Act.

(2) The Government may, by order, revoke an order under this section.

Amendments

1   Section 23A inserted by Criminal Justice (Miscellaneous Provisions) Act 1997, s 17(b).

24   [...]¹

Amendments

1   Section 24 repealed by Children Act 2001, s 5 and Sch 2.

25   Disposal of property in possession of Garda Síochána

An order may be made under section 1 of the Police Property Act, 1897, for the disposal of property in the possession of the Garda Síochána although no person has been charged with an offence in connection with it.

26   Repeals

[...]¹

Amendments

1   Section 26 repealed by Courts (Supplemental Provisions) Act 1961, Sch 1.

27   Short Title

This Act may be cited as the Criminal Justice Act, 1951.

FIRST SCHEDULE

Section 2.

INDICTABLE OFFENCES WHICH MAY BE DEALT WITH SUMMARILY BY THE DISTRICT
COURT.

Ref. No.   Offence

(1)   (2)

1.   An offence in the nature of a public mischief.

2.   An indictable offence consisting of any form of obstruction of the administration of justice or the enforcement of the law.

3.   Perjury.

4. Not or unlawful assembly, where the Court is of opinion that the act constituting the offence was not done in furtherance of an organised conspiracy or, if so done, that the conspiracy is at an end.

5. Assault occasioning actual bodily harm.

6. [...]¹.

7. An offence under section 16 of the Plate Assay (Ireland) Act, 1807 as amended by section 2 of the Plate Assay (Amendment) Act 1931.

[8. [...]²

9. An offence under section 38 of the Offences against the Person Act, 1861.

10. An offence under section 60 of the Offences against the Person Act, 1861.

11. [...]²

12. An offence under section 11 of the Criminal Law Amendment Act, 1885, where the accused person is over the age of sixteen years and the person with whom the act is alleged to have been committed is either under the age of sixteen or is an idiot, an imbecile or a feeble-minded person.

13. An offence under the Forgery Act, 1913.

14. [...]²

15. [...]²

16. An offence under section 24 of the Enforcement of Court Orders Act, 1926.

17. An offence under section 11 of the Wireless Telegraphy Act, 1926.

18. [...]³.

19. Attempted carnal knowledge constituting an offence under sections 1(2), 2(2) or 4 of the Criminal Law Amendment Act, 1935.

20. [...].⁴

21. An attempt to commit an offence which the District Court has, by virtue of any enactment (including this Act), jurisdiction to try summarily.

[22. An offence under section 13 of the Debtors (Ireland) Act, 1872.

23. An offence under sections 20, 21, 22, 23 or 51 of the Malicious Damage Act, 1861.]⁵

[24. An offence under section 7(2) of the Criminal Law Act, 1997.]⁶

[25. An offence under section 8 of the Criminal Law Act, 1997.]⁷

[26. The offence at common law of breach of the peace.]⁸

Amendments

1   Paragraph 6 repealed by Criminal Law (Rape) (Amendment) Act 1990, s 21 and Sch.

2   Paragraphs 8, 11, 14 and 15 repealed by Criminal Justice (Theft And Fraud Offences) Act 2001, Sch 1.

3   Paragraph 18 deleted by Criminal Procedure Act 1967, s 19(b).

4   Paragraph 20 repealed by Criminal Justice (Theft and Fraud Offences) Act 2001.

5   Paragraphs 22 and 23 inserted by Criminal Procedure Act 1967, s 19(c).

6   Paragraph 24 inserted by Criminal Law Act 1997, s 7(7).

7   Paragraph 25 inserted by Criminal Law Act 1997, s 8(1).

8   Paragraph 26 inserted by Criminal Procedure Act 2010, s 38.

SECOND SCHEDULE

Section 26

ENACTMENTS REPEALED

[…]¹

Amendments

1   Sch 2 repealed by Courts (Supplemental Provisions) Act 1961, Sch 1.

Criminal Justice Act 1960

Number 27 of 1960

ARRANGEMENT OF SECTIONS

Section

1. Definitions.

2. Temporary release of persons from prisons and from Saint Patrick's Institution.

3. Temporary release of criminal lunatics.

4. Conditions in relation to temporary release.

5. Power to suspend currency of sentence in respect of period of temporary release.

6. Persons unlawfully at large.

7. Arrest of persons unlawfully at large.

8. Extension of powers in relation to the places of confinement of criminal lunatics.

9. Remand or committal for trial or sentence of certain young persons to remand institutions.

10. Power of Minister to transfer a person detained under section 9.

11. Lawful custody of persons detained under sections 9 and 10.

12. Discontinuance of use of term "Borstal."

13. Sentencing of certain young persons to detention in Saint Patrick's Institution.

14. Expenses.

15. Short title.

AN ACT TO AMEND CRIMINAL LAW AND ADMINISTRATION. [26th July, 1960.]

BE IT ENACTED BY THE OIREACHTAS AS FOLLOWS:—

1   Definitions

In this Act—

"remand institution" means an institution (other than a prison) whose use for the purposes of this Act has been approved of by the Minister;

"the Central Mental Hospital" means the Central Criminal Lunatic Asylum established in pursuance of the Central Criminal Lunatic Asylum (Ireland) Act, 1845;

"district mental hospital" has the meaning assigned to it by the Mental Treatment Act, 1945;

"the Minister" means the Minister for Justice;

"Saint Patrick's Institution" means the institution called and known as "Saint Patricks" and situate at North Circular Road, Dublin.

2   Temporary release of persons from prisons and from Saint Patrick's Institution

[(1) The Minister may direct that such person as is specified in the direction (being a person who is serving a sentence of imprisonment) shall be released from prison for such temporary period, and subject to such conditions, as may be specified in the direction [(including, if appropriate, any condition under section 108 of the Criminal Justice Act 2006)]² or rules under this section applying to that person—

    (a) for the purpose of—

        (i)   assessing the person's ability to reintegrate into society upon such release,

        (ii) preparing him for release upon the expiration of his sentence of imprisonment, or upon his being discharged from prison before such expiration, or

        (iii) assisting the Garda Síochána in the prevention, detection or investigation of offences, or the apprehension of a person guilty of an offence or suspected of having committed an offence,

    (b) where there exist circumstances that, in the opinion of the Minister, justify his temporary release on—

        (i)   grounds of health, or

        (ii) other humanitarian grounds,

    (c) where, in the opinion of the Minister, it is necessary or expedient in order to—

        (i)   ensure the good government of the prison concerned, or

        (ii) maintain good order in, and humane and just management of, the prison concerned, or

    (d) where the Minister is of the opinion that the person has been rehabilitated and would, upon being released, be capable of reintegrating into society.

(2) The Minister shall, before giving a direction under this section, have regard to—

    (a) the nature and gravity of the offence to which the sentence of imprisonment being served by the person relates.

    (b) the sentence of imprisonment concerned and any recommendations of the court that imposed that sentence in relation thereto,

    (c) the period of the sentence of imprisonment served by the person,

    (d) the potential threat to the safety and security of members of the public (including the victim of the offence to which the sentence of imprisonment being served by the person relates) should the person be released from prison,

    (e) any offence of which the person was convicted before being convicted of the offence to which the sentence of imprisonment being served by him relates,

    (f) the risk of the person failing to return to prison upon the expiration of any period of temporary release,

    (g) the conduct of the person while in custody, while previously the subject of a direction under this section, or during a period of temporary release to which rules under this section, made before the coming into operation of the Criminal Justice (Temporary Release of Prisoners) Act 2003, applied,

    (h) any report of, or recommendation made by—

        (i)   the governor of, or person for the time being performing the functions of governor in relation to, the prison concerned,

        (ii) the Garda Síochána,

        (iii) a probation and welfare officer, or

    (iv) any other person whom the Minister considers would be of assistance in enabling him to make a decision as to whether to give a direction under subsection (1) that relates to the person concerned.

  (i) the risk of the person committing an offence during any period of temporary release,

  (j) the risk of the person failing to comply with any conditions attaching to his temporary release, and

  (k) the likelihood that any period of temporary release might accelerate the person's reintegration into society or improve his prospects of obtaining employment.

(3) The Minister shall not give a direction under this section in respect of a person—

  (a) if he is of the opinion that, for reasons connected with any one or more of the matters referred to in subsection (2), it would not be appropriate to so do,

  (b) where the release of that person from prison is prohibited by or under any enactment, whether passed before or after the passing of this Act, or

  (c) where the person has been charged with, or convicted of, an offence and is in custody pursuant to an order of a court remanding him to appear at a future sitting of a court.

(4) A direction under this section shall be given to the governor of, or person for the time being performing the functions of governor in relation to, the prison concerned.

(5) The governor of, or person for the time being performing the functions of governor in relation to, the prison concerned to whom a direction under this section is given shall comply with that direction, and shall make and keep a record in writing of that direction.

(6) Without prejudice to subsection (1), the release of a person pursuant to a direction under this section shall not confer an entitlement on that person to further such release.

(7) (a) The Minister may make rules for the purpose of enabling this section to have full effect and such rules may contain such incidental, supplementary and consequential provisions as the Minister considers to be necessary or expedient.

  (b) Rules under this section may specify conditions to which all persons released pursuant to a direction under this section shall be subject or conditions to which all persons belonging to such classes of persons as are specified in the rules shall be subject.

(8) Every rule under this section shall be laid before each House of the Oireachtas as soon as may be after it is made, and if a resolution annulling the rule is passed by either such House within the next 21 days on which that House has sat after the rule is laid before it, the rule shall be annulled accordingly but without prejudice to the validity of anything previously done thereunder.

(9) This section shall not affect the operation of the Criminal Justice (Release of Prisoners) Act 1998.

(10) In this section, 'probation and welfare officer' means a person appointed by the Minister to be—

  (a) a welfare officer,

  (b) a probation officer, or

  (c) a probation and welfare officer.

(11) In this section—

  (a) references to a person who is serving a sentence of imprisonment shall be construed as including references to—

    (i) a person being detained in a place provided under section 2 of the Prisons Act 1970, and

    (ii) a person serving a sentence of detention in St. Patrick's Institution,

    and sentence of imprisonment shall be construed accordingly,

    and

  (b) references to a prison shall be construed as including references to a place provided under the said section 2 and that Institution.]¹

Amendments

1   Section 2 inserted by Criminal Justice (Temporary Release Of Prisoners) Act 2003, s 1.

2   Words inserted by Criminal Justice Act 2006, s 110.

3   Temporary release of criminal lunatics

(1) In this section—

"criminal lunatic" means a person who is detained in a district mental hospital or in the Central Mental Hospital by warrant, order or direction of the Government or the Minister or under the provisions of section 91 of the Army Act, 1881, or of the Defence Act, 1954, and, if he is undergoing a sentence of penal servitude or imprisonment, or of detention in Saint Patrick's Institution, whose sentence has not expired;

"person in charge" means—

  (a) in relation to a criminal lunatic detained in a district mental hospital, the resident medical superintendent thereof, and

  (b) in relation to a criminal lunatic detained in the Central Mental Hospital, the Resident Physician and Governor thereof.

(2) A criminal lunatic who, in the opinion of the person in charge, is not dangerous to himself or to others may, with the consent of the Minister, be released temporarily by the person in charge subject to such conditions (if any) as he may, with the consent of the Minister, impose.

(3) (a) The consent of the Minister to the release of a criminal lunatic under this section may be given in relation to a particular release or in relation to the release from time to time during a specified period of that criminal lunatic.

  (b) The consent of the Minister to the imposition of conditions in relation to the release of a criminal lunatic under this section may relate to the imposition of conditions in relation to a particular release of that criminal lunatic or to the imposition of conditions in relation to the release from time to time during a specified period of that criminal lunatic.

4 Conditions in relation to temporary release

(1) Where the release of a person under section 2 or section 3 of this Act is made subject to conditions, the conditions shall be communicated to the person at the time of his release by notice in writing.

(2) A person temporarily released under section 2 or section 3 of this Act shall comply with any conditions to which his release is made subject.

5 Power to suspend currency of sentence in respect of period of temporary release

The currency of the sentence, if any, of a person temporarily released under section 2 or section 3 of this Act may, at the time of release or at any time during or after the period of release, be suspended by the Minister, if he so thinks fit, in respect of the whole or part of the period.

6 Persons unlawfully at large

(1) A person who, by reason of having been temporarily released under section 2 or section 3 of this Act, is at large shall be deemed to be unlawfully at large if—

(a) the period for which he was temporarily released has expired, or

(b) a condition to which his release was made subject has been broken.

(2) A person who is unlawfully at large shall be guilty of an offence under this section and on summary conviction thereof shall be liable to imprisonment for a term not exceeding six months.

(3) Where, by reason of the breach of a condition to which his release under section 2 or section 3 of this Act was made subject, a person is deemed to be unlawfully at large and is arrested under section 7 of this Act, the period for which he was temporarily released shall thereupon be deemed to have expired.

(4) The currency of the sentence of a person who is unlawfully at large for any period shall be suspended in respect of the whole of that period.

7 Arrest of persons unlawfully at large

A member of the Garda Síochána may arrest without warrant a person whom he suspects to be unlawfully at large and may take such person to the place in which he is required in accordance with law to be detained.

8 Extension of powers in relation to the places of confinement of criminal lunatics

[…]¹

Amendments

1 Section 8 repealed by Criminal Law (Insanity) Act 2006, s 25 and Sch 2.

---

9   Remand or committal for trial or sentence of certain young persons to remand institutions

(1) Where a statute or instrument made under statute confers a power to remand in custody or to commit in custody for trial or for sentence a person who is not less than sixteen nor more than twenty-one years of age, the power shall be deemed to include a power to remand or commit the person in custody to a remand institution and the statute or instrument, as the case may be, shall have effect accordingly.

(2) For the purposes of subsection (1) of this section, the power conferred by section 10 of the Criminal Justice Administration Act, 1914, to commit to prison shall be deemed to be a power to commit in custody for sentence.

(3) A person shall not be detained under this section or under section 10 of this Act in a remand institution which is conducted otherwise than in accordance with the religion to which the person belongs.

10   Power of Minister to transfer a person detained under section 9

(1) Subject to subsection (2) of this section and subsection (3) of section 9 of this Act, the Minister may, if he thinks it proper to do so, direct that a person detained under section 9 of this Act or this section in a remand institution be transferred to and detained for the unexpired part of the period of remand or committal, as the case may be, in another remand institution, in a prison or in Saint Patrick's Institution.

(2) The Minister shall not give a direction under this section in respect of a person unless he has been so requested by the person or by the person in charge of the institution in which he is detained.

(3) When a direction is given under this section in relation to a person, he shall be transferred as soon as may be to the institution or prison specified in the direction and shall be detained there for the unexpired part of the period for which he was remanded or committed.

11   Lawful custody of persons detained under sections 9 and 10

(1) Subject to subsection (3) of this section, a person who is detained in a remand institution pursuant to section 9 of this Act shall be deemed to be in the lawful custody of the person for the time being in charge of the institution during and until the expiration of the period for which he was remanded or committed, or, if it should sooner happen, until he is transferred under section 10 of this Act.

(2) Subject to subsection (3) of this section, a person who is transferred under section 10 of this Act to an institution (being a remand institution or Saint Patrick's Institution) or to a prison shall be deemed to be in the lawful custody of the person in charge of the institution or the governor of the prison, as the case may be, from the time he is transferred until the expiration of the period for which he was remanded or committed or, if it should sooner happen, until he is transferred again under the said section 10.

(3) A person who, during a period of detention pursuant to section 9 or section 10 of this Act, is absent without permission from the place of detention shall be deemed to have escaped from lawful custody and the foregoing provisions of this section shall not apply in relation to the period during which he is so absent.

12   Discontinuance of use of term "Borstal"

On the commencement of this Act, the use of the term "Borstal" shall be discontinued and, accordingly, references in any statute or instrument made under statute to a Borstal Institution or to Borstal Institutions shall thenceforth be construed as references to Saint Patrick's Institution.

13   Sentencing of certain young persons to detention in Saint Patrick's Institution

(1) Where a person who is not less than seventeen nor more than twenty-one years of age is convicted of an offence for which he is liable to be sentenced to a term of penal servitude or imprisonment, he may, in lieu of being so sentenced, be sentenced to be detained in Saint Patrick's Institution for a period not exceeding the term for which he might have been sentenced to penal servitude or imprisonment, as the case may be.

(2) Where a person who is less than seventeen but not less than sixteen years of age is convicted of an offence for which he would, if he were not less than seventeen years of age, be liable to be sentenced to a term of penal servitude or imprisonment and the court considers that none of the other methods in which the case may legally be dealt with is suitable, he may be sentenced to be detained in Saint Patrick's Institution for a period not exceeding the term for which he might, if he were not less than seventeen years of age, be sentenced to penal servitude or imprisonment, as the case may be.

(3) The Minister may make regulations providing for the rule and management of and the constitution of a visiting committee for Saint Patrick's Institution in so far as it is being used for the detention of persons sentenced under this section and for the classification, treatment, employment and control of such persons and may, by the regulations, apply, to such extent and subject to such modifications, if any, as may be specified therein—

[(a)   the Prisons Acts 1826 to 2007 (other than section 12 of the General Prisons (Ireland) Act 1877, the Prisons (Ireland) Act 1907 and section 8 of the Penal Servitude Act 1891) and rules thereunder, whether made before or after the commencement of this Act,

(aa)   rules made under section 35 of the Prisons Act 2007, and][1]

(b)   regulations made, whether before or after the commencement of this Act, under subsection (2) of section 4 of the Prevention of Crime Act, 1908,

in relation to Saint Patrick's Institution in its use aforesaid.

Amendments

1   Subsection (3)(a) substituted and (3)(aa) inserted by Prisons Act 2007, s 41.

---

14   Expenses

The expenses incurred by the Minister in the administration of this Act shall, to such extent as may be sanctioned by the Minister for Finance, be paid out of moneys provided by the Oireachtas.

15   Short title

This Act may be cited as the Criminal Justice Act, 1960.

Courts (Supplemental Provisions) Act 1961

Number 39 of 1961

ARRANGEMENT OF SECTIONS

PART I
PRELIMINARY AND GENERAL

1   Short title and commencement.

2   Interpretation generally.

3   Repeals and saving.

PART II
SUPREME COURT, HIGH COURT, CHIEF JUSTICE, PRESIDENT OF THE HIGH COURT, CENTRAL CRIMINAL COURT AND COURT OF CRIMINAL APPEAL

SUPREME COURT HIGH COURT

4   Number of ordinary judges of Supreme Court and High Court.

5   Qualifications of judges of Supreme Court and High Court.

6   Pensions of judges of Supreme Court and High Court.

7   General jurisdiction of Supreme Court.

8   General Jurisdiction of High Court.

9   Jurisdiction of High Court in lunacy and minor matters.

CHIEF JUSTICE AND PRESIDENT OF THE HIGH COURT

10   Jurisdiction of Chief Justice and President of the High Court.

CENTRAL CRIMINAL COURT

11   The Central Criminal Court.

COURT OF CRIMINAL APPEAL

12   Jurisdiction of Court of Criminal Appeal.

HIGH COURT CIRCUITS

13   High Court Circuit.

EXERCISE OF JURISDICTION

14   Jurisdiction to be exercised pursuant to rules of court (Supreme Court High Court, Chief Justice, President of the High Court Central Criminal Court and Court of Criminal Appeal).

PART III
CIRCUIT COURT

15   Definitions (Part III).

16   Number of ordinary judges of Circuit Court.

17   Qualifications of judges of Circuit Court.

18   Age of retirement of judge of Circuit Court.

19   Pensions of judges of Circuit Court.

20   Circuits and assignment of judges to circuits.

21   Circuit Court to be a court of record.

22   Jurisdiction of Circuit Court except in applications for new on-licences and in indictable, offences.

23   Jurisdiction of Cork Circuit Court Judge in admiralty causes and in bankruptcy.

24   Jurisdiction of Circuit Court in applications for new on-licences.

25   Jurisdiction of Circuit Court in indictable offences.

25A   "Exercise of jurisdiction by Circuit Court judges in indictable offences.

26   Transfer of trials in criminal cases by judge of the Circuit Court.

27   Jurisdiction to be exercised pursuant to rules of court (Circuit Court, Cork Local Admiralty Court and Cork Local Bankruptcy Court).

Part IV
District Court

General Provisions

28   Number of justices of District Court.

29   Qualifications of justices of District Court and interpretation of section 2 of the Act of 1949, as applied by section 48 of this Act.

30   Age of retirement of justice of District Courts.

31   Pensions of justices of District Court.

32   District court areas and districts and assignment of justices to districts.

32A   Exercise of certain powers by judge of District Court outside district court district.

33   Jurisdiction of District Court.

34   Jurisdiction to be exercised pursuant to rules of court (District Court).

Provisions relating to the President of the District Court and to the Dublin Metropolitan District

35   Qualification for appointment as president of the District Court and assignment.

36   General powers of President of the District Court.

37   Abolition of Divisions of Dublin Metropolitan Justices.

38   Principal Justices of the Dublin Metropolitan District.

39   Number of justices of Dublin in Metropolitan District.

40   Places at which business of Dublin Metropolitan District is to be transacted.

41   Number of sitting days in each week for justices assigned Dublin Metropolitan District.

42   Business of District Court in Dublin Metropolitan District.

43   Restriction of section 26 of Act of 1953.

44   Ex officio members of District Court Rules Committee.

PART V
MISCELLANEOUS PROVISIONS

45 Administration of justice otherwise than in public.

46 Provisions in relation to remuneration and pensions of judges and justices.

46A Remuneration to be adjusted automatically by reference to salary increases in Civil Service.

47 Interest on judgment debts.

48 Application of enactments relating to existing courts and judges and officers thereof, and rules of court.

49 Preservation of continuity of administration and enforcement of justice.

50 Appeals from District Court in criminal cases against sentence only.

51 Extension of section 2 of the Summary Jurisdiction Act, 1857.

52 Case stated for High Court on question of law.

53 Application of section 26 of Hire-Purchase (Amendment) Act, 1960.

54 Jurisdiction to bind to the peace or to good behaviour.

55 Offices and officers, etc. under Court Officers Acts, 1926 to 1951.

56 Power to continue county registrars in office after reaching age of Sixty-five years.

57 Pension of Master of the High Court, Taxing Master and county registrar.

58 Special provisions for person who, on the operative date, holds the office of Master of the High Court, Taxing-Master or County registrar.

59 Officers of Cork Local Admiralty Court and Cork Local Bankruptcy Court.

60 Right of audience of solicitors in Circuit Court, Cork Local Admiralty Court and Cork Local Bankruptcy Court.

61 Solicitors and commissioners for oaths.

FIRST SCHEDULE

SECOND SCHEDULE

THIRD SCHEDULE

FOURTH SCHEDULE

FIFTH SCHEDULE

SIXTH SCHEDULE

SEVENTH SCHEDULE

EIGHTH SCHEDULE

AN ACT TO PROVIDE, IN RELATION TO THE COURTS TO BE ESTABLISHED BY THE COURTS (ESTABLISHMENT AND CONSTITUTION) ACT, 1961, AND THE JUDGES AND OFFICERS OF THOSE COURTS, FOR CERTAIN MATTERS NECESSARY TO SUPPLEMENT THAT ACT, TO CONFER JURISDICTION ON THE JUDGE OF THE CIRCUIT COURT ASSIGNED TO THE CORK CIRCUIT IN ADMIRALTY CAUSES AND IN

BANKRUPTCY, TO REPEAL CERTAIN ENACTMENTS, AND TO PROVIDE FOR CERTAIN OTHER MATTERS CONNECTED WITH THE MATTERS AFORESAID. [16th August, 1961.]

BE IT ENACTED BY THE OIREACHTAS AS FOLLOWS:—

PART I
PRELIMINARY AND GENERAL

1   Short title and commencement

(1) The Act may be cited as the Courts (Supplemental Provisions) Act, 1961.

(2) This Act shall come into operation on the date on which the Principal Act comes into operation and immediately after the coming into operation of the Principal Act.

2   Interpretation generally

(1) In this Act—

"the Act of 1924" means the Courts of Justice Act, 1924;

"the Act of 1926" means the Court Officers Act, 1926;

"the Act of 1936" means the Courts of Justice Act, 1936;

"the Act of 1945" means the Court Officers Act, 1945;

"the Act of 1946" means the Courts of Justice (District Court) Act, 1946;

"the Act of 1947" means the Courts of Justice Act, 1947;

"the Act of 1949" means the Courts of Justice (District Court) Act, 1949;

"the Act of 1953" means the Courts of Justice Act, 1953;

"the Circuit Court" means the Court established by section 4 of the Principal Act;

"the Court of Criminal Appeal" means the Court established by section 3 of the Principal Act;

"the District Court" means the Court established by section 5 of the Principal Act;

"the Dublin Metropolitan District" means the district styled and known as the Dublin Metropolitan District under section 64 of the Act of 1936;

"enactment" includes a charter and any instrument made under an enactment;

"the existing Chief Justice" means the judge of the existing Supreme Court who, by virtue of section 5 of the Act of 1924, was immediately before the operative date, president of that Court;

"the existing Circuit Court" means the Circuit Court of Justice constituted by section 37 of the Act of 1924;

"the existing Court of Criminal Appeal" means the Court of Criminal Appeal constituted by section 8 of the Act of 1924;

"the existing District Court" means the District Court of Justice constituted by section 67 of the Act of 1924;

"the existing High Court" means the High Court of Justice constituted by section 4 of the Act of 1924;

"the existing President of the Circuit Court" means the judge of the existing Circuit Court who, immediately before the operative date, held the office created by section 9 of the Act of 1947;

"the existing President of the High Court" means the judge of the existing High Court who, by virtue of section 4 of the Act of 1924, was, immediately before the operative date, president of that Court;

"the existing Supreme Court" means the Supreme Court of Justice constituted by section 5 of the Act of 1924;

"the High Court" means the Court established by section 2 of the Principal Act;

"justice of the District Court" includes, except where the context otherwise requires, the President of the District Court;

["market value' means, in relation to land, the price that would have been obtained in respect of the unencumbranced fee simple were the land to have been sold on the open market, in the year immediately preceding the bringing of the proceedings concerned, in such manner and subject to such conditions as might reasonably be calculated to have resulted in the vendor obtaining the best price for the land.][1]

"the Minister" means the Minister for Justice;

"the operative date" means the date on which this Act comes into operation;

"the Principal Act" means the Courts (Establishment and Constitution) Act, 1961 (No. 39 of 1961);

"State authority" means any authority being—

(a) a Minister of State, or

(b) the Commissioners of Public Works in Ireland, or

(c) the Irish Land Commission, or

(d) the Revenue Commissioners, or

(e) the Attorney General;

"the Supreme Court" means the Court established by section 1 of the Principal Act.

(2) Except where the context otherwise requires, any reference in this Act to any other enactment shall be construed as a reference to that enactment as amended, adapted or applied by or under any other enactment, including this Act.

Amendments

1   Definition inserted by Civil Liability and Courts Act 2004, s 45(1).

---

3   Repeals and saving

The enactments mentioned in column (2) of the First Schedule to this Act are hereby repealed to the extent mentioned in column (3) of that Schedule, but, without prejudice to subsection (1) of section 21 of the Interpretation Act, 1937, such of those enactments as relate to the pensions of the judges and justices of the courts established by the Act of 1924 shall, notwithstanding the repeal thereof, continue to apply to any person who, having been a judge of the existing Supreme Court existing High Court or existing Circuit Court or a justice of the existing District Court retired or retires from office before the operative date.

PART II

SUPREME COURT, HIGH COURT, CHIEF JUSTICE, PRESIDENT OF THE HIGH COURT, CENTRAL CRIMINAL COURT AND COURT OF CRIMINAL APPEAL

Supreme Court High Court

4   Number of ordinary judges of Supreme Court and High Court

Text not reproduced here.

5   Qualifications of judges of Supreme Court and High Court

Text not reproduced here.

6   Pensions of judges of Supreme Court and High Court

Text not reproduced here.

7   General jurisdiction of Supreme Court

Text not reproduced here.

8   General Jurisdiction of High Court

Text not reproduced here.

9   Jurisdiction of High Court in lunacy and minor matters

Text not reproduced here.

10   Jurisdiction of Chief Justice and President of the High Court

Text not reproduced here.

Central Criminal Court

11   The Central Criminal Court

(1) The High Court exercising the criminal jurisdiction with which it is invested shall be known as An Phríomh-Chúirt Choiriúil (The Central Criminal Court) and is in this Act referred to as the Central Criminal Court.

(2) (a)   The jurisdiction exercisable by the Central Criminal Court shall be exercisable by a judge or judges of the High Court (including the President of the High Court) nominated from time to time by the President of the High Court.

  (b)   The jurisdiction of the Court shall be exercisable by each judge for the time being so nominated save that, where the President of the High Court directs that two or more such judges shall sit together for the purpose of a particular case, the jurisdiction of the Court for that purpose shall be exercised by those judges sitting together.

(3) Every person lawfully brought before the Central Criminal Court may be indicted before and tried and sentenced by that Court, wherever it may be sitting, in like manner in all respects as if the crime with which such person is charged had been committed in the county or county borough in which the said Court is sitting.

(4) References in any other enactment (whether passed before or after this Act) to the Central Criminal Court shall be construed as references to the High Court exercising the criminal jurisdiction with which it is invested.

Court of Criminal Appeal

12   Jurisdiction of Court of Criminal Appeal

(1) The Court of Criminal Appeal shall be a superior court of record and shall, for the purposes of this Act and subject to the enactments applied by section 48 of this Act, have full power to determine any questions necessary to be determined for the purpose of doing justice in the case before it.

(2) There shall be vested in the Court of Criminal Appeal all jurisdiction which, by virtue, of any enactment which is applied by section 48 of this Act, was, immediately before the operative date, vested in or capable of being exercised by the existing Court of Criminal Appeal.

(3) In subsection (2) of section 44 of the Offences Against the State Act, 1939, the reference to section 30 of the Act of 1924 shall be construed as a reference to subsection (1) of this section.

High Court Circuits

13   High Court Circuit

Text not reproduced here.

Exercise of Jurisdiction

14   Jurisdiction to be exercised pursuant to rules of court (Supreme Court High Court, Chief Justice, President of the High Court Central Criminal Court and Court of Criminal Appeal).

(1) In this section "rules of court" means rules made under section 36 of the Act of 1924, as applied by section 48 of this Act.

(2) The jurisdiction which is [...][1] vested in or exercisable by the Supreme Court, the High Court, the Chief justice, the President of the High Court, the Central Criminal court and the Court of Criminal Appeal respectively shall be exercised so far as regards pleading, practice and procedure, generally, including liability to costs, in the manner provided by rules of court, and, where no provision is contained in such rules and so long as there is no rule with reference thereto, it shall be exercised as nearly as possible in the same manner as it might have been exercised by the respective existing courts or judges by which or by whom such jurisdiction was, immediately before the operative date, respectively exercisable.

(3) Rules of court may, in relation to proceedings and matters (not being criminal proceedings or matters or matters relating to the liberty of the person) in the High Court and Supreme Court, authorise the Master of the High Court and other principal officers, within the meaning of the Court Officers Acts 1926 to 1951, to exercise functions, powers and jurisdiction in uncontested cases and to take accounts, conduct inquiries and make orders of an interlocutory nature.Part III Circuit Court.

Amendments

1   Words "by virtue of this Act" were repealed by the Courts Act 1971, s 24.

15   Definitions (Part III)

Text not reproduced here.

16   Number of ordinary judges of Circuit Court

Text not reproduced here.

17   Qualifications of judges of Circuit Court

Text not reproduced here.

18   Age of retirement of judge of Circuit Court

Text not reproduced here.

19   Pensions of judges of Circuit Court

Text not reproduced here.

20   Circuits and assignment of judges to circuits

Text not reproduced here.

21   Circuit Court to be a court of record

Text not reproduced here.

22   Jurisdiction of Circuit Court except in applications for new on-licences and in indictable, offences

Text not reproduced here.

23   Jurisdiction of Cork Circuit Court Judge in admiralty causes and in bankruptcy

Text not reproduced here.

24   Jurisdiction of Circuit Court in applications for new on-licences

Text not reproduced here.

25   Jurisdiction of Circuit Court in indictable offences

(1) Subject to subsection (2) of this section, the Circuit Court shall have and may exercise every jurisdiction as respects indictable offences for the time being vested in the Central Criminal Court and every person lawfully brought before the Circuit Court in exercise of such jurisdiction may be indicted before and tried and, if convicted, sentenced by the Circuit Court accordingly.

(2) The jurisdiction conferred on the Circuit Court by subsection (1) of this section shall not extend to treason, an offence under section 2 or 3 of the Treason Act, 1939, an offence under

section 6, 7 or 8 of the Offences Against the State Act, 1939, murder, attempt to murder, conspiracy to murder, or piracy, including an offence by an accessory before or after the fact.

(3) The jurisdiction vested in the Circuit Court by subsection (1) of this section shall be exercised by the judge of the circuit in which the offence charged has been committed or in which the accused person has been arrested or resides.

(4) In section 6 of the Courts of justice Act, 1926, as applied by section 48 of this Act, and in subsection (1) of section 14 of the Wireless Telegraphy Act 1926, the references to section 53 of the Act of 1924 shall be construed as references to subsection (3) of this section [and section 25A of this Act.]¹

Amendments

1   Words inserted by Criminal Justice Act 2006, s 179.

[25A   Exercise of jurisdiction by Circuit Court judges in indictable offences.

(1) Where, in respect of an offence committed in the State—

  (a) the accused person does not reside in the State,

  (b) he or she was not arrested for and charged with the offence in the State, and

  (c) either—

      (i)   the offence was committed in more than one circuit, or

      (ii) it is known that it was committed in one of not more than three circuits, but the particular circuit concerned is not known,

then, for the purposes of section 25(3) of this Act, the offence shall be deemed to have been committed in each of the circuits concerned and a judge of any of the circuits concerned may deal with the case.

(2) Where the circumstances of an offence committed in the State fall within paragraphs (a) and (b), but not (c), of subsection (1) of this section and the circuit in which the offence was committed is not known, then, for the purposes of section 25(3) of this Act, the offence shall be deemed to have been committed in the Dublin Circuit.

(3) A case does not fall within this section unless it is shown that reasonable efforts have been made to ascertain the whereabouts of the accused person for the purposes of arresting him or her for and charging him or her with the offence concerned.

(4) Where a judge of a circuit exercises jurisdiction in relation to an indictable offence by virtue of this section, the judge or any other judge assigned to the circuit shall have jurisdiction in relation to the offence until the conclusion of proceedings in respect of it in the Circuit Court notwithstanding that it is later established that, but for this subsection, he or she would not have had jurisdiction in relation to the offence.

(5) In this section 'offence' means an indictable offence as respects which jurisdiction is vested in the Circuit Court by section 25 of this Act.]¹

Amendments

1 Section 25A inserted by Criminal Justice Act 2006, s 179.

26 Transfer of trials in criminal cases by judge of the Circuit Court

(1) A judge of the Circuit Court may, if he thinks fit transfer the trial of a criminal issue from the place in his circuit where it is required by law to be held to any other place in that circuit, and, in that event, the trial shall be held at the place to which it is transferred with a jury drawn from the jury district or other area prescribed for trials by the Circuit Court sitting in the outer place.

(2) An order of a judge of the Circuit Court under subsection of this section—

    (a) may be made only on the application of the Attorney General or an accused person,

    (b) may provide for matters ancillary or incidental to the transfer, and

    (c) shall be final and unappealable.

27 Jurisdiction to be exercised pursuant to rules of court (Circuit Court, Cork Local Admiralty Court and Cork Local Bankruptcy Court)

Text not reproduced here.

PART IV
DISTRICT COURT

General Provisions

28 Number of justices of District Court

Text not reproduced here.

29 Qualifications of justices of District Court and interpretation of section 2 of the Act of 1949, as applied by section 48 of this Act

Text not reproduced here.

30 Age of retirement of justice of District Courts

Text not reproduced here.

31 Pensions of justices of District Court

Text not reproduced here.

32 District court areas and districts and assignment of justices to districts

Text not reproduced here.

[32A Exercise of certain powers by judge of District Court outside district court district

Text not reproduced here.

33   Jurisdiction of District Court

Text not reproduced here.

34   Jurisdiction to be exercised pursuant to rules of court (District Court)

Text not reproduced here.

35   Qualification for appointment as president of the District Court and assignment

Text not reproduced here.

36   General powers of President of the District Court

Text not reproduced here.

37   Abolition of Divisions of Dublin Metropolitan Justices

Text not reproduced here.

38   Principal Justices of the Dublin Metropolitan District

Text not reproduced here.

39   Number of judges permanently assigned to districts.

Text not reproduced here.

40   Places at which business of Dublin Metropolitan District is to be transacted

Text not reproduced here.

41   Number of sitting days in each week for justices assigned Dublin Metropolitan District

Text not reproduced here.

42   Business of District Court in Dublin Metropolitan District

Text not reproduced here.

43   Restriction of section 26 of Act of 1953

Text not reproduced here.

44   Ex officio members of District Court Rules Committee

Text not reproduced here.

PART V

MISCELLANEOUS PROVISIONS

45   Administration of justice otherwise than in public

(1) Justice may be administered otherwise than in public in any of the following cases:

(a) applications of an urgent nature for relief by way of habeas corpus, bail, prohibition or injunction;

(b) matrimonial causes and matters;

   (c) lunacy and minor matters;

   (d) proceedings involving the disclosure of a secret manufacturing process;

(2) The cases prescribed by subsection (1) of this section shall be in addition to any other cases prescribed by any Act of the Oireachtas.

(3) Any provision contained in any statute of the Parliament of the former United Kingdom or of the Oireachtas of Saorstát Éireann which provided for the administration of justice otherwise than in public and which is not in force solely by reason of its being inconsistent with the provisions of the Constitution of Saorstát Éireann or the Constitution, as the case may be, shall have full force and effect.

46   Provisions in relation to remuneration and pensions of judges and justices

Text not reproduced here.

[46A   Remuneration to be adjusted automatically by reference to salary increases in Civil Service

Text not reproduced here.

47   Interest on judgment debts.

Text not reproduced here.

48   Application of enactments relating to existing courts and judges and officers thereof, and rules of court.

Text not reproduced here.

49   Preservation of continuity of administration and enforcement of justice

Text not reproduced here.

50   Appeals from District Court in criminal cases against sentence only

Where—

   (a) an order is made in a criminal case by a justice of the District Court convicting a person and sentencing him to pay a penal or other sum or to do anything at any expense or to undergo a term of imprisonment or to be detained in Saint Patrick's Institution, and

   (b) an appeal is taken against the order, and

   (c) either—

      (i) the notice of appeal states that the appeal is against so much only of the order as relates to the sentence, or

     (ii) the appellant, on the hearing of the appeal, indicates that he desires to appeal against so much only of the order as relates to the sentence,

then, notwithstanding any rule of law, the Circuit Court shall not, on the hearing of the appeal, re-hear the case except to such extent as shall be necessary to enable the court to adjudicate on the question of sentence.

51   Extension of section 2 of the Summary Jurisdiction Act, 1857

(1) Section 2 of the Summary Jurisdiction Act, 1857, is hereby extended so as to enable any party to any proceedings whatsoever heard and determined by a justice of the District Court

(other than proceedings relating to an indictable offence which was not dealt with summarily by the court) if dissatisfied with such determination as being erroneous on a point of law, to apply in writing within fourteen days after such determination to the said justice to state and sign a case setting forth the facts and the grounds of such determination for the opinion thereon of the High Court.

(2) Upon the making of an application under section 2 of the Summary Jurisdiction Act, 1857, as extended by subsection (1) of this section, for a case stated, the determination in respect of which the application is made shall be suspended—

(a) where the justice of the District Court to whom the application is made grants the application, until the case stated has been heard and determined, and

(b) where he refuses to grant the application, until he so refuses.

(3) The references in sections 6, 8, 9, 10 and, 14 of the Summary Jurisdiction Act, 1857, to that Act shall be construed as references to that Act as extended by subsection (1) of this section.

(4) In section 2 of the Summary Jurisdiction Act, 1857, and in this section, "party" means any person who was, entitled to be heard and was heard in the proceedings in which the determination in respect of which an application for a case stated is made was given.

52   Case stated for High Court on question of law

(1) A justice of the District Court shall, if requested by any person who has been heard in any proceedings whatsoever before him (other than proceedings relating to an indictable offence which is not being dealt with summarily by the court) unless he consider the request frivolous, and may (without request) refer any question of law arising in such proceedings to the High Court for determination.

(2) An appeal shall lie by leave of the High Court to the Supreme Court from every determination of the High Court on a question of law referred to the High Court under subsection (1) of this section.

53   Application of section 26 of Hire-Purchase (Amendment) Act, 1960

Text not reproduced here.

54   Jurisdiction to bind to the peace or to good behaviour

The jurisdiction formerly exercisable by justices of the peace to make an order binding a person to the peace or to good behaviour or to both the peace and good behaviour and requiring him to enter into a recognizance in that behalf may be exercised by—

(a) a judge of the Supreme Court or the High Court, or

(b) a judge of the Circuit Court within the circuit to which he is for the time being assigned, or

(c) a justice of the District Court within the district to which he is for the time being assigned.

55   Offices and officers, etc. under Court Officers Acts, 1926 to 1951.

Text not reproduced here.

56 Power to continue county registrars in office after reaching age of Sixty-five years

Text not reproduced here.

57 Pension of Master of the High Court, Taxing Master and county registrar

Text not reproduced here.

58 Special provisions for person who, on the operative date, holds the office of Master of the High Court, Taxing-Master or County registrar

Text not reproduced here.

59 Officers of Cork Local Admiralty Court and Cork Local Bankruptcy Court

Text not reproduced here.

60 Right of audience of solicitors in Circuit Court, Cork Local Admiralty Court and Cork Local Bankruptcy Court

Text not reproduced here.

61 Solicitors and commissioners for oaths

Text not reproduced here.

FIRST SCHEDULE

Section 3

ENACTMENTS REPEALED

Session and Chapter or Number and Year	Short Title	Extent of Repeal
(1)	(2)	(3)
5 & 6 Vic. c. 24.	Dublin Police Act, 1842	Section 68
43 & 44 Vic. c. 39.	Lunacy (Ireland) Act, 1880	The whole Act.
6 Edw. 7. c. 37.	Labourers (Ireland) Act, 1906.	In subsection (1) of section 31, all words from "and the Local Government Board" to the end of the subsection.
No. 10 of 1924	Courts of Justice Act, 1924	Section 2; in section 3, the definition of "Central Criminal Court"; sections 4, 5, 6, 7, 8, 11, 13, 14, 16,17 and 18; subsections (1) and (3) of section 19; in section 20, the words "From and after the commencement of this Act"; sections 21 and 22; in section 27, the words "From and after the commencement of this Act":

Session and Chapter or Number and Year	Short Title	Extent of Repeal
No. 10 of 1924 (*contd*)		sections 30, 37,41,43, 45,46, 47, 48, 49, 50, 51, 52, 53, 55, 56 and 57; in section 60, all words from "Any judgment" to the end of the section; sections 67, 69, 70 and 74; in section 78, all words from "and the provisions" to the end of the section; sections 82, 83 89, 93, 98, 99,100, 102, 103 and 104; the Schedule.
No. 1 of 1926	Courts of Justice Act, 1926	Sections 2, 3, 4 and 7.
No. 27 of 1926	Court Officers Act 1926	Subsection (2) of section 1; in section 2, the definitions of "the Chief Justice" and "court"; subsections (1) and (2) of section 3; in subsection (6) of section 3, the words from "but such age" to the end of the subsection; sections 4, 5, 6, 7, 10, 11, 13, 14, 19, 20, 21, 22, 25 and 26; in subsection (1) of section 28, the words "the Central Office and"; subsection (2) of section 28; section 30; in subsection (6) of section 35, from the words "but such age" to the end of the subsection; in subsection (1) of section 38, the words" or, where a local bankruptcy court formerly existed, the registrar, or any other officer of that court except the official assignee"; sections 45, 49 and 50;
No. 27 of 1926 (*contd*)		in subsection (1) of section 51, the words "after the appointed day"; subsection (2) of section 51 section 55; subsection (4) of section 59; section 62; subsections (1), (2), (3), (4) and (6) of section 63; section 64.
No. 29 of 1927	Courts of Justice Act, 1927.	The whole Act

Session and Chapter or Number and Year	Short Title	Extent of Repeal
No. 15 of 1928.	Courts of Justice Act 1928	In subsection (1) of section 1, the definition of "the Chief Justice"; subsection (2) of section 1; sections 2, 3, 4, 8, 9, 13, 14, 15 and 22; the Schedule
No. 35 of 1928.	Courts of Justice (No. 2) Act 1928	The whole Act.
No. 40 of 1931.	Courts of Justice (No. 2) Act 1931.	The whole Act
No. 48 of 1936	Courts of Justice Act 1936.	Sections 3, 4, 5 and 6; sub-section (1) of section 7; sections 8, 9, 15, 17, 18, 19, 25, 26, 27 and 28; in sub-section (3) of section 31, the words "on the commencement of this Part of this Act and ",as on and from such commencement,"; subsection (1) of section 33; in sub section,(2) of section 33, the words "At any time after the commencement of this Part of this Act"; sections 45, 48 and 50; subsections (2) and (4) of section 51; sections 54 and 56; paragraph (c) of subsection (3) of section 64 the First Schedule.
No. 25 of 1945.	Court Officers Act, 1945.	Sections 2, 3, 4, 5, 7 and 8.
No. 21 of 1946.	Courts of Justice (District Court) Act 1946.	In section 2, all definitions except the definitions of "Justice" and "the Minister"; sections 3, 4, 5, 6, 7, 8, 9, 10, 11, 12, 13, 14, 15, 17, 18, 19 and 22; the Schedule.
No. 20 of 1947	Courts of Justice Act 1947	Sections 2, 4, 5, 6, 7 and 8 subsections (1) and (2) of section 9; in subsection (3) of section 9, the words "shall be appointed from amongst the Circuit judges by the President acting on the advice of the Government and"; subsection (4) of section 9; sections 13, 14, 15, 17, 18 and 20; the Schedule.

Session and Chapter or Number and Year	Short Title	Extent of Repeal
No. 8 of 1949.	Courts of Justice (District Court) Act, 1949.	Sections 3 and 4; the Schedule.
No. 2 of 1951.	Criminal Justice Act 1951	Sections 19 and 26, the Second Schedule.
No. 32 of 1953.	Courts of Justice Act, 1953	Sections 3, 4, 6, 7, 8, 9, 10, 11, 16, 17 and 18; subsection (1) of section 19; sections 20, 21, 22, 23, 24, 25 and 32; the Schedule.
No. 35 of 1959.	Courts of Justice Act, 1959.	The whole Act.
No. 15 of 1960.	Hire-Purchase (Amendment) Act, 1960	Paragraph (a) of subsection (1) of section 19; paragraph (a) of subsection (2) of section 19. Sections 6, 19 and 31.

SECOND SCHEDULE
PENSIONS OF JUDGES OF COURTS ESTABLISHED BY THE PRINCIPAL ACT

Text not reproduced here.

THIRD SCHEDULE

CIVIL PROCEEDINGS IN RESPECT OF WHICH THE JURISDICTION OF THE HIGH COURT IS, WITH QUANTITATIVE LIMITATIONS, CONFERRED ON THE CIRCUIT COURT, AND JUDGES OF THE CIRCUIT COURT BY WHOM THE JURISDICTION IS TO BE EXERCISED

Text not reproduced here.

FOURTH SCHEDULE
JURISDICTION OF THE CIRCUIT COURT UNDER CERTAIN BRITISH STATUTES AND SAORSTÁT ÉIREANN STATUTES, AND JUDGES OF THE CIRCUIT COURT BY WHOM THE JURISDICTION TO BE EXERCISED

Text not reproduced here.

FIFTH SCHEDULE
ADAPTATIONS (IN RELATION TO THE CIRCUIT COURT AND THE JUDGES THEREOF) OR CERTAIN BRITISH STATUTES RELATING TO FORMER COUNTY COURTS, COURTS OF QUARTER SESSIONS AND JUDGES THEREOF

Text not reproduced here.

SIXTH SCHEDULE
ASSIGNMENT OF JUSTICE OF DISTRICT COURT TO DISTRICT COURT DISTRICTS

Text not reproduced here.

SEVENTH SCHEDULE
EXISTING COURTS AND CORRESPONDING ESTABLISHED BY THE PRINCIPAL ACT, AND JUDGES OF EXISTING COURTS AND CORRESPONDING JUDGES OF COURTS ESTABLISHED BY THE PRINCIPAL ACT

Text not reproduced here.

EIGHTH SCHEDULE
PROVISIONS IN RELATION TO OFFICES AND OFFICERS TO BE ATTACHED TO THE HIGH COURT, THE SUPREME COURT AND THE PRESIDENT OF THE HIGH COURT

Text not reproduced here.

Criminal Justice (Legal Aid) Act 1962

Number 12 of 1962

ARRANGEMENT OF SECTIONS

Section

1. Definitions.

2. Legal aid (District Court) certificate.

3. Legal aid (trial on indictment) certificate.

4. Legal aid (appeal) certificate.

5. Legal aid (case stated) certificate.

6. Legal aid (Supreme Court) certificate.

6A Legal aid (monitoring order) certificate.

6B Legal aid (protection of persons order) certificate.

6C Legal aid (re- trial order) certificate.

7. Payment of expenses of legal aid out of moneys provided by Oireachtas.

8. Restriction of section 34 of Courts of Justice Act, 1924, and section 5 of Courts of Justice Act, 1928.

9. Statement as to means.

10. Regulations.

11. Penalty for false or misleading statements.

12. Commencement.

13. Expenses.

14. Short Title.

AN ACT TO MAKE PROVISION FOR THE GRANT BY THE STATE OF FREE LEGAL AID TO POOR PERSONS IN CERTAIN CRIMINAL CASES. [20th June, 1962.]

BE IT ENACTED BY THE OIREACHTAS AS FOLLOWS:—

1   Definitions

In this Act, except where the context otherwise requires—

"justice" means justice of the District Court and includes the President of the District Court;

"the Minister" means the Minister for Justice.

2   Legal aid (District Court) certificate

[(1) If it appears to the District Court before which a person is charged with an offence or an alternative court within the meaning of section 5 of the Criminal Justice (Miscellaneous Provisions) Act, 1997 before which a person is appearing—

    (a) that the means of the person before it are insufficient to enable him to obtain legal aid, and

297

(b) that by reason of the gravity of the offence with which he is charged or of exceptional circumstances it is essential in the interests of justice that he should have legal aid in the preparation and conduct of his defence before it,

the said District Court or the alternative court, as may be appropriate, shall, on application being made to it in that behalf, grant a certificate, in respect of him, for free legal aid (in this Act referred to as a legal aid (District Court) certificate) and thereupon he shall be entitled to such aid and to have a solicitor and (where he is charged with murder and the said District Court or the alternative court, as the case may be, thinks fit) counsel assigned to him for that purpose in such manner as may be prescribed by regulations under section 10 of this Act.][1]

(2) A decision of the District Court in relation to an application under this section shall be final and shall not be appealable.

Amendments

1   Subsection (1) substituted by Criminal Justice (Miscellaneous Provisions) Act 1997, s 5(6).

2A

[...][1]

Amendments

1   Section 2A (inserted by Criminal Evidence Act 1992, s 15(4)(a)) repealed by Criminal Justice Act 1999, s 12(1).

---

3   Legal aid (trial on indictment) certificate

(1) Where—
  (a) a person is [sent forward for trial][1] for an indictable offence, and
  (b) a certificate for free legal aid (in this Act referred to as a legal aid (trial on indictment) certificate) is granted in respect of him by the District Court, upon his being [sent forward for trial][1], or by the judge of the court before which he is to be or is being tried,

the person shall be entitled to free legal aid in the preparation and conduct of his defence at the trial and to have a solicitor and counsel assigned to him for that purpose in such manner as may be prescribed by regulations under section 10 of this Act.

(2) A legal aid (trial on indictment) certificate shall be granted in respect of a person [sent forward for trial][1] for an indictable offence if (but only if)—
  (a) application is made therefor,
  (b) it appears to the District Court or the judge of the court before which the person is to be or is being tried that the means of the person are insufficient to enable him to obtain legal aid, and

(c) either—

    (i) [the person is charged with murder, or]²

    (ii) it appears to the District Court or the judge of the court before which the person is to be or is being tried (as the case may be) that, having regard to all the circumstances of the case (including the nature of such defence (if any) as may have been set up), it is essential in the interests of justice that the person should have legal aid in the preparation and conduct of his defence at the trial.

Amendments

1   Words substituted by Criminal Justice Act 1999, s 12(2)(a).

2   Subsection (3)(c)(i) substituted by Criminal Justice Act 1999, s 12(2)(b).

4   Legal aid (appeal) certificate

(1) Where—

    (a) a person is convicted of an offence, and

    (b) a certificate for free legal aid (in this Act referred to as a legal aid (appeal) certificate) is granted in respect of him by the District Court or by the judge of the court before which he was tried or under subsection (3) of this section,

the person shall be entitled to free legal aid in the preparation and conduct of an appeal from the conviction or the penalty (if any) imposed on conviction and to have a solicitor and (where the appeal lies to the Court of Criminal Appeal) counsel assigned to him for that purpose in such manner as may be prescribed by regulations under section 10 of this Act.

(2) A legal aid (appeal) certificate shall be granted in respect of a person convicted of an offence if (but only if)—

    (a) application is made therefor,

    (b) it appears to the District Court or the judge of the court before which the person was tried that his means are insufficient to enable him to obtain legal aid, and

    (c) either—

        (i) the conviction is of murder, or

        (ii) it appears to the District Court or the judge of the court before which the person was tried that, by reason of the serious nature of the offence or of exceptional circumstances, it is essential in the interests of justice that the person should have legal aid in the preparation and conduct of an appeal.

(3) Where a person is, on being convicted of an offence, refused a legal aid (appeal) certificate, he may apply for the certificate to the court to which an appeal from the conviction lies either—

    (a) by letter addressed to the registrar of that court setting out the facts of the case and the grounds of the application, or

    (b) to the court itself,

and the court shall grant the certificate if (but only if)—

(i)   it appears to the court that the means of the person are insufficient to enable him to obtain legal aid, and

(ii) either—

(I)   the conviction is of murder, or

(II) it appears to the court that, by reason of the serious nature of the offence or of exceptional circumstances, it is essential in the interests of justice that the convicted person should have legal aid in the preparation and conduct of an appeal.

5   Legal aid (case stated) certificate

(1) Where—

(a)   a person is charged with an offence before the District Court or the Circuit Court or appeals to the Circuit Court against a conviction of an offence by the District Court and the justice or judge (as the case may be) of the court before which the charge or appeal (as the case may be) is heard refers a question of law arising in the proceedings to the High Court or Supreme Court (as the case may be) by way of case stated or the justice states a case in relation to the proceedings for the opinion of the High Court, and

(b)   a certificate for free legal aid (in this Act referred to as a legal aid (case stated) certificate) is granted in respect of the person by the court before which the charge or appeal (as the case may be) is heard or under subsection (3) of this section,

the person shall be entitled to free legal aid in the preparation and conduct of his case in relation to the case stated and to have a solicitor and counsel assigned to him for that purpose in such manner as may be prescribed by regulations under section 10 of this Act.

(2) Where a person is charged with an offence before the District Court or the Circuit Court or appeals to the Circuit Court against a conviction of an offence by the District Court and the justice or judge (as the case may be) of the court before which the charge or appeal (as the case may be) is heard refers a question of law arising in the proceedings to the High Court or Supreme Court (as the case may be) by way of case stated or the justice states a case in relation to the proceedings for the opinion of the High Court, a legal aid (case stated) certificate shall be granted in respect of the person if (but only if)—

(a)   application is made therefor,

(b)   it appears to the court before which the charge or appeal (as the case may be) is heard that the means of the person are insufficient to enable him to obtain legal aid, and

(c)   it appears to the court before which the charge or appeal (as the case may be) is heard that, by reason of the serious nature of the offence with which the person is charged or of exceptional circumstances, it is essential in the interests of justice that a legal aid (case stated) certificate should be granted in respect of the person.

(3) Where, in relation to a case stated, a person is refused a legal aid (case stated) certificate by the District Court or Circuit Court, he may apply for the certificate to the court in which the case stated is to be heard either—

(a)   by letter addressed to the registrar of that court setting out the facts of the case and the grounds of the application, or

(b)   to the court itself,

and the court shall grant the certificate if (but only if)—

(i) it appears to the court that the means of the person are insufficient to enable him to obtain legal aid, and

(ii) it appears to the court that, by reason of the serious nature of the offence with which the person is charged or of exceptional circumstances, it is essential in the interests of justice that a legal aid (case stated) certificate should be granted in respect of the person.

6 Legal aid (Supreme Court) certificate

(1) Where—

(a) a person is charged with an offence,

(b) an appeal is brought to the Supreme Court from a determination of the Court of Criminal Appeal in relation to the offence or the penalty (if any) imposed in respect thereof or from a determination of the High Court on a case stated by a justice in relation to the proceedings in the District Court in regard to the offence or in relation to a question of law arising in those proceedings, and

(c) a certificate for free legal aid (in this Act referred to as a legal aid (Supreme Court) certificate) is granted in respect of the person charged with the offence to which the appeal relates by the Court of Criminal Appeal or the High Court (as the case may be) or under subsection (3) of this section,

the person shall be entitled to free legal aid in the preparation and conduct of his case in relation to the appeal and to have a solicitor and counsel assigned to him for that purpose in such manner as may be prescribed by regulations under section 10 of this Act.

(2) A legal aid (Supreme Court) certificate shall be granted if (but only if)—

(a) application is made therefor,

(b) it appears to the Court of Criminal Appeal or the High Court (as the case may be) that the means of the person charged with the offence are insufficient to enable him to obtain legal aid, and

(c) in the case of an appeal from a determination of the High Court on a case stated by a justice, it appears to the High Court that, by reason of the serious nature of the offence with which the person is charged or of exceptional circumstances, it is essential in the interests of justice that a legal aid (Supreme Court) certificate should be granted in respect of the person.

(3) Where a person is refused a legal aid (Supreme Court) certificate, he may apply for the certificate to the Supreme Court either—

(a) by letter addressed to the registrar of the Supreme Court setting out the facts of the case and the grounds of the application, or

(b) to the Supreme Court itself,

and the Court shall grant the certificate if (but only if)—

(i) it appears to the Court that the means of the person are insufficient to enable him to obtain legal aid, and

(ii) in the case of an appeal from a determination of the High Court on a case stated by a justice, it appears to the Supreme Court that, by reason of the serious nature of the offence with which the person is charged or of exceptional circumstances, it is essential in the interests of justice that a legal aid (Supreme Court) certificate should be granted in respect of the person.

[6A   Legal aid (monitoring order) certificate

(1) Where—

   (a) a monitoring order has been made in relation to a person, and

   (b) a certificate for free legal aid (in this Act referred to as a 'legal aid (monitoring order) certificate') is granted in respect of him or her by the court to which an application is made to vary or revoke the order,

the person shall be entitled to free legal aid in the preparation and conduct of an application under section 26(8) of the Criminal Justice Act 2007 to vary or revoke the order and to have a solicitor and, if the court considers it appropriate, counsel assigned to him or her for that purpose in such manner as may be prescribed by regulations under section 10 of this Act.

(2) A legal aid (monitoring order) certificate shall be granted in relation to a person in respect of whom a monitoring order has been made if (but only if)—

   (a) application is made therefor,

   (b) it appears to the court to which the application is made to vary or revoke the order that—

     (i) the means of the person are insufficient to enable him or her to obtain legal aid, and

     (ii) by reason of the conditions specified in the order or of exceptional circumstances, it is essential in the interests of justice that the person should have legal aid in the preparation and conduct of the application to vary or revoke the order.

(3) In this section 'monitoring order' has the meaning it has in section 26 of the Criminal Justice Act 2007.

6B   Legal aid (protection of persons order) certificate

(1) Where—

   (a) a protection of persons order has been made in relation to a person, and

   (b) a certificate for free legal aid (in this Act referred to as a 'legal aid (protection of persons order) certificate') is granted in respect of him or her by the court to which an application is made to vary or revoke the order,

the person shall be entitled to free legal aid in the preparation and conduct of an application under section 26(8) of the Criminal Justice Act 2007 to vary or revoke the order and to have a solicitor and, if the court considers it appropriate, counsel assigned to him or her for that purpose in such manner as may be prescribed by regulations under section 10 of this Act.

(2) A legal aid (protection of persons order) certificate shall be granted in respect of a person in relation to whom a protection of persons order has been made if (but only if)—

   (a) application is made therefor,

   (b) it appears to the court to which the application is made to vary or revoke the order that—

     (i) the means of the person are insufficient to enable him or her to obtain legal aid, and

    (ii) by reason of the conditions specified in the order or of exception; circumstances, it is essential in the interests of justice that the person should have legal aid in the preparation and conduct of the application to vary or revoke the order.

(3) In this section 'protection of persons order' has the meaning it has in section 26 of the Criminal Justice Act 2007.]¹

Amendments

1   Section 6A and 6B inserted by Criminal Justice Act 2007, s 27(a).

[6C   Legal aid (re- trial order) certificate

(1) Where—

    (a) an application for a re-trial order has been made in relation to a person, and

    (b) a certificate for free legal aid (in this Act referred to as a 'legal aid (re-trial order) certificate') is granted in respect of him or her by the Court of Criminal Appeal, the person shall be entitled to free legal aid in the preparation and conduct of his or her case in relation to an application under section 8 or 9 of the Criminal Procedure Act 2010 and to have a solicitor and counsel assigned to him or her for that purpose in such manner as may be prescribed by regulations under section 10 of this Act.

(2) A legal aid (re-trial order) certificate shall be granted in relation to a person in respect of whom an application under section 8 or 9 of the Criminal Procedure Act 2010 has been made if (but only if)—

    (a) an application is made therefor,

    (b) it appears to the Court of Criminal Appeal that—

        (i) the means of the person are insufficient to enable him or her to obtain legal aid, and

        (ii) it is essential in the interests of justice that the person should have legal aid in the preparation and conduct of his or her case in relation to the application for a re-trial order.

(3) In this section 'application for a retrial order' has the meaning it has in section 7 of the Criminal Procedure Act 2010.]¹

Amendments

1   Section 6C inserted by Criminal Procedure Act 2010, s 11(a).

7   Payment of expenses of legal aid out of moneys provided by Oireachtas

(1) Where a legal aid (District Court) certificate or a legal aid (trial on indictment) certificate has been granted in respect of a person, any fees, costs or other expenses properly incurred in

nducting the defence to which the certificate relates shall, subject to the section 10 of this Act, be paid out of moneys provided by the Oireachtas.

aid (appeal) certificate, a legal aid (case stated) certificate or a legal aid (Supreme Court) certificate has been granted in respect of a person, any fees, costs or other expenses properly incurred in preparing and conducting the person's case in relation to the appeal or case stated (as the case may be) to which the certificate relates shall, subject to the regulations under section 10 of this Act, be paid out of moneys provided by the Oireachtas.

[(3) Where a legal aid (monitoring order) certificate or a legal aid (protection of persons order) certificate has been granted in respect of a person, any fees, costs or other expenses properly incurred in preparing and conducting the person's application to vary or revoke the monitoring order or the protection of persons order to which the certificate relates shall, subject to the regulations under section 10 of this Act, be paid out of moneys provided by the Oireachtas.][1]

[(4) Where a legal aid (re-trial order) certificate has been granted in respect of a person, any fees, costs or other expenses properly incurred in preparing and conducting the person's case in relation to the application to which the certificate relates shall, subject to the regulations under section 10 of this Act, be paid out of moneys provided by the Oireachtas.][2]

Amendments

1   Subsection (3) inserted by Criminal Justice Act 2007, s 27(b).

2   Subsection (4) inserted by Criminal Procedure Act 2010, s 11(b).

---

8   **Restriction of section 34 of Courts of Justice Act, 1924, and section 5 of Courts of Justice Act, 1928**   *Both repealed S13. Crim. Proc. Act 43*

(1) Where a legal aid (trial on indictment) certificate is granted in respect of a person, the Court of Criminal Appeal shall not have jurisdiction under section 34 of the Courts of Justice Act, 1924, or section 5 of the Courts of Justice Act, 1928, to award costs to the person in respect of court proceedings in relation to which the certificate applies.

(2) Where a legal aid (appeal) certificate is granted in respect of a person, the Court of Criminal Appeal shall not have jurisdiction under the said section 34 or the said section 5 to award costs to the person in respect of court proceedings in relation to which the certificate applies.

9   **Statement as to means**

(1) Before a person is granted a legal aid certificate he may be required by the court or judge, as the case may be, granting the certificate to furnish a written statement in such form as may be prescribed by the Minister by regulations under section 10 of this Act about matters relevant for determining whether his means are insufficient to enable him to obtain legal aid.

(2) In this and in the next following section "legal aid certificate" means a legal aid (District Court) certificate, [...][1] a legal aid (trial on indictment) certificate, a legal aid (appeal) certificate, a legal aid (case stated) certificate[, a legal aid (Supreme Court) certificate, a

legal aid (monitoring order) certificate[", a legal aid (protection of persons order) certificate or a legal aid (re-trial order) certificate.][2]

Amendments

1   Words deleted (inserted by Criminal Evidence Act 1992, s 15(4)(b)) by Criminal Justice Act 1999, s 12(3).

2   Words inserted by Criminal Justice Act 2007, s 27(c) and further amended by Criminal Procedure Act 2010, s 11(c).

10   Regulations

(1) The Minister may make regulations for carrying this Act into effect and the regulations may, in particular, prescribe—

  (a)   the form of legal aid certificates,

  (b)   the rates or scales of payment of any fees, costs or other expenses payable out of moneys provided by the Oireachtas pursuant to such certificates,

  (c)   the manner in which solicitors and counsel are to be assigned pursuant to such certificates.

  (d)   (i)   a requirement that a solicitor who has notified a county registrar in accordance with the Criminal Justice (Legal Aid) Regulations, 1965 (S.I. No. 12 of 1965), of his willingness to act for persons to whom legal aid certificates are granted must, when required to do so by the Minister, furnish to the County Registrar a certificate issued by the Collector-General (within the meaning of section 851 of the Taxes Consolidation Act, 1997) in respect of that solicitor certifying that he has complied with all the obligations imposed on him by the Tax Acts, the Capital Gains Tax Acts and the Value-Added Tax Act, 1972, and the enactments amending or extending that Act (and any instruments made under those Acts) in relation to—

      (I)   the payment or remittance of the taxes, interest and penalties required to be paid or remitted, and

      (II)   the delivery of returns,

    (ii)   a requirement that a barrister, the willingness of whom to act for persons to whom legal aid certificates are granted has been notified to the Minister by the General Council of the Bar of Ireland in accordance with the Criminal Justice (Legal Aid) Regulations, 1965, must, when required to do so by the Minister, furnish to the Minister a certificate issued by the Collector-General (within the meaning of section 851 of the Taxes Consolidation Act, 1997) in respect of that barrister certifying that he has complied with all the obligations imposed on him by the Tax Acts, the Capital Gains Tax Acts and the Value-Added Tax Act, 1972, and the enactments amending or extending that Act (and any instruments made under those Acts) in relation to—

      (I)   the payment or remittance of the taxes, interest and penalties required to be paid or remitted, and

      (II)   the delivery of returns,

(e) the conditions that must be satisfied before a certificate referred to in paragraph (d) of this subsection may be issued by the Collector-General (within the meaning aforesaid),

(f) matters consequential on, or incidental to, a requirement or condition prescribed under paragraph (d) or (e) of this subsection (which may include a provision enabling the deletion from any list kept pursuant to regulations under this subsection of the name of a solicitor or barrister who has failed to comply with a requirement prescribed under the said paragraph (d)).][1]

(2) Regulations under this section in relation to the matters specified in paragraph (b) of subsection (1) of this section shall not be made without the consent of the Minister for Finance.

(3) Every regulation made by the Minister under this section shall be laid before each House of the Oireachtas as soon as may be after it is made and, if a resolution annulling the regulation is passed by either such House within the next subsequent twenty-one days on which that House has sat after the regulation is laid before it, the regulation shall be annulled accordingly but without prejudice to anything previously done thereunder.

Amendments

1   Subsections (1)(d)–(f) inserted by Finance Act 1998, s 132.

11   Penalty for false or misleading statements

(1) A person who, for the purpose of obtaining free legal aid under this Act, whether for himself or some other person, knowingly makes a false statement or false representation either verbally or in writing or knowingly conceals any material fact shall be guilty of an offence and shall be liable on summary conviction to a fine not exceeding one hundred pounds or to imprisonment for a term not exceeding six months or to both the fine and the imprisonment.

(2) Upon conviction of a person of an offence under this section, the court by which the person is convicted may, if in the circumstances of the case the court so thinks fit, order the person to pay to the Minister the whole or part (as the court considers appropriate) of any sum paid under section 7 of this Act in respect of the free legal aid in relation to which the offence was committed, and any sum paid to the Minister pursuant to this section shall be paid into or disposed of for the benefit of the Exchequer in accordance with the directions of the Minister for Finance.

12   Commencement

This Act shall come into operation on such day as the Minister may appoint by order.

13   Expenses

The expenses incurred by the Minister in the administration of this Act shall, to such extent as may be sanctioned by the Minister for Finance, be defrayed out of moneys provided by the Oireachtas.

14   Short Title

This Act may be cited as the Criminal Justice (Legal Aid) Act 1962.

Criminal Justice Act 1964

Number 5 of 1964

ARRANGEMENT OF SECTIONS

Section

1. Death penalty restricted.

2. Punishment in place of death.

3. Procedure in capital murder cases.

4. Malice.

5. Amendment of Offences Against the Person Act, 1861.

6. Amendment of Piracy Act, 1837.

7. Amendment of Juries Act, 1927.

8. Amendment of Treason Act, 1939.

9. Amendment of Defence Act, 1954.

10. Amendment of Geneva Conventions Act, 1962.

11. Short title.

AN ACT TO AMEND THE LAW AS TO THE IMPOSITION OF THE DEATH PENALTY AND AS TO MALICE IN THE CASE OF MURDER. [25th March, 1964.]

BE IT ENACTED BY THE OIREACHTAS AS FOLLOWS:—

1–3   [...]¹

Amendments

1   Sections 1–3 repealed by Criminal Justice Act 1990, s 9 and Sch 2.

---

4   Malice

(1) Where a person kills another unlawfully the killing shall not be murder unless the accused person intended to kill, or cause serious injury to, some person, whether the person actually killed or not.

(2) The accused person shall be presumed to have intended the natural and probable consequences of his conduct; but this presumption may be rebutted.

5–11   [...]¹

Amendments

1   Sections 5–10 repealed by Criminal Justice Act 1990, s 9 and Sch 2.

---

11 Short title

This Act may be cited as the Criminal Justice Act, 1964.

Firearms Act 1964

Number 1 of 1964

ARRANGEMENT OF SECTIONS

Section

1. Interpretation.
2. Extension of Principal Act to airguns.
3. Temporary prohibition of game shooting.
4. Temporary custody of firearms by Garda Síochána in interests of public safety.
5. Contravention of orders under sections 3 and 4.
6. Provisions in relation to orders under sections 3 and 4.
7. Disposal of certain firearms and ammunition in the possession of the Garda Síochána.
8. Disposal of firearms in certain circumstances.
9. Renewal of firearm certificate.
10. Period of validity of firearm certificate granted by Minister.
11. Change of firearm to which firearm certificate relates.
12. Limited use of shot-gun.
13. Sale of firearms by auctioneers.
14. Amendment of section 1 of Principal Act.
15. Amendment of section 2 of Principal Act.
16. Amendment of section 3 of Principal Act.
17. Amendment of section 8 of Principal Act.
18. Amendment of section 9 of Principal Act.
19. Amendment of section 10 of Principal Act.
20. Amendment of section 16 of Principal Act.
21. Amendment of section 17 of Principal Act.
22. Amendment of section 21 of Principal Act.
23. Amendment of section 24 of Principal Act.
24. Onus of proof.
25. Extension of sections 23 and 28 of Larceny Act, 1916.
26. Possession of firearm while taking vehicle without authority.
27. Prohibition of use of firearms to resist arrest or aid escape.
27A Possession of firearm or ammunition in suspicious circumstances
27B Carrying firearm with criminal intent
27C Provisions relating to minimum sentences under Firearms Acts 1925 to 2006.
28. Repeals.
29. Short title and collective citation.

AN ACT TO AMEND AND EXTEND THE FIREARMS ACT, 1925. [28th January, 1964.]

BE IT ENACTED BY THE OIREACHTAS AS FOLLOWS:—

1   Interpretation

(1) In this Act—

["the Commissioner" means the Commissioner of the Garda Síochána or a member of the Garda Síochána, or members of a particular rank in the Garda Síochána, not below the rank of superintendent appointed in writing by the Commissioner for the purpose of performing any of the Commissioner's functions under this Act;

"firearm" includes a restricted firearm, unless otherwise provided or the context otherwise requires;

"the Minister" means the Minister for Justice, Equality and Law Reform;][1]

 "the Principal Act" means the Firearms Act, 1925;

"public place" means any place to which the public have access whether as of right or by permission and whether subject to or free of charge;

"Superintendent" means a Superintendent of the Garda Síochána and includes an Inspector of the Garda Síochána acting as a Superintendent.

(2) In this Act and in the Principal Act, references to the Principal Act shall, where the context so requires or permits, be construed as references to that Act as amended by this Act.

(3) This Act shall be construed as one with the Principal Act.

Amendments

1   Definitions substituted by Criminal Justice Act 2006, s 52.

---

2   Extension of Principal Act to airguns

[…][1]

Amendments

1   Section 2 repealed by Firearms and Offensive Weapons Act 1990, s 4(2).

---

3   Temporary prohibition of game shooting

(1) The Minister may, on its being represented to him by the Minister for Lands that it is necessary to do so in the interests of the preservation of [protected wild animals or protected wild birds within the meaning of the Wildlife Act, 1976],[1] make an order prohibiting the use or carriage of firearms or of firearms of such class or classes as may be specified in the order in a public place or on any lands either throughout the State or in such area or areas as may be

specified in the order during such period, not exceeding one month, as may be specified in the order.

(2) The Minister may by order, made after consultation with the Minister for Lands, amend or revoke an order under this section, including an order under this subsection[, but an order under this subsection shall not extend for more than a month a period mentioned in subsection (1) of this section.]²

(3) An order under this section shall not apply in relation to the use or carriage of firearms by members of the Defence Forces or the Garda Síochána or to the use or carriage of a firearm by a person to whom the Superintendent of any district has granted a permit which is in force to use and carry a firearm for a purpose (other than the shooting of [such protected wild animals or wild birds]³) specified in the permit in that district during a period specified in the permit, if the firearm is being used and carried in accordance with the terms of the permit.

(4) (a) Whenever an order under subsection (1) of this section is in force in relation to any district, the Superintendent of that district may, in his absolute discretion, grant to any person a permit to use and carry in that district for a purpose (other than the shooting of [such protected wild animals or wild birds]³) specified in the permit during a period specified in the permit a firearm to the use or carriage of which the order applies.

(b) The Superintendent of any district may revoke a permit granted under this section in relation to that district.

Amendments

1   Words substituted by Wildlife Act 1976, s 65(a).
2   Words substituted by Wildlife Act 1976, s 65(b).
3   Words substituted by Wildlife Act 1976, s 65(c).

4   Temporary custody of firearms by Garda Síochána in interests of public safety

(1) The Minister may, if satisfied that it is necessary to do so in the interests of the public safety, [or public security]¹ make an order requiring every person residing in an area specified in the order and having possession of any firearm or ammunition or of a firearm or ammunition of such class or classes as may be specified in the order to surrender it on or before a date specified in the order to the Garda Síochána.

(2) An order under subsection (1) of this section shall remain in force for such period not exceeding one month as may be specified in the order.

(3) The Minister may by order amend or revoke an order under this section, including an order under this subsection.

(4) Whenever an order under subsection (1) of this section is in force a member of the Garda Síochána may seize a firearm or ammunition to which the order applies found in the area specified in the order after the date on or before which the firearm or ammunition is required by the order to be surrendered to the Garda Síochána and the Garda Síochána may, while the order remains in force, retain possession of any firearm or ammunition seized by or surrendered to them in pursuance of the order.

(5) As soon as may be after the time at which an order under subsection (1) of this section ceases to be in force, the Garda Síochána shall, subject to the provisions of the Principal Act, return any firearms or ammunition surrendered to or seized by them pursuant to the order to the owners thereof.

(6) An order under subsection (1) of this section shall not apply in relation to firearms or ammunition in the possession of members of the Defence Forces or the Garda Síochána.

Amendments

1   Words inserted by European Communities (Acquisition and Possession of Weapons and Ammunition) Regulations 1993 (SI 362/1993), reg 12.

5   Contravention of orders under sections 3 and 4

A person who contravenes a provision of an order under section 3 or section 4 of this Act shall be guilty of an offence under the Principal Act.

6   Provisions in relation to orders under sections 3 and 4

(1) An order under section 3 or section 4 of this Act shall be laid before each House of the Oireachtas as soon as may be after it is made and if a resolution annulling the order is passed by either such House within the next twenty-one days on which that House has sat after the order is laid before it, the order shall be annulled accordingly, but without prejudice to the validity of anything previously done thereunder.

(2) Whenever an order is made under section 3 or section 4 of this Act, notice of the making of the order and of its effect shall be published in at least one newspaper circulating in the area or each area to which the order applies.

7   Disposal of certain firearms and ammunition in the possession of the Garda Síochána

(1) References in this section to a firearm or ammunition that has come into the possession of the Garda Síochána are references to a firearm or ammunition that has come into the possession of the Garda Síochána before the passing of this Act pursuant to section 6 of the Principal Act or otherwise.

(2) The Commissioner may cause to be published in each daily newspaper published in the State a notice stating that any firearm or ammunition that has come into the possession of the Garda Síochána may be sold or destroyed unless the owner thereof makes claim and establishes his title thereto within the period of three months beginning on the date of the publication of the notice.

(3) Where a notice is published pursuant to subsection (2) of this section—

   (a)   the Commissioner shall cause to be sent by post to every person of whose address the Garda Síochána are aware and who is believed to be the owner of a firearm or ammunition that has come into the possession of the Garda Síochána a notice stating that the firearm or ammunition may be sold or destroyed unless the person makes claim and establishes his title thereto within the period of three months beginning on the date of the publication of the notice referred to in subsection (2) of this section,

(b) where the address of the person believed to be the owner is unknown or the Commissioner is of opinion that a notice as aforesaid would not be understood by such person, the Commissioner may, at his discretion, cause the notice to be sent by post or otherwise given to any member of the family of such person or to such other person, if any, as he may, in the particular circumstances, think appropriate.

(4) Where a notice is published pursuant to subsection (2) of this section and, in cases where it is appropriate, notice is given pursuant to subsection (3) of this section—

(a) a person who makes claim and establishes his title to a firearm or ammunition that has come into the possession of the Garda Síochána within the period specified in the notice published pursuant to subsection (2) of this section may, subject to the provisions of the Principal Act, cause the firearm or ammunition to be removed from the custody of the Garda Síochána within that period, and

(b) the Commissioner may cause to be sold any firearm or ammunition that has come into the possession of the Garda Síochána and is not claimed and removed from the custody of the Garda Síochána or to which title is not established to the satisfaction of the Commissioner within the period referred to in paragraph (a) of this subsection and shall, as soon as may be, cause the proceeds of the sale to be paid to the owner or, if the owner cannot be ascertained, for the benefit of the Exchequer, and

(c) the Commissioner may cause to be destroyed any firearm or ammunition that has been offered for sale under paragraph (b) of this subsection and has not been sold, if, in the opinion of the Commissioner, the firearm or ammunition is unlikely to be sold if offered for sale again and shall cause to be sent to any person who is believed to be the owner of the firearm or ammunition or (where appropriate) to another person in accordance with paragraph (b) of subsection (3) of this section a notice informing the person to whom it is sent of such destruction.

8   Disposal of firearms in certain circumstances

The following section is hereby substituted for section 6 of the Principal Act:

[...][1]

Amendments

1   See Firearms Act 1925, s 6.

---

9   Renewal of firearm certificate

[(1) The Commissioner may from time to time renew a firearm certificate granted by him or her.

(2) The superintendent of the district where the holder of such a certificate resides may from time to time renew such a certificate.

(3) The superintendent of a district where the holder of a firearm certificate resides may from time to time renew a firearm certificate which has been granted by a superintendent.

(4) An inspector or sergeant of the Garda Síochána in the district where the holder of a firearm certificate issued by a superintendent resides may from time to time renew the certificate.

(5) A superintendent, or other member of the Garda Síochána, who is authorised under this section to renew a firearm certificate ("an authorised member") may refuse to renew it, or vary any conditions to which it is subject under section 4(2)(g) of the Principal Act, only if prior sanction to do so in the particular case has been given by the Commissioner or superintendent, as the case may be.

[(6) An application for renewal of a firearm certificate shall be in the prescribed form.]²

(7) A renewal of a firearm certificate shall be in the prescribed form.

(8) Before renewing a firearm certificate, an authorised member shall be of opinion that the conditions to which it is subject have been complied with and will continue to be complied with during the period for which the certificate is renewed.

(9) On the renewal of a firearm certificate, an authorised member may, subject to subsection (5) of this section, vary any conditions to which the certificate is subject under section 4(2)(g) of the Principal Act, if of opinion that such a variation is necessary in the interests of public safety or security.]¹

Amendments

1   Section 9 substituted by Criminal Justice Act 2006, s 53.
2   Subsection (6) substituted by Criminal Justice (Miscellaneous Provisions) Act 2009, s 37.

10   Period of validity of firearm certificate granted by Minister

[...]¹

Amendments

1   Section 10 repealed by Firearms (Firearm Certificates For Non-Residents) Act 2000, s 7.

11   Change of firearm to which firearm certificate relates

(1) Subject to subsection (3) of this section, [the Minister or the Commissioner may substitute for the description of a firearm in a firearm certificate granted by him or her]¹ the description of another firearm and, upon such substitution, the certificate shall have effect in relation to that other firearm and shall not have effect in relation to the first-mentioned firearm.

(2) Subject to subsection (3) of this section, the Superintendent of any district or any member of the Garda Síochána in any district duly authorised to do so by the Superintendent of that district may substitute for the description of a firearm [(other than a restricted firearm)]¹ in a

firearm certificate held by a person residing in that district the description of another [such][1] firearm and, upon such substitution, the certificate shall have effect in relation to that other firearm and shall not have effect in relation to the first-mentioned firearm.

(3) A substitution under this section in a firearm certificate shall not be effected unless the rate of excise duty chargeable in respect of a renewal of the certificate after the substitution does not exceed the rate chargeable immediately before such substitution.

Amendments

1   Words amended by Criminal Justice Act 2006, s 54.

12   Limited use of shot-gun

[...][1]

Amendments

1   Section 12 repealed by Criminal Justice Act 2006, s 30(15).

13   Sale of firearms by auctioneers

(1) Notwithstanding anything contained in section 10 of the Principal Act, an auctioneer who stands authorised under this section may sell, expose for sale and have in his possession for sale, by auction in the ordinary course of his business as an auctioneer, a firearm or ammunition: Provided that in the case of a sale, the firearm or ammunition is not delivered to the purchaser until he produces to the auctioneer a firearm certificate which is in force authorising him to purchase the firearm or ammunition or proves that he is lawfully entitled to have possession of the firearm or ammunition without having a firearm certificate therefor.

(2) The Superintendent of any district may authorise in writing an auctioneer in that district to sell, expose for sale and have in his possession for sale, by auction a firearm or ammunition during such period, not exceeding one year, as may be specified in the authorisation.

(3) A Superintendent shall not grant an authorisation under this section to an auctioneer unless he is satisfied, having regard to all the circumstances (including the provision made or to be made for the storage of the firearms and ammunition to which the authorisation, if granted, would relate), that the sale, exposing for sale or possession of firearms or ammunition in pursuance of the authorisation will not endanger the public safety or the peace.

(4) A Superintendent may impose in relation to the grant of an authorisation under this section such conditions (if any) as he considers necessary to prevent danger to the public and, where a condition is imposed, it shall be specified in the authorisation.

(5) An authorisation under this section may be revoked at any time by the Superintendent of the district in which it was granted.

(6) A person who contravenes a condition imposed in relation to the grant of an authorisation under this section shall be guilty of an offence under the Principal Act.

[(7) In this section, references to a firearm and ammunition do not include references to a restricted firearm or restricted ammunition.

(8) This section is without prejudice to subsections (4A) to (4G) of section 10 of the Principal Act.][1]

Amendments

1   Subsections (7) and (8) inserted by Criminal Justice Act 2006, s 55.

14   Amendment of section 1 of Principal Act

Section 1 of the Principal Act is hereby amended by the insertion after subsection (2) of the following subsection:[1]

Amendments

1   See Firearms Act 1925, s 1.

15   Amendment of section 2 of Principal Act

Section 2 of the Principal Act is hereby amended by—

    (a)   the insertion in paragraph (g) of subsection (3) after "humane killer" of "or ammunition therefor", and

    (b)   the insertion after subsection (3) of the following subsection:[1]

Amendments

1   See Firearms Act 1925, s 2.

16   Amendment of section 3 of Principal Act

Section 3 of the Principal Act is hereby amended by—

    (a)   the substitution of "before the 31st day of July in any year" for "during the month of July" in subsection (3), and

    (b)   the substitution for subsection (4) of the following subsection—[1]

Amendments

1 See Firearms Act 1925, s 3.

17 Amendment of section 8 of Principal Act

Section 8 of the Principal Act is hereby amended by—

(a) the substitution of "sixteen years" for "fifteen years" in paragraph (a) of subsection (1),

(b) the deletion of paragraphs (d) and (e) of subsection (1) and the insertion of the following paragraphs:[1]

Amendments

1 See Firearms Act 1925, s 8.

18 Amendment of section 9 of Principal Act

Section 9 of the Principal Act is hereby amended by the deletion in subsection (3) of "the number of registered firearms dealers in the neighbourhood in which the applicant proposes to carry on business,".

19 Amendment of section 10 of Principal Act

Section 10 of the Principal Act is hereby amended by—

(a) the substitution of "any person" for "any firearms dealer" and "such person" for "such firearms dealer" in subsection (2), and

(b) the substitution for subsection (4) of the following subsection:[1]

(c) the insertion in paragraph (b) of subsection (6) after "letting on hire" of ", giving" and after "hiring" of ", receiving".

Amendments

1 See Firearms Act 1925, s 10.

20 Amendment of section 16 of Principal Act,

Section 16 of the Principal Act is hereby amended by the insertion in subsection (4) before "the firearm" of "or consigning for export".

21   Amendment of section 17 of Principal Act

(1) The restriction imposed by section 17 of the Principal Act on the importation into the State of firearms shall not apply in relation to the importation of a firearm by the holder of a firearm certificate in respect of the firearm which is in force.

(2) The said section 17 is hereby amended by—

   (a)   the deletion in subsection (3) of "(not exceeding six months)", and

   (b)   the deletion in subsection (4) of "(not being more than one month)".

Amendments

1   Section 21 repealed by Criminal Justice (Miscellaneous Provisions) Act 2009, s 38 which is not yet in operation (February 2011).

22   Amendment of section 21 of Principal Act

Section 21 of the Principal Act is hereby amended by the substitution of the following subsection for subsection (6):[1]

Amendments

1   See Firearms Act 1925, s 21.

23   Amendment of section 24 of Principal Act

Section 24 of the Principal Act is hereby amended by the substitution of "forty-eight hours" for "twenty-four hours" in subsection (2).

24   Onus of proof

(1) Where, in a prosecution for an offence under the Principal Act, the existence or non-existence of a firearm certificate, a licence under section 17 of the Principal Act, an authorisation under section 2 of the Principal Act, a permit under section 3 of this Act or an authorisation under section 13 of this Act is material, it shall not be necessary to prove that the certificate, licence, authorisation or permit does not exist.

(2) Where, in a prosecution for an offence under the Principal Act, possession, use or carriage of a firearm or ammunition by a person is proved, it shall not be necessary to prove that the person was not entitled to have in his possession, use or carry a firearm or ammunition.

25   Extension of section [...][1] 28 of Larceny Act, 1916

(1) In section 28 of the Larceny Act, 1916, "offensive weapon" shall include a firearm that is not loaded and an imitation firearm.

(2) In this section and the next two sections "imitation firearm" means anything which is not a firearm but has the appearance of being a firearm.

Amendments

1   Words 'section 23' deleted by Criminal Law (Jurisdiction) Act 1976, s 21.

26   Possession of firearm while taking vehicle without authority

[(1) A person who contravenes subsection (1) of section 112 of the Road Traffic Act 1961 and who at the time of the contravention has with him or her a firearm or imitation firearm is guilty of an offence.

(2) A person guilty of an offence under this section is liable on conviction on indictment—

(a) to imprisonment for a term not exceeding 14 years or such shorter term as the court may determine, subject to subsections (4) to (6) of this section or, where subsection (8) of this section applies, to that subsection, and

(b) at the court's discretion, to a fine of such amount as the court considers appropriate.

(3) The court, in imposing sentence on a person for an offence under this section, may, in particular, have regard to whether the person has a previous conviction for an offence under the Firearms Acts 1925 to 2006, the Offences against the State Acts 1939 to 1998 or the Criminal Justice (Terrorist Offences) Act 2005.

(4) Where a person (other than a person under the age of 18 years) is convicted of an offence under this section, the court shall, in imposing sentence, specify a term of imprisonment of not less than 5 years as the minimum term of imprisonment to be served by the person.

[(4A) The purpose of subsections (5) and (6) of this section is to provide that in view of the harm caused to society by the unlawful possession and use of firearms, a court, in imposing sentence on a person (other than a person under the age of 18 years) for an offence under this section, shall specify as the minimum term of imprisonment to be served by the person a term of not less than 5 years, unless the court determines that by reason of exceptional and specific circumstances relating to the offence, or the person convicted of it, it would be unjust in all the circumstances to do so.][2]

(5) Subsection (4) of this section does not apply where the court is satisfied that there are exceptional and specific circumstances relating to the offence, or to the person convicted of it, which would make the minimum term unjust in all the circumstances, and for this purpose the court may[, subject to subsection (6),][3] have regard to any matters it considers appropriate, including—

(a) whether the person pleaded guilty to the offence and, if so—

(i)   the stage at which the intention to plead guilty was indicated, and

(ii) the circumstances in which the indication was given,

and

(b) whether the person materially assisted in the investigation of the offence.

(6) The court, in considering for the purposes of subsection (5) of this section whether a sentence of not less than 5 years imprisonment is unjust in all the circumstances, may have regard, in particular, to—

(a) whether the person convicted of the offence has a previous conviction for an offence under the Firearms Acts 1925 to 2006, the Offences Against the State Acts 1939 to 1998 or the Criminal Justice (Terrorist Offences) Act 2005, and

(b) whether the public interest in preventing the unlawful possession or use of firearms would be served by the imposition of a lesser sentence.

(7) Subsections (4) to (6) of this section apply and have effect only in relation to a person convicted of a first offence under this section (other than a person who falls under subsection (8)(b) of this section), and accordingly references in those first-mentioned subsections to an offence under this section are to be construed as references to a first such offence.

(8) Where a person (except a person under the age of 18 years)—

(a) is convicted of a second or subsequent offence under this section,

(b) is convicted of a first offence under this section and has been convicted of an offence under section 15 of the Principal Act, section 27, 27A or 27B of this Act or section 12A of the Firearms and Offensive Weapons Act 1990,

the court shall, in imposing sentence, specify a term of imprisonment of not less than 5 years as the minimum term of imprisonment to be served by the person.

(9) In proceedings for an offence under this section it is a good defence for the defendant to show that he or she had the firearm or imitation firearm for a lawful purpose when doing the act alleged to constitute the offence under subsection (1) of the said section 112.

(10) Section 27C of this Act applies in relation to proceedings for an offence under this section and any minimum term of imprisonment imposed under subsection (4) or (8) of this section in those proceedings.]¹

Amendments

1 Section 26 substituted by Criminal Justice Act 2006, s 57.

2 Subsection (4A) inserted by Criminal Justice Act 2007, s 36(a).

3 Words inserted by Criminal Justice Act 2007, s 36(b).

27   Prohibition of use of firearms to resist arrest or aid escape

[(1) A person shall not use or produce a firearm or imitation firearm—

(a) for the purpose of or while resisting the arrest of the person or of another person by a member of the Garda Síochána, or

(b) for the purpose of aiding, or in the course of, the escape or rescue of the person or of another person from lawful custody.

(2) A person who contravenes subsection (1) of this section is guilty of an offence and liable on conviction on indictment—

(a) to imprisonment for life or such shorter term as the court may determine, subject to subsections (4) to (6) of this section or, where subsection (8) of this section applies, to that subsection, and

(b) at the court's discretion, to a fine of such amount as the court considers appropriate.

(3) The court, in imposing sentence on a person for an offence under this section, may, in particular, have regard to whether the person has a previous conviction for an offence under the Firearms Acts 1925 to 2006, the Offences against the State Acts 1939 to 1998 or the Criminal Justice (Terrorist Offences) Act 2005.

(4) Where a person (other than a person under the age of 18 years) is convicted of an offence under this section, the court shall, in imposing sentence, specify a term of imprisonment of not less than 10 years as the minimum term of imprisonment to be served by the person.

[(4A) The purpose of subsections (5) and (6) of this section is to provide that in view of the harm caused to society by the unlawful possession and use of firearms, a court, in imposing sentence on a person (other than a person under the age of 18 years) for an offence under this section, shall specify as the minimum term of imprisonment to be served by the person a term of not less than 10 years, unless the court determines that by reason of exceptional and specific circumstances relating to the offence, or the person convicted of it, it would be unjust in all the circumstances to do so.][2]

(5) Subsection (4) of this section does not apply where the court is satisfied that there are exceptional and specific circumstances relating to the offence, or to the person convicted of it, which would make the minimum term unjust in all the circumstances, and for this purpose the court may[, subject to subsection (6),][3] have regard to any matters it considers appropriate, including—

    (a) whether the person pleaded guilty to the offence and, if so—

        (i) the stage at which the intention to plead guilty was indicated, and

        (ii) the circumstances in which the indication was given,

        and

    (b) whether the person materially assisted in the investigation of the offence.

(6) The court, in considering for the purposes of subsection (5) of this section whether a sentence of not less than 10 years imprisonment is unjust in all the circumstances, may have regard, in particular, to—

    (a) whether the person convicted of the offence has a previous conviction for an offence under the Firearms Acts 1925 to 2006, the Offences Against the State Acts 1939 to 1998 or the Criminal Justice (Terrorist Offences) Act 2005, and

    (b) whether the public interest in preventing the unlawful possession or use of firearms would be served by the imposition of a lesser sentence.

(7) Subsections (4) to (6) of this section apply and have effect only in relation to a person convicted of a first offence under this section (other than a person who falls under subsection (8)(b) of this section), and accordingly references in those first-mentioned subsections to an offence under this section are to be construed as references to a first such offence.

(8) Where a person (except a person under the age of 18 years)—

    (a) is convicted of a second or subsequent offence under this section,

    (b) is convicted of a first offence under this section and has been convicted of an offence under section 15 of the Principal Act, section 26, 27A or 27B of this Act or section 12A of the Firearms and Offensive Weapons Act 1990,

the court shall, in imposing sentence, specify a term of imprisonment of not less than 10 years as the minimum term of imprisonment to be served by the person.

(9) Section 27C of this Act applies in relation to proceedings for an offence under this section and any minimum term of imprisonment imposed under subsection (4) or (8) of this section in those proceedings.]¹

Amendments

1   Section 27 substituted by Criminal Justice Act 2006, s 58.
2   Subsection (4A) inserted by Criminal Justice Act 2007, s 37(a).
3   Words inserted by Criminal Justice Act 2007, s 37(b).

[27A   Possession of firearm or ammunition in suspicious circumstances

(1) It is an offence for a person to possess or control a firearm [or ammunition]² in circumstances that give rise to a reasonable inference that the person does not possess or control it for a lawful purpose, unless the person possesses or controls it for such a purpose.

(2) A person guilty of an offence under this section is liable on conviction on indictment—

(a)   to imprisonment for a term not exceeding 14 years or such shorter term as the court may determine, subject to subsections (4) to (6) of this section or, where subsection (8) of this section applies, to that subsection, and

(b)   at the court's discretion, to a fine of such amount as the court considers appropriate.

(3) The court, in imposing sentence on a person for an offence under this section, may, in particular, have regard to whether the person has a previous conviction for an offence under the Firearms Acts 1925 to 2006, the Offences against the State Acts 1939 to 1998 or the Criminal Justice (Terrorist Offences) Act 2005.

(4) Where a person (other than a person under the age of 18 years) is convicted of an offence under this section, the court shall, in imposing sentence, specify a term of imprisonment of not less than 5 years as the minimum term of imprisonment to be served by the person.

[(4A) The purpose of subsections (5) and (6) of this section is to provide that in view of the harm caused to society by the unlawful possession and use of firearms, a court, in imposing sentence on a person (other than a person under the age of 18 years) for an offence under this section, shall specify as the minimum term of imprisonment to be served by the person a term of not less than 5 years, unless the court determines that by reason of exceptional and specific circumstances relating to the offence, or the person convicted of it, it would be unjust in all the circumstances to do so.]³

(5) Subsection (4) of this section does not apply where the court is satisfied that there are exceptional and specific circumstances relating to the offence, or the person convicted of it, which would make the minimum term unjust in all the circumstances, and for this purpose the court may[, subject to subsection (6),]⁴ have regard to any matters it considers appropriate, including—

(a)   whether the person pleaded guilty to the offence and, if so—

(i)   the stage at which the intention to plead guilty was indicated, and

(ii)   the circumstances in which the indication was given,

and

(b)   whether the person materially assisted in the investigation of the offence.

(6) The court, in considering for the purposes of subsection (5) of this section whether a sentence of not less than 5 years imprisonment is unjust in all the circumstances, may have regard, in particular, to—

(a)   whether the person convicted of the offence has a previous conviction for an offence under the Firearms Acts 1925 to 2006, the Offences Against the State Acts 1939 to 1998 or the Criminal Justice (Terrorist Offences) Act 2005, and

(b)   whether the public interest in preventing the unlawful possession or use of firearms would be served by the imposition of a lesser sentence.

(7) Subsections (4) to (6) of this section apply and have effect only in relation to a person convicted of a first offence under this section (other than a person who falls under subsection (8)(b) of this section), and accordingly references in those first-mentioned subsections to an offence under this section are to be construed as references to a first such offence.

(8) Where a person (except a person under the age of 18 years)—

(a)   is convicted of a second or subsequent offence under this section,

(b)   is convicted of a first offence under this section and has been convicted of an offence under section 15 of the Principal Act, section 26, 27 or 27B of this Act or section 12A of the Firearms and Offensive Weapons Act 1990,

the court shall, in imposing sentence, specify a term of imprisonment of not less than 5 years as the minimum term of imprisonment to be served by the person.

(9) Section 27C of this Act applies in relation to proceedings for an offence under this section and any minimum term of imprisonment imposed under subsection (4) or (8) of this section in those proceedings.

(10) In the application of section 2 of the Criminal Law (Jurisdiction) Act 1976 to this section, it shall be presumed, unless the contrary is shown, that a purpose that is unlawful in the State is unlawful in Northern Ireland.][1]

Amendments

1   Section 27A substituted by Criminal Justice Act 2006, s 59.

2   Words inserted by Criminal Justice Act 2007, s 38(a).

3   Subsection (4A) inserted by Criminal Justice Act 2007, s 38(b).

4   Words inserted by Criminal Justice Act 2007, s 38(c).

[27B   Carrying firearm with criminal intent

(1) It is an offence for a person to have with him or her a firearm, or an imitation firearm, with intent—

(a)   to commit an indictable offence, or

(b)   to resist or prevent the arrest of the person or another person,

in either case while the person has the firearm or imitation firearm with him or her.

(2) A person guilty of an offence under this section is liable on conviction on indictment—

(a) to imprisonment for a term not exceeding 14 years or such shorter term as the court may determine, subject to subsections (4) to (6) of this section or, where subsection (8) of this section applies, to that subsection, and

(b) at the court's discretion, to a fine of such amount as the court considers appropriate.

(3) The court, in imposing sentence on a person for an offence under this section, may, in particular, have regard to whether the person has a previous conviction for an offence under the Firearms Acts 1925 to 2006, the Offences against the State Acts 1939 to 1998 or the Criminal Justice (Terrorist Offences) Act 2005.

(4) Where a person (other than a person under the age of 18 years) is convicted of an offence under this section, the court shall, in imposing sentence, specify a term of imprisonment of not less than 5 years as the minimum term of imprisonment to be served by the person.

[(4A) The purpose of subsections (5) and (6) of this section is to provide that in view of the harm caused to society by the unlawful possession and use of firearms, a court, in imposing sentence on a person (other than a person under the age of 18 years) for an offence under this section, shall specify as the minimum term of imprisonment to be served by the person a term of not less than 5 years, unless the court determines that by reason of exceptional and specific circumstances relating to the offence, or the person convicted of it, it would be unjust in all the circumstances to do so.]²

(5) Subsection (4) of this section does not apply where the court is satisfied that there are exceptional and specific circumstances relating to the offence, or the person convicted of it, which would make the minimum term unjust in all the circumstances, and for this purpose the court may[, subject to subsection (6),]³ have regard to any matters it considers appropriate, including—

(a) whether the person pleaded guilty to the offence and, if so—

(i) the stage at which the intention to plead guilty was indicated, and

(ii) the circumstances in which the indication was given,

and

(b) whether the person materially assisted in the investigation of the offence.

(6) The court, in considering for the purposes of subsection (5) of this section whether a sentence of not less than 5 years imprisonment is unjust in all the circumstances, may also have regard, in particular, to—

(a) whether the person convicted of the offence has a previous conviction for an offence under the Firearms Acts 1925 to 2006, the Offences Against the State Acts 1939 to 1998 or the Criminal Justice (Terrorist Offences) Act 2005, and

(b) whether the public interest in preventing the unlawful possession or use of firearms would be served by the imposition of a lesser sentence.

(7) Subsections (4) to (6) of this section apply and have effect only in relation to a person convicted of a first offence under this section (other than a person who falls under subsection (8)(b) of this section), and accordingly references in those first-mentioned subsections to an offence under this section are to be construed as references to a first such offence.

(8) Where a person (except a person under the age of 18 years)—

(a) is convicted of a second or subsequent offence under this section,

(b) is convicted of a first offence under this section and has been convicted of an offence under section 15 of the Principal Act, section 26, 27 or 27A of this Act or section 12A of the Firearms and Offensive Weapons Act 1990,

the court shall, in imposing sentence, specify a term of imprisonment of not less than 5 years as the minimum term of imprisonment to be served by the person.

(9) In proceedings for an offence under this section proof that the accused had a firearm or imitation firearm with him or her and intended to commit an indictable offence or to resist or prevent arrest is evidence that the accused intended to have it with him or her while doing so.

(10) Section 27C of this Act applies in relation to proceedings for an offence under this section and any minimum term of imprisonment imposed under subsection (4) or (8) of this section in those proceedings.]¹

Amendments

1   Section 27B substituted by Criminal Justice Act 2006, s 60.

2   Subsection (4A) inserted by Criminal Justice Act 2007, s 39(a).

3   Words inserted by Criminal Justice Act 2007, s 39(b).

[27C   Provisions relating to minimum sentences under Firearms Acts 1925 to 2006

(1) In this section, "minimum term of imprisonment" means a term specified by a court under—

(a) section 15 of the Principal Act,

(b) section 26, 27, 27A or 27B of this Act, and

(c) section 12A of the Firearms and Offensive Weapons Act 1990,

less any reduction in the period of imprisonment under subsection (3) of this section.

(2) The power to commute or remit punishment conferred by section 23 of the Criminal Justice Act 1951 does not apply in relation to a minimum term of imprisonment.

(3) The rules or practice whereby prisoners generally may earn remission of sentence by industry and good conduct apply in relation to a person serving such a minimum term.

(4) Any powers conferred by rules made under section 2 of the Criminal Justice Act 1960, as applied by section 4 of the Prisons Act 1970, to release temporarily a person serving a sentence of imprisonment shall not be exercised during a minimum term of imprisonment, unless for grave reason of a humanitarian nature, and any release so granted shall be only of such limited duration as is justified by that reason.]¹

Amendments

1   Section 27C inserted by Criminal Justice Act 2006, s 61.

28 Repeals

(1) Subsection (5) of section 3, section 14 and subsection (2) of section 17 of the Principal Act are hereby repealed.

(2) Where, immediately before the passing of this Act, there was in force an authorisation under section 14 of the Principal Act there shall, upon such passing, be deemed to be in force a firearm certificate relating to the weapon to which the authorisation related granted by a Superintendent.

(3) An occasional licence granted under subsection (2) of section 17 of the Principal Act in relation to a prohibited weapon, and in force immediately before such passing, shall, upon such passing, be deemed to be an occasional licence granted under subsection (4) of the said section 17 in relation to that weapon.

29 Short title and collective citation

(1) This Act may be cited as the Firearms Act, 1964.

(2) The Firearms Act, 1925, and this Act may be cited together as the Firearms Acts, 1925 and 1964.

Extradition Act 1965

Number 17 of 1965

ARRANGEMENT OF SECTIONS

PART I
PRELIMINARY

1   Short title.

2   Commencement.

3   Interpretation.

4   Laying of orders before Houses of Oireachtas.

5   Expenses.

6   Repeals.

7   Transitory provisions.

PART II
EXTRADITION GENERALLY

8   Application of Part II.

9   Obligation to extradite.

10   Extraditable offences.

11   Political offences.

12   Military offences.

13   Revenue offences.

14   Irish citizens.

15   Place of commission.

16   Pending proceedings for the same offence.

17   Non bis in idem.

18   Lapse of time.

19   Capital punishment.

20   Rule of speciality.

21   Re-extradition to a third country.

22   Evidence of commission of offence by person claimed.

23   Request for extradition.

24   Conflicting requests.

25   Documents to support request.

26   Warrant of arrest.

27   Provisional arrest.

28   Exercise of jurisdiction of [High Court].

29   Committal or discharge of person whose extradition is requested.

30   Removal of committed person to hospital or other place.

31   Lapse of time before surrender.

32   Postponement of surrender.

33   Surrender of prisoner under order of Minister.

34   Discharge of prisoner if not conveyed out of State.

35   General power of Minister to release.

36   Seizure and handing over of property.

37   Evidence of documents.

38   Offences committed abroad by Irish citizens.

39   Rule of speciality as applied by the State.

40   Transit.

PART III
ENDORSEMENT AND EXECUTION OF CERTAIN WARRANTS

41–55 ...

SCHEDULE

AN ACT TO AMEND THE LAW RELATING TO EXTRADITION. [19th July, 1965.]

BE IT ENACTED BY THE OIREACHTAS AS FOLLOWS:—

PART I
PRELIMINARY

1   Short title

This Act may be cited as the Extradition Act, 1965.

2   Commencement

This Act shall come into operation on such day as the Minister by order appoints.

3   Interpretation

(1) In this Act—

"act" includes omission;

["country" includes—

(a)   a place or territory for whose external relations a country, other than that place or territory, is (in whole or in part) responsible, and

(b)   a place or territory for whose external relations the government of a country, other than the government of that place or territory, is (in whole or in part) responsible.]¹

"detention order", in relation to another country, means any order involving deprivation of liberty which has been made by a criminal court in that country in addition to or instead of a prison sentence;

"diplomatic agent" means an ambassador extraordinary and plenipotentiary, envoy extraordinary and minister plenipotentiary or chargé d'affaires;

"extradition" means the surrender of a person under the provisions of Part II to a country in relation to which that Part applies;

"extradition agreement" has the meaning assigned to it by subsection (1) of section 8;

"extradition provisions" means the provisions of an extradition agreement or of an order under section 8 applying Part II otherwise than in pursuance of an extradition agreement;

"habeas corpus proceedings" means proceedings (including proceedings on appeal) under section 4.2° of Article 40 of the Constitution;

"imprisonment", in relation to the State, includes penal servitude and detention in Saint Patrick's Institution and, in relation to any other country, includes deprivation of liberty under a detention order;

"justice of the [High Court]"[2] includes the President of the [High Court];

[...];[3]

"the Minister" means the Minister for Justice;

"person claimed" means a person whose extradition is requested;

["political offence" does not include any of the following:

    (a) the taking or attempted taking of the life of a Head of State or a member of his family;

    (b) an offence within the scope of the United Nations Convention against Illicit Traffic in Narcotic Drugs and Psychotropic Substances done at Vienna on the 20th of December, 1988;

    (c) an offence within the scope of the International Convention for the Suppression of Terrorist Bombings adopted by resolution 52/164 of the General Assembly of the United Nations on 15 December 1997;

    (d) an offence within the scope of the International Convention for the Suppression of the Financing of Terrorism adopted by resolution 54/109 of the General Assembly of the United Nations on 9 December 1999;][4]

"remand institution" means an institution (other than a prison) within the meaning of the Criminal Justice Act, 1960;

"requested country" means a country which is requested to surrender a person to the State for prosecution or punishment for an offence;

"requesting country" means a country which requests extradition;

["revenue offence", in relation to any country or place outside the State, means an offence in connection with taxes, duties or exchange control but does not include an offence involving the use or threat of force or perjury or the forging of a document issued under statutory authority or an offence alleged to have been committed by an officer of the revenue of that country or place in his capacity as such officer or an offence within the scope of Article 3 of the United Nations Convention Against Illicit Traffic in Narcotic Drugs and Psychotropic Substances done at Vienna on the 20th day of December 1988;][5]

"Saint Patrick's Institution" has the meaning assigned to it in the Criminal Justice Act, 1960;

"sentence" includes detention order.

["torture" has the meaning assigned to it by the Criminal Justice (United Nations Convention against Torture) Act, 2000.][6]

[(1A) For the purposes of the amendments to this Act effected by Part 2 of the Extradition (European Union Conventions) Act 2001, 'Convention country' means—

    (a) a country designated under section 4(1) of that Act, or

    (b) in such provisions of this Act as are specified in an order under subsection (1A) (inserted by section 52 of the European Arrest Warrant Act 2003) of section 4 of the Extradition (European Union Conventions) Act 2001, a country designated by that order, to which the provisions so specified apply.

(1B) For the purposes of the amendments to this Act effected by Part 3 of the Extradition (European Union Conventions) Act 2001, 'Convention country' means—

    (a) a country designated under section 10(1) of that Act, or

    (b) in such provisions of this Act as are specified in an order under subsection (1A) (inserted by section 52 of the European Arrest Warrant Act 2003) of section 10 of the Extradition (European Union Conventions) Act 2001, a country designated by that order, to which the provisions so specified apply.][7]

[(1C) For the purposes of this Act and the Convention of 1996, the Central Authority in the State shall be the Minister.][8]

(2) This Act applies, except where otherwise provided, in relation to an offence whether committed or alleged to have been committed before or after the passing of this Act.

Amendments

1   Definition inserted by European Arrest Warrant Act 2003, s 47(a) and later substituted by Criminal Justice (Terrorist Offences) Act 2005, s 57(2).

2   Amended by Extradition (European Union Conventions) Act 2001, s 20(1)(a) – "High Court" substituted for "District Court" in each place it occurs throughout the Act.

3   Definition 'judge of the District Court assigned to the Dublin Metropolitan District' deleted by Extradition (European Union Conventions) Act 2001, s 20(c).

4   Definition substituted by Criminal Justice (Terrorist Offences) Act 2005, s 57(1).

5   Definition substituted by Extradition (European Union Conventions) Act 2001, s 13(a).

6   Definition inserted by Criminal Justice (United Nations Convention Against Torture) Act 2000, s 7(a).

7   Subsections (1A) and (1B) inserted by Extradition (European Union Conventions) Act 2001, s 3 and 9 and later substituted by European Arrest Warrant Act 2003, s 47(b) and (c).

8   Subsection (1C) inserted by Extradition (European Union Conventions) Act 2001, s 9.

4   Laying of orders before Houses of Oireachtas

[Every order under section 8 of this Act made after the commencement of section 48 of the European Arrest Warrant Act 2003 shall be laid before each House of the Oireachtas as soon as may be after it is made and, if a resolution annulling the order is passed by either such House within the next 21 days on which that House sits after the order is laid before it, the order shall be annulled accordingly, but without prejudice to the validity of anything previously done thereunder.][1]

Amendments

1   Section 4 substituted by European Arrest Warrant Act 2003, s 48.

5   Expenses

The expenses incurred by the Minister in the administration of this Act shall, to such extent as may be sanctioned by the Minister for Finance, be paid out of moneys provided by the Oireachtas.

6   Repeals

(1) Each of the enactments specified in the Schedule to this Act is hereby repealed to the extent set out in the third column of that Schedule.

(2) Rule 74(3) of the District Court Rules, 1948, shall cease to have effect.

7   Transitory provisions

(1) Any order made under section 2 of the Extradition Act, 1870, and in force immediately before the commencement of this Act shall continue in force and be deemed to be an order made under subsection (1) of section 8 and the arrangement to which it relates shall be deemed to be an extradition agreement.

(2) An order to which subsection (1) applies shall, if not sooner revoked under section 8, expire on the 1st day of January, 1972.

[**7A**   A person arrested under Part II or III of this Act shall not be admitted to bail except by order of the High Court.][1]

Amendments

1   Section 7A inserted by Extradition (Amendment) Act 1994, s 5.

[**7B**   (1) In proceedings under this Act, evidence as to any matter to which such proceedings relate may be given by affidavit or by a statement in writing that purports to have been sworn—

    (a)   by the deponent in a place other than the State, and

    (b)   in the presence of a person duly authorised under the law of the place concerned to attest to the swearing of such a statement by a deponent,

howsoever such a statement is described under the law of that place.

(2) In proceedings referred to in subsection (1), the High Court may, if it considers that the interests of justice so require, direct that oral evidence of the matters described in the affidavit or statement concerned be given, and the court may, for the purpose of receiving oral evidence, adjourn the proceedings to a later date.][1]

Amendments

1   Section 7B inserted by Extradition (European Union Conventions) Act 2001, s 22.

PART II
EXTRADITION GENERALLY

8   Application of Part II

[(1) Where by any international agreement or convention to which the State is a party an arrangement (in this Act referred to as an extradition agreement) is made with another country for the surrender by each country to the other of persons wanted for prosecution or punishment or where the Minister is satisfied that reciprocal facilities to that effect will be afforded by another country, the Minister for Foreign Affairs may, after consultation with the Minister, by order apply this Part—

   (a)   in relation to that country, or

   (b)   in relation to a place or territory for whose external relations that country is (in whole or in part) responsible.

(1A) Where at any time after the making of an order under subsection (1), a country becomes a party to an extradition agreement to which that order applies, the Minister for Foreign Affairs may, after consultation with the Minister, by order so declare, and this Part shall, upon the making of the second-mentioned order, apply—

   (a)   to that country, or

   (b)   if that country became a party to the extradition agreement concerned for the purpose only of its applying in relation to a place or territory for whose external relations that country is (in whole or in part) responsible, to that place or territory.]¹

(2) Where the Government have made an arrangement amending an extradition agreement the [Minister for Foreign Affairs may, after consultation with the Minister,]² by order so declare and the extradition agreement shall thereupon have effect as so amended.

[(3) An order relating to an extradition agreement (other than an order under subsection (1A) (inserted by section 23(a) of the Extradition (European Union Conventions) Act 2001)) shall recite or embody the terms of the agreement and shall be evidence of the making of the agreement and of its terms.

(3A) An order under subsection (1A) shall in relation to the extradition agreement concerned recite or embody the terms of any reservation or declaration entered to that agreement by a country to which the order applies, and shall be evidence of the reservation or declaration (if any) and of its terms.

(3B) An order under subsection (2) shall recite or embody the terms of the amendment and shall be evidence of the making of the arrangement amending the extradition agreement concerned and of the terms of the amendment.]³

(4) An order applying this Part in relation to any country otherwise than in pursuance of an extradition agreement, may be made subject to such conditions, exceptions and qualifications as may be specified in the order.

(5) Every extradition agreement and every order applying this Part otherwise than in pursuance of an extradition agreement shall, subject to the provisions of this Part, have the force of law in accordance with its terms.

(6) The [Minister for Foreign Affairs may, after consultation with the Minister,]⁴ by order revoke or amend an order under this section.

(7) On the revocation of an order applying this Part in relation to any country, this Part shall cease to apply in relation to that country.

[(8) A notice of the making of each order under this section shall be published in Iris Oifigiúil as soon as may be after it is made.]⁵

[(9) An order under this section in force immediately before the commencement of the European Arrest Warrant Act 2003 shall continue in force after such commencement as if made under this section (as amended by section 49 of that Act), and may be amended or revoked accordingly.]⁶

Amendments

1   Subsection (1) and (1A) substituted by Criminal Justice (Terrorist Offences) Act 2005. s 57(3)

2   Subsection (2) amended by European Arrest Warrant Act 2003, s 49(c).

3   Subsection (3) substituted and subsections (3A) and (3B) inserted by Extradition (European Union Conventions) Act 2001, s 23(b).

4   Subsection (6) amended by European Arrest Warrant Act 2003, s 49(d).

5   Subsection (8) amended by Extradition (European Union Conventions) Act 2001, s 23(c).

6   Subsection (9) substituted by European Arrest Warrant Act 2003, s 49(e).

9   Obligation to extradite

Where a country in relation to which this Part applies duly requests the surrender of a person who is being proceeded against in that country for an offence or who is wanted by that country for the carrying out of a sentence, that person shall, subject to and in accordance with the provisions of this Part, be surrendered to that country.

10   Extraditable offences

(1) Subject to subsection (2), extradition shall be granted only in respect of an offence which is punishable under the laws of the requesting country and of the State by imprisonment for a maximum period of at least one year or by a more severe penalty and for which, if there has been a conviction and sentence in the requesting country, imprisonment for a period of at least four months or a more severe penalty has been imposed.

[(1A) Subject to subsection (2A), extradition to a requesting country that is a Convention country shall be granted only in respect of an offence that is punishable—

    (a)   under the laws of that country, by imprisonment or detention for a maximum period of not less than one year or by a more severe penalty, and

    (b)   under the laws of the State, by imprisonment or detention for a maximum period of not less than 6 months or by a more severe penalty, and for which, if there has been a conviction and sentence in the requesting country, imprisonment for a period of not less than 4 months or a more severe penalty has been imposed.][1]

(2) If a request is made for extradition in respect of an offence to which subsection (1) applies and the request includes also any other offence which is punishable under the laws of the requesting country and of the State but does not comply with the conditions as to the period of imprisonment which may be, or has been, imposed, then extradition may, subject to the provisions of this Part, be granted also in respect of the latter offence.

[(2A) If a request is made by a Convention country for extradition for—

    (a)   an offence to which subsection (1A) applies, and

    (b)   an offence punishable under the laws of that country and of the State in respect of which there is a failure to comply with subsection (1A),

extradition may, subject to this Part, be granted in respect of the second-mentioned offence, but where extradition is refused for the first-mentioned offence it shall be refused for the second-mentioned offence also.][2]

[(3) In this section 'an offence punishable under the laws of the State' means—

    (a)   an act that, if committed in the State on the day on which the request for extradition is made, would constitute an offence, or

    (b)   in the case of an offence under the law of a requesting country consisting of the commission of one or more acts including any act committed in the State (in this paragraph referred to as 'the act concerned'), such one or more acts, being acts that, if committed in the State on the day on which the act concerned was committed or alleged to have been committed would constitute an offence,

and cognate words shall be construed accordingly.][3]

[(4) In this section 'an offence punishable under the laws of the requesting country' means an offence punishable under the laws of the requesting country on—

    (a)   the day on which the offence was committed or is alleged to have been committed, and

    (b)   the day on which the request for extradition is made,

and cognate words shall be construed accordingly.][4]

Amendments

1   Subsection (1A) inserted by Extradition (European Union Conventions) Act 2001, s 11(a).

2   Subsection (2A) inserted by Extradition (European Union Conventions) Act 2001, s 11(b).

3   Subsection (3) substituted by Extradition (European Union Conventions) Act 2001, s 11(c).

4   Subsection (4) inserted by Extradition (European Union Conventions) Act 2001, s 11(d).

11   Political offences

(1) Extradition shall not be granted for an offence which is a political offence or an offence connected with a political offence.

(2) The same rule shall apply if there are substantial grounds for believing that a request for extradition for an ordinary criminal offence has been made for the purpose of prosecuting or punishing a person on account of his race, religion, nationality or political opinion or that that person's position may be prejudiced for any of these reasons.

[(2A) The same rule shall apply if there are substantial grounds for believing that if the request for extradition is granted the person claimed may be subjected to torture.][1]

[(3) (a)   This subsection applies to an offence of which a person is accused or has been convicted outside the State and the act constituting which would, if done within the State, constitute an offence under—

  (i)   section 3 (grave breaches of Scheduled Conventions) of the Geneva Conventions Act 1962, as amended by section 3 of the Geneva Conventions (Amendment) Act 1998, and

  (ii)   section 7 (genocide, crimes against humanity and war crimes) or 8 (ancillary offences) of the International Criminal Court Act 2006.

  (b)   For the purposes of this Part and without prejudice to section 3 (certain offences not to be regarded as political offences) of the Extradition (European Convention on the Suppression of Terrorism) Act 1987, an offence to which this subsection applies shall not be regarded as a political offence or an offence connected with a political offence.][2]

Amendments

1   Subsection (2A) inserted Criminal Justice (United Nations Convention Against Torture) Act 2000, s 7(b).

2   Subsection (3) inserted by International Criminal Court Act 2006, s 66 and Sch 3.

12   Military offences

Extradition shall not be granted for offences under military law which are not offences under ordinary criminal law.

13   Revenue offences

[Extradition shall not be granted for revenue offences unless the relevant extradition provisions otherwise provide.][1]

Amendments

1   Section 13 substituted by Extradition (European Union Conventions) Act 2001, s 13.

14   Irish citizens

[Extradition shall not be granted where a person claimed is a citizen of Ireland, unless the relevant extradition provisions or this Act otherwise provide.][1]

Amendments

1   Section 14 substituted by Extradition (European Union Conventions) Act 2001, s 6(a).

15   Place of commission

Extradition shall not be granted where the offence for which it is requested is regarded under the law of the State as having been committed in the State.

16   Pending proceedings for the same offence

Extradition shall not be granted where a prosecution is pending in the State against the person claimed for the offence for which extradition is requested.

17   Non bis in idem

(1) Extradition shall not be granted if final judgment has been passed in the State or in a third country upon the person claimed in respect of the offence for which extradition is requested.

(2) Extradition may be refused by the Minister for an offence which is also an offence under the law of the State if the Attorney General has decided either not to institute or to terminate proceedings against the person claimed in respect of the offence.

18   Lapse of time

Extradition shall not be granted when the person claimed has, according to the law of either the requesting country or the State, become immune by reason of lapse of time from prosecution or punishment.

[18A   (1) Extradition shall not be granted where the person claimed has been granted a pardon under Article 13.6 of the Constitution in respect of an offence consisting of an act that constitutes in whole or in part the offence under the law of the requesting country in respect of which extradition is sought.

(2) Extradition shall not be granted where the person claimed has, in accordance with the law of the requesting country, become immune, by virtue of any amnesty or pardon, from prosecution or punishment for the offence concerned.

(3) Extradition shall not be granted where the person claimed has, by virtue of any Act of the Oireachtas, become immune from prosecution or punishment for any offence consisting of an act that constitutes in whole or in part the offence under the law of the requesting country in respect of which extradition is sought.][1]

Amendments

1   Section 18A inserted by Extradition (European Union Conventions) Act 2001, s 14.

19   Capital punishment

Extradition shall not be granted for an offence which is punishable by the requesting country but is of a category for which the death penalty the law of the State or is not generally carried out unless the request assurance as the Minister considers sufficient that the death penalty w

20   Rule of speciality

(1) [Subject to subsection (1A) (inserted by section 15(b) of the Extradition (European Union Conventions) Act, 2001), extradition shall not be granted unless provision is made by the law of the requesting country or by the extradition agreement—]¹

(a)   that the person claimed shall not be proceeded against, sentenced or detained with a view to the carrying out of a sentence or detention order, or otherwise restricted in his personal freedom, for any offence committed prior to his surrender other than that for which his extradition is requested, except in the following cases—

    (i)   [subject to section 20A (inserted by section 7(b) of the Extradition (European Union Conventions) Act, 2001), with the consent of the Minister, or]²

    (ii) where that person, having had an opportunity to leave the territory of that country, has not done so within forty-five days of his final discharge in respect of the offence for which he was extradited or has returned to the territory of that country after leaving it, and

(b)   that where the description of the offence charged in the requesting country is altered in the course of proceedings, he shall only be proceeded against or sentenced in so far as the offence under its new description is shown by its constituent elements to be an offence which would allow extradition.

[(1A) Extradition to a Convention country of a person claimed shall not be refused on the grounds only that it is intended—

(a)   to proceed against him in that country for an offence alleged to have been committed by him before his surrender (other than an offence to which the request for extradition relates) provided that—

    (i)   upon conviction he is not liable to a term of imprisonment or detention, or

    (ii) in circumstances where upon conviction he is liable to a term of imprisonment or detention and such other penalty as does not involve a restriction of his personal liberty, the High Court is satisfied that the said other penalty only will be imposed should he be convicted of the offence concerned,

(b)   to impose in the Convention country concerned a penalty (other than a penalty consisting of the restriction of the person's liberty) including a financial penalty in respect of an offence—

    (i)   of which the person claimed has been convicted,

    (ii) that was committed before his surrender, and

    (iii) that is not an offence to which the request relates,

notwithstanding that where such person fails or refuses to pay the penalty concerned (or, in the case of a penalty that is not a financial penalty, fails or refuses to submit to any measure or comply with any requirements of which the penalty consists), he may under the law of that Convention country be detained or otherwise deprived of his personal liberty, or

(c) to proceed against or detain him in the Convention country concerned for the purpose of executing a sentence or order of detention in respect of an offence—

    (i) of which the person claimed has been convicted,

    (ii) that was committed before his surrender, and

    (iii) that is not an offence to which the request relates,

or otherwise restrict his personal liberty as a consequence of being convicted of such offence, provided that—

    (I) after his surrender he consents to such execution or to his personal liberty being so restricted and, in the case of an Irish citizen, the Minister so consents also, and

    (II) under the law of the Convention country, such consent shall be given before the competent judicial authority in that country and be recorded in accordance with the law of that country.][3]

(2) Notwithstanding anything in subsection (1), the fact that the law of the requesting country permits the taking of any measures necessary to remove the person from its territory or any measures necessary under its law, including proceedings by default, to prevent any legal effects of lapse of time shall not of itself prevent his extradition.

(3) The consent of the Minister shall not be given unless a request for consent is submitted by the requesting country, supported by the documents mentioned in section 25 and a legal record of any statement made by the extradited person in respect of the offence concerned.

(4) The consent of the Minister shall be given if the offence for which it is requested is itself one for which there is an obligation to grant extradition.

Amendments

1   Words substituted by Extradition (European Union Conventions) Act 2001, s 15(a).

2   Subsection (1)(a)(i) substituted by Extradition (European Union Conventions) Act 2001, s 7(a).

3   Subsection (1A) inserted by Extradition (European Union Conventions) Act 2001, s 15(b).

[20A   (1) The Minister may, where a person whose extradition is sought by a Convention country consents—

(a) under section 29A to his being surrendered to that country, and

(b) voluntarily before the High Court to the Minister giving his consent under section 20(1)(a)(i), and is aware of the consequences of the Minister so doing,

give his consent under the said section 20(1)(a)(i).

(2) A person who has consented in accordance with subsection (1) to the Minister giving his consent under section 20(1)(a)(i) may at any time thereafter, but before the giving of such consent by the Minister, withdraw his consent, and if the person so withdraws his consent the Minister shall not give his consent under section 20(1)(a)(i).

(3) The Minister shall not give his consent under section 20(1)(a)(i) in accordance with this section on a day that is before the day on which he makes an order under section 33 in respect of the person concerned.]¹

Amendments

1 Section 20A inserted by Extradition (European Union Conventions) Act 2001, s 7(b).

21 Re-extradition to a third country

(1) Extradition shall not be granted unless provision is made by the law of the requesting country or by the extradition agreement that that country shall not surrender to another country a person surrendered to the requesting country and sought by the other country for an offence committed before his surrender to the requesting country, except in the following cases—

    (a) with the consent of the Minister, or

    (b) where that person, having had an opportunity to leave the territory of that country, has not done so within forty-five days of his final discharge in respect of the offence for which he was extradited or has returned to the territory of that country after leaving it.

(2) Before acceding to a request for consent to the extradition of a person to whom subsection (1) applies, the Minister may request the production of the documents mentioned in section 25.

(3) A person who has been surrendered to the State by a requested country shall not be surrendered to a third country for an offence committed before his surrender, except in the following cases—

    [(a) with the consent of the requested country signified under the seal of a minister of state, ministry or department of state of that country or such other person as performs in that country functions the same as or similar to those performed by the Minister under this Act, as may be appropriate, which seal shall be judicially noticed, or]¹

    (b) where that person, having had an opportunity to leave the State, has not done so within forty-five days of his final discharge in respect of the offence for which he was surrendered to the State or has returned to the State after leaving it.

Amendments

1 Section 21(3)(a) substituted by Extradition (European Union Conventions) Act 2001, s 25(a).

22 Evidence of commission of offence by person claimed

Where the relevant extradition provisions require the production by the requesting country of evidence as to the commission by the person claimed of the offence for which extradition is requested, extradition shall not be granted unless sufficient evidence is produced to satisfy the requirement.

23   Request for extradition

A request for the extradition of any person shall be made in writing and shall be communicated by—

    (a) a diplomatic agent of the requesting country, accredited to the State, or

    (b) any other means provided in the relevant extradition provisions.

[23A   (1) For the purposes of a request for extradition from a Convention country, a facsimile copy of a document to which paragraph (a), (b), (c), (d) or (e) of section 25(1) applies may be transmitted by the Central Authority of the Convention country concerned to the Central Authority in the State by means of the use of a facsimile machine fitted with a cryptographic device that is in operation during the transmission.

(2) The facsimile copy of a document transmitted in accordance with subsection (1) shall include—

    (a) a copy of a certificate of the Central Authority of the Convention country concerned stating that the copy of the document so transmitted corresponds to the original document,

    (b) a description of the pagination of that document, and

    (c) a statement that the cryptographic device fitted to the facsimile machine that was used to transmit that facsimile copy was in operation during the transmission concerned.

(3) If the Central Authority in the State is not satisfied that the facsimile copy of a document transmitted to him in accordance with subsection (1) corresponds to the document of which it purports to be a facsimile copy, he may require the Central Authority of the requesting country to cause the original document or a true copy thereof to be provided to him by—

    (a) a diplomatic agent of the requesting country, accredited to the State, or

    (b) any other means agreed by the Central Authority in the State and the Central Authority of the Convention country concerned,

within such period as he may specify.]¹

Amendments

1   Section 23A inserted by Extradition (European Union Conventions) Act 2001, s 18.

---

24   Conflicting requests

If extradition is requested concurrently by more than one country, either for the same offence or for different offences, the Minister shall decide which, if any, of the requests is to be proceeded with under this Part, having regard to all the circumstances and especially the relative seriousness and place of commission of the offences, the respective dates of the requests, the nationality of the person claimed and the possibility of subsequent surrender to another country.

25 Documents to support request

(1) A request for extradition shall be supported by the following documents—

    (a) the original or an authenticated copy of the conviction and sentence or detention order immediately enforceable or, as the case may be, of the warrant of arrest or other order having the same effect and issued in accordance with the procedure laid down in the law of the requesting country;

    (b) a statement of each offence for which extradition is requested specifying, as accurately as possible, the time and place of commission, its legal description and a reference to the relevant provisions of the law of the requesting country;

    (c) a copy of the relevant enactments of the requesting country or, where this is not possible, a statement of the relevant law;

    (d) as accurate a description as possible of the person claimed, together with any other information which will help to establish his identity and nationality, and

    (e) any other document required under the relevant extradition provisions.

[(2) For the purposes of a request for extradition from a Convention country, a document shall be deemed to be an authenticated copy if it has been certified as a true copy by the judicial authority that issued the original or by an officer of the Central Authority of the Convention country concerned duly authorised to so do.][1]

Amendments

1   Subsection (2) inserted by Extradition (European Union Conventions) Act 2001, s 17(a).

---

26 Warrant of arrest

[(1) (a) If the Minister receives a request made in accordance with this Part for the extradition of any person, he shall, subject to the provisions of this section, certify that the request has been made.

    (b) On production to a [judge of the High Court] of a certificate of the Minister under paragraph (a) stating that a request referred to in that paragraph has been made, the judge shall issue a warrant for the arrest of the person concerned unless a warrant for his arrest has been issued under section 27.][1]

[(2) A warrant issued under this section may be executed by any member of the Garda Síochána in any part of the State and may be so executed notwithstanding that it is not in the possession of the member at the time; and the warrant shall be shown to, and a copy of same given to, the person arrested at the time of such arrest or, if the warrant is not then in the possession of the member, within 24 hours thereafter.][2]

(3) If the Minister is of opinion that the information communicated to him in pursuance of section 25 is insufficient, he may request in the requesting country to furnish such further information as he thinks proper and may fix a time-limit for the receipt thereof.

(4) The Minister may refuse extradition if he is of opinion that the case is one in which extradition is prohibited under any provision of this Part or under the relevant extradition, provisions.

[(5) A person arrested under a warrant issued under this section shall be brought as soon as may be before a [judge of the High Court.

(6) Where a person has been arrested under a warrant issued under this section, then, in any proceedings it shall be presumed, unless the contrary is proved, that a request for the extradition of the person has been duly made and has been duly received by the Minister.][3]

Amendments

1   Subsection (1) substituted by Extradition (Amendment) Act 1994, s 7.
2   Subsection (2) substituted by Extradition (Amendment) Act 1994, s 6.
2   Subsection (5) substituted and subsection (6) inserted by Extradition (Amendment) Act 1994, s 7.

---

27   Provisional arrest

[(1) A judge of the [High Court] may, without a certificate of the Minister under section 26(1)(a), issue a warrant for the arrest of any person on the sworn information of a member of the Garda Síochána not below the rank of inspector that a request for the provisional arrest of that person has been made, on the ground of urgency, on behalf of a country in relation to which this Part applies and on being satisfied that the request complies with the requirements of this section.][1]

(2) A request for the provisional arrest of any person shall—

   (a) state that one of the documents mentioned in paragraph (a) of section 25 exists in respect of that person and that it is intended to send a request for his extradition,

   (b) specify the nature of the offence and the time at which and the place where the offence is alleged to have been committed, and

   (c) give a description of the person whose arrest is sought.

[(2A) A request for the provisional arrest of a person made on behalf of a requesting country that is a Convention country shall—

   (a) state that one of the documents mentioned in paragraph (a) of section 25(1) exists in respect of that person,

   (b) be accompanied by a statement of the offences to which the request relates specifying the nature and description under the law of the requesting country of the offences concerned,

   (c) specify the circumstances in which the offences were committed or alleged to have been committed including the time and place of their commission or alleged commission, and the degree of involvement or alleged degree of involvement of the person to whom the request relates in their commission or alleged commission, and

   (d) specify the penalties to which that person would be liable if convicted of the offences concerned or, where he has been convicted of those offences, the penalties that have been imposed or, where he has been convicted of those offences but not yet sentenced, the penalties to which he is liable,

hereafter in this section referred to as 'information furnished under subsection (2A)'.

(2B) A member of the Garda Síochána not below the rank of inspector shall provide a person, who is provisionally arrested pursuant to a warrant issued on foot of a request to which subsection (2A) applies, with the information furnished under subsection (2A) and shall inform him of his right to consent to his surrender under section 29A(1) (inserted by section 6(b) of the Extradition (European Union Conventions) Act, 2001) and inquire of him whether he wishes to so consent.][2]

(3) A request for provisional arrest may be transmitted by post or telegraph or by any other means affording evidence in writing.

[(3A) For the purposes of this section an alert shall be deemed to constitute a request for provisional arrest of the person named therein and the provisions of subsection (2) of this section shall not apply.

(3B) (a) The Director of Public Prosecutions shall be a judicial authority for the purposes of requesting the entry of an alert in the SIS for the arrest and extradition of the person named therein.

    (b) The issue of a request for extradition by the Director of Public Prosecutions shall be deemed to constitute a request by the Director of Public Prosecutions for entry of an alert in the SIS for the arrest and extradition of the person named therein.][3]

[(4) A warrant issued under this section may be executed by any member of the Garda Síochána in any part of the State and may be so executed notwithstanding that it is not in the possession of the member at the time; and the warrant shall be shown to, and a copy of same given to, the person arrested at the time of such arrest or, if the warrant is not then in the possession of the member, within 24 hours thereafter.][4]

(5) Where a justice issues a warrant under subsection (1) he shall forthwith inform the Minister of the issue of the warrant and the Minister may, if he thinks fit, order the warrant to be cancelled and the person arrested thereunder released.

[(6) A person arrested under a warrant issued under this section shall, unless the warrant is cancelled under subsection (5), be brought as soon as may be before a judge of the High Court and the judge shall remand the said person in custody or on bail pending—

    (a) the receipt by him of a certificate of the Minister under section 26(1)(a) (inserted by section 7(a) of the Act of 1994) stating that the request for extradition has been duly made, or

    (b) (in circumstances where the person is remanded in custody) the release of that person under section 35,

and for those purposes the judge shall have the same powers of remand as if that person were brought before him charged with an indictable offence.][5]

[(7) If, within the period of 18 days after such person's arrest, no such certificate is produced, he shall be released.][6]

(8) The release of any person under subsection (5) or (7) shall not prejudice his re-arrest and extradition if a request for his extradition is afterwards made.

[(9) A warrant for the arrest of a person may be issued under subsection (1) notwithstanding that, previously—

    (a) a warrant for the arrest of that person has been issued, or

    (b) the issue of such a warrant has been refused.

(10) Where an information is sworn by a member of the Garda Síochána not below the rank of inspector before a judge of the [High Court] stating that a request for the provisional arrest of a person has been made, on the ground of urgency, on behalf of a country in relation to which this Part applies, then, in any proceedings it shall be presumed, unless the contrary is proved, that a request for the provisional arrest of the person has been made on the ground of urgency on behalf of a country in relation to which this Part applies.

(11) Where a person has been arrested under a warrant issued under this section and a certificate of the Minister under section 26(1)(a) stating that a request for the extradition of the person has been duly made, has been produced to a [judge of the High Court], then, in any proceedings it shall be presumed, unless the contrary is proved, that a request in accordance with this Part for the extradition of the person has been duly made and has been duly received by the Minister.][7]

[(12) In this section—

"alert" means an alert entered in the SIS for the arrest and extradition, on foot of an extradition warrant, of the person named therein;

"Council Decision" means Council Decision 2007/533/JHA of 12 June 2007 on the establishment, operation and use of the second generation Schengen Information System;

"Schengen Convention" means the Convention implementing the Schengen Agreement of 14 June 1985 between the Governments of the States of the Benelux Economic Union, the Federal Republic of Germany and the French Republic on the gradual abolition of checks at their common borders done at Schengen on 19 June 1990 and includes any amendment to or modification of that Convention whether before or after the passing of this Act but does not include the Council Decision;

"SIS" means the system referred to in Title IV of the Schengen Convention or, as appropriate, the system established under Chapter 1 of the Council Decision.][8]

Amendments

1 Subsection (1) substituted by Extradition (Amendment) Act 1994, s 8(a).
2 Subsection (2A) and (2B) inserted by Extradition (European Union Conventions) Act 2001, s 5.
3 Subsection (3A) and (3B) inserted by Criminal Justice (Miscellaneous Provisions) Act 2009, s 24(a).
4 Subsection (4) substituted by Extradition (Amendment) Act 1994, s 6.
5 Subsection (6) substituted by Extradition (European Union Conventions) Act 2001, s 20(d).
6 Subsection (7) substituted by Extradition (Amendment) Act 1994, s 8(b).
7 Subsections (9)–(11) inserted by Extradition (Amendment) Act 1994, s 8(c).
8 Subsection (12) inserted by Criminal Justice (Miscellaneous Provisions) Act 2009, s 24(b).

28   Exercise of jurisdiction of District Court

[…][1]

Amendments

1   Section 28 repealed by Extradition (Amendment) Act 1994, Sch 2.

29   Committal or discharge of person whose extradition is requested

(1) Where a person is before the [High Court] under section 26 or 27 and the Court is satisfied that—

(a)   the extradition of that person has been duly requested, and

(b)   this Part applies in relation to the requesting country, and

(c)   extradition of the person claimed is not prohibited by this Part or by the relevant extradition provisions, and

(d)   the documents required to support a request for extradition under section 25 have been produced,

the Court shall make an order committing that person to a prison (or, if he is not more than twenty-one years of age, to a remand institution) there to await the order of the Minister for his extradition.

[(2) Subject to section 7A (inserted by the Extradition (Amendment) Act, 1994), the Court shall have the same powers of adjournment and remand as if the person concerned were brought before the court charged with an indictable offence.][1]

(3) The Court, on making an order under subsection (1), shall—

(a)   inform the person to whom it relates that he will not be surrendered, except with his consent, until after the expiration of fifteen days from the date of his committal and inform him also of the provisions of section 4.2° of Article 40 of the Constitution (which relates to the making of a complaint to the High Court by or on behalf of any person alleging that that person is unlawfully detained), and

(b)   cause a certificate of the committal to be sent forthwith to the Minister.

(4) Where the person claimed is not committed under subsection (1) the Court shall order him to be discharged.

[(5) No appeal shall lie to the Supreme Court from an order of the High Court under this section, except on a point of law.][2]

(6) Sections 10 and 11 of the Criminal Justice Act, 1960, shall apply to a person committed to a remand institution under this section.

Amendments

1   Subsection (2) substituted by Extradition (Amendment) Act 1994, s 9.

2   Subsection (5) substituted by Extradition (European Union Conventions) Act 2001, s 20(f).

[**29A**   (1) Where a person is brought before the High Court—

  (a) under section 26, pursuant to a request from a Convention country for his extradition, or

  (b) under section 27, pursuant to a request from a Convention country for his provisional arrest,

he may consent to his being surrendered to the Convention country concerned.

(2) Notwithstanding section 29, where a person is brought before the High Court under section 27, pursuant to a request from a Convention country to which this Part applies for the provisional arrest of that person, and the court is satisfied that—

  (a) there has been compliance with subsection (2A) of the said section 27 (inserted by section 5 of the Extradition (European Union Conventions) Act, 2001),

  (b) it is intended that a request will be made by or on behalf of the Convention country for the person's extradition, unless he consents to being surrendered,

  (c) the person consents voluntarily to his being surrendered to the Convention country and is aware of the consequences of his so consenting,

  (d) extradition of the person claimed is not prohibited by this Part or by the relevant extradition provisions,

  (e) where the person claimed is a citizen of Ireland, the Minister consents to the person being surrendered to the Convention country concerned,

the court shall make an order committing that person to a prison (or, if he is not more than 21 years of age, to a remand institution) there to await the order of the Minister for his extradition.

(3) Notwithstanding section 29, where a person is brought before the High Court under section 26, pursuant to a request from a Convention country for the extradition of that person, and the court is satisfied that—

  (a) the extradition of that person has been duly requested,

  (b) this Part applies in relation to that Convention country,

  (c) extradition of the person claimed is not prohibited by this Part or by the relevant extradition provisions,

  (d) the documents required to support a request for extradition under section 25 have been produced,

  (e) the person consents voluntarily to his being surrendered to the Convention country and is aware of the consequences of his so consenting, and

  (f) where the person is a citizen of Ireland, the Minister consents to the person being surrendered to the Convention country concerned,

the court shall make an order committing that person to a prison (or, if he is not more than 21 years of age, to a remand institution) there to await the order of the Minister for his extradition.

(4) Where a person consents to his being surrendered under subsection (1), the High Court shall record in writing the giving of such consent and shall cause a copy thereof to be sent forthwith to the Minister.

(5) (a) If a person arrested under section 27 consents under subsection (1) to his being surrendered to the Convention country concerned, the Minister shall so inform that country not later than 10 days after the person is so arrested.

(b) Where a person arrested under section 27 does not consent under the said subsection to his being surrendered to the Convention country concerned, the Minister shall so inform that country not later than 10 days after the person is so arrested.

(6) A person who has consented under subsection (1) to his being surrendered to the Convention country concerned may, at any time thereafter but before the making of an order by the Minister under section 33, withdraw his consent and, if he withdraws his consent, the period between the giving of such consent before the High Court and the withdrawal of such consent by him shall not be taken into account for the purpose of calculating the period of 18 days specified in section 27(7).

(7) Where a person in respect of whom the High Court has made an order of committal under subsection (2) withdraws his consent to being surrendered to the Convention country concerned, he shall, as soon as may be after a request for his extradition has been received by the Minister from that Convention country, be brought before the High Court and the court shall affirm the said order of committal provided that, in relation to that request, there has been compliance with this Act.

(8) Subsection (2) of section 29 (inserted by section 9 of the Act of 1994) and subsections (4) and (6) of that section shall apply for the purposes of this section, subject to the modification that references in subsection (4) to subsection (1) shall be construed as references to subsection (2) or (3) of this section.]¹

Amendments

1   Section 29A inserted by Extradition (European Union Conventions) Act 2001, s 6(b).

30   Removal of committed person to hospital or other place

The Minister may by order cause a person committed under section 29 to he removed to a hospital or any other place if the Minister thinks it necessary so to do in the interests of his health and that person shall, while detained in that hospital or place, be in lawful custody.

31   Lapse of time before surrender

[A person committed under section 29 shall not be surrendered, except with his consent, given before a [judge of the High Court], to the requesting country until the expiration of 15 days from the date of his committal or until the conclusion of any habeas corpus proceedings brought by him or on his behalf, whichever is the later.]¹

Amendments

1   Section 31 substituted by Extradition (Amendment) Act 1994, s 4(1)(a).

32   Postponement of surrender

The Minister may postpone the surrender of a person claimed in order that he may be proceeded against in the State, or (if he has already been convicted) in order that he may serve any sentence imposed on him in the State, for an offence other than that for which his extradition is requested.

33   Surrender of prisoner under order of Minister

(1) Subject to sections 31 and 32, the Minister may, if the person committed is not discharged by the decision of the High Court in habeas corpus proceedings, by order direct the person to be surrendered to such other person as in his opinion is duly authorised by the requesting country to receive him and he shall be surrendered accordingly.

(2) Any person to whom an order under subsection (1) directs a person to be surrendered may receive, hold in custody, and convey out of the State the person so surrendered and if the person so surrendered escapes from any custody to which he has been delivered in pursuance of the said order he shall be liable to be retaken in the same manner as any person who escapes from lawful custody.

(3) The Minister shall not make an order under subsection (1) if he is of the opinion that the extradition of the person whose surrender is requested would involve transit through any territory where there is reason to believe that his life or his freedom may be threatened by reason of his race, religion, nationality or political opinion[, or that he may be subjected to torture.]¹

Amendments

1   Words inserted by Criminal Justice (United Nations Convention Against Torture) Act 2000, s 7(c).

[33A   (1) Where the High Court makes an order under section 29A (inserted by section 6(b) of the Extradition (European Union Conventions) Act, 2001) in relation to a person whose surrender is sought by a Convention country, the Minister shall, not later than 20 days after the giving by that person of his consent to being surrendered to that country before that Court, so notify the Convention country in writing.

(2) Subject to subsection (3), the Minister shall make an order under section 33 in respect of a person to whom subsection (1) applies not later than 20 days after the giving of notification to the Convention country concerned under the said subsection (1).

(3) Where, for reasons beyond the control of the Minister, the Minister is unable to comply with subsection (2), he shall so notify the Convention country concerned and shall make an order under the said section 33 on such day as may be agreed by the Minister and that country.

(4) Where a day for the making of an order under section 33 is agreed in accordance with subsection (3), the person whose surrender is sought shall be surrendered to the Convention country concerned not later than 20 days after such day and if surrender is not effected before the expiration of such period of 20 days the person shall be released.

(5) Subsections (1), (2), (3) and (4) shall not apply where the Minister proposes to postpone the surrender of a person claimed in accordance with section 32.

Amendments

1   Section 33A inserted by Extradition (European Union Conventions) Act 2001, s 8.

---

34   Discharge of prisoner if not conveyed out of State

(1) Subject to section 32 and to subsection (2) of this section, if any person awaiting his surrender under this Part is not surrendered and conveyed out of the State within one month after the committal, or within one month after the conclusion of habeas corpus proceedings brought by him or on his behalf, whichever is the later, the High Court may, on application made by or on behalf of that person and upon proof that reasonable notice of the intention to make the application has been given to the Minister, order the person to be discharged from custody.

(2) Where, on application to the High Court under subsection (1), the Court is satisfied—

    (a) that the state of health of the person claimed or other circumstances beyond the control of the State or the requesting country have prevented the person claimed from being conveyed out of the State, and

    (b) that it is likely that within a reasonable time such circumstances will no longer prevent his removal,

the Court may fix a period within which he may be surrendered and he shall be released if not conveyed out of the State within that period.

35   General power of Minister to release

(1) Whenever the Minister is of opinion, in relation to a person who is for the time being on remand or awaiting his surrender under this Part, that extradition is prohibited under any provision of this Part or of the relevant extradition provisions, the Minister may at any time refuse extradition and shall thereupon order the person, if in custody, to be released.

(2) In case it appears to the Minister that the request or intended request for extradition is not being proceeded with, the Minister may order that the said person, if in custody, shall be released.

36   Seizure and handing over of property

(1) A member of the Garda Síochána executing a warrant under section 26 or 27 may seize and retain any property—

    (a) which appears to him to be reasonably required as evidence for the purpose of proving the offence alleged, or

    (b) which appears to him to have been acquired as a result of the alleged offence and which—

        (i)   is found at the time of arrest in the possession of the person arrested under the warrant, or

        (ii) is discovered subsequently.

(2) Subject to the provisions of this section, any property seized under subsection (1) shall, if an order is issued by the Minister under section 33 for the surrender of the person claimed, be handed over to any person who appears to the Minister to be duly authorised by the requesting country to receive it as soon as may be after the issue of the order and the said property shall be so handed over notwithstanding that the extradition in question cannot be carried out by reason of the death or escape of the person claimed.

(3) Any property so seized may, if any criminal proceedings to which the property relates are pending in the State, be retained in the State in accordance with law until the conclusion of the said proceedings or may, if the Minister so directs, be handed over on condition that the requesting country shall return the property.

(4) Nothing in this section shall prejudice or derogate from any rights that may lawfully have been acquired by the State or any person in the State in any property to be handed over under this section and where any such rights exist the property shall not be handed over except upon condition that the requesting country shall return it as soon as may be after the trial of the person surrendered and without charge to the State or person having such rights.

37   Evidence of documents

[(1) In proceedings to which this Part applies, a document supporting a request for extradition from a requesting country (other than a Convention country) shall be received in evidence without further proof if it purports—

    (a)   to be signed by a judge, magistrate or officer of the requesting country, and

    (b)   to be certified by being sealed with the seal of a minister of state, ministry, department of state or such other person as performs in that country functions the same as or similar to those performed by the Minister under this Act, as may be appropriate, and judicial notice shall be taken of such seal.

(2) In proceedings to which this Part applies, a document purporting to be a copy of a document supporting a request for extradition from a Convention country shall, subject to subsection (3), be received in evidence without further proof.

(3) In proceedings to which this Part applies, a document that purports to be certified by—

    (a)   the judicial authority in a Convention country that issued the original, or

    (b)   an officer of the Central Authority of such a country duly authorised to so do,

to be a true copy of a conviction and sentence or detention order immediately enforceable or, as the case may be, the warrant of arrest or other order having the same effect and issued in accordance with the procedure laid down in the law of that country, shall be received in evidence without further proof, and where the seal of the judicial authority or Central Authority concerned has been affixed to the document, judicial notice shall be taken of that seal.][1]

Amendments

1   Section 37 substituted by Extradition (European Union Conventions) Act 2001, s 17(b).

---

38   Offences committed abroad by Irish citizens

(1) Where any citizen of Ireland does any act outside the State which constitutes an offence for which he would be liable to extradition but for the fact that he is a citizen of Ireland he shall be guilty of the like offence and be liable on conviction to the like punishment as if the act were done within the State.

(2) No proceedings for an offence under subsection (1) shall be taken except by direction of the Attorney General, given following a request to that effect made in the manner provided for in section 23 by the country within whose territory the act is alleged to have been committed.

(3) This section shall apply only to acts committed after the commencement of this Act.

(4) For the purpose of the exercise of jurisdiction, in relation to an offence to which subsection (1) applies, by any court of competent jurisdiction the act constituting the offence shall be deemed to have been committed within the area of the Dublin Metropolitan District.

39   Rule of speciality as applied by the State

(1) This section applies to a person who has been surrendered to the State by a requested country.

[(2) Subject to subsection (2A) (inserted by section 16(b) of the Extradition (European Union Conventions) Act, 2001), a person to whom this section applies shall not be proceeded against, sentenced or imprisoned or otherwise restricted in his personal freedom for any offence committed before his surrender other than that for which he was surrendered, except in the following cases—][1]

    (a) with the consent of the requested country, signified under the seal of a [minister of state, ministry or department of state of that country or such other person as performs in that country functions the same as or similar to those performed by the Minister under this Act, as may be appropriate,][2] which seal shall be judicially noticed, or

    (b) where that person, having had an opportunity to leave the State, has not done so within forty-five days of his final discharge in respect of the offence for which he was surrendered or has returned to the State after leaving it.

[(2A) A person to whom this section applies, who has been surrendered to the State by a Convention country pursuant to a request for his extradition from the Central Authority in the State, may—

    (a) be proceeded against for an offence alleged to have been committed by him before his surrender (other than that for which he has been surrendered) provided that—

        (i) upon conviction he is not liable to a term of imprisonment or detention,

        (ii) in circumstances where, upon conviction, he would be liable to a term of imprisonment or detention or such penalty as does not involve a restriction of his personal liberty, the said other penalty only shall be imposed should he be convicted of the offence concerned,

    (b) be subjected to a penalty (other than a penalty consisting of the restriction of his personal liberty) including a financial penalty, where apart from this section the law so provides in respect of an offence—

(i) of which he has been convicted,

(ii) that was committed before his surrender, and

(iii) that is not an offence for which he has been surrendered,

notwithstanding that where such person fails or refuses to pay the penalty concerned (or, in the case of a penalty that is not a financial penalty, fails or refuses to comply with the order of the court by which the penalty has been imposed), he may in accordance with law and apart from this section be detained or otherwise deprived of his personal liberty, or

(c) be proceeded against or, where apart from this section the law so provides, be detained for the purpose of executing a sentence of imprisonment or detention in respect of an offence—

(i) of which he has been convicted,

(ii) that was committed before his surrender, and

(iii) that is not an offence for which he has been surrendered,

or, where apart from this section the law so provides, be otherwise restricted in his personal liberty as a consequence of being convicted of such offence, provided that he has consented to such execution or his personal liberty being so restricted before the High Court which shall, upon being satisfied that the person so consents voluntarily and is aware of the consequences of his so consenting, record that consent.][3]

(3) Where the description of the offence charged is altered in the course of proceedings, he shall only be proceeded against or sentenced in so far as the offence under its new description is shown by its constituent elements to be an offence for which he would be liable to be surrendered to the State.

Amendments

1   Words substituted by Extradition (European Union Conventions) Act 2001, s 16(a).

2   Words amended by Extradition (European Union Conventions) Act 2001, s 25(b).

3   Subsection (2A) inserted by Extradition (European Union Conventions) Act 2001, s 16(b).

---

40   Transit

[(1) Transit through the State of a person being conveyed from one country to another upon his surrender pursuant to an agreement in the nature of an extradition agreement may, subject to—

(a) any relevant extradition provisions,

(b) such conditions, if any, as the Minister thinks proper, and

(c) in circumstances where the country to which he is being conveyed is a Convention country, compliance with subsection (1A) (inserted by section 19(b) of the Extradition (European Union Conventions) Act, 2001),

be granted by the Minister upon a request to that effect by the country to which he is being conveyed.][1]

[(1A) Where a request to which subsection (1) applies is made by a Convention country, the following information shall be provided by or on behalf of the Central Authority in that country in writing to the Central Authority in the State, that is to say:

    (a) such information as will enable the person to be identified by the Central Authority in the State,

    (b) whether—

        (i) there exists an arrest warrant or other document having the same effect as an arrest warrant under the law of the Convention country issued by a judicial authority in that country in respect of the person, or

        (ii) the person has been convicted in the Convention country of an offence in respect of which he has been surrendered,

    (c) the nature, and description under the law of the Convention country, of the offence in respect of which the person has been surrendered, and

    (d) a description of the circumstances in which the offence—

        (i) was committed, or

        (ii) where the person has not yet been convicted of the offence concerned, is alleged to have been committed,

and the date and place of its commission or alleged commission, as may be appropriate.][2]

(2) The Minister may arrange for the supervision of such transit by the Garda Síochána and the person concerned shall be deemed to be in the custody of any member of the Garda Síochána accompanying him pursuant to such arrangement.

[(2A)(a) This subsection applies to an aircraft that has taken off from a place (other than the State) and that is scheduled to land in a place (other than the State) and on board which there is a person who is being conveyed to a Convention country upon his surrender to that country pursuant to an agreement in the nature of an extradition agreement.

    (b) Where an aircraft to which this subsection applies, for whatever reason, lands in the State, the Central Authority of the Convention country referred to in paragraph (a) shall, upon its landing or as soon as may be after it lands, comply with subsection (1A) and the said subsection (1A) shall apply subject to any necessary modifications.

    (c) While an aircraft to which this subsection applies is in the State, a person referred to in paragraph (a) who is on board that aircraft shall be deemed to be in transit through the State and subsection (2) shall apply accordingly.][3]

Amendments

1   Subsection (1) substituted by Extradition (European Union Conventions) Act 2001, s 19(a).

2   Subsection (1A) inserted by Extradition (European Union Conventions) Act 2001, s 19(b).

3   Subsection (2A) inserted by Extradition (European Union Conventions) Act 2001, s 19(c).

PART III

ENDORSEMENT AND EXECUTION OF CERTAIN WARRANTS

41–55

Amendments

1   Part III is repealed by European Arrest Warrant Act 2003, s 50.

SCHEDULE

Section 6

REPEALS

Session and Chapter	Short Title	Extent of Repeal
11 & 12 Vict. c. 42.	Indictable Offences Act, 1848.	Sections 12 and 15.
11 & 12 Vict. c. 43.	Summary Jurisdiction Act, 1848.	Section 3.
12 & 13 Vict. c. 69.	Indictable Offences (Ir.) Act, 1849.	Sections 12, 13, 14 and 15.
14 & 15 Vict. c. 93.	Petty Sessions (Ir.) Act, 1851.	Subsection (3) of section 27; section 29.
31 & 32 Vict. c. 107.	Indictable Offences Act Amendment Act, 1868.	The whole Act.
33 & 34 Vict c. 52.	Extradition Act, 1870.	The whole Act, except section 24.
36 & 37 Vict. c. 60.	Extradition Act, 1873.	The whole Act, except section 5.
36 & 37 Vict. c. 88.	Slave Trade Act, 1873.	Section 27.
44 & 45 Vict. c. 69.	Fugitive Offenders Act, 1881.	The whole Act.
58 & 59 Vict. c. 33.	Extradition Act, 1895.	The whole Act.
6 Edw. 7. c. 15.	Extradition Act, 1906.	The whole Act.
5 & 6 Geo. 5 c. 39.	Fugitive Offenders (Protected States) Act, 1915.	The whole Act.

Criminal Procedure Act 1967

Number 12 of 1967

ARRANGEMENT OF SECTIONS

PART I

PRELIMINARY

1   Short title.

2   Commencement.

3   Repeals.

4   Interpretation.

[PART IA

PROCEEDINGS RELATING TO INDICTABLE OFFENCES

4A   Accused to be sent forward for trial

4B   Service of documents on accused, etc

4C   Additional documents

4D   Examination of exhibits

4E   Application by accused for dismissal of charge

4F   Taking of evidence by District Court

4G   Admissibility of deposition or videorecording

4H   Legal Aid

4I   Power to exclude public

4J   Proceedings not to be published or broadcast

4K   Witness order

4L   Witness summons

4M   Amendment of charges

4N   Joinder of unrelated charges

4O   Correction of defect in charge

4P   Transfer of proceedings from Circuit Court to Central Criminal Court

4Q   Jurisdiction of Circuit Court to remand accused to alternative circuit and hear applications][1]

Amendments

1   Part 1A inserted by Criminal Justice Act 1999, s 9.

PART II
PRELIMINARY EXAMINATION OF INDICTABLE OFFENCES IN THE DISTRICT COURT

5   Procedure.

6   Documents to be served on accused.

7   Preliminary examination.

8   Decision on preliminary examination.

9   Witness order.

10   Witness summons.

11   Additional documents.

12   Waiver by accused of preliminary examination.

13   Procedure where accused pleads guilty in District Court to indictable offence.

14   Further power to take depositions.

15   Deposition as evidence.

16   Power to exclude public.

17   Prohibition of publication of proceedings.

18   Inclusion of further counts in indictment.

19   Amendment of Criminal Justice Act, 1951, and Criminal Justice (Legal Aid) Act, 1962.

20   Consent of Attorney General.

PART III
REMAND

21   Power to remand.

22   Remand in custody or on bail by the District Court.

23   Form of recognisance.

24   Period of remand.

25   Remand to custody of Garda Síochána.

26   Acceptance of deposit in lieu of sureties.

27   Sufficiency of bailsmen.

28   Provisions as to admission to bail.

29   Bail in case of treason, murder and certain other offences.

30   Endorsement on warrants as to release on bail.

31   Release on bail in certain cases by members of Garda Síochána.

32   Proceedings to estreat recognisance.

33   Arrest of accused about to abscond.

PART IV
MISCELLANEOUS

34   Reference of question of law to Supreme Court.

35 Amendment of section 52 of Extradition Act, 1965.

36 Explanation of "imprisonment" in Part III of Extradition Act, 1965.

37 Offences under the law of Scotland.

38 Offences under the laws of the Channel Islands.

SCHEDULE

AN ACT TO ESTABLISH A NEW PROCEDURE FOR THE PRELIMINARY EXAMINATION OF INDICTABLE OFFENCES AND FOR THIS AND OTHER PURPOSES TO AMEND CRIMINAL LAW AND ADMINISTRATION. [13th June, 1967]

BE IT ENACTED BY THE OIREACHTAS AS FOLLOWS:—

PART I
PRELIMINARY

1   Short title

This Act may be cited as the Criminal Procedure Act, 1967.

2   Commencement

Section 3 and Parts II and III shall come into operation on such day as the Minister for Justice by order appoints.

3   Repeals

Each of the enactments mentioned in the Schedule is hereby repealed to the extent specified in the third column.

[4   Interpretation

(1) In this Act 'the prosecutor' means, in relation to an offence—

  (a) in Part IA and section 13, the Director of Public Prosecutions, and

  (b) in Parts II and III, other than section 13—

   (i)   the Director of Public Prosecutions,

   (ii) a person prosecuting the offence at the suit of the Director of Public Prosecutions, or

   (iii) a person authorised by law to prosecute the offence.

(2) Notwithstanding subsection (1), references to the prosecutor in Parts IA, II and III shall be construed, in relation to offences for which proceedings may not be [instituted or continued except by the Attorney General.]²]¹

Amendments

1   Section 4 substituted by Criminal Justice Act 1999, s 8.

2   Words substituted by Criminal Procedure Act 2010, s 37.

[PART IA
PROCEEDINGS RELATING TO INDICTABLE OFFENCES][1]

Amendments

1   Part IA (sections 4A–4Q) inserted by Criminal Justice Act 1999, s 9.

4A   Accused to be sent forward for trial

(1) Where an accused person is before the District Court charged with an indictable offence, the Court shall send the accused forward for trial to the court before which he is to stand trial (the trial court) unless—

   (a)   the case is being tried summarily,

   (b)   the case is being dealt with under section 13, or

   (c)   the accused is unfit to plead.

(2) The accused shall not be sent forward for trial under subsection (1) without the consent of the prosecutor.

(3) Where the prosecutor refuses to give a consent required under subsection (2) in relation to an indictable offence, the District Court shall strike out the proceedings against the accused in relation to that offence.

(4) The striking out of proceedings under subsection (3) shall not prejudice the institution of proceedings against the accused by the prosecutor.

(5) The accused shall not be sent forward for trial under subsection (1) until the documents mentioned in section 4B(1) have been served on the accused.

4B   Service of documents on accused, etc

[(1) (a)   Subject to subsection (3), the prosecutor shall cause the documents specified in paragraph (b) to be served on the accused or his or her solicitor (if any) not later than 42 days from the date on which—

     (i)   the accused, on being informed by the District Court of his or her right to be tried by a jury, objects to being tried summarily or the prosecutor informs the court that he or she does not consent to the person being tried summarily for the offence concerned or,

     (ii)   in the case of an offence in respect of which the prosecutor may elect to prosecute either summarily or on indictment, the prosecutor elects to try the offence on indictment, or

     (iii) the District Court determines that the facts alleged do not constitute a minor offence and are not fit to be tried summarily.

   (b)   The documents referred to in paragraph (a) are:

     (i)   a statement of the charges against the accused;

     (ii)   a copy of any sworn information in writing upon which the proceedings were initiated;

     (iii) a list of the witnesses the prosecutor proposes to call at the trial;

     (iv)   a statement of the evidence that is expected to be given by each of them;

(v) a copy of any document containing information which it is proposed to give in evidence by virtue of Part II of the Criminal Evidence Act 1992;

(vi) where appropriate, a copy of a certificate under section 6(1) of that Act;

(vii) a list of the exhibits (if any).]¹

(2) As soon as the documents mentioned in subsection (1) are served, the prosecutor shall furnish copies of them to the District Court.

(3) On application by the prosecutor, the District Court may extend the period within which the documents mentioned in subsection (1) are to be served if it is satisfied that—

(a) there is good reason for doing so, and

(b) it would be in the interests of justice to do so.

(4) An application may be made and an extension may be granted under subsection (3) before or after the expiry of—

(a) the period of 42 days mentioned in subsection (1), or

(b) any extension of that period granted under subsection (3).

(5) Where it refuses to grant an extension, the District Court shall strike out the proceedings against the accused in relation to the offence.

(6) The striking out of proceedings under subsection (5) shall not prejudice the institution of any proceedings against the accused by the prosecutor.

Amendments

1   Subsection 1 substituted by Criminal Procedure Act 2010, s 37.

4C   Additional documents

(1) At any time after service of the documents mentioned in section 4B(1), the prosecutor shall cause the following documents to be served on the accused or his solicitor, if any:

(a) a list of any further witnesses the prosecutor proposes to call at the trial;

(b) a statement of the evidence that is expected to be given by each witness whose name appears on the list of further witnesses;

(c) a statement of any further evidence that is expected to be given by any witness whose name appears on the list already served under section 4B(1)(c);

(d) any notice of intention to give information contained in a document in evidence under section 7(1)(b) of the Criminal Evidence Act, 1992, together with a copy of the document;

(e) where appropriate, a copy of a certificate under section 6(1) of the Criminal Evidence Act, 1992;

(f) a copy of any deposition taken under section 4F;

(g) a list of any further exhibits.

(2) As soon as any documents are served in accordance with this section, the prosecutor shall furnish copies of them to the trial Court.

4D Examination of exhibits

The accused shall have the right to inspect all exhibits mentioned in the list of exhibits served on the accused or his solicitor under section 4B or 4C.

4E Application by accused for dismissal of charge

(1) At any time after the accused is sent forward for trial, the accused may apply to the trial court to dismiss one or more of the charges against the accused.

(2) Notice of an application under subsection (1) shall be given to the prosecutor not less than 14 days before the date on which the application is due to be heard.

(3) The trial court may, in the interests of justice, determine that less than 14 days notice of an application under subsection (1) may be given to the prosecutor.

(4) If it appears to the trial court that there is not a sufficient case to put the accused on trial for any charge to which the application relates, the court shall dismiss the charge.

(5) (a) Oral evidence may be given on an application under subsection (1) only if it appears to the trial court that such evidence is required in the interests of justice.

(b) In paragraph (a) 'oral evidence'

includes—

(i) any evidence given through a live television link pursuant to Part III of the Criminal Evidence Act, 1992, or section 39 of the Criminal Justice Act, 1999, or

(ii) a videorecording of any evidence given through a live television link pursuant to that Part or section in proceedings under [section 4F, or]¹

[(iii) any other videorecording, or an audiorecording, which may be admitted by the trial court as evidence of any fact stated in it.]²

(6) Where the trial court is satisfied that it is in the interests of justice that any document required under this Part to be served on the accused or his solicitor be served at the hearing of an application under this section—

(a) the prosecutor shall serve the document on the accused or his solicitor, if any, at the hearing, and

(b) the court may, if it considers it appropriate to do so, adjourn the hearing for that purpose.

(7) Where a charge is dismissed by the trial court under subsection (4), the prosecutor may, within 21 days after the dismissal date, appeal against the dismissal to the Court of Criminal Appeal.

(8) On an appeal under subsection (7), the Court of Criminal Appeal may—

(a) affirm the decision of the trial court, or

(b) quash the decision of the trial court, in which case the trial of the accused may proceed as if the charge had never been dismissed.

Amendments

1 Subsection (5)(b)(ii) amended by Criminal Justice Act 2006, s 20(a).

2 Subsection (5)(b)(iii) inserted by Criminal Justice Act 2006, s 20(b).

4F   Taking of evidence by District Court

(1) At any time after the accused is sent forward for trial, the prosecutor or the accused may apply to the trial court for an order requiring a person to appear before a judge of the District Court so that the person's evidence may be taken either—

    (a)   by way of sworn deposition, or

    (b)   in case the person's evidence is to be given through a live television link pursuant to Part III of the Criminal Evidence Act, 1992, or section 39 of the Criminal Justice Act, 1999, through such a link.

whether or not the person's name appears in the list of witnesses served on the accused under section 4B or 4C.

(2) If satisfied that it would be in the interests of justice to do so, the trial court may order a person who is the subject of an application under subsection (1) to attend before a judge of the District Court in the district court district—

    (a)   in which the offence was committed, or

    (b)   in which the accused was arrested or resides,

so that the judge may take the person's evidence accordingly.

(3) The following rules shall apply to the taking of evidence under this section—

    (a)   when the evidence is being taken, both the accused and a judge of the District Court shall be present;

    (b)   before it is taken, the judge shall inform the accused of the circumstances in which it may be admitted in evidence at the accused's trial;

    (c)   the witness may be cross-examined and re-examined;

    (d)   where the evidence is taken by way of sworn deposition, the deposition and any cross-examination and re-examination of the deponent shall be recorded, read to the deponent and signed by the deponent and the judge.

(4) A judge of the District Court shall have the same powers for—

    (a)   enforcing compliance by a prospective witness with this section or with an order under this section, and

    (b)   securing the attendance of the accused,

as the District Court has in relation to witnesses in criminal proceedings.

4G   Admissibility of deposition or videorecording

(1) A deposition taken under section 4F may be considered by the trial court on an application under section 4E(1).

(2) Such a deposition may be admitted in evidence at the trial of the accused if it is proved that—

    (a)   the witness—

        (i)   is dead,

        (ii)   is unable to attend to give evidence at the trial,

        (iii) is prevented from so attending, or

        (iv)   does not give evidence at the trial through fear or intimidation,

    (b)   the accused was present at the taking of the evidence, and

    (c)   an opportunity was given to crossexamine and re-examine the witness;

unless the court is of opinion that to do so would not be in the interests of justice.

(3) Subject to section 16 (admissibility at trial of videorecording of evidence given by witness under 17) of the Criminal Evidence Act, 1992, a videorecording of evidence given through a live television link in proceedings under section 4F shall, if the accused was present at the taking of the evidence and an opportunity was given to cross-examine and re-examine the witness, be admissible at the trial of the offence with which the accused is charged as evidence of any fact stated therein of which direct oral evidence by the witness would be admissible, unless the court is of opinion that in the interests of justice the videorecording ought not to be so admitted.

4H   Legal Aid

(1) The provision for legal aid made by section 2 of the Criminal Justice (Legal Aid) Act, 1962, shall extend to the accused in relation to all proceedings conducted under this Part before the District Court.

(2) The provision for legal aid made by section 3 of the Criminal Justice (Legal Aid) Act, 1962, shall extend to the accused in relation to all proceedings conducted under this Part before the trial court, the Court of Criminal Appeal or an alternative court referred to in section 4Q.

4I   Power to exclude public

(1) Subject to this section and any other enactment, a proceeding under this Part shall be conducted in open court.

(2) Where a court conducting a proceeding under this Part is satisfied, because of the nature or circumstances of the case or otherwise in the interests of justice, that it is desirable to do so, it may exclude from the court during the proceeding—

    (a)   the public or any portion of the public, or

    (b)   any particular person or persons,

except bona fide representatives of the Press.

(3) Subsection (2) is without prejudice to the right of a parent, relative or friend of the accused or of an injured party to remain in court in any case to which section 20(4) of the Criminal Justice Act, 1951, or section 6 of the Criminal Law (Rape) Act, 1981 (as substituted by section 11 of the Criminal Law (Rape) (Amendment) Act, 1990) applies.

4J   Proceedings not to be published or broadcast

(1) No person shall publish or broadcast or cause to be published or broadcast any information about a proceeding under this Part other than—

    (a)   a statement of—

        (i)   the fact that the proceeding has been brought by a named person in relation to a specified charge against a named person, and

        (ii)   any decision resulting from the proceeding,

    and

    (b)   in the case of an application under section 4E for the dismissal of a charge against the accused, any information that the judge hearing the application permits to be published or broadcast at the request of the accused.

(2) If, on application by the prosecutor, it appears to a judge of the District Court that a person has contravened subsection (1), the judge may certify to that effect to the High Court.

(3) On receiving a certificate under subsection (2), the High Court may—

    (a)   inquire into the matter to which the certificate relates, and

    (b)   after hearing any witnesses and after considering any statement that may be offered in defence of the person alleged to have contravened subsection (1), punish, or take steps for the punishment of, that person in the like manner as if he had been guilty of contempt of the Court.

(4) This section shall not affect—

    (a)   the operation of any other enactment that imposes further restrictions on the extent to which information relating to court proceedings may be published or broadcast, or

    (b)   any power conferred on a court by such an enactment to make an order authorising the publication or broadcast of such information.

(5) In this section—

'broadcast' means the transmission, relaying or distribution by wireless telegraphy of communications, sounds, signs, visual images or signals, intended for direct reception by the general public whether or not such communications, sounds, signs, visual images or signals are actually received;

'publish' means publish to the public or a portion of the public.

4K   Witness order

(1) The trial court may, in relation to the trial of the accused, make an order requiring a person whose statement of evidence was served on the accused or whose deposition was taken to—

    (a)   attend before the trial court and give evidence at the trial of the accused, and

    (b)   produce to that court any document or thing specified in the order.

(2) A person who without just excuse disobeys a witness order shall be guilty of contempt of the trial court.

(3) If, on application by the prosecutor or the accused, the trial court is satisfied by evidence on oath that any person is unlikely to comply with a witness order, the court—

    (a)   may bind the person by recognisance to appear at the trial,

    (b)   if the person refuses to be so bound, may, by warrant, commit him to custody until the trial or until he enters into a recognisance, and

    (c)   shall have the same powers for enforcing the person's attendance before the trial court for the purposes of this subsection as that court has in relation to witnesses in criminal proceedings.

(4) In this section, 'witness order' means an order made under subsection (1).

4L   Witness summons

(1) On application by the prosecutor or the accused, a summons may be issued out of the trial court requiring the person to whom the summons is directed to—

    (a)   attend before the trial court and give evidence at the trial of the accused, and

    (b)   produce to that court any document or thing specified in the summons, unless the court is satisfied that the person proposed to be summoned cannot give any material evidence or, as the case may be, produce any document or thing likely to be material evidence.

(2) A person who without just excuse disobeys a witness summons shall be guilty of contempt of the court out of which the summons was issued.

(3) This section is without prejudice to any other powers for enforcing the attendance of witnesses at the trial.

(4) In this section, 'witness summons' means a summons issued under subsection (1).

4M   Amendment of charges

Where the accused has been sent forward for trial in accordance with this Part, the indictment against the accused may include, either in substitution for or in addition to counts charging the offence for which he has been sent forward, any counts that—

(a)   are founded on any of the documents served on the accused under section 4B or 4C, and

(b)   may lawfully be joined in the same indictment.

4N   Joinder of unrelated charges

Where the accused has been sent forward for trial in accordance with this Part, the indictment against the accused may, with the consent of the accused and notwithstanding any other enactment, include counts that—

(a)   charge an offence justiciable within the State, other than the offence for which the accused was sent forward, and

(b)   are not founded on the documents served on the accused under section 4B or 4C,

and section 25(3) of the Courts (Supplemental Provisions) Act, 1961, shall be construed accordingly.

4O   Correction of defect in charge

Where the accused has been sent forward for trial in accordance with this Part, the trial court may correct any defect in a charge against the accused unless it considers that the correction would result in injustice.

4P   Transfer of proceedings from Circuit Court to Central Criminal Court

Where, after being sent forward for trial in accordance with this Part to the Circuit Court for an indictable offence (the original offence), the accused is sent forward for trial to the Central Criminal Court for another indictable offence connected with or arising from the circumstances that gave rise to the original offence, the Circuit Court may, unless it considers it would not be in the interests of justice to do so, transfer the trial of the original offence to the Central Criminal Court.

4Q   Jurisdiction of Circuit Court to remand accused to alternative circuit and hear applications

(1) Notwithstanding any other enactment, where the accused has been sent forward for trial in accordance with this Part to the Circuit Court, it may remand the accused in custody to appear at a sitting of the Circuit Court ('alternative court') in the circuit of the Circuit Court

in which is situated the prison or place of detention where the accused is to be held in custody.

(2) If the accused is remanded under this section to a sitting of an alternative court—

    (a) the alternative court may, from time to time as occasion requires, further remand the accused, in custody or on bail, to that court or another alternative court,

    (b) a reference in section 4B(3) or (5), 4E or 4P to the trial court shall be read as a reference to the alternative court to which the accused is remanded, and

    (c) the alternative court shall have the same power to correct any defect in the charge against the accused as the trial court has under section 4O.

(3) An alternative court shall, for the purposes of the trial of the offence, remand the accused to a sitting of the Circuit Court in the circuit of the Circuit Court—

    (a) in which the offence was committed, or

    (b) in which the accused was arrested or resides.

PART II
[GUILTY PLEAS AND OTHER MATTERS][1]

Amendments

1   Title to Part II substituted by Criminal Justice Act 1999, s 10(1).

5–12   [...][1]

Amendments

1   Sections 5–12 repealed by Criminal Justice Act 1999, s 10(2).

---

13   Procedure where accused pleads guilty in District Court to indictable offence

[(1) This section applies to all indictable offences except the following— an offence under the Treason Act, 1939, murder, attempt to murder, conspiracy to murder, piracy, an offence under section 7 (genocide, crimes against humanity and war crimes) or 8 (ancillary offences) of the International Criminal Court Act 2006, an offence under the Criminal Justice (United Nations Convention against Torture) Act, 2000, the offence of murder under section 2 of the Criminal Justice (Safety of United Nations Workers) Act, 2000, or the offence of killing or attempted killing under paragraph (h) or (j) of section 2(1) of the Maritime Security Act 2004, the offence of murder under section 6 or 11 of the Criminal Justice (Terrorist Offences) Act 2005, or an offence under section 71, 71A, 72 or 73 of the Criminal Justice Act 2006 or an attempt to commit such offence, or an attempt or conspiracy to commit that offence or a grave breach such as is referred to in section 3(1)(i) of the Geneva Conventions Act, 1962, including an offence by an accessory before or after the fact.][1]

[(2) If at any time the District Court ascertains that a person charged with an offence to which this section applies wishes to plead guilty and the court is satisfied that he understands the nature of the offence and the facts alleged, the Court—

   (a) may, with the consent of the prosecutor, deal with the offence summarily, in which case the accused shall be liable to the penalties provided for in subsection (3), or

   (b) if the accused signs a plea of guilty, may, subject to subsection (2A), send him forward for sentence with that plea to that court to which, but for that plea, he would have been sent forward for trial.

(2A) The accused shall not be sent forward for sentence under this section without the consent of the prosecutor.]²

(3) (a) On conviction by the District Court for an offence dealt with summarily under subsection (2)(a), the accused shall be liable to a fine not exceeding [£1000]³ or, at the discretion of the Court, to imprisonment for a term not exceeding twelve months, or to both such fine and imprisonment.

   (b) [...]⁴

(4) (a) Where a person is sent forward for sentence under this section he may withdraw his written plea and plead not guilty to the charge.

   [(b) In that event—

      (i) the court shall enter a plea of not guilty, which shall have the same effect in all respects as if the accused had been sent forward for trial to that court on that charge in accordance with Part IA,

      (ii) the prosecutor shall cause to be served on the accused any documents that under section 4B or 4C are required to be served and have not already been served, and

      (iii) the period referred to in section 4B(1) shall run from the date on which the not guilty plea is entered.]⁵

(5) This section shall not affect the jurisdiction of the Court under section 2 of the Criminal Justice Act, 1951.

Amendments

1 "genocide" substituted in s 13(1) (as amended by s 6 of the Genocide Act 1973, s 8 of the Criminal Justice (United Nations Convention against Torture) Act 2000, s 7 of the Criminal Justice (Safety of United Nations Workers) Act 2000 and s 59(a) of the Criminal Justice (Terrorist Offences) Act 2005), by International Criminal Court Act 2006, s 66 and Sch 3 and further amended by Criminal Justice (Amendment) Act 2009, s 17.

2 Subsection (2) substituted and (2A) inserted by Criminal Justice Act 1999, s 10(3).

3 Amended by Criminal Justice Act 1984, s 17.

4 Subsection 3(b) repealed by Broadcasting and Wireless Telegraphy Act 1988, s 12.

5 Subsection (4)(b) substituted by Criminal Justice Act 1999, s 10(4).

14–18

[...]¹

Amendments

1   Section 14–18 repealed by Criminal Justice Act 1999, s 10(5).

19   Amendment of Criminal Justice Act, 1951, and Criminal Justice (Legal Aid) Act, 1962

(1) Section 2(2) of the Criminal Justice Act, 1951, is hereby amended by the substitution, for paragraph (b), of the following paragraph:

[…][1]

(2) The First Schedule to the Criminal Justice Act, 1951 (which specifies the indictable offences which may be tried summarily with the consent of the accused) is hereby amended—

(a) by the deletion of the matter set out at reference numbers 8, 14 and 15 and the insertion of—[1]

(b) by the deletion of the matter set out at reference number 18;

(c) by the insertion of the following additional references:[1]

(3) […][2]

Amendments

1   See the amended Act.

2   Subsection (3) repealed by Criminal Procedure (Amendment) Act 1973, s 3

20   Consent of Attorney General

The consent of the Attorney General under any provision of this Part may be conveyed in writing signed by the Attorney General or orally by a person prosecuting at the suit of the Attorney General or appearing on his behalf.

PART III
REMAND

21   Power to remand

Where an accused person is before the District Court in connection with an offence the Court may, subject to the provisions of this Part, remand the accused from time to time as occasion requires.

22   Remand in custody or on bail by the District Court

(1) Where the District Court remands a person or sends him forward for trial or sentence, the Court may—

(a) commit him to prison or other lawful custody, or

(b) release him conditionally on his entering into a recognisance, with or without sureties.

In this Part, references to "custody" are to a committal under paragraph (a) and references to "bail" are to a conditional release under paragraph (b).

[(1A) The Court may admit a person to bail without imposing a condition in the recognisance as to payment of moneys into court by the person if it considers it appropriate to do so, having regard to the circumstances of the case, including the means of the person and the nature of the offence in relation to which the person is in custody.][1]

[(1B) A recognisance to which subsection (1) applies may be taken by—

(a) any judge of the District Court, or

(b) any District Court clerk.][2]

[(2) The Court may, instead of taking a recognisance from a person in accordance with subsection (1)—

(a) determine the conditions to be contained in the recognisance, including the amount of any moneys to be paid into court under it, with a view to its being subsequently taken, and

(b) in the meantime commit the person concerned to custody in accordance with paragraph (a) of that subsection.][3]

[(3) A recognisance to which subsection (2) applies may be taken by—

(a) any judge of the District Court,

(b) any District Court clerk,

(c) a peace commissioner designated for that purpose by order of the Minister for Justice, Equality and Law Reform,

(d) the governor of a prison, or

(e) a prison officer designated for that purpose by the governor of a prison.][4]

(4) Where a person is brought before the Court after remand under subsection (1) the Court may further remand him.

[(5) In this section ' prison ' has the same meaning as it has in the Prisons Act 2007.][5]

Amendments

1 Subsection (1A) inserted by Criminal Justice Act 2007, s 18(a).

2 Subsection (1B) inserted by Court and Court Officers Act 2009, s 25.

3 Subsection (2) substituted by Criminal Justice Act 2007, s 18(b).

4 Subsection (3) substituted by Criminal Procedure (Amendment) Act 2007, s 1(a).

5 Subsection (5) inserted by Criminal Procedure (Amendment) Act 2007, s 1(b).

---

23   Form of recognisance

(1) Where a person is remanded on bail under section 22 the recognisance shall be conditioned for his appearance before the Court at the end of the period of remand and at

every place and time to which during the course of the proceedings the hearing may be adjourned.

(2) The fixing at any time of the time for the next appearance shall be deemed to be a remand.

(3) Nothing in subsection (1) or (2) shall deprive the Court of power at any subsequent hearing to remand him afresh.

24   Period of remand

[(1) The Court shall not remand a person, on the occasion of that person's first appearance before the Court charged with a particular offence, for a period exceeding eight days, except where this section otherwise provides.

(2) The Court may remand a person on bail for a period that is longer than eight days if the person and the prosecutor consent.

(3) The Court may remand a person in custody (other than on the occasion of that person's first appearance before the Court charged with a particular offence) for a period not exceeding fifteen days, save that where the Court is of opinion that in all the circumstances it would be unreasonable to remand the person in custody for a period of fifteen days, the period of remand shall be such period of less than fifteen days as the Court considers appropriate.

(4) The Court may remand a person in custody (other than on the occasion of that person's first appearance before the Court charged with a particular offence), for a period exceeding fifteen days but not exceeding thirty days, if the person and the prosecutor consent.

(5) [(a)   If the Court is satisfied that a person who has been remanded in custody is unable to be brought before the Court at the expiration of the period of remand—

     (i)   by reason of illness or accident, or

     (ii)   for any other good and sufficient reason,

the Court may, in that person's absence, remand the person for such further period, which may exceed fifteen days, as the Court considers reasonable.][2]

   (b)   If the Court is satisfied that a person who has been remanded on bail is unable by reason of illness or accident to appear before the Court at the expiration of the period of remand, the Court may, in that person's absence, remand that person for such further period, which may exceed eight days, as the Court considers reasonable.

(6) (a)   Where a person has been remanded in custody and there is no sitting of the Court on the day to which he has been remanded, that person shall stand so remanded to the sitting of the Court next held in the same District Court District.

   (b)   Where a person has been remanded on bail and there is no sitting of the Court on the day to which he has been remanded, that person shall stand so remanded to the sitting of the Court next held in the same District Court Area.][1]

Amendments

1   Section 24 substituted by Criminal Justice (Miscellaneous Provisions) Act 1997, s 4.

2   Subsection (5)(a) substituted by Criminal Procedure Act 2010, s 37(c).

---

25 Remand to custody of Garda Síochána

(1) The Court may, where it remands a person in custody for a period not exceeding four days, commit him to the custody of a member of the Garda Síochána.

(2) Outside the Dublin Metropolitan Police District the Court, before so remanding him, shall satisfy itself that suitable facilities are available for the custody of such person during the period of remand.

26 Acceptance of deposit in lieu of sureties

Where a justice of the District Court [...]¹ decides to admit to bail a person charged with an offence, he may direct that a sum of money equivalent to the amount of bail be accepted in lieu of a surety or sureties.

Amendments

1 Words deleted by Bail Act 1997, s 11(a).

27 Sufficiency of bailsmen

[...]¹

Amendments

1 Section 27 repealed by Bail Act 1997, s 12.

28 Provisions as to admission to bail

(1) A justice of the District Court [...]¹ shall admit to bail a person charged before him with an offence, other than an offence to which section 29 applies, if it appears to him to be a case in which bail ought to be allowed.

(2) Refusal of bail at a particular appearance before the District Court shall not prevent a renewal of the application for bail at a subsequent appearance or while the accused is in custody awaiting trial.

[(3) (a) An applicant for bail or the prosecutor may appeal to the High Court if dissatisfied with a refusal or grant of the application for bail or, where bail is granted, with any matter relating to the bail.

(b) Where the applicant has been remanded in custody by the District Court and the offence with which the applicant is charged is triable by the Circuit Court, the High Court may transfer the appeal to the judge of the Circuit Court for the circuit in which the prison or place of detention to which the applicant has been remanded is situated.

(c) The judge of the Circuit Court referred to in paragraph (b) shall exercise jurisdiction in respect of the appeal.

(d) An appeal against a decision by the Circuit Court under this section lies to the High Court at the instance of the applicant or prosecutor.]²

(4) When a justice [...]³ grants bail to an accused person who is in custody that person shall, on completion of the recognisance, be released if he is in custody for no other cause than the offence in respect of which bail is granted.

Amendments

1   Words deleted by Bail Act 1997, s 11(b)(i).
2   Subsection (3) substituted by Criminal Justice Act 2007, s 19.
3   Words deleted by Bail Act 1997, s 11(b)(ii).

29   Bail in case of treason, murder and certain other offences

(1) This section applies to each of the following offences—

(a)   treason,

(b)   an offence under section 2 or 3 of the Treason Act, 1939,

(c)   an offence under section 6, 7 or 8 of the Offences Against the State Act, 1939,

(d)   a grave breach such as is referred to in section 3(1)(i) of the Geneva Conventions Act, 1962,

(e)   an offence under section 9 of the Official Secrets Act, 1963, or an offence under Part II of that Act committed in a manner prejudicial to the safety or preservation of the State,

(f)   murder, attempt to murder, conspiracy to murder or piracy, including an accessory before or after the fact.

[(g)   an offence under section 3, as amended, of the Geneva Conventions Act 1962 or an offence under section 7 or 8 of the International Criminal Court Act 2006]¹

[(h)   an offence under the Criminal Justice (United Nations Convention against Torture) Act, 2000.]²

[(i)   the offence of murder under section 2 of the Criminal Justice (Safety of United Nations Workers) Act, 2000, or an attempt or conspiracy to commit that offence.]³

[(j)   the offence of killing or attempted killing under paragraph (h) or (j) of section 2(1) of the Maritime Security Act 2004.]⁴

[(k)   the offence of murder under section 6 or 11 of the Criminal Justice (Terrorist Offences) Act 2005 or an attempt to commit such offence.]⁵

[(l)   an offence under section 71, [71A], 72 or 73 of the Criminal Justice Act 2006.]⁶

(2) A person charged with an offence to which this section applies shall not be admitted to bail except by order of the High Court.

(3) If in the course of proceedings, including proceedings on appeal, in relation to the grant of bail to a person charged with an offence under paragraph (a), (b), (c) or (e) of subsection (1), application is made by the prosecutor, on the ground that the publication of any evidence or statement to be given or made during any part of the hearing would be prejudicial to the safety or preservation of the State, that that part of the proceedings should be in camera, the

Court shall make an order to that effect, but the decision of the Court shall be announced in public.

Amendments

1 Paragraph (g) substituted by International Criminal Court Act 2006, s 66 and Sch 3.
2 Paragraph (h) inserted by Criminal Justice (United Nations Convention Against Torture) Act 2000, s 8.
3 Paragraph (i) inserted by Criminal Justice (Safety of United Nations Workers) Act 2000, s 7(b).
3 Paragraph (j) inserted by Maritime Security Act 2004, s 10.
4 Paragraph (k) inserted by Criminal Justice (Terrorist Offences) Act 2005, s 59(b).
5 Paragraph (l) inserted by Criminal Justice Act 2006, s 78 and amended by inserting '71A' by Criminal Justice (Amendment) Act 2009, s 17.

30 Endorsement on warrants as to release on bail

[...]¹

Amendments

1 Section 30 repealed by Bail Act 1997, s 12.

31 Release on bail in certain cases by members of Garda Síochána

[(1) Whenever a person is brought in custody to a Garda Síochána station by a member of the Garda Síochána, the sergeant or other member in charge of the station may, if he considers it prudent to do so and no warrant directing the detention of that person is in force, release him on bail and for that purpose take from him a recognisance, with or without sureties, for his due appearance—

    (a) before the District Court at the next sitting thereof in the District Court Area in which that person has been arrested or at any subsequent sitting thereof in that District Court Area during the period of thirty days immediately following such next sitting, or

    (b) in the case of the District Court in the Dublin Metropolitan District, before the next sitting of that Court or at any subsequent sitting thereof during the period of thirty days immediately following such next sitting.]¹

(2) The recognisance may be estreated in the like manner as a recognisance entered into before a justice is estreated.

[(3) If the recognisance is conditioned for the payment of a sum of money, that sum may be accepted in lieu of a surety or sureties.]²

[(3A) Any recognisance taken under this section, or any sum of money accepted under this section in lieu of a surety or sureties, shall be given, by the member of the Garda Síochána taking the said recognisance or receiving the said sum of money, to the District Court clerk for the District Court Area in which the sitting of the Court to which the person has been remanded is situated.]³

(4) This section does not apply to a person arrested under section 251 of the Defence Act, 1954, on suspicion of being a deserter or an absentee without leave from the Defence Forces.

[(5) The provisions of this section are without prejudice to the provisions of section 94 of the Children Act, 1908.]⁴

Amendments

1   Subsection (1) substituted by Criminal Justice (Miscellaneous Provisions) Act 1997, s 3(a).

2   Subsection (3) substituted by Criminal Justice Act 2007, s 20.

3   Subsection (3A) inserted by Criminal Justice (Miscellaneous Provisions) Act 1997, s 3(c).

3   Subsection (5) inserted by Criminal Justice (Miscellaneous Provisions) Act 1997, s 3(d).

32   Proceedings to estreat recognisance

Where a person has failed to appear before a court in accordance with his recognisance, any proceedings to estreat the recognisance shall be taken in that court.

33   Arrest of accused about to abscond

[...]¹

Amendments

1   Section 33 repealed by Bail Act 1997, s 12.

PART IV
MISCELLANEOUS

34   [Reference of question of law to Supreme Court.

(1) Where a person tried on indictment is acquitted (whether in respect of the whole or part of the indictment) the Attorney General in any case or, if he or she is the prosecuting authority in the trial, the Director of Public Prosecutions may, without prejudice to the verdict or decision in favour of the accused person, refer a question of law arising during the trial to the Supreme Court for determination.

(2) Where a question of law is referred to the Supreme Court under subsection (1), the statement of the question shall be settled by the Attorney General or the Director of Public Prosecutions, as may be appropriate, after consultation with the trial judge concerned or, in the case of a Special Criminal Court, with the member of that Court who pronounced the decision of the Court in the trial concerned following consultation by that member with the

other members of the Court concerned and shall include any observations which the judge or that member, as may be appropriate, may wish to add.

(3) For the purpose of considering a question referred to it under this section, the Supreme Court shall hear argument—

    (a) by, or by counsel on behalf of, the Attorney General or the Director of Public Prosecutions, as may be appropriate,

    (b) if the acquitted person so wishes, by counsel on his or her behalf or, with the leave of the Court, by the acquitted person himself or herself, and

    (c) if counsel are assigned under subsection (4), such counsel.

(4) The Supreme Court shall assign counsel to argue in support of the decision if—

    (a) the acquitted person waives his or her right to be represented or heard under subsection (3)(b), or

    (b) notwithstanding the fact that the acquitted person exercises his or her right to be represented or heard under subsection (3)(b), the Court considers it desirable in the public interest to do so.

(5) The Supreme Court shall ensure, in so far as it is reasonably practicable to do so, that the identity of the acquitted person in proceedings under this section is not disclosed in connection with the proceedings unless the person agrees to the use of his or her name in the proceedings.

(6) If the acquitted person wishes to be represented in proceedings before the Supreme Court under this section and a legal aid (Supreme Court) certificate is granted under subsection (7), or is deemed to have been granted under subsection (8), in respect of him or her, he or she shall be entitled to free legal aid in the preparation and presentation of any argument that he or she wishes to make to the Court and to have a solicitor and counsel assigned to him or her for that purpose in the manner prescribed by regulations under section 10 of the Criminal Justice (Legal Aid) Act 1962.

(7) The acquitted person may, in relation to proceedings under this section, apply for a legal aid (Supreme Court) certificate to the Supreme Court either—

    (a) by letter addressed to the registrar of the Supreme Court setting out the facts of the case and the grounds of the application, or

    (b) to the Supreme Court itself,

and the Court shall grant the certificate if (but only if) it appears to the Court that the means of the person are insufficient to enable him or her to obtain legal aid.

(8) If a legal aid (trial on indictment) certificate was granted in respect of the acquitted person in relation to the trial on indictment concerned, a legal aid (Supreme Court) certificate shall be deemed to have been granted in respect of him or her in relation to proceedings under this section.

(9) In this section 'legal aid (Supreme Court) certificate' and 'legal aid (trial on indictment) certificate' have the meanings they have in the Criminal Justice (Legal Aid) Act 1962.][1]

Amendments

1   Section 34 substituted by Criminal Justice Act 2006, s 21.

35   Amendment of section 52 of Extradition Act, 1965

Section 52 of the Extradition Act, 1965, is hereby amended by the insertion of the following subsection:[1]

Amendments

1   See the amended Act.

36   Explanation of "imprisonment" in Part III of Extradition Act, 1965

In order to remove doubts it is hereby declared that references to imprisonment in Part III of the Extradition Act, 1965, whether in relation to the State or to any other place, include references to any form of lawful custody of the person affected.

37   Offences under the law of Scotland

[...][1]

Amendments

1   Section 37 repealed by Criminal Justice Act 1999, s 32.

38   Offences under the laws of the Channel Islands

(1) This section applies in relation to the Channel Islands, namely, Jersey and the Bailiwick of Guernsey.

(2) For the purposes of Part III of the Extradition Act, 1965, an offence punishable under the law of Jersey or of any part of the Bailiwick of Guernsey by death or by imprisonment for a maximum period of at least six months shall be treated as being an indictable offence and not also a summary offence if it is certified by the Attorney General for Jersey or Guernsey, as the case may be, that the offence is an indictable offence and that it is punishable by death or by such imprisonment.

(3) A certificate appearing to be given by the appropriate Attorney General may without further evidence—

(a) be accepted by the Commissioner of the Garda Síochána,

(b) be admitted in any proceedings, unless the court sees good reason to the contrary,

as evidence of the matters so certified.

(4) In this section "Attorney General" includes a person for the time being exercising the functions of that office.

(5) This section shall be construed as one with Part III of the Extradition Act, 1965.

SCHEDULE

ENACTMENTS REPEALED

Section 3.

Session and Chapter or Number and Year	Short title	Extent of repeal
12 & 13 Vict. c. 69.	Indictable Offences (Ireland) Act, 1849.	In section 16, the words "within the Jurisdiction of such Justice", and "for the Prosecution". Sections 17 to 25 and 27.
14 & 15 Vict. c. 93.	Petty Sessions (Ireland) Act, 1851.	Section 9(2). In section 13 the words "within the Jurisdiction of such Justice" and "for the Prosecution". Sections 13(6), 14 to 17 and 19.
4 & 5 Geo. 5 c. 58.	Criminal Justice Administration Act, 1914	Sections 19, 20, 21 and 43(1)(d).
No. 48 of 1936.	Courts of Justice Act, 1936.	In section 62, the words "to receive informations in relation to such charge or".
No. 2 of 1951.	Criminal Justice Act, 1951.	Section 3. In section 4, the words "or for an indictable offence dealt with under section 3 of this Act". Sections 9 and 14. Section 20(1),(2).

Criminal Law Act 1976

Number 32 of 1976

ARRANGEMENT OF SECTIONS

1   Definitions.

2   Penalties for certain offences under Act of 1939.

3   Incitement or invitation to join etc. an unlawful organisation.

4   Amendment of section 25 of Act of 1939.

5   Search warrants relating to commission of offences under Act of 1939 etc.

6   Escape from custody.

7   Power of Garda Síochána in relation to certain arrested persons.

8   Power of Garda Síochána to search vehicles and persons in vehicles.

9   Power to retain articles seized.

10   Prohibition of possession of photographs etc. of certain buildings.

11   Certain offences to be felonies.

12   Prohibition of giving certain false information.

13   Offence committed while serving sentence.

14   Restriction of meaning of "document" in sections 13 and 14 of Act of 1939.

15   Power of Defence Forces to arrest and search in certain circumstances.

16   Short title and application.

AN ACT TO AMEND THE CRIMINAL LAW. [24th September, 1976]

BE IT ENACTED BY THE OIREACHTAS AS FOLLOWS:

1   Definitions

In this Act—

"the Act of 1939" means the Offences against the State Act, 1939;

"the Defence Forces" means the Permanent Defence Force within the meaning of the Defence Act, 1954;

"prison" includes Saint Patrick's Institution, any place provided under section 2 of the Prisons Act, 1970, any place in which persons are kept in military custody pursuant to section 2 of the Prisons Act, 1972, or any place specified to be used as a prison under section 3 of that Act, and "governor" and "prison officer" shall be construed accordingly;

"unlawful organisation" means an organisation which is an unlawful organisation within the meaning and for the purposes of the Act of 1939.

2   Penalties for certain offences under Act of 1939

(1) The maximum penalty for a felony under section 6 of the Act of 1939 shall be imprisonment for 20 years and accordingly, section 6(1) of that Act is hereby amended by the substitution of "to imprisonment for a term not exceeding 20 years" for "to suffer penal

servitude for a term not exceeding ten years or to imprisonment for a term not exceeding two years".

(2) The maximum penalty for a misdemeanour under section 6 of the Act of 1939 shall be imprisonment for 20 years and, accordingly, section 6(2) of that Act is hereby amended by the substitution of "imprisonment for a term not exceeding 20 years" for "imprisonment for a term not exceeding two years".

(3) The maximum penalty for a felony under section 7 of the Act of 1939 shall be imprisonment for 20 years and, accordingly, section 7(1) of that Act is hereby amended by the substitution of "to imprisonment for a term not exceeding 20 years" for "to suffer penal servitude for a term not exceeding seven years or to imprisonment for a term not exceeding two years".

(4) The maximum penalty for a misdemeanour under section 7 of the Act of 1939 shall be imprisonment for 20 years and, accordingly, section 7(2) of that Act is hereby amended by the substitution of "imprisonment for a term not exceeding 20 years" for "imprisonment for a term not exceeding two years".

(5) The maximum penalty for an offence under section 15 of the Act of 1939 shall be imprisonment for 15 years and, accordingly, section 15(3) of that Act is hereby amended by the substitution of "15 years" for "two years".

(6) The maximum penalty for an offence under section 21 of the Act of 1939 shall be, in the case of a conviction on indictment, imprisonment for 7 years and, accordingly, section 21(2) of that Act is hereby amended by the substitution in paragraph (b) of "7 years" for "two years".

(7) The maximum penalty for an offence under section 27 of the Act of 1939 shall be a fine of £500 or imprisonment for 12 months or both and, accordingly, section 27(4) of that Act is hereby amended by the substitution of "£500" for "fifty pounds" and "12 months" for "three months"

3   Incitement or invitation to join etc. an unlawful organisation

Any person who recruits another person for an unlawful organisation or who incites or invites another person (or other persons generally) to join an unlawful organisation or to take part in, support or assist its activities shall be guilty of an offence and shall be liable on conviction on indictment to imprisonment for a term not exceeding 10 years.

4   Amendment of section 25 of Act of 1939

Section 25 of the Act of 1939 is hereby amended—

(a) by the substitution of "12 months" for "three months" in subsections (1) and (2), and

(b) by the addition of the following subsection:[1]

Amendments

1   See the amended Act.

---

5   Search warrants relating to commission of offences under Act of 1939 etc.

The following section is hereby substituted for section 29 of the Act of 1939:[1]

Amendments

1   See the amended Act.

6   Escape from custody

(1) Any person who—

(a) aids any person in escaping or attempting to escape from lawful custody or, with intent to facilitate the escape of any person from lawful custody or enable a person after escape to remain unlawfully at large, or with intent to cause injury to persons or property in a place where a person is in lawful custody, conveys any article or thing into or out of such a place or to a person in such a place or places any article or thing inside or outside such a place, or

(b) makes, or takes part in, any arrangement for the purpose of enabling a person to escape from lawful custody, facilitating such an escape, enabling a person after escape to remain unlawfully at large, or causing injury to persons or property in a place where a person is in lawful custody,

shall be guilty of an offence and shall be liable on conviction on indictment to imprisonment for a term not exceeding 10 years.

(2) Any person who, contrary to any rules or regulations in force in relation to a prison, conveys or attempts to convey any article or thing into or out of the prison or to a person in the prison, or places any article or thing in any place inside or outside the prison with intent that it shall come into the possession of a person in the prison, shall be guilty of an offence and shall be liable—

(a) on summary conviction, to a fine not exceeding [€3,000][1] or to imprisonment for a term not exceeding 12 months, or to both, or

(b) on conviction on indictment, to imprisonment for a term not exceeding 5 years.

(3) A prison officer may in the interests of security search any person at any time while he is in a prison or while he is in the custody of the governor of a prison.

Amendments

1   Amount amended by Criminal Justice Act 2006, s 196.

7   Power of Garda Síochána in relation to certain arrested persons

(1) Where a person is in custody under the provisions of section 30 of the Act of 1939 or section 2 of the Emergency Powers Act, 1976, a member of the Garda Síochána may do all or any of the following in respect of him:

(a) demand of him his name and address;

(b) search him or cause him to be searched;

(c) photograph him or cause him to be photographed;

(d) take, or cause to be taken, his fingerprints and palm prints;

(e) ...¹

(f) seize and retain for testing anything that he has in his possession.

(2) Any person who obstructs or attempts to obstruct any member of the Garda Síochána or any other person acting under the powers conferred by subsection (1) of this section, or who fails or refuses to give his name and address when demanded, or gives a name or address which is false or misleading, shall be guilty of an offence and shall be liable—

(a) on summary conviction, to a fine not exceeding [£1000]² or to imprisonment for a term not exceeding 12 months, or to both, or

(b) [...]²

Amendments

1 Subsection (1)(e) repealed by Criminal Justice (Forensic Evidence) Act 1990, s 6.

2 Words inserted and para (b) deleted by Criminal Justice Act 1984, s 6(5).

8 Power of Garda Síochána to search vehicles and persons in vehicles

(1) This section applies to:

(a) an offence under the Act of 1939 or an offence that is for the time being a scheduled offence for the purposes of Part V of that Act;

(b) an offence under section 2 or 3 of the Criminal Law (Jurisdiction) Act, 1976;

(c) murder, manslaughter or an offence under section 18 of the Offences against the Person Act, 1861;

(d) an offence under section 23, 23A or 23B of the Larceny Act, 1916,

(e) an offence of malicious damage to property involving the use of fire or of any explosive substance (within the meaning of section 7(1)(e) of this Act);

(f) an offence under the Firearms Acts, 1925 to 1971;

(g) escape from lawful custody;

(h) an offence under section 11 of the Air Navigation and Transport Act, 1973, or under section 10 of the Criminal Law (Jurisdiction) Act, 1976;

[(i) an offence under this Act,

(j) an offence under section 12(1) of the Firearms and Offensive Weapons Act, 1990,

(k) an offence under section 112(2) of the Road Traffic Act, 1961 (substituted by section 3(7) of the Road Traffic (Amendment) Act, 1984),

(l) an offence under section 2 of the Illegal Immigrants (Trafficking) Act, 2000.]¹

(2) Where a member of the Garda Síochána who with reasonable cause suspects that an offence to which this section applies has been, is being or is about to be committed requires a person to stop a vehicle with a view to ascertaining whether—

(a) any person in or accompanying the vehicle has committed, is committing or is about to commit the offence, or

(b) evidence relating to the commission or intended commission of the offence by any person is in or on the vehicle or on any person in or accompanying it,

he may search the vehicle, and if (whether before or after the commencement of the search) he suspects with reasonable cause that any of the facts mentioned in paragraph (a) or (b) above exists, he may search any person in or accompanying the vehicle.

(3) A member of the Garda Síochána may use reasonable force in order to compel a person to comply with a requirement to stop a vehicle, and such force may include the placing of a barrier or other device in the path of vehicles.

(4) Any reference in subsection (1) of this section to an offence includes a reference to attempting or conspiring to commit the offence.

Amendments

1   Subsections (1)((i)–(l) substituted by Illegal Immigrants (Trafficking) Act 2000, s 6.

9   Power to retain articles seized

(1) Where in the course of exercising any powers under this Act or in the course of a search carried out under any other power, a member of the Garda Síochána, a prison officer or a member of the Defence Forces finds or comes into possession of anything which he believes to be evidence of any offence or suspected offence, it may be seized and retained for use as evidence in any criminal proceedings, or in any proceedings in relation to a breach of prison discipline, for such period from the date of seizure as is reasonable or, if proceedings are commenced in which the thing so seized is required for use in evidence, until the conclusion of the proceedings, and thereafter the Police (Property) Act, 1897, shall apply to the thing so seized in the same manner as that Act applies to property which has come into the possession of the Garda Síochána in the circumstances mentioned in that Act.

(2) If it is represented or appears to a person proposing to seize or retain a document under this section that the document was, or may have been, made for the purpose of obtaining, giving or communicating legal advice from or by a barrister or solicitor, that person shall not seize or retain the document unless he suspects with reasonable cause that the document was not made, or is not intended, solely for any of the purposes aforesaid.

10   Prohibition of possession of photographs etc. of certain buildings.

(1) A person in lawful custody in any prison, Garda station or courthouse shall not have in his possession any photograph, film, illustration, drawing, sketch, map, plan or other representation of or note concerning any part of the interior or exterior of any prison, Garda station or courthouse without the permission of the governor (if he is in a prison), of the member of the Garda Síochána in charge (if he is in a Garda station) or of the court before which the person in question is appearing or is to appear (if he is in a courthouse), and any such person who has any such representation or note in his possession without that permission shall, unless he has it in his possession when taken into custody and discloses that fact on being informed that possession of any such representation or note without permission is forbidden, be guilty of an offence.

(2) (a) A person who is in or in the precincts of a prison, Garda station or courthouse and while there intends to visit or meet, or has visited or met, a person in lawful custody in that prison, station or courthouse shall not have in his possession any representation or note which is referred to in subsection (1) of this section without the permission specified in that subsection, and any person who has any such representation or note in his possession without that permission shall be guilty of an offence if he has been informed orally or by written notice that possession of any such representation or note without that permission is forbidden.

    (b) Notwithstanding paragraph (a) of this subsection, if a person applies for the permission specified in subsection (1) of this section at the first available opportunity after arrival at the prison, Garda station or courthouse, he shall not be guilty of an offence under this subsection unless and until the permission is refused and he continues to retain possession of the representation or note.

(3) Nothing in this section shall make it unlawful for a person to have in his possession in a courthouse any representation or note which is referred to in subsection (1) of this section and is intended for production, use or reference in any proceedings that are taking place, are about to take place or have taken place in that courthouse.

(4) A person guilty of an offence under this section shall be liable—

    (a) on summary conviction, to a fine not exceeding £500 or to imprisonment for a term not exceeding 12 months, or to both, or

    (b) on conviction on indictment, to imprisonment for a term not exceeding 5 years.

11   Certain offences to be felonies

(1) The offences of kidnapping and false imprisonment and an offence under section 10 of the Criminal Law (Jurisdiction) Act, 1976, shall be felonies.

(2) [...][1]

Amendments

1   Subsection (2) repealed by Non-Fatal Offences Against The Person Act 1997, s 31 and Sch.

---

12   Prohibition of giving certain false information

Any person who—

    (a) knowingly makes a false report or statement tending to show that an offence has been committed, whether by himself or another person, or tending to give rise to apprehension for the safety of persons or property, or

    (b) knowingly makes a false report or statement tending to show that he has information material to any inquiries by the Garda Síochána and thereby causes the time of the Garda Síochána to be wastefully employed,

shall be guilty of an offence and shall be liable—

    (i) on summary conviction, to a fine not exceeding £500 or to imprisonment for a term not exceeding 12 months, or to both, or

    (ii) on conviction on indictment, to imprisonment for a term not exceeding 5 years.

13   Offence committed while serving sentence

(1) Any sentence of penal servitude or imprisonment or of detention in Saint Patrick's Institution passed on a person for an offence committed while he is serving any such sentence shall be consecutive on the sentence that he is serving or, if he is serving or is due to serve more than one sentence, on the sentence last due to expire, so however that, where two or more consecutive sentences as required by this section are passed by the District Court, the aggregate term of imprisonment or detention in respect of those consecutive sentences shall not exceed [two years].[1]

(2) Subsection (1) of this section shall not apply in any case where the sentence being served or to be passed is a sentence of penal servitude for life or imprisonment for life.

(3) Subsection (1) of this section shall apply notwithstanding any thing contained in section 5 of the Criminal Justice Act, 1951.

Amendments

1   Words inserted by Criminal Justice Act 1984, s 12.

14   Restriction of meaning of "document" in sections 13 and 14 of Act of 1939

In sections 13 and 14 of the Act of 1939, "document" does not include any of the things specified in the amendment of the definition of "document" made by section 5 of the Offences against the State (Amendment) Act, 1972.

15   Power of Defence Forces to arrest and search in certain circumstances

(1) The powers conferred by subsections (3) and (4) of this section may be exercised only in accordance with subsection (2) of this section.

(2) Whenever a member of the Garda Síochána not below the rank of superintendent requests an officer of the Defence Forces to make members of the Defence Forces available for the purpose of the exercise of the powers conferred by subsections (3) and (4) of this section during a period specified in the request, the officer may make—

(a)   himself and one or more members of the Defence Forces under his command, or

(b)   one or more members of the Defence Forces under his command,

available for the purpose aforesaid, and a member of the Defence Forces made available as aforesaid may, while on duty in uniform during the period specified in the request, exercise the powers conferred by the said subsections (3) and (4).

(3) (a)   A member of the Defence Forces who with reasonable cause suspects that an offence to which section 8 of this Act applies has been, is being or is about to be committed may require a person to stop a vehicle with a view to ascertaining whether—

(i)   any person in or accompanying the vehicle has committed is committing or is about to commit the offence, or.

(ii)   evidence relating to the commission or intended commission of the offence by any person is in or on the vehicle or on any person in or accompanying it, and he may search the vehicle and if (whether before or after the commencement of the search) he suspects with reasonable cause that any of the facts mentioned in subparagraph (i) or (ii) above exists, he may search any person in or accompanying the vehicle.

(b) A member of the Defence Forces may use reasonable force in order to compel a person to comply with a requirement to stop a vehicle, and such force may include the placing of a barrier or other device in the path of vehicles.

(4) (a) A member of the Defence Forces may arrest without warrant a person whom he, with reasonable cause, suspects to be in the act of committing, of having committed or of being about to commit an offence to which section 8 of this Act applies and in relation to which a member of the Garda Síochána would be entitled, if he so suspected, to arrest the person.

(b) For the purpose of arresting a person under this subsection, a member of the Defence Forces shall have the same power to enter and search any building or part of a building or any vehicle, vessel, aircraft or hovercraft or any other place as a member of the Garda Síochána would have in like circumstances.

(c) This subsection shall not prejudice any power of arrest conferred by law apart from this subsection.

(5) A person arrested under this section shall, as soon as may be, be delivered into the custody of the Garda Síochána or released and shall in any event, if he has not then been so delivered, be released upon the expiration of 6 hours from the time of his arrest.

(6) A person effecting an arrest under this section complies with any rule of law requiring him to state the ground of arrest if he states that he is effecting an arrest as a member of the Defence Forces because he suspects the person being arrested of being in the act of committing, of having committed or of being about to commit, as the case may be, an offence to which section 8 of this Act applies.

(7) (a) Where a power conferred by subsection (3) or (4) of this section is exercised, a certificate signed by an officer of the Defence Forces not below the rank of commandant and stating—

(i) that a request was made under subsection (2) of this section on a specified date by a member of the Garda Síochána not below the rank of superintendent named in the certificate to an officer of the Defence Forces named in the certificate,

(ii) that the power aforesaid was exercised by the officer named in the certificate or, as the case may be, by a member or members of the Defence Forces under his command or by that officer and a member or members of the Defence Forces under his command, and that, at the time of such exercise, those exercising the power were on duty in uniform and had been made available pursuant to the request aforesaid, and

(iii) that the power aforesaid was exercised during the period specified in the request,

shall, without proof of the signature of the person purporting to have signed the certificate or that he was an officer of the Defence Forces not below the rank of commandant, be evidence in any proceedings of the matters certified in and by the certificate.

(b) Where a power conferred by subsection (3) or (4) of this section is exercised, a certificate signed by a member of the Garda Síochána not below the rank of superintendent and stating that a request was made under subsection (2) of this section on a specified date by a member of the Garda Síochána not below the rank of superintendent named in the certificate to an officer of the Defence Forces named in the certificate shall, without proof of the signature of the person purporting to have signed the certificate or that he was a member of the Garda Síochána not below the rank of superintendent, be evidence in any proceedings of the matters certified in and by the certificate.

(8) This section shall have effect only as long as the Emergency Powers Act, 1976 is in force.

16   Short title and application

(1) This Act may be cited as the Criminal Law Act, 1976.

(2) Sections 2 and 11 of this Act shall not apply in relation to offences committed before the passing of this Act and the reference in section 13(1) of this Act to an offence is a reference to an offence committed after such passing.

Juries Act 1976

Number 4 of 1976

ARRANGEMENT OF SECTIONS

PART I
PRELIMINARY

1   Short title.

2   Interpretation.

3   Expenses.

4   Repeals.

PART II
QUALIFICATION AND LIABILITY FOR SERVICE AS A JUROR

5   Jury districts.

6   Qualification and liability for jury service.

7   Ineligibility.

8   Disqualification.

9   Excusal from service.

PART III
SELECTION AND SERVICE OF JURORS

10   Supply of electoral registers.

11   Empanelling of jurors.

12   Summoning of jurors.

13   Service of jury summons.

14   Summoning of jurors to make up deficiency.

15   Selection of jury from panel.

16   Inspection of jury panel.

17   Mode of swearing a jury.

18   Administration of oath to jurors.

19   Forms of oaths to be taken by jurors.

20   Challenges without cause shown.

21   Challenges for cause shown.

22   View by jury.

23   Death or discharge of juror during trial.

24   Discontinuance of juror's service.

25   Separation of juries during trial.

26   Non-effect of appeals as to electoral register on jury service.

PART IV
GENERAL

27   Administrative instructions.

28   Person standing mute.

29   Jury service by employees and apprentices.

30   Commission de lunatico inquirendo.

31   Liability to serve on coroner's jury.

32   Non-application of provisions to coroners' inquests.

33   Restriction of functions of sheriff.

PART V
OFFENCES

34   Failure of juror to attend court etc.

35   False statements by or on behalf of juror.

36   Service by ineligible or disqualified person.

37   Refusal to be sworn as a juror.

FIRST SCHEDULE
PERSONS INELIGIBILE AND PERSONS EXCUSABLE AS OF RIGHT

SECOND SCHEDULE
REPEALS

AN ACT TO AMEND THE LAW RELATING TO JURIES [2nd March, 1976]

BE IT ENACTED BY THE OIREACHTAS AS FOLLOWS:

PART I
PRELIMINARY

1   Short title

This Act may be cited as the Juries Act, 1976.

2   Interpretation

(1) In this Act—

"county" means an administrative county;

"jury summons" means a summons under section 12;

"the Minister" means the Minister for Justice.

(2) References in this Act to any enactment shall be construed as references to that enactment as amended or extended by any subsequent enactment, including this Act.

(3) (a) A reference in this Act to a section or Schedule means a reference to a section of, or a Schedule to, this Act, unless it is indicated that reference to some other enactment is intended.

(b) A reference in this Act to a subsection is a reference to the subsection of the section in which the reference occurs unless it is indicated that reference to some other provision is intended.

3   Expenses

The expenses incurred by the Minister in the administration of this Act shall, to such extent as may be sanctioned by the Minister for Finance, be paid out of moneys provided by the Oireachtas.

4   Repeals

Each enactment mentioned in the Second Schedule is hereby repealed to the extent specified in column (3) of that Schedule.

PART II

QUALIFICATION AND LIABILITY FOR SERVICE AS A JUROR

5   Jury districts

(1) Subject to the provisions of this section, each county shall be a jury district and for this purpose the county boroughs of [and the county borough of Dublin and the counties of South Dublin, Fingal and Dun Laoghaire-Rathdown shall form one jury district]¹, Cork, Limerick and Waterford shall be deemed to form part of the counties of [and the county borough of Dublin and the counties of South Dublin, Fingal and Dun Laoghaire-Rathdown shall form one jury district]¹, Cork, Limerick and Waterford respectively.

(2) The Minister may by order divide a county into two or more jury districts or limit a jury district to a part or parts of a county.

(3) The Minister may by order revoke or vary an order under this section.

(4) Every issue that is triable with a jury shall be triable with a jury called from a panel of jurors drawn from the jury district in which the court is sitting.

Amendments

1   Words amended by Local Government (Dublin) Act 1993, s 28.

---

6   Qualification and liability for jury service

Subject to the provisions of this Act, every citizen aged eighteen years or upwards [...]¹ who is entered in a register of Dáil electors in a jury district shall be qualified and liable to serve as a juror for the trial of all or any issues which are for the time being triable with a jury drawn from that jury district, unless he is for the time being ineligible or disqualified for jury service.

Amendments

1   Words deleted by Civil Law (Miscellaneous Provisions) Act 2008, s 54.

---

7   Ineligibility

The persons specified in Part I of the First Schedule shall be ineligible for jury service.

8   Disqualification

A person shall be disqualified for jury service if on conviction of an offence in any part of Ireland—

(a)   he has at any time been sentenced to imprisonment or penal servitude for life or for a term of five years or more or to detention under section 103 of the Children Act, 1908, or under the corresponding law of Northern Ireland, or

(b)   he has at any time in the last ten years—

(i)   served any part of a sentence of imprisonment or penal servitude, being, in the case of imprisonment, a sentence for a term of at least three months, or

(ii)   served any part of a sentence of detention in Saint Patrick's Institution or in a corresponding institution in Northern Ireland, being a sentence for a term of at least three months.

9   Excusal from service

(1) A county registrar shall excuse any person whom he has summoned as a juror under this Act if—

(a)   that person is one of the persons specified in Part II of the First Schedule and informs the county registrar of his wish to be excused, or

(b)   that person shows to the satisfaction of the county registrar that he has served on a jury, or duly attended to serve on a jury, in the three years ending with the service of the summons on him, or

(c)   that person shows to the satisfaction of the county registrar that, at the conclusion of a trial, a judge of any court has excused him from jury service for a period that has not terminated.

(2) A county registrar may excuse any person whom he has summoned as a juror from attendance during the whole or any part of the sittings in question if that person shows to the registrar's satisfaction that there is good reason why he should be so excused.

(3) If a person summoned as a juror under this Act is unable, owing to illness or any other reason, to make any representation to a county registrar under subsection (1) or (2), another person may make the representation on his behalf.

(4) A person whom the county registrar has refused to excuse may appeal against the refusal to the court at which he has been summoned to attend.

(5) The procedure for the appeal, including the designation of the judge to hear the appeal, and the time within which and the manner in which it should be brought, shall be as provided

by directions of the President of the High Court and the President of the Circuit Court respectively.

(6) The decision of the court shall be final.

(7) When a person is required to be in attendance as a juror at a court during a sitting, the judge shall have the same duty or discretion, as the case may be, as that imposed or conferred on the county registrar under this section to excuse that person from attendance or further attendance. The judge may also, for good reason, excuse the juror during the course of a trial from further service as a juror in the trial.

(8) The judge of any court may, at the conclusion of a trial of an exceptionally exacting nature, excuse the members of the jury from jury service for such period as the judge may think fit.

PART III
SELECTION AND SERVICE OF JURORS

10   Supply of electoral registers

For the purpose of enabling county registrars to empanel and summon jurors, every county council and corporation of a county borough, as registration authority under section 7(1) of the Electoral Act, 1963, shall as soon as practicable after the passing of this Act deliver to the county registrar for the county such number of copies of the then current register of Dáil electors for the county or county borough as the county registrar may require and shall do likewise as soon as practicable after the publication of every similar register thereafter.

11   Empanelling of jurors

Each county registrar, using a procedure of random or other non-discriminatory selection, shall draw up a panel of jurors for [one or more courts within a jury district]¹ from the register or registers delivered to him under section 10 (omitting persons whom he knows or believes not to be qualified as jurors).

Amendments

1   Words substituted by Civil Law (Miscellaneous Provisions) Act 2008, s 55.

---

12   Summoning of jurors

[(1) Each county registrar shall cause a written summons, in such form as the Minister may by regulations prescribe, to be served on every person whom the registrar has selected as a juror requiring the person—

    (a)   to attend as a juror at the court in question or other place specified in the summons for the reception of jurors on the day and at the time specified in the summons, and

    (b)   to thereafter attend at that court or place, as the case may be, or such other court or place as the court may direct, at such times as are directed by—

        (i)   the court, or

        (ii)   the registrar in any case where the registrar is authorised to do so by the court.]¹

(2) A jury summons served on a person under this section shall be accompanied by a notice informing him—

(a) of the effect of sections 6, 7, 8, 9(1), 35 and 36, and

(b) that he may make representations to the county registrar with a view to obtaining a withdrawal of the summons, if for any reason he is not qualified for jury service or wishes or is entitled to be excused.

Amendments

1   Subsection (1) substituted by Civil Law (Miscellaneous Provisions) Act 2008, s 56.

13   Service of jury summons

(1) A jury summons may be sent by post or delivered by hand.

(2) For the purposes of section 18 of the Interpretation Act, 1937, a letter containing a jury summons shall be deemed to be properly addressed if it is addressed to the juror at, his address as shown in the current register of Dáil electors.

(3) In any proceedings for an offence of non-attendance in compliance with a jury summons or of not being available when called upon to serve as a juror—

(a) a certificate by the county registrar or an officer acting on his behalf that the registrar or officer posted a letter containing the summons addressed as provided in subsection (2) shall be evidence of the fact so certified;

(b) a certificate by the county registrar or an officer acting on his behalf or a member of the Garda Síochána that he personally delivered the summons to the juror on a specified date shall be evidence of the fact so certified, and

[(c) a certificate by—

(i) the registrar or other officer acting as registrar of a court, or

(ii) a member of the staff of the Courts Service duly authorised in that behalf by the Chief Executive Officer of the Courts Service,

present when a person summoned to attend as a juror in that court failed to answer to his or her name at the time it was called out in that court or at the place specified in the summons shall be evidence, unless the contrary is proved, that that person failed to attend in compliance with the summons, or was not available when called on to serve, as the case may be.]¹

(4) A document purporting to be a certificate under this section of a county registrar, or officer acting on his behalf, officer of a court or member of the Garda Síochána and to be signed by him shall be deemed, for the purposes of this section, to be such a certificate and to be so signed unless the contrary is proved.

Amendments

1   Subsection (3)(c) substituted by Civil Law (Miscellaneous Provisions) Act 2008, s 57.

14   Summoning of jurors to make up deficiency

(1) If it appears to a judge of a court that a jury to try any issue before the court will or may be incomplete, the judge may require any persons (being person; qualified and liable to serve as jurors in that court) to he summoned by the county registrar in order to make up the number needed.

(2) The judge shall specify the area from which persons may be summoned (which may be the area in the vicinity of the court) and the method of summons, whether by written notice or otherwise.

(3) Section 9 shall apply to persons summoned under this section except that there shall not be an appeal from the county registrar.

(4) The names of persons summoned under this section shall be added to the panel of jurors.

15   Selection of jury from panel

(1) The selection of persons empanelled as jurors to serve on a particular jury shall be made by balloting in open court.

(2) The power of summoning jurors under section 14 may be exercised after balloting has begun, as well as earlier, and if it is exercised after balloting has begun the judge may dispense with balloting for persons summoned under that section.

(3) Before the selection is begun the judge shall warn the jurors present that they must not serve if they are ineligible or disqualified and as to the penalty under section 36 for doing so; and he shall invite any person who knows that he is not qualified to serve or who is in doubt as to whether he is qualified or who may have an interest in or connection with the case or the parties to communicate the fact to the judge (either orally or otherwise as the judge may direct or authorise) if he is selected on the ballot.

(4) The foreman shall be such member as the jurors shall choose and the choice shall be made at such time as the judge may direct or, in the absence of a direction, before the jury bring in their verdict or make any other communication to the judge.

16   Inspection of jury panel

(1) Every person shall be entitled to reasonable facilities to inspect a panel of jurors free of charge and a party to any proceedings, civil or criminal, to be tried with a jury shall be entitled to a copy free of charge on application to the county registrar.

(2) The rights under subsection (1) shall be exercisable at any time between the issue of the summonses and the close of the trial or the time when it is no longer possible to have a trial with a jury.

(3) The panel referred to in subsection (1) is the panel as prepared for and in advance of the sittings, including any supplemental panel so prepared, and it shall not be necessary to indicate in it that any of the persons in it have been excused in the meantime, or to include any persons summoned under section 14.

(4) The right to inspect the panel shall, however, include a right to be shown, on request, all alterations to the panel and the names of any persons summoned under section 14 and, on request, to be told of any excusals.

17   Mode of swearing a jury

(1) When swearing a juror the registrar or other officer acting as registrar shall call out the juror's name and direct him to take the Testament in his hand and shall administer the oath to him in accordance with sections 18 and 19.

(2) The jurors shall be sworn separately.

(3) Any juror who objects to be sworn in the ordinary manner shall make his objection immediately after his name is called out and before the administration of the oath to him has begun.

(4) Every challenge of a juror shall be made immediately after his name is called out and before the administration of the oath to him has begun.

(5) If any juror refuses to be sworn or insists on being sworn in a manner not authorised by this Act or otherwise by law, he shall not be included in the jury then being sworn.

(6) For the purposes of this section the administration of an oath shall be deemed to be begun when the registrar or other officer begins to say the words of the oath to the juror being sworn.

(7) In this section and in the next following section the word "Testament" means, in the case of a person of the Christian faith, the New Testament and, in the case of a person of the Jewish faith, the Old Testament.

18   Administration of oath to jurors

(1) The ordinary manner of administering the oath shall be as follows:

> The juror to be sworn shall hold the Testament in his uplifted hand and the registrar or other officer shall say to the juror the words "I swear by Almighty God that....." followed by the appropriate form of oath provided by section 19 and the juror shall repeat after him the words so spoken by him.

(2) The Oaths Act, 1888 (which provides for the making of an affirmation instead of an oath) and also every Act for the time being in force authorising an oath to be taken in a court in any particular manner shall apply to the oaths required by this Act to be taken by jurors.

(3) A juror who states that he has a religious belief but that he is neither of the Christian nor of the Jewish faith may, if the judge so permits, be sworn in any manner that the juror states to be binding on him.

(4) The oath shall be administered to every juror in the ordinary manner without question unless the juror appears to be physically incapable of taking the oath in that manner or objects to taking the oath in that manner and satisfies the judge that he is entitled to take the oath in some other manner.

19   Forms of oaths to be taken by jurors

(1) Whenever the issue to be tried is whether an accused person is or is not guilty of an offence, the form of oath to be administered to the jurors shall, be as follows:

> "I will well and truly try the issue whether the accused is (or are) guilty or not guilty of the offence (or the several offences) charged in the indictment preferred against him (or her or them) and a true verdict give according to the evidence."

(2) [...]¹

(3) Whenever the issue to be tried is not one of the issues hereinbefore expressly provided for, the form of oath to be administered to the jurors shall be as follows:

"I will well and truly try all such issues as shall be given to me to try and true verdicts give according to the evidence."

Amendments

1   Subsection (2) repealed by Criminal Law (Insanity) Act 2006, s 25 and Sch 2.

20   Challenges without cause shown

(1) In every trial of a civil issue which is tried with a jury each party may challenge without cause shown seven jurors and no more.

(2) In every trial of a criminal issue which is tried with a jury the prosecution and each accused person may challenge without cause shown seven jurors and no more.

(3) Whenever a juror is lawfully challenged without cause shown, he shall not be included in the jury.

21   Challenges for cause shown

(1) In every trial of a civil issue which is tried with a jury any party may challenge for cause shown any number of jurors.

(2) In every trial of a criminal issue which is tried with a jury the prosecution and each accused person may challenge for cause shown any number of jurors.

(3) Whenever a juror is challenged for cause shown, such cause shall be shown immediately upon the challenge being made and the judge shall then allow or disallow the challenge as he shall think proper.

(4) Whenever a juror is challenged for cause shown and such challenge is allowed by the judge, the juror shall not be included in the jury.

22   View by jury

(1) In the trial of any issue with a jury the judge may, at any time after the jurors have been sworn and before they have given their verdict, by order direct that the jurors shall have a view of any place specified in the order which in the opinion of the judge it is expedient for the purposes of the trial that the jurors should see, and when any such order is made the judge may adjourn the trial at such stage and for such time as appears to him to be convenient for the execution of the order.

(2) In the trial of a civil issue, an order under this section shall be made only on the application of one of the parties and the expenses of the conveyance of the jurors to and from the place specified in the order shall be paid in the first instance by the party on whose application the order was made but shall be included in the costs of that party and be ultimately borne accordingly.

(3) In the trial of a criminal issue, an order under this section shall be made only on the application of the prosecution or of the accused person or of one or more of the accused persons and the expenses of the conveyance of the jurors to and from the place specified in

the order shall be paid by the county registrar or other officer acting as registrar to the court during the trial out of moneys to be provided by the Oireachtas.

(4) Whenever a judge makes an order under this section, he shall give such directions as appear to him to be expedient for the purpose of preventing undue communication with the jurors during the execution of the order.

23   Death or discharge of juror during trial

Whenever in the course of the trial of any issue a juror dies or is discharged by the judge owing to his being incapable through illness or any other cause of continuing to act as a juror, or under section 9(7) or 24, the jury shall, unless the judge otherwise directs or the number of jurors is thereby reduced below ten, be considered as remaining properly constituted for all the purposes of the trial and the trial shall proceed and a verdict may be found accordingly.

24   Discontinuance of juror's service

In any trial with a jury the judge way at any stage direct that any person summoned or sworn as a juror shall not serve, or shall not continue to serve, as a juror if the judge considers that for any stated reason it is desirable in the interests of justice that he should give that direction.

25   Separation of juries during trial

[(1) In any trial with a jury—

    (a) the jurors may, at any time before they retire to consider their verdict, separate unless the judge otherwise directs, and

    (b) the jurors may, after they retire to consider their verdict, only separate for such period or periods as the judge directs.

(2) A direction under subsection (1)(b) may be given in respect of a jury whether or not the jury is present when the direction is given.][1]

Amendments

1   Subsection (3)(c) substituted by Civil Law (Miscellaneous Provisions) Act 2008, s 58.

---

26   Non-effect of appeals as to electoral register on jury service

The qualification or liability of a person to serve as a juror shall not be affected by the fact that an appeal is pending under section 8 of the Electoral Act, 1963 (which relates to appeals regarding the register of electors).

PART IV

GENERAL

27   Administrative instructions

With a view to securing consistency in the administration of this Act, the Minister may issue instructions to county registrars with regard to the practice and the procedure to be adopted by them in the discharge of their duties under this Act; but nothing in this section shall authorise the Minister to issue any instruction as to whether particular persons should or should not be summoned for service as jurors or, if summoned, should or should not be excused from attendance in accordance with the summons.

28 Person standing mute

Whenever a person charged with an offence to be tried with a jury stands mute when called upon to plead, the issue whether he is mute of malice or by the visitation of God shall be decided by the judge and, if the judge is not satisfied that he is mute by the visitation of God, the judge shall direct a plea of not guilty to be entered for him.

29 Jury service by employees and apprentices

(1) For the purposes of any contract of service or apprenticeship or any agreement collateral thereto (including a contract or agreement entered into before the passing of this Act), a person shall be treated as employed or apprenticed during any period when he is absent from his employment or apprenticeship in order to comply with a jury summons.

(2) Any provision contained in any such contract or agreement shall be void in so far as it would have the effect of excluding or limiting any liability of the employer in respect of the payment of salary or wages to the employee or apprentice during any such absence.

30 Commission de lunatico inquirendo

Whenever a panel of jurors is lawfully in attendance before a commissioner under a commission de lunatico inquirendo, then, for the purposes of this Act, the commissioner shall be deemed to be a court and also a judge of the court.

31 Liability to serve on coroner's jury

Every citizen of the age of eighteen years or upwards [...][1] residing in a coroner's district shall be qualified and liable to serve on the jury at any coroner's inquest held in that district unless he is ineligible or disqualified under this Act for jury service or is among the persons specified in Part II of the First Schedule.

Amendments

1   Words deleted by Civil Law (Miscellaneous Provisions) Act 2008, s 59.

---

32 Non-application of provisions to coroners' inquests

Nothing in this Act except section 31 shall apply to a coroner's inquest, and in this Act the word "jury" does not include a jury at such an inquest and the word "juror" does not include a juror serving on such a jury.

33 Restriction of functions of sheriff

The powers and duties conferred and imposed on a county registrar under this Act shall be exercised and performed by him notwithstanding anything in section 12 of the Court Officers Act, 1945 (which refers to the duties of sheriffs) or in any order made thereunder.

PART V

OFFENCES

34   Failure of juror to attend court etc

(1) Any person who, having been duly summoned as a juror, fails without reasonable excuse to attend in compliance with the summons or to attend on any day when required by the court shall be guilty of an offence and shall be liable on summary conviction to a fine not exceeding [€500].[1]

(2) A juror who, having attended in pursuance of a summons, is not available when called upon to serve as a juror, or is unfit for service by reason of drink or drugs, shall be guilty of an offence and shall be liable on summary conviction to a fine not exceeding [€500].[1]

(3) Except in a cast to which section 14 applies, a person shall not be guilty of an offence under subsection (1) in respect of failure to attend in compliance with a summons unless the summons was served at least fourteen days before the date specified therein for his first attendance.

Amendments

1   Amounts amended by Civil Law (Miscellaneous Provisions) Act 2008, s 60.

35   False statements by or on behalf of juror

(1) If any person who has been duly summoned as a juror makes or causes or permits to be made on his behalf a false representation to the county registrar or any person acting on his behalf, or to a judge, with the intention of evading jury service, he shall be guilty of an offence and shall be liable on summary conviction to a fine not exceeding [€500].[1]

(2) If any person makes or causes or permits to be made on behalf of another person duly summoned as a juror a false representation in order to enable that other person to evade jury service, he shall be guilty of an offence and shall be liable on summary conviction to a fine not exceeding [€500].[1]

(3) If any person refuses without reasonable excuse to answer, or gives an answer known to him to be false in a material particular, or recklessly gives an answer that is false in a material particular, when questioned by a judge of a court for the purpose of determining whether that person is qualified to serve as a juror, he shall be guilty of an offence and shall be liable on summary conviction to a fine not exceeding [€500].[1]

Amendments

1   Amounts amended by Civil Law (Miscellaneous Provisions) Act 2008, s 61.

36   Service by ineligible or disqualified person

(1) Any person who serves on a jury knowing that he is ineligible for service shall be guilty of an offence and shall be liable on summary conviction to a fine not exceeding [€500].[1]

(2) Any person who serves on a jury knowing that he is disqualified shall be guilty of an offence and shall be liable on summary conviction to a fine not exceeding [€2,000].[1]

Amendments

1   Amounts amended by Civil Law (Miscellaneous Provisions) Act 2008, s 62.

37   Refusal to be sworn as a juror

Any person who, on being called upon to be sworn as a juror, refuses to be sworn in a manner authorised by this Act or otherwise by law shall be guilty of an offence and shall be liable on summary conviction to a fine not exceeding [€500].[1]

Amendments

1   Amounts amended by Civil Law (Miscellaneous Provisions) Act 2008, s 63.

FIRST SCHEDULE
PERSONS INELIGIBLE AND PERSONS EXCUSABLE AS OF RIGHT
Sections 7, 9, 31.

PART I
PERSONS INELIGIBLE

Uachtarán na h-Éireann.

Persons concerned with administration of justice

Persons holding or who have at any time held any judicial office within the meaning of the Courts (Establishment and Constitution) Act 1961 (No. 38).

Coroners, deputy coroners and persons appointed under section 5(2) of the Local Authorities (Officers and Employees) Act 1926 (No. 39) to fill the office of coroner temporarily.

The Attorney General and members of his staff.

The Director of Public Prosecutions and members of his staff.

Barristers and solicitors actually practising as such.

Solicitors' apprentices, solicitors' clerks and other persons employed on work of a legal character in solicitors' offices.

Officers attached to a court or to the President of the High Court and officers and other persons employed in any office attached to a court or attached to the President of the High Court.

Persons employed from time to time in any court for the purpose of taking a record of the proceedings of the court.

Members of the Garda Síochána.

Prison officers and other persons employed in any prison, Saint Patrick's Institution or any place provided under section 2 of the Prisons Act 1970 (No. 11) or in any place in which persons are kept in military custody pursuant to section 2 of the Prisons Act 1972 (No. 7) or in any place specified to be used as a prison under section 3 of the latter Act, chaplains and medical officers of, and members of visiting committees for, any such establishment or place.

Persons employed in the welfare service of the Department of Justice.

A person in charge of, or employed in, a forensic science laboratory.

Members of the Defence Forces

Every member of the Permanent Defence Force, including the Army Nursing Service.

Every member of the Reserve Defence Force during any period during which he is in receipt of pay for any service or duty as a member of the Reserve Defence Force.

[*Other persons*

Persons who have—

    (a)   an incapacity to read, or

    (b)   an enduring impairment,

such that it is not practicable for them to perform the duties of a juror.][1]

Amendments

1   Section substituted by Civil Law (Miscellaneous Provisions) Act 2008, s 64.

PART II
PERSONS EXCUSABLE AS OF RIGHT

Members of either House of the Oireachtas.

Members of the Council of State.

The Comptroller and Auditor General.

The Clerk of Dáil Éireann.

The Clerk of Seanad Éireann.

A person in Holy Orders.

A regular minister of any religious denomination or community.

Vowed members of any religious order living in a monastery, convent or other religious community.

The following persons if actually practising their profession and registered (including provisionally or temporarily registered), enrolled or certified under the statutory provisions relating to that profession:

        Medical practitioners;

        Dentists;

        Nurses;

        Midwives;

Veterinary surgeons;

Pharmaceutical chemists.

A member of the staff of either House of the Oireachtas on a certificate from the Clerk of that House that it would be contrary to the public interest for the member to have to serve as a juror because he performs essential and urgent services of public importance that cannot reasonably be performed by another or postponed.

Heads of Government Departments and Offices and any civil servant on a certificate from the head of his Department or Office that it would be contrary to the public interest for the civil servant to have to serve as a juror because he performs essential and urgent services of public importance that cannot reasonably be performed by another or postponed.

Any civilian employed by the Minister for Defence under section 30(1)(g) of the Defence Act 1954 (No. 18) on a certificate from the Secretary of the Department of Defence that it would be contrary to the public interest for the civilian to have to serve as a juror because he performs essential and urgent services of public importance that cannot reasonably be performed by another or postponed.

Chief officers of local authorities for the purposes of the Local Government Act 1941 (No. 23), health boards established under the Health Act 1970 (No. 1) and harbour authorities within the meaning of the Harbours Act 1946 (No. 9) and any employee of a local authority, health board or harbour authority on a certificate from its chief officer that it would be contrary to the public interest for the employee to have to serve as a juror because he performs essential and urgent services of public importance that cannot reasonably be performed by another or postponed.

The head or principal teacher of the college of a university, of a school or other educational institution, and any professor, lecturer or member of the teaching staff of any such institution on a certificate from such head or principal teacher that the person concerned performs services in the institution that cannot reasonably be performed by another or postponed.

Whole-time students at any such educational institution as is mentioned in the preceding paragraph.

The secretary to the Commissioners of Irish Lights and any person in the employment of the Commissioners on a certificate from the secretary that the person concerned performs services for the Commissioners that cannot reasonably be performed by another or postponed.

Masters of vessels duly licensed pilots and duly licensed aircraft commanders.

Persons aged sixty-five years or upwards [....].[1]

Amendments

1   Words deleted by Civil Law (Miscellaneous Provisions) Act 2008, s 64.

SECOND SCHEDULE
REPEALS

Section 4.

Number and Year	Short Title	Extent of repeal
(1)	(2)	(3)
1908, c.48	Post Office Act, 1908.	In section 43, the words "or on any jury or inquest,".
1919, c.71	Sex Disqualification (Removal) Act, 1919.	So much of section 1 as empowers a judge to order an all-male or all-female jury.
No. 23 of 1927	Juries Act, 1927.	The whole Act.
No. 27 of 1930	Local Government (Dublin Act) 1930.	Section 23(4).
No. 48 of 1936	Courts of Justice Act, 1936.	Section 80.
No. 21 of 1940	Local Government (Dublin) (Amendment) Act, 1940.	Section 9(3).
No. 24 of 1945	Juries Act, 1945.	The whole Act.
No. 18 of 1954	Defence Act, 1954.	Section 105.
No. 11 of 1961	Juries Act, 1961.	The whole Act.
No. 9 of 1962	Coroners Act, 1962.	Sections 42 and 59.
No. 19 of 1963	Electoral Act, 1963.	In section 7(1), the words "after consultation with the Minister for Justice,". Sections 7(2)(b), (6) and (8) and 8(5).
No. 5 of 1964	Criminal Justice Act, 1964.	Section 7.

Misuse of Drugs Act 1977

Number 12 of 1977

ARRANGEMENT OF SECTIONS

1   Interpretation.

2   Controlled drugs.

3   Restriction on possession of controlled drugs.

4   Regulations permitting possession of controlled drugs.

5   Regulations to prevent misuse of controlled drugs.

6   Directions prohibiting prescribing, supply etc. of controlled drugs by practitioners or pharmacists convicted of offences.

7   Special directions prohibiting prescribing etc. of controlled drug in certain cases.

8   Investigation of cases where Minister considers there are grounds for special direction.

9   Prohibition of prescribing etc. in cases of urgency.

10   Investigation on initiative of Dental Board, Medical Registration Council or Veterinary Council.

11   Appeals.

12   Regulations (committees and panels).

13   Additional powers in relation to certain controlled drugs.

14   Licences etc.

15   Possession of controlled drugs for unlawful sale or supply.

15A   Offence relating to possession of drugs with value of £10,000 or more.

15B   Importation of controlled drugs in excess of certain value.

15C   Supply of controlled drugs into prisons and places of detention.

16   Prohibition of certain activities etc. relating to opium.

17   Prohibition of cultivation of opium poppy or cannabis plant.

18   Forged or fraudulently altered prescriptions.

19   Occupiers etc. permitting certain activities to take place on land, vehicle or vessel to be guilty of an offence.

20   Offences relating to acts outside the State.

21   Attempts etc. and miscellaneous other offences.

22   Onus of proof.

23   Power of Garda Síochána to search persons, vehicles, vessels or aircraft.

24   Powers to inspect and demand production of drugs, books or documents.

25   Power of arrest.

26   Search warrants.

27   Penalties.

28   Power of court to remand persons convicted under section 3, 15, 16, 17 or 18 and to obtain a report and in certain cases to arrange for the medical treatment or for the care of such persons.

29   Defences generally.

30   Forfeiture.

31   Offences in relation to bodies corporate.

32   Poisons for purposes of Pharmacy Acts, 1875 to 1962.

33   Amendment of Poisons Act, 1961.

34   Amendment of section 2 of Pharmacy Act, 1962.

35   Amendment of Pharmacopoeia Act, 1931.

36   Amendment of section 65 of Health Act, 1947.

37   Service etc. of notices.

38   Regulations generally; laying of orders.

39   Expenses.

40   Collection and disposal of moneys payable under Act.

41   Repeal of Dangerous Drugs Act, 1934, and transitional provision.

42   Miscellaneous repeals and transitional provisions.

43   Short title, commencement and collective citations.

An Act to prevent the misuse of certain dangerous or otherwise harmful drugs, to enable the Minister for Health to make for that purpose certain regulations in relation to such drugs, to enable that Minister to provide that certain substances shall be poisons for the purposes of the Pharmacy Acts, 1875 to 1962, to amend the Pharmacopoeia Act, 1931, the Poisons Act, 1961, the Pharmacy Act, 1962, and the Health Acts, 1947 to 1970, to repeal the Dangerous Drugs Act, 1934, and section 78 of the Health Act, 1970, and to make certain other provisions in relation to the foregoing. [16th May, 1977]

BE IT ENACTED BY THE OIREACHTAS AS FOLLOWS:

1   Interpretation

(1) In this Act—

["business" includes a profession;][1]

["cannabis" (except in "cannabis resin") means any plant of the genus *Cannabis* or any part of any such plant (by whatever name designated) but includes neither cannabis resin nor any of the following products after separation from the rest of any such plant, namely—

    (a)   mature stalk of any such plant,

    (b)   fibre produced from such mature stalk, or

    (c)   seed of any such plant;';][2]

"cannabis resin" means the separated resin, whether crude or purified, obtained from any plant of the genus *Cannabis*;

"the Dental Board" means the Dental Board established under the Dentists Act, 1928;

"duly issued prescription" has the meaning assigned to it by section 18 of this Act;

"forged prescription" has the meaning assigned to it by section 18 of this Act;

["Irish Medicines Board" means the Irish Medicines Board established under section 3 of the Irish Medicines Board Act 1995;][3]

"land" includes land covered wholly or partly with water;

"the Medical Registration Council" means the Medical Registration Council established under the Medical Practitioners Acts, 1927 to 1961;

"the Minister" means the Minister for Health;

["opium poppy" means a plant of the species *Papaver somniferum L* or *Papaver bracteatum Lindl*][4];

"pharmacist" means a registered pharmaceutical chemist, a registered dispensing chemist and druggist and a registered druggist;

"prepared opium" means opium prepared for smoking and includes dross and any other residues remaining after opium has been smoked;

"practitioner" means a registered medical practitioner, a registered dentist [, a registered veterinary surgeon and a registered nurse][5];

"prescribed" means prescribed by regulations made by the Minister under this Act;

"registered dentist" means a person registered in the register established under the Dentists Act, 1928;

"registered dispensing chemist and druggist" means a person registered in the register of dispensing chemists and druggists established under the Pharmacy Act, 1951;

"registered druggist" means a person registered in the register of registered druggists in Ireland established under the Pharmacy Act (Ireland), 1875, Amendment Act, 1890;

"registered medical practitioner" means a person registered in the register established under the Medical Practitioners Act, 1927;

["registered nurse" means a person whose name is entered in the register of nurses maintained by An Bord Altranais under section 27 of the Nurses Act 1985;][6]

"registered pharmaceutical chemist" means a person registered in the register of pharmaceutical chemists for Ireland established under the Pharmacy Act (Ireland), 1875;

"registered veterinary surgeon" means a person registered in the register established under the Veterinary Surgeons Act, 1931;

"registration authority" means such one of the following as the context requires namely, the Dental Board, the Medical Registration Council and the Veterinary Council;

"the respondent" in relation to a reference under section 8 or section 9 of this Act means the practitioner in respect of whom the reference is made;

"special direction" has the meaning assigned to it by section 7(2) of this Act;

"supply" includes giving without payment;

["temporary direction" means a direction under section 9 of this Act][7];

["vessel" includes a hovercraft;][8]

"the Veterinary Council" means the Veterinary Council established under the Veterinary Surgeons Act, 1931.

(2) For the purposes of this Act any controlled drug, pipe, utensil or document of which a person has control and which is in the custody of another who is either under the person's control or, though not under the person's control, acts on his behalf, whether as an agent or otherwise, shall be regarded as being in the possession of the person, and the provisions of section 16 and section 18 together with the provisions of this Act relating to the possession of controlled drugs shall be construed and have effect in accordance with the foregoing.

Amendments

1   Definition of "business" inserted by Irish Medicines Board (Miscellaneous Provisions) Act 2006, s 3(a).

2   Definition of "cannabis" substituted by Misuse of Drugs Act 1984, s 2(a).

3   Definition of "Irish Medicines Board" inserted by Irish Medicines Board (Miscellaneous Provisions) Act 2006, s 3(b).

4   Definition of "opium resin" substituted by Misuse of Drugs Act 1984, s 2(b).

5   Definition of "practitioner" amended by Irish Medicines Board (Miscellaneous Provisions) Act 2006, s 3(c).

6   Definition of "registered nurse" inserted by Irish Medicines Board (Miscellaneous Provisions) Act 2006, s 3(d).

7   Definition of "temporary direction" substituted by Misuse of Drugs Act 1984, s 2(c).

8   Definition of "vessel" inserted by Misuse of Drugs Act 1984, s 2(d).

2   Controlled drugs

(1) In this Act "controlled drug" means any substance, product or preparation (other than a substance, product or preparation specified in an order under subsection (3) of this section which is for the time being in force) which is either specified in the Schedule to this Act or is for the time being declared pursuant to subsection (2) of this section to be a controlled drug for the purposes of this Act.

(2) The Government may by order declare any substance, product or preparation (not being a substance, product or preparation specified in the Schedule to this Act) to be a controlled drug for the purposes of this Act and so long as an order under this subsection is in force, this Act shall have effect as regards any substance, product or preparation specified in the order as if the substance, product or preparation were specified in the said Schedule.

(3) The Government may by order declare that the provisions of this Act shall not apply in relation to a substance, product or preparation specified both in the order and in the Schedule to this Act, and so long as an order under this subsection is in force, this Act shall not apply in relation to a substance, product or preparation specified in the order.

(4) The Government may by order amend or revoke an order under this section (including an order made under this subsection).

Note

The following SIs declare certain substances to be controlled drugs: SI 251/1987, SI 328/1993, SI 43/2003, SI 78/2004, SI 55/2006, SI 121/2009.

3   Restriction on possession of controlled drugs

(1) Subject to subsection (3) of this section and section 4(3) of this Act, a person shall not have a controlled drug in his possession.

(2) A person who has a controlled drug in his possession in contravention of subsection (1) of this section shall be guilty of an offence.

(3) The Minister may by order declare that subsection (1) of this section shall not apply to a controlled drug specified in the order, and for so long as an order under this subsection is in force the prohibition contained in the said subsection (1) shall not apply to a drug which is a controlled drug specified in the order.

(4) The Minister may by order amend or revoke an order under this section (including an order made under this subsection).

Note

The following SIs list products or substances to which s 3(1) does not apply: SI 29/1979, SI 341/1993, SI 326/1998, SI 91/2004, SI 54/2006.

4   Regulations permitting possession of controlled drugs

(1) The Minister may make regulations enabling any person, or persons of a prescribed class or description, in prescribed circumstances or for prescribed purposes, to possess a controlled drug subject to such conditions (if any), or subject to and in accordance with such licence, as may be prescribed.

(2) Subject to section 13 of this Act, the Minister shall exercise his power to make regulations under this section so as to secure that it is not unlawful under this Act for a practitioner or pharmacist to have a controlled drug in his possession for the purpose of his profession or business.

(3) It shall be lawful for any person, or a person of a class or description specified in regulations under this section, to have in his possession in prescribed circumstances or for prescribed purposes, as may be appropriate, a controlled drug specified therein, provided that any conditions specified in the regulations or attached to a licence granted under this Act and applicable in the particular case are complied with by him.

5   Regulations to prevent misuse of controlled drugs

(1) For the purpose of preventing the misuse of controlled drugs, the Minister may make regulations—

(a) prohibiting absolutely, or permitting subject to such conditions or exceptions as may be specified in the regulations, or subject to any licence, permit or other form of authority as may be so specified—

    (i) the manufacture, production or preparation of controlled drugs,

    (ii) the importation or exportation of controlled drugs,

    (iii) the supply, the offering to supply or the distribution of controlled drugs,

    (iv) the transportation of controlled drugs,

(b) requiring prescribed documents to be used in a prescribed manner in relation to prescribed transactions concerning controlled drugs and requiring copies of such documents to be furnished to prescribed persons, or to persons of a prescribed class or description,

(c) requiring prescribed precautions to be taken for the purpose of ensuring the safe custody of controlled drugs,

(d) requiring prescribed records to be kept in relation to controlled drugs and regulations under this section may specify the manner in which the records are to be kept and maintained and such regulations may also provide for the furnishing of information relating to such records in such circumstances and in such manner as may be prescribed,

(e) providing for the inspection by prescribed persons of precautions taken or records kept in pursuance of regulations under this section,

[(f) subject to subsection (1A) of this section, regulating the issue by—

    (i) registered medical practitioners, registered dentists or registered veterinary surgeons, or

    (ii) registered nurses, or registered nurses belonging to a class of registered nurses,

of prescriptions for controlled drugs and the supply of controlled drugs on prescription,][1]

(g) requiring persons dispensing prescriptions for controlled drugs to furnish to the Minister such information relating to those prescriptions as may be prescribed,

(h) regulating or controlling the packaging and labelling of controlled drugs and such regulations may in particular require prescribed particulars relating to controlled drugs or a prescribed statement (including a warning or caution) relating to such drugs to be printed either on the outside of any packet or container used in the sale, supply or distribution of controlled drugs or on a label attached to such packet or container,

(i) requiring that any controlled drugs which, because of their condition or for any other reason, are not intended to be used shall be destroyed or disposed of in a prescribed manner,

(j) requiring any manufacturer, manufacturer's agent or wholesaler who wishes to withdraw a controlled drug from public sale to give six months notice of such proposed withdrawal unless the Minister is satisfied that it is in the public interest that such controlled drug should be withdrawn at such shorter notice as the Minister may determine.

[(1A) The Minister shall only exercise the power to make regulations under subsection (1)(f) of this section in the case of registered nurses, or registered nurses belonging to a class of registered nurses, if the Minister, after having had regard to the nature and purpose of the controlled drug concerned (including any deleterious effects which may arise from the misuse thereof), is satisfied that it is reasonably safe to permit the issue by registered nurses, or registered nurses belonging to a class of registered nurses, of prescriptions for that drug.][2]

(2) Subject to section 13 of this Act, the Minister shall exercise his power to make regulations under this section so as to secure that it is not unlawful under this Act for—

    (a) a practitioner [(other than a registered nurse)][3], for the purpose of his profession, to prescribe, administer, manufacture, compound or supply a controlled drug,

    (b) a pharmacist, for the purpose of his profession or business, to [....][4] manufacture, compound or supply a controlled drug,

provided that nothing in this subsection shall be construed as enabling the Minister to make regulations under this Act authorising a registered druggist to keep open shop for the compounding or dispensing of medical prescriptions.

[(3) Subject to section 13 of this Act, the Minister may exercise the Minister's power to make regulations under this section so as to secure that it is not unlawful under this Act for a practitioner who is a registered nurse, or a practitioner who is a registered nurse belonging to a class of registered nurses, for the purpose of the practitioner's profession as a registered nurse, to prescribe, administer, manufacture, compound or supply a controlled drug if the Minister, after having had regard to the nature and purpose of the controlled drug (including any deleterious effects which may arise from the misuse thereof), is satisfied that it is reasonably safe to permit the practitioner, for the purpose of the practitioner's profession as a registered nurse, to prescribe, administer, manufacture, compound or supply that controlled drug.][5]

Amendments

1   Subsection 1(f) substituted by Irish Medicines Board (Miscellaneous Provisions) Act 2006, s 4(a).

2   Subsection (1A) inserted by Irish Medicines Board (Miscellaneous Provisions) Act 2006, s 4(b).

3   Words inserted by Irish Medicines Board (Miscellaneous Provisions) Act 2006, s 4(c).

4   Words deleted by Misuse of Drugs Act 1984, s 15(a).

5   Subsection (3) inserted by Irish Medicines Board (Miscellaneous Provisions) Act 2006, s 4(d).

6   Directions prohibiting prescribing, supply etc. of controlled drugs by practitioners or pharmacists convicted of offences

(1) Where a practitioner or pharmacist has after the commencement of this subsection been convicted of—

    (a) an offence under this Act, or

    (b) an offence against the Customs Acts in relation to the importation or exportation of a controlled drug,

the Minister may give a direction under subsection (2) of this section in respect of that person.

[(1A) Where a relevant person has after the commencement of this subsection been convicted of—

   (a) an offence under this Act, or
   (b) an offence against the Customs Acts in relation to the importation or exportation of a controlled drug,

the Minister may give a direction under subsection (2) of this section in respect of that person.]¹

(2) A direction under this subsection shall—

   (a) in case the direction relates to a practitioner, be a direction prohibiting him from having in his possession, prescribing, administering, manufacturing, compounding and supplying and from authorising the administration and supply of such controlled drugs as may be specified in the direction,
   (b) in case the direction relates to a pharmacist [or relevant person, be a direction prohibiting the pharmacist or relevant person, as the case may be, from having in the pharmacist's or relevant person's, as the case may be,]² possession, manufacturing, compounding and supplying and from supervising and controlling the manufacture, compounding and supply of such controlled drugs as may be specified in the direction.

(3) The Minister may at any time give a direction cancelling or suspending any direction given by him under subsection (2) of this section, or cancelling any direction of his under this subsection by which a direction so given is suspended.

(4) The Minister shall cause a copy of any direction given by him under this section to be served on the person to whom it applies and shall cause notice of any such direction to be published in the *Iris Oifigiúil* and in such other manner (if any) as the Minister may consider appropriate.

(5) A direction under this section shall take effect when a copy of it is served on the person to whom it applies.

(6) Any person who contravenes a direction given under this section shall be guilty of an offence.

[(7) In this section, "relevant person" means—

   (a) a person, not being a pharmacist, keeping open shop for the dispensing or compounding of medical prescriptions in accordance with the provisions of the Pharmacy Acts 1875 to 1977, or
   (b) any director, manager, secretary or other official of a person referred to in paragraph (a) of this definition which is a body corporate.]³

Amendments

1   Subsection (1A) inserted by Irish Medicines Board (Miscellaneous Provisions) Act 2006, s 5(a).
2   Subsection (2)(b) amended by Irish Medicines Board (Miscellaneous Provisions) Act 2006, s 5(b).
3   Subsection (7) inserted by Irish Medicines Board (Miscellaneous Provisions) Act 2006, s 5(c).

7   Special directions prohibiting prescribing etc. of controlled drug in certain cases

(1) If the Minister believes that a practitioner is or has been, after the commencement of this section, prescribing, administering or supplying, or authorising the administration or supply of any controlled drug in an irresponsible manner, subject to the provisions of this Act, he may give a direction in respect of the practitioner prohibiting him prescribing, administering or supplying or authorising the administration or supply of such controlled drugs as may be specified in the direction.

(2) A direction given pursuant to this section (in this Act subsequently referred to as a special direction) shall come into force when a copy of it is given to the practitioner to whom it relates and, subject to subsection (3) of this section and section 11(1) of this Act, the special direction shall remain in operation until it is cancelled.

(3) The Minister may, [...]¹ suspend the operation of a special direction.

(4) The Minister may, [...]¹ cancel a special direction.

(5) Where the Minister suspends the operation of or cancels a special direction, he shall cause notice to that effect to be given to the practitioner to whom the special direction applies and, as soon as may be, cause notice of the suspension or cancellation to be published in the *Iris Oifigiúil*.

(6) A person who contravenes a special direction shall be guilty of an offence.

Amendments

1   Words repealed by Misuse of Drugs Act 1984, s 15(b).

---

8   Investigation of cases where Minister considers there are grounds for special direction

[(1) If the Minister considers that there may be grounds for giving a special direction, he shall forthwith establish a committee of inquiry, constituted in accordance with any regulations under section 12 of this Act which apply to it, and as soon as may be after such committee is established he shall refer the matter in question to the committee for investigation and when making the reference send to the committee a statement of such grounds, and it shall be the duty of the committee in accordance with this section to investigate the matter referred to it and to report on it to the Minister.

(2) Where the Minister sends a statement of grounds to a committee of inquiry established pursuant to this section, he shall at the same time send to the respondent a copy of the statement and invite him to submit to the committee in writing, within the period of twenty-one days commencing on the date on which the statement is sent to the committee, any representations relating to the matter to be investigated which he may then wish to make.

(3) (a)   Where a committee of inquiry is established under this section, a meeting of the committee of inquiry shall be convened by the Minister who shall at the same time fix a day for the meeting, being a day which is neither earlier than the seventh day after the expiration of the period referred to in subsection (2) of this section nor later than the twenty-first day after such expiration.

(b)   Where the Minister convenes a meeting under this subsection, he shall at the same time send to the respondent not less than seven days' notice in writing of the date, place and time fixed by the Minister for the meeting and the notice shall also notify the respondent that he may make representations to, and if he so wishes appear in person before, the committee of inquiry concerned, be assisted by another person (whether so appearing or not) in making such representations or have such representations made by another person (whether so appearing or not) acting on his behalf.

(4) A committee of inquiry established under this section shall report to the Minister on its investigation as soon as may be and shall state in the report whether or not they recommend the giving of a special direction as regards the matter being investigated, and in case the committee recommends the giving of such a direction they shall indicate in their report either the controlled drugs which the committee considers should be specified in the relevant special direction or that the committee considers that such direction should apply to all controlled drugs.

(5) Having considered the report of the committee of inquiry established under this section, the Minister may—

(a)   decide to give in respect of the respondent a special direction specifying all or any of the controlled drugs indicated in a recommendation of the committee, or

(b)   decide not to give a special direction, and in case the Minister pursuant to this section decides not to give a special direction, he shall notify the respondent accordingly.

(6) Where the Minister gives a special direction, he shall, as soon as may be, cause a copy of the special direction to be served on the respondent and shall cause a copy of the direction to be published in the *Iris Oifigiúil* and in such other manner (if any) as the Minister may consider appropriate.

(7) Where the Minister gives a special direction, he shall send a copy of the report received by him from the relevant committee of inquiry and the special direction to the respondent and also to—

(a)   in case the respondent is a registered dentist, the Dental Board,

(b)   in case the respondent is a registered medical practitioner, the Medical Council,

(c)   in case the respondent is a registered veterinary surgeon, the Veterinary Council,][1]

[(d)   in case the practitioner concerned is a registered nurse, to An Bord Altranais.][2]

Amendments

1   Section 8 was substituted by Misuse of Drugs Act 1984, s 3.

2   Subsection 8(7)(d) was inserted by Irish Medicines Board (Miscellaneous Provisions) Act 2006, s 6.

---

9   Prohibition of prescribing etc. in cases of urgency

[(1) Where the Minister refers a matter for investigation to a committee of inquiry established under section 8 of this Act, he may give a direction under this section in respect of the respondent prohibiting his prescribing, administering or supplying or authorising the administration or supply of such controlled drugs as may be specified in the direction, and such direction shall come into force on the expiration of the period of seven days beginning on the day on which a copy of the direction is sent by the Minister to the respondent unless, not later than the seventh day following the day on which such copy is so sent, the respondent satisfies the Minister that the direction should not come into force.

(2) In case a copy of a temporary direction is sent by the Minister, the Minister shall at the same time send to the respondent a notice in writing stating that the respondent may, within the time limit specified in subsection (1) of this section, make representations to the Minister stating why the temporary direction should not come into force.

(3) A temporary direction shall remain in force until the expiration of the period of twenty-eight days beginning on the day on which it is given or until the Minister makes a decision under section 8(5) of this Act as regards the relevant case, whichever first occurs.

(4) The Minister may extend or further extend, in either case for a period not exceeding twenty-eight days, the period during which a particular temporary direction is to remain in force.

(5) Where a temporary direction is given, extended or further extended, the Minister shall, as soon as may be, cause a notice of the temporary direction, its extension or further extension, as may be appropriate, to be published in the *Iris Oifigiúil* and in such other manner (if any) as the Minister may consider appropriate.]¹

Amendments

1   Section 9 was substituted by Misuse of Drugs Act 1984, s 4.

---

10   **Investigation on initiative of Dental Board, Medical Registration Council or Veterinary Council**

[...]¹

Amendments

1   Section 10 repealed by Misuse of Drugs Act 1984, s 15(c).

---

11   **Appeals**

(1) Any practitioner or pharmacist who is aggrieved by a direction under section 6(2) of this Act, a special direction or a temporary direction may, not later than three weeks after the day on which the direction under the said section 6(2), special direction or temporary direction, as the case may be, comes into force, appeal to the High Court, and that Court may—

    (a) by interim order suspend the operation of the direction under the said section 6(2), special direction or temporary direction, either generally or in a particular respect, until the final determination of the proceedings,

(b) confirm the direction under the said section 6(2), special direction or temporary direction with or without modification or cancel it.

(2) Where a direction under section 6(2) of this Act, special direction or temporary direction is suspended or cancelled or confirmed with modifications by the High Court, the order of the Court shall not prejudice the validity of anything done on foot of the direction prior to the making of the order.

(3) Where a direction under section 6(2) of this Act, special direction or temporary direction is suspended or cancelled by the High Court, the Minister shall as soon as may be cause notice thereof to be published in the *Iris Oifigiúil.*

12 Regulations (committees and panels)

(1) The Minister may, after consultation with any registered authority concerned, make regulations in relation to the constitution and procedure of committees of inquiry, [...]¹ established pursuant to section 8 [...]¹ of this Act.

(2) Subject to the provisions of this Act and to any regulations made by the Minister under this section and which apply to it, a committee [...]² referred to in subsection (1) of this section may regulate its procedure and business.

Amendments

1   Words repealed by Misuse of Drugs Act 1984, s 15(d).

2   Words repealed by Misuse of Drugs Act 1984, s 15(e).

---

13 Additional powers in relation to certain controlled drugs

(1) If in the case of any controlled drug the Minister is of the opinion that it is in the public interest—

(a) for the manufacture, production, preparation, sale, supply, distribution and possession of that drug to be either wholly unlawful or unlawful except for purposes of research or for other special purposes specified in an order under this section, or

(b) for it to be unlawful for any person who is either a practitioner or a pharmacist to ˙ have in his possession or to do in relation to that drug any of the things mentioned in section 5(2) of this Act except under a licence or other authority issued by the Minister,

he may by order designate that drug as a drug to which this subsection applies, and while there is in force an order under this section designating a controlled drug as one to which this subsection applies, section 4(2) of this Act and the said section 5(2) shall not apply as regards that drug.

(2) The Minister may by order revoke or amend any order under this section (including an order under this subsection).

14 Licences etc

(1) The [Irish Medicines Board][1] may grant licences or issue permits or authorisations for any of the purposes of this Act, attach conditions to any such licence, permit or authorisation, vary such conditions and revoke any such licence, permit or authorisation.

(2) The Minister may make regulations requiring the payment of prescribed fees in respect of the grant or issue under this section of a licence, permit or authorisation.

[(3) A licence, permit or authorisation—

  (a) granted or issued by the Minister under subsection (1) (including granted or issued by way of being renewed) at any time before the commencement of this subsection, and

  (b) in force immediately before that commencement, shall, on and after that commencement

but subject to the conditions, if any, attached under subsection (1) to it and in force immediately before that commencement, continue in force, unless sooner revoked under subsection (1), for the unexpired portion of the period of validity, if any, which it had left to run immediately before that commencement as if, on that commencement, the Irish Medicines Board had, under subsection (1)—

  (c) granted or issued that licence, permit or authorisation, and

  (d) attached to that licence, permit or authorisation those conditions, if any,

and the provisions of this Act shall apply to the licence, permit or authorisation accordingly.][2]

Amendments

1 Words repealed by Irish Medicines Board (Miscellaneous Provisions) Act 2006, s 7(a).

2 Subsection (3) inserted by Irish Medicines Board (Miscellaneous Provisions) Act 2006, s 7(b).

15 Possession of controlled drugs for unlawful sale or supply

(1) Any person who has in his possession, whether lawfully or not, a controlled drug for the purpose of selling or otherwise supplying it to another in contravention of regulations under section 5 of this Act, shall be guilty of an offence.

(2) Subject to section 29(3) of this Act, in any proceedings for an offence under subsection (1) of this section, where it is proved that a person was in possession of a controlled drug and the court, having regard to the quantity of the controlled drug which the person possessed or to such other matter as the court considers relevant, is satisfied that it is reasonable to assume that the controlled drug was not intended for the immediate personal use of the person, he shall be presumed, until the court is satisfied to the contrary, to have been in possession of the controlled drug for the purpose of selling or otherwise supplying it to another in contravention of regulations under section 5 of this Act.

[15A Offence relating to possession of drugs with value of £10,000 or more

(1) A person shall be guilty of an offence under this section where—

(a) the person has in his possession, whether lawfully or not, one or more controlled drugs for the purpose of selling or otherwise supplying the drug or drugs to another in contravention of regulations under section 5 of this Act, and

(b) at any time while the drug or drugs are in the person's possession the market value of the controlled drug or the aggregate of the market values of the controlled drugs, as the case may be, amounts to [€13,000]² or more.

(2) Subject to section 29(3) of this Act (as amended by section 6 of the Criminal Justice Act, 1999), in any proceedings for an offence under this section, where—

(a) it is proved that a person was in possession of a controlled drug, and

(b) the court, having regard to the quantity of the controlled drug which the person possessed or to such other matters that the court considers relevant, is satisfied that it is reasonable to assume that the controlled drug was not intended for his immediate personal use,

he shall be presumed, until the court is satisfied to the contrary, to have been in possession of the controlled drug for the purpose of selling or otherwise supplying it to another in contravention of regulations under section 5 of this Act.

(3) If the court is satisfied that a member of the Garda Síochána or an officer of customs and excise has knowledge of the unlawful sale or supply of controlled drugs, that member or officer, as the case may be, shall be entitled in any proceedings for an offence under this section to be heard and to give evidence as to—

(a) the market value of the controlled drug concerned, or

(b) the aggregate of the market values of the controlled drugs concerned.

[(3A) In any proceedings for an offence under this section, it shall not be necessary for the prosecutor to prove that a person knew that at any time while the controlled drug or drugs concerned were in the person's possession that the market value of that drug or the aggregate of the market values of those drugs, as the case may be, amounted to €13,000 or more or that he or she was reckless in that regard.]³

(4) No proceedings may be instituted under this section except by or with the consent of the Director of Public Prosecutions.

(5) In this section—

'market value', in relation to a controlled drug, means the price that drug could be expected to fetch on the market for the unlawful sale or supply of controlled drugs;

'an officer of customs and excise' has the same meaning as in section 6 of the Criminal Justice (Drug Trafficking) Act, 1996.]¹

Amendments

1   Section 15A was inserted by Criminal Justice Act 1999, s 4.

2   "£10,000" changed to "€13,000" in accordance with the Euro Changeover (Amounts) Act 2001.

3   Subsection (3A) inserted by Criminal Justice Act 2006, s 81(1).

[15B   Importation of controlled drugs in excess of certain value.

(1) A person shall be guilty of an offence where—

(a) the person imports one or more controlled drugs in contravention of regulations under section 5 of this Act, and

(b) at or about the time the drug or drugs are imported the market value of the controlled drug or the aggregate of the market values of the controlled drugs, as the case may be, amounts to €13,000 or more.

(2) If the court is satisfied that a member of the Garda Síochána or an officer of customs and excise has knowledge of the unlawful sale or supply of controlled drugs, that member or officer, as the case may be, shall be entitled in any proceedings for an offence under this section to be heard and to give evidence as to—

(a) the market value of the controlled drug concerned, or

(b) the aggregate of the market values of the controlled drugs concerned.

(3) In any proceedings for an offence under this section, it shall not be necessary for the prosecutor to prove that a person knew that at the time the person imported the controlled drug or drugs concerned that the market value of that drug or the aggregate of the market values of those drugs, as the case may be, amounted to €13,000 or more or that he or she was reckless in that regard.

(4) No proceedings may be instituted under this section except by or with the consent of the Director of Public Prosecutions.

(5) In this section 'market value' and 'an officer of customs and excise' have the meanings they have in section 15A of this Act.][1]

Amendments

1   Section 15B was inserted by Criminal Justice Act 2006, s 82.

[15C   Supply of controlled drugs into prisons and places of detention

(1) A person shall be guilty of an offence where—

(a) the person, other than in accordance with regulations made under section 4 of this Act, conveys a controlled drug into a prison, children detention school or remand centre or to a person in the prison, school or centre,

(b) the person, other than in accordance with regulations made under section 4 of this Act, places a controlled drug in any place inside or outside a prison, children detention school or remand centre with intent that it shall come into the possession of a person in the prison, school or centre,

(c) the person throws or projects a controlled drug into a prison, children detention school or remand centre, or

(d) the person, while in the vicinity of a prison, children detention school or remand centre, has in his or her possession a controlled drug with intent to commit an act referred to in paragraph (a), (b) or (c) of this subsection.

(2) A person may be guilty of an offence under subsection (1) of this section irrespective of the quantity of the controlled drug concerned.

(3) Subject to section 29(3) of this Act, in any proceedings for an offence under subsection (1)(d) of this section, where—

> (a) it is proved that a person was in possession of a controlled drug in the vicinity of a prison, children detention school or remand centre, as the case may be, and
>
> (b) the court (or the jury, as the case may be), having regard to all the circumstances including the person's proximity to the prison, school or centre, as the case may be, the packaging (if any) of the controlled drug and the time of the day or night concerned, is satisfied that it is reasonable to assume that the controlled drug was not intended for his or her immediate personal use,

he or she shall be presumed, until the court (or the jury, as the case may be) is satisfied to the contrary, to have been in possession of the controlled drug with intent to commit an act referred to in paragraph (a) or (b) or, as the case may be, (c) of subsection (1) of this section.

(4) In any proceedings for an offence under subsection (1) of this section, it shall not be necessary for the prosecutor to prove that the controlled drug concerned was intended to come into the possession of any particular person in the prison, children detention school or remand centre, as the case may be.

(5) If a prison officer or an authorised member of the staff of a children detention school or remand centre reasonably suspects that a person has committed or is committing an offence under this section, he or she may, for the purpose of detecting the commission of such an offence, search the person at any time while he or she is in the prison, school or centre, as the case may be.

(6) A prison officer or an authorised member of the staff of a children detention school or remand centre may, for the purpose of performing his or her functions under subsection (5) of this section, have a controlled drug in his or her possession.

(7) A person guilty of an offence under this section shall be liable—

> (a) on summary conviction, to a fine not exceeding €3,000 or imprisonment for a term not exceeding 12 months or both, or
>
> (b) on conviction on indictment, to a fine or imprisonment for a term not exceeding 10 years or both.

(8) In this section—

> 'an authorised member of the staff'—
>
> > (a) in relation to a children detention school, means a member of the staff of the school who is authorised in writing for the purposes of this section by the Director (within the meaning of section 157 of the Children Act 2001) of the school, and
> >
> > (b) in relation to a remand centre, means a member of the staff of the centre who is authorised in writing for the purposes of this section by the owners or, as the case may be, the managers of the centre;
>
> 'children detention school' and 'remand centre' have the meanings they have in section 3(1) of the Children Act 2001;
>
> 'prison' means a place of custody administered by the Minister for Justice, Equality and Law Reform and includes Saint Patrick's Institution and a place of detention

provided under section 2 of the Prisons Act 1970, and 'prison officer', in relation to a prison, shall be construed accordingly.]¹

Amendments

1   Section 15C was inserted by Criminal Justice Act 2006, s 83.

16   Prohibition of certain activities etc. relating to opium

(1) A person shall not—

- (a)   smoke or otherwise use prepared opium,
- (b)   frequent a place used for the purpose of smoking or otherwise using prepared opium, or
- (c)   have in his possession—
  - (i)   any pipes or other utensils made or adapted for use in connection with the smoking of opium being, pipes or utensils which have been used by him or with his knowledge and permission in that connection or which he intends to use or permit others to use in that connection, or
  - (ii)   any utensils which have been used by him or with his knowledge and permission in connection with the preparation of opium for smoking.

(2) A person who contravenes a provision of subsection (1) of this section shall be guilty of an offence.

17   Prohibition of cultivation of opium poppy or cannabis plant

[(1) A person shall not cultivate opium poppy [for the production of opium],² any plant of the genus *Cannabis* or any plant of the genus *Erythroxylon* except under and in accordance with a licence issued in that behalf [under section 14(1)]².

(2) Every person who cultivates opium poppy [for the production of opium],³ a plant of the genus *Cannabis* or a plant of the genus *Erythroxylon* in contravention of subsection (1) of this section shall be guilty of an offence.]¹

Amendments

1   Section 17 was substituted by Misuse of Drugs Act 1984, s 11(1).

2   Words inserted by Irish Medicines Board (Miscellaneous Provisions) Act 2006, 8(a).

3   Words inserted by Irish Medicines Board (Miscellaneous Provisions) Act 2006, 8(b).

18   Forged or fraudulently altered prescriptions

(1) A person shall not forge a document purporting to be a prescription issued by a practitioner (which document is in this Act referred to as a forged prescription).

(2) A person shall not with intent to deceive either alter or use a prescription which has been duly issued by a practitioner (which document is in this Act referred to as a duly issued prescription).

(3) A person shall not have in his possession either a forged prescription or a duly issued prescription which has been altered with intent to deceive.

(4) The Minister may by regulations declare that in circumstances specified in the regulations subsection (3) of this section shall not apply in relation to persons who are of a prescribed class or description, and for so long as regulations under this subsection are in force the said subsection (3) shall be construed in accordance with and have effect subject to the regulations.

(5) A person who contravenes a provision of this section shall be guilty of an offence.

19   Occupiers etc. permitting certain activities to take place on land, vehicle or vessel to be guilty of an offence

(1) A person who is the occupier or is in control or is concerned in the management of any land, vehicle or vessel and who knowingly permits or suffers any of the following to take place on the land, vehicle or vessel, namely—

  (a) the cultivation contrary to section 17 of this Act of opium poppy or any plant of the genus *Cannabis*,[1]
  (b) the preparation of opium for smoking,
  (c) the preparation of cannabis for smoking,
  (d) the smoking of cannabis, cannabis resin or prepared opium,
  (e) the manufacture, production or preparation of a controlled drug in contravention of regulations made under section 5 of this Act,
  (f) the importation or exportation of a controlled drug in contravention of such regulations,
  (g) the sale, supply or distribution of a controlled drug in contravention of such regulations,
  (h) any attempt so to contravene such regulations, or
  (i) the possession of a controlled drug in contravention of section 3 of this Act,

shall be guilty of an offence.

(2) In any proceedings for an offence under subsection (1) of this section, where it is proved that an activity or contravention mentioned in the said subsection (1) took place on particular land or on a particular vehicle or vessel and that the defendant was, at the time of the alleged offence, the occupier of, or in control or concerned in the management of the land, vehicle or vessel, as the case may be, it shall be presumed until the court is satisfied to the contrary that the activity or contravention took place with the knowledge of the defendant.[1]

Amendments

1   Section 19 amended by Misuse of Drugs Act 1984, s 11(2) which reads:

    'Section 19 of the Principal Act shall be construed and have effect as if the reference in subsection (1)(a) thereof to the cultivation contrary to section 17 of that Act of opium poppy included a reference to the cultivation contrary to the said section 17, as amended by subsection (1) of this section, of any plant of the genus *Erythroxylon.*'

20   Offences relating to acts outside the State

(1) Any person who aids, abets, counsels or induces the commission in a place outside the State of an offence punishable under a corresponding law in force in that place shall be guilty of an offence.

(2) In this section "a corresponding law" means a law stated in a certificate purporting to be issued by or on behalf of the government of a country outside the State to be a law providing for the control or regulation in that country of the manufacture, production, supply, use, exportation or importation of dangerous or otherwise harmful drugs in pursuance of any treaty, convention, protocol or other agreement between states and prepared or implemented by, or under the auspices of the League of Nations or the United Nations Organisation and which for the time being is in force.

(3) Any statement in a certificate mentioned in subsection (2) of this section as to the effect of the law mentioned in the certificate or any such statement that any facts constitute an offence against the law so mentioned shall, for the purposes of any proceedings under this Act, be evidence of the matters stated.

21   Attempts etc. and miscellaneous other offences

(1) A person who attempts to commit an offence under this Act, or who aids, abets, counsels or procures the commission of an offence under this Act, or who solicits or incites any other person to commit an offence under this Act shall be guilty of an offence.

(2) Any person who, whether by act or omission, contravenes or fails to comply with regulations under this Act shall be guilty of an offence.

(3) A person who, in purported compliance with any obligation to give information to which he is subject by virtue of regulations made under this Act, gives any information which he knows to be false in a material particular or recklessly gives information which is so false shall be guilty of an offence.

(4) Any person who by act or omission impedes or obstructs a member of the Garda Síochána or a person duly authorised under this Act in the lawful exercise of a power conferred by this Act shall be guilty of an offence and if, in the case of a continuing offence, the impediment or obstruction is continued after conviction, he shall be guilty of a further offence.

(5) Any person who conceals from a person lawfully exercising a power under section 24 of this Act any controlled drug, or who without reasonable excuse fails to produce any book, record or other document which he has been duly required to produce under that section, shall be guilty of an offence.

(6) Any person who contravenes a condition attached to a licence, permit or authorisation granted or issued by the Minister under this Act (other than section 24) or under regulations made under this Act shall be guilty of an offence.

(7) Any person who, for the purpose of obtaining, whether for himself or another, the grant, issue or renewal of a licence, permit or authorisation under this Act or under regulations made under this Act—

(a) makes any statement or gives information which he knows to be false in a material particular or recklessly gives information which is so false, or

(b) produces or otherwise makes use of any book, record or other document which to his knowledge contains any statement or information which he knows to be false in a material particular,

shall be guilty of an offence.

22 Onus of proof

(1) In any proceedings for an offence under this Act, it shall not be necessary to negative by evidence the existence of any—

(a) order made under section 2 [or 3]¹ of this Act,

(b) licence, permit or authorisation under this Act,

and accordingly the onus of proving the existence of any such licence, permit or authorisation shall be on the person seeking to avail himself thereof.

(2) In any proceedings for an offence under this Act it shall not be necessary for the prosecutor to prove that at the time of the offence—

(a) a defendant was not a person to whom regulations made under section 4 of this Act applied,

(b) a defendant was a person to whom an exception under regulations made under section 5 of this Act applied, and

in case a defendant claims that—

(i) by virtue of the said section 4 he had lawfully in his possession a controlled drug,

(ii) he is a person to whom such an exception applied,

the onus of proving such lawful possession, or that he is such a person, as may be appropriate, shall be on the defendant.

Amendments

1 Words inserted by Misuse of Drugs Act 1984, s 14(a).

23 Power of Garda Síochána to search persons, vehicles, vessels or aircraft

(1) A member of the Garda Síochána who with reasonable cause suspects that a person is in possession in contravention of this Act of a controlled drug, may without warrant—

(a) search the person and, if he considers it necessary for that purpose, detain the person for such time as is reasonably necessary for making the search,

(b) search any vehicle, vessel or aircraft in which he suspects that such drug may be found [,and any substance, article or other thing on or in the vehicle, vessel or aircraft]¹ and for the purpose of carrying out the search may, if he thinks fit, require the person who for the time being is in control of such vehicle, vessel or aircraft to bring it to a stop and when stopped to refrain from moving it, or in case such vehicle, vessel or aircraft is already stationary, to refrain from moving it, or

(c) [examine (by opening or otherwise) and]² seize and detain anything found in the course of a search under this section which with such cause appears to him to be something which might be required as evidence in proceedings for a this Act.

[(1A) Where a member of the Garda Síochána decides to search a person under this section, he may require the person to accompany him to a Garda Station for the purpose of being so searched at that station. *No object.*

(1B) Where a member of the Garda Síochána decides to search a vehicle, vessel or aircraft under this section he may as regards the person who appears to him to be the owner or in control or charge for the time being of the vehicle, vessel or aircraft make any one or more or all of the following requirements:

(a) require such person, pending the commencement of the search, not to remove from the vehicle, vessel or aircraft, as may be appropriate, any substance, article or other thing,

(b) in case the decision relates to a vehicle and the place at which he finds the vehicle is in his reasonable opinion unsuitable for such search, require such person forthwith to take the vehicle or cause it to be taken to a place which he considers suitable for such search and which is specified by him,

(c) require the person to be in or on or to accompany the vehicle, vessel or aircraft, as may be appropriate, for so long as the requirement under this paragraph remains in force.

(1C) Where there is a failure to comply with a requirement made under this section the following provisions shall apply—

(a) in case the requirement was made under subsection (1A) of this section, the member of the Garda Síochána concerned may arrest without warrant the person of whom the requirement was made, and

(b) in case the requirement is a requirement mentioned in paragraph (b) of subsection (1B) of this section, such member may take the vehicle concerned, or cause it to be taken, to a place which he considers suitable for a search under this section.

(1D) Where a requirement is made of a person under this section—

(a) in case the requirement is a requirement mentioned in paragraph (c) of subsection (1B) of this section, if at any time while the requirement is in force the person of whom it was made is neither in nor on nor accompanying the vehicle, vessel or aircraft, as may be appropriate, in relation to which the requirement was made, he shall be guilty of an offence,

(b) in case of any other requirement under this section the person who fails to comply with the requirement shall be guilty of an offence.

(1E) A requirement mentioned in paragraph (c) of subsection (1B) of this section shall remain in force until the search in relation to which it is made is completed.

(1F) Where a requirement described in paragraph (a) of subsection (1B) of this section is made of a person, the search in relation to which the requirement is made shall be carried out as soon as is practicable.][3]

(2) Nothing in this section shall operate to prejudice any power to search, or to seize or detain property which may be exercised by a member of the Garda Síochána apart from this section.

Amendments

1 Words inserted by Misuse of Drugs Act 1984, s 12(a).
2 Words inserted by Misuse of Drugs Act 1984, s 12(b).
3 Subsections (1A)–(1F) inserted by Misuse of Drugs Act 1984, s 12(c).

24   Powers to inspect and demand production of drugs, books or documents

(1) For the purpose of enforcing this Act and regulations made thereunder, a member of the Garda Síochána or a person authorised in [writing in that behalf by the Minister or the Irish Medicines Board][1] may at all reasonable times—

  (a) enter any building or other premises in which a person carries on business as a producer, manufacturer, seller or distributor of controlled drugs [or as a practitioner][2],

  (b) require any such person, or any person employed in connection with such a business, to produce any controlled drugs which are in his possession or under his control,

  (c) require any such person, or any person so employed, to produce any books, records or other documents [(including any data within the meaning of the Data Protection Acts 1988 and 2003)][3] which relate to transactions concerning controlled drugs and which are in his possession or under his control, and

  (d) inspect any controlled drug, book, record or other document produced in pursuance of a requirement under this section.

[(2) For the purposes of enforcing this Act and any statutory instruments made thereunder, and without prejudice to the generality of subsection (1) of this section, a person authorised in writing in that behalf by the Council of the Pharmaceutical Society of Ireland may at all reasonable times—

  (a) enter any building or premises in which a person keeps open shop for the dispensing or compounding of medical prescriptions,

  (b) require any such person, or any person employed in connection with keeping such open shop for the dispensing or compounding of medical prescriptions, to produce any controlled drugs which are in his possession or under his control,

  (c) require any such person, or any person so employed, to produce any books, records or other documents (including any data within the meaning of the Data Protection Acts 1988 and 2003) which relate to transactions concerning controlled drugs and which are in his possession or under his control, and

  (d) inspect any controlled drug, book, record or other document produced in pursuance of a requirement under this section.][4]

(3) Where the Minister or the Irish Medicines Board authorises a person under subsection (1) of this section, then the Minister or the Irish Medicines Board, as the case may be, shall furnish the person with a warrant of his authorisation.

(4) Where the Pharmaceutical Society of Ireland authorises a person under subsection (2) of this section, then it shall furnish the person with a warrant of his authorisation.

(5) Where—

    (a) a person has been authorised by the Minister under subsection (1) of this section at any time before the commencement of this subsection,

    (b) the authorisation is still in force immediately before that commencement, and

    (c) either—

        (i) the person has, before that commencement, been issued with a certificate of his authorisation, or

        (ii) the person has not, before that commencement, been issued with a certificate of his authorisation,

    then the Minister shall—

    (d) in a case falling within paragraph (c)(i) of this subsection, furnish the person with a warrant of his authorisation upon the surrender of his certificate of authorisation,

    (e) in a case falling within paragraph (c)(ii) of this subsection, as soon as reasonably practicable after that commencement, furnish the person with a warrant of his authorisation.

(6) Where a person authorised under subsection (1) or (2) of this section—

    (a) claims to exercise a power by virtue of that authorisation, and

    (b) is required by a person in relation to whom the power is proposed to be exercised, to produce evidence of that authorisation,

then the person so authorised shall not exercise that power until he has produced the warrant of authorisation furnished under this section to the person in relation to whom the power is proposed to be exercised.

(7) A certificate of authorisation referred to in subsection (5)(c)(i) of this section which has not been surrendered as referred to in subsection (5)(d) of this section shall be deemed to be a warrant of authorisation furnished under this section to the person to whom the certificate of authorisation was furnished, and subsection (6) of this section shall be construed accordingly.][4]

Amendments

1   Words inserted by Irish Medicines Board (Miscellaneous Provisions) Act 2006, s 9(a)(i).

2   Words inserted by Irish Medicines Board (Miscellaneous Provisions) Act 2006, s 9(a)(ii).

3   Words inserted by Irish Medicines Board (Miscellaneous Provisions) Act 2006, s 9(a)(iii).

4   Subsection (2) substituted and subsections (3)–(7) inserted by Irish Medicines Board (Miscellaneous Provisions) Act 2006, s 9(b).

---

25   Power of arrest

(1) Where with reasonable cause a member of the Garda Síochána suspects that an offence under section 15 of this Act has been committed and so suspects a person of having committed the offence, he may arrest the person without warrant.

ere with reasonable cause a member of the Garda Síochána,

(a) suspects that an offence under this Act, other than an offence under section 15, has been committed or attempted, and

(b) suspects a person of having committed the offence or having made the attempt, then if the member,

(c) with reasonable cause suspects that the person unless he is arrested either will abscond for the purposes of evading justice or will obstruct the course of justice, or

(d) having enquired of the person, has reasonable doubts as to the person's identity or place of abode, or

(e) having enquired of the person, knows that the person does not ordinarily reside in the State, or has reasonable doubts as to whether the person so resides.

he may arrest the person without warrant.

26   Search warrants

(1) If a Justice of the District Court or a Peace Commissioner is satisfied by information on oath of a member of the Garda Síochána [or if, subject to the provisions of subsection (2) of section 8 of the Criminal Justice (Drug Trafficking) Act, 1996, a member of the Garda Síochána not below the rank of superintendent is satisfied]¹ that there is reasonable ground for suspecting that—

(a) a person is in possession in contravention of this Act on any premises or other land of a controlled drug, a forged prescription or a duly issued prescription which has been wrongfully altered and that such drug or prescription is on a particular premises [or other land]², or

[(aa) opium poppy, a plant of the genus *Cannabis* or a plant of the genus *Erythroxylon* is being cultivated contrary to section 17 of this Act on or in any premises or other land, or]³

(b) a document directly or indirectly relating to, or connected with, a transaction or dealing which was, or an intended transaction or dealing which would if carried out be, an offence under this Act, or in the case of a transaction or dealing carried out or intended to be carried out in a place outside the State, an offence against a provision of a corresponding law within the meaning of section 20 of this Act and in force in that place, is in the possession of a person on any premises,

[such Justice, Commissioner or, as the case may be, member]⁴ may issue a search warrant mentioned in subsection (2) of this section.

[(2) A search warrant issued under this section shall be expressed and operate to authorise a named member of the Garda Síochána, accompanied by such other members of the Garda Síochána and such other persons as may be necessary, at any time or times within one month of the date of issue of the warrant, to enter (if need be by force) the premises or other land named in the warrant, to search such premises or other land and any persons found therein, to examine any substance, article or other thing found thereon or therein, to inspect any book, record or other document found thereon and, if there is reasonable ground for suspecting that an offence is being or has been committed under this Act in relation to a substance, article or other thing found on such premises or other land or that a document so found is a document mentioned in subsection (1)(b) of this section or is a record or other document which the member has reasonable cause to believe to be a document which may be required as evidence in proceedings for an offence under this Act, to seize and detain the substance, article, document or other thing, as the case may be.]⁵

[(3) Where any premises or other land is entered pursuant to a warrant issued under this section, the member of the Garda Síochána named in the warrant may do either or both of the following:

(a) arrest without warrant any person or persons found on such premises or other land for the purpose of searching him or them,

(b) so arrest any such person or persons and keep him or them, as may be appropriate, under arrest until such time as such of the powers of search or examination as he wishes to exercise pursuant to the warrant have been exercised by him.

(4) In this section—

'land' includes any structure on land;

'structure' means building, structure or any other thing constructed, erected, placed or made on, in or under any land.]⁶

Amendments

1 Words inserted by Criminal Justice (Drug Trafficking) Act 1996, s 8(1)(a).
2 Words inserted by Misuse of Drugs Act 1984, s 13(a).
3 Subsection (1)(aa) inserted by Misuse of Drugs Act 1984, s 13(b).
4 Words substituted by Criminal Justice (Drug Trafficking) Act 1996, s 8(1)(b).
5 Subsection (2) substituted by Misuse of Drugs Act 1984, s 13(c).
6 Subsections (3)–(4) inserted by Misuse of Drugs Act 1984, s 13(c).

27   Penalties

[(1) Subject to section 28 of this Act, every person guilty of an offence under section 3 of this Act shall be liable—

(a) where the relevant controlled drug is cannabis or cannabis resin and the court is satisfied that the person was in possession of such drug for his personal use:

(i) in the case of a first offence,

(I) on summary conviction, to a fine not exceeding £300, or

(II) on conviction on indictment, to a fine not exceeding £500,

(ii) in the case of a second offence,

(I) on summary conviction, to a fine not exceeding £400, or

(II) on conviction on indictment, to a fine not exceeding £1,000,

(iii) in the case of a third or subsequent offence,

(I) on summary conviction, to a fine not exceeding £1,000 or, at the discretion of the court, to imprisonment for a term not exceeding twelve months, or to both the fine and the imprisonment, or

(II) on conviction on indictment, to a fine of such amount as the court considers appropriate or, at the discretion of the court, to imprisonment for a term not exceeding three years, or to both the fine and the imprisonment;

(b) in any other case—

    (i) on summary conviction, to a fine not exceeding £1,000 or, at the discretion of the court, to imprisonment for a term not exceeding twelve months, or to both the fine and the imprisonment, or

    (ii) on conviction on indictment, to a fine of such amount as the court considers appropriate or, at the discretion of the court, to imprisonment for a term not exceeding seven years, or to both the fine and the imprisonment.

(2) Subject to section 28 of this Act, every person guilty of an offence under section 6, 7, 16, 17, 19 or 20 of this Act shall be liable—

    (a) on summary conviction, to a fine not exceeding £1,000 or, at the discretion of the court, to imprisonment for a term not exceeding twelve months, or to both the fine and the imprisonment, or

    (b) on conviction on indictment, to a fine of such amount as the court considers appropriate or, at the discretion of the court, to imprisonment for a term not exceeding fourteen years, or to both the fine and the imprisonment.

(3) Subject to section 28 of this Act, every person guilty of an offence under section 15 of this Act shall be liable—

    (a) on summary conviction, to a fine not exceeding £1,000 or, at the discretion of the court, to imprisonment for a term not exceeding twelve months, or to both the fine and the imprisonment, or

    (b) on conviction on indictment, to a fine of such amount as the court considers appropriate or, at the discretion of the court, to imprisonment for life or such lesser period as the court shall determine, or, at such discretion, to both such fine and such lesser period of imprisonment.

[(3A) Every person guilty of an offence under section 15A or 15B of this Act shall be liable, on conviction on indictment—

    (a) to imprisonment for life or such shorter term as the court may determine, subject to subsections (3C) and (3D) of this section or, where subsection (3F) of this section applies, to that subsection, and

    (b) at the court's discretion, to a fine of such amount as the court considers appropriate.

(3B) The court, in imposing sentence on a person for an offence under section 15A or 15B of this Act, may, in particular, have regard to whether the person has a previous conviction for a drug trafficking offence.

(3C) Where a person (other than a person under the age of 18 years) is convicted of an offence under section 15A or 15B of this Act, the court shall, in imposing sentence, specify a term of not less than 10 years as the minimum term of imprisonment to be served by the person.

(3D) (a) The purpose of this subsection is to provide that in view of the harm caused to society by drug trafficking, a court, in imposing sentence on a person (other than a person under the age of 18 years) for an offence under section 15A or 15B of this Act, shall specify a term of not less than 10 years as the minimum term of imprisonment to be served by the person, unless the court determines that by reason of exceptional and specific circumstances relating to the offence, or the person convicted of the offence, it would be unjust in all the circumstances to do so.

(b) Subsection (3C) of this section shall not apply where the court is satisfied that there are exceptional and specific circumstances relating to the offence, or the person convicted of the offence, which would make a sentence of not less than 10 years imprisonment unjust in all the circumstances and for that purpose the court may, subject to this subsection, have regard to any matters it considers appropriate, including—

  (i) whether that person pleaded guilty to the offence and, if so—

    (I) the stage at which he or she indicated the intention to plead guilty, and

    (II) the circumstances in which the indication was given, and

  (ii) whether that person materially assisted in the investigation of the offence.

(c) The court, in considering for the purposes of paragraph (b) of this subsection whether a sentence of not less than 10 years imprisonment is unjust in all the circumstances, may have regard, in particular, to—

  (i) whether the person convicted of the offence concerned was previously convicted of a drug trafficking offence, and

  (ii) whether the public interest in preventing drug trafficking would be served by the imposition of a lesser sentence.

(3E) Subsections (3C) and (3D) of this section apply and have effect only in relation to a person convicted of a first offence under section 15A or 15B of this Act (other than a person who falls under paragraph (b) of subsection (3F) of this section), and accordingly references in those first-mentioned subsections to an offence under section 15A or 15B of this Act are to be construed as references to a first such offence.

(3F) Where a person (other than a person under the age of 18 years)—

  (a) is convicted of a second or subsequent offence under section 15A or 15B of this Act, or

  (b) is convicted of a first offence under one of those sections and has been convicted under the other of those sections,

the court shall, in imposing sentence, specify a term of not less than 10 years as the minimum term of imprisonment to be served by the person.

(3G) The power conferred by section 23 of the Criminal Justice Act 1951 to commute or remit a punishment shall not, in the case of a person serving a sentence imposed under subsection (3A) of this section, be exercised before the expiry of the minimum term specified by the court under subsection (3C) or (3F), as may be appropriate, of this section less any reduction of that term under subsection (3H) of this section.

(3H) The rules or practice whereby prisoners generally may earn remission of sentence by industry and good conduct shall apply in the case of a person serving a sentence imposed under subsection (3A) of this section and the minimum term specified by the court under subsection (3C) of this section shall be reduced by the amount of any remission so earned by the person.

(3I) Any powers conferred by rules made under section 2 of the Criminal Justice Act 1960 to release temporarily a person serving a sentence of imprisonment shall not, in the case of a person serving a sentence imposed under subsection (3A) of this section, be exercised during the term for which the commutation or remission of his or her punishment is prohibited by

ₗon (3G) of this section unless for a grave reason of a humanitarian nature, and any
rₑₗₑ₋ so granted shall be only of such limited duration as is justified by such reason.

(3J) In imposing a sentence on a person convicted of an offence under section 15A or 15B of this Act, a court—

    (a) may inquire whether at the time of the commission of the offence the person was addicted to one or more controlled drugs, and

    (b) if satisfied that the person was so addicted at that time and that the addiction was a substantial factor leading to the commission of the offence, may list the sentence for review after the expiry of not less than one-half of the term specified by the court under subsection (3C) or (3F), as may be appropriate, of this section.

(3K) On reviewing a sentence listed under subsection (3J)(b) of this section, the court—

    (a) may suspend the remainder of the sentence on any conditions it considers fit, and

    (b) in deciding whether to exercise its powers under this subsection, may have regard to any matters it considers appropriate.

(3L) Paragraph (a) of section 13(2) of the Criminal Procedure Act 1967 shall not apply in relation to an offence under section 15A or 15B of this Act, but each of those offences shall be deemed for the purposes of paragraph (b) of section 13(2) of that Act to be an offence to which section 13 of that Act applies.

(3M) The reference in subsection (3I) of this section to section 2 of the Criminal Justice Act 1960 shall be construed to include that section as applied by section 4 of the Prisons Act 1970.

(3N) In subsections (3B) and (3D) of this section 'drug trafficking offence' has the meaning it has in section 3(1) of the Criminal Justice Act 1994 and in subsection (3D) of this section 'drug trafficking' has the meaning it has in the said section 3(1).]²

(4) Subject to section 28 of this Act, every person guilty of an offence under section 18 of this Act shall be liable—

    (a) on summary conviction, to a fine not exceeding £400 or, at the discretion of the court, to imprisonment for a term not exceeding six months, or to both the fine and the imprisonment, or

    (b) on conviction on indictment, to a fine of such amount as the court considers appropriate or, at the discretion of the court, to imprisonment for a term not exceeding three years, or to both the fine and the imprisonment.

(5) Every person guilty of an offence under section 21(1) of this Act shall be liable to be punished on summary conviction as if he were guilty of the substantive offence and in case a penalty on conviction on indictment is provided by this Act in relation to the substantive offence, he shall be liable to be proceeded against on indictment and, if convicted, punished as it he were convicted on indictment of the substantive offence.

(6) Every person guilty of an offence under section 21(2) of this Act shall be liable—

    (a) in case the regulation in relation to which the offence was committed is a regulation made pursuant to section 5(a) of this Act, other than a regulation regulating the transportation of controlled drugs,

        (i) on summary conviction, to a fine not exceeding £1,000 or, at the discretion of the court, to imprisonment for a term not exceeding twelve months, or to both the fine and the imprisonment, or

> > (ii) on conviction on indictment, to a fine of such amount as the court considers appropriate or, at the discretion of the court, to imprisonment for a term not exceeding fourteen years, or to both the fine and the imprisonment, and

> (b) in case the regulation in relation to which the offence was committed is a regulation made otherwise than under the said section 5(1)(a) or is a regulation regulating the transportation of controlled drugs—

> > (i) on summary conviction, to a fine not exceeding £500 or, at the discretion of the court, to imprisonment for a term not exceeding six months, or to both the fine and the imprisonment, or

> > (ii) on conviction on indictment, to a fine of such amount as the court considers appropriate, or at the discretion of the court, to imprisonment for a term not exceeding two years, or to both the fine and the imprisonment.

(7) Every person guilty of an offence under section 21 of this Act, other than an offence mentioned in subsection (1) or subsection (2) of that section, shall be liable on summary conviction to a fine not exceeding £400 or, at the discretion of the court, to imprisonment for a term not exceeding six months, or to both the fine and the imprisonment.

(8) Every person guilty of an offence under paragraph (a) or (b) of subsection (1D) of section 23 of this Act, as amended by section 12 of the Misuse of Drugs Act, 1984, shall be liable on summary conviction to a fine not exceeding £200.

(9) Every person guilty of an offence under section 5 of the Misuse of Drugs Act, 1984, shall on summary conviction be liable—

> (a) in case the offence is an offence under subsection (2) of that section, to a fine not exceeding £1,000,

> (b) in any other case, to a fine not exceeding £500.

(10) ....

(11) ....]¹

(12) In this section—

> "relevant controlled drug" means the controlled drug in relation to which the offence was committed;

> "substantive offence" means the offence under this Act to which the attempt or, as the case may be, the aiding, abetting, counselling, procuring, soliciting or incitement was directed.

Amendments

1   Subsections (1)–(9) were substituted and sub-ss (10)–(11) were deleted by Misuse of Drugs Act 1984, s 6.

2   Subsections (3A)–(3J) inserted by Criminal Justice Act 1999, s 5, amended by Criminal Justice Act 2006, s 84 and sub-ss (3A)–(3N) were substituted by Criminal Justice Act 2007, s 33.

Power of court to remand persons convicted under section 3, 15, 16, 17 or 18 and to obtain a report and in certain cases to arrange for the medical treatment or for the care of such persons

(1) (a) Where a person is convicted of an offence under section 3 of this Act, other than a first or second offence in relation to which a penalty may be imposed under section 27(a) of this Act, or an offence under section 15 or 16 of this Act, or of attempting to commit any such offence, [if, having regard to the circumstances of the case, the court considers it appropriate so to do, the court may]¹ remand the person for such period as it considers necessary for the purposes of this section (being a period not exceeding eight days in the case of a remand in custody), and request [the Health Service Executive]², [probation and welfare]³ officer or other body or person, considered by the court to be appropriate, to—

    (i) cause to be furnished to the court a medical report in writing on the convicted person together with such recommendations (if any) as to medical treatment which the person making the report considers appropriate to the needs [, arising because of his being dependent on drugs,]⁴ of the convicted person, and

    (ii) furnish to the court a report in writing as to the vocational and educational circumstances and social background of the convicted person together with such recommendations (if any) as to care which the body or person making the report considers appropriate to the said needs.

  (b) Where a person is convicted of a first or second offence under section 3 of this Act in relation to which a penalty may be imposed under the said section 27(1)(a) or an offence under section 17 or 18 of this Act, or of attempting to commit any such offence, and the court, having regard to the circumstances of the case, considers it appropriate so to do, the court may remand the person [on bail or, unless a penalty falls to be imposed on the person under paragraph (a) of section 27(1) of this Act, in custody]⁵ for such period as it considers necessary for the purposes of this section, and request [the Health Service Executive]², [probation and welfare]³ officer or other body or person, considered by the court to be appropriate, to—

    (i) cause to be furnished to the court a medical report in writing on the convicted person together with such recommendations (if any) as to medical treatment which the person making the report considers appropriate to the needs [, arising because of his being dependent on drugs,]⁴ of the convicted person, and

    (ii) furnish to the court a report in writing as to the vocational and educational circumstances and social background of the convicted person together with such recommendations (if any) as to care which the body or person making the report considers appropriate to the said needs.

(2) Having considered the reports furnished pursuant to subsection (1) of this section, the court shall, if in its opinion the welfare of the convicted person warrants its so doing, instead of imposing a penalty under section 27 of this Act, but subject to subsection (8) of this section either—

(a) permit the person concerned to enter into a recognisance containing such of the following conditions as the court considers appropriate having regard to the circumstances of the case and the welfare of the person, namely—

    (i) a condition that the person concerned be placed under the supervision of such body (including [the Health Service Executive][2],) or person as may be named in the order and during a period specified in the order,

   [(ia) in case the person concerned is placed under such supervision, a condition requiring such person, at the place at which he normally resides or at such other place as may be specified in the order and during such period and at such intervals as shall be so specified, to receive visits from and permit visits by—

      (I) in case such person is placed under the supervision of a body, an officer of that body,

     (II) in case such person is placed under the supervision of a person, that person,][6]

   (ii) a condition requiring such person to undergo medical [or other][7] treatment recommended in the report,

  (iii) a condition requiring such person for such treatment to attend or remain in a hospital, clinic or other place specified in the order for a period so specified,

  (iv) a condition requiring the person to attend a specified course of education, instruction or training, being a course which, if undergone by such person, would, in the opinion of the court, improve his vocational opportunities or social circumstances, facilitate his social rehabilitation or reduce the likelihood of his committing a further offence under this Act, or

(b) order that the person be detained in custody in a designated custodial treatment centre for a period not exceeding the maximum period of imprisonment which the court may impose in respect of the offence to which the conviction relates, or one year, whichever is the shorter.

(3) A court may, if it thinks fit, consider otherwise than in public—

(a) a report under subsection (1) of this section,

(b) whether or not it will permit a person to enter into a recognisance mentioned in subsection (2) of this section, or

(c) whether or not it will make an order referred to in paragraph (b) of subsection (2) of this section.

(4) In any proceedings in which a report furnished under subsection (1) of this section is considered, the court may, if it believes that it is in the interests of the person concerned not to know the contents of the report, withhold from him the report, but the foregoing shall not be construed as preventing any barrister or solicitor who appears on such person's behalf in the proceedings seeing the report or, if thought fit, questioning or commenting on any of its contents in the proceedings.

(5) Where it is alleged to the court that a person has been in breach of a recognisance entered into by him under subsection (2) of this section, the court, notwithstanding the decision by it under the said subsection (2), may direct that the person be brought before the court, and, if satisfied that the person has been in breach of the recognisance, may estreat the recognisance and, subject to subsection (8) of this section, either make in respect of the person an order

to in paragraph (b) of subsection (2) of this section or proceed to deal with the case
... rdance with the provisions of section 27 of this Act as if the decision had not been
made.

(6) If at any time during a period of detention in a designated custodial treatment centre it
appears to the court, on an application made by or on behalf either of the prosecutor or the
person who is being detained, or on receipt of a message, in a form approved of by the
Minister, from an authorised medical practitioner [or the person who is for the time being in
charge of such centre]⁸, that the person being detained under this Act is not then, or may not
then be, in further need of the treatment or care of which the court formerly considered him
to be in need, or that his continued detention in custody in the designated custodial treatment
centre is not then, or may not then be, in his best interests or in the best interests of other
persons in that centre, the court, notwithstanding its decision under subsection (2) of this
section, may order the person to be brought before the court.

(7) Where a person is brought before the court pursuant to an order under subsection (6) of
this section, the court may inquire into the case and hear such evidence as it considers
relevant, and if, having considered the circumstances of the case, the court is satisfied that
the person is not then in further need of the treatment or care referred to in subsection (6) of
this section, or that his continued detention in custody in the designated custodial treatment
centre would not be in his best interests or in the best interests of other persons in that centre,
the court, notwithstanding its decision under subsection (2) of this section, may revoke the
relevant order made by it under the said subsection (2) and, subject to subsection (8) of this
section,

(a) permit the person to enter into a recognisance described in the said subsection (2) if
the court is of the opinion that the welfare of the person warrants its so doing, or

(b) order the person to be detained for a period not exceeding the unexpired portion of
the period specified in the revoked order in a custodial treatment centre other than
that so specified, or

(c) decide not to impose any penalty under section 27 of this Act, or

(d) where it considers it appropriate so to do and subject to subsection (9) of this
section, proceed to deal with the offence in accordance with section 27 of this Act.

(8) The court shall not under this section either,

(a) permit a person to enter into a recognisance containing a condition requiring him
for [medical or other treatment]⁹ to remain in a specified hospital, clinic or other
place, or

(b) order a person to be detained in a custodial treatment centre,

unless, after consultation with, or consideration of a report of, either [the medical practitioner
or other person]⁹ in charge of the hospital, clinic, custodial treatment centre or other place
concerned or a [medical practitioner or other person]⁸ nominated by [the medical practitioner
or other person]⁹ so in charge, the court is satisfied that the giving or making of the
permission or order would be an appropriate course having regard to the needs of the person
and would not prejudicially affect the ability of such hospital, clinic, custodial treatment
centre or other place to provide for the treatment or care of persons.

(9) In case a court decides, pursuant to subsection (7) of this section, to impose a sentence of
imprisonment under section 27 of this Act, the period of imprisonment which may be so
imposed shall not exceed the period by which the maximum term of imprisonment which

that court could otherwise have imposed under the said section 27 for the offence of which the person was convicted exceeds the period already spent by him in custody on foot of the order revoked by the court.

(10) The Minister may by order designate an institution which in his opinion is suitable for the medical treatment or the care of persons in respect of whom an order may be made under this section, or a specified part of such an institution, as a designated custodial treatment centre for the purpose of this section.

(11) In this section—

> "authorised medical practitioner" means a registered medical practitioner authorised for the purposes of this section by the Minister in writing or a registered medical practitioner of a class specified by the Minister as being authorised for the said purposes;
>
> ["probation and welfare officer" means an officer employed in the probation and welfare service of the Department of Justice;][10]
>
> [...].[11]

Amendments

1   Words substituted by Misuse of Drugs Act 1984, s 14(b).
2   Words amended by Health Act 2004, s 75 and Sch 6.
3   Words substituted by Misuse of Drugs Act 1984, s 14(d).
4   Words inserted by Misuse of Drugs Act 1984, s 14(c).
5   Words substituted by Misuse of Drugs Act 1984, s 14(e).
6   Subparagraph (ia) inserted by Misuse of Drugs Act 1984, s 14(f).
7   Words inserted by Misuse of Drugs Act 1984, s 14(g).
8   Words inserted by Misuse of Drugs Act 1984, s 14(h).
9   Words substituted by Misuse of Drugs Act 1984, s 14(i).
10 Definition of "probation and welfare officer" inserted by Misuse of Drugs Act 1984, s 14(j).
11 Definition deleted by Health Act 2004, s 75 and Sch 6.

29   Defences generally

[(1) In any proceedings for an offence under this Act or an offence under section 34 of the Criminal Justice Act, 1994 in which it is proved that the defendant had in his possession or supplied a controlled drug, the defendant shall not be acquitted of the offence charged by reason only of proving that he neither knew nor suspected nor had reason to suspect that the substance, product or preparation in question was the particular controlled drug alleged.][1]

(2) In any such proceedings in which it is proved that the defendant had in his possession a controlled drug, or a forged prescription, or a duly issued prescription altered with intent to deceive, it shall be a defence to prove that—

(a)   he did not know and had no reasonable grounds for suspecting—

(i)   that what he had in his possession was a controlled drug or such a prescription, as may be appropriate, or

    (ii) that he was in possession of a controlled drug or such a prescription, as may be appropriate, or

(b) he believed the substance, product or preparation to be a controlled drug, or a controlled drug of a particular class or description, and that, if the substance, product or preparation had in fact been that controlled drug or a controlled drug of that class or description, he would not at the material time have been committing an offence under this Act, or

(c) knowing or suspecting it to be such a drug or prescription, he took or retained possession of it for the purpose of—

    (i) preventing another from committing or continuing to commit an offence in relation to the drug or document, as may be appropriate, or

    (ii) delivering it into the custody of a person lawfully entitled to take custody of it,

and that as soon as practicable he took all such steps as were reasonably open to him to destroy the drug or document or to deliver it into the custody of such a person.

[(3) In any proceedings for an offence under section 15 or 15A, or subsection (1)(d) of section 15C, of this Act, a defendant may rebut the presumption raised by subsection (2) of the said section 15 or 15A or subsection (3) of the said section 15C, as the case may be, by showing that at the time of the alleged offence, he or she was by virtue of regulations made under section 4 of this Act lawfully in possession of the controlled drug or drugs to which the proceedings relate.][2]

(4) In any proceedings for an offence under section 19 of this Act it shall be a defence to show that the defendant took steps to prevent the occurrence or continuance of the activity or contravention to which the alleged offence relates and that, in the particular circumstances, the steps were taken as soon as practicable and were reasonable.

(5) In any proceedings for an offence under section 16, 17 or 21(2) of this Act, it shall be a defence for the defendant to prove that he neither knew of nor suspected nor had reason to suspect the existence of some fact alleged by the prosecutor which it is necessary for the prosecutor to prove if he is to be convicted of the offence charged.

(6) In any proceedings for an attempt to commit an offence under this Act the defences mentioned in subsection (2) or (5) of this section shall, with the necessary modifications, be open to the defendant.

(7) Subject to subsection (1) of this section nothing in this section shall prevent a person raising a defence which, apart from this section, would be open to him to raise in proceedings for an offence under this Act.

Amendments

1 Subsection (1) was substituted by Criminal Justice Act 1994, s 34(5).

2 Subsection (3) was substituted by Criminal Justice Act 1999, s 6 and further substituted by Criminal Justice Act 2006, s 85.

30   Forfeiture

[(1) Subject to subsection (2) of this section, a court by which a person is convicted of an offence under this Act or a drug trafficking offence (within the meaning of the Criminal Justice Act, 1994), may order anything shown to the satisfaction of the court to relate to the offence to be forfeited and either destroyed or dealt with in such other manner as the court thinks fit.]¹

(2) A court shall not order anything to be forfeited under this section if a person claiming to be the owner of or otherwise interested in it applies to be heard by the court, unless an opportunity has been given to him to show cause why the order should not be made.

Amendments

1   Subsection (1) substituted by Criminal Justice Act 1994, s 62.

31   Offences in relation to bodies corporate

Where an offence under this Act is committed by a body corporate or by a person purporting to act on behalf of a body corporate and is proved to have been so committed with the consent, connivance or approval of, or to have been facilitated by any neglect on the part of, any director, manager, secretary or other official of such body, such person shall also be guilty of the offence.

32   Poisons for purposes of Pharmacy Acts, 1875 to 1962

[...]¹

Amendments

1   Section 32 repealed by Pharmacy Act 2007, s 4(1) and Sch 4.

33   Amendment of Poisons Act, 1961

(1) The Poisons Act, 1961, shall be amended as follows:
    (a)   section 4(1) is hereby amended by—
          (i)   the addition of "and one of whom is a person with knowledge and experience of the manufacture of preparations containing poisons" to paragraph (b), and
          (ii) the insertion of the following paragraph after paragraph (c),
                "(cc) one person who is a fellow, ordinary member or licentiate of the Institute of Chemistry of Ireland;";
    (b)   section 14(3) is hereby amended by the substitution of the following paragraphs for paragraphs (j) to (l):
          "(j) provide for the enforcement and execution of the provisions of the regulations—

    (i)   by officers of the Minister,

    (ii)   with the consent of the Minister for Agriculture, by officers of that Minister,

    (iii) by the Pharmaceutical Society of Ireland and its officers, and

    (iv) by health boards and their officers,

(k) enable any such officer (with, in the case of an officer of the Minister or the Minister for Agriculture, a written authorisation of whichever of those Ministers is appropriate, in the case of an officer of the Pharmaceutical Society of Ireland, a written authorisation of that Society, and in the case of an officer of a health board, a written authorisation of the board), at all reasonable times, for the purpose of ascertaining whether or not there is or has been a contravention of the regulations, to enter premises of a class or description specified in the regulations and to inspect any substance or article which is so specified and require the production of and inspect, and if he thinks fit take copies of any entry in, any book, record or other document which is of a class or description so specified,

(l) provide for the taking (without payment) by such officers, with such authorisation, of samples of poisons or such substances for test, examination or analysis,

(m) prescribe the certificate or other evidence to be given of the result of any such test, examination or analysis and the classes of person by whom such certificate or evidence is to be given,

(n) provide that any certificate or other evidence specified under paragraph (m) of this subsection and given in respect of the test, examination or analysis of a sample shall with regard to that sample be evidence for all purposes of the result,

(o) provide for the prosecution of offences under section 17 of this Act in relation to the regulations by the Minister, the Pharmaceutical Society of Ireland or health boards, and

(p) provide for matters ancillary to the foregoing matters.";

(c) the following new section is hereby inserted after section 15:

"Evidence of result of certain tests, examinations or analyses.

"15A.—Whenever regulations made under this Act provide that a certificate or other evidence is to be evidence for all purposes of a result of a test, examination or analysis of a sample, such certificate or other evidence shall until the contrary is shown, in relation to that sample, be accepted by a court as sufficient evidence of the result of the test, examination or analysis.".

(2) Regulations under section 14 or section 15 of the Poisons Act, 1961, may provide that a substance which is declared to be a poison for the purposes of those regulations or a provision thereof, shall, for the purposes of whichever of the said sections is appropriate and the regulations or provision to which the declaration relates, be regarded in circumstances specified in the regulations as not being the subject of the declaration.

34   Amendment of section 2 of Pharmacy Act, 1962

Section 2 of the Pharmacy Act, 1962, is hereby amended by the substitution of the following subsection for subsection (4):

"(4) It shall not be a contravention of subsection (2) of this section for a person to keep open shop for the sale of a substance which is declared to be a poison for the purposes of regulations made under section 14 of the Poisons Act, 1961, if the person is a person, or a member of a class of persons, by whom pursuant to such regulations the substance may be sold or offered or kept for sale.".

35   Amendment of Pharmacopoeia Act, 1931

(1) The Pharmacopoeia Act, 1931, is hereby amended as follows:

(a) section 2(1) shall be construed and have effect as if the reference therein to the Council were a reference to the Minister for Health;

(b) the following subsection shall be substituted for subsection (2) of section 2:

"(2) The Minister for Health may by regulations make such modifications (by way of deletion, addition or amendment) in the British Pharmacopoeia for the time being in force in Great Britain as he thinks fit.";

(c) the following subsection shall be substituted for subsection (2) of section 3:

"(2) A certificate endorsed on a book purporting to be a copy of the British Pharmacopoeia and purporting to be signed by an officer of the Minister for Health that such book is a copy of the British Pharmacopoeia in force in Great Britain on a specified day or days, or during a specified period, shall in any legal proceedings until the contrary is shown be admitted as evidence of the facts so certified, and in such proceedings it shall not be necessary to prove the signature of the person purporting to sign the certificate or that the person was an officer of the said Minister."; and

(d) the following new section shall be inserted after section 4:

"Regulations.

4A.—Every regulation made under this Act shall be laid before each House of the Oireachtas as soon as may be after it is made and, if a resolution annulling the regulation is passed by either such House within the next twenty-one days on which that House has sat after the regulation is laid before it, the regulation shall be annulled accordingly, but without prejudice to anything previously done thereunder.".

(2) As on and from the specified day section 4 of the Pharmacopoeia Act, 1931, shall be construed and have effect as if—

(a) "or the European Pharmacopoeia" were inserted after "Saorstát Éireann Pharmacopoeia " in subsection (1), and

(b) the following subsection were added to the section:

"(3) In this section 'the European Pharmacopoeia' means the Pharmacopoeia elaborated under the auspices of the Council of Europe in pursuance of the Convention in that behalf done at Strasbourg on the 22nd day of July, 1964.".

(3) In this section "the specified day" means the day specified for the purposes of this section in a notice published by the Minister in the *Iris Oifigiúil*.

36   Amendment of section 65 of Health Act, 1947

Section 65 of the Health Act, 1947, as amended by section 39 of the Health Act, 1953, and section 6 of the Health Act, 1970, is hereby amended by—

(a) the substitution of the following paragraphs for paragraph (j) of subsection (3):

   "(j) the enforcement and execution of the regulations—

      (i)   by officers of the Minister,

      (ii)   by health boards and their officers,

      (iii) with the consent of the Minister for Finance, by officers of Customs and Excise,

      (iv)   with the consent of the Minister for Industry and Commerce, by officers of that Minister,

      (v)   by the Pharmaceutical Society of Ireland and its officers;

   (k) the enabling for the purpose of ascertaining whether or not there is or has been a contravention of the regulations, of any such officer (with, in the case of an officer of the Minister or the Minister for Industry and Commerce or an officer of Customs and Excise, a written authorisation of whichever of those Ministers or the Minister for Finance is appropriate, in the case of an officer of a health board, a written authorisation of the board and in the case of an officer of the Pharmaceutical Society of Ireland, a written authorisation of that Society), at all reasonable times to enter any premises which are of a class or description specified in the regulations and to inspect or examine any substance or article which is of a class or description so specified and require the production of and inspect, and if he thinks fit, to take copies of any entry in, any book, record or other document which is of a prescribed class or description;

   (l) the taking (without payment) by such officers, with such authorisation, of samples of such substances or articles for test, examination or analysis;

   (m) the prescribing of the certificate or other evidence to be given of the result of any such test, examination or analysis and the classes of person by whom such certificate or evidence is to be given; and

   (n) providing that any certificate or other evidence specified under paragraph (m) of this subsection and given in respect of the test, examination or analysis of a sample shall with regard to that sample be evidence for all purposes of the result.", and

(b) the substitution of the following subsection for subsection (5):

   "(5) An offence under this section may be prosecuted by the Minister, the Pharmaceutical Society of Ireland or by the health board in whose functional area the offence is committed.".

37   Service etc. of notices

(1) Where a notice or other document is required or authorised by this Act or by regulations under this Act to be served on or given or sent to a person, it may be served on or given or sent to him—

(a) by delivering it to him,

(b) in the case of a person other than a body corporate, by sending it by post in an envelope addressed to him at the address at which he ordinarily resides or carries on business, or

(c) in the case of a body corporate, by sending it by post in an envelope addressed to the secretary or principal officer of the body at the address at which the body carries on business.

(2) For the purposes of subsection (1) of this section, a company registered under the Companies Act, 1963, shall be deemed to carry on business at its registered offices and every other body corporate and every unincorporated body of persons shall be deemed to carry on business at its principal office or place of business.

38   Regulations generally; laying of orders

(1) The Minister may make regulations for prescribing any matter referred to in this Act as prescribed, provided that in so far as any such regulations provide for the charging of fees they shall only be made with the consent of the Minister for Finance.

(2) Regulations under this Act may apply to controlled drugs generally, to controlled drugs of a prescribed class or description, or to one or more prescribed controlled drugs.

(3) Every regulation and every order made under this Act (other than an order under section 8(8) or an order referred to in section 11 or section 28) shall be laid before each House of the Oireachtas as soon as may be after it is made and, if a resolution annulling the regulation or order is passed by either such House within the next twenty-one days on which that House has sat after the regulation or order is laid before it, the regulation or order, as the case may be, shall be annulled accordingly but without prejudice to the validity of anything previously done thereunder.

39   Expenses

The expenses incurred by the Minister in the administration of this Act shall, to such extent as may be sanctioned by the Minister for Finance, be paid out of moneys provided by the Oireachtas.

40   Collection and disposal of moneys payable under Act

(1) All moneys payable under regulations under this Act shall be collected and taken in such manner as the Minister for Finance may from time to time direct and shall be paid into or disposed of for the benefit of the Exchequer in accordance with the directions of the Minister for Finance.

(2) The Public Offices Fees Act, 1879, shall not apply in respect of moneys mentioned in subsection (1) of this section and payable to the Minister.

41   Repeal of Dangerous Drugs Act, 1934, and transitional provision

(1) The Dangerous Drugs Act, 1934, is hereby repealed.

(2) In case a provision of this Act other than subsection (1) of this section, comes into force on a day which is earlier than the day on which the said subsection (1) comes into force, the following provisions shall have effect, namely, as regards the period beginning on the day on which the first-mentioned provision comes into force and ending on the day on which the said subsection (1) comes into force, an act or omission which is an offence under this Act shall not be an offence under the Dangerous Drugs Act, 1934.

42   Miscellaneous repeals and transitional provisions

(1) The following are hereby repealed:

(a)   (i) "by the General Council of Medical Education and Registration of the United Kingdom " in section 1 of the Pharmacopoeia Act, 1931, and

    (ii) section 2(3) of that Act; and

(b) section 78 of the Health Act, 1970.

(2) Notwithstanding subsection (1) of this section, the Minister may by regulations provide—

(a) that a register specified in the regulations and kept by him under regulations made under section 78 of the Health Act, 1970, shall be included in and shall be deemed to be part of a register to be kept by him for the purposes of regulations under this Act, or

(b) that any person, being a person whose name was, immediately before the commencement of this section, on a register specified in the regulations and kept by the Minister under the said section 78, shall be deemed to have been granted, issued or given, as may be appropriate, such licence, permit or other form of authority under this Act as may be specified in the regulations.

(3) Notwithstanding section 41(1) of this Act, the Minister may by regulations provide that any person who was, immediately before the commencement of this section, the holder of a licence, permit or other authority granted, issued or given under the Dangerous Drugs Act, 1934, shall be deemed to have been granted, issued or given, as may be appropriate, such licence, permit or other form of authority under this Act as may be specified in the regulations.

(4) Regulations made under this section which include provisions mentioned in paragraph (b) of subsection (2) or in subsection (3) of this section may also include—

(a) provisions deeming any such licence, permit or other form of authority to have been granted, issued or given subject to conditions specified in the regulations, and

(b) provisions enabling the Minister in specified circumstances to direct that provisions of regulations under this section shall cease to apply in relation to a particular person.

(5) Where the Minister duly gives a direction referred to in subsection (4)(b) of this section, the provisions specified in the direction shall in accordance with the direction cease to apply in relation to the person to whom the direction relates.

43   Short title, commencement and collective citations

(1) This Act may be cited as the Misuse of Drugs Act, 1977.

(2) Subsection (1) of this section and section 41(2) of this Act shall come into operation on the passing hereof and the other purposes and provisions of this Act shall come into operation on such day or days as may be fixed therefor by any order or orders of the Minister, either generally or with reference to any particular such purpose or provision and different days may be so fixed for different such purposes and different such provisions of this Act.

(3) The Pharmacy Acts, 1875 to 1962, and sections 32 and 34 of this Act may be cited together as the Pharmacy Acts, 1875 to 1977.

(4) The Pharmacopoeia Act, 1931, section 35 of this Act, and section 42 of this Act in so far as it amends that Act, may be cited together as the Pharmacopoeia Acts, 1931 and 1977.

(5) The Health Acts, 1947 to 1970, section 36 of this Act, and section 42 of this Act in so far as it amends those Acts, may be cited together as the Health Acts, 1947 to 1977.

(6) The Poisons Act, 1961, and section 33 of this Act may be cited together as the Poisons Acts, 1961 and 1977.

SCHEDULE

CONTROLLED DRUGS

1. Acetorphine

       Acetyldihydrocodeine.

       Acetylmethadol.

       Allylprodine.

       Alphacetylmethadol.

       Alphameprodine.

       Alphamethadol.

       Alphaprodine.

       Amphetamine.

       Amylobarbitone.

       Anileridine.

       Benzethidine.

       Benzphetamine.

       Benzylmorphine (3-benzylmorphine).

       Betacetylmethadol.

       Betameprodine.

       Betamethadol.

       Betaprodine.

       Bezitramide.

       Bufotenine.

       Cannabinol, except where contained in cannabis or cannabis resin.

       Cannabinol derivatives.

       Cannabis and cannabis resin.

       Chlorphentermine.

       Clonitazene.

       Coca leaf.

       Cocaine.

       Codeine.

       Codoxime.

       Desomorphine.

       Dexamphetamine.

       Dextromoramide.

       Diamorphine.

       Diampromide.

       Diethylthiambutene.

       Difenoxin.

       Dihydrocodeine.

       Dihydromorphine.

Dimenoxadole.

Dimepheptanol.

Dimethylthiambutene.

Dioxaphetyl butyrate.

Diphenoxylate.

Dipipanone.

Drotebanol.

Ecgonine, and any derivative of ecgonine which is convertible to ecgonine or to cocaine.

Ethylmethylthiambutene.

Ethylmorphine (3-ethylmorphine).

Etonitazene.

Etorphine.

Etoxeridine.

Fentanyl.

Furethidine.

Hydrocodone.

Hydromorphinol.

Hydromorphone.

Hydroxypethidine.

Isomethadone.

Ketobemidone.

Levomethorphan.

Levomoramide.

Levophenacylmorphan.

Levorphanol.

Lysergamide.

Lysergide and other N-alkyl derivatives of lysergamide.

Mephentermine.

Mescaline.

Metazocine.

Methadone.

Methaqualone.

Methylamphetamine.

Methyldesorphine.

Methyldihydromorphine (6-methyldihydromorphine).

Methylphenidate.

Metopon.

Morpheridine.

Morphine.

Morphine methobromide, morphine N-oxide and other pentavalent nitrogen morphine derivatives.

Myrophine.

Nicocodine.

Nicodicodine (6-nicotinoyldihydrocodeine).

Nicomorphine.

Noracymethadol.

Norcodeine.

Norlevorphanol.

Normethadone.

Normorphine.

Norpipanone.

Opium, whether raw, prepared or medicinal.

Oxycodone.

Oxymorphone.

Pentobarbitone.

Pethidine.

Phenadoxone.

Phenampromide.

Phenazocine.

Phendimetrazine.

Phenmetrazine.

Phenobarbitone.

Phenomorphan.

Phenoperidine.

Pholcodine.

Piminodine.

Pipradrol.

Piritramide.

Poppy straw and concentrate of poppy straw.

Proheptazine.

Properidine.

Propiram.

Psilocin.

Quinalbarbitone.

Racemethorphan.

Racemoramide.

Racemorphan.

Thebacon.

Thebaine.

Trimeperidine.

4-Cyano-2-dimethylamino-4, 4-diphenylbutane.

4-Cyano-1-methyl-4-phenylpiperidine.

N, N-Diethyltryptamine.

N, N-Dimethyltryptamine.

2, 5-Dimethoxy- *a*, 4-dimethyl-phenethylamine.

1-Methyl-4-phenylpiperidine-4-carboxylic acid.

2-Methyl-3-morpholino-1, 1-diphenylpropanecarboxylic acid.

4-Phenylpiperidine-4-carboxylic acid ethyl ester.

2. Any stereoisomeric form of a substance or product specified in paragraph 1 of this Schedule not being dextromethorphan or dextrorphan.

3. Any ester or ether of a substance or product specified in paragraph 1 or 2 of this Schedule.

4. Any salt of a substance or product specified in paragraph 1, 2 or 3 of this Schedule.

5. Any preparation or product containing any proportion of a substance or product specified in paragraph 1, 2, 3 or 4 of this Schedule.

6. In this Schedule—

"cannabinol derivatives" means the following substances, except where contained in cannabis or cannabis resin, namely, tetrahydro derivatives of cannabinol and 3-alkyl homologues of cannabinol or of its tetrahydro derivatives;

"coca leaf" means the leaf of any plant of the genus *Erythroxylon* from whose leaves cocaine can be extracted either directly or by chemical transformation;

"concentrate of poppy straw" means the material produced when poppy straw has entered into a process for the concentration of its alkaloids;

"medicinal opium" means raw opium which has undergone the process necessary to adapt it for medicinal use in accordance with the requirements of the Irish Pharmacopoeia, whether it is in the form of powder or is granulated or is in any other form, and whether it is or is not mixed with neutral substances;

"poppy straw" means all parts, except the seeds, of the opium poppy, after mowing;

"raw opium" includes powdered or granulated opium but does not include medicinal opium.

Criminal Law (Rape) Act 1981

Number 10 of 1981

ARRANGEMENT OF SECTIONS

Section

1. Interpretation.

2. Meaning of "rape".

3. Restrictions on evidence at trials for rape offences.

4. Proceedings under Part IA of the Criminal Procedure Act, 1967.

4A Legal representation for complainants.

5. Trials of juveniles.

6. Exclusion of the public.

7. Anonymity of complainants.

8. Anonymity of accused.

9. Trials by court-martial.

10. Punishment of indecent assault on female.

11. Penalty for publication of unauthorised matter.

12. Summary jurisdiction.

13. Short title and commencement.

AN ACT TO AMEND THE LAW RELATING TO RAPE AND INDECENT ASSAULT ON FEMALES. [6th May, 1981]

BE IT ENACTED BY THE OIREACHTAS AS FOLLOWS:

1   Interpretation

(1) In this Act—

'aggravated sexual assault', 'rape under section 4' and 'sexual assault' have the meanings respectively assigned to them by the Criminal Law (Rape) (Amendment) Act, 1990;

'complainant' means a person in relation to whom a sexual assault offence is alleged to have been committed;

'a rape offence' means any of the following, namely, rape, attempted rape, burglary with intent to commit rape, aiding, abetting, counselling and procuring rape, attempted rape or burglary with intent to commit rape, and incitement to rape and, other than in sections 2(2) and 8 of this Act, rape under section 4. attempted rape under section 4. aiding, abetting, counselling and procuring rape under section 4 or attempted rape under section 4 and incitement to rape under section 4;

'a sexual assault offence' means a rape offence and any of the following, namely, aggravated sexual assault, attempted aggravated sexual assault, sexual assault, attempted sexual assault, aiding, abetting, counselling and procuring aggravated sexual assault, attempted aggravated sexual assault, sexual assault or attempted sexual assault, incitement to aggravated sexual assault or sexual assault and conspiracy to commit any of the foregoing offences.]¹

(2) In this Act references to sexual intercourse shall be construed as references to carnal knowledge as defined in section 63 of the Offences against the Person Act, 1861, so far as it relates to natural intercourse (under which such intercourse is deemed complete on proof of penetration only).

(3) In this Act "man" and "woman" include respectively a male and a female person of any age; [...]².

Amendments

1   Subsection (1) substituted by Criminal Law (Rape) (Amendment) Act 1990, s 12.

2   Words repealed by Criminal Law (Rape) (Amendment) Act 1990, s 21 and Sch.

---

2   Meaning of "rape"

(1) A man commits rape if—

  (a) he has [...]¹ sexual intercourse with a woman who at the time of the intercourse does not consent to it, and

  (b) at that time he knows that she does not consent to the intercourse or he is reckless as to whether she does or does not consent to it,

and references to rape in this Act and any other enactment shall be construed accordingly.

(2) It is hereby declared that if at a trial for a rape offence the jury has to consider whether a man believed that a woman was consenting to sexual intercourse, the presence or absence of reasonable grounds for such a belief is a matter to which the jury is to have regard, in conjunction with any other relevant matters, in considering whether he so believed.

Amendments

1   Word 'unalwful' deleted by Criminal Law (Rape) (Amendment) Act 1990, s 21 and Sch.

---

3   Restrictions on evidence at trials for rape offences

[(1) If at a trial any person is for the time being charged with a sexual assault offence to which he pleads not guilty, then, except with the leave of the judge, no evidence shall be adduced and no question shall be asked in cross-examination at the trial, by or on behalf of any accused person at the trial, about any sexual experience (other than that to which the charge relates) of a complainant with any person; and in relation to a sexual assault tried summarily pursuant to section 12—

  (a) subsection (2)(a) shall have effect as if the words 'in the absence of the jury' were omitted,

  (b) subsection (2)(b) shall have effect as if for the references to the jury there were substituted references to the court, and

    (c)   this section (other than this paragraph) and subsections (3) and (4) of section 7 shall have effect as if for the references to the judge there were substituted references to the court.]¹

(2) (a) The judge shall not give leave in pursuance of subsection (1) for any evidence or question except on an application made to him, in the absence of the jury, by or on behalf of an accused person.

    (b) The judge shall give leave if, and only if, he is satisfied that it would be unfair to the accused person to refuse to allow the evidence to be adduced or the question to be asked, that is to say, if he is satisfied that, on the assumption that if the evidence or question was not allowed the jury might reasonably be satisfied beyond reasonable doubt that the accused person is guilty, the effect of allowing the evidence or question might reasonably be that they would not be so satisfied.

(3) If, notwithstanding that the judge has given leave in accordance with this section for any evidence to be adduced or question to be asked in cross-examination, it appears to the judge that any question asked or proposed to be asked (whether in the course of so adducing evidence or of cross-examination) in reliance on the leave which he has given is not or may not be such as may properly be asked in accordance with that leave, he may direct that the question shall not be asked or, if asked, that it shall not be answered except in accordance with his leave given on a fresh application under this section.

(4) Nothing in this section authorises evidence to be adduced or a question to be asked which cannot be adduced or asked apart from this section.

Amendments

1   Subsection (1) substituted by Criminal Law (Rape) (Amendment) Act 1990, s 13.

[4   **Proceedings under Part IA of the Criminal Procedure Act, 1967.**

(1) In a proceeding under Part IA of the Criminal Procedure Act, 1967, relating to—

    (a) the dismissal of a charge of a sexual assault offence, or

    (b) the taking of a person's evidence by way of deposition in the case of a sexual assault offence.

then, except with leave of the judge conducting the proceeding, evidence shall not be adduced and a question shall not be asked which, if the proceeding were a trial such as is mentioned in section 3(1), could not be adduced or asked without leave in pursuance of that section.

(2) On an application for leave the judge shall—

    (a) refuse leave unless he is satisfied that leave in respect of the evidence or question would be likely to be given at such a trial, or

    (b) give leave if he is so satisfied.

(3) Section 3(3) shall apply to an application under subsection (2) of this section.".

Amendments

1   Section 4 substituted by Criminal Justice Act 1999, s 15.

[4A   Legal representation for complainants

(1) Where an application under section 3 or 4 is made by or on behalf of an accused person who is for the time being charged with an offence to which this section applies, the complainant shall be entitled to be heard in relation to the application and, for this purpose, to be legally represented during the hearing of the application.

(2) Notice of intention to make an application under section 3 or 4 shall be given to the prosecution by or on behalf of the accused person before, or as soon as practicable after, the commencement of the trial for the offence concerned or, as the case may be, the commencement of the proceeding concerned referred to in section 4(1).

(3) The prosecution shall, as soon as practicable after the receipt by it of such a notice, notify the complainant of his or her entitlement to be heard in relation to the said application and to be legally represented, for that purpose, during the course of the application.

(4) The judge shall not hear the said application without first being satisfied that subsections (2) and (3) have been complied with.

(5) If the period between the complainant's being notified, under subsection (3), of his or her entitlements under this section and the making of the said application is not, in the judge's opinion, such as to have afforded the complainant a reasonable opportunity to arrange legal representation of the kind referred to in this section, the judge shall postpone the hearing of the application (and, for this purpose, may adjourn the trial or proceeding concerned) for a period that the judge considers will afford the complainant such an opportunity.

(6) This section applies to a rape offence[, an offence under the Criminal Law (Sexual Offences) Act 2006]² [an offence under section 6 of the Criminal Law (Sexual Offences) Act 1993]³ and any of the following, namely, aggravated sexual assault, attempted aggravated sexual assault, aiding, abetting, counselling and procuring aggravated sexual assault or attempted aggravated sexual assault, incitement to aggravated sexual assault and conspiring to commit any of the foregoing offences.]¹

Amendments

1   Section 4A inserted by Sex Offenders Act 2001, s 34.
2   Words inserted by Criminal Law (Sexual Offences) Act 2006, s 6(2).
3   Words inserted by Criminal Law (Sexual Offences) (Amendment) Act 2007, s 3.

5   Trials of juveniles

Where a person charged with a [sexual assault offence]¹ is tried for that offence summarily in pursuance of [section 75 (which provides for the summary trial in certain cases of persons under the age of 18 years who are charged with indictable offences) of the Children Act, 2001]—²

  (a) sections 2(2) and 3(2)(b) shall have effect as if for the references to the jury there were substituted references to the court,

  (b) section 3(2)(a) shall have effect as if the words "in the absence of the jury" were omitted, and

  (c) section 3. subsections (3) and (4) of section 7 and subsections (2), (4) and (5) of section 8 shall have effect as if for the references to the judge there were substituted references to the court.

Amendments

1   Words amended by Criminal Law (Rape) (Amendment) Act 1990, s 17(1).

2   Words inserted by Children Act 2001, s 266.

6   Exclusion of the public

[(1) Subject to subsections (2), (3) and (4), in any proceedings for a rape offence or the offence of aggravated sexual assault or attempted aggravated sexual assault or of aiding, abetting, counselling or procuring the offence of aggravated sexual assault or attempted aggravated sexual assault or of incitement to the offence of aggravated sexual assault or conspiracy to commit any of the foregoing offences, the judge, the justice or the court, as the case may be, shall exclude from the court during the hearing all persons except officers of the court, persons directly concerned in the proceedings, bona fide representatives of the Press and such other persons (if any) as the judge, the justice or the court, as the case may be, may in his or its discretion permit to remain.

(2) Subject to subsection (3), during the hearing of an application under section 3 (including that section as applied by section 5) or under section 4(2), the judge, the justice or the court, as the case may be, shall exclude from the court all persons except officers of the court and persons directly concerned in the proceedings.

(3) Subsections (1) and (2) are without prejudice to the right of a parent, relative or friend of the complainant or, where the accused is not of full age, of the accused to remain in court.

(4) In any proceedings to which subsection (1) applies the verdict or decision and the sentence (if any) shall be announced in public.]¹

Amendments

1   Section 6 substituted by Criminal Law (Rape) (Amendment) Act 1990, s 11.

7   Anonymity of complainants

(1) Subject to subsection (8)(a), after a person is charged with a [sexual assault offence]¹ no matter likely to lead members of the public to identify a [person]² as the complainant in

relation to that charge shall be published in a written publication available to the public or be broadcast except as authorised by a direction given in pursuance of this section.

(2) If, at any stage before the commencement of a trial of a person for a [sexual assault offence]¹, he or another person against whom the complainant may be expected to give evidence at the trial applies to a judge of the High Court or Circuit Court for a direction in pursuance of this subsection and satisfies the judge—

(a) that the direction is required for the purpose of inducing persons to come forward who are likely to be needed as witnesses at the trial, and

(b) that the conduct of the applicant's defence at the trial is likely to be adversely affected if the direction is not given,

the judge shall direct that subsection (1) shall not, by virtue of the charge alleging the offence aforesaid, apply to such matter relating to the complainant as is specified in the direction.

(3) If at a trial of a person for a [sexual assault offence]¹ he or another person who is also charged at the trial applies to the judge for a direction in pursuance of this subsection and satisfies the judge—

(a) that the direction is required for the purpose of inducing persons to come forward who are likely to be needed as witnesses at the trial,

(b) that the conduct of the applicant's defence at the trial is likely to be adversely affected if the direction is not given, and

(c) that there was good reason for his not having made an application under subsection (2) before the commencement of the trial,

the judge shall direct that subsection (1) shall not, by virtue of the charge alleging the offence aforesaid, apply to such matter relating to the complainant as is specified in the direction.

(4) If at a trial for a [sexual assault offence]¹ the judge is satisfied that the effect of subsection (1) is to impose a substantial and unreasonable restriction on the reporting of proceedings at the trial and that it is in the public interest to remove or relax the restriction, he shall direct that that subsection shall not apply to such matter relating to the complainant as is specified in the direction; but a direction shall not be given in pursuance of this subsection by reason only of [the outcome of]³ an accused person at the trial.

(5) If a person who has been convicted of an offence and given notice of appeal against the conviction, or, on conviction on indictment, notice of an application for leave so to appeal, applies to the appellate court for a direction in pursuance of this subsection and satisfies the court—

(a) that the direction is required for the purpose of obtaining evidence in support of the appeal, and

(b) that the applicant is likely to suffer injustice if the direction is not given,

the court shall direct that subsection (1) shall not apply to such matter relating to a specified complainant and [sexual assault offence]¹ as is specified in the direction.

(6) If any matter is published or broadcast in contravention of subsection (1), the following persons, namely—

(a) in the case of a publication in a newspaper or periodical, any proprietor, any editor and any publisher of the newspaper or periodical,

(b) in the case of any other publication, the person who publishes it, and

(c) in the case of a broadcast, any body corporate which transmits or provides the programme in which the broadcast is made and any person having functions in relation to the programme corresponding to those of an editor of a newspaper,

shall be guilty of an offence.

(7) In this section—

"a broadcast" means a broadcast by wireless telegraphy of sound or visual images intended for general reception, and cognate expressions shall be construed accordingly;

"written publication" includes a film, a sound track and any other record in permanent form but does not include an indictment or other document prepared for use in particular legal proceedings.

(8) Nothing in this section—

(a) prohibits the publication or broadcasting of matter consisting only of a report of legal proceedings other than proceedings at, or intended to lead to, or on an appeal arising out of, a trial at which the accused is charged with a [sexual assault offence][1], or

(b) affects any prohibition or restriction imposed by virtue of any other enactment upon a publication or broadcast.

(9) A direction in pursuance of this section does not affect the operation of subsection (1) at any time before the direction is given.

(10) If, after the commencement of a trial of a person for a [sexual assault offence][1], a new trial of the person for that offence is ordered, the commencement of any previous trial of that person for that offence shall be disregarded for the purposes of subsections (2) and (3).

Amendments

1   Words amended by Criminal Law (Rape) (Amendment) Act 1990, s 17(2)(c).

2   Words amended by Criminal Law (Rape) (Amendment) Act 1990, s 17(2)(a).

3   Words amended by Criminal Law (Rape) (Amendment) Act 1990, s 17(2)(b).

---

8   Anonymity of accused

(1) After a person is charged with a rape offence no matter likely to lead members of the public to identify him as the person against whom the charge is made shall be published in a written publication available to the public or be broadcast except—

(a) as authorised by a direction given in pursuance of this section or by virtue of section 7(8)(a) as applied by subsection (6) of this section, or

(b) after he has been convicted of the offence.

[(2) If a person charged with a rape offence applies in that behalf to a judge of the High Court before the commencement of the trial or to the judge at the trial, the judge shall direct that subsection (1) shall not apply to the person in relation to the charge:

Provided that, if it appears to the judge that, if the direction were given, the publication of any matter in pursuance of the direction might enable members of the public to identify a person as the complainant in relation to the charge, the judge shall not give the direction unless he is satisfied that a direction could properly be given in relation to that person in pursuance of section 7.][1]

(3) If, at any stage before the commencement of a trial of a person for a rape offence, another person who is to be charged with a rape offence at the trial applies to a judge of the High Court [...]² for a direction in pursuance of this subsection and satisfies the judge—

(a) that the direction is required for the purpose of inducing persons to come forward who are likely to be needed as witnesses at the trial, and

(b) that the conduct of the applicant's defence at the trial is likely to be adversely affected if the direction is not given,

the judge shall direct that subsection (1) shall not, by virtue of the charge alleging the offence aforesaid, apply to such matter relating to the first-mentioned person as is specified in the direction.

(4) If at a trial of a person for a rape offence another person who is also charged at the trial applies to the judge for a direction in pursuance of this subsection and satisfies the judge—

(a) that the direction is required for the purpose of inducing persons to come forward who are likely to be needed as witnesses at the trial,

(b) that the conduct of the applicant's defence is likely to be adversely affected if the direction is not given, and

(c) that there was good reason for his not having made an application under subsection (3) before the commencement of the trial,

the judge shall direct that subsection (1) shall not, by virtue of the charge alleging the offence aforesaid, apply to such matter relating to the first-mentioned person as is specified in the direction.

(5) If at a trial at which a person is charged with a rape offence the judge is satisfied that the effect of subsection (1) is to impose a substantial and unreasonable restriction on the reporting of proceedings at the trial and that it is in the public interest to remove or relax the restriction in respect of that person, the judge shall direct that subsection (1) shall not, by virtue of the charge alleging the offence aforesaid, apply to such matter relating to that person as is specified in the direction.

(6) Subsections (6) to (9) of section 7 shall have effect for the purposes of this section as if for references to that section there were substituted references to this section.

(7) If, after the commencement of a trial of a person for a rape offence, a new trial of the person for that offence is ordered, the commencement of any previous trial of that person for that offence shall be disregarded for the purposes of subsections (2), (3) and (4).

[(8) If, at any time after a person is charged with a rape offence, the Director of Public Prosecutions applies in that behalf to a judge of the High Court, the judge, if he is satisfied that it is in the public interest to do so, shall direct that subsection (1) shall not apply to such matter relating to the person charged with the offence as is specified in the direction.]³

Amendments

1   Subsection (2) substituted by Criminal Law (Rape) (Amendment) Act 1990, s 14(a).

2   Words deleted by Criminal Law (Rape) (Amendment) Act 1990, s 21 and Sch.

3   Subsection (8) inserted by Criminal Law (Rape) (Amendment) Act 1990, s 14(b).

9   Trials by court-martial

(1) This Act applies to the trial of a [sexual assault offence]¹ by court-martial with the necessary modifications.

(2) In particular—

    (a) for the references to a judge in section 7(2) or section 8(3) and for the references to a justice of the District Court in section 8(2) there shall be substituted references to the convening authority, and

  [(aa) n section 8(8) for the reference to the Director of Public Prosecutions there shall be substituted a reference to the convening authority and for the references to a judge of the High Court there shall be substituted references to a superior authority; and, for the purposes of this paragraph, each of the following shall be a superior authority:

      (i) the Minister for Defence,

      (ii) the Adjutant-General of the Defence Forces,

      (iii) any general officer or flag officer (within the meaning, in each case, of the Defence Act, 1954) appointed by the Minister for Defence for the purpose, and]²

    (b) for references in section 3 and for other references in section 7 or 8 to a judge there shall be substituted references to the court-martial.

Amendments

1   Words amended by Criminal Law (Rape) (Amendment) Act 1990, s 17(1).

2   Subsection (2)(aa) inserted by Criminal Law (Rape) (Amendment) Act 1990, s 15.

10   Punishment of indecent assault on female

[…]¹

Amendments

1   Section 10 repealed by Criminal Law (Rape) (Amendment) Act 1990, s 21 and Sch.

11   Penalty for publication of unauthorised matter

(1) A person guilty of an offence under section 7(6) (including an offence under that section as applied by section 8(6)) shall be liable on conviction on indictment to a fine not exceeding £10,000 or, at the discretion of the court, to imprisonment for a term not exceeding 3 years or to both such fine and such imprisonment.

(2) (a) Where an offence to which subsection (1) relates and which has been committed by a body corporate is proved to have been committed with the consent or connivance of, or to be attributable to any neglect on the part of, any director, manager, secretary or other similar officer of the body corporate or any person who was

purporting to act in any such capacity, he as well as the body corporate shall be guilty of that offence and be liable to be proceeded against and punished accordingly.

(b) Where the affairs of a body corporate are managed by its members, paragraph (a) shall apply in relation to the acts and defaults of a member in connection with his functions of management as if he were a director of the body corporate.

(3) Where a person is charged with an offence to which subsection (1) relates it shall be a defence to prove that at the time of the alleged offence he was not aware, and neither suspected nor had reason to suspect, that the publication or broadcast in question was of such matter as is mentioned in section 7(1) or section 8(1), as the case may be.

12   Summary jurisdiction

(1) A justice of the District Court shall have jurisdiction to try summarily [a sexual assault or an an offence to which section 11 relates][1] if—

(i) the justice is of opinion that the facts proved or alleged against a defendant charged with such an offence constitute a minor offence fit to be tried summarily,

(ii) the Director of Public Prosecutions consents, and

(iii) the defendant (on being informed by the justice of his right to be tried by a jury) does not object to being tried summarily,

and, upon conviction under this subsection, the said defendant shall be liable to a fine not exceeding [£1000][1] or, at the discretion of the court, to imprisonment for a term not exceeding 12 months or to both such fine and such imprisonment.

(2) Section 13 of the Criminal Procedure Act, 1967 (which provides for the procedure where a person pleads guilty in the District Court to an indictable offence) shall apply in relation to an offence mentioned in subsection (1) as if, in lieu of the penalties specified in subsection (3) of the said section 13, there were specified therein the penalties provided for by subsection (1) of this section and the reference in subsection (2)(a) of the said section 13 to the penalties provided for in subsection (3) of that section shall be construed accordingly.

(3) ....[2]

Amendments

1   Words substituted by Criminal Law (Rape) (Amendment) Act 1990, s 16.

2   Subsection (3) repealed by Criminal Law (Rape) (Amendment) Act 1990, s 21 and Sch.

---

13   Short title and commencement

(1) This Act may be cited as the Criminal Law (Rape) Act, 1981.

(2) This Act shall come into operation one month after the date of its passing.

(3) Section 3 (including that section as applied by sections 5 and 9) and section 4 shall not have effect in relation to a trial or preliminary examination which begins before the commencement of this Act and sections 7 and 8 shall not have effect in relation to a charge alleging a rape offence which is made before such commencement.

(4) Section 10 and, in so far as it relates to an offence under section 10. section 12 shall not have effect in relation to an offence committed before the commencement of this Act.

Criminal Justice (Community Service) Act 1983

Number 23 of 1983

ARRANGEMENT OF SECTIONS

Section

1. Interpretation.

2. Persons to whom Act applies.

3. Community service order.

4. Conditions required for making of community service order.

5. Previsions regarding more than one community service order.

6. Provisions consequential on making of community service order.

7. Requirements under community service order and failure to comply with such requirements.

8. Alternative methods of dealing with offence under section 7(4).

9. Extension of time for performance of work under community service order.

10. Change of residence by offender.

11. Revocation of community service order.

12. Jurisdiction.

13. Power to summon or order arrest.

14. Regulations.

15. Expenses.

16. Short title and commencement.

AN ACT TO MAKE FURTHER PROVISION FOR DEALING WITH PERSONS CONVICTED OF CERTAIN OFFENCES AND TO PROVIDE FOR CONNECTED MATTERS. [13th July, 1983]

BE IT ENACTED BY THE OIREACHTAS AS FOLLOWS:

1   Interpretation

(1) In this Act—

["Act of 2010"means the Fines Act 2010;][1]

"community service order" has the meaning assigned to it by section 3;

"court" does not include a Special Criminal Court;

"district of residence" has the meaning assigned to it by section 6;

["fine" has the same meaning as it has in section 2 (amended by subparagraph (iii) of section 19(a) of the Act of 2010) of the Courts (No. 2) Act 1986;][1]

"the Minister" means the Minister for Justice;

"offender" has the meaning assigned to it by section 2;

459

"probation and welfare officer" means a person appointed by the Minister to be a probation and welfare officer or to be a welfare officer or probation officer;

"relevant officer" means a probation and welfare officer discharging functions under this Act.

(2) A reference in this Act to a section is to a section of this Act and a reference to a subsection is to a subsection of the section in which the reference occurs.

Amendments

1   Definitions inserted by Fines Act 2010, s 18(a), which has not yet come into operation (February 2011).

2   Persons to whom Act applies

(1) This Act applies to a person (in this Act referred to as an "offender") who is of or over the age of 16 years and is convicted of an offence for which, in the opinion of the court, the appropriate sentence would but for this Act be one [...]¹, of imprisonment or of detention in Saint Patrick's Institution, [in any children detention centre designated under section 150 of the Children Act, 2001, or in a children detention school,]² but does not apply where any such sentence is fixed by law.

[(2) This Act also applies to a person (in this Act also referred to as an 'offender') who—

(a)   has attained the age of 16 years, and

(b)   stands convicted of an offence in respect of which the court has imposed a fine that the offender has failed to pay by the due date for payment.

(3) In this section 'due date for payment' means, in relation to a fine—

(a)   the date specified by the court that imposed the fine as being the date by which the fine is required to be paid, or

(b)   where a direction is given under section 15 of the Act of 2010, the date by which the final instalment of the fine is required to be paid in accordance with that direction.]³

Amendments

1   Words deleted by Criminal Law Act 1997, s 16 and Sch 3.

2   Words inserted by Children Act 2001, s 154. However CJA 2006, s 158 and Sch 4 subsequently deletes the definition of 'children detention centre' and all references to 'children detention centre' in the Childrens Act 2001.

3   Subsections (2) and (3) inserted by Fines Act 2010, s 18(b), which has not yet come into operation (February 2011).

3   Community service order

(1) Subject to section 4, the court by or before which an offender is convicted may, instead of dealing with him in any other way, make, in respect of the offence of which he is convicted, an order (in this Act referred to as a "community service order") under this section.

[(1A) Where a court is satisfied that—

-   (a) a receiver appointed under section 16 of the Act of 2010 has been unable to recover—
    -   (i) the fine imposed by it in relation to an offender to whom subsection (2) of section 2 applies, or
    -   (ii) a sum or sums from the sale of property belonging to that offender sufficient to pay that fine,

    and
-   (b) that, in relation to the offender, the provisions of section 4 have been complied with, it may make an order (in this Act also referred to as a 'community service order') in accordance with this section.]¹

(2) A community service order shall require the offender to perform, in accordance with this Act, unpaid work for such number of hours as are specified in the order and are not less than 40 and not more than 240.²

(3) Nothing in this section shall be construed as preventing a court which makes a community service order from making, in relation to the offence in respect of which the order is made, an order under any other enactment for—

-   (a) the revocation of any licence,
-   (b) the imposition of any disqualification or endorsement,
-   (c) the forfeiture, confiscation, seizure, restitution or disposal of any property, or
-   (d) the payment of compensation, costs or expenses.

Amendments

1   Subsection (1A) inserted by Fines Act 2010, s 18(c)(i) which has not yet come into operation (February 2011).

2   Subsection (2) substituted by Fines Act 2010, s 18(c)(ii) which has not yet come into operation (February 2011). See the amending Act.

---

4   Conditions required for making of community service order

(1) A court shall not make a community service order unless the following conditions have been complied with:

-   (a) the court is satisfied, after considering the offender's circumstances and a report about him by a probation and welfare officer (including, if the court thinks it necessary, hearing evidence from such an officer), that the offender is a suitable person to perform work under such an order and that arrangements can be made for him to perform such work, and
-   (b) the offender has consented.

(2) Before making a community service order in respect of an offender the court shall explain to him—

   (a)   the effect of the order and, in particular, the requirements of sections 7(1) and 7(2),

   (b)   the consequences which may follow under sections 7(4) and 8 if he fails to comply with any of those requirements, and

   (c)   that under this Act the District Court may review the order on the application of either the offender or a relevant officer.

5   **Provisions regarding more than one community service order**

(1) Notwithstanding subsections (2) and (3), where more than one community service order is in force in respect of an offender at any time, the total number of hours which the offender is required to work under such orders shall not exceed 240.

(2) Where a court makes community service orders in respect of two or more offences of which the offender has been convicted by or before the court, the court may direct that the hours of work specified in any of those orders shall be concurrent with or additional to those specified in any other of those orders.

[(2A) The hours of work specified in a community service order under subsection (1A) (inserted by section 18 of the Act of 2010) of section 3 shall be additional to any hours of work specified in any other community service order made in respect of the offender.

(2B) In determining the number of hours of work to specify in a community service order under subsection (1A) of section 3 the court shall take account of—

   (a)   any sum or sums paid by the offender concerned in satisfaction of part of the fine, and

   (b)   any part of the fine, or any sum or sums from the proceeds of the sale of property of the offender sufficient to pay part only of that fine, recovered by the receiver appointed under section 16 of the Act of 2010.][1]

(3) Where a court makes a community service order and there is in force in respect of the offender at the time of the making of that order another such order (whether made by the same or a different court) the court making the later order may direct in that order that the hours of work specified therein shall be concurrent with or additional to those specified in the earlier order.

Amendments

1   Subsections (2A) and (2B) inserted by Fines Act 2010, s 18(d), which has not yet come into operation (February 2011).

---

6   **Provisions consequential on making of community service order**

(1) A community service order shall specify the district court district (in this Act referred to as the "district of residence") in which the offender resides or will reside while performing work under the order.

(2) The court by which a community service order is made shall cause certified copies of the order to be sent—

(a) to the justice of the District Court assigned to the district of residence, and

(b) to a specified relevant officer in the district of residence, who shall give a copy to the offender.

7 Requirements under community service order and failure to comply with such requirements

(1) An offender in respect of whom a community service order is in force shall—

(a) report to a relevant officer as directed from time to time by or on behalf of the officer referred to in section 6(2) or 10(2) or by or on behalf of an officer discharging functions previously discharged by that officer,

(b) perform satisfactorily for the number of hours specified in the order such work at such times as he may be directed by or on behalf of the relevant officer to whom he is required to report under this subsection or by or on behalf of an officer discharging functions previously discharged by that officer, and

(c) notify the officer to whom he is required to report under this subsection of any change of address.

(2) Subject to section 9, the work to be performed under a community service order shall be performed in the period of one year beginning on the date of the order but, unless revoked, the order shall remain in force until the offender has worked under it for the number of hours specified in it.

(3) Directions given under subsection (1)(b) shall, so far as practicable, avoid any interference with the times the offender normally works or attends a school or other educational or training establishment.

(4) An offender who fails, without reasonable excuse, to comply with a requirement of subsection (1) shall be guilty of an offence and, without prejudice to the continuance in force of the community service order, shall be liable on summary conviction to a fine not exceeding £300.

(5) An offence under subsection (4) may be prosecuted by a relevant officer.

[(6) Subsection (4) shall not apply to an offender to whom subsection (2) of section 2 applies.][1]

Amendments

1 Subsection (6) inserted by Fines Act 2010, s 18(e), which has not yet come into operation (February 2011).

---

8 Alternative methods of dealing with offence under section 7(4)

(1) Where an offender is convicted of an offence under section 7(4), the court, in lieu of imposing a fine under that section, may—

(a) if the community service order was made by the District Court in the district of residence, either revoke the order or revoke it and deal with the offender for the offence in respect of which the order was made in any manner in which he could have been dealt with for that offence if the order had not been made, or

(b) if the community service order was made by the District Court in a district court district other than the district of residence or by another court, remand the offender to the District Court in that other district or to that other court to be dealt with in accordance with subsection (2).

(2) Where, by virtue of subsection (1)(b), an offender in respect of whom a community service order is in force is brought or appears before a court, the court shall either revoke the order or revoke it and deal with the offender for the offence in respect of which the order was made in any manner in which he could have been dealt with for that offence if the order had not been made.

9   Extension of time for performance of work under community service order

Where a community service order is in force and, on application by the offender or a relevant officer, it appears to the District Court that it would be in the interests of justice, having regard to circumstances which have arisen since the order was made, to extend the period of one year specified in section 7(2), the court may, in relation to the order, extend that period.

10   Change of residence by offender

(1) Where a community service order is in force and, on application to the District Court by the offender or a relevant officer, the court is satisfied that the offender proposes to change, or has changed, his residence from the district of residence to another district court district and it appears to the court that arrangements can be made in that other district for the offender to perform work under the order, the court may amend the order by substituting the other district for the district of residence, and the district so substituted shall be deemed to be the district of residence for the purposes of this Act.

(2) Where a community service order is amended under this section, the court shall cause certified copies of the order as so amended to be sent to a specified relevant officer in the district of residence, who shall give a copy to the offender.

11   Revocation of community service order

(1) Where a community service order is in force and, on application by the offender or a relevant officer, it appears to the District Court that it would be in the interests of justice, having regard to circumstances which have arisen since the order was made, that the order should be revoked or that the offender should be dealt with in some other manner for the offence in respect of which the order was made, the court may—

(a) if the order was made by the District Court in the district of residence, either revoke the order or revoke it and deal with the offender for that offence in any manner in which he could have been dealt with for that offence if the order had not been made, or

(b) if the order was made by the District Court in a district court district other than the district of residence or by another court, remand the offender to the District Court in that other district or to that other court to be dealt with in accordance with subsection (2).

(2) Where, by virtue of subsection (1)(b), an offender in respect of whom a community service order is in force is brought or appears before a court and it appears to the court to be in the interests of justice, having regard to circumstances which have arisen since the order was made, to revoke the order or to revoke it and deal with the offender for the offence in

respect of which the order was made in some other manner in which he could have been dealt with for that offence if the order had not been made, the court may either revoke the order or revoke it and so deal with the offender.

12   Jurisdiction

(1) The jurisdiction vested in the Circuit Court by this Act in respect of proceedings to which sections 8(2) and 11(2) relate shall be exercised by the judge of the circuit where the community service order was made.

(2) The jurisdiction vested in the District Court by this Act—

(a) in respect of proceedings under section 7(4), in respect of proceedings to which section 8(1) relates and in respect of applications under sections 9, 10(1) and 11(1), shall be exercised by the justice for the time being assigned to the district of residence, and

(b) in respect of proceedings to which sections 8(2) and 11(2) relate, shall be exercised by the justice for the time being assigned to the district court district where the community service order was made.

13   Power to summon or order arrest

Where the District Court proposes to exercise its powers under section 9, 10 or 11(1) otherwise than on application by the offender, it shall summon him to appear before the court and, if he does not appear in answer to the summons, may issue a warrant for his arrest.

14   Regulations

(1) The Minister may make regulations for the purpose of giving effect to this Act.

(2) Without prejudice to the generality of subsection (1), regulations under this section may—

(a) provide for regulating the performance of work under community service orders,

(b) limit the number of hours of work to be done under such an order on any one day,

(c) make provision regarding the reckoning of time worked under such orders,

(d) make provision for the payment of travelling and other expenses in connection with the performance of work under such orders, and

(e) provide for records to be kept of the work done under such orders.

(3) Regulations made under this section shall be laid before each House of the Oireachtas as soon as may be after they are made and, if a resolution annulling the regulations is passed by either such House within the next twenty-one days on which that House has sat after the regulations are laid before it, the regulations shall be annulled accordingly, but without prejudice to the validity of anything previously done thereunder.

15   Expenses

The expenses incurred by the Minister in the administration of this Act shall, to such extent as may be sanctioned by the Minister for Finance, be paid out of moneys provided by the Oireachtas.

16   Short title and commencement

This Act may be cited as the Criminal Justice (Community Service) Act, 1983, and shall come into operation on such day as the Minister appoints by order.

Misuse of Drugs Act 1984

Number 18 of 1984

ARRANGEMENT OF SECTIONS

Section

1. Definition.

2. New definitions of 'cannabis' and 'opium poppy' and other amendments of section 1(1) of Principal Act.

3. Investigation of case where Minister considers there are grounds for special direction.

4. Temporary direction pending investigation under section 8.

5. Printing etc. of certain books etc., communication of certain information and possession of certain documents an offence.

6. Penalties.

7. Penalties for offences under Customs Acts relating to controlled drugs.

8. Power of court to remand person convicted of offence to which section 7 applies and to obtain a report and in certain cases to arrange for the medical or other treatment or for the care of such person.

9. Offences to which section 7 applies; presumption, defences, etc.

10. Evidential value of certain certificates.

11. Amendment of sections 17 and 19 of Principal Act.

12. Amendment of section 23 of Principal Act.

13. Amendment of section 26 of Principal Act.

14. Miscellaneous amendments of Principal Act.

15. Repeals.

16. Short title, commencement, collective citation and construction.

An Act to Amend and Extend the Law Relating to the Misuse of Certain Dangerous or Otherwise Harmful Drugs. [18th July, 1984]

BE IT ENACTED BY THE OIREACHTAS AS FOLLOWS:

1   Definition

In this Act 'the Principal Act' means the Misuse of Drugs Act, 1977.

2   New definition of 'cannabis' and 'opium poppy' and other amendments of section 1(1) of Principal Act

Section 1(1) of the Principal Act is hereby amended by—

    (a) [...];[1]

    (b) [...];[2]

    (c) [...];[3]

    (d) [...];[4]

Amendments

1 Subsection (a) substituted definition of "cannabis" in Misuse of Drugs Act 1977, s 1(1).

2 Subsection (b) substituted definition of "opium poppy" in Misuse of Drugs Act 1977, s 1(1).

3 Subsection (c) substituted definition of "temporary direction" in Misuse of Drugs Act 1977, s 1(1).

4 Subsection (d) substituted definition of "vessel" in Misuse of Drugs Act 1977, s 1(1).

3 Investigation of case where Minister considers there are grounds for special direction

(a) [...].[1]

Amendments

1 Section 3 substituted Misuse of Drugs Act 1977, s 8.

4 Temporary direction pending investigation under section 8

(a) [...].[1]

Amendments

1 Section 4 substituted Misuse of Drugs Act 1977, s 9.

5 Printing etc. of certain books etc., communication of certain information and possession of certain documents an offence.

(1) (a) A person shall not print, publish, cause or procure to be printed or published, sell or expose or offer or keep for sale, distribute or offer or keep for distribution, any book, periodical or other publication which and possession of either—

   (i) advocates or encourages, or might reasonably be supposed to advocate or encourage, whether expressly or by implication, the use of any controlled drug prescribed for the purposes of this section, or any product or preparation containing any such controlled drug, otherwise than in the course of professional treatment by a practitioner, or

   (ii) contains any advertisement advertising any use of a pipe, utensil or other thing for use by persons, for or in connection with the use of a controlled drug so prescribed or such a product or preparation, which is a use other than a use described in paragraph (b) of this subsection.

   (b) The use lastly referred to in paragraph (a) of this subsection is a use (being the use of a pipe, utensil or other thing)—

> (i) which is described in the relevant advertisement, and
>
> (ii) which any person reading the relevant advertisement would—
>
> > (I) take to be a use relating to a controlled drug prescribed for the purposes of this section or a product or preparation containing such a controlled drug, and
> >
> > (II) take to be, and only to be, a use to be availed of in the course of professional treatment by a practitioner.

(2) A person who contravenes subsection (1) of this section shall be guilty of an offence under this subsection.

(3) If any person, for the purpose of enabling or assisting another person to obtain, otherwise than on foot of a prescription issued by a practitioner, a controlled drug prescribed for the purposes of this section or a product or preparation containing such a drug communicates to that person any information, he shall be guilty of an offence under this subsection.

(4) If a person, with intent to commit or to aid, abet, cause or procure the commission of an offence under subsection (3) of this section, has in his possession or under his control any document of such a nature that the dissemination of copies thereof would constitute such an offence, he shall be guilty of an offence under this subsection.

(5) In any proceedings for an offence under subsection (2) of this section it shall be a defence for the defendant to prove that—

> (a) at the time of the alleged offence he carried on the business of selling or distributing books, periodicals or other publications, and
>
> (b) the act alleged to constitute such offence was committed by him in the ordinary course of his said business, and
>
> (c) he could not by the exercise of reasonable care have known or ascertained the contents of the book, periodical or other publication in respect of which such act was committed.

(6) Where in proceedings for an offence under subsection (4) of this section it is proved that the defendant had at the time of the alleged offence in his possession or under his control a document described in the said subsection (4), then, unless there is sufficient other evidence to raise an issue as to whether the defendant so had the document with the intent referred to in the said subsection (4), he shall be treated as having had at such time the document in his possession or under his control with such intent.

6   Penalties

> […].[1]

Amendments

1   Section 6 substituted new sub-ss (1)–(9) for Misuse of Drugs Act 1977, s 27(1)–(11).

---

7   Penalties for offences under Customs Acts relating to controlled drugs

(1) Where a person is convicted of an offence to which this section applies, subject to section 8 of this Act, the person shall, in lieu of the penalties specified in the enactments relating to the customs which are for the time being in force, be liable to—

(a) where the court is satisfied that the relevant controlled drug was imported by the person for the purpose of selling or otherwise supplying it to another in contravention of regulations under section 5 of the Principal Act which are for the time being in force

    (i) on summary conviction, the penalty specified in paragraph (a) of subsection (3) (inserted by section 6 of this Act) of section 27 of the Principal Act,

    (ii) on conviction on indictment, the penalty specified in paragraph (b) of the said subsection (3),

(b) where the relevant controlled drug is cannabis or cannabis resin and the court is satisfied that the person imported such drug for his personal use:

    (i) in the case of a first offence,

        (I) on summary conviction, to a fine not exceeding £300, or

        (II) on conviction on indictment, to a fine not exceeding £500,

    (ii) in the case of a second offence,

        (I) on summary conviction, to a fine not exceeding £400, or

        (II) on conviction on indictment, to a fine not exceeding £1,000,

    (iii) in the case of a third or subsequent offence,

        (I) on summary conviction, to a fine not exceeding £1,000 or, at the discretion of the court, to imprisonment for a term not exceeding twelve months, or to both the fine and the imprisonment, or

        (II) on conviction on indictment, to a fine of such amount as the court considers appropriate or, at the discretion of the court, to imprisonment for a term not exceeding three years, or to both the fine and the imprisonment,

(c) in any other case—

    (i) on summary conviction, to a fine not exceeding £1,000 or, at the discretion of the court, to imprisonment for a term not exceeding twelve months, or to both the fine and the imprisonment, or

    (ii) on conviction on indictment, to a fine of such amount as the court considers appropriate or, at the discretion of the court, to imprisonment for a term not exceeding seven years, or to both the fine and the imprisonment.

(2) This section applies to an offence against the Customs Acts in relation to the importation or exportation of a controlled drug.

8   Power of court to remand person convicted of offence to which section 7 applies and to obtain a report and in certain cases to arrange for the medical or other treatment or for the care of such person

(1) Where a person is convicted of an offence to which section 7 of this Act applies, if, having regard to the circumstances of the case, the court considers it appropriate so to do, the court may remand the person for such period as it considers necessary for the purposes of this section (being a period not exceeding eight days in the case of a remand in custody) and

request a health board, probation and welfare officer employed in the probation and welfare service of the Department of Justice or such other person or body, considered by the court to be appropriate to furnish to the court—

(a) a medical report described in subparagraph (i), as amended by section 14 of this Act, of Section 28(1)(a) of The Principal Act, and

(b) a report described in subparagraph (ii), as so amended, of the said section 28(1)(a).

(2) Where the court makes a request under subsection (1) of this section, subsections (2) to (9) of section 28, as amended by section 14 of this Act, of the Principal Act, shall with the necessary modifications apply as regards the relevant case, and without prejudice to the generality of the foregoing—

(a) each of the references in the said subsections (2) to (9) to section 27 of the Principal Act shall be construed as a reference to that section as applied by this subsection,

(b) the references to a report in subsections (3) and (4) of the said section 28 shall each be construed as including a reference to a report furnished under subsection (1) of this section,

(c) the reference in subsection (6) of the said section 28 to a person's being detained under The Principal Act shall be construed as a reference to detention imposed by virtue of this subsection,

(d) references in subsection (6) or (7) of the said section 28 to a decision or order under subsection (2) of that section shall be construed as including references to a decision or order under the said subsection (2) as applied by this subsection.

9   Offences to which section 7 applies; presumption, defences, etc

(1) Subject to subsection (4) of this section, in any proceedings for an offence to which section 7 of this Act applies, where it is proved that a person imported a controlled drug and the court, having regard to the quantity of the controlled drug which the person imported and to such other matter as the court considers relevant, is satisfied that it is reasonable to assume that the controlled drug was not intended for the immediate personal use of the person, then for the purposes of section 7(1)(a) of this Act, he shall be regarded by the court, until the court is satisfied to the contrary, as having imported the controlled drug for the purpose of selling or otherwise supplying it to another in contravention of regulations referred to in that section.

(2) In any proceedings for an offence to which section 7 of this Act applies, the defendant shall not be acquitted of the offence charged by reason only of proving that he neither knew nor suspected nor had reason to suspect that the substance, product or preparation in question was the particular controlled drug alleged.

(3) In proceedings for an offence to which section 7 of this Act applies in which it is proved that the defendant imported or exported the relevant controlled drug in contravention of the Customs Acts, it shall be a defence to prove that

(a) he did not know and had no reasonable ground for suspecting that what he so imported or exported, as may be appropriate, was a controlled drug, or

(b) he believed the relevant substance, product or preparation to be a controlled drug, or a controlled drug of a particular class or description, and that, if the substance, product or preparation had in fact been that controlled drug or a controlled drug of that class or description, he would not at the material time have been committing an offence against the Customs Acts.

(4) In any proceedings for an offence to which section 7 of this Act applies a defendant may rebut the presumption raised by subsection (1) of this section by showing that at the time of the alleged offence he was by virtue of regulations made under section 4 of the Principal Act lawfully in possession of the controlled drug to which the proceedings relate.

(5) In any proceedings for an attempt to commit an offence to which section 7 of this Act applies the defences mentioned in subsection (3) of this section shall, with the necessary modifications, be open to the defendant.

(6) Subject to subsection (2) of this section, nothing in this section shall prevent a person raising a defence which, apart from this section, would be open to him to raise in proceedings for an offence to which section 7 of this Act applies.

10   Evidential value of certain certificates

In any proceedings for an offence under The Principal Act or section 5 of this Act, the production of a certificate purporting to be signed by an officer of the Forensic Science Laboratory of the Department of Justice and relating to an examination, inspection, test or analysis, as the case may be, specified in the certificate of a controlled drug or other substance, product or preparation so specified shall, until the contrary is proved, be evidence of any fact thereby certified without proof of any signature thereon or that any such signature is that of such an officer.

11   Amendment sections 17 and 19 of Principal Act

(1) […].[1]

(2) Section 19 of the Principal Act shall be construed and have effect as if the reference in subsection (1)(a) thereof to the cultivation contrary to section 17 of that Act of opium poppy included a reference to the cultivation contrary to the said section 17, as amended by subsection (1) of this section, of any plant of the genus *Erythroxylon*.

Amendments

1   Subsection (1) substituted Misuse of Drugs Act 1977, s 17(1) and (2).

---

12   Amendment of section 23 of the Principal Act

Section 23 of the Principal Act is hereby amended by—

(a) the insertion of '(and any substance, article or other thing on or in the vehicle, vessel or aircraft)' before 'and for the purpose' in paragraph (b) of subsection (1);

(b) the insertion of 'examine (by opening or otherwise) and' before 'seize' in paragraph (c) of subsection (1);

(c) […].[1]

and the said paragraphs (b) and (c), as so amended, are set out in paragraphs 1 and 2, respectively, of the Table to this section.

TABLE

1. (b) search any vehicle, vessel or aircraft in which he suspects that such drug may be found (and any substance, article or other thing on or in the vehicle, vessel or aircraft) and for the purpose of carrying out the search may, if he thinks fit, require the person who for the time being is in control of such vehicle, vessel or aircraft to bring it to a stop and when stopped to refrain from moving it, or in case such vehicle, vessel or aircraft is already stationary, to refrain from moving it, or

2. (c) examine (by opening or otherwise) and seize and detain anything found in the course of a search under this section which with such cause appears to him to be something which might be required as evidence in proceedings for an offence under this Act.

Amendments

1   Section 12(c) inserted Misuse of Drugs Act 1977, s 23(1A)–(1F).

13   Amendment of section 26 of Principal Act

Section 26 of the Principal Act is hereby amended by—

(a)   the insertion of 'or other land' after 'premises' in paragraph (a);

(b)   [...];[1]

(c)   [...];[2]

and the said paragraph (a), as so amended, is set out in the Table to this section.

TABLE

(a) a person is in possession in contravention of this Act on any premises or other land of a controlled drug, a forged prescription or a duly issued prescription which has been wrongfully altered and that such drug or prescription is on a particular premises or other land, or

Amendments

1   Subsection (b) inserted Misuse of Drugs Act 1977, s 26(aa).

2   Subsection (c) substituted sub-s (2) and inserted sub-ss (3) and (4) in s 26 of the Misuse of Drugs Act 1977.

14   Miscellaneous amendments of Principal Act

The Principal Act is hereby amended by—

(a)   the insertion of 'or 3' after 'section 2' in paragraph (a) of section 22(1);

(b)   the substitution of 'if, having regard to the circumstances of the case, the court considers it appropriate so to do, the court may' for 'the court shall' in paragraph (a) of section 28(1);

(c) the insertion of ', arising because of his being dependent on drugs,' after 'needs' in both subparagraph (i) of section 28(1)(a) and subparagraph (i) of section 28(1)(b);

(d) the substitution of 'probation and welfare' for 'court welfare' in section 28(1)(a);

(e) the substitution of 'on bail or, unless a penalty falls to be imposed on the person under paragraph (a) of section 27(1) of this Act, in custody' and 'probation and welfare' for 'on bail' and 'court welfare', respectively, in section 28(1)(b);

(f) [...]¹;

(g) the insertion of 'or other' before 'treatment' in subparagraph (ii) of section 28(2)(a);

(h) the insertion of 'or the person who is for the time being in charge of such centre' after 'medical practitioner' in subsection (6) of section 28;

(i) the substitution in subsection (8) of section 28 of 'medical or other treatment' for 'medical treatment and 'the medical practitioner or other person' for 'the medical practitioner' in each place where it occurs; and

(j) [...],²

and the said paragraph (a) of the said section 22(1), the said section 28(1), the said subparagraph (ii), the said subsection (6) and the said subsection (8), as amended by this section, are set out in paragraphs 1, 2, 3, 4 and 5, respectively, of the Table to this section.

Amendments

1 Subsection (f) inserted Misuse of Drugs Act 1977, s 28(a)(ia).

2 Subsection (j) inserted a definition of 'probation and welfare officer' in Misuse of Drugs Act 1977, s 28(11).

TABLE

1. (a) order made under section 2 or 3 of this Act.

2. (1)(a) Where a person is convicted of an offence under section 3 of this Act, other than a first or second offence in relation to which a penalty may be imposed under section 27(a) of this Act, or an offence under section 15 or 16 of this Act, or of attempting to commit any such offence, if, having regard to the circumstances of the case, the court considers it appropriate so to do, the court may remand the person for such period as it considers necessary for the purposes of this section (being a period not exceeding eight days in the case of a remand in custody), and request a health board, probation and welfare officer or other body or person, considered by the court to be appropriate, to—

(i) cause to be furnished to the court a medical report in writing on the convicted person together with such recommendations (if any) as to medical treatment which the person making the report considers so appropriate to the needs, arising because of his being dependent on drugs, of the convicted person, and

(ii) furnish to the court a report in writing as to the vocational and educational circumstances and social background of the convicted person together with such recommendations (if any) as to care which the body or person making the report considers appropriate to the said needs.

(b) Where a person is convicted of a first or second offence under section 3 of this Act in relation to which a penalty may be imposed under the said section 27(1)(a) or an offence under section 17 or 18 of this Act, or of attempting to commit any such offence, and the court, having regard to the circumstances of the case, considers it appropriate so to do, the court may remand the person on bail or, unless a penalty falls to be imposed on the person under paragraph (a) of section 27(1) of this Act, in custody for such period as it considers necessary for the purposes of this section, and request a health board, probation and welfare officer or other body or person, considered by the court to be appropriate, to—

    (i)   cause to be furnished to the court a medical report in writing on the convicted person together with such recommendations (if any) as to medical treatment which the person making the report considers appropriate to the needs, arising because of his being dependent on drugs, of the convicted person, and

    (ii) furnish to the court a report in writing as to the vocational and educational circumstances and social background of the convicted person together with such recommendations (if any) as to care

which the body or person making the report considers appropriate to the said needs.

3. (ii) a condition requiring such person to undergo medical or other treatment recommended in the report,

4. (6) If at any time during a period of detention in a designated custodial treatment centre it appears to the court, on an application made by or on behalf either of the prosecutor or the person who is being detained, or on receipt of a message, in a form approved of by the Minister, from an authorised medical practitioner or the person who is for the time being in charge of such centre, that the person being detained under this Act is not then, or may not then be, in further need of the treatment or care of which the court formerly considered him to be in need, or that his continued detention in custody in the designated custodial treatment centre is not then, or may not then be, in his best interests or in the best interests of other persons in that centre, the court, notwithstanding its decision under subsection (2) of this section, may order the person to be brought before the court.

5.(8) The court shall not under this section either, (a) permit a person to enter into a recognisance containing a condition requiring him for medical or other treatment to remain in a specified hospital, clinic or other place, or(b) order a person to be detained in a custodial treatment centre, unless, after consultation with, or consideration of a report of, either the medical practitioner or other person in charge of the hospital, clinic, custodial treatment centre or other place concerned or a medical practitioner or other person nominated by the medical practitioner or other person so in charge, the court is satisfied that the giving or making of the permission or order would be an appropriate course having regard to the needs of the person and would not prejudicially affect the ability of such hospital, clinic, custodial treatment centre or other place to provide for the treatment or care of persons.

15   Repeals

The following provisions of The Principal Act are hereby repealed—

    (a)   the words 'import, export, transport,' in section 5(2)(b);

    (b)   the words 'after consultation with the registration authority concerned,' in both subsection (3) and subsection (4) of section 7;

    (c)   section 10;

(d)   the words 'advisory committees or advisory panels' and 'or 9' in section 12(1);and

(e)   the words 'or advisory panel' in section 12(2).

16   Short title, commencement, collective citation and construction

(1) This Act may be cited as the Misuse of Drugs Act, 1984.

(2) This Act shall come into operation on such day or days as may be fixed therefor by order or orders of the Minister, either generally or with reference to any particular purpose or provision of this Act, and different days may be so fixed for different such purposes or provisions.

(3) The Principal Act and this Act may be cited together as the Misuse of Drugs Acts, 1977 and 1984, and shall be construed together as one Act.

Criminal Justice Act 1984

Number 22 of 1984

ARRANGEMENT OF SECTIONS

Section

1.   Commencement.

2.   Duration of certain sections.

3.   Interpretation.

DETENTION OF ARRESTED PERSONS IN GARDA SÍOCHÁNA CUSTODY IN CERTAIN CIRCUMSTANCES

4.   Detention after arrest.

5.   Access to solicitor and notification of detention.

6.   Powers of Garda Síochána in relation to detained person.

6A   Use of reasonable force in certain circumstances.

7.   Regulations regarding treatment of persons in custody.

8.   Destruction of records.

9.   Application to persons in custody under section 30 of Offences against the State Act, 1939.

10.   Rearrest.

OFFENCES COMMITTED WHILE ON BAIL AND OTHER OFFENCES

11.   Offences committed while on bail: consecutive sentences.

12.   Increase of aggregate term of imprisonment in certain cases.

13.   Failure to surrender to bail.

14.   Increase of penalties for certain firearms offences.

15.   Withholding information regarding firearms or ammunition.

16.   Withholding information regarding stolen property, etc.

17.   Maximum fine on summary conviction of certain indictable offences.

INFERENCES FROM ACCUSED'S FAILURE TO ACCOUNT FOR CERTAIN MATTERS

18.   Inferences from failure, refusal to account for objects, marks, etc.

19.   Inferences from accused's presence at a particular place.

TRIAL PROCEDURE

20.   Notice of alibi in trials on indictment.

21.   Proof by written statement.

22.   Proof by formal admission.

23.   Abolition of right of accused to make unsworn statement.

24.   Order of closing speeches.

25.   Majority verdicts.

MISCELLANEOUS

26   Proceedings after arrest.

27.   Electronic recording of questioning.

28.   Taking of fingerprints, palmprints or photographs of person dealt with under Probation of Offenders Act, 1907, or convicted.

29.   Application of Act to courts-martial.

30.   Laying of regulations before Houses of Oireachtas.

31.   Expenses.

32.   Short title.

AN ACT TO AMEND CRIMINAL LAW AND PROCEDURE. [6th December, 1984]

BE IT ENACTED BY THE OIREACHTAS AS FOLLOWS:

1   Commencement

(1) This Act shall come into operation on such day or days as may be fixed therefor by order or orders of the Minister for Justice either generally or with reference to any particular purpose or provision and different days may be so fixed for different purposes and different provisions of this Act.

(2) An order shall not be made under subsection (1) in respect of any of the following sections namely, sections 4 to 6, 8 to 10, 15, 16, 18 and 19 until provisions relating to the investigation of complaints from the public against [members (within the meaning of the Garda Síochána (Complaints) Act, 1986)]¹ and the adjudication by a body other than the Garda Síochána of such complaints have been enacted by the Oireachtas and have come into operation and until regulations under section 7 have been made.

(3) Sections 12 and 14 shall not apply in relation to offences committed before the commencement of the section concerned.

Amendments

1   Words substituted by Garda Síochána (Complaints) Act 1986, s 16.

2   Duration of certain sections

Each of the following sections, namely, sections 4 to 66, 8 to 10, 15, 16, 18 and 19 shall cease to be in operation at the expiry of four years from the commencement of that section unless a resolution has been passed by each House of the Oireachtas resolving that that section should continue in operation.

3   Interpretation

(1) In this Act, except where the context otherwise requires—

"the Act of 1939" means the Offences against the State Act, 1939;

"imprisonment" includes penal servitude and detention in Saint Patrick's Institution;

"place" includes any building or part of a building, vehicle, vessel, aircraft or hovercraft and any other place whatsoever.

(2) Any reference in this Act to any other enactment shall, except so far as the context otherwise requires, be construed as a reference to that enactment as amended by or under any other enactment, including this Act.

(3) In this Act, a reference to a section is to a section of this Act and a reference to a subsection or paragraph is to the subsection or paragraph of the provision in which the reference occurs, unless it is indicated that reference to some other enactment or provision, as may be appropriate, is intended.

DETENTION OF ARRESTED PERSONS IN GARDA SÍOCHÁNA CUSTODY IN CERTAIN CIRCUMSTANCES

4 Detention after arrest

(1) This section applies to any offence for which a person of full age and capacity and not previously convicted may, [under or by virtue of any enactment or the common law][1], be punished by imprisonment for a term of five years or by a more severe penalty and to an attempt to commit any such offence.

[(2) (a) Where a member of the Garda Síochána arrests without warrant, whether in a Garda Síochána station or elsewhere, a person whom he or she, with reasonable cause, suspects of having committed an offence to which this section applies, the person—

    (i) if not already in a Garda Síochána station, may be taken to and detained in a Garda Síochána station, or

    (ii) if he or she is arrested in a Garda Síochána station, may be detained in the station,

for such period as is authorised by this section if the member of the Garda Síochána in charge of the station to which the person is taken on arrest or in which he or she is arrested has at the time of the person's arrival at the station or his or her arrest in the station, as may be appropriate, reasonable grounds for believing that his or her detention is necessary for the proper investigation of the offence.

  (b) Where a member of the Garda Síochána arrests a person pursuant to an authority of a judge of the District Court under section 10(1), the person may be taken to and detained in a Garda Síochána station for such period as is authorised by this section if the member of the Garda Síochána in charge of the station to which the person is taken on arrest has at the time of the person's arrival at the station reasonable grounds for believing that his or her detention is necessary for the proper investigation of the offence.][2]

(3) (a) The period for which a person so arrested may be detained shall, subject to the provisions of this section, not exceed six hours from the time of his arrest.

  (b) An officer of the Garda Síochána not below the rank of superintendent may direct that a person detained pursuant to subsection (2) be detained for a further period not exceeding six hours if he has reasonable grounds for believing that such further detention is necessary for the proper investigation of the offence.

[(bb)   A member of the Garda Síochána not below the rank of chief superintendent may direct that a person detained pursuant to a direction under paragraph (b) be detained for a further period not exceeding twelve hours if he or she has reasonable grounds for believing that such further detention is necessary for the proper investigation of the offence concerned.]³

   (c)   A direction under paragraph (b) [or (bb)]⁴ may be given orally or in writing and if given orally shall be recorded in writing as soon as practicable.

(4) If at any time during the detention of a person pursuant to this section there are no longer reasonable grounds for suspecting that he has committed an offence to which this section applies, he shall be released from custody forthwith unless his detention is authorised apart from this Act.

[(5) If at any time during the detention of a person pursuant to this section there are no longer reasonable grounds for believing that his detention is necessary for the proper investigation of the offence to which the detention relates, he shall, [subject to subsection (5A)], be released from custody forthwith unless he is charged or caused to be charged with an offence and is brought before a court as soon as may be in connection with such charge or his detention is authorised apart from this Act.]⁵

(5A)(a) If a person is being detained pursuant to this section in a Garda Síochána station between midnight and 8 a.m. and the member in charge of the station is of opinion that any questioning of that person for the purpose of the investigation should be suspended in order to afford him reasonable time to rest, and that person consents in writing to such suspension, the member may give him a notice in writing (which shall specify the time at which it is given) that the investigation (so far as it involves questioning of him) is suspended until such time as is specified in the notice and shall ask him to sign the notice as an acknowledgement that he has received it; and, if the notice is given, the period between the giving thereof and the time specified therein (not being a time later than 8 a.m.) shall be excluded in reckoning a period of detention permitted by this section and the powers conferred by section 6 shall not be exercised during the period so excluded:

         Provided that not more than one notice under this paragraph shall be given to a person during any period between midnight and 8 a.m.

  (b)   A notice under paragraph (a) may, for serious reasons, be withdrawn by a subsequent notice given in like manner, and in that event any time subsequent to the giving of the second notice shall not be excluded under that paragraph.

  (c)   A member of the Garda Síochána when giving a notice to any person under paragraph (a) or (b) shall explain to him orally the effect of the notice.

  (d)   The following particulars shall be entered in the records of the Garda Síochána station without delay—

     (i)   the time of the giving of a notice under paragraph (a) and the time specified therein as the time up to which the questioning is being suspended,

    (ii)   whether the person being detained acknowledged that he received the notice, and

   (iii)   the time of the giving of any notice under paragraph (b).

  (e)   Records kept in pursuance of paragraph (d) shall be preserved for at least twelve months and, if any proceedings are taken against the person in question for the offence in respect of which he was detained, until the conclusion of the proceedings (including any appeal or retrial).[6]

(7) (a) Subject to paragraph (b), subsection (2) shall not apply to a person below the age of twelve years.

(b) If the member in charge of the Garda Síochána station in which a person is detained has reasonable grounds for believing that the person is not below the age of twelve years the subsection shall apply to him as if he were of that age, provided that, where such member ascertains or has reasonable grounds for believing that the person is below that age, he shall be released from custody forthwith unless his detention is authorised apart from this Act.

(8) Where it appears to a member of the Garda Síochána that a person arrested in the circumstances mentioned in subsection (2) is in need of medical attention, or where during his detention it comes to notice that he is in need of such attention, and he is taken for that purpose to a hospital or other suitable place, the time before his arrival at the station or the time during which he is absent from the station, as the case may be, shall be excluded in reckoning a period of detention permitted by this section.

[(8A) Where a person detained pursuant to subsection (2) is taken to a court in connection with an application relating to the lawfulness of his detention, the time during which he is absent from the station for that purpose shall be excluded in reckoning a period of detention permitted by this section.][7]

[(8B) (a) Where a medical practitioner—

(i) has, at the request of a member of the Garda Síochána, assessed the condition of a person detained pursuant to subsection (2), and

(ii) certifies that the person, although the person's condition is not such as to require the person's hospitalisation, is unfit for any questioning for the purpose of the investigation for a specified period,

no questioning of the person shall take place during that period and that period shall be excluded in reckoning a period of detention permitted by this section.

(b) The period that may be specified in a certificate provided under paragraph (a) by a medical practitioner shall not exceed 6 hours.

(c) A certificate may be provided under paragraph (a) on one occasion only in respect of the particular person detained pursuant to subsection (2).][8]

(9) To avoid doubt, it is hereby declared that a person who is being detained pursuant to subsection (2) in connection with an offence shall in no case be held in detention (whether for the investigation of that or any other offence) [for longer than twenty-four hours][9] from the time of his arrest, not including any period which is to be excluded under subsection [(8), (8A) and (8B)][10] in reckoning a period of detention.

(10) Nothing in this section shall affect the operation of section 30 of the Act of 1939.

(11) The powers conferred by this section are without prejudice to any powers exercisable by a member of the Garda Síochána in relation to offences other than offences to which this section applies.

Amendments

1   Words substituted by Criminal Justice Act 2006, s 9(a).

2   Subsection (2) substituted by Criminal Justice Act 2006, s 9(b).

3   Subsection (3)(bb) inserted by Criminal Justice Act 2006, s 9(c).

4   Words substituted by Criminal Justice Act 2006, s 9(c)(ii).

5   Subsection (5) substituted by Criminal Justice (Miscellaneous Provisions) Act 1997, s 2(b). and further amended by Criminal Justice Act 1999, s 34(a) by the substitution of "subject to subsection (5A)" for "subject to subsection (6)".

6   Subsection (6) renumbered as subsection (5A) by Criminal Justice Act 1999, s 34(b) and subsequently deleted by Criminal Justice (Miscellaneous Provisions) Act 2009, s 47(a) which is not yet in operation (February 2011). See the amending Act.

7   Subsection (8A) inserted by Criminal Justice (Miscellaneous Provisions) Act 1997, s 2(c).

8   Subsection (8B) inserted by Criminal Justice (Amendment) Act 2009, s 24(1)(a).

9   Words substituted by Criminal Justice Act 2006, s 9(d).

10 Words substituted by Criminal Justice (Miscellaneous Provisions) Act 1997, s 2(d), and deleted by Criminal Justice (Miscellaneous Provisions) Act 2009, s 47(b).

5   Access to solicitor and notification of detention

(1) Where a person not below the age of [eighteen years][1] is detained in a Garda Síochána station pursuant to section 4, the member of the Garda Síochána in charge of the station shall inform him or cause him to be informed without delay that he is entitled to consult a solicitor and to have notification of his detention and of the station where he is being detained sent to one other person reasonably named by him and shall, on request, cause the solicitor and the named person to be notified accordingly as soon as practicable.

[…][2]

(3) If and for so long as the member of the Garda Síochána in charge of a Garda Síochána station in which a person is detained pursuant to section 4 has reasonable grounds for believing that the person is not below the age of [eighteen years][1], the provisions of subsection (1) shall apply as if he were of that age.

Amendments

1   Words substituted by Children Act 2001, s 67.

2   Subsection (2) repealed by Children Act 2001, s 67.

6   Powers of Garda Síochána in relation to detained person

(1) Where a person is detained pursuant to section 4, a member of the Garda Síochána may—

    (a)   demand of him his name and address;

    (b)   search him or cause him to be searched;

(c) photograph him or cause him to be photographed;

(d) take, or cause to be taken, his fingerprints and palm prints;

(e) ...¹

(f) seize and retain for testing anything that he has in his possession.

[(1A) Where photographs or fingerprints and palm prints, taken pursuant to subsection (1), are lost or damaged or are otherwise imperfect, they may be taken on a second or further occasion.]²

[(2) The powers conferred by subsections (1)(c), (1)(d) or (1A) shall not be exercised except on the authority of a member of the Garda Síochána not below the rank of inspector.]³

(3) Subsection (1)(b) does not empower a member of the Garda Síochána to require a person to remove his underclothing, except where such member, with reasonable cause, suspects that he has concealed on his person a controlled drug (within the meaning of section 2 of the Misuse of Drugs Act, 1977) or an explosive substance and a member of the Garda Síochána not below the rank of superintendent so authorises.

(4) Any person who obstructs or attempts to obstruct any member of the Garda Síochána or any other person acting under the powers conferred by subsection (1) or who fails or refuses to give his name and address when demanded, or gives a name or address which is false or misleading, shall be guilty of an offence and shall be liable on summary conviction to a fine not exceeding [€3,000]⁴ or to imprisonment for a term not exceeding 12 months or to both.

(5) Section 7(2) of the Criminal Law Act, 1976, is hereby amended by the substitution in paragraph (a), for "£500", of "£1,000" and by the deletion of paragraph (b).

Amendments

1 Subsection (1)(e) repealed by Criminal Justice (Forensic Evidence) Act 1990, s 6.

2 Subsection (1A) inserted by Criminal Justice Act 2007, s 48(a)(i).

3 Subsection (2) substituted by Criminal Justice Act 2007, s 48(a)(ii).

4 Amount substituted by Criminal Justice Act 2006, s 13(a).

[6A   Use of reasonable force in certain circumstances

(1) Without prejudice to the generality of section 6, a member of the Garda Síochána may, where—

(a) a person is detained under section 4, and

(b) he or she fails or refuses to allow his or her photograph or fingerprints and palm prints to be taken pursuant to section 6,

use such force as he or she reasonably considers to be necessary to take the photograph or fingerprints and palm prints.

(2) (a) Such a power shall not be exercised except on the authority of a member of the Garda Síochána not below the rank of superintendent.

(b) An authorisation pursuant to paragraph (a) may be given orally or in writing and if given orally shall be confirmed in writing as soon as practicable.

(3) Where a member of the Garda Síochána intends to exercise a power conferred by subsection (1), he or she shall inform the person—

    (a)   of that intention, and

    (b)   that an authorisation to do so has been given pursuant to subsection (2)(a).

(4) Photographs or fingerprints and palm prints taken pursuant to this section shall be taken in the presence of a member of the Garda Síochána not below the rank of inspector.

(5) The taking of such photographs and fingerprints and palm prints shall be video-recorded.]¹

Amendments

1   Section 6A inserted by Criminal Justice Act 2007, s 48(b).

---

7   Regulations regarding treatment of persons in custody

(1) The Minister shall make regulations providing for the treatment of persons in custody in Garda Síochána stations.

(2) The regulations shall include provision for the assignment to custody the member of the Garda Síochána in charge of a Garda Síochána station, or to some other member, of responsibility for overseeing the application of the regulations at that station, without prejudice to the responsibilities and duties of any other member of the Garda Síochána.

(3) A failure on the part of any member of the Garda Síochána to observe any provision of the regulations shall not of itself render that person liable to any criminal or civil proceedings or of itself affect the lawfulness of the custody of the detained person or the admissibility in evidence of any statement made by him.

(4) A failure on the part of any member of the Garda Síochána to observe any provision of the regulations shall render him liable to disciplinary proceedings.

(5) A draft of every regulation proposed to be made under this section shall be laid before each House of the Oireachtas and the regulation shall not be made until a resolution approving the draft has been passed by each such House.

8   Destruction of records

[(1) Where a person (in this section referred to as 'the requester') has had records taken in pursuance of powers conferred by section 6 or 6A of this Act or section 12 of the Act of 2006, and proceedings for an offence to which section 4 applies—

    (a)   are not instituted against the requester within the period of twelve months from the date of the taking of the records, and the failure to institute such proceedings within that period is not due to the fact that he or she has absconded or cannot be found, or

    (b)   have been so instituted and—

        (i)   the requester is acquitted,

        (ii)   the charge against the requester in respect of the offence concerned is dismissed under section 4E of the Criminal Procedure Act 1967, or

        (iii)   the proceedings are discontinued,

he or she may request the Commissioner to have the records concerned destroyed or their use limited.

(2) For the purposes of subsection (1)(b)(ii), a charge against the requester in respect of the offence concerned shall be regarded as dismissed when—

    (a) the time for bringing an appeal against the dismissal has expired,

    (b) any such appeal has been withdrawn or abandoned, or

    (c) on any such appeal, the dismissal is upheld.

(3) Such a request shall be made in writing to the Commissioner and shall—

    (a) contain sufficient particulars in relation to the request to enable the records to be identified, and

    (b) set out the reasons for the request.

(4) The Commissioner shall, as soon as may be, acknowledge receipt of the request in writing.

(5) The Commissioner shall, as soon as may be but not later than 4 weeks after receipt of the request, decide whether to grant or refuse to grant the request or whether to grant it in part and shall cause the requester to be notified in writing of the decision and the date on which it was made.

(6) Where the Commissioner decides to refuse the request or grant it only in part, the requester may within 8 weeks beginning on the date of the decision, appeal to the District Court against the decision.

(7) An appeal under subsection (6) shall—

    (a) be on notice to the other party to the proceedings,

    (b) set out reasons for the appeal, and

    (c) be heard otherwise than in public.

(8) On appeal, the court may have regard in particular to—

    (a) the results of analysis (if any) of the records concerned,

    (b) any previous convictions of the requester, and

    (c) whether, in all the circumstances, it would be unjust not to allow the appeal.

(9) The court may make such order as it sees fit on the appeal, including an order—

    (a) for the destruction of the records, or

    (b) an order authorising their retention for such purpose or period as it may direct.

(10) An appeal from a refusal or grant of an order of destruction of the District Court shall lie to a judge of the Circuit Court at the instance of the requester or the Commissioner, and the appeal shall be heard otherwise than in public.

(11) Where an order for the destruction of any records is made under this section, the Commissioner shall cause the requester to be notified in writing as soon as the records have been destroyed.

(12) The jurisdiction conferred on the District Court under this section shall be exercised by the judge of that Court assigned to the district court district where the requester resides.

(13) Nothing in this section shall—

    (a) prevent or restrict the exercise of powers conferred by section 6 or 6A of this Act or section 12 of the Act of 2006, or

(b) pending the conclusion of proceedings under this section, prevent or restrict use of the records for the purpose of other proceedings or of a criminal investigation.

(14) This section does not apply to records taken inpursuance of powers conferred by section 6 of this Act or section 12 of the Act of 2006 before the commencement of this section.

(15) In this section—

"Act of 2006" means Criminal Justice Act 2006;

"Commissioner" means the Commissioner of the Garda Síochána;

"records" means a photograph (including a negative), fingerprints and palm prints taken in pursuance of the powers conferred by section 6 or 6A of this Act or section 12 of the Act of 2006 and every copy and related record thereof.]¹

Amendments

1   Section 8 substituted by Criminal Justice Act 2007, s 49.

---

9   Application to persons in custody under section 30 of Offences against the State Act, 1939

Sections 4(8), [4(8A)],¹ [4(8B)],² 5, 6(2), [6(3), 6A, 18, 19 and 19A]³ shall apply, with the necessary modifications, in relation to persons in custody under section 30 of the Act of 1939 and to the powers conferred by section 7 of the Criminal Law Act, 1976, as they apply to persons detained pursuant to section 4 of this Act.

Amendments

1   Words inserted by Criminal Justice Act 2007, s 55(a).

2   Words inserted by Criminal Justice (Amendment) Act 2009, s 24(2).

3   Words substituted by Criminal Justice Act 2007, s 55(b).

---

10   Rearrest

[(1) Where a person arrested on suspicion of having committed an offence is detained pursuant to section 4 and is released without any charge having been made against him, he shall not—

(a) be arrested again in connection with the offence to which the detention related, or

(b) be arrested for any other offence of which, at the time of the first arrest, the member of the Garda Síochána by whom he was arrested suspected, or ought reasonably to have suspected him of having committed,

except on the authority of a warrant issued by a judge of the District Court who is satisfied on information supplied on oath by a member of the Garda Síochána not below the rank of superintendent that either of the following cases apply, namely:

(i) further information has come to the knowledge of the Garda Síochána since the person's release as to his suspected participation in the offence for which his arrest is sought, or

(ii) notwithstanding that the Garda Síochána had knowledge, prior to the person's release, of the person's suspected participation in the offence for which his arrest is sought, the questioning of the person in relation to that offence, prior to his release, would not have been in the interests of the proper investigation of the offence.

A person arrested under that authority shall be dealt with pursuant to section 4.

(1A) An application for a warrant under this section shall be heard otherwise than in public.]¹

(2) Notwithstanding anything in subsection (1), a person to whom that subsection relates may be arrested for any offence for the purpose of charging him with that offence forthwith.

(3) Where a person who has been arrested under section 30 of the Act of 1939 in connection with an offence is released without any charge having been made against him, he shall not be detained pursuant to section 4—

(a) in connection with the first-mentioned offence, or

(b) in connection with any other offence of which, at the time of his arrest for the first-mentioned offence, the member of the Garda Síochána by whom he was arrested suspected him or ought reasonably to have suspected him.

Amendments

1 Subsection (1) substituted and (1A) inserted by Criminal Justice (Amendment) Act 2009, s 24(3).

OFFENCES COMMITTED WHILE ON BAIL AND OTHER OFFENCES

11   Offences committed while on bail: consecutive sentences

[(1) Any sentence of imprisonment passed on a person for an offence—

(a) committed while on bail, whether committed before or after the commencement of section 22 of the Criminal Justice Act 2007, or

(b) committed after such commencement while the person is unlawfully at large after the issue of a warrant for his or her arrest for non-compliance with a condition of the recognisance concerned,

shall be consecutive on any sentence passed on him or her for a previous offence or, if he or she is sentenced in respect of two or more previous offences, on the sentence last due to expire, so however that, where two or more consecutive sentences as required by this section are passed by the District Court, the aggregate term of imprisonment in respect of those consecutive sentences shall not exceed 2 years.]¹

(2) Subsection (1) shall not apply where any such sentence is one of imprisonment for life or is a sentence of detention under section 103 of the Children Act, 1908.

(3) Subsection (1) shall apply notwithstanding anything contained in section 5 of the Criminal Justice Act, 1951.

[(4) Where a court—

(a)   is determining the sentence to be imposed on a person for an offence committed while he or she was on bail,

and

(b)   is required by subsection (1) to impose two or more consecutive sentences,

then, the fact that the offence was committed while the person was on bail shall be treated for the purpose of determining the sentence as an aggravating factor and the court shall (except where the sentence for the previous offence is one of imprisonment for life or where the court considers that there are exceptional circumstances justifying its not doing so) impose a sentence that is greater than that which would have been imposed in the absence of such a factor.][2]

Amendments

1   Subsection (1) substituted by Criminal Justice Act 2007, s 22.

2   Subsection (4) inserted by Bail Act 1997, s 10.

12   Increase of aggregate term of imprisonment in certain cases

(1) Section 5 of the Criminal Justice Act, 1951 (which provides that, where two or more sentences passed by the District Court are ordered to run consecutively, the aggregate term of imprisonment shall not exceed twelve months) is hereby amended by the substitution, for "twelve months", of "two years". In that section "imprisonment" shall include detention in Saint Patrick's Institution.

(2) Section 13(1) of the Criminal Law Act, 1976 (which provides for consecutive sentences in the case of an offence committed by a person while he is serving a sentence) is hereby amended by the substitution, for "twelve months", of "two years".

13   Failure to surrender bail

(1) If a person who has been released on bail in criminal proceedings fails to appear before a court in accordance with his recognisance, he shall be guilty of an offence and shall be liable on summary conviction to a fine not exceeding [€5,000][1] or to imprisonment for a term not exceeding twelve months or to both.

(2) It shall be a defence in any proceedings for an offence under subsection (1) for the accused to show that he had a reasonable excuse for not so appearing.

(3) For the purpose of section 11 an offence under this section shall be treated as an offence committed while on bail.

(4) Where a person has failed to appear before a court in answer to his bail and the court has directed that a warrant be issued for the arrest of that person by reason of his failure to answer his bail, a member of the Garda Síochána may arrest such a person notwithstanding that he does not have the warrant in his possession at the time of the arrest.

(5) Where a person is arrested pursuant to subsection (4) the member arresting him shall as soon as practicable produce and serve on the said person the said warrant.

[(6) Notwithstanding section 10(4) of the Petty Sessions (Ireland) Act 1851, summary proceedings for an offence under this section may be instituted within 12 months from the date on which the offence was committed.]²

Amendments

1   Amounts amended by Criminal Justice Act 2007, s 23(a).

2   Subsection (6) inserted by Criminal Justice Act 2007, s 23(b).

14   Increase of penalties for certain offences

(1) Section 15 of the Firearms Act, 1925, as amended by section 21(4) of the Criminal Law (Jurisdiction) Act, 1976 (possessing firearm or ammunition with intent to endanger life or cause serious injury to property) is hereby amended by the substitution, for "imprisonment for a term not exceeding fourteen years", of "imprisonment for life".

(2) Section 26(1) of the Firearms Act, 1964, as amended by section 21(6)(b) of the Criminal Law (Jurisdiction) Act, 1976 (possession of firearm while taking vehicle without authority) is hereby amended by the substitution, for "seven years", of "fourteen years".

(3) Section 27(2) of the Firearms Act, 1964, as amended by section 21(6)(c) of the Criminal Law (Jurisdiction) Act, 1976 (use of firearm to resist arrest or aid escape) is hereby amended by the substitution for "imprisonment for a term not exceeding fourteen years", of "imprisonment for life".

(4) Section 27A(1) of the Firearms Act, 1964, inserted by section 8 of the Criminal Law (Jurisdiction) Act, 1976 (possession of firearm or ammunition in suspicious circumstances) is hereby amended by the substitution, for "five years", of "ten years".

(5) Section 27B(1) of the Firearms Act, 1964, inserted by section 9 of the Criminal Law (Jurisdiction) Act, 1976 (carrying firearm with criminal intent) is hereby amended by the substitution, for "ten years", of "fourteen years".

15   Withholding information regarding firearms or ammunition

(1) Where a member of the Garda Síochána—

(a)   finds a person in possession of any firearm or ammunition,

(b)   has reasonable grounds for believing that the person is in possession of the firearm or ammunition in contravention of the criminal law, and

(c)   informs that person of his belief,

he may require that person to give him any information which is in his possession, or which he can obtain by taking reasonable steps, as to how he came by the firearm or ammunition and as to any previous dealings with it, whether by himself or by any other person.

(2) If that person fails or refuses, without reasonable excuse, to give the information or gives information that he knows to be false or misleading, he shall be guilty of an offence and shall be liable on summary conviction to a fine not exceeding [€5,000]¹ or to imprisonment for a term not exceeding twelve months or to both.

(3) Subsection (2) shall not have effect unless the accused when required to give the information was told in ordinary language by the member of the Garda Síochána what the effect of his failure or refusal might be.

(4) Any information given by a person in compliance with a requirement under subsection (1) shall not be admissible in evidence against that person or his spouse in any proceedings, civil or criminal, other than proceedings for an offence under subsection (2).

Amendments

1   Words amended by Criminal Justice Act 2006, s 62 and further amended by Criminal Justice Act 2007, s 48(c).

16   Withholding information regarding stolen property, etc

Amendments

1   Section 16 repealed by Criminal Justice (Theft And Fraud Offences) Act 2001, Sch 1.

17   Maximum fine on summary conviction of certain indictable offences

Section 4(1) of the Criminal Justice Act, 1951, and section 13(3)(a) of the Criminal Procedure Act, 1967 (each of which provides for a maximum fine of £100 on summary conviction of certain indictable offences) are hereby amended by the substitution, in each of those provisions, of "£1,000" for "£100".

INFERENCES FROM ACCUSED'S FAILURE TO ACCOUNT FOR CERTAIN MATTERS

18   Inferences from failure, refusal to account for objects, marks, etc

[(1) Where in any proceedings against a person for an arrestable offence evidence is given that the accused—

    (a) at any time before he or she was charged with the offence, on being questioned by a member of the Garda Síochána in relation to the offence, or

    (b) when being charged with the offence or informed by a member of the Garda Síochána that he or she might be prosecuted for it,

was requested by the member to account for any object, substance or mark, or any mark on any such object, that was—

    (i)   on his or her person,

    (ii)   in or on his or her clothing or footwear,

    (iii) otherwise in his or her possession, or

    (iv) in any place in which he or she was during any specified period,

and which the member reasonably believes may be attributable to the participation of the accused in the commission of the offence and the member informed the accused that he or she so believes, and the accused failed or refused to give an account, being an account which in the circumstances at the time clearly called for an explanation from him or her when so questioned, charged or informed, as the case may be, then, the court, in determining whether a charge should be dismissed under Part IA of the Criminal Procedure Act 1967 or whether there is a case to answer and the court (or, subject to the judge's directions, the jury) in determining whether the accused is guilty of the offence charged (or of any other offence of which he or she could lawfully be convicted on that charge) may draw such inferences from the failure or refusal as appear proper; and the failure or refusal may, on the basis of such inferences, be treated as, or as capable of amounting to, corroboration of any evidence in relation to which the failure or refusal is material.

(2) A person shall not be convicted of an offence solely or mainly on an inference drawn from a failure or refusal to account for a matter to which subsection (1) applies.

(3) Subsection (1) shall not have effect unless—

  (a) the accused was told in ordinary language when being questioned, charged or informed, as the case may be, what the effect of the failure or refusal to account for a matter to which that subsection applies might be, and

  (b) the accused was afforded a reasonable opportunity to consult a solicitor before such failure or refusal occurred.

(4) Nothing in this section shall, in any proceedings—

  (a) prejudice the admissibility in evidence of the silence or other reaction of the accused in the face of anything said in his or her presence relating to the conduct in respect of which he or she is charged in so far as evidence thereof would be admissible apart from this section,

  (b) be taken to preclude the drawing of any inference from the silence or other reaction of the accused which could properly be drawn apart from this section, or

  (c) be taken to preclude the drawing of any inference from a failure or refusal to account for the presence of an object, substance or mark or for the condition of clothing or footwear which could properly be drawn apart from this section.

(5) The court (or, subject to the judge's directions, the jury) shall, for the purposes of drawing an inference under this section, have regard to whenever, if appropriate, the account of the matter concerned was first given by the accused.

(6) This section shall not apply in relation to the questioning of a person by a member of the Garda Síochána unless it is recorded by electronic or similar means or the person consents in writing to it not being so recorded.

(7) Subsection (1) shall apply to the condition of clothing or footwear as it applies to a substance or mark thereon.

(8) References in subsection (1) to evidence shall, in relation to the hearing of an application under Part IA of the Criminal Procedure Act 1967 for the dismissal of a charge, be taken to include a statement of the evidence to be given by a witness at the trial.

(9) In this section 'arrestable offence' has the meaning it has in section 2 (as amended by section 8 of the Criminal Justice Act 2006) of the Criminal Law Act 1997.]¹

Amendments

1   Section 18 substituted by Criminal Justice Act 2007, s 28(1).

Note

Criminal Justice Act 2007, s 28(2) and (3) provides that:

> (2) A person shall not be convicted of an offence solely or mainly on an inference drawn from a failure or refusal to account for a matter to which subsection (1) applies.
>
> (3) Subsection (1) shall not have effect unless—
>
> (a) the accused was told in ordinary language when being questioned, charged or informed, as the case may be, what the effect of the failure or refusal to account for a matter to which that subsection applies might be, and
>
> (b) the accused was afforded a reasonable opportunity to consult a solicitor before such failure or refusal occurred.

---

19   Inferences from accused's presence at a particular place

[(1) Where in any proceedings against a person for an arrestable offence evidence is given that the accused—

(a) at any time before he or she was charged with the offence, on being questioned by a member of the Garda Síochána in relation to the offence, or

(b) when being charged with the offence or informed by a member of the Garda Síochána that he or she might be prosecuted for it,

was requested by the member to account for his or her presence at a particular place at or about the time the offence is alleged to have been committed, and the member reasonably believes that the presence of the accused at that place and at that time may be attributable to his or her participation in the commission of the offence and the member informed the accused that he or she so believes, and the accused failed or refused to give an account, being an account which in the circumstances at the time clearly called for an explanation from him or her when so questioned, charged or informed, as the case may be, then, the court, in determining whether a charge should be dismissed under Part IA of the Criminal Procedure Act 1967 or whether there is a case to answer and the court (or, subject to the judge's directions, the jury) in determining whether the accused is guilty of the offence charged (or of any other offence of which he or she could lawfully be convicted on that charge) may draw such inferences from the failure or refusal as appear proper; and the failure or refusal may, on the basis of such inferences, be treated as, or as capable of amounting to, corroboration of any evidence in relation to which the failure or refusal is material.

(2) A person shall not be convicted of an offence solely or mainly on an inference drawn from a failure or refusal to account for his or her presence at a particular place under subsection (1).

(3) Subsection (1) shall not have effect unless—

(a) the accused was told in ordinary language when being questioned, charged or informed, as the case may be, what the effect of the failure or refusal to account for his or her presence at a particular place might be, and

(b) the accused was afforded a reasonable opportunity to consult a solicitor before such failure or refusal occurred.

(4) Nothing in this section shall, in any proceedings—

(a) prejudice the admissibility in evidence of the silence or other reaction of the accused in the face of anything said in his or her presence relating to the conduct in respect of which he or she is charged in so far as evidence thereof would be admissible apart from this section,

(b) be taken to preclude the drawing of any inference from the silence or other reaction of the accused which could properly be drawn apart from this section, or

(c) be taken to preclude the drawing of any inference from the failure or refusal of a person to account for his or her presence which could properly be drawn apart from this section.

(5) The court (or, subject to the judge's directions, the jury) shall, for the purposes of drawing an inference under this section, have regard to whenever, if appropriate, the account of his or her presence at a particular place concerned was first given by the accused.

(6) This section shall not apply in relation to the questioning of a person by a member of the Garda Síochána unless it is recorded by electronic or similar means or the person consents in writing to it not being so recorded.

(7) References in subsection (1) to evidence shall, in relation to the hearing of an application under Part IA of the Criminal Procedure Act 1967 for the dismissal of a charge, be taken to include a statement of the evidence to be given by a witness at the trial.

(8) In this section 'arrestable offence' has the meaning it has in section 2 (as amended by section 8 of the Criminal Justice Act 2006) of the Criminal Law Act 1997][1]

Amendments

1   Subsection 19 substituted by Criminal Justice Act 2007, s 29(1).

Note

Criminal Justice Act 2007, s 29(2) and (3) provides that:

(2) A person shall not be convicted of an offence solely or mainly on an inference drawn from a failure or refusal to account for his or her presence at a particular place under subsection (1).

(3) Subsection (1) shall not have effect unless—

(a) the accused was told in ordinary language when being questioned, charged or informed, as the case may be, what the effect of the failure or refusal to account for his or her presence at a particular place might be, and

(b) the accused was afforded a reasonable opportunity to consult a solicitor before such failure or refusal occurred.

[19A   (1) Where in any proceedings against a person for an arrestable offence evidence is given that the accused—

(a) at any time before he or she was charged with the offence, on being questioned by a member of the Garda Síochána in relation to the offence, or

(b) when being charged with the offence or informed by a member of the Garda Síochána that he or she might be prosecuted for it, failed to mention any fact relied on in his or her defence in those proceedings, being a fact which in the circumstances existing at the time clearly called for an explanation from him or her when so questioned, charged or informed, as the case may be, then, the court, in determining whether a charge should be dismissed under Part IA of the Criminal Procedure Act 1967 or whether there is a case to answer and the court (or, subject to the judge's directions, the jury) in determining whether the accused is guilty of the offence charged (or of any other offence of which he or she could lawfully be convicted on that charge) may draw such inferences from the failure as appear proper; and the failure may, on the basis of such inferences, be treated as, or as capable of amounting to, corroboration of any evidence in relation to which the failure is material.

(2) A person shall not be convicted of an offence solely or mainly on an inference drawn from a failure to mention a fact to which subsection (1) applies.

(3) Subsection (1) shall not have effect unless—

   (a) the accused was told in ordinary language when being questioned, charged or informed, as the case may be, what the effect of the failure to mention a fact to which that subsection applies might be, and

   (b) the accused was afforded a reasonable opportunity to consult a solicitor before such failure occurred.

(4) Nothing in this section shall, in any proceedings—

   (a) prejudice the admissibility in evidence of the silence or other reaction of the accused in the face of anything said in his or her presence relating to the conduct in respect of which he or she is charged in so far as evidence thereof would be admissible apart from this section, or

   (b) be taken to preclude the drawing of any inference from the silence or other reaction of the accused which could properly be drawn apart from this section.

(5) The court (or, subject to the judge's directions, the jury) shall, for the purposes of drawing an inference under this section, have regard to when the fact concerned was first mentioned by the accused.

(6) This section shall not apply in relation to the questioning of a person by a member of the Garda Síochána unless it is recorded by electronic or similar means or the person consents in writing to it not being so recorded.

(7) Subject to section 7 of the Criminal Justice (Drug Trafficking) Act 1996 and section 5 of the Offences Against the State (Amendment) Act 1998, this section shall not apply in relation to a failure to mention a fact if the failure occurred before the commencement of this section.

(8) References in subsection (1) to evidence shall, in relation to the hearing of an application under Part IA of the Criminal Procedure Act 1967 for the dismissal of a charge, be taken to include a statement of the evidence to be given by a witness at the trial.

(9) In this section 'arrestable offence' has the meaning it has in section 2 (as amended by section 8 of the Criminal Justice Act 2006) of the Criminal Law Act 1997.]¹

Amendments

1 Section 19A inserted by Criminal Justice Act 2007, s 30.

TRIAL PROCEDURE

20   Notice of alibi in trials on indictment

(1) On a trial on indictment for an offence committed after the commencement of this section the accused shall not without the leave of the court adduce evidence in support of an alibi unless, before the end of the prescribed period, he gives notice of particulars of the alibi.

(2) Without prejudice to subsection (1), on any such trial the accused shall not without the leave of the court call any other person (in this section referred to as the witness) to give such evidence unless—

(a)   the notice under that subsection includes the name and address of the witness or, if the name or address is not known to the accused at the time he gives the notice, any information in his possession which might be of material assistance in finding the witness,

(b)   if the name or the address is not included in that notice, the court is satisfied that the accused, before giving the notice, took and thereafter continued to take all reasonable steps to secure that the name or address would be ascertained,

(c)   if the name or the address is not included in that notice, but the accused subsequently discovers the name or address or receives other information which might be of material assistance in finding the witness, he gives notice forthwith of the name, address or other information, as the case may be, and

(d)   if the accused is notified by or on behalf of the prosecution that the witness has not been traced by the name or at the address given, he gives notice forthwith of any such information which is then in his possession or, on subsequently receiving any such information, gives notice of it forthwith.

(3) The court shall not refuse leave under this section if it appears to the court that the accused was not informed of the requirements of this section—

(a)   by the District Court when he was sent forward for trial, or

(b)   by the trial court when, on being sent forward by the District Court for sentence, he changed his plea to one of not guilty, or

(c)   where he was brought before a Special Criminal Court for trial under section 47 of the Act of 1939, by the Court when it fixed the date of trial.

(4) Any evidence tendered to disprove an alibi may, subject to any directions by the court as to the time it is to be given, be given before or after evidence is given in support of the alibi.

(5) Any notice purporting to be given under this section on behalf of the accused by his solicitor shall, unless the contrary is proved, be deemed to be given with the authority of the accused.

[(6) A notice under subsection (1) or under paragraph (c) or (d) of subsection (2) shall be given in writing to the solicitor for the prosecution.]¹

(7) A notice required by this section to be given to the solicitor for the prosecution may be given by delivering it to him or by leaving it at his office or by sending it to him by registered post at his office.

(8) In this section—

"evidence in support of an alibi" means evidence tending to show that by reason of the presence of the accused at a particular place or in a particular area at a particular time he was not, or was unlikely to have been, at the place where the offence is alleged to have been committed at the time of its alleged commission;

"the prescribed period" means—

    [(a) the period of fourteen days after the date the accused is, in accordance with section 4B(1) of the Criminal Procedure Act, 1967, served with the documents referred to in that section, or]²

    (b) ...³

    [(c) where the accused, on being sent forward for sentence, changes his plea to not guilty, the period of fourteen days after the accused is, in accordance with section 13(4)(b) of the Criminal Procedure Act, 1967, served with the documents referred to in section 4B(1) of that Act, or]⁴

    (d) where the accused is brought before a Special Criminal Court for trial under section 47 of the Act of 1939, such period as is fixed by the Court when the Court fixes the date of trial.

Amendments

1   Subsection (6) substituted by Criminal Justice Act 1999, s 16(3).

2   Paragraph (a) substituted by Criminal Justice Act 1999, s 16(3).

3   Paragraph (b) deleted by Criminal Justice Act 1999, s 16(3).

4   Paragraph (c) substituted by Criminal Justice Act 1999, s 16(3).

21   Proof by written statement

(1) In any proceedings against a person for an offence[, other than the hearing of an application under Part IA of the Criminal Procedure Act, 1967[, for the dismissal of the charge]¹, a written statement by any person shall, if such of the conditions mentioned in subsection (2) as are applicable are satisfied, be admissible as evidence to the like extent as oral evidence to the like effect by that person.

(2) The said conditions are:

    (a) the statement purports to be signed by the person who made it;

    (b) the statement contains a declaration by that person to the effect that it is true to the best of his knowledge and belief and that he made the statement knowing that, if it were tendered in evidence, he would be liable to prosecution if he stated in it anything which he knew to be false or did not believe to be true;

    (c) a copy of the statement is served, by or on behalf of the party proposing to tender it in evidence, on each of the other parties to the proceedings; and

(d) none of the other parties or their solicitors, within twenty-one days from the service of the copy of the statement, serves on the party so proposing a notice objecting to the statement being tendered in evidence under this section.

(3) The conditions mentioned in paragraphs (c) and (d) of subsection (2) shall not apply if the parties agree at the hearing or the parties or their solicitors agree before the hearing that the statement shall be so tendered.

(4) The following provisions shall also have effect in relation to any written statement tendered in evidence under this section:

(a) if the statement is made by a person under the age of twenty-one years, it shall give his age;

(b) if it is made by a person who cannot read it, it shall be read to him before he signs it and shall be accompanied by a declaration by the person who so read the statement to the effect that it was so read; and

(c) if it refers to any other document as an exhibit, the copy served on any other party to the proceedings under subsection (2)(c) shall be accompanied by a copy of that document or by such information as may be necessary in order to enable the party on whom it is served to inspect that document or a copy thereof.

(5) Notwithstanding that a written statement made by any person may be admissible as evidence by virtue of this section—

(a) the party by whom or on whose behalf a copy of the statement was served may call that person to give evidence, and

(b) the court may, of its own motion or on the application of any party to the proceedings, require that person to attend before the court and give evidence.

(6) An application under subsection (5)(b) may be made before the hearing in a case in which the proceedings are in the Central Criminal Court, the Circuit Court or the Special Criminal Court and, for this purpose, the powers of the Central Criminal Court shall be exercisable by any judge of the High Court and the powers of the Circuit Court shall be exercisable by any judge of that court.

(7) So much of any statement as is admitted as evidence by virtue of this section shall, unless the court otherwise directs, be read aloud at the hearing.

(8) Any document or object referred to as an exhibit and identified in a written statement tendered in evidence under this section shall be treated as if it had been produced as an exhibit and identified in court by the maker of the statement.

(9) A document required by this section to be served on any person may, subject to subsection (10), be served—

(a) by delivering it to him or to his solicitor,

(b) by addressing it to him and leaving it at his usual or last known residence or place of business or by addressing it to his solicitor and leaving it at the solicitor's office,

(c) by sending it by registered post to him at his usual or last known residence or place of business or to his solicitor at the solicitor's office, or

(d) in the case of a body corporate, by delivering it to the secretary or clerk of the body at its registered or principal office or sending it by registered post to the secretary or clerk of that body at that office.

(10) A document required by this section to be served on an accused shall, if the accused is not represented by a solicitor, be served personally on the accused.

(11) Where—

   (a) a statement is tendered in evidence by virtue of this section, and

   (b) the person by whom the statement was made has stated in it anything which he knew to be false or did not believe to be true,

he shall be guilty of an offence and shall be liable on summary conviction to a fine not exceeding £1,000 or to imprisonment for a term not exceeding twelve months or to both, or on conviction on indictment to a fine not exceeding £2,000 or to imprisonment for a term not exceeding five years or to both.

(12) This section shall also apply to a written statement made outside the State with the omission from subsection (2)(b) of the words from "and that he made the statement to the end of the paragraph, and the omission of subsection (11).

Amendments

1   Words substituted by Criminal Justice Act 1999, s 16(4).

---

22   Proof by formal admission

(1) Subject to the provisions of this section, any fact of which oral evidence may be given in any criminal proceedings may be admitted for the purpose of those proceedings by or on behalf of the prosecution or the accused, and the admission by any party of any such fact under this section shall as against that party be conclusive evidence in those proceedings of the fact admitted.

(2) An admission under this section—

   (a) may be made before or at the hearing,

   (b) if made otherwise than in court, shall be in writing,

   (c) if made in writing by an individual, shall be signed by the person making it and, if so made by a body corporate, shall be signed by a director or manager, or the secretary or clerk or some other similar officer of the body corporate,

   (d) if made on behalf of an accused who is an individual, shall be made by his counsel or solicitor,

   (e) if made at any stage before the hearing by an accused who is an individual, must be approved by his counsel or solicitor either at the time it was made or subsequently,

and any signature referred to in paragraph (c) shall be taken to be that of the person whose signature it appears to be unless the contrary is shown.

(3) An admission under this section for the purpose of proceedings relating to any matter shall be treated as an admission for the purpose of any subsequent criminal proceedings relating to that matter (including any appeal or retrial).

(4) An admission under this section may with the leave of the court be withdrawn in the proceedings for the purpose of which it is made or any subsequent criminal proceedings relating to the same matter.

23   Abolition of right of accused to make unsworn statement

(1) In any proceedings against a person for an offence the accused shall not be entitled to make a statement without being sworn and, accordingly, if he gives evidence, he shall do so on oath and be liable to cross-examination, but this shall not—

(a) affect the right of the accused, if not represented by counsel or a solicitor, to address the court or jury otherwise than on oath on any matter on which, if he were so represented, his counsel or solicitor could address the court or jury on his behalf,

(b) affect any trial, or the preliminary examination of any indictable offence, commenced before the commencement of this section.

(2) Nothing in subsection (1) shall prevent the accused from making a statement without being sworn—

(a) if it is one which he is required by law to make personally, or

(b) if he makes it by way of mitigation before the court passes sentence upon him.

(3) The following provisions are hereby repealed:

(a) paragraph (h) of the proviso to section 1 of the Criminal Justice (Evidence) Act, 1924, and

(b) section 7(4) of the Criminal Procedure Act, 1967, and, in section 8(2) of that Act, the words from "proceed in accordance with" to "paragraph (a),".

24   Order of closing speeches

(1) Notwithstanding any rule of law or practice, and notwithstanding anything contained in section 2 of the Criminal Procedure Act, 1865, the procedure at a trial on indictment as to the closing speeches for the prosecution and for the defence shall be as follows:

(a) the prosecution shall have the right to a closing speech in all cases except where the accused is not represented by counsel or a solicitor and does not call any witness (other than a witness to character only), and the defence shall have the right to a closing speech in all cases, and

(b) the closing speech for the defence shall be made after that for the prosecution.

(2) Section 3 of the Criminal Justice (Evidence) Act, 1924, is hereby repealed.

25   Majority verdicts

(1) The verdict of a jury in criminal proceedings need not be unanimous in a case where there are not fewer than eleven jurors if ten of them agree on the verdict.

(2) The court shall not accept a verdict of guilty unless the foreman of the jury has stated in open court whether the verdict is unanimous or is by a majority in accordance with subsection (1) and, in the latter event, the number of jurors who agreed to the verdict.

(3) The court shall not accept a verdict by virtue of subsection (1) unless it appears to the court that the jury have had such period of time for deliberation as the court thinks reasonable having regard to the nature and complexity of the case; and the court shall not in any event accept such a verdict unless it appears to the court that the jury have had at least two hours for deliberation.

(4) The court shall cause the verdict of the jury to be taken in such a way that, where the verdict is one of not guilty, it shall not be indicated whether the verdict was unanimous or by a majority.

(5) This section shall not affect the trial of any offence for which the court is required, upon the conviction of the accused, to sentence him to death or any trial commenced before the commencement of this section.

MISCELLANEOUS

26   Proceedings after arrest

The following section shall be substituted for section 15 of the Criminal Justice Act, 1951:[1]

Amendments

1   See the amended Act.

---

27   Electronic recording of questioning

(1) The Minister for Justice may by regulations provide for the recording by electronic or other similar means of the questioning of persons by members of the Garda Síochána at Garda Síochána stations or elsewhere in connection with the investigation of offences.

(2) The regulations may be made so as to apply generally or to questioning at such places, to such extent, in relation to such offences or in such circumstances, as may be prescribed therein.

(3) The regulations shall include provision for the preservation, for such time and in such manner as may be prescribed therein, of every recording made in accordance with the regulations.

(4) Any failure to comply with a provision of the regulations shall not by itself render a person liable to civil or criminal proceedings, and (without prejudice to the power of the court to exclude evidence at its discretion) shall not by itself render inadmissible in evidence anything said during such questioning.

28   [Taking of fingerprints, palmprints or photographs of person dealt with under Probation of Offenders Act, 1907, or convicted

(1) Where a person, on being prosecuted for an indictable offence, is the subject of an order under subsection (1) or (2) of section 1 of the Probation of Offenders Act, 1907, or is convicted and otherwise dealt with, a member of the Garda Síochána may—

   (a)   at any convenient place, take the fingerprints, palmprints or photograph of that person, within 7 days of the making of such order or his being convicted, or

   (b)   require, in writing, that person to attend, within 7 days of the making of such order or his being convicted, at a named Garda Síochána station for the purpose of having his fingerprints, palmprints or photograph taken:

Provided that where a person has made it impracticable for his fingerprints, palmprints or photograph to be taken within the said period of 7 days, a member of the Garda Síochána may require (or in the case of a person attending a Garda Síochána station pursuant to a requirement under this section, further require) in writing, that person to attend at a named Garda Síochána station on a specified day for the purpose of having his fingerprints, palmprints or photograph taken.

500

(2) A member of the Garda Síochána may take the fingerprints, palmprints or photograph of a person on his attendance at a Garda Síochána station pursuant to a requirement under this section.

(3) The provisions of section 8 shall apply to fingerprints, palmprints or photographs taken pursuant to this section of a person who is the subject of an order under subsection (1) or (2) of section 1 of the Probation of Offenders Act, 1907, as they apply to fingerprints, palmprints or photographs taken in pursuance of the powers conferred by section 6.

(4) Any person who refuses to comply with a requirement under this section or to allow his fingerprints, palmprints or photograph to be taken pursuant to this section shall be guilty of an offence and shall be liable on summary conviction to a fine not exceeding [€3,000] or to imprisonment for a term not exceeding 12 months or to both.]¹

Amendments

1 Section 28 substituted by Criminal Justice (Miscellaneous Provisions) Act 1997, s 12 and further amended by Criminal Justice Act 2006, s 13(c).

29 Application of Act to courts-martial

The provisions of this Act relating to criminal proceedings shall not apply in relation to a trial by court-martial except so far as any such provision is so applied by regulations made by the Minister for Defence, with such modifications, if any, as may be prescribed by the regulations.

30 Laying of regulations before Houses of Oireachtas

Every regulation made under this Act (other than a regulation under section 7) shall be laid before each House of the Oireachtas as soon as may be after such regulation is made and, if a resolution annulling such regulation is passed by either House of the Oireachtas within the next subsequent twenty-one days on which that House has sat after such regulation has been laid before it, such regulation shall be annulled accordingly, but without prejudice to the validity of anything previously done under such regulation.

31 Expenses

The expenses incurred by the Minister for Justice in the administration of this Act shall, to such extent as may be sanctioned by the Minister for Finance, be paid out of moneys provided by the Oireachtas.

32 Short title

This Act may be cited as the Criminal Justice Act, 1984.

Courts (No 3) Act 1986

Number 33 of 1986

ARRANGEMENT OF SECTIONS

Section

1.   Issue of summonses in relation to offences.

2.   Short title, collective citation and construction.

AN ACT TO AMEND AND EXTEND THE COURTS (SUPPLEMENTAL PROVISIONS) ACTS, 1961 TO 1986. [19th December, 1986]

BE IT ENACTED BY THE OIREACHTAS AS FOLLOWS:

1   Issue of summonses in relation to offences

[(1) Proceedings in the District Court in respect of an offence may be commenced by the issuing, as a matter of administrative procedure, of a document (in this section referred to as a 'summons') to the prosecutor by the appropriate office.

(2) The issue of a summons may, in addition to being effected by any method by which the issue of a summons could be effected immediately before the enactment of section 49 of the Act of 2004, be effected by transmitting it by electronic means to the person who applied for it or a person acting on his or her behalf.

(3) An application for the issue of a summons may be made to the appropriate office by or on behalf of the Attorney General, the Director of Public Prosecutions, a member of the Garda Síochána or any person authorised by or under an enactment to bring and prosecute proceedings for the offence concerned.

(4) The making of an application referred to in subsection (3) of this section may, in addition to being effected by any method by which the making of an application for a summons could be effected immediately before the enactment of section 49 of the Act of 2004, be effected by transmitting it to the appropriate office by electronic means.

(5) Where an application for the issue of a summons is made to—

   (a) an office referred to in paragraph (a) of the definition of 'appropriate office' in this section, the summons may, instead of its being issued by that office, be issued by an office referred to in paragraph (b) of that definition, or

   (b) an office referred to in paragraph (b) of that definition, the summons may, instead of its being issued by that office, be issued by an office referred to in paragraph (a) of that definition.

(6) A summons shall—

   (a) specify the name of the person who applied for the issue of the summons,

   (b) specify the application date as respects the summons,

   (c) state shortly and in ordinary language particulars of the alleged offence, the name of the person alleged to have committed the offence and the address (if known) at which he or she ordinarily resides,

    (d) notify that person that he or she will be accused of that offence at a sitting of the District Court specified by reference to its date and location and, insofar as is practicable, its time, and

    (e) specify the name of an appropriate District Court clerk.

(7) For the avoidance of doubt, particulars of the penalty to which a person guilty of the offence concerned would be liable are not required to be stated in a summons.

(8) Where the issue of a summons is effected in accordance with subsection (2) of this section, references to an original summons in any enactment relating to the service of summonses (whether the references employ the word 'summons' or the expression 'original document') shall be construed as references to a true copy of the summons.

(9) In any proceedings—

    (a) a document purporting to be a summons shall be deemed to be a summons duly applied for and issued, and

    (b) the date specified in the summons as being the application date shall be deemed to be such date,

unless the contrary is shown.

(10) In any proceedings in which the issue of a summons was effected in accordance with subsection (2) of this section, a true copy of the summons shall, unless the contrary is shown, be evidence of the summons concerned.

(11) A summons duly issued under this Act shall be deemed for all purposes to be a summons duly issued pursuant to the law in force immediately before the passing of this Act.

(12) Any provision made by or under any enactment passed before the passing of this Act relating to the time for making a complaint in relation to an offence shall apply, with any necessary modifications, in relation to an application under subsection (3) of this section.

(13) The procedures provided for in this section in relation to applications for, and the issue of, summonses are without prejudice to any other procedures in force immediately before the passing of this Act whereby proceedings in respect of an offence can be commenced and, accordingly, any of those other procedures may be adopted, where appropriate, as if this Act had not been passed.

(14) In this section—

"Act of 2004" means the *Civil Liability and Courts Act 2004*;

"application date" means, in relation to a summons, the date on which the application for the issue of the summons was received by the appropriate office;

"appropriate District Court clerk" means, in relation to a summons, a District Court clerk assigned to any district court area in the district court district in which a judge of the District Court has jurisdiction in relation to the offence to which the summons relates;

"appropriate office" means, in relation to a summons—

    (a) the office of any District Court clerk assigned to any district court area in the district court district in which a judge of the District Court has jurisdiction in relation to the offence to which the summons relates, or

    (b) any office of the Courts Service designated by the Courts Service for the purpose of receiving applications referred to in subsection (3) of this section;

["electronic means", in relation to an application for a summons or the issue of a summons, includes the use of an information system (within the meaning of section 2 of the Electronic Commerce Act 2000) under the control of a person other than—

    (a) the person who applied for the summons or a person acting on his or her behalf, or

    (b) the appropriate office;][2]

"prosecutor" includes a person acting on behalf of the prosecutor;

"summons" has the meaning assigned to it by subsection (1);

"true copy" means, in relation to a summons the issue of which was effected in accordance with subsection (2), a document that purports to be a reproduction in writing of the summons certified by the prosecutor as being a true copy thereof.][1]

Amendments

1   Section (1) substituted by Civil Liability and Courts Act 2004, s 49.

2   Definition inserted by Civil Law (Miscellaneous Provisions) Act 2008, s 19.

2   Short title, collective citation and construction

(1) This Act may be cited as the Courts (No. 3) Act, 1986.

(2) The collective citation "the Courts (Supplemental Provisions) Acts, 1961 to 1986" shall include this Act and the said Courts (Supplemental Provisions) Acts, 1961 to 1986, shall be construed together as one.

Firearms and Offensive Weapons Act 1990

Number 12 of 1990

ARRANGEMENT OF SECTIONS

PART I
PRELIMINARY

1.   Short title and commencement.

2.   Interpretation.

PART II
AMENDMENTS TO FIREARMS ACTS

3.   Collective citation and construction.

4.   Extension of Firearms Acts to crossbows and stun guns.

5.   Amendment of section 10 of Firearms Act, 1925.

6.   Authorisation to hold defective firearm without firearm certificate.

7.   Possession, sale, etc., of silencers.

8.   Reckless discharge of firearm.

8A   Other amendments to Firearms Acts.

PART III
OFFENSIVE WEAPONS

9.   Possession of knives and other articles.

9A   Possession of a realistic imitation firearm in a public place.

9B   Authorisation of use of realistic imitation firearms at specified venues, theatres, etc.

9C   Register of dealers in realistic imitation firearms to be kept.

9D   Restrictions on import, manufacture and sale of realistic imitation firearms.

9E   Removal of names from register of dealers in realistic imitation firearms.

9F   Inspection of stock of dealer in realistic imitation firearms.

9G   Power by order to restrict sale of certain realistic imitation firearms from specified date.

9H   Power by order to require certain descriptions of imitation firearms to conform to certain specifications.

9I   Tax clearance.

10.   Trespassing with a knife, weapon of offence or other article.

11.   Production of article capable of inflicting serious injury.

12.   Power to prohibit manufacture, importation, sale, hire or loan of offensive weapons.

12A   Shortening barrel of shot-gun or rifle.

13.   Forfeiture of weapons and other articles.

14.   Power of arrest without warrant.

15.   Search warrants.

16.   Power of search without warrant.

17.   Extension of section 8 of Criminal Law Act, 1976.

18.   Repeal of portion of section 4 of Vagrancy Act, 1824.

AN ACT TO AMEND AND EXTEND THE FIREARMS ACTS, 1925 TO 1971, TO CONTROL THE AVAILABILITY AND POSSESSION OF OFFENSIVE WEAPONS AND OTHER ARTICLES AND TO PROVIDE FOR CERTAIN OTHER MATTERS CONNECTED WITH THE MATTERS AFORESAID. [12th June, 1990]

BE IT ENACTED BY THE OIREACHTAS AS FOLLOWS:

PART I
PRELIMINARY

1   Short title and commencement

(1) This Act may be cited as the Firearms and Offensive Weapons Act, 1990.

(2) This Act (other than Part II) shall come into operation on the date of its passing.

(3) Part II of this Act shall come into operation on such day or days as may be fixed therefor by order or orders of the Minister either generally or with reference to any particular provision, and different days may be so fixed for different provisions of that Part.

2   Interpretation

(1) In this Act "the Minister" means the Minister for Justice.

(2) In this Act a reference to a section is a reference to a section of this Act unless it is indicated that reference to some other enactment is intended and a reference to a subsection is a reference to the subsection of the section in which the reference occurs, unless it is indicated that reference to some other section is intended.

(3) A reference in this Act to any enactment shall be construed as a reference to that enactment as amended or adapted by or under any subsequent enactment.

PART II
AMENDMENTS TO FIREARMS ACTS

3   Collective citation and construction

(1) The Firearms Acts, 1925 to 1971, and this Part may be cited together as the Firearms Acts, 1925 to 1990.

(2) The Firearms Acts, 1925 to 1971 (other than the Firearms (Proofing) Act, 1968) and this Part shall be construed together as one.

4   Extension of Firearms Acts to crossbows and stun guns

[...]¹

Amendments

1 Section 4 repealed by Criminal Justice Act 2006, s 63.

5 Amendment of section 10 of Firearms Act, 1925

The Firearms Act, 1925, is hereby amended by the insertion in section 10 after subsection (3) of the following subsection:[1]

Amendments

1 See the amended Act.

6 Authorisation to hold defective firearm without firearm certificate

(1) The superintendent of the Garda Síochána of a district may grant an authorisation in writing to a person resident in the district, not being a person disentitled under the Firearms Acts, 1925 to 1990, to hold a firearm certificate, to have in his possession, without a firearm certificate, a firearm where he is satisfied that the firearm would not be a firearm but for [paragraph (f) of the definition of "firearm" in section 1(1) of the Principal Act][1] and that the person has a good reason for wishing to keep it and may be permitted to do so without danger to the public safety or the peace.

(2) The superintendent of the district where the holder of an authorisation under this section resides may, at any time, attach to the authorisation any conditions, whether as regards safe custody or otherwise, which he considers necessary and may at any time revoke the authorisation.

Amendments

1 Words substituted by Criminal Justice Act 2006, s 63.

7 Possession, sale, etc., of silencers

(1) A person shall be guilty of an offence if he has in his possession or sells or transfers to another person a silencer unless the possession, sale or transfer is authorised in writing by the superintendent of the district in which the first-mentioned person resides.

(2) A superintendent shall not grant an authorisation under this section unless he is satisfied that the person who is to have possession of the silencer or to whom it is to be sold or transferred is the holder of a firearm certificate for a firearm to which the silencer can be fitted and that—

    (a) having regard to all the circumstances, the possession, sale or transfer concerned will not endanger the public safety or the peace, and

(b) the person has a special need that is, in the opinion of the superintendent, sufficient to justify the granting of the authorisation for the silencer.

(3) The superintendent of the district where the holder of an authorisation under this section resides may, at any time, attach to the authorisation such conditions as he considers necessary for the purpose of preventing danger to the public or to the peace or of ensuring that the silencer is used only to satisfy the special need for which the authorisation was granted.

(4) An authorisation under this section may be granted for such period not exceeding one year as is specified in the authorisation and may be revoked by the superintendent of the district where its holder resides.

(5) A person who contravenes a condition attached to an authorisation under this section shall be guilty of an offence.

(6) A person guilty of an offence under this section shall be liable—

(a) on summary conviction, to a fine not exceeding [€5,000][2] or to imprisonment for a term not exceeding one year or to both, or

(b) on conviction on indictment, to a fine or to imprisonment for a term not exceeding [7 years][2] or to both.

(7) This section does not apply in relation to a person specified in paragraph (b), (c) or (d) of subsection (3) of section 2 of the Firearms Act, 1925, or paragraph (a) or (b) of subsection (4) (inserted by the Firearms Act, 1964) of that section.

(8) In this section—

"silencer" means a silencer specified in [paragraph (g)(ii) of the definition of "firearm" in section 1(1) of the Principal Act][1];

"superintendent" means a superintendent of the Garda Síochána.

Amendments

1   Words substituted by Criminal Justice Act 2006, s 63.

2   Words substituted by Criminal Justice Act 2006, s 64 and Sch 1.

---

8   Reckless discharge of firearm

A person who discharges a firearm being reckless as to whether any person will be injured or not, shall be guilty of an offence, whether any such injury is caused or not, and shall be liable—

(a) on summary conviction, to a fine not exceeding [€5,000][1] or to imprisonment for a term not exceeding twelve months or to both, or

(b) on conviction on indictment, to a fine or to imprisonment for a term not exceeding [7 years][1] or to both.

Amendments

1 Words substituted by Criminal Justice Act 2006, s 64 and Sch 1.

[8A   Other amendments to Firearms Acts

Each provision of the Firearms Acts 1925 to 2006 specified in Schedule 1 to the Criminal Justice Act 2006 is amended in the manner specified in the third and fourth columns opposite the mention of that provision in the first column of that Schedule.]¹

Amendments

1 Section 8A inserted by Criminal Justice Act 2006, s 64.

PART III
OFFENSIVE WEAPONS

9   Possession of knives and other articles

(1) Subject to subsections (2) and (3), where a person has with him in any public place any knife or any other article which has a blade or which is sharply pointed, he shall be guilty of an offence.

(2) It shall be a defence for a person charged with an offence under subsection (1) to prove that he had good reason or lawful authority for having the article with him in a public place.

(3) Without prejudice to the generality of subsection (2), it shall be a defence for a person charged with an offence under subsection (1) to prove that he had the article with him for use at work or for a recreational purpose.

(4) Where a person, without lawful authority or reasonable excuse (the onus of proving which shall lie on him), has with him in any public place—

    (a) any flick-knife, or

    (b) any other article whatsoever made or adapted for use for causing injury to or incapacitating a person,

he shall be guilty of an offence.

(5) Where a person has with him in any public place any article intended by him unlawfully to cause injury to, incapacitate or intimidate any person either in a particular eventuality or otherwise, he shall be guilty of an offence.

(6) In a prosecution for an offence under subsection (5), it shall not be necessary for the prosecution to allege or prove that the intent to cause injury, incapacitate or intimidate was intent to cause injury to, incapacitate or intimidate a particular person; and if, having regard to all the circumstances (including the type of the article alleged to have been intended to cause injury, incapacitate or intimidate, the time of the day or night, and the place), the court (or the jury as the case may be) thinks it reasonable to do so, it may regard possession of the

article as sufficient evidence of intent in the absence of any adequate explanation by the accused.

(7) [(a) A person guilty of an offence under subsection (1) shall be liable—

    (i) on summary conviction, to a fine not exceeding €5,000 or to imprisonment for a term not exceeding twelve months or to both, or

    (ii) on conviction on indictment, to a fine or to imprisonment for a term not exceeding five years or to both.]¹

  (b) A person guilty of an offence under subsection (4) or (5) shall be liable—

    (i) on summary conviction, to a fine not exceeding [€5,000]² or to imprisonment for a term not exceeding twelve months or to both, or

    (ii) on conviction on indictment, to a fine or to imprisonment for a term not exceeding five years or to both.

(8) In this section "public place" includes any highway and any other premises or place to which at the material time the public have or are permitted to have access, whether on payment or otherwise, and includes any club premises and any train, vessel or vehicle used for the carriage of persons for reward.

(9) In this section "flick-knife" means a knife—

  (a) which has a blade which opens when hand pressure is applied to a button, spring, lever or other device in or attached to the handle, or

  (b) which has a blade which is released from the handle or sheath by the force of gravity or the application of centrifugal force and when released is locked in an open position by means of a button, spring, lever or other device.

Amendments

1   Subsection 7(a) substituted by Criminal Justice (Miscellaneous Provisions) Act 2009, s 39.

2   Words substituted by Criminal Justice Act, 2006, s 64 and Sch 1.

[9A   Possession of a realistic imitation firearm in a public place

(1) Where a person, without lawful authority or reasonable excuse (the onus of proving which shall lie on him or her), has a realistic imitation firearm with him or her in any public place, that person shall be guilty of an offence.

(2) A person guilty of an offence under this section shall be liable:

    (i) on summary conviction to a fine not exceeding €5,000 or to imprisonment for a term not exceeding twelve months or to both, or

    (ii) on conviction on indictment, to a fine or to imprisonment for a term not exceeding five years or to both.

(3) In this section "public place" includes any highway and any other premises or place to which at the material time the public have or are permitted to have access, whether on payment or otherwise, and includes any club premises and any train, vessel or vehicle used for the carriage of persons for reward.

(4) In this section and in sections 9B to 9G "realistic imitation firearm" means a device that appears to the ordinary observer so realistic as to make it indistinguishable from a firearm.

9B **Authorisation of use of realistic imitation firearms at specified venues, theatres, etc**

(1) The Superintendent of any district may authorise in writing the possession, use or carriage of realistic imitation firearms in that district at a specified location during such period, not exceeding one year, as may be specified in the authorisation.

(2) A Superintendent shall not grant an authorisation under this section unless he or she is satisfied having regard to all the circumstances (including the provision made or to be made for the storage of realistic imitation firearms to which the authorisation (if granted) would relate and the supervision of their use) that the possession, use or carriage, as the case may be, of realistic imitation firearms in pursuance of the authorisation will not endanger the public safety or the peace.

(3) Where it is proposed to grant an authorisation under this section in respect of a specified location, the authorisation shall be granted to the person in charge of the specified location and where there is a contravention of a condition imposed in relation to the grant of such an authorisation and the contravention is proved to have been committed with the consent or approval of or to have been facilitated by any neglect on the part of the person to whom the authorisation is granted, that person shall be guilty of an offence under this Act.

(4) A Superintendent may impose in relation to the grant of an authorisation under this section such conditions (if any) as he considers necessary to prevent danger to the public and, where a condition is imposed, it shall be specified in the authorisation.

(5) An authorisation under this section may be revoked at any time by the Superintendent of the District in which it is granted.

(6) A person who contravenes a condition imposed in relation to the grant of an authorisation under this section shall be guilty of an offence and shall be liable on summary conviction to a fine of up to €5,000 or up to 12 months imprisonment.

9C **Register of dealers in realistic imitation firearms to be kept**

(1) The Minister shall cause a register of dealers in realistic imitation firearms to be established and kept.

(2) Any person who—

(a) applies, in accordance with the provisions of this section, to be registered in the register of dealers in realistic imitation firearms,

(b) pays the fee, if any, prescribed by regulations made by the Minister under this section, and

(c) satisfies the Minister that he or she is immediately about to carry on business as a dealer in realistic imitation firearms in premises suitable for that business,

may be registered in such register, but when considering any such application for registration the Minister shall have regard to the character of the applicant, and generally to the public safety and the preservation of the peace.

(3) The registration of a person in the register of dealers in realistic imitation firearms shall continue in force for a period of 3 years from the date of the registration, unless previously

revoked and, if renewed, for a further period of 3 years from the expiration of that period or, as the case may be, of any subsequent such period for which the registration was renewed.

(4) Every registered dealer in realistic imitation firearms shall be entitled to renew his or her registration in the register of dealers in realistic imitation firearms at any time within one month before the expiration of his existing registration or renewal on application therefor in accordance with the provisions of this section and payment of the fee, if any, prescribed by regulations made by the Minister under this section.

(5) Every application for registration in the register of dealers in realistic imitation firearms or for renewal of such registration shall be made to the Minister in the form and manner prescribed by regulations made by the Minister under this section and shall contain the prescribed particulars (if any) so prescribed.

(6) Every person registered in the register of dealers in realistic imitation firearms shall be entitled on such registration and on every renewal thereof to obtain from the Minister a certificate in writing of such registration or renewal.

(7) An application for registration in the register of dealers in realistic firearms dealers or for renewal of such registration shall be refused if granting it would, in the opinion of the Minister, prejudice public safety or security.

(8) The Minister, after consultation with the Commissioner, may by regulations specify minimum standards to be complied with in relation to premises in which a dealer in realistic imitation firearms carries on business or proposes to do so.

(9) The minimum standards shall be determined by reference to—

    (a)   the security of the premises,

    (b)   the location of the premises,

    (c)   their safety,

    (d)   their standard of construction,

    (e)   window displays, and

    (f)   types of merchandise,

and having regard to their use for, as the case may be, the manufacture, repair, testing or sale of imitation firearms.

(10) Applicants for registration or renewal shall satisfy the Minister that their premises comply with the minimum standards specified in any regulations under subsection (8) of this section.

(11) Without prejudice to subsection (2) of this section, the following persons are declared to be disentitled to be registered in the register of dealers in realistic imitation firearms:

    (a)   a person under the age of 21 years;

    (b)   a person of unsound mind;

    (c)   a person who has been sentenced to imprisonment for an offence under the Firearms Acts 1925 to 2009, the Offences Against the State Acts 1939 to 1998 or the Criminal Justice (Terrorist Offences) Act 2005;

    (d)   a person who is bound by a recognisance to keep the peace or be of good behaviour, a condition of which is that the person shall not possess, use or carry a firearm or ammunition.

(12) Every regulation made under this section shall be laid before each House of the Oireachtas as soon as may be after it is made and, if a resolution annulling the regulation is

passed by either such House within the next 21 days on which that House sits after the regulation is laid before it, the regulation shall be annulled accordingly but without prejudice to anything previously done thereunder.

9D   **Restrictions on import, manufacture and sale of realistic imitation firearms**

(1) On and after the date of commencement of section 40 of the Criminal Justice (Miscellaneous Provisions) Act 2009 it is an offence for any person to import, manufacture, sell, repair, test, expose for sale, or have in his possession for sale, repair or test by way of trade or business, any realistic imitation firearm unless such person is registered in the register of dealers in realistic imitation firearms.

(2) On and after the date of commencement of section 40 of the Criminal Justice (Miscellaneous Provisions) Act 2009 it is an offence for a person to sell a realistic imitation firearm to a person under the age of 16 years.

(3) A person guilty of an offence under this section shall be liable:

(a)   on summary conviction to a fine not exceeding €5,000 or to imprisonment for a term not exceeding twelve months or both, or

(b)   on conviction on indictment, to a fine or to imprisonment for a term not exceeding five years or both.

9E   **Removal of names from register of dealers in realistic imitation firearms**

(1) The Minister may at the request of any person who is registered in the register of dealers in realistic imitation firearms remove the name of such person from the register.

(2) If and when the Minister is satisfied that any person who is registered in the register of dealers in realistic imitation firearms—

(a)   no longer carries on business as a dealer in realistic imitation firearms, or

(b)   no longer has a place of business as such dealer in realistic imitation firearms in the State, or

(c)   cannot any longer be permitted to carry on such business without danger to the public safety or to the peace, or

(d)   has become a person who is declared under section 9C(11) of this Act to be disentitled to be registered in the register of dealers in realistic imitation firearms,

the Minister may remove the name of such person from the register.

(3) A person whose name is removed under this section from the register of dealers in realistic imitation firearms shall, on such removal, forthwith deliver up to the Minister the person's certificate of registration or renewal.

(4) A person who contravenes subsection (3) of this section is guilty of an offence and on summary conviction is liable to a fine not exceeding €3,000.

9F   **Inspection of stock of dealer in realistic imitation firearms**

(1) Any member of the Garda Síochána may at all reasonable times enter the premises of any registered dealer in realistic imitation firearms and there inspect any imitation firearms and any materials used in the manufacture, repair or test thereof found on such premises.

(2) Every person who obstructs or impedes any member of the Garda Síochána in the exercise of any of the powers conferred on him by this section shall be guilty of an offence

under this section and shall be liable on summary conviction thereof to a fine not exceeding €1,000 or imprisonment for a term not exceeding 6 months or both.

9G   Power by order to restrict sale of certain realistic imitation firearms from specified date

(1) Notwithstanding section 9D(1), the Minister may, if he or she considers that realistic imitation firearms represent a threat to public safety and security, and following consultation with the Commissioner, by order set a date or dates after which it is an offence for a person to import, manufacture, sell, repair, test, expose for sale or have in his or her possession for sale, repair or testing by way of trade or business any realistic imitation firearm or to do any one or more of the foregoing as may be specified in the order.

(2) Any order made under this section shall be laid before each House of the Oireachtas as soon as may be after it is made and, if a resolution annulling the order is passed by either such House within the next 21 days on which that House sits after the order is laid before it, the order shall be annulled accordingly but without prejudice to anything previously done thereunder.

(3) A person guilty of an offence under this section shall be liable:

   (a) on summary conviction to a fine not exceeding €5,000 or to imprisonment for a term not exceeding twelve months or both, or

   (b) on conviction on indictment, to a fine or to imprisonment for a term not exceeding five years or both.

9H   Power by order to require certain descriptions of imitation firearms to conform to certain specifications

(1) The Minister may, if he or she considers that certain imitation firearms represent a threat to public safety and security, and following consultation with the Commissioner, by order set a date or dates after which it is an offence for a person to import, manufacture, sell, repair, test, expose for sale or have in his or her possession for sale, repair or testing by way of trade or business certain descriptions of imitation firearms unless the imitation firearms conform to certain specifications set out in the order.

(2) In this section "imitation firearm" means anything which is not a firearm but has the appearance of being a firearm.

(3) Any order made under this section shall be laid before each House of the Oireachtas as soon as may be after it is made and, if a resolution annulling the order is passed by either such House within the next 21 days on which that House sits after the order is laid before it, the order shall be annulled accordingly but without prejudice to anything previously done thereunder.

(4) A person guilty of an offence under this section shall be liable:

   (a) on summary conviction to a fine not exceeding €5,000 or to imprisonment for a term not exceeding twelve months or both, or

   (b) on conviction on indictment, to a fine or to imprisonment for a term not exceeding five years or both.

9I   Tax clearance

(1) In this section—

"Act of 1997" means the Taxes Consolidation Act 1997;

"Collector-General" means the Collector-General appointed under section 851 of the Act of 1997;

"tax clearance certificate" means a certificate under section 1095 (as substituted by section 127(b) of the Finance Act 2002) of the Act of 1997.

(2) The Minister shall refuse to register a person in the register of dealers in realistic imitation firearms or renew any such registration in respect of that person if that person is a person in relation to whom a tax clearance certificate is not in force.

(3) The Minister may nevertheless register a person in the register of dealers in realistic imitation firearms or renew any such registration in respect of that person if—

(a) the person has, at least four months before applying for such registration or renewal, applied for a tax clearance certificate and it has been refused and an appeal against the refusal has been made under section 1094(7) of the Act of 1997 but not determined, and

(b) the Minister would, but for subsection (2), have registered that person in the register of dealers in realistic imitation firearms or renewed any such registration in respect of the person.

(4) Where an appeal referred to in subsection (3) is made but is not successful, any registration or renewal of registration under that subsection shall expire 7 days after the appeal is determined or, where appropriate, finally determined.

(5) The Collector-General shall notify the Minister of any appeal against a refusal of an application for a tax clearance certificate and of the determination or, as appropriate, final determination of any such appeal.][1]

Amendments

1   Section 9A–I inserted by Criminal Justice (Miscellaneous Provisions) Act 2009, s 40.

---

10   Trespassing with a knife, weapon of offence or other article

(1) Where a person is on any premises as defined in subsection (2) as a trespasser, he shall be guilty of an offence if he has with him—

(a) any knife or other article to which section 9(1) applies, or

(b) any weapon of offence (as defined in subsection (2)).

(2) In this section—

"premises" means any building, any part of a building and any land ancillary to a building;

"weapon of offence" means any article made or adapted for use for causing injury to or incapacitating a person, or intended by the person having it with him for such use.

(3) A person guilty of an offence under this section shall be liable—

(a) on summary conviction, to a fine not exceeding [€5,000][1] or to imprisonment for a term not exceeding twelve months or to both, or

(b) on conviction on indictment, to a fine or to imprisonment for a term not exceeding 5 years or to both.

Amendments

1   Words substituted by Criminal Justice Act 2006, s 64 and Sch 1.

11   Production of article capable of inflicting serious injury

Where a person, while committing or appearing to be about to commit an offence, or in the course of a dispute or fight, produces in a manner likely unlawfully to intimidate another person any article capable of inflicting serious injury, he shall be guilty of an offence and shall be liable—

   (a)   on summary conviction, to a fine not exceeding [€5,000][1] or to imprisonment for a term not exceeding twelve months or to both, or

   (b)   on conviction on indictment, to a fine or to imprisonment for a term not exceeding five years or to both.

Amendments

1   Words substituted by Criminal Justice Act 2006, s 64 and Sch 1.

12   Power to prohibit manufacture, importation, sale, hire or loan of offensive weapons

(1) Any person who—

   (a)   manufactures, sells or hires, or offers or exposes for sale or hire, or by way of business repairs or modifies, or

   (b)   has in his possession for the purpose of sale or hire or for the purpose of repair or modification by way of business, or

   (c)   puts on display, or lends or gives to any other person,

a weapon to which this section applies shall be guilty of an offence.

(2) Where an offence under subsection (1) is committed by a body corporate and is proved to have been so committed with the consent or connivance of or to be attributable to any neglect on the part of a director, manager, secretary or other officer of the body corporate, the director, manager, secretary or other officer or any person purporting to act in such capacity shall also be guilty of an offence.

(3) A person guilty of an offence under this section shall be liable—

   (a)   on summary conviction, to a fine not exceeding [€5,000][1] or to imprisonment for a term not exceeding twelve months or to both, or

   (b)   on conviction on indictment, to a fine or to imprisonment for a term not exceeding [7 years][1] or to both.

(4) The Minister may by order direct that this section shall apply to any description of weapon specified in the order except any firearm subject to the Firearms Acts, 1925 to 1990.

(5) The Minister may by order amend or revoke an order made under this section.

(6) The importation of a weapon to which this section applies is hereby prohibited.

(7) Every order made under this section shall be laid before each House of the Oireachtas as soon as may be after it is made and, if a resolution annulling the order is passed by either such House within the next 21 days on which that House has sat after the order is laid before it, the order shall be annulled accordingly, but without prejudice to the validity of anything previously done thereunder.

Amendments

1   Words substituted by Criminal Justice Act 2006, s 64 and Sch 1.

[12A   Shortening barrel of shot-gun or rifle

(1) Subject to subsection (2), a person who shortens the barrel of—

    (a) a shot-gun to a length of less than 61 centimetres, or

    (b) a rifle to a length of less than 50 centimetres,

is guilty of an offence.

(2) It is not an offence under subsection (1) for a registered firearms dealer to shorten the barrel of a shot-gun or rifle to a length of less than 61 or 50 centimetres respectively if the sole purpose of doing so is to replace a defective part of the barrel with a barrel of not less than 61 or 50 centimetres, as the case may be.

(3) It is an offence for a person to convert into a firearm anything which resembles a firearm but is not capable of discharging a projectile.

(4) Subject to subsection (5), it is an offence to modify a firearm so as to render its reloading mechanism fully automatic or to increase its calibre, irrespective of whether the firearm, as so modified, is a restricted firearm.

(5) Subsection (4) does not apply to a firearm designed and manufactured so as to enable barrels of different calibres to be attached to it.

(6) It is an offence for a person (except a registered firearms dealer) to possess without lawful authority or reasonable excuse—

    (a) a shot-gun the barrel of which is less than 61 centimetres in length,

    (b) a rifle the barrel of which is less than 50 centimetres in length,

    (c) a converted firearm mentioned in subsection (3), or

    (d) a firearm which has been modified as described in subsection (4).

(7) A person who is guilty of an offence under this section is liable on conviction on indictment—

    (a) to imprisonment for a term not exceeding 10 years or such shorter term as the court may determine, subject to subsections (9) to (11) of this section or, where subsection (13) of this section applies, to that subsection, and

    (b) at the court's discretion, to a fine of such amount as the court considers appropriate.

(8) The court, in imposing sentence on a person for an offence under this section, may, in particular, have regard to whether the person has a previous conviction for an offence under

the Firearms Acts 1925 to 2006, the Offences against the State Acts 1939 to 1998 or the Criminal Justice (Terrorist Offences) Act 2005.

(9) Where a person (other than a person under the age of 18 years) is convicted of an offence under this section, the court shall, in imposing sentence, specify a term of imprisonment of not less than 5 years (in this section referred to as the "minimum term of imprisonment") as the minimum term of imprisonment to be served by the person.

[(9A) The purpose of subsections (10) and (11) is to provide that in view of the harm caused to society by the unlawful possession and use of firearms, a court, in imposing sentence on a person (other than a person under the age of 18 years) for an offence under this section, shall specify as the minimum term of imprisonment to be served by the person a term of not less than 5 years, unless the court determines that by reason of exceptional and specific circumstances relating to the offence, or the person convicted of it, it would be unjust in all the circumstances to do so.]²

(10) Subsection (9) does not apply where the court is satisfied that there are exceptional and specific circumstances relating to the offence, or to the person convicted of it, which would make the minimum term of imprisonment unjust in all the circumstances, and for this purpose the court may[, subject to subsection (11),]³ have regard to any matters it considers appropriate, including—

    (a)   whether the person pleaded guilty to the offence and, if so—

        (i)   the stage at which the intention to plead guilty was indicated, and

        (ii)   the circumstances in which the indication was given,

    and

    (b)   whether the person materially assisted in the investigation of the offence.

(11) The court, in considering for the purposes of subsection (10) of this section whether a sentence of not less than 5 years imprisonment is unjust in all the circumstances, may have regard, in particular, to—

    (a)   whether the person convicted of the offence has a previous conviction for an offence under the Firearms Acts 1925 to 2006, the Offences Against the State Acts 1939 to 1998 or the Criminal Justice (Terrorist Offences) Act 2005, and

    (b)   whether the public interest in preventing the unlawful possession or use of firearms would be served by the imposition of a lesser sentence.

(12) Subsections (9) to (11) of this section apply and have effect only in relation to a person convicted of a first offence under this section (other than a person who falls under subsection (13)(b) of this section), and accordingly references in those first-mentioned subsections to an offence under this section are to be construed as references to a first such offence.

(13) Where a person (except a person under the age of 18 years)—

    (a)   is convicted of a second or subsequent offence under this section,

    (b)   is convicted of a first offence under this section and has been convicted of an offence under section 15 of the Principal Act or section 26, [27], 27A or 27B of the Firearms Act 1964,

the court shall, in imposing sentence, specify a term of imprisonment of not less than 5 years as the minimum term of imprisonment to be served by the person.

(14) Section 27C of the Firearms Act 1964 applies in relation to proceedings for an offence under this section and any minimum term of imprisonment imposed under subsection (9) or (13) in those proceedings.]¹

Amendments

1   Section 12A inserted by Criminal Justice Act 2006, s 65.
2   Subsection (9A) inserted by Criminal Justice Act 2007, s 40(a).
3   Words inserted by Criminal Justice Act 2007, s 40(b).
4   Words inserted by Criminal Justice Act 2007, s 40(c).

13   Forfeiture of weapons and other articles

(1) Where a person is convicted of an offence under this Part, the court by or before which he is convicted may order any article in respect of which the offence was committed to be forfeited and either destroyed or otherwise disposed of in such manner as the court may determine.

(2) An order under this section shall not take effect until the ordinary time for instituting an appeal against the conviction or order concerned has expired or, where such an appeal is instituted, until it or any further appeal is finally decided or abandoned or the ordinary time for instituting any further appeal has expired.

14   Power of arrest without warrant

A member of the Garda Síochána may arrest without warrant any person who is, or whom the member, with reasonable cause, suspects to be, in the act of committing an offence under section 9, 10 or 11.

15   Search warrants

If a justice of the District Court or a Peace Commissioner is satisfied on the sworn information of a member of the Garda Síochána that there are reasonable grounds for suspecting that an offence under section 12 has been or is being committed on any premises, he may issue a warrant under his hand authorising a specified member of the Garda Síochána, accompanied by such other members of the Garda Síochána as the member thinks necessary, at any time or times within one month from the date of the issue of the warrant, on production if so requested of the warrant, to enter, if need be by force, and search the premises specified in the warrant and to seize anything found there that he believes on reasonable grounds may be required to be used in evidence in any proceedings for an offence under section 12 or an offence under the Customs Acts in relation to the importation into the State of a weapon to which section 12 applies.

16   Power of search without warrant

[(1) If a member of the Garda Síochána suspects with reasonable cause that a person has with him or her in any public place (within the meaning of section 9(8)) any article in contravention of section 9 or 9A (inserted by section 40 of the Criminal Justice (Miscellaneous Provisions) Act 2009), he may:

(a) search the person and, if he or she considers it necessary for that purpose, detain the person for such time as is reasonably necessary for carrying out the search,

(b) search any vehicle, vessel or aircraft in which he or she suspects that such article may be found and for the purpose of carrying out the search may, if he or she thinks fit, require the person who for the time being is in possession or control of such vehicle, vessel or aircraft to bring it to a stop and when stopped to refrain from moving it, or in case such vehicle, vessel or aircraft is already stationary, to refrain from moving it, or

(c) seize and detain anything found in the course of a search under this section that appears to him or her to be something that might be required as evidence in proceedings for an offence under section 9 or 9A.

(2) Nothing in this section shall operate to prejudice any powers to search, seize or detain property that may be exercisable by a member of the Garda Síochána apart from this section.][1]

Amendments

1   Section 16 substituted by Criminal Justice (Miscellaneous Provisions) Act 2009, s 41.

---

17   Extension of section 8 of Criminal Law Act, 1976

Section 8 of the Criminal Law Act, 1976, is hereby amended by the insertion in subsection (1) after paragraph (i) of the following paragraph:[1]

Amendments

1   See the amended Act.

---

18   Repeal of portion of section 4 of Vagrancy Act, 1824

Section 4 of the Vagrancy Act, 1824 (as extended to Ireland by section 15 of the Prevention of Crimes Act, 1871), is hereby amended by the deletion of "or being armed with any gun, pistol, hanger, cutlass, bludgeon, or other offensive weapon," and "and every such gun, pistol, hanger, cutlass, bludgeon, or other offensive weapon,".

Criminal Justice Act 1990

Number 16 of 1990

ARRANGEMENT OF SECTIONS

Section

1. Abolition of death penalty.

2. Sentence for treason and murder.

3. Special provision in relation to certain murders and attempts.

4. Minimum period of imprisonment for treason and murder, and attempts, to which section 3 applies.

5. Restrictions on power to commute or remit punishment or grant temporary release.

6. Procedure in cases of murder, and attempts, to which section 3 applies.

7. Consequential amendments.

8. Transitional provisions.

9. Repeals.

10. Short title.

FIRST SCHEDULE
CONSEQUENTIAL AMENDMENTS

SECOND SCHEDULE
ENACTMENTS REPEALED

AN ACT TO ABOLISH THE DEATH PENALTY AND SUBSTITUTE IMPRISONMENT FOR LIFE, TO PROVIDE THAT A MINIMUM PERIOD OF IMPRISONMENT SHALL BE SERVED BY PERSONS CONVICTED OF TREASON OR OF CERTAIN CATEGORIES OF MURDER OR ATTEMPTS TO COMMIT ANY SUCH MURDER AND TO PROVIDE FOR OTHER CONNECTED MATTERS. [11th July, 1990]

BE IT ENACTED BY THE OIREACHTAS AS FOLLOWS:

1   Abolition of death penalty

No person shall suffer death for any offence.

2   Sentence for treason and murder

A person convicted of treason or murder shall be sentenced to imprisonment for life.

3   Special provision in relation to certain murders and attempts

(1) This section applies to—

    (a) murder of a member of the Garda Síochána acting in the course of his duty,

    (b) murder of a prison officer acting in the course of his duty,

    (c) murder done in the course or furtherance of an offence under section 6, 7, 8 or 9 of the Offences against the State Act, 1939, or in the course or furtherance of the activities of an unlawful organisation within the meaning of section 18 (other than paragraph (f)) of that Act, and

(d) murder, committed within the State for a political motive, of the head of a foreign State or of a member of the government of, or a diplomatic officer of, a foreign State,

and to an attempt to commit any such murder.

(2) (a) Subject to paragraph (b), murder to which this section applies, and an attempt to commit such a murder, shall be a distinct offence from murder and from an attempt to commit murder and a person shall not be convicted of murder to which this section applies or of an attempt to commit such a murder unless it is proved that he knew of the existence of each ingredient of the offence specified in the relevant paragraph of subsection (1) or was reckless as to whether or not that ingredient existed.

(b) Save as otherwise provided by this Act, the law and procedure relating to murder and an attempt to commit murder shall apply to the offence.

(3) In this section—

"diplomatic officer" means a member of the staff of a diplomatic mission of a foreign State having diplomatic rank;

"prison" means any place for which rules or regulations may be made under the Prisons Acts, 1826 to 1980, section 7 of the Offences against the State (Amendment) Act, 1940, section 233 of the Defence Act, 1954, section 2 of the Prisoners of War and Enemy Aliens Act, 1956, or section 13 of the Criminal Justice Act, 1960;

["prison officer" includes any member of the staff of a prison and any person having the custody of, or having duties relating to the custody of, a person in relation to whom an order of a court committing that person to a prison is for the time being in force;][1]

Amendments

1   Definition substituted by Prisons Act 2007, s 41(3).

---

4   Minimum period of imprisonment for treason and murder, and attempts, to which section 3 applies

Where a person (other than a child or young person) is convicted of treason or of a murder or attempt to commit a murder to which section 3 applies, the court—

(a) in the case of treason or murder, shall in passing sentence specify as the minimum period of imprisonment to be served by that person a period of not less than forty years,

(b) in the case of an attempt to commit murder, shall pass a sentence of imprisonment of not less than twenty years and specify a period of not less than twenty years as the minimum period of imprisonment to be served by that person.

5   Restrictions on power to commute or remit punishment or grant temporary release

(1) The power conferred by section 23 of the Criminal Justice Act, 1951, to commute or remit a punishment shall not, in the case of a person serving a sentence passed on him on conviction of treason or of murder to which section 3 applies or an attempt to commit such a murder, be exercisable before the expiration of the minimum period specified by the court under section 4 less any reduction of that period under subsection (2) of this section.

(2) The rules or practice whereby prisoners generally may earn remission of sentence by industry and good conduct shall apply in the case of a person serving a sentence passed on him on conviction of treason or of murder to which section 3 applies or an attempt to commit such a murder as if he had been sentenced to a term of imprisonment equal to the minimum period specified by the court under section 4, and that period shall be reduced by the amount of any remission which he has so earned.

(3) Any power conferred by rules made under section 2 of the Criminal Justice Act, 1960 (including that section as applied by section 4 of the Prisons Act, 1970), to release temporarily a person serving a sentence of imprisonment shall not, in the case of a person serving a sentence passed on him on conviction of treason or of murder to which section 3 applies or an attempt to commit such a murder, be exercisable during the period for which the commutation or remission of his punishment is prohibited by subsection (1) of this section unless for grave reasons of a humanitarian nature, and any release so granted shall be only of such limited duration as is justified by those reasons.

6   Procedure in cases of murder, and attempts, to which section 3 applies

(1) Where a person is accused of murder to which section 3 applies or of any attempt to commit such a murder, he shall be charged in the indictment with murder to which that section applies or, as the case may be, with an attempt to commit such a murder.

(2) [...]¹

(3) [...]¹

Amendments

1   Subsections (2) and (3) repealed by Criminal Law Act 1997, s 16 and Sch 3.

---

7   Consequential amendments

The enactments mentioned in the First Schedule are hereby amended in the manner specified therein.

8   Transitional provisions

(1) An offence of treason, capital murder or attempt to commit a capital murder, being an offence committed wholly or partly before the passing of this Act, shall be dealt with under the law in force before such passing, except that—

(a) if the offender is convicted of treason or capital murder, he shall be sentenced as provided for by this Act as if, in the case of capital murder, the murder were murder to which section 3 applies, and

(b) if he is convicted of attempted capital murder, he shall be sentenced as if he had been convicted of attempted murder.

(2) If, on an appeal against a conviction before the passing of this Act, of treason or capital murder the conviction is confirmed, the appeal court shall impose sentence as provided for by this Act as if, in the case of capital murder, the murder were murder to which section 3 applies.

9   Repeals

(1) The enactments mentioned in the Second Schedule are hereby repealed to the extent specified therein.

(2) The repeal by this Act of section 1 of the Offences against the Person Act, 1861, shall not affect the operation of sections 64 to 68 of that Act.

10   Short title

This Act may be cited as the Criminal Justice Act, 1990.

FIRST SCHEDULE
CONSEQUENTIAL AMENDMENTS

Section 7

1. In section 2 of the Piracy Act, 1837, "and on conviction thereof shall be sentenced to imprisonment for life" shall be inserted at the end of the section.

2. Section 103 of the Children Act, 1908, shall have effect in relation to a child or young person who is convicted of an offence for which an adult would be required to be sentenced to imprisonment for life as it had effect before the passing of this Act in relation to a child or young person convicted of an offence for which an adult would have been required to be sentenced to death.

3. Section 1 of the Treason Act, 1939, shall be amended as follows:

(a) in subsections (1) and (2) "be sentenced on conviction thereof to imprisonment for life" shall be substituted for "be liable on conviction thereof to suffer death", and

(b) in subsection (3) "murder to which section 3 of the Criminal Justice Act, 1990, applies" shall be substituted for "capital murder" (inserted therein by the Criminal Justice Act, 1964).

4. The Defence Act, 1954, shall be amended as follows:

(a) in section 50(2) "death," shall be deleted;

(b) in sections 124 and 125 "imprisonment for life" shall be substituted for "death";

(c) in section 126(2)(iii) "for any term not exceeding two years" shall be inserted after "imprisonment";

(d) in sections 127 and 128 "imprisonment for life" shall be substituted for "death";

(e) in sections 133, 134, 135(1)(b), 136, 137(1), 140, 141, 142(b), 142A(1)(ii), 143, 144, 145, 146, 147, 148, 150, 152, 153, 156, 157, 159(1), 160, 161(2), 162, 163, 164(1), 165, 166, 167 and 168(1) "for any term not exceeding two years" shall be inserted after "imprisonment";

(f) the following section shall be substituted for section 169:

"Offences punishable by ordinary law.

169.—(1) Subject to the provisions of this Act, every person who, while he is subject to military law, commits any of the offences referred to in this section shall be deemed to be guilty of an offence against military law and, if charged under this section with any such offence (in this Act referred to as a civil offence) shall be liable to be tried by court-martial.

(2) Where a person charged under this section is convicted by a court-martial of treason or murder, he shall be sentenced to imprisonment for life.

(3) Where a person charged under this section is convicted by a court-martial of an offence other than treason or murder, he shall be liable to be punished as follows:

(a) if he is convicted of manslaughter, be liable to suffer penal servitude or any less punishment awardable by a court-martial;

(b) if he is convicted of rape, be liable to suffer penal servitude or any less punishment awardable by a court-martial;

(c) if he is convicted of an act of genocide which would be punishable under the Genocide Act, 1973, be liable—

(i)   in case the offence consists of the killing of any person, to imprisonment for life, or

(ii) in any other case, to imprisonment for a term not exceeding fourteen years;

(d) if he is convicted of any offence not before in this section particularly specified which when committed in the State is punishable by the ordinary criminal law of the State, be liable, whether the offence is committed in the State or elsewhere, either to suffer any punishment assigned for such offence by law of the State or, if he is subject to military law as an officer, dismissal with ignominy from the Defence Forces or any less punishment awardable by a court-martial or, if he is subject to military law as a man, imprisonment for any term not exceeding two years or any less punishment awardable by a court-martial.";

(g) the following section shall be inserted after section 169:

"Trial by court-martial of treason and certain murders and attempts.

169A.—(1) A person subject to military law who is accused of murder which is alleged to be murder to which section 3 of the Criminal Justice Act, 1990, applies or of an attempt to commit such a murder and is to be tried by court-martial shall be charged with murder to which that section applies or, as the case may be, with an attempt to commit such a murder, and the following provisions of that Act, namely—

(a) section 4, with the substitution of 'court-martial' for 'court', and

(b) subsection (2) of section 6, with the substitution of 'charged with' for 'indicted for',

shall apply and have effect in relation to the trial.

(2) The said section 4 shall apply and have effect, in relation to the trial of a person subject to military law who is accused of treason, with the substitution of 'court-martial' for 'court'.";

(h) in section 192(2)(d) "for any term not exceeding two years" shall be inserted after "imprisonment";

(i) in section 198, subsection (2) shall be deleted;

(j) in sections 209(1) and 210(1) "Imprisonment for life" shall be substituted for "Death";

(k) in section 210(6) "imprisonment for life or" shall be inserted before "penal servitude" in each place where those words occur;

(l) in subsections (7) and (10) of section 210 "for any term not exceeding two years" shall be inserted after "imprisonment";

(m) [...]¹;

(n) in section 220, subsection (2) shall be deleted and, in subsection (3), "imprisonment on conviction of treason or of murder, or attempted murder, to which section 3 of the Criminal Justice Act, 1990, applies" shall be substituted for "death";

(o) in section 221(1) "(other than a sentence of death)" shall be deleted and the following proviso added:

"Provided that—

(i) the said power of mitigation or remission shall not, in the case of a sentence of imprisonment passed on a person on conviction of treason or of murder, or attempted murder, to which section 3 of the Criminal Justice Act, 1990, applies, be exercisable before the expiration of the minimum period specified by the court-martial under section 4 of that Act, as applied by section 169A of this Act, less any reduction of that period under paragraph (ii) of this proviso, and

(ii) the rules or practice whereby prisoners generally may earn remission of sentence by industry and good conduct shall apply in the case of a person serving a sentence passed on him on conviction of treason or of murder, or attempted murder, to which the said section 3 applies as if he had been sentenced to a term of imprisonment equal to the minimum period specified by the court-martial under the said section 4, as applied by section 169A of this Act, and that period shall be reduced by the amount of any remission which he has so earned.";

(p) in section 222, paragraph (a) and "in any other case" in paragraph (b) shall be deleted;

(q) the following subsection shall be added to section 223:

"(10) This section shall not apply to a sentence of imprisonment on conviction of treason or of murder, or attempted murder, to which section 3 of the Criminal Justice Act, 1990, applies.";

(r) section 227 shall be deleted;

(s) the following subsection shall be inserted in section 228 after subsection (1):

"(1A) Where a sentence of imprisonment for life is passed by a court-martial and confirmed, the military prisoner shall, as soon as practicable, be committed to a public prison to undergo his sentence according to law, and subsections (2) to (7) of this section shall have effect in relation to him—

    (a) as if each reference therein to a military convict were a reference to a military prisoner and each reference to a penal servitude prison a reference to a public prison, and

    (b) as if the reference in the said subsection (7) to penal servitude were a reference to imprisonment.";

(t) ...²

(u) the following subsection shall be inserted in section 233 after subsection (2):

"(2A) Any power conferred by rules under this section to release a person temporarily shall not, in the case of a person serving a sentence passed on him on conviction of treason or of murder, or attempted murder, to which section 3 of the Criminal Justice Act, 1990, applies, be exercisable during the period for which the power to mitigate or remit his punishment is prohibited by paragraph (i) of the proviso (inserted by that Act) to section 221(1) of this Act unless for grave reasons of a humanitarian nature, and any such release shall be only of such limited duration as is justified by those reasons.".

5. In the Courts-Martial Appeals Act, 1983 —

    (a) in sections 26, 28(2)(c) and 28(3)(ii)(I) "a capital offence or murder" shall be replaced in each case by "an offence for which a person would be required on conviction to be sentenced to imprisonment for life";

    (b) in section 27(2)(c) "a capital charge or a charge of murder" shall be replaced by "a charge of an offence for which a person would be required on conviction to be sentenced to imprisonment for life".

Amendments

1   Paragraph 4(m) deleted by Criminal Law Act 1997, s 13 and Sch 1.

2   Paragraph 4(t) repealed by Criminal Law Act 1997, s 16 and Sch 3.

SECOND SCHEDULE
ENACTMENTS REPEALED

Section 9

Chapter or Number and Year	Short Title	Extent of Repeal
(1)	(2)	(3)
C. 100.	Offences against the Person Act, 1861.	Sections 1 to 3. In section 71, the words "otherwise than with death".
C. 24.	Capital Punishment Amendment Act, 1868.	The whole Act.
C. 78.	Juries Procedure (Ireland) Act, 1876.	Section 13.

Chapter or Number and Year	Short Title	Extent of Repeal
(1)	(2)	(3)
C. 49.	General Prisons (Ireland) Act, 1877.	Proviso in section 40.
No. 27 of 1926.	Court Officers Act, 1926.	Section 53.
No. 15 of 1928.	Courts of Justice Act, 1928.	In subsection (1) of section 6, the words "death or". Subsection (2) of section 6.
No. 2 of 1951.	Criminal Justice Act, 1951.	In subsection (1) of section 23, the words "Except in capital cases,".
No. 27 of 1956.	Prisoners of War and Enemy Aliens Act, 1956.	Subsection (1) of section 5.
No. 11 of 1962.	Geneva Conventions Act, 1962.	In subsection (1)(b) of section 6 and in subsection (1) of section 8, the words "to death or". In subsection (2) of section 8, the words "remains a sentence of death, or".
No. 5 of 1964.	Criminal Justice Act, 1964.	The whole Act, except sections 4 and 11.
No. 28 of 1973.	Genocide Act, 1973.	Section 4.
No. 14 of 1976.	Criminal Law (Jurisdiction) Act, 1976.	Subsection (6) of section 20.
No. 19 of 1983.	Courts-Martial Appeals Act, 1983.	Section 21.
No. 1 of 1987.	Extradition (European Convention on the Suppression of Terrorism) Act, 1987.	Subsection (4) of section 6.

Criminal Law (Rape) (Amendment) Act 1990

Number 32 of 1990

ARRANGEMENT OF SECTIONS

1. Interpretation
2. Sexual assault
3. Aggravated sexual assault
4. Rape under section 4
5. Abolition of marital exemption in relation to rape
6. Capacity to commit offences of a sexual nature
7. Corroboration of evidence in proceedings in relation to offences of a sexual nature
8. Alternative verdicts
9. Consent
10. Trial of persons for certain offences by Central Criminal Court
11. Exclusion of the public from hearings
12. Amendment of section 1 of Principal Act
13. Amendment of section 3 of Principal Act
14. Amendment of section 8 of Principal Act
15. Amendment of section 9 of Principal Act
16. Amendment of section 12 of Principal Act
17. Miscellaneous amendments of Principal Act
18. Amendment of section 18 of Criminal Law Amendment Act, 1935
19. Amendment of Defence Act, 1954
20. Amendment of Criminal Procedure Act, 1967
21. Repeals
22. Short title, collective citation, construction, commencement and transitional provision

SCHEDULE

ENACTMENTS REPEALED

AN ACT TO AMEND THE LAW RELATING TO RAPE AND CERTAIN OTHER SEXUAL OFFENCES AND FOR THAT PURPOSE TO AMEND THE CRIMINAL LAW (RAPE) ACT, 1981, AND CERTAIN OTHER ENACTMENTS. [18th December, 1990]

BE IT ENACTED BY THE OIREACHTAS AS FOLLOWS:

1   Interpretation

(1) In this Act—

"aggravated sexual assault" has the meaning assigned to it by section 3;

"rape under section 4" has the meaning assigned to it by section 4;

"the Principal Act" means the Criminal Law (Rape) Act, 1981;

"sexual assault" has the meaning assigned to it by section 2.

(2) (a) In this Act and in the Principal Act a reference to a section is a reference to a section of the Act in which the reference occurs unless it is indicated that reference to some other enactment is intended.

    (b) In this Act and in the Principal Act a reference to a subsection, paragraph or subparagraph is a reference to the subsection, paragraph or subparagraph of the provision in which the reference occurs unless it is indicated that reference to some other provision is intended.

    (c) In this Act and in the Principal Act a reference to any enactment shall be construed as a reference to that enactment as amended or adapted by or under any subsequent enactment.

2   Sexual assault

(1) The offence of indecent assault upon any male person and the offence of indecent assault upon any female person shall be known as sexual assault.

[(2)(a)   A person guilty of sexual assault shall be liable on conviction on indictment—

    (i) in case the person on whom the assault was committed was a child, to imprisonment for a term not exceeding 14 years, and

    (ii) in any other case, to imprisonment for a term not exceeding 10 years.

    (b) In this subsection 'child' means a person under 17 years of age.][1]

(3) Sexual assault shall be a felony.

Amendments

1   Subsection (2) substituted by Sex Offenders Act 2001, s 37.

---

3   Aggravated sexual assault

(1) In this Act "aggravated sexual assault" means a sexual assault that involves serious violence or the threat of serious violence or is such as to cause injury, humiliation or degradation of a grave nature to the person assaulted.

(2) A person guilty of aggravated sexual assault shall be liable on conviction on indictment to imprisonment for life.

(3) Aggravated sexual assault shall be a felony.

4   Rape under section 4

(1) In this Act "rape under section 4 " means a sexual assault that includes—

    (a) penetration (however slight) of the anus or mouth by the penis, or

    (b) penetration (however slight) of the vagina by any object held or manipulated by another person.

(2) A person guilty of rape under section 4 shall be liable on conviction on indictment to imprisonment for life.

(3) Rape under section 4 shall be a felony.

5   Abolition of marital exemption in relation to rape

(1) Any rule of law by virtue of which a husband cannot be guilty of the rape of his wife is hereby abolished.

(2) Criminal proceedings against a man in respect of the rape by him of his wife shall not be instituted except by or with the consent of the Director of Public Prosecutions.

6   Capacity to commit offences of a sexual nature

Any rule of law by virtue of which a male person is treated by reason of his age as being physically incapable of committing an offence of a sexual nature is hereby abolished.

7   Corroboration of evidence in proceedings in relation to offences of a sexual nature

(1) Subject to any enactment relating to the corroboration of evidence in criminal proceedings, where at the trial on indictment of a person charged with an offence of a sexual nature evidence is given by the person in relation to whom the offence is alleged to have been committed and, by reason only of the nature of the charge, there would, but for this section, be a requirement that the jury be given a warning about the danger of convicting the person on the uncorroborated evidence of that other person, it shall be for the judge to decide in his discretion, having regard to all the evidence given, whether the jury should be given the warning; and accordingly any rule of law or practice by virtue of which there is such a requirement as aforesaid is hereby abolished.

(2) If a judge decides, in his discretion, to give such a warning as aforesaid, it shall not be necessary to use any particular form of words to do so.

8   Alternative verdicts

(1) A person indicted for rape may, if the evidence does not warrant a conviction for rape but warrants a conviction for rape under section 4 or aggravated sexual assault or sexual assault, be found guilty of rape under section 4 or of aggravated sexual assault or of sexual assault, as may be appropriate.

(2) A person indicted for rape may, if the evidence does not warrant a conviction for rape but warrants a conviction for an offence under [section 2 or 3 of the Criminal Law (Sexual Offences) Act 2006,][1] or under section 3 of the Criminal Law Amendment Act, 1885, be found guilty of an offence under the said section 1, 2 or 3, as may be appropriate.

(3) A person indicted for rape under section 4 may, if the evidence does not warrant a conviction for rape under section 4 but warrants a conviction for aggravated sexual assault or for sexual assault, be found guilty of aggravated sexual assault or of sexual assault, as may be appropriate.

(4) A person indicted for aggravated sexual assault may, if the evidence does not warrant a conviction for aggravated sexual assault but warrants a conviction for sexual assault, be found guilty of sexual assault.

(5) A person indicted for an offence made felony by [section 2 of the Criminal Law (Sexual Offences) Act 2006][1], may, if the evidence does not warrant a conviction for the felony or an attempt to commit the felony but warrants a conviction for an offence under [section 3 of the Criminal Law (Sexual Offences) Act 2006],[1] or section 3 of the Criminal Law Amendment Act, 1885, or rape under section 4 or aggravated sexual assault or sexual assault, be found

guilty of an offence under [the said section 3 or section 3 of the Criminal Law (Sexual Offences) Act 2006]¹ or of rape under section 4 or of aggravated sexual assault or of sexual assault, as may be appropriate.

Amendments

1   Words inserted by Criminal Law (Sexual Offences) Act 2006, s 7.

9   Consent

It is hereby declared that in relation to an offence that consists of or includes the doing of an act to a person without the consent of that person any failure or omission by that person to offer resistance to the act does not of itself constitute consent to the act.

10   Trial of persons for certain offences by Central Criminal Court

A person indicted for a rape offence or the offence of aggravated sexual assault or attempted aggravated sexual assault or of aiding, abetting, counselling or procuring the offence of aggravated sexual assault or attempted aggravated sexual assault or of incitement to the offence of aggravated sexual assault or conspiracy to commit any of the foregoing offences shall be tried by the Central Criminal Court.

11   Exclusion of the public from hearings

The following section shall be substituted for section 6 of the Principal Act:¹

Amendments

1   See the amended Act.

12   Amendment of section 1 of Principal Act

Section 1 of the Principal Act is hereby amended by the substitution of the following subsection for subsection (1):¹

Amendments

1   See the amended Act.

13   Amendment of section 3 of Principal Act

Section 3 of the Principal Act is hereby amended by the substitution of the following subsection for subsection (1):¹

Amendments

1   See the amended Act.

14   Amendment of section 8 of Principal Act

Section 8 of the Principal Act is hereby amended—

    (a) by the substitution of the following subsection for subsection (2):[1] and

    (b) by the insertion of the following subsection after subsection (7):[1]

Amendments

1   See the amended Act.

15   Amendment of section 9 of Principal Act

Section 9(2) of the Principal Act is hereby amended by the insertion after paragraph (a) of the following paragraph:[1]

Amendments

1   See the amended Act.

16   Amendment of section 12 of Principal Act

Section 12(1) of the Principal Act is hereby amended by—

    (a) the substitution of "a sexual assault or an offence to which section 11 relates" for "an offence to which section 10 or 11 relates", and

    (b) the substitution of "£1,000" for "£500".

17   Miscellaneous amendments of Principal Act

(1) Sections 4(1), 5 and 9(1) of the Principal Act are hereby amended by the substitution of "sexual assault offence" for "rape offence".

(2) Section 7 of the Principal Act is hereby amended by—

    (a) the substitution of "person" for "woman" in subsection (1), and

    (b) the substitution of "the outcome of" for "an acquittal of the accused person at" in subsection (4), and

    (c) the substitution of "sexual assault offence" for "rape offence" in subsections (1), (2), (3), (4), (5), (8)(a) and (10).

18   Amendment of section 18 of Criminal Law Amendment Act, 1935

Section 18 of the Criminal Law Amendment Act, 1935, is hereby amended by the substitution of "£500" for "two pounds" and "6 months or to both" for "one month".

19   Amendment of Defence Act, 1954

The Defence Act, 1954, is hereby amended by—

(a) the insertion in [section 169(3)(b)][1], after "rape", of ", rape under section 4 (within the meaning of the Criminal Law (Rape) (Amendment) Act, 1990) or aggravated sexual assault (within the meaning of the Criminal Law (Rape) (Amendment) Act, 1990)", and

(b) the substitution in section 192(3) of ", rape, rape under section 4 (within the meaning of the Criminal Law (Rape) (Amendment) Act, 1990) or aggravated sexual assault (within the meaning of the Criminal Law (Rape) (Amendment) Act, 1990)" for "or rape".

Amendments

1   Words substituted by Criminal Law Act 1997, s 13 and Sch 1, para 9.

---

20   Amendment of Criminal Procedure Act, 1967

(a) Paragraph (a) of subsection (2) of section 13 of the Criminal Procedure Act, 1967, shall not apply in relation to rape, rape under section 4 (within the meaning of the Criminal Law (Rape) (Amendment) Act, 1990) or aggravated sexual assault (within the meaning of the Criminal Law (Rape) (Amendment) Act, 1990).

(b) Notwithstanding paragraph (a), the offences referred to therein shall be deemed, for the purposes of paragraph (b) of the said subsection (2), to be offences to which the said section 13 applies.

21   Repeals

The enactments specified in column (3) of the Schedule to this Act are hereby repealed to the extent specified in column (4) of that Schedule.

22   Short title, collective citation, construction, commencement and transitional provision

(1) This Act may be cited as the Criminal Law (Rape) (Amendment) Act, 1990.

(2) The Criminal Law (Rape) Act, 1981, and this Act may be cited together as the Criminal Law (Rape) Acts, 1981 and 1990, and shall be construed together as one.

(3) This Act shall come into operation one month after the date of its passing.

(4) (a) Sections 2, 3, 4, 5, 6, 8, 12, 16, 19 and 21 (insofar as it relates to reference numbers 3 and 4 in the Schedule to this Act) shall not have effect in relation to an offence committed before the commencement of this Act.

(b) Sections 7, 11, 13, 15 and 17(1) shall not have effect in relation to a trial or preliminary examination that begins before such commencement.

(c)   (i)   Subject to subparagraph (ii), section 10 shall not have effect in relation to a case in which, before such commencement, a person has been sent forward for trial to the Circuit Court.

    (ii)   In a case to which subparagraph (i) applies, an application by a person charged or the Director of Public Prosecutions, made before the commencement of the trial concerned, to a judge of the Circuit Court sitting in the circuit where it is to take place for its transfer to the Central Criminal Court shall be granted.

(d)   Section 20 shall not have effect in relation to a charge that is made before such commencement.

SCHEDULE

ENACTMENTS REPEALED

Section 21

Ref No	Session and Chapter or Number and Year	Short Title	Extent of Repeal
(1)	(2)	(3)	(4)
1	24 & 25 Vic., c. 100	Offences against the Person Act, 1861	In section 62, the words ", or of any indecent assault upon any male person".
2	48 & 49 Vic., c. 69	Criminal Law Amendment Act, 1885	Section 9.
3	1935, No. 6	Criminal Law Amendment Act, 1935	Section 3.
4	1951, No. 2	Criminal Justice Act, 1951	In the First Schedule, the matter at reference number 6.
5	1981, No. 10	Criminal Law (Rape) Act, 1981	In section 1(3), the words "but this does not affect any rule of law by virtue of which a male person is treated by reason of his age as being incapable of committing an offence of any particular kind"; In section 2(1)(a), the word "unlawful"; In section 8(3), the words "or the Circuit Court"; Section 10; Section 12(3).

Criminal Justice (Forensic Evidence) Act 1990

Number 34 of 1990

ARRANGEMENT OF SECTIONS

Section

1. Interpretation.

2. Power to take bodily samples.

3. Inferences from refusal to consent to taking a sample.

4. Destruction of records and samples.

5. Regulations regarding taking of samples.

6. Repeals.

7. Expenses.

8. Short title and commencement.

AN ACT TO AMEND AND EXTEND THE LAW TO AUTHORISE THE TAKING OF BODILY SAMPLES FOR FORENSIC TESTING FROM PERSONS SUSPECTED OF CERTAIN CRIMINAL OFFENCES. [24th December, 1990]

BE IT ENACTED BY THE OIREACHTAS AS FOLLOWS:

1   Interpretation

In this Act—

"appropriate consent" has the meaning assigned to it by section 2(10) of this Act;

"the Minister" means the Minister for Justice;

"prescribed" means prescribed by regulations made by the Minister under section 5 of this Act;

"prison" means any place for which rules or regulations may be made under the Prisons Acts, 1826 to 1980, or section 13 of the Criminal Justice Act, 1960;

"registered dentist" means a person whose name is entered for the time being on the Register of Dentists maintained under the Dentists Act, 1985;

"registered medical practitioner" has the meaning assigned to it by 20 section 2 of the Medical Practitioners Act, 1978;

"samples" means the samples or other things referred to in section 2(1)(a) to (e) of this Act.

2   Power to take bodily samples

(1) Subject to the provisions of [subsections (4) to (8A)]¹ of this section, where a person is in custody under the provisions of section 30 of the Offences against the State Act, 1939, [section 4 of the Criminal Justice Act, 1984, section 2 of the Criminal Justice (Drug Trafficking) Act, 1996 or section 50 of the Criminal Justice Act 2007]², a member of the Garda Síochána may take, or cause to be taken, from that person for the purpose of forensic testing all or any of the following samples, namely—

(a) a sample of—
  (i) blood,
  (ii) pubic hair,
  (iii) urine,
  (iv) saliva,
  (v) hair other than pubic hair,
  (vi) a nail,
  (vii) any material found under a nail,
[(b) a swab from any part of the body including the mouth but not from any other body orifice or a genital region,]¹
[(c) a swab from a body orifice, other than the mouth, or a genital region,]¹
(d) a dental impression,
(e) a footprint or similar impression of any part of the person's body other than a part of his hand [...]¹.

[(1A) A reference in subsection (1) of this section to the mouth shall be read as including a reference to the inside of the mouth.]³

(2) Subject to [the provisions of subsections (3) to (8A)]⁴ of this section, where a person is in prison, a member of the Garda Síochána may take, or cause to be taken, from that person for the purpose of forensic testing all or any of the samples specified in subsection (1) of this section.

(3) The power conferred by subsection (2) of this section shall only be exercisable—

(a) where the sample to be taken is required in connection with an offence other than the offence in respect of which the person is in prison or an offence of which he could be convicted on an indictment alleging that offence, and

(b) where the sample to be taken is required in connection with an investigation in respect of the commission of an offence under the Offences against the State Act, 1939, or an offence which is for the time being a scheduled offence for the purposes of Part V of that Act or an offence to which section 4 of the Criminal Justice Act, 1984, applies [or a drug trafficking offence within the meaning of section 3(1) of the Criminal Justice Act, 1994 or an offence to which section 50 of the Criminal Justice Act 2007 applies.]⁵

(4) A sample may be taken under this section only if—

(a) a member of the Garda Síochána not below the rank of superintendent authorises it to be taken, and

(b) in the case of a sample mentioned in [subparagraph (i), (ii) or (iii) of paragraph (a) of subsection (1) of this section],⁶ or in paragraph (c) or (d) of the said subsection (1), the appropriate consent has been given in writing.

(5) An authorisation to take a sample under this section shall not be given unless the member of the Garda Síochána giving it has reasonable grounds—

(a) for suspecting the involvement of the person from whom the sample is to be taken—

  (i) in a case where the person is in custody, in the offence in respect of which he is in custody, or

(ii) in a case where the person is in prison, in the commission of an offence under the Offences against the State Act, 1939, or an offence which is for the time being a scheduled offence for the purposes of Part V of that Act or an offence to which section 4 of the Criminal Justice Act, 1984, applies [or a drug trafficking offence within the meaning of section 3(1) of the Criminal Justice Act 1994 or an offence to which section 50 of the Criminal Justice Act 2007 applies.][7]

and

(b) for believing that the sample will tend to confirm or disprove the involvement of the person from whom the sample is to be taken in the said offence.

(6) Before a member of the Garda Síochána takes, or causes to be taken, a sample under subsection (1) of this section, or seeks the consent of the person from whom the sample is required to the taking of such a sample, the member shall inform the person—

(a) of the nature of the offence in which it is suspected that that person has been involved,

(b) that an authorisation has been given under subsection (4)(a) of this section and of the grounds on which it has been given, and

(c) that the results of any tests on the sample may be given in evidence in any proceedings.

(7) An authorisation under subsection (4)(a) of this section may be given orally but, if it is given orally, it shall be confirmed in writing as soon as is practicable.

(8) A sample of a kind specified in subparagraph (i) or (ii) of paragraph (a) of subsection (1) of this section or in paragraph (c) of the said subsection (1) may be taken only by a registered medical practitioner and a dental impression may be taken only by a registered dentist or a registered medical practitioner.

[(8A) Where a sample of hair other than pubic hair is taken in accordance with this section—

(a) the sample may be taken by plucking hairs with their roots and, in so far as it is reasonably practicable, the hairs shall be plucked singly, and

(b) no more hairs shall be plucked than the person taking the sample reasonably considers to be necessary to constitute a sufficient sample for the purpose of forensic testing.][8]

(9) A person who obstructs or attempts to obstruct any member of the Garda Síochána or any other person acting under the powers conferred by subsection (1) of this section shall be guilty of an offence and shall be liable on summary conviction to a fine not exceeding [€3,000][9] or to imprisonment for a term not exceeding 12 months or to both.

(10) In this Act "appropriate consent" means—

(a) in the case of a person who has attained the age of 17 years, the consent of that person,

(b) in the case of a person who has not attained the age of 17 years but has attained the age of 14 years, the consent of that person and of a parent or guardian of that person, and

(c) in the case of a person who has not attained the age of 14 years, the consent of a parent or guardian of that person.

(11) The powers conferred by this section are without prejudice to any other powers exercisable by a member of the Garda Síochána.

Amendments

1   Subsection (1) amended by Criminal Justice Act 2006, s 14(a)(i).
2   Words substituted by Criminal Justice (Drug Trafficking) Act 1996, s 3(a)(i) and further substituted by Criminal Justice Act 2007, 53(a)(i).
3   Subsection (1A) inserted by Criminal Justice Act 2006, s 14(a)(ii).
4   Subsection (2) amended by Criminal Justice Act 2006, s 14(a)(iii).
5   Subsection (3) amended by Criminal Justice (Drug Trafficking) Act 1996, s 3(a)(ii) and further amended Criminal Justice Act 2007, s 53(a)(ii).
6   Subsection (4) amended by Criminal Justice Act 2006, s 14(a)(iv).
7   Subsection (5) amended by Criminal Justice Act 2006, s 14(a)(v) and further amended Criminal Justice Act 2007, s 53(a)(iii).
8   Subsection (8A) inserted by Criminal Justice Act 2006, s 14(a)(vi).
9   Subsection (9) amended by Criminal Justice Act 2006, s 14(a)(vii).

---

3   **Inferences from refusal to consent to taking a sample**

(1) Where a consent required under section 2 of this Act is refused without good cause, in any proceedings against a person for an offence—

    (a)   the court, in determining—

        [(i)   whether a charge against that person should be dismissed under Part IA of the Criminal Procedure Act, 1967, or][1]

        (ii)   whether there is a case to answer, and

    (b)   the court (or, subject to the judge's directions, the jury), in determining whether that person is guilty of the offence charged (or of any other offence of which he could lawfully be convicted on that charge),

may draw such inferences, if any, from the refusal as appear proper; and the refusal may, on the basis of such inferences, be treated as, or as being capable of amounting to, corroboration of any evidence in relation to which the refusal is material, but a person shall not be convicted of an offence solely on an inference drawn from such refusal.

(2) The reference in subsection (1) of this section to evidence shall[, in relation to the hearing of an application under Part IA of the Criminal Procedure Act, 1967 for the dismissal of a charge][2], be taken to include a statement of the evidence to be given by a witness at the trial.

(3) Subsection (1) of this section shall not have effect in relation to an accused unless he has been told in ordinary language by a member of the Garda Síochána when seeking his consent that the sample was required for the purpose of forensic testing, that his consent was necessary and, if his consent was not given, what the effect of a refusal by him of such consent could be.

(4) This section shall not apply—

    (a)   to a person who has not attained the age of 14 years, or

    (b)   in a case where an appropriate consent has been refused by a parent or guardian.

Amendments

1   Subsection (1)(a)(i) substituted by Criminal Justice Act 1999, s 17(1).
2   Words substituted by Criminal Justice Act 1999, s 17(2).

4   Destruction of records and samples

(1) Subject to subsection (5) of this section, every record identifying the person from whom a sample has been taken pursuant to section 2 of this Act shall, if not previously destroyed, be destroyed as this section directs and every sample identified by such record shall be destroyed in like manner.

(2) Where proceedings for any offence in respect of which a person could be detained under section 30 of the Offences against the State Act, 1939, [section 4 of the Criminal Justice Act, 1984, section 2 of the Criminal Justice (Drug Trafficking) Act 1996 or section 50 of the Criminal Justice Act 2007]¹, are not instituted against the person from whom the sample was taken [within twelve months from the taking of the sample]² and the failure to institute the proceedings within that period is not due to the fact that he has absconded or cannot be found, the destruction of the record and the sample identified by such record shall be carried out on the expiration of that period unless an order has been made under subsection (5) of this section.

[(3) Where proceedings have been so instituted and—

(a)   the person is acquitted,

(b)   the charge against the person in respect of the offence concerned is dismissed under section 4E of the Criminal Procedure Act 1967, or

(c)   the proceedings are discontinued,

the destruction of the record and the sample identified by such record shall be carried out on the expiration of twenty-one days after the acquittal, dismissal or discontinuance, as the case may be, unless an order has been made under subsection (5) of this section.

(3A) For the purposes of subsection (3)(b) of this section, a charge against the person in respect of the offence concerned shall be regarded as dismissed when—

(a)   the time for bringing an appeal against the dismissal has expired,

(b)   any such appeal has been withdrawn or abandoned, or

(c)   on any such appeal, the dismissal is upheld.]³

(4)   (a)   Where a person from whom a sample has been taken is the subject of an order under subsection (1) or (2) of section 1 of the Probation of Offenders Act, 1907, the destruction of the said sample and every record identifying such sample shall be carried out on the expiration of 3 years from the making of the order; provided that he has not been convicted of an offence to which section 4 of the Criminal Justice Act, 1984, applies during that period.

      (b)   Paragraph (a) of this subsection shall not apply to an order under section 1(2) of the Probation of Offenders Act, 1907, discharged on the appeal of a person against conviction if on appeal his conviction is affirmed.

(5) If a court is satisfied, on an application being made to it by or on behalf of the Director of Public Prosecutions or the person from whom the sample was taken, that there is good reason why records and samples to which this section applies should not be destroyed under this section, it may make an order authorising the retention of such records and samples for such purpose or period as it may direct.

Amendments

1   Words amended by Criminal Justice (Drug Trafficking) Act 1996, s 3(b) and further amended by Criminal Justice Act 2007, s 53(b).

2   Words substituted by Criminal Justice Act 2006, s 14(b)(i).

3   Subsection (3) substituted and subsection (3A) inserted by Criminal Justice Act 2006, s 14(b)(ii).

5   Regulations regarding taking of samples

(1) The Minister shall make regulations relating to the taking of samples for the purposes of this Act.

(2) Without prejudice to the generality of subsection (1) of this section, the regulations shall—

    (a) make provision for the recording in the records of a Garda Síochána station of—

        (i)   an authorisation to take a sample given under section 2(4)(a) of this Act and any consent given under section 2(4)(b) of this Act,

        (ii) a refusal to consent to the taking of a sample in cases where consent is to be given under section 2(4)(b) of this Act,

        (iii) particulars of the time and manner of the taking of a sample pursuant to this Act, [...][1]

    [(aa) make provision for—

        (i)   the manner in which samples may be taken,

        (ii) the location and physical conditions in which samples may be taken, and

        (iii) the persons (including members of the Garda Síochána), and the number of such persons, who may be present when samples are taken, and].[1]

    (b) make provision for the taking of samples from persons who have not attained the age of 17 years.

(3) Every regulation made under this section shall be laid before each House of the Oireachtas as soon as may be after it is made and, if a resolution annulling the regulation is passed by either such House within the next twenty-one days on which that House has sat after the regulation has been laid before it, the regulation shall be annulled accordingly, but without prejudice to the validity of anything previously done thereunder.

Amendments

1   Subsection (2)(a) amended by the deletion of the word 'and' and subection (2)(aa) inserted by Criminal Justice Act 2006, s 14(c).

6 Repeals

Section 7(1)(e) of the Criminal Law Act, 1976, and section 6(1)(e) of the Criminal Justice Act, 1984, are hereby repealed.

7 Expenses

The expenses incurred by the Minister in the administration of this Act shall, to such extent as may be sanctioned by the Minister for Finance, be paid out of moneys provided by the Oireachtas.

8 Short title and commencement

(1) This Act may be cited as, the Criminal Justice (Forensic Evidence) Act, 1990.

(2) This Act shall come into operation on such day as may be fixed therefor by order of the Minister.

Courts Act 1991

Number 20 of 1991

ARRANGEMENT OF SECTIONS

Section

1. Interpretation.

2. Extension of jurisdiction of Circuit Court.

3. Extension of jurisdiction of Circuit Court under Registration of Title Act, 1964.

4. Extension of jurisdiction of District Court.

5. Extension of jurisdiction of District Court in interpleader by under-sheriffs.

6. Extension of jurisdiction of District Court under Hire-Purchase Acts, 1946 and 1960.

7. Extension of jurisdiction of District Court in cases of detinue.

8. Extension of jurisdiction of District Court under Family Home Protection Act, 1976.

9. Extension of jurisdiction of Circuit Court and District Court under Hotel Proprietors Act, 1963.

10. Extension of jurisdiction of Circuit Court and District Court under Local Government (Water Pollution) Act, 1977.

11. Extension of jurisdiction of Circuit Court and District Court under Family Law (Maintenance of Spouses and Children) Act, 1976.

12. Extension of jurisdiction of Circuit Court and District Court under Guardianship of Infants Act, 1964.

13. Extension of jurisdiction of Circuit Court and District Court under Family Law Act, 1981.

14. Amendment of Act of 1981.

15. Remittal or transfer of certain actions.

16. Variation by order of certain monetary limits.

17. Number of ordinary judges of High Court.

18. Number of judges of Circuit Court.

19. Number of justices of District Court.

20. Permanent assignment of justices of District Court to districts.

21. Amendment of Courts (Establishment and Constitution) Act, 1961.

22. Service of summonses.

23. Short title, collective citation and commencement.

AN ACT TO AMEND AND EXTEND THE COURTS OF JUSTICE ACTS, 1924 TO 1961, THE COURTS (ESTABLISHMENT AND CONSTITUTION) ACT, 1961, AND THE COURTS (SUPPLEMENTAL PROVISIONS) ACTS, 1961 TO 1988, AND TO PROVIDE FOR OTHER MATTERS RELATING TO THE COURTS. [15th July, 1991]

BE IT ENACTED BY THE OIREACHTAS AS FOLLOWS:

1   **Interpretation**

(1) In this Act—

"the Act of 1851" means the Petty Sessions (Ireland) Act, 1851;

"the Act of 1924" means the Courts of Justice Act, 1924;

"the Act of 1936" means the Courts of Justice Act, 1936;

"the Act of 1961" means the Courts (Supplemental Provisions) Act, 1961;

"the Act of 1977" means the Courts Act, 1977;

"the Act of 1981" means the Courts Act, 1981;

"the Act of 1985" means the Courts Act, 1985.

(2) A reference in this Act to any other enactment shall, except so far as the context otherwise requires, be construed as a reference to that enactment as amended or applied by or under any other enactment including this Act.

2   **Extension of jurisdiction of Circuit Court**

Text not reproduced here.

3   **Extension of jurisdiction of Circuit Court under Registration of Title Act, 1964**

Text not reproduced here.

4   **Extension of jurisdiction of District Court**

Text not reproduced here.

5   **Extension of jurisdiction of District Court in interpleader by under-sheriffs**

Text not reproduced here.

6   **Extension of jurisdiction of District Court under Hire-Purchase Acts, 1946 and 1960**

Text not reproduced here.

7   **Extension of jurisdiction of District Court in cases of detinue**

Text not reproduced here.

8   **Extension of jurisdiction of District Court under Family Home Protection Act, 1976**

Text not reproduced here.

9   **Extension of jurisdiction of Circuit Court and District Court under Hotel Proprietors Act, 1963.**

Text not reproduced here.

10   **Extension of jurisdiction of Circuit Court and District Court under Local Government (Water Pollution) Act, 1977**

Text not reproduced here.

11   Extension of jurisdiction of Circuit Court and District Court under Family Law (Maintenance of Spouses and Children) Act, 1976

Text not reproduced here.

12   Extension of jurisdiction of Circuit Court and District Court under Guardianship of Infants Act, 1964

Text not reproduced here.

13   Extension of jurisdiction of Circuit Court and District Court under Family Law Act, 1981

Text not reproduced here.

14   Amendment of Act of 1981

Text not reproduced here.

15   Remittal or transfer of certain actions

Text not reproduced here.

16   Variation by order of certain monetary limits

Text not reproduced here.

17   Number of ordinary judges of High Court

Text not reproduced here.

18   Number of judges of Circuit Court

Text not reproduced here.

19   Number of justices of District Court

Section 1 of the Act of 1977 is hereby amended by the substitution of "45" for "thirty-nine" in subsection (3).

20   Permanent assignment of justices of District Court to districts

The Sixth Schedule to the Act of 1961 is hereby amended in paragraph 2(1) by the substitution for clause (b) (inserted by the Act of 1977) of the following:[1]

Amendments

1   See the amended Act.

21   Amendment of Courts (Establishment and Constitution) Act, 1961

(1) The Courts (Establishment and Constitution) Act, 1961, is hereby amended—

(a) in section 5, by the substitution in subsection (2)(b) of "Judge of the District Court" for "Justice of the District Court", and

(b) in section 6—

(i)   by the substitution in subsection (1)(b) of "judge of the District Court" for "justice of the District Court", and

(ii) by the substitution in subsection (6) of "judge" for "justice".

(2) References in any statute or instrument made under statute to a justice of the District Court shall be construed as references to a judge of the District Court.

22   Service of summonses

(1) Notwithstanding section 12 of the Act of 1851 and without prejudice to the provisions of any Act authorising the service of summonses in any particular manner in particular cases, a summons issued in a case of summary jurisdiction under section 11(2) or 13 of the Act of 1851 or section 1 of the Act of 1986 may be served upon the person to whom it is directed—

(a)   by sending, by registered prepaid post, a copy thereof in an envelope addressed to him at his last known residence or most usual place of abode or at his place of business in the State,

(b)   by sending, by any other system of recorded delivery prepaid post specified in rules of court, a copy thereof in such an envelope as aforesaid, or

(c)   by delivery by hand, by a person other than the person on whose behalf it purports to be issued authorised in that behalf by rules of court, of a copy thereof in such an envelope as aforesaid.

(2) Service of a summons upon a person pursuant to subsection (1) of this section shall, upon proof that a copy of the summons was placed in an envelope and that the envelope was addressed, recorded, prepaid and sent or was delivered in accordance with the provisions of the said subsection (1), be deemed to be good service of the summons upon the person unless it is proved, whether in pursuance of an application under subsection (6) of this section or otherwise, that the person did not receive notice of the summons or of the hearing to which the summons relates.

(3) Where service of a summons upon a person is effected by a means provided for in subsection (1)(a) or (b) of this section—

(a)   the summons shall, subject to subsection (2) of this section, be deemed to be served upon the person at the time at which the envelope containing a copy of the summons would be delivered in the ordinary course of post,

(b)   the placing of a copy of the summons in the envelope and the addressing, recording, prepaying and sending, in accordance with the provisions of subsection (1)(a) or (b) of this section, of the envelope may be proved by a statutory declaration (which shall be endorsed upon the original summons and shall be made, not earlier than 10 days after the day on which the envelope is posted, by the person who posted the envelope) exhibiting the record of posting of the envelope aforesaid and stating, if it be the case, that the original summons was duly issued at the time of posting and that the envelope has not been returned undelivered to the sender, and

(c)   the time, date and place of posting of the envelope shall be endorsed upon the original summons.

(4) Where a summons has been issued under section 11(2) of the Act of 1851 or section 1 of the Act of 1986 and served upon the person to whom it is directed by a means of service provided for in subsection (1) of this section and that person neither appears at the time and place specified in the summons nor at the hearing of the complaint or accusation to which the

summons relates, the District Court may, if it considers it undesirable in the interests of justice, whether because of the gravity of the offence or otherwise, to continue the hearing in the absence of the person, adjourn the hearing to such time and place as the Court may direct to enable the person to be notified in such manner as the Court may direct of the adjourned hearing.[a]

(5) Where the District Court has adjourned the hearing of a complaint or accusation under subsection (4) of this section and the person to whom the summons concerned is directed does not appear at the adjourned hearing, the District Court may, [...][1] if the Court is satisfied that reasonable notice of the adjourned hearing was given to the person in accordance with the said subsection (4), issue a warrant for the arrest and bringing of the person before it to answer the said complaint or accusation or proceed to hear the complaint or accusation in the absence of the person.

(6) (a)   Where a summons has been issued under section 11(2) of the Act of 1851 or section 1 of the Act of 1986 and the District Court has proceeded to hear the complaint or accusation to which the summons relates, the person to whom the summons is directed may, if he did not receive notice of the summons or of the hearing to which the summons relates, within 21 days after the said summons or hearing comes to his notice or such further period as the District Court may, having regard to the circumstances, allow, apply to the District Court to have the proceedings set aside.[b]

   (b)   Notice of an application under paragraph (a) of this subsection shall—

      (i)   be lodged with the District Court clerk for the District Court area in which the hearing to which the summons relates has taken place,

      (ii)   be in the form prescribed by rules of court,

      (iii)   state that the applicant did not receive notice of the summons or of the hearing to which the summons relates until a time specified in the notice of the said application, being a time after the commencement of the hearing to which the summons relates,

   and the hearing of the application shall not take place before the expiration of a period of 21 days from the date of such lodgment as aforesaid or such shorter period as the District Court may allow.

   (c)   A person who, in connection with an application under this subsection, makes a statement that he knows to be false or misleading in a material respect shall be guilty of an offence and shall be liable on summary conviction to a fine not exceeding £500 or to 3 months imprisonment or to both.

(7) The District Court may, on the hearing of an application under subsection (6) of this section, grant or refuse to grant the application and may direct that the complaint or accusation to which it relates be heard again at such time and place as the Court may direct.

(8) The rule-making authority for the time being for the District Court may make rules for carrying this section into effect.

(9) In this section—

"the Act of 1986" means the Courts (No. 3) Act, 1986;

"a case of summary jurisdiction" means a case which may be heard or disposed of only summarily or under section 6 of the Criminal Justice Act, 1951;

"District Court area" shall include the Dublin Metropolitan District.

Amendments

1   Words deleted by Criminal Procedure Act 2010, s 36.

Note

a   SI 116/1992, reg 4 provides that:

4.   Where, in a case of summary jurisdiction, the Court adjourns pursuant to section 22(4) of the Act the hearing of a complaint or an accusation to which a particular summons relates and requires the person to whom the summons was directed to be notified of the adjourned hearing, the Clerk shall, unless the Court otherwise directs, issue and serve upon the person a notice in the Form 1 in the schedule hereto. Service shall be effected at least fourteen days before the date of the adjourned hearing and in such manner as the Court may direct. The original notice, with the details of service endorsed thereon, shall be retained by the Clerk and produced to the Court at said hearing.

b   SI 116/1992, reg 5 provides that:

5.   (1) An application pursuant to section 22(6)(a) of the Act to have proceedings set aside may be made at any sitting of the Court for the transaction of summary business for the court area wherein the hearing to which the relevant summons relates has taken place. Where such application is not made within 21 days after the said summons or hearing comes to the notice of the applicant, a further period within which to make the application may be sought *ex parte* at any sitting of the Court for the said court area

---

23   Short title, collective citation and commencement

(1) This Act may be cited as the Courts Act, 1991.

(2) The Courts (Supplemental Provisions) Acts, 1961 to 1988, and this Act may be cited together as the Courts (Supplemental Provisions) Acts, 1961 to 1991.

(3) Sections 2 to 4(b) and 5 to 14 of this Act shall come into operation on the day that is 1 month after the date of the passing of this Act, but shall not apply in relation to proceedings in any court instituted before that day.

(4) Sections 4(c), 15 and 21 of this Act shall come into operation on the day that is 3 months after the date of the passing of this Act, but shall not apply in relation to proceedings in any court instituted before that day.

(5) Section 22 of this Act shall come into operation on the day that is 3 months after the date of the passing of this Act.

Criminal Damage Act 1991

Number 31 of 1991

ARRANGEMENT OF SECTIONS

Section

1. Interpretation.
2. Damaging property.
3. Threat to damage property.
4. Possessing any thing with intent to damage property.
5. Unauthorised accessing of data.
6. "Without lawful excuse".
7. Proceedings.
8. Jurisdiction of District Court.
9. Compensation order.
10. Suspension of compensation order pending appeal.
11. Effect of compensation order on civil proceedings.
12. Arrest without warrant.
13. Search warrant.
14. Minor and consequential changes in existing law.
15. Repeal.
16. Short title and commencement.

AN ACT TO AMEND THE LAW RELATING TO OFFENCES OF DAMAGE TO PROPERTY AND TO PROVIDE FOR CONNECTED MATTERS. [27th December, 1991]

BE IT ENACTED BY THE OIREACHTAS AS FOLLOWS:

1   Interpretation

(1) In this Act—

"compensation order" has the meaning assigned to it by section 9(1);

"to damage" includes—

    (a) in relation to property other than data (but including a storage medium in which data are kept), to destroy, deface, dismantle or, whether temporarily or otherwise, render inoperable or unfit for use or prevent or impair the operation of,

    (b) in relation to data—

        (i) to add to, alter, corrupt, erase or move to another storage medium or to a different location in the storage medium in which they are kept (whether or not property other than data is damaged thereby), or

        (ii) to do any act that contributes towards causing such addition, alteration, corruption, erasure or movement,

    (c) to do any act within the State that damages property outside the State,

553

(d) to do any act outside the State that damages property within the State, and

(e) to make an omission causing damage,

and cognate words shall be construed accordingly;

"data" means information in a form in which it can be accessed by means of a computer and includes a program;

"property" means—

(a) property of a tangible nature, whether real or personal, including money and animals that are capable of being stolen, and

(b) data.

(2) Property shall be treated for the purposes of this Act as belonging to any person—

(a) having lawful custody or control of it,

(b) having in it any proprietary right or interest (not being an equitable interest arising only from an agreement to transfer or grant an interest), or

(c) having a charge over it.

(3) Where, as respects an offence under section 2, 3(a) or 4(a)—

(a) the property concerned is a family home within the meaning of the Family Home Protection Act, 1976 [or a dwelling, within the meaning of section 2(2) of the Family Home Protection Act, 1976, as amended by section 54(1)(a) of the Family Law Act, 1995, in which a person, who is a party to a marriage that has been dissolved under the Family Law (Divorce) Act, 1996, or under the law of a country or jurisdiction other than the State, being a divorce that is entitled to be recognised as valid in the State, ordinarily resided with his or her former spouse, before the dissolution,][1]

and

(b) the person charged—

[(i) is the spouse of a person who resides, or is entitled to reside, in the home or is a party to a marriage that has been dissolved under the Family Law (Divorce) Act, 1996, or under the law of a country or jurisdiction other than the State, being a divorce that is entitled to be recognised as valid in the State, and.][2]

(ii) is the subject of a protection order or barring order (within the meaning in each case of the Family Law (Protection of Spouses and Children) Act, 1981) or is excluded from the home pursuant to an order under section 16(a) of the Judicial Separation and Family Law Reform Act, 1989, or any other order of a court,

sections 2, 3(a) and 4(a) shall have effect as if the references therein to any property belonging to another, however expressed, were references to the home.

(4) Where property is subject to a trust, the persons to whom the property belongs shall be treated for the purposes of this Act as including any person having a right to enforce the trust.

(5) Property of a corporation sole shall be treated for the purposes of this Act as belonging to the corporation notwithstanding a vacancy in it.

(6) In this Act—

(a) a reference to any enactment shall, unless the context otherwise requires, be construed as a reference to that enactment as amended or extended by or under any subsequent enactment including this Act,

(b) a reference to a section is a reference to a section of this Act unless it is indicated that reference to some other enactment is intended,

(c) a reference to a subsection, paragraph or subparagraph is a reference to the subsection, paragraph or subparagraph of the provision in which the reference occurs unless it is indicated that reference to some other provision is intended.

Amendments

1 Words inserted by Family Law (Divorce) Act 1996, s 48(a).

2 Subsection (3)(b)(i) substituted by Family Law (Divorce) Act 1996, s 48(a).

2   Damaging property

(1) A person who without lawful excuse damages any property belonging to another intending to damage any such property or being reckless as to whether any such property would be damaged shall be guilty of an offence.

(2) A person who without lawful excuse damages any property, whether belonging to himself or another—

(a) intending to damage any property or being reckless as to whether any property would be damaged, and

(b) intending by the damage to endanger the life of another or being reckless as to whether the life of another would be thereby endangered,

shall be guilty of an offence.

(3) A person who damages any property, whether belonging to himself or another, with intent to defraud shall be guilty of an offence.

(4) An offence committed under this section by damaging property by fire shall be charged as arson.

(5) A person guilty of an offence under this section shall be liable—

(a) on summary conviction, to a fine not exceeding £1,000 or imprisonment for a term not exceeding 12 months or both, and

(b) on conviction on indictment—

(i) in case the person is guilty of arson under subsection (1) or (3) or of an offence under subsection (2) (whether arson or not), to a fine or imprisonment for life or both, and

(ii) in case the person is guilty of any other offence under this section, to a fine not exceeding £10,000 or imprisonment for a term not exceeding 10 years or both.

(6) For the purposes of this section a person is reckless if he has foreseen that the particular kind of damage that in fact was done might be done and yet has gone on to take the risk of it.

3   Threat to damage property

A person who without lawful excuse makes to another a threat, intending that that other would fear it would be carried out—

(a) to damage any property belonging to that other or a third person, or

(b) to damage his own property in a way which he knows is likely to endanger the life of that other or a third person,

shall be guilty of an offence and shall be liable—

(i) on summary conviction, to a fine not exceeding £1,000 or imprisonment for a term not exceeding 12 months or both, and

(ii) on conviction on indictment, to a fine not exceeding £10,000 or imprisonment for a term not exceeding 10 years or both.

4 Possessing any thing with intent to damaged property

A person (in this section referred to as the possessor) who has any thing in his custody or under his control intending without lawful excuse to use it or cause or permit another to use it—

(a) to damage any property belonging to some other person, or

(b) to damage his own or the intended user's property—

(i) in a way which he knows is likely to endanger the life of a person other than the possessor, or

(ii) with intent to defraud,

shall be guilty of an offence and shall be liable—

(A) on summary conviction, to a fine not exceeding £1,000 or imprisonment for a term not exceeding 12 months or both, and

(B) on conviction on indictment, to a fine not exceeding £10,000 or imprisonment for a term not exceeding 10 years or both.

5 Unauthorised accessing of data

(1) A person who without lawful excuse operates a computer—

(a) within the State with intent to access any data kept either within or outside the State, or

(b) outside the State with intent to access any data kept within the State,

shall, whether or not he accesses any data, be guilty of an offence and shall be liable on summary conviction to a fine not exceeding £500 or imprisonment for a term not exceeding 3 months or both.

(2) Subsection (1) applies whether or not the person intended to access any particular data or any particular category of data or data kept by any particular person.

6 "Without lawful excuse"

(1) This section applies to—

(a) any offence under section 2(1) or 5,

(b) any offence under section 3 other than one involving a threat by the person charged to damage property in a way which he knows is likely to endanger the life of another, and

(c) any offence under section 4 other than one involving an intent by the person charged to use, or cause or permit the use of, something in his custody or under his control to damage property in such a way as aforesaid.

(2) A person charged with an offence to which this section applies shall, whether or not he would be treated for the purposes of this Act as having a lawful excuse apart from this subsection, be treated for those purposes as having a lawful excuse—

(a) if at the time of the act or acts alleged to constitute the offence he believed that the person or persons whom he believed to be entitled to consent to or authorise the damage to (or, in the case of an offence under section 5, the accessing of) the property in question had consented, or would have consented to or authorised it if he or they had known of the damage or the accessing and its circumstances,

(b) in the case of an offence under section 5, if he is himself the person entitled to consent to or authorise accessing of the data concerned, or

[(c) if he damaged or threatened to damage the property in question or, in the case of an offence under section 4, intended to use or cause or permit the use of something to damage it, in order to protect himself or another or property belonging to himself or another or a right or interest in property which was or which he believed to be vested in himself or another and the act or acts alleged to constitute the offence were reasonable in the circumstances as he believed them to be.]¹

(3) For the purposes of this section it is immaterial whether a belief is justified or not if it is honestly held.

(4) For the purposes of subsection (2) a right or interest in property includes any right or privilege in or over land, whether created by grant, licence or otherwise.

(5) This section shall not be construed as casting doubt on any defence recognised by law as a defence to criminal charges.

Amendments

1 Subsection (2)(c) substituted by Non-Fatal Offences Against The Person Act 1997, s 21.

7 Proceedings

(1) Proceedings for an offence under section 2 or 5 alleged to have been committed by a person outside the State in relation to data kept within the State or other property so situate may be taken, and the offence may for all incidental purposes be treated as having been committed, in any place in the State.

(2) (a) Where a person is charged with an offence under section 2, 3 or 4 in relation to property belonging to another—

(i) it shall not be necessary to name the person to whom the property belongs, and

(ii) it shall be presumed, until the contrary is shown, that the property belongs to another.

(b) Where a person is charged with an offence under section 2 in relation to such property as aforesaid, it shall also be presumed, until the contrary is shown, that the person entitled to consent to or authorise the damage concerned had not consented to or authorised it, unless the property concerned is data and the person charged is an employee or agent of the person keeping the data.

(c) Paragraph (b) shall apply in relation to a person charged with an offence under section 5 as if the reference to damage were a reference to access and with any necessary modifications.

(3) A person charged with an offence under section 2 in relation to data or an attempt to commit such an offence may, if the evidence does not warrant a conviction for the offence charged but warrants a conviction for an offence under section 5, be found guilty of that offence.

8   Jurisdiction of District Court

No rule of law ousting the jurisdiction of the District Court to try offences where a dispute of title to property is involved shall preclude that court from trying offences under this Act.

9–11   [...][1]

Amendments

1   Sections 9, 10 and 11 of the Criminal Damage Act 1991, are repealed by Criminal Justice Act 1993, s 13.

---

12   Arrest without warrant

(1) This section applies to an offence under this Act other than section 5 or 13(4).

(2) Any person may arrest without warrant anyone who is or whom he, with reasonable cause, suspects to be in the act of committing an offence to which this section applies.

(3) Where an offence to which this section applies has been committed, any person may arrest without warrant anyone who is or whom he, with reasonable cause, suspects to be guilty of the offence.

(4) Where a member of the Garda Síochána, with reasonable cause, suspects that an offence to which this section applies or an offence under section 13(4) has been committed, he may arrest without warrant anyone whom he, with reasonable cause, suspects to be guilty of the offence.

(5) A member of the Garda Síochána may arrest without warrant anyone who is or whom he, with reasonable cause, suspects to be about to commit an offence to which this section applies.

(6) For the purpose of arresting a person under any power conferred by this section a member of the Garda Síochána may enter (if need be, by force) and search any place where that person is or where the member, with reasonable cause, suspects him to be.

(7) This section shall apply to an attempt to commit an offence as it applies to the commission of that offence.

(8) This section shall not prejudice any power of arrest conferred by law apart from this section.

13   Search warrant

(1) If a judge of the District Court is satisfied by information on oath of a member of the Garda Síochána that there is reasonable cause to believe that any person has in his custody or under his control or on his premises any thing and that it has been used, or is intended for use, without lawful excuse—

    (a) to damage property belonging to another,

    (b) to damage any property in a way likely to endanger the life of another or with intent to defraud, or

    (c) to access, or with intent to access, data,

the judge may issue a search warrant mentioned in subsection (2).

(2) A search warrant issued under this section shall be expressed and operate to authorise a named member of the Garda Síochána, accompanied by such other members of the Garda Síochána as may be necessary, at any time or times within one month of the date of issue of the warrant, to enter if need be by force the premises named in the warrant, to search the premises and any persons found therein, to seize and detain anything which he believes to have been used or to be intended for use as aforesaid and, if the property concerned is data or the search warrant has been issued on a ground referred to in subsection (1)(c), to operate, or cause to be operated by a person accompanying him for that purpose, any equipment in the premises for processing data, inspect any data found there and extract information therefrom, whether by the operation of such equipment or otherwise.

(3) The Police (Property) Act, 1897, shall apply to property which has come into the possession of the Garda Síochána under this section as it applies to property which has come into the possession of the Garda Síochána in the circumstances mentioned in that Act.

(4) A person who—

    (a) obstructs or impedes a member of the Garda Síochána acting under the authority of a search warrant issued under this section, or

    (b) is found on or at the premises specified in the warrant by a member of the Garda Síochána acting as aforesaid and who fails or refuses to give the member his name and address when required by the member to do so or gives him a name or address that is false or misleading,

shall be guilty of an offence and shall be liable on summary conviction—

    (i) in the case of an offence under paragraph (a), to a fine not exceeding £1,000 or imprisonment not exceeding 12 months or both, and

    (ii) in the case of an offence under paragraph (b), to a fine not exceeding £500.

14   Minor and consequential changes in existing law

(1) The common law offence of arson is hereby abolished.

(2) The Malicious Damage Act, 1861, is hereby amended—

    (a) by the substitution in section 37, for "Electric or Magnetic Telegraph", of "telegraph (within the meaning of the Telegraph Acts, 1863 to 1916)", and

    (b) by the substitution—

        (i) in section 40, for the words from "shall be liable" to the end of the section, and

(ii) in section 41, for the words from "shall, on conviction thereof" to the end of the section,

of "shall be liable—

(a) on summary conviction, to a fine not exceeding £1,000 or imprisonment for a term not exceeding 12 months or both, and

(b) on conviction on indictment, to a fine not exceeding £10,000 or imprisonment for a term not exceeding 10 years or both.".

(3) The abolition by subsection (1) of the common law offence of arson shall not affect the operation of section 2 of, and paragraph 3 of the Schedule to, the Criminal Law (Jurisdiction) Act, 1976, and the repeal by section 15 of sections 1 to 7 of the Malicious Damage Act, 1861, shall not affect the operation of those sections for the purposes of the said section 2 and paragraph 6 of the said Schedule; and accordingly the said section 2 and the said Schedule shall have effect as if subsection (1) and section 15 had not been enacted.

(4) On the commencement of this subsection—

(a) subsection (3) shall cease to have effect,

(b) section 21(2) of, and paragraph 3 of the Schedule to, the Criminal Law (Jurisdiction) Act, 1976, shall be repealed, and

(c) the following paragraphs shall be substituted for paragraph 6 of the said Schedule:—[1]

Amendments

1 See the amended Act.

15 Repeal

The Malicious Damage Act, 1861 (except sections 35 to 38, 40, 41, 47, 48, 58 and 72), is hereby repealed.

16 Short title and commencement

(1) This Act may be cited as the Criminal Damage Act, 1991.

(2) This Act (except section 14(4)) shall come into operation one month after the date of its passing.

(3) Section 14(4) shall come into operation on such day as may be fixed therefor by order made by the Minister for Justice.

Criminal Evidence Act 1992

Number 12 of 1992

ARRANGEMENT OF SECTIONS

PART I
PRELIMINARY

Section

1. Short title and commencement.
2. Interpretation (general).
3. Repeals.

PART II
ADMISSIBILITY OF DOCUMENTARY EVIDENCE

4. Definition (Part II).
5. Admissibility of documentary evidence.
6. Evidence of admissibility.
7. Notice of documentary evidence.
8. Admission and weight of documentary evidence.
9. Evidence as to credibility of supplier of information.
10. Amendment of Criminal Procedure Act, 1967.
11. Evidence of resolution of Dáil or Seanad.

PART III
EVIDENCE IN CERTAIN PROCEEDINGS

12. Offences to which Part III applies.
13. Evidence through television link.
14. Evidence through intermediary.
15. Procedure in relation to certain offences
16. Videorecording as evidence at trial.
17. Transfer of proceedings.
18. Identification evidence.
19. Application of Part III to persons with mental handicap.

PART IV
COMPETENCE AND COMPELLABILITY OF SPOUSES AND FORMER SPOUSES TO GIVE EVIDENCE

20. Definitions (Part IV).
21. Competence of spouses and former spouses to give evidence.
22. Compellability to give evidence at instance of prosecution.
23. Compellability to give evidence at instance of accused.

24.   Compellability to give evidence at instance of co-accused.

25.   Saving.

26.   Right to marital privacy.

PART V
MISCELLANEOUS

27.   Oath or affirmation not necessary for child etc., witness.

28.   Abolition of requirement of corroboration for unsworn evidence of child, etc.

29.   Evidence through television link by persons outside State.

30.   Copies of documents in evidence.

SCHEDULE
ENACTMENTS REPEALED

AN ACT TO AMEND THE LAW OF EVIDENCE IN RELATION TO CRIMINAL PROCEEDINGS AND TO PROVIDE FOR CONNECTED MATTERS. [7th July, 1992]

BE IT ENACTED BY THE OIREACHTAS AS FOLLOWS:

PART I
PRELIMINARY

1   Short title and commencement

(1) This Act may be cited as the Criminal Evidence Act, 1992.

(2) This Act (except Part III and section 29) shall come into operation three months after the date of its passing.

(3) Part III and section 29 shall come into operation on such day or days as may be fixed therefor by order or orders of the Minister for Justice and different days may be so fixed for different purposes and different provisions; and, in particular, any of the provisions of sections 13 to 16 and section 29 may be brought into operation on different days for different courts and for different circuits and district court districts.

(4) (a)   The provisions of this Act (other than Part III (except sections 15, 16(1)(b) and 18) and section 29) shall not apply to criminal proceedings instituted before the commencement of the provisions concerned.

    (b)   For the purposes of paragraph (a) criminal proceedings are instituted—

        (i)   when a summons or warrant of arrest is issued in respect of an offence,

        (ii)   when a person is arrested without a warrant, or

        (iii) when a person is remanded for trial pursuant to [Chapter IV of Part V.][1]

Amendments

1   Words substituted by Defence (Amendment) Act 2007, Sch 4.

---

2 Interpretation (general)

(1) In this Act—

"the Act of 1935" means the Criminal Law Amendment Act, 1935;

"court" includes court-martial;

"criminal proceedings" includes proceedings before a court-martial and proceedings on appeal;

"document" includes—

(i) a map, plan, graph, drawing or photograph, or

(ii) a reproduction in permanent legible form, by a computer or other means (including enlarging), of information in non-legible form;

"information" includes any representation of fact, whether in words or otherwise;

"information in non-legible form" includes information on microfilm, microfiche, magnetic tape or disk;

["sexual offence" means rape, an offence under section 3 of the Criminal Law (Sexual Offences) Act, 1993, sexual assault (within the meaning of section 2 of the Criminal Law (Rape) (Amendment) Act, 1990), aggravated sexual assault (within the meaning of section 3 of that Act), rape under section 4 of the Criminal Law (Rape) (Amendment) Act, 1990 or an offence under—

(a) section 3 (as amended by section 8 of the Act of 1935) or 6 (as amended by section 9 of the Act of 1935) of the Criminal Law Amendment Act, 1885,

[(aa) section 6 (inserted by section 2 of the Criminal Law (Sexual Offences) (Amendment) Act 2007) of the Criminal Law (Sexual Offences) Act 1993;][2]

(b) section 4 of the Criminal Law (Sexual Offences) Act, 1993,

(c) section 1 (as amended by section 12 of the Criminal Justice Act, 1993 and section 5 of the Criminal Law (Incest Proceedings) Act, 1995) or 2 (as amended by section 12 of the Act of 1935) of the Punishment of Incest Act, 1908,

(d) section 17 (as amended by section 11 of the Act of 1935) of the Children Act, 1908,

[(e) the Criminal Law (Sexual Offences) Act 2006, or][3]

(f) section 5 of the Criminal Law (Sexual Offences) Act, 1993,

excluding an attempt to commit any such offence;][1]

"videorecording" means any recording, on any medium, from which a moving image may by any means be produced and includes the accompanying soundtrack (if any), and cognate words shall be construed accordingly.

(2) Nothing in Part II or in section 30 shall prejudice the admissibility in evidence in any criminal proceedings of information contained in a document that is otherwise so admissible.

(3) Where in any criminal proceedings the age of a person at any time is material for the purposes of any provision of this Act, his age at that time shall for the purposes of that provision be deemed, unless the contrary is proved, to be or to have been that which appears to the court to be or to have been his age at that time.

(4) In this Act—

(a) a reference to a Part or section is to a Part or section of this Act, unless it is indicated that reference to some other enactment is intended,

(b) a reference to a subsection or paragraph is to the subsection or paragraph of the provision in which the reference occurs, unless it is indicated that reference to some other provision is intended.

(5) A reference in this Act to any enactment shall be construed as a reference to that enactment as amended, adapted or extended by or under any subsequent enactment (including this Act).

Amendments

1   Definition of 'sexual offences' substituted by Criminal Justice (Miscellaneous Provisions) Act 1997, s 16 and amended by Criminal Law (Sexual Offences) (Amendment) Act 2007, s 2.

2   Paragraph inserted by Criminal Law (Sexual Offences) (Amendment) Act 2007, s 4.

3   Paragraph substituted by Criminal Law (Human Trafficking) Act 2008, s 12(a)(ii).

---

3   Repeals

The enactments specified in the Schedule to this Act are hereby repealed to the extent specified in column (3) thereof.

PART II
ADMISSIBILITY OF DOCUMENTARY EVIDENCE

4   Definition (Part II)

In this Part "business" includes any trade, profession or other occupation carried on, for reward or otherwise, either within or outside the State and includes also the performance of functions by or on behalf of—

(a) any person or body remunerated or financed wholly or partly out of moneys provided by the Oireachtas,

(b) any institution of the European Communities,

(c) any national or local authority in a jurisdiction outside the State, or

(d) any international organisation.

5   Admissibility of documentary evidence

(1) Subject to this Part, information contained in a document shall be admissible in any criminal proceedings as evidence of any fact therein of which direct oral evidence would be admissible if the information—

(a) was compiled in the ordinary course of a business,

(b) was supplied by a person (whether or not he so compiled it and is identifiable) who had, or may reasonably be supposed to have had, personal knowledge of the matters dealt with, and

(c) in the case of information in non-legible form that has been reproduced in permanent legible form, was reproduced in the course of the normal operation of the reproduction system concerned.

(2) Subsection (1) shall apply whether the information was supplied directly or indirectly but, if it was supplied indirectly, only if each person (whether or not he is identifiable) through whom it was supplied received it in the ordinary course of a business.

(3) Subsection (1) shall not apply to—

    (a)   information that is privileged from disclosure in criminal proceedings,

    (b)   information supplied by a person who would not be compellable to give evidence at the instance of the party wishing to give the information in evidence by virtue of this section, or

    (c)   subject to subsection (4), information compiled for the purposes or in contemplation of any—

        (i)   criminal investigation,

        (ii)   investigation or inquiry carried out pursuant to or under any enactment,

        (iii)   civil or criminal proceedings, or

        (iv)   proceedings of a disciplinary nature.

(4) Subsection (3)(c) shall not apply where—

    (a)   (i)   the information contained in the document was compiled in the presence of a judge of the District Court and supplied on oath by a person in respect of whom an offence was alleged to have been committed and who is ordinarily resident outside the State,

        (ii)   either [section 4F][1] (which deals with the taking of a deposition in the presence of such a judge and the accused) of the Criminal Procedure Act, 1967, could not be invoked or it was not practicable to do so, and

        (iii)   the person in respect of whom the offence was alleged to have been committed either has died or is outside the State and it is not reasonably practicable to secure his attendance at the criminal proceedings concerned,

        or

    (b)   the document containing the information is—

        (i)   a map, plan, drawing or photograph (including any explanatory material in or accompanying the document concerned),

        (ii)   a record of a direction given by a member of the Garda Síochána pursuant to any enactment,

        [(iia)   a record of the receipt, handling, transmission or storage of anything by the Forensic Science Laboratory of the Department of Justice, Equality and Law Reform in connection with the performance of its functions to examine and analyse things or samples of things for the purposes of criminal investigations or proceedings or both,][2]

        (iii)   a record of the receipt, handling, transmission, examination or analysis of any thing by any person acting on behalf of any party to the proceedings, or

        (iv)   a record by a registered medical practitioner of an examination of a living or dead person.

(5) Without prejudice to subsection (1)—

    (a)   where a document purports to be a birth certificate issued in pursuance of the Births and Deaths Registration Acts, 1863 to 1987, and

(b) a person is named therein as father or mother of the person to whose birth the certificate relates,

the document shall be admissible in any criminal proceedings as evidence of the relationship indicated therein.

(6) Where information is admissible in evidence by virtue of this section but is expressed in terms that are not intelligible to the average person without explanation, an explanation of the information shall also be admissible in evidence if either—

(a) it is given orally by a person who is competent to do so, or

(b) it is contained in a document and the document purports to be signed by such a person.

Amendments

1 Words substituted by Criminal Justice Act 1999, s 18(1).

2 Subsection (4)(b)(iia) inserted by Criminal Justice Act 2006, s 188.

---

6 Evidence of admissibility

(1) In relation to information contained in a document which a party to criminal proceedings wishes to give in evidence by virtue of section 5, a certificate—

(a) stating that the information was compiled in the ordinary course of a specified business,

(b) stating that the information is not of a kind mentioned in paragraph (a) or (b) of section 5(3),

(c) either stating that the information was not compiled for the purposes or in contemplation of any investigation, inquiry or proceedings referred to in section 5(3)(c) or, as the case may be, specifying which of the provisions of section 5(4) applies in relation to the document containing the information,

(d) stating that the information was supplied, either directly or, as the case may be, indirectly through an intermediary or intermediaries (who, or each of whom, received it in the ordinary course of a specified business), by a person who had, or may reasonably be supposed to have had, personal knowledge of the matters dealt with in the information and, where the intermediary, intermediaries or person can be identified, specifying them,

(e) in case the information is information in non-legible form that has been reproduced in permanent legible form, stating that the reproduction was effected in the course of the normal operation of a specified system,

(f) where appropriate, stating that the person who supplied the information cannot reasonably be expected to have any, or any adequate, recollection of the matters dealt with in the information, having regard to the time that has elapsed since he supplied it or to any other specified circumstances,

(g) unless the date on which the information was compiled is already shown on the document, specifying the date (or, if that date is not known, the approximate date) on which it was compiled,

(h) stating any other matter that is relevant to the admissibility in evidence of the information and is required by rules of court to be certified for the purposes of this subsection,

and purporting to be signed by a person who occupies a position in relation to the management of the business in the course of which the information was compiled or who is otherwise in a position to give the certificate shall be evidence of any matter stated or specified therein.

(2) For the purposes of subsection (1) it shall be sufficient for a matter to be stated or specified to the best of the knowledge and belief of the person stating or specifying it.

(3) Notwithstanding that a certificate may have been given pursuant to subsection (1), the court—

(a) shall, where a notice has been served pursuant to section 7(2) objecting to the admissibility in evidence of the whole or any specified part of the information concerned, and

(b) may, in any other case,

require oral evidence to be given of any matter stated or specified in the certificate.

(4) If any person in a certificate given in evidence in any proceedings by virtue of subsection (1) makes a statement material in those proceedings which he knows to be false or does not believe to be true, he shall be guilty of an offence and shall be liable—

(a) on summary conviction, to a fine not exceeding £500 or imprisonment for a term not exceeding 6 months or both, or

(b) on conviction on indictment, to a fine or imprisonment for a term not exceeding 2 years or both.

7   Notice of documentary evidence

(1) Information in a document shall not, without the leave of the court, be admissible in evidence by virtue of section 5 at a trial unless—

(a) a copy of the document and, where appropriate, of a certificate pursuant to section 6(1) has been served on the accused [pursuant to section 4B(1) or 4C(1) of the Criminal Procedure Act, 1967][1], or

(b) not later than 21 days before the commencement of the trial, a notice of intention so to give the information in evidence, together with a copy of the document and, where appropriate, of the certificate, is served by or on behalf of the party proposing to give it in evidence on each of the other parties to the proceedings.

(2) A party to the proceedings on whom a notice has been served pursuant to subsection (1) shall not, without the leave of the court, object to the admissibility in evidence of the whole or any specified part of the information concerned unless, not later than 7 days before the commencement of the trial, a notice objecting to its admissibility is served by or on behalf of that party on each of the other parties to the proceedings.

(3) A document required by this section to be served on any person may, subject to subsection (4), be served—

(a) by delivering it to him or to his solicitor,

(b) by addressing it to him and leaving it at his usual or last known residence or place of business or by addressing it to his solicitor and leaving it at the solicitor's office,

(c) by sending it by registered post to him at his usual or last known residence or place of business or to his solicitor at the solicitor's office, or

(d) in the case of a body corporate, by delivering it to the secretary or clerk of the body at its registered or principal office or sending it by registered post to the secretary or clerk of that body at that office.

(4) A document required by this section to be served on an accused shall be served personally on him if he is not represented by a solicitor.

Amendments

1 Words substituted by Criminal Justice Act 1999, s 18(2).

8   Admission and weight of documentary evidence

(1) In any criminal proceedings information or any part thereof that is admissible in evidence by virtue of section 5 shall not be admitted if the court is of opinion that in the interests of justice the information or that part ought not to be admitted.

(2) In considering whether in the interests of justice all or any part of such information ought not to be admitted in evidence the court shall have regard to all the circumstances, including—

(a) whether or not, having regard to the contents and source of the information and the circumstances in which it was compiled, it is a reasonable inference that the information is reliable,

(b) whether or not, having regard to the nature and source of the document containing the information and to any other circumstances that appear to the court to be relevant, it is a reasonable inference that the document is authentic, and

(c) any risk, having regard in particular to whether it is likely to be possible to controvert the information where the person who supplied it does not attend to give oral evidence in the proceedings, that its admission or exclusion will result in unfairness to the accused or, if there is more than one, to any of them.

(3) In estimating the weight, if any, to be attached to information given in evidence by virtue of this Part, regard shall be had to all the circumstances from which any inference can reasonably be drawn as to its accuracy or otherwise.

9   Evidence as to credibility of supplier of information

Where information is given in evidence by virtue of this Part—

(a) any evidence which, if the person who originally supplied the information had been called as a witness, would have been admissible as relevant to his credibility as a witness shall be admissible for that purpose,

(b) evidence may, with the leave of the court, be given of any matter which, if that person had been called as a witness, could have been put to him in cross-examination as relevant to his credibility as a witness but of which evidence could not have been adduced by the cross-examining party, and

(c) evidence tending to prove that that person, whether before or after supplying the information, made (whether orally or not) a statement which is inconsistent with it shall, if not already admissible by virtue of section 5, be admissible for the purpose of showing that he has contradicted himself.

10   Amendment of Criminal Procedure Act, 1967

The Criminal Procedure Act, 1967, is hereby amended—

(a) by the substitution, for paragraphs (d) and (e) of section 6(1) of that Act (which provides for the service of documents on an accused), of the following paragraphs:[1]

(b) by the substitution, for section 11 of that Act (which provides for service of additional documents on an accused after he has been sent forward for trial), of the following section:[1]

Amendments

1 See the amended Act.

11   Evidence of resolution of Dáil or Seanad

In any criminal proceedings evidence of the passing of a resolution by either House of the Oireachtas, whether before or after the commencement of this section, may be given by the production of a copy of the Journal of the proceedings of that House relating to the resolution and purporting to have been published by the Stationery Office.

PART III

EVIDENCE IN CERTAIN PROCEEDINGS

12   Offences to which Part III applies

[This Part applies to—

(a) a sexual offence,

(b) an offence involving violence or the threat of violence to a person,

(c) an offence under section 3, 4, 5 or 6 of the Child Trafficking and Pornography Act 1998,

(d) an offence under section 2, 4 or 7 of the Criminal Law (Human Trafficking) Act 2008, or

(e) an offence consisting of attempting or conspiring to commit, or of aiding or abetting, counselling, procuring or inciting the commission of, an offence mentioned in paragraph (a), (b), (c) or (d).][1]

Amendments

1 Section 12 substituted by Criminal Law (Human Trafficking) Act 2008, s 12(b).

13   Evidence through television link

(1) In any proceedings [(including proceedings under section 4E or 4F of the Criminal Procedure Act, 1967)]¹ for an offence to which this Part applies a person other than the accused may give evidence, whether from within or outside the State, through a live television link—

  (a) if the person is under [18 years]² of age, unless the court sees good reason to the contrary,

  (b) in any other case, with the leave of the court.

(2) Evidence given under subsection (1) shall be videorecorded.

(3) While evidence is being given through a live television link pursuant to subsection (1) (except through an intermediary pursuant to section 14(1)), neither the judge, nor the barrister or solicitor concerned in the examination of the witness, shall wear a wig or gown.

Amendments

1   Words inserted by Criminal Justice Act 1999, s 18(3).

2   Words substituted by Children Act 2001, s 257(3).

14   Evidence through intermediary

(1) Where—

  (a) a person is accused of an offence to which this Part applies, and

  (b) a person under [18 years]¹ of age is giving, or is to give, evidence through a live television link,

the court may, on the application of the prosecution or the accused, if satisfied that, having regard to the age or mental condition of the witness, the interests of justice require that any questions to be put to the witness be put through an intermediary, direct that any such questions be so put.

(2) Questions put to a witness through an intermediary under this section shall be either in the words used by the questioner or so as to convey to the witness in a way which is appropriate to his age and mental condition the meaning of the questions being asked.

(3) An intermediary referred to in subsection (1) shall be appointed by the court and shall be a person who, in its opinion, is competent to act as such.

Amendments

1   Words substituted by Children Act 2001, s 257(3).

[15   Procedure in relation to certain offences

(1) Where—

(a)   under Part IA of the Criminal Procedure Act, 1967, the prosecutor consents to the sending forward for trial of an accused person who is charged with an offence to which this Part applies,

(b)   the person in respect of whom the offence is alleged to have been committed is under [18 years]² of age on the date consent is given to the accused being sent forward for trial, and

(c)   it is proposed that a videorecording of a statement made by the person referred to in paragraph (b) of this subsection during an interview as mentioned in section 16(1)(b) shall be given in evidence pursuant to that section,

the prosecutor shall, in addition to causing the documents mentioned in section 4B(1) of that Act to be served on the accused—

(i)   notify the accused that it is proposed so to give evidence, and

(ii)   give the accused an opportunity of seeing the videorecording of the interview.

(2) If the person in respect of whom the offence is alleged to have been committed is available for cross-examination at the hearing of an application under section 4E of the Criminal Procedure Act, 1967, the judge hearing the application may consider any statement made in relation to that offence by that person on a videorecording mentioned in section 16(1)(b) of this Act.

(3) If the accused consents, an edited version of the videorecording of an interview mentioned in section 16(1)(b), may, with leave of the judge hearing an application referred to in subsection (2) of this section, be shown at the hearing of the application, and, in that event, subsection (2) and section 16(1)(b) shall apply in relation to that version as it applies in relation to the original videorecording.]¹

Amendments

1   Section 15 substituted by Criminal Justice Act 1999, s 19.

2   Words substituted by Children Act 2001, s 257(3).

---

16   Videorecording as evidence at trial

(1) Subject to subsection (2)—

[(a)   a videorecording of any evidence given, in relation to an offence to which this Part applies, by a person under [18 years]¹ of age through a live television link in proceedings under Part IA of the Criminal Procedure Act, 1967, and]¹

(b)   a videorecording of any statement made by a person under 14 years of age (being a person in respect of whom such an offence is alleged to have been committed) during an interview with a member of the Garda Síochána or any other person who is competent for the purpose,

shall be admissible at the trial of the offence as evidence of any fact stated therein of which direct oral evidence by him would be admissible:

[Provided that, in the case of a videorecording mentioned in paragraph (b), the person whose statement was videorecorded is available at the trial for crossexamination.]²

(2) (a) Any such videorecording or any part thereof shall not be admitted in evidence as aforesaid if the court is of opinion that in the interests of justice the videorecording concerned or that part ought not to be so admitted.

    (b) In considering whether in the interests of justice such videorecording or any part thereof ought not to be admitted in evidence, the court shall have regard to all the circumstances, including any risk that its admission will result in unfairness to the accused or, if there is more than one, to any of them.

(3) In estimating the weight, if any, to be attached to any statement contained in such a videorecording regard shall be had to all the circumstances from which any inference can reasonably be drawn as to its accuracy or otherwise.

(4) In this section "statement" includes any representation of fact, whether in words or otherwise.

Amendments

1   Subsection (1)(a) substituted by Criminal Justice Act 1999, s 20(a) and further amended by words substituted by Children Act 2001, s 257(3).

2   Words substituted by Criminal Justice Act 1999, s 20(b).

---

17   Transfer of proceedings

In any proceedings for an offence to which this Part applies in any circuit or district court district in relation to which any of the provisions of sections 13 to 16 or section 29 is not in operation the court concerned may, if in its opinion it is desirable that evidence be given in the proceedings through a live television link or by means of a videorecording, by order transfer the proceedings to a circuit or district court district in relation to which those provisions are in operation and, where such an order is made, the jurisdiction of the court to which the proceedings have been transferred may be exercised—

(a) in the case of the Circuit Court, by the judge of the circuit concerned, and

(b) in the case of the District Court, by the judge of that court for the time being assigned to the district court district concerned.

18   Identification evidence

Where—

(a) a person is accused of an offence to which this Part applies, and

(b) evidence is given by a person (in this section referred to as "the witness") through a live television link pursuant to section 13(1),

    then—

    (i) in case evidence is given that the accused was known to the witness before the date on which the offence is alleged to have been committed, the witness shall not be required to identify the accused at the trial of the offence, unless the court in the interests of justice directs otherwise, and

(ii) in any other case, evidence by a person other than the witness that the witness identified the accused at an identification parade as being the offender shall be admissible as evidence that the accused was so indentified.

19   Application of Part III to persons with mental handicap

The references in sections 13(1)(a), 14(1)(b), 15(1)(b) and 16(1)(a) to a person under [18 years][1] of age and the reference in section 16(1)(b) to a person under 14 years of age shall include references to a person with mental handicap who has reached the age concerned.

Amendments

1   Words substituted by Children Act 2001, s 257(3).

PART IV

COMPETENCE AND COMPELLABILITY OF SPOUSES AND FORMER SPOUSES TO GIVE EVIDENCE

20   Definitions (Part IV)

In this Part—

["decree of divorce" means a decree under section 5 of the Family Law (Divorce) Act, 1996 or any decree that was granted under the law of a country or jurisdiction other than the State and is recognised in the State;][1]

"decree of judicial separation" includes a decree of divorce a mensa et thoro or any decree made by a court outside the State and recognised in the State as having the like effect;

["former spouse" includes a person who, in respect of his or her marriage to an accused—

(a)   has been granted a decree of judicial separation, or

(b)   has entered into a separation agreement, or

(c)   has been granted a decree of divorce;][2]

Amendments

1   Definition inserted by Family Law (Divorce) Act 1996, s 49(a).

2   Definition substituted by Family Law (Divorce) Act 1996, s 49(b).

21   Competence of spouses and former spouses to give evidence

In any criminal proceedings the spouse or a former spouse of an accused shall be competent to give evidence at the instance—

(a)   subject to section 25, of the prosecution, and

(b)   of the accused or any person charged with him in the same proceedings.

22   Compellability to give evidence at instance of prosecution

(1) In any criminal proceedings the spouse of an accused shall, subject to section 25, be compellable to give evidence at the instance of the prosecution only in the case of an offence which—

    (a) involves violence, or the threat of violence, to—

       (i)   the spouse,

       (ii) a child of the spouse or of the accused, or

       (iii) any person who was at the material time under the age of [18 years]¹,

    (b) is a sexual offence alleged to have been committed in relation to a person referred to in subparagraph (ii) or (iii) of paragraph (a), or

    (c) consists of attempting or conspiring to commit, or of aiding, abetting, counselling, procuring or inciting the commission of, an offence falling within paragraph (a) or (b).

(2) In any criminal proceedings a former spouse of an accused shall, subject to section 25, be compellable to give evidence at the instance of the prosecution unless—

    (a) the offence charged is alleged to have been committed at a time when the marriage was subsisting and no decree of judicial separation or separation agreement was in force, and

    (b) it is not an offence mentioned in subsection (1).

(3) The reference in subsection (1) to a child of the spouse or the accused shall include a reference to—

    (a) a child who has been adopted by the spouse or the accused under the Adoption Acts, 1952 to 1991, or, in the case of a child whose adoption by the spouse or the accused has been effected outside the State, whose adoption is recognised in the State by virtue of those Acts, and

    (b) a person in relation to whom the spouse or the accused is in loco parentis.

Amendments

1   Words substituted by Children Act 2001, s 257(3).

---

23   Compellability to give evidence at instance of accused

Subject to section 25, in any criminal proceedings the spouse or a former spouse of an accused shall be compellable to give evidence at the instance of the accused.

24   Compellability to give evidence at instance of co-accused

(1) Subject to section 25, in any criminal proceedings—

    (a) the spouse of an accused shall be compellable to give evidence at the instance of any person charged with the accused in the same proceedings only in the case of an offence mentioned in section 22(1),

    (b) a former spouse of an accused shall be compellable to give evidence at the instance of any person charged with the accused in the same proceedings unless—

(i) the offence charged is alleged to have been committed at a time when the marriage was subsisting and no decree of judicial separation or separation agreement was in force, and

(ii) it is not an offence mentioned in section 22(1).

(2) Subsection (1) is without prejudice to the power of a court to order separate trials of persons charged in the same proceedings if it appears to it to be desirable in the interests of justice to do so.

25   Saving

Where persons (being either a husband and wife or persons who were formerly husband and wife) are charged in the same proceedings, neither shall at the trial be competent by virtue of section 21(a) to give evidence at the instance of the prosecution, or be compellable by virtue of section 22, 23 or 24 to give evidence, unless the person concerned is not, or is no longer, liable to be convicted at the trial as a result of pleading guilty or for any other reason.

26   Right to marital privacy

Nothing in this Part shall affect any right of a spouse or former spouse in respect of marital privacy.

PART V
MISCELLANEOUS

27   Oath or affirmation not necessary for child etc., witness

(1) Notwithstanding any enactment, in any criminal proceedings the evidence of a person under 14 years of age may be received otherwise than on oath or affirmation if the court is satisfied that he is capable of giving an intelligible account of events which are relevant to those proceedings.

(2) If any person whose evidence is received as aforesaid makes a statement material in the proceedings concerned which he knows to be false or does not believe to be true, he shall be guilty of an offence and on conviction shall be liable to be dealt with as if he had been guilty of perjury.

(3) Subsection (1) shall apply to a person with mental handicap who has reached the age of 14 years as it applies to a person under that age.

28   Abolition of requirement of corroboration for unsworn evidence of child, etc

(1) The requirement in section 30 of the Children Act, 1908, of corroboration of unsworn evidence of a child given under that section is hereby abolished.

(2) (a) Any requirement that at a trial on indictment the jury be given a warning by the judge about convicting the accused on the uncorroborated evidence of a child is also hereby abolished in relation to cases where such a warning is required by reason only that the evidence is the evidence of a child and it shall be for the judge to decide, in his discretion, having regard to all the evidence given, whether the jury should be given the warning.

(b) If a judge decides, in his discretion, to give such a warning as aforesaid, it shall not be necessary to use any particular form of words to do so.

(3) Unsworn evidence received by virtue of section 27 may corroborate evidence (sworn or unsworn) given by any other person.

29   Evidence through television link by persons outside State

[(1) Without prejudice to section 13(1), in any criminal proceedings or proceedings under the Extradition Acts, 1965 to 2001, a person other than the accused or the person whose extradition is being sought, as the case may be, may, with the leave of the court, give evidence through a live television link.]¹

(2) Evidence given under subsection (1) shall be videorecorded.

(3) Any person who while giving evidence pursuant to subsection (1) makes a statement material in the proceedings which he knows to be false or does not believe to be true shall, whatever his nationality, be guilty of perjury.

(4) Proceedings for an offence under subsection (3) may be taken, and the offence may for all incidental purposes be treated as having been committed, in any place in the State.

Amendments

1   Subsection (1) substituted by Extradition (European Union Conventions) Act 2001, s 24.

30   Copies of documents in evidence

(1) Where information contained in a document is admissible in evidence in criminal proceedings, the information may be given in evidence, whether or not the document is still in existence, by producing a copy of the document, or of the material part of it, authenticated in such manner as the court may approve.

(2) It is immaterial for the purposes of subsection (1) how many removes there are between the copy and the original, or by what means (which may include facsimile transmission) the copy produced or any intermediate copy was made.

(3) In subsection (1) "document" includes a film, sound recording or videorecording.

SCHEDULE
ENACTMENTS REPEALED

Section 3.

Session and Chapter or Number and Year	Short Title	Extent of Repeal
(1)	(2)	(3)
16 & 17 Vict., c. 83	Evidence Amendment Act, 1853	Section 3
35 & 36 Vict., c. 94	Licensing Act, 1872	In paragraph 4 of section 51, the words "and in all cases of summary proceedings under this Act, the defendant and his wife shall be competent to give evidence"

Session and Chapter or Number and Year	Short Title	Extent of Repeal
(1)	**(2)**	**(3)**
38 & 39 Vict., c. 63	Sale of Food and Drugs Act, 1875	In section 21, the words "and the defendant may, if he think fit, tender himself and his wife to be examined on his behalf, and he or she shall, if he so desires, be examined accordingly"
38 & 39 Vict., c. 86	Conspiracy, and Protection of Property Act, 1875	Section 11
40 & 41 Vict., c. 14	Evidence Act, 1877	The whole Act
46 & 47 Vict., c. 3	Explosive Substances Act, 1883	Section 4(2)
46 & 47 Vict., c. 51	Corrupt and Illegal Practices Prevention Act, 1883	Section 53(2)
48 & 49 Vict., c. 69	Criminal Law Amendment Act, 1885	Section 20
50 & 51 Vict., c. 28	Merchandise Marks Act, 1887	Paragraph (1) of section 10
55 & 56 Vict., c. 4	Betting and Loans (Infants) Act, 1892	Section 6
60 & 61 Vict., c. 60	Chaff-Cutting Machines (Accidents) Act, 1897	Section 5
8 Edw. 7, c. 24	Summary Jurisdiction (Ireland) Act, 1908	Section 12
8 Edw. 7, c. 67	Children Act, 1908	Sections 30 and 133(28)
2 & 3 Geo. 5, c. 20	Criminal Law Amendment Act, 1912	Section 7(6)
4 & 5 Geo. 5, c. 58	Criminal Justice Administration Act, 1914	Section 28(2)
No. 37 of 1924	Criminal Justice (Evidence) Act, 1924	In section 1, the words ", and the wife or husband, as the case may be, of the person so charged,", where they first occur, and paragraphs (c) and (d) of the proviso Section 4(1) Schedule

Session and Chapter or Number and Year	Short Title	Extent of Repeal
(1)	(2)	(3)
No. 5 of 1957	Married Women's Status Act, 1957	Section 9(4)
No. 7 of 1988	Social Welfare Act, 1988	Section 20(7)

Criminal Justice Act 1993

Number 6 of 1993

ARRANGEMENT OF SECTIONS

Section

1. Interpretation.
2. Review of certain sentences.
3. Appeal on point of law to Supreme Court.
4. Minor and consequential provisions.
5. Effect of certain offences on persons in respect of whom committed.
5A
5B
6. Compensation order.
7. Payment of compensation to District Court clerks for transmission, and attachment of earnings orders.
8. Suspension of compensation order pending appeal.
9. Effect of compensation order on civil proceedings.
10. Service of documents.
11. Amendment of Criminal Procedure Act, 1967.
12. Amendment of Punishment of Incest Act, 1908.
13. Repeals.
14. Short title and commencement.

AN ACT TO ENABLE THE COURT OF CRIMINAL APPEAL TO REVIEW UNDULY LENIENT SENTENCES, TO MAKE OTHER PROVISION IN RELATION TO SENTENCING, TO PROVIDE FOR THE PAYMENT BY OFFENDERS OF COMPENSATION FOR INJURY OR LOSS RESULTING FROM THEIR OFFENCES, TO AMEND THE CRIMINAL PROCEDURE ACT, 1967, AND THE PUNISHMENT OF INCEST ACT, 1908, AND TO PROVIDE FOR CONNECTED MATTERS. [3rd April, 1993]

BE IT ENACTED BY THE OIREACHTAS AS FOLLOWS:

1   Interpretation

(1) In this Act, unless the context otherwise requires—

"compensation order" and "injured party" have the meanings assigned to them by section 6;

"imprisonment" includes detention in Saint Patrick's Institution;

"sentence" includes a sentence of imprisonment and any other order made by a court in dealing with a convicted person other than—

    (a) an order under section 17 of the Lunacy (Ireland) Act, 1821, or section 2(2) of the Trial of Lunatics Act, 1883, or

(b) an order postponing sentence for the purpose of obtaining a medical or psychiatric report or a report by a probation officer;

"sentencing court" means the court referred to in section 2(1).

(2) References in sections 2(1) and 4(1) to conviction of a person on indictment include references to conviction of a person after signing a plea of guilty and being sent forward for sentence under section 13(2)(b) of the Criminal Procedure Act, 1967.

(3) This Act shall not apply to sentences imposed on persons convicted before its commencement.

(4) In this Act—

(a) a reference to a section is a reference to a section of this Act, unless it is indicated that reference to some other enactment is intended, and

(b) a reference to a subsection or paragraph is a reference to the subsection or paragraph of the provision in which the reference occurs, unless it is indicated that reference to some other provision is intended.

2   Review of certain sentences

(1) If it appears to the Director of Public Prosecutions that a sentence imposed by a court (in this Act referred to as the "sentencing court") on conviction of a person on indictment was unduly lenient, he may apply to the Court of Criminal Appeal to review the sentence.

(2) An application under this section shall be made, on notice given to the convicted person, within 28 days[, or such longer period not exceeding 56 days as the Court may, on application to it in that behalf, determine,]¹ from the day on which the sentence was imposed.

(3) On such an application, the Court may either—

(a) quash the sentence and in place of it impose on the convicted person such sentence as it considers appropriate, being a sentence which could have been imposed on him by the sentencing court concerned, or

(b) refuse the application.

(4) Section 6 of the Prosecution of Offences Act, 1974 (which prohibits certain communications in relation to criminal proceedings), shall apply, with any necessary modifications, to communications made to the persons mentioned in that section for the purpose of influencing the making of a decision in relation to an application under this section as it applies to such communications made for the purpose of making a decision to withdraw or not to initiate criminal proceedings or any particular charge in criminal proceedings.

Amendments

1   Words inserted by Criminal Justice Act 2006, s 23.

---

3   Appeal on point of law to Supreme Court

(1) An appeal shall lie to the Supreme Court by the convicted person or the Director of Public Prosecutions from the determination of the Court of Criminal Appeal of an application under section 2 if that Court, the Attorney General or the Director of Public Prosecutions certifies

that the determination involves a point of law of exceptional public importance and that it is desirable in the public interest that an appeal should be taken to the Supreme Court.

(2) The Supreme Court may, for the purposes of its decision on such an appeal, either—

    (a) remit the case to the Court of Criminal Appeal to deal with, or

    (b) deal with it itself and for that purpose exercise any powers of that Court,

and that Court or the Supreme Court, as may be appropriate, may, if necessary, quash any sentence imposed by the Court of Criminal Appeal and in place of it impose on the convicted person such sentence as it considers appropriate, being a sentence which could have been imposed on him by the sentencing court concerned.

4   Minor and consequential provisions

(1) The registrar of a court which has imposed a sentence on conviction of a person on indictment shall—

    (a) give to the Director of Public Prosecutions, on request, a copy of any reports or other relevant documents that were considered by the court before it imposed the sentence, and

    (b) if the sentence has become the subject of an application under section 2, give a copy of those documents to the Court of Criminal Appeal and the convicted person.

(2) Where an application has been made to the Court of Criminal Appeal under section 2 or an appeal has been made to the Supreme Court under section 3 —

    (a) a legal aid (appeal) certificate or, as the case may be, a legal aid (Supreme Court) certificate shall be deemed, for the purposes of the Criminal Justice (Legal Aid) Act, 1962, to have been granted in respect of the person whose sentence is the subject of the application or appeal, and

    (b) the person shall be entitled to free legal aid in the preparation and conduct of his case before the Court of Criminal Appeal or the Supreme Court and to have a solicitor and counsel assigned to him for that purpose in the manner prescribed by regulations under section 10 of that Act.

5   Effect of certain offences on persons in respect of whom committed

[(1) This section applies to—

    (a) a sexual offence within the meaning of the Criminal Evidence Act 1992,

    (b) an offence involving violence or the threat of violence to a person,

    (c) an offence under the Non-Fatal Offences Against the Person Act 1997, and

    (d) an offence consisting of attempting or conspiring to commit, or aiding, abetting, counselling, procuring or inciting the commission of, an offence mentioned in paragraph (a), (b) or (c).

(2) (a) When imposing sentence on a person for an offence to which this section applies, a court shall take into account, and may, where necessary, receive evidence or submissions concerning, any effect (whether long-term or otherwise) of the offence on the person in respect of whom the offence was committed.

    (b) For the purposes of paragraph (a), a 'person in respect of whom the offence was committed' includes, where, as a result of the offence, that person has died, is ill or is otherwise incapacitated, a family member of that person.

(3) (a)   When imposing sentence on a person for an offence to which this section applies, a court shall, upon application by the person in respect of whom such offence was committed, hear the evidence of the person in respect of whom the offence was committed as to the effect of the offence on such person.

  (b)   For the purpose of paragraph (a), where the person in respect of whom the offence was committed—

    (i)   is a child under the age of 14 years, the child, or his or her parent or guardian, may give evidence as to the effect of the offence concerned on that child,

    (ii)   is—

      (I)   a person with a mental disorder (not resulting from the offence concerned), the person or a family member,

      (II)   a person with a mental disorder (not resulting from the offence concerned), who is a child, the person or his or her parent or guardian,

      may give evidence as to the effect of the offence concerned on that person,

    (iii)   is a person who is ill or is otherwise incapacitated as a result of the offence, a family member of the person may give evidence as to the effect of the offence concerned on that person and on his or her family members,

    (iv)   has died as a result of the offence, a family member of the person may give evidence as to the effect of the offence concerned—

      (I)   on the person between the commission of the offence and his or her death (where relevant), and

      (II)   on the family members of the person who has died.

  (c)   A person who has been convicted of an offence to which this section applies may not give evidence pursuant to paragraph (b) in respect of that offence.

  (d)   Where more than one family member seeks to avail of paragraph (b), the court may direct the family members to nominate one or more family members for the purpose of that paragraph.

  (e)   Where the court directs the family members to nominate one or more family members pursuant to paragraph

  (d)   and the family members are unable to reach agreement, the court may, having regard to the degree of relationship between the family members and the person in respect of whom the offence was committed, nominate one or more family members as it considers appropriate.

(4) Where no evidence is given pursuant to subsection (3), the court shall not draw an inference that the offence had little or no effect (whether long-term or otherwise) on the person in respect of whom the offence was committed or, where appropriate, on his or her family members.

(5) (a)   The court may, in the interests of justice, order that information relating to the evidence given under subsection (3) or a part of it shall not be published or broadcast.

  (b)   If any matter is published or broadcast in contravention of paragraph (a), the following persons, namely—

    (i)   in the case of a publication in a newspaper or periodical, any proprietor, any editor and any publisher of the newspaper or periodical,

    (ii)   in the case of any other publication, the person who publishes it, and

      (iii) in the case of a broadcast, any person who transmits or provides the programme in which the broadcast is made and any person having functions in relation to the programme corresponding to those of the editor of a newspaper,

shall be guilty of an offence.

  (c) A person guilty of an offence under paragraph (b) shall be liable—

      (i) on summary conviction, to a fine not exceeding €5,000 or to imprisonment for a term not exceeding 12 months or to both, or

      (ii) on conviction on indictment, to a fine not exceeding €50,000 or to imprisonment for a term not exceeding 3 years or to both.

  (d) Where an offence under paragraph (b) is committed by a body corporate and is proved to have been so committed with the consent, connivance or approval of or to be attributable to any neglect on the part of a person being a director, manager, secretary or other officer of the body corporate or any other person who was acting or purporting to act in any such capacity, that person as well as the body corporate shall be guilty of an offence and be liable to be proceeded against and punished as if he or she were guilty of the first-mentioned offence.

  (e) Where the affairs of a body corporate are managed by its members, paragraph (d) shall apply in relation to the acts and defaults of a member in connection with his or her functions of management as if he or she were a director or manager of the body corporate.

(6) In this section and in sections 5A and 5B, unless the context otherwise requires—

'broadcast' has the meaning it has in section 2 of the Broadcasting Act 2009;

'child' means a person under the age of 18;

'family member' means—

  (a) a spouse or partner of the person,

  (b) a child, grandchild, parent, grandparent, brother, sister, uncle, aunt, nephew or niece of the person,

  (c) a person who is acting in loco parentis to the person,

  (d) a dependant of the person, or

  (e) any other person whom the court considers to have had a close connection with the person;

'guardian', in relation to a child, has the meaning it has in the Children Act 2001;

'mental disorder' includes a mental illness, mental disability, dementia or any disease of the mind;

'publish' means publish, other than by way of broadcast, to the public or a portion of the public.]¹

Amendments

1   Section 5 substituted by Criminal Procedure Act 2010, s 4.

[5A

(1) (a) A child or a person with a mental disorder in respect of whom an offence to which section 5 applies was committed, may give evidence pursuant to section 5(3), whether from within or outside the State, through a live television link unless the court sees good reason to the contrary.

   (b) Any other person in respect of whom an offence to which section 5 applies was committed may, with the leave of the court, give evidence pursuant to section 5(3), whether from within or outside the State, through a live television link.

(2) Evidence given under subsection (1) shall be video-recorded.

(3) While evidence is being given pursuant to subsection (1) (except through an intermediary pursuant to section 5B(1)), neither the judge, nor the barrister or solicitor concerned in the examination of the witness, shall wear a wig or gown.]¹

Amendments

1   Section 5A inserted by Criminal Procedure Act 2010, s 5.

[5B   (1) Where a child or a person with a mental disorder is giving, or is to give evidence through a live television link, pursuant to section 5A, the court may, on the application of the prosecution or the accused, if satisfied that, having regard to the age or mental condition of the witness, the interests of justice require that any questions to be put to the witness be put through an intermediary, direct that any such questions be so put.

(2) Questions put to a witness through an intermediary under this section shall be either in the words used by the questioner or so as to convey to the witness in a way which is appropriate to his or her age and mental condition, the meaning of the questions being asked.

(3) An intermediary referred to in subsection (1) shall be appointed by the court and shall be a person who, in its opinion, is competent to act as such.]¹

Amendments

1   Section 5B inserted by Criminal Procedure Act 2010, s 6.

6   Compensation order

(1) Subject to the provisions of this section, on conviction of any person of an offence, the court, instead of or in addition to dealing with him in any other way, may, unless it sees reason to the contrary, make (on application or otherwise) an order (in this Act referred to as a "compensation order") requiring him to pay compensation in respect of any personal injury or loss resulting from that offence (or any other offence that is taken into consideration by the court in determining sentence) to any person (in this Act referred to as the "injured party") who has suffered such injury or loss.

(2) The compensation payable under a compensation order (including a compensation order made against a parent or guardian of the convicted person and notwithstanding, in such a case, any other statutory limitation as to amount) shall be of such amount (not exceeding, in the case of such an order made by the District Court, such amount as may stand prescribed for the time being by law as the limit of that Court's jurisdiction in tort) as the court considers appropriate, having regard to any evidence and to any representations that are made by or on behalf of the convicted person, the injured party or the prosecutor, and shall not exceed the amount of the damages that, in the opinion of the court, the injured party would be entitled to recover in a civil action against the convicted person in respect of the injury or loss concerned.

(3) Where the commission of the offence by the convicted person involved the taking of property out of the possession of the injured party and the property has been recovered, any loss occurring to the injured party by reason of the property being damaged while out of his possession shall be treated for the purposes of subsection (1) as having resulted from the offence, irrespective of how the damage was caused or who caused it.

(4) A compensation order shall not be made in respect of an injury or loss that results from the use of a mechanically propelled vehicle (within the meaning of the Road Traffic Act, 1961) in a public place unless it appears to the court that—

    (a) it is in respect of an injury or loss as respects which the use of the vehicle by the convicted person was in breach of section 56 (which provides for the compulsory insurance of mechanically propelled vehicles) of that Act, or

    (b) it is in respect of a loss which is treated by subsection (3) as having resulted from the offence,

and, where a compensation order is made in respect of injury or loss resulting from such use, the amount of the compensation may include an amount representing the whole or part of any loss of or reduction in preferential rates of insurance resulting from such use.

(5) In determining whether to make a compensation order against a person, and in determining the amount of the compensation, the court shall have regard—

    (a) to his means, or

    (b) in a case to which section 99 of the Children Act, 1908 (which empowers a court to require a parent or guardian to pay any fine, damages or costs imposed on or awarded against a child or young person), applies, to the means of the parent or guardian,

so far as they appear or are known to the court and for that purpose the court may require the convicted person or his parent or guardian, as the case may be, to give evidence as to his means and financial commitments.

(6) A compensation order may provide for payment of the compensation by such instalments and at such times as the court shall in all the circumstances consider reasonable.

(7) Where the court considers—

    (a) that it would be appropriate both to impose a fine and to make a compensation order, but

    (b) that the convicted person has insufficient means to pay both an appropriate fine and appropriate compensation, the court may, if it is satisfied that the means are sufficient to justify its doing so, make a compensation order and, if it is satisfied that it is appropriate to do so having regard to the means that would remain after compliance with the order, impose a fine.

(8) At any time after a compensation order has ceased to be suspended by virtue of section 8 and before it has been complied with or fully complied with, the District Court (or, where the amount payable under the order exceeds such amount as may stand prescribed for the time being by law as the limit of that Court's jurisdiction in tort, the court which made the order) may—

(a) on the application of the convicted person concerned and on being satisfied that the injured party concerned has been given an opportunity of making representations to the Court on the issue and having regard to any such representations that are made by him or on his behalf, reduce the amount remaining to be paid, vary any instalment payable, or direct that no payments or further payments be made, under the order if it appears to the Court that, because of a substantial reduction in the means of the convicted person, his means are insufficient to satisfy the order in full, or

(b) on the application of the injured party concerned and on being satisfied that the convicted person concerned has been given an opportunity of making representations to the Court on the issue and having regard to any such representations that are made by him or on his behalf, increase the amount to be paid, the amount of any instalment or the number of instalments payable, under the order if it appears to the Court that—

   (i) because of a substantial increase in the means of the convicted person, his means are sufficient for the relevant purposes aforesaid, and

   (ii) any increased amount to be paid under the order would not exceed—

      (I) the amount of the damages that the injured party concerned would be entitled to recover in a civil action against the convicted person in respect of the injury or loss concerned, or

      (II) such amount as may stand prescribed for the time being by law as the limit of the Court's jurisdiction in tort,

   whichever is the lesser.

(9) The references to damages in the aforesaid section 99 shall be construed as if they included references to compensation under a compensation order and subsections (5) and (6) of that section shall not apply in relation to a compensation order.

(10) This section is without prejudice to any other enactment which provides for the payment of compensation by a person convicted of an offence or otherwise proved to have committed an offence.

(11) The making of a compensation order against a parent or guardian of a convicted person shall not of itself give rise to any other liability on the part of the parent or guardian in respect of the injury or loss.

(12) In this section—

(a) in a case where death has resulted from an offence specified in subsection (1)—

   "loss" means any matter (including mental distress resulting from the death and funeral expenses) for which damages could be awarded in respect of the death by virtue of Part V of the Civil Liability Act, 1961, "injured party" includes a dependant (within the meaning of the said Part V) of the deceased person concerned,

(b) references to conviction of a person include references to dealing with a person under section 1(1) of the Probation of Offenders Act, 1907, and

(c) the third reference in subsection (1), the second reference in subsection (2) and the references in subsections (7)(b) and (8) (other than paragraph (b)(ii)) to a convicted person, however expressed, include, in a case to which the aforesaid section 99 applies, references to his parent or guardian.

(13) In assessing for the purposes of this section the means of a person, the court shall take into account his financial commitments.

7   Payment of compensation to District Court clerks for transmission, and attachment of earnings orders

(1) Subject to subsection (2), payments under a compensation order or an order under section 6(8) shall be made, for transmission to the injured party concerned, to such District Court clerk as may be determined from time to time by the court which made the order.

(2) For the purposes of subsection (1) and of securing compliance with compensation orders and orders under section 6(8)—

(a) subsections (2), (4), (5) and (6) of section 9 (which relates to the transmission of maintenance order payments through District Court clerks),

(b) Part III (which relates to attachment of earnings), and

(c) section 29 (which amends the Enforcement of Court Orders Act, 1940),

of the Family Law (Maintenance of Spouses and Children) Act, 1976, shall apply to those orders with the following modifications and any other necessary modifications, that is to say:

(i) in the said subsections (2) and (4)—

   (I) the references to payments shall be construed as including payments under a compensation order or an order under section 6(8) to a District Court clerk pursuant to subsection (1), and

   (II) the references to the maintenance creditor shall be construed as references to the injured party,

(ii) in the said Part III—

   (I) in section 10—

      (A) subparagraphs (i) and (ii) of subsection (1)(a) shall not apply,

      (B) the reference to the District Court in subsection (1)(a)(iii)(I) shall be construed as a reference to a court, and

      (C) in subsection (2), paragraph (a) shall be deleted and the following paragraph shall be substituted for paragraph (b): "(b) in any other case, to the District Court clerk specified by the attachment of earnings order for transmission to the injured party concerned",

   (II) the references to an antecedent order shall be construed as references to a compensation order and an order under section 6(8),

   (III) the references to the maintenance creditor shall be construed as references to the injured party, and

(IV) the references to the maintenance debtor shall be construed as references to the convicted person or, in a case to which section 99 of the Children Act, 1908, applies, to his parent or guardian,

and

(iii) in the said section 29 the reference to a maintenance order shall be construed as including a reference to a compensation order and an order under section 6(8).

8   Suspension of compensation order pending appeal

(1) The operation of a compensation order shall be suspended—

(a) in any case, until the ordinary time for giving notice of an appeal or of an application for leave to appeal (whether against the conviction to which the order relates or the sentence) has expired, and

(b) in a case where the notice aforesaid is given within that time or such extended time as the court to which the appeal is brought may allow, until the appeal or any further appeal therefrom is finally determined or abandoned or the ordinary time for instituting any further appeal has expired.

(2) Where the operation of a compensation order is suspended under subsection (1)(b), the order shall not take effect if the conviction concerned is reversed on appeal.

(3) A court hearing an appeal against conviction or sentence may annul or vary the compensation order concerned.

(4) A person against whom a compensation order is made may appeal against the order to the court to which an appeal against the conviction concerned may be brought and subsections (1)(b) and (3) shall apply in relation to an appeal under this subsection as they apply, or would apply, to an appeal against the conviction.

(5) Where a compensation order has been made against a person in respect of an offence taken into consideration in determining his sentence, the order shall cease to have effect if he successfully appeals against his conviction of the offence, or, if more than one, all the offences, of which he was convicted in the proceedings in which the order was made.

(6) In this section references to conviction of a person include references to dealing with a person under section 1(1) of the Probation of Offenders Act, 1907.

9   Effect of compensation order on civil proceedings

Where—

(a) a compensation order has been made in favour of a person, and

(b) damages in respect of the injury or loss concerned fall to be assessed in civil proceedings,

then—

(i) if the damages, as so assessed, exceed any amount paid under the compensation order, the damages awarded shall not exceed the amount of that excess, and

(ii) if any amount paid under the compensation order exceeds the damages, as so assessed, the court may order that the amount of the excess be repaid by that person to the person against whom the compensation order was made,

and, upon the award of damages or, as the case may be, the making of the order by the court, the compensation order shall cease to have effect.

10   Service of documents

(1) A document required by section 2 or 4 of this Act to be given to a convicted person may, subject to subsection (3), be so given—

    (a) by delivering it to him or to his solicitor,

    (b) by addressing it to him and leaving it at his usual or last known residence or place of business or by addressing it to his solicitor and leaving it at the solicitor's office,

    (c) by sending it by registered post to him at his usual or last known residence or place of business or to his solicitor at the solicitor's office, or

    (d) in the case of a body corporate, by delivering it, or sending it by registered post, to the secretary or other officer of the body at its registered or principal office.

(2) For the purposes of subsection (1) the solicitor retained to appear on behalf of the convicted person at his trial shall be deemed to continue to be retained on his behalf unless he is discharged by the Court of Criminal Appeal.

(3) A document required by section 2 or 4 of this Act to be given to a convicted person shall be given personally to him if he was not represented by a solicitor at his trial or if his solicitor has been so discharged.

11   Amendment of Criminal Procedure Act, 1967

[…]¹

Amendments

1   Section 11 repealed by Criminal Justice Act 1999, s 22.

---

12   Amendment of Punishment of Incest Act, 1908

Section 1 (incest by males) of the Punishment of Incest Act, 1908, is hereby amended by the substitution for "liable, at the discretion of the court, to be kept in penal servitude for any term not less than three years, and not exceeding seven years, or to be imprisoned for any time not exceeding two years with or without hard labour" of "liable to imprisonment for a term not exceeding 20 years".

13   Repeals

Sections 9, 10 and 11 of the Criminal Damage Act, 1991, are hereby repealed.

14   Short title and commencement

(1) This Act may be cited as the Criminal Justice Act, 1993.

(2) This Act shall come into operation one month after the date of its passing.

Criminal Law (Sexual Offences) Act 1993

Number 20 of 1993

ARRANGEMENT OF SECTIONS

1. Interpretation
2. Abolition of offence of buggery between persons
3. Buggery of persons under 17 years of age
4. Gross indecency with males under 17 years of age
5. Protection of mentally impaired persons
6. Soliciting or importuning for purposes of commission of sexual offence
7. Soliciting or importuning for purposes of prostitution
8. Loitering for purposes of prostitution
9. Organisation of prostitution
10. Living on earnings of prostitution
11. Brothel keeping
12. Amendment of section 19 of Criminal Law Amendment Act, 1935 (search of brothels)
13. Powers of arrest
14. Repeals
15. Short title and collective citation

SCHEDULE

ENACTMENTS REPEALED

AN ACT TO AMEND THE LAW IN RELATION TO SEXUAL OFFENCES AND FOR THAT PURPOSE TO AMEND THE OFFENCES AGAINST THE PERSON ACT, 1861, IN RELATION TO BUGGERY; TO AMEND THE CRIMINAL LAW AMENDMENT ACTS, 1885 TO 1935; TO REPEAL THE VAGRANCY ACT, 1898, AND CERTAIN PROVISIONS OF CERTAIN OTHER ENACTMENTS RELATING TO SEXUAL OFFENCES AND TO PROVIDE FOR CONNECTED MATTERS. [7th July, 1993]

BE IT ENACTED BY THE OIREACHTAS AS FOLLOWS:

1   Interpretation

(1) In this Act—

"motor vehicle" means a mechanically propelled vehicle intended or adapted for use on roads;

"public place" means any place to which the public have access whether as of right or by permission and whether subject to or free of charge;

"solicits or importunes" includes soliciting or importuning from or in a motor vehicle, and cognate words shall be construed accordingly;

591

"street" includes any road, bridge, lane, footway, subway, square, court, alley or passsage, whether a thoroughfare or not, which is for the time being open to the public; and the doorways, entrances and gardens abutting on a street and any ground or car-park adjoining and open to a street, shall be treated as forming part of a street.

(2) In this Act a person solicits or importunes for the purposes of prostitution where the person—

    (a)   offers his or her services as a prostitute to another person,

    (b)   solicits or importunes another person for the purpose of obtaining that other person's services as a prostitute, or

    (c)   solicits or importunes another person on behalf of a person for the purposes of prostitution.

(3) In this Act references to sexual intercourse shall be construed as references to carnal knowledge as defined in section 63 of the Offences against the Person Act, 1861.

(4) In this Act and in any other enactment, whether passed before or after this Act, a reference to a prostitute includes a reference to a male person who is a prostitute and a reference to prostitution shall be construed accordingly.

(5) In this Act a reference to a subsection is a reference to the subsection of the provision in which the reference occurs unless it is indicated that reference to some other provision is intended.

2   Abolition of offence of buggery between persons

Subject to sections 3 and 5 of this Act, any rule of law by virtue of which buggery between persons is an offence is hereby abolished.

3   Buggery of persons under 17 years of age

[...]¹

Amendments

1   Section 3 repealed by Criminal Law (Sexual Offences) Act 2006, s 8 and Sch.

---

4   Gross indecency with males under 17 years of age

[...]¹

Amendments

1   Section 4 repealed by Criminal Law (Sexual Offences) Act 2006, s 8 and Sch.

---

5   Protection of mentally impaired persons

(1) A person who—

    (a)   has or attempts to have sexual intercourse, or

    (b)   commits or attempts to commit an act of buggery,

with a person who is mentally impaired (other than a person to whom he is married or to whom he believes with reasonable cause he is married) shall be guilty of an offence and shall be liable on conviction on indictment to—

    (i)   in the case of having sexual intercourse or committing an act of buggery, imprisonment for a term not exceeding 10 years, and

    (ii) in the case of an attempt to have sexual intercourse or an attempt to commit an act of buggery, imprisonment for a term not exceeding 3 years in the case of a first conviction, and in the case of a second or any subsequent conviction imprisonment for a term not exceeding 5 years.

(2) A male person who commits or attempts to commit an act of gross indecency with another male person who is mentally impaired shall be guilty of an offence and shall be liable on conviction on indictment to imprisonment for a term not exceeding 2 years.

(3) In any proceedings under this section it shall be a defence for the accused to show that at the time of the alleged commission of the offence he did not know and had no reason to suspect that the person in respect of whom he is charged was mentally impaired.

(4) Proceedings against a person charged with an offence under this section shall not be taken except by or with the consent of the Director of Public Prosecutions.

(5) In this section "mentally impaired" means suffering from a disorder of the mind, whether through mental handicap or mental illness, which is of such a nature or degree as to render a person incapable of living an independent life or of guarding against serious exploitation.

6   Soliciting or importuning for purposes of commission of sexual offence

[(1) A person who solicits or importunes a child (whether or not for the purposes of prostitution) for the purposes of the commission of an act that would constitute an offence—

    (a) under section 2 or 3 of the Criminal Law (Sexual Offences) Act 2006, or

    (b) referred to in section 2 of the Act of 1990,

shall be guilty of an offence.

(2) A person who solicits or importunes a person who is mentally impaired (whether or not for the purposes of prostitution) for the purposes of the commission of an act that would constitute an offence—

    (a) under section 5 of this Act, or

    (b) referred to in section 2 of the Act of 1990,

shall be guilty of an offence.

(3) A person guilty of an offence under this section shall be liable—

    (a) on summary conviction to a fine not exceeding €5,000, or imprisonment for a term not exceeding 12 months, or to both, or

    (b) on conviction on indictment to a fine, or imprisonment for a term not exceeding 5 years, or to both.

(4) In this section—

"Act of 1990" means the Criminal Law (Rape) (Amendment) Act 1990;

"child" means a person under the age of 17 years;

"mentally impaired" has the same meaning as it has in section 5 of this Act.][1]

Amendments

1   Section 6 substituted by Criminal Law (Sexual Offences) (Amendment) Act 2007, s 2.

7   Soliciting or importuning for purposes of prostitution

A person who in a street or public place solicits or importunes another person or other persons for the purposes of prostitution shall be guilty of an offence and shall be liable on summary conviction to a fine not exceeding—

(a)   £250, in the case of a first conviction,

(b   £500, in the case of a second conviction, or

(c)   £500 or to imprisonment for a term not exceeding 4 weeks or to both, in the case of a third or any subsequent conviction.

8   Loitering for purposes of prostitution

(1) A member of the Garda Síochána who has reasonable cause to suspect that a person is loitering in a street or public place in order to solicit or importune another person or other persons for the purposes of prostitution may direct that person to leave immediately that street or public place.

(2) A person who without reasonable cause fails to comply with a direction under subsection (1) shall be guilty of an offence and shall be liable on summary conviction to a fine not exceeding—

(a)   £250, in the case of a first conviction,

(b)   £500, in the case of a second conviction, or

(c)   £500 or to imprisonment for a term not exceeding 4 weeks or to both, in the case of a third or any subsequent conviction.

(3) In this section "loitering" includes loitering in a motor vehicle.

9   Organisation of prostitution

A person who for gain—

(a)   controls or directs the activities of a prostitute in respect of prostitution,

(b)   organises prostitution by controlling or directing the activities of more than one prostitute for that purpose, or

(c)   compels or coerces a person to be a prostitute,

shall be guilty of an offence and shall be liable—

(i)   on summary conviction to a fine not exceeding £1,000 or to imprisonment for a term not exceeding 6 months or to both, or

(ii) on conviction on indictment to a fine not exceeding £10,000 or to imprisonment for a term not exceeding 5 years or to both.

10   Living on earnings of prostitution

(1) A person who knowingly lives in whole or in part on the earnings of the prostitution of another person and aids and abets that prostitution shall be guilty of an offence and shall be

liable on summary conviction to a fine not exceeding £1,000 or to imprisonment for a term not exceeding 6 months or to both.

(2) If a judge of the District Court is satisfied on the sworn information of a member of the Garda Síochána not below the rank of sergeant that there are reasonable grounds for suspecting that any premises or any part of a premises is used by a person for the purposes of prostitution, and that any person residing in or frequenting the premises or part of the premises is living in whole or in part on the earnings of the prostitution of another person, he may issue a warrant under his hand authorising any member of the Garda Síochána, accompanied by other members of the Garda Síochána, at any time or times within one month from the date of issue of the warrant, on production if so requested of the warrant, to enter, if need be by force, and search the premises and arrest that person.

(3) A person who obstructs or interferes with a member of the Garda Síochána acting under the authority of a warrant under subsection (2) shall be guilty of an offence and shall be liable on summary conviction to a fine not exceeding £1,000 or to imprisonment for a term not exceeding 6 months or to both.

11 Brothel keeping

A person who—

(a) keeps or manages or acts or assists in the management of a brothel,

(b) being the tenant, lessee, occupier or person in charge of a premises, knowingly permits such premises or any part thereof to be used as a brothel or for the purposes of habitual prostitution, or

(c) being the lessor or landlord of any premises or the agent of such lessor or landlord, lets such premises or any part thereof with the knowledge that such premises or some part thereof are or is to be used as a brothel, or is wilfully a party to the continued use of such premises or any part thereof as a brothel,

shall be guilty of an offence and shall be liable—

(i) on summary conviction to a fine not exceeding £1,000 or to imprisonment for a term not exceeding 6 months or to both, or

(ii) on conviction on indictment to a fine not exceeding £10,000 or to imprisonment for a term not exceeding 5 years or to both.

12 Amendment of section 19 of Criminal Law Amendment Act, 1935 (search of brothels)

Section 19 of the Criminal Law Amendment Act, 1935, is hereby amended by—

(a) the substitution of "sergeant" for "inspector" in each place it occurs, and

(b) the substitution in subsection (4) of "£500" for "five pounds".

13 Powers of arrest

(1) If a member of the Garda Síochána reasonably suspects that a person has committed an offence under section 4, 6, 7, 8(2) or 10(3) of this Act he may—

(a) arrest that person without warrant, or

(b) require him to give his name and address and, if the person fails or refuses to do so or gives a name or address that the member reasonably suspects to be false or misleading, the member may arrest that person without warrant.

(2) A person who fails or refuses to give his name or address when required under subsection (1), or gives a name or address which is false or misleading, shall be guilty of an offence and shall be liable on summary conviction to a fine not exceeding £500.

14   Repeals

The enactments specified in column (2) of the Schedule to this Act are hereby repealed to the extent specified in column (3) of that Schedule.

15   Short title and collective citation

(1) This Act may be cited as the Criminal Law (Sexual Offences) Act, 1993.

(2) The Criminal Law Amendment Acts, 1885 to 1935, and this Act may be cited together as the Criminal Law (Sexual Offences) Acts, 1885 to 1993.

SCHEDULE
ENACTMENTS REPEALED

Section 14.

Session and Chapter or Year and Number	Short Title	Extent of Repeal
(1)	(2)	(3)
5 & 6 Vict., c. 24	Dublin Police Act, 1842	Paragraph 11 of section 14.
10 & 11 Vict., c. 89	Town Police Clauses Act, 1847	In section 28 the words "Every common Prostitute or Nightwalker loitering and importuning Passengers for the Purpose of Prostitution:".
17 & 18 Vict., c. 103	Towns Improvement (Ireland) Act, 1854	In section 72 the words "Every common Prostitute or Nightwalker loitering and importuning Passengers for the Purpose of Prostitution, or being otherwise offensive, shall be liable to a fine not exceeding Forty Shillings:".
24 & 25 Vict., c. 100	Offences against the Person Act, 1861	Sections 61 and 62 (save in so far as they apply to buggery or attempted buggery with animals).
48 & 49 Vict., c. 69	Criminal Law Amendment Act, 1885	Section 11.
61 & 62 Vict., c. 39	Vagrancy Act, 1898	The whole Act.

Session and Chapter or Year and Number	Short Title	Extent of Repeal
(1)	(2)	(3)
2 & 3 Geo. 5, c. 20	Criminal Law Amendment Act, 1912	Sections 3 and 7.
1935, No. 6	Criminal Law Amendment Act, 1935	Sections 4, 13 and 16.

Criminal Law (Suicide) Act 1993

Number 11 of 1993

ARRANGEMENT OF SECTIONS

1. Short title and commencement
2. Suicide
3. Repeal

AN ACT TO ABOLISH THE OFFENCE OF SUICIDE, TO MAKE IT AN OFFENCE TO BE AN ACCOMPLICE TO SUICIDE AND TO REPEAL SECTION 9 OF THE SUMMARY JURISDICTION (IRELAND) AMENDMENT ACT, 1871. [9th June, 1993]

BE IT ENACTED BY THE OIREACHTAS AS FOLLOWS:

1 Short title and commencement

(1) This Act may be cited as the Criminal Law (Suicide) Act, 1993.

(2) This Act shall come into operation one month after the date of its passing.

2 Suicide

(1) Suicide shall cease to be a crime.

(2) A person who aids, abets, counsels or procures the suicide of another, or an attempt by another to commit suicide, shall be guilty of an offence and shall be liable on conviction on indictment to imprisonment for a term not exceeding fourteen years.

(3) If, on the trial of an indictment for murder, murder to which section 3 of the Criminal Justice Act, 1990 applies or manslaughter, it is proved that the person charged aided, abetted, counselled or procured the suicide of the person alleged to have been killed, he may be found guilty of an offence under this section.

(4) No proceedings shall be instituted for an offence under this section except by or with the consent of the Director of Public Prosecutions.

3 Repeal

Section 9 of the Summary Jurisdiction (Ireland) Amendment Act, 1871 (amended by section 85 of the Courts of Justice Act, 1936) is hereby repealed.

Criminal Procedure Act 1993

Number 40 of 1993

ARRANGEMENT OF SECTIONS

1. Interpretation
2. Review by Court of Criminal Appeal of alleged miscarriage of justice or excessive sentence
3. Jurisdiction of Court of Criminal Appeal in relation to appeals
4. Re-trial
5. Summary determination
6. Application to Courts-Martial Appeal Court
7. Petition for grant of pardon
8. Committee to inquire into alleged miscarriages of justice
9. Compensation for miscarriage of justice
10. Uncorroborated confession
11. Appeal from Central Criminal Court
12. Expenses
13. Repeals
14. Short title

SCHEDULE
ENACTMENTS REPEALED

AN ACT TO PROVIDE FOR JUDICIAL REVIEW OF CERTAIN CONVICTIONS AND SENTENCES, FOR PRESENTATION OF PETITIONS FOR THE GRANT OF PARDON ON THE GROUNDS OF MISCARRIAGE OF JUSTICE, FOR PAYMENT OF COMPENSATION BY THE STATE TO OR IN RESPECT OF PERSONS CONVICTED AS A RESULT OF A MISCARRIAGE OF JUSTICE AND FOR CONNECTED MATTERS. [29th December, 1993]

BE IT ENACTED BY THE OIREACHTAS AS FOLLOWS:

1   Interpretation

(1) In this Act—

"the Court" means the Court of Criminal Appeal but, in sections 2 to 5 and 7, as modified by section 6, also includes the Courts-Martial Appeal Court;

"legal aid certificate" means a certificate granted under the appropriate provision of the Criminal Justice (Legal Aid) Act, 1962.

(2) In this Act—

    (a) a reference to a section is to a section of this Act, unless it is indicated that reference to some other enactment is intended,

(b) a reference to a subsection or paragraph is to the subsection or paragraph of the provision in which the reference occurs, unless it is indicated that reference to some other provision is intended.

(3) A reference in this Act to any enactment shall be construed as a reference to that enactment as amended or adapted by or under any subsequent enactment.

2   Review by Court of Criminal Appeal of alleged miscarriage of justice or excessive sentence

(1) A person—

    (a) who has been convicted of an offence either—

        (i) on indictment, or

        (ii) after signing a plea of guilty and being sent forward for sentence under section 13(2)(b) of the Criminal Procedure Act, 1967, and

    who, after appeal to the Court including an application for leave to appeal, and any subsequent re-trial, stands convicted of an offence to which this paragraph applies, and

    (b) who alleges that a new or newly-discovered fact shows that there has been a miscarriage of justice in relation to the conviction or that the sentence imposed is excessive,

may, if no further proceedings are pending in relation to the appeal, apply to the Court for an order quashing the conviction or reviewing the sentence.

(2) An application under subsection (1) shall be treated for all purposes as an appeal to the Court against the conviction or sentence.

(3) In subsection (1)(b) the reference to a new fact is to a fact known to the convicted person at the time of the trial or appeal proceedings the significance of which was appreciated by him, where he alleges that there is a reasonable explanation for his failure to adduce evidence of that fact.

(4) The reference in subsection (1)(b) to a newly-discovered fact is to a fact discovered by or coming to the notice of the convicted person after the relevant appeal proceedings have been finally determined or a fact the significance of which was not appreciated by the convicted person or his advisers during the trial or appeal proceedings.

(5) Where—

    (a) after an application by a convicted person under subsection (1) and any subsequent re-trial the person stands convicted of an offence, and

    (b) the person alleges that a fact discovered by him or coming to his notice after the hearing of the application and any subsequent re-trial or a fact the significance of which was not appreciated by him or his advisers during the hearing of the application and any subsequent re-trial shows that there has been a miscarriage of justice in relation to the conviction, or that the sentence was excessive,

he may apply to the Court for an order quashing the conviction or reviewing the sentence and his application shall be treated as if it were an application under that subsection.

3   Jurisdiction of Court of Criminal Appeal in relation to appeals

(1) On the hearing of an appeal against conviction of an offence the Court may—

(a) affirm the conviction (and may do so, notwithstanding that it is of opinion that a point raised in the appeal might be decided in favour of the appellant, if it considers that no miscarriage of justice has actually occurred), or *Same as 5(1) 1928 Act (B)*

(b) quash the conviction and make no further order, or

(c) quash the conviction and order the applicant to be re-tried for the offence, or

(d) quash the conviction and, if it appears to the Court that the appellant could have been found guilty of some other offence and that the jury must have been satisfied of facts which proved him guilty of the other offence—

  (i) substitute for the verdict a verdict of guilty of the other offence, and

  (ii) impose such sentence in substitution for the sentence imposed at the trial as may be authorised by law for the other offence, not being a sentence of greater severity.

(2) On the hearing of an appeal against sentence for an offence the Court may quash the sentence and in place of it impose such sentence or make such order as it considers appropriate, being a sentence or order which could have been imposed on the convicted person for the offence at the court of trial.

(3) The Court, on the hearing of an appeal or, as the case may be, of an application for leave to appeal, against a conviction or sentence may—

(a) where the appeal is based on new or additional evidence, direct the Commissioner of the Garda Síochána to have such inquiries carried out as the Court considers necessary or expedient for the purpose of determining whether further evidence ought to be adduced;

(b) order the production of any document, exhibit or other thing connected with the proceedings;

(c) order any person who would have been a compellable witness in the proceedings from which the appeal lies to attend for examination and be examined before the Court, whether or not he was called in those proceedings;

(d) receive the evidence, if tendered, of any witness;

(e) generally make such order as may be necessary for the purpose of doing justice in the case before the Court. *inc. power to award Costs. Conmey*

(4) For the purposes of this section, the Court may order the examination of any witness whose attendance might be required under this section to be conducted, in a manner provided by rules of court, before any judge or officer of the Court or other person appointed by the Court for the purpose, and allow the admission of any depositions so taken as evidence before the Court.

(5) The reference in subsection (1)(d) to a jury shall, where the trial was before a court sitting without a jury, be construed as a reference to that court.

(6) Section 32 of the Courts of Justice Act, 1924, is hereby amended by the addition after "pending the determination of his appeal" of "or application for leave to appeal".

(7) A legal aid certificate which was granted in relation to the trial of an accused person who has been ordered by the Court under this section to be re-tried shall have effect as if it had been granted also in relation to his re-trial.

(8) The references in section 44(2) of the Offences Against the State Act, 1939, to section 34 of the Criminal Justice Act, 1924, and section 5 of the Criminal Justice Act, 1928, shall be construed as references to this section.

4   Re-trial

*Incorporates / Replicates
S. S(1)(iz) 1928 C.J. Act*

(1) Where a person is ordered under this Act to be re-tried for an offence he may, notwithstanding any rule of law, be again indicted and tried and, if found guilty, sentenced for that offence.

(2) In a case to which subsection (1) relates the Court may—

(a) . where a legal aid certificate does not apply in respect thereof, order that the costs of the appeal and of the new trial, in whole or in part, be paid by the State, unless the Court is of opinion that the necessity for the appeal and the new trial has been contributed to by the defence,

(b) order that the accused be detained in custody or be admitted to bail pending the re-trial on such terms as the Court thinks proper,

(c) order that any property or money forfeited, restored or paid by virtue of the conviction or of any order made on the conviction be retained pending the re-trial.

5   Summary determination

(1) If it appears to the registrar of the Court that a notice of an application for leave to appeal does not show any substantial ground of appeal or, in the case of an application under section 2, that the application does not disclose a prima facie case that a miscarriage of justice has occurred in relation to the conviction or that the sentence is excessive, he may, without calling for the report of the official stenographer, refer the application to the Court for summary determination; and where the case is so referred the Court may, if it considers that the application is frivolous or vexatious and can be determined without adjourning it for a full hearing, dismiss it summarily, without calling on anyone to attend the hearing or to appear on behalf of the prosecution.

(2) The jurisdiction of the Court under subsection (1) may be exercised by a single judge of the Court and an appeal may be made to the Court by the convicted person against the summary determination of an application.

6   Application to Courts-Martial Appeal Court

(1) References in sections 2 to 5 and 7 to the Court shall include references to the Courts-Martial Appeal Court, and those provisions shall have effect in relation to that court with the necessary modifications.

(2) For the purposes of subsection (1)—

(a) the references in section 2 to a conviction or sentence shall be construed as references to a conviction or sentence of a court-martial;

(b) the reference in section 3 to the jury shall be construed as a reference to the court-martial;

(c) the references in section 3 to the trial shall be construed as references to the court-martial;

(d) the reference in section 3(3) to the Commissioner of the Garda Síochána shall be construed as a reference to the Adjutant-General of the Defence Forces;

(e) the reference in section 4(1) to any rule of law shall include a reference to anything in the Defence Act, 1954.

(3) The Superior Courts Rules Committee may, with the concurrence of the Minister for Justice, make rules of court for the purposes of this section.

7 Petition for grant of pardon

(1) If a person—

    (a) who has been convicted of an offence,

    (b) who after appeal against the conviction stands convicted of an offence, and

    (c) who alleges that a new or newly-discovered fact shows that a miscarriage of justice has occurred in relation to the conviction,

petitions the Minister for Justice with a view to the Government advising the President to grant a pardon under Article 13.6 of the Constitution and no further proceedings are pending in relation to the appeal, the following provisions of this section shall apply.

(2) The Minister for Justice shall make or cause to be made such inquiries as he considers necessary and—

    (a) if he is of opinion either—

        (i) that the matters dealt with in the petition could appropriately be dealt with by way of an application to the Court pursuant to section 2, or

        (ii) that a case has not been made out that a miscarriage of justice has occurred and that no useful purpose would be served by further investigation,

    shall inform the petitioner accordingly and take no further action, and

    (b) in any other case, shall recommend to the Government either—

        (i) that it should advise the President to grant a pardon in respect of the offence of which the applicant was convicted, or

        (ii) that it should appoint a committee pursuant to section 8 to inquire into and report on the case.

(3) In subsection (1)(c) the reference to a new fact is to a fact known to the convicted person at the time of the trial or appeal proceedings the significance of which was appreciated by him, where he alleges that there is a reasonable explanation for his failure to adduce evidence of that fact.

(4) The reference in subsection (1)(c) to a newly-discovered fact is to a fact discovered by or coming to the notice of the convicted person after the relevant appeal proceedings have been finally determined or a fact the significance of which was not appreciated by the convicted person or his advisers during the trial or appeal proceedings.

(5) References in subsections (1) and (2) to the Minister for Justice shall, in relation to a conviction by court-martial, be construed as references to the Minister for Defence.

(6) Nothing in this section shall affect any functions of the Minister for Justice in relation to a petition to him from a person other than a person mentioned in subsection (1) with a view to the Government advising the President to grant a pardon under Article 13.6 of the Constitution.

8 Committee to inquire into alleged miscarriages of justice

(1) The Government, for the purpose of enabling it to decide whether or not to advise the President to exercise the right of pardon conferred by Article 13.6 of the Constitution, may establish a committee to inquire into any or all of the matters dealt with in a petition for the grant of a pardon by the President and to report whether, in the opinion of the committee, the President should be so advised.

(2) The committee shall be a tribunal within the meaning of the Tribunals of Inquiry (Evidence) Acts, 1921 and 1979.

(3) Where a committee consists of more than one member, the Government shall designate one of the members to be its chairman.

(4) The person constituting the committee (or, where the committee consists of more than one member, its chairman) shall be either a judge or former judge or a practising barrister or solicitor of not less than ten years standing.

(5) A committee may receive such evidence and other information as it sees fit, whether or not that evidence or information is or would be admissible in a court of law.

9   Compensation for miscarriage of justice

(1) Where a person has been convicted of an offence and either—

    (a)   (i)   his conviction has been quashed by the Court on an application under section 2 or on appeal, or he has been acquitted in any re-trial, and

          (ii)   the Court or the court of re-trial, as the case may be, has certified that a newly-discovered fact shows that there has been a miscarriage of justice,

    or

    (b)   (i)   he has been pardoned as a result of a petition under section 7, and

          (ii)   the Minister for Justice is of opinion that a newly-discovered fact shows that there has been a miscarriage of justice,

the Minister shall, subject to subsections (2) and (3), pay compensation to the convicted person or, if he is dead, to his legal personal representatives unless the non-disclosure of the fact in time is wholly or partly attributable to the convicted person.

(2) A person to whom subsection (1) relates shall have the option of applying for compensation or of instituting an action for damages arising out of the conviction.

(3) No payment of compensation under this section shall be made unless an application for such compensation has been made to the Minister for Justice.

(4) The compensation shall be of such amount as may be determined by the Minister for Justice.

(5) Any person who is dissatisfied with the amount of compensation determined by the Minister may apply to the High Court to determine the amount which the Minister shall pay under this section and the award of the High Court shall be final.

(6) In subsection (1) "newly-discovered fact" means—

    (a)   where a conviction was quashed by the Court on an application under section 2 or a convicted person was pardoned as a result of a petition under section 7, or has been acquitted in any re-trial, a fact which was discovered by him or came to his notice after the relevant appeal proceedings had been finally determined or a fact the significance of which was not appreciated by the convicted person or his advisers during the trial or appeal proceedings, and

    (b)   where a conviction was quashed by that Court on appeal, a fact which was discovered by the convicted person or came to his notice after the conviction to which the appeal relates or a fact the significance of which was not appreciated by the convicted person or his advisers during the trial.

10   Uncorroborated confession

(1) Where at a trial of a person on indictment evidence is given of a confession made by that person and that evidence is not corroborated, the judge shall advise the jury to have due regard to the absence of corroboration.

(2) It shall not be necessary for a judge to use any particular form of words under this section.

11   Appeal from Central Criminal Court

[...]¹

Amendments

1   Section 11 repealed by Courts and Court Officers Act 1995, Sch 1, Pt 2.

---

12   Expenses

The expenses incurred in the administration of this Act shall, to such extent as may be sanctioned by the Minister for Finance, be paid out of moneys provided by the Oireachtas.

13   Repeals

The enactments referred to in column (2) of the Schedule to this Act are hereby repealed to the extent mentioned in column (3) of the Schedule .

14   Short title

This Act may be cited as the Criminal Procedure Act, 1993.

SCHEDULE

ENACTMENTS REPEALED

Section 13

No. and Year	Short Title	Extent of Repeal
(1)	(2)	(3)
No. 10 of 1924	Courts of Justice Act, 1924	Section 34
No. 15 of 1928	Courts of Justice Act, 1928	Section 5
No. 19 of 1983	Courts-Martial Appeals Act, 1983	Section 18

Criminal Justice (Public Order) Act 1994

Number 2 of 1994

ARRANGEMENT OF SECTIONS

PART I
PRELIMINARY AND GENERAL

1   Short title, collective citation and commencement.

2   Interpretation (general).

PART II
OFFENCES RELATING TO PUBLIC ORDER

3   Interpretation (Part II).

4   Intoxication in public place.

5   Disorderly conduct in public place.

6   Threatening, abusive or insulting behaviour in public place.

7   Distribution or display in public place of material which is threatening, abusive, insulting or obscene.

8   Failure to comply with direction of member of Garda Síochána.

9   Wilful obstruction.

10   Increase of penalty for common assault, etc.

11   Entering building, etc., with intent to commit an offence.

12   Amendment of Vagrancy Act, 1824.

13   Trespass on building, etc.

14   Riot.

15   Violent disorder.

16   Affray.

17   Blackmail, extortion and demanding money with menaces.

18   Assault with intent to cause bodily harm or commit indictable offence.

19   Assault or obstruction of peace officer.

PART III
CROWD CONTROL AT PUBLIC EVENTS

20   Interpretation (Part III).

21   Control of access to certain events, etc.

22   Surrender and seizure of intoxicating liquor, etc.

PART IV
MISCELLANEOUS AND REPEALS

23   Prohibition of advertising of brothels and prostitution.

23A Fixed charge offences.

23B   Application of section 23A in relation to offence under section 4.

24   Arrest without warrant.

25   Continuance of existing powers of Garda Síochána.

26   Repeals.

SCHEDULE

AN ACT TO ABOLISH CERTAIN COMMON LAW OFFENCES RELATING TO PUBLIC ORDER AND TO PROVIDE CERTAIN STATUTORY OFFENCES RELATING TO PUBLIC ORDER IN LIEU THEREOF, TO PROVIDE FOR ADDITIONAL POWERS OF CROWD CONTROL BY MEMBERS OF THE GARDA SÍOCHÁNA IN, OR OF CONTROL BY SUCH MEMBERS OF ACCESS TO, THE VICINITY OF CERTAIN EVENTS AND TO PROVIDE FOR OFFENCES RELATING THERETO, TO PROVIDE FOR OTHER MATTERS RELATING TO PUBLIC ORDER AND TO FINES AND TERMS OF IMPRISONMENT IN RESPECT OF CERTAIN OFFENCES AND FOR THOSE AND OTHER PURPOSES TO AMEND THE CRIMINAL LAW AND ADMINISTRATION. [3rd March, 1994]

BE IT ENACTED BY THE OIREACHTAS AS FOLLOWS:

PART I
PRELIMINARY AND GENERAL

1   Short title, collective citation and commencement

(1) This Act may be cited as the Criminal Justice (Public Order) Act, 1994.

(2) The Vagrancy Acts, 1824 and 1988, and section 12 may be cited together as the Vagrancy Acts, 1824 to 1994.

(3) This Act shall come into operation one month after its passing.

2   Interpretation (general)

(1) A reference in this Act to a Part or to a section is a reference to a Part or section of this Act unless it is indicated that a reference to some other Act is intended.

(2) A reference in this Act to a subsection or to a paragraph is to the subsection or paragraph of the provision in which the reference occurs unless it is indicated that a reference to some other provision is intended.

PART II
OFFENCES RELATING TO PUBLIC ORDER

3   Interpretation (Part II)

In this Part, except where the context otherwise requires—

"dwelling" includes a building, vehicle or vessel ordinarily used for habitation;

"private place" means a place that is not a public place;

"public place" includes—

(a) any highway,

(b) any outdoor area to which at the material time members of the public have or are permitted to have access, whether as of right or as a trespasser or otherwise, and which is used for public recreational purposes,

(c) any cemetery or churchyard,

(d) any premises or other place to which at the material time members of the public have or are permitted to have access, whether as of right or by express or implied permission, or whether on payment or otherwise, and

(e) any train, vessel or vehicle used for the carriage of persons for reward.

4   Intoxication in public place

(1) It shall be an offence for any person to be present in any public place while intoxicated to such an extent as would give rise to a reasonable apprehension that he might endanger himself or any other person in his vicinity.

(2) A person who is guilty of an offence under this section shall be liable on summary conviction to a fine not exceeding [€500].[1]

(3) Where a member of the Garda Síochána suspects, with reasonable cause, that an offence under this section or under section 5 or 6 is being committed, the member concerned may seize, obtain or remove, without warrant, any bottle or container, together with its contents, which—

(a) is in the possession, in a place other than a place used as a dwelling, of a person by whom such member suspects the offence to have been committed, and

(b) such member suspects, with reasonable cause, contains an intoxicating substance:

Provided that, in the application of this subsection to section 5 or 6, any such bottle or container, together with its contents, may only be so seized, obtained or removed where the member of the Garda Síochána suspects, with reasonable cause, that the bottle or container or its contents, is relevant to the offence under section 5 or 6 which the member suspects is being committed.

(4) In this section—

["bottle or container" means a bottle or container irrespective of whether—

(a) the bottle or container is opened or unopened, and

(b) any or all of the contents of the bottle or container have been or are being consumed,

and includes the contents of the bottle or container, but does not include a bottle or container for a substance which is in the possession of the person concerned for a purpose other than the intoxication of that or any other person;][2]

"intoxicated" means under the intoxicating influence of any alcoholic drink, drug, solvent or other substance or a combination of substances and cognate words shall be construed accordingly.

Amendments

1   Amount amended by Intoxicating Liquor Act 2008, s 22 and Sch 2.

2   Definition substituted by Intoxicating Liquor Act 2008, s 18.

5   Disorderly conduct in public place

(1) It shall be an offence for any person in a public place to engage in offensive conduct—

   (a) between the hours of 12 o'clock midnight and 7 o'clock in the morning next following, or

   (b) at any other time, after having been requested by a member of the Garda Síochána to desist.

(2) A person who is guilty of an offence under this section shall be liable on summary conviction to a fine not exceeding [€1,000.]¹

(3) In this section "offensive conduct" means any unreasonable behaviour which, having regard to all the circumstances, is likely to cause serious offence or serious annoyance to any person who is, or might reasonably be expected to be, aware of such behaviour.

Amendments

1   Amount amended by Intoxicating Liquor Act 2008, s 22 and Sch 2.

6   Threatening, abusive or insulting behaviour in public place

(1) It shall be an offence for any person in a public place to use or engage in any threatening, abusive or insulting words or behaviour with intent to provoke a breach of the peace or being reckless as to whether a breach of the peace may be occasioned.

(2) A person who is guilty of an offence under this section shall be liable on summary conviction to a fine not exceeding [€1,000]¹ or to imprisonment for a term not exceeding 3 months or to both.

Amendments

1   Amount amended by Intoxicating Liquor Act 2008, s 22 and Sch 2.

7   Distribution or display in public place of material which is threatening, abusive, insulting or obscene

(1) It shall be an offence for any person in a public place to distribute or display any writing, sign or visible representation which is threatening, abusive, insulting or obscene with intent

to provoke a breach of the peace or being reckless as to whether a breach of the peace may be occasioned.

(2) A person who is guilty of an offence under this section shall be liable on summary conviction to a fine not exceeding [€1,000][1] or to imprisonment for a term not exceeding 3 months or to both.

Amendments

1   Amount amended by Intoxicating Liquor Act 2008, s 22 and Sch 2.

8   Failure to comply with direction of member of Garda Síochána

(1) Where a member of the Garda Síochána finds a person in a public place and suspects, with reasonable cause, that such person—

(a)   is or has been acting in a manner contrary to the provisions of section 4, 5, 6, 7 or 9, or

(b)   without lawful authority or reasonable excuse, is acting in a manner which consists of loitering in a public place in circumstances, which may include the company of other persons, that give rise to a reasonable apprehension for the safety of persons or the safety of property or for the maintenance of the public peace, the member may direct the person so suspected to do either or both of the following, that is to say:

(i)   desist from acting in such a manner, and

(ii)   leave immediately the vicinity of the place concerned in a peaceable or orderly manner.

(2) It shall be an offence for any person, without lawful authority or reasonable excuse, to fail to comply with a direction given by a member of the Garda Síochána under this section.

(3) A person who is guilty of an offence under this section shall be liable on summary conviction to a fine not exceeding [€1,000][1] or to imprisonment for a term not exceeding 6 months or to both.

Amendments

1   Amount amended by Intoxicating Liquor Act 2008, s 22 and Sch 2.

[8A   Power to direct persons who are in possession of intoxicating substances, etc

(1) This section applies where a member of the Garda Síochána believes with reasonable cause that—

(a)   a person is in a relevant place alone or accompanied by other persons,

(b)   a bottle or container which contains an intoxicating substance is in the possession of the relevant person, and

   (c)   the relevant person is acting in that place, or the relevant person and some or all of the accompanying persons are acting in that place, in a manner that—

      (i)   gives rise to a reasonable apprehension for the safety of persons or the safety of property or for the maintenance of the public peace, or

     (ii)   is causing, or gives rise to a reasonable apprehension is likely to cause, annoyance and nuisance to another person or persons or interference with that other person's or persons' peaceful possession and enjoyment by that other person or persons of his or her, or their, as the case may be, property.

(2) Where this section applies, the member may—

   (a)   seek an explanation from the relevant person as to all or any of the matters to which the relevant belief relates, and

   (b)   do one or more of the following, if the relevant person fails or refuses to give such an explanation or if such an explanation is given, and in either case the member remains of the relevant belief:

      (i)   request the relevant person to immediately give the bottle or container to the member (or to another member of the Garda Síochána accompanying the member) and at the same time as the request is made give to the relevant person a warning in ordinary language that a failure or refusal to comply with the request may lead to the seizure of the bottle or container or to his or her arrest or to both (or words to the like effect);

     (ii)   if the relevant person fails or refuses to comply with the request, seize, detain and remove, without warrant, the bottle or container with the use, if necessary, of such force as is reasonable in the circumstances;

    (iii)   direct the relevant person and, if appropriate, some or all of the accompanying persons, to desist from acting in the manner referred to in paragraph (c) of subsection (1);

    (iv)   direct the relevant person and, if appropriate, some or all of the accompanying persons, to leave immediately the place in a peaceable or orderly manner;

     (v)   request the relevant person to provide the member with his or her name and address.

(3) Where—

   (a)   a person fails or refuses to comply with a request made by the member under subparagraph (i) or (v) of paragraph (b) of subsection (2),

   (b)   a person fails or refuses to comply with a direction given by the member under subparagraph (iii) or (iv) of paragraph (b) of subsection (2), or

   (c)   the member has reasonable grounds for believing that the name or address provided to the member, in compliance with a request made by the member under subparagraph (v) of paragraph (b) of subsection (2), is false or misleading,

the member may arrest such person without warrant.

(4) A person who—

   (a)   fails or refuses to comply with a request made by the member under subparagraph (i) or (v) of paragraph (b) of subsection (2), or

(b) in purported compliance with a request made by the member under subparagraph
(v) of paragraph (b) of subsection (2), provides to the member a name or address
which is false or misleading,

shall be guilty of an offence and shall be liable on summary conviction to a fine not
exceeding €500.

(5) It shall be an offence for any person, without lawful authority or reasonable excuse, to fail
to comply with a direction given by the member under subparagraph (iii) or (iv) of paragraph
(b) of subsection (2).

(6) A person who is guilty of an offence under subsection (5) shall be liable on summary
conviction to a fine not exceeding €1,000.

(7) Where the member or another member of the Garda Síochána has been given, or has
seized, detained and removed, a bottle or container pursuant to this section, the member
shall—

(a) dispose of the bottle or container in such manner as he or she considers appropriate,
and

(b) make and retain, or cause to be made and retained, a record in writing of the
manner, date and place of such disposal.

(8) Nothing in this section shall prejudice the operation of the other provisions of this Act or
of the Criminal Justice (Public Order) Act 2003.

(9) In this section—

"bottle or container" means a bottle or container irrespective of whether—

(a) the bottle or container is opened or unopened, and

(b) any or all of the contents of the bottle or container have been or are being
consumed,

and includes the contents of the bottle or container;

"relevant belief", in relation to a member of the Garda Síochána, means the belief referred to
in subsection (1) of the member;

"relevant person" means the person first-mentioned in paragraph (a) of subsection (1);

"relevant place" means a place other than a place used as a private dwelling.

8B   Power of entry for purposes of section 8A, etc

A member of the Garda Síochána may enter without warrant a place other than a place used
as a private dwelling if the member has reasonable grounds for believing that—

(a) the matters specified in paragraphs (a), (b) and (c) of subsection (1) of section 8A,
or

(b) the matters specified in paragraphs (a), (b) and (c) of subsection (1) of section 37A
(inserted by section 14 of the Intoxicating Liquor Act 2008),

are occurring in such place.][1]

Amendments

1   Sections 8A and 8B inserted by Intoxicating Liquor Act 2008, s 19.

---

9   Wilful obstruction

Any person who, without lawful authority or reasonable excuse, wilfully prevents or interrupts the free passage of any person or vehicle in any public place shall be liable on summary conviction to a fine not exceeding [€400][1].

Amendments

1   Amount amended by Intoxicating Liquor Act 2008, s 22 and Sch 2.

10   Increase of penalty for common assault, etc

The Criminal Justice Act, 1951, is hereby amended by the substitution for subsection (2) of section 11 of the following:[1]

Amendments

1   See the amended Act.

11   Entering building, etc., with intent to commit an offence

(1) It shall be an offence for a person—

(a)   to enter any building or the curtilage of any building or any part of such building or curtilage as a trespasser, or

(b)   to be within the vicinity of any such building or curtilage or part of such building or curtilage for the purpose of trespassing thereon,

in circumstances giving rise to the reasonable inference that such entry or presence was with intent to commit an offence or with intent to unlawfully interfere with any property situate therein.

(2) A person who is guilty of an offence under this section shall be liable on summary conviction to a fine not exceeding [€2,500][1] or to imprisonment for a term not exceeding 6 months or to both.

Amendments

1   Amount amended by Intoxicating Liquor Act 2008, s 22 and Sch 2.

12   Amendment of Vagrancy Act, 1824

Section 4 (as applied to Ireland by the Prevention of Crimes Act, 1871) of the Vagrancy Act, 1824, is hereby amended by the deletion of "every person being found in or upon any dwelling house, warehouse, coach-house, stable, or outhouse, or in any enclosed yard, garden or area, for any unlawful purpose;".

13   Trespass on building, etc

(1) It shall be an offence for a person, without reasonable excuse, to trespass on any building or the curtilage thereof in such a manner as causes or is likely to cause fear in another person.

(2) (a) Where a member of the Garda Síochána finds a person in a place to which subsection (1) relates and suspects, with reasonable cause, that such person is or has been acting in a manner contrary to the provisions of that subsection, then the member may direct the person so suspected to do either or both of the following, that is to say:

  (i) desist from acting in such a manner, and

  (ii) leave immediately the vicinity of the place concerned in a peaceable or orderly manner.

  (b) It shall be an offence for any person, without lawful authority or reasonable excuse, to fail to comply with a direction given by a member of the Garda Síochána under this section.

(3) (a) A person who is guilty of an offence under subsection (1) shall be liable on summary conviction to a fine not exceeding [€2,500][1] or to imprisonment for a term not exceeding 12 months or to both.

  (b) A person who is guilty of an offence under subsection (2) shall be liable on summary conviction to a fine not exceeding [€1,000][1] or to imprisonment for a term not exceeding 6 months or to both.

Amendments

1   Amount amended by Intoxicating Liquor Act 2008, s 22 and Sch 2.

14   Riot

(1) Where—

  (a) 12 or more persons who are present together at any place (whether that place is a public place or a private place or both) use or threaten to use unlawful violence for a common purpose, and

  (b) the conduct of those persons, taken together, is such as would cause a person of reasonable firmness present at that place to fear for his or another person's safety,

then, each of the persons using unlawful violence for the common purpose shall be guilty of the offence of riot.

(2) For the purposes of this section—

  (a) it shall be immaterial whether or not the 12 or more persons use or threaten to use unlawful violence simultaneously at any place;

  (b) the common purpose may be inferred from conduct;

  (c) no person of reasonable firmness need actually be, or be likely to be, present at that place.

(3) A person guilty of an offence of riot shall be liable on conviction on indictment to a fine or to imprisonment for a term not exceeding 10 years or to both.

(4) The common law offence of riot is hereby abolished.

15   Violent disorder

(1) Where—

    (a) three or more persons who are present together at any place (whether that place is a public place or a private place or both) use or threaten to use unlawful violence, and

    (b) the conduct of those persons, taken together, is such as would cause a person of reasonable firmness present at that place to fear for his or another person's safety,

then, each of the persons using or threatening to use unlawful violence shall be guilty of the offence of violent disorder.

(2) For the purposes of this section—

    (a) it shall be immaterial whether or not the three or more persons use or threaten to use unlawful violence simultaneously;

    (b) no person of reasonable firmness need actually be, or be likely to be, present at that place.

(3) A person shall not be convicted of the offence of violent disorder unless the person intends to use or threaten to use violence or is aware that his conduct may be violent or threaten violence.

(4) A person guilty of an offence of violent disorder shall be liable on conviction on indictment to a fine or to imprisonment for a term not exceeding 10 years or to both.

(5) A reference, however expressed, in any enactment passed before the commencement of this Act—

    (a) to the common law offence of riot, or

    (b) to the common law offence of riot and to tumult,

shall be construed as a reference to the offence of violent disorder.

(6) The common law offence of rout and the common law offence of unlawful assembly are hereby abolished.

16   Affray

(1) Where—

    (a) two or more persons at any place (whether that place is a public place or a private place or both) use or threaten to use violence towards each other, and

    (b) the violence so used or threatened by one of those persons is unlawful, and

    (c) the conduct of those persons taken together is such as would cause a person of reasonable firmness present at that place to fear for his or another person's safety,

then, each such person who uses or threatens to use unlawful violence shall be guilty of the offence of affray.

(2) For the purposes of this section—

    (a) a threat cannot be made by words alone;

    (b) no person of reasonable firmness need actually be, or be likely to be, present at the place where the use or threat of violence occurred.

(3) A person shall not be convicted of the offence of affray unless the person intends to use or threaten to use violence or is aware that his conduct may be violent or threaten violence.

(4) A person guilty of an offence of affray shall be liable—

(a) on summary conviction to a fine not exceeding [€1,000]¹ or to imprisonment for a term not exceeding 12 months or to both,

(b) on conviction on indictment to a fine or to imprisonment for a term not exceeding 5 years or to both.

(5) The common law offence of affray is hereby abolished.

Amendments

1   Amount amended by Intoxicating Liquor Act 2008, s 22 and Sch 2.

17   Blackmail, extortion and demanding money with menaces

(1) It shall be an offence for any person who, with a view to gain for himself or another or with intent to cause loss to another, makes any unwarranted demand with menaces.

(2) For the purposes of this section—

(a) a demand with menaces shall be unwarranted unless the person making it does so in the belief—

(i)   that he has reasonable grounds for making the demand, and

(ii)   that the use of the menaces is a proper means of reinforcing the demand;

(b) the nature of the act or omission demanded shall be immaterial and it shall also be immaterial whether or not the menaces relate to action to be taken by the person making the demand.

(3) A person guilty of an offence under this section shall be liable—

(a) on summary conviction to a fine not exceeding [€2,500]¹ or to imprisonment for a term not exceeding 12 months or to both,

(b) on conviction on indictment to a fine or to imprisonment for a term not exceeding 14 years or to both.

Amendments

1   Amount amended by Intoxicating Liquor Act 2008, s 22 and Sch 2.

18   Assault with intent to cause bodily harm or commit indictable offence

(1) Any person who assaults any person with intent to cause bodily harm or to commit an indictable offence shall be guilty of an offence.

(2) A person guilty of an offence under this section shall be liable—

(a) on summary conviction, to a fine not exceeding [€2,500]¹ or to imprisonment for a term not exceeding 12 months or to both,

(b) on conviction on indictment, to a fine or to imprisonment for a term not exceeding 5 years or to both.

Amendments

1 Amount amended by Intoxicating Liquor Act 2008, s 22 and Sch 2.

19   Assault or obstruction of peace officer

[(1) Any person who assaults or threatens to assault—

(a) a person providing medical services at or in a hospital, or

(b) a person assisting such a person, or

(c) a peace officer acting in the execution of a peace officer's duty, knowing that he or she is, or being reckless as to whether he or she is, a peace officer so acting, or

(d) any other person acting in aid of a peace officer, or

(e) any other person with intent to resist or prevent the lawful apprehension or detention of himself or herself or any other person for any offence,

shall be guilty of an offence.][1]

(2) A person guilty of an offence under subsection (1) shall be liable—

(a) having elected for summary disposal of the offence, on summary conviction, to a fine not exceeding [€5,000][2] or to imprisonment for a term not exceeding 12 months, or to both,

(b) on conviction on indictment, to a fine or to imprisonment for a term not exceeding [7 years][2] or to both.

[(3) Any person who resists or wilfully obstructs or impedes—

(a) a person providing medical services at or in a hospital, knowing that he or she is, or being reckless as to whether he or she is, a person providing medical services, or

(b) a person assisting such a person, or

(c) a peace officer acting in the execution of a peace officer's duty, knowing that he or she is or being reckless as to whether he or she is, a peace officer so acting, or

(d) a person assisting a peace officer in the execution of his or her duty,

shall be guilty of an offence.][3]

(4) A person guilty of an offence under subsection (3) shall be liable on summary conviction to a fine not exceeding [€2,500][4] or to imprisonment for a term not exceeding 6 months or to both.

(5) The provisions of this section are in addition to and not in substitution of any provision in any other enactment relating to assault or obstruction of a peace officer.

(6) In this section—

["hospital" includes the lands, buildings and premises connected with and used wholly or mainly for the purposes of a hospital;

"medical services" means services provided by—

(a) doctors, dentists, psychiatrists, nurses, midwives, pharmacists, health and social care professionals (within the meaning of the Health and Social Care Professionals Act 2005) or other persons in the provision of treatment and care for persons at or in a hospital, or

(b)   persons acting under direction of those persons;][5]

"peace officer" means a member of the Garda Síochána, a prison officer[, a member of the fire brigade, ambulance personnel][6] or a member of the Defence Forces;

"prison" means any place for which rules or regulations may be made under the Prisons Acts, 1826 to 1980, section 7 of the Offences against the State (Amendment) Act, 1940, section 233 of the Defence Act, 1954, section 2 of the Prisoners of War and Enemy Aliens Act, 1956, or section 13 of the Criminal Justice Act, 1960;

["prison officer" includes any member of the staff of a prison and any person having the custody of, or having duties relating to the custody of, a person in relation to whom an order of a court committing that person to a prison is for the time being in force;][7]

Amendments

1   Subsection (1) substituted and amended by Criminal Justice Act 2006, s 185(a).

2   Subsection (2) amended by Criminal Justice Act 2006, s 185(b).

3   Subsection (3) amended by Criminal Justice Act 2006, s 185(c).

4   Definition inserted by Criminal Justice Act 2006, s 185(d).

5   Definitions amended by Criminal Justice Act 2006, s 185(e)(i).

6   Definition amended by Criminal Justice Act 2006, s 185(e)(ii).

7   Definition substituted by Prisons Act 2007, s 41(4).

[PART IIA

OFFENCES RELATING TO ENTERING AND OCCUPYING LAND WITHOUT CONSENT

Amendments

1   Part IIA [ss 19A–19H inserted by Housing (Miscellaneous Provisions) Act 2002, s 24.

19A   Interpretation (Part IIA)

(1) In this Part, except where the context otherwise requires—

"Commissioner" means the Commissioner of the Garda Síochána;

"consent duly given" means consent given by—

(a)   in the case of lands referred to in subsection (2)(a), the relevant statutory body,

(b)   in the case of lands referred to in subsection (2)(b), the relevant trustees, and

(c)   in any other case, the owner concerned;

"health board" means

(a)   a health board established under the Health Act, 1970,

(b)   the Eastern Regional Health Authority, or

(c)   an Area Health Board established under the Health (Eastern Regional Health Authority) Act, 1999;

"local authority" means a county council, a city council or a town council for the purposes of the Local Government Act, 2001;

"object" includes any temporary dwelling (within the meaning of section 69 of the Roads Act, 1993) and an animal of any kind or description;

"owner" means—

(a)   in relation to land, the person lawfully entitled—

    (i)   to possession, and

    (ii)   to the immediate use and enjoyment,

of the land as the owner, lessee, ten-and or otherwise, or any person acting on behalf of that person;

(b)   in relation to land referred to in paragraph (a) or (b) of subsection (2), the relevant statutory body or trustees, as the case may be;

"statutory body" means—

(a)   a Minister of the Government,

(b)   the Commissioners of Public Works in Ireland,

(c)   a local authority,

(d)   a harbour authority within the meaning of the Harbours Act, 1946, or a company established pursuant to section 7 of the Harbours Act, 1996,

(e)   a health board,

(f)   a vocational education committee within the meaning of the Vocational Education Acts, 1930 to 1999,

(g)   any other body established—

    (i)   by or under any enactment (other than the Companies Acts, 1963 to 2001), or

    (ii)   under the Companies Acts, 1963 to 2001, in pursuance of powers conferred by or under another enactment,

and financed wholly or partly by means of moneys provided, or loans made or guaranteed, by a Minister of the Government or the issue of shares held by or on behalf of a Minister of the Government, and subsidiary of any such body.

(2) In this part a reference to land includes—

(a)   land provided or maintained by a statutory body primarily for the amenity or recreation of the public or any class of persons (including any park, open space, car park, playing field or other space provided for recreational, community or conservation purposes) or is land within the curtilage of any public building,

(b)   land held by trustees for the benefit of the public or any class of the public, and

(c)   land covered by water.

19B   Extent of application (Part IIA), etc

(1) This Part does not apply to any public road within the meaning of the Roads Act, 1993.

(2) This Part is without prejudice to any other enactment (including any other provision of this Act) or any rule of law.

19C   Entry on and occupation of land or bringing onto or placing an object on land without consent

(1) A person, without the duly given consent of the owner, shall not—

    (a) enter and occupy any land, or

    (b) bring onto or place on any land any object,

where such entry or occupation or the bringing onto or placing on the land of such object is likely to—

    (i)   substantially damage the land,

    (ii) substantially and prejudicially affect any amenity in respect of the land,

    (iii) prevent persons entitled to use the land or any amenity in respect of the land from making reasonable use of the land or amenity,

    (iv) otherwise render the land or any amenity in respect of the land, or the lawful use of the land or any amenity in respect of the land, unsanitary or unsafe,

    (v) substantially interfere with the land, any amenity in respect of the land, the lawful use of the land or any amenity in respect of the land.

(2) A person who contravenes subsection (1) shall be guilty of an offence.

(3) Where a member of the Garda Síochána has reason to believe that a person is committing or has committed an offence under subsection (1) the member—

    (a) may demand of the person his or her name and address,

    (b) may direct the person to leave the land concerned and to remove from the land any object that belongs to the person or that is under his or her control, and

    (c) shall inform the person of the nature of the offence in respect of which it is suspected that person has been involved and the statutory consequences of failing to comply with a demand or direction under this subsection.

19D   Refusing or failing to give name or address or failure to comply with direction

Where a person—

    (a) refuses or fails to give his or her name and address to a member of the Garda Síochána when demanded under section 19C, or gives to the member a name or address that is false or misleading, or

    (b) fails to comply with a direction under that section,

he or she shall be guilty of an offence.

19E   Arrest without warrant

A member of the Garda Síochána may arrest without warrant a person—

    (a) who fails or refuses to give his or her name and address when demanded under section 19C(3)(a) or gives a name or address which the member has reasonable grounds for believing is false or misleading,

    (b) who fails to comply with a direction given under section 19C(3)(b), or

    (c) whom the member finds committing an offence under section 19C(1).

19F   Removal, storage and disposal of object

(1) Where a person fails to comply with a direction under section 19C(3)(b), a member of the Garda Síochána may remove or cause to be removed any object which the member has reason to believe was brought onto or placed on the land in contravention of section 19C(1) and may store or cause to be stored such object so removed.

(2) Any person who obstructs or impedes or assists a person to obstruct or impede a member of the Garda Síochana in the execution of his or her duty under this section shall be guilty of an offence.

(3) Where an object has been removed under this section without the presence or knowledge of any person claiming to own, occupy, control or otherwise retain it, the Commissioner shall serve or cause to be served upon each such person whose name and address can be ascertained by reasonable enquiry, a notice informing the person where the object may be claimed and recovered, requiring the person to claim and recover it within one month of the date of service of the notice and informing him or her of the statutory consequences of his or her failure to do so.

(4) An object removed and stored under this section shall be given to a person claiming possession of the object if, but only if, he or she makes a declaration in writing that he or she is the owner of the object or is authorised by its owner to claim it or is, for a specified reason, otherwise entitled to possession of it and, at the discretion of the Commissioner, the person pays the amount of any expenditure reasonably incurred in removing and storing the object.

(5) The Commissioner may dispose of, or cause to be disposed of, an object removed and stored under this section if—

    (a)   the owner of the object fails to claim it and remove it from the place where it is stored within one month of the date on which a notice under subsection (3) was served on him or her, or

    (b)   the name and address of the owner of the object cannot be ascertained by reasonable enquiry.

(6) Where the Commissioner becomes entitled to dispose of or cause to be disposed of an object under subsection (5) and the object is, in his or her opinion, capable of being sold, the Commissioner shall be entitled to sell or cause to be sold the object for the best price reasonably obtainable and upon doing so shall pay or cause to be paid to the person who was the owner of the object at the time of its removal, where the name and address of the owner can be ascertained by reasonable enquiry, a sum equal to the proceeds of such sale after deducting therefrom any expenditure reasonably incurred in its removal, storage and sale.

19G   Penalties and proceedings

(1) A person guilty of an offence under this Part shall be liable on summary conviction to a fine not exceeding [€4,000][1] or to a term of imprisonment not exceeding one month or to both.

(2) In any proceedings for an offence under this Part it shall be presumed until the contrary is shown that consent under this Part was not given.

Amendments

1   Amount amended by Intoxicating Liquor Act 2008, s 22 and Sch 2.

19H   Jurisdiction of District Court

(1) Notwithstanding any statutory provision or rule of law to the contrary, the jurisdiction of the District Court shall not, in summary proceedings in relation to an offence under this Part, be ousted by reason solely of a question of title to land being brought into issue.

(2) Where in summary proceedings in relation to an offence under this Part a question of title to land is brought into issue, the decision of a justice of the District Court in the proceedings or on the question shall not operate as an estoppel in, or a bar to, proceedings in any court in relation to the land.]

PART III
CROWD CONTROL AT PUBLIC EVENTS

20   Interpretation (Part III)

In this Part—

"container" does not include a container for any medicinal product;

"disposable container" includes—

(a) any bottle, can or other portable container or any part thereof (including any crushed or broken portable container or part thereof) for holding any drink which, when empty, is of a kind normally discarded or returned to, or left to be recovered by, the supplier, and

(b) any crate or packaging designed to hold more than one such bottle, can or other portable container;

"event" has the meaning assigned to it by section 21 (1);

"intoxicating liquor" includes any container containing intoxicating liquor, whether or not a disposable container.

21   Control of access to certain events, etc

(1) If it appears to a member of the Garda Síochána not below the rank of superintendent that it is necessary in the interests of safety or for the purpose of preserving order to restrict the access of persons to a place where an event is taking or is about to take place which attracts, or is likely to attract, a large assembly of persons (in this Part referred to as the "event"), he may authorise any member of the Garda Síochána to erect or cause to be erected a barrier or a series of barriers on any road, street, lane, alley or other means of access to such a place in a position not more than one mile therefrom for the purpose of regulating the access of persons or vehicles thereto.

(2) Where a barrier has been erected in accordance with subsection (1), a member of the Garda Síochána in uniform may by oral or manual direction or by the exhibition of any notice or sign, or any combination thereof—

(a) divert persons generally or particularly and whether in or on vehicles or on foot to another means of access to the event, including a means of access to that event on foot only, or

(b) where possession of a ticket is required for entrance to the event, prohibit a person whether in or on vehicles or on foot from crossing or passing the barrier towards the event where the person has no such ticket, or

(c) indicate that to proceed beyond the barrier while in possession of any intoxicating liquor, disposable drinks container or offensive article will render such liquor, container or article liable to confiscation.

(3) A member of the Garda Síochána shall not prohibit a person from crossing or passing a barrier erected under this section save for the purpose of diverting the person to another means of access to the event, if it appears to the member that the person is seeking to do so for the purpose only of—

(a) going to his dwelling or place of business or work in the vicinity of the event, or

(b) going for any other lawful purpose to any place in the vicinity of the event other than the place where the event is taking place or is about to take place.

(4) A person who—

(a) fails to obey a direction given by a member of the Garda Síochána under subsection (2) for the purposes of paragraph (a) or (b) thereof, or

(b) fails to comply with the terms of a notice or sign exhibited under subsection (2) for the purposes of paragraph (a) or (b) thereof,

shall be guilty of an offence.

(5) A person guilty of an offence under this section shall be liable on summary conviction to a fine not exceeding [€1,000.]¹

Amendments

1   Amount amended by Intoxicating Liquor Act 2008, s 22 and Sch 2.

---

22   Surrender and seizure of intoxicating liquor, etc

(1) Where in relation to an event—

(a) a barrier has been erected under section 21 and it appears to a member of the Garda Síochána that a person on foot or in a vehicle is seeking to cross or pass the barrier, or has crossed or passed the barrier, for the purpose of going to the place where the event is taking place or is about to take place, or

(b) it appears to a member of the Garda Síochána that a person is about to enter, or has entered, the place where the event is taking place or is about to take place,

and the person has, or the member of the Garda Síochána suspects with reasonable cause that the person has, in his possession—

(i) any intoxicating liquor, or

(ii) any disposable container, or

(iii) any other article which, having regard to the circumstances or the nature of the event, could be used to cause injury,

the member may exercise any one or more of the following powers—

(I) search or cause to be searched that person or any vehicle in or on which he may be in order to ascertain whether he has with him any such liquor, container or other article,

(II) refuse to allow that person to proceed to the event or to proceed further, as the case may be, unless that person surrenders permanently to a member of the Garda Síochána as directed by the member such liquor, container or other article.

(2) Where a member of the Garda Síochána refuses to allow a person to proceed to the event or to proceed further by virtue of subsection (1)(II) and the person does not surrender the alcoholic liquor, disposable container or other article concerned, the member may require the person to leave the vicinity in an orderly and peaceful manner as directed by the member.

(3) A person who, without lawful authority or reasonable excuse, fails to comply with a requirement under subsection (2) shall be guilty of an offence.

(4) A person guilty of an offence under this section shall be liable on summary conviction to a fine not exceeding [€1,000.]¹

Amendments

1 Amount amended by Intoxicating Liquor Act 2008, s 22 and Sch 2.

PART IV

MISCELLANEOUS AND REPEALS

23   Prohibition of advertising of brothels and prostitution

(1) A person who publishes or causes to be published or distributes or causes to be distributed an advertisement which advertises a brothel or the services of a prostitute in the State or any premises or service in the State in terms, circumstances or manner which gives rise to the reasonable inference that the premises is a brothel or that the service is one of prostitution shall be guilty of an offence.

(2) A person who is guilty of an offence under subsection (1) shall be liable—

(a) on summary conviction to a fine not exceeding [€2,500.]¹,

(b) on conviction on indictment to a fine not exceeding [€25,000.]¹

(3) In any proceedings for an offence under subsection (1) it shall be a defence for the accused to show that he is a person whose business it is to publish or distribute or to arrange for the publication or distribution of advertisements and that he received the advertisement in question for publication or distribution in the ordinary course of business and did not know and had no reason to suspect that the advertisement related to a brothel or to the services of a prostitute.

(4) Where an offence under subsection (1) is committed by a body corporate or by a person purporting to act on behalf of a body corporate or an unincorporated body of persons and is proved to have been committed with the consent or approval of, or to have been attributable to any neglect on the part of, any person who, when the offence was committed, was a director, member of the committee of management or other controlling authority of the body concerned, or the manager, secretary or other officer of the body, or who was purporting to act in any such capacity, that person, as well as the body, shall be guilty of an offence and shall be liable to be proceeded against and punished as if that person were guilty of the first-mentioned offence.

(5) In this section—

"advertisement" includes every form of advertising or promotion, whether in a publication or by the display of notices or posters or by the means of circulars, leaflets, pamphlets or cards or other documents or by way of radio, television, computer monitor, telephone, facsimile transmission, photography or cinematography or other like means of communication;

"distribute" means distribute to the public or a section of the public and cognate words shall be construed accordingly;

"publish" means publish to the public or a section of the public and cognate words shall be construed accordingly.

Amendments

1   Amount amended by Intoxicating Liquor Act 2008, s 22 and Sch 2.

[23A   Fixed charge offences

(1) A member of the Garda Síochána who has reasonable grounds for believing that a person is committing, or has committed, an offence under section 5 (in this section referred to as a 'fixed charge offence') may serve on the person personally or by post the notice referred to in subsection (5) or cause it to be so served.

(2) A member of the Garda Síochána may, for the purposes of subsection (1)—

    (a)   request the person concerned to give his or her name and address and to verify the information given, and

    (b)   if not satisfied with the name and address or any verification given, request that the person accompany the member to a Garda Síochána station for the purpose of confirming the person's name and address.

(3) A person who—

    (a)   does not give his or her name and address when requested to do so under subsection (2)(a) or gives a name or address that is false or misleading, or

    (b)   does not comply with a request by a member of the Garda Síochána under subsection (2)(b),

is guilty of an offence and is liable on summary conviction to a fine not exceeding €1,500.

(4) A member of the Garda Síochána who is of opinion that a person is committing, or has committed, an offence under subsection (3) may arrest the person without warrant.

(5) The notice referred to in subsection (1) shall be in the prescribed form and shall state—

    (a)   that the person on whom it is served is alleged to have committed the fixed charge offence concerned,

    (b)   when and where it is alleged to have been committed,

    (c)   that a prosecution for it will not be instituted if—

        (i)   during the period of 28 days beginning on the date of the notice, the person pays [in accordance with the notice]² the prescribed amount, or

(ii) within 28 days beginning on the expiration of that period, the person [pays in accordance with the notice]² an amount which is 50 per cent greater than the prescribed amount,

and

(d) that in default of such payment the person will be prosecuted for the alleged offence.

(6) A payment referred to in subsection (5) shall be accompanied by the notice referred to in that subsection.

(7) Where a notice is served under subsection (1)—

(a) a person to whom the notice applies may make a payment in accordance with subsections (5)(c) and (6),

[(b) the payment shall be received in accordance with the notice and the person receiving the payment shall issue a receipt for it,]³

(c) a payment so received shall not be recoverable by the person who made it, and

(d) a prosecution in respect of the alleged fixed charge offence to which the notice relates shall not be instituted during the periods specified in subsection (5)(c) or, if a payment is made in accordance with that subsection and subsection (6), at all.

[(8) (a) In a prosecution for a fixed charge offence it shall be presumed until the contrary is shown that—

(i) the relevant notice under this section has been served or caused to be served, and

(ii) a payment pursuant to the relevant notice under this section accompanied by the notice, duly completed (unless the notice provides for payment without the notice accompanying the payment), has not been made.]⁴

(9) (a) The Minister may make regulations prescribing anything which is referred to in this section as prescribed.

(b) Different amounts may be prescribed for a fixed charge offence under this section and an offence under section 4 which is deemed by section 23B(4) to be a fixed charge offence.

(c) Regulations made under this section may contain such incidental, supplementary and consequential provisions as appear to the Minister to be necessary for the purposes of the regulations.

(10) In this section—

"Minister" means Minister for Justice, Equality and Law Reform;

"person" means a person of not less than 18 years of age.]¹

Amendments

1   Section 23A inserted by Criminal Justice Act 2006, s 184.
2   Words in sub-s (5) substituted by Intoxicating Liquor Act 2008, s 20(a).
3   Subsection (7)(b) substituted by Intoxicating Liquor Act 2008, s 20(b).
4   Subsection (8)(a) substituted by Intoxicating Liquor Act 2008, s 20(c).

[23B   Application of section 23A in relation to offence under section 4

(1) This section applies to a person of not less than 18 years of age who is suspected, with reasonable cause, by a member of the Garda Síochána of committing, or of having committed, an offence under section 4.

(2) Where—

   (a) a person to whom this section applies is arrested and brought to a Garda Síochána station, and

   (b) he or she is a person whom the member of the Garda Síochána in charge of the station is authorised by section 31 of the Criminal Procedure Act 1967 to release on bail,

the member may, instead of releasing the person on bail, release him or her unconditionally [after—

   (i) serving on the person personally a notice in the prescribed form stating the matters specified in section 23A(5) or causing it to be so served, or

   (ii) informing him or her that such notice will be served on him or her by post.]²

(3) Where a person to whom this section applies is not arrested, the member of the Garda Síochána referred to in subsection (1) may serve on the person personally or by post a notice in the prescribed form stating the matters specified in section 23A(5) or cause it to be so served.

(4) On the service of a notice under subsection (2) or (3) the offence under section 4 is thereupon deemed to be a fixed charge offence, and subsections (5) to (10) of section 23A apply and have effect accordingly in relation to it.]¹

Amendments

1   Section 23B inserted by Criminal Justice Act 2006, s 184.

2   Words in sub-s (2) substituted by Intoxicating Liquor Act 2008, s 21.

---

24   Arrest without warrant

(1) Where a member of the Garda Síochána finds any person committing an offence under a relevant provision, the member may arrest such person without warrant.

(2) Where a member of the Garda Síochána is of the opinion that an offence has been committed under a relevant provision, the member may—

   (a) demand the name and address of any person whom the member suspects, with reasonable cause, has committed, or whom the member finds committing, such an offence, and

   (b) arrest without warrant any such person who fails or refuses to give his name and address when demanded, or gives a name or address which the member has reasonable grounds for believing is false or misleading.

(3) Any person who fails or refuses to give his name and address when demanded by virtue of subsection (2), or gives a name or address when so demanded which is false or misleading, shall be guilty of an offence.

(4) A person guilty of an offence under subsection (3) shall be liable on summary conviction to a fine not exceeding [€1,000]¹ or to a term of imprisonment not exceeding 6 months or to both.

(5) In this section "relevant provision" means section 4, 6, 7, 8, 11, 13, 14, 15, 16, 17, 18 or 19.

Amendments

1   Amount amended by Intoxicating Liquor Act 2008, s 22 and Sch 2.

---

25   Continuance of existing powers of Garda Síochána

Any power conferred on a member of the Garda Síochána by this Act is without prejudice to any other power exercisable by such a member.

26   Repeals

The Acts specified in the Schedule to this Act are hereby repealed to the extent specified in the third column of that Schedule.

SCHEDULE
ENACTMENTS REPEALED

Section 26.

Session and Chapter	Short Title	Extent of Repeal
6 & 7 Will. 4, c. 29	Dublin Police Act, 1836	Section 9.
5 & 6 Vict., c. 24	Dublin Police Act, 1842	Paragraph numbered 13 of section 14.
13 & 14 Vict., c. 92	Summary Jurisdiction Ireland) Act, 1851	Paragraph numbered 3 of section 13.
24 & 25 Vict., c. 100	Offences against the Person Act, 1861	Section 38.
34 & 35 Vict., c. 112	Prevention of Crimes Act, 1871	Section 12.
6 & 7 Geo. 5, c. 50	Larceny Act, 1916	Sections 29 to 31.

Criminal Justice Act 1994

Number 15 of 1994

ARRANGEMENT OF SECTIONS

PART I
PRELIMINARY

Section
1. Short title.
2. Commencement.
3. Interpretation.

PART II
CONFISCATION

4. Confiscation orders: drug trafficking offences.
5. Assessing the proceeds of drug trafficking.
6. Amount to be recovered under confiscation order made under section 4.
7. Re-assessment of whether defendant has benefited from drug trafficking.
8. Revised assessment of proceeds of drug trafficking.
9. Confiscation orders: offences other than drug trafficking offences.
10. Statements relevant to making confiscation orders.
11. Provision of information by defendant.
12. Supplementary provisions concerning confiscation orders.
13. Power of High Court where defendant has died or is absent.
14. Effect of conviction where High Court has acted under section 13.
15. Appeal against confiscation order.
16. Variation of confiscation orders.
17. Variation of confiscation orders made by virtue of section 13.
18. Increase in value of realisable property.

PART III
ENFORCEMENT, ETC. OF CONFISCATION ORDERS

19. Enforcement of confiscation orders.
20. Realisation of property.
21. Interest on sums unpaid under confiscation orders.
22. Application of proceeds of realisation.
23. Cases in which restraint orders may be made.
24. Restraint orders.
25. Registration of restraint orders.
26. Exercise of powers by High Court or receiver.

27.   Receivers: supplementary provisions.

28.   Bankruptcy of defendant, etc.

29.   Property subject to restraint order dealt with by Official Assignee.

30.   Winding up of company holding realisable property.

PART IV
MONEY LAUNDERING

31.   Money laundering, etc.

32.   Measures to be taken to prevent money laundering.

PART V
DRUG TRAFFICKING OFFENCES AT SEA

33.   Drug trafficking offences on Irish ships.

34.   Ships used for drug trafficking.

35.   Enforcement powers in respect of ships.

36.   Jurisdiction and prosecutions in relation to offences on ships.

37.   Convention states.

PART VI
DRUG TRAFFICKING MONEY IMPORTED OR EXPORTED IN CASH

38.   Seizure and detention.

39.   Forfeiture of cash seized under section 38.

40.   Appeal against section 39 order.

41.   Interest.

42.   Procedure.

43.   Interpretation of Part VI.

44.   Prescribed sum for purposes of section 38.

45.   Disposal of cash etc. forfeited under section 39.

PART VII
INTERNATIONAL CO-OPERATION

[...]

PART VIII
SUPPLEMENTARY

57.   Disclosure of information.

57A Designation of certain states or territorial units

58.   Offences of prejudicing investigation.

59.   Offences by bodies corporate.

60.   Voidance of dispositions designed to frustrate confiscation, etc.

61.   Forfeiture orders.

62. Forfeiture for drug offences.

63. Order to make material available.

64. Authority for search.

65. Compensation.

66. Compensation, etc. where absconder is acquitted.

67. Power to discharge confiscation order and order compensation when absconder returns.

68. Expenses.

FIRST SCHEDULE
ENFORCEMENT POWERS IN RESPECT OF SHIPS

SECOND SCHEDULE
TAKING OF EVIDENCE FOR USE OUTSIDE STATE

AN ACT TO MAKE PROVISION FOR THE RECOVERY OF THE PROCEEDS OF DRUG TRAFFICKING AND OTHER OFFENCES, TO CREATE AN OFFENCE OF MONEY LAUNDERING, TO MAKE PROVISION FOR INTERNATIONAL CO-OPERATION IN RESPECT OF CERTAIN CRIMINAL LAW ENFORCEMENT PROCEDURES AND FOR FORFEITURE OF PROPERTY USED IN THE COMMISSION OF CRIME AND TO PROVIDE FOR RELATED MATTERS. [30th June, 1994]

BE IT ENACTED BY THE OIREACHTAS AS FOLLOWS:

PART I
PRELIMINARY

1   Short title

This Act may be cited as the Criminal Justice Act, 1994.

2   Commencement

This Act shall come into operation on such day or days as may be appointed by order or orders of the Minister, either generally or with reference to a particular purpose or provision, and different days may be so appointed for different purposes and different provisions of this Act.

3   Interpretation

(1) In this Act—

["Act of 2005" means the Criminal Justice (Terrorist Offences) Act 2005;][1]

"benefited from drug trafficking" shall be construed in accordance with section 4(5) of this Act;

"benefited from an offence other than a drug trafficking offence" shall be construed in accordance with section 9(4) of this Act;

["confiscation order" means an order made under section 4(4), 8A(5) or 9(1) of this Act;][2]

"controlled drug" has the same meaning as in section 2 of the Misuse of Drugs Act, 1977;

"Convention state" means a state other than the State that is a party to the United Nations Convention against Illicit Traffic in Narcotic Drugs and Psychotropic Substances done at Vienna on the 20th day of December, 1988;

"corresponding law" has the same meaning as in section 20(2) of the Misuse of Drugs Act, 1977;

"dealing with property" shall be construed in accordance with section 24(8) of this Act;

["defendant" means, for the purposes of any provision of this Act relating to confiscation, and subject to section 23(2)(*a*) of this Act, a person against whom proceedings for the relevant drug trafficking offence, offence of financing terrorism or other offence have been instituted;]³

"drug trafficking" means doing or being concerned in any of the following, whether in the State or elsewhere, that is to say—

(a) producing or supplying a controlled drug where the production or supply contravenes any regulations made under section 5 of the Misuse of Drugs Act, 1977, and in force at the material time (whether before or after the commencement of the relevant provision of this Act) or a corresponding law,

(b) transporting or storing a controlled drug where possession of the drug contravenes section 3 of that Act or a corresponding law,

(c) importing or exporting a controlled drug where the importation or exportation contravenes any such regulations as mentioned in paragraph (a) of this definition or a corresponding law,

[(d) engaging in any conduct (whether or not in the State) in relation to property obtained, whether directly or indirectly, from anything done in relation to a controlled drug, being conduct that—

(i) is an offence under Part 2 of the Criminal Justice (Money Laundering and Terrorist Financing) Act 2010 ("Part 2 of the Act of 2010") or would have been an offence under that Part if the Part had been in operation at the time when the conduct was engaged in, or

(ii) in the case of conduct in a place outside of the State, other than conduct referred to in subparagraph (i)—

(I) would be an offence under Part 2 of the Act of 2010 if done in corresponding circumstances in the State, or

(II) would have been an offence under that Part if done in corresponding circumstances in the State and if the Part had been in operation at the time when the conduct was engaged in, or]⁴

(e) using any ship for illicit traffic in controlled drugs in contravention of section 33 or 34 of this Act;

"drug trafficking offence" means any of the following—

(a) an offence under any regulations made under section 5 of the Misuse of Drugs Act, 1977, involving the manufacture, production, preparation, importation, exportation, supply, offering to supply, distribution or transportation of a controlled drug,

(b) an offence under section 15 of that Act of possession of a controlled drug for unlawful sale or supply,

[(bb) an offence under section 15A of that Act;]⁵

[(bbb)   an offence under section 15B (importation of controlled drugs in excess of certain value) of that Act,]⁶

(c)   an offence under section 20 of that Act (assisting in or inducing the commission outside the State of an offence punishable under a corresponding law),

(d)   an offence under the Customs Acts in relation to the importation or exportation of a controlled drug or in relation to the fraudulent evasion of any prohibition, restriction or obligation in relation to such importation or exportation,

(e)   [an offence under Part 2 of the Criminal Justice (Money Laundering and Terrorist Financing) Act 2010, or under section 31 of this Act (as in force before the commencement of that Part), in relation to the proceeds of drug trafficking,]⁷

(f)   an offence under section 33 or 34 of this Act, or

(g)   an offence of aiding, abetting, counselling or procuring the commission of any of the offences mentioned in paragraphs (a) to (f) of this definition or of attempting or conspiring to commit any such offence or inciting another person to do so;

"enforcement officer" has the meaning assigned to it by paragraph 1 of the First Schedule to this Act;

"forfeiture order" means an order made under section 61 of this Act;

["funds" has the meaning given by section 12 of the Act of 2005;

"funds subject to confiscation" has the meaning given by section 8A(2) of this Act;]⁸

"interest", in relation to property, includes right;

"Irish ship" has the same meaning as in section 9 of the Mercantile Marine Act, 1955;

"Minister" means the Minister for Justice;

["offence of financing terrorism" means an offence under section 13 of the Act of 2005;]⁸

["outer limit of the territorial seas" has the meaning given to that expression by the Maritime Jurisdiction Acts 1959 to 1988;]⁹

"premises" includes any building or any part of a building and any vehicle, vessel or structure;

["proceeds", in relation to an offence of financing terrorism, means any funds derived from or obtained, directly or indirectly, through the commission of that offence, including payments and rewards;]⁸

"proceeds of drug trafficking" has the meaning assigned to it by section 5(1)(a) of this Act;

["property" includes money and all other property, real or personal, heritable or moveable, including choses-in-action and other intangible or incorporeal property and, in relation to an offence of financing terrorism, includes funds;]¹⁰

"realisable property" means—

(a)   any property held by the defendant, and

(b)   any property held by a person to whom the defendant has directly or indirectly made a gift caught by this Act,

but does not include property which is the subject of—

(a)   an order under section 30 of the Misuse of Drugs Act, 1977 (forfeiture orders), or

(b)   an order under section 61 of this Act;

"receiver" means a person appointed as a receiver under section 20(2) or 24(7) of this Act;

"[freezing order]¹¹" has the meaning assigned to it by section 24 of this Act;

["ship" includes a hovercraft or submersible craft, any vessel used in navigation and any other floating craft of any description;][12]

["value of funds subject to confiscation" has the meaning given by section 8B(1) of this Act;][13]

"value of proceeds of drug trafficking" has the meaning assigned to it by section 5(1)(b) of this Act.

(2) For the purposes of this Act the amount that might be realised at the time a confiscation order is made against the defendant is—

    (a) the aggregate of the values at that time of all the realisable property held by the defendant, less

    (b) where there are obligations having priority at that time, the aggregate of the amounts payable in pursuance of such obligations,

together with the aggregate of the values at that time of all gifts caught by this Act.

(3) Subject to the provisions of subsections (4) to (12) of this section, for the purposes of this Act the value of property (other than cash) in relation to any person holding the property—

    (a) where any other person holds an interest in the property, is—

        (i) the market value of the first-mentioned person's beneficial interest in the property, less

        (ii) the amount required to discharge any incumbrance on that interest,

        and

    (b) in any other case, is its market value.

(4) References in this Act to the value at any time (referred to in subsection (5) of this section as "the material time") of a person's proceeds of drug trafficking or, as the case may be, of any property obtained by a person as a result of or in connection with the commission of an offence other than a drug trafficking offence are references to—

    (a) the value of the said proceeds or property to the recipient when he obtained them or it, adjusted to take account of subsequent changes in the value of money, or

    (b) where subsection (5) of this section applies, the value there mentioned,

whichever is the greater.

(5) If at the material time the recipient holds—

    (a) the proceeds or property which he obtained (not being cash), or

    (b) property which, in whole or in part, directly or indirectly represents in his hands the proceeds or property which he obtained,

the value referred to in subsection (4)(b) of this section is the value to him at the material time of the proceeds or property mentioned in paragraph (a) of this subsection or, as the case may be, of the proceeds or property mentioned in paragraph (b) of this subsection, so far as it so represents the proceeds or property which he obtained.

(6) Subject to subsection (12) of this section, references in this Act to the value at any time (referred to in subsection (7) of this section as "the material time") of a gift caught by this Act or to a payment or reward are references to—

    (a) the value of the gift, payment or reward to the recipient when he received it adjusted to take account of subsequent changes in the value of money, or

    (b) where subsection (7) of this section applies, the value there mentioned, whichever is the greater.

(7) Subject to subsection (12) of this section, if at the material time the recipient holds—

    (a) the property which he received (not being cash), or

    (b) property which, in whole or in part, directly or indirectly represents in his hands the property which he received,

the value referred to in subsection (6) of this section is the value to him at the material time of the property mentioned in paragraph (a) of this subsection or, as the case may be, of the property mentioned in paragraph (b) of this subsection so far as it so represents the property which he received.

(8) For the purposes of subsection (2) of this section, an obligation has priority at any time if it is an obligation of the defendant to—

    (a) pay an amount due in respect of a fine, or other order of a court, imposed or made on conviction of an offence, where the fine was imposed or order made before the confiscation order, or

    (b) pay any sum which would be included among the preferential payments (within the meaning of the Bankruptcy Act, 1988) in the defendant's bankruptcy commencing on the date of the confiscation order or winding up under an order of the court made on that date.

(9) For the purposes of the provisions of this Act relating to drug trafficking, a gift (including a gift made before the commencement of section 4 of this Act) is caught by this Act if—

    (a) it was made by the defendant at any time since the beginning of the period of 6 years ending when the proceedings were instituted against him, or

    (b) it was made by the defendant at any time and was a gift of property—

        (i) which was received by the defendant in connection with drug trafficking carried on by him or another, or

        (ii) which in whole or in part directly or indirectly represented in the defendant's hands property received by him in that connection.

[(9A) For the purposes of the provisions of this Act relating to an offence of financing terrorism, a gift (including a gift made before the commencement of section 8A of this Act) is caught by this Act if—

    (a) it was made by the defendant at any time since the beginning of a period of 6 years ending when proceedings in respect of that offence were instituted against the defendant, or

    (b) it was made by the defendant at any time and was a gift of property—

        (i) which was received by the defendant in connection with an offence of financing terrorism committed by the defendant or another person, or

        (ii) which in whole or in part directly or indirectly represented in the defendant's hands funds received by the defendant in connection with an offence of financing terrorism.][14]

(10) For the purposes of the provisions of this Act relating to offences other than drug trafficking offences, a gift (including a gift made before the commencement of section 9 of this Act) is caught by this Act if—

    (a) it was made by the defendant at any time after the commission of the offence or, if more than one, the earliest of the offences to which the proceedings for the time being relate, and

    (b) the court considers it appropriate in all the circumstances to take the gift into account.

(11) The reference in subsection (10) of this section to an offence to which the proceedings for the time being relate includes, where the proceedings have resulted in the conviction of the defendant, a reference to any offence which the court takes into consideration when determining his sentence.

(12) For the purposes of this Act—

    (a) the circumstances in which the defendant is to be treated as making a gift include those where he transfers property to another person directly or indirectly for a consideration the value of which is significantly less than the value of the consideration provided by the defendant, and

    (b) in those circumstances, subsections (2) to (11) of this section shall apply as if the defendant had made a gift of such share in the property as bears to the whole property the same proportion as the difference between the values referred to in paragraph (a) of this subsection bears to the value of the consideration provided by the defendant.

(13) This Act applies to property wherever situated.

(14) A reference in this Act to an offence includes a reference to an offence committed before the commencement of the provision of this Act in which the reference occurs, but nothing in this Act imposes any duty or confers any power on any court in connection with proceedings against a person for an offence instituted before the commencement of the provision of this Act in which the reference occurs.

(15) A reference in this Act to property obtained, or to a pecuniary advantage derived, in connection with drug trafficking or the commission of an offence includes references to property obtained, or to a pecuniary advantage derived, both in that connection and in some other connection.

(16) The following provisions shall have effect for the interpretation of this Act, namely,

    (a) property is held by any person if he holds any interest in it,

    (b) references to property held by a person include a reference to property vested in his trustee within the meaning of Part V of the Bankruptcy Act, 1988 or liquidator,

    (c) references to an interest held by a person beneficially in property include a reference to an interest which would be held by him beneficially if the property were not so vested,

    (d) property is transferred by one person to another if the first person transfers or grants to the other any interest in the property,

    (e) proceedings for an offence are instituted—

        (i) when a summons or warrant for arrest is issued in respect of that offence,

        (ii) when a person is charged with the offence after being taken into custody without a warrant,

    and where the application of this section would result in there being more than one time for the institution of proceedings, they shall be taken to have been instituted at the earliest of those times,

(f) proceedings for an offence are concluded—

    [(i)   (I)   when the defendant is acquitted on all counts, or

            (II)   where the provisions of section 23 of the Criminal Procedure Act 2010 apply to the proceedings—

                (A)   when the time period for an appeal under that section has expired and no appeal has been made,

                (B)   where an appeal has been made but no re-trial is ordered, at the conclusion of the appeal proceedings under the section, or

                (C)   where a re-trial has been ordered, at the conclusion of the re-trial;][15]

    (ii)   if he is convicted on one or more counts, but no application for a confiscation order is made against him or the court decides not to make a confiscation order in his case; or

    (iii)   if a confiscation order is made against him in connection with those proceedings, when the order is satisfied,

(g) [an application under section 7, 8D or 13 of this Act][16] is concluded—

    (i)   if the court decides not to make a confiscation order against the defendant, when it makes that decision; or

    (ii)   if a confiscation order is made against the defendant as a result of that application, when the order is satisfied,

(h) [an application under section 8, 8E or 18 of this Act][17] is concluded—

    (i)   if the court decides not to vary the confiscation order in question, when it makes that decision; or

    (ii)   if the court varies the confiscation order as a result of the application, when the order is satisfied,

(i) a confiscation order is satisfied when no amount is due under it,

(j) an order is subject to appeal until (disregarding any power of a court to grant leave to appeal out of time) there is no further possibility of an appeal on which the order could be varied or set aside.

[(16A) References in this Act (other than section 9) to an offence in respect of which a confiscation order might be made under section 9 of this Act shall be construed as references to an indictable offence (other than a drug trafficking offence), irrespective of whether a person has been convicted of it on indictment.][18]

(17) In this Act, a reference to any enactment shall be construed as a reference to that enactment as amended or adapted by or under any subsequent enactment (including this Act).

Amendments

1   Definition inserted by Criminal Justice (Terrorist Offences) Act 2005, s 21(a).

2   Definition substituted by Criminal Justice (Terrorist Offences) Act 2005, s 21(b).

3   Definition substituted by Criminal Justice (Terrorist Offences) Act 2005, s 21(c).

4   Paragraph (d) of "drug trafficking" substituted by Criminal Justice (Money Laundering and Terrorist Financing) Act 2010, s 117(2).

5   Paragraph (bb) of "drug trafficking offence" inserted by Criminal Justice Act 1999, s 7.

6   Paragraph (bbb) of "drug trafficking offence" inserted by Criminal Justice Act 2006, s 86.

7   Paragraph (e) of "drug trafficking offence" substituted by Criminal Justice (Money Laundering and Terrorist Financing) Act 2010, s 117(3).

8   Definitions inserted by Criminal Justice (Terrorist Offences) Act 2005, s 21(d).

9   Definition inserted by Criminal Justice (Illicit Traffic by Sea) Act 2003, s 28(a)(i).

10 Definition substituted by Criminal Justice (Terrorist Offences) Act 2005, s 21(e).

11 Words substituted for "restraint order" by Criminal Justice (Mutual Assistance) Act 2008, s 105(a).

12 Definition inserted by Criminal Justice (Illicit Traffic by Sea) Act 2003, s 28(a)(ii).

13 Definition inserted by Criminal Justice (Terrorist Offences) Act 2005, s 21(f).

14 Subsection (9A) inserted by Criminal Justice (Terrorist Offences) Act 2005, s 21(g).

15 Subsection (16)(f)(i) substituted by Criminal Procedure Act 2010, s 27.

16 Words substituted for 'an application under section 7 or 13 of this Act' by Criminal Justice Terrorist Offences) Act 2005, s 21(h).

17 Words substituted for 'an application under section 8 or 18 of this Act' by Criminal Justice Terrorist Offences) Act 2005, s 21(i).

18 Subsection (16A) inserted by Criminal Justice (Mutual Assistance) Act 2008, s 105(c).

PART II
CONFISCATION

4   Confiscation orders: drug trafficking offences

[(1) Where a person has been sentenced or otherwise dealt with by a court in respect of one or more drug trafficking offences of which he has been convicted on indictment, the court shall, subject to subsections (2) and (3), determine whether the person has benefited from drug trafficking.

(2) A court may decide not to make a determination under subsection (1) of this section where, following such preliminary inquiries, if any, as it may make, it is satisfied that having regard to—

(a) the present means of the convicted person, and

(b) all of the other circumstances of the case, including the matters which are to be taken into account under section 12(3) of this Act,

the amount, if any, which might be recovered under any confiscation order which might be made would not be sufficient to justify proceeding with consideration of the making of such an order.

(3) The duty of a court to make a determination under subsection (1) of this section shall not apply if the convicted person has died or absconded, and accordingly the provisions of section 13 of this Act shall apply in such a case.]¹

(4) If the court determines that the person in question has benefited from drug trafficking, the court shall determine in accordance with section 6 of this Act the amount to be recovered

in his case by virtue of this section and shall make a confiscation order under this section requiring the person concerned to pay that amount.

(5) For the purposes of this Act, a person who has at any time (whether before or after the commencement of this section) received any payment or other reward in connection with drug trafficking carried on by him or another has benefited from drug trafficking.

(6) The standard of proof required to determine any question arising under this Act as to—

    (a) whether a person has benefited from drug trafficking, or

    (b) the amount to be recovered in his case by virtue of this section,

shall be that applicable in civil proceedings.

Amendments

1   Subsections (1)–(3) substituted by Criminal Justice Act 1999, s 25.

---

5   Assessing the proceeds of drug trafficking

(1) For the purposes of this Act—

    (a) any payments or other rewards received by a person at any time (whether before or after the commencement of section 4 of this Act) in connection with drug trafficking carried on by him or another are his proceeds of drug trafficking, and

    (b) the value of his proceeds of drug trafficking is the aggregate of the values of the payments or other rewards.

(2) The court shall, for the purpose of determining whether the defendant has benefited from drug trafficking and, if he has, of assessing the value of his proceeds of drug trafficking, make the assumptions set out in subsection (4) of this section except that the court shall not make any of the said assumptions if—

    (a) the assumption is shown to be incorrect in the case of the defendant, or

    (b) it is satisfied that there would be a serious risk of injustice in his case if the assumption were to be made.

(3) Where the court does not apply one or more of the assumptions set out in subsection (4) of this section it shall state its reasons.

(4) The assumptions referred to in subsection (2) of this section are—

    (a) that any property appearing to the court—

        (i) to have been held by the defendant at any time since his conviction, or

        (ii) to have been transferred to him at any time since the beginning of the period of 6 years ending when the proceedings were instituted against him,

    was received by him, at the earliest time at which he appears to the court to have held it, as a payment or reward in connection with drug trafficking carried on by him,

    (b) that any expenditure of his since the beginning of that period was met out of payments received by him in connection with drug trafficking carried on by him, and

(c) that, for the purpose of valuing any property received or assumed to have been received by him at any time as such a reward, he received the property free of any other interests in it.

(5) For the purpose of assessing the value of the defendant's proceeds of drug trafficking in a case where a confiscation order has previously been made against him, the court shall not take into account any of his proceeds of drug trafficking that are shown to the court to have been taken into account in determining the amount to be recovered under that order.

6   Amount to be recovered under confiscation order made under section 4

(1) Subject to subsection (2) of this section, where a confiscation order has been made under section 4 of this Act, the amount to be recovered under the order shall be equal to the amount assessed by the court to be the value of the defendant's proceeds of drug trafficking.

(2) If the court is satisfied that the amount that might be realised at the time the confiscation order is made is less than the amount the court assesses to be the value of his proceeds of drug trafficking, the amount to be recovered in the defendant's case under the confiscation order shall be the amount appearing to the court to be the amount that might be so realised.

7   Re-assessment of whether defendant has benefited from drug trafficking

[(1) This section applies where a court has—

(a) determined under section 4 of this Act that a defendant has not benefited from drug trafficking, or

(b) decided under section 4(2) of this Act not to make a determination as to whether a convicted person has benefited from drug trafficking.][1]

(2) If the Director of Public Prosecutions has evidence—

[(a) which was not considered by the court in making, or in deciding not to make, the determination referred to in subsection (1) of this section, but][2],

(b) which the Director of Public Prosecutions believes would have led the court to determine that the defendant had benefited from drug trafficking if it had been considered by the court, he may make, or cause to be made, an application to the court for it to consider that evidence.

(3) If, having considered the evidence, the court is satisfied that it would have determined that the defendant had benefited from drug trafficking if that evidence had been available to it, the court—

(a) shall—

[(i) make a determination or a fresh determination, as the case may be, of whether the defendant has benefited from drug trafficking; and][3]

(ii) make a determination under section 4(4) of this Act of the amount to be recovered by virtue of that section; and

(b) may make a confiscation order under section 4(4) of this Act.

[(4) In considering an application under this section, the court may take into account any payment or other reward received by the defendant on or after the determination, or the decision not to make a determination, referred to in subsection (1) of this section, but only if the Director of Public Prosecutions shows that it was received by the defendant in connection with drug trafficking carried on by the defendant or another person on or before that date.][4]

(5) In considering any evidence under this section which relates to any payments or reward to which subsection (4) of this section applies, the court shall not make the assumptions which would otherwise be required by section 5 of this Act.

(6) No application shall be entertained by the court under this section if it is made after the end of the period of six years beginning with the date on which the defendant was convicted.

Amendments

1   Subsection (1) substituted by Criminal Justice Act 1999, s 26(a).

2   Subsection (2)(a) substituted by Criminal Justice Act 1999, s 26(b).

3   Subsection (3)(a)(i) substituted by Criminal Justice Act 1999, s 26(c).

3   Subsection (4) substituted by Criminal Justice Act 1999, s 26(d).

---

8   Revised assessment of proceeds of drug trafficking

(1) This section applies where a court has made a determination under section 4(4) of this Act of the amount to be recovered in a particular case by virtue of that section referred to in this section as "the current determination".

(2) Where the Director of Public Prosecutions is of the opinion that the real value of the defendant's proceeds of drug trafficking was greater than their assessed value, the Director of Public Prosecutions may make, or cause to be made, an application to the court for the evidence on which he has formed his opinion to be considered by the court.

(3) In subsection (2) of this section—

"assessed value" means the value of the defendant's proceeds of drug trafficking as assessed by the court under section 6(1) of this Act; and

"real value" means the value of the defendant's proceeds of drug trafficking which took place—

    (a)   in the period by reference to which the current determination was made;
    or

    (b)   in any earlier period.

(4) If, having considered the evidence, the court is satisfied that the real value of the defendant's proceeds of drug trafficking is greater than their assessed value (whether because the real value was higher at the time of the current determination than was thought or because the value of the proceeds in question has subsequently increased), the court shall make a fresh determination under section 4(4) of this Act of the amount to be recovered by virtue of that section.

(5) Any determination under section 4(4) of this Act by virtue of this section shall be by reference to the amount that might be realised at the time when the determination is made.

(6) For any determination under section 4(4) of this Act by virtue of this section, section 5(5) of this Act shall not apply in relation to any of the defendant's proceeds of drug trafficking taken into account in respect of the current determination.

(7) In relation to any such determination—

(a) section 3(2) of this Act shall have effect as if for "a confiscation order is made against the defendant" there were substituted "of the determination";

(b) sections 3(8), 10(5)(a) and 12(4) of this Act shall have effect as if for "confiscation order" there were substituted "determination"; and

(c) section 6(2) of this Act shall have effect as if for "confiscation order is made" there were substituted "determination is made".

(8) The court may take into account any payment or other reward received by the defendant on or after the date of the current determination, but only if the Director of Public Prosecutions shows that it was received by the defendant in connection with drug trafficking carried on by the defendant or another on or before that date.

(9) In considering any evidence under this section which relates to any payment or reward to which subsection (8) of this section applies, the court shall not make the assumptions which would otherwise be required by section 5 of this Act.

(10) If, as a result of making the fresh determination required by subsection (4) of this section, the amount to be recovered exceeds the amount set by the current determination, the court may substitute for the amount to be recovered under the confiscation order which was made by reference to the current determination such greater amount as it thinks just in all circumstances of the case.

(11) No application shall be entertained by the court under this section if it is made after the end of the period of six years beginning with the date on which the defendant was convicted.

[8A   Confiscation orders relating to offence of financing terrorism

(1) Where a person has been sentenced or otherwise dealt with by a court in respect of one or more offences of financing terrorism of which that person has been convicted, the Director of Public Prosecutions may make, or cause to be made, an application to the court to determine whether the convicted person holds funds subject to confiscation.

(2) For the purposes of this Act, funds subject to confiscation are—

(a) funds used or allocated for use in connection with an offence of financing terrorism, or

(b) funds that are the proceeds of such an offence.

(3) An application under subsection (1) of this section may be made at the conclusion of the proceedings at which the person is sentenced or otherwise dealt with or at a later stage in the proceedings.

(4) An application under subsection (1) of this section shall not be made unless it appears to the Director of Public Prosecutions that the person in question holds funds subject to confiscation.

(5) If the court determines that the person in question holds funds subject to confiscation, the court shall—

(a) determine in accordance with section 8C of this Act the amount to be recovered in that person's case by virtue of this section, and

(b) make a confiscation order under this section requiring the person to pay that amount.

(6) The standard of proof applicable in civil proceedings is the standard required to determine a question arising under this Act as to—

(a)   whether a person holds funds subject to confiscation, and

(b)   the amount to be recovered in that person's case by virtue of this section.]¹

Amendments

1   Section 8A inserted by Criminal Justice (Terrorist Offences) Act 2005, s 22.

[8B   Assessing the value of funds subject to confiscation

(1) For the purposes of this Act, the value of the funds that are subject to confiscation is the aggregate of the values of those funds held by the defendant.

(2) For the purpose of assessing the value of funds subject to confiscation, the court shall, subject to subsection (3) of this section, make the following assumptions:

(a)   that any funds appearing to the court—

   (i)   to have been held by the defendant at any time since the conviction, or

   (ii)   to have been transferred to the defendant at any time since the beginning of the period of six years ending when the proceedings were instituted against the defendant,

   were received or collected by the defendant, at the earliest time at which the defendant appears to the court to have held them, for use (whether or not used) in connection with the offence of financing terrorism or as the proceeds of such offence;

(b)   that any expenditure of the defendant since the beginning of that period was met out of funds subject to confiscation;

(c)   that the funds subject to confiscation are held by the defendant free of any other interests in them.

(3) The court shall not make an assumption set out in subsection (2) of this section if—

(a)   that assumption is shown to be incorrect in the case of the defendant, or

(b)   the court is satisfied that there would be a serious risk of injustice in that case were the assumption made.

(4) Where the court does not apply one or more of the assumptions set out in subsection (2) of this section, it shall state its reasons.

(5) For the purpose of assessing the value of funds subject to confiscation in a case where a confiscation order has previously been made against the defendant, the court shall not take into account any of that defendant's funds subject to confiscation that are shown to the court to have been taken into account in determining the amount to be recovered under the confiscation order.]¹

Amendments

1   Section 8B inserted by Criminal Justice (Terrorist Offences) Act 2005, s 22.

[8C   Amount to be recovered under a confiscation order made under section 8A

(1) Subject to subsection (2) of this section, where a confiscation order has been made under section 8A of this Act, the amount to be recovered under the order shall be equal to the amount assessed by the court to be the value of the defendant's funds subject to confiscation.

(2) If the court is satisfied that the amount that might be realised at the time the confiscation order is made is less than the amount the court assesses to be the value of the funds subject to confiscation, the amount to be recovered in the defendant's case under the confiscation order shall be the amount appearing to the court to be the amount that might be so realised.][1]

Amendments

1   Section 8C inserted by Criminal Justice (Terrorist Offences) Act 2005, s 22.

[8D   Re-assessment of whether defendant holds funds subject to confiscation

(1) This section applies where an application has previously been made to the court under section 8A of this Act and the court has determined that the defendant did not hold funds subject to confiscation.

(2) The Director of Public Prosecutions may make, or cause to be made, an application to the court for it to consider evidence—

(a) which was not considered by the court in making the determination referred to in subsection (1) of this section, and

(b) which, had it been considered, the Director of Public Prosecutions believes would have led the court to determine that the defendant held funds subject to confiscation.

(3) If, having considered the evidence, the court is satisfied that, had that evidence been available to it, it would have determined that the defendant held funds subject to confiscation, the court—

    (a) shall—

        (i) make a fresh determination of whether the defendant holds funds subject to confiscation, and

        (ii) make a determination under section 8A(5) of this Act of the amount to be recovered by virtue of that section,

    and

    (b) may make a confiscation order under section 8A(5) of this Act.

(4) In considering an application under this section, the court may take into account any funds held by the defendant on or after the date of the determination referred to in subsection (1) of this section, but only if the Director of Public Prosecutions shows that the funds relate to an offence of financing terrorism committed on or before that date by the defendant or another person.

(5) In considering any evidence under this section relating to any funds to which subsection (4) applies, the court shall not make the assumptions which would otherwise be required under section 8B of this Act.

(6) No application shall be entertained by the court under this section if it is made after the end of the period of six years beginning with the date on which the defendant was convicted.]¹

Amendments

1   Section 8D inserted by Criminal Justice (Terrorist Offences) Act 2005, s 22.

[8E   Revised assessment of funds subject to confiscation

(1) This section applies where a court has made a determination (referred to in this section as 'the current determination') under section 8A(5) of this Act of the amount to be recovered in a particular case by virtue of that section.

(2) Where the Director of Public Prosecutions is of the opinion that the real value of the defendant's funds subject to confiscation was greater than their assessed value, the Director of Public Prosecutions may make, or cause to be made, an application to the court for the evidence on which that opinion was formed to be considered by the court.

(3) In subsections (2) and (4) of this section—

'assessed value' means the value of the defendant's funds subject to confiscation as assessed by the court under section 8C(1) of this Act;

'real value' means the value of the defendant's funds subject to confiscation which relate to an offence of financing terrorism committed either in the period by reference to which the current determination was made or in any earlier period.

(4) If, having considered the evidence, the court is satisfied that the real value of the defendant's funds subject to confiscation is greater than their assessed value (whether because their real value was higher at the time of the current determination than was thought or because the value of the funds subject to confiscation has subsequently increased), the court shall make a fresh determination under section 8A(5) of this Act of the amount to be recovered by virtue of that section.

(5) Any determination under section 8A(5) of this Act by virtue of this section shall be by reference to the amount that might be realised at the time the determination is made.

(6) For any determination under section 8A(5) of this Act by virtue of this section, section 8B(5) of this Act shall not apply in relation to any of the defendant's funds subject to confiscation that were taken into account in respect of the current determination.

(7) In relation to a determination under section 8A(5) of this Act by virtue of this section—

   (a)   section 3(2) of this Act shall have effect as if for 'a confiscation order is made against the defendant' there were substituted 'of the determination',

   (b)   sections 3(8), 10(5)(*a*) and 12(4) of this Act shall have effect as if for 'confiscation order' there were substituted 'determination', and

   (c)   section 8C(2) of this Act shall have effect as if for 'confiscation order is made' there were substituted 'determination is made'.

(8) The court may take into account any funds held by the defendant on or after the date of the current determination, but only if the Director of Public Prosecutions shows that the

funds relate to an offence of financing terrorism committed before that date by the defendant or another person.

(9) In considering any evidence relating to any funds to which subsection (8) applies, the court shall not make the assumptions which would otherwise be required by section 8B of this Act.

(10) If, as a result of making the fresh determination required by subsection (4) of this section, the amount to be recovered exceeds the amount set by the current determination, the court may substitute for the amount to be recovered under the confiscation order which was made by reference to the current determination such greater amount as it thinks just in all the circumstances of the case.

(11) No application shall be entertained by the court under this section if it is made after the end of the period of six years beginning with the date on which the defendant was convicted.][1]

Amendments

1   Section 8E inserted by Criminal Justice (Terrorist Offences) Act 2005, s 22.

---

9   Confiscation orders: offences other than drug trafficking offences

(1) Where a person has been sentenced or otherwise dealt with in respect of an offence[, other than a drug trafficking offence or an offence of financing terrorism,][1] of which he has been convicted on indictment, then, if an application is made, or caused to be made, to the court by the Director of Public Prosecutions the court may, subject to the provisions of this section, make a confiscation order under this section requiring the person concerned to pay such sum as the court thinks fit.

(2) An application under this section may be made if it appears to the Director of Public Prosecutions that the person concerned has benefited from the offence of which he is convicted or from that offence taken together with some other offence [(not being a drug trafficking offence or an offence of financing terrorism)][2] of which he is convicted in the same proceedings or which the court has taken into consideration in determining his sentence.

(3) An application under subsection (1) of this section may be made at the conclusion of the proceedings at which the person is sentenced or otherwise dealt with or may be made at a later stage.

(4) For the purposes of this Act, a person benefits from an offence[, other than a drug trafficking offence or an offence of financing terrorism,][3] if he obtains property as a result of or in connection with the commission of that offence and his benefit is the value of the property so obtained.

(5) Where a person derives a pecuniary advantage as a result of or in connection with the commission of an offence, he is to be treated for the purposes of this section as if he had obtained as a result of or in connection with the commission of the offence a sum of money equal to the value of the pecuniary advantage.

(6) The amount to be recovered by an order under this section shall not exceed—

(a) the amount of the benefit or pecuniary advantage which the court is satisfied that a person has obtained, or

(b) the amount appearing to the court to be the amount that might be realised at the time the order is made,

whichever is the less.

(7) The standard of proof required to determine any question arising under this Act as to—

(a) whether a person has benefited as mentioned in subsection (2) of this section, or

(b) the amount to be recovered in his case by virtue of this section,

shall be that applicable in civil proceedings.

Amendments

1 Words substituted for ', other than a drug trafficking offence,' by Criminal Justice (Terrorist Offences) Act 2005, s 23(a).

2 Words substituted for '(not being a drug trafficking offence)' by Criminal Justice (Terrorist Offences) Act 2005, s 23(b).

3 Words substituted for 'other than a drug trafficking offence' by Criminal Justice (Terrorist Offences) Act 2005, s 23(c).

10   Statements relevant to making confiscation orders

[(1) Where a defendant accepts to any extent an allegation in a statement that—

(a) is tendered by or on behalf of the Director of Public Prosecutions to a court that is engaged in a determination under section 4 of this Act as to whether a person has benefited from drug trafficking or as to any amount to be recovered by virtue of that section or to a court that is considering an application under section 7, 8, 8A, 8D, 8E or 9 of this Act, and

(b) concerns any matter relevant—

    (i) to the determination of whether the defendant—

        (I) in the case of a conviction for a drug trafficking offence, has benefited from drug trafficking,

        (II) in the case of a conviction for an offence of financing terrorism, holds funds subject to confiscation, or

        (III) in the case of a conviction for an offence other than a drug trafficking offence or an offence of financing terrorism, has benefited as mentioned in section 9(4) of this Act,

    or

    (ii) to the assessment of the value of the defendant's proceeds of drug trafficking, the value of the funds subject to confiscation or the value of the defendant's benefits as mentioned in section 9(4) of this Act, as the case may be,

the court may, for the purposes of that determination or assessment, treat the defendant's acceptance as conclusive of the matters to which it relates.][1]

(2) Nothing in this section shall prevent the Director of Public Prosecutions from making more than one statement.

(3) Where—

    (a) a statement is tendered under subsection (1) or (2) of this section, and

    (b) the court is satisfied that a copy of that statement has been served on the defendant,

the court may require the defendant to indicate to what extent he accepts each allegation in the statement and, so far as he does not accept any such allegation, to indicate any matters he proposes to rely on to refute such allegation.

[(4) A defendant who fails in any respect to comply with a requirement under subsection (3) of this section may be treated for the purposes of this section as accepting every allegation in the statement other than—

    (a) any allegation in respect of which the defendant has complied with the requirement, and

    (b) any allegation that—

        (i)   in the case of a conviction for one or more drug trafficking offences, the defendant has benefited from drug trafficking or that any payment or reward was received by the defendant in connection with drug trafficking carried on by the defendant or another person,

        (ii) in the case of a conviction for one or more offences of financing terrorism, the defendant holds funds subject to confiscation, or

        (iii) in the case of a conviction for one or more offences, other than a drug trafficking offence or an offence of financing terrorism, the defendant benefited from the offence or property was obtained from the defendant as a result of or in connection with the commission of an offence.][2]

(5) Where—

    (a) there is tendered to the court by the defendant a statement as to any matters relevant to determining the amount that might be realised at the time the confiscation order is made, and

    (b) the Director of Public Prosecutions accepts to any extent any allegation in the statement,

the court may, for the purposes of that determination, treat that acceptance as conclusive of the matters to which it relates.

(6) Nothing in this section shall prevent a defendant from making more than one statement.

(7) An allegation may be accepted or a matter indicated for the purposes of this section—

    (a) orally before the court,

    (b) in writing in accordance with rules of court, or

    (c) as the court may direct.

[(8) No acceptance by the defendant under this section of an allegation that—

    (a) any payment or other reward was received by the defendant in connection with drug trafficking carried on by the defendant or another person,

    (b) the defendant holds funds subject to confiscation, or

    (c) the defendant has benefited from an offence other than a drug trafficking offence or an offence of financing terrorism,

shall be admissible in evidence in any proceedings for an offence.][3]

Amendments

1   Subsection (1)(a) substituted by Criminal Justice Act 1999, s 27, then entire sub-s (1) substituted by Criminal Justice (Terrorist Offences) Act 2005, s 24(a).

2   Subsection (4) substituted by Criminal Justice (Terrorist Offences) Act 2005, s 24(b).

3   Subsection (8) substituted by Criminal Justice (Terrorist Offences) Act 2005, s 24(c).

11   Provision of information by defendant

[(1) This section applies where—

    (a)   a court is engaged in a determination under section 4 of this Act as to whether a convicted person has benefited from drug trafficking or as to any amount to be recovered by virtue of that section, or

    (b)   [an application has been made to a court under section 7, 8, 8A, 8D, 8E or 9 of this Act.]¹]²

(2) For the purpose of obtaining information to assist it in carrying out its functions, the court may, at any time, order the defendant to give it such information as may be specified in the order.

(3) An order under subsection (2) of this section may require all, or any specified part, of the required information to be given to the court in such manner, and before such date, as may be specified in the order.

(4) If the defendant fails, without reasonable excuse, to comply with any order under this section, the court may draw such inference from that failure as it considers appropriate.

(5) Where the Director of Public Prosecutions accepts to any extent any allegation made by the defendant in giving to the court information required by an order under this section, the court may treat that acceptance as conclusive of the matters to which it relates.

(6) For the purposes of this section, an allegation may be accepted in such manner as the court may direct.

[(7) A defendant who—

    (a)   fails, without reasonable excuse, to comply with an order under this section, or

    (b)   gives to the court, in purported compliance with this section, information which the defendant knows or has reason to believe is false or misleading,

shall be guilty of an offence.

(8) A person guilty of an offence under this section shall be liable—

    (a)   on summary conviction, to imprisonment for a term not exceeding 12 months or to a fine not exceeding £1,500 or to both, or

    (b)   on conviction on indictment, to imprisonment for a term not exceeding five years or to a fine or to both.

(9) Information that is specified in an order under this section and is given to the court in compliance with that order shall not be admissible in evidence in any proceedings for an offence, other than an offence under this section.]³

Amendments

1   Subsection 11(1)(b) substituted by Criminal Justice (Terrorist Offences) Act 2005, s 25(b).

2   Subsection (1) substituted by Criminal Justice Act 1999, s 28(1).

3   Subsections (7)–(9) inserted by Criminal Justice Act 1999, s 28(2).

12   Supplementary provisions concerning confiscation orders

(1) When considering whether to make a confiscation order under section 9 of this Act [(but not when considering whether to make such an order under section 4 or 8A of this Act)]¹, the court may take into account any information placed before it showing that a victim of an offence to which the proceedings relate has instituted, or intends to institute, civil proceedings against the defendant in respect of loss, injury or damage sustained in connection with the offence.

(2) Where a court makes a confiscation order, it may direct that payment of the amount to be recovered in respect of the order shall be made forthwith or at some other time specified in the order.

(3) Where a court makes a confiscation order against a defendant in any proceedings, it shall, in respect of any offence of which he is convicted in those proceedings, take account of—

    (a)   any fine imposed on him,

    (b)   any order involving any payment by him, or

    (c)   any forfeiture order made under section 30 of the Misuse of Drugs Act, 1977, or section 61 of this Act.

(4) If the court is satisfied as to any matter relevant for determining the amount that might be realised at the time the confiscation order is made (whether by an acceptance under section 10 of this Act or otherwise), the court may issue a certificate giving the opinion of the court as to the matters concerned and shall do so if satisfied that the amount that might be realised at the time the confiscation order is made is less than the amount the court assesses to be—

    (a)   (in the case of a conviction for a drug trafficking offence or offences) the value of the defendant's proceeds of drug trafficking, or

    [(b)   (in the case of a conviction for one or more offences of financing terrorism) the value of the defendant's funds subject to confiscation, or

    (c)   (in the case of a conviction for an offence or offences other than a drug trafficking offence or an offence of financing terrorism) the value of the defendant's benefit from the offence or offences in respect of which the order may be made.]²

Amendments

1   Words substituted for '(but not when considering whether to make an order under section 4 of this Act)' by Criminal Justice (Terrorist Offences) Act 2005, s 26(a).

2   Subsection (4)(b) substituted and (4)(c) inserted by Criminal Justice (Terrorist Offences) Act 2005, s 26(b).

13   Power of High Court where defendant has died or is absent

(1) Subsection (2) of this section applies where a person has been convicted on indictment of one or more offences.

[(2) The High Court may exercise the powers of a court under section 4, 8A or 9 of this Act to make a confiscation order against the defendant in the case of a conviction for a drug trafficking offence, an offence of financing terrorism or an offence other than a drug trafficking offence or an offence of financing terrorism if—

(a) the Director of Public Prosecutions asks the High Court to proceed under this section, and

(b) the High Court is satisfied that the defendant has died or absconded.]¹

(3) Subsection (4) of this section applies where proceedings for one or more offences in respect of which a confiscation order may be made under this Act have been instituted against a person but have not been concluded.

[(4) The High Court may exercise the powers of a court under section [4, 8A or 9 of this Act to make a confiscation order against the defendant if—

(a) the relevant proceedings have been instituted in respect of a drug trafficking offence, an offence of financing terrorism or an offence other than a drug trafficking offence or an offence of financing terrorism,

(b) the Director of Public Prosecutions asks the High Court to proceed under this section, and

(c) the High Court is satisfied that the defendant has absconded.]²

(5) The power conferred by subsection (4) of this section may not be exercised at any time before the end of the period of two years beginning with the date which is, in the opinion of the court, the date on which the defendant absconded save where it appears to the High Court that it would be reasonable in the circumstances.

(6) In any proceedings on an application under this section—

[(a) sections 5(2), 8B(2), 10(3) and 10(4) of this Act shall not apply,]³

(b) the court shall not make a confiscation order against a person who has absconded unless it is satisfied that the Director of Public Prosecutions has taken reasonable steps to contact him, and

(c) any person appearing to the court to be likely to be affected by the making of a confiscation order by the court shall be entitled to appear before the court and make representations.

Amendments

1   Subsection (2) substituted by Criminal Justice (Terrorist Offences) Act 2005, s 27(a).
2   Subsection (4) substituted by Criminal Justice (Terrorist Offences) Act 2005, s 27(b).
3   Subsection (6)(a) substituted by Criminal Justice (Terrorist Offences) Act 2005, s 27(c).

14 Effect of conviction where High Court has acted under section 13

Where the High Court has made a confiscation order by virtue of section 13 of this Act, the court shall, in respect of the offence or any of the offences concerned take account of the following, namely:

(a) any fine imposed on him,

(b) any order involving any payment by him, or

(c) any forfeiture order made under section 30 of the Misuse of Drugs Act, 1977, or under section 61 of this Act.

15 Appeal against confiscation order

(1) An appeal against the making of a confiscation order shall lie to the Court of Criminal Appeal.

(2) If it upholds the appeal, in whole or in part, the court may, on an application by a person who held property which was realisable property, order compensation to be paid to the applicant if—

(a) it is satisfied that the applicant has suffered loss as a result of the making of the confiscation order; and

(b) having regard to all the circumstances of the case, the court considers it to be appropriate.

(3) The amount of compensation to be paid under this section shall be such as the court considers just in all the circumstances of the case.

16 Variation of confiscation orders

(1) If, on an application by the defendant or by the Director of Public Prosecutions in respect of a confiscation order, the High Court is satisfied that the value of the realisable property is inadequate for the payment of any amount remaining to be recovered under the order, the court shall substitute for the amount to be recovered under the order such lesser amount as the court thinks just in all the circumstances of the case.

(2) For the purposes of subsection (1) of this section—

(a) in the case of realisable property held by a person who has been adjudged bankrupt the court shall take into account the extent to which any property held by him may be distributed among creditors, and

(b) the court may disregard any inadequacy in the value of the realisable property which appears to the court to be attributable wholly or partly to anything done by the defendant for the purpose of preserving any property held by a person to whom the defendant had directly or indirectly made a gift caught by this Act from any risk of realisation under this Act.

17 Variation of confiscation orders made by virtue of section 13

(1) This section applies where—

(a) the High Court has made a confiscation order by virtue of section 13(4) of this Act, and

(b) the defendant has ceased to be an absconder.

(2) If, on an application by the defendant or the Director of Public Prosecutions in respect of the confiscation order, the High Court is satisfied that—

[(a) the value of the defendant's—
    (i) proceeds of drug trafficking,
    (ii) funds subject to confiscation, or
    (iii) benefit as mentioned in section 9(4) of this Act,
    as the case may be, in the period by reference to which the determination in question was made ('the original value'), or]¹
(b) the amount that might have been realised at the time the confiscation order was made,

was less than the amount ordered to be paid under the confiscation order, the court—
[(i) may make a fresh determination of the value of the defendant's—
    (I) proceeds under section 4 of this Act, in the case of a drug trafficking offence,
    (II) funds subject to confiscation under section 8A of this Act, in the case of an offence of financing terrorism, and
    (III) benefit under section 9 of this Act, in the case of an offence other than a drug trafficking offence or an offence of financing terrorism, and]²
(ii) may, if it considers it just in all the circumstances, vary the amount to be recovered under the confiscation order.

(3) For any determination under section 4 of this Act by virtue of this section, section 5(5) shall not apply in relation to any of the defendant's proceeds of drug trafficking taken into account in determining the original value.

[(3A) For any determination under section 8A of this Act by virtue of this section, section 8B(5) shall not apply in relation to any of the defendant's funds subject to confiscation that were taken into account in determining the original value.]³

(4) Where the court varies a confiscation order under this section it may, on an application by a person who held property which was realisable property, order compensation to be paid to the applicant if—
(a) it is satisfied that the applicant has suffered loss as a result of the making of the confiscation order; and
(b) having regard to all the circumstances of the case, the court considers it to be appropriate.

(5) The amount of compensation to be paid under this section shall be such as the court considers just in all the circumstances of the case.

(6) No application shall be entertained by the court under this section if it is made after the end of the period of six years beginning with the date on which the confiscation order was made.

Amendments

1 Subsection (2)(a) substituted by Criminal Justice (Terrorist Offences) Act 2005, s 28(a).
2 Subsection (2)(i) substituted by Criminal Justice (Terrorist Offences) Act 2005, s 28(b).
3 Subsection (3A) inserted by Criminal Justice (Terrorist Offences) Act 2005, s 28(c).

18   Increase in value of realisable property

[(1) This section shall have effect where the amount which a person is ordered to pay by a confiscation order is less than the amount assessed to be the value of the person's—

    (a) proceeds of drug trafficking, in the case of a drug trafficking offence,

    (b) funds subject to confiscation, in the case of an offence of financing terrorism, or

    (c) benefit obtained from an offence other than a drug trafficking offence or an offence of financing terrorism.]¹

(2) If, on an application made by the Director of Public Prosecutions, the High Court is satisfied that the amount ("the first amount") that might be realised in the case of the person in question is greater than the amount taken into account in making the confiscation order (whether it was greater than was thought when the order was made or has subsequently increased), the court may substitute for the first amount such amount (not exceeding the amount assessed as the value referred to in subsection (1) of this section) as appears to the court to be appropriate having regard to the amount now shown to be realisable.

Amendments

1   Subsection (1) substituted by Criminal Justice (Terrorist Offences) Act 2005, s 29.

PART III

ENFORCEMENT, ETC. OF CONFISCATION ORDERS

19   Enforcement of confiscation orders

(1) Where a court makes a confiscation order, then (without prejudice to the provisions of section 22 of this Act enabling property of the defendant in the hands of a receiver appointed under this Act to be applied in satisfaction of the confiscation order) the order may be enforced by the Director of Public Prosecutions at any time after it is made (or, if the order provides for payment at a later time, then at any time after the later time) as if it were a judgment of the High Court for the payment to the State of the sum specified in the order (or of any lesser sum remaining due under the order), save that nothing in this subsection shall enable a person to be imprisoned.

(2) Subject to subsection (3) of this section, if, at any time after payment of a sum due under a confiscation order has become enforceable in the manner provided for by subsection (1) of this section, it is reported to the High Court, by the Director of Public Prosecutions that any such sum or any part thereof remains unpaid, the court may, without prejudice to the validity of anything previously done under the order or to the power to enforce the order in the future in accordance with subsection (1) of this section, order that the defendant shall be imprisoned for a period not exceeding that set out in the second column of the table to this section opposite to the amount set out therein of the confiscation order remaining unpaid.

(3) An order under subsection (2) of this section shall not be made unless the defendant has been given a reasonable opportunity to make any representations to the court that the order should not be made and the court has taken into account any representations so made and any representations made by the Director of Public Prosecutions in reply.

(4) Any term of imprisonment imposed under subsection (2) of this section shall commence on the expiration of any term of imprisonment for which the defendant is liable under the sentence for the offence in question or otherwise, but shall be reduced in proportion to any sum or sums paid or recovered from time to time under the confiscation order.

[TABLE]¹

Amount outstanding under confiscation order	Period of imprisonment
Not exceeding £650	45 days
Exceeding £650 but not exceeding £1,300	3 months
Exceeding £1,300 but not exceeding £3,250	4 months
Exceeding £3,250 but not exceeding £6,500	6 months
Exceeding £6,500 but not exceeding £13,000	9 months
Exceeding £13,000 but not exceeding £26,000	12 months
Exceeding £26,000 but not exceeding £65,000	18 months
Exceeding £65,000 but not exceeding £130,000	2 years
Exceeding £130,000 but not exceeding £325,000	3 years
Exceeding £325,000 but not exceeding £1,300,000	5 years
Exceeding £1,300,000	10 years

Amendments

1 Table substituted by Criminal Justice (Mutual Assistance) Act 2008, s 105(d).

20 Realisation of property

(1) Where—

(a) a confiscation order is made under this Act,

(b) the confiscation order is not subject to appeal, and

(c) the confiscation order has not been satisfied,

the High Court may, on an application by the Director of Public Prosecutions, exercise the powers conferred by subsections (2) to (6) of this section.

(2) The court may appoint a person to be a receiver in respect of realisable property.

(3) The court may empower a receiver appointed under subsection (2) of this section or under section 24 of this Act to take possession of the property subject to such conditions or exceptions as may be specified by the court.

(4) The court may order any person having possession or control of realisable property to give possession of it to the receiver.

(5) The court may empower the receiver to realise any realisable property in such manner as the court may direct.

(6) The court may order any person holding an interest in realisable property to make such payment to the receiver in respect of any beneficial interest held by the defendant or, as the case may be, the recipient of any gift caught by this Act as the court may direct and the court may, on the payment being made, by order transfer, grant or extinguish any interest in the property.

(7) The court shall not, in respect of any property, exercise the powers conferred by subsection (3), (4), (5) or (6) of this section unless a reasonable opportunity has been given for persons holding any interest in the property to make representations to the court.

21   Interest on sums unpaid under confiscation orders

(1) Subject to subsection (2) of this section, if any sum required to be paid by a person under a confiscation order is not paid when it is required to be paid (whether forthwith on the making of an order or at the time specified by the court), that person shall be liable to pay interest on that sum for the period for which it remains unpaid and the amount of the interest shall for the purposes of enforcement be treated as part of the amount to be recovered from him under the confiscation order.

(2) The amount of interest payable under subsection (1) of this section shall be disregarded for the purposes of calculating the term of imprisonment to be imposed by virtue of section 19 of this Act.

(3) The rate of interest payable under subsection (1) of this section shall be that for the time being applying to a High Court civil judgment debt.

22   Application of proceeds of realisation

(1) Money paid or recovered in respect of a confiscation order (including any variation of such an order) may, to the extent necessary, be applied to meet expenses incurred in exercising any powers under this Act and the remuneration of any person employed for that purpose.

(2) Money paid or recovered in respect of a confiscation order shall, following the payment of any expenses or remuneration in accordance with subsection (1) of this section, be applied towards satisfaction of the confiscation order and paid into or disposed of for the benefit of the Exchequer in accordance with the directions of the Minister for Finance.

23   Cases in which restraint orders may be made

[(1) The powers conferred on the High Court by section 24 of this Act shall be exercisable—

    (a) where—

        (i)   proceedings have been instituted in the State against the defendant for a drug trafficking offence, an offence of financing terrorism or an indictable offence (other than a drug trafficking offence or an offence of financing terrorism) or an application has been made in respect of the defendant under section 7, 8, 8D, 8E, 13 or 18 of this Act,

        (ii) the proceedings or application have not been concluded, and

        (iii) either a confiscation order has been made or it appears to the Court that there are reasonable grounds for thinking that a confiscation order may be made in the proceedings or that, in the case of an application under section 7, 8, 8D, 8E, 13 or 18 of this Act, the Court will be satisfied as mentioned in section 7(3), 8(4), 8D(3), 8E(4), 13(2), 13(4) or 18(2) of this Act,

or

(b) where—

  (i) the Court is satisfied that proceedings are to be instituted against a person for a drug trafficking offence, an offence of financing terrorism or an offence in respect of which a confiscation order might be made under section 9 of this Act or that an application of a kind mentioned in paragraph (*a*)(i) of this subsection is to be made in respect of a person, and

  (ii) it appears to the Court that a confiscation order may be made in connection with the offence or that a court will be satisfied as mentioned in paragraph (*a*)(iii) of this subsection.]¹

(2) For the purposes of section 24 of this Act, at any time when those powers are exercisable before proceedings have been instituted—

  (a) references in this Act to the defendant shall be construed as references to the person referred to in subsection (1)(b)(i) of this section, and

  [(b) references in this Act to realisable property shall be construed as if, immediately before that time, proceedings had been instituted against the person referred to in subsection (1)(*b*)(i) of this section for a drug trafficking offence, an offence of financing terrorism or an offence in respect of which a confiscation order might be made under section 9 of this Act.]²

(3) Where the court has made an order under section 24 of this Act by virtue of subsection (1)(b) of this section, the court shall discharge the order if proceedings in respect of the offence are not instituted or the relevant application is not made within such time as the court considers reasonable.

Amendments

1   Subsection (1) substituted by Criminal Justice (Terrorist Offences) Act 2005, s 30(a).
2   Subsection (2)(b) substituted by Criminal Justice (Terrorist Offences) Act 2005, s 30(b).

24   [Freezing orders]¹

(1) The High Court may by order (in this Act referred to as a "[freezing order]¹") prohibit any person from dealing with any realisable property, subject to such conditions and exceptions as may be specified in that order.

(2) Without prejudice to the generality of subsection (1) of this section, a [freezing order]¹ may make such provision as the court thinks fit for living expenses and legal expenses.

(3) A [freezing order]¹ may apply—

  (a) to all realisable property held by a specified person, whether the property is described in the order or not, and

  (b) to realisable property held by a specified person, being property transferred to him after the making of the order.

(4) A [freezing order]¹—

  (a) may be made only on an application by the Director of Public Prosecutions, which may be made ex parte and otherwise than in public, and

(b)   shall provide for notice to be given to persons affected by the order.

(5) A [freezing order]¹—

  (a)   may be discharged or varied in relation to any property, and

  (b)   shall be discharged on the conclusion of the proceedings or of the application in question.

(6) An application for the discharge or variation of a [freezing order]¹ may be made by any person affected by it.

(7) Where the High Court has made a [freezing order]¹, the court may at any time appoint a receiver—

  (a)   to take possession of any realisable property, and

  (b)   in accordance with the court's directions, to manage or otherwise deal with any property in respect of which he is appointed,

subject to such exceptions and conditions as may be specified by the court, and may require any person having possession or control of property in respect of which a receiver is appointed under this section to give possession of it to the receiver.

(8) For the purposes of this Act, dealing with property held by any person includes (without prejudice to the generality of the expression)—

  (a)   where a debt is owed to that person, making a payment to any person in reduction of the amount of the debt, and

  (b)   removing the property from the State.

(9) Where the High Court has made a [freezing order]¹, a member of the Garda Síochána or an officer of customs and excise may, for the purpose of preventing any realisable property being removed from the State, seize the property.

(10) Property seized under subsection (9) of this section shall be dealt with in accordance with the court's directions.

Amendments

1   Words substituted for "restraint order" by Criminal Justice (Mutual Assistance) Act 2008, s 105(a).

---

25   Registration of [freezing orders]¹

(1) Where a [freezing order]¹ is made, the registrar of the High Court shall, in the case of registered land, furnish the Registrar of Titles with notice of the order and the Registrar of Titles shall thereupon cause an entry to be made in the register under the Registration of Title Act, 1964, inhibiting, until such time as the order is discharged, any dealing with any registered land or charge which appears to be affected by the order.

(2) Where notice of an order has been given under subsection (1) of this section and the order is varied, the registrar of the High Court shall furnish the Registrar of Titles with notice to that effect and the Registrar of Titles shall thereupon cause the entry made under subsection (1) of this section to be varied to that effect.

(3) Where notice of an order has been given under subsection (1) of this section and the order is discharged, the registrar of the High Court shall furnish the Registrar of Titles with notice to that effect and the Registrar of Titles shall cancel the entry made under subsection (1) of this section.

(4) Where a [freezing order][1] is made, the registrar of the High Court shall, in the case of unregistered land, furnish the Registrar of Deeds with notice of the order and the Registrar of Deeds shall thereupon cause the notice to be registered in the Registry of Deeds pursuant to the Registration of Deeds Act, 1707.

(5) Where notice of an order has been given under subsection (4) of this section and the order is varied, the registrar of the High Court shall furnish the Registrar of Deeds with notice to that effect and the Registrar of Deeds shall thereupon cause the entry made under subsection (4) of this section to be varied to that effect.

(6) Where notice of an order has been given under subsection (4) of this section and the order is discharged, the registrar of the High Court shall furnish the Registrar of Deeds with notice to that effect and the Registrar of Deeds shall thereupon cancel the entry made under subsection (4) of this section.

(7) Where a [freezing order][1] is made which applies to an interest in a company or to the property of a company, the registrar of the High Court shall furnish the Registrar of Companies with notice of the order and the Registrar of Companies shall thereupon cause the notice to be entered in the Register of Companies maintained under the Companies Acts, 1963 to 1990.

(8) Where notice of an order has been given under subsection (7) of this section and the order is varied, the registrar of the High Court shall furnish the Registrar of Companies with notice to that effect and the Registrar of Companies shall thereupon cause the entry made under subsection (7) of this section to be varied to that effect.

(9) Where notice of an order has been given under subsection (7) of this section and the order is discharged, the registrar of the High Court shall furnish the Registrar of Companies with notice to that effect and the Registrar of Companies shall thereupon cancel the entry made under subsection (7) of this section.

Amendments

1   Words substituted for "restraint order" by Criminal Justice (Mutual Assistance) Act 2008, s 105(a).

---

26   Exercise of powers by High Court or receiver

(1) This section applies to the powers conferred on the High Court by section 20 or 24 of this Act or on a receiver appointed under either of those sections.

(2) Subject to the provisions of this section, the powers shall be exercised with a view to making available, for satisfying the confiscation order or, as the case may be, any confiscation order that may be made in the defendant's case, the value for the time being of realisable property held by any person by the realisation of such property.

(3) In the case of realisable property held by a person to whom the defendant has directly or indirectly made a gift caught by this Act, the powers shall be exercised with a view to realising no more than the value for the time being of the gift.

(4) The powers shall be exercised with a view to allowing any person, other than the defendant or the recipient of any such gift, to retain or recover the value of any property held by him.

(5) In exercising the powers no account shall be taken of any obligations of the defendant or of the recipient of any such gift that conflict with the obligation to satisfy the confiscation order.

27 Receivers: supplementary provisions

Where a receiver takes any action—

    (a) in relation to property which is not realisable property, being action which he would be entitled to take if it were such property,

    (b) believing, and having reasonable grounds for believing, that he is entitled to take that action in relation to that property,

he shall not be liable to any person in respect of any loss or damage resulting from his action except in so far as the loss or damage is caused by his negligence.

28 Bankruptcy of defendant, etc

(1) Where a person who holds realisable property is adjudicated bankrupt—

    (a) property for the time being subject to a [freezing order][1] made before the order adjudicating him bankrupt, and

    (b) any proceeds of property realised by virtue of section 20(5) or (6) or 24(7) of this Act, for the time being in the hands of a receiver,

is excluded from the property of the bankrupt for the purposes of the Bankruptcy Act, 1988.

(2) Where a person has been adjudicated bankrupt, the powers conferred on the High Court or on a receiver by section 20 or 24 of this Act shall not be exercised in relation to property of the bankrupt for the purposes of the said Act of 1988.

(3) Where a person is adjudicated bankrupt and has directly or indirectly made a gift caught by this Act—

    (a) no decision as to whether the gift is void shall be made under section 57, 58 or 59 of the said Act of 1988 in respect of the making of the gift at any time when—

        (i) proceedings for an offence in respect of which a confiscation order might be made have been instituted against him and have not been concluded, or

        [(ii) an application has been made in respect of the defendant under section 7, 8, 8D, 8E, 13 or 18 of this Act and has not been concluded, or][2]

        (iii) property of the person to whom the gift was made is subject to a [freezing order][1],

    and

    (b) any decision as to whether it is void made under any of those sections after the conclusion of the proceedings or of the application shall take into account any realisation under this Act of property held by the person to whom the gift was made.

(4) In any case in which a petition in bankruptcy was presented, or an adjudication in bankruptcy was made, before 1st January, 1989, this section shall have effect with the modification that for references to the property of the bankrupt for the purposes of the said Act of 1988 there shall be substituted references to the property of the bankrupt vesting in the assignees for the purposes of the law of bankruptcy existing before that date.

Amendments

1 Words substituted for "restraint order" by Criminal Justice (Mutual Assistance) Act 2008, s 105(a).

2 Subparagraph (3)(a)(ii) substituted by Criminal Justice (Terrorist Offences) Act 2005, s 31.

29   Property subject to [freezing order][1] dealt with by Official Assignee

(1) Without prejudice to the generality of any provision of any other enactment, where—

(a) the Official Assignee or a trustee appointed under the provisions of Part V of the Bankruptcy Act, 1988, seizes or disposes of any property in relation to which his functions are not exercisable because it is for the time being subject to a [freezing order][1], and

(b) at the time of the seizure or disposal he believes, and has reasonable grounds for believing, that he is entitled (whether in pursuance of an order of the court or otherwise) to seize or dispose of that property,

he shall not be liable to any person in respect of any loss or damage resulting from the seizure or disposal except in so far as the loss or damage is caused by his negligence in so acting, and he shall have a lien on the property, or the proceeds of its sale, for such of his expenses as were incurred in connection with the bankruptcy or other proceedings in relation to which the seizure or disposal purported to take place and for so much of his remuneration as may reasonably be assigned for his acting in connection with those proceedings.

(2) Where the Official Assignee or a trustee appointed as aforesaid incurs expenses in respect of such property as is mentioned in paragraph (a) of subsection (1) of this section and in so doing does not know and has no reasonable grounds to believe that the property is for the time being subject to a [freezing order][1], he shall be entitled (whether or not he has seized or disposed of that property so as to have a lien) to payment of those expenses under section 22 of this Act.

Amendments

1 Words substituted for "restraint order" by Criminal Justice (Mutual Assistance) Act 2008, s 105(a).

30   Winding up of company holding realisable property

(1) Where realisable property is held by a company and an order for the winding up of the company has been made or a resolution has been passed by the company for a voluntary

winding up, the functions of the liquidator (or any provisional liquidator) shall not be exercisable in relation to—

(a) property for the time being subject to a [freezing order]¹ made before the relevant time, and

(b) any proceeds of property realised by virtue of section 20(5) or (6) or 24 (7) of this Act for the time being in the hands of a receiver.

(2) Where, in the case of a company, such an order has been made or such a resolution has been passed, the powers conferred by section 20 or 24 of this Act on the High Court or on a receiver shall not be exercised in relation to any realisable property held by the company in relation to which the functions of the liquidator are exercisable—

(a) so as to inhibit him from exercising those functions for the purpose of distributing any property held by the company to the company's creditors, or

(b) so as to prevent the payment out of any property of expenses (including the remuneration of the liquidator or any provisional liquidator) properly incurred in the winding up in respect of the property.

(3) In this section—

"company" means any company which may be wound up under the Companies Acts, 1963 to 1990;

"relevant time" means—

(a) where no order for the winding up of the company has been made, the time of the passing of the resolution for voluntary winding up,

(b) where such an order has been made and, before the presentation of the petition for the winding up of the company by the court, such a resolution had been passed by the company, the time of the passing of the resolution, and

(c) in any other case where such an order has been made, the time of the making of the order.

Amendments

1   Words substituted for "restraint order" by Criminal Justice (Mutual Assistance) Act 2008, s 105(a).

PART IV
MONEY LAUNDERING

31   Money laundering, etc

[...]¹

Amendments

1   Section 31 repealed by Criminal Justice (Money Laundering and Terrorist Financing) Act 2010, s 4(1).

---

32   Measures to be taken to prevent money laundering

[...]¹

Amendments

1   Section 32 repealed by Criminal Justice (Money Laundering and Terrorist Financing) Act 2010, s 4(1).

[32A   Revenue offence

...]¹

Amendments

1   Section 32A inserted by Criminal Justice (Mutual Assistance) Act 2008, s 105(e) and repealed by Criminal Justice (Money Laundering and Terrorist Financing) Act 2010, s 4(1).

PART V
DRUG TRAFFICKING OFFENCES AT SEA

33   Drug trafficking offences on Irish ships

[(1) A person is guilty of a drug trafficking offence if the person does, on an Irish ship, a ship registered in a Convention state or a ship not registered in any country or territory, any act which, if done in the State, would constitute such an offence.

(2) This section is without prejudice to section 34 of this Act.]¹

Amendments

1   Section 33 substituted by Criminal Justice (Illicit Traffic by Sea) Act 2003, s 28(b).

---

34   Ships used for drug trafficking

(1) This section applies to an Irish ship, a ship registered in a Convention state and a ship not registered in any country or territory.

(2) A person shall be guilty of an offence if, on a ship to which this section applies, wherever it may be, he—

   (a) has a controlled drug in his possession, or

   (b) is in any way knowingly concerned in the carrying or concealing of a controlled drug on the ship, knowing or having reasonable grounds to suspect that the drug is intended to be imported or has been exported contrary to any regulations made by the Minister for Health under section 5(1)(a)(ii) of the Misuse of Drugs Act, 1977, or the law of any state outside the State.

(3) A certificate purporting to be issued by or on behalf of the government of any state other than the State to the effect that the importation or exportation of a controlled drug is prohibited by the law of that state shall in a prosecution under this section be evidence of the matters stated in that certificate without further proof.

(4) A person guilty of an offence under this section shall be liable—

    (a) on summary conviction, to a fine not exceeding £1,000 or to imprisonment for a term not exceeding 12 months or to both, or

    (b) on conviction on indictment, to a fine or to imprisonment for a term not exceeding 7 years or to both.

(5) Section 29(1) of the Misuse of Drugs Act, 1977 (defences generally) is hereby amended by the substitution therefor of the following subsection:

[...]¹

Amendments

1   See the amended Act.

---

35   **Enforcement powers in respect of ships**

(1) The powers conferred on an enforcement officer by the First Schedule to this Act shall be exercisable in relation to any ship to which section 33 or 34 of this Act applies for the purpose of detecting and the taking of appropriate action in respect of the offences mentioned in those sections.

(2) The powers conferred by subsection (1) of this section shall not be exercised outside the [outer limit]¹ of the territorial seas of the State in relation to a ship registered in a Convention state except with the authority of the Minister for Foreign Affairs and he shall not give his authority unless that state has in relation to that ship—

    (a) requested the assistance of the State for the purpose mentioned in subsection (1) of this section, or

    (b) authorised the State to act for that purpose.

(3) In giving his authority pursuant to a request or authorisation from a Convention state, the Minister for Foreign Affairs shall impose such conditions or limitations on the exercise of the powers as may be necessary to give effect to any conditions or limitations imposed by that state.

(4) The Minister for Foreign Affairs may, either of his own motion or in response to a request from a Convention state, authorise a Convention state to exercise, in relation to an Irish ship, powers corresponding to those conferred on enforcement officers by the First Schedule to this Act but subject to such conditions or limitations, if any, as he may impose.

(5) Subsection (4) of this section shall be without prejudice to any agreement made, or which may be made, on behalf of the State whereby the State undertakes not to object to the

exercise by any other state in relation to an Irish ship of powers corresponding to those conferred by the First Schedule to this Act.

(6) The powers conferred by the First Schedule to this Act shall not be exercised in the territorial seas of any state other than the State without the authority of the Minister for Foreign Affairs and he shall not give his authority unless that state has consented to the exercise of those powers.

[(7) Where an enforcement officer is acting under the powers conferred by subsection (1) of this section with the authority of the Minister for Foreign Affairs given under subsection (2) of this section, any person who does or fails to do any act in relation to the officer, which if done or not done in the State in relation to another person would constitute an offence, shall be guilty of that offence.

(8) Requests under this section may be transmitted by facsimile transmission or other electronic means.][2]

Amendment

1   Words substituted for "landward limits" by Criminal Justice (Illicit Traffic by Sea) Act 2003, s 28(c)(i).

2   Subsections (7) and (8) inserted by Criminal Justice (Illicit Traffic by Sea) Act 2003, s 28(c)(ii).

---

36   Jurisdiction and prosecutions in relation to offences on ships

(1) Proceedings under section 33 or 34 of this Act or the First Schedule to this Act in respect of an offence on a ship may be taken in any place in the State and the offence may for all incidental purposes be treated as having been committed in that place.

(2) No such proceedings shall be instituted except by or with the consent of the Director of Public Prosecutions.

(3) Without prejudice to subsection (2) of this section, no proceedings for an offence under section 34 of this Act alleged to have been committed outside the [outer limit][1] of the territorial seas of the State on a ship registered in a Convention state shall be instituted except in pursuance of the exercise, with the authority of the Minister for Foreign Affairs, of the powers conferred by the First Schedule to this Act.

(4) [Section 90 of the Sea-Fisheries and Maritime Jurisdiction Act 2006][2] (consent of Minister for Foreign Affairs for prosecutions for certain offences on foreign ships), shall not apply to the proceedings to which subsection (3) of this section relates.

Amendment

1   Words substituted for "landward limits" by Criminal Justice (Illicit Traffic by Sea) Act 2003, s 28(d).

2   Words substituted for "Section 11 of the Maritime Jurisdiction Act 1959" by Sea-Fisheries and Maritime Jurisdiction Act 2006, s 93(6).

---

37   Convention states

(1) The Minister for Foreign Affairs may by order declare that any state specified in the order is a Convention state.

(2) An order that is in force under subsection (1) of this section shall be evidence that any state specified in the order is a Convention state.

(3) The Minister for Foreign Affairs may by order amend or revoke an order under this section including an order under this subsection.

(4) An order under this section shall, as soon as may be after it is made, be laid before each House of the Oireachtas.

Note

SI 289/2005 declares the following countries to be a Convention state for purposes of this Act; "Republic of Albania, Principality of Andorra, Republic of Austria, Republic of Benin, Central African Republic, Union of the Comoros, Republic of the Congo, Cook Islands, Republic of Djibouti, State of Eritrea, Republic of Estonia, Georgia, Republic of Iceland, Republic of Indonesia, Republic of Iraq, State of Israel, Republic of Kazakhstan, State of Kuwait, Lao People's Democratic Republic, Republic of Lithuania, Republic of Maldives, Republic of Mauritius, Federated States of Micronesia, Mongolia, Republic of Mozambique, New Zealand, Republic of Korea, Republic of Rwanda, Republic of San Marino, Serbia and Montenegro, Republic of Singapore, Republic of South Africa, Kingdom of Thailand, Socialist Republic of Vietnam."

PART VI
[SEARCH FOR, SEIZURE AND DISPOSAL OF MONEY GAINED FROM, OR FOR USE IN, CRIMINAL CONDUCT][1]

Amendment

1   Words substituted for "Drug Trafficking Money Imported or Exported in Cash" by Proceeds of Crime (Amendment) Act 2005, s 19.

---

38   Seizure and detention

[(1) A member of the Garda Síochána or an officer of customs and excise may search a person if the member or officer has reasonable grounds for suspecting that—

  (a)   the person is importing or exporting, or intends or is about to import or export, an amount of cash which is not less than the prescribed sum, and

(b) the cash directly or indirectly represents the proceeds of crime or is intended by any person for use in connection with any criminal conduct.

(1A) A member of the Garda Síochána or an officer of the Revenue Commissioners may seize and in accordance with this section detain any cash (including cash found during a search under subsection (1)) if—

    (a) its amount is not less than the prescribed sum, and

    (b) he or she has reasonable grounds for suspecting that it directly or indirectly represents the proceeds of crime or is intended by any person for use in any criminal conduct.]¹

(2) Cash seized by virtue of this section shall not be detained for more than forty-eight hours unless its detention beyond forty-eight hours is authorised by an order made by a judge of the District Court and no such order shall be made unless the judge is satisfied—

    (a) that there are reasonable grounds for the suspicion mentioned in subsection (1) of this section, and

    (b) that detention of the cash beyond forty-eight hours is justified while its origin or derivation is further investigated or consideration is given to the institution (whether in the State or elsewhere) of criminal proceedings against any person for an offence with which the cash is connected.

(3) Any order under subsection (2) of this section shall authorise the continued detention of the cash to which it relates for such period, not exceeding three months beginning with the date of the order, as may be specified in the order, and a judge of the District Court, if satisfied as to the matters mentioned in that subsection, may thereafter from time to time by order authorise the further detention of the cash but so that—

    (a) no period of detention specified in such an order, shall exceed three months beginning with the date of the order; and

    (b) the total period of detention shall not exceed two years from the date of the order under subsection (2) of this section.

[(3A) Where an application is made under section 39(1) for an order for the forfeiture of cash detained under this section, the cash shall, notwithstanding subsection (3), continue to be so detained until the application is finally determined.]²

(4) Any application for an order under subsection (2) or (3) of this section may be made by a member of the Garda Síochána or an officer of customs and excise.

(5) At any time while cash is detained by virtue of the foregoing provisions of this section a judge of the District Court may direct its release if satisfied—

    (a) on an application made by the person from whom it was seized or a person by or on whose behalf it was being imported or exported, that there are no, or are no longer, any such grounds for its detention as are mentioned in subsection (2) of this section, or

    (b) on an application made by any other person, that detention of the cash is not for that or any other reason justified.

(6) If at a time when any cash is being detained by virtue of the foregoing provisions of this section—

    (a) an application for its forfeiture is made under section 39 of this Act; or

    (b) proceedings are instituted (whether in the State or elsewhere) against any person for an offence with which the cash is connected, the cash shall not be released until any proceedings pursuant to the application or, as the case may be, the proceedings for that offence have been concluded.

Amendments

1   Subsection (1) substituted and sub-s (1A) inserted by Proceeds of Crime (Amendment) Act 2005, s 20(a).

2   Subsection (3A) inserted by Proceeds of Crime (Amendment) Act 2005, s 20(b).

Note

The prescribed sum is £5,000 by virtue of SI 167/1996.

39   Forfeiture of cash seized under section 38

(1) A judge of the Circuit Court may order the forfeiture of any cash which has been seized under section 38 of this Act if satisfied, on an application made while the cash is detained under that section, that the cash directly or indirectly represents [the proceeds of crime or is intended by any person for use in connection with any criminal conduct][1].

(2) Any application under this section shall be made, or caused to be made, by the Director of Public Prosecutions.

(3) The standard of proof in proceedings on an application under this section shall be that applicable to civil proceedings; and an order may be made under this section whether or not proceedings are brought against any person for an offence with which the cash in question is connected.

Amendments

1   Words substituted for "any person's proceeds of, or is intended by any person for use in, drug trafficking" by Proceeds of Crime (Amendment) Act 2005, s 21.

40   Appeal against section 39 order

(1) This section applies where an order for the forfeiture of cash (in this section known as "the section 39 order") is made under section 39 of this Act.

(2) Any party to the proceedings in which the section 39 order is made (other than the Director of Public Prosecutions) may, before the end of the period of 30 days beginning with the date on which it is made, appeal in respect of the order to the High Court.

(3) An appeal under this section shall be by way of a rehearing.

(4) On an application made by the appellant to a judge of the Circuit Court at any time, the judge may order the release of so much of the cash to which the section 39 order relates as he considers appropriate to enable the appellant to meet his legal expenses in connection with the appeal.

(5) When hearing an appeal under this section the High Court may make such order as it considers appropriate.

(6) If it upholds the appeal, the judge may order the release of the cash, or (as the case may be) the remaining cash, together with any accrued interest.

(7) Section 39(3) of this Act shall apply in relation to a rehearing on an appeal under this section as it applies to proceedings under section 39 of this Act.

41 Interest

Cash seized under this Part of this Act and detained for more than forty-eight hours shall, unless required as evidence of an offence, be held in an interest-bearing account and the interest accruing on any such cash shall be added to that cash on its forfeiture or release.

42 Procedure

(1) An order under section 38(2) of this Act shall provide for notice to be given to persons affected by the order.

(2) Provision may be made by rules of court with respect to applications or appeals to any court under this Part of this Act, for the giving of notice of such applications or appeals to persons affected, for the joinder of such persons as parties and generally with respect to the procedure under this Part of this Act before any court.

43 Interpretation of Part VI

[(1) In this Part of this Act—

"cash" includes notes and coins in any currency, postal orders, cheques of any kind (including travellers' cheques), bank drafts, bearer bonds and bearer shares;

"criminal conduct" means any conduct which—

    (a) constitutes an offence or more than one offence, or

    (b) where the conduct occurs outside the State, constitutes an offence under the law of the state or territory concerned and would constitute an offence or more than one offence if it occurred within the State;

"exported", in relation to any cash, includes its being brought to any place in the State for the purpose of being exported;

"proceeds of crime" has the meaning given to that expression by section 1(1) (as amended by section 3 of the Proceeds of Crime (Amendment) Act 2005) of the Proceeds of Crime Act 1996.][1]

(2) In section 38 of this Act "the prescribed sum" means such sum as may for the time being be prescribed for the purposes of that section by any regulations made under section 44 of this Act.

Amendments

1   Subsection (1) substituted by Proceeds of Crime (Amendment) Act 2005, s 22.

44   Prescribed sum for purposes of section 38

(1) The Minister may by regulations prescribe a sum for the purposes of section 38 of this Act and in determining under that section whether an amount of foreign currency is not less than the prescribed sum that amount shall be converted at the prevailing rate of exchange.

(2) Where it is proposed to make regulations under subsection (1) of this section, a draft of the regulations shall be laid before each House of the Oireachtas and the regulations shall not be made until a resolution approving of such draft has been passed by each such House.

45   Disposal of cash etc. forfeited under section 39

Any money representing cash which is forfeited under this Part of this Act or accrued interest thereon shall, following the payment of any expenses or remuneration that may have arisen in relation to such forfeiture, be paid into or disposed of for the benefit of the Exchequer in accordance with the directions of the Minister for Finance.

PART VII

INTERNATIONAL CO-OPERATION

[...]¹

Amendments

1   Part VII repealed with saver by Criminal Justice (Mutual Assistance) Act 2008, s 10(a). The repealing is without prejudice to the Criminal Justice (Mutual Assistance) Act 2008, s 11.

PART VIII

SUPPLEMENTARY

57   Disclosure of information

[...]¹

(7) Where a person or body—

    (a)   [...]¹

    (b)   discloses in good faith to a member of the Garda Síochána or any person concerned [in the investigation or prosecution of a drug trafficking offence, an offence of financing terrorism or an offence in respect of which a confiscation order might be made under section 9 of this Act]² a suspicion, or any matter on which such a suspicion is based, that any property—

        (i)   has been obtained as a result of or in connection with the commission of any such offence, or

        (ii)   derives from property so obtained,

the disclosure shall not be treated as a breach of any restriction upon the disclosure of information imposed by statute or otherwise and shall not involve the person or body making the disclosure (including their directors, employees and officers) in liability of any kind.

Amendments

1   Subsections (1)–(6) and (7)(a) repealed by Criminal Justice (Money Laundering and Terrorist Financing) Act 2010, s 4(1).

2   Words substituted for "in the investigation or prosecution of a drug trafficking offence or an offence in respect of which a confiscation order might be made under section 9 of this Act" by Criminal Justice (Terrorist Offences) Act 2005, s 36(c).

[57A   Designation of certain states or territorial units

...]¹

Amendments

1   Section 57A inserted by Criminal Justice (Theft and Fraud Offences) Act, 2001, s 23 and repealed by Criminal Justice (Money Laundering and Terrorist Financing) Act 2010, s 4(1).

58   Offences of prejudicing investigation

(1) Where, in relation to [an investigation into drug trafficking, into whether a person holds funds subject to confiscation or into whether a person has benefited from an offence in respect of which a confiscation order might be made]¹, an order under section 63 of this Act has been made, or has been applied for and has not been refused, or a warrant under section 55 or 64 of this Act has been issued, a person who, knowing or suspecting that the investigation is taking place, makes any disclosure which is likely to prejudice the investigation shall be guilty of an offence.

(2) [...]².

(3) In proceedings against a person for an offence under this section, it is a defence for that person to prove—

(a)   that he did not know or suspect that the disclosure to which the proceedings relate was likely to prejudice the investigation, or

(b)   that he had lawful authority or reasonable excuse for making the disclosure.

(4) A person guilty of an offence under this section shall be liable—

(a)   on summary conviction, to a fine not exceeding £1,000 or to imprisonment for a term not exceeding 12 months or to both, or

(b)   on conviction on indictment, to a fine or to imprisonment for a term not exceeding 5 years or to both.

Amendments

1   Words substituted for "an investigation into drug trafficking or into whether a person has benefited from an offence in respect of which a confiscation order might be made" by Criminal Justice (Terrorist Offences) Act 2005, s 37(a).

s 57A

,dies corporate

...ınder this Act has been committed by a body corporate and is proved to ha. ...ed with the consent or connivance of or to be attributable to any neglect on the part ... son, being a director, manager, secretary or other officer of the body corporate, or a person who was purporting to act in any such capacity, that person, as well as the body corporate, shall be guilty of the offence and shall be liable to be proceeded against and punished accordingly.

(2) Where the affairs of a body corporate are managed by its members, subsection (1) of this section shall apply in relation to the acts and defaults of a member in connection with his functions of management as if he were a director or manager of the body corporate.

60   Voidance of dispositions designed to frustrate confiscation, etc

Where any property of whatever kind and wherever situated, or any interest in such property, becomes subject to confiscation, forfeiture or any measure of [restraint (including a freezing order)]¹ or control by virtue of any provision of this Act (including any provision for giving effect to orders made under the law of any country or territory outside the State) or of any action taken under any such provision, no purported disposition of the property or interest, and no other action purporting to be taken in respect of it, by or on behalf of any owner or other person having or claiming to have any interest in it (whether as beneficial owner or trustee or in any other capacity) in reliance on the law of any country or territory outside the State shall have effect so as to prevent the confiscation, forfeiture or measure from taking effect as provided by this Act.

Amendments

1   Words "restraint (including a freezing order)" substituted for "restraint" by Criminal Justice (Mutual Assistance) Act 2008, s 105(f).

61   Forfeiture orders

(1) Subject to the following provisions of this section, where a person is convicted of an offence, and—

(a) the court by or before which he is convicted is satisfied that any property which has been lawfully seized from him or which was in his possession or under his control at the time when he was apprehended for the offence or when a summons in respect of it was issued—

(i) has been used for the purpose of committing, or facilitating the commission of, any offence, or

(ii) was intended by him to be used for that purpose,

or

(b) the offence, or an offence which the court has taken determining his sentence, consists of unlawful possession c

    (i) has been lawfully seized from him, or

    (ii) was in his possession or under his control at 1 apprehended for the offence of which he has be(summons in respect of that offence was issued,

the court may make an order under this section (referred to in this Act as a "forfeiture order") in respect of that property, and may do so whether or not it also deals with the offender in respect of the offence in any other way.

[(1A) Where—

(a) a person has been convicted of an offence under section 3 or 4 of the Explosive Substances Act, 1883, section 15 of the Firearms Act, 1925, [section 27A of the Firearms Act 1964 or section 6 of the Act of 2005]², and

(b) a forfeiture order may be made in the case of that person by virtue of subsection (1) of this section in respect of property to which that subsection applies,

the court shall, subject to subsection (5) of this section, make the forfeiture order, unless, having regard to the matters mentioned in subsection (2) of this section and to the nature and degree of seriousness of the offence of which the person has been convicted, it is satisfied that there would be a serious risk of injustice if it made the order.]¹

(2) In considering whether to make a forfeiture order in respect of any property a court shall have regard—

(a) to the value of the property, and

(b) to the likely financial and other effects on the offender of the making of the order (taken together with any other order that the court contemplates making).

(3) Facilitating the commission of an offence shall be taken for the purposes of this section to include the taking of any steps after it has been committed for the purpose of disposing of any property to which the offence relates or of avoiding, or enabling any other person to avoid, apprehension or detection.

(4) An order under this section shall operate to deprive the offender of his rights, if any, in the property to which it relates, and the property shall (if not already in their possession) be taken into the possession of the Garda Síochána.

(5) A court shall not order property to be forfeited under this section if a person claiming to be the owner of it or otherwise interested in it applies to be heard by the court, unless an opportunity has been given to him to show cause why the order should not be made.

[(5A) A court may, in making a forfeiture order, include such provisions in that order, or, as the case may require, may make an order supplemental to that order that contains such provisions, as appear to it to be necessary to protect any interest in the property, the subject of the forfeiture order, of a person other than the offender.]³

(6) An order under this section shall not take effect until the ordinary time for instituting an appeal against the conviction or order concerned has expired or, where such an appeal is instituted, until it or any further appeal is finally decided or abandoned or the ordinary time for instituting any further appeal has expired.

(7) The Police Property Act, 1897, shall apply, with the following modifications, to property which is in the possession of the Garda Síochána by virtue of this section, that is to say:

no application shall be made under section 1(1) of that Act by any claimant of the property after the expiration of 6 months from the date on which the order in respect of the property was made under this section, and

(b) no such application shall succeed unless the claimant satisfies the court either that he had not consented to the offender having possession of the property or that he did not know, and had no reason to suspect, that the property was likely to be used for a purpose mentioned in subsection (1) of this section.

(8) In relation to property which is in the possession of the Garda Síochána by virtue of this section, the power to make regulations under section 2(1) of the Police Property Act, 1897 (disposal of property in cases where the owner of the property has not been ascertained etc.), shall include power to make regulations for disposal in cases where no application by a claimant of the property has been made within the period specified in subsection (7)(a) of this section or no such application has succeeded.

(9) Nothing in this section shall affect the provisions of any enactment whereby property is, or may be ordered to be, forfeited as a result of a conviction for an offence.

Amendments

1   Subsection (1A) inserted by Offences Against the State (Amendment) Act 1998, s 17(a).

2   Words substituted for "or section 27A of the Firearms Act, 1964" by Criminal Justice (Terrorist Offences) Act 2005, s 38.

3   Subsection (5A) inserted by Offences Against the State (Amendment) Act 1998, s 17(b).

---

62   Forfeiture for drug offences

Section 30(1) of the Misuse of Drugs Act, 1977 (forfeiture on conviction of an offence under that Act) is hereby amended by the substitution therefor of the following subsection:

[...]¹

Amendments

1   See the amended Act.

---

63   Order to make material available

[(1) For the purposes of an investigation into whether a person has engaged in criminal conduct or criminal proceedings in relation thereto, a member of the Garda Síochána may apply for an order under subsection (3) of this section in relation to any particular material or material of a particular description to a judge of the District Court for the district where the material is situated.

(2) On such an application the judge may make an order under subsection (3) of this section, if satisfied—

(a)   that there are reasonable grounds for suspectting that the person has engaged in criminal conduct,

(b)   that the material concerned is likely to be of substantial value (whether by itself or together with other material) for the purposes of such investigation or proceedings, and

(c)   that there are reasonable grounds for believing that material should be produced or that access to it should be given, having regard to the benefit likely to accrue to the investigation or proceedings and any other relevant circumstances.

(3) An order under this subsection—

(a)   shall require any person who appears to the judge to be in possession of the material—

(i)   to produce it to a named member of the Garda Síochána so that he or she may take it away, or

(ii)   to give the member access to it within 7 days, unless it appears to the judge that another period would be appropriate in the particular circumstances of the case,

(b)   may, if the order relates to material at any place and on application by the member concerned, require any person who appears to the judge to be entitled to grant entry to the place to allow the member to enter it to obtain access to the material,

(c)   shall authorise the member, if the person so required to grant entry to the place does not do so—

(i)   to enter the place, accompanied by such other members or persons or both as the member thinks necessary, on production if so requested of the order and, if necessary, by the use of reasonable force,

(ii)   to search the place and any persons present there,

(iii)   to take away the material, and

(iv)   to take such other steps as appear to the member to be necessary for preserving the material and preventing interference with it.

(4) Where the material consists of information contained in a computer, an order under subsection (3) of this section shall have effect as an order to produce the material, or to give access to it, in a form which is legible and comprehensible or can be made so and in which it can be taken away.

(5) Such an order—

(a)   in so far as it may empower a member to take away a document or to be given access to it, shall authorise him or her to make a copy of it and to take the copy away,

(b)   shall not confer any right to production of, or access to, any material subject to legal privilege, and

(c)   subject to paragraph (b) of this subsection and subsection (10) of this section, shall have effect notwithstanding any other obligation as to secrecy or other restriction on disclosure of information imposed by statute or otherwise.

(6) Any material taken away by a member under this section may be retained by him or her for use as evidence in any proceedings.

(7) A judge of the District Court may at a sitting of the Court vary or discharge an order under this section on the application of a member or any person to whom the order relates.

(8) A member searching a place under the authority of an order under this section may—

    (a) require any person present at the place where the search is being carried out to give his or her name and address to the member, and

    (b) arrest without warrant any person who—

        (i) obstructs or attempts to obstruct the member in the carrying out of his or her duties,

        (ii) fails to comply with a requirement under paragraph (*a*) of this subsection, or

        (iii) gives a name or address which the member has reasonable cause to believe is false or misleading.

(9) A person who—

    (a) obstructs or attempts to obstruct a member acting under the authority of an order under this section,

    (b) fails to comply with a requirement under subsection (3)(a) of this section, or

    (c) gives a false or misleading name or address to a member,

shall be guilty of an offence and liable on summary conviction to a fine not exceeding €2,500 or imprisonment for a term not exceeding 6 months or both.

(10) Where—

    (a) material has been supplied to a Government department or other authority by or on behalf of the government of another state, and

    (b) an undertaking was given that the material would be used only for a particular purpose or purposes,

an order under subsection (3) of this section shall not have the effect of requiring or permitting the production of, or the giving of access to, the material for any other purpose without the consent of that government.

(11) In this section—

"criminal conduct" means—

    (a) drug trafficking,

    (b) the commission of an indictable offence or more than one such offence,

    (c) holding funds subject to confiscation,

    (d) benefiting from—

        (i) drug trafficking,

        (ii) an indictable offence or more than one such offence,

        (iii) assets or proceeds deriving from criminal conduct or the receipt or control of such assets or proceeds, including conduct which occurs outside the State and which would constitute an indictable offence or more than one such offence—

            (I) if it occurred in the State, and

            (II) if it constituted an offence or more than one such offence under the law of the state or territory concerned.][1]

Amendments

1   Section 63 substituted by Criminal Justice (Mutual Assistance) Act 2008, s 105(g).

[**63A   Furnishing of certain information by Revenue Commissioners, etc.**

(1) In this section—

"relevant investigation" means an investigation of a kind referred to in subsection (1) of section 63 of this Act;

"relevant person" means—

(a)   a member of the Garda Síochána not below the rank of Chief Superintendent, or

(b)   the head of any body, or any member of that body nominated by the head of the body, being a body established by or under statute or by the Government, the purpose. or one of the principal purposes of which is—

   (i)   the identification of the assets of persons which derive or are suspected to derive, directly or indirectly, from criminal activity,

   (ii)   the taking of appropriate action under the law to deprive or to deny those persons of the assets or the benefit of such assets, in whole or in part, as may be appropriate, and

   (iii)   the pursuit of any investigation or the doing of any other preparatory work in relation to any proceedings arising from the objectives mentioned in subparagraphs (i) and (ii).

(2) If, having regard to information obtained from a relevant person or otherwise, the Revenue Commissioners have reasonable grounds—

(a)   for suspecting that a person may have derived profits or gains from an unlawful source or activity, and

(b)   for forming the opinion that—

   (i)   information in their possession is likely to be of value to a relevant investigation which may be, or may have been, initiated, and

   (ii)   it is in the public interest that the information should be produced or that access to it should be given,

   then, the Revenue Commissioners shall, subject to subsection (4) of this section and notwithstanding any obligation as to secrecy or other restriction upon disclosure of information imposed by or under any statute or otherwise, produce, or provide access to, such information to a relevant person.

(3) (a)   The Revenue Commissioners may authorise any officer of the Revenue Commissioners serving in a grade not lower than that of Principal Officer or its equivalent to perform any acts and discharge any functions authorised by this section to be performed or discharged by the Revenue Commissioners and references in this section, other than in this subsection, to the Revenue Commissioners shall, with any necessary modifications, be construed as including references to an officer so authorised.

(b) The Revenue Commissioners may by notice in writing revoke an authorisation given by them under this section, without prejudice to the validity of anything previously done thereunder.

(c) In any proceedings arising out of a relevant investigation, a certificate signed by a Revenue Commissioner or an officer authorised under paragraph (a) of this subsection, as the case may be, certifying that information specified in the certificate has been produced to or access to such information has been provided to a relevant person shall, unless the contrary is proved, be evidence without further proof of the matters stated therein or of the signature thereon.

(4) Where information has been supplied to the Revenue Commissioners by or on behalf of the government of another state in accordance with an undertaking (express or implied) on the part of the Revenue Commissioners that the material will be used only for a particular purpose or purposes, no action under this section shall have the effect of requiring or permitting the production of, or the provision of access to, the information for a purpose other than one permitted in accordance with the undertaking and the information shall not, without the consent of the other state, be further disclosed or used otherwise than in accordance with the undertaking.]¹

Amendments

1   Section 63A inserted by Disclosure of Certain Information for Taxation and Other Purposes Act 1996, s 1.

---

64   Authority for search

[(1) A member of the Garda Síochána may apply to a judge of the District Court for a warrant under this section in relation to specified premises for the purposes of an investigation into any of the following matters:

(a) drug trafficking;

(b) the commission of an offence of financing terrorism;

(c) the commission of an offence under section 31 of this Act;

(d) whether a person has benefited from drug trafficking;

(e) whether a person holds funds subject to confiscation;

(f) whether a person has benefited from an offence in respect of which a confiscation order might be made under section 9 of this Act.]¹

(2) On an application being made under subsection (1) of this section, the judge may issue a warrant authorising a specified member of the Garda Síochána, accompanied by such other [persons]² as the member thinks necessary, to enter, by force if necessary, and search the premises if he is satisfied—

(a) that an order made under section 63 of this Act in relation to material on the premises has not been complied with, or

(b) that the conditions in subsection (3) of this section are fulfilled, or

(c) that the conditions in subsection (4) of this section are fulfilled.

(3) The conditions referred to in subsection (2)(b) of this section are—

[(a) that there are reasonable grounds for suspecting that a specified person—

  (i) has carried on drug trafficking,

  (ii) has committed an offence of financing terrorism,

  (iii) has committed an offence under section 31 of this Act,

  (iv) has benefited from drug trafficking,

  (v) holds funds subject to confiscation, or

  (vi) has benefited from an offence in respect of which a confiscation order might be made under section 9 of this Act, and][3]

(b) that the conditions in section 63(4)(b) and (c) of this Act are fulfilled in relation to any material on the premises, and

(c) that it would not be appropriate to make an order under that section in relation to the material because—

  (i) it is not practicable to communicate with any person entitled to produce the material, or

  (ii) it is not practicable to communicate with any person entitled to grant access to the material or entitled to grant entry to the premises on which the material is situated, or

  (iii) the investigation for the purpose of which the application is made might be seriously prejudiced unless a member of the Garda Síochána could secure immediate access to the material.

(4) The conditions referred to in subsection (2)(c) of this section are—

[(a) that there are reasonable grounds for suspecting that a specified person—

  (i) has carried on drug trafficking,

  (ii) has committed an offence of financing terrorism,

  (iii) has committed an offence under section 31 of this Act,

  (iv) has benefited from drug trafficking,

  (v) holds funds subject to confiscation, or

  (vi) has benefited from an offence in respect of which a confiscation order might be made under section 9 of this Act, and

(b) that there are reasonable grounds for suspecting that there is on the premises material that—

  (i) relates to the specified person or to—

    (I) drug trafficking,

    (II) an offence of financing terrorism,

    (III) an offence under section 31 of this Act, or

    (IV) an offence in respect of which a confiscation order might be made under section 9 of this Act,

    and

  (ii) is likely to be of substantial value (whether by itself or together with other material) to the investigation for the purpose of which the application is made, and

  (iii) cannot be particularised at the time of the application, and][4]

(c) that—
- (i) it is not practicable to communicate with any person entitled to grant entry to the premises, or
- (ii) entry to the premises will not be granted unless a warrant is produced, or
- (iii) the investigation for the purpose of which the application is made might be seriously prejudiced unless a member of the Garda Síochána arriving at the premises could secure immediate entry to them.

(5) Where a member of the Garda Síochána has entered premises in the execution of a warrant issued under this section, he may seize and retain any material, other than items subject to legal privilege, which is likely to be of substantial value (whether by itself or together with other material) to the investigation for the purpose of which the warrant was issued.

Amendments

1   Subsection (1) substituted by Criminal Justice (Terrorist Offences) Act 2005, s 40(a).
2   Word substituted for "members of the Garda Síochána" by Disclosure of Certain Information for Taxation and Other Purposes Act 1996, s 4.
3   Subsection (3)(a) substituted by Criminal Justice (Terrorist Offences) Act 2005, s 40(b).
4   Subsection (4)(a) and (b) substituted by Criminal Justice (Terrorist Offences) Act 2005, s 40(c).

---

65   Compensation

(1) [If proceedings are instituted against a person for a drug trafficking offence, an offence of financing terrorism, an offence in respect of which a compensation order might be made under section 9 of this Act, or for more than one of any of those offences][1] and either—
- (a) the proceedings do not result in his conviction for any such offence, or
- (b) where he is convicted of one or more such offences—
  - (i) the conviction or convictions concerned are quashed, or
  - (ii) he is pardoned by the President in respect of the conviction or convictions concerned,

the High Court may, on an application by a person who held property which was realisable property, order compensation to be paid to the applicant if, having regard to all the circumstances, it considers it appropriate to make such an order.

(2) The court shall not order compensation to be paid in any case under this section unless the court is satisfied—
- (a) that there has been some serious default on the part of a person concerned in the investigation or prosecution of the offence concerned, and
- (b) that the applicant has suffered loss in consequence of anything done in relation to the property by or in pursuance of an order under this Act.

(3) The court shall not order compensation to be paid under this section in any case where it appears to the court that the proceedings would have been instituted or continued even if the serious default had not occurred.

(4) The court may order compensation to be paid under this section to a person with an interest in property affected by a confiscation order or a [freezing order]² notwithstanding that he is not the person who was the subject of the relevant investigation or prosecution.

(5) The compensation to be paid under this section shall be such amount as the court thinks just in all the circumstances of the case.

Amendments

1   Words substituted for "If proceedings are instituted against a person for a drug trafficking offence or offences or for an offence or offences in respect of which a confiscation order might be made under section 9 of this Act" by Criminal Justice (Terrorist Offences) Act 2005, s 41.

2   Words substituted for "restraint order" by Criminal Justice (Mutual Assistance) Act 2008, s 105(a).

---

66   Compensation, etc. where absconder is acquitted

(1) This section applies where—

   (a)   the High Court has made a confiscation order in the exercise of its powers under section 13(4) of this Act, and

   (b)   the defendant is subsequently tried for the offence or offences concerned and acquitted on all counts.

(2) The court by which the defendant is acquitted shall cancel the confiscation order.

(3) The High Court may, on the application of a person who held property which was realisable property, order compensation to be paid to the applicant if it is satisfied that the applicant has suffered loss as a result of the making of the confiscation order.

(4) The amount of compensation to be paid under this section shall be such as the court considers just n all the circumstances of the case.

(5) Where the court cancels a confiscation order under this section it may make such consequential or incidental order as it considers appropriate in connection with the cancellation.

67   Power to discharge confiscation order and order compensation when absconder returns

(1) This section applies where—

   (a)   the High Court has made a confiscation order by virtue of section 13(4) of this Act in relation to an absconder,

   (b)   the defendant has ceased to be an absconder, and

   (c)   section 66 of this Act does not apply.

(2) The High Court may, on the application of the defendant, cancel the confiscation order if it is satisfied that—

   (a)   there has been undue delay in continuing the proceedings in respect of which the power under section 13(4) of this Act was exercised; or

   (b)   the Director of Public Prosecutions does not intend to proceed with the prosecution.

(3) Where the High Court cancels a confiscation order under this section it may, on the application of a person who held property which was realisable property, order compensation to be paid to the applicant if it is satisfied that the applicant has suffered loss as a result of the making of the confiscation order.

(4) The amount of compensation to be paid under this section shall be such as the court considers just in all the circumstances of the case.

(5) Where the court cancels a confiscation order under this section it may make such consequential or incidental order as it considers appropriate in connection with the cancellation.

68   Expenses

The expenses incurred in the administration of this Act shall, to such extent as may be sanctioned by the Minister for Finance, be paid out of moneys provided by the Oireachtas.

FIRST SCHEDULE
ENFORCEMENT POWERS IN RESPECT OF SHIPS

Section 35.

Preliminary

1. (1) In this Schedule—

"an enforcement officer" means—

  (a) a member of the Garda Síochána,

  (b) an officer of customs and excise,

  (c) a member of the Naval Service of the Defence Forces not below the rank of petty officer, and

  (d) any other person of a description specified in an order made for the purposes of this Schedule by the Minister;

"the ship" means the ship in relation to which the powers conferred by this Schedule are exercised.

(2) An order under this Schedule (including an order made under this subparagraph) may be amended or revoked by the Minister.

(3) Every order made under this Schedule shall be laid before each House of the Oireachtas as soon as may be after it is made and, if a resolution annulling the order is passed by either such House within the next 21 days on which that House has sat after the order is laid before it, the order shall be annulled accordingly, but without prejudice to the validity of anything previously done thereunder.

Power to stop, board, divert and detain a ship

2. (1) An enforcement officer may stop a ship, board it and, if he thinks it necessary for the exercise of his functions, require it to be taken to a port in the State and detain it there.

(2) Where an enforcement officer is exercising his powers with the authority of the Minister for Foreign Affairs given under section 35 of this Act, the officer may require the ship to be taken to a port in the Convention state in question or, if that state has so requested, in any other country or territory willing to receive it.

686

(3) For any of the purposes of this Schedule an enforcement officer may require the master or any member of the crew to take such action as may be necessary.

(4) If an enforcement officer detains a ship, he shall serve on the master a notice in writing that it is to be detained until the notice is withdrawn by the service on him of a further notice in writing signed by an enforcement officer.

Power to search and obtain information

3. (1) An enforcement officer may search the ship, anyone on it and anything on it including its cargo.

(2) An enforcement officer may require any person on the ship to give information concerning himself or anything on the ship.

(3) Without prejudice to the generality of the powers conferred by this paragraph, an enforcement officer may—

    (a) open any container,

    (b) make tests and take samples of anything on the ship,

    (c) require the production of documents, books or records relating to the ship or anything on it,

    (d) make photographs or copies of anything whose production he has power to require.

Powers in respect of suspected offence

4. If an enforcement officer has reasonable grounds to suspect that [a drug trafficking offence][1] has been committed on a ship to which that section applies he may—

    (a) arrest without warrant anyone whom he has reasonable grounds for suspecting to be guilty of the offence, and

    (b) seize and detain anything found on the ship which appears to him to be evidence of the offence,

and section 9(1) of the Criminal Law Act, 1976, shall apply in relation to anything seized under this paragraph.

Amendments

1   Words substituted for "an offence mentioned in section 33 or 34 of this Act" by Criminal Justice (Illicit Traffic by Sea) Act 2003, s 28(e).

Assistants

5. (1) An enforcement officer may take with him, to assist him in exercising his powers—

    (a) any other persons, and

    (b) any equipment or materials.

(2) A person whom an enforcement officer takes with him to assist him may perform any of the officer's functions but only under the officer's supervision.

Use of reasonable force

6. An enforcement officer may use reasonable force, if necessary, in the performance of his functions.

Evidence of authority

7. An enforcement officer shall, if required, produce evidence of his authority.

Protection of officers

8. An enforcement officer shall not be liable in any civil or criminal proceedings for anything done in the purported performance of his functions under this Schedule if the court is satisfied that the act was done in good faith and that there were reasonable grounds for doing it.

Offences

9. (1) A person shall be guilty of an offence if he—

   (a) intentionally obstructs an enforcement officer in the performance of any of his functions under this Schedule,

   (b) fails without reasonable excuse to comply with a requirement made by an enforcement officer in the performance of those functions, or

   (c) in purporting to give information required by an officer for the performance of those functions—

   (i) makes a statement which he knows to be false in a material particular or recklessly makes a statement which is false in a material particular, or

   (ii) intentionally fails to disclose any material particular.

(2) A person guilty of an offence under this paragraph shall be liable—

   (a) on summary conviction, to a fine not exceeding £1,000 or to imprisonment for a term not exceeding 12 months or to both, or

   (b) on conviction on indictment, to a fine not exceeding £5,000 or to a term of imprisonment not exceeding 5 years or to both.

SECOND SCHEDULE

TAKING OF EVIDENCE FOR USE OUTSIDE STATE

[...]¹

Amendments

1 Second Schedule repealed with saver by Criminal Justice (Mutual Assistance) Act 2008, s 10(a). The repealing is without prejudice to the Criminal Justice (Mutual Assistance) Act 2008, s 11.

Criminal Law (Incest Proceedings) Act 1995

Number 12 of 1995

ARRANGEMENT OF SECTIONS

1. "Act of 1908"

2. Exclusion of public from hearings of proceedings under Act of 1908

3. Anonymity of person charged with offence under Act of 1908 and person to whom offence relates

4. Provisions in relation to offences under section 3

5. Amendment of section 1 of Act of 1908

6. Repeal of section 5 of Act of 1908

7. Short title

AN ACT TO AMEND THE PUNISHMENT OF INCEST ACT, 1908, AND TO PROVIDE FOR RELATED MATTERS. [5th July, 1995]

BE IT ENACTED BY THE OIREACHTAS AS FOLLOWS:

1   "Act of 1908"

In this Act "the Act of 1908" means the Punishment of Incest Act, 1908.

2   Exclusion of public from hearings of proceedings under Act of 1908

(1) In any proceedings for an offence under the Act of 1908, the judge or the court, as the case may be, shall exclude from the court during the hearing all persons except officers of the court, persons directly concerned in the proceedings, bona fide representatives of the press and such other persons (if any) as the judge or the court, as the case may be, may, in his, her or its discretion, permit to remain.

(2) In any proceedings to which subsection (1) of this section applies the verdict or decision and the sentence (if any) shall be announced in public.

3   Anonymity of person charged with offence under Act of 1908 and person to whom offence relates

(1) After a person is charged with an offence under the Act of 1908, no matter likely to lead members of the public to identify that person as the person charged or to identify any other person as a person in relation to whom the offence is alleged to have been committed shall be published in a written publication available to the public or broadcast.

(2) If any matter is published or broadcast in contravention of subsection (1) of this section, the following persons shall be guilty of an offence namely:

    (a) in the case of matter published in a newspaper or periodical publication, the proprietor, the editor and the publisher thereof,

    (b) in the case of matter published in any other written publication, the publisher thereof, and

(c)   in the case of matter broadcast, any person who transmits or provides the programme in which the broadcast is made and any person who performs functions in relation to the programme corresponding to those of the editor of a newspaper.

(3) Nothing in this section shall be construed as—

(a)   prohibiting the publication or broadcasting of matter consisting only of a report of legal proceedings other than proceedings at, or intended to lead to, or an appeal arising out of, a trial of a person for an offence under the Act of 1908, or

(b)   affecting any prohibition or restriction imposed by virtue of any other enactment upon the publication or broadcasting of any matter.

(4) In the section—

"broadcast" means broadcast by wireless telegraphy of sound or visual images intended for general reception, and cognate words shall be construed accordingly;

"written publication" includes a film, or a recording (whether of sound or images or both) in permanent form but does not include an indictment or other document prepared for use in particular legal proceedings.

4   Provisions in relation to offences under section 3

(1) A person guilty of an offence under section 3 of this Act shall be liable—

(a)   on conviction on indictment, to a fine not exceeding £10,000 or to imprisonment for a term not exceeding 3 years or to both, or

(b)   on summary conviction, to a fine not exceeding £1,500 or to imprisonment for a term not exceeding 12 months or to both.

(2)   (a)   Where an offence under section 3 of this Act has been committed by a body corporate and is proved to have been committed with the consent or connivance of or to be attributable to any neglect on the part of a person, being a director, manager, secretary or other officer of the body corporate, or a person who was purporting to act in any such capacity, that person as well as the body corporate shall be guilty of an offence and be liable to be proceeded against and punished as if he or she were guilty of the first-mentioned offence.

(b)   Where the affairs of a body corporate are managed by its members, paragraph (a) of this subsection shall apply in relation to the acts and defaults of a member in connection with his or her functions of management as if he or she were a director or manager of the body corporate.

(3) It shall be a defence for a person who is charged with an offence under section 3 of this Act to prove that at the time of the alleged offence the person was not aware, and neither suspected nor had reason to suspect, that the matter alleged to have been published or broadcast was matter specified in the said section 3 .

5   Amendment of section 1 of Act of 1908

Section 1 of the Act of 1908 is hereby amended—

(a)   in subsection (1), by the substitution of "life" for "a term not exceeding 20 years" (inserted by the Criminal Justice Act, 1993) and "felony" for "misdemeanour", and

(b)   by the deletion of subsection (3).

6   Repeal of section 5 of Act of 1908

Section 5 of the Act of 1908 is hereby repealed.

7   Short title

This Act may be cited as the Criminal Law (Incest Proceedings) Act, 1995.

Domestic Violence Act 1996

Number 1 of 1996

ARRANGEMENT OF SECTIONS

1. Interpretation
2. Safety order
3. Barring order
4. Interim barring order
5. Protection order
6. Power of health board to apply for certain orders
7. Power to make orders, etc., under Child Care Act, 1991
8. Application of section 9(2) of Family Home Protection Act, 1976, to certain orders
9. Hearing of applications under various Acts together
10. Taking effect of orders
11. Copies of orders to be given to certain persons
12. Effect of appeal from order
13. Discharge of order
14. Exercise of jurisdiction by court
15. Rules of court
16. Hearing of civil proceedings, etc
17. Offences
18. Arrest without warrant
19. Costs
20. Amendment of Judicial Separation and Family Law Reform Act, 1989
21. Amendment of Family Law Act, 1995
22. Saving provisions
23. Repeal and transitional provisions
24. Expenses
25. Commencement
26. Short title

AN ACT TO MAKE PROVISION FOR THE PROTECTION OF A SPOUSE AND ANY CHILDREN OR OTHER DEPENDENT PERSONS, AND OF PERSONS IN OTHER DOMESTIC RELATIONSHIPS, WHOSE SAFETY OR WELFARE REQUIRES IT BECAUSE OF THE CONDUCT OF ANOTHER PERSON IN THE DOMESTIC RELATIONSHIP CONCERNED AND FOR THAT PURPOSE TO REPEAL AND RE-ENACT WITH AMENDMENTS THE PROVISIONS OF THE FAMILY LAW (PROTECTION OF SPOUSES AND CHILDREN) ACT, 1981, TO PROVIDE FOR ARREST WITHOUT WARRANT IN CERTAIN CIRCUMSTANCES, TO PROVIDE FOR THE HEARING AT THE SAME TIME

OF CERTAIN APPLICATIONS TO A COURT UNDER MORE THAN ONE ENACTMENT FOR ORDERS RELATING TO DOMESTIC RELATIONSHIPS AND TO PROVIDE FOR OTHER CONNECTED MATTERS. [27th February, 1996]

BE IT ENACTED BY THE OIREACHTAS AS FOLLOWS:

1   Interpretation

(1) In this Act, except where the context otherwise requires—

"applicant", where appropriate, has the meaning assigned by either section 2 or 3 or by both of those sections and where an interim barring order has been made the applicant for the barring order to which the interim barring order relates shall be deemed to be the applicant for the interim barring order and where a protection order has been made the applicant for the safety order or the barring order to which the protection order relates shall be deemed to be the applicant for that protection order;

"barring order" has the meaning assigned by section 3;

"civil proceedings under this Act" means—

(a) proceedings for the making, variation or discharge of a safety order or a barring order,

(b) proceedings, consequent on the making of an application for a barring order, for the making, variation or discharge of an interim barring order which relates to the application,

(c) proceedings, consequent on the making of an application for a safety order or barring order, for the making, variation or discharge of a protection order which relates to the application,

(d) any proceedings by way of appeal or case stated which are related to proceedings to which paragraph (a), (b) or (c) applies;

"the court" means the Circuit Court or the District Court;

"dependent person", in relation to the applicant or the respondent or both of them, as the case may be, means any child—

(a) of the applicant and the respondent or adopted by both the applicant and the respondent under the Adoption Acts, 1952 to 1991, or under an adoption deemed to have been effected by a valid adoption order by virtue of section 2, 3, 4 or 5 of the Adoption Act, 1991, or in relation to whom both the applicant and the respondent are in loco parentis, or

(b) of the applicant or adopted by the applicant under the Adoption Acts, 1952 to 1991, or under an adoption deemed to have been effected by a valid adoption order by virtue of section 2, 3, 4 or 5 of the Adoption Act, 1991, or in relation to whom the applicant is in loco parentis, or

(c) of the respondent or adopted by the respondent under the Adoption Acts, 1952 to 1991, or under an adoption deemed to have been effected by a valid adoption order by virtue of section 2, 3, 4 or 5 of the Adoption Act, 1991, or in relation to whom the respondent is in loco parentis, and the applicant, while not in the same relationship to that child for the purposes of this paragraph as the respondent is in, is in respect of that child a person to whom paragraph (b) of this definition relates, who is not of full age or if the child has attained full age has a physical or mental disability to such extent that it is not reasonably possible for the child to live independently of the applicant;

"full age" has the same meaning as it has in the Age of Majority Act, 1985;

"functions" includes powers and duties;

[...]¹;

"interim barring order" has the meaning assigned by section 4;

"protection order" has the meaning assigned by section 5;

"respondent", where appropriate, has the meaning assigned by either section 2 or 3 or by both of those sections and where an interim barring order has been made the respondent to the application for the barring order to which the interim barring order relates shall be deemed to be the respondent to the interim barring order and where a protection order has been made the respondent to the application for the safety order or the barring order to which the protection order relates shall be deemed to be the respondent to that protection order;

"safety order" has the meaning assigned by section 2;

"welfare" includes the physical and psychological welfare of the person in question.

(2) (a) A reference in this Act to a section is a reference to a section of this Act unless it is indicated that a reference to some other Act is intended.

    (b) A reference in this Act to a subsection or to a paragraph is to the subsection or paragraph of the provision in which the reference occurs unless it is indicated that reference to some other provision is intended.

(3) Any reference in this Act to any other enactment shall, except where the context otherwise requires, be construed as a reference to that enactment as amended by or under any other enactment including this Act.

Amendments

1   Definition of 'health board' deleted by Health Act 2004, Sch 6, Pt 14.

2   Safety order

(1) (a) In this section—

    "the applicant" means a person, other than a health board, who has applied or on whose behalf [the Health Service Executive]¹ has applied by virtue of section 6 for a safety order against another person (in this section referred to as "the respondent") and the person so applying or on whose behalf [the Health Service Executive]¹ has so applied—

      (i)   is the spouse of the respondent, or

      (ii) is not the spouse of the respondent but has lived with the respondent as husband or wife for a period of at least six months in aggregate during the period of twelve months immediately prior to the application for the safety order, or

(iii) is a parent of the respondent and the respondent is a person of full age who is not, in relation to the parent, a dependent person, or

(iv) being of full age resides with the respondent in a relationship the basis of which is not primarily contractual;

"kindred", in respect of two or more persons, means the relationship of each of those persons to the other person or to the rest of those persons by blood, adoption or marriage.

(b) In deciding whether or not a person is residing with another person in a relationship the basis of which is not primarily contractual, the court shall have regard to—

    (i) the length of time those persons have been residing together,

    (ii) the nature of any duties performed by either person for the other person or for any kindred person of that other person,

    (iii) the absence of any profit or of any significant profit made by either person from any monetary or other consideration given by the other person in respect of residing at the place concerned,

    (iv) such other matters as the court considers appropriate in the circumstances.

(2) Where the court, on application to it, is of the opinion that there are reasonable grounds for believing that the safety or welfare of the applicant or any dependent person so requires, it may, subject to section 7, by order (in this Act referred to as a "safety order") direct that the respondent to the application—

(a) shall not use or threaten to use violence against, molest or put in fear the applicant or that dependent person, and

(b) if he or she is residing at a place other than the place where the applicant or that dependent person resides, shall not watch or beset the place where the applicant or that dependent person resides,

and the court may make such order subject to such exceptions and conditions as it may specify.

(3) Where a safety order has been made, any of the following may apply to have it varied, that is to say:

(a) if the application for the order was made by [the Health Service Executive]¹ in respect of any dependent person by virtue of section 6 —

    (i) [the Health Service Executive]¹,

    (ii) the person referred to in subsection (1)(c) of that section, or

    (iii) the respondent to that application;

(b) if the application for the order was made by [the Health Service Executive]¹ in any other case by virtue of section 6 —

    (i) [the Health Service Executive]¹,

    (ii) the person who was the applicant for the order, or

    (iii) the respondent to that application;

(c) in any other case—

    (i) the person who was the applicant for the order, or

    (ii) the person who was the respondent to the application for the order, and the court upon hearing any such application shall make such order as it considers appropriate in the circumstances.

(4) For the purposes of subsection (3), a safety order made by a court on appeal from another court shall be treated as if it had been made by that other court.

(5) A safety order, if made by the District Court or by the Circuit Court on appeal from the District Court, shall, subject to subsection (6)(a) and section 13, expire five years after the date of its making or on the expiration of such shorter period as the court may provide for in the order.

(6) (a) On or before the expiration of a safety order to which subsection (5) relates, a further safety order may be made by the District Court or by the Circuit Court on appeal from the District Court for a period of five years, or such shorter period as the court may provide for in the order, with effect from the expiration of the first-mentioned order.

(b) On or before the expiration of a safety order to which paragraph (a) does not relate, a further safety order may be made with effect from the expiration of the first-mentioned safety order.

(7) Notwithstanding subsection (5), so much of a safety order as was made for the benefit of a dependent person shall expire in accordance with such order or upon such person ceasing to be a dependent person, whichever first occurs.

(8) The court shall not make a safety order on an application for a barring order unless there is also an application for a safety order before the court concerning the same matter.

Amendments

1   Words substituted by Health Act 2004, Sch 6, Pt 14.

3   Barring order

(1) In this section "the applicant" means a person, other than [the Health Service Executive][1], who has applied or on whose behalf [the Health Service Executive][1] has applied by virtue of section 6 for a barring order against another person (in this section referred to as "the respondent") and the person so applying or on whose behalf [the Health Service Executive][1] has so applied—

(a)   is the spouse of the respondent, or

(b)   is not the spouse of the respondent but has lived with the respondent as husband or wife for a period of at least six months in aggregate during the period of nine months immediately prior to the application for the barring order, or

(c)   is a parent of the respondent and the respondent is a person of full age who is not, in relation to the parent, a dependent person.

(2) (a)   Where the court, on application to it, is of the opinion that there are reasonable grounds for believing that the safety or welfare of the applicant or any dependent person so requires, it may, subject to section 7 and having taken into account any order made or to be made to which paragraph (a) or (d) of subsection (2) of section 9 relates, by order (in this Act referred to as a "barring order")—

(i)   direct the respondent, if residing at a place where the applicant or that dependent person resides, to leave such place, and

697

(ii) whether the respondent is or is not residing at a place where the applicant or that dependent person resides, prohibit that respondent from entering such place until further order of the court or until such other time as the court shall specify.

(b) In deciding whether or not to grant a barring order the court shall have regard to the safety and welfare of any dependent person in respect of whom the respondent is a parent or in loco parentis, where such dependent person is residing at the place to which the order, if made, would relate.

(3) A barring order may, if the court thinks fit, prohibit the respondent from doing one or more of the following, that is to say:

(a) using or threatening to use violence against the applicant or any dependent person;

(b) molesting or putting in fear the applicant or any dependent person;

(c) attending at or in the vicinity of, or watching or besetting a place where, the applicant or any dependent person resides;

and shall be subject to such exceptions and conditions as the court may specify.

(4) (a) In respect of a person who is an applicant by virtue of paragraph (b) or (c) of subsection (1), the court shall not make a barring order in respect of the place where the applicant or dependent person resides where the respondent has a legal or beneficial interest in that place but—

(i) the applicant has no such interest, or

(ii) the applicant's interest is, in the opinion of the court, less than that of the respondent.

(b) Where in proceedings to which this section applies the applicant states the belief, in respect of the place to which paragraph (a) relates, that he or she has a legal or beneficial interest in that place which is not less than that of the respondent, then such belief shall be admissible in evidence.

(5) Without prejudice to section 22, nothing in this Act shall be construed as affecting the rights of any person, other than the applicant or the respondent, who has a legal or beneficial interest in a place in respect of which the court has made an order under this section.

(6) Where a barring order has been made, any of the following may apply to have it varied, that is to say:

(a) if the application for the order was made by [the Health Service Executive][1] in respect of any dependent person by virtue of section 6 —

(i) [the Health Service Executive][1],

(ii) the person referred to in subsection (1)(c) of that section, or

(iii) the respondent to that application;

(b) if the application for the order was made by [the Health Service Executive][1] in any other case by virtue of section 6—

(i) [the Health Service Executive][1],

(ii) the person who was the applicant for the order, or

(iii) the respondent to that application;

(c) in any other case—

(i) the person who was the applicant for the order, or

(ii) the person who was the respondent to the application for the order, and the court upon hearing any such application shall make such order as it considers appropriate in the circumstances.

(7) For the purposes of subsection (6), a barring order made by a court on appeal from another court shall be treated as if it had been made by that other court.

(8) A barring order, if made by the District Court or by the Circuit Court on appeal from the District Court, shall, subject to subsection (9)(a) and section 13, expire three years after the date of its making or on the expiration of such shorter period as the court may provide for in the order.

(9) (a) On or before the expiration of a barring order to which subsection (8) relates, a further barring order may be made by the District Court or by the Circuit Court on appeal from the District Court for a period of three years, or such shorter period as the court may provide for in the order, with effect from the expiration of the first-mentioned order.

    (b) On or before the expiration of a barring order to which paragraph (a) does not relate, a further barring order may be made with effect from the expiration of the first-mentioned barring order.

(10) Notwithstanding subsection (8), so much of a barring order as was made for the benefit of a dependent person shall expire in accordance with such order or upon such person ceasing to be a dependent person, whichever first occurs.

(11) The court shall not make a barring order on an application for a safety order unless there is also an application for a barring order before the court concerning the same matter.

(12) For the purposes of subsections (2) and (3), an applicant or a dependent person who would, but for the conduct of the respondent, be residing at a place shall be treated as residing at such place.

[(13) Where, by reason only of either or both of the following, that is to say, a barring order and an interim barring order, an applicant who is not the spouse of the respondent has not lived with the respondent as husband or wife for a period of at least six months in aggregate during the period of nine months immediately prior to the application for a further barring order under subsection (9), the applicant shall be deemed, for the purposes of this section, to have lived with the respondent as husband or wife for a period of at least six months in aggregate during the period of nine months immediately prior to the application.][2]

Amendments

1   Words substituted by Health Act 2004, Sch 6, Pt 14.

2   Paragraph (13) inserted by Family Law (Miscellaneous Provisions) Act 1997, s 4.

---

4   Interim barring order

(1) If, on the making of an application for a barring order or between the making of such application and its determination, the court is of the opinion that there are reasonable grounds for believing that—

    (a) there is an immediate risk of significant harm to the applicant or any dependent person if the order is not made immediately, and

(b) the granting of a protection order would not be sufficient to protect the applicant or any dependent person,

the court may, subject to section 7 and having taken into account any order made or to be made to which paragraph (a)or (d)of subsection (2)of section 9 relates, by order (in this Act referred to as an "interim barring order")—

    (i) direct the respondent, if residing at a place where the applicant or that dependent person resides, to leave such place, and

    (ii) whether the respondent is or is not residing at a place where the applicant or that dependent person resides, prohibit that respondent from entering such place until further order of the court or until such other time as the court shall specify.

(2) Subsections (3), (4), (5), (6), (7) and (12) of section 3 shall apply to an interim barring order as they apply to a barring order.

[(3) (a) An interim barring order may be made ex parte where, having regard to the circumstances of the particular case, the court considers it necessary or expedient to do so in the interests of justice.

    (b) The application for such an order shall be grounded on an affidavit or information sworn by the applicant.

    (c) If an interim barring order is made ex parte—

        (i) a note of evidence given by the applicant shall be prepared forthwith—

            (I) by the judge,

            (II) by the applicant or the applicant's solicitor and approved by the judge, or

            (III) as otherwise directed by the judge,

        and

        (ii) a copy of the order, affidavit or information and note shall be served on the respondent as soon as practicable.

    (d) The order shall have effect for a period, not exceeding 8 working days, to be specified in the order, unless, on application by the applicant for the barring order and on notice to the respondent, the interim barring order is confirmed within that period by order of the court.

    (e) The order shall contain a statement of the effect of paragraph (d).

    (f) In paragraph (d) 'working days' means days other than Saturdays, Sundays or public holidays (within the meaning of the Organisation of Working Time Act, 1997).][1]

(4) An interim barring order shall cease to have effect on the determination by the court of the application for a barring order.

(5) Notwithstanding subsection (4), so much of an interim barring order as was made for the benefit of a dependent person shall cease to have effect in accordance with that subsection or upon such person ceasing to be a dependent person, whichever first occurs.

Amendments

1   Subsection (3) substituted by Domestic Violence (Amendment) Act 2002, s 1(a).

5   Protection order

(1) If, on the making of an application for a safety order or a barring order or between the making of such an application and its determination, the court is of the opinion that there are reasonable grounds for believing that the safety or welfare of the applicant for the order concerned or of any dependent person so requires, the court may by order (in this Act referred to as a "protection order") direct that the respondent to the application—

(a)   shall not use or threaten to use violence against, molest or put in fear the applicant or that dependent person, and

(b)   if he or she is residing at a place other than the place where the applicant or that dependent person resides, shall not watch or beset the place where the applicant or that dependent person resides,

and the court may make the protection order subject to such exceptions and conditions as it may specify.

(2) Where a protection order has been made, any of the following may apply to have it varied, that is to say:

(a)   if the application for the order was made by [the Health Service Executive][1] in respect of any dependent person by virtue of section 6 —

(i)   [the Health Service Executive][1],

(ii)   the person referred to in subsection (1)(c) of that section, or

(iii)   the respondent to that application;

(b)   if the application for the order was made by a health board in any other case by virtue of section 6 —

(i)   [the Health Service Executive][1],

(ii)   the person who was the applicant for the order, or

(iii)   the respondent to that application;

(c)   in any other case—

(i)   the person who was the applicant for the order, or

(ii)   the person who was the respondent to the application for the order,

and the court upon hearing any such application shall make such order as it considers appropriate in the circumstances.

(3) For the purposes of subsection (2), a protection order made by a court on appeal from another court shall be treated as if it had been made by that other court.

[(4) A protection order may be made ex parte.][2]

(5) A protection order shall cease to have effect on the determination by the court of the application for a safety order or a barring order.

(6) Notwithstanding subsection (5), so much of a protection order as was made for the benefit of a dependent person shall cease to have effect in accordance with that subsection or upon such person ceasing to be a dependent person, whichever first occurs.

(7) For the purposes of this section, an applicant or a dependent person who would, but for the conduct of the respondent, be residing at a place shall be treated as residing at such place.

Amendments

1   Words substituted by Health Act 2004, Sch 6, Pt 14.

2   Subsection (4) substituted by Domestic Violence (Amendment) Act 2002, s 1(b).

6   Power of health board to apply for certain orders

(1) Subject to subsections (2), (3) and (4), this section shall apply where [the Health Service Executive][1]—

   (a)   becomes aware of an alleged incident or series of incidents which in its opinion puts into doubt the safety or welfare of a person (in this section referred to as the "aggrieved person"),

   (b)   has reasonable cause to believe that the aggrieved person has been subjected to molestation, violence or threatened violence or otherwise put in fear of his or her safety or welfare,

   (c)   is of the opinion that there are reasonable grounds for believing that, where appropriate in the circumstances, a person would be deterred or prevented as a consequence of molestation, violence or threatened violence by the respondent or fear of the respondent from pursuing an application for a safety order or a barring order on his or her own behalf or on behalf of a dependent person, and

   (d)   considers, having ascertained as far as is reasonably practicable the wishes of the aggrieved person or, where the aggrieved person is a dependent person, of the person to whom paragraph (c) relates in respect of such dependent person, that it is appropriate in all the circumstances to apply for a safety order or a barring order or both in accordance with this Act on behalf of the aggrieved person.

(2) [The Health Service Executive][1] may apply to the court on behalf of the aggrieved person for a safety order or a barring order for which the aggrieved person or, where the aggrieved person is a dependent person, the person to whom subsection (1)(c) relates in respect of such dependent person could have applied.

(3) Where an application is made by [the Health Service Executive][1] by virtue of this section, the court shall, in determining whether, and if so to what extent, to exercise any of its functions under section 2, 3, 4, 5 or 13, have regard to any wishes expressed by—

   (a)   the aggrieved person, or

   (b)   where the aggrieved person is a dependent person, the person to whom subsection (1)(c) relates in respect of such dependent person and, where the court considers it appropriate, such dependent person.

(4) The provisions of paragraphs (a) and (b) of subsection (1) need not be complied with—

    (a)   where the application relates to an aggrieved person who is a dependent person, or

    (b)   in respect of so much of an application as relates to an aggrieved person where such person is a dependent person,

if the court is of the opinion that there is reasonable cause to believe that—

    (i)   such dependent person has been or is being assaulted, ill-treated, sexually abused or seriously neglected, or

    (ii)   such dependent person's health, development or welfare has been, is being or is likely to be avoidably impaired or seriously neglected,

and that if the order is made the likelihood of harm to such dependent person will not arise or will be materially diminished.

(5) The court shall not make a barring order or an interim barring order where the aggrieved person is a dependent person unless [the Health Service Executive][1] satisfies the court that the person to whom subsection (1)(c) relates in respect of such dependent person is willing and able to provide reasonable care for such dependent person.

(6) [...][2]

Amendments

1   Words substituted by Health Act 2004, Sch 6, Pt 14.
2   Subsection (6) deleted by Health Act 2004, Sch 6, Pt 14.

---

7   Power to make orders, etc., under Child Care Act, 1991

(1) Where in proceedings for any order under this Act, other than proceedings to which section 6 relates, it appears to the court that it may be appropriate for a care order or a supervision order to be made under the Child Care Act, 1991, with respect to a dependent person concerned in the proceedings, the court may, of its own motion or on the application of any person concerned, adjourn the proceedings and direct [the Health Service Executive][1] for the area in which such dependent person resides or is for the time being to undertake an investigation or, as the case may be, further investigations of such dependent person's circumstances.

(2) Where proceedings are adjourned and the court gives a direction under subsection(1), the court may give such directions under the Child Care Act, 1991, as it sees fit as to the care and custody of, and may make a supervision order under that Act in respect of, the dependent person concerned pending the outcome of the investigation by [the Health Service Executive][1] concerned.

(3) Where the court gives a direction under subsection (1) in respect of a dependent person, [the Health Service Executive][1] concerned shall undertake an investigation of such dependent person's circumstances and shall consider if it should—

    (a)   apply for a care order or a supervision order under the Child Care Act, 1991,

    (b)   provide services or assistance for such dependent person's family, or

    (c)   take any other action in respect of such dependent person.

(4) Where [the Health Service Executive]¹ undertakes an investigation under this section and decides not to apply for a care order or supervision order under the Child Care Act, 1991, with respect to the dependent person concerned, it shall inform the court of—

    (a) its reasons for so deciding,

    (b) any service or assistance it has provided, or intends to provide, for such dependent person and his or her family, and

    (c) any other action which it has taken, or proposes to take, with respect to such dependent person.

Amendments

1   Words substituted by Health Act 2004, Sch 6, Pt 14.

---

8   **Application of section 9(2) of Family Home Protection Act, 1976, to certain orders**

(1) Subsection (2) of section 9 (which restricts the right of a spouse to dispose of or remove household chattels pending the determination of matrimonial proceedings) of the Family Home Protection Act, 1976, shall apply between the making of an application, against the spouse of the applicant, for a barring order or a safety order and its determination, and if an order is made, while such order is in force, as it applies between the institution and final determination of matrimonial proceedings to which that section relates.

(2) For the avoidance of doubt, it is hereby declared that the court which is empowered under subsection (2)(b) of section 9 of the Family Home Protection Act, 1976, to grant permission for any disposition or removal of household chattels (being household chattels within the meaning of that section) is, notwithstanding anything in section 10 of that Act, the court before which the proceedings (including any proceedings for a barring order or a safety order) have been instituted.

9   **Hearing of applications under various Acts together**

(1) Where an application is made to the court for an order under this Act, the court may, on application to it in the same proceedings and without the institution of proceedings under the Act concerned, if it appears to the court to be proper to do so, make one or more of the orders referred to in subsection (2).

(2) The provisions to which subsection (1)relates are as follows, that is to say:

    (a) an order under section 11 (as amended by the Status of Children Act, 1987) of the Guardianship of Infants Act, 1964;

    (b) an order under section 5, 5A, 6, 7 or 21A of the Family Law (Maintenance of Spouses and Children) Act, 1976 (as amended by the Status of Children Act, 1987);

    (c) an order under section 5 or 9 of the Family Home Protection Act, 1976;

    (d) an order under the Child Care Act, 1991.

10   **Taking effect of orders**

(1) A safety order, barring order, interim barring order or protection order shall take effect on notification of its making being given to the respondent.

(2) Oral communication to the respondent by or on behalf of the applicant of the fact that a safety order, barring order, interim barring order or protection order has been made, together with production of a copy of the order, shall, without prejudice to the sufficiency of any other form of notification, be taken to be sufficient notification to the respondent of the making of the order.

(3) If the respondent is present at a sitting of the court at which the safety order, barring order, interim barring order or protection order is made, that respondent shall be taken for the purposes of subsection (1) to have been notified of its making.

(4) An order varying a safety order, barring order, interim barring order or protection order shall take effect on notification of its making being given to the person who was the other party in the proceedings for the making of the safety order or barring order and for this purpose subsections (2) and (3) shall apply with the necessary modifications.

11   Copies of orders to be given to certain persons

(1) The court, on making, varying or discharging a safety order or a protection order, shall cause a copy of the order in question to be given or sent as soon as practicable—

   (a)   to the applicant for the safety order or, in respect of a protection order, the applicant for the safety order or barring order concerned,

   (b)   to the respondent to the application for the safety order or, in respect of a protection order, the respondent to the application for the safety order or barring order concerned,

   (c)   where [the Health Service Executive][1] by virtue of section 6 made the application for the safety order or, in respect of a protection order, for the safety order or barring order, to [the Health Service Executive][1],

   (d)   to the member of the Garda Síochána in charge of the Garda Síochána station for the area in which the person for whose benefit the safety order or protection order was made resides, and

   (e)   where the order in question is a variation or discharge of a safety order or a protection order and the person for whose benefit the order was made had previously resided elsewhere, to the member of the Garda Síochána in charge of the Garda Síochána station for the area in which that person had so resided but only if that member had previously been sent under this subsection a copy of such safety order or protection order or any order relating thereto.

(2) The court on making, varying or discharging a barring order or an interim barring order shall cause a copy of the order in question to be given or sent as soon as practicable to—

   (a)   the applicant for the barring order,

   (b)   the respondent to the application for the barring order,

   (c)   where [the Health Service Executive][1] by virtue of section 6 made the application for the barring order concerned, [the Health Service Executive][1],

   (d)   the member of the Garda Síochána in charge of the Garda Síochána station for the area in which is situate the place in relation to which the application for the barring order was made, and

   (e)   where the order in question is a variation or discharge of a barring order or an interim barring order and the place in respect of which the previous order was made is elsewhere, to the member of the Garda Síochána in charge of the Garda Síochána station for the area in which is situated that place but only if that member had previously been sent under this subsection a copy of such barring order or interim barring order or any order relating thereto.

(3) The court—

(a) on making a barring order, a safety order, an interim barring order or a protection order on the application of, or on behalf of, a person who is not of full age, or

(b) on varying or discharging an order to which paragraph (a) relates,

shall cause a copy of the order in question to be given or sent as soon as practicable to [the Health Service Executive]¹ for the area in which the person resides.

(4) The validity of any order to which this section relates shall not be affected by non-compliance with the other provisions of this section.

Amendments

1 Words substituted by Health Act 2004, Sch 6, Pt 14.

12 Effect of appeal from order

(1) An appeal from a safety order or a barring order shall, if the court that made the order or the court to which the appeal is brought so determines (but not otherwise), stay the operation of the order on such terms (if any) as may be imposed by the court making the determination.

(2) An appeal from a protection order or an interim barring order shall not stay the operation of the order.

13 Discharge of orders

(1) Where a safety order, barring order, interim barring order or protection order has been made, any of the following may apply to the court that made the order to have the order discharged, that is to say:

(a) if the application for the order was made by [the Health Service Executive]¹ in respect of any dependent person by virtue of section 6 —

(i) [the Health Service Executive]¹,

(ii) the person referred to in subsection (1)(c) of that section, or

(iii) the respondent to that application;

(b) if the application for the order was made by [the Health Service Executive]¹ in any other case by virtue of section 6 —

(i) [the Health Service Executive]¹,

(ii) the person who was the applicant for the order, or

(iii) the respondent to that application;

(c) in any other case—

(i) the person who was the applicant for the order, or

(ii) the person who was the respondent to the application for the order, and thereupon the court shall discharge the order if it is of the opinion that the safety and welfare of the applicant or such dependent person for whose protection the order was made does not require that the order should continue in force.

(2) On determination of any matrimonial cause or matter between the applicant and the respondent or of any proceedings between them under the Guardianship of Infants Act, 1964, the court determining any such cause, matter or proceedings may, if it thinks fit, discharge any safety order, barring order, interim barring order or protection order.

(3) For the purposes of this section, an order made by a court on appeal from another court shall be treated as if it had been made by that other court.

Amendments

1   Words substituted by Health Act 2004, Sch 6, Pt 14.

14   Exercise of jurisdiction by court

(1) The jurisdiction of the court in respect of civil proceedings under this Act may be exercised—

    (a) as regards the Circuit Court, by the judge of the circuit, and

    (b) as regards the District Court, by the judge of the District Court for the time being assigned to the district court district,

where the applicant resides or, if the application is for a barring order, where there is situate the place in relation to which that application was made.

(2) For the purposes of subsection (1), the court may treat any person concerned as residing at a place where that person would, but for the conduct of the respondent, be residing at.

(3) Where a judge of the District Court to whom subsection (1) relates is not immediately available, the jurisdiction of the District Court under that subsection may be exercised by any judge of the District Court.

15   Rules of court

(1) For the purpose of ensuring the expeditious hearing of applications under this Act, rules of court may make provision for the service of documents otherwise than under section 7 (as amended by section 22 of the Courts Act, 1971) of the Courts Act, 1964, in circumstances to which that section relates.

(2) This section is without prejudice to section 17 of the Interpretation Act, 1937, which provides for rules of court.

16   Hearing of civil proceedings, etc

(1) Civil proceedings under this Act shall be heard otherwise than in public.

(2) Where under section 9 the court hears together applications under several enactments, then the court shall as far as is practicable comply with the requirements relating to the hearing of applications under each of those enactments and the other relevant provisions of those Acts shall apply accordingly.

(3) (a) Civil proceedings under this Act before the District Court shall be as informal as is practicable and consistent with the administration of justice.

    (b) District Court judges hearing and determining civil proceedings under this Act and barristers and solicitors appearing in such proceedings shall not wear wigs or gowns.

(4) Civil proceedings under this Act before the Circuit Court shall be heard by the Circuit Family Court and, accordingly, the provisions of section 32 and subsection (1) and (2) of section 33 of the Judicial Separation and Family Law Reform Act, 1989, shall apply to such proceedings.

(5) The proceedings to which subsections (3) and (4) of section 33 of the Judicial Separation and Family Law Reform Act, 1989, apply shall be deemed to include civil proceedings under this Act.

17   Offences

(1) A respondent who—

    (a) contravenes a safety order, a barring order, an interim barring order or a protection order, or

    (b) while a barring order or interim barring order is in force refuses to permit the applicant or any dependent person to enter in and remain in the place to which the order relates or does any act for the purpose of preventing the applicant or such dependent person from so doing,

shall be guilty of an offence and shall be liable on summary conviction to a fine not exceeding £1,500 or, at the discretion of the court, to imprisonment for a term not exceeding 12 months, or to both.

(2) Subsection (1) is without prejudice to the law as to contempt of court or any other liability, whether civil or criminal, that may be incurred by the respondent concerned.

18   Arrest without warrant

(1) (a) Where a member of the Garda Síochána has reasonable cause for believing that, in respect of an order under this Act, an offence is being or has been committed under section 17 the member may, on complaint being made to him or her by or on behalf of the person who was the applicant to which the order relates, arrest the respondent concerned without warrant.

    (b) For the purpose of arresting a respondent under paragraph (a), a member of the Garda Síochána may enter, if need be by force, and search any place where the member, with reasonable cause, suspects the respondent to be.

(2) Where a member of the Garda Síochána has reasonable cause for believing that a person (in this section referred to as "the first-mentioned person") is committing or has committed—

    (a) an assault occasioning actual bodily harm, or

    (b) an offence under section 20 (which relates to unlawfully and maliciously wounding or inflicting any grievous bodily harm) of the Offences against the Person Act, 1861,

against a person (in this section referred to as "the second-mentioned person") in circumstances which in the opinion of the member could give rise to the second-mentioned person applying for, or on whose behalf another person could in accordance with this Act apply for, a safety order or a barring order, then the member may—

> (i) arrest the first-mentioned person without warrant, and
>
> (ii) for the purpose of making such an arrest, enter, if need be by force, and search any place where the member, with reasonable cause, suspects the first-mentioned person to be.

19   Costs

The costs of any civil proceedings under this Act shall be in Costs, the discretion of the court.

20   Amendment of Judicial Separation and Family Law Reform Act, 1989

The Judicial Separation and Family Law Reform Act, 1989, is hereby amended—

> (a) in section 11, by the substitution of the following paragraph for paragraph (a):

"(a) a safety order, barring order, interim barring order or protection order pursuant to section 2, 3, 4 or 5, respectively, of the Domestic Violence Act, 1996;",

> (b) in section 16, by the substitution of the following paragraph for paragraph (e):

"(e) an order under section 2, 3, 4 or 5 of the Domestic Violence Act, 1996;",

> and

> (c) in section 19, by the substitution of "the Domestic Violence Act, 1996" for "the Family Law (Protection of Spouses and Children) Act, 1981 ".

21   Amendment of Family Law Act, 1995

The Family Law Act, 1995, is hereby amended—

> (a) in section 2, by the deletion of the definition of "the Act of 1981" and the insertion of the following definition after the definition of "the Act of 1989" in subsection (1):

"'the Act of 1996' means the Domestic Violence Act, 1996;",

> (b) in section 6, by the substitution of the following paragraph for paragraph (a):

"(a) an order under section 2, 3, 4 or 5 of the Act of 1996,",

> (c) in section 10, by the substitution of the following paragraph for paragraph (d) of subsection (1):

"(d) an order under section 2, 3, 4 or 5 of the Act of 1996,",

> and

> (d) in section 47, by the substitution of the following paragraph for paragraph (d) of subsection (6):

"(d) under the Act of 1996,".

22   Saving provisions

(1) Where, by reason only of an interim barring order or a barring order, a person is not residing at a place during any period, that person shall be deemed, for the purposes of any rights under the Statutes of Limitation, 1957 and 1991, the Landlord and Tenant Acts, 1967 to 1994, and the Housing (Private Rented Dwellings) Acts, 1982 and 1983, to be residing at that place during that period.

(2) Except in so far as the exercise by a respondent of a right to occupy the place to which a barring order or an interim barring order relates is suspended by virtue of the order, the order shall not affect any estate or interest in that place of that respondent or any other person.

23 Repeal and transitional provisions

(1) The Family Law (Protection of Spouses and Children) Act, 1981 (in this section referred to as "the Act of 1981"), is hereby repealed.

(2) (a) Subject to paragraph (b), this Act shall apply to a barring order made under the Act of 1981 and which is in force, or stayed by virtue of section 10 of that Act, at the commencement of this Act as if it were an order made under section 3.

   (b) For the purposes of a barring order to which paragraph (a) relates, the reference in section 3(8) to the expiration of three years after the date of its making shall be construed as a reference to twelve months after the date of its making.

(3) An application made to the court under the Act of 1981 for a barring order and not determined before the commencement of this Act shall be treated as if it had been made under section 3.

(4) This Act shall apply to a protection order made under the Act of 1981 and which is in force at the commencement of this Act as if it were an order made under section 5.

24 Expenses

The expenses incurred by the Minister for Equality and Law Reform, the Minister for Health and the Minister for Justice in the administration of this Act shall, to such extent as may be sanctioned by the Minister for Finance, be paid out of moneys provided by the Oireachtas.

25 Commencement

(1) Subject to subsection (2), this Act shall come into operation one month after the date of its passing.

(2) Section 6 and so much of the other provisions of this Act as relate to that section shall come into operation on the 1st day of January, 1997.

26 Short title

This Act may be cited as the Domestic Violence Act, 1996.

Criminal Justice (Drug Trafficking) Act 1996

Number 29 of 1996

ARRANGEMENT OF SECTIONS

Section

1. Interpretation.
2. Powers of detention.
3. Amendment of Act of 1990.
4. Rearrest.
5. Application of certain provisions of Act of 1984.
6. Regulations regarding officers of customs and excise.
7. Inferences from failure of accused to mention particular facts.
8. Search warrants.
9. Amendment of Public Dance Halls Act, 1935.
10. Expenses.
11. Duration of certain sections.
12. Short title and commencement.

AN ACT TO MAKE PROVISION FOR ADDITIONAL POWERS OF DETENTION BY THE GARDA SÍOCHÁNA OF SUSPECTED DRUG TRAFFICKERS FOLLOWING ARREST, TO MAKE PROVISION FOR THE ISSUANCE OF SEARCH WARRANTS BY CERTAIN MEMBERS OF THE GARDA SÍOCHÁNA IN THE CASE OF SUSPECTED DRUG TRAFFICKING OFFENCES AND FOR THE ATTENDANCE OF OFFICERS OF CUSTOMS AND EXCISE AT, AND THE PARTICIPATION OF SUCH OFFICERS IN, THE QUESTIONING OF CERTAIN ARRESTED PERSONS BY THE GARDA SÍOCHÁNA AND TO PROVIDE FOR RELATED MATTERS. [31st July, 1996]

BE IT ENACTED BY THE OIREACHTAS AS FOLLOWS:

1   Interpretation

(1) In this Act—

"controlled drug" has the meaning it has in section 2 of the Act of 1977;

"drug trafficking offence" has the meaning it has in section 3(1) of the Criminal Justice Act, 1994;

[…]¹

"the Minister" means the Minister for Justice;

"place of detention" shall be construed in accordance with section 2(9)(a);

"the Act of 1939" means the Offences against the State Act, 1939;

"the Act of 1977" means the Misuse of Drugs Act, 1977;

"the Act of 1984" means the Criminal Justice Act, 1984;

"the Act of 1990" means the Criminal Justice (Forensic Evidence) Act, 1990.

(2) In this Act a reference to an offence shall, where the context so requires, be construed as a reference to a suspected offence.

(3) In this Act a reference to any other enactment shall, save where the context otherwise requires, be construed as a reference to that enactment as amended, adapted or extended by or under any subsequent enactment, including this Act.

(4) In this Act, a reference to a section is a reference to a section of this Act and a reference to a subsection or paragraph is a reference to a subsection or paragraph of the provision in which the reference occurs, unless it is indicated that reference to some other enactment or provision is intended.

Amendments

1   Definition deleted by Criminal Justice Act 1999, s 35.

2   Powers of detention

(1) [(a)   Where a member of the Garda Síochána arrests without warrant, whether in a Garda Síochána station or elsewhere, a person (an 'arrested person') whom he or she, with reasonable cause, suspects of having committed a drug trafficking offence, the arrested person—

    (i)   if not already in a Garda Síochána station, may be taken to and detained in a Garda Síochána station, or

    (ii)   if he or she is arrested in a Garda Síochána station, may be detained in the station,

for a period or periods authorised by subsection (2) if the member of the Garda Síochána in charge of the station to which the arrested person is taken on arrest or in which he or she is arrested has at the time of the arrested person's arrival at the station or his or her arrest in the station, as may be appropriate, reasonable grounds for believing that his or her detention is necessary for the proper investigation of the offence.]¹

  (b)   Without prejudice to paragraph (a), where a member of the Garda Síochána suspects an arrested person of concealing in his or her person a controlled drug, that person may—

    (i)   be taken to a place of detention, and

    (ii)   if a member of the Garda Síochána not below the rank of inspector who is not investigating the drug trafficking offence has, at the time of that person's arrival there, reasonable grounds for believing that his or her detention is necessary for the proper investigation of the drug trafficking offence, be detained in that place of detention for a period or periods authorised by subsection (2).

(2) (a)   The period for which a person may be detained under subsection (1) shall, subject to the provisions of this subsection, not exceed 6 hours from the time of his or her arrest.

(b) An officer of the Garda Síochána not below the rank of [superintendent]² may direct that a person detained under subsection (1) be detained for a further period not exceeding 18 hours if he or she has reasonable grounds for believing that such further detention is necessary for the proper investigation of the offence concerned.

(c) An officer of the Garda Síochána not below the rank of chief superintendent may direct that a person detained pursuant to a direction under paragraph (b) be detained for a further period not exceeding 24 hours, if he or she has reasonable grounds for believing that such further detention is necessary for the proper investigation of the offence concerned.

(d) A direction under paragraph (b) or (c) may be given orally or in writing and, if given orally, shall be recorded in writing as soon as practicable.

(e) Where a direction has been given under paragraph (b) or (c), the fact that the direction was given, the date and time when it was given and the name and rank of the officer of the Garda Síochána who gave it shall be recorded.

(f) The direction or, if it was given orally, the written record of it shall be signed by the officer giving it and—

    (i) shall state the date and time when it was given, the officer's name and rank and that the officer had reasonable grounds for believing that such further detention was necessary for the proper investigation of the offence concerned, and

    (ii) shall be attached to and form part of the custody record (within the meaning of the Criminal Justice Act, 1984 (Treatment of Persons in Custody in Garda Síochána Stations) Regulations, 1987) in respect of the person concerned.

(g) (i) An officer of the Garda Síochána not below the rank of chief superintendent may apply to a judge of the Circuit Court or a judge of the District Court for a warrant authorising the detention of a person detained pursuant to a direction under paragraph (c) for a further period not exceeding 72 hours if he or she has reasonable grounds for believing that such further detention is necessary for the proper investigation of the offence concerned.

    (ii) On an application under subparagraph (i) the judge concerned shall issue a warrant authorising the detention of the person to whom the application relates for a further period not exceeding 72 hours if, but only if, the judge is satisfied that such further detention is necessary for the proper investigation of the offence concerned and that the investigation is being conducted diligently and expeditiously.

(h) (i) An officer of the Garda Síochána not below the rank of chief superintendent may apply to a judge of the Circuit Court or a judge of the District Court for a warrant authorising the detention of a person detained under a warrant issued pursuant to paragraph (g)(ii) for a further period not exceeding 48 hours, if he or she has reasonable grounds for believing that such further detention is necessary for the proper investigation of the offence concerned.

    (ii) On an application under subparagraph (i) the judge concerned shall issue a warrant authorising the detention of the person to whom the application relates for a further period not exceeding 48 hours if, but only if, the judge is satisfied that such further detention is necessary for the proper investigation of the offence concerned and that the investigation is being conducted diligently and expeditiously.

(3) On an application under subsection (2) the person to whom the application relates shall be produced before the judge concerned and the judge shall hear any submissions made and consider any evidence adduced by or on behalf of the person and the officer of the Garda Síochána making the application.

[(3A) (a) Without prejudice to paragraph (b), where a judge hearing an application under subsection (2) is satisfied, in order to avoid a risk of prejudice to the investigation concerned, that it is desirable to do so, he or she may—

   (i)   direct that the application be heard otherwise than in public, or

   (ii) exclude from the Court during the hearing all persons except officers of the Court, persons directly concerned in the proceedings, bona fide representatives of the Press and such other persons as the Court may permit to remain.

 (b) On the hearing of an application under subsection (2), the judge may, of his or her own motion or on application by the officer of the Garda Síochána making the application under subsection (2), where it appears that—

   (i)   particular evidence to be given by any member of the Garda Síochána during the hearing (including evidence by way of answer to a question asked of the member in cross-examination) concerns steps that have been, or may be taken, in the course of any inquiry or investigation being conducted by the Garda Síochána with respect to the suspected involvement of the person to whom the application relates, or any other person, in the commission of the offence to which the detention relates or any other offence, and

   (ii) the nature of those steps is such that the giving of that evidence concerning them could prejudice, in a material respect, the proper conducting of any foregoing inquiry or investigation,

   direct that, in the public interest, the particular evidence shall be given in the absence of every person, including the person to whom the application relates and any legal representative (whether of that person or the applicant), other than—

   (I)   the member or members whose attendance is necessary for the purpose of giving the evidence to the judge; and

   (II) if the judge deems it appropriate, such one or more of the clerks or registrars of the Court as the judge determines.

 (c) If, having heard such evidence given in that manner, the judge considers the disclosure of the matters to which that evidence relates would not have the effect referred to in paragraph (b)(ii), the judge shall direct the evidence to be re-given in the presence of all the other persons (or, as the case may be, those of them not otherwise excluded from the Court under paragraph (a)).

 (d) No person shall publish or broadcast or cause to be published or broadcast any information about an application under subsection (2) other than a statement of—

   (i)   the fact that the application has been made by the Garda Síochána in relation to a particular investigation, and

   (ii) any decision resulting from the application.

(e) If any matter is published or broadcast in contravention of paragraph (d), the following persons, namely—

   (i) in the case of a publication in a newspaper or periodical, any proprietor, any editor and any publisher of the newspaper or periodical,

   (ii) in the case of any other publication, the person who publishes it, and

   (iii) in the case of a broadcast, any person who transmits or provides the programme in which the broadcast is made and any person having functions in relation to the programme corresponding to those of the editor of a newspaper,

   shall be guilty of an offence and shall be liable—

   (I) on summary conviction to a fine not exceeding €5,000 or imprisonment for a term not exceeding 12 months or both, or

   (II) on conviction on indictment, to a fine not exceeding €50,000 or imprisonment for a term not exceeding 3 years or both.

(f) Where an offence under this subsection has been committed by a body corporate and is proved to have been committed with the consent or connivance of or to be attributable to any neglect on the part of a person being a director, manager, secretary or other officer of the body corporate, or a person who was purporting to act in any such capacity, that person as well as the body corporate shall be guilty of an offence and be liable to be proceeded against and punished as if he or she were guilty of the first-mentioned offence.

(g) Where the affairs of a body corporate are managed by its members, paragraph (f) shall apply in relation to the acts and defaults of a member in connection with his or her functions of management as if he or she were a director or manager of the body corporate.

(h) In this subsection—

   "broadcast" means the transmission, relaying or distribution by wireless telegraphy, cable or the internet of communications, sounds, signs, visual images or signals, intended for direct reception by the general public whether such communications, sounds, signs, visual images or signals are actually received or not;

   "publish" means publish, other than by way of broadcast, to the public or a portion of the public.

(3B) Save where any rule of law requires such an issue to be determined by the Court, in an application under subsection (2) no issue as to the lawfulness of the arrest or detention of the person to whom the application relates may be raised.

(3C)(a) In an application under subsection (2) it shall not be necessary for a member of the Garda Síochána, other than the officer making the application, to give oral evidence for the purposes of the application and the latter officer may testify in relation to any matter within the knowledge of another member of the Garda Síochána that is relevant to the application notwithstanding that it is not within the personal knowledge of the officer.

(b) However, the Court hearing such an application may, if it considers it be in the interests of justice to do so, direct that another member of the Garda Síochána give oral evidence and the Court may adjourn the hearing of the application for the purpose of receiving such evidence.][3]

(4) When issuing a warrant under subsection (2) the judge concerned may order that the person concerned be brought before a judge of the Circuit Court or a judge of the District Court at a specified time or times during the period of detention specified in the warrant and if, upon the person's being so brought before such a judge, he or she is not satisfied that the person's detention is justified, the judge shall revoke the warrant and order the immediate release from custody of the person.

(5) If at any time during the detention of a person pursuant to this section there are no longer reasonable grounds for believing that his or her detention is necessary for the proper investigation of the offence to which the detention relates, he or she shall, subject to subsection (6), be released from custody forthwith unless he or she is charged or caused to be charged with an offence and is brought before a court as soon as may be in connection with such charge or his or her detention is authorised apart from this Act.

(6) If at any time during the detention of a person pursuant to this section a member of the Garda Síochána, with reasonable cause, suspects that person of having committed a drug trafficking offence other than the offence to which the detention relates and—

    (a)   the member of the Garda Síochána then in charge of the Garda Síochána station, or

    (b)   in case the person is being detained in a place of detention, a member of the Garda Síochána not below the rank of inspector who is not investigating the offence to which the detention relates or the other offence,

has reasonable grounds for believing that the continued detention of the person is necessary for the proper investigation of that other offence, the person may continue to be detained in relation to the other offence as if that offence was the offence for which the person was originally detained.

(7) To avoid doubt, it is hereby declared that a person shall not be detained pursuant to this section for more than 168 hours from the time of his or her arrest, not including any period which is to be excluded under section 4(8) of the Act of 1984 (as applied by section 5) in reckoning a period of detention.

[(7A) Notwithstanding subsections (2) and (7), if—

    (a)   an application is to be made, or is made, under subsection (2) for a warrant authorising the detention for a further period of a person detained under that subsection, and

    (b)   the period of detention under that subsection has not expired at the time of the arrival of the person concerned at the court house for the purposes of the hearing of the application but would, but for this subsection, expire before, or during the hearing (including, if such should occur, any adjournment of the hearing),

it shall be deemed not to expire until the final determination of the application; and, for purposes of this subsection—

    (i)   a certificate signed by the court clerk or registrar in attendance at the court house concerned stating the time of the arrival of the person concerned at that court house shall be evidence, until the contrary is shown, of the time of that person's arrival there;

    (ii)   "court house" includes any venue at which the hearing of the application takes place.]⁴

(8) Nothing in this section shall affect the operation of section 30 of the Act of 1939 or section 4 of the Act of 1984.

(9) (a) The Minister may make regulations prescribing specified places as places where a person may be detained pursuant to subsection (1)(b), and a place for the time being standing so specified is referred to in this Act as a "place of detention".

(b) Section 7 of the Act of 1984 and any regulations made thereunder shall, with any necessary modifications, apply in relation to places of detention as they apply in relation to Garda Síochána stations.

(10) Every regulation made under this section shall be laid before each House of the Oireachtas as soon as may be after it is made and, if a resolution annulling the regulation is passed by either such House within the next 21 days on which that House has sat after the regulation is laid before it, the regulation shall be annulled accordingly, but without prejudice to the validity of anything previously done thereunder.

Amendments

1   Subsection (1)(a) substituted by Criminal Justice Act 2006, s 10(a).

2   Subsection (2)(b) amended by Criminal Justice (Amendment) Act 2009, s 22(1)(a) by substituting 'superintendent' for 'chief superintendent'.

3   Subsections (3A)–(3C) inserted by Criminal Justice (Amendment) Act 2009, s 22(1)(b).

4   Subsection (7A) (inserted by Criminal Justice Act 2006, s 10(a)(ii)) substituted by Criminal Justice (Amendment) Act 2009, s 22(1)(c).

3   Amendment of Act of 1990

The Act of 1990 is hereby amended—

(a) in section 2—

(i) by the substitution in subsection (1) for "or section 4 of the Criminal Justice Act, 1984," of "section 4 of the Criminal Justice Act, 1984, or section 2 of the Criminal Justice (Drug Trafficking) Act, 1996,", and

(ii) by the insertion in paragraph (b) of subsection (3) after "applies" of "or a drug trafficking offence within the meaning of section 3(1) of the Criminal Justice Act, 1994 ",

and

(b) in section 4, by the substitution in subsection (2) thereof for "or section 4 of the Criminal Justice Act, 1984," of " section 4 of the Criminal Justice Act, 1984, or section 2 of the Criminal Justice (Drug Trafficking) Act, 1996,".

4   Rearrest

[(1) Where a person arrested on suspicion of having committed an offence is detained pursuant to section 2 and is released without any charge having been made against him or her, he or she shall not—

(a) be arrested again in connection with the offence to which the detention related, or

(b) be arrested for any other offence of which, at the time of the first arrest, the member of the Garda Síochána by whom he or she was arrested suspected, or ought reasonably to have suspected, him or her of having committed, except on the authority of a warrant issued by a judge of the Circuit Court or the District Court who is satisfied on information supplied on oath by a member of the Garda Síochána not below the rank of superintendent that either of the following cases apply, namely—

    (i) further information has come to the knowledge of the Garda Síochána since the person's release as to the person's suspected participation in the offence for which his or her arrest is sought,

    (ii) notwithstanding that the Garda Síochána had knowledge, prior to his or her release, of the person's suspected participation in the offence for which his or her arrest is sought, the questioning of the person in relation to that offence, prior to his or her release, would not have been in the interests of the proper investigation of the offence.

(1A) An application for a warrant under this section shall be heard otherwise than in public.]¹

(2) When issuing a warrant under subsection (1), the judge concerned may order that the person concerned be brought before a judge of the Circuit Court or a judge of the District Court on arrest or at any specified time or times during the period of detention authorised by section 2 as applied by subsection (3) and if, upon the person's being so brought before such a judge, he or she is not satisfied that the person's detention is justified, the judge shall revoke the warrant and order the immediate release from custody of the person.

(3) Section 2 shall apply to a person arrested in connection with an offence to which that section relates under a warrant issued pursuant to subsection (1), as it applies to a person to whom that section applies, with the following and any other necessary modifications:

    [(a) the substitution for paragraph (a) in subsection (1) of the following paragraph:

        "(a) Where a member of the Garda Síochána arrests a person (an "arrested person") under a warrant issued pursuant to section 4(1), the arrested person may be taken to and detained in a Garda Síochána station for a period or periods authorised by subsection (2) if the member of the Garda Síochána in charge of the station to which the arrested person is taken on arrest has at the time of the arrested person's arrival at the station reasonable grounds for believing that his or her detention is necessary for the proper investigation of the offence.

        (b) An officer of the Garda Síochána not below the rank of chief superintendent may apply to a judge of the Circuit Court or a judge of the District Court for a warrant authorising the detention of a person detained under paragraph (b) for a further period not exceeding 24 hours if he or she has reasonable grounds for believing that such further detention is necessary for the proper investigation of the offence concerned.

        (c) On an application under paragraph (c) the judge concerned shall issue a warrant authorising the detention of the person to whom the application relates for a further period not exceeding 24 hours if, but only if, the judge is satisfied that such further detention is necessary for the proper investigation of the offence concerned and that the investigation is being conducted diligently and expeditiously.",]²

    and

    (b) the substitution in paragraph (g)(i) of subsection (2) for "pursuant to a direction under paragraph (c)" of "under a warrant issued pursuant to paragraph (d)".

(4) A person arrested in connection with an offence other than one to which section 2 relates, under a warrant issued pursuant to subsection (1), shall, subject to subsection (2), be dealt with under section 4 of the Act of 1984 in like manner as a person arrested without warrant to whom the said section 4 applies.

(5) Notwithstanding subsection (1), a person to whom that subsection relates may be arrested for any offence for the purpose of charging him or her with that offence forthwith.

(6) Where a person who has been arrested under section 30 of the Act of 1939 or detained under section 4 of the Act of 1984 in connection with an offence is released without any charge having been made against him or her, he or she shall not be detained pursuant to section 2 —

    (a)   in connection with the first-mentioned offence, or

    (b)   in connection with an offence to which section 2 relates which, at the time of the first arrest, the member of the Garda Síochána by whom he or she was arrested suspected, or ought reasonably to have suspected, him or her of having committed.

Amendments

1   Subsection (1) substituted and (1A) inserted by Criminal Justice (Amendment) Act 2009, s 22(2).

2   Subsection (3)(a) inserted para (a) (with (a) and (b) renumbered as (b) and (c)) by Criminal Justice Act 2006, s 10(b).

5   Application of certain provisions of Act of 1984

Sections 4(4), 4(7), 4(8), [4(8A)][1] [4(8B)][2], 4(11), 5, 6(1) to (4), [6A, 8, 18, 19 and 19A][1] of the Act of 1984 shall apply with any necessary modifications in relation to persons detained under section 2 as they apply to persons detained under section 4 of the Act of 1984.

Amendments

1   Words inserted by Criminal Justice Act 2007, s 54.

2   Words inserted by Criminal Justice (Amendment) Act 2009, s 22(3).

6   Regulations regarding officers of customs and excise

(1) The Minister may, following consultation with the Minister for Finance, make regulations providing for the attendance of an officer of customs and excise at, and the participation of such an officer in, the questioning of a person detained under section 2 or under section 4 of the Act of 1984 in relation to a drug trafficking offence.

(2) An officer of customs and excise may not commit any act or make any omission which, if committed or made by a member of the Garda Síochána, would be a contravention of any regulation made under section 7 of the Act of 1984.

(3) An act committed or omission made by an officer of customs and excise which, if committed or made by a member of the Garda Síochána would be a contravention of any regulation made under the said section 7 shall not of itself render the officer liable to any criminal or civil proceedings or of itself affect the lawfulness of the custody of the detained person or the admissibility in evidence of any statement made by him or her.

(4) In this section "an officer of customs and excise" means a person appointed by the Revenue Commissioners under the Customs Acts and under the statutes which relate to the duties of excise or any instrument relating to duties of excise made under statute.

(5) A draft of every regulation proposed to be made under this section shall be laid before each House of the Oireachtas and the regulations shall not be made until a resolution approving of the draft has been passed by each such House.

7   Inferences from failure of accused to mention particular facts

[...]¹

Amendments

1   Section 7 repealed with saver by Criminal Justice Act 2007, s 3 and Sch 1.

Note

Criminal Justice Act 2007, s 3 provides:

(1) Subject to subsection (2), the enactments specified in Schedule 1 are repealed to the extent specified in column 3 of that Schedule.

(2) The repeal by subsection (1) of the enactments specified in Schedule 1 does not affect the application of those enactments to a failure to mention a fact to which those enactments relate if the failure occurred before the repeal comes into operation, and those enactments apply to such a failure as if they had not been repealed.

---

8   Search warrants

(1) Subsection (1) of section 26 of the Act of 1977 is hereby amended—

    (a) by the insertion after "Garda Síochána" of "or if, subject to the provisions of subsection (2) of section 8 of the Criminal Justice (Drug Trafficking) Act, 1996, a member of the Garda Síochána not below the rank of superintendent is satisfied", and

    (b) by the substitution for "such Justice or Commissioner" of "such Justice, Commissioner or, as the case may be, member".

(2) A member of the Garda Síochána not below the rank of superintendent shall not issue a search warrant under the said section 26 unless he or she is satisfied—

    (a) that the warrant is necessary for the proper investigation of a drug trafficking offence, and

    (b) that circumstances of urgency giving rise to the need for the immediate issue of the search warrant would render it impracticable to apply to a judge of the District

Court or a Peace Commissioner under the said section 26 for the issue of the warrant.

(3) Notwithstanding subsection (2) of section 26 of the Act of 1977, a search warrant issued by a member of the Garda Síochána not below the rank of superintendent under subsection (1) of that section shall cease to have effect after a period of 24 hours has elapsed from the time of the issue of the warrant.

9   Amendment of Public Dance Halls Act, 1935

The Public Dance Halls Act, 1935, is hereby amended by the insertion after section 13 of the following section:

> "13A.—(1) Any member of the Garda Síochána whether in uniform or not may enter any place in respect of which a public dancing licence is for the time being in force at any time while such place is being used for public dancing or at any other reasonable time and there make such inspection, examination and inquiry as he shall think proper for the prevention or detection of a drug trafficking offence within the meaning of section 3(1) of the Criminal Justice Act, 1994.
>
> (2) Every person who shall prevent or attempt to prevent a member of the Garda Síochána from exercising, or obstruct or attempt to obstruct any such member in the exercise of, a power vested in such member by virtue of this section shall be guilty of an offence under this section and shall be liable on summary conviction thereof to a fine not exceeding £1,000.".

10   Expenses

The expenses incurred by the Minister in the administration of this Act shall, to such extent as may be sanctioned by the Minister for Finance, be paid out of moneys provided by the Oireachtas.

11   Duration of certain sections

[…][1]

Amendments

1   Section 11 repealed by Criminal Justice (Amendment) Act 2009, s 22(4).

12   Short title and commencement

(1) This Act may be cited as the Criminal Justice (Drug Trafficking) Act, 1996.

(2) This Act shall come into operation on such day or days as may be fixed therefor by order or orders made by the Minister for Justice either generally or with reference to any particular purpose or provision and different days may be so fixed for different purposes and different provisions of this Act.

Proceeds of Crime Act 1996

Number 30 of 1996

ARRANGEMENT OF SECTIONS

1. Interpretation
2. Interim order
3. Interlocutory order
4. Disposal order
4A Consent disposal order.
5. Ancillary orders and provision in relation to certain profits or gains, etc
6. Order in relation to property the subject of interim order or interlocutory order
7. Receiver
8. Provisions in relation to evidence and proceedings under Act
9. Affidavit specifying property and income of respondent
10. Registration of interim orders and interlocutory orders
11. Bankruptcy of respondent, etc
12. Property subject to interim order, interlocutory order or disposal order dealt with by Official Assignee
13. Winding up of company in possession or control of property the subject of interim order, interlocutory order or disposal order
14. Immunity from proceedings
15. Seizure of certain property
16. Compensation
16A Admissibility of certain documents
16B Corrupt enrichment order
17. Expenses
18. Short title

AN ACT TO ENABLE THE HIGH COURT, AS RESPECTS THE PROCEEDS OF CRIME, TO MAKE ORDERS FOR THE PRESERVATION AND, WHERE APPROPRIATE, THE DISPOSAL OF THE PROPERTY CONCERNED AND TO PROVIDE FOR RELATED MATTERS. [4th August, 1996]

BE IT ENACTED BY THE OIREACHTAS AS FOLLOWS:

1   Interpretation

(1) In this Act, save where the context otherwise requires—

["the applicant" means a person, being a member, an authorised officer or the Criminal Assets Bureau, who has applied to the Court for the making of an interim order or an interlocutory order and, in relation to such an order that is in force, means, as appropriate, any member, any authorised officer or the Criminal Assets Bureau;]¹

"authorised officer" means an officer of the Revenue Commissioners authorised in writing by the Revenue Commissioners to perform the functions conferred by this Act on authorised officers;

["consent disposal order" means an order under section 3(1A) or 4A(1);]²

"the Court" means the High Court;

["criminal conduct" means any conduct—

(a) which constitutes an offence or more than one offence, or

(b) which occurs outside the State and which would constitute an offence or more than one offence—

    (i) if it occurred within the State,

    (ii) if it constituted an offence under the law of the state or territory concerned, and

    (iii) if, at the time when an application is being made for an interim order or interlocutory order, any property obtained or received at any time (whether before or after the passing of this Act) by or as a result of or in connection with the conduct is situated within the State;]²

"dealing", in relation to property in the possession or control of a person, includes—

(a) where a debt is owed to that person, making a payment to any person in reduction of the amount of the debt,

(b) removing the property from the State, and

(c) in the case of money or other property held for the person by another person, paying or releasing or transferring it to the person or to any other person;

"disposal order" means an order under section 4;

"interest", in relation to property, includes right;

"interim order" means an order under section 2;

"interlocutory order" means an order under section 3;

"member" means a member of the Garda Síochána not below the rank of Chief Superintendent;

"the Minister" means the Minister for Finance;

["proceeds of crime" means any property obtained or received at any time (whether before or after the passing of this Act) by or as a result of or in connection with criminal conduct;

"property", in relation to proceeds of crime, includes—

(a) money and all other property, real or personal, heritable or moveable,

(b) choses in action and other intangible or incorporeal property, and

(c) property situated outside the State where—

    (i) the respondent is domiciled, resident or present in the State, and

    (ii) all or any part of the criminal conduct concerned occurs therein,

and references to property shall be construed as including references to any interest in property;

"the respondent" means a person, wherever domiciled, resident or present, in respect of whom an interim order or interlocutory order, or an application for such an order, has been made and includes any person who, but for this Act, would become entitled, on the death of the first-mentioned person, to any property to which such an order relates (being an order that is in force and is in respect of that person);]¹

[(1A) (a) For the avoidance of doubt, a person shall be deemed for the purposes of this Act to be in possession or control of property notwithstanding that it (or any part of it)—

    (i)   s lawfully in the possession of any member of the Garda Síochána, any officer of the Revenue Commissioners or any other person, having been lawfully seized or otherwise taken by any such member, officer or person,

    (ii) is subject to an interim order or interlocutory order or any other order of a court which—

        (I)   prohibits any person from disposing of or otherwise dealing with it or diminishing its value, or

        (II)   contains any conditions or restrictions in that regard,

        or is to the like effect,

        or

    (iii) is subject to a letting agreement, the subject of a trust or otherwise occupied by another person or is inaccessible,

and references in this Act to the possession or control of property shall be construed accordingly.

   (b) Paragraph (a)(ii) is without prejudice to sections 11(2) and 13(2).]³

(2) In this Act—

   (a) a reference to a section is a reference to a section of this Act unless it is indicated that reference to some other provision is intended, and

   (b) a reference to a subsection, paragraph or subparagraph is a reference to a subsection, paragraph or subparagraph of the provision in which the reference occurs, unless it is indicated that reference to some other provision is intended, and

   (c) a reference to any enactment shall be construed as a reference to that enactment as amended, adapted or extended by or under any subsequent enactment.

Amendments

1   Definitions substituted by Proceeds of Crime (Amendment) Act 2005, s 3(a)(i).

2   Definitions inserted by Proceeds of Crime (Amendment) Act 2005, s 3(a)(ii).

3   Subsection (1A) inserted by Proceeds of Crime (Amendment) Act 2005, s 3(b).

2   Interim order

[(1) Where it is shown to the satisfaction of the Court on application to it ex parte in that behalf by a member, an authorised officer or the Criminal Assets Bureau —]¹

   (a) that a person is in possession or control of—

      (i)   specified property and that the property constitutes, directly or indirectly, proceeds of crime, or

(ii) specified property that was acquired, in whole or in part, with or in connection with property that, directly or indirectly, constitutes proceeds of crime,

and

(b) that the value of the property or, as the case may be, the total value of the property referred to in both subparagraphs (i) and (ii), of paragraph (a) is not less than [€13,000],[2]

the Court may make an order ("an interim order") prohibiting the person or any other specified person or any other person having notice of the order from disposing of or otherwise dealing with the whole or, if appropriate, a specified part of the property or diminishing its value during the period of 21 days from the date of the making of the order.

(2) An interim order—

(a) may contain such provisions, conditions and restrictions as the Court considers necessary or expedient, and

(b) shall provide for notice of it to be given to the respondent and any other person who appears to be or is affected by it unless the Court is satisfied that it is not reasonably possible to ascertain his, her or their whereabouts.

(3) Where an interim order is in force, the Court, on application to it in that behalf by the respondent or any other person claiming ownership of any of the property concerned may, if it is shown to the satisfaction of the Court that—

(a) the property concerned or a part of it is not property to which subparagraph (i) or (ii) of subsection (1)(a) applies, or

(b) the value of the property to which those subparagraphs apply is less than [€13,000][2],

discharge or, as may be appropriate, vary the order.

[(3A) Without prejudice to sections 3(7) and 6, where an interim order is in force, the Court may, on application to it in that behalf by the applicant or any other person, vary the order to such extent as may be necessary to permit—

(a) the enforcement of any order of a court for the payment by the respondent of any sum, including any sum in respect of costs,

(b) the recovery by a county registrar or sheriff of income tax due by the respondent pursuant to a certificate issued by the Collector-General under section 962 of the Taxes Consolidation Act 1997, together with the fees and expenses provided for in that section, or

(c) the institution of proceedings for, or relating to, the recovery of any other sum owed by the respondent.][3]

(4) The Court shall, on application to it in that behalf at any time by the applicant, discharge an interim order.

(5) Subject to subsections (3) and (4), an interim order shall continue in force until the expiration of the period of 21 days from the date of its making and shall then lapse unless an application for the making of an interlocutory order in respect of any of the property concerned is brought during that period and, if such an application is brought, the interim order shall lapse upon—

(a) the determination of the application,

(b) the expiration of the ordinary time for bringing an appeal from the determination,

(c) if such an appeal is brought, the determination or abandonment of it or of any further appeal or the expiration of the ordinary time for bringing any further appeal,

whichever is the latest.

(6) Notice of an application under this section shall be given—

(a) in case the application is under subsection (3), by the respondent or other person making the application to the applicant,

[(b) in case the application is under subsection (3A) or (4), by the applicant or other person making the application to the respondent, unless the Court is satisfied that it is not reasonably possible to ascertain the respondent's whereabouts,]⁴

and, in either case, to any other person in relation to whom the Court directs that notice of the application be given to him or her.

[(7) An application under subsection (1) may be made by originating motion.]⁵

Amendments

1   Subsection (1) amended by Proceeds of Crime (Amendment) Act 2005, s 4(a).

2   Amount amended by Euro Changeover (Amounts) Act 2001, Schs 3 and 4.

3   Subsection (3A) inserted by Proceeds of Crime (Amendment) Act 2005, s 4(b).

4   Subsection (6)(b) substituted by Proceeds of Crime (Amendment) Act 2005, s 4(c).

5   Subsection (7) inserted by Proceeds of Crime (Amendment) Act 2005, s 4(d).

---

3   Interlocutory order

[(1) Where, on application to it in that behalf by a member, an authorised officer or the Criminal Assets Bureau, it appears to the Court on evidence tendered by the applicant, which may consist of or include evidence admissible by virtue of section 8—]¹

(a) that a person is in possession or control of—

(i) specified property and that the property constitutes, directly or indirectly, proceeds of crime, or

(ii) specified property that was acquired, in whole or in part, with or in connection with property that, directly or indirectly, constitutes proceeds of crime,

and

(b) that the value of the property or, as the case may be, the total value of the property referred to in both subparagraphs (i) and (ii) of paragraph (a) is not less than [€13,000]²,

[the Court shall, subject to subsection (1A), make]¹ an order ("an interlocutory order") prohibiting the respondent or any other specified person or any other person having notice of the order from disposing of or otherwise dealing with the whole or, if appropriate, a specified part of the property or diminishing its value, unless, it is shown to the satisfaction of the Court, on evidence tendered by the respondent or any other person—

(I)   that that particular property does not constitute, directly or indirectly, proceeds of crime and was not acquired, in whole or in part, with or in connection with property that, directly or indirectly, constitutes proceeds of crime, or

(II) that the value of all the property to which the order would relate is less than [€13,000]²:

Provided, however, that the Court shall not make the order if it is satisfied that there would be a serious risk of injustice.

[(1A) On such an application the Court, with the consent of all the parties concerned, may make a consent disposal order, and section 4A shall apply and have effect accordingly.]³

(2) An interlocutory order—

(a)   may contain such provisions, conditions and restrictions as the Court considers necessary or expedient, and

(b)   shall provide for notice of it to be given to the respondent and any other person who appears to be or is affected by it unless the Court is satisfied that it is not reasonably possible to ascertain his, her or their whereabouts.

(3) Where an interlocutory order is in force, the Court, on application to it in that behalf at any time by the respondent or any other person claiming ownership of any of the property concerned, may, if it is shown to the satisfaction of the Court that the property or a specified part of it is property to which paragraph (I) of subsection (1) applies, or that the order causes any other injustice, discharge or, as may be appropriate, vary the order.

[(3A) Without prejudice to subsection (7) and section 6, where an interlocutory order is in force, the Court may, on application to it in that behalf by the applicant or any other person, vary the order to such extent as may be necessary to permit—

(a)   the enforcement of any order of a court for the payment by the respondent of any sum, including any sum in respect of costs,

(b)   the recovery by a county registrar or sheriff of income tax due by the respondent pursuant to a certificate issued by the Collector-General under section 962 of the Taxes Consolidation Act 1997, together with the fees and expenses provided for in that section, or

(c)   the institution of proceedings for, or relating to, the recovery of any other sum owed by the respondent.]⁴

(4) The Court shall, on application to it in that behalf at any time by the applicant, discharge an interlocutory order.

(5) Subject to subsections (3) and (4), an interlocutory order shall continue in force until—

(a)   the determination of an application for a disposal order in relation to the property concerned,

(b)   the expiration of the ordinary time for bringing an appeal from that determination,

(c)   if such an appeal is brought, it or any further appeal is determined or abandoned or the ordinary time for bringing any further appeal has expired,

whichever is the latest, and shall then lapse.

(6) Notice of an application under this section shall be given—

[(a) in case the application is under subsection (1), (3A) or (4), by the applicant or other person making the application to the respondent, unless the Court is satisfied that it is not reasonably possible to ascertain the respondent's whereabouts,]⁵

(b)   in case the application is under subsection (3), by the respondent or other person making the application to the applicant,

and, in either case, to any other person in relation to whom the Court directs that notice of the application be given to him or her.

(7) Where a forfeiture order, or a confiscation order, under the Criminal Justice Act, 1994, or a forfeiture order under the Misuse of Drugs Act, 1977, relates to any property that is the subject of an interim order, or an interlocutory order, that is in force, ("the specified property"), the interim order or, as the case may be, the interlocutory order shall—

(a)   if it relates only to the specified property, stand discharged, and

(b)   if it relates also to other property, stand varied by the exclusion from it of the specified property.

[(8) An application under subsection (1) may be made by originating motion.]⁶

Amendments

1   Subsection (1) amended by Proceeds of Crime (Amendment) Act 2005, s 5(a).

2   Amount amended by Euro Changeover (Amounts) Act 2001, Schs 3 and 4.

3   Subsection (1A) inserted by Proceeds of Crime (Amendment) Act 2005, s 5(b).

4   Subsection (3A) inserted by Proceeds of Crime (Amendment) Act 2005, s 5(c).

5   Subsection (6)(a) substituted by Proceeds of Crime (Amendment) Act 2005, s 5(d).

6   Subsection (8) inserted by Proceeds of Crime (Amendment) Act 2005, s 5(e).

---

4   Disposal order

(1) Subject to subsection (2), where an interlocutory order has been in force for not less than 7 years in relation to specified property, the Court, on application to it in that behalf by the applicant, may make an order ("a disposal order") directing that the whole or, if appropriate, a specified part of the property be transferred, subject to such terms and conditions as the Court may specify, to the Minister or to such other person as the Court may determine.

(2) Subject to subsections (6) and (8), the Court shall make a disposal order in relation to any property the subject of an application under subsection (1) unless it is shown to its satisfaction that that particular property does not constitute, directly or indirectly, proceeds of crime and was not acquired, in whole or in part, with or in connection with property that, directly or indirectly, constitutes proceeds of crime.

(3) The applicant shall give notice to the respondent (unless the Court is satisfied that it is not reasonably possible to ascertain his or her whereabouts), and to such other (if any) persons as the Court may direct of an application under this section.

(4) A disposal order shall operate to deprive the respondent of his or her rights (if any) in or to the property to which it relates and, upon the making of the order, the property shall stand transferred to the Minister or other person to whom it relates.

(5) The Minister may sell or otherwise dispose of any property transferred to him or her under this section, and any proceeds of such a disposition and any moneys transferred to him

or her under this section shall be paid into or disposed of for the benefit of the Exchequer by the Minister.

(6) In proceedings under subsection (1), before deciding whether to make a disposal order, the Court shall give an opportunity to be heard by the Court and to show cause why the order should not be made to any person claiming ownership of any of the property concerned.

(7) The Court, if it considers it appropriate to do so in the interests of justice, on the application of the respondent or, if the whereabouts of the respondent cannot be ascertained, on its own initiative, may adjourn the hearing of an application under subsection (1) for such period not exceeding 2 years as it considers reasonable.

(8) The Court shall not make a disposal order if it is satisfied that there would be a serious risk of injustice.

[(9) An application under subsection (1) may be made by originating motion.]¹

Amendments

1   Subsection (9) inserted by Proceeds of Crime (Amendment) Act 2005, s 6.

[4A   Consent disposal order

(1) Where in relation to any property—

> (a)   an interlocutory order has been in force for a period of less than 7 years, and
>
> (b)   an application is made to the Court with the consent of all the parties concerned,

the Court may make an order (a 'consent disposal order') directing that the whole or a specified part of the property be transferred to the Minister or to such other person as the Court may determine, subject to such terms and conditions as it may specify.

(2) A consent disposal order operates to deprive the respondent of his or her rights (if any) in or to the property to which the order relates and, on its being made, the property stands transferred to the Minister or that other person.

(3) The Minister—

> (a)   may sell or otherwise dispose of any property transferred to him or her under this section, and
>
> (b)   shall pay into or dispose of for the benefit of the Exchequer the proceeds of any such disposition as well as any moneys so transferred.

(4) Before deciding whether to make a consent disposal order, the Court shall give to any person claiming ownership of any of the property concerned an opportunity to show cause why such an order should not be made.

(5) The Court shall not make a consent disposal order if it is satisfied that there would be a serious risk of injustice if it did so.

(6) Sections 3(7) and 16 apply, with any necessary modifications, in relation to a consent disposal order as they apply in relation to an interlocutory order.

(7) This section is without prejudice to section 3(1A).]¹

Amendments

1   Section 4A inserted by Proceeds of Crime (Amendment) Act 2005, s 7.

5   Ancillary orders and provision in relation to certain profits or gains, etc

(1) At any time while an interim order or an interlocutory order is in force, the Court may, on application to it in that behalf by the applicant, make such orders as it considers necessary or expedient to enable the order aforesaid to have full effect.

(2) Notice of an application under this section shall be given by the applicant to the respondent unless the Court is satisfied that it is not reasonably possible to ascertain his or her whereabouts and to any other person in relation to whom the Court directs that notice of the application be given to him or her.

(3) An interim order, an interlocutory order or a disposal order may be expressed to apply to any profit or gain or interest, dividend or other payment or any other property payable or arising, after the making of the order, in connection with any other property to which the order relates.

6   Order in relation to property the subject of interim order or interlocutory order

(1) At any time while an interim order or an interlocutory order is in force, the Court may, on application to it in that behalf by the respondent or any other person affected by the order, make such orders as it considers appropriate in relation to any of the property concerned if it considers it essential to do so for the purpose of enabling—

    [(a)   the respondent or that other person to discharge the reasonable living and other necessary expenses (including legal expenses in or in relation to proceedings under this Act) incurred or to be incurred by or in respect of the respondent and his or her dependants or that other person, or][1]

    (b)   the respondent or that other person to carry on a business, trade, profession or other occupation to which any of that property relates.

(2) An order under this section may contain such conditions and restrictions as the Court considers necessary or expedient for the purpose of protecting the value of the property concerned and avoiding any unnecessary diminution thereof.

(3) Notice of an application under this section shall be given by the person making the application to the applicant and any other person in relation to whom the Court directs that notice of the application be given to him or her.

Amendments

1   Subsection (1)(a) substituted by Proceeds of Crime (Amendment) Act 2005, s 8.

7 Receiver

(1) Where an interim order or an interlocutory order is in force, the Court may at any time appoint a receiver—

(a) to take possession of any property to which the order relates,

(b) in accordance with the Court's directions, to manage, keep possession or dispose of or otherwise deal with any property in respect of which he or she is appointed, subject to such exceptions and conditions (if any) as may be specified by the Court, and may require any person having possession or control of property in respect of which the receiver is appointed to give possession of it to the receiver.

(2) Where a receiver takes any action under this section—

(a) in relation to property which is not property the subject of an interim order or an interlocutory order, being action which he or she would be entitled to take if it were such property, and

(b) believing, and having reasonable grounds for believing, that he or she is entitled to take that action in relation to that property,

he or she shall not be liable to any person in respect of any loss or damage resulting from such action except in so far as the loss or damage is caused by his or her negligence.

8 Provisions in relation to evidence and proceedings under Act

(1) Where a member or an authorised officer states—

(a) in proceedings under section 2, on affidavit or, if the Court so directs, in oral evidence, or

[(b) in proceedings under section 3, on affidavit or, where the respondent requires the deponent to be produced for cross-examination or the court so directs, in oral evidence,]¹

and that the value of the property or, as the case may be, the total value of the property referred to in both paragraphs (i) and (ii) is not less than [€13,000]², then, if the Court is satisfied that there are reasonable grounds for the belief aforesaid, the statement shall be evidence of the matter referred to in paragraph (i) or in paragraph (ii) or in both, as may be appropriate, and of the value of the property.

(2) The standard of proof required to determine any question arising under this Act shall be that applicable to civil proceedings.

(3) Proceedings under this Act in relation to an interim order shall be heard otherwise than in public and any other proceedings under this Act may, if the respondent or any other party to the proceedings (other than the applicant) so requests and the Court considers it proper, be heard otherwise than in public.

(4) The Court may, if it considers it appropriate to do so, prohibit the publication of such information as it may determine in relation to proceedings under this Act, including information in relation to applications for, the making or refusal of and the contents of orders under this Act and the persons to whom they relate.

(5) Production to the Court in proceedings under this Act of a document purporting to authorise a person, who is described therein as an officer of the Revenue Commissioners, to perform the functions conferred on authorised officers by this Act and to be signed by a Revenue Commissioner shall be evidence that the person is an authorised officer.

[(6) In any proceedings under this Act a document purporting to be a document issued by the Criminal Assets Bureau and to be signed on its behalf shall be deemed, unless the contrary is shown, to be such a document and to be so signed.]³

Amendments

1   Subsection (1)(b) substituted by Proceeds of Crime (Amendment) Act 2005, s 9(a).

2   Amount amended by Euro Changeover (Amounts) Act 2001, Schs 3 and 4.

3   Subsection (6) inserted by Proceeds of Crime (Amendment) Act 2005, s 9(b).

9   Affidavit specifying property and income of respondent

(1) At any time during proceedings under section 2 or 3 or while an interim order or an interlocutory order is in force, the Court or, as appropriate, in the case of an appeal in such proceedings, the Supreme Court may by order direct the respondent to file an affidavit in the Central Office of the High Court specifying—

    (a)   the property of which the respondent is in possession or control, or

    (b)   the income, and the sources of the income, of the respondent during such period (not exceeding 10 years) ending on the date of the application for the order as the court concerned may specify,

or both.

[(2) Such an affidavit is not admissible in evidence in any criminal proceedings against that person or his or her spouse, except any such proceedings for perjury arising from statements in the affidavit.]¹

Amendments

1   Section 9 renumbered as s 9(1) and sub-s (2) inserted by Proceeds of Crime (Amendment) Act 2005, s 11.

10   Registration of interim orders and interlocutory orders

(1) Where an interim order or an interlocutory order is made, the registrar of the Court shall, in the case of registered land, furnish the Registrar of Titles with notice of the order and the Registrar of Titles shall thereupon cause an entry to be made in the appropriate register under the Registration of Title Act, 1964, inhibiting, until such time as the order lapses, is discharged or is varied so as to exclude the registered land or any charge thereon from the application of the order, any dealing with any registered land or charge which appears to be affected by the order.

(2) Where notice of an order has been given under subsection (1) and the order is varied in relation to registered land, the registrar of the Court shall furnish the Registrar of Titles with notice to that effect and the Registrar of Titles shall thereupon cause the entry made under subsection (1) of this section to be varied to that effect.

(3) Where notice of an order has been given under subsection (1) and the order is discharged or lapses, the registrar of the High Court shall furnish the Registrar of Titles with notice to that effect and the Registrar of Titles shall cancel the entry made under subsection (1).

(4) Where an interim order or an interlocutory order is made, the registrar of the Court shall, in the case of unregistered land, furnish the Registrar of Deeds with notice of the order and the Registrar of Deeds shall thereupon cause the notice to be registered in the Registry of Deeds pursuant to the Registration of Deeds Act, 1707.

(5) Where notice of an order has been given under subsection (4) and the order is varied, the registrar of the Court shall furnish the Registrar of Deeds with notice to that effect and the Registrar of Deeds shall thereupon cause the notice registered under subsection (4) to be varied to that effect.

(6) Where notice of an order has been given under subsection (4) and the order is discharged or lapses, the registrar of the Court shall furnish the Registrar of Deeds with notice to that effect and the Registrar of Deeds shall thereupon cancel the registration made under subsection (4).

(7) Where an interim order or an interlocutory order is made which applies to an interest in a company or to the property of a company, the registrar of the Court shall furnish the Registrar of Companies with notice of the order and the Registrar of Companies shall thereupon cause the notice to be entered in the Register of Companies maintained under the Companies Acts, 1963 to 1990.

(8) Where notice of an order has been given under subsection (7) and the order is varied, the registrar of the Court shall furnish the Registrar of Companies with notice to that effect and the Registrar of Companies shall thereupon cause the notice entered under subsection (7) to be varied to that effect.

(9) Where notice of an order has been given under subsection (7) and the order is discharged or lapses, the registrar of the Court shall furnish the Registrar of Companies with notice to that effect and the Registrar of Companies shall thereupon cancel the entry made under subsection (7).

11   Bankruptcy of respondent, etc

(1) Where a person who is in possession or control of property is adjudicated bankrupt, property subject to an interim order, an interlocutory order, or a disposal order, made before the order adjudicating the person bankrupt, is excluded from the property of the bankrupt for the purposes of the Bankruptcy Act, 1988.

(2) Where a person has been adjudicated bankrupt, the powers conferred on the Court by section 2 or 3 shall not be exercised in relation to property of the bankrupt for the purposes of the said Act of 1988.

(3) In any case in which a petition in bankruptcy was presented, or an adjudication in bankruptcy was made, before the 1st day of January, 1989, this section shall have effect with the modification that, for the references in subsections (1) and (2) to the property of the bankrupt for the purposes of the Act aforesaid, there shall be substituted references to the property of the bankrupt vesting in the assignees for the purposes of the law of bankruptcy existing before that date.

12   **Property subject to interim order, interlocutory order or disposal order dealt with by Official Assignee**

(1) Without prejudice to the generality of any provision of any other enactment, where—

    (a) the Official Assignee or a trustee appointed under the provisions of Part V of the Bankruptcy Act, 1988, seizes or disposes of any property in relation to which his or her functions are not exercisable because it is subject to an interim order, an interlocutory order or a disposal order, and

    (b) at the time of the seizure or disposal he or she believes, and has reasonable grounds for believing, that he or she is entitled (whether in pursuance of an order of a court or otherwise) to seize or dispose of that property,

he or she shall not be liable to any person in respect of any loss or damage resulting from the seizure or disposal except in so far as the loss or damage is caused by his or her negligence in so acting, and he or she shall have a lien on the property, or the proceeds of its sale, for such of his or her expenses as were incurred in connection with the bankruptcy or other proceedings in relation to which the seizure or disposal purported to take place and for so much of his or her remuneration as may reasonably be assigned for his or her acting in connection with those proceedings.

(2) Where the Official Assignee or a trustee appointed as aforesaid incurs expenses in respect of such property as is mentioned in subsection (1)(a) and in so doing does not know and has no reasonable grounds to believe that the property is for the time being subject to an order under this Act, he or she shall be entitled (whether or not he or she has seized or disposed of that property so as to have a lien) to payment of those expenses.

13   **Winding up of company in possession or control of property the subject of interim order, interlocutory order or disposal order**

(1) Where property the subject of an interim order, an interlocutory order or a disposal order made before the relevant time is in the possession or control of a company and an order for the winding up of the company has been made or a resolution has been passed by the company for a voluntary winding up, the functions of the liquidator (or any provisional liquidator) shall not be exercisable in relation to the property.

(2) Where, in the case of a company, an order for its winding up has been made or such a resolution has been passed, the powers conferred by section 2 or 3 on the Court shall not be exercised in relation to any property held by the company in relation to which the functions of the liquidator are exercisable—

    (a) so as to inhibit him or her from exercising those functions for the purpose of distributing any property held by the company to the company's creditors, or

    (b) so as to prevent the payment out of any property of expenses (including the remuneration of the liquidator or any provisional liquidator) properly incurred in the winding up in respect of the property.

(3) In this section—

"company" means any company which may be wound up under the Companies Acts, 1963 to 1990;

"relevant time" means—

    (a) where no order for the winding up of the company has been made, the time of the passing of the resolution for voluntary winding up,

(b) where such an order has been made and, before the presentation of the petition for the winding up of the company by the court, such a resolution had been passed by the company, the time of the passing of the resolution, and

(c) in any other case where such an order has been made, the time of the making of the order.

14   Immunity from proceedings

No action or proceedings of any kind shall lie against a bank, building society or other financial institution or any other person in any court in respect of any act or omission done or made in compliance with an order under this Act.

15   Seizure of certain property

(1) Where an order under this Act is in force, a member of the Garda Síochána or an officer of customs and excise may, for the purpose of preventing any property the subject of the order being removed from the State, seize the property.

(2) Property seized under this section shall be dealt with in accordance with the directions of the Court.

16   Compensation

(1) Where—

(a) an interim order is discharged or lapses and an interlocutory order in relation to the matter is not made or, if made, is discharged (otherwise than pursuant to section 3(7)),

(b) an interlocutory order is discharged (otherwise than pursuant to section 3(7)) or lapses and a disposal order in relation to the matter is not made or, if made, is discharged,

(c) an interim order or an interlocutory order is varied (otherwise than pursuant to section 3(7)) or a disposal order is varied on appeal,

the Court may, on application to it in that behalf by a person who shows to the satisfaction of the Court that—

(i) he or she is the owner of any property to which—

(I) an order referred to in paragraph (a) or (b) related, or

(II) an order referred to in paragraph (c) had related but, by reason of its being varied by a court, has ceased to relate,

and

(ii) the property does not constitute, directly or indirectly, proceeds of crime or was not acquired, in whole or in part, with or in connection with property that, directly or indirectly, constitutes proceeds of crime, award to the person such (if any) compensation payable by the Minister as it considers just in the circumstances in respect of any loss incurred by the person by reason of the order concerned.

(2) The Minister shall be given notice of, and be entitled to be heard in, any proceedings under this section.

[16A   Admissibility of certain documents

(1) The following documents are admissible in any proceedings under this Act, without further proof, as evidence of any fact therein of which direct oral evidence would be admissible:

    (a) a document constituting part of the records of a business or a copy of such a document;

    (b) a deed;

    (c) a document purporting to be signed by a person on behalf of a business and stating—

        (i) either—

            (I) that a designated document or documents constitutes or constitute part of the records of the business or is or are a copy or copies of such a document or documents, or

            (II) that there is no entry or other reference in those records in relation to a specified matter, and

        (ii) that the person has personal knowledge of the matters referred to in subparagraph (i).

(2) Evidence that is admissible by virtue of subsection (1) shall not be admitted if the Court is of the opinion that in the interests of justice it ought not to be admitted.

(3) This section is without prejudice to any other enactment or any rule of law authorising the admission of documentary evidence.

(4) In this section—

'business' includes—

    (a) an undertaking not carried on for profit, and

    (b) a public authority;

'deed' means any document by which an estate or interest in land is created, transferred, charged or otherwise affected and includes a contract for the sale of land;

'document' includes a reproduction in legible form of a record in non-legible form;

'public authority' has the meaning given to it by section 2(1) of the Local Government Act 2001 and includes a local authority within the meaning of that section;

'records' includes records in non-legible form and any reproduction thereof in legible form.][1]

Amendments

1   Section 16A inserted by Proceeds of Crime (Amendment) Act 2005, s 12.

[16B   Corrupt enrichment order

(1) For the purposes of this section—

    (a) a person is corruptly enriched if he or she derives a pecuniary or other advantage or benefit as a result of or in connection with corrupt conduct, wherever the conduct occurred;

(b) 'corrupt conduct' is any conduct which at the time it occurred was an offence under the Prevention of Corruption Acts 1889 to 2001, the Official Secrets Act 1963 or the Ethics in Public Office Act 1995;

(c) 'property' includes—

(i) money and all other property, real or personal, heritable or moveable,

(ii) choses in action and other intangible or incorporeal property, and

(iii) property situated outside the State,

and references to property shall be construed as including references to any interest in property.

(2) Where, on application to it in that behalf by the applicant, it appears to the Court, on evidence tendered by the applicant, consisting of or including evidence admissible by virtue of subsection (5), that a person (a 'defendant') has been corruptly enriched, the Court may make an order (a 'corrupt enrichment order') directing the defendant to pay to the Minister or such other person as the Court may specify an amount equivalent to the amount by which it determines that the defendant has been so enriched.

(3) Where—

(a) the defendant is in a position to benefit others in the exercise of his or her official functions,

(b) another person has benefited from the exercise, and

(c) the defendant does not account satisfactorily for his or her property or for the resources, income or source of income from which it was acquired,

it shall be presumed, until the contrary is shown, that the defendant has engaged in corrupt conduct.

(4) In any proceedings under this section the Court may, on application to it *ex parte* in that behalf by the applicant, make an order prohibiting the defendant or any other person having notice of the order from disposing of or otherwise dealing with specified property of the defendant or diminishing its value during a period specified by the Court.

(5) Where in any such proceedings a member or an authorised officer states on affidavit or, where the respondent requires the deponent to be produced for cross-examination or the Court so directs, in oral evidence that he or she believes that the defendant—

(a) has derived a specified pecuniary or other advantage or benefit as a result of or in connection with corrupt conduct,

(b) is in possession or control of specified property and that the property or a part of it was acquired, directly or indirectly, as a result of or in connection with corrupt conduct, or

(c) is in possession or control of specified property and that the property or a part of it was acquired, directly or indirectly, with or in connection with the property referred to in paragraph (b),

then, if the Court is satisfied that there are reasonable grounds for the belief aforesaid, the statement shall be evidence of the matters referred to in any or all of paragraphs (*a*) to (*c*), as may be appropriate.

(6) (a) In any such proceedings, on an application to it in that behalf by the applicant, the Court may make an order directing the defendant to file an affidavit specifying—

(i) the property owned by the defendant, or

      (ii)   the income and sources of income of the defendant, or

      (iii)   both such property and such income or sources.

  (b)   Such an affidavit is not admissible in evidence in any criminal proceedings against the defendant or his or her spouse, except any such proceedings for perjury arising from statements in the affidavit.

(7) Sections 14 to 14C [of the Criminal Assets Bureau Act 1996][2] shall apply, with the necessary modifications, in relation to assets or proceeds deriving from unjust enrichment as they apply to assets or proceeds deriving from criminal conduct.

(8) The standard of proof required to determine any question arising in proceedings under this section as to whether a person has been corruptly enriched and, if so, as to the amount of such enrichment shall be that applicable in civil proceedings.

(9) The rules of court applicable in civil proceedings shall apply in relation to proceedings under this section.][1]

Amendments

1   Section 16B inserted by Proceeds of Crime (Amendment) Act 2005, s 12.

2   Subsection 7 amended by Criminal Justice Act 2006, s 189.

---

17   Expenses

The expenses incurred by the Minister and (to such extent as may be sanctioned by the Minister) by the Garda Síochána and the Revenue Commissioners in the administration of this Act shall be paid out of moneys provided by the Oireachtas.

18   Short title

This Act may be cited as the Proceeds of Crime Act, 1996.

Criminal Assets Bureau Act 1996

Number 31 of 1996

Section

1. Interpretation.

2. Establishment day.

3. Establishment of Bureau.

4. Objectives of Bureau.

5. Functions of Bureau.

6. Conferral of additional functions on Bureau.

7. Chief Bureau Officer.

8. Bureau officers.

9. Staff of Bureau.

10. Anonymity.

11. Identification.

12. Obstruction.

13. Intimidation.

14. Search warrants.

14A Order to make material available.

14B Disclosure prejudicial to making available of material under section 14A.

14C Property held in trust.

15. Assault.

16. Arrest.

17. Prosecution of offences under section 13 or 15.

18. Special leave and compensation, etc.

19. Advances by Minister to Bureau and audit of accounts of Bureau by Comptroller and Auditor General.

20. Accounting for tax.

21. Reports and information to Minister.

22. Expenses.

23. Amendment of section 19A (anonymity) of Finance Act, 1983.

24. Amendment of certain taxation provisions.

25. Amendment of section 5 (enquiries or action by inspector or other officer) of the Waiver of Certain Tax, Interest and Penalties Act, 1993.

26. Short title.

AN ACT TO MAKE PROVISION FOR THE ESTABLISHMENT OF A BODY TO BE KNOWN AS THE CRIMINAL ASSETS BUREAU AND TO DEFINE ITS FUNCTIONS AND TO AMEND THE FINANCE ACT, 1983, AND THE WAIVER OF CERTAIN TAX, INTEREST AND PENALTIES ACT, 1993, AND TO PROVIDE FOR RELATED MATTERS. [11th October, 1996]

BE IT ENACTED BY THE OIREACHTAS AS FOLLOWS:

1   Interpretation

(1) In this Act—

"the Bureau" means the Criminal Assets Bureau established by section 3;

"the bureau legal officer" means the legal officer of the Bureau;

"bureau officer" means a person appointed as a bureau officer under section 8;

"the Chief Bureau Officer" means the chief officer of the Bureau;

"the Commissioner" means the Commissioner of the Garda Síochána;

"the establishment day" means the day appointed by the Minister under section 2;

["criminal conduct" means any conduct which—

     (a)   constitutes an offence or more than one offence, or

     (b)   where the conduct occurs outside the State, constitutes an offence under the law of the state or territory concerned and would constitute an offence or more than one offence if it occurred within the State;]¹

"Garda functions" means any power or duty conferred on any member of the Garda Síochána by or under any enactment (including an enactment passed after the passing of this Act) or the common law;

"member of the family", in relation to an individual who is a bureau officer or a member of the staff of the Bureau, means the spouse, parent, grandparent, step-parent, child (including a step-child or an adopted child), grandchild, brother, sister, half-brother, half-sister, uncle, aunt, nephew or niece of the individual or of the individual's spouse, or any person who is cohabiting or residing with the individual;

"the Minister" means the Minister for Justice;

["place" includes a dwelling;]¹

"proceedings" includes any hearing before the Appeal Commissioners (within the meaning of the Revenue Acts) or before an appeals officer or the Social Welfare Tribunal under the Social Welfare Acts or a hearing before any committee of the Houses of the Oireachtas;

"Revenue Acts" means—

     (a)   the Customs Acts,

     (b)   the statutes relating to the duties of excise and to the management of those duties,

     (c)   the Tax Acts,

     (d)   the Capital Gains Tax Acts,

     (e)   the Value-Added Tax Act, 1972,

     (f)   the Capital Acquisitions Tax Act, 1976,

     (g)   the statutes relating to stamp duty and to the management of that duty,

     (h)   Part VI of the Finance Act, 1983,

     (i)   Chapter IV of Part II of the Finance Act, 1992,

and any instruments made thereunder and any instruments made under any other enactment and relating to tax;

"tax" means any tax, duty, levy or charge under the care and management of the Revenue Commissioners.

(2) In this Act—

    (a) a reference to a section is a reference to a section of this Act unless it is indicated that reference to some other enactment is intended,

    (b) a reference to a subsection, paragraph or subparagraph is a reference to the subsection, paragraph or subparagraph of the provision in which the reference occurs unless it is indicated that reference to some other provision is intended, and

    (c) a reference to an enactment shall be construed as a reference to that enactment as amended or extended by any other enactment.

Amendments

1   Definitions inserted by Proceeds of Crime (Amendment) Act 2005, s 13.

2   Establishment day

The Minister may, after consultation with the Minister for Finance, by order appoint a day to be the establishment day for the purposes of this Act.

3   Establishment of Bureau

(1) On the establishment day there shall stand established a body to be known as the Criminal Assets Bureau, and in this Act referred to as "the Bureau", to perform the functions conferred on it by or under this Act.

(2) The Bureau shall be a body corporate with perpetual succession and an official seal and power to sue and be sued in its corporate name and to acquire, hold and dispose of land or an interest in land and to acquire, hold and dispose of any other property.

4   Objectives of Bureau

Subject to the provisions of this Act, the objectives of the Bureau shall be—

    (a) the identification of the assets, wherever situated, of persons which derive or are suspected to derive, directly or indirectly, from [criminal conduct,][1]

    (b) the taking of appropriate action under the law to deprive or to deny those persons of the assets or the benefit of such assets, in whole or in part, as may be appropriate, and

    (c) the pursuit of any investigation or the doing of any other preparatory work in relation to any proceedings arising from the objectives mentioned in paragraphs (a) and (b).

Amendments

1 Words substituted by Proceeds of Crime (Amendment) Act 2005, s 14.

5 Functions of Bureau

(1) Without prejudice to the generality of section 4, the functions of the Bureau, operating through its bureau officers, shall be the taking of all necessary actions—

 (a) in accordance with Garda functions, for the purposes of, the confiscation, restraint of use, freezing, preservation or seizure of assets identified as deriving, or suspected to derive, directly or indirectly, from [criminal conduct,][1]

 (b) under the Revenue Acts or any provision of any other enactment, whether passed before or after the passing of this Act, which relates to revenue, to ensure that the proceeds of [criminal conduct][1] or suspected [criminal conduct][1] are subjected to tax and that the Revenue Acts, where appropriate, are fully applied in relation to such proceeds or activities, as the case may be,

 (c) under the Social Welfare Acts for the investigation and determination, as appropriate, of any claim for or in respect of benefit (within the meaning of section 204 of the Social Welfare (Consolidation) Act, 1993) by any person engaged in criminal activity, and

 (d) at the request of the Minister for Social Welfare, to investigate and determine, as appropriate, any claim for or in respect of a benefit, within the meaning of section 204 of the Social Welfare (Consolidation) Act, 1993, where the Minister for Social Welfare certifies that there are reasonable grounds for believing that, in the case of a particular investigation, officers of the Minister for Social Welfare may be subject to threats or other forms of intimidation,

and such actions include, where appropriate, subject to any international agreement, cooperation with any police force, or any authority, being [an authority with functions related to the recovery of proceeds of crime,][2] a tax authority or social security authority, of a territory or state other than the State.

(2) In relation to the matters referred to in subsection (1), nothing in this Act shall be construed as affecting or restricting in any way—

 (a) the powers or duties of the Garda Síochána, the Revenue Commissioners or the Minister for Social Welfare, or

 (b) the functions of the Attorney General, the Director of Public Prosecutions or the Chief State Solicitor.

Amendments

1 Words substituted by Proceeds of Crime (Amendment) Act 2005, s 15(a).

2 Words inserted by Proceeds of Crime (Amendment) Act 2005, s 15(b).

6   Conferral of additional functions on Bureau

(1) The Minister may, if the Minister so thinks fit, and after consultation with the Minister for Finance, by order—

(a) confer on the Bureau or its bureau officers such additional functions connected with the objectives and functions for the time being of the Bureau, and

(b) make such provision as the Minister considers necessary or expedient in relation to matters ancillary to or arising out of the conferral on the Bureau or its bureau officers of functions under this section or the performance by the Bureau or its bureau officers of functions so conferred.

(2) The Minister may by order amend or revoke an order under this section (including an order under this subsection).

(3) Every order made by the Minister under this section shall be laid before each House of the Oireachtas as soon as may be after it is made and, if a resolution annulling the order is passed by either such House within the next 21 days on which that House has sat after the order is laid before it, the order shall be annulled accordingly, but without prejudice to the validity of anything previously done thereunder.

(4) In this section "functions" includes powers and duties.

7   Chief Bureau Officer

(1) There shall be a chief officer of the Bureau who shall be known, and is referred to in this Act, as the Chief Bureau Officer.

(2) The Commissioner shall, from time to time, appoint to the Bureau the Chief Bureau Officer and may, at any time, remove the Chief Bureau Officer from his or her appointment with the Bureau.

(3) The Chief Bureau Officer shall carry on and manage and control generally the administration and business of the Bureau.

(4) The Chief Bureau Officer shall be responsible to the Commissioner for the performance of the functions of the Bureau.

(5) (a) In the event of incapacity through illness, or absence otherwise, of the Chief Bureau Officer, the Commissioner may appoint to the Bureau a person, who shall be known, and is referred to in this section, as the Acting Chief Bureau Officer, to perform the functions of the Chief Bureau Officer.

(b) The Commissioner may, at any time, remove the Acting Chief Bureau Officer from his or her appointment with the Bureau and shall, in any event, remove the Acting Chief Bureau Officer from that appointment upon being satisfied that the incapacity or absence of the Chief Bureau Officer has ceased and that the Chief Bureau Officer has resumed the performance of the functions of Chief Bureau Officer.

(c) Subsections (3) and (4) and paragraph (a) shall apply to the Acting Chief Bureau Officer as they apply to the Chief Bureau Officer.

(6) The Chief Bureau Officer shall be appointed from amongst the members of the Garda Síochána of the rank of Chief Superintendent.

(7) For the purposes of this Act other than subsections (1), (3) and (9) of section 8, the Chief Bureau Officer or Acting Chief Bureau Officer, as the case may be, shall be a bureau officer.

8   Bureau officers

(1) (a) The Minister may appoint, with the consent of the Minister for Finance, such and so
          many—

          (i)   members of the Garda Síochána nominated for the purposes of this Act by the
                Commissioner,

          (ii) officers of the Revenue Commissioners nominated for the purposes of this
                Act by the Revenue Commissioners, and

          (iii) officers of the Minister for Social Welfare nominated for the purposes of this
                Act by that Minister,

          To be bureau officers for the purposes of this Act.

     (b) An appointment under this subsection shall be confirmed in writing, at the time of
          the appointment or as soon as may be thereafter, specifying the date of the
          appointment.

(2) The powers and duties vested in a bureau officer for the purposes of this Act, shall,
subject to subsections subject to [subsections (5), (6), (6A), (6B), (6C) and (7),]¹ be the
powers and duties vested in the bureau officer, as the case may be, by virtue of—

     (a) being a member of the Garda Síochána,

     (b) the Revenue Acts or, any provision of any other enactment, whether passed before
          or after the passing of this Act, which relates to revenue, including any
          authorisation or nomination made thereunder, or

     (c) the Social Welfare Acts, including any appointment made thereunder,

and such exercise or performance of any power or duty for the purposes of this Act shall be
exercised or performed in the name of the Bureau.

(3) A bureau officer, when exercising or performing any powers or duties for the purposes of
this Act, shall be under the direction and control of the Chief Bureau Officer.

(4) Where in any case a bureau officer (other than the Chief Bureau Officer) who, prior to
being appointed a bureau officer, was required to exercise or perform any power or duty on
the direction of any other person, it shall be lawful for the bureau officer to exercise or
perform such power or duty for the purposes of this Act on the direction of the Chief Bureau
Officer.

(5) A bureau officer may exercise or perform his or her powers or duties on foot of any
information received by him or her from another bureau officer or on foot of any action taken
by that other bureau officer in the exercise or performance of that other bureau officer's
powers or duties for the purposes of this Act, and any information, documents or other
material obtained by bureau officers under this subsection shall be admitted in evidence in
any subsequent proceedings.

(6) (a) A bureau officer may be accompanied or assisted in the exercise or performance of
          that bureau officer's powers or duties by such other persons (including bureau
          officers) as the first-mentioned bureau officer considers necessary.

     (b) A bureau officer may take with him or her, to assist him or her in the exercise or
          performance of his or her powers or duties, any equipment or materials as that
          bureau officer considers necessary.

(c) A bureau officer who assists another bureau officer under paragraph (a) shall have and be conferred with the powers and duties of the first-mentioned bureau officer for the purposes of that assistance only.

(d) Information, documents or other material obtained by any bureau officer under paragraph (a) or (c) may be admitted in evidence in any subsequent proceedings.

[(6A) Without prejudice to the generality of subsection (6), a bureau officer who is an officer of the Revenue Commissioners or an officer of the Minister for Social and Family Affairs may, if and for so long as he or she is accompanied by a bureau officer who is a member of the Garda Síochána, attend at, and participate in, the questioning of a person detained pursuant to—

(a) section 4 of the Criminal Justice Act 1984, or

(b) section 2 of the Criminal Justice (Drug Trafficking) Act 1996 (including that section as applied by section 4 of that Act),

in connection with the investigation of an offence but only if the second-mentioned bureau officer requests the first-mentioned bureau officer to do so and the second-mentioned bureau officer is satisfied that the attendance at, and participation in, such questioning of the first-mentioned bureau officer is necessary for the proper investigation of the offence concerned.

(6B) A bureau officer who attends at, and participates in, the questioning of a person in accordance with subsection (6A) may not commit any act or make any omission which, if committed or made by a member of the Garda Síochána, would be a contravention of any regulation made under section 7 of the Criminal Justice Act 1984.

(6C) An act committed or omission made by a bureau officer who attends at, and participates in, the questioning of a person in accordance with subsection (6A) which, if committed or made by a member of the Garda Síochána, would be a contravention of any regulation made under the said section 7 shall not of itself render the bureau officer liable to any criminal or civil proceedings or of itself affect the lawfulness of the custody of the detained person or the admissibility in evidence of any statement made by him or her.][2]

(7) [Subject to section 5(1), any information][3] or material obtained by a bureau officer for the purposes of this Act may only be disclosed by the bureau officer to—

(a) another bureau officer or a member of the staff of the Bureau,

(b) any member of the Garda Síochána for the purposes of Garda functions,

(c) any officer of the Revenue Commissioners for the purposes of the Revenue Acts or any provision of any other enactment, whether passed before or after the passing of this Act, which relates to revenue,

(d) any officer of the Minister for Social Welfare for the purposes of the Social Welfare Acts, or

(e) with the consent of the Chief Bureau Officer, any other officer of another Minister of the Government or of a local authority (within the meaning of the Local Government Act, 1941) for the purposes of that other officer exercising or performing his or her powers or duties,

and information, documents or other material obtained by a bureau officer or any other person under the provisions of this subsection shall be admitted in evidence in any subsequent proceedings.

(8) A member of the Garda Síochána, an officer of the Revenue Commissioners or an officer of the Minister for Social Welfare, who is a bureau officer, notwithstanding his or her

appointment as such, shall continue to be vested with and may exercise or perform the powers or duties of a member of the Garda Síochána, an officer of the Revenue Commissioners or an officer of the Minister for Social Welfare, as the case may be, for purposes other than the purposes of this Act, as well as for the purposes of this Act.

(9) The Chief Bureau Officer may, at his or her absolute discretion, at any time, with the consent of the Commissioner, remove any bureau officer from the Bureau whereupon his or her appointment as a bureau officer shall cease.

(10) Nothing in this section shall affect the powers and duties of a member of the Garda Síochána, an officer of the Revenue Commissioners or an officer of the Minister for Social Welfare, who is not a bureau officer.

Amendments

1   Words substituted by Criminal Justice Act 2007, s 58(a).

2   Subsections (6A), (6B) and (6C) inserted by Criminal Justice Act 2007, s 58(b).

3   Words in sub-s (7) substituted by Criminal Justice (Mutual Assistance) Act 2008, s 106.

9   Staff of Bureau

(1) (a) The Minister may, with the consent of the Attorney General and of the Minister for Finance, appoint a person to be the bureau legal officer, who shall be a member of the staff of the Bureau and who shall report directly to the Chief Bureau Officer, to assist the Bureau in the pursuit of its objectives and functions.

     (b) The Minister may, with the consent of the Minister for Finance and after such consultation as may be appropriate with the Commissioner, appoint such, and such number of persons to be professional or technical members of the staff of the Bureau, other than the bureau legal officer, and any such member will assist the bureau officers in the exercise and performance of their powers and duties.

(2) A professional or technical member of the staff of the Bureau, including the bureau legal officer, shall perform his or her functions at the direction of the Chief Bureau Officer.

(3) The Minister may, with the consent of the Attorney General and of the Minister for Finance, at any time remove the bureau legal officer from being a member of the staff of the Bureau whereupon his or her appointment as bureau legal officer shall cease.

(4) The Commissioner may, with the consent of the Minister, at any time remove any professional or technical member of the staff of the Bureau, other than the bureau legal officer, from being a member of the staff of the Bureau whereupon his or her appointment as a member of the staff shall cease.

(5) (a) A professional or technical member of the staff of the Bureau, including the bureau legal officer, shall hold his or her office or employment on such terms and conditions (including terms and conditions relating to remuneration and superannuation) as the Minister may, with the consent of the Minister for Finance, and in the case of the bureau legal officer with the consent also of the Attorney General, determine.

(b) A professional or technical member of the staff of the Bureau, including the bureau legal officer, shall be paid, out of the moneys at the disposal of the Bureau, such remuneration and allowances for expenses incurred by him or her as the Minister may, with the consent of the Minister for Finance, determine.

10 Anonymity

(1) Notwithstanding any requirement made by or under any enactment or any other requirement in administrative and operational procedures, including internal procedures, all reasonable care shall be taken to ensure that the identity of a bureau officer, who is an officer of the Revenue Commissioners or an officer of the Minister for Social Welfare or the identity of any member of the staff of the Bureau, shall not be revealed.

(2) Where a bureau officer who is an officer of the Revenue Commissioners or an officer of the Minister for Social Welfare may, apart from this section, be required under the Revenue Acts or the Social Welfare Acts, as the case may be, for the purposes of exercising or performing his or her powers or duties under those Acts, to produce or show any written authority or warrant of appointment under those Acts or otherwise to identify himself or herself, the bureau officer shall—

(a) not be required to produce or show any such authority or warrant of appointment or to so identify himself or herself, for the purposes of exercising or performing his or her powers or duties under those Acts, and

(b) be accompanied by a bureau officer who is a member of the Garda Síochána and the bureau officer who is a member of the Garda Síochána shall on request by a person affected identify himself or herself as a member of the Garda Síochána, and shall state that he or she is accompanied by a bureau officer.

(3) Where, in pursuance of the functions of the Bureau, a member of the staff of the Bureau accompanies or assists a bureau officer in the exercise or performance of the bureau officer's powers or duties, the member of the staff shall be accompanied by a bureau officer who is a member of the Garda Síochána and the bureau officer who is a member of the Garda Síochána shall on request by a person affected identify himself or herself as a member of the Garda Síochána, and shall state that he or she is accompanied by a member of the staff of the Bureau.

(4) Where a bureau officer—

(a) who is an officer of the Revenue Commissioners exercises or performs any of his or her powers or duties under the Revenue Acts or any provision of any other enactment, whether passed before or after the passing of this Act, which relates to revenue, in writing, or

(b) who is an officer of the Minister for Social Welfare exercises or performs any of his or her powers or duties under the Social Welfare Acts in writing,

such exercise or performance of his or her powers or duties shall be done in the name of the Bureau and not in the name of the individual bureau officer involved, notwithstanding any provision to the contrary in any of those enactments.

(5) Any document relating to proceedings arising out of the exercise or performance by a bureau officer of his or her powers or duties shall not reveal the identity of any bureau officer who is an officer of the Revenue Commissioners or an officer of the Minister for Social

Welfare or of any member of the staff of the Bureau, provided that where such document is adduced in evidence, subsection (7) shall apply.

(6) In any proceedings the identity of any bureau officer who is an officer of the Revenue Commissioners or an officer of the Minister for Social Welfare or of any member of the staff of the Bureau other than that he or she is a bureau officer or the member of such staff, shall not be revealed other than, in the case of a hearing before a court, to the judge hearing the case, or in any other case the person in charge of the hearing, provided that, where the identity of such a bureau officer or member of the staff of the Bureau is relevant to the evidence adduced in the proceedings, subsection (7) shall apply.

(7) In any proceedings where a bureau officer or a member of the staff of the Bureau may be required to give evidence, whether by affidavit or certificate, or oral evidence—

    (a) the judge, in the case of proceedings before a court, or

    (b) the person in charge of the proceedings, in any other case,

may, on the application of the Chief Bureau Officer, if satisfied that there are reasonable grounds in the public interest to do so, give such directions for the preservation of the anonymity of the bureau officer or member of the staff of the Bureau as he or she thinks fit, including directions as to—

    (i) the restriction of the circulation of affidavits or certificates,

    (ii) the deletion from affidavits or certificates of the name and address of any bureau officer or member of the staff of the Bureau, including the deponent and certifier, or

    (iii) the giving of evidence in the hearing but not the sight of any person.

(8) In this section "member of the staff of the Bureau" means a member of the staff of the Bureau appointed under section 9.

11   Identification

(1) A person who publishes or causes to be published—

    (a) the fact that an individual—

        (i) being or having been an officer of the Revenue Commissioners or an officer of the Minister for Social Welfare, is or was a bureau officer, or

        (ii) is or was a member of the staff of the Bureau,

    (b) the fact that an individual is a member of the family of—

        (i) a bureau officer,

        (ii) a former bureau officer,

        (iii) a member of the staff of the Bureau, or

        (iv) a former member of the staff of the Bureau,

        or

    (c) the address of any place as being the address where any—

        (i) bureau officer,

        (ii) former bureau officer,

        (iii) member of the staff of the Bureau,

        (iv) former member of the staff of the Bureau, or

(v) member of the family of any bureau officer, former bureau officer, member of the staff of the Bureau or former member of the staff of the Bureau, resides,

shall be guilty of an offence under this section.

(2) A person guilty of an offence under this section shall be liable—

(a) on summary conviction, to a fine not exceeding [€3,000],[1] or to imprisonment for a term not exceeding 12 months, or to both, or

(b) on conviction on indictment, to a fine not exceeding £50,000, or to imprisonment for a term not exceeding 3 years, or to both.

(3) In this section references to bureau officer, former bureau officer, member of the staff of the Bureau and former member of the staff of the Bureau do not include references to the Chief Bureau Officer, the Acting Chief Bureau Officer or the bureau legal officer.

Amendments

1 "€3,000" substituted for "£1,500" by Proceeds of Crime (Amendment) Act 2005, s 17.

12 Obstruction

(1) A person who delays, obstructs, impedes, interferes with or resists a bureau officer in the exercise or performance of his or her powers or duties under Garda functions, the Revenue Acts or the Social Welfare Acts or a member of the staff of the Bureau in accompanying or assisting a bureau officer shall be guilty of an offence.

(2) A person guilty of an offence under this section shall be liable—

(a) on summary conviction, to a fine not exceeding [€3,000][1], or to imprisonment for a term not exceeding 12 months, or to both, or

(b) on conviction on indictment, to a fine not exceeding £10,000, or to imprisonment for a term not exceeding 3 years, or to both.

Amendments

1 "€3,000" substituted for "£1,500" by Proceeds of Crime (Amendment) Act 2005, s 17.

13 Intimidation

(1) A person who utters or sends threats to or, in any way, intimidates or menaces a bureau officer or a member of the staff of the Bureau or any member of the family of a bureau officer or of a member of the staff of the Bureau shall be guilty of an offence.

(2) A person guilty of an offence under this section shall be liable—

(a) on summary conviction, to a fine not exceeding [€3,000][1], or to imprisonment for a term not exceeding 12 months, or to both, or

(b) on conviction on indictment, to a fine not exceeding £100,000, or to imprisonment for a term not exceeding 10 years, or to both.

Amendments

1   "€3,000" substituted for "£1,500" by Proceeds of Crime (Amendment) Act 2005, s 17.

---

14   Search warrants

[(1) If a judge of the District Court is satisfied by information on oath of a bureau officer who is a member of the Garda Síochána that there are reasonable grounds for suspecting that evidence of or relating to assets or proceeds deriving from criminal conduct, or to their identity or whereabouts, is to be found in any place, the judge may issue a warrant for the search of that place and any person found at that place.]¹

(2) A bureau officer who is a member of the Garda Síochána not below the rank of superintendent may, subject to subsection (3), if he or she is satisfied that there are reasonable grounds for suspecting that evidence of or relating to assets or proceeds deriving from [criminal conduct]², or to their identity or whereabouts, is to be found in any place, issue a warrant for the search of that place and any person found at that place.

(3) A bureau officer who is a member of the Garda Síochána not below the rank of superintendent shall not issue a search warrant under this section unless he or she is satisfied that circumstances of urgency giving rise to the need for the immediate issue of the search warrant would render it impracticable to apply to a judge of the District Court under this section for a search warrant.

(4) Subject to subsection (5), a warrant under this section shall be expressed to and shall operate to authorise a named bureau officer who is a member of the Garda Síochána, accompanied by such other persons as the bureau officer thinks necessary, to enter, [within a period to be specified in the warrant]³ (if necessary by the use of reasonable force), the place named in the warrant, and to search it and any person found at that place and seize and retain [any material (other than material subject to legal privilege) found at that place, or any such material]³ found in the possession of a person found present at that place at the time of the search, which the officer believes to be evidence of or relating to assets or proceeds deriving from [criminal conduct]², or to their identity or whereabouts.

[(4A) The period to be specified in the warrant shall be one week, unless it appears to the judge that another period, not exceeding 14 days, would be appropriate in the particular circumstances of the case.]⁴

(5) Notwithstanding subsection (4), a search warrant issued under [subsection (2)]⁵ shall cease to have effect after a period of 24 hours has elapsed from the time of the issue of the warrant.

[(5A) The authority conferred by subsection (4) to seize and retain any material includes, in the case of a document or record, authority—

(a) to make and retain a copy of the document or record, and

(b) where necessary, to seize and retain any computer or other storage medium in which any record is kept.]⁵

(6) A bureau officer who is a member of the Garda Síochána acting under the authority of a warrant under this section may—

(a) require any person present at the place where the search is carried out to give to the officer the person's name and address, and

(b) arrest without warrant any person who—

    (i) obstructs or attempts to obstruct that officer or any person accompanying that officer in the carrying out of his or her duties,

    (ii) fails to comply with a requirement under paragraph (a), or

    (iii) gives a name or address which the officer has reasonable cause for believing is false or misleading.

[(6A) A bureau officer who is a member of the Garda Síochána acting under the authority of a warrant under this section may—

(a) operate any computer at the place which is being searched or cause it to be operated by a person accompanying the member for that purpose, and

(b) require any person at that place who appears to the member to have lawful access to the information in the computer—

    (i) to give to the member any password necessary to operate it,

    (ii) otherwise to enable the member to examine the information accessible by the computer in a form in which it is visible and legible, or

    (iii) to produce the information to the member in a form in which it can be removed and in which it is, or can be made, visible and legible,]⁶

(7) A person who obstructs or attempts to obstruct a person acting under the authority of a warrant under this section, who fails to comply with a requirement under subsection (6)(a) or who gives a false or misleading name or address to a bureau officer who is a member of the Garda Síochána, shall be guilty of an offence and shall be liable on summary conviction to a fine not exceeding [€3,000]⁷, or to imprisonment for a period not exceeding 6 months, or to both.

(8) The power to issue a warrant under this section is in addition to and not in substitution for any other power to issue a warrant for the search of any place or person.

[(9) In this section—

"computer at the place which is being searched" includes any other computer, whether at that place or at any other place, which is lawfully accessible by means of that computer, and

"material" includes a copy of the material and a document or record.]⁸

Amendments

1   Subsection (1) substituted by Criminal Justice Act, 2006, s 190.

2   Words substituted by Proceeds of Crime (Amendment) Act 2005, s 16(a).

3   Words substituted by Proceeds of Crime (Amendment) Act 2005, s 16(b).

3   Subsection (4A) inserted by Proceeds of Crime (Amendment) Act 2005, s 16(c).

4   Words substituted by Proceeds of Crime (Amendment) Act 2005, s 16(d).

5   Subsection (5A) inserted by Proceeds of Crime (Amendment) Act 2005, s 16(e).

6   Subsection (6A) inserted by Proceeds of Crime (Amendment) Act 2005, s 16(f).

7   "€3,000" substituted for "£1,500" by Proceeds of Crime (Amendment) Act 2005, s 17.
8   Subsection (9) substituted by Proceeds of Crime (Amendment) Act 2005, s 16(g).

[14A   Order to make material available

(1) For the purposes of an investigation into whether a person has benefited from assets or proceeds deriving from criminal conduct or is in receipt of or controls such assets or proceeds a bureau officer who is a member of the Garda Síochána may apply to a judge of the District Court for an order under this section in relation to making available any particular material or material of a particular description.

(2) On such an application the judge, if satisfied—

    (a)   that there are reasonable grounds for suspecting that the person has benefited from such assets or proceeds or is in receipt of or controls such assets or proceeds, and

    (b)   that the material concerned is required for the purposes of such an investigation,

may order that any person who appears to him or her to be in possession of the material shall—

    (i)   produce the material to the member so that he or she may take it away, or

    (ii) give the member access to it within a period to be specified in the order.

(3) The period to be so specified shall be one week, unless it appears to the judge that another period would be appropriate in the particular circumstances of the case.

(4) (a)   An order under this section in relation to material in any place may, on the application of the member concerned, require any person who appears to the judge to be entitled to grant entry to the place to allow the member to enter it to obtain access to the material.

    (b)   Where a person required under paragraph (a) to allow the member to enter a place does not allow him or her to do so, section 14 shall have effect, with any necessary modifications, as if a warrant had been issued under that section authorising him or her to search the place and any person found there.

(5) Where such material consists of information contained in a computer, the order shall have effect as an order to produce the material, or to give access to it, in a form in which it is visible and legible and in which it can be taken away.

(6) The order—

    (a)   in so far as it may empower a member of the Garda Síochána to take away a document or to be given access to it, shall authorise him or her to make a copy of it and to take the copy away,

    (b)   shall not confer any right to production of, or access to, any material subject to legal privilege, and

    (c)   shall have effect notwithstanding any other obligation as to secrecy or other restriction on disclosure of information imposed by statute or otherwise.

(7) Any material taken away by a member of the Garda Síochána under this section may be retained by him or her for use as evidence in any proceedings.

(8) A judge of the District Court may vary or discharge an order under this section on the application of any person to whom an order under this section relates or a member of the Garda Síochána.

(9) A person who without reasonable excuse fails or refuses to comply with any requirement of an order under this section is guilty of an offence and liable—

    (a) on summary conviction, to a fine not exceeding €3,000 or to imprisonment for a term not exceeding 12 months or to both, or

    (b) on conviction on indictment, to a fine or to imprisonment for a term not exceeding 5 years or to both.

14B   Disclosure prejudicial to making available of material under section 14A

(1) A person who, knowing or suspecting that an application is to be made, or has been made, under section 14A for an order in relation to making available any particular material or material of a particular description, makes any disclosure which is likely to prejudice the making available of the material in accordance with the order is guilty of an offence.

(2) In proceedings against a person for an offence under this section it is a defence to prove that the person—

    (a) did not know or suspect that the disclosure to which the proceedings relate was likely to prejudice the making available of the material concerned, or

    (b) had lawful authority or reasonable excuse for making the disclosure.

(3) A person guilty of an offence under this section is liable—

    (a) on summary conviction, to a fine not exceeding €3,000 or to imprisonment for a term not exceeding 12 months or to both, or

    (b) on conviction on indictment, to a fine or to imprisonment for a term not exceeding 5 years or to both.

14C   Property held in trust

(1) For the purposes of an investigation into whether a person has benefited from assets or proceeds deriving from criminal conduct or is in receipt of or controls such assets or proceeds the Chief Bureau Officer or an authorised officer may apply to a judge of the High Court for an order under this section in relation to obtaining information regarding any trust in which the person may have an interest or with which he or she may be otherwise connected.

(2) On such an application the judge, if satisfied—

    (a) that there are reasonable grounds for suspecting that a person—

        (i) has benefited from assets or proceeds deriving from criminal conduct or is in receipt of or controls such assets or proceeds, and

        (ii) has some interest in or other connection with the trust,

    (b) that the information concerned is required for the purposes of such an investigation, and

    (c) that there are reasonable grounds for believing that it is in the public interest that the information should be disclosed for the purposes of the investigation, having regard to the benefit likely to accrue to the investigation and any other relevant circumstances,

may order the trustees of the trust and any other persons (including the suspected person) to disclose to the Chief Bureau Officer or an authorised officer such information as he or she may require in relation to the trust, including the identity of the settlor and any or all of the trustees and beneficiaries.

(3) An order under this section—

(a) shall not confer any right to production of, or access to, any information subject to legal privilege, and

(b) shall have effect notwithstanding any other obligation as to secrecy or other restriction on disclosure of information imposed by statute or otherwise.

(4) A judge of the High Court may vary or discharge an order under this section on the application of any person to whom it relates or a member of the Garda Síochána.

(5) A trustee or other person who without reasonable excuse fails or refuses to comply with an order under this section or gives information which is false or misleading is guilty of an offence and liable—

(a) on summary conviction, to a fine not exceeding €3,000 or to imprisonment for a term not exceeding 12 months or to both, or

(b) on conviction on indictment, to a fine or to imprisonment for a term not exceeding 5 years or to both.

(6) Any information given by a person in compliance with an order under this section is not admissible in evidence in any criminal proceedings against the person or his or her spouse, except in any proceedings for an offence under subsection (5).

(7) In this section 'information' includes—

(a) a document or record, and

(b) information in non-legible form.][1]

Amendments

1   Sections 4A, 4B and 4C inserted by Proceeds of Crime (Amendment) Act 2005, s 18.

15   Assault

(1) A person who assaults or attempts to assault a bureau officer or a member of the staff of the Bureau or any member of the family of a bureau officer or of a member of the staff of the Bureau shall be guilty of an offence.

(2) A person guilty of an offence under this section shall be liable—

(a) on summary conviction, to a fine not exceeding [€3,000][1], or to imprisonment for a term not exceeding 12 months, or to both, or

(b) on conviction on indictment, to a fine not exceeding £100,000, or to imprisonment for a term not exceeding 10 years, or to both.

Amendments

1   "€3,000" substituted for "£1,500" by Proceeds of Crime (Amendment) Act 2005, s 17.

16   Arrest

(1) Where a bureau officer who is a member of the Garda Síochána has reasonable cause to suspect that a person is committing or has committed an offence under section 12, 13 or 15 or under section 94 of the Finance Act, 1983, the bureau officer may—

    (a)   arrest that person without warrant, or

    (b)   require the person to give his or her name and address, and if the person fails or refuses to do so or gives a name or address which the bureau officer reasonably suspects to be false or misleading, the bureau officer may arrest that person without warrant.

(2) A person who fails or refuses to give his or her name or address when required under this section or gives a name or address which is false or misleading, shall be guilty of an offence and shall be liable on summary conviction to a fine not exceeding [€3,000][1].

Amendments

1   "€3,000" substituted for "£1,500" by Proceeds of Crime (Amendment) Act 2005, s 17.

17   Prosecution of offences under section 13 or 15

Where a person is charged with an offence under section 13 or 15, no further proceedings in the matter (other than any remand in custody or on bail) shall be taken except by or with the consent of the Director of Public Prosecutions.

18   Special leave and compensation, etc

(1) Any person appointed to the Bureau as a bureau officer or appointed under section 9 or seconded to the Bureau as a member of the staff of the Bureau from the civil service (within the meaning of the Civil Service Regulation Act, 1956) shall, on being so appointed or seconded, be granted special leave with pay from any office or employment exercised by the person at the time.

(2) The Bureau shall, out of the moneys at its disposal, reimburse any Minister of the Government, the Revenue Commissioners or other person paid out of moneys provided by the Oireachtas for the full cost of the expenditure incurred by such Minister of the Government, the Revenue Commissioners or other person paid out of moneys provided by the Oireachtas, in respect of any person appointed or seconded to the Bureau for the full duration of that appointment.

(3) The provisions of the Garda Síochána (Compensation) Act, 1941, and the Garda Síochána (Compensation) (Amendment) Act, 1945, shall, with any necessary modifications, apply to—

    (a)   bureau officers and members of the staff of the Bureau, and

    (b)   the Chief State Solicitor and solicitors employed in the Office of the Chief State Solicitor, in respect of injuries maliciously inflicted on them because of anything done or to be done by any of them in a professional capacity for or on behalf of the Bureau,

as they apply to members of the Garda Síochána.

19   Advances by Minister to Bureau and audit of accounts of Bureau by Comptroller and Auditor General

(1) The Minister may, from time to time, with the consent of the Minister for Finance, make advances to the Bureau, out of moneys provided by the Oireachtas, in such manner and such sums as the Minister may determine for the purposes of expenditure by the Bureau in the performance of its functions.

(2) The First Schedule to the Comptroller and Auditor General (Amendment) Act, 1993, is hereby amended by the insertion before "Criminal Injuries Compensation Tribunal" of "Criminal Assets Bureau".

(3) The person who from time to time has been appointed by the Minister for Finance under the Exchequer and Audit Departments Act, 1866, as the Accounting Officer for the Vote for the Office of the Minister shall prepare in a format prescribed by the Minister for Finance an account of the moneys provided to the Bureau by the Oireachtas in any financial year and submit it for examination to the Comptroller and Auditor General not later than 90 days after the end of that financial year.

(4) All of the duties specified in section 19 of the Comptroller and Auditor General (Amendment) Act, 1993, shall apply to the Accounting Officer for the Vote for the Office of the Minister in regard to the income, expenditure and assets of the Bureau.

20   Accounting for tax

On payment to the Bureau of tax in accordance with the provisions of section 5(1)(b), the Bureau shall forthwith—

    (a) lodge the tax paid to the General Account of the Revenue Commissioners in the Central Bank of Ireland, and

    (b) transmit to the Collector-General particulars of the tax assessed and payment received in respect thereof.

21   Reports and information to Minister

(1) As soon as may be, but not later than 6 months, after the end of each year, the Bureau shall through the Commissioner present a report to the Minister of its activities during that year and the Minister shall cause copies of the report to be laid before each House of the Oireachtas.

(2) Each report under subsection (1) shall include information in such form and regarding such matters as the Minister may direct.

(3) The Bureau shall, whenever so requested by the Minister through the Commissioner, furnish to the Minister through the Commissioner information as to the general operations of the Bureau.

22   Expenses

The expenses incurred by the Minister in the administration of this Act shall, to such extent as may be sanctioned by the Minister for Finance, be paid out of moneys provided by the Oireachtas.

23   Amendment of section 19A (anonymity) of Finance Act, 1983

[...]¹

Amendments

1   Section 23 repealed by Taxes Consolidation Act 1997, Sch 30.

24   Amendment of certain taxation provisions

[...]¹

(3) [...]²

(4) The proviso to subsection (7) (as amended by the Disclosure of Certain Information for Taxation and Other Purposes Act, 1996) of section 39 of the Capital Acquisitions Tax Act, 1976, is hereby deleted.

(5) Subsection (2) (as amended by the Disclosure of Certain Information for Taxation and Other Purposes Act, 1996) of section 104 of the Finance Act, 1983, is hereby amended by the substitution of the following proviso for the proviso to that subsection:

> "Provided that the Commissioners may withdraw an assessment made under this subsection and make an assessment of the amount of tax payable on the basis of a return which, in their opinion, represents reasonable compliance with their requirements and which is delivered to the Commissioners within 30 days after the date of the assessment made by the Commissioners pursuant to this subsection.".

Amendments

1   Subsections (1) and (2) repealed by Taxes Consolidation Act 1997, Sch 30.

2   Subsection (3) repealed by Stamp Duties Consolidation Act 1999, Sch 3

25   Amendment of section 5 (enquiries or action by inspector or other officer) of the Waiver of Certain Tax, Interest and Penalties Act, 1993

Section 5 of the Waiver of Certain Tax, Interest and Penalties Act, 1993, is hereby amended in subsection (1), by the substitution for "arrears of tax, as the case may be" of "arrears of tax, as the case may be, or that the declaration made by the individual under section 2(3)(a)(iv) is false".

26   Short title

This Act may be cited as the Criminal Assets Bureau Act, 1996.

Criminal Justice (Miscellaneous Provisions) Act 1997

Number 4 of 1997

ARRANGEMENT OF SECTIONS

Section

1.   Interpretation.

2.   Amendment of section 4 of Criminal Justice Act, 1984.

3.   Station bail.

4.   Extending periods of remand in custody.

5.   Jurisdiction of District Court and place of remand.

6.   Certificates of evidence relating to certain matters.

7.   Recording of evidence.

8.   Consent of Director of Public Prosecutions to summary disposal of certain offences.

9.   Consent of Director of Public Prosecutions to other offences being taken into consideration in awarding punishment.

10.   Search warrants in relation to serious offences.

11.   Electronic recording of fingerprints and palmprints.

12.   Amendment of section 28 of Criminal Justice Act, 1984.

13.   Extension of section 8 of Criminal Law Act, 1976.

14.   Amendment of section 32 of Act of 1994.

15.   Amendment of Act of 1994.

16.   Amendment of section 2 of Criminal Evidence Act, 1992.

17.   Amendment of section 23 of Act of 1951.

18.   Amendment of section 15 of Act of 1951.

19.   Power to make Prison Rules.

20.   Amendment of Courts Act, 1971.

21.   Commencement.

22.   Expenses.

23.   Repeal of enactments.

24.   Short title.

FIRST SCHEDULE

SECOND SCHEDULE

AN ACT TO AMEND THE LAW RELATING TO PROCEEDINGS IN CRIMINAL MATTERS IN THE DISTRICT COURT, FOR THAT AND OTHER PURPOSES TO AMEND THE COURTS OF JUSTICE ACT, 1924, THE CRIMINAL JUSTICE ACT, 1951, THE CRIMINAL PROCEDURE ACT, 1967, AND OTHER ENACTMENTS, TO GIVE EFFECT TO ARTICLE 11 OF COUNCIL DIRECTIVE 91/308/EEC OF 10 JUNE 1991 OF THE COUNCIL OF THE EUROPEAN COMMUNITIES ON PREVENTION OF THE USE OF THE FINANCIAL

SYSTEM FOR THE PURPOSE OF MONEY LAUNDERING, TO MAKE PROVISION FOR THE AFFIXING OF A SEAL TO ORDERS OF THE DISTRICT COURT, TO ENABLE THE MINISTER FOR JUSTICE TO MAKE RULES FOR THE REGULATION AND GOOD GOVERNMENT OF PRISONS, AND TO PROVIDE FOR RELATED MATTERS. [4th March, 1997]

BE IT ENACTED BY THE OIREACHTAS AS FOLLOWS:

1   Interpretation

(1) In this Act—

"Act of 1924" means the Courts of Justice Act, 1924;

"Act of 1951" means the Criminal Justice Act, 1951;

"Act of 1967" means the Criminal Procedure Act, 1967;

"Act of 1994" means the Criminal Justice Act, 1994;

"member" means a member of the Garda Síochána.

(2) A reference in this Act to a subsection, paragraph or subparagraph is a reference to the subsection, paragraph or subparagraph of the provision in which the reference occurs, unless it is indicated that reference to some other provision is intended.

(3) A reference in this Act to an enactment shall be construed as a reference to that enactment as amended or adapted, whether before or after the commencement of this section, by or under any subsequent enactment, including this Act.

2   Amendment of section 4 of Criminal Justice Act, 1984

The Criminal Justice Act, 1984, is hereby amended, in section 4—

    (a) by the insertion in subsection (2), after "without warrant", of "or pursuant to an authority of a judge of the District Court under section 10(1)",

    (b) by the substitution of the following subsections for subsection (5):[1]

    (c) by the insertion, after subsection (8), of the following subsection:[1]

    (d) by the substitution, in subsection (9), of "subsection (6), (8) or (8A)" for "subsection (6) or (8)".

Amendments

1   See the amended Act.

---

3   Station bail

Section 31 of the Act of 1967 is hereby amended by—

    (a) the substitution of the following subsection for subsection (1):[1]

    (b) the deletion of the second sentence in subsection (3),

    (c) the insertion of the following subsection:[1]

    (d) by the insertion of the following subsection:[1]

Amendments

1 See the amended Act.

4 Extending periods of remand in custody

The Act of 1967 is hereby amended by the substitution of the following section for section 24 (amended by section 8(2) of the Courts (No 2) Act, 1986):[1]

Amendments

1 See the amended Act.

5 Jurisdiction of District Court and place of remand

(1) Notwithstanding section 27(3) of the Courts of Justice Act, 1953, the court before which a person first appears charged with a particular offence or a judge of the District Court exercising jurisdiction under subsection (2) of section 79 of the Act of 1924 (inserted by section 41 of the Courts and Court Officers Act, 1995) may remand that person in custody to appear at a sitting of the District Court ("alternative court") in the District Court District in which the prison or place of detention where he or she is to be held in custody is situated or a District Court District adjoining the first-mentioned District Court District.

(2) The alternative court may, from time to time, as occasion requires, further remand a person, referred to in subsection (1) of the said section 79, in custody or on bail, to that court or to another alternative court.

[(3) An alternative court shall, for the purposes of the trial of a person, remand the person to a sitting of the court in the District Court District—

    (a) in which the offence to which the trial relates was committed, or

    (b) in which the person resides or was arrested.][1]

(4) The said section 79 is hereby amended by the substitution of the following subsection for subsection (3):

    "(3) A judge of the District Court exercising jurisdiction under subsection (2) shall not have jurisdiction to—

        (a) conduct a preliminary examination under the provisions of the Criminal Procedure Act, 1967, or

        (b) try an accused for an offence, unless that jurisdiction is exercised in the District Court District—

            (i) in which the offence was committed, or

            (ii) in which the accused resides or was arrested.".

(5) Subsection (4) of the said section 79 shall not apply to an alternative court.

(6) Section 2 of the Criminal Justice (Legal Aid) Act, 1962, is hereby amended by the substitution of the following subsection for subsection (1):[2]

Amendments

1   Subsection (3) substituted by Criminal Justice Act 1999, s 21.

2   See the amended Act.

6   Certificates of evidence relating to certain matters

(1) Where a person, who has been arrested otherwise than under a warrant, first appears before the District Court charged with an offence, a certificate purporting to be signed by a member and stating that that member did, at a specified time and place, any one or more of the following namely—

(a)   arrested that person for a specified offence,

(b)   charged that person with a specified offence, or

(c)   cautioned that person upon his or her being arrested for, or charged with, a specified offence,

shall be admissible as evidence of the matters stated in the certificate.

(2) In any criminal proceedings a certificate purporting to be signed by a member and stating that—

(a)   that member did any one or more of the following namely—

  (i)   commenced duty, or replaced a specified member on duty, at a specified time at a place—

    (I)   where the offence to which such proceedings relate is alleged to have been committed,

    (II)   adjacent to the place referred to in clause I of this subparagraph, or

    (III) containing evidence of the offence to which the proceedings relate,

    or

  (ii) remained on duty at a place referred to in subparagraph (i) until a specified time or until replaced at a specified time by a specified member,

  or

(b)   in relation to a place referred to in paragraph (a) no person entered upon that place during a specified period without the permission of that member and that no evidence at that place was disturbed while he or she was on duty at that place,

shall be admissible as evidence of the matters stated in the certificate.

(3) Where a person enters upon a place referred to in paragraph (a) of subsection (2) at a time when a member is on duty at that place, a certificate referred to in the said subsection shall state the name of that person and the purpose for which that person was permitted to enter upon that place.

(4) In any criminal proceedings the court may, if it considers that the interests of justice so require, direct that oral evidence of the matters stated in a certificate under this section be given, and the court may for the purpose of receiving oral evidence adjourn the proceedings to a later date.

(5) A certificate under this section shall be tendered in evidence by a member not below the rank of sergeant.

(6) Upon the laying of a charge sheet and recognisance before the District Court, the court shall require the person (if any) present and to whom the charge sheet and recognisance relate, to identify himself or herself, and accordingly, on being so required, the person shall identify himself or herself, as the case may be, to the court.

(7) The Minister for Justice may, by regulations, prescribe the form of a certificate under this section.

7 Recording of evidence

The Act of 1924 is hereby amended by the substitution of the following section for section 33:

"33. (1) The appeal, in case such certificate or leave to appeal is granted, shall be heard and determined by the Court of Criminal Appeal ('the court') on—

(a) a record of the proceedings at the trial and on a transcript thereof verified by the judge before whom the case was tried, and

(b) where the trial judge is of opinion that the record or transcript referred to in paragraph (a) of this subsection does not reflect what took place during the trial, a report by him as to the defects which he considers such record or transcript, as the case may be, contains,

with power to the court to hear new or additional evidence, and to refer any matter for report by the said judge.

(2) Where the court is of opinion that either the record or the transcript thereof is defective in any material particular, it may determine the appeal in such manner as it considers, in all the circumstances, appropriate.

(3) In this section, 'record' includes, in addition to a record in writing—

(a) shorthand notes, or a disc, tape, soundtrack or other device in which information, sounds or signals are embodied so as to be capable (with or without the aid of some other instrument) of being reproduced in legible or audible form,

(b) a film tape or other device in which visual images are embodied so as to be capable (with or without the aid of some other instrument) of being reproduced in visual form, and

(c) a photograph.

(4) Section 97 of the Act of 1924 is hereby repealed.".

8 Consent of Director of Public Prosecutions to summary disposal of certain offences

Section 2 of the Act of 1951 (amended by section 19 of the Act of 1967) is hereby amended by the substitution of the following subsection for subsection (2):[1]

Amendments

1   See the amended Act.

9   Consent of Director of Public Prosecutions to other offences being taken into consideration in awarding punishment

Section 8 of the Act of 1951 is hereby amended by the substitution of the following subsection for subsection (1):[1]

Amendments

1   See the amended Act.

10   Search warrants in relation to arrestable offences

[(1) If a judge of the District Court is satisfied by information on oath of a member not below the rank of sergeant that there are reasonable grounds for suspecting that evidence of, or relating to, the commission of an arrestable offence is to be found in any place, the judge may issue a warrant for the search of that place and any persons found at that place.

(2) A search warrant under this section shall be expressed, and shall operate, to authorise a named member, accompanied by such other members or persons or both as the member thinks necessary—

(a)   to enter, at any time or times within one week of the date of issue of the warrant, on production if so requested of the warrant, and if necessary by the use of reasonable force, the place named in the warrant,

(b)   to search it and any persons found at that place, and

(c)   to seize anything found at that place, or anything found in the possession of a person present at that place at the time of the search, that that member reasonably believes to be evidence of, or relating to, the commission of an arrestable offence.

(3) A member acting under the authority of a search warrant under this section may—

(a)   require any person present at the place where the search is being carried out to give to the member his or her name and address, and

(b)   arrest without warrant any person who—

(i)   obstructs or attempts to obstruct the member in the carrying out of his or her duties,

(ii)   fails to comply with a requirement under paragraph (a), or

(iii) gives a name or address which the member has reasonable cause for believing is false or misleading.

(4) A person who obstructs or attempts to obstruct a member acting under the authority of a search warrant under this section, who fails to comply with a requirement under subsection (3)(a) or who gives a false or misleading name or address to a member shall be guilty of an

offence and shall be liable on summary conviction to a fine not exceeding €3,000 or imprisonment for a term not exceeding 6 months or both.

(5) The power to issue a warrant under this section is without prejudice to any other power conferred by statute to issue a warrant for the search of any place or person.

(6) In this section—

"arrestable offence" has the meaning it has in section 2 (as amended by section 8 of the Criminal Justice Act 2006) of the Criminal Law Act 1997;

"place" means a physical location and includes—

    (a) a dwelling, residence, building or abode,

    (b) a vehicle, whether mechanically propelled or not,

    (c) a vessel, whether sea-going or not,

    (d) an aircraft, whether capable of operation or not, and

    (e) a hovercraft.][1]

Amendments

1   Section 10 substituted by Criminal Justice Act 2006, s 6(1)(a).

Note

Criminal Justice Act 2006, s 6(2) contains the following saver:

> (2) This section shall not affect the validity of a warrant issued under section 10 of the Criminal Justice (Miscellaneous Provisions) Act 1997 before the commencement of this section and such a warrant shall continue in force in accordance with its terms after such commencement.

11   Electronic recording of fingerprints and palmprints

(1) A power under any enactment, whether passed before or after the passing of this Act, to take the fingerprints or palmprints of any person shall include the power to record an image of that person's fingerprints or palmprints by electronic means or in any other manner.

(2) A photograph, or an image of any fingerprint or palmprint attached to or contained in a certificate purporting to be signed by the member who took such photograph or recorded such image and stating that—

    (a) the said photograph is that of a specified person, or

    (b) the said image is that of the fingerprint or palmprint, as the case may be, of a specified person,

and was taken or recorded, as the case may be, by the said member, shall, unless the contrary is proved, be evidence of the matters stated in the certificate.

12   Amendment of section 28 of Criminal Justice Act, 1984

The Criminal Justice Act, 1984, is hereby amended by the substitution of the following section for section 28:[1]

Amendments

1   See the amended Act.

13   Extension of section 8 of Criminal Law Act, 1976

Section 8 of the Criminal Law Act, 1976, is hereby amended by the insertion subsection (1), after paragraph (j), of the following paragraph:[1]

Amendments

1   See the amended Act.

14   Amendment of section 32 of Act of 1994

Section 32 of the Act of 1994 is hereby amended by the insertion of the following subsections:[1]

Amendments

1   See the amended Act.

15   Amendment of Act of 1994

[...][1]

Amendments

1   Section 15 repealed by Criminal Justice (Mutual Assistance) Act 2008, s 10.

16   Amendment of section 2 of Criminal Evidence Act, 1992

Section 2 of the Criminal Evidence Act, 1992, is hereby amended by the substitution of the following definition for the definition of "sexual offence":[1]

Amendments

1   See the amended Act.

17   Amendment of section 23 of Act of 1951

The Act of 1951 is hereby amended by—

(a) the deletion of subsection (3) of section 23, and

(b) the insertion of the following section:[1]

Amendments

1 See the amended Act.

18   Amendment of section 15 of Act of 1951

The Act of 1951 is hereby amended by the substitution of the following section for section 15 (substituted by section 26 of the Criminal Justice Act, 1984):[1]

Amendments

1 See the amended Act.

19   Power to make Prison Rules

[…][1]

Amendments

1 Section 19 repealed by Prisons Act 2007, s 42(c).

20   Amendment of Courts Act, 1971

The Courts Act, 1971, is hereby amended by—

(a) the insertion of the following section:

"District Court seal.

13A. (1) The District Court shall, as soon as may be after the passing of the Criminal Justice (Miscellaneous Provisions) Act, 1997, provide itself with one or, as may be appropriate, more than one seal—

(a)   in respect of each District Court Area, and

(b)   in respect of the Dublin Metropolitan District,

for use in the District Court Area concerned or the Dublin Metropolitan District, as the case may be.

(2) A seal under this section shall be inscribed with the number of the District Court District and the name of the District Court Area to which it relates or, in the case of the Dublin Metropolitan District, with the name of that District.

(3) Where there is more than one seal in respect of a District Court Area each such seal shall, in addition to the number it is required to bear under subsection (2), bear a number distinguishing it from all other seals in respect of that District Court Area.

(4) Each seal in respect of the Dublin Metropolitan District shall, in addition to the name it is required to bear under subsection (2), bear a number distinguishing it from all other seals in respect of that District.

(5) Rules of court may make provision for the custody of a seal under this section.",

and

(b)   the substitution of the following section for section 14:

"14.(1) In any legal proceedings regard shall not be had to any record, relating to a decision of a judge of the District Court in any case of summary jurisdiction, other than an order which, when an order is required, shall be drawn up by the District Court clerk and either—

(a)   signed by the judge who made the order, or

(b)   affixed with the seal of the District Court in respect of the District Court Area in which the order was made or, where the order was made by a judge of the District Court sitting in the Dublin Metropolitan District, affixed with the seal of that District,

or a copy thereof certified in accordance with rules of court.

(2) A seal of the District Court when affixed to an order drawn up in accordance with this section shall be authenticated by the signature of the judge who made the order or the District Court clerk who drew up the order.".

21   Commencement

Sections 3 to 10, 12 and 18 shall come into operation one month after the passing of this Act.

22   Expenses

The expenses incurred by the Minister for Justice in the administration of this Act, shall, to such extent as may be sanctioned by the Minister for Finance, be paid out of moneys provided by the Oireachtas.

23   Repeal of enactments

The enactments specified in the Second Schedule to this Act are hereby repealed.

24   Short title

This Act may be cited as the Criminal Justice (Miscellaneous Provisions) Act, 1997.

FIRST SCHEDULE

Amendments

1   Schedule 1 deleted by Criminal Justice Act 2006, s 6(b).

SECOND SCHEDULE

Section 23

Number and Year	Enactment
(1)	(2)
40 & 41 Vict. c.49	Section 12 of the General Prisons (Ireland) Act, 1877
54 & 55 Vict. c.69	Section 8 of the Penal Servitude (Ireland) Act, 1891
7 Edw. 7. c.19	Section 1 of the Prisons (Ireland) Act, 1907

Criminal Law Act 1997

Number 14 of 1997

ARRANGEMENT OF SECTIONS

1.   Commencement.

2.   Interpretation.

3.   Abolition of distinction between felony and misdemeanour.

4.   Arrest without warrant.

5.   Arrest on warrant or order of committal.

6.   Entry and search of premises to effect an arrest.

7.   Penalties for assisting offenders.

8.   Penalty for concealing offence.

9.   Trial of offences.

10.   Powers of dealing with offenders.

11.   Abolition of penal servitude, hard labour and prison divisions.

12.   Abolition of corporal punishment.

13.   Amendment of particular enactments.

14.   Amendment of Defence Act, 1954.

15.   Savings and other general provisions.

16.   Repeals.

17.   Short title.

FIRST SCHEDULE

AMENDMENT OF PARTICULAR ENACTMENTS

SECOND SCHEDULE

AMENDMENT OF DEFENCE ACT 1954

THIRD SCHEDULE

ENACTMENTS REPEALED

AN ACT TO ABOLISH ALL DISTINCTIONS BETWEEN FELONY AND MISDEMEANOUR AND TO AMEND AND SIMPLIFY THE LAW IN RESPECT OF MATTERS ARISING FROM OR RELATED TO ANY SUCH DISTINCTION, TO ABOLISH PENAL SERVITUDE, HARD LABOUR, PRISON DIVISIONS AND CORPORAL PUNISHMENT, AND TO PROVIDE FOR CERTAIN OTHER MATTERS CONNECTED WITH THE MATTERS AFORESAID.
[22nd April, 1997]

BE IT ENACTED BY THE OIREACHTAS AS FOLLOWS:

ement

into operation three months after the date of its passing.

ion

(1) in this Act, and in any amendment made by this Act in any other enactment—

"arrestable offence" means an offence for which a person of full capacity and not previously convicted may, [under or by virtue of any enactment or the common law][1], be punished by imprisonment for a term of five years or by a more severe penalty and includes an attempt to commit any such offence;

"fixed by law", in relation to a sentence for an arrestable offence, means a sentence which the court is required by law to impose on an offender, being a person of full capacity.

(2) Any reference in this Act to any other enactment shall, except so far as the context otherwise requires, be construed as a reference to that enactment as amended by or under any other enactment, including this Act.

(3) In this Act, a reference to a section is to a section of this Act and a reference to a subsection or paragraph is to the subsection or paragraph of the provision in which the reference occurs, unless it is indicated that reference to some other enactment or provision, as may be appropriate, is intended.

Amendments

1   Words substituted by Criminal Justice Act 2006, s 8.

---

3   Abolition of distinction between felony and misdemeanour

(1) All distinctions between felony and misdemeanour are hereby abolished.

(2) Subject to the provisions of this Act, on all matters on which a distinction has previously been made between felony and misdemeanour, including mode of trial, the law and practice in relation to all offences (including piracy) shall be the law and practice applicable at the commencement of this Act in relation to misdemeanour.

4   Arrest without warrant

(1) Subject to subsections (4) and (5), any person may arrest without warrant anyone who is or whom he or she, with reasonable cause, suspects to be in the act of committing an arrestable offence.

(2) Subject to subsections (4) and (5), where an arrestable offence has been committed, any person may arrest without warrant anyone who is or whom he or she, with reasonable cause, suspects to be guilty of the offence.

(3) Where a member of the Garda Síochána, with reasonable cause, suspects that an arrestable offence has been committed, he or she may arrest without warrant anyone whom the member, with reasonable cause, suspects to be guilty of the offence.

(4) An arrest other than by a member of the Garda Síochána may only be effected by a person under subsection (1) or (2) where he or she, with reasonable cause, suspects that the person

to be arrested by him or her would otherwise attempt to avoid, or member of the Garda Síochána.

(5) A person who is arrested pursuant to this section by a person o Garda Síochána shall be transferred into the custody of the Garda practicable.

(6) This section shall not affect the operation of any enactment restricting the insti proceedings for an offence or prejudice any power of arrest conferred by law apart from this section.

5   Arrest on warrant or order of committal

A warrant for the arrest of a person or an order of committal may be executed by a member of the Garda Síochána notwithstanding that it is not in the member's possession at the time; but the warrant or order shall be shown to him or her as soon as practicable.

6   Entry and search of premises to effect an arrest

(1) For the purpose of arresting a person on foot of a warrant of arrest or an order of committal, a member of the Garda Síochána may enter (if need be, by use of reasonable force) and search any premises (including a dwelling) where the person is or where the member, with reasonable cause, suspects that person to be, and such warrant or order may be executed in accordance with section 5.

(2) For the purpose of arresting a person without a warrant for an arrestable offence a member of the Garda Síochána may enter (if need be, by use of reasonable force) and search any premises (including a dwelling) where that person is or where the member, with reasonable cause, suspects that person to be, and where the premises is a dwelling the member shall not, unless acting with the consent of an occupier of the dwelling or other person who appears to the member to be in charge of the dwelling, enter that dwelling unless—

(a) he or she or another such member has observed the person within or entering the dwelling, or

(b) he or she, with reasonable cause, suspects that before a warrant of arrest could be obtained the person will either abscond for the purpose of avoiding justice or will obstruct the course of justice, or

(c) he or she, with reasonable cause, suspects that before a warrant of arrest could be obtained the person would commit an arrestable offence, or

(d) the person ordinarily resides at that dwelling. ,

(3) Without prejudice to any express amendment or repeal made by this Act, this section shall not affect the operation of any enactment or rule of law relating to powers of search or powers of arrest.

7   Penalties for assisting offenders

(1) Any person who aids, abets, counsels or procures the commission of an indictable offence shall be liable to be indicted, tried and punished as a principal offender.

[(1A) Any person who, outside the State, aids, abets, counsels or procures the commission of an indictable offence in the State shall be liable to be indicted, tried and punished as a principal offender if—

the person does so on board an Irish ship,

(b)   the person does so on an aircraft registered in the State,

(c)   the person is an Irish citizen, or

(d)   the person is ordinarily resident in the State.]¹

(2) Where a person has committed an arrestable offence, any other person who, knowing or believing him or her to be guilty of the offence or of some other arrestable offence, does without reasonable excuse any act[, whether in or outside the State,]² with intent to impede his or her apprehension or prosecution shall be guilty of an offence.

[(2A) A person shall be guilty of an offence under subsection (2) for doing an act outside the State only if—

(a)   the person does so on board an Irish ship,

(b)   the person does so on an aircraft registered in the State,

(c)   the person is an Irish citizen, or

(d)   the person is ordinarily resident in the State.]³

(3) If, upon the trial on indictment of an arrestable offence, it is proved that the offence charged, or some other offence of which the accused might on that charge be found guilty, was committed but it is not proved that the accused was guilty of it, the accused may be found guilty of an offence under subsection (2) of which it is proved that he or she is guilty in relation to the offence charged, or that other offence.

(4) A person committing an offence under subsection (2) with intent to impede another person's apprehension or prosecution shall be liable on conviction on indictment to imprisonment according to the gravity of the offence that the other person has committed or attempted to commit, as follows:

(a)   if that offence is one for which the sentence is fixed by law, or for which the maximum sentence is imprisonment for life, he or she shall be liable to imprisonment for a term not exceeding ten years;

(b)   if it is one for which a person of full capacity and not previously convicted may be sentenced to imprisonment for a term of fourteen years, he or she shall be liable to imprisonment for a term not exceeding seven years;

(c)   if it is not one included in paragraph (a) or (b) but is one for which a person of full capacity and not previously convicted may be sentenced to imprisonment for a term of ten years, he or she shall be liable to imprisonment for a term not exceeding five years;

(d)   in any other case, he or she shall be liable to imprisonment for a term not exceeding three years.

(5) Where a person is charged with an offence under subsection (2), no further proceedings in the matter (other than any remand in custody or on bail) shall be taken except by or with the consent of the Director of Public Prosecutions.

(6) The references in the following provisions, namely subsection (1) of section 13 (which relates to a plea of guilty in the District Court of an indictable offence) and subsection (1)(f) of section 29 (which relates to bail in the case of certain offences) of the Criminal Procedure Act, 1967, to an accessory before or after the fact shall be construed as references to aiding, abetting, counselling or procuring[the commission of an offence, and to an offence under subsection (2).

(7) The First Schedule to the Criminal Justice Act, 1951 (which specifies the indictable offences which may be tried summarily with the consent of the accused) is hereby amended by the insertion of the following reference:⁴

[(8) A person who has his or her principal residence in the State for the 12 months immediately preceding the commission of an offence referred to in subsection (1A) or an offence under subsection (2) is, for the purposes of subsection (1A)(d) or (in the case of an offence under subsection (2)) subsection (2A)(d), taken to be ordinarily resident in the State on the date of the commission of the offence.

(9) In this section ' Irish ship' has the meaning it has in section 9 of the Mercantile Marine Act 1955.]⁵

Amendments

1   Subsection (1A) inserted by Criminal Justice (Amendment) Act 2009, s 19(1).
2   Words inserted by Criminal Justice (Amendment) Act 2009, s 19(2)(a).
3   Subsection (2A) inserted by Criminal Justice (Amendment) Act 2009, s 19(2)(b).
4   See the amended Act.
5   Subsections (8) and (9) inserted by Criminal Justice (Amendment) Act 2009, s 19(2)(c).

8   Penalty for concealing offence

(1) Where a person has committed an arrestable offence, any other person who, knowing or believing that the offence or some other arrestable offence has been committed and that he or she has information which might be of material assistance in securing the prosecution or conviction of an offender for it, [accepts (or agrees to accept), whether in or outside the State, for not disclosing that information any consideration]¹ other than the making good of loss or injury caused by the offence, or the making of reasonable compensation for that loss or injury, shall be guilty of an offence and shall be liable on conviction on indictment to imprisonment for a term not exceeding three years.

[(1A) A person shall be guilty of an offence under subsection (1) for conduct that the person engages in outside the State only if—

   (a)   the conduct takes place on board an Irish ship,
   (b)   the conduct takes place on an aircraft registered in the State,
   (c)   the person is an Irish citizen, or
   (d)   the person is ordinarily resident in the State.]²

(2) No proceedings shall be instituted for an offence under this section except by or with the consent of the Director of Public Prosecutions.

(3) The compounding of an offence shall not be an offence otherwise than under this section.

(4) The First Schedule to the Criminal Justice Act, 1951 (which specifies the indictable offences which may be tried summarily with the consent of the accused) is hereby amended by the insertion of the following reference:³

[(5) A person who has his or her principal residence in the State for the 12 months immediately preceding the commission of an offence under subsection (1) is, for the purposes of subsection (1A)(d), ordinarily resident in the State on the date of the commission of the offence.

(6) In this section ' Irish ship' has the same meaning as it has in section 7.]⁴

Amendments

1   Words substituted by Criminal Justice (Amendment) Act 2009, s 19(3).

2   Subsection (1A) inserted by Criminal Justice (Amendment) Act 2009, s 19(4).

3   See the amended Act.

4   Subsections (5) and (6) inserted by Criminal Justice (Amendment) Act 2009, s 19(4)(b).

---

9   Trial of offences

(1) Where a person is arraigned on an indictment—

   (a)   he or she shall in all cases be entitled to make a plea of not guilty in addition to any demurrer or special plea;

   (b)   he or she may plead not guilty of the offence specifically charged in the indictment but guilty of another offence of which he or she might be found guilty on that indictment;

   (c)   if he or she stands mute of malice or will not answer directly to the indictment, the court shall order a plea of not guilty to be entered on his or her behalf, and he or she shall then be treated as having pleaded not guilty.

(2) If, on an indictment for murder, the evidence does not warrant a conviction for murder but warrants a conviction for any of the following offences—

   [(a)   manslaughter, or causing serious harm with intent to do so, or]¹

   (b)   any offence of which the accused may be found guilty by virtue of an enactment specifically so providing (including section 7(3)), or

   (c)   an attempt to commit murder, or an attempt to commit any other offence under this section of which the accused might be found guilty, or

   (d)   an offence under the Criminal Law (Suicide) Act, 1993,

the accused may be found guilty of such offence but may not on that indictment be found guilty of any offence not specified in any of the foregoing paragraphs.

(3) If, on an indictment for murder to which section 3 of the Criminal Justice Act, 1990, applies or for an attempt to commit such murder, the evidence does not warrant a conviction for such murder but warrants a conviction for murder or for any offence mentioned in paragraph (a), (b), (c) or (d) of subsection (2), the accused may be found guilty of murder or of any offence so mentioned but may not on that indictment be found guilty of any offence not specified in any of the foregoing paragraphs.

(4) Where, on a person's trial on indictment for any offence except treason, murder to which section 3 of the Criminal Justice Act, 1990, applies or murder, the evidence does not warrant a conviction for the offence specifically charged in the indictment, but the allegations in the indictment amount to or include (expressly or by implication) an allegation of another

offence, that person may be found guilty of that other offence or of an offe.
she could be found guilty on an indictment specifically charging that other

(5) An allegation of an offence to which subsection (4) relates shall be take
allegation of attempting to commit that offence; and where a person is charg
with attempting to commit an offence or with any assault or other act pr~ımınary to an
offence, but not with the completed offence, then (subject to the discretion of a court sitting
with a jury to discharge the jury with a view to the preferment of an indictment for the
completed offence) the accused may be convicted of the offence charged notwithstanding
that he or she is shown to be guilty of the completed offence.

(6) Where a person arraigned on an indictment pleads not guilty of an offence charged in the
indictment but guilty of some other offence of which the accused might be found guilty on
that charge, and he or she is convicted on that plea of guilty without trial for the offence of
which the accused has pleaded not guilty, then (whether or not the two offences are
separately charged in distinct counts) conviction of the one offence shall be an acquittal of
the other.

(7) Where a person charged on an indictment with any offence is convicted of some other
offence of which he or she might be found guilty on that charge, conviction of that offence
shall be an acquittal of the offence charged.

(8) Subsections (1) to (5) shall apply to an indictment containing more than one count as if
each count were a separate indictment.

Amendments

1   Subsection (2)(a) substituted by Non-Fatal Offences Against The Person Act 1997, s 29.

10   Powers of dealing with offenders

(1) Where a person is convicted on indictment of an offence against any enactment and is for
that offence liable to be sentenced to imprisonment but the sentence is not by any enactment
either limited to a specified term or expressed to extend to imprisonment for life, the person
so convicted shall be liable to imprisonment for not more than two years.

(2) A person convicted on indictment of an attempt to commit an offence for which a
maximum term of imprisonment or a maximum fine is provided by an enactment shall not be
sentenced to imprisonment for a term longer, or a fine larger, than that which could be
imposed for the completed offence.

(3) Where a person is convicted on indictment of any offence other than an offence for which
the sentence is fixed by law, the court, if not precluded from doing so by its exercise of some
other power, may impose a fine in lieu of or in addition to dealing with the offender in any
other way in which the court has power to deal with him or her, subject however to any
enactment limiting the amount of the fine that may be imposed or requiring the offender to
be dealt with in a particular way.

(4) Notwithstanding anything in any enactment whereby power is conferred on a court, on
the conviction of a person of an offence, to bind the offender over to keep the peace or to be

good behaviour, that power may be exercised without sentencing the offender to a fine or to imprisonment.

(5) A person sent forward to a court for sentence under section 13(2) of the Criminal Procedure Act, 1967 with a plea of guilty of an offence may be dealt with in all respects as if he or she had been convicted on indictment of the offence by that court.

11   Abolition of penal servitude, hard labour and prison divisions

(1) No person shall be sentenced by a court to penal servitude.

(2) Every enactment conferring a power on a court to pass a sentence of penal servitude in any case shall be treated as an enactment empowering that court to pass a sentence of imprisonment for a term not exceeding the maximum term of penal servitude for which a sentence could have been passed in that case immediately before the commencement of this Act, and accordingly, in the case of any enactment in force on the 5th day of August, 1891, being the date on which section 1 (repealed by this Act) of the Penal Servitude Act, 1891, came into operation, whereby a court had, immediately before the commencement of this Act, power to pass a sentence of penal servitude, the maximum term of imprisonment shall not exceed five years or any greater term authorised by the enactment.

(3) No person shall be sentenced by a court to imprisonment with hard labour; and every enactment conferring a power on a court to pass a sentence of imprisonment with hard labour in any case shall operate so as to empower that court to pass a sentence of imprisonment for a term not exceeding the term for which a sentence of imprisonment with hard labour could have been passed in that case immediately before the commencement of this Act; and so far as any enactment in force immediately before the commencement of this Act requires or permits prisoners to be kept to hard labour it shall cease to have effect; and accordingly the expressions "with or without hard labour", "with hard labour", "without hard labour" and corresponding expressions, wherever occurring in any enactment prescribing the punishment for an offence, are hereby repealed.

(4) So far as any enactment provides that a person sentenced to imprisonment or committed to prison is or may be directed to be treated as an offender of a particular division, or to be placed in a separate division, it shall cease to have effect.

(5) Any person who, immediately before the commencement of this Act, was undergoing or liable to undergo a term of penal servitude shall, if that person is or ought to be in custody at such commencement, be treated thereafter as if he or she were undergoing or liable to undergo imprisonment and not penal servitude for that term.

(6) Any person who has been sentenced to imprisonment with hard labour for a term which has not expired at the commencement of this Act shall, for the remainder of that term, be treated as though he or she had been sentenced to imprisonment without hard labour.

12   Abolition of corporal punishment

(1) No person shall be sentenced by a court to whipping, and so far as any enactment confers power on a court to pass a sentence of whipping it shall cease to have effect.

(2) Corporal punishment shall not be inflicted in any place to which the Prisons Acts, 1826 to 1980, or section 13 of the Criminal Justice Act, 1960, apply.

13 Amendment of particular enactments

The enactments mentioned in the First Schedule to this Act are hereby amended in accordance with the provisions of that Schedule.

14 Amendment of Defence Act, 1954

(1) The Defence Act, 1954, is hereby amended in accordance with the provisions of the Second Schedule to this Act.

(2) This section, the Second Schedule to this Act and the Defence Acts, 1954 to 1993, may be cited together as the Defence Acts, 1954 to 1997.

15 Savings and other general provisions

(1) Except as provided by the following subsections, this Act, in so far as it affects any matter of procedure or evidence or the jurisdiction or powers of any court in relation to offences, shall have effect in relation to proceedings on indictment for an offence committed before the commencement of this Act if the person charged is arraigned after that commencement.

(2) Where a person is arraigned after the commencement of this Act on an indictment for a felony committed before that commencement, then, for the purposes of trial on that indictment, the offence shall be deemed always to have been a misdemeanour and, notwithstanding that the indictment is framed as an indictment for felony, shall be deemed to be charged as a misdemeanour in the indictment.

(3) On an indictment signed before the commencement of this Act, a person may be found guilty of any offence of which he or she could have been found guilty on that indictment if this Act had not been passed, but not of any other offence; and a person tried by a court-martial ordered or convened before that commencement may be found guilty of any offence of which he or she could have been found guilty if this Act had not been passed, but not of any other offence.

(4) For the purpose of Article 15.13 of the Constitution and for that purpose only, offences which were felonies immediately before the commencement of this Act shall continue to be treated as felonies and, accordingly, for all other purposes any rule of law or enactment whereby an offence is, or is regarded as, a felony shall be construed as relating to an indictable offence.

(5) Without prejudice to any express amendment or repeal made by this Act—

(a) nothing in this Act shall affect the operation of any reference to an offence in the enactments specially relating to that offence by reason only of the reference being in terms no longer applicable after the commencement of this Act;

(b) any enactment referring to felonious stealing or to felonious taking shall be read as referring merely to stealing;

(c) nothing in this Act shall affect the punishment provided for an offence by the enactments specially relating to that offence.

16 Repeals

Each of the enactments mentioned in the Third Schedule to this Act is hereby repealed to the extent specified in the third column of that Schedule.

17 Short title

This Act may be cited as the Criminal Law Act, 1997.

FIRST SCHEDULE

AMENDMENT OF PARTICULAR ENACTMENTS

Section 13

1. In the Slave Trade Act, 1824, as amended by section 1 of the Slave Trade Act, 1843—

   (a) in sections 3, 5, 6, 7, 8 and 11, "and their procurers, counsellors, aiders, and abettors" shall be deleted;

   (b) in section 9, for "piracy, felony, and robbery" there shall be substituted "an offence, and shall be liable to imprisonment for life", and for the references to British subjects there shall be substituted references to Irish citizens;

   (c) in section 10, for the words from "and their procurers" to the end of that section there shall be substituted "shall be guilty of an offence and shall be liable to imprisonment for a term not exceeding fourteen years";

   (d) in section 12, "piracies, felonies, robberies, and" shall be deleted.

2. In section 8 of the Carriers Act, 1830 (under which the protection given by that Act to common carriers does not extend to the felonious acts of their servants) for "the felonious acts" there shall be substituted "any theft, embezzlement or forgery".

3. In the proviso to section 30 of the Town Police Clauses Act, 1847 (which provides that a person liable to a penalty under that section for wilfully setting or causing to be set a chimney on fire shall not be exempt from liability to be indicted for felony) for "felony" there shall be substituted "any other offence".

4. In section 10 of the Offences against the Person Act, 1861 (which provides for the trial of murder or manslaughter where any person dies in a country after being feloniously stricken out of it or vice versa) for "feloniously", in both places where the word occurs, there shall be substituted "criminally".

5. In section 6, subsection (2), of the Criminal Law Amendment Act, 1885 (as amended by section 9 of the Criminal Law Amendment Act, 1935) (as to defilement of young persons) "of or above the age of fifteen and" shall be deleted.

6. (1) The Larceny Act, 1916, shall be amended in accordance with the provisions of this paragraph.

(2) Section 35 (accessories and abettors) shall be repealed.

(3) Section 37(4) shall be deleted.

(4) Section 41(3) (arrest without warrant) shall be deleted.

(5) In section 44(1) (verdict), "acquit the defendant of robbery and" and, in section 44(3), "acquit the defendant of stealing and" shall be deleted.

7. The Criminal Law Amendment Act, 1935, shall be amended as follows: in section 2(1) and 2(2) (defilement of girl between fifteen and seventeen years of age), "of or over the age of fifteen years and" shall be deleted.

8. In the Criminal Justice Act, 1990, paragraph 4(m) of the First Schedule shall be deleted.

9. Section 19(a) of the Criminal Law (Rape) (Amendment) Act, 1990, shall be amended by the deletion of "section 169(b)" and the substitution of "section 169(3)(b)".

10. In section 3(c) and (d) of the Criminal Law (Sexual Offences) Act, 1993, "of or over the age of 15 years and" shall be deleted.

SECOND SCHEDULE
AMENDMENT OF DEFENCE ACT, 1954

Section 14

1. In section 2 there shall be deleted—

(a) "the expression 'military convict' means a person under sentence of penal servitude passed by a court-martial;", and

(b) "the expression 'penal servitude prison' means any prison or place in which a person convicted and sentenced to penal servitude by a civil court may be lawfully confined;".

2. In section 40(2) "military convict," shall be deleted in each place where the words occur.

3. In section 50(2) "penal servitude or" shall be deleted.

4. In sections 120(3), 206(1), 222, 223(1), 223(2), 223(3), 223(4), 230 and 240(1)(i) "penal servitude," shall be deleted.

5. In sections 126(2)(i), 127, 131, 135(1)(b), 145, 149, 151, 154(1), 155 and 158, "imprisonment for a term not exceeding seven years" shall be substituted for "penal servitude".

6. In sections 129, 130, 132, 135(1)(a), 169(3)(a) and 169(3)(b) "imprisonment for life" shall be substituted for "penal servitude".

7. In section 192(2)(d) "for a term of two years" shall be inserted after "imprisonment" in place of the words "for any term not exceeding two years" (inserted by paragraph 4(h) of the First Schedule to the Criminal Justice Act, 1990).

8. In section 208(2)(a) ", without hard labour," shall be deleted and "or, in either case, to be fined" shall be inserted after "twenty-one days".

9. In item A of the Scale in section 209(1) (as amended by paragraph 4(j) of the First Schedule to the Criminal Justice Act, 1990) after "Imprisonment for life" there shall be inserted "or any specified period" and items B and C shall be deleted.

10. In section 209(5) "penal servitude or" wherever occurring shall be deleted.

11. In item A of the Scale in section 210(1) (as amended by paragraph 4(j) of the First Schedule to the Criminal Justice Act, 1990) after "Imprisonment for life" there shall be inserted "or any specified period" and items B and C shall be deleted.

12. In section 210(6) "imprisonment for a term exceeding two years" shall be substituted for "imprisonment for life or penal servitude" wherever occurring.

13. In section 212 "be served concurrently with the term then unexpired of the former sentence and on completion of either sentence any balance of the other sentence shall be served" shall be substituted for "not exceed such term as will make up a period of two consecutive years including the term then unexpired of the former sentence".

14. In section 223(7) "penal servitude," (where occurring after "is sentenced to") and ", and where the sentence for such other offence is a sentence of penal servitude, then, whether or not that sentence is suspended, any previous sentence of imprisonment or detention which has been suspended shall be avoided" shall be deleted and "any sentences of" shall be substituted for "imprisonment or" (where occurring after "the aggregate term of").

15. Sections 224(2)(c)(iii) and 228 shall be deleted.

16. In section 229 the following subsection shall be substituted for subsection (1):

"(1) Where a sentence of imprisonment is passed by a court-martial and confirmed, the military prisoner shall undergo sentence as follows:

(a) if the sentence is for a term exceeding two years, he or she shall, as soon as practicable, be committed to a public prison to undergo sentence;

(b) if the sentence is for a term not exceeding two years, he or she shall undergo sentence either in a military prison or detention barrack or in other service custody or in a public prison, or partly in one way and partly in another.".

17. In section 229(8) ", kept to hard labour" shall be deleted.

18. In section 234 "an offence" shall be substituted for "felony" and ", with or without hard labour," shall be deleted.

19. In section 239(1) "military convict or", "convict or" and "convict," and in section 239(2) "a military convict or" shall be deleted.

THIRD SCHEDULE
ENACTMENTS REPEALED

Section 16

Session and Chapter or Number and Year	Short Title	Extent of Repeal
7 Will. 3, c. 17	Sunday Observance Act, 1695	The whole Act
9 Anne, c. 6	Criminal Evidence Act, 1710	The whole Act
21 & 22 Geo. 3, c. 11	Habeas Corpus Act, 1781	In section 2, the words from "and if any person or persons" to the end of the section
26 Geo. 3, c. 24	Forcible Entry Act, 1786	The whole Act
27 Geo. 3, c. 15	Riot Act, 1787	The whole Act
55 Geo. 3, c. 91	Criminal Costs (Dublin) Act, 1815	The whole Act
1 Geo. 4, c. 57	Whipping Act, 1820	The whole Act
1 & 2 Geo. 4, c. 88	Rescue Act, 1821	The whole Act
3 Geo. 4, c. 114	Hard Labour Act, 1822	The whole Act

Session and Chapter or Number and Year	Short Title	Extent of Repeal
5 Geo. 4, c. 83, as extended to Ireland by 34 and 35 Vict., c. 112, s. 15	Vagrancy Act, 1824	In section 4, the words "or having upon him or her any instrument, with intent to commit any felonious act" and the words from "every suspected person or reputed thief" to "intent to commit felony", and the words "and every such instrument as aforesaid, shall, by the conviction of the offender, become forfeited to the King's Majesty"
7 Geo. 4, c. 9	Hard Labour (Ireland) Act, 1826	The whole Act
9 Geo. 4, c. 32	Civil Rights of Convicts Act, 1828	The whole Act
6 & 7 Will. 4, c. 114	Trials for Felony Act, 1836	The whole Act
6 & 7 Will. 4, c. 116	Grand Jury (Ireland) Act, 1836	Sections 35,105 and 108
3 & 4 Vict., c. 90	Infant Felons Act, 1840	The whole Act
5 & 6 Vict., c. 61	South Australia Act, 1842	The whole Act
7 & 8 Vict., c. 106	County Dublin Grand Jury Act, 1844	Sections 40 and 43
14 & 15 Vict., c. 19	Prevention of Offences Act, 1851	Sections 5 and 14
14 & 15 Vict., c. 100	Criminal Procedure Act, 1851	Sections 9,12 and 29
19 & 20 Vict., c. 68	Prisons (Ireland) Act, 1856	Section 14
20 & 21 Vict., c. 3	Penal Servitude Act, 1857	The whole Act
24 & 25 Vict., c. 94	Accessories and Abettors Act, 1861	The whole Act
24 & 25 Vict., c. 96	Larceny Act, 1861	In section 21, "only, or to be imprisoned and kept to hard labour" and "there to be kept to hard labour" In section 26, ", with or without hard labour, and with or without solitary confinement"

Session and Chapter or Number and Year	Short Title	Extent of Repeal
24 & 25 Vict., c. 96 (contd)		Sections 98 and 104 In section 115, "deemed to be offences of the same nature, and" In section 117, "fine the offender, and" and the words from "and in case of any felony" to "authorized", where next occurring Sections 119 and 121
24 & 25 Vict., c. 97	Malicious Damage Act, 1861	In section 72, "deemed to be offences of the same nature and"
24 & 25 Vict., c. 98	Forgery Act, 1861	Sections 47, 48 and 49 In section 50, "deemed to be offences of the same nature and" In section 51, "fine the offender, and to" and the words from "and in all cases of felonies" to "authorized", where next occurring Section 54
24 & 25 Vict., c. 99	Coinage Offences Act, 1861	Section 35 In section 36, "deemed to be offences of the same nature and" In section 38, "fine the offender, and" and the words from "and in case of any felony" to "authorized", where next occurring
24 & 25 Vict., c. 100	Offences against the Person Act, 1861	Sections 7 and 8 In sections 9 and 10, "or of being accessory to murder or manslaughter" Sections 11 to 15

Session and Chapter or Number and Year	Short Title	Extent of Repeal
24 & 25 Vict., c. 100 (contd)		In section 18, the words from "or shoot" to "at any person" where those words secondly occur, the words from "in any" to "person, or" and the word "other" Section 19 In section 46, the words from "shall find" to "felony, or" and the word "other" Sections 66 and 67 In section 68, "deemed to be offences of the same nature, and". Section 70 In section 71, "fine the offender, and" and the words from "and in case of any felony" to "authorized", where next occurring Sections 74, 75 and 77
25 & 26 Vict., c. 18	Whipping Act, 1862	The whole Act
26 & 27 Vict., c. 44	Garrotters Act, 1863	The whole Act
27 & 28 Vict., c. 47	Penal Servitude Act, 1864	The whole Act
28 & 29 Vict., c. 18	Criminal Procedure Act, 1865	In sections 1 and 2, "for felony or misdemeanour"
33 & 34 Vict., c. 23	Forfeiture Act, 1870	The whole Act
34 & 35 Vict., c. 112	Prevention of Crimes Act, 1871	Sections 3, 4, 5, 6, 7, 8 and 9 Section 15, except insofar as it applies section 4 of the Vagrancy Act, 1824, to Ireland In the proviso to section 17, paragraph 4 Sections 20 and 22
35 & 36 Vict., c. 57	Debtors Act (Ireland), 1872	Section 17
39 & 40 Vict., c. 23	Prevention of Crimes Amendment Act, 1876	The whole Act

Session and Chapter or Number and Year	Short Title	Extent of Repeal
40 & 41 Vict., c. 49	General Prisons (Ireland) Act, 1877	In section 47, "in which prisoners sentenced to imprisonment without hard labour shall be confined", the word "such" and the word "respectively" Section 49 In section 54, the words from "No prisoner" to the end of the section
42 & 43 Vict., c. 55	Prevention of Crime Act, 1879	The whole Act
47 & 48 Vict., c. 19	Summary Jurisdiction over Children (Ireland) Act, 1884	In section 4, paragraph (d) of subsection (1)
48 & 49 Vict., c. 69	Criminal Law Amendment Act, 1885	Section 18
52 & 53 Vict., c. 69	Public Bodies Corrupt Practices Act, 1889	Section 5
54 & 55 Vict., c. 69	Penal Servitude Act, 1891	Sections 1 to 7 In section 8, the words from "and all" to "of this section"
57 & 58 Vict., c. 60	Merchant Shipping Act, 1894	Section 700
61 & 62 Vict., c. 41	Prison Act, 1898	Section 6, as extended to Ireland by section 43(8) of the Criminal Justice Administration Act, 1914
6 Edw. 7, c. 34	Prevention of Corruption Act, 1906	Section 2(4)
8 Edw. 7, c. 59	Prevention of Crime Act, 1908	Part II In section 18 all references to Part II; paragraphs (e) and (f) Schedule

Session and Chapter or Number and Year	Short Title	Extent of Repeal
3 & 4 Geo. 5, c. 27	Forgery Act, 1913	In section 4(1) and (2) the words from "which" to "in force"
		In section 6(1) "of the like degree (whether felony or misdemeanour)"
		Section 11
		Section 12(1)
		In section 12(2), paragraphs (a) and (b)
4 & 5 Geo. 5, c. 58	Criminal Justice Administration Act, 1914	Sections 16, 26 and 36
		In section 43(1), the references to those sections
		In section 43(8), the reference to section 6 of the Prison Act, 1898
No. 11 of 1925	Prisons (Visiting Committees) Act, 1925	Section 4
No. 6 of 1957	Statute of Limitations, 1957	In section 48(1), paragraph (b) "or"; paragraph (c)
No. 1 of 1963	Official Secrets Act, 1963	Section 15
No. 19 of 1983	Courts-Martial Appeals Act, 1983	In section 16(a), "penal servitude"
No. 23 of 1983	Criminal Justice (Community Service) Act, 1983	In section 2, "of penal servitude"
No. 16 of 1990	Criminal Justice Act, 1990	Subsections (2) and (3) of section 6 and paragraph 4(t) of the First Schedule
No. 23 of 1992	Electoral Act, 1992	In section 41(j), ", whether with or without hard labour, or of penal servitude for any period"
No. 8 of 1994	Local Government Act, 1994	In section 6(1)(k), "whether with or without hard labour, or of penal servitude for any period"

Bail Act 1997

Number 16 of 1997

ARRANGEMENT OF SECTIONS

Section

1. Interpretation.

1A Statement by applicants for bail charged with serious offences.

2. Refusal of bail.

2A Evidence in applications for bail under section 2.

3. Renewal of bail application.

4. Evidence of previous criminal record.

5. Payment of moneys into court, etc.

6. Conditions of bail.

6A. Application of section 6 in relation to certain appellants.

6B. Electronic monitoring of certain persons admitted to bail.

6C Evidence of electronic monitoring.

6D Arrangements for electronic monitoring.

7. Sufficiency of bailspersons.

8. Endorsement on warrants as to release on bail.

9. Estreatment of recognisance and forfeiture of moneys paid into court.

10. Amendment of Criminal Justice Act, 1984.

11. Amendment of Act of 1967.

11A Regulations.

12. Repeals.

13. Short title and commencement.

AN ACT TO MAKE FURTHER PROVISION IN RELATION TO BAIL, TO AMEND THE CRIMINAL PROCEDURE ACT, 1967, AND TO PROVIDE FOR RELATED MATTERS. [5th May, 1997]

BE IT ENACTED BY THE OIREACHTAS AS FOLLOWS:

1   Interpretation

(1) In this Act, except when the context otherwise requires—

"the Act of 1967" means the Criminal Procedure Act, 1967;

["authorised person" means a person who is appointed in writing by the Minister, or a person who is one of a prescribed class of persons, to be an authorised person for the purposes of sections 6B and 6C;][1]

"court" means any court exercising criminal jurisdiction but does not include court martial;

"criminal record", in relation to a person, means a record of the previous convictions of the person for offences (if any);

["Minister" means Minister for Justice, Equality and Law Reform;

"prescribed" means prescribed by regulations made by the Minister;]¹

"serious offence" means an offence specified in the Schedule for which a person of full capacity and not previously convicted may be punished by a term of imprisonment for a term of 5 years or by a more severe penalty.

(2) In this Act—

    (a) a reference to a section is a reference to a section of this Act, unless it is indicated that reference to some other enactment is intended,

    (b) a reference to a subsection, paragraph or subparagraph is a reference to a subsection, paragraph or subparagraph of the provision in which the reference occurs unless it is indicated that reference to some other provision is intended,

    (c) a reference to any enactment shall be construed as a reference to that enactment as amended, adapted or extended by or under any subsequent enactment.

Amendments

1   Definitions inserted by Criminal Justice Act 2007, s 5.

[1A   Statement by applicants for bail charged with serious offences

(1) A person who is charged with a serious offence and applies for bail (in this section referred to as 'the applicant') shall, subject to subsections (4) and (5)(c), furnish to the prosecutor a written statement duly signed by the applicant and containing the following information relating to the applicant:

    (a) his or her name and any other name or names previously used;

    (b) his or her current occupation and any previous occupation or occupations within the immediately preceding 3 years;

    (c) his or her source or sources of income within the immediately preceding 3 years;

    (d) his or her property, whether wholly or partially owned by, or under the control of, the applicant and whether within or outside the State;

    (e) any previous conviction or convictions of the applicant for a serious offence;

    (f) any previous conviction or convictions of the applicant for an offence or offences committed while on bail;

    (g) any previous application or applications by the person for bail, indicating whether or not it was granted and, if granted, the conditions to which the recognisance was subject.

(2) The statement shall be in the prescribed form or a form to the like effect.

(3) The statement shall be furnished to the prosecutor—

    (a) where written notice of the application for bail is not required, as soon as reasonably practicable before the application is made, or

    (b) where such notice is required, on service of the notice.

(4) The requirement in subsection (1) to furnish a statement may be dispensed with where—

    (a) the prosecutor states an intention to consent to the grant of bail, or

    (b) the applicant and prosecutor consent to dispensing with the requirement.

(5) The court may by order:

    (a) extend the period for production by the applicant of the statement;

    (b) adjourn the hearing of the application pending production of the statement;

    (c) dispense with the need to comply with subsection (1) if satisfied that there is good and sufficient reason for doing so;

    (d) impose such conditions as it considers just in any order made by it under this section.

(6) The statement shall be received in evidence without further proof in proceedings under this section if it purports to be signed by the applicant.

(7) In proceedings under this section any witness may, with the leave of the court, be examined on the content of the statement.

(8) No information relating to the statement or any part of it shall be published in a written publication available to the public or be broadcast, unless the court otherwise directs.

(9) The court may, if it considers that publication of any examination of the applicant in relation to the statement or any part of it or of any submissions made to the court may prejudice the applicant's right to a fair trial, by order direct that no information relating to the examination or submissions be published in a written publication available to the public or be broadcast.

(10) The court, when making an order under subsection (9), may specify the duration of the order and may at any time vary or set aside the order.

(11) An applicant who knowingly gives false or misleading information or conceals any material fact, either in the statement or in evidence in proceedings under this section, is guilty of an offence and liable on summary conviction to a fine not exceeding €5,000 or imprisonment for a term not exceeding 12 months or both.

(12) Any information contained in the statement is not admissible in evidence in any other proceedings or matter, except in proceedings against the applicant under subsection (11).

(13) The court may consider an application for bail, notwithstanding a failure by the applicant to furnish the statement.

(14) Nothing in this section limits the jurisdiction of a court to grant bail.

(15) Subsection (2) of section 4 applies in relation to the hearing of evidence in relation to the statement and subsections (4) to (7) of that section apply in relation to a contravention of subsection (8) or (9) of this section, in each case with the necessary modifications.

(16) In this section ' property ' means—

    (a) cash, money in an account in a financial institution, cheques, bank drafts and transferable securities (including shares, warrants and debentures),

    (b) land,

    (c) mechanically propelled vehicles, and

    (d) any other asset exceeding €3,000 in value.][1]

Amendments

1 Section 1A inserted by Criminal Justice Act 2007, s 6.

2 Refusal of bail

(1) Where an application for bail is made by a person charged with a serious offence, a court may refuse the application if the court is satisfied that such refusal is reasonably considered necessary to prevent the commission of a serious offence by that person.

(2) In exercising its jurisdiction under subsection (1), a court shall take into account and may, where necessary, receive evidence or submissions concerning—

(a) the nature and degree of seriousness of the offence with which the accused person is charged and the sentence likely to be imposed on conviction,

(b) the nature and degree of seriousness of the offence apprehended and the sentence likely to be imposed on conviction,

(c) the nature and strength of the evidence in support of the charge,

(d) any conviction of the accused person for an offence committed while he or she was on bail,

(e) any previous convictions of the accused person including any conviction the subject of an appeal (which has neither been determined nor withdrawn) to a court,

(f) any other offence in respect of which the accused person is charged and is awaiting trial,

and, where it has taken account of one or more of the foregoing, it may also take into account the fact that the accused person is addicted to a controlled drug within the meaning of the Misuse of Drugs Act, 1977.

(3) In determining whether the refusal of an application for bail is reasonably considered necessary to prevent the commission of a serious offence by a person, it shall not be necessary for a court to be satisfied that the commission of a specific offence by that person is apprehended.

[2A Evidence in applications for bail under section 2

(1) Where a member of the Garda Síochána not below the rank of chief superintendent, in giving evidence in proceedings under section 2, states that he or she believes that refusal of the application is reasonably necessary to prevent the commission of a serious offence by that person, the statement is admissible as evidence that refusal of the application is reasonably necessary for that purpose.

(2) Evidence given by such a member in the proceedings is not admissible in any criminal proceedings against the applicant.

(3) The court may, if it considers that publication of evidence given by such a member under subsection (1) or of any part of it may prejudice the accused person's right to a fair trial, by order direct that no information relating to the evidence or that part, or to any examination of the member, be published in a written publication or be broadcast.

(4) The court, when making an order under subsection (3), may specify the duration of the order and may at any time vary or set aside the order as it sees fit and subject to such conditions as it may impose.

(5) Subsection (2) of section 4 applies in relation to the hearing of the evidence of the member and subsections (4) to (7) of that section apply in relation to a contravention of subsection (3) of this section, in each case with the necessary modifications.

(6) Nothing in this section is to be construed as prejudicing the admission in proceedings under section 2 of other evidence of belief, or of evidence of opinion, whether tendered by any member of the Garda Síochána or other person.

(7) Nothing in this section limits the jurisdiction of a court to grant bail.][1]

Amendments

1   Section 2A inserted by Criminal Justice Act 2007, s 7.

3   Renewal of bail application

(1) Where an application by a person for bail—

   (a) has been refused by a court under section 2, and

   (b) the trial of the person for the offence concerned has not commenced within 4 months from the date of such refusal,

then, the person may renew his or her application for bail to that court on the ground of delay by the prosecutor in proceeding with his or her trial, and the court shall, if satisfied that the interests of justice so require, release the person on bail.

(2) In determining whether to grant or refuse an application under subsection (1), a court may receive evidence or submissions concerning the delay in proceeding with the trial of the person concerned.

(3) Nothing in this section shall affect the operation of section 24 of the Act of 1967.

4   Evidence of previous criminal record

(1) In any proceedings in relation to an application referred to in section 2(1), the previous criminal record of the person applying for bail shall not be referred to in a manner which may prejudice his or her right to a fair trial.

(2) In any such proceedings as aforesaid, a court may—

   (a) direct that the proceedings shall be heard otherwise than in public, or

   (b) exclude from the court during the hearing all persons except officers of the court, persons directly concerned in the proceedings, bona fide representatives of the Press and such other persons if any as the court may permit to remain.

(3) In any report of any such proceedings as aforesaid, no information relating to the criminal record of the person applying for bail shall be published in a written publication available to the public or be broadcast.

(4) If any matter is published or broadcast in contravention of subsection (3), the following persons, namely—

(a) in the case of a publication in a newspaper or periodical, any proprietor, any editor and any publisher of the newspaper or periodical,

(b) in the case of any other publication, the person who publishes it, and

(c) in the case of a broadcast, any person who transmits or provides the programme in which the broadcast is made and any person having functions in relation to the programme corresponding to those of the editor of a newspaper,

shall be guilty of an offence and shall be liable—

(i) on summary conviction to a fine not exceeding £1,500 or to imprisonment for a term not exceeding 12 months or to both, or

(ii) on conviction on indictment, to a fine not exceeding £10,000 or to imprisonment for a term not exceeding 3 years or to both.

(5) In this section—

"a broadcast" means the transmission, relaying or distribution by wireless telegraphy of communications, sounds, signs, visual images or signals intended for direct reception by the general public whether such communications, sounds, signs, visual images or signals are actually received or not;

"written publication" includes a film, a sound track and any other record in permanent form (including a record that is not in a legible form but which is capable of being reproduced in a legible form) but does not include an indictment or other document prepared for use in particular legal proceedings.

(6) Where an offence under this section has been committed by a body corporate and is proved to have been committed with the consent or connivance of or to be attributable to any neglect on the part of a person being a director, manager, secretary or other officer of the body corporate, or a person who was purporting to act in any such capacity, that person as well as the body corporate shall be guilty of an offence and be liable to be proceeded against and punished as if he or she were guilty of the first-mentioned offence.

(7) Where the affairs of a body corporate are managed by its members, subsection (6) shall apply in relation to the acts and defaults of a member in connection with his or her functions of management as if he or she were a director or manager of the body corporate.

5   Payment of moneys into court, etc

(1) Where a court admits a person who is in custody to bail[, the court may, having regard to the circumstances of the case, including the means of the person and the nature of the offence in relation to which the person is in custody, order that]¹ the person shall not be released until—

(a) an amount equal to one third, or

(b) such greater amount as the court may determine,

of [any moneys to be paid into court under a recognisance]² entered into by a person in connection therewith has been paid into court by the person.

(2) [(a) Where a court requires payment of moneys into court by a person or any surety as a condition of a recognisance, it may accept as security, in lieu of such payment, any instrument that it considers to be adequate evidence of the title of a person to property (other than land or any estate, right or interest in or over land).]³

(b) Where a bank, building society, credit union or post office deposit book is accepted as security by a court by virtue of paragraph (a), the court shall make an order directing the bank, building society or credit union concerned or An Post, as the case may be, not to permit the moneys on deposit to be reduced below—

    (i)   an amount equal to the amount required to be paid into court, or

    (ii) the amount then on deposit,

whichever is the lesser.

(3) Where a person charged with an offence is admitted to bail by a court and—

    (a) he or she is discharged in relation to that offence pursuant to section 8(5) of the Act of 1967 or otherwise,

    (b) a nolle prosequi is entered by the prosecutor in respect of the offence, or

    (c) he or she is convicted or found not guilty of the offence charged or of some other offence of which the accused might on that charge be found guilty,

and if the conditions of any [moneys paid]⁴ entered into by a person in connection therewith have been duly complied with, the court before which the accused person was bound by his or her recognisance to appear shall make an order that [the amount (if any) of any recognisance paid into court]⁵ by any person in connection therewith shall be repaid to the person and shall discharge any order made under subsection (2) and release any security accepted by the court under that subsection.

[(4) This section shall not apply in relation to a person under the age of 18 years]⁶

[(5) The payment of an amount of moneys under a recognisance for transmission to the court to a person specified in section 22(3) of the Act of 1967 shall be deemed to be a payment into court for the purposes of this section and references in this section and in section 22 of the Act of 1967 to the payment of an amount of moneys into court and to moneys paid or to be paid into court shall be construed accordingly.]⁷

Amendments

1   Words inserted by Courts and Court Officers Act 2001, s 33(a)(i).

2   Words substituted by Criminal Justice Act 2007, s 8(a).

3   Subsection (2)(a) substituted by Criminal Justice Act 2007, s 8(b).

4   Words substituted by Criminal Justice Act 2007, s 8(c).

5   Words substituted by Courts and Court Officers Act 2001, s 33(a)(ii).

6   Subsection (4) inserted by Children Act 2001, s 89.

7   Subsection (5) inserted by Criminal Justice (Miscellaneous Provisions) Act 2009, s 48(a).

6   Conditions of bail

(1) Where an accused person is admitted to bail on his or her entering into a recognisance—

    [(a) the recognisance shall, in addition to the condition requiring his or her appearance before the court at the end of the period of remand of the accused person, be subject to the condition that the accused person shall not commit an offence while on bail,]¹ and

    (b) the recognisance may be subject to such conditions as the court considers appropriate having regard to the circumstances of the case, including but without prejudice to the generality of the foregoing, any one or more of the following conditions:

   (i) that the accused person resides or remains in a particular district or place in the State,

  (ii) that the accused person reports to a specified Garda Síochána Station at specified intervals,

 (iii) that the accused person surrenders any passport or travel document in his or her possession or, if he or she is not in possession of a passport or travel document, that he or she refrains from applying for a passport or travel document,

 (iv) that the accused person refrains from attending at such premises or other place as the court may specify,

  (v) that the accused person refrains from having any contact with such person or persons as the court may specify.

(2) Where an accused person is admitted to bail by a court on his or her entering into a recognisance with or without a surety or sureties, the court shall direct that a copy of the recognisance containing the conditions of the recognisance be given to the accused person and to the surety or sureties (if any).

(3) Where an accused person is admitted to bail by a court on his or her entering into a recognisance subject to one or more of the conditions referred to in subsection (1)(b), that court may, on the application to it in that behalf at any time by the accused person, if it considers it appropriate to do so, vary (whether by the alteration, addition or revocation of a condition) a condition.

[(3A) A recognisance referred to in subsection (3) shall contain a statement that the accused person may apply to the court at any time to vary or revoke a condition of the recognisance.]²

(4) The prosecutor shall be given notice of, and be entitled to be heard in, any proceedings under subsection (3).

(5) Where a person charged with an offence is admitted to bail by a court on his or her entering into a recognisance with or without a surety or sureties, the court may, on the application to it in that behalf by a surety or sureties of the accused person or of a member of the Garda Síochána and upon information being made in writing and on oath by or on behalf of such surety or member that the accused is about to contravene any of the conditions of the recognisance, issue a warrant for the arrest of the accused person.

(6) A member of the Garda Síochána may arrest a person pursuant to subsection (5) notwithstanding that he or she does not have the warrant concerned in his or her possession at the time of the arrest.

(7) Where a person is arrested pursuant to subsection (6), the member arresting him or her shall, as soon as practicable produce and serve on the person the warrant concerned.

(8) A person arrested pursuant to subsection (6), shall, as soon as practicable, be brought before the court that made the order directing that the recognisance be entered into.

(9) Where a person is brought before a court pursuant to subsection (8), the court may commit the person to prison to await his or her trial or until he or she enters a fresh recognisance or, if he or she is on remand, further remand him or her.

Amendments

1   Subsection (1)(a) substituted by Criminal Justice Act 2007, s 9(a).

2   Subsection (3A) inserted by Criminal Justice Act 2007, s 9(b).

[6A   Application of section 6 in relation to certain appellants

Section 6 applies in relation to recognisances entered into by persons appealing against sentences of imprisonment imposed by the District Court with the following modifications:

(a) by the substitution of the following paragraph for paragraph (a) of subsection (1):

'(a) the recognisance shall be subject to the following conditions, namely, that the appellant shall—

(i)   prosecute the appeal,

(ii) attend the sittings of the Circuit Court until the appeal has been determined, and

(iii) not commit an offence while on bail,';

(b) references in that section to an accused person or a person charged with an offence are to be construed as references to persons so appealing;

(c) the reference to a court in subsection (8) is to be construed as a reference to the District Court;

and with any other necessary modifications.][1]

Amendments

1   Section 6A inserted by Criminal Justice Act 2007, s 10.

[6B   Electronic monitoring of certain persons admitted to bail

(1) Subject to subsection (2), where a person (in this section referred to as 'the person') who—

(a) is charged with a serious offence or is appealing against a sentence of imprisonment imposed by the District Court, and

(b) is admitted to bail on entering into a recognisance which is subject to any of the conditions mentioned in subparagraphs (i) and (iv) of section 6(1)(b),

the court may make the recognisance subject to the following further conditions:

(i)   that the person's movements while on bail are monitored electronically so that his or her compliance or non-compliance with a condition mentioned in any of the said subparagraphs can be established;

(ii) that for that purpose the person has an electronic monitoring device attached to his or her person, either continuously or for such periods as may be specified; and

> (iii) that an authorised person is responsible for monitoring the person's compliance or non-compliance with any condition mentioned in the said subparagraphs or in paragraph (ii) of this subsection.

(2) A recognisance shall not be made subject to the further conditions mentioned in subsection (1)—

> (a) if the person is to reside or remain in a particular place, without the consent of the owner of the place or of an adult person habitually residing there, or, as the case may be, of the person in charge of the place, and
>
> (b) unless the person agrees to comply with those further conditions.

(3) The court shall direct that a copy of the recognisance containing the conditions to which it is subject be given to—

> (a) the person and any surety,
>
> (b) the member in charge of the Garda Síochána station for the place where the person is residing while the recognisance is in force, and
>
> (c) if an authorised person is to be responsible for monitoring the person's movements electronically, the authorised person.

(4) The court, on application to it by a person whose recognisance is subject to one or more of the conditions or further conditions referred to in subsection (1), may, if it considers it appropriate to do so, vary a condition of the recognisance, whether by altering or revoking it or by adding a further condition to it.

(5) A recognisance referred to in subsection (3) shall contain a statement that the accused person may apply to the court at any time to vary or revoke a condition of the recognisance.

(6) The prosecutor shall be given notice of, and be entitled to be heard in, any proceedings under subsection (4).

(7) Without prejudice to section 6(5), the court may issue a warrant for the arrest of the person on information being made in writing and on oath by an authorised person, any surety or a member of the Garda Síochána that he or she is about to contravene any of the further conditions referred to in paragraph (i) or (ii) of subsection (1).

(8) Subsections (6) to (9) of section 6 apply, with the necessary modifications, in relation to a warrant issued under subsection (7) of this section as if the warrant had been issued under subsection (5) of that section.

(9) This section does not apply in relation to a person under the age of 18 years.]¹

Amendments

1   Section 6B inserted by Criminal Justice Act 2007, s 11.

[6C   Evidence of electronic monitoring

(1) Where the movements of a person are subject to electronic monitoring as a condition of the recognisance entered into by the person, evidence of his or her—

> (a) presence or absence in or from a particular district or place at a particular time, or
>
> (b) compliance or non-compliance with a condition imposed under section 6B(1)(ii) in relation to the wearing of an electronic monitoring device,

may, subject to this section, be given in any proceedings by the production of the following documents:

  (i) a statement purporting to be generated automatically or otherwise by a prescribed device by which the person's whereabouts were electronically monitored;

  (ii) a certificate—

    (I) that the statement relates to the whereabouts of the person at the dates and times shown in it, and

    (II) purporting to be signed by an authorised person who is responsible for monitoring electronically the accused person's compliance with a condition mentioned in subparagraph (i) or (iv) of section 6(1)(b) or in section 6B(1).

(2) Subject to subsection (3), in any proceedings the statement and certificate mentioned in paragraphs (i) and (ii) of subsection (1) are admissible as evidence of the facts contained in them, unless the contrary is shown.

(3) Neither the statement nor the certificate is so admissible unless a copy of it has been served on the person concerned before the commencement of the proceedings concerned.]¹

Amendments

1   Section 6C inserted by Criminal Justice Act 2007, s 12.

[6D   Arrangements for electronic monitoring

The Minister may, with the consent of the Minister for Finance, make such arrangements, including contractual arrangements, as he or she considers appropriate with such persons as he or she thinks fit for monitoring electronically the compliance or non-compliance of persons with a condition mentioned in subparagraph (i) or (iv) of section 6(1)(b) or in section 6B(1)(ii).]¹

Amendments

1   Section 6D inserted by Criminal Justice Act 2007, s 13.

7   Sufficiency of bailspersons

(1) A court shall in every case satisfy itself as to the sufficiency and suitability of any person proposed to be accepted as a surety for the purpose of bail.

(2) In determining the sufficiency and suitability of a person proposed to be accepted as a surety, a court shall have regard to and may, where necessary, receive evidence or submissions concerning:

  (a) the financial resources of the person,

  (b) the character and antecedents of the person,

  (c) any previous convictions of the person, and

  (d) the relationship of the person to the accused person.

8 Endorsement on warrants as to release on bail

(1) Where a court issues a warrant for the arrest of a person, the court may direct that the person named in the warrant be on arrest released on his or her entering into a recognisance, with or without a surety or sureties, conditioned for his or her appearance before a court on such date and at such time and place as may be specified in the endorsement, and the endorsement shall fix the amounts in which the person and his or her surety or sureties [amounts]¹ (if any) are to be bound and shall specify any other conditions of the recognisance.

(2) Where such an endorsement is made, the member of the Garda Síochána in charge of the Garda Síochána Station to which on arrest the person named in the warrant is brought shall discharge him or her upon his or her entering into a [any moneys conditioned to be paid under a recognisance]¹, with or without surety or sureties, approved by that member and[, if the court, having regard to the circumstances of the case, including the means of the person and the nature of the offence to which the warrant relates, so orders]² upon the payment of—

(a) an amount equal to one third, or

(b) such greater amount as the court may determine,

of any recognisance entered into by a person.

(3) Any moneys paid to a member of the Garda Síochána under subsection (2) shall be deposited by him or her with the district court clerk for the district court area [where the courthouse at which the arrested person is conditioned to appear is situate.]¹

(4) This section shall not apply to a person arrested under section 251 of the Defence Act, 1954, on suspicion of his or her being a deserter or an absentee without leave from the Defence Forces.

Amendments

1 Words inserted by Criminal Justice Act 2007, s 14.

2 Words inserted by Courts and Court Officers Act 2001, s 33(b).

---

9 Estreatment of recognisance and forfeiture of moneys paid into court

[(1) Where an accused person or a person who is appealing against a sentence of imprisonment imposed by the District Court (in either case referred to in this section as ' the person') is admitted to bail on entering into a recognisance conditioned for his or her appearance before a specified court on a specified date at a specified time and place, and the person—

(a) fails to appear in accordance with the recognisance, or

(b) is brought before the court in accordance with subsection (7) and the court is satisfied that the person has contravened a condition of the recognisance,

the court may order—

(i) that any moneys conditioned to be paid under the recognisance by the person or any surety be estreated in such amount and within such period as the court thinks fit,

(ii) that any sums paid into court by the person or any surety be forfeited in such amount or amounts as the court thinks fit,

(iii) where a bank, building society, credit union or an An Post deposit book has been accepted as security for the amount of the recognisance, that the entity concerned pay into court that amount, or such lesser amount as the court thinks fit, from the moneys held by the person or any surety on deposit therein, and

(iv) where necessary for estreatment, that a receiver be appointed to take possession or control of the property of the person or any surety and to manage or otherwise deal with it in accordance with the directions of the court.

(2) Where a receiver—

(a) appointed under subsection (1) takes any action under this section in relation to property, and

(b) believes, and has reasonable grounds for believing, that he or she is entitled to take that action in relation to the property,

he or she shall not be liable to any person in respect of any loss or damage resulting from the action, except in so far as the loss or damage is caused by his or her negligence.

(3) Money recovered by the receiver may, to the extent necessary, be applied to meet expenses incurred in the performance of his or her functions and the remuneration of any person employed in that connection.

(4) The court may, on the application of a member of the Garda Síochána and on information being made in writing and on oath by or on behalf of the member that the person has contravened a condition of the recognisance (other than the condition referred to in subsection (1) that he or she appear before a specified court on a specified date at a specified place), issue a warrant for the arrest of the person.

(5) A member of the Garda Síochána may arrest the person pursuant to a warrant issued under subsection (4) notwithstanding that the member does not have the warrant concerned in his or her possession at the time of the arrest.

(6) Where subsection (5) applies, the member shall serve the warrant on the arrested person as soon as practicable.

(7) The arrested person shall be brought as soon as practicable before the court.

(8) Where a warrant has been issued under subsection (4), the person and any surety remain bound by their recognisances, and any money paid into court in connection therewith shall not be released before the conclusion of any proceedings under this section.

(9) Where the court makes an order under subsection (1), notice shall be given to the person and any surety stating that an application to vary or discharge the order may be made to the court within 21 days from the date of the issue of the notice.

(10) On such an application, the court may vary or discharge the order if satisfied that compliance with it would cause undue hardship to the person or any surety.

(11) The prosecutor shall be given notice of, and be entitled to be heard in, any application under subsection (10).

(12) Subject to subsection (13), if an order under subparagraph (i) of subsection (1) or any variation of it under subsection (10) is not complied with, a warrant of committal of the person or any surety for such non-compliance shall be issued by the court and, for the purpose of determining the term of imprisonment to be served by the person or surety, the

warrant shall be treated as if it were a warrant for imprisonment for the non-payment of a fine equivalent to the amount estreated under the said subparagraph (i) of subsection (1).

(13) Where the person referred to in subsection (12) is a child within the meaning of section 110 of the Children Act 2001, non-compliance with an order under subparagraph (i) of subsection (1) or with any variation of it under subsection (10) shall be treated as a default in payment of a fine, costs or compensation under the said section 110 and the provisions of that section shall apply accordingly.]¹

Amendments

1   Section 9 substituted by Criminal Justice (Miscellaneous Provisions) Act 2009, s 48(b).

10   Amendment of Criminal Justice Act, 1984

Section 11 of the Criminal Justice Act, 1984, is hereby amended by the insertion of the following subsection after subsection (3):¹

Amendments

1   See the amended Act.

11   Amendment of Act of 1967

The Act of 1967 is hereby amended—

(a) in section 26, by the deletion of "or peace commissioner",

(b) in section 28—

(i)   by the deletion in subsection (1) of "or a peace commissioner", and

(ii) by the deletion in subsection (4) of "or a peace commissioner", and

(c) in section 33, by the deletion in subsection (1) of "or a peace commissioner".

[11A   Regulations

(1) The Minister may make regulations prescribing any matter or thing which is referred to in this Act as prescribed or for the purpose of enabling any provision of this Act to have full effect.

(2) The regulations may include such consequential, incidental or supplementary provisions as may be necessary for that purpose.

(3) Regulations under this section shall be laid before each House of the Oireachtas as soon as may be after they are made and, if a resolution annulling them is passed by either such House within the next 21 days on which that House has sat after they are laid before it, the regulations shall be annulled accordingly, but without prejudice to the validity of anything previously done thereunder.]¹

Amendments

1   Section 11A inserted by Criminal Justice Act 2007, s 16.

12   Repeals

Sections 27, 30 and 33 of the Act of 1967 are hereby repealed.

13   Short title and commencement

(1) This Act may be cited as the Bail Act, 1997.

(2) This Act shall come into operation on such day or days as, by order or orders made by the Minister for Justice under this section, may be fixed therefor, either generally or with reference to any particular purpose or provision, and different days may be so fixed for different purposes and different provisions.

SCHEDULE

COMMON LAW OFFENCES

Section 1 .

1.   Murder.

2.   Manslaughter.

3.   ...[1]

4.   ...[1]

5.   ...[1]

6.   Rape.

[Genocide, crimes against humanity, war crimes and ancillary offences

6A.   An offence under section 7 or 8 of the International Criminal Court Act 2006.][2]

Offences against the person

7.   [Any offence under the following provisions of the Non-Fatal Offences against the Person Act, 1997—

    (a)   section 3 (assault causing harm);

    (b)   section 4 (causing harm);

    (c)   section 5 (threats to kill or cause serious harm);

    (d)   section 6 (syringe, etc. attacks);

    (e)   section 7(1) (offence of possession of syringe, etc. in certain circumstances);

    (f)   section 8 (placing or abandoning syringe);

    (g)   section 9 (coercion);

    (h)   section 10 (harassment);

    (i)   section 13 (endangerment);

(j)   section 14 (endangering traffic);

(k)   section 15 (false imprisonment);

(l)   section 16 (abduction of child by parent, etc.);

(m)   section 17 (abduction of child by other persons).]¹

[7A.   Any offence under section 3 of the Criminal Justice Act 1990 (certain murders and attempts).]³

8.   Any offence under the following provisions of the Criminal Justice (Public Order) Act, 1994—

(a)   section 18 (assault with intent to cause bodily harm or commit indictable offence);

(b)   section 19 (assault or obstruction of peace officer).

[8A.   An offence under the Criminal Law (Human Trafficking) Act 2008.]⁴

Sexual offences

9.   Any offence under section 1 (incest by males) and section 2 (incest by female of or over 17 years) of the Punishment of Incest Act, 1908.

[10.   An offence under the Criminal Law (Sexual Offences) Act 2006.]⁵

11.   Any offence under the following provisions of the Criminal Law (Rape) (Amendment) Act, 1990 —

(a)   section 2 (sexual assault);

(b)   section 3 (aggravated sexual assault);

(c)   section 4 (rape under section 4).

12.   Any offence under the following provisions of the Criminal Law (Sexual Offences) Act, 1993 —

(a)   section 3 (buggery of persons under 17 years of age);

(b)   section 5 (protection of mentally impaired persons);

(c)   sections 9 and 11 (organisation etc. of prostitution).

[12A. Any offence under the following provisions of the Child Trafficking and Pornography Act, 1998—

(a)   section 3 (child trafficking and taking, etc., child for sexual exploitation);

(b)   section 5 (producing, distributing, etc., child pornography).]⁶

[12B. An offence under section 6 (inserted by section 2 of the Criminal Law (Sexual Offences) (Amendment) Act 2007) of the Criminal Law (Sexual Offences) Act 1993.]⁷

Explosives

13.   Any offence under the following provisions of the Explosive Substances Act, 1883—

(a)   section 2 (causing explosion likely to endanger life or damage property);

(b)   section 3 (possession etc. of explosive substances);

(c)   section 4 (making or possessing explosives in suspicious circumstances).

Firearms

[14. Any offence under the following provisions of the Firearms Act 1925 :

    (a)   section 2 (restrictions on possession, use, and carriage of firearms);

    (b)   section 3 (applications for, and form and effect of, firearm certificates);

    (c)   section 4A(18) (authorisation of rifle or pistol clubs or shooting ranges);

    (d)   section 10A (reloading of ammunition);

    (e)   section 15 (possession of firearms with intent to endanger life);

    (f)   section 25 (punishments).][8]

15. Any offence under the following provisions of the Firearms Act, 1964—

    (a)   section 26 (possession of firearm while taking vehicle without authority);

    (b)   section 27 (use of firearm to resist arrest or aid escape);

    (c)   section 27A (possession of firearm or ammunition in suspicious circumstances);

    (d)   section 27B (carrying firearm with criminal intent).

[16. Any offence under the following provisions of the Firearms and Offensive Weapons Act 1990:

    (a)   section 7 (possession, sale, etc., of silencers);

    (b)   section 8 (reckless discharge of firearm);

    (c   section 9 (possession of knives and other articles);

    (d)   section 10 (trespassing with a knife, weapon of offence or other article);

    (e)   section 11 (production of article capable of inflicting serious injury);

    (f)   section 12 (power to prohibit manufacture, importation, sale, hire or loan of offensive weapons);

    (g)   section 12A (shortening barrel of shotgun or rifle).][9]

[16A. Any offence under section 3 of the Firearms (Firearm Certificates for Non-Residents) Act 2000 (prohibition of false information and alteration of firearm certificates).][10]

Robbery and burglary

17. [Any offence under the Criminal Justice (Theft and Fraud Offences) Act, 2001.][11]

18. Any offence under the following provisions of the Criminal Damage Act, 1991—

    (a)   section 2 (damaging property);

    (b)   section 3 (threat to damage property);

    (c)   section 4 (possessing any thing with intent to damage property).

[Offences relating to passports

18A. An offence under any paragraph of section 20(1) of the Passports Act 2008.][12]

Road Traffic Act offences

19. Any offence under the following provisions of the Road Traffic Act, 1961 —

    (a)   section 53 (dangerous driving causing death or serious bodily harm);

    (b)   section 112 (taking vehicle without authority).

Offences in relation to aircraft and vehicles

20.   Any offence under section 11 of the Air Navigation and Transport Act, 1973 (unlawful seizure of aircraft).

21.   Any offence under section 3 of the Air Navigation and Transport Act, 1975 (unlawful acts against the safety of aviation).

22.   Any offence under section 10 of the Criminal Law (Jurisdiction) Act, 1976 (unlawful seizure of vehicles).

[Maritime security offences

22A.—Any offence under section 2 of the Maritime Security Act 2004.][13]

Forgery etc. offences

[…][14]

Offences against the State

[25.   Any offence under the provisions of the Offences against the State Acts, 1939 to 1998.][15]

26.   Treason.

Drugs offences

27.   A drug trafficking offence within the meaning of section 3(1) of the Criminal Justice Act, 1994 .

[27A. Any offence under section 2 of the Illegal Immigrants (Trafficking) Act, 2000.][16]

Public order offences

28.   Any offence under the following provisions of the Criminal Justice (Public Order) Act, 1994—

(a)   section 14 (riot);

(b)   section 15 (violent disorder);

[(c)   section 16 (affray), and

(d)   section 17 (blackmail, extortion and demanding money with menaces).][17]

[Organised Crime

28A. An offence under section 71, 72 or 73 of the Criminal Justice Act 2006.] [18]

Accomplices

29.   References in this Schedule to an offence include references to participation as an accomplice of a person who commits the offence.

Attempts and conspiracy

[30.   An offence of attempting or conspiring to commit, or inciting the commission of, any offence mentioned in this Schedule.][19]

[Torture

31. Any offence under the Criminal Justice (United Nations Convention against Torture) Act 2000.][20]

[Offences against United Nations workers

32. Any offence under the Criminal Justice (Safety of United Nations Workers) Act, 2000.][21]

[Suppression of Terrorism

33. Any offence under the Criminal Justice (Terrorist Offences) Act 2005.][22]

[Offences under the Prisons Act 2007

34. Any offence under section 36 of the Prisons Act 2007.][18]

[Money Laundering

35. Any offence under Part 2 of the Criminal Justice (Money Laundering and Terrorist Financing) Act 2010.][24]

Offences relating to psychoactive substances

36. Any offence under the following provisions of the Criminal Justice (Psychoactive Substances) Act 2010—

    (a) section 3 (prohibition of sale, etc. of psychoactive substances);

    (b) section 4 (prohibition of sale of certain objects);

    (c) section 5 (prohibition of advertising of psychoactive substances, etc.);

    (d) section 8(6) (failure or refusal to comply with a prohibition order);

    (e) section 10(8) (failure or refusal to comply with a closure order).[25]

Amendments

1 Paragraphs 3, 4 and 5 deleted and para 7 substituted by Non-Fatal Offences Against The Person Act, 1997, s 30.

2 Paragraph 6A inserted by International Criminal Court Act 2006. s 66 and Sch 3.

3 Paragraph 7A inserted by Criminal Justice (Miscellaneous Provisions) Act 2009, s 48(c)(i).

4 Paragraph 8A inserted by Criminal Law (Human Trafficking) Act 2008, s 14.

5 Paragraph 10 substituted by Criminal Law (Sexual Offences) Act 2006, s 7(4).

6 Paragraph 12A inserted by substituted by Child Trafficking And Pornography Act 1998, s 12.

7 Paragraph 12B inserted by Criminal Law (Sexual Offences) (Amendment) Act 2007, s 4(3).

8 Paragraph 14 substituted by Criminal Justice Act 2007, s 17(a).

9 Paragraph 16 substituted by Criminal Justice Act 2007, s 17(b).

10 Paragraph 16A inserted by Criminal Justice Act 2007, s 17(c).

11 Paragraph 17 substituted by Criminal Justice (Theft And Fraud Offences) Act 2001, s 64.

12 Paragraph 18A inserted by Passports Act 2008, s 20(1).

13 Paragraph 22A inserted by Maritime Security Act 2004, s 12.

14 Paragraphs 23 and 24 deleted by Criminal Justice (Theft And Fraud Offences) Act 2001, s 64.

15 Paragraph 25 substituted by Offences Against the State (Amendment) Act 1998, s 16.

16 Paragraph 27A inserted by Illegal Immigrants (Trafficking) Act 2000, s 8.

17 Paragraph 28 amended by Criminal Justice (Miscellaneous Provisions) Act 2009, s 48(c)(ii).

18 Paragraph 28A (inserted by Criminal Justice Act 2006, s 79) substituted by Criminal Justice (Miscellaneous Provisions) Act 2009, s 48(c)(iii), which is not yet in operation (February 2011). See the amending Act. This paragraph is further amended by Criminal Justice (Amendment) Act 2009, s 15.

19 Paragraph 30 substituted by Criminal Justice Act 2007, s 17(d).

20 Paragraph 31 inserted by Criminal Justice (United Nations Convention against Torture) Act 2000, s 10.

21 Paragraph 32 inserted by Criminal Justice (Safety of United Nations Workers) Act 2000, s 9.

22 Paragraph 33 inserted by Criminal Justice (Terrorist Offences) Act 2005, s 60.

23 Paragraph 34 inserted by Criminal Justice (Miscellaneous Provisions) Act 2009, s 48(c)(iv).

24 Paragraph 35 inserted by Criminal Justice (Money Laundering and Terrorist Financing) Act 2010, s 113.

25 Paragraph 36 inserted by Criminal Justice (Psychoactive Substances) Act 2010, s 23.

Non-Fatal Offences Against the Person Act 1997

Number 26 of 1997

ARRANGEMENT OF SECTIONS

1.   Interpretation.

2.   Assault.

3.   Assault causing harm.

4.   Causing serious harm.

5.   Threats to kill or cause serious harm.

6.   Syringe, etc., attacks.

7.   Offence of possession of syringe, etc., in certain circumstances and seizure thereof by member of Garda Síochána.

8.   Placing or abandoning syringe.

9.   Coercion.

10.   Harassment.

11.   Demands for payment of debt causing alarm, etc.

12.   Poisoning.

13.   Endangerment.

14.   Endangering traffic.

15.   False imprisonment.

16.   Abduction of child by parent, etc.

17.   Abduction of child by other persons.

18.   Justifiable use of force; protection of person or property, prevention of crime, etc.

19.   Justifiable use of force in effecting or assisting lawful arrest.

20.   Meaning of "use of force" and related provisions.

21.   Amendment of section 6 of the Criminal Damage Act, 1991.

22.   General defences, etc.

23.   Consent by minor over 16 years to surgical, medical and dental treatment.

24.   Abolition of common law rule in respect of immunity of teachers from criminal liability for punishing pupils.

25.   Evidential value of certain certificates signed by medical practitioners.

26.   Amendment of Schedule to Criminal Law (Jurisdiction) Act, 1976.

27.   Amendment of First Schedule to Extradition (Amendment) Act, 1994.

28.   Abolition of common law offences of assault and battery, kidnapping and false imprisonment.

29.   Amendment of section 9 of Criminal Law Act, 1997.

30.   Amendment of Schedule to Bail Act, 1997.

31.   Repeals.

32.   Short title and commencement.

SCHEDULE

ENACTMENTS REPEALED

AN ACT TO REVISE THE LAW RELATING TO THE MAIN NON-FATAL OFFENCES AGAINST THE PERSON AND TO PROVIDE FOR CONNECTED MATTERS. [19th May, 1997]

BE IT ENACTED BY THE OIREACHTAS AS FOLLOWS:

1   Interpretation

(1) In this Act—

"contaminated blood" means blood which is contaminated with any disease, virus, agent or organism which if passed into the blood stream of another could infect the other with a life threatening or potentially life threatening disease;

"contaminated fluid" means fluid or substance which is contaminated with any disease, virus, agent or organism which if passed into the blood stream of another could infect the other with a life threatening or potentially life threatening disease;

"contaminated syringe" means a syringe which has in it or on it contaminated blood or contaminated fluid;

"harm" means harm to body or mind and includes pain and unconsciousness;

"member of the family" in relation to a person, means the spouse, a child (including stepchild or adopted child), grandchild, parent, grandparent, step-parent, brother, sister, halfbrother, half-sister, uncle, aunt, nephew or niece of the person or any person cohabiting or residing with him or her;

"property" means property of a tangible nature, whether real or personal, including money and animals that are capable of being stolen;

"public place" includes any street, seashore, park, land or field, highway and any other premises or place to which at the material time the public have or are permitted to have access, whether on payment or otherwise, and includes any train, vessel, aircraft or vehicle used for the carriage of persons for reward;

"serious harm" means injury which creates a substantial risk of death or which causes serious disfigurement or substantial loss or impairment of the mobility of the body as a whole or of the function of any particular bodily member or organ;

"street" includes any road, bridge, lane, footway, subway, square, court, alley or passage, whether a thoroughfare or not, which is for the time being open to the public; and the doorways, entrances and gardens abutting on a street and any ground or car-park adjoining and open to a street, shall be treated as forming part of a street;

"syringe" includes any part of a syringe or a needle or any sharp instrument capable of piercing skin and passing onto or into a person blood or any fluid or substance resembling blood.

(2) For the purposes of sections 17, 18 and 19 it is immaterial whether a belief is justified or not if it is honestly held but the presence or absence of reasonable grounds for the belief is a matter to which the court or the jury is to have regard, in conjunction with any other relevant matters, in considering whether the person honestly held the belief.

(3) In this Act—

    (a) a reference to any enactment shall, unless the context otherwise requires, be construed as a reference to that enactment as amended or extended by or under any subsequent enactment including this Act,

    (b) a reference to a section is a reference to a section of this Act unless it is indicated that reference to some other enactment is intended,

    (c) a reference to a subsection, paragraph or subparagraph is a reference to the subsection, paragraph or subparagraph of the provision in which the reference occurs unless it is indicated that reference to some other provision is intended.

2   Assault

(1) A person shall be guilty of the offence of assault who, without lawful excuse, intentionally or recklessly—

    (a) directly or indirectly applies force to or causes an impact on the body of another, or

    (b) causes another to believe on reasonable grounds that he or she is likely immediately to be subjected to any such force or impact,

without the consent of the other.

(2) In subsection (1)(a), "force" includes—

    (a) application of heat, light, electric current, noise or any other form of energy, and

    (b) application of matter in solid liquid or gaseous form.

(3) No such offence is committed if the force or impact, not being intended or likely to cause injury, is in the circumstances such as is generally acceptable in the ordinary conduct of daily life and the defendant does not know or believe that it is in fact unacceptable to the other person.

(4) A person guilty of an offence under this section shall be liable on summary conviction to a fine not exceeding £1,500 or to imprisonment for a term not exceeding 6 months or to both.

3   Assault causing harm

(1) A person who assaults another causing him or her harm shall be guilty of an offence.

(2) A person guilty of an offence under this section shall be liable—

    (a) on summary conviction, to imprisonment for a term not exceeding 12 months or to a fine not exceeding £1,500 or to both, or

    (b) on conviction on indictment to a fine or to imprisonment for a term not exceeding 5 years or to both.

4   Causing serious harm

(1) A person who intentionally or recklessly causes serious harm to another shall be guilty of an offence.

(2) A person guilty of an offence under this section shall be liable on conviction on indictment to a fine or to imprisonment for life or to both.

5   **Threats to kill or cause serious harm**

(1) A person who, without lawful excuse, makes to another a threat, by any means intending the other to believe it will be carried out, to kill or cause serious harm to that other or a third person shall be guilty of an offence,

(2) A person guilty of an offence under this section shall be liable—

     (a)   on summary conviction to a fine not exceeding £1,500 or to imprisonment for a term not exceeding 12 months or to both, or

     (b)   on conviction on indictment to a fine or to imprisonment for a term not exceeding 10 years or to both.

6   **Syringe, etc., attacks**

(1) A person who—

     (a)   injures another by piercing the skin of that other with a syringe, or

     (b)   threatens to so injure another with a syringe,

with the intention of or where there is a likelihood of causing that other to believe that he or she may become infected with disease as a result of the injury caused or threatened shall be guilty of an offence.

(2) A person who—

     (a)   sprays, pours or puts onto another blood or any fluid or substance resembling blood, or

     (b)   threatens to spray, pour or put onto another blood or any fluid or substance resembling blood,

with the intention of or where there is a likelihood of causing that other to believe that he or she may become infected with disease as a result of the action caused or threatened shall be guilty of an offence.

(3) A person who in committing or attempting to commit an offence under subsection (1) or (2)—

     (a)   injures a third person with a syringe by piercing his or her skin, or

     (b)   sprays, pours or puts onto a third person blood or any fluid or substance resembling blood,

resulting in the third person believing that he or she may become infected with disease as a result of the injury or action caused shall be guilty of an offence.

(4) A person guilty of an offence under subsection (1), (2) or (3) shall be liable—

     (a)   on summary conviction to a fine not exceeding £1,500 or to imprisonment for a term not exceeding 12 months or to both, or

     (b)   on conviction on indictment to a fine or to imprisonment for a term not exceeding 10 years or to both.

(5) (a)   A person who intentionally injures another by piercing the skin of that other with a contaminated syringe shall be guilty of an offence.

     (b)   A person who intentionally sprays, pours or puts onto another contaminated blood shall be guilty of an offence.

     (c)   A person who in committing or attempting to commit an offence under paragraph (a) or (b)—

(i) injures a third person with a contaminated syringe by piercing his or her skin, or

(ii) sprays, pours or puts onto a third person contaminated blood,

shall be guilty of an offence.

(d) A person guilty of an offence under this subsection shall be liable on conviction on indictment to imprisonment for life.

7 Offence of possession of syringe, etc., in certain circumstances and seizure thereof by member of Garda Síochána

(1) A person who has with him or her in any place—

    (a) a syringe, or

    (b) any blood in a container,

intended by him or her unlawfully to cause or threaten to cause injury to or to intimidate another shall be guilty of an offence.

(2) A member of the Garda Síochána who has reasonable cause to suspect that a person has with him or her in a public place a syringe, or any blood in a container intended by him or her unlawfully to cause or to threaten to cause injury to or to intimidate another, may stop and question and if necessary (if need be by using reasonable force) search such person and the member may seize and detain any syringe or such container found on the person or in the immediate vicinity of the person, unless the person gives to the member reasonable excuse for having the syringe or container with him or her, and, where a syringe or such a container is so found, require the name and address of the person.

(3) A member of the Garda Síochána may arrest without warrant a person who—

    (a) fails to stop when required under subsection (2), or

    (b) fails or refuses to give his or her name or address when required under subsection (2) or gives a name or address which the member has reasonable cause to believe is false or misleading, or

    (c) obstructs or attempts to obstruct the member or any person accompanying that member in the carrying out of the member's duties under subsection (2).

(4) A person who, without reasonable excuse, fails to stop or fails to give his or her name or address when required to under subsection (2) or gives a name or address which is false or misleading or obstructs or interferes with a member of the Garda Síochána acting under that subsection shall be guilty of an offence and shall be liable on summary conviction to a fine not exceeding £1,500 or to imprisonment for a term not exceeding 6 months, or to both.

(5) In a prosecution for an offence under subsection (1), it shall not be necessary for the prosecution to allege or prove that the intent to threaten or cause injury to or intimidate was intent to threaten or cause injury to or intimidate a particular person; and if, having regard to all the circumstances (including the contents of the syringe, if any, the time of the day or night, and the place), the court (or the jury as the case may be) thinks it reasonable to do so, it shall regard possession of the syringe or container as sufficient evidence of intent in the absence of any adequate explanation by the accused.

(6) In this section "blood" includes any fluid or substance resembling blood.

(7) A person guilty of an offence under subsection (1) shall be liable—

    (a) on summary conviction, to a fine not exceeding £1,500 or to imprisonment for a term not exceeding 12 months or to both, or

   (b) on conviction on indictment, to a fine or to imprisonment for a term not exceeding 7 years or to both.

8   **Placing or abandoning syringe**

(1) Subject to subsection (3), a person who places or abandons a syringe in any place in such a manner that it is likely to injure another and does injure another or is likely to injure, cause a threat to or frighten another shall be guilty of an offence.

(2) A person who intentionally places a contaminated syringe in any place in such a manner that it injures another shall be guilty of an offence.

(3) Subsection (1) does not apply to a person placing a syringe in any place whilst administering or assisting in lawful medical, dental or veterinary procedures.

(4) In a prosecution for an offence under subsection (1) where it is alleged a syringe is placed in a place being a private dwelling at which the accused normally resides, it shall be a defence for the accused to show that he or she did not intentionally place the syringe in such a manner that it injured or was likely to injure or cause a threat to or frighten another, as the case may be.

(5) A person guilty of an offence under subsection (1) shall be liable—

   (a) on summary conviction to a fine not exceeding £1,500 or to imprisonment for a term not exceeding 12 months or to both, or

   (b) on conviction on indictment to a fine or to imprisonment for a term not exceeding 7 years or to both.

(6) A person guilty of an offence under subsection (2) shall be liable on conviction on indictment to imprisonment for life.

9   **Coercion**

(1) A person who, with a view to compel another to abstain from doing or to do any act which that other has a lawful right to do or to abstain from doing, wrongfully and without lawful authority—

   (a) uses violence to or intimidates that other person or a member of the family of the other, or

   (b) injures or damages the property of that other, or

   (c) persistently follows that other about from place to place, or

   (d) watches or besets the premises or other place where that other resides, works or carries on business, or happens to be, or the approach to such premises or place, or

   (e) follows that other with one or more other persons in a disorderly manner in or through any public place,

shall be guilty of an offence.

(2) For the purpose of this section attending at or near the premises or place where a person resides, works, carries on business or happens to be, or the approach to such premises or place, in order merely to obtain or communicate information, shall not be deemed a watching or besetting within the meaning of subsection (1)(d).

(3) A person guilty of an offence under this section shall be liable—

   (a) on summary conviction to a fine not exceeding £1,500 or to imprisonment for a term not exceeding 12 months or to both, or

(b) on conviction on indictment to a fine or to imprisonment for a term not exceeding 5 years or to both.

10   Harassment

(1) Any person who, without lawful authority or reasonable excuse, by any means including by use of the telephone, harasses another by persistently following, watching, pestering, besetting or communicating with him or her, shall be guilty of an offence.

(2) For the purposes of this section a person harasses another where—

(a) he or she, by his or her acts intentionally or recklessly, seriously interferes with the other's peace and privacy or causes alarm, distress or harm to the other, and

(b) his or her acts are such that a reasonable person would realise that the acts would seriously interfere with the other's peace and privacy or cause alarm, distress or harm to the other.

(3) Where a person is guilty of an offence under subsection (1), the court may, in addition to or as an alternative to any other penalty, order that the person shall not, for such period as the court may specify, communicate by any means with the other person or that the person shall not approach within such distance as the court shall specify of the place of residence or employment of the other person.

(4) A person who fails to comply with the terms of an order under subsection (3) shall be guilty of an offence.

(5) If on the evidence the court is not satisfied that the person should be convicted of an offence under subsection (1), the court may nevertheless make an order under subsection (3) upon an application to it in that behalf if, having regard to the evidence, the court is satisfied that it is in the interests of justice so to do.

(6) A person guilty of an offence under this section shall be liable—

(a) on summary conviction to a fine not exceeding £1,500 or to imprisonment for a term not exceeding 12 months or to both, or

(b) on conviction on indictment to a fine or to imprisonment for a term not exceeding 7 years or to both.

11   Demands for payment of debt causing alarm, etc

(1) A person who makes any demand for payment of a debt shall be guilty of an offence if—

(a) the demands by reason of their frequency are calculated to subject the debtor or a member of the family of the debtor to alarm, distress or humiliation, or

(b) the person falsely represents that criminal proceedings lie for non-payment of the debt, or

(c) the person falsely represents that he or she is authorised in some official capacity to enforce payment, or

(d) the person utters a document falsely represented to have an official character.

(2) A person guilty of an offence under this section shall be liable on summary conviction to a fine not exceeding £1,500.

12   Poisoning

(1) A person shall be guilty of an offence if, knowing that the other does not consent to what is being done, he or she intentionally or recklessly administers to or causes to be taken by

another a substance which he or she knows to be capable of interfering substantially with the other's bodily functions.

(2) For the purpose of this section a substance capable of inducing unconsciousness or sleep is capable of interfering substantially with bodily functions.

(3) A person guilty of an offence under this section shall be liable—

    (a) on summary conviction to a fine not exceeding £1,500 or to imprisonment for a term not exceeding 12 months or to both, or

    (b) on conviction on indictment to a fine or to imprisonment for a term not exceeding 3 years or to both.

13   Endangerment

(1) A person shall be guilty of an offence who intentionally or recklessly engages in conduct which creates a substantial risk of death or serious harm to another.

(2) A person guilty of an offence under this section shall be liable—

    (a) on summary conviction to a fine not exceeding £1,500 or to imprisonment for a term not exceeding 12 months or to both, or

    (b) on conviction on indictment, to a fine or to imprisonment for a term not exceeding 7 years or to both.

14   Endangering traffic

(1) A person shall be guilty of an offence who—

    (a) intentionally places or throws any dangerous obstruction upon a railway, road, street, waterway or public place or interferes with any machinery, signal, equipment or other device for the direction, control or regulation of traffic thereon, or interferes with or throws anything at or on any conveyance used or to be used thereon, and

    (b) is aware that injury to the person or damage to property may be caused thereby, or is reckless in that regard.

(2) In this section—

"conveyance" means any conveyance constructed or adapted for the carriage of a person or persons or of goods by land or water;

"railway" means a railway, a tramway, or a light railway or any part of a railway, tramway or light railway;

"waterway" means any route upon water used by any conveyance.

(3) A person guilty of an offence under this section shall be liable—

    (a) on summary conviction to a fine not exceeding £1,500 or to S.14 imprisonment for a term not exceeding 12 months or to both, or

    (b) on conviction on indictment to a fine or to imprisonment for a term not exceeding 7 years or to both.

15   False imprisonment

(1) A person shall be guilty of the offence of false imprisonment who intentionally or recklessly—

    (a) takes or detains, or

    (b) causes to be taken or detained, or

    (c) otherwise restricts the personal liberty of,

another without that other's consent.

(2) For the purposes of this section, a person acts without the consent of another if the person obtains the other's consent by force or threat of force, or by deception causing the other to believe that he or she is under legal compulsion to consent.

(3) A person guilty of an offence under this section shall be liable—

    (a) on summary conviction, to a fine not exceeding £1,500 or to imprisonment for a term not exceeding 12 months or to both, or

    (b) on conviction on indictment, to imprisonment for life.

16   Abduction of child by parent, etc

(1) A person to whom this section applies shall be guilty of an offence, who takes, sends or keeps a child under the age of 16 years out of the State or causes a child under that age to be so taken, sent or kept—

    (a) in defiance of a court order, or

    (b) without the consent of each person who is a parent, or guardian or person to whom custody of the child has been granted by a court unless the consent of a court was obtained.

(2) This section applies to a parent, guardian or a person to whom custody of the child has been granted by a court but does not apply to a parent who is not a guardian of the child.

(3) It shall be a defence to a charge under this section that the defendant—

    (a) has been unable to communicate with the persons referred to in subsection (1)(b) but believes they would consent if they were aware of the relevant circumstances; or

    (b) did not intend to deprive others having rights of guardianship or custody in relation to the child of those rights.

(4) A person guilty of an offence under this section shall be liable—

    (a) on summary conviction to a fine not exceeding £1,500 or to imprisonment for a term not exceeding 12 months or to both, or

    (b) on conviction on indictment to a fine or to imprisonment for a term not exceeding 7 years or to both.

(5) Any proceedings under this section shall not be instituted except by or with the consent of the Director of Public Prosecutions.

17   Abduction of child by other persons

(1) A person, other than a person to whom section 16 applies, shall be guilty of an offence who, without lawful authority or reasonable excuse, intentionally takes or detains a child under the age of 16 years or causes a child under that age to be so taken or detained—

    (a) so as to remove the child from the lawful control of any person having lawful control of the child; or

    (b) so as to keep him or her out of the lawful control of any person entitled to lawful control of the child.

(2) It shall be a defence to a charge under this section that the defendant believed that the child had attained the age of 16 years.

(3) A person guilty of an offence under this section shall be liable—

    (a) on summary conviction to a fine not exceeding £1,500 or to imprisonment for a term not exceeding 12 months or to both, or

    (b) on conviction on indictment to a fine or to imprisonment for a term not exceeding 7 years or to both.

18   Justifiable use of force; protection of person or property, prevention of crime, etc

(1) The use of force by a person for any of the following purposes, if only such as is reasonable in the circumstances as he or she believes them to be, does not constitute an offence—

    (a) to protect himself or herself or a member of the family of that person or another from injury, assault or detention caused by a criminal act; or

    (b) to protect himself or herself or (with the authority of that other) another from trespass to the person; or

    (c) to protect his or her property from appropriation, destruction or damage caused by a criminal act or from trespass or infringement; or

    (d) to protect property belonging to another from appropriation, destruction or damage caused by a criminal act or (with the authority of that other) from trespass or infringement; or

    (e) to prevent crime or a breach of the peace.

(2) "use of force" in subsection (1) is defined and extended by section 20 .

(3) For the purposes of this section an act involves a "crime" or is "criminal" although the person committing it, if charged with an offence in respect of it, would be acquitted on the ground that—

    (a) he or she was under 7 years of age; or

    (b) he or she acted under duress, whether by threats or of circumstances; or

    (c) his or her act was involuntary; or

    (d) he or she was in a state of intoxication; or

    (e) he or she was insane, so as not to be responsible, according to law, for the act.

(4) The references in subsection (1) to protecting a person and property from anything include protecting the person or property from its continuing; and the reference to preventing crime or a breach of the peace shall be similarly construed.

(5) For the purposes of this section the question whether the act against which force is used is of a kind mentioned in any of the paragraphs (a) to (e) of subsection (1) shall be determined according to the circumstances as the person using the force believes them to be.

(6) Notwithstanding subsection (1), a person who believes circumstances to exist which would justify or excuse the use of force under that subsection has no defence if he or she knows that the force is used against a member of the Garda Síochána acting in the course of the member's duty or a person so assisting such member, unless he or she believes the force to be immediately necessary to prevent harm to himself or herself or another.

(7) The defence provided by this section does not apply to a person who causes conduct or a state of affairs with a view to using force to resist or terminate it:

But the defence may apply although the occasion for the use of force arises only because the person does something he or she may lawfully do, knowing that such an occasion will arise.

(8) Property shall be treated for the purposes of subsection (1)(c) and (d) as belonging to any person—

    (a) having the custody or control of it;

    (b) having in it any proprietary right or interest (not being an equitable interest arising only from an agreement to transfer or grant an interest); or

    (c) having a charge on it;

and where property is subject to a trust, the persons to whom it belongs shall be treated as including any person having a right to enforce the trust.

Property of a corporation sole shall be treated for the purposes of the aforesaid provisions as belonging to the corporation notwithstanding a vacancy in the corporation.

19   Justifiable use of force in effecting or assisting lawful arrest

(1) The use of force by a person in effecting or assisting in a lawful arrest, if only such as is reasonable in the circumstances as he or she believes them to be, does not constitute an offence.

(2) "use of force" in subsection (1) is defined and extended by section 20 .

(3) For the purposes of this section the question as to whether the arrest is lawful shall be determined according to the circumstances as the person using the force believed them to be.

20   Meaning of "use of force" and related provisions

(1) For the purposes of sections 18 and 19—

    (a) a person uses force in relation to another person or property not only when he or she applies force to, but also where he or she causes an impact on, the body of that person or that property;

    (b) a person shall be treated as using force in relation to another person if—

        (i) he or she threatens that person with its use, or

        (ii) he or she detains that person without actually using it; and

    (c) a person shall be treated as using force in relation to property if he or she threatens a person with its use in relation to property.

(2) Sections 18 and 19 shall apply in relation to acts immediately preparatory to the use of force as they apply in relation to acts in which force is used.

(3) A threat of force may be reasonable although the actual use of force may not be.

(4) The fact that a person had an opportunity to retreat before using force shall be taken into account, in conjunction with other relevant evidence, in determining whether the use of force was reasonable.

21   Amendment of section 6 of the Criminal Damage Act, 1991

Section 6(2) of the Criminal Damage Act, 1991, is hereby amended by the substitution for paragraph (c) of the following paragraph:[1]

Amendments

1   See the amended Act.

22   General defences, etc

(1) The provisions of this Act have effect subject to any enactment or rule of law providing a defence, or providing lawful authority, justification or excuse for an act or omission.

(2) Notwithstanding subsection (1) any defence available under the common law in respect of the use of force within the meaning of section 18 or 19, or an act immediately preparatory to the use of force, for the purposes mentioned in section 18(1) or 19(1) is hereby abolished.

23   Consent by minor over 16 years to surgical, medical and dental treatment

(1) The consent of a minor who has attained the age of 16 years to any surgical, medical or dental treatment which, in the absence of consent, would constitute a trespass to his or her person, shall be as effective as it would be if he or she were of full age; and where a minor has by virtue of this section given an effective consent to any treatment it shall not be necessary to obtain any consent for it from his or her parent or guardian.

(2) In this section "surgical, medical or dental treatment" includes any procedure undertaken for the purposes of diagnosis, and this section applies to any procedure (including, in particular, the administration of an anaesthetic) which is ancillary to any treatment as it applies to that treatment.

(3) Nothing in this section shall be construed as making ineffective any consent which would have been effective if this section had not been enacted.

24   Abolition of common law rule in respect of immunity of teachers from criminal liability for punishing pupils

The rule of law under which teachers are immune from criminal liability in respect of physical chastisement of pupils is hereby abolished.

25   Evidential value of certain certificates signed by medical practitioners

(1) In any proceedings for an offence alleging the causing of harm or serious harm to a person, the production of a certificate purporting to be signed by a registered medical practitioner and relating to an examination of that person, shall unless the contrary is proved, be evidence of any fact thereby certified without proof of any signature thereon or that any such signature is that of such practitioner.

(2) In this section "registered medical practitioner" means a person registered in the General Register of Medical Practitioners established under section 26 of the Medical Practitioners Act, 1978.

26   Amendment of Schedule to Criminal Law (Jurisdiction) Act, 1976

The Schedule to the Criminal Law (Jurisdiction) Act, 1976, is hereby amended—

    (a)   by the deletion, in paragraph 5, of "False imprisonment.", and

    (b)   by the substitution for paragraph 7 of the following:[1]

Amendments

1   See the amended Act.

---

27   Amendment of First Schedule to Extradition (Amendment) Act, 1994

The First Schedule to the Extradition (Amendment) Act, 1994, is hereby amended—
- (a) by the deletion, in paragraph 4, of "False imprisonment.",
- (b) by the deletion, in paragraph 5, of "Assault occasioning actual bodily harm.", and
- (c) the substitution for paragraph 6 of the following:

    "6. Any offence under the following provisions of the Non-Fatal Offences against the Person Act, 1997—
    - (a)   section 3 (assault causing harm);
    - (b)   section 4 (causing serious harm);
    - (c)   section 15 (false imprisonment).".

28   Abolition of common law offences of assault and battery, kidnapping and false imprisonment

(1) The following common law offences are hereby abolished—
- (a) assault and battery,
- (b) assault occasioning actual bodily harm,
- (c) kidnapping, and
- (d) false imprisonment.

(2) The abolition of the common law offence of kidnapping shall not affect the operation of section 2 of, and paragraph 4 of the Schedule to, the Criminal Law (Jurisdiction) Act, 1976, and accordingly the said section 2 and the said Schedule shall have effect as if subsection (1)(c) had not been enacted.

29   Amendment of section 9 of Criminal Law Act, 1997

Section 9 of the Criminal Law Act, 1997, is hereby amended by the substitution for paragraph (a) of subsection (2) of the following paragraph:[1]

Amendments

1   See the amended Act.

---

30   Amendment of Schedule to Bail Act, 1997

The Schedule to the Bail Act, 1997, is hereby amended by—
- (a) the deletion in paragraph 3 of "Assault occasioning actual bodily harm.",
- (b) the deletion in paragraph 4 of "Kidnapping.",
- (c) the deletion in paragraph 5 of "False imprisonment.", and
- (d) the substitution for the matter contained in paragraph 7 of the following:

"Any offence under the following provisions of the Non-Fatal Offences against the Person Act, 1997—

(a)   section 3 (assault causing harm);

(b)   section 4 (causing harm);

(c)   section 5 (threats to kill or cause serious harm);

(d)   section 6 (syringe, etc. attacks);

(e)   section 7(1) (offence of possession of syringe, etc. in certain circumstances);

(f)   section 8 (placing or abandoning syringe);

(g)   section 9 (coercion);

(h)   section 10 (harassment);

(i)   section 13 (endangerment);

(j)   section 14 (endangering traffic);

(k)   section 15 (false imprisonment);

(l)   section 16 (abduction of child by parent, etc.);

(m)   section 17 (abduction of child by other persons).".

31   Repeals

Each enactment specified in column (2) of the Schedule to this Act is hereby repealed to the extent specified in column (3) of that Schedule.

32   Short title and commencement

(1) This Act may be cited as the Non-Fatal Offences against the Person Act, 1997.

(2) This Act (other than sections 6, 7, 8 and 10) shall come into operation 3 months after the date of its passing.

(3) Sections 6, 7, 8 and 10 shall come into operation on the day after the date of the passing of this Act.

SCHEDULE
ENACTMENTS REPEALED

Section 31

Session and Chapter or Number and Year	Short Title	Extent of Repeal
(1)	(2)	(3)
24 & 25 Vict., c.100	Offences against the Person Act, 1861	Sections 16 to 26, 28 to 34, 36, 37, 39, 40, 42, 46, 47, 53 to 56, 64, 65 and 73
38 & 39 Vict., c.86	Conspiracy and Protection of Property Act, 1875	Sections 6 and 7
48 & 49 Vict., c.69	Criminal Law Amendment Act, 1885	Paragraph (3) of section 3 and sections 7 and 8
No. 2 of 1951	Criminal Justice Act, 1951	Section 11
No. 32 of 1976	Criminal Law Act, 1976	Subsection (2) of section 11

Child Trafficking And Pornography Act 1998

Number 22 of 1998

Arrangement of Sections

Section

1.   Short title and commencement.

2.   Interpretation.

3.   Child trafficking and taking, etc., child for sexual exploitation.

4.   Allowing child to be used for child pornography.

5.   Producing, distributing, etc., child pornography.

6.   Possession of child pornography.

7.   Entry, search and seizure.

8.   Forfeiture.

9.   Offences by bodies corporate.

10.   Amendment of Criminal Evidence Act, 1992.

11.   Amendment of Sexual Offences (Jurisdiction) Act, 1996.

12.   Amendment of Bail Act, 1997.

AN ACT TO PROHIBIT TRAFFICKING IN, OR THE USE OF, CHILDREN FOR THE PURPOSES OF THEIR SEXUAL EXPLOITATION AND THE PRODUCTION, DISSEMINATION, HANDLING OR POSSESSION OF CHILD PORNOGRAPHY, AND TO PROVIDE FOR RELATED MATTERS. [29th June, 1998]

BE IT ENACTED BY THE OIREACHTAS AS FOLLOWS:

1   Short title and commencement

(1) This Act may be cited as the Child Trafficking and Pornography Act, 1998.

(2) This Act shall come into operation one month after the date of its passing.

2   Interpretation

(1) In this Act, except where the context otherwise requires—

"audio representation" includes—

    (a) any such representation by means of tape, computer disk or other thing from which such a representation can be produced, and

    (b) any tape, computer disk or other thing on which any such representation is recorded;

"child" means a person under the age of 17 years;

"child pornography" means—

    (a) any visual representation—

        (i) that shows or, in the case of a document, relates to a person who is or is depicted as being a child and who is engaged in or is depicted as being engaged in explicit sexual activity,

    (ii) that shows or, in the case of a document, relates to a person who is or is depicted as being a child and who is or is depicted as witnessing any such activity by any person or persons, or

    (iii) whose dominant characteristic is the depiction, for a sexual purpose, of the genital or anal region of a child,

(b) any audio representation of a person who is or is represented as being a child and who is engaged in or is represented as being engaged in explicit sexual activity,

(c) any visual or audio representation that advocates, encourages or counsels any sexual activity with children which is an offence under any enactment, or

(d) any visual representation or description of, or information relating to, a child that indicates or implies that the child is available to be used for the purpose of sexual exploitation within the meaning of section 3,

irrespective of how or through what medium the representation, description or information has been produced, transmitted or conveyed and, without prejudice to the generality of the foregoing, includes any representation, description or information produced by or from computer-graphics or by any other electronic or mechanical means but does not include—

(I) any book or periodical publication which has been examined by the Censorship of Publications Board and in respect of which a prohibition order under the Censorship of Publications Acts, 1929 to 1967, is not for the time being in force,

(II) any film in respect of which a general certificate or a limited certificate under the Censorship of Films Acts, 1923 to 1992, is in force, or

(III) any video work in respect of which a supply certificate under the Video Recordings Acts, 1989 and 1992, is in force;

"document" includes—

(a) any book, periodical or pamphlet, and

(b) where appropriate, any tape, computer disk or other thing on which data capable of conversion into any such document is stored;

"photographic representation" includes the negative as well as the positive version;

"visual representation" includes—

(a) any photographic, film or video representation, any accompanying sound or any document,

(b) any copy of any such representation or document, and

(c) any tape, computer disk or other thing on which the visual representation and any accompanying sound are recorded.

(2) The reference in paragraph (a) of the definition of child pornography to a person shall be construed as including a reference to a figure resembling a person that has been generated or modified by computer-graphics or otherwise, and in such a case the fact, if it is a fact, that some of the principal characteristics shown are those of an adult shall be disregarded if the predominant impression conveyed is that the figure shown is a child.

(4) For the purposes of this Act, except where the context otherwise requires—

(a) a reference to a section is to a section of this Act,

(b) a reference to a subsection or paragraph is to the subsection or paragraph of the provision in which the reference occurs,

(c) a reference to any enactment shall be construed as a reference to that enactment as amended, adapted or extended, whether before or after the passing of this Act, by or under any subsequent enactment.

3   Child trafficking and taking, etc., child for sexual exploitation

[(1) A person who trafficks a child for the purposes of the sexual exploitation of the child shall be guilty of an offence and shall be liable upon conviction on indictment—

(a) to imprisonment for life or a lesser term, and

(b) at the discretion of the court, to a fine.

(2) A person who—

(a) sexually exploits a child, or

(b) takes, detains, or restricts the personal liberty of, a child for the purpose of his or her sexual exploitation,

shall be guilty of an offence and shall be liable upon conviction on indictment—

(i) to imprisonment for life or a lesser term, and

(ii) at the discretion of the court, to a fine.]¹

[(2A) Any person who within the State—

(a) intentionally meets, or travels with the intention of meeting, a child, having met or communicated with that child on 2 or more previous occasions, and

(b) does so for the purpose of doing anything that would constitute sexual exploitation of the child,

shall be guilty of an offence and shall be liable on conviction on indictment to imprisonment for a term not exceeding 14 years.

(2B) Any person, being a citizen of the State or being ordinarily resident in the State, who outside the State—

(a) intentionally meets, or travels with the intention of meeting, a child, having met or communicated with that child on 2 or more previous occasions, and

(b) does so for the purpose of doing anything that would constitute sexual exploitation of the child,

shall be guilty of an offence and shall be liable on conviction on indictment to imprisonment for a term not exceeding 14 years.]²

[(3) A person who causes another person to commit an offence under subsection (1) or (2) shall be guilty of an offence and shall be liable upon conviction on indictment—

(a) to imprisonment for life or a lesser term, and

(b) at the discretion of the court, to a fine.

(4) A person who attempts to commit an offence under subsection (1), (2) or (3) shall be guilty of an offence and shall be liable upon conviction on indictment—

(a) to imprisonment for life or a lesser term, and

(b) at the discretion of the court, to a fine.

(5) In this section—

"child" means a person under the age of 18 years;

"sexual exploitation" means, in relation to a child—

(a) inviting, inducing or coercing the child to engage in prostitution or the production of child pornography,

(b) the prostitution of the child or the use of the child for the production of child pornography,

(c) the commission of an offence specified in the Schedule to the Sex Offenders Act 2001 against the child; causing another person to commit such an offence against the child; or inviting, inducing or coercing the child to commit such an offence against another person,

(d) inviting, inducing or coercing the child to engage or participate in any sexual, indecent or obscene act, or

(e) inviting, inducing or coercing the child to observe any sexual, indecent or obscene act, for the purpose of corrupting or depraving the child,

and 'sexually exploits' shall be construed accordingly;

"trafficks" means, in relation to a child—

(a) procures, recruits, transports or harbours the child, or—

(i) transfers the child to,

(ii) places the child in the custody, care or charge, or under the control, of, or

(iii) otherwise delivers the child to,

another person,

(b) causes the child to enter or leave the State or to travel within the State,

(c) takes custody of the child or takes the child—

(i) into one's care or charge, or

(ii) under one's control,

or

(d) provides the child with accommodation or employment.][3]

Amendments

1   Subsections (1) and (2) substituted by Criminal Law (Human Trafficking) Act 2008, s 3(a).

2   Subsections (2A) and (2B) inserted by Criminal Law (Sexual Offences) (Amendment) Act 2007, s 6(a).

3   Subsection (3) substituted and subsections (4) and (5) inserted by Criminal Law (Human Trafficking) Act 2008, s 3(b).

4   Allowing child to be used for child pornography

(1) Without prejudice to section 3, any person who, having the custody, charge or care of a child, allows the child to be used for the production of child pornography shall be guilty of an offence and shall be liable on conviction on indictment to a fine not exceeding £25,000 or to imprisonment for a term not exceeding 14 years or both.

(2) For the purposes of this section—

(a) any person who is the parent or guardian of a child or who is liable to maintain a child shall be presumed to have the custody of the child and, as between parents, one parent shall not be deemed to have ceased to have the custody of the child by reason only that he or she has deserted, or does not reside with, the other parent and child,

(b) any person to whose charge a child is committed by any person who has the custody of the child shall be presumed to have charge of the child, and

(c) any person exercising authority over or having actual control of a child shall be presumed to have care of the child.

5   Producing, distributing, etc., child pornography

(1) Subject to sections 6(2) and 6(3), any person who—

(a) knowingly produces, distributes, prints or publishes any child pornography,

(b) knowingly imports, exports, sells or shows any child pornography,

(c) knowingly publishes or distributes any advertisement likely to be understood as conveying that the advertiser or any other person produces, distributes, prints, publishes, imports, exports, sells or shows any child pornography,

(d) encourages or knowingly causes or facilitates any activity mentioned in paragraph (a), (b) or (c), or

(e) knowingly possesses any child pornography for the purpose of distributing, publishing, exporting, selling or showing it,

shall be guilty of an offence and shall be liable—

(i) on summary conviction to a fine not exceeding £1,500 or to imprisonment for a term not exceeding 12 months or both, or

(ii) on conviction on indictment to a fine or to imprisonment for a term not exceeding 14 years or both.

(2) In this section "distributes", in relation to child pornography, includes parting with possession of it to, or exposing or offering it for acquisition by, another person, and the reference to "distributing" in that context shall be construed accordingly.

6   Possession of child pornography

(1) Without prejudice to section 5(1)(e) and subject to subsections (2) and (3), any person who knowingly possesses any child pornography shall be guilty of an offence and shall be liable—

(a) on summary conviction to a fine not exceeding £1,500 or to imprisonment for a term not exceeding 12 months or both, or

(b) on conviction on indictment to a fine not exceeding £5,000 or to imprisonment for a term not exceeding 5 years or both.

(2) Section 5(1) and subsection (1) shall not apply to a person who possesses child pornography—

(a) in the exercise of functions under the Censorship of Films Acts, 1923 to 1992, the Censorship of Publications Acts, 1929 to 1967, or the Video Recordings Acts, 1989 and 1992, or

(b) for the purpose of the prevention, investigation or prosecution of offences under this Act.

(3) Without prejudice to subsection (2), it shall be a defence in a prosecution for an offence under section 5(1) or subsection (1) for the accused to prove that he or she possessed the child pornography concerned for the purposes of bona fide research.

7 Entry, search and seizure

(1) Where, on the sworn information of a member of the Garda Síochána not below the rank of sergeant, a judge of the District Court is satisfied that there are reasonable grounds for suspecting that evidence of or relating to an offence under section 3, 4, 5 or 6 is to be found at a place specified in the information, the judge may issue a warrant for the search of that place and any persons found at that place.

(2) A warrant issued under this section shall authorise a named member of the Garda Síochána, alone or accompanied by such other members of the Garda Síochána and such other persons as may be necessary—

    (a) to enter, within 7 days from the date of the warrant, and if necessary by the use of reasonable force, the place named in the warrant,

    (b) to search it and any persons found there, and

    (c) to seize anything found there, or anything found in the possession of a person present there at the time of the search, which that member reasonably believes to be evidence of or relating to an offence under section 3, 4, 5 or 6.

(3) A member of the Garda Síochána acting in accordance with a warrant issued under this section may require any person found at the place where the search is carried out to give the member his or her name and address.

(4) Any person who—

    (a) obstructs or attempts to obstruct any member of the Garda Síochána acting in accordance with a warrant issued under subsection (1),

    (b) fails or refuses to comply with a requirement under this section, or

    (c) gives a name or address which is false or misleading,

shall be guilty of an offence and shall be liable on summary conviction to a fine not exceeding £1,500 or to imprisonment for a term not exceeding 12 months or both.

(5) A member of the Garda Síochána may arrest without warrant any person whom the member suspects of having committed an offence under subsection (4).

(6) In this section "place" includes any dwelling, any building or part of a building and any vehicle, vessel or structure.

8 Forfeiture

(1) The court by or before which a person is convicted of an offence under section 3, 4, 5 or 6 may order—

    (a) anything seized pursuant to section 7, or

    (b) anything shown to the satisfaction of the court to relate to the offence,

to be forfeited and either destroyed or otherwise disposed of in such manner as the court may determine.

(2) A court shall not order anything to be forfeited under this section if a person claiming to be the owner of it or otherwise interested in it applies to be heard by the court, unless the opportunity has been given to him or her to show cause why the order should not be made.

(3) An order under this section shall not take effect until the ordinary time for instituting an appeal against the conviction or order concerned has expired or, where such an appeal is instituted, until it or any further appeal is finally decided or abandoned or the ordinary time for instituting any further appeal has expired.

9   Offences by bodies corporate

(1) Where an offence under section 3, 4, 5 or 6 is committed by a body corporate and is proved to have been committed with the consent or connivance of, or to be attributable to any neglect on the part of, any person, being a director, manager, secretary or other similar officer of such body or a person who was purporting to act in any such capacity, that person as well as the body corporate shall be guilty of an offence and shall be liable to be proceeded against and punished as if he or she were guilty of the first-mentioned offence.

(2) Where the affairs of a body corporate are managed by its members, subsection (1) shall apply in relation to the acts and defaults of a member of that body in connection with the member's functions of management as if he or she were a director or manager of it.

10   Amendment of Criminal Evidence Act, 1992

The Criminal Evidence Act, 1992, is hereby amended in section 12—

(a)   by the deletion of "or" in paragraph (b) where it last occurs and by the substitution of "paragraph (a) or (b), or" for "paragraph (a) or (b)." in paragraph (c), and

(b)   by the insertion of the following paragraph after paragraph (c):[1]

Amendments

1   See the amended Act.

---

11   Amendment of Sexual Offences (Jurisdiction) Act, 1996

The Sexual Offences (Jurisdiction) Act, 1996, is hereby amended in the Schedule thereto by the insertion of the following paragraphs after paragraph 9:

"10. Section 3 of the Child Trafficking and Pornography Act, 1998.

11. Section 4 of the Child Trafficking and Pornography Act, 1998.".

12   Amendment of Bail Act, 1997

The Bail Act, 1997, is hereby amended in the Schedule thereto by the insertion of the following paragraph after paragraph 12:[1]

Amendments

1   See the amended Act.

[13   Nothing in this Act prevents—

(a) the giving of or compliance with a direction under section 3 of the Committees of the Houses of the Oireachtas (Compellability, Privileges and Immunities of Witnesses) Act 1997, or

(b) the possession, distribution, printing, publication or showing by either House of the Oireachtas, a committee (within the meaning of that Act) or any person of child pornography for the purposes of, or in connection with, the performance of any function conferred by the Constitution or by law on those Houses or conferred by a resolution of either of those Houses or resolutions of both of them on such a committee.][1]

Amendments

1   Section 13 inserted by Child Trafficking and Pornography (Amendment) Act 2004, s 1.

Criminal Justice Act 1999

Number 10 of 1999

ARRANGEMENT OF SECTIONS

PART I
PRELIMINARY AND GENERAL

Section

1. Interpretation.
2. Citation and commencement.
3. Expenses.

PART II
AMENDMENTS TO PROVIDE FOR NEW DRUG RELATED OFFENCE

4. Amendment of Act of 1977.
5. Amendment of penalty provisions of Act of 1977.
6. Amendment of defence provisions of Act of 1977.
7. Amendment of Act of 1994.

PART III
AMENDMENTS TO ABOLISH PRELIMINARY EXAMINATIONS

8. Amendment of section 4 of Act of 1967.
9. Insertion of Part IA in Act of 1967.
10. Amendment or repeal of other provisions of Act of 1967.
11. Amendment of Offences against the State Act, 1939.
12. Amendment of Act of 1962.
13. Amendment of Act of 1973.
14. Amendment of Criminal Law (Jurisdiction) Act, 1976.
15. Amendment of Act of 1981.
16. Amendment of Act of 1984.
17. Amendment of Act of 1990.
18. Amendment of sections 5, 7 and 13 of Act of 1992.
19. Amendment of section 15 of Act of 1992.
20. Amendment of section 16 of Act of 1992.
21. Amendment of Act of 1997.
22. Repeal of other enactments.
23. Transitional provision.
24. Amendment of section 3 of Offences against the State (Amendment) Act, 1998.

PART IV
AMENDMENTS RELATING TO CONFISCATION ORDERS

25. Amendment of section 4 of Act of 1994.

26. Amendment of section 7 of Act of 1994.

27. Amendment of section 10 of Act of 1994.

28. Amendment of section 11 of Act of 1994.

PART V
GUILTY PLEAS AND CERTIFICATE EVIDENCE

29. Guilty pleas.

30. Certificate evidence relating to custody of exhibits.

PART VI
EXTRADITION AND OTHER MATTERS

31. Offences under the law of Northern Ireland.

32. Offences under the law of Scotland.

33. Amendment of Extradition Acts, 1965 to 1994.

34. Amendment of Act of 1984.

35. Amendment of Criminal Justice (Drug Trafficking) Act, 1996.

36. Amendment of section 15 of Offences against the State (Amendment) Act, 1998.

37. Amendment of section 18 of Offences against the State (Amendment) Act, 1998.

38. Abolition of "year and a day" rule.

39. Witnesses in fear or subject to intimidation.

40. Relocated witnesses.

41. Intimidation etc. of witnesses, jurors and others.

42. Arrest and detention of prisoners in connection with investigation of other offences.

AN ACT TO CREATE A NEW DRUG OFFENCE, TO AMEND THE LAW RELATING TO PROCEEDINGS IN CRIMINAL MATTERS, TO AMEND THE LAW RELATING TO ENFORCEMENT OF PENALTIES AGAINST DRUG TRAFFICKERS, TO ESTABLISH RULES RELATING TO THE SENTENCING OF PERSONS WHO HAVE ENTERED GUILTY PLEAS, TO PROVIDE FOR EVIDENCE BY CERTIFICATE IN RELATION TO EXHIBITS, TO AMEND THE LAW RELATING TO THE CERTIFICATION, FOR EXTRADITION PURPOSES, OF CERTAIN OFFENCES UNDER THE LAW OF NORTHERN IRELAND AND SCOTLAND AND THE LAW DEFINING THE JUDGES WHO HAVE JURISDICTION TO HEAR EXTRADITION MATTERS, TO ABOLISH THE "YEAR AND A DAY" RULE, TO AMEND SECTION 4 OF THE CRIMINAL JUSTICE ACT, 1984, TO AMEND THE OFFENCES AGAINST THE STATE (AMENDMENT) ACT, 1998, TO PROVIDE FOR THE GIVING OF EVIDENCE THROUGH A LIVE TELEVISION LINK BY WITNESSES IN FEAR OR SUBJECT TO INTIMIDATION, FOR THE PROTECTION OF THE WHEREABOUTS AND IDENTITY OF WITNESSES UNDER A GARDA SÍOCHÁNA WITNESS PROTECTION PROGRAMME, FOR THE OFFENCE OF INTIMIDATION OF

WITNESSES, JURORS AND OTHER PERSONS AND FOR THE ARREST AND DETENTION OF PRISONERS IN CONNECTION WITH THE INVESTIGATION OF OFFENCES AND TO PROVIDE FOR OTHER RELATED MATTERS. [26th May, 1999]

BE IT ENACTED BY THE OIREACHTAS AS FOLLOWS:

PART I
PRELIMINARY AND GENERAL

1   Interpretation

(1) In this Act—

"the Act of 1962" means the Criminal Justice (Legal Aid) Act, 1962;

"the Act of 1967" means the Criminal Procedure Act, 1967;

"the Act of 1973" means the Criminal Procedure (Amendment) Act, 1973;

"the Act of 1977" means the Misuse of Drugs Act, 1977;

"the Act of 1981" means the Criminal Law (Rape) Act, 1981;

"the Act of 1984" means the Criminal Justice Act, 1984;

"the Act of 1990" means the Criminal Justice (Forensic Evidence) Act, 1990;

"the Act of 1992" means the Criminal Evidence Act, 1992;

"the Act of 1994" means the Criminal Justice Act, 1994;

"the Act of 1997" means the Criminal Justice (Miscellaneous Provisions) Act, 1997;

"the Minister" means the Minister for Justice, Equality and Law Reform.

(2) A reference in this Act to any other enactment is to that enactment as amended, adapted or extended by or under any subsequent enactment including this Act.

2   Citation and commencement

(1) This Act may be cited as the Criminal Justice Act, 1999.

(2) This Act, other than Part VI, shall come into operation on such day or days as, by order or orders made by the Minister, may be fixed therefor either generally or with reference to any particular purpose or provision, and different days may be so fixed for different purposes or different provisions.

3   Expenses

The expenses incurred by the Minister in the administration of this Act shall, to such extent as may be sanctioned by the Minister for Finance, be paid out of moneys provided by the Oireachtas.

PART II
AMENDMENTS TO PROVIDE FOR NEW DRUG RELATED OFFENCE

4   Amendment of Act of 1977

The Act of 1977 is hereby amended by the insertion after section 15 of the following section:[1]

Amendments

1   See the amended Act.

5   Amendment of penalty provisions of Act of 1977

Section 27 of the Act of 1977 is hereby amended by the insertion after subsection (3) of the following subsections:[1]

Amendments

1   See the amended Act.

6   Amendment of defence provisions of Act of 1977

Section 29 of the Act of 1977 is hereby amended by the substitution of the following subsection for subsection (3):[1]

Amendments

1   See the amended Act.

7   Amendment of Act of 1994

Section 3(1) of the Act of 1994 is hereby amended in the definition of "drug trafficking offence" by the insertion of the following paragraph after paragraph (b):[1]

Amendments

1   See the amended Act.

PART III
AMENDMENTS TO ABOLISH PRELIMINARY EXAMINATIONS

8   Amendment of section 4 of Act of 1967

The Act of 1967 is hereby amended by the substitution of the following section for section 4:[1]

Amendments

1   See the amended Act.

9   Insertion of Part IA in Act of 1967

The Act of 1967 is hereby amended by the insertion after section 4 of the following Part:[1]

Amendments

1   See the amended Act.

10   Amendment or repeal of other provisions of Act of 1967

(1) Part II of the Act of 1967 is hereby amended by the substitution of the following title for the title to that Part:

  "Guilty Pleas and Other Matters".

(2) Sections 5 to 12 of the Act of 1967 are hereby repealed.

(3) Section 13 of the Act of 1967 is hereby amended by the substitution of the following subsections for subsection (2):[1]

(4) Section 13(4) of the Act of 1967 is hereby amended by the substitution of the following paragraph for paragraph (b):[1]

(5) Sections 14 to 18 of the Act of 1967 are hereby repealed.

Amendments

1   See the amended Act.

11   Amendment of Offences against the State Act, 1939

Sections 45(2) and 46(2) of the Offences against the State Act, 1939, are amended by the deletion of "receives informations in relation to such charge and".

12   Amendment of Act of 1962

(1) Section 2A of the Act of 1962 (as inserted by section 15(4) of the Act of 1992) is hereby repealed.

(2) Section 3 of the Act of 1962 is hereby amended—

  (a) in subsections (1) and (2) by the substitution of "sent forward for trial" for "returned for trial", wherever the latter phrase appears, and

  (b) in subsection (2)(c) by the substitution of the following subparagraph for subparagraph (i):

  "(i) the person is charged with murder, or".

(3) Section 9(2) of the Act of 1962 (as amended by section 15 of the Act of 1992) is hereby amended by the deletion of "a legal aid (preliminary examination) certificate,".

13 Amendment of Act of 1973

(1) The Act of 1973 is hereby amended by the substitution of the following section for section 2:

> "Correction of defect in charge after accused is sent forward for sentence.
>
> 2.—Where under section 13(2) of the Criminal Procedure Act, 1967, an accused person is sent forward for sentence on any charge with a plea of guilty—
>
> (a) any defect in the charge may be corrected by the court to which the accused has been sent forward, and
>
> (b) the plea of guilty shall be treated as a plea of guilty to the charge so corrected,
>
> unless such correction would, in the opinion of the court, result in injustice.".

(2) Section 3(2) of the Act of 1973 is amended by the substitution of "as if he had been sent forward for trial" for "as if he had been returned for trial".

14 Amendment of Criminal Law (Jurisdiction) Act, 1976

The Criminal Law (Jurisdiction) Act, 1976 is hereby amended by the substitution of the following section for section 18:[1]

Amendments

1 See the amended Act.

---

15 Amendment of Act of 1981

The Act of 1981 is hereby amended by the substitution of the following section for section 4:[1]

Amendments

1 See the amended Act.

---

16 Amendment of Act of 1984

(1) Sections 18(1) and 19(1) of the Act of 1984 are hereby amended by the substitution of "in determining whether a charge should be dismissed under Part IA of the Criminal Procedure Act, 1967" for "in determining whether to send forward the accused for trial".

(2) Sections 18(2) and 19(2) of the Act of 1984 are hereby amended by the substitution of ", in relation to the hearing of an application under Part IA of the Criminal Procedure Act, 1967, for the dismissal of a charge," for ", in relation to the preliminary examination of a charge,".

(3) Section 20 of the Act of 1984 is hereby amended—

(a) by the substitution of the following subsection for subsection (6):[1]

(b) in subsection (8) by the substitution of the following paragraph for paragraph (a) of the definition of "prescribed period":[1]

(c) in subsection (8) by the deletion of paragraph (b) of the definition of "prescribed period", and

(d) in subsection (8) by the substitution of the following for paragraph (c) of the definition of "prescribed period":

(4) Section 21(1) of the Act of 1984 is hereby amended by the substitution of ", other than the hearing of an application under Part IA of the Criminal Procedure Act, 1967, for the dismissal of a charge," for ", other than the preliminary examination of an indictable offence,".

Amendments

1 See the amended Act.

17 Amendment of Act of 1990

(1) Section 3(1)(a) of the Act of 1990 is hereby amended by the substitution of the following subparagraph for subparagraph (i):[1]

(2) Section 3(2) of the Act of 1990 is hereby amended by the substitution of ", in relation to the hearing of an application under Part IA of the Criminal Procedure Act, 1967, for the dismissal of a charge," for ", in relation to the preliminary examination of a charge,".

Amendments

1 See the amended Act.

18

Amendment of sections 5, 7 and 13 of Act of 1992

(1) Section 5(4)(a)(ii) of the Act of 1992 is hereby amended by the substitution of "section 4F" for "section 14".

(2) Section 7(1)(a) of the Act of 1992 is hereby amended by the substitution of "pursuant to section 4B(1) or 4C(1) of the Criminal Procedure Act, 1967," for "pursuant to section 6(1) of the Criminal Procedure Act, 1967,".

(3) Section 13(1) of the Act of 1992 is hereby amended by the insertion, after "proceedings", of "(including proceedings under section 4E or 4F of the Criminal Procedure Act, 1967)".

19 Amendment of section 15 of Act of 1992

The Act of 1992 is hereby amended by the substitution of the following section for section 15:[1]

Amendments

1   See the amended Act.

20   Amendment of section 16 of Act of 1992

Section 16(1) of the Act of 1992 is hereby amended—

   (a) by the substitution of the following paragraph for paragraph (a):[1]

   (b) by the substitution of the following for the proviso:[1]

Amendments

1   See the amended Act.

21   Amendment of Act of 1997

Section 5 of the Act of 1997 is hereby amended by the substitution of the following subsection for subsection (3):[1]

Amendments

1   See the amended Act.

22   Repeal of other enactments

The following enactments are hereby repealed:

   (a) section 79(3)(a) of the Courts of Justice Act, 1924 (as substituted by the Act of 1997);

   (b) section 8(1) of the Courts (No. 2) Act, 1986;

   (c) section 11 of the Criminal Justice Act, 1993.

23   Transitional provision

If, before the commencement of this Part, any steps have been taken under Part II of the Act of 1967 in relation to the prosecution of an accused person, the applicable provisions of the enactments amended or repealed by this Part shall continue to apply to all matters connected with or arising out of the prosecution of the accused, as if those enactments had not been so amended or repealed.

24   Amendment of section 3 of Offences against the State (Amendment) Act, 1998

Section 3 of the Offences against the State (Amendment) Act, 1998, is hereby amended—

   (a) by the substitution of the following subsection for subsection (5):

      "(5) A notice under subsection (1) or under paragraph (c) or (d) of subsection (2) shall be given in writing to the solicitor for the prosecution.",

(b) in subsection (7) by the substitution of the following for paragraph (a):

"(a) the period of fourteen days after the date the accused is, in accordance with section 4B(1) of the Criminal Procedure Act, 1967, served with the documents mentioned in that section, or",

(c) in subsection (7) by the deletion of paragraph (b), and

(d) in subsection (7) by the substitution of the following for paragraph (c):

"(c) where the accused, on being sent forward for sentence, changes his or her plea to not guilty, the period of fourteen days after the date the accused is, in accordance with section 13(4)(b) of the Criminal Procedure Act, 1967, served with the documents mentioned in section 4B(1) of that Act, or".

PART IV
AMENDMENTS RELATING TO CONFISCATION ORDERS

25   Amendment of section 4 of Act of 1994

Section 4 of the Act of 1994 is hereby amended by the substitution of the following subsections for subsections (1) to (3):[1]

Amendments

1   See the amended Act.

26   Amendment of section 7 of Act of 1994

Section 7 of the Act of 1994 is hereby amended—

(a) by the substitution of the following subsection for subsection (1):[1]

(b) in subsection (2) by the substitution of the following paragraph for paragraph (a):[1]

(c) in subsection (3)(a) by the substitution of the following subparagraph for subparagraph (i):[1]

(d) by the substitution of the following subsection for subsection (4):[1]

Amendments

1   See the amended Act.

27   Amendment of section 10 of Act of 1994

Section 10(1)(a) of the Act of 1994 is hereby amended by the substitution of the following for everything before subparagraph (i):[1]

Amendments

1 See the amended Act.

28 Amendment of section 11 of Act of 1994

(1) Section 11 of the Act of 1994 is hereby amended by the substitution of the following subsection for subsection (1):[1]

(2) Section 11 of the Act of 1994 is hereby amended by the insertion of the following subsections:[1]

Amendments

1 See the amended Act.

PART V
GUILTY PLEAS AND CERTIFICATE EVIDENCE

29 Guilty pleas

(1) In determining what sentence to pass on a person who has pleaded guilty to an offence, other than an offence for which the sentence is fixed by law, a court, if it considers it appropriate to do so, shall take into account—

(a) the stage in the proceedings for the offence at which the person indicated an intention to plead guilty, and

(b) the circumstances in which this indication was given.

(2) To avoid doubt, it is hereby declared that subsection (1) shall not preclude a court from passing the maximum sentence prescribed by law for an offence if, notwithstanding the plea of guilty, the court is satisfied that there are exceptional circumstances relating to the offence which warrant the maximum sentence.

(3) In this section, "fixed by law", in relation to a sentence for an offence, means a sentence which a court is required by law to impose on a person of full capacity who is guilty of the offence.

30 Certificate evidence relating to custody of exhibits

(1) In any criminal proceedings, a certificate purporting to be signed by a member of the Garda Síochána and stating that the member had custody of an exhibit at a specified place or for a specified period or purpose shall be admissible as evidence of the matters stated in the certificate.

(2) In any criminal proceedings, the court may—

(a) if it considers that the interests of justice so require, direct that oral evidence be given of the matters stated in a certificate under this section, and

(b) adjourn the proceedings to a later date for the purpose of receiving the oral evidence.

(3) A certificate under this section shall be tendered in evidence by a member of the Garda Síochána not below the rank of sergeant.

(4) The Minister may, by regulations, prescribe the form of a certificate under this section.

PART VI
EXTRADITION AND OTHER MATTERS

31   Offences under the law of Northern Ireland

(1) For the purposes of Part III of the Extradition Act, 1965, an offence punishable under the law of Northern Ireland by imprisonment for a maximum period of at least 6 months and triable either summarily or on indictment at the election of the prosecution shall be treated as follows:

(a) as an indictable offence and not also as a summary offence, if it is certified by the Director of Public Prosecutions for Northern Ireland that the offence is so punishable and triable and that it will not be or, as the case may be, has not been prosecuted summarily;

(b) as a summary offence, if it is certified by the Director of Public Prosecutions for Northern Ireland that the offence is so punishable and triable and that it will be or, as the case may be, has been prosecuted summarily.

(2) A certificate appearing to be given by the Director of Public Prosecutions for Northern Ireland and certifying as to the matters mentioned in paragraph (a) or (b) of subsection (1) may, without further evidence—

(a) be accepted by the Commissioner of the Garda Síochána, and

(b) be admitted in any proceedings, unless the court sees good reason to the contrary, as evidence of the matters so certified.

(3) In this section "Director of Public Prosecutions" includes a person for the time being exercising the functions of that office.

(4) This section shall be construed as one with Part III of the Extradition Act, 1965.

32   Offences under the law of Scotland

(1) For the purposes of Part III of the Extradition Act, 1965—

(a) an offence punishable under the law of Scotland by imprisonment for a maximum period of at least 6 months shall be treated as an indictable offence and not also as a summary offence if it is certified by a Procurator Fiscal that the offence is an indictable offence so punishable and that it will not be or, as the case may be, has not been prosecuted summarily, and

(b) an offence punishable under the law of Scotland by imprisonment for a maximum period of at least 6 months shall be treated as a summary offence if it is certified by a Procurator Fiscal that the offence will be or, as the case may be, has been prosecuted summarily, and that it is so punishable.

(2) A certificate appearing to be given by a Procurator Fiscal and certifying as to the matters mentioned in paragraph (a) or (b) of subsection (1) may, without further evidence—

(a) be accepted by the Commissioner of the Garda Síochána, and

(b) be admitted in any proceedings, unless the court sees good reason to the contrary, as evidence of the matters so certified.

(3) In this section "Procurator Fiscal" includes a Depute.

(4) This section shall be construed as one with Part III of the Extradition Act, 1965.

(5) Section 37 of the Act of 1967 is hereby repealed.

33   Amendment of Extradition Acts, 1965 to 1994

(1) Section 3 of the Extradition Act, 1965, is hereby amended in the definition of "judge of the District Court assigned to the Dublin Metropolitan District" (inserted by the Extradition (Amendment) Act, 1994) by the deletion of "nominated for the purposes of this Act by the President of the District Court".

(2) Section 4 of the Extradition (Amendment) Act, 1994, is hereby amended by the deletion of subsection (2).

34

Amendment of Act of 1984

Section 4 of the Act of 1984 is hereby amended—

(a) by the substitution, in subsection (5) (as inserted by the Act of 1997), of "subject to subsection (5A)" for "subject to subsection (6)", and

(b) by the renumbering of subsection (6) (as inserted by the Act of 1997) as subsection (5A).

35   Amendment of Criminal Justice (Drug Trafficking) Act, 1996

Section 1 of the Criminal Justice (Drug Trafficking) Act, 1996, is hereby amended by the deletion of the definition of "judge of the District Court".

36   Amendment of section 15 of Offences against the State (Amendment) Act, 1998

Section 15 of the Offences against the State (Amendment) Act, 1998, is hereby amended by the substitution of the following subsection for subsection (3):

> "(3) Section 3 of the Explosive Substances Act, 1883, inserted by section 4 of the Criminal Law (Jurisdiction) Act, 1976, is hereby amended by the substitution of 'shall be liable to a fine or imprisonment' for 'shall be liable to imprisonment'.".

37   Amendment of section 18 of Offences against the State (Amendment) Act, 1998

Section 18 of the Offences against the State (Amendment) Act, 1998, is hereby amended by the substitution of the following subsection for subsection (2):

> "(2) A section referred to in subsection (1) may, by resolution of each House of the Oireachtas passed before the expiry of the section, be continued in operation from time to time for such period, not exceeding twelve months, as is specified in the resolutions.".

38   Abolition of "year and a day" rule

(1) In this section, "the 'year and a day' rule" means the rule of law that an act or omission is conclusively presumed not to have caused a person's death if more than a year and a day elapsed between the act or omission and the death.

(2) The "year and a day" rule is hereby abolished for all purposes, including—

(a) for the purposes of offences involving the death of a person, and

(b) for the purpose of determining whether a person committed suicide.

(3) Subsection (2) does not affect the continued application of the "year and a day" rule to any case where the act or omission, or the last of the acts or omissions, that caused the death occurred before the day on which this Act is passed.

39   Witnesses in fear or subject to intimidation

(1) Subject to subsection (2), in any proceedings on indictment for an offence (including proceedings under Part IA of the Act of 1967) a person other than the accused may, with the leave of the court, give evidence through a live television link.

(2) A court shall not grant leave under subsection (1) unless it is satisfied that the person is likely to be in fear or subject to intimidation in giving evidence otherwise.

(3) Evidence given under subsection (1) shall be videorecorded.

(4) In any proceedings referred to in subsection (1) in any circuit or district court district where the court is satisfied that leave should be granted for evidence to be given through a live television link pursuant to subsection (1) but the necessary facilities for doing so are not available in that circuit or district, the court may by order transfer the proceedings to a circuit or district court district where such facilities are available and, where such an order is made, the jurisdiction of the court to which the proceedings have been transferred may be exercised—

(a) in the case of the Circuit Court, by the judge of the circuit concerned, and

(b) in the case of the District Court, by the judge of that court for the time being assigned to the district court district concerned.

(5) Where evidence is given by a person ("the witness") through a live television link pursuant to subsection (1)—

(a) in case evidence is given that the accused was known to the witness before the date on which the offence in question is alleged to have been committed, the witness shall not be required to identify the accused, unless the court in the interests of justice directs otherwise, and

(b) in any other case, evidence by a person other than the witness that the witness identified the accused as being the offender at an identification parade or by other means shall be admissible as evidence that the accused was so identified.

(6) This section is without prejudice to any other enactment providing for the giving of evidence through a live television link.

40   Relocated Witnesses

(1) A person who without lawful authority makes enquiries or takes any other steps whatever, whether within or outside the State, for the purpose of discovering—

(a) the whereabouts of a person whom he or she knows, or reasonably suspects, to be a relocated witness, or

(b) any new name or other particulars related to any new identity provided for such a witness,

shall be guilty of an offence.

(2) A person who without lawful authority discloses, whether within or outside the State, to any other person any information (including information lawfully obtained pursuant to subsection (1)) concerning—

    (a) the whereabouts of a person whom he or she knows, or reasonably suspects, to be a relocated witness, or

    (b) any new name or other particulars related to any new identity provided for such a person,

shall be guilty of an offence.

(3) In this section "relocated witness" means any person who intends to give or has given evidence in proceedings for an offence and who as a consequence has moved residence, under any programme operated by the Garda Síochána for the protection of witnesses, to any place, whether within or outside the State.

(4) In this section "lawful authority" means the authority of—

    (a) a court in any proceedings involving the relocated witness, or

    (b) a member of the Garda Síochána not below the rank of chief superintendent.

(5) A court shall give authority pursuant to subsection (1) or (2) only if it is satisfied—

    (a) that to do so would be in the interests of justice, and

    (b) that another way of proceeding which would not prejudice the continued participation of the relocated witness in the programme aforesaid, including, without prejudice to the generality of the foregoing, the transmission of any documents required to be served on the witness to the Commissioner of the Garda Síochána for the purpose of effecting such service, is not available.

(6) A person guilty of an offence under this section shall be liable—

    (a) on summary conviction, to a fine not exceeding £1,500 or imprisonment for a term not exceeding 12 months or both, and

    (b) on conviction on indictment, to a fine or imprisonment for a term not exceeding five years or both.

41   Intimidation etc. of witnesses, jurors and others

(1) Without prejudice to any provision made by any other enactment or rule of law, a person—

    (a) [who (whether in or outside the State) harms]¹ or threatens, menaces or in any other way intimidates or puts in fear another person who is assisting in the investigation by the Garda Síochána of an offence or is a witness or potential witness or a juror or potential juror in proceedings for an offence, or a member of his or her family,

    (b) with the intention thereby of causing the investigation or the course of justice to be obstructed, perverted or interfered with,

shall be guilty of an offence.

(2) In this section, "potential juror" means a person who, at the time an offence under this section is alleged to have been committed, has been summoned for jury service but has not been empanelled as a juror to serve on a particular jury.

(3) In proceedings for an offence under this section, proof to the satisfaction of the court or jury, as the case may be, that the accused did an act referred to in subsection (1)(a) shall be evidence that the act was done with the intention required by subsection (1)(b).

[(3A) A person shall be guilty of an offence under this section for conduct that the person engages in outside the State only if—

(a) the conduct takes place on board an Irish ship (within the meaning of section 9 of the Mercantile Marine Act 1955),

(b) the conduct takes place on an aircraft registered in the State,

(c) the person is an Irish citizen, or

(d) the person is ordinarily resident in the State.

(3B) A person who has his or her principal residence in the State for the 12 months immediately preceding the commission of an offence under subsection (1) is, for the purposes of subsection (3A)(d), ordinarily resident in the State on the date of the commission of the offence.]²

(4) In subsection (1) the reference to a member of a person's family includes a reference to—

(a) the person's spouse,

(b) a parent, grandparent, step-parent, child (including a step-child or an adopted child), grandchild, brother, sister, half-brother, half-sister, uncle, aunt, nephew or niece of the person or his or her spouse, or

(c) any person who is cohabiting or residing with him or her.

(5) A person guilty of an offence under this section shall be liable—

(a) on summary conviction, to a fine not exceeding £1,500 or imprisonment for a term not exceeding 12 months or both, and

(b) on conviction on indictment, to a fine or imprisonment for a term not exceeding [15 years]³ or both.

Amendments

1   Words substituted by Criminal Justice (Amendment) Act 2009, s 20(a).

2   Subsections (3A) and (3B) inserted by Criminal Justice (Amendment) Act 2009, s 20(b).

3   Words substituted by Criminal Justice (Amendment) Act 2009, s 16.

42   Arrest and detention of prisoners in connection with investigation of other offences

(1) In this section—

"offence" means an arrestable offence as defined in section 2 of the Criminal Law Act, 1997;

"prison" means a place of custody administered by the Minister for Justice, Equality and Law Reform;

"prisoner" means a person who is in prison on foot of a sentence of imprisonment, on committal awaiting trial, on remand or otherwise.

[(2) A member of an Garda Síochána may arrest a prisoner on the authority of a judge of the District Court who is satisfied, on information supplied on oath by a member of the Garda Síochána not below the rank of superintendent, that the following conditions are fulfilled:

(a) there are reasonable grounds for suspecting that the prisoner has committed an offence or offences other than the offence or offences in connection with which he or she is imprisoned;

(b) the arrest of the prisoner is necessary for the proper investigation of the offence or offences that he or she is suspected of having committed; and

(c) where the prisoner has previously been arrested for the same offence or offences, whether prior to his or her imprisonment or under this section, further information has come to the knowledge of the Garda Síochána since that arrest as to the prisoner's suspected participation in the offence or offences for which his or her arrest is sought.][1]

(3) A person arrested under this section—

(a) shall be taken forthwith to a Garda Station and may, subject to subsection (5), be detained there for such period as is authorised under section 4 of the Act of 1984, and

(b) shall, subject to this section, be dealt with as though he or she had been detained under that section.

(4) Section 4(4), (5), (5A) and 10 of the Act of 1984 shall not apply to a person arrested and detained under this section.

(5) If at any time during the detention of a person under this section there are no longer reasonable grounds for—

(a) suspecting that the person has committed [the offence or offences in respect of which he or she was arrested][2] under this section, or

(b) believing that his or her detention is necessary for [the proper investigation of that offence or those offences][2],

the detention shall be terminated forthwith.

(6) On termination of the detention in accordance with subsection (5) or by reason of the expiry of the period referred to in subsection (3)(a) the member of the Garda Síochána in charge of the Garda Station where the person is detained shall transfer him or her, or cause him or her to be transferred, forthwith back into the custody of the governor of the prison where the person was imprisoned at the time of the arrest.

(7) This section shall not prejudice any power conferred by law apart from this section in relation to the arrest, detention or transfer of prisoners.

Amendments

1   Subsection (2) substituted by Criminal Justice Act 2006, s 11(a).

2   Subsection (5) amended by Criminal Justice Act 2006, s 11(b).

Sex Offenders Act 2001

Number 18 of 2001

ARRANGEMENT OF SECTIONS

PART 1
PRELIMINARY AND GENERAL

1. Short title and commencement.
2. Interpretation (general).
3. Sexual offences for purposes of Act.
4. Regulations.
5. Expenses.

PART 2
OBLIGATIONS OF SEX OFFENDERS TO NOTIFY CERTAIN INFORMATION

6. "relevant date".
7. Persons subject to the requirements of this Part.
8. Period for which person is subject to requirements of this Part and related matters.
9. Supply of information to facilitate compliance with this Part.
10. Notification requirements.
11. Discharge from obligation to comply with requirements of this Part.
12. Offences in connection with notification requirements.
13. Application of this Part to persons convicted outside State.
14. Certificate as evidence of person's being subject to requirements of this Part.

PART 3
SEX OFFENDERS ORDERS

15. Definitions (Part 3).
16. Sex offender orders.
17. Taking effect of sex offender order.
18. Effect of appeal from order.
19. Discharge or variation of sex offender order.
20. Court jurisdiction and venue.
21. Provisions in relation to evidence and proceedings under this Part.
22. Offence in respect of contravention of sex offender order.
23. Rules of court.
24. Amendment of Civil Legal Aid Act, 1995.

PART 4
PROVISION OF INFORMATION FOR EMPLOYMENT PURPOSES

25. Interpretation (Part 4).
26. Failure to inform employer, etc., of sexual offence conviction.

PART 5

POST-RELEASE SUPERVISION FOR SEX OFFENDERS

27. Interpretation (Part 5).

28. Duty of court to consider imposition of sentence involving post-release supervision.

29. Power of court to impose sentence involving post-release supervision.

30. Additional provisions which may be included in sentence involving post-release supervision.

31. Duty of court to explain effect of sentence to offender.

32. Discharge or variation of requirements relating to supervision period.

33. Non-compliance with requirements relating to supervision period.

PART 6

MISCELLANEOUS

34. Amendment of Criminal Law (Rape) Act, 1981.

35. Further amendments of Civil Legal Aid Act, 1995.

36. Proof of foreign conviction in certain cases.

37. Amendment of section 2 of Act of 1990.

SCHEDULE

SEXUAL OFFENCES FOR PURPOSES OF ACT

AN ACT TO REQUIRE, IN THE INTERESTS OF THE COMMON GOOD, THE NOTIFICATION OF INFORMATION TO THE GARDA SÍOCHÁNA BY PERSONS WHO HAVE COMMITTED CERTAIN SEXUAL OFFENCES; IN THOSE INTERESTS TO IMPOSE, OR ENABLE THE IMPOSITION OF, CERTAIN OTHER REQUIREMENTS ON SUCH PERSONS (INCLUDING REQUIREMENTS THE PURPOSE OF WHICH IS TO ASSIST IN THEIR REHABILITATION); TO ENABLE CERTAIN COMPLAINANTS TO BE HEARD AND LEGALLY REPRESENTED IN RELATION TO APPLICATIONS UNDER SECTION 3 OR 4 OF THE CRIMINAL LAW (RAPE) ACT, 1981, TO AMEND SECTION 2 OF THE CRIMINAL LAW (RAPE) (AMENDMENT) ACT, 1990, AND TO PROVIDE FOR RELATED MATTERS. [30th June, 2001]

BE IT ENACTED BY THE OIREACHTAS AS FOLLOWS:

PART 1

PRELIMINARY AND GENERAL

1   Short title and commencement.

(1) This Act may be cited as the Sex Offenders Act, 2001.

(2) This Act shall come into operation on such day or days as the Minister may appoint by order or orders either generally or with reference to any particular purpose or provision and different days may be so appointed for different purposes or different provisions.

2   Interpretation (general)

(1) In this Act, unless the context otherwise requires—

"Act of 1861" means the Offences against the Person Act, 1861;

"Act of 1908" means the Punishment of Incest Act, 1908;

"Act of 1935" means the Criminal Law Amendment Act, 1935;

"Act of 1990" means the Criminal Law (Rape) (Amendment) Act, 1990;

"Act of 1993" means the Criminal Law (Sexual Offences) Act, 1993;

"conviction" (other than in sections 12, 22, 26(8) and 33) includes a finding of guilty but insane and "convicted" and cognate expressions shall be construed accordingly;

"court" means any court exercising criminal jurisdiction and includes court-martial;

"imprisonment" includes detention in Saint Patrick's Institution or the Central Mental Hospital and "prison" shall be construed accordingly;

"Minister" means the Minister for Justice, Equality and Law Reform;

"remission from the sentence" means, in relation to the sentence imposed on a person, the remission which the person may earn from the sentence under the rules or practice whereby prisoners generally may earn remission of sentence by industry and good conduct;

"sentence" includes a sentence of imprisonment and any other order made by a court in dealing with a convicted person, including—

  (a) an order under section 2(2) of the Trial of Lunatics Act, 1883, and

  (b) an order postponing sentence;

"sexual offence" shall be construed in accordance with section 3.

(2) In this Act—

  (a) a reference to a Part, section or Schedule is to a Part or section of, or a Schedule to, this Act, unless it is indicated that reference to some other enactment is intended,

  (b) a reference to a subsection or paragraph is to the subsection or paragraph of the provision in which the reference occurs unless it is indicated that reference to some other provision is intended.

(3) A reference in this Act to any enactment shall be construed as a reference to that enactment as amended, adapted or extended by or under any enactment.

3   Sexual offences for purposes of Act.

(1) Each of the offences referred to in the Schedule shall, subject to subsections (2) and (3), be a sexual offence for the purposes of this Act.

(2) An offence referred to in—

  [(a) paragraph 2 of the Schedule (sexual assault or indecent assault), other than an offence of sexual assault or indecent assault of a person who, at the time of the commission of the offence, was mentally impaired,][1]

  (b) paragraph 5 of the Schedule (incest by males),

  (c) paragraph 6 of the Schedule (incest by females of or over 17 years of age), or

  (d) paragraph 18, 19 or 20 of the Schedule in so far as it relates to an offence referred to in paragraph (a), (b) or (c),

shall not be a sexual offence for the purposes of this Act if—

   (i) the victim of or, as the case may be, the other party to the offence was aged, at the date of the offence's commission, 17 years or more, and

[(ii) the person guilty of the offence—

     (I) is, for the time being, the subject of an order of the court remanding him or her on bail or in custody pending the passing of sentence, or

    (II) has not, in respect of the offence, been sentenced to any punishment involving deprivation of liberty for a limited or unlimited period of time or been made subject to any measure involving such deprivation of liberty.]²

(3) An offence referred to in—

  (a) paragraph 8 of the Schedule (defilement of girl between 15 and 17 years of age),

  (b) paragraph 11 of the Schedule (buggery of persons under 17 years of age),

  (c) paragraph 12 of the Schedule (gross indecency with males under 17 years of age), or

  (d) paragraph 18, 19 or 20 of the Schedule in so far as it relates to an offence referred to in paragraph (a), (b) or (c),

shall not be a sexual offence for the purposes of this Act if—

  (i) the victim of or, as the case may be, the other party to the offence was aged, at the date of the offence's commission, 15 years or more but less than 17 years, and

  (ii) the person guilty of the offence was aged, at that date, not more than 3 years older than that victim or other party.

[(4) In this section 'mentally impaired' has the same meaning as it has in section 5 of the Criminal Law (Sexual Offences) Act 1993.]³

Amendments

1   Subsection (2)(a) substituted by Criminal Law (Human Trafficking) Act 2008, s 13(a)(i).

2   Paragraph (ii) substituted by Criminal Law (Human Trafficking) Act 2008, s 13(a)(ii).

3   Subsection (4) inserted by Criminal Law (Human Trafficking) Act 2008, s 13(a)(iii).

---

4   Regulations

(1) The Minister may make regulations prescribing any matter or thing which is referred to in this Act as prescribed or to be prescribed or for the purpose of enabling any provision of this Act to have full effect.

(2) Every regulation under this section shall be laid before each House of the Oireachtas as soon as may be after it is made and, if a resolution annulling the regulation is passed by either such House within the next 21 days on which that House has sat after the regulation is laid before it, the regulation shall be annulled accordingly, but without prejudice to the validity of anything previously done thereunder.

5   Expenses

The expenses incurred by the Minister in the administration of this Act shall, to such extent as may be sanctioned by the Minister for Finance, be paid out of moneys provided by the Oireachtas.

PART 2

OBLIGATIONS OF SEX OFFENDERS TO NOTIFY CERTAIN INFORMATION

6   "relevant date"

In this Part, "relevant date" means the date of conviction for the sexual offence concerned.

7   Persons subject to the requirements of this Part

(1) Without prejudice to subsection (2) and section 13 and 16(7), a person is subject to the requirements of this Part if he or she is convicted of a sexual offence after the commencement of this Part.

(2) A person is also subject to the requirements of this Part if he or she has been convicted of a sexual offence before the commencement of this Part and, at that commencement, either—

   (a) the sentence to be imposed on the person in respect of the offence has yet to be determined, or

   (b) a sentence has been imposed on the person in respect of the offence and—
       (i)   the person is serving the sentence in prison,
       (ii) the person is temporarily released under section 2 or 3 of the Criminal Justice Act, 1960, or
       (iii) the sentence is otherwise still in force or current.

8   Period for which person is subject to requirements of this Part and related matters

(1) A person who, by reason of section 7, is subject to the requirements of this Part shall be so subject for the period referred to in subsection (3) or, in the case of a person referred to in section 7(2), so much (if any) of that period as falls after the commencement of this Part.

(2) Subsection (1) is subject to section 11.

(3) The period mentioned in subsection (1) is the period, beginning with the relevant date, of—

   (a) an indefinite duration if the sentence imposed on the person in respect of the offence concerned is one of imprisonment for life or for a term of more than 2 years,

   (b) 10 years if the sentence imposed on the person in respect of the offence concerned is one of imprisonment for a term of more than 6 months but not more than 2 years,

   (c) 7 years if the sentence imposed on the person in respect of the offence concerned is one of imprisonment for a term of 6 months or less, or

   (d) 5 years if the sentence imposed on the person—
       (i)   is one of imprisonment for any term, the operation of the whole of which is suspended (but, if the operation of that term is revived by the court, whichever of the preceding paragraphs is appropriate shall apply instead of this subparagraph), or
       (ii) is otherwise than one of imprisonment.

(4) If—

   (a) a sentence is imposed on a person in respect of a sexual offence, and

   (b) at the time of sentencing the person is aged under 18 years, subsection (3) shall have effect in relation to that person as if for the references to 10 years, 7 years and

5 years in that subsection there were substituted references to 5 years, 3½ years and 2½ years, respectively.

(5) If a sentence of imprisonment for any term is imposed on the person referred to in subsection (1) in respect of the offence concerned and the operation of a part of that term is suspended—

    (a) the part of that term the operation of which is not suspended shall be regarded as the term of imprisonment imposed on that person for the purposes of subsection (3) (but, if the operation of the first-mentioned part of that term is revived by the court, whichever of paragraphs (a), (b) and (c) of subsection (3) is appropriate shall apply without regard to this paragraph),

    (b) the preceding paragraph extends to a case in which that suspension is provided for subsequent to the imposition of the sentence.

(6) If a person is or has been sentenced in respect of 2 or more sexual offences and the sentences imposed are consecutive or partly concurrent then subsection (3) shall have effect as if—

    (a) in the case of consecutive sentences, the sentence imposed in respect of each of the offences were or had been a sentence equal to the aggregate of those sentences,

    (b) in the case of partly concurrent sentences, the sentence imposed in respect of each of the offences were or had been a sentence equal to the aggregate of those sentences after making such deduction as is necessary to ensure that no period of time is counted more than once.

(7) Without prejudice to section 11, a person shall cease to be subject to the requirements of this Part if the conviction in respect of the offence concerned is quashed on appeal or otherwise.

(8) A reference in this section to a sentence imposed on a person shall, if the sentence is varied on appeal, be construed as a reference to the sentence as so varied and, accordingly, the period for which a person is subject to the requirements of this Part, by reason of this section, shall stand reduced or increased, as the case may be, in the event that such a variation is made which results in the sentence falling into a different paragraph of subsection (3) than it did before the variation.

9   Supply of information to facilitate compliance with this Part.

The person for the time being in charge of the place where a person subject to the requirements of this Part is ordered to be imprisoned in respect of an offence (whether or not the offence that gave rise to the person's being subject to those requirements) shall notify in writing—

    (a) before the date on which the sentence of imprisonment imposed on the person in respect of the first-mentioned offence expires or, as the case may be, the person's remission from the sentence begins ("the date of release"), the person that he or she is subject to the requirements of this Part, and

    (b) at least 10 days before the date of release, the Commissioner of the Garda Síochána of the fact that that expiry or remission will occur in relation to the person.

10   Notification requirements

(1) A person who is subject to the requirements of this Part shall, before the end of the period of 7 days beginning with the relevant date, or, if that date is prior to the commencement of this Part, that commencement, notify to the Garda Síochána—

(a) his or her name and, where he or she also uses one or more other names, each of those names, and

(b) his or her home address.

(2) A person who is subject to those requirements shall also, before the end of the period of 7 days beginning with—

(a) the person's using a name which is not the name, or one of the names, last previously notified by him or her to the Garda Síochána under this section,

(b) any change of his or her home address,

(c) the person's having resided or stayed, for a qualifying period, at any place in the State, the address of which has not been notified to the Garda Síochána under this section as being his or her current home address, or

(d) the person's returning to an address in the State, having, immediately prior to such return, been outside the State for a continuous period of 7 days or more, notify that name, the effect of that change, the address of that place or, as the case may be, the fact of that return to the Garda Síochána.

(3) If a person who is subject to the requirements of this Part intends to leave the State for a continuous period of 7 days or more he or she shall notify the Garda Síochána of that intention and, if known, the address of the place outside the State he or she intends to reside or stay at.

(4) If a person who is subject to the requirements of this Part is outside the State for a continuous period of 7 days or more and did not intend, on leaving the State, to be outside the State for such a continuous period, the person shall, subject to subsection (5), notify the Garda Síochána, before the expiry of a further period of 7 days, reckoned from the 7th day that he or she is so outside the State, of that fact and the address of the place at which he or she is residing or staying outside the State.

(5) Subsection (4) shall not apply if the person concerned has returned to the State before the expiry of the further period of 7 days mentioned in that subsection.

(6) A notification given to the Garda Síochána by any person shall not be regarded as complying with subsection (1), (2), (3) or (4) unless it also states the person's—

(a) date of birth,

(b) name on the relevant date and, where he or she used one or more other names on that date, each of those names, and

(c) home address on the relevant date.

(7) For the purpose of determining any period for the purposes of subsection (1), (2), (3) or (4), there shall be disregarded any time when the person concerned is—

(a) remanded in custody,

(b) serving a sentence in prison, or

(c) temporarily released under section 2 or 3 of the Criminal Justice Act, 1960.

(8) A person may give a notification under this section—

(a) by attending in person at any Garda Síochána station which is a divisional or district headquarters and notifying orally a member of the Garda Síochána at the station of the matters concerned,

(b) by sending, by post, a written notification of the matters concerned to any Garda Síochána station which is such a headquarters, or

(c) by such other means as may be prescribed.

(9) Proof of the sending by post of such a notification shall, in any proceedings for an offence under section 12(1)(a), lie on the defendant.

(10) A notification under this section shall be acknowledged in writing and that acknowledgement shall be in such form as may be prescribed.

(11) In this section—

"home address", in relation to any person, means the address of his or her sole or main residence or, if he or she has no such residence, his or her most usual place of abode or, if he or she has no such abode, the place which he or she regularly visits;

"qualifying period" means—

(a) a period of 7 days, or

(b) 2 or more periods, in any period of 12 months, which (taken together) amount to 7 days.

11   Discharge from obligation to comply with requirements of this Part

(1) A person who, by reason of sections 7 and 8, is subject to the requirements of this Part for a period of an indefinite duration may apply to the court for an order discharging the person from the obligation to comply with those requirements on the ground that the interests of the common good are no longer served by his or her continuing to be subject to them.

(2) An application under this section shall not be made before the expiration of the period of 10 years from the date of the applicant's release from prison.

(3) The applicant shall, not later than the beginning of such period before the making of the application as may be prescribed, notify the superintendent of the Garda Síochána of the district in which he or she ordinarily resides or has his or her most usual place of abode of his or her intention to make an application under this section.

(4) That superintendent or any other member of the Garda Síochána shall be entitled to appear and be heard at the hearing of that application.

(5) On the hearing of an application under this section, the court shall, if satisfied that the interests of the common good would no longer be served by the applicant's continuing to be subject to the requirements of this Part, make an order discharging the applicant from the obligation to comply with those requirements.

(6) In considering an application under this section, the court may require to be adduced, in such form as it thinks appropriate, evidence (including expert evidence) with regard to whether or not the interests of the common good would any longer be served by the applicant's continuing to be subject to the requirements of this Part.

(7) If the court makes an order discharging the applicant from the obligation to comply with the requirements of this Part, the court shall cause the Garda Síochána to be notified, in writing, of that discharge.

(8) The jurisdiction of the court in respect of an application under this section may be exercised by the judge of the circuit where the applicant ordinarily resides or has his or her most usual place of abode.

(9) Proceedings under this section shall be heard otherwise than in public.

(10) In this section—

"applicant" means the person referred to in subsection (1);

"court" means the Circuit Court;

"date of the applicant's release from prison" means the date on which the applicant's sentence of imprisonment referred to in section 8(3) expires or, as the case may be, his or her remission from the sentence begins.

12   Offences in connection with notification requirements

(1) A person who—

    (a)   fails, without reasonable excuse, to comply with subsection (1), (2), (3) or (4) of section 10, or

    (b)   notifies to the Garda Síochána, in purported compliance with that subsection (1), (2), (3) or (4), any information which he or she knows to be false or misleading in any respect,

shall be guilty of an offence.

(2) A person is guilty of an offence under subsection (1)(a) on the day on which he or she first fails, without reasonable excuse, to comply with subsection (1), (2), (3) or (4), as the case may be, of section 10 and continues to be guilty of it throughout any period during which the failure continues; but a person shall not be prosecuted under that provision more than once in respect of the same failure.

[(3) A person guilty of an offence under this section shall be liable—

    (a)   on summary conviction, to a fine not exceeding €5,000, or imprisonment for a term not exceeding 12 months, or both, or

    (b)   on conviction on indictment to a fine not exceeding €10,000, or imprisonment for a term not exceeding 5 years, or both.][1]

(4) In proceedings for an offence under subsection (1)(a) a statement on oath by a member of the Garda Síochána referred to in subsection (5) that no notification of the matters concerned was given by the defendant to the Garda Síochána by any of the means referred to in section 10(8) shall, until the contrary is shown, be evidence that no such notification was given by the defendant.

(5) The member of the Garda Síochána referred to in subsection (4) is a member not below the rank of sergeant who, from his or her evidence to the court, the court is satisfied—

    (a)   is familiar with the systems operated by the Garda Síochána for recording the fact that particular information has been received by them, and

    (b)   has made all proper inquiries in ascertaining whether a notification by the defendant of the matters concerned was received by the Garda Síochána.

Amendments

1   Subsection (3) substituted by Criminal Law (Human Trafficking) Act 2008, s 13(b).

13   Application of this Part to persons convicted outside State.

(1) If—

   (a) a person has been convicted, in a place other than the State of an offence,

   (b) the act constituting the offence concerned would, if done in the State, constitute a sexual offence (within the meaning of this Act) under the law of the State, and either—

   (i) the person would, accordingly, be subject to the requirements of this Part by reason of subsection (1) or (2) of section 7, or

   (ii) at the commencement of this Part, the person, as a person who has been convicted of the first-mentioned offence in paragraph (a), is required, under the law of the first-mentioned place in that paragraph (however that requirement is described in that law), to notify to the police in that place information of a similar nature to that required to be notified by a person otherwise subject to the requirements of this Part,

   and

   (c) the person is, at the time of the conviction, or thereafter becomes, resident in the State,

that person shall be deemed to be subject to the requirements of this Part and this Part shall, subject to subsection (2), apply accordingly.

(2) For the purposes of such application, section 10 shall have effect as if for subsection (1) there was substituted the following subsection:

   "(1) A person who is subject to the requirements of this Part shall, before the end of the period of 7 days beginning with—

   (a) in case the person is already resident in the State upon his or her so first returning and paragraph (c) does not apply, the date on which the person first returns to the State after being convicted of the offence concerned,

   (b) in case the person is not so resident and paragraph (c) does not apply, the date on which the person first becomes resident in the State after being convicted of the offence concerned, or

   (c) in case the date on which the person so first returns to, or becomes resident in, the State is prior to the commencement of this Part, the commencement of this Part, notify to the Garda Síochána—

   (i) his or her name and, where he or she also uses one or more other names, each of those names, and

   (ii) his or her home address.".

(3) For the purposes of this section, a person shall be deemed to be resident in the State if he or she is ordinarily resident, or has his or her principal residence, in the State, or is in the State for a qualifying period.

(4) Where a person to whom this section applies is charged with an offence under section 12, he or she shall, whether or not he or she would be treated for the purposes of section 12 as having a reasonable excuse apart from this subsection, be treated for those purposes as having a reasonable excuse if he or she believed that the act constituting the offence referred to in subsection (1) would not, if done in the State, constitute any sexual offence (within the meaning of this Act) under the law of the State.

(5) For the purposes of subsection (4), it is immaterial whether a belief is justified or not if it is honestly held.

(6) In this section—

"police" means, in relation to the first-mentioned place in subsection (1), any police force in that place, or a member thereof, whether that force is organised at a national, regional or local level;

"qualifying period" has the same meaning as it has in section 10.

14   Certificate as evidence of persons being subject to requirements of this Part

(1) If the conviction, after the commencement of this Part, of a person for an offence gives rise to his or her becoming subject to the requirements of this Part, the court before which he or she is convicted of the offence shall forthwith, after the conviction, issue to each of the persons referred to in subsection (5) a certificate stating—

    (a)   that the person has been convicted of the offence,

    (b)   the sentence, if any, imposed on the person in respect of the offence, and

    (c)   that the person has become subject to the requirements of this Part.

(2) If a sentence is imposed on a person in respect of the offence referred to in subsection (1) after a certificate relating to that offence has been issued under that subsection, the court which imposed the sentence shall forthwith, after the imposition of the sentence, issue to each of the persons referred to in subsection (5) a certificate stating the sentence that has been imposed on the person.

(3) If—

    (a)   the conviction referred to in subsection (1) is quashed on appeal or otherwise, or

    (b)   the sentence imposed on foot of that conviction is varied on appeal or otherwise,

the court which quashes the conviction or varies the sentence shall forthwith, after the quashing of the conviction or the variation of the sentence, issue to each of the persons referred to in subsection (5) a certificate stating that the conviction has been quashed or stating the variation that has been made in the sentence.

(4) A certificate purporting to be issued under subsection (1), (2) or (3) shall, in any proceedings, be evidence of the matters stated in it without proof of the signature of the officer of the court purporting to sign it or that that person was authorised to sign it.

(5) The persons referred to in subsections (1), (2) and (3) are—

    (a)   the Garda Síochána,

    (b)   the person convicted of the offence concerned, and

    (c)   where appropriate, the person for the time being in charge of the place where the convicted person is ordered to be imprisoned or, as the case may be, the probation and welfare service (within the meaning of Part 5).

(6) The mode of proving a conviction or sentence authorised by subsection (4) shall be in addition to, and not in substitution for, any other authorised mode of proving such conviction or sentence.

(7) Rules of court may make provision in relation to the form of certificates under this section and the manner in which they may be issued.

PART 3

SEX OFFENDERS ORDERS

15   Definitions (Part 3)

In this Part, unless the context otherwise requires—

"applicant" means a member of the Garda Síochána not below the rank referred to in section 16 who has applied to the court for the making of a sex offender order and, in relation to such an order that is in force, means any member of the Garda Síochána;

"court" means the Circuit Court;

"respondent" means a person in respect of whom an application for a sex offender order has been made or in respect of whom such an order has been made;

"sex offender order" has the meaning assigned to it by section 16.

16   Sex offender orders

(1) If, on application to it in that behalf by a member of the Garda Síochána not below the rank of Chief Superintendent, it appears to the court, on evidence tendered by the applicant, that the conditions specified in subsection (2) are satisfied in respect of the respondent, the court may make an order (in this Act referred to as a "sex offender order") prohibiting the respondent from doing one or more things specified in the order.

(2) The conditions mentioned in subsection (1) are that—

    (a) the respondent has been convicted, before or after the commencement of this Part, either—

        (i) in the State of a sexual offence, or

        (ii) in a place outside the State of an offence and the act constituting that offence would, if done in the State, constitute a sexual offence (within the meaning of this Act) under the law of the State,

    and

    (b) the respondent has, at a time referred to in subsection (3), acted on one or more occasions in such a way as to give reasonable grounds for believing that an order under this section is necessary to protect the public from serious harm from him or her.

(3) The time mentioned in paragraph (b) of subsection (2) is any time subsequent to the date of the respondent's release from prison or, as the case may be, the date on which the sentence imposed on the respondent in respect of the offence referred to in that subsection otherwise ceases to be in force, being in either case a time after the commencement of this Part.

(4) A sex offender order shall contain only such prohibitions on the respondent's doing a thing or things as the court considers necessary for the purpose of protecting the public from serious harm from the respondent.

(5) References in this section to protecting the public from serious harm from the respondent shall be construed as references to protecting a member or members of the public from death or serious personal injury, whether physical or psychological, which would be occasioned if the respondent were to commit a sexual offence at a time subsequent to the making of the application under this section.

(6) A sex offender order shall continue in force until the expiration of—

    (a)   5 years from the date of notification of its making being given to the respondent, or

    (b)   such longer period as the court may provide for in the order.

(7) For so long as a sex offender order is in force, Part 2 shall have effect as if—

    (a)   the respondent were subject to the requirements of that Part, and

    (b)   "relevant date" (within the meaning of that Part) were the date on which notification of the making of the sex offender order has been given to the respondent.

(8) Subsection (7) shall not operate to prevent a respondent's remaining subject to the requirements of Part 2, on the date that the sex offender order concerned ceases to be in force, if, by reason of the operation of section 7 and 8 (including those sections as applied by section 13), he or she would remain so subject to those requirements.

(9) The reference in subsection (3) to the date of the respondent's release from prison is a reference to the date on which the sentence of imprisonment imposed on the respondent in respect of the offence referred to in subsection (2) (if such be the sentence imposed) expires or, as the case may be, the respondent's remission from the sentence begins.

17   Taking effect of sex offender order

(1) A sex offender order shall take effect on notification of its making being given to the respondent.

(2) Oral communication to the respondent by or on behalf of the applicant of the fact that a sex offender order has been made, together with production of a copy of the order, shall, without prejudice to the sufficiency of any other form of notification, be taken to be sufficient notification to the respondent of the making of the order.

(3) If the respondent is present at the sitting of the court at which the sex offender order is made, he or she shall be taken for the purposes of subsection (1) to have been notified of its making.

18   Effect of appeal from order

An appeal from a sex offender order shall, if the court that made the order or the court to which the appeal is brought so determines (but not otherwise), stay the operation of the order on such terms (if any) as may be imposed by the court making the determination.

19   Discharge or variation of sex offender order

(1) Where a sex offender order is in force, the court, on application to it in that behalf at any time by the respondent, may, if it is shown to the satisfaction of the court that—

    (a)   the protection of the public from serious harm from the respondent does not require that the order should continue in force, or

    (b)   the order's effect for the time being is the cause of injustice,

discharge or, as may be appropriate, vary the order.

(2) The court shall, on application to it in that behalf at any time by the applicant, discharge a sex offender order.

(3) The reference in subsection (1) to protecting the public from serious harm from the respondent shall be construed in accordance with section 16(5).

20   Court jurisdiction and venue

(1) The jurisdiction of the court in respect of civil proceedings under this Part may be exercised by the judge of the circuit where the respondent ordinarily resides or carries on any profession, business or occupation or by the judge of the circuit where the respondent is alleged to have acted in such a way as to give reasonable grounds for believing that the making of a sex offender order is or, as the case may be, was necessary.

(2) For the avoidance of doubt, subsection (1) applies in the case of section 19 notwithstanding that the sex offender order concerned was made by the High Court on appeal from a decision of the court refusing to make such an order.

21   Provisions in relation to evidence and proceedings under this Part.

(1) The standard of proof required to determine any question relating to the making, varying, or discharge of a sex offender order shall be that applicable to civil proceedings.

(2) Proceedings under this Part (other than under section 22) in relation to a sex offender order shall be heard otherwise than in public.

22   Offence in respect of contravention of sex offender order.

A respondent who, without reasonable excuse, contravenes a sex offender order shall be guilty of an offence and shall be liable—

    (a)   on summary conviction, to a fine not exceeding £1,500 or imprisonment for a term not exceeding 12 months or both, or

    (b)   on conviction on indictment, to a fine or imprisonment for a term not exceeding 5 years or both.

23   Rules of court

(1) For the purpose of ensuring the expeditious hearing of applications under this Part, rules of court may make provision for the service of documents otherwise than under section 7 of the Courts Act, 1964 (as amended by section 22 of the Courts Act, 1971), in circumstances to which that section 7 relates.

(2) Rules of court shall provide for the documentation required for the commencement of proceedings under this Part.

(3) This section is without prejudice to section 17 of the Interpretation Act, 1937, which provides for rules of court.

24   Amendment of Civil Legal Aid Act, 1995

Section 28 of the Civil Legal Aid Act, 1995, is hereby amended by the substitution of the following subsection for subsection (3):

    "(3) Where the proceedings the subject matter of the application under this section concern—

    (a)   the welfare of (including the custody of or access to) a child, or

    (b)   a sex offender order (within the meaning of the Sex Offenders Act, 2001), paragraphs (c) and (e) of subsection (2) shall not apply.".

PART 4
PROVISION OF INFORMATION FOR EMPLOYMENT PURPOSES

25   Interpretation (Part 4)

(1) In this Part—

"child" means a person who is less than 18 years of age;

"contract of employment" means—

(a)   a contract of service or apprenticeship, or

(b)   any other contract whereby an individual agrees with another person, who is carrying on the business of an employment agency within the meaning of the Employment Agency Act, 1971, and is acting in the course of that business, to do or perform personally any work or service for a third person (whether or not the third person is a party to the contract),

whether the contract is express or implied and if express, whether it is oral or in writing;

"mentally impaired" has the meaning assigned to it by section 5 of the Act of 1993;

"State work or a service" means work done or a service performed by a person who—

(a)   holds office under, or is otherwise in the service of the State (including as a civil servant, within the meaning of the Civil Service Regulation Act, 1956),

(b)   is a member of the Garda Síochána or the Defence Forces,

(c)   is an officer or servant of a local authority for the purposes of the Local Government Act, 1941, or

(d)   is an officer or servant of a harbour authority or vocational education committee, or

(e)   is an employee of the Health Service Executive.][1]

(2) In this Part a reference to a person applying to another person includes a reference to the person applying to another person without that other's having requested or solicited the making of the application.

Amendments

1   Paragraph (d) substituted and para (e) inserted by Health Act 2004, s 75 and Sch 6.

---

26   Failure to inform employer, etc., of sexual offence conviction

(1) In this section "relevant work" means work or a service (including State work or a service) a necessary and regular part of which consists, mainly, of the person referred to in subsection (3), (5) or (6) having unsupervised access to, or contact with, a child or children or a mentally impaired person or persons.

(2) A person referred to in subsection (3) shall be guilty of an offence if he or she—

(a)   applies to another person to be employed by that person to do relevant work,

(b)   enters into a contract of employment to do relevant work,

(c) applies to another person to do relevant work on that other person's behalf (whether in return for payment or for any other consideration or not), or

(d) enters into a contract for services to do relevant work, without, during the course of the application or before entering into the contract, informing the other person or the other party to the contract of the fact that he or she has been convicted of the offence referred to in subsection (3).

(3) The person mentioned in subsection (2) is a person who has been convicted, before or after the commencement of this Part, either—

(a) in the State of a sexual offence, or

(b) in a place outside the State of an offence and the act constituting that offence would, if done in the State, constitute a sexual offence (within the meaning of this Act) under the law of the State.

(4) In proceedings for an offence under subsection (2) it shall be a defence for the accused to prove that he or she neither knew nor could reasonably be expected to have known that the work to which the application or contract referred to in subsection (2) related was relevant work (within the meaning of this section).

(5) A person convicted, before or after the commencement of this Part, of an offence referred to in subsection (3) who—

(a) does a thing referred to in any of paragraphs (a) to (d) of subsection (2) (and, in the case of paragraph (a) or (c) of that subsection, commences to do the work concerned), and

(b) at the time he or she does such a thing, neither knows nor can reasonably be expected to know that the work concerned is relevant work (within the meaning of this section),

shall inform the other person or the other party to the contract referred to in subsection (2) of the fact that he or she has been convicted of that offence as soon as may be after he or she becomes aware of the fact that the work concerned is relevant work.

(6) A person who—

(a) does a thing referred to in any of paragraphs (a) to (d) of subsection (2) (and, in the case of paragraph (a) or (c) of that subsection, commences to do the work concerned), and

(b) is subsequently convicted of an offence referred to in subsection (3),

shall, unless, at the time of the conviction, the work he or she has applied to do is wholly completed or the contract he or she has entered into has expired or ceased to be in force, inform the person on whose behalf the work is being done or the other party to the contract, as soon as may be after the conviction, of the fact that he or she has been so convicted.

(7) A person who fails to comply with subsection (5) or (6) shall be guilty of an offence.

(8) A person guilty of an offence under subsection (2) or (7) shall be liable—

(a) on summary conviction, to a fine not exceeding £1,500 or imprisonment for a term not exceeding 12 months or both, or

(b) on conviction on indictment, to a fine not exceeding £10,000 or imprisonment for a term not exceeding 5 years or both.

PART 5

POST-RELEASE SUPERVISION FOR SEX OFFENDERS

27   Interpretation (Part 5)

(1) In this Part—

"probation and welfare officer" means a person appointed by the Minister to be a probation and welfare officer or to be a welfare officer or probation officer;

"probation and welfare service" means the probation and welfare service of the Department of Justice, Equality and Law Reform;

"sentence involving post-release supervision" shall be construed in accordance with section 29(1);

"sex offender" means a person who, after the commencement of this Part, is convicted of a sexual offence for which, in the opinion of the court before which the person appears, the appropriate sentence is, apart from the provisions of this Part, one of imprisonment for any term (whether in addition to the imposition of a fine or not);

"supervision period" shall be construed in accordance with section 29(1);

"supervision period conditions" means the conditions referred to in section 29(1)(b) or 30 that relate to the sex offender concerned.

(2) References in this Part to protecting the public from serious harm from a sex offender shall be construed as references to protecting a member or members of the public from death or serious personal injury, whether physical or psychological, which would be occasioned if the offender were to commit a sexual offence after he or she has been released into the community.

28   Duty of court to consider imposition of sentence involving post-release supervision

(1) In determining the sentence to be imposed on a sex offender in respect of the sexual offence concerned, the court shall consider whether to impose a sentence involving post-release supervision.

(2) In considering that matter, the court shall have regard to—

    (a) the need for a period, after the offender has been released into the community, during which his or her conduct is supervised by a responsible person,

    (b) the need to protect the public from serious harm from the offender,

    (c) the need to prevent the commission by the offender of further sexual offences, and

    (d) the need to rehabilitate or further rehabilitate the offender.

(3) For the purposes of this section, the court may, if it thinks it necessary to do so, receive evidence or submissions from any person concerned.

29   Power of court to impose sentence involving post-release supervision

(1) A court may impose on a sex offender in respect of the sexual offence concerned a sentence involving post-release supervision, that is to say a sentence which consists of—

    (a) the imposition of a sentence of imprisonment for a specified term (whether in addition to the imposition of a fine or not), and

    (b) a provision that during a specified period ("the supervision period") commencing on the date of the offender's release from prison, the offender shall be under the supervision of a probation and welfare officer and requiring the offender to comply with such conditions as are specified in the sentence for securing that supervision.

(2) The aggregate of the sentence of imprisonment referred to in subsection (1)(a) and the supervision period shall not exceed the duration of the maximum term of imprisonment that may be imposed in respect of the sexual offence concerned.

(3) The term of the sentence of imprisonment referred to in subsection (1)(a) shall not be less than the term the court would have imposed if it had considered the matter apart from the provisions of this Part.

(4) In determining the period to be specified as the supervision period, the matters to which the court shall have regard shall include the matters referred to in paragraphs (a) to (d) of section 28(2).

(5) The reference in this section to the date of the offender's release from prison is a reference to the date on which the offender's sentence of imprisonment referred to in subsection (1)(a) expires or, as the case may be, the offender's remission from the sentence begins.

30   Additional provisions which may be included in sentence involving post-release supervision

(1) In addition to the conditions referred to in section 29(1)(b), a sentence involving post-release supervision may include such conditions as the court considers appropriate for the purposes of paragraphs (a) to (d) of section 28(2) and having regard to the needs of the sex offender.

(2) Without prejudice to the generality of subsection (1), there may be included in a sentence involving post-release supervision—

    (a) a condition prohibiting the sex offender from doing such one or more things as the court considers necessary for the purpose of protecting the public from serious harm from the offender, and

    (b) a condition requiring the sex offender to receive psychological counselling or other appropriate treatment provided by the probation and welfare service or any other body which it appears to the court, having regard to any submissions made to it on behalf of the probation and welfare service, is an appropriate body to provide such counselling or treatment.

(3) A condition referred to in subsection (1) or (2) shall have effect during the whole or a specified part of the supervision period as the court considers appropriate and specifies in the sentence concerned.

31   Duty of court to explain effect of sentence to offender

In imposing a sentence involving post-release supervision on a sex offender, the court shall explain to him or her—

    (a) the effect of the sentence,

    (b) the consequences provided for under section 33 if he or she fails to comply with any of the supervision period conditions, and

    (c) that under this Act the court may vary or discharge any of those conditions on the application of either the offender or a probation and welfare officer.

32 Discharge or variation of requirements relating to supervision period

At any time after the supervision period has commenced the court may, on the application of—

(a) the offender on whom the sentence involving post-release supervision concerned was imposed, or

(b) a probation and welfare officer,

discharge all of the supervision period conditions (and the supervision period shall lapse accordingly) or vary or discharge one or more of those conditions if, having regard to the circumstances which have arisen since the sentence was imposed, it considers—

(i) it would be in the interests of justice to do so, and

(ii) the protection of the public from serious harm from the offender no longer requires that those conditions should continue in force or, as appropriate, that they should continue in force in the form in which they stand at the date of the making of the application.

33 Non-compliance with requirements relating to supervision period

(1) A sex offender who fails, without reasonable excuse, to comply with any of the supervision period conditions shall be guilty of an offence and shall be liable on summary conviction to a fine not exceeding £1,500 or imprisonment for a term not exceeding 12 months or both.

(2) Subject to subsection (3), the conviction of a sex offender for an offence under this section shall not prevent the supervision period conditions from continuing to have effect.

(3) If a sentence of imprisonment is imposed on a sex offender for an offence under this section, that sentence shall, for the period the offender spends in prison on foot of that sentence, operate to suspend the supervision period conditions and the period for which those conditions are so suspended shall not be reckoned in calculating the date on which the supervision period expires.

[(4) Proceedings for an offence under subsection (1) may be brought and prosecuted by a probation and welfare officer.][1]

Amendments

1   Subsection (4) inserted by Criminal Law (Human Trafficking) Act 2008, s 13(c).

PART 6
MISCELLANEOUS

34 Amendment of Criminal Law (Rape) Act, 1981

The Criminal Law (Rape) Act, 1981, is hereby amended by the insertion after section 4 of the following section:[1]

Amendments

1   See the amended Act.

---

35   Further amendments of Civil Legal Aid Act, 1995

(1) In this section "the Act of 1995" means the Civil Legal Aid Act, 1995.

(2) In addition to the meaning assigned to that expression by section 27 of the Act of 1995, "legal aid" in the Act of 1995 means representation by a solicitor or barrister, engaged by the Legal Aid Board under section 11 of that Act, on behalf of a complainant in relation to an application referred to in section 4A of the Criminal Law (Rape) Act, 1981, that concerns the complainant.

(3) Section 28 of the Act of 1995 is hereby amended by the insertion of the following subsection after subsection (5):

> "(5A) Notwithstanding any other provision of this Act, the Board shall grant a legal aid certificate to a complainant for the purpose of his or her being represented in relation to an application referred to in section 4A of the Criminal Law (Rape) Act, 1981, that concerns him or her.".

36   Proof of foreign conviction in certain cases

(1) In proceedings against a person for an offence under—

(a)   section 12 (where the person is a person referred to in section 13(1)), or

(b)   section 26 (where the person is a person referred to in subsection (2), (5) or (6) of that section and falls within subsection (3)(b) of that section),

the production to the court of a document that satisfies the condition referred to in subsection (2) and which purports to contain either or both—

(i)   particulars of the conviction in a state, other than the State, of that person for an offence and of the act constituting the offence,

(ii)   a statement that, on a specified date, that person was subject to the first-mentioned requirement in section 13(1)(b)(ii),

shall, without further proof, be evidence, until the contrary is shown, of the matters stated in it.

(2) The condition mentioned in subsection (1) is that the document concerned purports to be signed or certified by a judge, magistrate or officer of the state referred to in that subsection and to be authenticated by the oath of some witness or by being sealed with the official seal of a minister of state of that state (judicial notice of which shall be taken by the court).

(3) That condition shall be regarded as being satisfied without proof of the signature or certification, and the authentication of it, that appears in or on the document.

37   Amendment of section 2 of Act of 1990

(1) Section 2 of the Act of 1990 is amended by the substitution of the following subsection for subsection (2):

"(2)(a) A person guilty of sexual assault shall be liable on conviction on indictment—

    (i)   in case the person on whom the assault was committed was a child, to imprisonment for a term not exceeding 14 years, and

    (ii) in any other case, to imprisonment for a term not exceeding 10 years.

   (b) In this subsection 'child' means a person under 17 years of age.

(2) The amendment effected by subsection (1) shall apply to sexual assaults committed after the commencement of this section.

SCHEDULE
SEXUAL OFFENCES FOR PURPOSES OF ACT

Section 3

1.   Rape.

2.   Sexual assault (whether the offence of which the person was convicted was known by that name or by the name "Indecent assault upon a female person" or "Indecent assault upon a male person").

3.   Aggravated sexual assault (within the meaning of section 3 of the Act of 1990).

4.   Rape under section 4 of the Act of 1990.

5.   An offence under section 1 of the Act of 1908 (incest by males).

6.   An offence under section 2 of the Act of 1908 (incest by females of or over 17 years of age).

[7.   An offence under the Criminal Law (Sexual Offences) Act 2006.][1]

8.   ....[2]

9.   The offence of buggery with a person or with an animal referred to in section 61 of the Act of 1861.

10.   The offence of an attempt to commit such buggery referred to in section 62 of the Act of 1861.

11.   An offence under section 3 of the Act of 1993 (buggery of persons under 17 years of age).

12   An offence under section 4 of the Act of 1993 (gross indecency with males under 17 years of age).

13.   An offence under section 11 of the Criminal Law Amendment Act, 1885 (acts of gross indecency).

14.   An offence under section 5 of the Act of 1993 (protection of mentally impaired persons).

15.   An offence under section 4 of the Act of 1935 (defilement of mentally impaired females).

16.   An offence under any of the following provisions of the Child Trafficking and Pornography Act, 1998 —

    (a) section 3 (child trafficking and taking, etc., child for sexual exploitation),

    (b) section 4 (allowing child to be used for child pornography),

    (c) section 5 (producing, distributing, etc., child pornography),

(d)   section 6 (possession of child pornography).

[16A. An offence under the Criminal Law (Human Trafficking) Act 2008 in so far as the offence is committed for the purposes of the sexual exploitation of a person.]³

17.   An offence under section 2 of the Sexual Offences (Jurisdiction) Act, 1996 (sexual offences committed outside the State).

18.   An offence consisting of attempting to commit an offence referred to in any of paragraphs 1 to 17 of this Schedule (other than such an offence that itself consists of an attempt to do a particular act).

19.   An offence consisting of aiding, abetting, counselling, procuring or inciting the commission of an offence referred to in any of paragraphs 1 to 18 of this Schedule.

20.   An offence consisting of conspiracy to commit an offence referred to in any foregoing paragraph of this Schedule.

[21.   An offence under section 6 (inserted by section 2 of the Criminal Law (Sexual Offences) (Amendment) Act 2007) of the Criminal Law (Sexual Offences) Act 1993.]⁴

Amendments

1   Paragraph 7 substituted by Criminal Law (Sexual Offences) Act 2006, s 7(5)(a).

2   Paragraph 8 deleted by Criminal Law (Sexual Offences) Act 2006, s 7(5)(b).

3   Paragraph 16A inserted by Criminal Law (Human Trafficking) Act 2008, s 13(d).

4   Paragraph 21 inserted by Criminal Law (Sexual Offences) (Amendment) Act 2007, s 4(4).

Children Act 2001

Number 24 of 2001

ARRANGEMENT OF SECTIONS

PART 1
PRELIMINARY

Section

1. Short title and collective citation.
2. Commencement.
3. Interpretation (general).
4. Laying of regulations before Houses of Oireachtas.
5. Repeals.
6. Expenses.

PART 2
FAMILY WELFARE CONFERENCES

7. Convening of family welfare conference.
8. Functions of conference.
9. Persons entitled to attend conference.
10. Procedure at conference.
11. Administrative services.
12. Notification of recommendations of conference.
13. Action by health board on recommendations.
14. Privilege.
15. Regulations.
15A Transitional provisions relating to Health Act 2004.

PART 3
AMENDMENT OF ACT OF 1991

16. Amendment (new Parts IVA and IVB) of Act of 1991.

PART 4
DIVERSION PROGRAMME

INTRODUCTORY

17. Interpretation (Part 4).
18. Principle.
19. Objective of Programme.
20. Diversion Programme.
21. Temporary incapacity of Director.

ADMISSION TO PROGRAMME

22. Report on child to Director.
23. Admission to Programme.
24. Decision to admit to Programme.

ADMINISTRATION OF CAUTIONS

25. Cautions.
26. Presence of victim at formal caution.

SUPERVISION OF CHILDREN ADMITTED TO PROGRAMME

27. Supervision.
28. Level of supervision.

HOLDING OF CONFERENCE IN RESPECT OF CHILD

29. "Conference".
30. Recommendation that conference be held.
31. Decision on holding conference.
32. Persons entitled to attend conference.
33. Location of conference.
34. Time limit for holding conference.
35. Notification to participants.
36. Views of those unable or unwilling to attend conference.
37. Procedure at conference.
38. Period or level of supervision.
39. Action plan.
40. Disagreement on action plan.
41. Report to Director.
42. Decision by Director on period or level of supervision.
43. Administrative services.

COMMITTEE TO MONITOR EFFECTIVENESS OF PROGRAMME

44. Review of effectiveness of Programme.
45. Vacancies in committee.

OTHER MATTERS RELATING TO THE PROGRAMME

46. Supplemental provisions.
47. Regulations (Part 4).
48. Inadmissibility of certain evidence.
49. Bar to proceedings.
50. Privilege.
51. Protection of identity of children.

PART 5
RESTRICTION ON CRIMINAL PROCEEDINGS AGAINST CERTAIN CHILDREN

52. Restriction on criminal proceedings against children
53. Duty of Garda Síochána in relation to certain under-age children.
54. Aiding, etc., under-age child to commit offence.

PART 6
TREATMENT OF CHILD SUSPECTS IN GARDA SÍOCHÁNA STATIONS

55. Treatment of child suspects.
56. Separation of children from adults in Garda Síochána station.
57. Notification to child.
58. Notification of arrest of child to parent or guardian.
59. Notification to [Health Executive Service].
60. Notification to solicitor.
61. Interviewing children.
62. Notification of proceedings to parent or guardian.
63. Notification of proceedings to adult relative or other adult.
64. Procedure by summons.
65. Notice to adult relative or other adult where proceeding by summons.
66. Provisions common to sections 56 to 63 and 65.
67. Amendment of section 5 of the Criminal Justice Act, 1984.
68. Release on bail by member of Garda Síochána.
69. Application of certain provisions to married child.
70. Regulations (Part 6).

PART 7
CHILDREN COURT

71. Children Court.
72. Requirement for transacting business in Children Court.
73. Arrangements for hearing of proceedings in Children Court.
74. Children charged with summary offences jointly with adults.
75. Jurisdiction to deal summarily with indictable offences.
76. Children charged with indictable offences jointly with adults.

PART 8
PROCEEDINGS IN COURT

76A. Powers of Court in criminal proceedings against child.
76B Assistance to Court by Health Service Executive.
76C Dismissal of case against child under 14 in certain circumstances.
77. Referral of case to health board.

78.   Family conference.

79.   Convening of family conference.

80.   Action plan.

81.   Report to Court by probation and welfare officer.

82.   Action by Court on report of probation and welfare officer.

83.   Failure to comply with action plan.

84.   Review of compliance with action plan.

85.   Application of provisions.

86.   Procedure at family conference.

87.   Administrative services to family conference.

88.   Remand in custody.

89.   Non-application of section 5 of Bail Act, 1997.

90.   Conditions of bail.

91.   Attendance at Court of parents or guardian.

92.   Conveyance to and from Court.

93.   Restrictions on reports of proceedings in which children are concerned.

94.   Persons entitled to be present at hearing.

PART 9
POWERS OF COURTS IN RELATION TO CHILD OFFENDERS

GENERAL

95.   Interpretation (Part 9).

96.   Principles relating to exercise of criminal jurisdiction over children.

97.   Construction of certain references.

98.   Orders on finding of guilt.

PROBATION OFFICER'S REPORTS

99.   Probation officer's report.

100. Remand for preparation of report or other reason.

101. Availability of child for preparation of report.

102. Immunity from liability for reports.

103. Access to reports.

104. Right to tender evidence on report.

105. Oral reports.

106. Power of court on receipt of report.

107. Regulations regarding reports.

FINES, COSTS AND COMPENSATION

108. Maximum fines.

109. Determination of amount of fine and costs.

110. Default in payment of fine, costs or compensation.

ORDERS IN RELATION TO PARENTS OR GUARDIAN

111. Parental supervision order.
112. Non-compliance with parental supervision order.
113. Compensation by parent or guardian.
114. Binding over of parent or guardian.

COMMUNITY SANCTIONS

115. Community sanction.
116. Imposition of community sanction.
117. Conditions to which community sanction may be made subject.
118. Day centres.
119. Power to vary day centre order.
120. Power to revoke day centre order.
121. Provisions where more than one day centre order.
122. Non-compliance with day centre order.
123. Duties of child under day centre order.
124. Probation (training or activities programme) order.
125. Probation (intensive supervision) order.
126. Probation (residential supervision) order.
127. Power to vary probation (residential supervision) order.
128. Failure to observe conditions of probation.
129. Suitable person (care and supervision) order.
130. Non-compliance with suitable person (care and supervision) order.
131. Mentor (family support) order.
132. Non-compliance with mentor (family support) order.
133. Restriction on movement order.
134. Variation of restriction on movement order.
135. Provisions regarding more than one restriction on movement order.
136. Non-compliance with restriction on movement order.
137. Dual order.
138. Expiry of community sanction.
139. Commission of offence while community sanction in force.
140. Effect of subsequent period of detention.
141. Regulations.

DETENTION

142. Detention orders.
143. Restriction on detention orders.

144. Deferment of detention order.

145. Alternative to detention where no place available in children detention school.

146. Finding of guilt during deferment.

147. Detention in accordance with age of child.

148. Document to be produced to Director of children detention school.

149. Period of detention in children detention school.

150. Places of detention.

151. Detention and supervision.

152. Transfer.

153. Rules governing places of detention.

154. Amendment of Criminal Justice (Community Service) Act, 1983.

155. Punishment of certain indictable offences.

156. Restriction on punishment of children.

156A Transitional provision.

156B Application of Prisons Acts, etc. rules to children detention schools.

PART 10
CHILDREN DETENTION SCHOOLS

GENERAL

157. Interpretation (Part 10).

158. Principal object of children detention schools.

159. Certified schools under Act of 1908.

159A Education of children in children detention school, residential centres, etc.

159B Transfer of property, rights and liabilities of certified industrial school on commencement of section 159(2).

160. Designation of children detention schools.

161. Provision of other places for detention of children.

162. Funding of such places.

163. Closure of schools.

BOARDS OF MANAGEMENT

164. Boards of management.

165. Functions of boards of management.

166. Additional functions.

167. Membership, etc., of boards of management.

168. Removal and resignation of members.

169. Casual vacancies.

170. Temporary substitutes.

171. Remuneration of members.

172. Funding of Board.

173. Accounts and audits.

174. Annual report and information.

175. Meetings and procedure.

176. Directions by Minister.

177. Membership of either House of Oireachtas or of European Parliament.

178. Non-disclosure of information.

179. Rules by boards of management.

DIRECTOR AND STAFF OF SCHOOLS

180. The Director.

181. Staff of children detention schools.

182. Transfer of staff.

183. Terms and conditions of transferred staff.

184. Superannuation of staff.

INSPECTION OF SCHOOLS

185. Inspector of children detention schools.

186. Functions of Inspector.

186A Investigation of matters arising in relation to children detention schools, etc.

187. Powers of Inspector.

188. Reports of inspections and investigations.

189. Annual report of Inspector.

190. Visiting panel.

191. Duties and powers of visiting panels.

192. Visits by judges.

OPERATION OF SCHOOLS

193. Obligation of Director to accept children.

194. Reception of children in schools.

195. Maximum number of detained children.

196. Sex and age of detained children.

197. Treatment of children.

198. Transfer between schools and places provided under section 161.

199. Provision as to religious observance.

200. Provision of medical treatment.

201. Discipline.

202. Permitted absence.

203. Other permitted absences.

204. Mobility trips.

205. Temporary leave.

206. Conditions of grant of temporary leave.

207. Supervision in community.

208. Voluntary aftercare.

209. Unconditional release.

210. Early discharge.

211. Order for production of child.

212. Responsible persons.

213. Duty to notify changes of address to school.

214. Lawful custody of detained children.

OFFENCES

215. Escape.

216. Helping child to escape.

217. Harbouring escaped child.

218. Unlawful entry or communication.

219. Bringing alcohol, etc., into schools.

OTHER MATTERS

220. Delegation of certain functions by Minister.

221. Regulations.

222. Pending proceedings.

223. Saving for certain acts.

224. Transitional provisions.

PART 11
SPECIAL RESIDENTIAL SERVICES BOARD

225. Interpretation (Part 11).

226. Special Residential Services Board.

226A Change of name of Board.

227. Functions of Board.

228. Assignment of other functions.

229. Policy directions.

230. Membership, etc., of Board.

231. Removal and resignation of members.

232. Temporary substitutes.

233. Casual vacancies.

234. Remuneration of members.

235. Application to Board of sections 175, 177 and 178.

236. Seal.

237. Chief Executive of Board.

238. Staff of Board.

239. Superannuation of staff.

240. Funding of Board.

241. Accounts and audits of Board.

242. Annual report and information.

243. Delegation of functions.

244. Regulations.

PART 12
PROTECTION OF CHILDREN

245. Interpretation (Part 12).

246. Cruelty to children.

247. Begging.

248. Allowing child to be in brothel.

249. Causing or encouraging sexual offence upon child.

250. Amendment of Criminal Law (Sexual Offences) Act, 1993.

251. Power to proceed in absence of child.

252. Anonymity of child in court proceedings.

253. Mode of charging offences.

254. Powers of arrest without warrant, etc.

255. Power to take deposition of child.

256. Presumption and determination of age of child victim.

257. Clearing of court in certain cases.

PART 13
MISCELLANEOUS

258. Non-disclosure of certain findings of guilt.

259. Duties of probation officers.

260. Interference with supervisor.

261. Powers of Garda Síochána.

262. Delegation by principal probation and welfare officer.

263. Temporary accommodation of children.

264. Research.

265. Right of appeal.

266. Amendment of section 5 of Criminal Law (Rape) Act, 1981.

267. Amendment of sections 17(2) and 59 of Act of 1991.

268. Children in care of health board.

269. Presumption and determination of age.

270. Safety of children at entertainments.

271. Exclusion of members of Defence Forces.

SCHEDULE 1
OFFENCES AGAINST CHILDREN

SCHEDULE 2
ENACTMENTS REPEALED

An Act to make further provision in relation to the care, protection and control of children and, in particular, to replace the Children Act, 1908, and other enactments relating to juvenile offenders, to amend and extend the Child Care Act, 1991, and to provide for related matters. [8th July, 2001]

Be it enacted by the Oireachtas as follows:

PART 1
PRELIMINARY

1   Short title and collective citation

(1) This Act may be cited as the Children Act, 2001.

(2) Part 2, section 267 and the Child Care Act, 1991, may be cited together as the Child Care Acts, 1991 and 2001.

2   Commencement

(1) This Act shall, subject to subsection (2), come into operation on such day or days as, by order or orders made by the Minister under this section, may be fixed either generally or with reference to any particular purpose or provision, and different days may be so fixed for different purposes and different provisions.

(2) (a) Parts 2 and 3 shall come into operation on such day or days as, by order or orders made by the Minister for Health and Children, may be fixed generally in relation to either or both of these Parts or with reference to any particular purpose or provision thereof, and different days may be so fixed for different purposes and different such provisions.

  [(aa) Part 5 shall come into operation 3 months after the passing of the Criminal Justice Act 2006.]¹

  (b) Section 77 shall come into operation on such day as the Minister, with the agreement of the Minister for Health and Children, may by order appoint.

  (c) [...]²

  (d) Part 10 shall come into operation on such day or days as, by order or orders made by the Minister [...]³, may be fixed either generally or with reference to any particular purpose or provision, and different days may be so fixed for different purposes and different provisions.

  (e) Part 11 shall come into operation on such day as the Minister for Health and Children, with the agreement of the Minister for Education and Science, may by order appoint.

[(f) The amendments made to Part 11 in sections 156 and 157 of, and paragraph 30 of Schedule 4 to, the Criminal Justice Act 2006 shall come into operation on such day or days as the Minister for Health and Children, with the agreement of the Minister for Justice, Equality and Law Reform, may by order or orders appoint.][4]

Amendments

1 Paragraph (aa) inserted by Criminal Justice Act 2006, s 121(a).

2 Paragraph (c) deleted by Criminal Justice Act 2006, s 121(b).

3 Words deleted by Criminal Justice Act 2006, s 121(c).

4 Paragraph (f) inserted by Criminal Justice Act 2006, s 121(d).

3   Interpretation (general)

(1) In this Act, unless the context otherwise requires—

"Act of 1907" means the Probation of Offenders Act, 1907;

"Act of 1951" means the Criminal Justice Act, 1951;

"Act of 1967" means the Criminal Procedure Act, 1967;

"Act of 1984" means the Criminal Justice Act, 1984;

"Act of 1991" means the Child Care Act, 1991;

"action plan", where it occurs in Part 4, has the meaning assigned to it by section 39 and, where it occurs in Part 8, has the meaning assigned to it by section 80(1) or 82(2)(a), as the case may be;

"adult" means any person of or over the age of 18 years;

[...][1]

["anti-social behaviour" is to be construed in accordance with section 257A(2)][2];

"child" means a person under the age of 18 years;

"children detention order" has the meaning assigned to it by section 142;

"children detention school" means—

    (a) any certified reformatory school or industrial school that becomes a children detention school by virtue of section 159, or

    (b) any place, school, premises or building designated by the Minister [...][2] pursuant to section 160 as a children detention school;

"Commissioner" means the Commissioner of the Garda Síochána;

"community sanction" has the meaning assigned to it by section 115;

"Court", in Parts 7 and 8, means the Children Court;

"criminal behaviour", in relation to a child, means the act or omission constituting an offence alleged to have been committed by the child;

"detention" means detention in a children detention school [....][2];

"family conference" means a conference convened by a probation and welfare officer pursuant to section 79;

"family welfare conference" means a conference convened by [the Health Service Executive] pursuant to section 7;

"Gaeltacht area" means an area for the time being determined to be a Gaeltacht area by order under section 2 of the Ministers and Secretaries (Amendment) Act, 1956;

"guardian" means—

(a) any legal guardian of a child,

(b) any person who, in the opinion of the court having cognisance of any case in relation to a child or in which the child is concerned, has for the time being the charge of or control over the child, or

(c) any person who has custody or care of a child by order of a court, but does not include [the Health Service Executive][1];

[...];[2]

"juvenile liaison officer" means a member of the Garda Síochána assigned by the Commissioner to perform the duties which he or she considers appropriate for such a member, including duties assigned under Part 4 or any regulations under that Part;

"legal guardian", in relation to a child, means any person who is the guardian of a child pursuant to the Guardianship of Infants Act, 1964, or who is appointed to be his or her guardian by deed or will or by order of a court;

"member in charge" means a member of the Garda Síochána who is in charge of a Garda Síochána station at a time when the member in charge of a station is required to do anything or cause anything to be done pursuant to this Act;

"Minister", when used without qualification, means, except in Parts 3 [....][2] and 11, the Minister for Justice, Equality and Law Reform;

"parents", in relation to a child, means—

(a) in case one parent has the sole custody, charge or care of the child, that parent,

(b) in case the child has been adopted under the Adoption Acts, 1952 to 1998 (or, if adopted outside the State, his or her adoption is recognised under the law of the State), the adopter or adopters or the surviving adopter, and

(c) in any other case, both parents;

"prescribed" means prescribed by regulations made by the Minister or the Minister for Health and Children, as appropriate;

"principal probation and welfare officer" means the principal probation and welfare officer of the probation and welfare service;

"probation and welfare officer" means a person appointed by the Minister to be a probation and welfare officer, or to be a welfare officer or probation officer;

"probation and welfare service" means the probation and welfare service of the Department of Justice, Equality and Law Reform;

"relative", in relation to a child, means a brother, sister, uncle or aunt, or a spouse of the brother, sister, uncle or aunt, or a grandparent or step-parent, of the child;

"remand centre" means a centre designated as such under section 88;

"Saint Patrick's Institution" has the same meaning as in the Criminal Justice Act, 1960;

"school" means a children detention school;

"summons" has the meaning assigned to it by section 1(1) of the Courts (No. 3) Act, 1986;

"superannuation benefits" means pensions, gratuities and other allowances payable on resignation, retirement or death;

"victim" means a person who through or by means of an offence committed by a child, suffers physical or emotional harm, or loss of or damage to property [and, in relation to anti-social behaviour by a child, means a person who suffers physical or emotional harm as a consequence of that behaviour]².

(2) Any reference in this Act to a finding of guilt, or cognate words, includes a conviction, where the context so requires.

(3) For the purposes of this Act—

(a) a reference to a Part, section or Schedule is to a Part, section or Schedule of this Act unless it is indicated that reference to some other provision is intended,

(b) a reference to a subsection, paragraph or subparagraph is to the subsection, paragraph or subparagraph of the provision in which the reference occurs, unless it is indicated that reference to some other provision is intended,

(c) a reference to any other enactment shall, unless the context otherwise requires, be construed as a reference to that enactment as amended or extended by or under any other enactment, including this Act.

Amendments

1   Words amended and defintion of "area" deleted by Health Act 2004, s 75 and Sch 7.

2   Definitions inserted by Criminal Justice Act 2006, s 122.

4   Laying of regulations before Houses of Oireachtas

Every regulation made by the Minister, [....]¹ or the Minister for Health and Children under this Act shall be laid before each House of the Oireachtas as soon as may be after it is made and, if a resolution annulling the regulation is passed by either such House within the next 21 days on which the House has sat after the regulation is laid before it, the regulation shall be annulled accordingly, but without prejudice to the validity of anything previously done thereunder.

Amendments

1   Words deleted by Criminal Justice Act 2006, s 158 and Sch 4.

5   Repeals

(1) The enactments specified in Schedule 2 are repealed to the extent specified in column (3) of that Schedule; but the repeal shall not affect any notice or certificate given or any appointment or rules made under any of the repealed enactments and every such notice, certificate, appointment and rules shall have effect as if given or made under this Act.

(2) Every order, regulation and rule made under any provision of an enactment repealed by this Act and in force immediately before such repeal shall continue in force under the corresponding provision, if any, of this Act, subject to such adaptations and modifications as the Minister, [...]¹ or the Minister for Health and Children may by regulations make for the purpose of bringing any such order, regulation or rule into conformity with this Act.

Amendments

1   Words deleted by Criminal Justice Act 2006, s 158 and Sch 4.

6   Expenses

Any expenses incurred by the Minister, [...]¹ or the Minister for Health and Children in the administration of this Act shall, to such extent as may be sanctioned by the Minister for Finance, be paid out of moneys provided by the Oireachtas.

Amendments

1   Words deleted by Criminal Justice Act 2006, s 158 and Sch 4.

PART 2
FAMILY WELFARE CONFERENCES

7   Convening of family welfare conference

(1) Where—

   (a)   [The Health Service Executive]¹ receives a direction from the Children Court under section 77 to convene a family welfare conference in respect of a child, or

   (b)   it appears to [the Health Service Executive that a child may require]¹ special care or protection which the child is unlikely to receive unless a court makes an order in respect of him or her under Part IVA (inserted by this Act) of the Act of 1991,

[the Health Service Executive]¹ shall appoint a person (in this Part referred to as a "coordinator") to convene on its behalf a family welfare conference in respect of the child.

(2) The coordinator shall act as chairperson of a family welfare conference.

(3) [The Health Service Executive]¹ may direct that a family welfare conference shall consider such matters in relation to the child as [the Health Service Executive]¹ considers appropriate.

Amendments

1   Amended by Health Act 2004, s 75 and Sch 7.

8   Functions of conference

(1) A family welfare conference shall—

   (a)   decide if a child in respect of whom the conference is being convened is in need of special care or protection which the child is unlikely to receive unless an order is made in respect of him or her under Part IVA (inserted by this Act) of the Act of 1991,

   (b)   if it decides that the child is in such need, recommend to the [Health Service Executive][1] that it should apply for an order under that Part, and

   (c)   if it does not so decide, make such recommendations to the [Health Service Executive][1] in relation to the care or protection of the child as the conference considers necessary, including, where appropriate, a recommendation that the [Health Service Executive][1] should apply for a care order or a supervision order under the Act of 1991 in respect of the child.

(2) Any recommendations made by a family welfare conference shall be agreed unanimously by those present at the conference, unless the disagreement of any person present is regarded by the coordinator as unreasonable, in which case the coordinator may dispense with that person's agreement.

(3) Where any such recommendations are not agreed unanimously (disregarding any disagreement mentioned in subsection (2)), the matter shall be referred to the [Health Service Executive][1] for determination.

Amendments

1   Amended by Health Act 2004, s 75 and Sch 7.

---

9   Persons entitled to attend conference

(1) The following persons shall be entitled to attend a family welfare conference—

   (a)   the child in respect of whom the conference is being convened,

   (b)   the parents or guardian of the child,

   (c)   any guardian ad litem appointed for the child,

   (d)   such other relatives of the child as may be determined by the coordinator, after consultation with the child and the child's parents or guardian,

   [(e)   an employee or employees of the Health Service Executive;][1]

   (f)   any other person who, in the opinion of the coordinator, after consultation with the child and his or her parents or guardian, would make a positive contribution to the conference because of the person's knowledge of the child or the child's family or because of his or her particular expertise.

(2) If, before or during a family welfare conference, the coordinator is of opinion that the presence or continued presence of any person is not in the best interests of the conference or the child, the coordinator may exclude that person from participation or further participation in the conference.

(3) The coordinator shall take all reasonable steps to ensure that notice of the time, date and place of a family welfare conference is given to every person who is entitled to attend.

(4) Failure to notify any person entitled to attend a family welfare conference, or failure of any such person to attend it, shall not invalidate its proceedings.

Amendments

1   Subsection (1)(e) substituted by Health Act 2004, s 75 and Sch 7.

10   Procedure at conference

(1) Subject to the provisions of this Part or any regulations under section 15, a family welfare conference may regulate its procedure in such manner as it thinks fit.

(2) Subject to any direction of the Children Court pursuant to section 77, a family welfare conference may be adjourned to a time and place to be determined by it.

(3) The coordinator of a family welfare conference shall ensure, as far as practicable, that any information and advice required by the conference to carry out its functions are made available to it.

11   Administrative services

[The Health Service Executive]¹ shall provide, or arrange for the provision of, such administrative services as may be necessary to enable a family welfare conference to discharge its functions.

Amendments

1   Amended by Health Act 2004, s 75 and Sch 7.

12   Notification of recommendations of conference

The coordinator of a family welfare conference shall notify the following persons or bodies in writing of any recommendations of the conference:

(a)   the child in respect of whom the conference was convened,

(b)   the parents or guardian of the child,

(c)   any guardian ad litem appointed for the child,

(d)   any other persons who attended the conference,

[(e)   the Health Service Executive,]¹

(f)   if the child was referred to the [Health Service Executive]¹ by another body, that body, and

(g)   any other body or persons who should, in the coordinator's opinion, be so notified.

Amendments

1 Amended and subsection (e) substituted by Health Act 2004, s 75 and Sch 7.

13 Action by Health Service Executive on recommendations

(1) On receipt of the recommendations of a family welfare conference, the [Health Service Executive][1] may—

(a) apply for an order under Part IVA (inserted by this Act) of the Act of 1991,

(b) apply for a care order or a supervision order under that Act, or

(c) provide any service or assistance for the child or his or her family as it considers appropriate, having regard to the recommendations of the conference.

(2) Where a family welfare conference has been convened following a direction of the Children Court under section 77, the [Health Service Executive][1] shall communicate with that Court in accordance with subsection (2) of that section.

Amendments

1 Amended by Health Act 2004, s 75 and Sch 7.

14 Privilege

(1) No evidence shall be admissible in any court of any information, statement or admission disclosed or made in the course of a family welfare conference.

(2) Subsection (1) does not apply to a record of decisions or recommendations of a family welfare conference.

(3) Section 51 shall apply, with the necessary modifications, in relation to publication of proceedings at a family welfare conference and the protection of the identity of a child in respect of whom such a conference is being held.

15 Regulations

The Minister for Health and Children may make regulations prescribing any or all of the following matters:

(a) the arrangements for convening a family welfare conference and the appointment and role of the coordinator,

(b) subject to section 9, the categories of persons who shall be entitled to attend such a conference and the conditions under which a person or category of persons may so attend, and

(c) the arrangements for notifying any other body or person of any recommendations of such a conference, or for the purposes of enabling any provision of this Part to have full effect and for its due administration.

[15A   Transitional provisions relating to Health Act 2004

(1) In this section, a provisions reference to a provision of this Act is to that provision as it was before it was amended by the Health Act 2004.

(2) Where a family welfare conference convened under section 7 on behalf of a health board has not discharged its functions before the establishment day of the Health Service Executive, the conference shall be deemed to have been convened on behalf of the Executive.

(3) Where a direction given by a health board under section 7(3) to a family welfare conference is not complied with before the establishment day of the Health Service Executive, the direction shall be deemed to have been given to the Executive.

(4) Where a recommendation has been made or a matter has been referred to a health board by a family welfare conference under section 8 and all matters relating to the child concerned have not been concluded under this Act or the Child Care Act 1991 before the establishment day of the Health Service Executive, the recommendation shall be deemed for the purposes of this Act and the Child Care Act 1991 to have been made or the matter referred to the Executive.][1]

Amendments

1   Section 15A inserted by Health Act 2004, s 75 and Sch 7.

PART 3
AMENDMENT OF ACT OF 1991

16   Amendment (new Parts IVA and IVB) of Act of 1991

Text not reproduced here.

Amendments

Part 3 (Section 16) amends the Child Care Act 1991.

PART 4
DIVERSION PROGRAMME

Introductory

17   Interpretation (Part 4)

(1) In this Part—

"caution" means either a formal caution or an informal caution, as appropriate;

"conference" has the meaning assigned to it by section 29;

"Director" means the member of the Garda Síochána assigned by the Commissioner pursuant to section 20;

"facilitator" has the meaning assigned to it by section 31(4);

"formal caution" and "informal caution" have the meanings assigned to them respectively by section 25(4);

"Programme" has the meaning assigned to it by section 18.

(2) A reference in this Part to the parents or guardian, or a parent or guardian, of a child shall be construed, unless the context otherwise requires, as including an adult relative of the child with whom the child is for the time being residing or who, in the opinion of the juvenile liaison officer supervising the child, is exercising, or could exercise, a beneficial influence on the child.

18   Principle

[Unless the interests of society otherwise require and subject to this Part, any child who—

(a)   has committed an offence, or

(b)   has behaved anti-socially,

and who accepts responsibility for his or her criminal or anti-social behaviour shall be considered for admission to a diversion programme (in this Part referred to as the Programme) having the objective set out in section 19.][1]

Amendments

1   Section 18 substituted by by Criminal Justice Act 2006, s 123.

19   Objective of Programme

[(1) The objective of the Programme is to divert any child who accepts responsibility for his or her criminal or anti-social behaviour from committing further offences or engaging in further anti-social behaviour.][1]

(2) The objective shall be achieved primarily by administering a caution to such a child and, where appropriate, by placing him or her under the supervision of a juvenile liaison officer and by convening a conference to be attended by the child, family members and other concerned persons.

Amendments

1   Section (1) substituted by Criminal Justice Act 2006, s 124.

20   Diversion Programme

(1) The Programme shall be carried on and managed, under the general superintendence and control of the Commissioner of the Garda Síochána, by a member of the Garda Síochána not

below the rank of superintendent who shall be assigned for that purpose by the Commissioner and is referred to in this Part as the Director.

(2) The Commissioner may assign duties other than those relating to the Programme to the Director during his or her period of assignment as Director.

21 Temporary incapacity of Director

(1) Whenever it appears to the Commissioner that the Director is, through absence, ill-health or other sufficient cause, temporarily unable to act, the Commissioner may appoint a member of the Garda Síochána not below the rank of inspector to act as the Director for such period (not exceeding the duration of the incapacity) as the Commissioner thinks proper, and references to the Director in this Part shall include the member so acting.

(2) The Director may, in writing, delegate any of the functions assigned to the Director under this Part to a member of the Garda Síochána not below the rank of inspector and may revoke any such delegation, and references to the Director in this Part shall include any member to whom any such functions are for the time being so delegated.

Admission to Programme

22 Report on child to Director

Where criminal [or anti-social][1] behaviour by a child comes to the notice of the Garda Síochána, the member of the Garda Síochána dealing with the child for that behaviour may prepare a report in the prescribed form as soon as practicable and submit it to the Director with a statement of any action that has been taken in relation to the child and a recommendation as to any further action, including admission to the Programme, that should, in the member's opinion, be taken in the matter.

Amendments

Words inserted by Criminal Justice Act 2006, s 158 and Sch 4.

---

23 Admission to Programme

(1) [Subject to subsection (6), a child][1] may be admitted to the Programme if he or she—

    (a) accepts responsibility for his or her criminal [or anti-social][1] behaviour, having had a reasonable opportunity to consult with his or her parents or guardian and obtained any legal advice sought by or on behalf of him or her,

    (b) consents to be cautioned and, where appropriate, to be supervised by a juvenile liaison officer, and

    (c) is of or over [is 10 years of age or over that age][1] and under 18 years of age, but paragraph (b) shall not apply where the Director is satisfied that the failure to agree to being cautioned or supervised is attributable to undue pressure being brought to bear on the child by any person and, in that event, the child shall be deemed to have consented for the purposes of that paragraph.

(2) The Director shall be satisfied that the admission of the child to the Programme would be appropriate, in the best interests of the child and not inconsistent with the interests of society and any victim.

(3) The criminal behaviour for which the child has accepted responsibility shall not be behaviour in respect of which admission to the Programme is excluded under any regulations made pursuant to section 47, unless the Director of Public Prosecutions directs otherwise in a notification to the Director.

(4) When the admission of a child to the Programme is being considered any views expressed by any victim in relation to the child's criminal [or anti-social][1] behaviour shall be given due consideration but the consent of the victim shall not be obligatory for such admission.

(5) For the purposes of subsection (1)(c), the age for admission to the Programme shall be the age of the child on the date on which the criminal [or anti-social][1] behaviour took place.

[(6) Notwithstanding subsection (1), a child aged 10 or 11 years shall be admitted to the Programme if—

    (a) he or she accepts responsibility for his or her criminal behaviour, having had a reasonable opportunity to consult with his or her parents or guardian and obtained any legal advice sought by or on behalf of him or her, and

    (b) subsections (2) to (5) apply in relation to the child.][1]

Amendments

1   Section 23 amended and sub-s (6) inserted by Criminal Justice Act 2006, s 125.

24   Decision to admit to Programme

(1) It shall be a function of the Director to decide whether to admit a child to the Programme and the category of caution to be administered to any child so admitted.

(2) Where the Director decides that a child should be admitted to the Programme, he or she shall direct a juvenile liaison officer to give notice in writing to the parents or guardian of the child specifying the criminal [or anti-social][1] behaviour in respect of which a caution is to be administered, whether the caution is to be formal or informal and the time and place where it is to be administered and stating that the parents or guardian are obliged to attend its administration.

(3) Every such notice shall be expressed in language designed to be understood by the parents or guardian of the child and shall be available in the Irish language to a child who is from a Gaeltacht area or whose first language is Irish.

Amendments

Words inserted by Criminal Justice Act 2006, s 158 and Sch 4.

Administration of cautions

25   Cautions

(1) A caution shall be administered to every child admitted to the Programme.

(2) A formal caution shall be administered in a Garda Síochána station or, in exceptional circumstances, elsewhere by—

   (a) a member of the Garda Síochána not below the rank of inspector, or

   (b) a juvenile liaison officer who has been trained in mediation skills, in the presence of the parents or guardian and, if the caution has been administered by such a member of the Garda Síochána, a juvenile liaison officer.

(3) An informal caution shall be administered by a juvenile liaison officer in a Garda Síochána station, in the child's normal place of residence or in exceptional circumstances elsewhere, in the presence of the parents or guardian of the child.

(4) In this section—

"formal caution" means a caution to be administered to a child where—

   (a) no previous caution has been administered, or

   (b) one or more than one informal or formal caution has been previously administered, and the Director considers that the child's criminal [or anti-social][1] behaviour was of such a nature that it could not be adequately dealt with by way of informal caution;

"informal caution" means a caution to be administered to a child where—

   (a) no previous caution has been administered, or

   (b) one or more than one informal caution has been previously administered, and the Director considers that the child's criminal [or anti-social][1] behaviour was not sufficiently serious to warrant a formal caution.

Amendments

Words inserted by Criminal Justice Act 2006, s 158 and Sch 4.

---

26   Presence of victim at formal caution

(1) The Director may invite any victim whose views in relation to the child's criminal [or anti-social][1] behaviour have been considered pursuant to section 23(4) to be present at the administration of a formal caution.

(2) Where any victim is so present, there shall be a discussion among those present about the child's criminal [or anti-social][1] behaviour.

(3) The member of the Garda Síochána administering the formal caution may invite the child—

   (a) to apologise, whether orally or in writing or both, to the victim, and

   (b) where appropriate, to make financial or other reparation to him or her.

Amendments

Words inserted by Criminal Justice Act 2006, s 158 and Sch 4.

Supervision of children admitted to Programme

27   Supervision

(1) (a)   Subject to paragraph (d), where a child has received a formal caution he or she shall be placed by the Director under the supervision of a juvenile liaison officer for a period of 12 months from the date of the administration of the caution.

   (b)   Subject to paragraph (c), where a child has received an informal caution he or she shall not be placed under the supervision of a juvenile liaison officer.

   (c)   Subject to paragraph (d), in exceptional circumstances, a child who has received an informal caution may be placed by the Director under the supervision of a juvenile liaison officer for a period of 6 months from the date of the administration of the caution.

   (d)   The periods referred to in paragraphs (a) and (c) may be varied by the Director in a manner consistent with any regulations under section 47 or pursuant to any recommendation arising from a conference.

(2) Where a child who is placed under the supervision of a juvenile liaison officer is subsequently found guilty of an offence the period of supervision shall terminate forthwith, if it has not terminated at the time of the finding of guilt.

28   Level of supervision

(1) The level of supervision to be applied in the case of any child shall, subject to section 42(1), be determined by the juvenile liaison officer who is supervising the child.

(2) The juvenile liaison officer shall have regard to the following matters when making a determination under subsection (1)—

   (a)   the seriousness of the child's criminal [or anti-social][1] behaviour,

   (b)   the level of support given to, and the level of control of, the child by the child's parents or guardian,

   (c)   the likelihood, in the opinion of the juvenile liaison officer, of the child's committing further offences [or engaging in further anti-social behaviour,][1] and

   (d)   any directions from the Director on the appropriate level of supervision in any case or in any case of a particular class.

Amendments

1   Words inserted by Criminal Justice Act 2006, s 158 and Sch 4.

Holding of conference in respect of child

29   "Conference"

In this Part "conference", in relation to a child, means a meeting held pursuant to this Part of persons concerned with the child's welfare, and such a conference shall have the following functions:

(a) to bring together the child in respect of whom the conference is being held, his or her parents or guardian, such other family members, relatives and other persons as appropriate and the facilitator with a view to—

    (i) establishing why the child became involved in the behaviour that gave rise to his or her admission to the Programme,

    (ii) discussing how the parents or guardian, family members, relatives or any other person could help to prevent the child from becoming involved in further such behaviour, and

    (iii) where appropriate, reviewing the child's behaviour since his or her admission to the Programme;

(b) as appropriate and in accordance with this Part, to mediate between the child and the victim;

(c) to formulate an action plan for the child; and

(d) to uphold the concerns of the victim and have due regard to his or her interests.

30 Recommendation that conference be held

(1) Where a child is placed under the supervision of a juvenile liaison officer, that officer may, if he or she so thinks proper, recommend in a written report to the Director that a conference be held in respect of the child.

(2) Without prejudice to any decision of the Director in a particular case, the agreement of a child's parent or guardian shall be required for, and the views of the child shall be ascertained on, the holding of a conference.

(3) (a) The juvenile liaison officer shall ascertain the views of any victim of the child's criminal [or anti-social][1] behaviour as to the possibility of a conference being held and as to whether the victim would be agreeable to attend any such conference.

    (b) Where the victim is a child, the juvenile liaison officer shall have regard to his or her best interests and shall also, where practicable, ascertain whether his or her parents or guardian would be agreeable that a conference be held and would attend it.

(4) The juvenile liaison officer shall, when he or she decides to make a recommendation pursuant to subsection (1), explain to the child concerned, and to his or her parent or guardian, the procedures and functions of a conference.

Amendments

1 Words inserted by Criminal Justice Act 2006, s 158 and Sch 4.

31 Decision on holding conference

(1) The Director, on receipt of a report pursuant to section 30 from a juvenile liaison officer, shall, having regard to subsections (2) and (3), decide whether or not a conference should be held.

(2) In deciding whether a conference should be held the Director shall have regard to—

(a) the report and recommendation of the juvenile liaison officer supervising the child concerned,

(b) whether in the Director's opinion a conference would be of assistance in preventing the commission by the child of further offences [or further criminal or anti-social behaviour by the child][1],

(c) the role and responsibilities of the child's parents or guardian and relatives,

(d) the views, if any, of the victim,

(e) whether the victim would attend the conference and, where the victim is a child, whether such attendance would be in his or her best interests,

(f) the interests of the community in which the child resides, and

(g) any other matter which the Director considers to be relevant.

(3) A conference shall not be held unless the child and the child's parents or guardian indicate that they will attend it.

(4) (a) Where the Director decides that a conference should be held, he or she shall appoint a person (in this Part referred to as a "facilitator") to convene the conference and a person to be its chairperson.

(b) The facilitator shall be either the juvenile liaison officer supervising the child or another member of the Garda Síochána.

(c) The chairperson shall be the facilitator, another member of the Garda Síochána or another person, with that other person's agreement.

(5) In any case where the Director decides that a conference should not be held he or she shall direct the juvenile liaison officer supervising the child to inform the child and the child's parent or guardian accordingly.

Amendments

1 Words inserted by Criminal Justice Act 2006, s 158 and Sch 4.

---

32   Persons entitled to attend conference

(1) The following persons shall be entitled to attend a conference:

(a) the child in respect of whom the conference is being held,

(b) the parents or guardian of the child and members of the child's family or relatives of the child, if the facilitator is of opinion that they or any one of them would make a positive contribution to it.

(2) A conference shall not be held unless at least one person invited by virtue of subsection (1)(b) is in attendance.

(3) The facilitator shall invite any other persons who in his or her opinion would make a positive contribution to the conference, including one or more representatives from any of the following bodies:

[(a) the Health Service Executive,][1]

(b) the probation and welfare service,

(c) the school attended by the child,

(d) the school attendance service,

(e) the Garda Síochána.

(4) The facilitator shall also invite to the conference any victim of the child's criminal [or anti-social]² behaviour and any relatives or friends of the victim whom the victim requests to have in attendance, unless the facilitator is of opinion that their attendance would not be in the best interests of the conference.

(5) The facilitator may invite to the conference any other person requested by the child or the child's family who in the facilitator's opinion would be of benefit to the conference and, with the agreement of the persons attending the conference and the Director, any person engaged in carrying out research on or evaluation of conferences or their equivalent inside or outside the State.

(6) If, in the course of a conference, the facilitator is of opinion that the continued presence of any person is not in the best interests of the conference or the child, the facilitator may exclude that person from further participation in the conference.

(7) A person shall not disclose confidential information obtained by him or her while participating (or as a result of having participated) as a member of a conference.

(8) A person who contravenes subsection (7) shall be guilty of an offence and shall be liable on summary conviction to a fine not exceeding [€1,904.61].

(9) In this section "confidential" means that which is expressed to be confidential either as regards particular information or information of a particular class or description.

Amendments

1   Subsection (3)(a) substituted by Health Act 2004, s 75 and Sch 7.

2   Words inserted by Criminal Justice Act 2006, s 158 and Sch 4.

---

33   Location of conference

The decision on where to hold a conference shall be made by the facilitator after hearing the views in that regard of the persons who are to attend it.

34   Time limit for holding conference

(1) A conference shall be held within the period during which the child concerned is under the supervision of a juvenile liaison officer.

(2) A conference may be held on more than one occasion but, subject to section 39(10), not outside the period referred to in subsection (1).

35   Notification to participants

(1) The facilitator shall take all reasonable steps to ensure that notice of the time, date and place of the conference is given to every person who is entitled or has been invited to attend and has indicated a willingness to attend or an interest in attending.

(2) Failure to notify any person entitled or invited to attend a conference or failure of any person so invited to attend it shall not of itself affect the validity of its proceedings unless the

facilitator is of opinion that any such failure is likely to affect materially the outcome of the conference.

36 Views of those unable or unwilling to attend conference

The facilitator shall take all reasonable steps to ascertain the views, if any, of any person who has been invited to attend the conference concerned but has notified the facilitator that he or she is, for any reason, unable or unwilling to do so and shall ensure that any views so ascertained are made known at the conference.

37 Procedure at conference

(1) Subject to the provisions of this Part and any regulations under section 47, a conference may regulate its procedure in such manner as it thinks fit.

(2) Subject to sections 33, 34 and 39(10), a conference may be adjourned to a time and place to be determined by it.

(3) The facilitator shall ensure, as far as practicable, that any information and advice required by the conference to carry out its functions are made available to it.

38 Period or level of supervision

A conference shall consider whether the period or level of supervision of the child in respect of whom the conference is being held should be varied in the light of the following matters:

    (a) the circumstances of the child as respects education, training or employment,

    (b) the child's leisure time activities,

    (c) the child's relationship with his or her family and the local community,

    (d) the child's attitude to his or her being supervised,

    (e) the child's progress under the supervision,

    (f) the child's attitude to his or her criminal [or anti-social][1] behaviour and, in particular, to the victim of that behaviour, whether or not the victim is present at the conference, and

    (g) any other matters that may be relevant in the particular case.

Amendments

1   Words inserted by Criminal Justice Act 2006, s 158 and Sch 4.

39 Action plan

(1) The parents or guardian of a child, when present at a conference in respect of the child (or in their absence a member of the child's family or a relative of the child), and the child may, with the assistance of the other persons present at the conference, formulate an action plan for the child.

(2) Any such action plan shall be agreed unanimously by those present at the conference, unless the disagreement of any person present is regarded by the facilitator as unreasonable, in which case that person's agreement to the plan shall not be necessary.

(3) An action plan may include provision for any one or more of the following matters:

(a) an apology, whether orally or in writing or both, by the child to any victim,

(b) financial or other reparation to any victim,

(c) participation by the child in an appropriate sporting or recreational activity,

(d) attendance of the child at a school or place of work,

(e) participation by the child in an appropriate training or educational course or a programme that does not interfere with any work or school schedule of the child,(f) the child being at home at specified times,

(g) the child staying away from specified places or a specified person or both,

(h) taking initiatives within the child's family and community that might help to prevent the commission by the child of further offences [or further criminal or anti-social behaviour by the child]¹, and

(i) any other matter that in the opinion of those present at the conference would be in the child's best interests or would make the child more aware of the consequences of his or her criminal [or anti-social]¹ behaviour.

(4) When the action plan and its duration have been agreed, the facilitator shall produce a written record of the plan in language that can be understood by the child.

(5) The action plan shall be signed by the child (where possible), the chairperson and one of the other persons present.

(6) The action plan shall come into operation on the date it is signed.

(7) A copy of the action plan shall be given or sent to the child by the chairperson.

(8) Those present at the conference may appoint one or more of their number to implement the action plan and monitor compliance with it.

(9) The chairperson shall, after consulting the other persons present, appoint a date, being a date after the period covered by the action plan has expired, for reconvening the conference to review compliance with the action plan.

(10) The reconvened conference shall be held not more than 6 months from the date on which the action plan was signed and may be held outside the period of the child's supervision by a juvenile liaison officer.

(11) The chairperson may reconvene the conference at an earlier date than that appointed under subsection (9) if it comes to his or her notice that the child is not complying with any of the terms of the action plan.

(12) The persons present at any conference reconvened pursuant to subsection (11) shall ascertain why the child is not complying with the action plan and shall encourage the child to comply with the plan or any amended version of it that they may agree upon.

(13) The provisions of subsections (4) to (7) shall apply to any action plan amended in accordance with subsection (12).

(14) Subject to subsection (10), a conference may be reconvened on any number of occasions to discuss any aspect of an action plan.

(15) Nothing in this section shall prevent any person or persons who implemented, and monitored compliance with, the action plan from continuing, with the agreement of the child, to implement and monitor compliance with the plan after the period covered by it has expired and it has been reviewed at a reconvened conference.

Amendments

1   Words inserted by Criminal Justice Act 2006, s 158 and Sch 4.

40   Disagreement on action plan

Failure to agree on the terms of an action plan shall not invalidate the proceedings of a conference.

41   Report to Director

As soon as practicable after a conference has been held the facilitator shall report to the Director on the following matters:

(a)   the terms of any action plan,

(b)   the matters discussed at the conference,

(c)   the views of those present, and

(d)   any views ascertained pursuant to section 36,

and shall recommend, having had regard to the views referred to in paragraphs (c) and (d), whether in his or her opinion the period and level of supervision of the child concerned should be varied and, if so, to what extent.

42   Decision by Director on period or level of supervision

(1) On receipt of a report submitted pursuant to section 41, the Director shall, where appropriate, decide whether the child's period or level of supervision should be varied and, if so, to what extent.

(2) Where the Director makes a decision pursuant to subsection (1), he or she shall inform the juvenile liaison officer supervising the child accordingly and that officer shall so inform the child and the child's parent or guardian as soon as practicable.

43   Administrative services

The Director shall provide such administrative services as may be necessary to enable a conference to discharge its functions.

Committee to monitor effectiveness of Programme

44   Review of effectiveness of Programme

(1) The Minister shall appoint a committee to monitor the effectiveness of the Programme, review all aspects of its operation and monitor the ongoing training needs of facilitators.

(2) The chairperson of the committee shall be an Assistant Commissioner of the Garda Síochána and it shall have 3 other members, of whom one shall be a chief superintendent of the Garda Síochána and the remaining two shall not be members of the Garda Síochána.

(3) The Minister shall consult with the Commissioner in relation to the appointment of members of the Garda Síochána to the committee.

(4) The committee shall have access to and may examine any documents relating to the operation of the Programme and may discuss any aspect of it with the Director and any other person concerned with its operation.

(5) The chairperson and other members of the committee shall be appointed for a term of 4 years and shall be eligible for reappointment.

(6) The committee shall make annually, by such date as the Minister may direct, a report to the Commissioner on its activities during the year and the Commissioner shall, as soon as may be, submit the report to the Minister.

(7) A copy of each such report shall be laid before each House of the Oireachtas by the Minister.

(8) Before laying a report before each House of the Oireachtas pursuant to subsection (7) the Minister may omit material from it where the omission is necessary to avoid the identification of any person.

(9) The terms and conditions of appointment of members of the committee and of any of their allowances or expenses shall be such as may be determined by the Minister with, in the case of any allowances or expenses, the consent of the Minister for Finance.

(10) Subject to the Freedom of Information Act, 1997, a person shall not disclose confidential information obtained by him or her while serving (or as a result of having served) as a member of the committee.

(11) A person who contravenes subsection (10) shall be guilty of an offence and shall be liable on summary conviction to a fine not exceeding [€1,904.61].

(12) In this section "confidential" means that which is expressed to be confidential either as regards particular information or information of a particular class or description.

45   Vacancies in committee

(1) Whenever a vacancy occurs in the membership of the committee appointed under section 44 for any reason, the Commissioner shall notify the Minister of the vacancy and the Minister shall, as soon as may be, appoint a person to fill the vacancy.

(2) Any person so appointed shall be appointed for the residue of the term of the person whom he or she replaces and shall be eligible for reappointment.

(3) If the vacancy occurs in relation to one of the members of the Garda Síochána on the committee, the Minister shall, after consultation with the Commissioner, appoint a member to fill the vacancy who is of the same rank as the member whom he or she replaces.

Other matters relating to the Programme

46   Supplemental provisions

(1) The Commissioner shall ensure that all members of the Garda Síochána who act as facilitators receive whatever training the Commissioner considers sufficient and appropriate for the proper and efficient discharge of their duties while they are acting in that capacity.

(2) Any powers conferred by this Part or any regulations under it on or in relation to any member of the Garda Síochána are without prejudice to any other powers which the member may have in relation to the commission or suspected commission of an offence.

(3) A failure on the part of any member of the Garda Síochána to observe any provision of this Part or of regulations under it shall not of itself render that member liable to any criminal or civil proceedings or of itself affect the lawfulness of the custody of a detained child or the admissibility in evidence of any statement made by such a child.

(4) A failure on the part of any member of the Garda Síochána to observe any provision of this Part or of regulations under it shall render the member liable to disciplinary proceedings.

47 Regulations (Part 4)

The Minister may make regulations prescribing—

    (a) the procedures to be followed when the Director is deciding—

        (i) whether or not a child should be admitted to the Programme,

        (ii) whether an informal or a formal caution should be administered to a child,

        (iii) whether the victim should be invited to the administration of a formal caution,

        (iv) whether to convene a conference in respect of any child who has been placed under supervision;

    (b) the level of supervision appropriate in any case or class of case;

    (c) any criminal behaviour of a serious nature in respect of which admission to the Programme shall be excluded; or

    (d) any other matter or thing which is referred to in this Part as prescribed; or for the purposes of enabling any provision of this Part to have full effect and for its due administration.

48 Inadmissibility of certain evidence

[(1) Subject to subsection (2), no evidence shall be admissible in any court in respect of—

    (a) any acceptance by a child of responsibility for criminal or anti-social behaviour in respect of which the child has been admitted to the Programme,

    (b) that behaviour, or

    (c) the child's involvement in the Programme.

(2) Where a court is considering the sentence (if any) to be imposed in respect of an offence committed by a child after the child's admission to the Programme, the prosecution may inform it of any of the matters referred to in subsection (1).

(3) Subsection (2) applies, with the necessary modifications, in relation to a child who has attained the age of 18 years.][1]

Amendments

1   Section 48 substituted by Criminal Justice Act 2006, s 126.

---

49 Bar to proceedings

[(1) A child shall not be prosecuted for the criminal behaviour, or any related behaviour, in respect of which he or she has been admitted to the Programme.

(2) A child who has been admitted to the Programme in respect of anti-social behaviour shall not be the subject of an application for an order under section 257D in relation to any such behaviour which occurred prior to such admission.][1]

Amendments

1   Section 49 substituted by Criminal Justice Act 2006, s 127.

50   Privilege

No evidence shall be admissible in any court of any information, statement or admission disclosed or made only in the course of a conference or of the contents of any report of a conference.

51   Protection of identity of children

(1) Subject to subsection (2), no report shall be published or included in a broadcast—

   (a)   in relation to the admission of a child to the Programme or the proceedings at any conference relating to the child, including the contents of any action plan for the child and of the report of the conference, or

   (b)   which reveals the name, address or school of the child or any other information, including any picture, which is likely to lead to identification of the child.

(2) Subsection (1) does not apply to the publication or broadcast of—

   (a)   statistical information relating to the Programme, and

   (b)   the results of any bona fide research relating to it.

(3) If any matter is published or broadcast in contravention of subsection (1), each of the following persons, namely—

   (a)   in the case of publication of the matter in a newspaper or periodical, any proprietor, any editor and any publisher of the newspaper or periodical,

   (b)   in the case of any other such publication, the person who publishes it, and

   (c)   in the case of any such broadcast, any body corporate which transmits or provides the programme in which the broadcast is made and any person having functions in relation to the programme corresponding to those of an editor of a newspaper, shall be guilty of an offence and shall be liable—

      (i)   on summary conviction, to a fine not exceeding [€1,904.61] or imprisonment for a term not exceeding 12 months or both, or

      (ii) on conviction on indictment, to a fine not exceeding [€12,697.38] or imprisonment for a term not exceeding 3 years or both.

(4) (a)   Where an offence under subsection (3)—

      (i)   has been committed by a body corporate, and

      (ii) is proved to have been committed with the consent or connivance of, or to be attributable to any neglect on the part of, any director, manager, secretary or other similar officer of the body corporate or any person who was purporting to act in any such capacity,

   he or she as well as the body corporate shall be guilty of the offence and be liable to be proceeded against and punished accordingly.

(b)   Where the affairs of a body corporate are managed by its members, paragraph (a) shall apply in relation to the acts and defaults of a member in connection with his or her functions of management as if he or she were a director of the body corporate.

(5) Where a person is charged with an offence under subsection (3), it shall be a defence to prove that at the time of the alleged offence the person was not aware, and neither suspected nor had reason to suspect, that the publication or broadcast in question was of a matter referred to in subsection (1).

(6) In this section—

"broadcast" means the transmission, relaying or distribution by wireless telegraphy of communications, sounds, signs, visual images or signals, intended for direct reception by the general public whether such communications, sounds, signs, visual images or signals are actually received or not;

"publish" means publish to the public or a section of the public, and cognate words shall be construed accordingly.

PART 5

RESTRICTION ON CRIMINAL PROCEEDINGS AGAINST CERTAIN CHILDREN[1]

Amendments

1   Title renamed by Criminal Justice Act 2006, s 128.

52   Restriction on criminal proceedings against children

[(1) Subject to subsection (2), a child under 12 years of age shall not be charged with an offence.

(2) Subsection (1) does not apply to a child aged 10 or 11 years who is charged with murder, manslaughter, rape, rape under section 4 of the Criminal Law (Rape) (Amendment) Act 1990 or aggravated sexual assault.

(3) The rebuttable presumption under any rule of law, namely, that a child who is not less than 7 but under 14 years of age is incapable of committing an offence because the child did not have the capacity to know that the act or omission concerned was wrong, is abolished.

(4) Where a child under 14 years of age is charged with an offence, no further proceedings in the matter (other than any remand in custody or on bail) shall be taken except by or with the consent of the Director of Public Prosecutions.][1]

Amendments

1   Section 52 substituted by Criminal Justice Act 2006, s 129.

53 Duty of Garda Síochána in relation to certain under-age children

[(1) Subject to subsections (2) and (3), where a member of the Garda Síochána has reasonable grounds for believing that a child under 12 years of age has committed an offence (except murder, manslaughter, rape, rape under section 4 of the Criminal Law (Rape) (Amendment) Act 1990 or aggravated sexual assault), the member shall endeavour to take the child to the child's parent or guardian or arrange for another such member to do so.][1]

(2) Where the child is taken to his or her parent or guardian and the member of the Garda Síochána so taking the child has reasonable grounds for believing that the child is not receiving adequate care or protection, the member shall inform [the Health Service Executive][2] of the name, address and age of the child and the circumstances in which he or she came to the notice of the Garda Síochána.

(3) Where it is not practicable for the child to be taken to his or her parent or guardian, the member of the Garda Síochána concerned may give the child, or arrange for the child to be given, into the custody of [the Health Service Executive].[2]

(4) Where the child comes to the notice of [the Health Service Executive][2] in accordance with subsection (2), or is given into its custody in accordance with subsection (3), and it appears to [the Health Service Executive][2] that the child requires care or protection which he or she is unlikely to receive unless a court makes a care order or a supervision order in respect of the child, it shall be the duty of [the Health Service Executive][2] to apply for a care order or a supervision order, as it thinks fit, in accordance with Part IV of the Act of 1991.

(5) Where, in relation to a child to whom subsection (1) applies, the member of the Garda Síochána concerned has reasonable grounds for believing—

(a) that there is an immediate and serious risk to the health or welfare of the child, and

(b) that it would not be sufficient for his or her protection from that risk to await the making of an application for an emergency care order by [the Health Service Executive] under section 13 of the Act of 1991,

the member may remove the child to safety, and Part III of the Act of 1991 shall then apply as if the removal were a removal under section 12 of that Act.

Amendments

1   Subsection (1) substituted by Criminal Justice Act 2006, s 130.
2   Words substituted by Health Act 2004, s 75 and Sch 7.

54 Aiding, etc., under-age child to commit offence

[...][1]

Amendments

1   Section 54 deleted by Criminal Justice Act 2006, s 158 and Sch 4.

PART 6

55   Treatment of child suspects

In any investigation relating to the commission or possible commission of an offence by children, members of the Garda Síochána shall act with due respect for the personal rights of the children and their dignity as human persons, for their vulnerability owing to their age and level of maturity and for the special needs of any of them who may be under a physical or mental disability, while complying with the obligation to prevent escapes from custody and continuing to act with diligence and determination in the investigation of crime and the protection and vindication of the personal rights of other persons.

56   Separation of children from adults in Garda Síochána station

The member in charge of a Garda Síochána station shall, as far as practicable, ensure that any child while detained in the station shall not associate with an adult who is so detained and shall not be kept in a cell unless there is no other secure accommodation available.

57   Notification to child

Where a child is arrested and brought to a Garda Síochána station on suspicion of having committed an offence, the member in charge of the station shall without delay inform the child or cause the child to be informed, in a manner and in language that is appropriate to the age and level of understanding of the child—

(a) of the offence in respect of which he or she has been arrested,

(b) that he or she is entitled to consult a solicitor and how this entitlement can be availed of, and

(c) that the child's parent or guardian is being—

   (i)   informed that the child is in custody in the station,

   (ii) given the information specified in paragraphs (a) and (b), and

   (iii) requested to attend at the station without delay.

58   Notification of arrest of child to parent or guardian

(1) When a child is arrested and brought to a Garda Síochána station on suspicion of having committed an offence, the member in charge of the station shall as soon as practicable—

(a) inform or cause to be informed a parent or guardian of the child—

   (i)   that the child is in custody in the station,

   (ii) in ordinary language and in the Irish language when dealing with a child from the Gaeltacht or a child whose first language is Irish, of the nature of the offence in respect of which the child has been arrested, and

   (iii) that the child is entitled to consult a solicitor and as to how this entitlement can be availed of; and

(b) request the parent or guardian to attend at the station without delay.

(2) (a) If the member in charge of the station—

   (i)   is unable to communicate with a parent or guardian of the child, or

   (ii) the parent or guardian indicates that he or she cannot or will not attend at the station within a reasonable time, the member shall inform the child or cause the child to be informed without delay of that fact and of the child's entitlement to have an adult relative or other adult reasonably named by him or her given the information specified in subsection (1)(a) and requested to attend at the station without delay.

(b) Subsection (1) shall apply in relation to a person named by a child pursuant to paragraph (a) as it applies in relation to a parent or guardian.

(3) Where the child is being transferred to another station or other place, the member in charge of the station from which the child is being transferred shall inform any person who has been informed under this section that the child is in custody, or cause him or her to be informed, of the transfer as soon as practicable.

59 Notification to [Health Executive Service][1]

(1) Where the member in charge of a Garda Síochána station has reasonable cause to believe that a child who is in custody in the station on suspicion of having committed an offence may be in need of care or protection, the member shall, as soon as practicable, inform or cause to be informed the [Health Executive Service][1] for the area in which the station is located accordingly, and the [Health Executive Service][1] shall send a representative to the station as soon as practicable.

(2) Where it is not practicable for the representative of the health board to attend at the station within a reasonable time, he or she shall at the first available opportunity attend at the station to ascertain why the member in charge had reasonable cause to believe that the child may be in need of care or protection.

(3) The health board shall, where appropriate, exercise its powers under the Act of 1991 in relation to the child.

[(4) The Minister, with the agreement of the Minister for Health and Children, may issue guidelines in relation to the practical operation of this section.][2]

Amendments

1   Words substituted by Health Act 2004, s 75 and Sch 7.

2   Subsection (4) substituted by Criminal Justice Act 2006, s 131.

---

60 Notification to solicitor

(1) Where a child who is in custody in a Garda Síochána station has asked for a solicitor, the member in charge of the station shall notify the solicitor or cause him or her to be notified accordingly as soon as practicable.

(2) Where the solicitor cannot be contacted within a reasonable time or is unwilling or unable to attend at the station, the child shall be so informed and given an opportunity to ask for another solicitor, and the member in charge shall notify or cause to be notified that other solicitor accordingly as soon as practicable.

(3) Subsections (1) and (2) shall also apply in relation to a request for a solicitor for the child by any parent, guardian, adult relative, any adult reasonably named by the child or other adult

(not being a member of the Garda Síochána) who is present, in accordance with section 61(1)(b), during the questioning of the child or the taking of a written statement.

(4) Where the child is being transferred to another station, the member in charge of the station from which the child is being transferred shall notify any solicitor who has been notified under this section or cause him or her to be notified of the transfer as soon as practicable.

(5) Where a solicitor (other than a named solicitor) has been requested by or on behalf of a child, the member in charge shall give the person making the request or cause him or her to be given the name of one or more than one solicitor whom the member in charge reasonably believes may be willing to attend at the station within a reasonable time.

61   Interviewing children

(1) Subject to subsections (2) to (4), a child who has been detained in a Garda Síochána station pursuant to any enactment shall not be questioned, or asked to make a written statement, in relation to an offence in respect of which he or she has been arrested unless in the presence of—

    (a) a parent or guardian, or

    (b) in his or her absence, another adult (not being a member of the Garda Síochána) nominated by the member in charge of the station.

(2) Notwithstanding subsection (1), the member in charge of the station may authorise the questioning of the child or the taking of a written statement in the absence of a parent or guardian, where the member has reasonable grounds for believing that to delay the questioning would involve a risk of death or injury to persons, serious loss of or damage to property, destruction of or interference with evidence or escape of accomplices.

(3) The member in charge of the station may authorise the exclusion of a parent or guardian during the questioning of the child or the taking of a written statement where—

    (a) the parent or guardian is the victim of, or has been arrested in respect of, the offence being investigated,

    (b) the member has reasonable grounds for suspecting the parent or guardian of complicity in the offence, or

    (c) the member has reasonable grounds for believing that the parent or guardian would, if present during the questioning or the taking of a written statement, be likely to obstruct the course of justice.

(4) The member in charge of the station may authorise the removal of a parent or guardian during the questioning of the child or the taking of a written statement where the member has reasonable grounds for believing that the conduct of the parent or guardian is such as to amount to an obstruction of the course of justice.

(5) Where the child or his or her parent or guardian asks for a solicitor, he or she shall not be asked to make a statement, either orally or in writing, in relation to an offence until a reasonable time for the attendance of the solicitor has elapsed.

(6) A child who is from a Gaeltacht area or whose first language is Irish shall be entitled to be questioned or to make a written statement in the Irish language, and any other child shall be entitled to make a written or oral statement in that language.

(7) In this section references to a parent or guardian include references to an adult relative of the child, an adult reasonably named by the child pursuant to section 58(2)(a) or the adult mentioned in subsection (1)(b).

62 Notification of proceedings to parent or guardian

(1) Where a child who is in custody in a Garda Síochána station is charged with an offence and the child's parent or guardian is present at the station, the member in charge of the station shall ensure that—

(a) a copy of the charge sheet containing particulars of the offence is handed to the parent or guardian, and

(b) as soon as practicable, a notification in writing is sent to the child's parents or guardian of—

(i) the time, date and place of the child's first appearance before the court, and

(ii) the provisions of section 91 concerning non-attendance, without reasonable excuse, of a parent or guardian at the court proceedings.

(2) Where the child's parent or guardian is not present at the station and his or her address is known, the member in charge of the station shall ensure that as soon as practicable—

(a) a copy of the charge sheet containing particulars of the offence is sent to the parents or guardian, and

(b) a notification in writing is sent to the parents or guardian of—

(i) the time, date and place of the child's first appearance before the court,

(ii) the provisions of section 91 concerning the nonattendance, without reasonable excuse, of a parent or guardian at the court proceedings,

(iii) whether or not a recognisance was taken from the child,

(iv) the name of any adult who attended at the station at the request of the child, and

(v) if the child consulted a solicitor, the solicitor's name and address.

63 Notification of proceedings to adult relative or other adult

(1) Where a child who is in custody in a Garda Síochána station is charged with an offence and the child's parent or guardian is not present at the station, the member in charge shall ensure that a copy of the charge sheet containing particulars of the offence is handed to an adult relative of the child who is so present.

(2) The member in charge of the station shall also ensure that as soon as practicable the adult relative is notified of the time, date and place of the child's first appearance before the court and, if the child has consulted a solicitor, of the solicitor's name and address.

(3) Where neither the parent or guardian nor any adult relative of the child is present at the station, the member in charge of the station may send a copy of the charge sheet and a notification of the time, date and place of the child's first appearance before the court to an adult relative.

(4) The duties of the member in charge under this section shall apply only where the member is of opinion that the child's parent or guardian would not be available to attend court with the child and that the adult relative in question is likely to be of assistance to, and provide support for, the child during the court proceedings.

(5) In this section "adult relative" includes any adult reasonably named by the child pursuant to section 58(2)(a).

64   Procedure by summons

(1) Where proceedings in respect of an offence alleged to have been committed by a child are to be commenced by the issue of a summons, the child's parents or guardian may be named in the summons and, if named, shall be required to appear at the sitting of the court specified in the summons.

(2) Where the summons names the child's parents or guardian, it shall also specify the provisions of section 91 concerning non-attendance, without reasonable excuse, of a parent or guardian at the specified sitting of the court.

65   Notice to adult relative or other adult where proceeding by summons

(1) Where proceedings in respect of an offence alleged to have been committed by a child are to be commenced by the issue of a summons and the whereabouts of his or her parents or guardian are unknown, a notice under this section may be issued to an adult relative of the child or other adult reasonably named by the child, whether or not the adult relative or other adult attended at the Garda Síochána station pursuant to section 58(2).

(2) A notice under this section shall be issued by the member of the Garda Síochána dealing with the child in respect of the offence for which the summons is being issued.

(3) The notice shall state the time, date and place of the sitting of the court in respect of which the summons was issued and shall contain particulars of the offence which the child is alleged to have committed.

(4) The notice shall issue only with the agreement of the child and where the member is of opinion that the adult concerned is likely to be of assistance to, and provide support for, the child during the court proceedings.

66   Provisions common to sections 56 to 63 and 65

(1) In this section "the relevant sections" means sections 56 to 63 and 65.

(2) A failure on the part of any member of the Garda Síochána to observe any provision of the relevant sections shall not of itself render that member liable to any criminal or civil proceedings or of itself affect the lawfulness of the custody of a detained child or of the admissibility in evidence of any statement made by the child.

(3) A failure on the part of any member of the Garda Síochána to observe any provision of the relevant sections shall render that member liable to disciplinary proceedings.

(4) The duties imposed by the relevant sections on members of the Garda Síochána in relation to the treatment of any child who is in custody in a Garda Síochána station are without prejudice to any other duties imposed on them in that respect by or under any other enactment.

(5) The provisions of the relevant sections shall not apply if and for so long as the member in charge of the Garda Síochána station in which a person is in custody has reasonable grounds for believing that the person is not below the age of 18 years.

67   Amendment of section 5 of the Criminal Justice Act, 1984

Section 5 (which provides for access to a solicitor and notification of detention) of the Act of 1984 is hereby amended by the deletion of subsection (2) of that section and the substitution of "eighteen years" for "seventeen years" where the latter expression occurs in subsections (1) and (3) thereof.

68 Release on bail by member of Garda Síochána

(1) When a child is arrested and brought to a Garda Síochána station by a member of the Garda Síochána, the member in charge of the station may, if he or she considers it prudent to do so and no warrant directing the detention of the child is in force, release the child on bail and for that purpose take, or arrange to have taken, from the child a recognisance, with or without sureties, for his or her due appearance—

(a) before the Children Court at its next sitting in the district court area in which the child has been arrested or at any subsequent sitting thereof in that district court area during the period of 30 days immediately following such next sitting, or

(b) in the case of the Children Court in the Dublin Metropolitan District, before the next sitting of that Court or any subsequent sitting thereof during the period of 30 days immediately following such next sitting.

(2) The recognisance referred to in subsection (1) may be taken from the child's parent or guardian and may be for the due appearance before the Children Court of the parent or guardian as well as of the child concerned.

(3) The recognisance may be estreated in like manner as a recognisance entered into before a judge of the District Court is estreated.

[(4) If the recognisance is conditioned for the payment of a sum of money, that sum may be accepted in lieu of a surety or sureties.]¹

(5) Any recognisance taken under this section, or any sum of money accepted under this section in lieu of a surety or sureties, shall be transmitted, by the person taking the recognisance or receiving the sum of money, to the district court clerk for the district court area in which the sitting of the Children Court before which the child is to appear is being held.

(6) This section does not apply in the case of an arrest of a child under section 251 (which deals with the arrest of suspected deserters and absentees) of the Defence Act, 1954.

(7) Section 31 (which deals with release on bail by members of the Garda Síochána) of the Criminal Procedure Act, 1967, shall cease to have effect in relation to a child.

Amendments

1   Subsection (4) substituted by Criminal Justice Act 2007, s 21.

69 Application of certain provisions to married child

In the application of this Part in relation to a child who is married—

(a) the references in sections 57, 58, 60(3), 61(7), 62 (except subsections (1)(b)(ii) and (2)(b)(ii)), 63, 65, 68(2) and 70(1)(b) to a parent or guardian of the child shall be construed as references to his or her spouse,

(b) the references in sections 58(2)(a), 60(3), 61(7), 63, 65 and 70(1)(b) to an adult relative of the child shall be construed as including references to his or her parent or guardian, and

(c) section 64 shall not have effect.

70   Regulations (Part 6)

(1) Further provision may be made by regulations in relation to—

(a) the treatment of children while in custody in Garda Síochána stations,

(b) the role of a parent, guardian or adult relative of a child or another adult (including any representative of [the Health Service Executive]¹) who is present in a Garda Síochána station pursuant to this Part while the child is in custody, and

(c) such other matters (if any) as may be necessary or expedient for the purpose of enabling this Part to have full effect and for its due administration.

(2) Pending the making of any regulations under subsection (1)(a), the references to seventeen years in Regulations 9 and 13 of the Criminal Justice Act, 1984 (Treatment of Persons in Custody in Garda Síochána Stations) Regulations, 1987, shall be construed and have effect as if they were references to eighteen years.

Amendments

1   Words amended by Health Act 2004, s 75 and Sch 7.

PART 7
CHILDREN COURT

71   Children Court

(1) (a) The District Court, when hearing charges against children or when hearing applications for orders relating to a child at which the attendance of the child is required or when exercising any other jurisdiction conferred on the Children Court by or under this or any other Act or by Part III, IV, IVA (inserted by this Act) or V of the Act of 1991, shall be known as the Children Court and is referred to as "the Court" in this Part and [Part 8 and 12A]¹.

(b) When exercising any such jurisdiction the Court shall sit in a different building or room from that in which sittings of any other court are held or on different days or at different times from those on or at which sittings of any such other court are held.

(2) So far as practicable sittings of the Court shall be so arranged that persons attending are not brought into contact with persons in attendance at a sitting of any other court.

(3) Where—

(a) in the course of any proceedings before the Court it appears to it that the person charged or to whom the proceedings relate is 18 years of age or upwards, or

(b) in the course of any proceedings before the District Court sitting otherwise than as the Children Court it appears to the District Court that the person charged or to whom the proceedings relate is under the age of 18 years, nothing in this section shall be construed as preventing the Court or the District Court, as the case may be, if it thinks it undesirable to adjourn the case, from proceeding to hear and determine it.

(4) The Court shall sit as often as may be necessary for the purpose of exercising any jurisdiction conferred on it by or under this or any other enactment.

(5) Any reference to a juvenile court in any enactment in force immediately before the commencement of this section shall be construed as a reference to the Court.

Amendments

1   Words inserted by Criminal Justice Act 2006, s 158 and Sch 4.

72   Requirement for transacting business in Children Court

(1) Subject to subsection (2), a judge of the District Court shall, before transacting business in the Children Court, participate in any relevant course of training or education which may be required by the President of the District Court.

(2) Subsection (1) shall apply only in relation to judges of the District Court appointed on or after 15 December, 1995.

73   Arrangements for hearing of proceedings in Children Court

(1) As far as practicable, the hearing of proceedings in the Court shall be arranged so that the time that the persons involved have to wait for the proceedings to be heard is kept to a minimum.

(2) The time stated in every summons requiring a person to appear before the Court shall be a time which the person preparing the summons reasonably expects that the proceedings in respect of which the summons is issued will be heard.

74   Children charged with summary offences jointly with adults

(1) Where—

   (a) a child is charged with a summary offence and the charge is made jointly against the child and one or more adults,

   (b) a child is charged with a summary offence and one or more adults are charged at the same time with aiding, abetting, counselling or procuring the commission of that offence,

   (c) a child is charged with aiding, abetting, counselling or procuring the commission of a summary offence with which one or more adults are charged at the same time, or

   (d) a child is charged with a summary offence arising out of circumstances which are the same as or connected with those giving rise to an offence with which one or more adults are charged at the same time,

the charge or charges against the child and the adult or adults shall be heard by the Court unless the Court considers that the charge or charges should be heard by the District Court sitting otherwise than as the Children Court.

[76B   Assistance to Court by Health Service Executive

(1) Where—

(a) a child who is charged with an offence is remanded on bail or, subject to section 88(10)(b), in custody, and

(b) it appears to the Court that the Health Service Executive may be of assistance to it in dealing with the case,

the Court may request the Executive to be represented in the proceedings.

(2) Where the child is remanded on bail, the request shall be made at least one week before the date of the resumption of the proceedings concerned.

(3) If, having heard the Health Service Executive's representative, the Court dismisses the case against the child on its merits, the Health Service Executive shall, where appropriate, exercise its powers under the Act of 1991 in relation to the child.]¹

Amendments

1   Section 76B inserted by Criminal Justice Act 2006, s 133.

[76C   Dismissal of case against child under 14 in certain circumstances

Where a child under 14 years of age is charged with an offence, the Court may, of its own motion or the application of any person, dismiss the case on its merits if, having had due regard to the child's age and level of maturity, it determines that the child did not have a full understanding of what was involved in the commission of the offence.]¹

Amendments

1   Section 76C inserted by Criminal Justice Act 2006, s 134.

77   Referral of case to health board

(1) Where, in any proceedings in which a child is charged with an offence, it appears to the Court that it may be appropriate for a care order or a supervision order to be made under the Act of 1991 with respect to the child, the Court may, of its own motion or on the application of any person—

(a) adjourn the proceedings and direct [the Health Service Executive]¹ to convene a family welfare conference in respect of the child, [if in the Court's view it is practicable for the Health Service Executive to hold such a conference having regard to the age of the child and his or her family and other circumstances,]²

(b) [...]³

(2) Where a family welfare conference has been held by [the Health Service Executive]¹ pursuant to a direction under subsection (1)(a)—

(a) if [the Health Service Executive]¹ applies under the Act of 1991 for a care order, a supervision order or a special care order with respect to the child, it shall inform the Court of the outcome of its application and of any other matter likely to be of assistance to the Court, or

(b) if it decides not to apply for any such order, it shall inform the Court of—

    (i) its reasons for so deciding,

    (ii) any service or assistance which it has provided, or intends to provide, for the child and his or her family, and

    (iii) any other action which it has taken, or intends to take, with respect to the child.

(3) The Court, on being informed by [the Health Service Executive]¹ of the matters mentioned in subsection (2), may, if satisfied that it is appropriate to do so, dismiss the charge against the child on its merits.

Amendments

1 Words amended by Health Act 2004, s 75 and Sch 7.

2 Words substituted by Child Care (Amendment) Act 2007, s 17(a).

3 Subsection (1)(b) deleted by Child Care (Amendment) Act 2007, s 17(b).

78 Family conference

(1) Where, in any proceedings in which a child is charged with an offence—

(a) the child accepts responsibility for his or her criminal behaviour, having had a reasonable opportunity to consult with his or her parents or guardian and obtained any legal advice sought by or on behalf of him or her,

(b) it appears to the Court that it is desirable that an action plan for the child should be formulated at a family conference, and

(c) the child and child's parent or guardian, or members of the child's family or relatives of the child who in the opinion of the Court could make a positive contribution at a family conference, agree to attend such a conference and to participate in its proceedings,

the Court may direct the probation and welfare service to arrange for the convening of a family conference in respect of the child and adjourn the proceedings until the conference has been held.

(2) The Court may direct that the conference consider such matters relating to the child as the Court considers appropriate.

79 Convening of family conference

A family conference shall be convened by a probation and welfare officer appointed for that purpose by the [Director of the Probation and Welfare Service]¹ and shall be held not later than 28 days after the date of the direction of the Court.

Amendments

1   Words substituted by by Criminal Justice Act 2006, s 137.

80   Action plan

(1) A family conference shall endeavour to formulate an action plan for the child in respect of whom it has been convened.

(2) Subsections (1) to (5) of section 39 shall apply and have effect in relation to such a plan, with the substitution in subsections (2), (4) and (5) of that section of references to a probation and welfare officer for the references to a facilitator or chairperson and with any other necessary modifications.

81   Report to Court by probation and welfare officer

The probation and welfare officer who was appointed to convene the family conference shall, as appropriate—

(a)   submit to the Court the action plan formulated at the conference,

(b)   inform the Court that the conference did not reach agreement on an action plan,

(c)   apply to the Court for an extension of the time for holding the conference, or

(d)   inform the Court that it has not been possible to hold the conference and that there is little likelihood of its being held.

82   Action by Court on report of probation and welfare officer

(1) Where an action plan is submitted to the Court pursuant to section 81(a), the Court may—

(a)   approve of the plan or amend it, and

(b)   order that the child concerned shall comply with it and be supervised by a probation and welfare officer while it is in operation.

(2) Where the probation and welfare officer reports to the Court pursuant to section 81(b) that the family conference did not reach agreement on an action plan, the Court may—

(a)   where it is of opinion that an action plan would be desirable and have a reasonable chance of success, formulate an action plan and order that the child concerned shall comply with it and be supervised by a probation and welfare officer while it is in operation, or

(b)   resume the proceedings in respect of the offence with which the child is charged.

(3) Where the probation and welfare officer applies to the Court pursuant to section 81(c) for an extension of the time for holding the family conference, or informs the Court pursuant to section 81(d) that there is little likelihood of its being held, the Court may—

(a)   where it is satisfied that there is a likelihood of the conference being held, grant an extension of time, not exceeding 28 days, for holding it, or

(b)   where it is not so satisfied, resume the proceedings in respect of the offence with which the child is charged.

(4) Where the Court makes an order pursuant to subsection (1)(b) or (2)(a) in relation to an action plan, it shall appoint a date for the Court to review compliance by the child with the plan, being a date not more than 6 months from the date of the order.

(5) An action plan formulated pursuant to subsection (1)(b) or (2)(a) shall be written in language that can be understood by the child and be signed by the child (or, where appropriate, a person mentioned in section 78(1)(c) on his or her behalf) and the supervising probation and welfare officer.

83   Failure to comply with action plan

Where the Court has ordered a child to comply with an action plan and, on application by the probation and welfare officer who convened the relevant family conference, it appears to the Court that the child has, without reasonable cause, failed to comply with the terms of the plan, the Court may resume the proceedings in respect of the offence with which the child is charged.

84   Review of compliance with action plan

At a resumed court sitting to review compliance with the action plan, the Court may resume the proceedings in respect of the offence with which the child is charged and, without prejudice to any other way of dealing with the case, may, if it is satisfied that the child has complied with the plan, dismiss the charge against the child on its merits.

85   Application of provisions

Sections 29, 30(3), 32, 33, 35, 36, 50 and 51 shall apply and have effect in relation to a family conference convened under this Part with the substitution, where appropriate, in those provisions of references to a probation and welfare officer for the references to a juvenile liaison officer, facilitator or chairperson and with any other necessary modifications.

86   Procedure at family conference

(1) Subject to the provisions of this Part or any direction given by the Court, a family conference may regulate its procedure in such manner as it thinks fit.

(2) A probation and welfare officer who convenes a family conference shall ensure, as far as practicable, that any information and advice required by the conference to carry out its functions are made available to it.

87   Administrative services to family conference

The [Director of the Probation and Welfare Service][1] shall provide such administrative services as may be necessary to enable a family conference to discharge its functions.

Amendments

1   Words substituted by by Criminal Justice Act 2006, s 137.

---

88   Remand in custody

[(1) Where the Court decides to remand in custody a child—

    (a) who is charged with or found guilty of one or more offences,

    (b) who is being sent forward for trial, or

    (c) in respect of whom the court has postponed a decision,

the following provisions of this section shall apply in relation to the child.

(2) The child shall be remanded to a place designated under this section as a remand centre.

(3) The Court shall explain the reasons for its decision in open court in language that is appropriate to the child's age and level of understanding.

(4) The Minister may by order designate as a remand centre any place, including part of a children detention school, which in the Minister's opinion is suitable for the custody of children who are remanded in custody under this section.

(5) The designation shall specify the sex and age of children who may be remanded to the remand centre concerned at any time.

(6) The Minister shall cause a copy of any order under this section to be sent to the President of the High Court, the President of the Circuit Court and the President of the District Court.

(7) A place may be designated as a remand centre only with the consent of its owners or, as the case may be, its managers.

(8) Where a remand centre is part of a children detention school, children remanded in custody to the centre shall, as far as practicable and where it is in the interests of the child, be kept separate from and not be allowed to associate with children in respect of whom a period of detention has been imposed.

(9) Where a remand centre is not part of a children detention school, the Minister shall appoint a board of management appointed to a children detention school under section 164 to manage the remand centre also in accordance with criteria laid down from time to time by the Minister.

(10) The Court shall not remand a child in custody under this section if the only reason for doing so is that—

    (a) the child is in need of care or protection, or

    (b) the Court wishes the Health Service Executive to assist it under section 76B in dealing with the case.

(11) Such matters as may be necessary or expedient for enabling remand centres to operate and be administered in accordance with this Act may be prescribed by the Minister.

(12) Notwithstanding the provisions of this section, males aged 16 or 17 years mentioned in subsection (1) may be remanded to Saint Patrick's Institution until places in a remand centre are available for males in that age group.

(13) A child remanded in custody to Saint Patrick's Institution may be transferred by the Minister to a remand centre.][1]

Amendments

1   Section 88 substituted by Criminal Justice Act 2006, s 135.

---

89   Non-application of section 5 of Bail Act, 1997

Section 5 (Payment of moneys into court) of the Bail Act, 1997, is amended by the addition of the following subsection:[1]

Amendments

1   See the amended Act.

---

90   Conditions of bail

(1) When releasing a child on bail the Court may, in the interests of the child, make the release subject to one or more than one of the following conditions:

   (a) that the child resides with his or her parents or guardian or such other specified adult as the Court considers appropriate,

   (b) that the child receives education or undergoes training, as appropriate,

   (c) that the child reports to a specified Garda Síochána station at a specified time at such intervals as the Court considers appropriate,

   (d) that the child does not associate with a specified individual or individuals,

   (e) that the child stays away from a specified building, place or locality except in such circumstances and at such times as the Court may specify,

   (f) such other conditions as the Court considers appropriate.

(2) Where a child who is released on bail does not comply with any condition to which the release was subject and is subsequently found guilty of an offence, the Court, in dealing with the child for the offence, may take into account the non-compliance in question and the circumstances in which it occurred.

(3) Subsection (2) is without prejudice to any other enactment which empowers a court to deal with offences committed by a person while on bail.

91   Attendance at Court of parents or guardian

(1) The parents or guardian of a child shall, subject to subsection (5), be required to attend at all stages of any proceedings—

   (a) against the child for an offence,

   (b) relating to a family conference in respect of the child, [...][1]

   (c) relating to any failure by the child to comply with a community sanction or any condition to which the sanction is [subject, or][1]

   [(d) under section 257D][1]

(2) Where the parents or guardian fail or neglect, without reasor
proceedings to which subsection (1) applies, the Court may a
issue a warrant for the arrest of the parents or guardian, and th
person to whom it is addressed to produce the parents or gu
time appointed for resuming the proceedings.

(3) Failure by the parents or guardian, without reasonable excuse, to ц
proceedings shall, subject to subsection (5), be treated for all purposes as n .
contempt in the face of the court.

(4) At the hearing of any proceedings in respect of the offence with which the child is
charged [or under section 257D][1], any parent or guardian who is required to attend the
proceedings may be examined in respect of any relevant matters.

(5) The Court may, at any stage of proceedings to which subsection (1) applies, excuse the
parents or a parent or the guardian of the child concerned from attendance at all or any part
of the proceedings in any case where the Court, either of its own motion or at the request of
any of the parties to the proceedings, is of opinion that the interests of justice would not be
served by such attendance.

(6) If in any such proceedings the whereabouts of the parents or guardian of the child
concerned are unknown, or neither a parent nor a guardian attends the proceedings for any
reason, the child may be accompanied during the proceedings by an adult relative or other
adult.

(7) This section does not apply to the parents of a child who is married.

Amendments

1 Subsections (1) and (4) amended by Criminal Justice Act 2006, s 138.

92 Conveyance to and from Court

Any child while being conveyed to or from the Court or while waiting before or after
attendance at the Court shall, as far as practicable, be prevented from associating with an
adult, not being a relative or spouse, who is charged with any offence other than an offence
with which the child is jointly charged.

93 Restrictions on reports of proceedings in which children are concerned

[(1) In relation to proceedings before any court concerning a child—

  (a) no report which reveals the name, address or school of any child concerned in the
      proceedings or includes any particulars likely to lead to the identification of any
      such child shall be published or included in a broadcast or any other form of
      communication, and

  (b) no still or moving picture of or including any such child or which is likely to lead to
      his or her identification shall be so published or included.

(2) A court may dispense, in whole or in part, with the requirements of this section in relation
to a child if satisfied that to do so is necessary—

  (a) where the child is charged with an offence—

    (i) to avoid injustice to the child,

    (ii) where the child is unlawfully at large, for the purpose of apprehending the child, or

    (iii) in the public interest,

  or

  (b) where the child is subject to an order under section 257D—

    (i) to avoid injustice to the child, or

    (ii) to ensure that the order is complied with.

(3) Where a court dispenses with any requirements of this section, it shall explain in open court the reasons for its decision.

(4) Subsections (3) to (6) of section 51 of this Act shall apply, with the necessary modifications, to matters published or included in a broadcast or other form of communication in contravention of subsection (1).

(5) This section shall apply in relation to proceedings on appeal from a court, including proceedings by way of case stated.

(6) This section shall not affect the provisions of any enactment concerning the anonymity of an accused or the law relating to contempt of court.]¹

Amendments

1   Section 93 substituted by Criminal Justice Act 2006, s 139.

---

94   Persons entitled to be present at hearing

(1) The Court shall exclude from the hearing of any proceedings before it all persons except—

  (a) officers of the Court,

  (b) the parents or guardian of the child concerned,

  (c) an adult relative of the child, or other adult who attends the Court pursuant to section 91(6),

  (d) persons directly concerned in the proceedings,

  (e) bona fide representatives of the Press, and

  (f) such other persons (if any) as the Court may at its discretion permit to remain.

(2) The order or decision of the Court (if any) in any such proceedings shall be announced in public.

PART 9

POWERS OF COURTS IN RELATION TO CHILD OFFENDERS

General

95   Interpretation (Part 9)

In this Part, unless the context otherwise requires—

"Act of 1970" means the Prisons Act, 1970;

"Act of 1983" means the Criminal Justice (Community Service) Act, 198

"children court district" has the same meaning as "district court district"

[...]¹

"compensation order" has the meaning assigned to it by section 6 of the Crimin...
Act, 1993;

"day centre" and "day centre order" have the meanings assigned to them by section 118;

"detention and supervision order" means an order under section 151;

"district" means either a children court district or a district court district, as the context requires;

"district of residence" means—

(a) in relation to an order under this Part affecting a child, the circuit or, as the case may be, the district in which the child resides or will reside while the order is in force, and

(b) in relation to a parental supervision order, the circuit or, as the case may be, the district in which the parents concerned reside or will reside while the order is in force;

"hostel residence" means a residence certified under section 126;

"parental supervision order" means an order under section 111;

"probation officer's report" has the meaning assigned to it by section 99;

"probation order" has the meaning assigned to it by section 2 of the Act of 1907.

Amendments

1 Definition deleted by Criminal Justice Act 2006, s 158 and Sch 4.

---

96   Principles relating to exercise of criminal jurisdiction over children

(1) Any court when dealing with children charged with offences shall have regard to—

(a) the principle that children have rights and freedom before the law equal to those enjoyed by adults and, in particular, a right to be heard and to participate in any proceedings of the court that can affect them, and

(b) the principle that criminal proceedings shall not be used solely to provide any assistance or service needed to care for or protect a child.

(2) Because it is desirable wherever possible—

(a) to allow the education, training or employment of children to proceed without interruption,

(b) to preserve and strengthen the relationship between children and their parents and other family members,

(c) to foster the ability of families to develop their own means of dealing with offending by their children, and

(d) to allow children reside in their own homes,

penalty imposed on a child for an offence should cause as little interference as possible with the child's legitimate activities and pursuits, should take the form most likely to maintain and promote the development of the child and should take the least restrictive form that is appropriate in the circumstances; in particular, a period of detention should be imposed only as a measure of last resort.

(3) A court may take into consideration as mitigating factors a child's age and level of maturity in determining the nature of any penalty imposed, unless the penalty is fixed by law.

(4) The penalty imposed on a child for an offence should be no greater than that which would be appropriate in the case of an adult who commits an offence of the same kind and may be less, where so provided for in this Part.

[(5) When dealing with a child charged with an offence, a court shall have due regard to the child's best interests, the interests of the victim of the offence and the protection of society.]¹

Amendments

1   Subsection (5) substituted by Criminal Justice Act 2006, s 136.

---

97   Construction of certain references

Any reference in an enactment, whether in force before or after the commencement of any relevant provision of this Act, to a person convicted, a conviction or a sentence shall, in the case of a child dealt with summarily by the Children Court, be construed as including a reference to a person found guilty of an offence, a finding of guilt or an order made upon such a finding, as the case may be.

98   Orders on finding of guilt

Where a court is satisfied of the guilt of a child charged with an offence it may, without prejudice to its general powers and in accordance with this Part, reprimand the child or deal with the case by making one or more than one of the following orders:

  (a) a conditional discharge order,

  (b) an order that the child pay a fine or costs,

  (c) an order that the parent or guardian be bound over,

  (d) a compensation order,

  (e) a parental supervision order,

  (f) an order that the parent or guardian pay compensation,

  (g) an order imposing a community sanction,

  (h) an order (the making of which may be deferred pursuant to section 144) that the child be detained in a children detention school [...]¹, including an order under section 155(1),

  (i) a detention and supervision order.

924

Amendments

1   Words deleted by Criminal Justice Act 2006, s 158 and Sch 4.

Probation Officer's Reports

99   Probation officer's report

(1) Subject to subsections (2) and (3), where a court is satisfied of the guilt of a child, it—

    (a) may in any case, and

    (b) shall, where it is of opinion that the appropriate decision would be to impose a community sanction, detention (whether or not deferred under section 144) or detention and supervision,

adjourn the proceedings, remand the child and request a probation and welfare officer to prepare a report in writing (a "probation officer's report") which—

    (i)   would assist the court in determining a suitable community sanction (if any) or another way of dealing with the child, and

    (ii) would contain information on such matters as may be prescribed, including any information specifically requested by the court.

(2) The probation officer's report shall, at the request of the court, indicate whether, and if so how, in his or her opinion any lack of care or control by the parents or guardian of the child concerned contributed to the behaviour which resulted in the child being found guilty of an offence.

(3) The court may, in addition, request that a victim impact report be furnished to it in respect of any victim of the child where it considers that such a report would assist it in dealing with the case.

(4) The court may decide not to request a probation officer's report where—

    (a) the penalty for the offence of which the child is guilty is fixed by law, or

    (b) (i)   the child was the subject of a probation officer's report prepared not more than 2 years previously,

        (ii) the attitude of the child to, and the circumstances of, the offence or offences to which that report relates are similar to his or her attitude to, and the circumstances of, the offence of which the child has been found guilty, and

        (iii) the previous report is available to the court and the court is satisfied that the material in it is sufficient to enable it to deal with the case.

(5) Where a court requests a report under this section, it may at any time summon as a witness any person whose evidence in its opinion would assist it in dealing with the case.

100   Remand for preparation of report or other reason

(1) Where the court is satisfied of the guilt of a child, it may defer taking a decision to allow time for the preparation of any report requested pursuant to this Part or for other sufficient reason and for that purpose may remand the child on bail, subject to such conditions as it may think fit, or, pursuant to section 88, in custody for, where appropriate, the minimum

period necessary for the preparation of any such report but not in any case exceeding 28 days.

(2) Notwithstanding subsection (1), where a child in respect of whom any such report is being prepared has been remanded on bail, the court may allow one extension of not more than 14 days for its preparation if satisfied, on application by the person preparing the report, that it is proper to do so.

(3) Any person responsible for making any such report shall make all reasonable endeavours to ensure that the report is lodged with the court at least 4 working days before the end of the period of remand.

101   Availability of child for preparation of report

(1) (a)   Where a court remands a child on bail to enable any report requested pursuant to this Part to be prepared, it may order—

    (i)   that in the meantime—

        (I)   the child shall reside at the residence of his or her parents, guardian, an adult relative or other adult who has undertaken to the court to care for the child, or

        (II)   where the child is already residing in a children's residential centre to which Part VIII of the Act of 1991 applies or in some other suitable place, the child shall continue to do so,

      and

    (ii)   that the child shall, for the purpose of facilitating the preparation of the report, attend, as the case may be—

        (I)   at the residence, centre or other suitable place, or

        (II)   at any day centre or other place specified in the order.

(b)   The time of the first such attendance at a day centre or other place shall be determined in accordance with subsection (3) and be specified in the order.

(c)   The times of subsequent attendances shall be determined in accordance with that subsection—

    (i)   in the case of such attendances at a day centre, by the person preparing the report, or

    (ii)   in the case of such attendances at another place, by the person in charge of that other place.

(2) An order under subsection (1)(a)(ii)(II) shall not be made unless the court is satisfied that the day centre or other place in question is reasonably accessible to the child concerned, having regard to the child's age, the means of access available to him or her and any other relevant circumstances.

(3) The times at which a child is required to attend at a day centre or other place pursuant to this section shall be determined having regard to the child's circumstances and shall be those—

(a)   at which the centre or place is available for that purpose, and

(b)   which are such as to avoid interference, as far as practicable, with any school or work schedules of the child.

102   Immunity from liability for reports

Any person who prepares or furnishes any report requested pursuant to this Part or who supplies any information for the purposes of preparing or furnishing it shall not be under any civil or criminal liability in respect of it unless the person has acted in bad faith in preparing or furnishing it or in supplying information for such purposes.

103   Access to reports

(1) A copy of any report furnished to a court pursuant to a request under this Part shall, subject to subsection (2), be made available, on request, by the clerk or other proper officer of the court to—

(a) the parents or guardian of the child concerned or, in their absence, an adult relative of the child or other adult accompanying the child during the proceedings,

(b) any counsel or solicitor representing the child,

(c) ...[1],

(d) every person entitled to appear and be heard at the proceedings to which the report relates and any counsel or solicitor appearing for any such person,

(e) where the court imposes a period of detention in a children detention school [...][2], the Director of the school [...][2], and

(f) any other person whom the court considers to have a proper interest in receiving a copy of the report.

(2) The court may order that the whole or any part of a report made available to any person pursuant to subsection (1) shall not be disclosed to any person specified in the order where it is satisfied that to do so would not be in the interests of the child or any other person to whom the report relates.

(3) Any copy of a report made available pursuant to subsection (1) shall, wherever possible, be supplied to the persons concerned in advance of the resumed sitting of the court.

Amendments

1   Paragraph (c) deleted by Criminal Justice Act 2006, s 158 and Sch 4.

2   Words deleted by Criminal Justice Act 2006, s 158 and Sch 4.

---

104   Right to tender evidence on report

Any person to whom a copy of a report has been made available pursuant to section 103 or who has been informed of its contents may tender evidence on any matter referred to in it.

105   Oral reports

The court may, unless any party to the proceedings objects, in exceptional circumstances direct that any report requested pursuant to this Part be made orally to the court.

106   Power of court on receipt of report

(1) Where the court has considered any report requested pursuant to this Part, it shall deal with the case in accordance with section 98.

(2) Before the court reaches a decision on the case, it may hear evidence from any person who prepared the report and from any person required under section 99(5) to attend the proceedings.

(3) The court shall also give a parent or guardian of the child concerned (or, if the child is married, his or her spouse), if present in court for the proceedings, or in his or her absence an adult relative or other adult accompanying the child, an opportunity to give evidence.

(4) The court may, on consideration of a probation officer's report, request such other report or reports in writing, including medical, psychiatric or psychological reports, as would in its opinion assist it in dealing with the case.

(5) The [Director of the Probation and Welfare Service]¹ shall arrange for the preparation of any such other report or reports, which shall contain information on such matters as may be prescribed and on any matter that may be specifically requested by the court.

Amendments

1   Words substituted by by Criminal Justice Act 2006, s 137.

107   Regulations regarding reports

(1) The Minister may prescribe such matters in relation to probation officers' reports or any other reports made pursuant to this Part as would in his or her opinion be of assistance to courts in dealing with cases under this Part.

(2) Without prejudice to the generality of subsection (1), the inclusion in probation officers' reports of information relating to the following matters, where appropriate, and such other matters (if any) as may be necessary or expedient for the purposes of any enabling provision of this Part to have full effect, may be prescribed—

(a)   the results of an interview with the child,

(b)   where it has been practicable for the probation and welfare officer concerned to interview the child's parent or guardian or any victim, the results of the interview,

(c)   the age, level of maturity, character, behaviour and attitude of the child and his or her willingness to make amends,

(d)   the educational circumstances and prospects of the child,

(e)   the child's friends and associates, and

(f)   the apparent motive for the child's behaviour and the likelihood of the child not committing further offences.

(3) Before prescribing any matter for which the Minister for Education and Science or the Minister for Health and Children has responsibility, the Minister shall obtain the agreement of that Minister.

Fines, costs and compensation

108   Maximum fines

Where a court is satisfied of the guilt of a child whom it has dealt with summarily for any offence and is of opinion that the appropriate penalty is or includes a fine, the fine shall not exceed half the amount which the District Court could impose on a person of full age and capacity on summary conviction for such an offence.

109   Determination of amount of fine and costs

(a) Subject to section 108, in determining the amount of a fine to be imposed on a child, and

(b) in determining whether to award costs against a child and the amount of any such costs, the court, among other considerations, shall have regard to the child's present and future means in so far as they appear or are

known to the court and for that purpose may require the child to give evidence as to those means and his or her financial commitments.

110   Default in payment of fine, costs or compensation

(1) Where a court orders a child to pay a fine, costs or compensation and the child is in default—

(a) the court shall not order that the child be detained in any case where, if the child were a person of full age and capacity, he or she would be liable to be committed to prison, and

(b) in lieu of such an order, the court may make one or more than one of the following orders:

(i)   in the case of a fine, an order reducing its amount,

(ii) an order allowing time, or further time, for payment of the fine, costs or compensation,

(iii) an order imposing a community sanction appropriate to the age of the child.

(2) An order under subsection (1)(b) shall be deemed for the purposes of this or any other Act to be an order made on a finding of guilt.

Orders in relation to parents or guardian

111   Parental supervision order

(1) In any proceedings in which a child is found guilty of an offence, the court may make an order for the supervision of the child's parents (a "parental supervision order") where it is satisfied that a wilful failure of the child's parents to take care of or control the child contributed to the child's criminal behaviour.

(2) Subject to subsection (3), the court may make a parental supervision order in addition to any other order it may make in relation to either the child or the child's parents.

(3) The court may not make an order under section 114 at the same time as a parental supervision order.

(4) Before making a parental supervision order, the court shall obtain and consider information about the parents' family and social circumstances and the likely effect of the order on those circumstances.

(5) A parental supervision order shall not be made without the parents of the child being given an opportunity to be heard.

(6) A parental supervision order may order the parents of the child to do any or all of the following:

(a) to undergo treatment for alcohol or other substance abuse, where facilities for such treatment are reasonably available,

(b) to participate in any course that is reasonably available for the improvement of parenting skills,

(c) adequately and properly to control or supervise the child to the best of their ability, except where the terms of any community sanction imposed on the child make such control or supervision impracticable,

(d) to comply with any other instructions of the court that would in its opinion assist in preventing the child from committing further offences.

(7) A parental supervision order shall be made for a period not exceeding 6 months.

(8) The court shall appoint a probation and welfare officer to supervise the parents, to assist them in complying with the order and to monitor compliance with it.

(9) When making a parental supervision order, the court shall have regard to any order it has made or is making in respect of the child concerned and, where any such order involves the supervision of the child by a probation and welfare officer, that officer shall also be appointed to supervise the child's parents.

(10) A parental supervision order shall specify—

(a) where appropriate, the address of any place where the parents may undergo treatment or participate in any course for the improvement of parenting skills,

(b) any particular requirements of the court in relation to the control or supervision of the child,

(c) any other instructions of the court, and

(d) the period during which the order is to be in force,

and the court shall explain to the parents in ordinary language the effects of the order and any requirements or instructions specified in it.

(11) Where for any reason the court considers that a parental supervision order should be made in respect of one parent only, the order may provide accordingly, notwithstanding that both parents have the custody, charge or care of the child.

(12) A parent who is the subject of a parental supervision order may appeal against the order.

112   Non-compliance with parental supervision order

(1) Where a parental supervision order is in force and it appears to the court, on application by the probation and welfare officer who is supervising the parents, that the parents have failed, without reasonable excuse (the proof of which shall lie on the parent or parents concerned), to comply with the order, the court may—

(a) if the order was made by a court in the district of residence, do one or more of the following:

(i) revoke the order,

(ii) make an order under section 114,

(iii) if it has not already done so, make an order under section 113, or

(iv) treat the failure to comply with the order for all purposes as if it were a contempt in the face of the court, or

(b) if the order was made by another court, remand the parents
that other court to be dealt with, and for that purpose paragι
relation to that court, with the necessary modifications.

(2) The matters which the court may take into account when making a
subsection (1) shall include the extent to which, and any period durin
complied with the parental supervision order.

(3) Where a court proposes to exercise its powers under subsection (1), it shall summon the parents to appear before it and, if the parents do not do so, may issue a warrant for their arrest.

(4) The jurisdiction vested in the Circuit Court in respect of proceedings to which subsection (1) relates shall be exercised by the judge for the time being assigned to the circuit where the parental supervision order was made.

(5) The jurisdiction vested in the Children Court or the District Court in respect of those proceedings shall be exercised by the judge for the time being assigned to the district of residence or, as the case may be, the district where the parental supervision order was made.

113   Compensation by parent or guardian

(1) Where a court is satisfied of the guilt of a child and that the appropriate way of dealing with the case is to make a compensation order (whether in addition to or instead of any other order), it may order that the compensation be paid by the parent or guardian of the child instead of by the child.

(2) The court may not order that the compensation be paid by a parent or guardian unless it is satisfied that a wilful failure of the parent or guardian to take care of or to control the child contributed to the child's criminal behaviour.

(3) An order may not be made under subsection (1) without giving the parent or guardian concerned an opportunity to be heard.

(4) Any sums imposed and ordered to be paid by a parent or guardian under this section may be recovered in like manner as if the order had been made on the conviction of the parent or guardian of the offence of which the child was found guilty.

(5) In determining whether to order a parent or guardian to pay compensation in accordance with subsection (1) and in determining the amount of the compensation, the court shall have regard to the present and future means of the parent or guardian in so far as they appear or are known to the court and for that purpose the court may require the parent or guardian to give evidence as to those means and his or her financial commitments.

(6) A parent or guardian who is the subject of a compensation order may appeal against the order.

(7) Notwithstanding anything in section 6 of the Criminal Justice Act, 1993, any sum ordered by a court to be paid under this section in respect of loss of or damage to property shall not be greater than the cost of its replacement or repair, as the case may be, and shall not include any loss or damage of a consequential nature.

(8) This section does not apply in relation to any person who is taking care of a child on behalf of [the Health Service Executive][1].

Amendmnts

Words amended by Health Act 2004, s 75 and Sch 7.

114   Binding over of parent or guardian

(1) Where a court is satisfied of the guilt of a child it may—

    (a)   order the parent or guardian, with his or her consent, to enter into a recognisance to exercise proper and adequate control over the child, and

    (b)   if the parent or guardian refuses to consent to such an order and the court considers the refusal unreasonable, treat the refusal for all purposes as if it were a contempt of court.

(2) An order under subsection (1)(a) may not require a parent or guardian to enter into a recognisance—

    (a)   for an amount exceeding [€317.43],

    (b)   where the child concerned will attain the age of 18 years within a period which is less than 3 years, for a period exceeding that period, or

    (c)   in any other case, for a period exceeding 3 years.

(3) Any rule of law relating to the forfeiture of recognisances shall apply to an order made under this section in relation to a recognisance entered into in pursuance of such an order as it applies to a recognisance to keep the peace or to be of good behaviour or both.

(4) A recognisance entered into by a parent or guardian in accordance with this section may be forfeited only if—

    (a)   the child concerned is found guilty by a court of another offence committed during the period of the recognisance, and

    (b)   the court is satisfied that the failure of the parent or guardian to exercise proper and adequate control over the child contributed to his or her committing that offence.

(5) In fixing the amount of a recognisance under this section, the court, among other considerations, shall have regard to the present and future means of the parent or guardian concerned in so far as they appear or are known to the court and for that purpose may require the parent or guardian to give evidence as to those means and his or her financial commitments.

(6) The parent or guardian may appeal against an order under this section.

(7) The court may vary or revoke an order made by it under this section if, on the application of the parent or guardian concerned, it appears to the court, having regard to any change in circumstances since the order was made, to be in the interests of justice to do so.

(8) An order under this section shall be in addition to or instead of any other order which the court may make.

(9) No order shall be made under this section without giving the parent or guardian an opportunity of being heard.

(10) When deciding whether to make an order under this section, the court, in addition to and without prejudice to any other consideration, shall have regard to the age and level of maturity of the child.

(11) This section does not apply in relation to any person who is taking care of a child on behalf of [the Health Service Executive]¹.

Amendments

Words amended by Health Act 2004, s 75 and Sch 7.

Community Sanctions

115   Community sanction

In this Part, **"community sanction"** means any of the orders referred to in paragraphs (a) to (j) which may be made by a court on being satisfied that a child is guilty of an offence—

    (a)   in the case of a child of 16 or 17 years of age, a community service order under section 3 of the Act of 1983,

    (b)   an order under section 118 (a day centre order),

    (c)   an order under section 2 of the Act of 1907 (a probation order),

    (d)   an order under section 124 (a probation (training or activities) order),

    (e)   an order under section 125 (a probation (intensive supervision) order),

    (f)   an order under section 126 (a probation (residential supervision) order),

    (g)   an order under section 129 (a suitable person (care and supervision) order),

    (h)   an order under section 131 (a mentor (family support) order),

    (i)   an order under section 133 (a restriction on movement order), or

    (j)   an order under section 137 (a dual order).

116   Imposition of community sanction

(1) Where a court—

    (a)   has considered a probation officer's report or any other report made pursuant to this Part,

    (b)   has heard the evidence of any person whose attendance it may have requested, including any person who made such a report, and

    (c)   has given the child's parent or guardian (or, if the child is married, his or her spouse), if present in court for the proceedings, or, if not so present, an adult relative of the child or other adult accompanying the child, an opportunity to give evidence,

it may make an order imposing on the child a community sanction, if it considers that the imposition of such a sanction would be the most suitable way of dealing with the case.

(2) Where the court intends to impose a community sanction it shall explain to the child in open court and in language appropriate to the level of understanding of the child—

    (a)   why a community sanction is being imposed,

    (b)   the terms of the sanction and any conditions to which it is being made subject,

(c) the expectation of the court that the child will be of good conduct while the community sanction is in force and the possible consequences for the child of his or her failure to comply with the sanction and any such conditions, and

(d) the expectation of the court that the child's parents or guardian, where appropriate, will help and encourage the child to comply with the sanction and any such conditions and not commit further offences.

(3) In any case where the court has explained to the child the matters referred to in subsection (2) and the child does not express his or her willingness to comply with the proposed community sanction and any conditions to which it is being made subject, the court may, instead of imposing such a sanction, deal with the case in any other manner in which it may be dealt with.

(4) Where a child fails to comply with a community sanction or any conditions to which it is subject or where for any reason a community sanction is revoked by the court, the court shall not make an order imposing a period of detention on the child unless it is satisfied that detention is the only suitable way of dealing with the child.

117   Conditions to which community sanction may be made subject

The conditions to which a community sanction imposed on a child may be made subject include conditions—

(a) requiring the child to attend school regularly,

(b) relating to the child's employment,

(c) aimed at preventing the child from committing further offences,

(d) relating to the child's place of residence,

(e) relating to the child undergoing counselling or medical treatment,

(f) limiting or prohibiting the child from associating with any specified person or with persons of any specified class,

(g) limiting the child's attendance at specified premises,

(h) prohibiting the consumption by the child of intoxicating liquor, and

(i) relating to such other matters as the court considers appropriate in relation to the child.

118   Day centres

(1) In this section—

"day centre" means a place to which subsection (2) applies;

"day centre order" means an order under subsection (5).

(2) For the purposes of this section the Minister shall provide or arrange for the provision of a sufficient number of places for use as day centres which shall be operated either by the probation and welfare service or by any body with the approval and assistance of that service.

(3) Before any place or part thereof may be used as a day centre, the [Director of the Probation and Welfare Service]1 shall inspect it and, if he or she considers that the place is suitable for such use, certify in writing accordingly.

(4) A certificate under subsection (3) shall remain in force for not more than one year from the date of its issue, unless it is cancelled by the [Director of the Probation and Welfare Service][1] before then on the ground that the place is no longer suitable for use as a day centre.

(5) (a) A court may by order direct that a child shall attend at a specified day centre for the purpose of participating in an occupation or activity, or receiving instruction, which is suitable and beneficial for him or her.

   (b) The child may participate in any such occupation or activity, or receive any such instruction, under supervision outside the day centre, and references in this section to attendance at a day centre include references to such participation or receiving outside it.

(6) The number of days a child shall be required to attend at a day centre pursuant to a day centre order shall be not more than 90, and attendance need not be on consecutive days.

(7) A child in respect of whom a day centre order has been made shall be under the supervision of a probation and welfare officer and while in attendance at a day centre shall be subject to the control, direction and supervision of the person in charge of the centre.

(8) A day centre order shall specify—

   (a) the name and address of the day centre which the child shall be required to attend while the order is in force,

   (b) the number of days that the child shall attend the centre,

   (c) the period of time during which attendance at the centre is required, being a period not exceeding 6 months, and

   (d) when and at what time the child is to report to the centre on the first occasion, and it may specify—

      (i) any programme of occupation, activity or instruction to be undertaken by the child,

      (ii) such other matters with respect to the child's attendance at the centre as the court determines, or

      (iii) such of the conditions provided for in section 117 as the court considers necessary for helping to improve the child's behaviour and to prevent him or her from committing further offences.

(9) When deciding on the number of days that the child shall attend at the day centre the court, in addition to and without prejudice to any other consideration, shall have regard to the child's age.

(10) A day centre order shall not be made unless the court is satisfied that the day centre to be specified in it is reasonably accessible to the child concerned or that arrangements can be made for the child's attendance at the centre, having regard to the child's age and sex, the means of access available to him or her and any other relevant circumstances.

(11) (a) The times at which a child is required to attend at a day centre shall, as far as practicable, be such as to avoid interference with any training the child is receiving, any attendance at a school or other educational establishment or any employment.

   (b) The first of those times shall be a time at which the centre is available for the attendance of the child, and the subsequent days and times shall be fixed by the person in charge of the day centre, having regard to the child's circumstances and the terms of the day centre order, without prejudice to the power of the court to direct that, as far as practicable, some of those times shall coincide with a specific event which it considers the child, for whatever reason, should refrain from taking part in or being present at.

(12) The person in charge of a day centre may, for good reason, excuse a child from attendance at the centre on a particular occasion or occasions.

(13) A child shall not, subject to subsection (14), be required to attend at a day centre on more than one occasion on any day or for more than 8 hours on any one day.

(14) Where the child participates in any occupation or activity, or receives any instruction, under supervision outside the day centre, subsection (13) shall not apply, and, where any such occupation, activity or instruction continues over more than one day, each such day shall count towards the number of days that the court has specified that the child shall attend at the centre.

(15) The person in charge of a day centre shall inform in writing the parent or guardian of the child of the days and times which the person in charge has fixed for the attendance of the child at the centre but in any case where a particular occupation, activity or instruction is arranged at short notice he or she may inform the parent or guardian orally.

(16) For the purpose of providing day centres the Minister may make arrangements, in agreement with any other Minister or any body, authority or person concerned, for the use of any premises, facilities or programmes provided by that Minister, body, authority or person.

(17) A day centre provided pursuant to arrangements made under subsection (16) may not necessarily—

    (a) be called a day centre even though it is a day centre for the purposes of this section, or

    (b) cater exclusively for children who have been found guilty of having committed offences.

(18) The probation and welfare service shall send a list of the day centres for the time being available for the reception of children to the President of the High Court, the President of the Circuit Court and the President of the District Court.

(19) On making a day centre order the court shall cause certified copies of the order to be sent to—

    (a) in case the order was not made by a judge of a court having jurisdiction in the district of residence, such a judge,

    (b) the person in charge of the day centre concerned,

    (c) the probation and welfare officer who is supervising the child, and

    (d) the parents or guardian of the child (or, if the child is married, his or her spouse) or, as appropriate, another adult in whose residence the child is residing while the order is in force.

(20) The person in charge of the day centre shall give a copy of the day centre order to the child.

Amendments

1   Words substituted by by Criminal Justice Act 2006, s 137.

---

119 Power to vary day centre order

(1) Where a day centre order is in force in respect of a child the Children Court, on application by the child or his or her parent or guardian or a probation and welfare officer, may vary the order if it appears to it that it would be in the interests of justice to do so, having regard to circumstances which have arisen since the order was made.

(2) An order varying a day centre order may—

    (a) vary the day or time specified for the child's first attendance at the relevant day centre,

    (b) if the Court is satisfied that the child proposes to change or has changed his or her residence, substitute for the day centre specified in the day centre order a day centre which the Court is satisfied is reasonably accessible to the child or at which arrangements can be made for the child's attendance, having regard to the child's age or sex, the means of access available to him or her and any other relevant circumstances, or

    (c) if the Court is satisfied that another day centre is providing a programme of occupation, activity or instruction more suited to the child's interests, substitute that day centre for the centre specified in the day centre order if the Court is satisfied that the substituted centre is reasonably accessible to the child or it appears to it that arrangements can be made for the child's attendance at that centre, having regard to his or her age, sex, the means of access available to the child and any other relevant circumstances.

(3) Where the Court is satisfied that the child proposes to change or has changed his or her residence and that there is no day centre reasonably accessible to the child's new or proposed new residence, the order varying the day centre order shall not require the child to attend at a day centre but shall require him or her to remain under the supervision of a probation and welfare officer for the duration of the day centre order.

(4) Where a day centre order is varied under this section, the Court shall cause certified copies of the order as so varied to be sent to—

    (a) the person in charge of the day centre specified in the order and of any day centre substituted for it pursuant to paragraph (b) or (c) of subsection (2),

    (b) the probation and welfare officer who is supervising the child, and

    (c) the parents or guardian of the child (or, if the child is married, his or her spouse) or, as appropriate, another adult in whose residence the child is residing while the day centre order, as so varied, is in force.

(5) The person in charge of the day centre shall give a copy of the day centre order, as so varied, to the child.

(6) The jurisdiction vested in the Court under this section shall be exercised by the judge for the time being assigned to the district of residence.

120 Power to revoke day centre order

(1) Where a day centre order is in force in respect of a child and it appears to a court, on application by the child or a probation and welfare officer, that it would be in the interests of justice, having regard to circumstances which have arisen since the order was made, that the order should be revoked or that the child should be dealt with in some other way for the offence in respect of which the order was made, the court may—

(a) if the order was made by a court in the district of residence, either—

    (i) revoke the order, or

    (ii) revoke it and deal with the child in another way, or

(b) if the order was made by another court, remand the child on bail to a sitting of that court to be dealt with, and for that purpose paragraph (a) shall apply in relation to that court, with the necessary modifications.

(2) The circumstances in which a day centre order may be revoked under subsection (1)(a)(i) shall include the progress the child has made, his or her satisfactory response to supervision and the discharge of any financial penalty.

(3) In dealing with a child under subsection (1)(a)(ii) a court shall take into account the extent to which the child has complied with the day centre order and any conditions to which it is subject.

(4) The jurisdiction vested in the court in respect of proceedings to which subsection (1) relates shall be exercised by the judge for the time being assigned to the district of residence or, as the case may be, the circuit or district where the day centre order was made.

(5) Where a court proposes to exercise its powers under subsection (1) otherwise than on an application by a child, it shall summon the child to appear before it and, if the child does not do so, may issue a warrant for his or her arrest.

121 Provisions where more than one day centre order

(1) Where more than one day centre order is in force in respect of a child at any time, the total number of days on which attendance by the child at the day centre is required under the orders shall, notwithstanding subsections (2) and (3), not exceed 90 days.

(2) Where a court makes day centre orders in respect of two or more offences of which the child has been found guilty, it may direct that the days of attendance specified in any of those orders shall be concurrent with or additional to those specified in any other of those orders.

(3) Where a court makes a day centre order and at the time of the making of the order there is in force in respect of the child another such order (whether made by the same or a different court), the court making the later order may direct in that order that the days of attendance specified therein shall be concurrent with or additional to those specified in the earlier order.

(4) In this section "attendance", in relation to a day centre, includes participation under supervision in any occupation, activity or instruction outside the centre.

122 Non-compliance with day centre order

(1) Where a day centre order in respect of a child is in force and it appears to a court, on application by the probation and welfare officer who is supervising the child, that the child has failed, without reasonable cause, to comply with the order or any condition to which it is subject, the court may—

(a) if the order was made by a court in the district of residence —

    (i) direct the child to comply with the order or any such condition in so far as it has not been complied with,

    (ii) revoke the order and substitute another day centre order or another community sanction, or

    (iii) revoke the order and deal with the case in any other way in which it could have been dealt with before the order was made, or

(b) if the order was made by another court, remand the child on bail to a sitting of that court to be dealt with, and for that purpose paragraph (a) shall apply in relation to that court, with the necessary modifications.

(2) The matters to be taken into account by the court in arriving at a decision pursuant to subsection (1) shall include the extent to which, and the period during which, the child has complied with the day centre order or any condition to which it is subject.

(3) Where the court proposes to exercise its powers under subsection (1), it shall summon the child to appear before it and, if the child does not do so, may issue a warrant for his or her arrest.

(4) The jurisdiction vested in the court under this section shall be exercised by the judge for the time being assigned to the district of residence or, as the case may be, the circuit or district where the day centre order was made.

123 Duties of child under day centre order

(1) A child in respect of whom a day centre order has been made shall be subject to the reasonable control, direction and supervision of the person in charge of a day centre, or a person authorised in that behalf by that person, while the child is—

(a) attending at a day centre or participating in any occupation or activity, or receiving any instruction, under supervision outside the centre, or

(b) travelling between the centre and a place outside the centre at which the child is directed or permitted to be.

(2) A child shall, while attending at the day centre—

(a) participate in such occupation or activities (whether physical or otherwise),

(b) attend such classes or groups of persons, or

(c) receive such instruction,

whether within or outside the centre, as the person in charge of the day centre, or a person authorised in that behalf by that person, considers to be in the interests of the child, having regard, where appropriate, to any directions of the court.

124 Probation (training or activities programme) order

(1) A court may order that a child shall undertake and complete a programme of training or specified activities in accordance with the provisions of this section.

(2) An order under this section shall for all purposes be a probation order, with the addition of such requirements as are imposed by this section.

(3) The order shall require the child concerned, as a condition of his or her recognisance, to undertake and complete a programme recommended to the court by a probation and welfare officer as being suitable for the development of the child and as helping to prevent the child from committing further offences through the attainment of positive social values; and for the duration of the programme the child shall comply with any instructions or directions given by or under the authority of the person or body managing the programme.

(4) The programme may be managed by the probation and welfare service or by any person or body recommended to the court by the [Director of the Probation and Welfare Service]1, whether or not the person or body is in receipt of any funding from the State, and it need not necessarily cater exclusively for children found guilty of offences.

(5) Where the programme is not managed by the probation and welfare service, the agreement of the person or body managing the programme shall be required for the admission of any child to it.

(6) An order under this section shall specify—

 (a) the programme to be undertaken and completed by the child,

 (b) the period during which the order is in force,

 (c) the first occasion on which the child shall attend the place where the programme is being organised so as to enable the person in charge of the programme to inform the child of the details of the programme, including the length of time it will take to complete, and

 (d) any other conditions that the child is required to observe while the order is in force, as provided for in section 2 of the Act of 1907 and section 117.

(7) Before making an order under this section the court shall be satisfied—

 (a) that a programme which is suitable for and reasonably accessible to the child is available,

 (b) that the child would benefit from it, and

 (c) where the programme is not managed by the probation and welfare service, that the person or body managing it agrees to accept the child.

(8) The court shall cause certified copies of its order to be sent to—

 (a) the person or body in charge of the programme,

 (b) the probation and welfare officer who is supervising the child, and

 (c) the parents or guardian of the child (or, if the child is married, his or her spouse) or, as appropriate, another adult with whom the child is residing while the order is in force.

(9) The person in charge of the programme shall give a copy of the order to the child.

Amendments

1 Words substituted by by Criminal Justice Act 2006, s 137.

---

125   Probation (intensive supervision) order

(1) A court may order that a child shall undergo intensive supervision in accordance with the provisions of this section.

(2) An order under this section shall for all purposes be a probation order, with the addition of such requirements as are imposed by this section.

(3) The order shall require the child concerned, as a condition of his or her recognisance—

 (a) to remain under the intensive supervision of a probation and welfare officer,

 (b) to reside at a specified residence during the period of intensive supervision, and

 (c) to undertake and complete an education or training programme, or to undergo a course of treatment, recommended to the court by a probation and welfare officer.

(4) Any such programme may be managed by the probation and welfare service or by any person or body recommended to the court by the [Director of the Probation and Welfare

Service][1], whether or not the person or body is in receipt of any funding from the State, and it need not cater exclusively for children found guilty of offences.

(5) Where the programme is not managed by the probation and welfare service, the agreement of the person or body managing the programme shall be required for the admission of any child to it.

(6) Subject to subsection (7), the period of intensive supervision shall—

    (a) commence on a date to be determined by the probation and welfare officer supervising the child,

    (b) not exceed 180 days, and

    (c) where it exceeds 90 days, be subject to review by the court after it has been in operation for 60 days.

(7) On a review of a period of intensive supervision in accordance with subsection (6)©, the court, having heard the child, his or her parents or guardian and the probation and welfare officer supervising the child, may—

    (a) reduce the period to 90 days, or

    (b) affirm it.

(8) During the time the order is in force the child shall comply with any instructions and directions given by the supervising probation and welfare officer.

(9) An order under this section shall specify—

    (a) the education or training programme to be undertaken and completed, or the course of treatment to be undergone, by the child concerned while the order is in force,

    (b) the period during which the order is in force,

    (c) the residence where the child is to reside while the order is in force, being the residence of the child's parents or guardian or, where that residence is not suitable or is unavailable for any reason, the residence of an adult recommended for that purpose by the probation and welfare service,

    (d) the name of the probation and welfare officer under whose supervision the child is to be placed and any provisions relating to the intensity of that supervision that the court considers appropriate, and

    (e) any other conditions that the child may be required to observe while the order is in force, as provided for in section 2 of the Act of 1907 and section 117.

(10) Before making an order under this section the court shall be satisfied—

    (a) that a probation and welfare officer is available for the intensive supervision of the child, and

    (b) that the child would benefit from that supervision and the programme or course of treatment referred to in subsection (3)(c).

(11) The court shall cause certified copies of its order to be sent to—

    (a) the person in charge of the programme or course of treatment,

    (b) the probation and welfare officer who is supervising the child, and

    (c) the parent or guardian of the child or, as appropriate, another adult with whom the child is residing while the order is in force.

(12) The person in charge of the programme or course of treatment shall give a copy of the order to the child.

Amendments

1   Words substituted by by Criminal Justice Act 2006, s 137.

126   Probation (residential supervision) order

(1) A court may order that a child shall reside in a hostel residence in accordance with the provisions of this section.

(2) An order under this section shall for all purposes be a probation order, with the addition of such requirements as are imposed by this section.

(3) The order shall require the child concerned, as a condition of his or her recognisance, to reside in any hostel residence provided by the probation and welfare service or recommended to the court by a probation and welfare officer on days to be determined by the probation and welfare officer supervising the child.

(4) A residence shall not be used as a hostel residence unless the [Director of the Probation and Welfare Service][1] has inspected it and a certificate by him or her that it is suitable for such use is in force.

(5) A certificate under subsection (4) shall remain in force for not more than one year from the date of its issue, unless it is cancelled by the [Director of the Probation and Welfare Service][1] before then on the ground that the residence is no longer suitable for use as a hostel residence.

(6) Where a hostel residence is not provided by the probation and welfare service, the agreement of the person or body providing it shall be required before an order is made under this section.

(7) An order under this section shall specify—

   (a)   the period, not exceeding one year, during which the order is in force,

   (b)   the name and address of the hostel residence concerned, and

   (c)   any other conditions that the child may be required to observe while the order is in force, as provided for in section 2 of the Act of 1907 and section 117.

(8) The child shall, while in the hostel residence, be subject to the control, direction and supervision of the person in charge of the residence.

(9) Subject to subsection (10), an order shall not be made under this section unless the court is satisfied that the hostel residence specified in it is reasonably close to the child's usual place of residence or to any place where the child is receiving education or training or is employed, and the court, in making such an order, shall have regard to the child's age, sex, means of access to his or her usual residence or any such place and any other relevant circumstances.

(10) Where the court is of opinion that it would be in the interests of a child to specify in the order a hostel residence that is not reasonably close to the child's usual place of residence and a suitable such hostel residence is available, it may specify that hostel in the order.

(11) The person in charge of the hostel residence, in consultation with the probation and welfare officer supervising a child, shall decide the times at which the child shall be required

to be in the hostel, having regard to the child's education, training or employment commitments and any other relevant circumstances, and any non-compliance with those times by the child, without good reason, shall be regarded as a breach of the order under this section.

(12) The court shall cause certified copies of its order to be sent to—

    (a) the person in charge of the hostel residence concerned,

    (b) the probation and welfare officer who is supervising the child, and

    (c) the parents or guardian of the child or, as appropriate, another adult with whom the child has been residing.

(13) The person in charge of the hostel residence shall give a copy of the order to the child.

Amendments

1   Words substituted by by Criminal Justice Act 2006, s 137.

---

127   Power to vary probation (residential supervision) order

(1) Where an order under section 126 is in force in respect of a child, the Children Court, on application by the child or his or her parent or guardian or a probation and welfare officer, may vary the order if it appears to it that it would be in the interests of justice to do so, having regard to circumstances which have arisen since the order was made.

(2) An order varying such an order may—

    (a) if the hostel residence specified in the order no longer complies with the requirements of section 126(9), substitute for that hostel residence another hostel residence which complies with those requirements,

    (b) in the case of a hostel residence specified in an order under section 126(10), substitute for the hostel residence so specified a hostel residence which complies with the requirements of section 126(9), if it appears to the Court that it would be in the interests of the child to reside in such a hostel residence.

(3) Where an order is varied under this section, the Court shall cause certified copies of the order as so varied to be sent to—

    (a) the person in charge of each hostel residence referred to in the order,

    (b) the probation and welfare officer who is supervising the child, and

    (c) the parents or guardian of the child or, as appropriate, another adult with whom the child was residing immediately before the order under section 126 was made.

(4) The person in charge of the hostel residence specified in the order under section 126 shall give a copy of the order, as so varied, to the child.

(5) The jurisdiction vested in the Court under this section shall be exercised by the judge for the time being assigned to the district of residence.

128   Failure to observe conditions of probation

(1) If a person who has failed to observe any condition of a recognisance under section 6 of the Act of 1907 is a child, the court may, in addition to its powers under that section—

(a) direct the child to comply with the condition in so far as it has not been complied with, or

(b) revoke the order and substitute another community sanction.

(2) Subsection (1) shall not apply to any recognisance under the Act of 1907 which was entered into before the commencement of this section.

129   Suitable person (care and supervision) order

(1) A court may by order assign a child to the care of a person, including a relative of the child concerned (a "suitable person"), in accordance with the provisions of this section.

(2) The court shall not make an order under this section unless the parents or guardian of the child have consented in writing to its being made and a probation and welfare officer has informed the court that a suitable person is available.

(3) An order under this section shall specify that the child shall ordinarily reside in the residence of the suitable person and shall also specify the period, not exceeding 2 years, for which the child shall so reside.

(4) While the order is in force the suitable person shall have the like control over the child as if he or she were the child's parent or guardian and shall do what is reasonable in all the circumstances of the case to safeguard or promote the child's health, development and welfare.

(5) The child shall be under the supervision of a probation and welfare officer while the order is in force.

(6) The order may specify such of the conditions provided for in section 117 as it considers necessary for helping to ensure that while the order is in force the child will be of good behaviour and will not commit any further offences.

(7) The court shall cause certified copies of its order to be sent to—

(a) where the order is not made by a judge of the court assigned to the district in which the suitable person resides, that judge,

(b) the parents or guardian of the child, and

(c) the probation and welfare officer who is supervising the child.

(8) The probation and welfare officer who is supervising the child shall give a copy of the order to the suitable person and the child.

(9) Where—

(a) on application by a probation and welfare officer to the court which made the order, the court is satisfied that its continuance in force—

(i) would not be in the interests of the suitable person or the child, or

(ii) is no longer necessary because of the progress made by the child,

(b) the parents or guardian of the child notify the court in writing that they are withdrawing their consent to the making of the order, or

(c) the suitable person applies to the court to have the order revoked, the court may, having regard to the period for which the order was in force and any other relevant circumstances—

(i) revoke the order,

(ii) revoke it and substitute another community sanction, or

(iii) revoke it and deal with the case in any other way in which it co'
dealt with before the order was made.

130   Non-compliance with suitable person (care and supervision) order

(1) Where an order under section 129 is in force and it appears to the court which made the order, on application by the probation and welfare officer who is supervising the child concerned, that the child has failed, without reasonable cause, to comply with the order or any condition to which it is subject, the court may—

(a) direct the child to comply with the order or any such condition in so far as it has not been complied with,

(b) revoke the order and substitute another order under section 129 or another community sanction, or

(c) revoke the order and deal with the case in any other way in which it could have been dealt with before the order was made.

(2) The matters to be taken into account by the court in arriving at a decision pursuant to subsection (1) shall include the extent to which, and the period during which, the child has complied with the order in question and any conditions to which it is subject.

(3) Where the court proposes to exercise its powers under subsection (1), it shall summon the child to appear before it and, if the child does not do so, may issue a warrant for his or her arrest.

131   Mentor (family support) order

(1) A court may by order assign a child to a person, including a relative of the child concerned (a "mentor"), to help, advise and support the child and the child's family in its efforts to prevent the child from committing further offences and to monitor the child's behaviour generally.

(2) An order under this section shall specify the period, not exceeding 2 years, during which the order shall remain in force and also specify that the child shall live with his or her parents or guardian at their normal place of residence during that period.

(3) A child in respect of whom an order under this section has been made shall, while the order is in force, be under the supervision of a probation and welfare officer who, in addition to his or her duty to supervise the child, shall help and advise the mentor in supporting the child and the child's family in its efforts to prevent the child from committing further offences.

(4) The court shall not make an order under this section unless—

(a) a probation and welfare officer has informed the court that a mentor is available, and

(b) the child and the child's parents or guardian consent to the making of the order and agree to cooperate with the mentor in accordance with its terms.

(5) The order may specify such of the conditions provided for in section 117 as the court considers necessary for helping to ensure that while the order is in force the child will be of good behaviour and will not commit any further offences.

(6) The court shall cause certified copies of its order to be sent to—

(a) the parents or guardian of the child, and

(b) the probation and welfare officer who is supervising the child.

(7) The probation and welfare officer who is supervising the child shall give a copy of the order to the mentor and to the child.

(8) Where—

    (a) on application by a probation and welfare officer to the court which made the order, the court is satisfied that its continuance in force—

        (i) would not be in the interests of the mentor or the child, or

        (ii) is no longer necessary because of the progress made by the child;

    (b) the parents or guardian of the child notify the court in writing that they are withdrawing their consent to the making of the order; or

    (c) the mentor applies to the court to have the order revoked,

the court may, having regard to the period for which the order was in force and any other relevant circumstances—

    (i) revoke the order,

    (ii) revoke it and substitute another community sanction, or

    (iii) revoke it and deal with the case in any other way in which it could have been dealt with before the order was made.

132   Non-compliance with mentor (family support) order

Section 130 shall apply, with any necessary modifications, to non-compliance with an order under section 131, or with any condition to which it is subject, as if for the references in section 130 to an order there were substituted references to an order under section 131.

133   Restriction on movement order

(1) A court may make either or both of the following orders in relation to a child:

    (a) an order that the child shall be at a specified residence between specified times during the period commencing at 7.00 p.m. on each day and ending at 6.00 a.m. on each following day,

    (b) an order that the child shall stay away from any specified premises, place or locality during specified days or between specified times, while the relevant order is in force.

(2) An order under subsection (1)(a) shall state—

    (a) the period, not exceeding 6 months, during which it is in force, and

    (b) the times between which the child concerned shall be at the specified residence.

(3) An order under subsection (1)(b) shall state—

    (a) the period, not exceeding 12 months, during which it is in force, and

    (b) the days on which or the times between which the child concerned shall stay away from the specified premises, place or locality.

(4) An order under this section may specify such of the conditions provided for in section 117 as the court considers necessary for helping to ensure that while the order is in force the child will be of good behaviour and will not commit any further offences.

(5) In determining for the purposes of subsection (1)(a) the times between which a child shall be at a specified residence the court shall have regard to the age and level of maturity of the child, the nature of the offence of which the child has been found guilty and any educational course, training or other activity in which the child is participating, and it shall ensure, as far

as practicable, that those times do not conflict with the practice by the child of his or her religion.

(6) In determining for the purposes of subsection (1)(b) the premises, place or locality, and the days or times, to be specified in an order under that subsection, the court shall have regard to the age and level of maturity of the child, the nature of the offence of which the child has been found guilty, the day or time that the child committed the offence, the place where the offence was committed and the likelihood of the child committing another offence in the same or similar premises, place or locality.

(7) The court shall cause certified copies of its order to be sent to—

    (a)   the child concerned,

    (b)   the child's parents or guardian or, where the residence specified in the order is not that of the parents or guardian, an adult living in the residence so specified,

    (c)   where the order has not been made by a judge of the court assigned to the district in which the child is to reside, such a judge, and

    (d)   the member in charge of the Garda Síochána station for the area where the child is to reside.

(8) An order under subsection (1)(b) may relate to one or more than one premises, place or locality.

134   Variation of restriction on movement order

(1) Where an order under section 133 is in force, the Children Court may, if it so thinks proper, on application by the child concerned or his or her parent or guardian or, where appropriate, an adult living in the residence specified in the order, vary the order by substituting another time or day or another residence for the time, day or residence specified in the order.

(2) The Court shall cause certified copies of the order as so varied to be sent to—

    (a)   the child concerned,

    (b)   the child's parents or guardian or, where the residence specified in the order is not that of the parents or guardian, an adult living in the residence so specified, and

    (c)   the member in charge of the Garda Síochána for the area where the child is to reside and, where appropriate, the area where the child was residing pursuant to the order under section 133.

(3) The jurisdiction vested in the Court under this section shall be exercised by the judge for the time being assigned to the district of residence.

135   Provisions regarding more than one restriction on movement order

(1) Where more than one order under section 133(1)(a) is in force in respect of a child at any time, the period during which a child is required to be at a specified residence shall, notwithstanding subsections (2) and (3), not exceed 6 months.

(2) Where a court makes orders under section 133(1)(a) in respect of two or more offences of which the child concerned has been found guilty, it may direct that the period for which the child is required by any of these orders to be at a specified residence shall be concurrent with or additional to that specified in any other of those orders.

(3) Where a court makes an order under section 133(1)(a) and at the time of the making of the order there is in force in respect of the child concerned another such order (whether made

by the same or a different court), the court making the later order may direct in that order that the period for which the child is required by that order to be at a specified residence shall be concurrent with or additional to that specified in the earlier order.

136   Non-compliance with restriction on movement order

[(1) A member of the Garda Síochána who finds a child in breach of an order under section 133 or of any condition to which it is subject may arrest the child without warrant.

(1A) Where it appears to a court that a child has failed, without reasonable cause, to comply with such an order or any condition to which it is subject, it may—

   (a)   if the order was made by a court in the district of residence—

      (i)   direct the child to comply with the order or any such condition in so far as it has not been complied with,

      (ii)   revoke the order and substitute another order under section 133 or another community sanction, or

      (iii)   revoke the order and deal with the case in any other way in which it could have been dealt with before the order was made,

      or

   (b)   if the order was made by another court, remand the child on bail to a sitting of that court to be dealt with, and for that purpose paragraph (a) shall apply in relation to that court, with the necessary modifications.]¹

(2) The matters to be taken into account by the court in arriving at a decision pursuant to subsection (1) shall include the extent to which, and the period during which, the child has complied with the order in question or any condition to which it is subject.

(3) [...]²

(4) The jurisdiction vested in the court under this section shall be exercised by the judge for the time being assigned to the district of residence or, as the case may be, the circuit or district where the order under section 133 was made.

Amendments

1   Subsection (1) substituted and (1A) inserted by Criminal Justice Act 2006, s 140(a).

2   Subsection (3) deleted by Criminal Justice Act 2006, s 140(b).

---

137   Dual order

(1) In this section "dual order" means an order which requires a child either—

   (a)   to be under the supervision of a probation and welfare officer for a specified period, or

   (b)   to attend at a day centre for a specified period not exceeding 90 days, and which also restricts the child's movements for a specified period not exceeding 6 months.

(2) The court may make a dual order where it is of opinion that neither supervision by a probation and welfare officer nor attendance at a day centre, including any conditions to which such supervision or attendance would be made subject, would of itself adequately reduce the likelihood of the child committing further offences.

(3) A dual order shall be deemed for all purposes—

(a) in so far as it imposes a requirement mentioned in subsection (1)(a), to be a probation order,

(b) in so far as it imposes a requirement mentioned in subsection (1)(b), to be a day centre order, and

(c) in so far as it restricts a child's movements, to be an order under section 133.

138 Expiry of community sanction

Every community sanction, other than an order under section 3 of the Act of 1983, shall, unless it sooner expires or the context otherwise requires, expire 6 months after the child in respect of whom the order was made attains the age of 18 years.

139 Commission of offence while community sanction in force

Where the court finds a child guilty of an offence, and the child is at that time subject to an order imposing a community sanction, the court may, in addition to or instead of any other powers available to it and subject to the provisions of this Part—

(a) revoke the order and make such other order imposing a community sanction on the child as the court thinks fit, or

(b) in addition to the order to which the child is already subject, make such other order as is mentioned in paragraph (a).

140 Effect of subsequent period of detention

An order which imposes a community sanction on a child for an offence and which is in force shall cease to be in force on the child commencing a period of detention for another offence.

141 Regulations

(1) The following matters may be prescribed:

(a) measures to prevent any risk to the health or welfare of any child on whom a community sanction has been imposed,

(b) procedures to be followed by a probation and welfare officer or any other person involved in supervising any such child,

(c) records to be kept in relation to any such child,

(d) such other matters (if any) as may be necessary or expedient for the purpose of enabling community sanctions to have full effect and for their due administration.

(2) The following matters may also be prescribed:

(a) the conditions under which children may be placed with suitable persons and under which mentors (within the meaning of section 131) may be assigned to support children and their families;

(b) the form of contract to be entered into by the [Director of the Probation and Welfare Service]1 with suitable persons and mentors;

(c) the supervision by a probation and welfare officer of—

(i) children placed with suitable persons and visits by the children to, and other contacts with, their parents or guardians and other members of their families and relatives,

    (ii) children to whom mentors have been assigned under section 131; and

  (d) such other matters in relation to—

    (i) placing children in the care of suitable persons by the court under section 129,

    (ii) regulating the powers, duties and functions of suitable persons and mentors under sections 129 and 131 respectively, and

    (iii) securing generally the welfare of such children and their future good behaviour, as may be necessary for the purposes of enabling sections 129 to 132 to have full effect.

Amendments

1   Words substituted by by Criminal Justice Act 2006, s 137.

Detention

142   Detention orders

A court may, in accordance with this Part, by order (in this Part referred to as a "children detention order") impose on a child a period of detention in a children detention school [...]¹ specified in the order.

Amendments

1   Words deleted by Criminal Justice Act 2006, s 158 and Sch 4.

143   Restriction on detention orders

(1) The court shall not make an order imposing a period of detention on a child unless it is satisfied that detention is the only suitable way of dealing with the child and [...]¹, that a place in a children detention school is available for him or her.

(2) Where an order is made under subsection (1), the court making the order shall give its reasons for doing so in open court.

Amendments

1   Words deleted by Criminal Justice Act 2006, s 158 and Sch 4.

144   Deferment of detention order

(1) Without prejudice to section 145, where a court—

  (a) has considered a probation officer's report or any other report made pursuant to this Part,

(b)   has heard the evidence of any person whose attendance it may have requested, including any person who made such a report,

(c)   has given the parent or guardian of the child concerned (or, if the child is married, his or her spouse), if present in court for the proceedings, or, if not so present, an adult relative of the child or other adult accompanying the child, an opportunity to give evidence, and

(d)   is of opinion that the appropriate way of dealing with the child would be to make a children detention order, it may defer making the order, in accordance with the provisions of this section, if a place is not available for the child in a children detention school or for any other sufficient reason.

(2) The court shall defer the making of a children detention order only if the court is satisfied that, having regard to the nature of the offence and the age, level of understanding, character and circumstances of the child concerned, it would be in the interests of justice to defer the making of the order.

(3) Where the making of a children detention order is deferred, the court shall adjourn the hearing and order that the child concerned be placed under the supervision of a probation and welfare officer.

(4) In case the making of the order has been deferred because a place for the child is not available in a children detention school, the court shall order that the Director of that school shall apply to the court to make the children detention order when such a place becomes available.

(5) In any other case, the court shall state in open court—

(a)   the period of detention that is being deferred,

(b)   the date of the resumed court hearing, and

(c)   that the court will take into account at that hearing the information in the probation and welfare officer's report concerning the child's conduct in the meantime and the other matters mentioned in subsection (7)(b).

(6) The court shall also explain to the child in open court in language appropriate to the level of understanding of the child—

(a)   why the making of the children detention order is being deferred and for what period,

(b)   any of the conditions referred to in section 117 which the court suggests should be complied with by the child during that period,

(c)   the expectation of the court that the child will be of good conduct during that period and the possible consequences for the child of his or her failure to comply with any such conditions, and

(d)   the expectation of the court that the child's parents or guardian, where appropriate, will help and encourage the child to comply with any such conditions and not commit further offences.

(7) (a)   The probation and welfare officer under whose supervision the child has been placed shall prepare a report on the child for consideration by the court at the resumed hearing.

(b)   The report shall contain information on the child's conduct after the finding of guilt, including the extent to which the child has complied with any conditions suggested by the court, on any change in the child's circumstances and on any

951

reparation by the child to the victim, together with any other information which the officer considers to be relevant.

(c) The officer shall make all reasonable endeavours to ensure that the report is lodged with the clerk or other proper officer of the court at least 4 working days before the date of the resumed hearing.

(8) The resumed court hearing shall take place not later than one year from the date of the adjourned hearing and may take place notwithstanding that the child has attained the age of 18 years in the meantime.

(9) At the resumed hearing the court shall consider the report prepared by the probation and welfare officer and, if the court thinks it necessary, hear evidence from the officer and shall by order—

(a) impose the period of detention which it had deferred or any shorter period,

(b) suspend the whole or any portion of a period of detention so imposed, or

(c) impose a community sanction appropriate to the age of the child concerned, and shall explain to the child in open court the reasons for its decision in language that the child understands.

(10) Where—

(a) the Director of a children detention school applies to the court pursuant to an order under subsection (4), and

(b) the court proposes to make a children detention order,

it may issue a summons requiring the child to appear before it and, if the child does not appear in answer to the summons, may issue a warrant for his or her arrest.

(11) Where the making of a children detention order has been deferred under this section it may not be further so deferred.

145   Alternative to detention where no place available in children detention school

Where—

(a) a court would impose a period of detention on a child [...]¹ if a place were available for the child in a children detention school,

(b) such a place is not available, and

(c) the court is satisfied that it would not be appropriate in the particular case to defer making a children detention order,

it may make, instead of a children detention order, an order imposing on the child the community sanction it considers most appropriate for the child.

Amendments

1   Words deleted by Criminal Justice Act 2006, s 158 and Sch 4.

---

146   Finding of guilt during deferment

A court which has deferred the making of a children detention order in relation to a child pursuant to section 144—

(a) may make the order before the expiration of the period of deferment if during that period the child is found guilty of any offence, and

(b) where it proposes to make such an order, whether on the date originally specified by the court or by virtue of paragraph (a) before that date, may issue a summons requiring the child to appear before it and, if the child does not do so, may issue a warrant for his or her arrest.

147 Detention in accordance with age of child

Amendments

1   Section 147 deleted by Criminal Justice Act 2006, s 158 and Sch 4.

148 Document to be produced to Director of children detention school

Where a child is ordered to be detained in a children detention school, a certified copy of the order shall be delivered with the child to the Director of the children detention school specified in the order and shall be sufficient authority for the detention of the child in the school for that period.

149 Period of detention in children detention school

[Where a child is found guilty of an offence in the Children Court, any term of detention in a children detention school imposed for the offence shall not be for a period longer than the term of detention or imprisonment which the court could impose on an adult who commits such an offence.][1]

Amendments

1   Section 149 substituted by Criminal Justice Act 2006, s 141.

150 Places of detention

Amendments

1   Section 150 deleted by Criminal Justice Act 2006, s 158 and Sch 4.

151 Detention and supervision

(1) Where a court is satisfied that detention is the only suitable way of dealing with a child [....],[1] it may, instead of making a children detention order, make a detention and supervision order.

(2) A detention and supervision order shall provide for detention in a [children detention school][2] followed by supervision in the community.

(3) Subject to subsection (4), half of the period for which a detention and supervision order is in force shall be spent by the child in detention in a [children detention school][2] and half under supervision in the community.

(4) Where the child is released from detention on earning remission of sentence by industry or good conduct or on being given temporary release under section 2 or 3 of the Act of 1960, supervision of the child in the community under the order shall be deemed to commence on the child's release.

(5) The supervision provided for in this section shall be by a probation and welfare officer.

(6) A detention and supervision order, in so far as it relates to detention, shall be deemed for all purposes to be a children detention order.

(7) A detention and supervision order may specify such of the conditions provided for in section 117 as the court considers necessary for helping to ensure that the child concerned would be of good behaviour and for reducing the likelihood of the child's committing any further offences.

(8) Section 130 shall apply, with any necessary modifications, to non-compliance with a detention and supervision order, or with any condition to which it is subject, as if for the references to an order in that section there were substituted references to a detention and supervision order.

Amendments

1   Words deleted by Criminal Justice Act 2006, s 158 and Sch 4.
2   Words substituted by Criminal Justice Act 2006, s 158 and Sch 4.

152   Transfer

[...][1]

Amendments

1   Section 152 deleted by Criminal Justice Act 2006, s 158 and Sch 4.

153   Rules governing places of detention

[...][1]

Amendments

1   Section 153 deleted by Criminal Justice Act 2006, s 158 and Sch 4.

154   Amendment of Criminal Justice (Community Service) Act, 1983

Section 2 of the Act of 1983 is hereby amended by the insertion of the following after "Saint Patrick's Institution"—

> [", in any children detention centre designated under section 150 of the Children Act, 2001,]¹ or in a children detention school".

Amendments

1   See the amended Act. Words deleted by Criminal Justice Act 2006, s 158 and Sch 4.

155   Punishment of certain indictable offences

[(1) Where—

  (a)   a child is convicted on indictment of an offence and sentenced to detention in a children detention school,

  (b)   the period of detention is served initially in such a school,

  (c)   the child has attained the age of 18 years before the period of detention has expired,

the person shall be transferred to a place of detention provided under section 2 of the Act of 1970 or a prison to serve the remainder of the period of detention.

(2) If, on attaining the age of 18 years, the person—

  (a)   is engaged in a particular course of education or in training which is not available in such a place of detention or in a prison, or

  (b)   is nearing the end of his or her period of detention in the school,

the person may continue to be detained in the school beyond that age for a period not exceeding 6 months.

(3) Notwithstanding any provision in any enactment, no child shall be transferred from a children detention school to a place of detention provided under section 2 of the Act of 1970 or a prison.]¹

(4) [...]²

(5) [...]²

(6) Any statutory provisions, rules or regulations applying to persons serving a sentence [...]³, in a place of detention provided for under section 2 of the Act of 1970 or in a prison shall, as appropriate, apply and have effect, with any necessary modifications, in relation to children transferred pursuant to this section.

(7) No sentence of detention imposed under subsection (1) for an offence shall be for longer than the term of imprisonment which the court could have imposed on a person of full age and capacity who is convicted of such an offence.

(8) Where a court imposes a period of detention exceeding 3 years, it shall give its reasons for doing so in open court.

Amendments

1   Subsections (1)–(3) substituted by Criminal Justice Act 2006, s 142(a).

2   Subsections (4)–(5) deleted by Criminal Justice Act 2006, s 142(b).

3   Words deleted by Criminal Justice Act 2006, s 142(c).

156   Restriction on punishment of children

No court shall pass a sentence of imprisonment on a child or commit a child to prison.

[156A   Transitional provision

(1) Notwithstanding anything in Part 9, males aged 16 and 17 years sentenced to detention may be detained in Saint Patrick's Institution or a place of detention until—

    (a) places suitable for the admission of children of those ages become available for designation as children detention schools under section 160, or

    (b) they have completed their period of detention.

(2) Subject to subsection (3), on or after the making of any such designation, any child serving a period of detention in Saint Patrick's Institution or a place of detention may be transferred to such a designated children detention school.

(3) A male aged 16 or 17 years may be transferred from Saint Patrick's Institution or a place of detention to a children detention school before such a designation is made and may later be transferred back to the Institution or place.

(4) A child who is serving a period of detention in St. Patrick's Institution or place of detention shall not have his or her period of detention varied by reason only of a transfer under subsection (2) or (3).

(5) In this section, "place of detention" means a place of detention provided under section 2 of the Act of 1970.][1]

Amendments

1   Section 156A inserted by Criminal Justice Act 2006, s 143.

[156B   Application of Prisons Acts, etc. rules to children detention schools

Pending the making of rules under section 179 for the management of children detention schools, the Prisons Acts 1826 to 1980 and any other enactments relating to or applying to St. Patrick's Institution or to persons serving sentences therein shall, except where they may be inconsistent with this Act, apply and have effect, with any necessary modifications, in relation to a children detention school and to persons detained therein as if the school were that Institution.][1]

Amendments

1   Section 156B inserted by Criminal Justice Act 2006, s 144.

PART 10
CHILDREN DETENTION SCHOOLS
General

157   Interpretation (Part 10)

In this Part, unless the context otherwise requires—

"Act of 1908" means the Children Act, 1908;

["authorised person" means a person authorised by the Minister under section 185]¹;

"board of management" has the meaning assigned to it by section 164;

"child" means a child found guilty or convicted of an offence by a court and in respect of whom a court has made a children detention order;

"Director" means a person appointed under section 180 as Director of a children detention school or, as the case may be, of more than one such school;

[...];²

[...];²

"responsible person", in relation to a child, means a relative of the child or a person in whose care the child is placed under this Act;

["staff" does not include teaching staff;]¹

"supervision in the community" has the meaning assigned to it by section 207.

Amendments

1   Definitions inserted by Criminal Justice Act 2006, s 145(a).

2   Definitions deleted by Criminal Justice Act 2006, s 145(b).

158   Principal object of children detention schools

It shall be the principal object of children detention schools to provide appropriate [appropriate educational, training and other programmes and facilities]¹ for children referred to them by a court and, by—

(a)   having regard to their health, safety, welfare and interests, including their physical, psychological and emotional wellbeing,

(b)   providing proper care, guidance and supervision for them,

(c)   preserving and developing satisfactory relationships between them and their families,

(d)   exercising proper moral and disciplinary influences on them, and

(e) recognising the personal, cultural and linguistic identity of

each of them, to promote their reintegration into society and prepare them to take their place in the community as persons who observe the law and are capable of making a positive and productive contribution to society.

Amendments

1 Words inserted by Criminal Justice Act 2006, s 158 and Sch 4.

159 Certified schools under Act of 1908

[(1) Subject to subsection (2), a certified reformatory school or industrial school under Part IV of the Act of 1908 shall, with the agreement of the Minister and the Minister for Education and Science, become a children detention school on the commencement of this section in relation to it.

(2) A certified industrial school under that Part shall, with the agreement of the Minister for Education and Science and the Minister for Health and Children and on the commencement of this section in relation to it, become premises provided and maintained by the Health Service Executive under section 38(2) of the Act of 1991 for the provision of residential care for children in care.

(3) On the commencement of this section in relation to a certified reformatory school or industrial school the functions relating to which stood vested in the Minister for Education and Science (other than the function of providing education and training and related programmes for children detained in it) immediately before such commencement, such functions shall—

(a) if the school becomes a children detention school, be vested in the Minister, or

(b) in the case referred to in subsection (2), be vested in the Health Service Executive.

(4) The lawfulness of the detention, and the period of detention, of a child who is detained in a certified reformatory or industrial school is not affected by the commencement of this section in relation to it.

(5) Any reference in any enactment to a reformatory school or an industrial school shall, on the commencement of this section in relation to it, be construed as a reference to a children detention school or, as the case may be, premises provided and maintained by the Health Service Executive under section 38(2) of the Act of 1991.][1]

Amendments

1 Section 159 substituted by Criminal Justice Act 2006, s 146.

[159A Education of children in children detention school, residential centres, etc

(1) In this section—

"Inspector" and "recognised school" have the meanings given to them in section 2 of the Education Act 1998;

"transferred premises" means a certified reformatory or an industrial school under Part IV of the Act of 1908 which, on the commencement of section 159 in relation to it, becomes a children detention school or premises provided and maintained by the Health Service Executive under section 38(2) of the Act of 1991;

"vocational education committee" means a committee established by section 7 of the Vocational Education Act 1930.

(2) Any recognised school forming part of transferred premises is dissolved.

(3) A vocational education committee in whose functional area transferred premises are situated shall provide for the education of children in those premises.

(4) Without prejudice to the generality of subsection (3), each vocational education committee shall, in respect of any such premises—

(a) plan, coordinate and review the provision of education and services ancillary thereto,

(b) ensure that the education provided therein meets the requirements of education policy as determined from time to time by the Minister for Education and Science,

(c) ensure that students have access to appropriate guidance to assist them in their educational and career choices,

(d) promote the moral, spiritual, social and personal development of the children concerned, and

(e) ensure that the needs of personnel involved in management functions and those in relation to staff development generally are identified and provided for.

(5) The functions of an Inspector within the meaning of the Education Act 1998 apply, with any necessary modifications, in relation to education facilities provided in respect of any transferred premises.

(6) A person who, immediately before the dissolution under this section of a recognised school, is a member of its teaching staff shall, on such dissolution, become an employee of the vocational education committee in whose functional area the recognised school is situated; and the rights and entitlements enjoyed by the person as such employee in respect of tenure, remuneration, fees, allowances, expenses and superannuation shall not, by virtue of the operation of this Act, be any less beneficial than the rights and entitlements enjoyed by that person immediately before the dissolution.][1]

Amendments

1   Section 159A inserted by Criminal Justice Act 2006, s 147.

[159B   Transfer of property, rights and liabilities of certified industrial school on commencement of section 159(2)

(1) In this section—

"board of management" in relation to a certified industrial school, includes managers of the school within the meaning of the Act of 1908;

"certified industrial school" means a certified industrial school under Part IV of the Act of 1908 which becomes transferred premises on the transfer day;

"land" includes any rights, liabilities, powers or privileges relating to or connected with the land;

"property" includes any rights or liabilities relating to or connected with the property;

"transfer day" means the day on which a certified industrial school becomes, by virtue of section 159(2), premises provided and maintained by the Health Service Executive under section 38(2) of the Act of 1991 for the provision of residential care for children in care;

"transferred premises" means premises which on the transfer day become premises so provided and maintained.

(2) On the transfer day—

(a) any land or other property, and any other rights or liabilities, vested in the Minister for Education and Science in relation to the certified industrial school concerned or in its board of management immediately before that day, except any rights or liabilities referred to in paragraph (b), is transferred to and vested in the Health Service Executive without any conveyance or assignment,

(b) any rights or liabilities—

(i) of the Minister for Education and Science in relation to the school or of its board of management, and

(ii) relating to or connected with members of its teaching staff or their teaching functions,

however arising immediately before that day are transferred to and vested without any assignment in the vocational education committee in whose functional area the transferred premises are situated.

(3) Any rights or liabilities transferred under this section may on and after the transfer day be sued on, recovered or enforced by or against the Health Service Executive or the vocational education committee concerned in its own name, and it shall not be necessary for the Executive or committee to give notice of the transfer to the person whose rights or liabilities are so transferred.

(4) Subject to subsection (5), where any proceedings to which the certified industrial school concerned or its board of management is a party are pending immediately before the transfer day, the Minister for Education and Science shall be substituted for the school or board as a party to the proceedings on and after that day, and the proceedings shall not abate by reason of the substitution.

(5) Where—

(a) the Minister for Education and Science is a party to proceedings pending immediately before the transfer day in relation to a certified industrial school or its board of management, whether by virtue of subsection (4) or otherwise, and

(b) the Minister and the Health Service Executive or vocational education committee concerned agree that the Executive or committee should be substituted for the Minister as a party to the proceedings,

the Executive or the committee shall notify the other parties to the proceedings accordingly, and the proceedings shall not abate by reason of the substitution.

(6) A person who was an employee of the certified industrial school concerned (other than a member of its teaching staff) immediately before the transfer day shall on that day become an employee of the Health Service Executive, and the rights and entitlements enjoyed by the

person as such employee in respect of his or her terms and conditions of employment, including remuneration, allowances and superannuation, shall not by virtue of the operation of this Act be any less beneficial than the rights and entitlements enjoyed by that person immediately before that day.

(7) The functions, including powers and duties, of the Minister for Health and Children under the Child Care Act 1991, as amended, and the Health Acts 1947 to 2006 in relation to premises provided and maintained under section 38(2) of the Act of 1991 by the Health Service Executive for the provision of residential care for children in care apply and have effect in relation to transferred premises.

(8) A child who is found guilty of an offence may not be ordered to be placed or detained in transferred premises.

(9) The Minister for Education and Science shall, before the commencement of section 159(2), direct the transfer of each child convicted of an offence or on remand in respect of an offence from any place which, on such commencement, becomes transferred premises to a certified reformatory or industrial school under Part IV of the Act of 1908 or a children detention school to serve the whole or any part of the unexpired residue of his or her period of detention.

(10) This section is without prejudice to section 159A.]¹

Amendments

1   Section 159B inserted by Criminal Justice Act 2006, s 148.

---

160   Designation of children detention schools

(1) The Minister may, with the agreement of its owners, provide any place, or any school or premises, for use as a children detention school and by order designate it as such a school.

(2) The Minister may arrange for the construction of any building for use as a children detention school and by order designate it as such a school.

(3) The Minister may direct one of his or her officers—

   (a)   to examine the structure, condition and environs of any place, school, premises or building referred to in subsections (1) and (2), and

   (b)   to report to the Minister on its suitability as a children detention school, and for that purpose the officer so directed may, with the Minister's approval, employ whatever expert help and advice he or she considers necessary.

(4) No order shall be made by the Minister under this section in relation to any place, school, premises or building unless, having considered a report under subsection (3), he or she is satisfied that it is suitable for use as a children detention school.

(5) An order under this section may be revoked by the Minister, including an order under this subsection.

(6) An order under this section shall be laid by the Minister before each House of the Oireachtas.

161 Provision of other places for detention of children

[(1) The Minister may enter into arrangements with any person or body for the provision by that person or body on behalf of the Minister of a place (except a prison) where children found guilty of offences can be detained.

(1A) Before entering into any such arrangements, the Minister shall be satisfied that the place provides treatment or other facilities not available in children detention schools.

(1B) The Minister may enter into arrangements under subsection (1) with more than one such person or body.

(1C) A child detained in a children detention school may be transferred to a place provided under subsection (1) with the agreement of the Minister and the person or body providing the place and, with such agreement, may be transferred back to that school.]¹

(2) The provisions of this Part relating to children detention schools shall, subject to subsection (3), apply to a place provided under subsection (1).

(3) Where a place is so provided, provisions as to its management, staffing and operation generally and the terms, conditions and rules under which it operates shall be subject to agreement between the persons managing it and the Minister.

(4) The powers of any court in relation to children detention schools shall apply also to a place provided under this section.

(5) Any such place need not cater exclusively for children found guilty of offences.

(6) The Minister shall cause the President of the High Court, the President of the Circuit Court and the President of the District Court to be notified of any arrangements entered into under subsection (1).

[(7) In this section, "place" includes part of a building.]²

Amendments

1   Subsection (1) substituted and (1A)–(1C) inserted by Criminal Justice Act 2006, s 149(a).

2   Subsection (7) inserted by Criminal Justice Act 2006, s 149(b).

162 Funding of such places

The Minister shall, on such terms and conditions as he or she thinks fit, make available to the persons managing any place provided for under section 161 such funds as are necessary for its operation—

(a) by a periodic contribution of funds,

(b) by a grant, or

(c) by a contribution in kind (whether by way of materials or labour or any other service).

163 Closure of schools

(1) Where the Minister is of opinion that a children detention school is no longer suitable for the detention of children or is no longer needed for that purpose, the Minister may make an

order declaring that the school shall cease to be such a school as and from a time specified in the order.

(2) Where a board of management of a children detention school, or the managers of a place to which section 161 applies, informs or inform the Minister that a school is temporarily unsuitable for the detention of children, the Minister may make an order declaring that the school is to cease to be such a school for a period to be specified in the order.

(3) Where a children detention school ceases for any time to be such a school pursuant to an order under this section, the children detained therein shall be placed out under supervision in the community or transferred to another children detention school in accordance with the provisions of this Part relating to such placing out or transfer.

(4) The Minister shall cause a copy of any order made under this section to be sent to the board of management, or the managers, of the school or place concerned, the President of the High Court, the President of the Circuit Court and the President of the District Court.

Boards of Management

164 Boards of management

(1) The Minister shall appoint a board of management to each children detention school or to more than one such school.

(2) The boards of management of certified reformatory schools and industrial schools which became children detention schools at the commencement of section 159 shall cease to exist on the appointment of boards of management to those schools under this section.

165 Functions of boards of management

(1) A board of management shall manage the children detention school or schools to which it has been appointed in accordance with criteria laid down from time to time by the Minister and, without prejudice to the generality of the foregoing, shall—

    (a) carry out any such policy in relation to children on remand or in detention as may be specified by the Minister,

    (b) cooperate and liaise with other bodies who are interested or engaged in assisting children who have been charged with offences or are at [risk, and][1]

    (c) [...][2]

    (d) perform the other functions assigned to it under this Part.

(2) Boards of management shall have all such powers as are necessary or expedient for the exercise of their functions.

Amendments

1 Subsection (1)(b) amended by Criminal Justice Act 2006, s 150(a).

2 Subsection (1)(c) deleted by Criminal Justice Act 2006, s 150(b).

---

166 Additional functions

(1) The Minister may by order assign such additional functions to one or more than one of the boards of management as the Minister considers to be incidental to or consequential on the functions assigned to them under other provisions of this Part.

(2) An order under this section may be amended or revoked by the Minister, including an order under this subsection.

167 Membership, etc., of boards of management

(1) Each board of management shall consist of a chairperson and 12 other members.

(2) (a) The Minister shall from time to time as occasion requires appoint a member of a board of management to be its chairperson.

   (b) Where the chairperson ceases during his or her term of office to be a member of the board, he or she shall thereupon also cease to be its chairperson.

   (c) The chairperson shall, unless he or she sooner dies, resigns, becomes disqualified or is removed from office, hold office as such chairperson until his or her term of office as a member of the board expires but, if reappointed as such a member, he or she shall be eligible for reappointment as chairperson.

(3) In appointing persons to be members of a board of management, the Minister shall have regard to the desirability of their having knowledge or experience of matters that come within the competence of such a board in the performance of its functions.

(4) Of the members of each board of management at least—

   (a) one shall be an officer of the Minister,

   (b) one shall be [an employee of the Health Service Executive]¹ nominated by the Minister for Health and Children,

   (c) one shall be an officer of the [Minister for Education and Science]² nominated by that Minister,

   (d) two shall be members of the staff of the children detention school or schools under the board's management, and

   (e) two shall be representative of persons living in the area of one or more than one of such schools.

(5) Members of a board of management shall be appointed for a term not exceeding 4 years and shall be eligible for reappointment.

(6) Members of a board of management shall act on a part-time basis.

Amendments

1 Words amended by Health Act 2004, s 75 and Sch 7.
2 Words inserted by Criminal Justice Act 2006, s 158 and Sch 4.

168 Removal and resignation of members

(1) The Minister may remove from office a member of a board of management who, in the opinion of the Minister, has become incapable through ill-health of effectively performing

his or her functions or has committed stated misbehaviour or whose removal appears to the Minister to be necessary for the effective performance by the board of its functions.

(2) A member of a board of management may at any time resign by letter addressed to the Minister, and the resignation shall take effect as and from the date on which the Minister receives the letter.

169   Casual vacancies

(1) If a member of a board of management dies, resigns, becomes disqualified or is removed from office, the Minister may appoint a person to be a member in his or her stead.

(2) A person so appointed shall hold office for the remainder of the term of office of the member whom he or she replaces and be eligible for reappointment.

170   Temporary substitutes

Whenever it appears to the Minister that any member of a board of management is, on account of illness or for other sufficient reason, temporarily unable to act, the Minister may appoint another person to act for that member for such period as the Minister thinks proper.

171   Remuneration of members

The chairperson and any other member of a board of management shall be paid, out of funds at the disposal of the board, such remuneration (if any) and such allowances for expenses as the Minister, with the approval of the Minister for Finance, may from time to time determine.

172   Funding of Board

For the purposes of expenditure by a board of management in the performance of its functions, the Minister may in each financial year, with the consent of the Minister for Finance, advance to the board out of moneys provided by the Oireachtas such sum or sums as the Minister, after consultation with the board, may determine.

173   Accounts and audits

(1) Each board of management shall—

(a) keep in such form and in respect of such accounting periods as may be approved of by the Minister, with the consent of the Minister for Finance, all proper and usual accounts (including an income and expenditure account and balance sheet) of the resources of the board and of all moneys received or expended by it,

(b) keep such special accounts as the Minister may from time to time direct, and

(c) where a board has been appointed to manage more than one children detention school, ensure that separate accounts are kept and presented to the board by each such school.

(2) (a) Accounts kept in pursuance of this section shall be submitted by each board of management to the Comptroller and Auditor General not later than 3 months after the end of each accounting year.

(b) A copy of the income and expenditure account and of the balance sheet and of such other (if any) of its accounts as the Minister may direct, together with a copy of the report of the Comptroller and Auditor General on the accounts, shall be presented by each board to the Minister as soon as may be.

(c)   The Minister shall cause copies of each of the documents aforesaid to be laid before each House of the Oireachtas.

174   Annual report and information

(1) Each board of management shall submit to the Minister an annual report which shall include information on the performance of its functions during the year to which it relates, information relating to the children detention school or schools under its management and such other information in such form as each board considers appropriate or as the Minister may direct.

(2) A report under subsection (1) shall be submitted to the Minister not later than 6 months after the end of the year to which it relates.

(3) Each board of management shall, at the request of the Minister, supply the Minister with such information relating to the performance of its functions as the Minister may from time to time specify.

(4) A copy of each report under subsection (1) shall be laid by the Minister before each House of the Oireachtas.

175   Meetings and procedure

(1) Each board of management shall hold such and so many meetings as may be necessary for the performance of its functions.

(2)   (a)   The chairperson of a board of management shall, if present, chair meetings of the board.

(b)   If and so long as the chairperson is not present or if the office of chairperson is vacant, the members who are present at a meeting of the board shall choose one of their number to chair the meeting concerned.

(c)   The chairperson and each other member present shall have a vote.

(d)   Every question shall be determined by a majority of the votes of the members present and voting on the question.

(e)   In the case of an equal division of votes, the chairperson or, in his or her absence, the member chosen to chair the meeting shall have a second or casting vote.

(f)   The quorum for a meeting shall be 6 or such greater number as the board may from time to time determine.

(3) A board of management may act notwithstanding one or more than one vacancy among its members and, subject to the provisions of this Part, shall determine its own procedure.

176   Directions by Minister

(1) The Minister may give directions to a board of management of a children detention school or the persons managing a place provided under section 161 in relation to their management of the school or place, and the board or persons shall comply with any such directions.

(2) Directions under subsection (1) shall not apply to any individual child detained in any such school or place.

177   Membership of either House of Oireachtas or of European Parliament

(1) Where a person who is a member of a board of management is—

    (a)   nominated as a member of Seanad Éireann, or

    (b)   elected as a member of either House of the Oireachtas or to the European Parliament, or

    (c)   regarded pursuant to Part XIII of the Second Schedule to the European Parliament Elections Act, 1997, as having been elected to the European Parliament to fill a vacancy,

the person shall thereupon cease to be a member of the board.

(2) Where a person employed by a board of management is—

    (a)   nominated as a member of Seanad Éireann, or

    (b)   elected as a member of either House of the Oireachtas or to the European Parliament, or

    (c)   regarded pursuant to Part XIII of the Second Schedule to the European Parliament Elections Act, 1997, as having been elected to the European Parliament to fill a vacancy, the person shall thereupon stand seconded from employment by the board and shall not be paid by, or be entitled to receive from, it any remuneration or allowance in respect of the period commencing on such nomination or election or when that person is so regarded as having been elected (as the case may be) and ending when that person ceases to be a member of either such House or such Parliament.

(3) A person who is for the time being entitled under the Standing Orders of either House of the Oireachtas to sit therein or who is a member of the European Parliament shall, while that person is so entitled or is such a member, be disqualified from becoming a member of a board of management or from employment in any capacity by it.

(4) Without prejudice to the generality of subsection (2), that subsection shall be construed as prohibiting, among other things, the reckoning of a period mentioned in that subsection as service with a board of management for the purposes of any superannuation benefits.

178   Non-disclosure of information

(1) Subject to subsection (2), a member of a board of management shall not disclose to any person who is not such a member any information relating to any person which the member has acquired as such member without that person's consent.

(2) Subsection (1) shall not apply in relation to any such disclosure of information to the Minister or his or her officers or to the Comptroller and Auditor General.

179   Rules by boards of management

(1) The board of management of a children detention school or schools may at any time [with the consent of the Minister][1], and shall whenever so required by the Minister, make rules—

    (a)   for the management of the school or schools under its management and the maintenance of discipline and good order generally therein, and

    (b)   without prejudice to the generality of the foregoing, setting out the procedures and conditions applicable to—

        (i)   the grant of mobility trips under section 204,

        (ii)   the grant of temporary leave under section 205, and

(iii) placing out under supervision in the community pursuant to section 207.

(2) The rules shall be consistent with this Part and any regulations made under it by the Minister or any criteria so laid down or general directions so given by him or her for the management of the school or schools concerned.

(3) A notice containing an abridged version of the rules shall be displayed in a conspicuous place in each children detention school, and a child on admission to such a school shall be given a document which contains information relating to the rules and the daily routine in the school and is written in language appropriate to the age of the children catered for in the school.

Amendments

1 Words inserted by Criminal Justice Act 2006, s 158 and Sch 4.

Director and staff of schools

180 The Director

(1) A board of management shall, from time to time as occasion requires, appoint a person to be responsible for the immediate control and supervision of a children detention school, or more than one such school under its management, and each person so appointed shall be known as the Director of the school or schools concerned.

(2) The appointment of a Director shall be on such terms and conditions as may be determined by the board of management concerned with the consent of the Minister and the Minister for Finance.

(3) A board of management shall, within 10 days after appointing a Director, notify the Minister of the Director's name.

(4) A Director shall not be a member of the board that appointed him or her.

(5) A Director shall perform such functions as may be assigned to him or her by the board of management concerned.

(6) Such functions of a Director as may be specified by him or her from time to time may, with the consent of the board, be performed by such member of the staff of the children detention school concerned as may be authorised in that behalf by the Director.

(7) The functions of a Director may be performed, during his or her absence or when the post of Director is vacant, by such member of the staff of the children detention school concerned as may from time to time be designated for that purpose by its board of management.

(8) Where a child is detained in a children detention school, the Director of the school shall—

(a) have the like control over the child as if he or she were the child's parent or guardian, and

(b) do what is reasonable (subject to the provisions of this Part) in all the circumstances of the case for the purpose of safeguarding or promoting the child's education, health, development or welfare.

181   Staff of children detention schools

(1) A board of management shall appoint such and so many persons to be members of the staff of the children detention school or schools under its management as the board, with the consent of the Minister and the Minister for Finance, from time to time thinks proper.

(2) A member of the staff of a children detention school shall be employed on such terms and conditions (including terms and conditions relating to remuneration and superannuation) as the board of management of the school, with the consent of the Minister and the Minister for Finance, may from time to time determine.

(3) (a)   The class or classes of staff of a children detention school, and the number of staff in each class, and

(b)   the grades in each such class, and the number of staff in each such grade, shall be determined by the board of management of the school with the consent of the Minister and the Minister for Finance.

182   Transfer of staff

Every person who, immediately before the commencement of section 159, was a Director or member of the staff of a certified reformatory school or industrial school which becomes a children detention school on such commencement shall thereupon become and be a member of the staff of that school.

183   Terms and conditions of transferred staff

(1) A person who is transferred under the provisions of this Act to a board of management shall not, while in the service of the board, save in accordance with a collective agreement negotiated with any recognised trade union or staff association, receive a lesser scale of pay or be made subject to less beneficial terms and conditions of service than the scale of pay to which that person was entitled and the terms and conditions of service to which he or she was subject immediately before the day on which he or she was so transferred.

(2) Until such time as the scale of pay and the terms and conditions of service of a person transferred under the provisions of this Act to a board of management are varied by the board, with the agreement of the Minister and the Minister for Finance, following consultation with any recognised trade unions or staff associations concerned, the scale of pay to which he or she was entitled and the terms and conditions of service, restrictions, requirements and obligations to which he or she was subject immediately before his or her transfer shall continue to apply to him or her and may be applied or imposed by the board while he or she is a member of its staff, and no such variation shall operate to worsen the scale of pay or the terms or conditions of service aforesaid applicable to such person immediately before the day on which he or she was so transferred, save in accordance with a collective agreement negotiated with any recognised trade union or staff association.

(3) In this section "recognised trade union or staff association" means a trade union or staff association recognised by the board of management concerned for the purposes of negotiations which are concerned with the remuneration, conditions of employment or working conditions of employees.

184   Superannuation of staff

(1) As soon as may be after its appointment, a board of management shall prepare and submit to the Minister a scheme or schemes for the granting of superannuation benefits to or in

respect of such of the staff (including the Director) of the children detention school or schools under its management as it thinks fit.

(2) Every such scheme shall fix the time and conditions of retirement for all persons to, or in respect of whom, superannuation benefits are payable under the scheme or schemes, and different times and conditions may be fixed in respect of different classes of persons.

(3) A board of management may at any time prepare and submit to the Minister a scheme amending or revoking a scheme previously submitted and approved of under this section.

(4) A scheme or amending scheme submitted by a board of management to the Minister under this section shall, if approved of by the Minister with the consent of the Minister for Finance, be carried out by the board in accordance with its terms.

(5) If any dispute arises as to the claim of any person to, or the amount of, any superannuation benefits in pursuance of a scheme or schemes under this section, such dispute shall be submitted to the Minister who shall refer it to the Minister for Finance whose decision shall be final.

(6) No superannuation benefits shall be granted by a board of management to or in respect of any of its staff (including the Director) who are members of a scheme under this section, nor shall any other arrangement be entered into for the provision of any superannuation benefits to such persons on ceasing to hold office, otherwise than in accordance with a scheme or schemes submitted and approved of under this section.

(7) Superannuation benefits granted under schemes under this section to persons transferred under section 182 and the terms and conditions relating to those benefits shall not be less favourable to those persons than those to which they were entitled immediately before the commencement of this section.

(8) Where at any time during the period beginning on the commencement of this section and ending immediately before the coming into operation of a scheme under this section, a superannuation benefit falls due for payment to or in respect of a person who was transferred under section 182, the benefit shall be calculated and paid by the relevant board of management in accordance with the scheme or such provisions in relation to superannuation as applied to the person immediately before the day this section comes into operation, and for that purpose that person's pensionable service with the board and previous pensionable service shall be aggregated.

(9) Every scheme submitted and approved of under this section shall be laid before each House of the Oireachtas as soon as may be after it is approved of and, if a resolution annulling the scheme is passed by either House within the next 21 days on which that House has sat after the scheme is laid before it, the scheme shall be annulled accordingly, but without prejudice to the validity of anything previously done thereunder.

Inspection of schools

185   Inspection of children detention schools

[(1) The Minister shall cause each children detention school to be inspected.

(2) An inspection shall be conducted by a person authorised in that behalf by the Minister.

(3) The person so authorised shall have expertise and experience in relation to the inspection of children's residential accommodation.]¹

Amendments

1 Section 185 substituted by Criminal Justice Act 2006, s 151.

186   Functions of authorised person

[(1) A person authorised under section 185 shall carry out inspections at least once every 12 months of each children detention school.

(2) Without prejudice to the generality of subsection (1), an authorised person shall, in carrying out an inspection of any such school, pay particular attention to—

    (a) the conditions in which the children are detained and the facilities available to them,

    (b) their health, safety and well-being,

    (c) policies and practice concerning the preservation and development of relationships between them and their families,

    (d) policies and practice concerning their discipline, care and protection, and

    (e) policies and practice in relation to the normal routine of the school.

(3) The authorised person may hear complaints by children who at any time were or who are detained in a children detention school, and for that and any other purpose—

    (a) may interview them and any member of the staff in the school concerned, and

    (b) shall have access to records, whether in legible or non-legible form, relating to the administration of the school and the children detained therein.

(4) Any interviews with children shall be with their consent and may, if they agree, take place in private.

(5) The authorised person—

    (a) shall not be an employee of any children detention school which the person inspects, and

    (b) shall be independent in the exercise of his or her functions in carrying out inspections.

(6) The authorised person shall submit a report to the Minister in relation to any inspection carried out under this section and publish the report at the same time as it is so submitted.

Amendments

1 Section 186 substituted by Criminal Justice Act 2006, s 152.

[186A   Investigation of matters arising in relation to children detention schools, etc.

(1) Where—

    (a) matters of concern in relation to a children detention school or place provided under section 161 are raised in a report of a person authorised under section 186 or otherwise, and

    (b) the Minister is satisfied that it would be desirable to investigate those matters, the Minister shall appoint a person (in this section referred to as an "Inspector") to investigate and report to him or her thereon.

(2) The Inspector shall carry out an investigation into the matters referred to in subsection (1) and such other matters relevant to them as he or she considers necessary for the purposes of the investigation.

(3) For those purposes, the Inspector may—

    (a) enter any children detention school or place provided under section 161,

    (b) examine the records, whether in legible or non-legible form, of the school or place, and

    (c) interview members of the staff of the school, including the Director, and members of its board of management or, as the case may be, members of the staff and managers of the place.

(4) The Inspector—

    (a) shall not be an employee of any children detention school which he or she inspects,

    (b) shall be independent in the exercise of his or her functions in carrying out inspections, and may interview any child who at any time was or who is detained in a children detention school.

(5) Any such interview shall be with the consent of the child concerned and may, if the child agrees, take place in private.

(6) The Inspector shall submit a report to the Minister in relation to the investigation.

(7) Each such report shall, where appropriate, contain recommendations which in the Inspector's opinion require to be implemented.

(8) A copy of each such report shall be laid by the Minister before each House of the Oireachtas.

(9) Before laying a report before each House of the Oireachtas pursuant to subsection (3), the Minister may omit material from it where the omission is necessary to avoid the identification of any person.

(10) An appointment of an Inspector shall be for a specified investigation, but the Minister may appoint the same person to carry out a further investigation or investigations as the Minister considers appropriate.

(11) The appointment of an Inspector shall be on such terms and conditions as may be determined by the Minister with, in the case of any terms and conditions relating to remuneration, the consent of the Minister for Finance.][1]

Amendments

1   Section 186A inserted by Criminal Justice Act 2006, s 153.

187   Powers of Inspector

[...][1]

Amendments

1   Section 187 deleted by Criminal Justice Act 2006, s 158 and Sch 4.

188   Reports of inspections and investigations

[...]¹

Amendments

1   Section 188 deleted by Criminal Justice Act 2006, s 158 and Sch 4.

189   Annual report of Inspector

[...]¹

Amendments

1   Section 189 deleted by Criminal Justice Act 2006, s 158 and Sch 4.

190   Visiting panel

(1) A visiting panel for children detention schools shall be established as soon as may be after the commencement of this section and shall consist of such number of persons, not being more than 8 or less than 6, as the Minister shall think proper.

(2) The members of the visiting panel shall be appointed by the Minister, and every member so appointed shall hold office as such member for such period not exceeding 3 years as the Minister shall think proper and specifies when appointing the member.

(3) In appointing members of the visiting panel, the Minister shall ensure that persons with knowledge or experience of matters relating to the welfare of children including their cultural and linguistic needs are adequately represented on it.

(4) The Minister may establish at any future time or times one or more than one additional visiting panel should the geographical situation of any of the schools justify such a course.

(5) The Minister may make rules setting out the duties and powers of visiting panels and the manner in which they shall perform the duties and exercise the powers imposed or conferred on them by this Part or by the rules.

191   Duties and powers of visiting panels

(1) A visiting panel appointed under section 190 shall observe such of the rules made by the Minister under that section as apply to it, and, subject to those rules, it shall be the duty of a visiting panel—

(a) to visit each children detention school from time to time and at frequent intervals and there to hear any complaint which may be made to it by any child residing in the school and, if so requested by the child, to hear any such complaint in private,

(b) to report to the Minister any abuses or irregularities observed or found by it in any school,

(c) to report to the Minister in relation to any repairs or structural alterations to any school which may appear to it to be needed, and

(d) to report to the Minister in relation to any other matter relating to any school either as instructed by the Minister or on its own initiative.

(2) A visiting panel and every member thereof shall be entitled at all times to visit either collectively or individually a children detention school in respect of which it is appointed and shall at all times have free access either collectively or individually to every such school and every part of it.

(3) The Minister may request the board of management of a children detention school to instruct the visiting panel to report to that board on any matter relating to the school.

(4) The board of management of such a school shall forward to the Minister any report made to it under this section, together with its views on the report.

(5) Copies of any such report and of the board of management's views on it shall be laid by the Minister before each House of the Oireachtas.

(6) Before laying a report before each House of the Oireachtas, the Minister may omit material from it where the omission is necessary to avoid the identification of any person.

192 Visits by judges

Any judge may visit any children detention school or any place provided under section 161 at any time.

Operation of schools

193 Obligation of Director to accept children

The Director of a children detention school shall accept any child ordered by a court to be detained in the school, unless the children detention order is, on its face, defective.

194 Reception of children in schools

(1) Subject to subsection (2), a children detention school shall be open at all times for the reception of children referred to it under this Part.

(2) The Minister may decide that subsection (1) shall not apply in respect of any school or any part of a school for a specified time where he or she is satisfied that, apart from those children who are eligible and suitable for placing out on supervision in the community under section 207, there are adequate and suitable alternative places available for children during that time in other schools.

(3) Where the Minister makes a decision pursuant to subsection (2), some or all of the children detained in the school the subject of the decision may be transferred to other schools in accordance with the provisions of this Part relating to such transfers or may be placed out on supervision in the community under section 207, if eligible and suitable for being so placed out.

195 Maximum number of detained children

(1) The Minister shall certify the maximum number of children who may be detained in each children detention school at any time.

(2) The Minister may vary any certificate under subsection (1), or vary any certificate varied under this subsection, where he or she is satisfied that such a variation is justified.

(3) The Minister shall cause a copy of any certificate or variation of any certificate under this section to be sent to the President of the High Court, the President of the Circuit Court, the President of the District Court and the Director of each children detention school.

196 Sex and age of detained children

(1) The Minister shall certify the sex and ages of children who may be detained in each children detention school at any time.

(2) The Minister may vary any certificate under subsection (1), or vary any certificate varied under this subsection, where he or she is satisfied that such a variation is justified.

(3) The Minister shall cause a copy of any certificate or variation of any certificate under this section to be sent to the President of the High Court, the President of the Circuit Court, the President of the District Court and the Director of each children detention school.

197 Treatment of children

The Minister shall decide which children detention schools shall provide any particular courses of specialised treatment which in his or her opinion should be available for children who may be in need of any such treatment and shall cause the President of the High Court, the President of the Circuit Court, the President of the District Court and the Director of each children detention school to be informed accordingly.

198 Transfer between schools

[(1) The Minister may direct the transfer of a child detained in a children detention school to another such school to serve the whole or any part of the remainder of the child's period of detention if—

    (a) the school to which the child is transferred caters, in accordance with the provisions of this Part, for that class of child, or

    (b) the Minister considers that the transfer is necessary in the interests of the good governance of children detention schools,

and, in either case, the school to which the child is transferred provides the conditions and facilities necessary for it to achieve its principal object in the case of the child.

(2) Before giving a direction under this section, the Minister shall consult the Directors of the children detention schools from and to which it is desired to transfer the child so as to ascertain whether the transfer would be in the child's interests or whether another course should be adopted in respect of the child.

(3) A direction under subsection (1) may be given at the request of the Director of a children detention school and, if so given, this section shall apply in relation to the direction with the necessary modifications.][1]

Amendments

1   Section 198 substituted by Criminal Justice Act 2006, s 154.

199   Provision as to religious observance

The Director of a children detention school shall ensure that each child detained in it shall, as far as practicable, be given the opportunity to receive religious assistance and instruction and the opportunity of practising his or her religion.

200   Provision of medical treatment

If it appears to the Director of a children detention school that a child detained in it requires medical attention that cannot properly be given in the school, the Director shall make arrangements for the child to be received into any hospital or other institution where he or she can receive the necessary attention, and that child, while so absent from the school, shall for the purposes of this Act be deemed to be in lawful custody.

201   Discipline

(1) Any child who breaches the rules of a children detention school may be disciplined on the instructions of the Director of the school in a way that is both reasonable and within the prescribed limits.

(2) Without prejudice to the power of the Minister to prescribe limits for the disciplining of children detained in children detention schools, the following forms of discipline shall be prohibited—

    (a)   corporal punishment or any other form of physical violence,

    (b)   deprivation of food or drink,

    (c)   treatment that could reasonably be expected to be detrimental to physical, psychological or emotional wellbeing, or

    (d)   treatment that is cruel, inhuman or degrading.

202   Permitted absence

(1) The Director of a children detention school may, by order in writing, permit a child to be absent from the school, whether or not accompanied—

    (a)   for the purpose of attending the funeral of a relative,

    (b)   for the purpose of visiting a relative who is seriously ill, or

    (c)   for any other purpose of exceptional importance that the Director thinks proper, being a purpose which the Director considers to be directly associated with the welfare or rehabilitation of the child concerned.

(2) The order shall specify the period for which the child may be absent from the school and the purpose for which it was made.

(3) A copy of the order shall be given to the child at or before the commencement of the absence.

(4) The order may be subject to any conditions, limitations or restrictions that the Director thinks appropriate to impose.

(5) The child to whom a copy of the order is given shall carry the copy at all times during the permitted absence.

(6) A failure, without reasonable excuse, by a child to return to the school when his or her period of permitted absence has expired shall be treated as a breach of the discipline of the school.

(7) A member of the Garda Síochána who detects any child in breach of subsection (6), or of any conditions, limitations or restrictions to which the order permitting the absence is subject, shall so inform the Director of the school concerned and return the child to the school.

(8) The period of a child's permitted absence from a school shall be deemed to be part of the child's period of detention in the school but, if a child fails to return to the school when the period of permitted absence has expired, the time that elapses thereafter shall be excluded in calculating the time during which he or she is to be detained.

203   Other permitted absences

(1) The Director of a children detention school may, by order in writing, permit a child to be absent from the school unaccompanied on a recurring basis or on one occasion only—

(a) for the purpose of seeking employment or engaging in employment or obtaining work experience,

(b) for the purpose of receiving additional training or education,

(c) for the purpose of participating in sport, recreation or entertainment in the community, or

(d) for any other purpose conducive to the reintegration of the child into the community.

(2) The Director may at any time before the end of a period of permitted absences under this section cancel the order permitting the absences.

(3) The Director of each children detention school shall keep the [Minister and][1] board of management of the school informed of the implementation of the [...][2] policy in relation to absences permitted under this section and section 202.

(4) The provisions of subsections (2) to (8) of section 202 shall, with the necessary modifications, apply in relation to an absence under this section as if it were an absence under that section.

Amendments

1   Words inserted by Criminal Justice Act 2006, s 158 and Sch 4.

2   Words deleted by Criminal Justice Act 2006, s 158 and Sch 4.

---

204   Mobility trips

(1) In this section "mobility trips" means authorised absences from a children detention school of children detained therein for the purpose of—

(a) assisting their reintegration into society by promoting their personal and social development, their awareness and appreciation in matters of culture, education and recreation, and

(b) where appropriate, the implementation of any necessary treatment or counselling directions.

(2) Each mobility trip shall be authorised by the Director of the children detention school concerned and shall be granted for a specified period.

(3) During a mobility trip the child shall be accompanied at all times by at least one member of the staff of the school.

(4) Before authorising any mobility trip, the Director shall be satisfied, on the basis of an assessment of the child's suitability for such trips, that the purpose of the mobility trip is appropriate for the child.

(5) The Minister may suspend, for a specified period, mobility trips for a particular child or for any children detention school where he or she is satisfied that they would not be in the best interests of the child or school or of society generally during that period.

(6) Any period specified in subsection (5) may be renewed on as many occasions as the Minister considers necessary until the circumstances that gave rise to the suspension of the mobility trips no longer apply.

(7) Any breach by a child of the rules governing the grant of mobility trips shall render that child ineligible for such trips for such period as the Director may determine.

(8) Absconding while on a mobility trip shall be treated as a breach of discipline of the school.

(9) The Director of each children detention school shall keep the [Minister and]¹ board of management of the school informed of the implementation of the [...]² rules in relation to the grant of mobility trips.

Amendments

1   Words inserted by Criminal Justice Act 2006, s 158 and Sch 4.
2   Words deleted by Criminal Justice Act 2006, s 158 and Sch 4.

---

205   Temporary leave

(1) The Director of each children detention school shall formulate a temporary leave programme for every child detained in the school for whom temporary leave is appropriate and ensure that every such programme is in accordance with the rules of the school's board of management in that regard.

(2) No temporary leave programme shall provide for temporary leave in the first one month of any child's period of detention.

(3) The Director may suspend, for a specified period, the temporary leave programme of any child or of the children in the school concerned where the Director is satisfied that temporary leave would not be in the best interests of the child or school or of society generally during that period.

(4) The Director may alter the temporary leave programme of any child where he or she is satisfied that to do so would be in the best interests of the child or of society generally.

(5) The one-month period referred to in subsection (2) need not necessarily have been served in one children detention school.

206 Conditions of grant of temporary leave

(1) A child while on temporary leave shall be in the care of his or her parents or guardian, or of a responsible person, who shall undertake to the Director of the children detention school concerned to supervise the child during the period of temporary leave.

(2) In deciding to grant temporary leave in any case, the Director shall be as satisfied as reasonably possible that the person who has undertaken to supervise the child will do so and, where a child has previously been granted temporary leave, the Director shall take into account how the child was supervised during that leave.

(3) Where a period of temporary leave involves a child being absent from the children detention school for one or more than one night, the child shall reside in the living accommodation of the person who has undertaken to supervise the child or in other accommodation with the prior approval of the Director, and, where that person so agrees, it shall be a condition of the leave that the child remain in that accommodation during a specified period between 7.00 p.m. on any day and 6.00 a.m. on the following day.

(4) Subject to subsection (3), where a child is so absent, a condition of the temporary leave may require the child to remain in the living accommodation of the person supervising the child or in such other accommodation, as the case may be, for different periods on different dates.

(5) Before the commencement of a period of temporary leave in respect of any child, the Director shall arrange for the member in charge of the Garda Síochána station for the area in which the child will reside during the period of the leave to be informed of the child's address, the period of the leave and, where appropriate, the periods during which the child is required to remain at that address.

(6) A member of the Garda Síochána who detects a child in breach of a condition specified in or pursuant to subsection (3) or (4) shall so inform the Director of the school concerned, return the child to the school in which he or she was detained when granted the temporary leave and inform the person who undertook to supervise the child accordingly as soon as practicable.

(7) A child who contravenes the rules governing temporary leave or, as the case may be, a condition specified in or pursuant to subsection (3) or (4) shall be ineligible for further temporary leave for such period as may be determined in accordance with the policy in that regard of the children detention school in which he or she was detained when granted the temporary leave.

(8) A failure, without reasonable excuse, by a child to return to the school on the expiry of the period of temporary leave shall be treated as a breach of the discipline of the school and of the rules governing temporary leave.

(9) The period of a child's absence from a school on temporary leave shall be deemed to be part of the child's period of detention in the school but, if a child fails to return to the school when the period of temporary leave has expired, the time that elapses thereafter shall be excluded in calculating the period during which he or she is to be detained.

(10) On the grant of temporary leave to a child, the Director shall specify in a notice in writing to the child—

    (a) the time of commencement and ending of the period of the leave, and

    (b) where appropriate, any condition specified in or pursuant to subsection (3) or (4).

207   Supervision in community

(1) Where a child is detained in a children detention school, the Director of the school may at any time, after consultation with the [Director of the Probation and Welfare Service]1, authorise the placing out of the child under supervision in the community to reside with his or her parents or guardian or a responsible person who is willing to receive and take charge of the child.

(2) Before authorising a placing out under subsection (1), the Director shall be satisfied that the child will continue to receive appropriate education or training while he or she is placed out and that the placing out conforms to the rules of the school's board of management in that regard.

(3) A child placed out under subsection (1) shall be under the supervision in the community of a probation and welfare officer.

(4) (a) An authorisation under subsection (1) shall be in writing and be signed by the Director and shall specify—

        (i) the name of the person who is willing to receive and take charge of the child, and

        (ii) any conditions imposed by the Director which he or she considers appropriate and which are consistent with any rules made by the board of management of the school under section 179.

    (b) The child shall comply with any conditions so specified.

(5) Where a child is placed out under this section, the Director shall ensure that at the time of the placing out—

    (a) the conditions of the child's placing out are communicated in writing to the child, to the person receiving and taking charge of the child and to the probation and welfare officer supervising the child in the community, and

    (b) the placing out and those conditions are notified to the member in charge of the Garda Síochána station for the area in which the child will be residing.

(6) A placing out under this section shall be in force until revoked or until the period of detention imposed by the court has expired, whichever is the sooner, and while it is in force the child shall be deemed to be under the care of the Director.

(7) The Director may at any time, after consultation with the [Director of the Probation and Welfare Service]1, revoke a placing out where—

    (a) he or she has reason to believe that it is necessary to do so for the protection or welfare of the child,

    (b) the child, without reasonable excuse, fails to comply with a condition imposed under subsection (4)(a)(ii), or

    (c) the child is not receiving appropriate education or training, and order the child to return to the school.

(8) Any child escaping from the person with whom he or she is placed out shall be liable to the same penalty as if he or she had escaped from the school itself.

(9) The period during which a child who is placed out is absent from a school shall be deemed to be part of the child's period of detention in the school but, if a child fails to return to the school when the placing out is revoked, the time that elapses thereafter shall be excluded in calculating the period during which he or she is to be detained.

(10) Where a member of the Garda Síochána has been notified that a child whose placing out has been revoked refuses or fails, without reasonable cause, to return to the school, the member may arrest the child without warrant and forthwith return the child to the school.

(11) Where a placing out of a child has been revoked and the child has returned or has been returned to the school, the Director of the school shall inform the member in charge of the Garda Síochána station for the area where the child resided accordingly.

(12) Where a child is found guilty of an offence committed while placed out, the placing out shall be deemed to be revoked.

Amendments

1 Words substituted by by Criminal Justice Act 2006, s 137.

208   Voluntary aftercare

(1) Where a child is released from a children detention school on the completion of his or her period of detention, the child may, with his or her consent, be placed under the supervision of a probation and welfare officer if the Director of the school considers, after consultation with the [Director of the Probation and Welfare Service]1, that to do so would further assist the child's reintegration into society and help to prevent the child from committing further offences.

(2) Subject to subsection (4), where a child is placed under supervision in accordance with subsection (1), the period of supervision shall continue for as long as the child consents and the probation and welfare officer supervising the child is satisfied that continuance of the supervision is in the child's interests.

(3) The probation and welfare officer supervising the child shall receive whatever assistance is necessary from the Director of the children detention school concerned to enable the officer to supervise the child effectively.

(4) Where a child is found guilty of an offence committed while under supervision in accordance with this section, the continuance of the supervision shall be reviewed by the [Director of the Probation and Welfare Service][1].

Amendments

1 Words substituted by by Criminal Justice Act 2006, s 137.

209 Unconditional release

Where a child is serving a period of detention in a children detention school, the Minister may at any time order the child's release from the school on compassionate grounds if he or she is satisfied on the basis of a report from the Director of the school, after consultation with the [Director of the Probation and Welfare Service][1], that exceptional circumstances exist which justify the release.

Amendments

1   Words substituted by by Criminal Justice Act 2006, s 137.

210 Early discharge

(1) A child detained in a children detention school may by order of the Director of the school be discharged from detention at any time during the period of 24 hours immediately preceding the time when the children detention order concerned would otherwise terminate.

(2) A child so detained whose detention would, but for this subsection, terminate on a Saturday, Sunday or public holiday may, by order of the Director, be discharged from detention on the last preceding day that is not a Saturday, Sunday or public holiday.

211 Order for production of child

(1) Where a child is detained in a children detention school, the Director of the school may, on proof to his or her satisfaction that the presence of the child at any place is required in the interests of justice, or for the purpose of any inquest or inquiry, in writing order that the child be taken to that place.

(2) A child taken from a children detention school under this section shall, while outside the school, be kept in such custody as the Director may determine and while in that custody shall be deemed to be in lawful custody.

212 Responsible persons

Where a child is in the care or charge of a responsible person under the provisions of section 206 or 207, the responsible person shall—

(a)   have the like control over the child as if he or she were the child's parent or guardian, and

(b)   do what is reasonable (subject to the provisions of this Act) in all the circumstances of the case for the purpose of safeguarding or promoting the child's education, health, development or welfare.

213 Duty to notify changes of address to school

(1) The parents or guardian of a child who is detained in a children detention school shall keep the Director of the school informed of their address.

(2) Where a child is transferred pursuant to section 198, the Director of the school or managers of a place from which the child is transferred shall, where practicable, inform the child's parents or guardian of the transfer, and until the parents or guardian have been so

informed their duty under subsection (1) shall be deemed to be duly discharged if they keep the Director of that school informed of their address.

214   Lawful custody of detained children

(1) Subject to section 215, a child in respect of whom a children detention order is in force shall be deemed to be in the lawful custody of the Director of the children detention school concerned while detained in the school and thereafter while being conveyed from or to the school, while placed out under supervision in the community or while on a permitted absence under section 202 or 203 or a mobility trip under section 204.

(2) [...]¹.

Amendments

1   Subsection (2) deleted by Criminal Justice Act 2006, s 158 and Sch 4.

Offences

215   Escape

(1) A child who has been ordered by a court to be detained in a children detention school and who—

(a)   escapes while being conveyed to or from the school, or

(b)   escapes or is otherwise absent without permission from the school or from any hospital or other institution in which the child is receiving medical attention,

shall commit the offence of escape from lawful custody and may at any time be arrested by a member of the Garda Síochána without warrant and returned to the school or, as the case may be, to the hospital or other institution concerned.

[(2) A child found guilty in the Children Court of an offence under subsection (1) may be sentenced to detention for a period not exceeding 3 months.]¹

(3) [...]¹

(4) Where a person who is found guilty of an offence under subsection (1) is 18 years of age or more, any period of detention imposed on him or her shall be served in a place of detention provided under section 2 of the Act of 1970 or in a prison.

(5) In calculating the period during which a person who, having escaped, is thereafter liable to be detained, the period during which he or she was absent from the children detention school shall not be reckoned as part of the person's period of detention in the school.

(6) Subject to the foregoing provisions of this section, an escape from a children detention school may be treated as a breach of the discipline of the school.

Amendments

1   Subsection (2) substituted, and (3) deleted, by Criminal Justice Act 2006, s 155.

216 Helping child to escape

A person who helps a child to escape or attempt to escape from lawful custody or to abscond from any person with whom the child is placed out on supervision in the community shall be guilty of an offence and shall be liable, on summary conviction, to a fine not exceeding [€952.3] or imprisonment for a term not exceeding 6 months or both.

217 Harbouring escaped child

Any person who knowingly harbours, maintains or conceals a child or otherwise prevents a child from returning to a children detention school or to any person with whom he or she has been placed out on supervision in the community shall be guilty of an offence and shall be liable, on summary conviction, to a fine not exceeding [€952.3] or imprisonment for a term not exceeding 6 months or both.

218 Unlawful entry or communication

A person who without lawful authority—

(a) enters or attempts to enter any children detention school, or

(b) communicates or attempts to communicate with any child detained therein, shall be guilty of an offence and shall be liable, on summary conviction, to a fine not exceeding [€317.43] or imprisonment for a term not exceeding 2 months or both.

219 Bringing alcohol, etc., into schools

A person who without lawful authority—

(a) brings or attempts to bring into a children detention school, or

(b) delivers or attempts to deliver to a child in any such school,

any alcohol or other prescribed thing, shall be guilty of an offence and shall be liable, on summary conviction, to a fine not exceeding [€317.43] or imprisonment for a term not exceeding 2 months or both.

Other matters

220 Delegation of certain functions by Minister

(1) The Minister may, subject to subsection (4), by instrument under his or her hand or seal delegate to a named officer of a specified grade, position or description any function of the Minister under this Part specified in the delegation and may revoke the delegation.

(2) A delegation of a function under subsection (1) is without prejudice to the right of the Minister to exercise it.

(3) Every delegated function shall be performed by the delegated officer subject to the general superintendence and control of the Minister and to such limitations (if any) as may be specified by the Minister either in the instrument of delegation or at any time thereafter.

(4) Subsection (1) does not apply to a function conferred on the Minister by sections 163 and 221.

(5) In this section "officer" means an officer of the Minister who is an established civil servant for the purposes of the Civil Service Regulation Act, 1956.

221   Regulations

(1) The Minister may make regulations, not inconsistent with this Part and any relevant international instruments to which the State is a party, for or with respect to any matter that is required or permitted by this Part to be prescribed or that is necessary or expedient to be prescribed for giving effect to this Part and, in particular, with respect to—

    (a) the promotion of the educational and social development of children detained in children detention schools,

    (b) the maintenance of the physical, psychological and emotional wellbeing of such children,

    (c) the provision of adequate and suitable accommodation for them,

    (d) the control and management of such schools and the maintenance of discipline and good order generally in them,

    (e) the inspection and investigation of such schools by the Inspector,

    (f) the conduct and functions of the Director and other members of the staff of such schools,

    (g) visits and other communications between children detained in such schools and their families, relatives and friends.

(2) Any such regulations may apply generally to children detention schools or apply to one or more than one such school or be limited in their application by reference to specified exceptions or factors or apply differently according to different factors of a specified kind.

(3) The Minister shall cause a copy of any such regulations to be sent to each board of management, who shall comply with them.

(4) The Minister may make regulations analogous to subsections (1) to (3) relating to any place provided under section 161 and for that purpose those subsections shall apply, with the necessary modifications, in relation to any such place.

222   Pending proceedings

Where, immediately before the commencement of section 159, the board of management or trustees of a certified reformatory school or industrial school to which on such commencement subsection (1) of that section applies, or any agent thereof acting on behalf of such a school, is a party to any proceedings pending in any court or tribunal, the name of the board of management appointed to the school under section 164 shall be substituted in those proceedings for the board of management, trustees or agent, as the case may be, and the proceedings shall not abate by reason of the substitution.

223   Saving for certain acts

Nothing in this Act shall affect the validity of any act that was done before the commencement of section 159 by or on behalf of a board of management or trustees of a certified reformatory school or industrial school to which on such commencement subsection (1) of that section applies, and every such act shall, if and in so far as it had effect immediately before such commencement, have effect on and after the commencement as if it had been done by or on behalf of the board of management appointed to the school under section 164.

224 Transitional provisions

(1) A child who is serving a period of detention in an institution which is a certified reformatory school or an industrial school in accordance with Part IV of the Act of 1908 shall not have his or her period of detention varied by reason only of an alteration of title or description of the said institution.

(2) Where a period of time specified in a provision of the Children Acts, 1908 to 1989, had not expired at the commencement of any corresponding provision of this Act, this Act shall have effect as if the corresponding provision had been in force when the period began to run.

PART 11
SPECIAL RESIDENTIAL SERVICES BOARD

225–244

Text not reproduced here.

PART 12
PROTECTION OF CHILDREN

245 Interpretation (Part 12)

(1) In this Part "registered medical practitioner" means a person registered in the General Register of Medical Practitioners established under the Medical Practitioners Acts, 1978 to 2000.

(2) For the purposes of this Part—

(a) any person who is the parent or guardian of a child or who is legally liable to maintain a child shall be presumed to have the custody of the child, and, as between parents, one parent shall not be deemed to have ceased to have the custody of the child by reason only that he or she has deserted or does not reside with, the other parent and child, and

(b) any person to whose charge a child is committed by any person who has the custody of the child shall be presumed to have charge of the child, and

(c) any person exercising authority over or having actual control of a child shall be presumed to have care of the child.

246 Cruelty to children

(1) It shall be an offence for any person who has the custody, charge or care of a child wilfully to assault, ill-treat, neglect, abandon or expose the child, or cause or procure or allow the child to be assaulted, ill-treated, neglected, abandoned or exposed, in a manner likely to cause unnecessary suffering or injury to the child's health or seriously to affect his or her wellbeing.

(2) A person found guilty of an offence under this section shall be liable—

(a) on summary conviction, to a fine not exceeding [€1,904.61] or imprisonment for a term not exceeding 12 months or both, or

(b) on conviction on indictment, to a fine not exceeding [€12,697.38] or imprisonment for a term not exceeding 7 years or both.

(3) A person may be convicted of an offence under this section—

(a) notwithstanding the death of the child in respect of whom the offence is committed, or

(b) notwithstanding that actual suffering or injury to the health of the child, or the likelihood of such suffering or injury, was obviated by the action of another person.

(4) On the trial of any person for the murder of a child of whom the person has the custody, charge or care, the court or the jury, as the case may be, may, if satisfied that the accused is guilty of an offence under this section in respect of the child, find the accused guilty of that offence.

(5) For the purposes of this section a person shall be deemed to have neglected a child in a manner likely to cause the child unnecessary suffering or injury to his or her health or seriously to affect his or her wellbeing if the person—

(a) fails to provide adequate food, clothing, heating, medical aid or accommodation for the child, or

(b) being unable to provide such food, clothing, heating, medical aid or accommodation, fails to take steps to have it provided under the enactments relating to health, social welfare or housing.

(6) In subsection (1) the reference to a child's health or wellbeing includes a reference to the child's physical, mental or emotional health or wellbeing.

(7) For the purposes of this section ill-treatment of a child includes any frightening, bullying or threatening of the child, and "ill-treat" shall be construed accordingly.

247   Begging

(1) A person is guilty of an offence if he or she causes or procures a child or, having the custody, charge or care of a child, allows the child to be in any street or public place, or to make house to house visits, for the purpose of begging or receiving alms or of inducing the giving of alms (whether or not there is any pretence of singing, playing, performing, offering anything for sale or otherwise).

(2) If a person who has the custody, charge or care of a child is charged with an offence under this section, and it is proved that the child was in any street, public place or house for any purpose referred to in subsection (1), the person shall be presumed to have allowed the child to be in the street, public place or house for that purpose, unless the contrary is proved.

(3) A person found guilty of an offence under this section shall be liable on summary conviction to a fine not exceeding—

(a) in the case of a first offence, [€317.43], or

(b) in the case of a second or any subsequent offence, [€634.87].

(4) In this section—

"house" includes any building occupied for residential or business purposes and any part of a building so occupied;

"public place" means any place to which the public have or are permitted to have access whether as of right or by permission and whether on payment or without payment;

"street" includes any road, bridge, lane, footway, subway, square, alley or passage, whether a thoroughfare or not, which is for the time being open to the public, and any ground or carpark adjoining and open to a street shall be treated as forming part of a street.

248 Allowing child to be in brothel

(1) A person is guilty of an offence if, having the custody, charge or care of a child, he or she allows the child to reside in or to frequent a brothel.

(2) A person found guilty of an offence under this section shall be liable on summary conviction to a fine not exceeding [€1,904.61] or imprisonment for a term not exceeding 12 months or both.

249 Causing or encouraging sexual offence upon child

(1) A person is guilty of an offence if, having the custody, charge or care of a child, he or she causes or encourages unlawful sexual intercourse or buggery with the child or causes or encourages the seduction or prostitution of, or a sexual assault on, the child.

(2) A person found guilty of an offence under this section shall be liable on conviction on indictment to a fine not exceeding [€31743.45] or imprisonment for a term not exceeding 10 years or both.

(3) For the purposes of this section a person shall be deemed to have caused or encouraged—

    (a) unlawful sexual intercourse or buggery with any child with whom unlawful sexual intercourse or buggery has taken place, or

    (b) the seduction or prostitution of a child who has been seduced or become a prostitute or a sexual assault on a child who has been sexually assaulted,

if the person has knowingly allowed the child to consort with, or to enter or continue in the employment of, any prostitute or keeper of a brothel.

(4) In this section—

"child" means a child under 17 years of age;

"keeper of a brothel" means a person referred to in section 11 (which relates to brothel keeping) of the Criminal Law (Sexual Offences) Act, 1993;

"sexual assault" has the meaning assigned to it by the Criminal Law (Rape) (Amendment) Act, 1990.

(5) References in this section to sexual intercourse shall be construed as references to carnal knowledge as defined in section 63 of the Offences against the Person Act, 1861.

250 Amendment of Criminal Law (Sexual Offences) Act, 1993

The Criminal Law (Sexual Offences) Act, 1993, is hereby amended by the substitution for section 6 of the following:

    "6. A person who solicits or importunes another person (whether or not for the purposes of prostitution) for the purposes of the commission of an act which would constitute an offence under section 3, 4 or 5 of this Act or section 1 or 2 of the Criminal Law Amendment Act, 1935, shall be guilty of an offence and shall be liable on summary conviction to a fine not exceeding [€1,904.61] or to imprisonment for a term not exceeding 12 months or to both.".

251 Power to proceed in absence of child

In any proceedings for an offence under this Part, or any offence mentioned in Schedule 1, it shall not be necessary for the child in respect of whom an offence is alleged to have been committed to be brought before a court or to be present for all or any part of the proceedings unless the court, either of its own motion or at the request of any of the parties to the proceedings, is satisfied that the presence of the child is necessary for the proper disposal of the case.

252   Anonymity of child in court proceedings

(1) Subject to subsection (2), in relation to any proceedings for an offence against a child or where a child is a witness in any such proceedings—

(a) no report which reveals the name, address or school of the child or includes any particulars likely to lead to his or her identification, and

(b) no picture which purports to be or include a picture of the child or which is likely to lead to his or her identification, shall be published or included in a broadcast.

(2) The court may dispense to any specified extent with the requirements of subsection (1) if it is satisfied that it is appropriate to do so in the interests of the child.

(3) Where the court dispenses with the requirements of subsection (1), the court shall explain in open court why it is satisfied it should do so.

(4) Subsections (3) to (6) of section 51 shall apply, with the necessary modifications, for the purposes of this section.

(5) Nothing in this section shall affect the law as to contempt of court.

253   Mode of charging offences

(1) Where a person is charged with committing any offence under this Part, or any offence mentioned in Schedule 1, in respect of two or more children, the same information or summons may charge the offence in respect of all or any of them, but the person charged shall not, if he or she is summarily convicted, be liable to a separate penalty in respect of each child except upon separate informations.

(2) The same information or summons may charge such a person—

(a) with the offences of assault, ill-treatment, neglect, abandonment or exposure together or separately, or

(b) with committing all or any of those offences in a manner likely to cause unnecessary suffering or injury to the child's health or seriously to affect his or her wellbeing, alternatively or together,

but when those offences are charged together the person charged shall not, if he or she is summarily convicted, be liable to a separate penalty for each.

(3) Where an offence under this Part or any offence mentioned in Schedule 1 charged against any person is a continuing offence, it shall not be necessary to specify in the information, summons or indictment the date of the acts or omissions constituting the offence.

254   Powers of arrest without warrant, etc

(1) Where a member of the Garda Síochána reasonably suspects—

(a) that an offence under this Part or any offence mentioned in Schedule 1 has been committed or attempted, and

(b) that a person has committed any such offence or attempted to commit it, the member may arrest the person without warrant if the member—

(i) reasonably suspects that unless the person is arrested he or she either will abscond for the purposes of evading justice or will obstruct the course of justice,

(ii) having enquired of the person, has reasonable doubts as to the person's identity or place of abode, or

(iii) has reasonable grounds for believing that there is an immediate and serious risk to the safety, health or wellbeing of the child concerned.

(2) Subsection (1) is without prejudice to any other powers exercisable by a member of the Garda Síochána.

(3) Section 68 (which empowers members of the Garda Síochána to release a child on bail in certain cases) shall apply to a child arrested under this section and section 31 of the Act of 1967 shall apply to an adult so arrested.

(4) Where a member of the Garda Síochána makes an arrest under this section and the member has reasonable grounds for believing that—

(a) there is an immediate and serious risk to the safety, health or wellbeing of the child, and

(b) it would not be sufficient for the protection of the child from such immediate and serious risk to await the making of an application for an emergency care order by [the Health Service Executive][1] under section 13 of the Act of 1991,

the member may remove the child to safety and the provisions of Part III of the Act of 1991 shall then apply as if the removal were a removal under section 12 of that Act.

(5) For the purpose of arresting a person under any power conferred by this section a member of the Garda Síochána, accompanied by such other members of the Garda Síochána or such other persons as may be necessary, may enter (if need be, by force) and search any place where the person is or the member reasonably suspects him or her to be.

Amendments

1 Words amended by Health Act 2004, s 75 and Sch 7.

---

255   Power to take deposition of child

(1) Without prejudice to section 4F of the Act of 1967, where a judge of the District Court is satisfied on the evidence of a registered medical practitioner that the attendance before a court of any child, in respect of whom an offence under this Part, or any offence mentioned in Schedule 1, is alleged to have been committed, would involve serious danger to the safety, health or wellbeing of the child, the judge may take the evidence either—

(a) by way of sworn deposition, or

(b) in case the evidence is to be given through a live television link pursuant to Part III of the Criminal Evidence Act, 1992, or section 39 of the Criminal Justice Act, 1999, through such a link.

(2) The rules mentioned in section 4F(3) of the Act of 1967 shall apply and have effect in relation to the taking of evidence under subsection (1).

(3) A deposition taken under subsection (1) or a videorecording of evidence given by a child under paragraph (b) of that subsection shall be deemed to have been taken under section 4F of the said Act of 1967, and section 4G (admissibility of deposition or videorecording) shall apply and have effect accordingly.

(4) Notwithstanding the provisions of this section, in any criminal proceedings for an offence under this Part or any offence mentioned in Schedule 1, the evidence of a child under 14 years of age may be taken or received otherwise than on oath or affirmation if the court is satisfied that the child is capable of giving an intelligible account of events which are relevant to those proceedings.

(5) If any child whose evidence is taken as aforesaid makes a statement material in the proceedings concerned which he or she knows to be false or does not believe to be true, the child shall be guilty of an offence and on being found guilty shall be liable to be dealt with as if he or she had been guilty of perjury.

256   Presumption and determination of age of child victim

(1) Where in a charge or indictment for an offence under this Part or any offence mentioned in Schedule 1, except an offence under the Criminal Law Amendment Act, 1885, or the Criminal Law Amendment Act, 1935—

(a) it is alleged that the person by or in respect of whom the offence was committed was a child or was under or had attained any specified age, and

(b) the person appears to the court to have been at the date of the commission of the alleged offence a child or to have been under or to have attained the specified age, as the case may be,

the person shall for the purposes of this Part be presumed, unless the contrary is proved, at that date to have been a child or to have been under or to have attained that age, as the case may be.

(2) Where a person is charged with an offence to which subsection (1) applies in respect of a person apparently under a specified age, it shall be a defence to prove that the person was of or over that age.

257   Clearing of court in certain cases

(1) Where in any proceedings for an offence a person who, in the opinion of the court, is a child is called as a witness, the court may exclude from the court during the taking of his or her evidence all persons except officers of the court, persons directly concerned in the proceedings, bona fide representatives of the Press and such other persons (if any) as the court may in its discretion permit to remain.

(2) The powers of a court under this section shall be in addition and without prejudice to any other power of the court to hear proceedings in camera or to exclude a witness until his or her evidence is required or to Part III (which relates to evidence through a television link in certain proceedings) of the Act of 1992.

(3) The said Part III and section 22 (which relates to compellability of spouses to give evidence at instance of prosecution in certain cases) of the Act of 1992 are hereby amended by the deletion of "17 years" wherever it occurs and the substitution of "18 years".

(4) In this section "the Act of 1992" means the Criminal Evidence Act, 1992.

[PART 12A
ANTI-SOCIAL BEHAVIOUR BY CHILDREN

257A   Interpretation (Part 12A)

(1) In this Part—

"behaviour order" means an order under section 257D;

"behaviour warning" shall be construed in accordance with section 257B;

"child" means a child who is at least 12 years of age and under the age of 18 years;

"good behaviour contract" has the meaning given to it in section 257C;

"Programme" means the diversion programme referred to in section 18.

(2) For the purposes of this Part, a child behaves in an anti-social manner if the child causes or, in the circumstances, is likely to cause, to one or more persons who are not of the same household as the child—

(a) harassment,

(b) significant or persistent alarm, distress, fear or intimidation, or

(c) significant or persistent impairment of their use or enjoyment of their property.

(3) This Part does not apply—

(a) to any behaviour of a child that takes place before this section comes into force, or

(b) to any act or omission of a child in respect of which criminal proceedings have been instituted against the child.]¹

Amendments

1 Title and s 257A inserted by Criminal Justice Act 2006, s 159.

[257B   Behaviour warning to child

(1) Subject to subsection (5), a member of the Garda Síochána may issue a behaviour warning to a child who has behaved in an anti-social manner.

(2) The behaviour warning may be issued orally or in writing and, if it is issued orally, shall be recorded in writing as soon as reasonably practicable and a written record of the behaviour warning shall be served on the child and his or her parents or guardian personally or by post.

(3) The behaviour warning or, if it is given orally, the written record of it shall—

(a) include a statement that the child has behaved in an anti-social manner and indicate what that behaviour is and when and where it took place,

(b) demand that the child cease the behaviour or otherwise address the behaviour in the manner specified in the warning, and

(c) include notice that—

(i) failure to comply with a demand under paragraph (b), or

(ii) issuance of a subsequent behaviour warning,

may result in an application being made for a behaviour order.

(4) The member of the Garda Síochána referred to in subsection (1) may require the child to give his or her name and address to the member for the purposes of the behaviour warning or the written record of it.

(5) A behaviour warning may not be issued more than one month after the time that—

(a) the behaviour took place, or

(b) in the case of persistent behaviour, the most recent known instance of that behaviour took place.

(6) Subject to subsection (7), a behaviour warning remains in force against the child to whom it is issued for 3 months from the date that it is issued.

(7) If an application is made under section 257D in respect of the child, the behaviour warning remains in force against the child until the application is determined by the Children Court.]¹

Amendments

1   Section 257B inserted by Criminal Justice Act 2006, s 160.

[257C   Meeting to discuss anti-social behaviour by child

(1) The superintendent in charge of a district, on receipt of a report from a member of the Garda Síochána in that district concerning the behaviour of a child, shall convene a meeting to discuss the child's behaviour if satisfied that—

    (a)   the child has behaved in an anti-social manner and is likely to continue doing so, and

    (b)   the child has previously behaved in an anti-social manner, but—

        (i)   has not received a warning in respect of previous anti-social behaviour, or

        (ii)   holding such a meeting would help to prevent further such behaviour by the child.

(2) A report under subsection (1) shall be prepared only after a behaviour warning has been given to the child by a member of the Garda Síochána in relation to the child's anti-social behaviour.

(3) The report shall include details of the behaviour warning.

(4) The following persons shall be asked to attend a meeting convened under subsection (1):

    (a)   the child;

    (b)   his or her parents or guardian;

    (c)   the member of the Garda Síochána who warned the child in relation to his or her anti-social behaviour;

    (d)   if the child is already participating in the Programme, a juvenile liaison officer.

(5) The superintendent may request the attendance at the meeting of such other person or persons as he or she considers would be of assistance to the child or the parents or guardian, including a member of the local policing forum (within the meaning of the Garda Síochána Act 2005).

(6) The meeting shall discuss the child's behaviour.

(7) Subject to subsection (8), at the meeting—

    (a)   the superintendent shall explain in simple language to the child and the parents or guardian what the offending behaviour is and the effect it is having on any other person or persons,

    (b)   the child shall be asked to acknowledge that the behaviour has occurred and to undertake to stop it,

(c) the parents or guardian shall be asked to acknowledge the child's behaviour and to undertake to take steps to prevent a recurrence,

(d) if the child and the parents or guardian agree to give those undertakings, a document (in this section referred to as a "good behaviour contract") incorporating the undertakings shall be prepared and, where practicable, be signed by the child and the parents or guardian.

(8) The functions of a superintendent under subsection (7) may, at his or her request, be performed by a member of the Garda Síochána not below the rank of inspector, and in that case the member shall provide the superintendent with a written report of the outcome of the meeting.

(9) A good behaviour contract shall expire at the end of a period not exceeding 6 months from the date of the meeting but may be renewed by the child and the parents or guardian for a further period of not more than 3 months.

(10) The superintendent may from time to time review the child's behaviour in the light of the undertaking given by him or her in the good behaviour contract.

(11) If the child—

(a) has behaved, or continues to behave, in breach of the undertaking, or

(b) in the opinion of the superintendent or the parent or guardian, is likely to so behave,

the superintendent may reconvene the meeting referred to in subsection (1) and renew the contract if the child and the parents so agree.

(12) A renewal of the contract under subsection (11) shall be for a period not exceeding—

(a) 6 months from the date of the original contract, or

(b) 9 months from the date of the original contract,

whichever is the shorter.

(13) Nothing in this section prevents a child being the subject of a further good behaviour contract if the child and the parents or guardian so agree.

(14) This subsection applies—

(a) where a superintendent, having considered a report referred to at subsection (1), does not consider that convening a meeting under this section would help to prevent anti-social behaviour by the child concerned, or

(b) where such a meeting has been convened and—

(i) a good behaviour contract was not prepared because the child or the parents or guardian refused to give the necessary undertaking, or

(ii) the child is in breach of an undertaking given by him or her in such a contract.

(15) Where subsection (14) applies, either—

(a) the child shall be admitted to the Programme, in which case Part 4 shall apply accordingly, with any necessary modifications, in relation to him or her, or

(b) the superintendent, if satisfied that the child's participation in the Programme would not be appropriate in the circumstances, shall apply to the Children Court for a behaviour order in respect of the child.][1]

Amendments

1   Section 257C inserted by Criminal Justice Act 2006, s 161.

[257D   Behaviour order for children over 12

(1) The Children Court may, on the application of a member of the Garda Síochána not below the rank of superintendent, make an order (in this Part referred to as a "behaviour order") prohibiting a child of or above the age of 12 years from doing anything specified in the order if the court is satisfied that—

  (a) the child, notwithstanding his or her participation in the procedures provided for in section 257C, has continued and is likely to continue to behave in an anti-social manner,

  (b) the order is necessary to prevent the child from continuing to behave in that manner,

  (c) having regard to the effect or likely effect of that behaviour on other persons, the order is reasonable and proportionate in the circumstances.

(2) The application shall indicate the extent of the child's participation in the procedures under section 257C.

(3) The Court may impose terms or conditions in the behaviour order that it considers appropriate.

(4) An order under this section may, for the purpose of protecting a person or persons from further anti-social behaviour by a child—

  (a) prohibit a child from behaving in a specified manner, and, where appropriate, from so behaving at or in the vicinity of a specified place,

  (b) require the child to comply with specified requirements, including requirements relating to—

    (i)   school attendance, and

    (ii) reporting to a member of the Garda Síochána, a teacher or other person in authority in a school,

  and

  (c) provide for the supervision of the child by a parent or guardian or any other specified person or authority with an interest in the child's welfare.

(5) The respondent child in an application under this section may not at any time be charged with, prosecuted or punished for an offence if the act or omission that constitutes the offence is the same behaviour that is the subject of the application and is to be determined by the court under subsection (1).

(6) Unless discharged under subsection (7), a behaviour order remains in force for no more than the lesser of the following:

  (a) 2 years from the date of the order;

  (b) the period specified in the order.

(7) The Court may vary or discharge a behaviour order on the application of the child concerned or his or her parents or guardian or of a member of the Garda Síochána not below the rank of superintendent.

(8) An applicant under subsection (1) or (7) shall give notice of the application—

    (a) where the applicant under either subsection is a member of the Garda Síochána, to the child and his or her parents or guardian, or

    (b) where the applicant under subsection (7) is the child, to the applicant under subsection (1) and the child's parents or guardian, and

    (c) where the applicant under subsection (7) is the child's parent or guardian, to the child and the applicant under subsection (1).

(9) The standard of proof in proceedings under this section is that applicable to civil proceedings.

(10) The jurisdiction conferred on the Court by this section may be exercised as follows:

    (a) in respect of subsections (1), (3) and (4), by a judge of the District Court for the time being assigned to the district court district in which the child resides at the time the application is made;

    (b) in respect of subsection (7), by a judge of the District Court for the time being assigned to the district court district in which the child subject to the behaviour order resides at the time the application is made.]¹

Amendments

1   Section 257D inserted by Criminal Justice Act 2006, s 162.

[257E   Appeal against behaviour order

(1) A child against whom a behaviour order has been made may, within 21 days from the date that the order is made, appeal the making of the order to the Circuit Court.

(2) An appellant under subsection (1) shall give notice of the appeal to the superintendent in charge of the Garda Síochána district in which the appellant resides.

(3) Notwithstanding the appeal, the behaviour order shall remain in force unless the court that made the order or the appeal court places a stay on it.

(4) An appeal under this section shall be in the nature of a rehearing of the application under section 257D and, for this purpose, subsections (1), (3) and (4) of that section apply in respect of the matter.

(5) If on appeal under this section, the appeal court makes a behaviour order, the provisions of section 257D(6) to (8) apply in respect of the matter.

(6) Notwithstanding the appeal period described in subsection (1), the Circuit Court may, on application by the child subject to the behaviour order or the child's parent or guardian, extend the appeal period if satisfied that exceptional circumstances exist which warrant the extension.

(7) The standard of proof in proceedings by this section is that applicable to civil proceedings.

(8) The jurisdiction conferred on the Circuit Court under this section may be exercised as follows:

(a) in respect of section 257D(1), (3) and (4) as those provisions apply to the Circuit Court under subsection (4) of this section, by a judge of the Circuit Court for the time being assigned to the circuit in which the appellant under this section resides at the time the appeal is commenced;

(b) in respect of section 257D(7) as it applies to the Circuit Court under subsection (5) of this section, by a judge of the Circuit Court for the time being assigned to the circuit in which the child subject to the behaviour order resides at the time the application is made;

(c) in respect of subsection (6) of this section, by a judge of the Circuit Court for the time being assigned to the circuit in which the child subject to the behaviour order resides at the time the application is made.]¹

Amendments

1   Section 257E inserted by Criminal Justice Act 2006, s 163.

[257F   Offences

(1) A child commits an offence who—

(a) fails to give a name and address when required to do so under section 257B(4) or gives a name or address that is false or misleading in response to that requirement, or

(b) without reasonable excuse, does not comply with a behaviour order to which the child is subject.

(2) A member of the Garda Síochána may arrest a child without warrant if the member has reasonable grounds to believe that the child has committed an offence under subsection (1)(b).

(3) A child who is guilty of an offence under this section is liable on summary conviction—

(a) in the case of an offence under subsection (1)(a), to a fine not exceeding €200, and

(b) in the case of an offence under subsection (1)(b), to a fine not exceeding €800 or detention in a children detention school for a period not exceeding 3 months or both.

(4) If a child is ordered to pay a fine and costs on conviction of an offence under subsection (1)(b), the aggregate of the fine and costs shall not exceed €1,500.]¹

Amendments

1   Section 257F inserted by Criminal Justice Act 2006, s 164.

[257G Legal aid

(1) Subject to subsection (2), a child who is the subject of an application for a behaviour order may be granted a certificate for free legal aid (in this Part referred to as a "legal aid (behaviour order) certificate") in preparation for and representation at the hearing of—

    (a) the application,

    (b) any application by the child or his or her parents or guardian to vary or discharge a behaviour order,

    (c) any appeal by the child against the making of the behaviour order, or

    (d) any proceedings in the High Court or Supreme Court arising out of the making of the application, the appeal or any subsequent proceedings.

(2) A legal aid (behaviour order) certificate may not be granted under subsection (1) unless it appears to the court hearing the application for the certificate—

    (a) that the means of the child concerned or of his or her parents or guardian are insufficient to enable him or her to obtain legal aid, and

    (b) that, by reason of the gravity of the alleged anti-social behaviour or of exceptional circumstances, it is essential in the interests of justice that the child should have legal aid in preparation for and representation at the hearing concerned.

(3) A child who is granted a legal aid (behaviour order) certificate is entitled—

    (a) to free legal aid in preparation for and representation at the hearing of the application for a behaviour order and any proceedings referred to in subsection (1)(b), (c) and (d), and

    (b) to have, in such manner as may be prescribed—

       (i) a solicitor assigned to the child in relation to the application for the behaviour order or any application to vary or discharge it,

       (ii) a solicitor assigned to the child in relation to any other such proceedings, and

       (iii) if the court granting the certificate considers it appropriate, a counsel assigned to the child in relation to any other proceedings referred to in subparagraph (ii).

(4) Where a legal aid (behaviour order) certificate is granted, any fees, costs or other expenses properly incurred in preparation for and representation at the proceedings concerned shall, subject to regulations under section 257H, be paid out of moneys provided by the Oireachtas.

(5) A child applying for a legal aid (behaviour order) certificate may be required by the court granting the certificate to furnish a written statement of his or her means and the means of his or her parents or guardian.

(6) A person who, for the purpose of obtaining free legal aid under this section, whether for himself or herself or for some other person, knowingly makes a false or misleading statement or representation either orally or in writing, or knowingly conceals any material fact, is guilty of an offence and liable on summary conviction to a fine not exceeding €2,500 or imprisonment for a term not exceeding 6 months or both.

(7) On conviction of a person for an offence under this section, the court by which the person is convicted may, if in the circumstances of the case it thinks fit, order the person to pay to the Minister the whole or part of any sum paid under subsection (4) in respect of the free legal aid in relation to which the offence was committed, and any sum so paid to the Minister

shall be paid into and disposed of for the benefit of the Exchequer in accordance with the directions of the Minister for Finance.]¹

Amendments

1   Section 257G inserted by Criminal Justice Act 2006, s 165.

[257H   Regulations (legal aid)

(1) The Minister may make regulations for carrying section 257G into effect.

(2) The regulations may, in particular, prescribe—

    (a)   the form of certificates granted under that section,

    (b)   the rates or scales of payment of any fees, costs or other expenses payable out of moneys provided by the Oireachtas pursuant to those certificates, and

    (c)   the manner in which solicitors and counsel are to be assigned pursuant to those certificates.

(3) Regulations in subsection (2)(b) shall not be made without the consent of the Minister for Finance.

(4) Pending the making of regulations under this section, the regulations under section 10 of the Criminal Justice (Legal Aid) Act 1962 shall apply and have effect, with the necessary modifications, in relation to certificates for free legal aid granted under section 257G of this Act as if they were certificates for free legal aid granted under the Criminal Justice (Legal Aid) Act 1962.]¹

Amendments

1   Section 257H inserted by Criminal Justice Act 2006, s 166.

PART 13

MISCELLANEOUS

258   Non-disclosure of certain findings of guilt

(1) Where a person has been found guilty of an offence, whether before or after the commencement of this section, and—

    (a)   the offence was committed before the person attained the age of 18 years,

    (b)   the offence is not an offence required to be tried by the Central Criminal Court,

    (c)   a period of not less than 3 years has elapsed since the finding of guilt, and

    (d)   the person has not been dealt with for an offence in that 3-year period, then, after the end of the 3-year period or, where the period ended before the commencement of this section, after the commencement of this section, the provisions of subsection (4) shall apply to the finding of guilt.

(2) This section shall not apply to a person who is found guilty of an offence unless he or she has served a period of detention or otherwise complied with any court order imposed on him or her in respect of the finding of guilt.

(3) Subsection (2) shall not prevent the application of this section to a person who—

(a) failed to pay a fine or other sum adjudged to be paid by, or imposed on, the person on a finding of guilt or breach of a condition of a recognisance to keep the peace or to be of good behaviour, or

(b) breached any condition or requirement applicable in relation to an order of a court which renders a person to whom it applies liable to be dealt with for the offence in respect of which the order was made.

(4) (a) A person to whom this section applies shall be treated for all purposes in law as a person who has not committed or been charged with or prosecuted for or found guilty of or dealt with for the offence or offences which were the subject of the finding of guilt; and, notwithstanding any other statutory provision or rule of law to the contrary but, subject as aforesaid—

(i) no evidence shall be admissible in any proceedings before a judicial authority to prove that any such person has committed or been charged with or prosecuted for or found guilty of or dealt with for any offence which was the subject of that finding, and

(ii) a person shall not, in any such proceedings, be asked, and, if asked, shall not be required to answer, any question relating to his or her past which cannot be answered without acknowledging or referring to a finding or findings to which this section refers or any circumstances ancillary thereto.

(b) Subject to any order made under paragraph (d), where a question seeking information with respect to a person's previous findings of guilt, offences, conduct or circumstances is put to him or her or to any other person otherwise than in proceedings before a judicial authority—

(i) the question shall be treated as not relating to findings to which this section applies or to any circumstances ancillary to such findings, and the answer thereto may be framed accordingly, and

(ii) the person questioned shall not be subjected to any liability or otherwise prejudiced in law by reason of any failure to acknowledge or disclose any such findings or any circumstances ancillary to the findings in his or her answer to the question.

(c) Subject to any order made under paragraph (d)—

(i) any obligation imposed on any person by any rule of law or by any agreement or arrangement to disclose any matters to any other person shall not extend to requiring him or her to disclose a finding to which this section applies or any circumstances ancillary to the finding (whether the finding is his or her own or another's), and

(ii) a finding to which this section applies, or any circumstances ancillary thereto or any failure to acknowledge or disclose a finding to which this section applies or any such circumstances, shall not be a proper ground for dismissing or excluding a person from any office, profession, occupation or employment, or for prejudicing him or her in any way in any occupation or employment.

(d) The Minister may by order make such provision as in his or her opinion is appropriate—

    (i) for excluding or modifying the application of either or both of subparagraphs (i) and (ii) of paragraph (b) in relation to questions put in such circumstances as may be specified in the order, or

    (ii) for exceptions from the provisions of paragraph (c) in relation to such cases, and findings of such a description, as may be so specified.

(5) An order under subsection (4)(d) may be amended or revoked by the Minister, including an order under this subsection.

(6) A draft of any order proposed to be made under this section shall be laid before each House of the Oireachtas and the order shall not be made until a resolution approving of the draft has been passed by each such House.

(7) For the purposes of this section any of the following circumstances are circumstances ancillary to a finding, that is to say:

(a) the offence or offences which were the subject of the finding,

(b) the conduct constituting that offence or those offences,

(c) any process or proceedings preliminary to the finding,

(d) any penalty imposed in respect of it,

(e) any proceedings (whether by way of appeal or otherwise) for reviewing any such finding or penalty,

(f) anything done in pursuance of or undergone in compliance with any such penalty.

(8) For the purposes of this section "proceedings before a judicial authority" includes, in addition to proceedings before a court, proceedings before any tribunal, body or person having power—

(a) by virtue of any statutory provision, law, custom or practice,

(b) under the rules governing any association, institution, profession, occupation or employment, or

(c) under any provision of an agreement providing for arbitration with respect to questions arising thereunder, to determine any question affecting the rights, privileges, obligations or liabilities of any person, or to receive evidence affecting the determination of any such question.

259 Duties of probation officers

While a child remains under the supervision of a probation and welfare officer pursuant to this Act, whether in accordance with an order of a court or otherwise, the officer shall, subject to the directions of the court, where appropriate, and in addition to the terms of and any conditions attaching to any particular placement—

(a) visit, assist, advise and befriend the child and, where feasible, the child's parents or guardian or other adult in whose residence the child may be residing,

(b) see that the child observes the terms and any conditions attaching to the supervision, and

(c) when necessary and appropriate, endeavour to find the child suitable employment and accommodation.

260 Interference with supervisor

Where a child is under the supervision of a probation and welfare officer or a juvenile liaison officer pursuant to this Act, it shall not be lawful for the child's parents or guardian to exercise, as respects the child, their rights and powers as parents or guardian in such a manner as to interfere with the supervision of the child by the probation and welfare officer or the juvenile liaison officer, as the case may be.

261 Powers of Garda Síochána

(1) Where, pursuant to this Act, a child is required to remain in a specified residence for specified periods, any member of the Garda Síochána may call to the residence, at any reasonable time within a period during which the child is required to remain there, for the purpose of establishing that the child is present in the residence at that time.

(2) The member may request any adult at the residence to produce the child to the member, and failure to do so shall give rise to an inference that the child is not at that time present in the residence.

(3) In any proceedings against a child for failure to comply with any term or condition of a court order that required the child to remain in a specified residence, a failure under subsection (2) to produce the child may be accepted by a court as evidence of noncompliance with the order.

(4) Such a failure to produce a child may also render the child, if detained in a children detention school, ineligible for temporary leave from the school in accordance with the rules of the school in that respect.

262 Delegation by principal probation and welfare officer

(1) The [Director of the Probation and Welfare Service]1 may, in writing, delegate to a named officer of the probation and welfare service of a specified grade, position or description any specified function of the [Director of the Probation and Welfare Service]1 under this Act and may revoke the delegation.

(2) The delegation of a function under this section is without prejudice to the right of the [Director of the Probation and Welfare Service]1 to continue to exercise the function.

(3) The performance of any function delegated under this section shall be subject to the general superintendence and control of the [Director of the Probation and Welfare Service]1 and to such limitations (if any) as may be specified in the instrument of delegation or at any time thereafter.

Amendments

1   Words substituted by by Criminal Justice Act 2006, s 137.

263 Temporary accommodation of children

(1) A child may be detained temporarily, but in no case for a period exceeding 24 hours, in a Garda Síochána station or in any other place, being a place designated for the purpose by the Minister, with the agreement of its owner—

  [(a)   while in transit to a court from a remand centre or children detention school]1

(b) while a case in which the child is involved is at hearing, or

[(c) while awaiting removal pursuant to this Act to a remand centre or children detention school.][1]

(2) The provisions of section 56 (separation of children from adults in Garda Síochána stations) shall apply to a child detained in a Garda Síochána station under subsection (1).

Amendments

1 Subsections substituted by Criminal Justice Act 2006, s 158 and Sch 4.

264 Research

The Minister may conduct or assist other persons in conducting research into any matter connected with children who are considered at risk of committing offences, who have admitted committing offences or who appear before the courts charged with offences.

65 Right of appeal

An appeal shall lie to the Circuit Court from an order of the Children Court or the District Court committing a child to a children detention school [...].[1]

Amendments

1 Words deleted by Criminal Justice Act 2006, s 158 and Sch 4.

266 Amendment of section 5 of Criminal Law (Rape) Act, 1981

Section 5 of the Criminal Law (Rape) Act, 1981, is hereby amended by the substitution of "section 75 (which provides for the summary trial in certain cases of persons under the age of 18 years who are charged with indictable offences) of the Children Act, 2001" for "the Summary Jurisdiction over Children (Ireland) Act, 1884, as amended by section 133(6) of the Children Act, 1908, and section 28 of the Children Act, 1941 (which provides for the summary trial in certain cases of persons under the age of 17 who are charged with indictable offences)".

267 Amendment of sections 17(2) and 59 of Act of 1991

(1) The Act of 1991 is hereby amended—

(a) in paragraphs (a) and (b) of section 17(2) (period in care of health board under interim care order), by the substitution of "twenty-eight days" for "eight days", and

(b) in section 59 (definitions for purposes of Part VIII), by the deletion of paragraph (c) from the definition of "children's residential centre".

(2) References in Part V (Jurisdiction and Procedure) of the Act of 1991 to Part IV of that Act shall be construed as including references to Parts IVA and IVB (inserted by section 16) thereof.

268   Children in care of health board

While a child is in the care of [the Health Service Executive][1] pursuant to any provision of this Act, [the Health Service Executive] shall—

(a)   have the like control over the child as if it were his or her parent, and

(b)   do what is reasonable (subject to the provisions of this Act) in all the circumstances of the case for the purpose of safeguarding or promoting the child's health, development or welfare.

Amendments

1   Words amended by Health Act 2004, s 75 and Sch 7.

269   Presumption and determination of age

Where a person who is charged with an offence is brought before a court and it appears to the court that the person is a child, the court shall make due inquiry as to the age of the person, and for that purpose shall take such evidence on oath as may be forthcoming at the hearing of the case, but an order or judgment of the court shall not be invalidated by any subsequent proof that the age of the person has not been correctly stated to the court, and the age presumed or declared by the court to be the age of the person so brought before it shall, for the purposes of this Act, be deemed to be the true age of that person.

270   Safety of children at entertainments

(1) Where—

(a)   an entertainment for children or any entertainment at which the majority of the persons attending are children is provided,

(b)   the number of children who attend the entertainment exceeds one hundred, and

(c)   access to any part of the building in which children are accommodated is by stairs, escalator, lift or other mechanical means,

it shall be the duty of the person who provides the entertainment—

(i)   to station and keep stationed wherever necessary a sufficient number of adult attendants, properly instructed as to their duties, so as to prevent more children or other persons being admitted to any such part of the building than that part can properly accommodate,

(ii)   to control the movement of the children and other persons admitted to any such part while entering and leaving, and

(iii) to take all other reasonable precautions for the safety of the children.

(2) Where the occupier of a building permits, for hire or reward, the building to be used for the purpose of an entertainment, he or she shall take all reasonable steps to ensure that the provisions of this section are complied with.

(3) If any person on whom any obligation is imposed by this section fails to fulfil it, he or she shall be liable, on summary conviction, in the case of a first offence, to a fine not exceeding [€634.87] or imprisonment for a term not exceeding 6 months or both and, in the case of a

second or subsequent offence, to a fine not exceeding [€1,904.61] or imprisonment for a term not exceeding 12 months or both.

(4) A member of the Garda Síochána may enter any building in which he or she has reason to believe that such an entertainment as aforesaid is being, or is about to be, provided with a view to seeing whether the provisions of this section are complied with.

(5) This section shall not apply to any entertainment given in a private residence.

Exclusion of members of Defence Forces

For the purposes of this Act, persons under 18 years of age who are enlisted members of the Defence Forces shall not be regarded as children in any case where they are subject to military law as governed by the Defence Acts, 1954 to 1998.

SCHEDULE 1
OFFENCES AGAINST CHILDREN

1.   The murder or manslaughter of a child.

2.   Any offence under the Criminal Law Amendment Act, 1885, in respect of a child.

3.   Any offence under the Punishment of Incest Act, 1908, in respect of a child.

[4.   Any offence under the Criminal Law (Sexual Offences) Act 2006.]¹

5.   Any offence under the Criminal Law (Rape) Act, 1981, in respect of a child.

6.   Any offence under the Criminal Law (Rape) (Amendment) Act, 1990, in respect of a child.

7.   Any offence under the Criminal Law (Sexual Offences) Act, 1993, in respect of a child.

8.   Any offence under the Non-Fatal Offences against the Person Act, 1997, in respect of a child.

9.   Any offence under the Child Trafficking and Pornography Act, 1998, in respect of a child.

10.   Any offence under the Dangerous Performances Acts, 1879 and 1897.

11.   Any other offence involving bodily injury to a child.

Amendments

1   Paragraph 4 substituted by Criminal Law (Sexual Offences) Act 2006, s 7.

SCHEDULE 2
ENACTMENTS REPEALED

Session and Chapter or Number and Year (1)	Short Title (2)	Extent of Repeal (3)
10 & 11 Vict., c. 84	Vagrancy (Ireland) Act, 1847	Section 3, the words "or causing or procuring or encouraging any child or children to do so".
24 & 25 Vict., c. 100	Offences against the Person Act, 1861	Section 27
31 & 32 Vict., c. 59	Irish Reformatory Schools Act, 1868	Section 25
47 & 48 Vict., c. 19	Summary Jurisdiction over Children (Ireland) Act, 1884	The whole Act
8 Edw. 7, c. 59	Prevention of Crime Act, 1908	Section 2
8 Edw. 7, c. 67	Children Act, 1908	The whole Act
10 Edw. 7, c. 25	Children Act (1908) Amendment Act, 1910	The whole Act
No. 10 of 1924	Courts of Justice Act, 1924	Section 80
No. 6 of 1935	Criminal Law Amendment Act, 1935	Section 11
No. 12 of 1941	Children Act, 1941	The whole Act
No. 6 of 1949	Children (Amendment) Act, 1949	The whole Act
No. 2 of 1951	Criminal Justice Act, 1951	Section 24
No. 28 of 1957	Children (Amendment) Act, 1957	The whole Act

Criminal Justice (Theft And Fraud Offences) Act 2001

Number 50 of 2001

ARRANGEMENT OF SECTIONS

PART 1
PRELIMINARY

Section

1.   Short title and commencement.

2.   Interpretation (general).

3.   Repeals, etc.

PART 2
THEFT AND RELATED OFFENCES

4.   Theft.

5.   Exceptions to theft.

6.   Making gain or causing loss by deception.

7.   Obtaining services by deception.

8.   Making off without payment.

9.   Unlawful use of computer.

10.   False accounting.

11.   Suppression, etc., of documents.

12.   Burglary.

13.   Aggravated burglary.

14.   Robbery.

15.   Possession of certain articles.

PART 3
HANDLING, ETC. STOLEN PROPERTY AND OTHER PROCEEDS OF CRIME

16.   Interpretation (Part 3).

17.   Handling stolen property.

18.   Possession of stolen property.

19.   Withholding information regarding stolen property.

20.   Scope of offences relating to stolen property.

21.   Amendment of section 31 of Criminal Justice Act, 1994.

22.   Amendment of section 56A of Criminal Justice Act, 1994.

23.   Amendment of Criminal Justice Act, 1994.

PART 4

FORGERY

24. Interpretation (Part 4).

25. Forgery.

26. Using false instrument.

27. Copying false instrument.

28. Using copy of false instrument.

29. Custody or control of certain false instruments, etc.

30. Meaning of "false" and "making".

31. Meaning of "prejudice" and "induce".

PART 5

COUNTERFEITING

32. Interpretation (Part 5).

33. Counterfeiting currency notes and coins.

34. Passing, etc. counterfeit currency notes or coins.

35. Custody or control of counterfeit currency notes and coins.

36. Materials and implements for counterfeiting.

37. Import and export of counterfeits.

38. Certain offences committed outside the State.

39. Measures to detect counterfeiting.

PART 6

CONVENTION ON PROTECTION OF EUROPEAN COMMUNITIES' FINANCIAL INTERESTS

40. Interpretation (Part 6).

41. Convention and Protocols to have force of law.

42. Fraud affecting European Communities' financial interests.

43. Active corruption.

44. Passive corruption.

45. Extra-territorial jurisdiction in case of certain offences.

46. Restriction on certain proceedings.

47. Extradition for revenue offences.

PART 7

INVESTIGATION OF OFFENCES

48. Search warrants.

49. Obstruction of Garda acting on warrant.

50. Forfeiture of seized property.

51. Concealing facts disclosed by documents.

52. Order to produce evidential material.

PART 8

TRIAL OF OFFENCES

53. Summary trial of indictable offences.

54. Trial procedure.

55. Alternative verdicts.

56. Orders for restitution.

57. Provision of information to juries.

PART 9

MISCELLANEOUS

58. Liability for offences by bodies corporate and unincorporated.

59. Reporting of offences.

60. Evidence in proceedings.

61. Jurisdiction of District Court in certain proceedings.

62. Amendment of section 9 of Married Women's Status Act, 1957.

63. Amendment of Defence Act, 1954.

64. Amendment of Bail Act, 1997.

65. Effect of Act and transitional provisions.

SCHEDULE 1

ENACTMENTS REPEALED

SCHEDULE 2

TEXT IN THE ENGLISH LANGUAGE OF THE CONVENTION DRAWN UP ON THE BASIS OF ARTICLE K.3 OF THE TREATY ON EUROPEAN UNION, ON THE PROTECTION OF THE EUROPEAN COMMUNITIES' FINANCIAL INTERESTS DONE AT BRUSSELS ON 26 JULY 1995

SCHEDULE 3

TEXT NOT REPRODUCED HERE

SCHEDULE 4

TEXT IN THE ENGLISH LANGUAGE OF THE PROTOCOL DRAWN UP ON THE BASIS OF ARTICLE K.3 OF THE TREATY ON EUROPEAN UNION TO THE CONVENTION ON THE PROTECTION OF THE EUROPEAN COMMUNITIES' FINANCIAL INTERESTS DONE AT BRUSSELS ON 27 SEPTEMBER 1996

SCHEDULE 5

TEXT NOT REPRODUCED HERE

SCHEDULE 6

TEXT IN THE ENGLISH LANGUAGE OF THE PROTOCOL DRAWN UP ON THE BASIS OF ARTICLE K.3 OF THE TREATY ON EUROPEAN UNION, ON THE INTERPRETATION, BY WAY OF PRELIMINARY RULINGS, BY THE COURT OF JUSTICE OF THE EUROPEAN

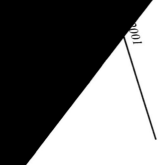

'ENTION ON THE PROTECTION OF THE EUROPEAN
RESTS DONE AT BRUSSELS ON **29 NOVEMBER 1996**

SCHEDULE 7
DT REPRODUCED HERE

SCHEDULE 8
F THE **PROTOCOL DRAWN UP ON THE BASIS OF**
UROPEAN **UNION, TO THE CONVENTION ON THE**
OPEAN **COMMUNITIES' FINANCIAL INTERESTS DONE AT**
BRUSSELS ON 19 JUNE 1997

SCHEDULE 9
TEXT NOT REPRODUCED HERE

AN ACT TO AMEND THE LAW RELATING TO STEALING AND RELATED OFFENCES AND THEIR INVESTIGATION AND TRIAL; TO GIVE THE FORCE OF LAW TO PROVISIONS OF THE CONVENTION ON THE PROTECTION OF THE EUROPEAN COMMUNITIES' FINANCIAL INTERESTS DONE AT BRUSSELS ON 26 JULY 1995 AND THE THREE PROTOCOLS TO THAT CONVENTION; AND TO PROVIDE FOR CONSEQUENTIAL AND RELATED MATTERS. [19th December, 2001]

BE IT ENACTED BY THE OIREACHTAS AS FOLLOWS:

PART 1
PRELIMINARY

1   Short title and commencement

(1) This Act may be cited as the Criminal Justice (Theft and Fraud Offences) Act, 2001.

(2) Subject to subsection (3), this Act shall come into operation on such day or days as may be appointed by order or orders made by the Minister, either generally or with reference to any particular purpose or provision, and different days may be so appointed for different purposes and different provisions of this Act.

(3) Parts 5 and 7 and sections 23, 53, 58 and 60(1) shall come into operation on the passing of this Act.

2   Interpretation (general)

(1) In this Act—

"appropriates" has the meaning given to it by section 4(5);

"deception" has the meaning given to it by subsection (2);

"dishonestly" means without a claim of right made in good faith;

"document" includes—

(a)   a map, plan, graph, drawing, photograph or record, or

(b)   a reproduction in permanent legible form, by a computer or other means (including enlarging), of information in non-legible form;

"gain" and "loss" have the meanings given to them by subsection (3);

"information in non-legible form" means information which is kept (by electronic means or otherwise) on microfilm, microfiche, magnetic tape or disk or in any other non-legible form;

"owner" and "ownership", in relation to property, have the meanings given to them by subsection (4);

"premises" includes a vehicle, vessel, aircraft or hovercraft or an installation in the territorial seas or in a designated area (within the meaning of the Continental Shelf Act, 1968) or a tent, caravan or other temporary or movable structure;

"property" means money and all other property, real or personal, including things in action and other intangible property;

"record" includes any information in non-legible form which is capable of being reproduced in permanent legible form;

"stealing" means committing an offence under section 4, and cognate words shall be construed accordingly;

"stolen property" includes property which has been unlawfully obtained otherwise than by stealing, and cognate words shall be construed accordingly;

"theft" has the meaning given to it by section 4(1); and

"unlawfully obtained" means obtained in circumstances constituting an offence, and cognate words shall be construed accordingly.

(2) For the purposes of this Act a person deceives if he or she—

    (a) creates or reinforces a false impression, including a false impression as to law, value or intention or other state of mind,

    (b) prevents another person from acquiring information which would affect that person's judgement of a transaction, or

    (c) fails to correct a false impression which the deceiver previously created or reinforced or which the deceiver knows to be influencing another to whom he or she stands in a fiduciary or confidential relationship,

and references to deception shall be construed accordingly.

(3) For the purposes of this Act—

    (a) "gain" and "loss" are to be construed as extending only to gain or loss in money or other property, whether any such gain or loss is temporary or permanent,

    (b) "gain" includes a gain by keeping what one has, as well as a gain by getting what one has not, and

    (c) "loss" includes a loss by not getting what one might get, as well as a loss by parting with what one has.

(4) For the purposes of this Act—

    (a) a person shall be regarded as owning property if he or she has possession or control of it, or has in it any proprietary right or interest (not being an equitable interest arising only from an agreement to transfer or grant an interest);

    (b) where property is subject to a trust, the persons who own it shall be regarded as including any person having a right to enforce the trust, and an intention to defeat the trust shall be regarded accordingly as an intention to deprive of the property any person having that right;

    (c) where a person receives property from or on behalf of another, and is under an obligation to that other person to retain and deal with that property or its proceeds in a particular way, that other person shall be regarded (as against the first-mentioned person) as the owner of the property;

(d) where a person gets property by another's mistake and is under an obligation to make restoration (in whole or in part) of the property or its proceeds or of the value thereof, then the person entitled to restoration shall to the extent of that obligation be regarded (as against the first-mentioned person) as the owner of the property or its proceeds or an amount equivalent to its value, and an intention not to make restoration shall be regarded accordingly as an intention to deprive that person of the property, proceeds or such amount;

(e) property of a corporation sole shall be regarded as belonging to the corporation notwithstanding a vacancy in the corporation,

and references to "owner" and "ownership" shall be construed accordingly.

(5) (a) A reference in this Act to a Part, section or Schedule is a reference to a Part, section or Schedule of this Act unless it is indicated that a reference to some other Act is intended.

(b) A reference in this Act to a subsection, paragraph or subparagraph is to the subsection, paragraph or subparagraph of the provision in which the reference occurs unless it is indicated that a reference to some other provision is intended.

(c) A reference in this Act to any enactment shall be construed as a reference to that enactment as amended, adapted or extended, whether before or after the passing of this Act, by or under any subsequent enactment.

3   Repeals, etc

(1) Subject to section 65, the Acts specified in Schedule 1 are Repeals, etc. repealed to the extent specified in the third column of that Schedule.

(2) Any offence at common law of larceny, burglary, robbery, cheating (except in relation to the public revenue), extortion under colour of office and forgery is abolished.

(3) The abolition of a common law offence mentioned in subsection (2) shall not affect proceedings for any such offence committed before its abolition.

PART 2
THEFT AND RELATED OFFENCES

4   Theft

(1) Subject to section 5, a person is guilty of theft if he or she dishonestly appropriates property without the consent of its owner and with the intention of depriving its owner of it.

(2) For the purposes of this section a person does not appropriate property without the consent of its owner if—

(a) the person believes that he or she has the owner's consent, or would have the owner's consent if the owner knew of the appropriation of the property and the circumstances in which it was appropriated, or

(b) (except where the property came to the person as trustee or personal representative) he or she appropriates the property in the belief that the owner cannot be discovered by taking reasonable steps,

but consent obtained by deception or intimidation is not consent for those purposes.

(3) (a) This subsection applies to a person who in the course of business holds property in trust for, or on behalf of, more than one owner.

(b) Where a person to whom this subsection applies appropriates some of the property so held to his or her own use or benefit, the person shall, for the purposes of subsection (1) but subject to subsection (2), be deemed to have appropriated the property or, as the case may be, a sum representing it without the consent of its owner or owners.

(c) If in any proceedings against a person to whom this subsection applies for theft of some or all of the property so held by him or her it is proved that—

(i) there is a deficiency in the property or a sum representing it, and

(ii) the person has failed to provide a satisfactory explanation for the whole or any part of the deficiency,

it shall be presumed, until the contrary is proved, for the purposes of subsection (1) but subject to subsection (2), that the person appropriated, without the consent of its owner or owners, the whole or that part of the deficiency.

(4) If at the trial of a person for theft the court or jury, as the case may be has to consider whether the person believed—

(a) that he or she had not acted dishonestly, or

(b) that the owner of the property concerned had consented or would have consented to its appropriation, or

(c) that the owner could not be discovered by taking reasonable steps,

the presence or absence of reasonable grounds for such a belief is a matter to which the court or jury shall have regard, in conjunction with any other relevant matters, in considering whether the person so believed.

(5) In this section—

"appropriates", in relation to property, means usurps or adversely interferes with the proprietary rights of the owner of the property;

"depriving" means temporarily or permanently depriving.

(6) A person guilty of theft is liable on conviction on indictment to a fine or imprisonment for a term not exceeding 10 years or both.

5   Exceptions to theft

(1) Where property or a right or interest in property is or purports to be transferred for value to a person acting in good faith, no later assumption by that person of rights which that person believes himself or herself to be acquiring shall, by reason of any defect in the transferor's title, amount to theft of the property.

(2) A person cannot steal land, or things forming part of land and severed from it by or under his or her directions, except where the person—

(a) being a trustee, personal representative or other person authorised by power of attorney or as liquidator of a company or otherwise to sell or dispose of land owned by another, appropriates the land or anything forming part of it by dealing with it in breach of the confidence reposed in him or her, or

(b) not being in possession of the land, appropriates anything forming part of the land by severing it or causing it to be severed, or after it has been severed, or

---

(c) being in possession of the land under a tenancy or licence, appropriates the whole or part of any fixture or structure let or licensed to be used with the land.

(3) For the purposes of subsection (2)—

(a) "land" does not include incorporeal hereditaments,

"tenancy" means a tenancy for years or any less period and includes an agreement for such a tenancy,

"licence" includes an agreement for a licence,

and

(b) a person who after the expiration of a tenancy or licence remains in possession of land shall be treated as having possession under the tenancy or licence, and "let" and "licensed" shall be construed accordingly.

(4) A person who picks mushrooms or any other fungus growing wild on any land, or who picks flowers, fruit or foliage from a plant (including any shrub or tree) growing wild on any land, does not (although not in possession of the land) steal what is picked, unless he or she does it for reward or for sale or other commercial purpose.

(5) Wild creatures, tamed or untamed, shall be regarded as property; but a person cannot steal a wild creature not tamed or ordinarily kept in captivity, or the carcase of any such creature, unless it has been reduced into possession by or on behalf of another person and possession of it has not since been lost or abandoned, or another person is in course of reducing it into possession.

6 Making gain or causing loss by deception

(1) A person who dishonestly, with the intention of making a gain for himself or herself or another, or of causing loss to another, by any deception induces another to do or refrain from doing an act is guilty of an offence.

(2) A person guilty of an offence under this section is liable on conviction on indictment to a fine or imprisonment for a term not exceeding 5 years or both.

7 Obtaining services by deception

(1) A person who dishonestly, with the intention of making a gain for himself or herself or another, or of causing loss to another, by any deception obtains services from another is guilty of an offence.

(2) For the purposes of this section a person obtains services from another where the other is induced to confer a benefit on some person by doing some act, or causing or permitting some act to be done, on the understanding that the benefit has been or will be paid for.

(3) Without prejudice to the generality of subsection (2), a person obtains services where the other is induced to make a loan, or to cause or permit a loan to be made, on the understanding that any payment (whether by way of interest or otherwise) will be or has been made in respect of the loan.

(4) A person guilty of an offence under this section is liable on conviction on indictment to a fine or imprisonment for a term not exceeding 5 years or both.

8 Making off without payment

(1) Subject to subsection (2), a person who, knowing that payment on the spot for any goods obtained or any service done is required or expected, dishonestly makes off without having

paid as required or expected and with the intention of avoiding payment on the spot is guilty of an offence.

(2) Subsection (1) shall not apply where the supply of the goods or the doing of the service is contrary to law or where the service done is such that payment is not legally enforceable.

(3) Subject to subsections (5) and (6), any person may arrest without warrant anyone who is or whom he or she, with reasonable cause, suspects to be in the act of committing an offence under this section.

(4) Where a member of the Garda Síochána, with reasonable cause, suspects that an offence under this section has been committed, he or she may arrest without warrant any person whom the member, with reasonable cause, suspects to be guilty of the offence.

(5) An arrest other than by a member of the Garda Síochána may be effected by a person under subsection (3) only where the person, with reasonable cause, suspects that the person to be arrested by him or her would otherwise attempt to avoid, or is avoiding, arrest by a member of the Garda Síochána.

(6) A person who is arrested pursuant to this section by a person other than a member of the Garda Síochána shall be transferred by that person into the custody of the Garda Síochána as soon as practicable.

(7) A person guilty of an offence under this section is liable on conviction on indictment to a fine not exceeding £3,000 or imprisonment for a term not exceeding 2 years or both.

9   Unlawful use of computer

(1) A person who dishonestly, whether within or outside the State, operates or causes to be operated a computer within the State with the intention of making a gain for himself or herself or another, or of causing loss to another, is guilty of an offence.

(2) A person guilty of an offence under this section is liable on conviction on indictment to a fine or imprisonment for a term not exceeding 10 years or both.

10   False accounting

(1) A person is guilty of an offence if he or she dishonestly, with the intention of making a gain for himself or herself or another, or of causing loss to another—

    (a)   destroys, defaces, conceals or falsifies any account or any document made or required for any accounting purpose,

    (b)   fails to make or complete any account or any such document, or

    (c)   in furnishing information for any purpose produces or makes use of any account, or any such document, which to his or her knowledge is or may be misleading, false or deceptive in a material particular.

(2) For the purposes of this section a person shall be treated as falsifying an account or other document if he or she—

    (a)   makes or concurs in making therein an entry which is or may be misleading, false or deceptive in a material particular, or

    (b)   omits or concurs in omitting a material particular therefrom.

(3) A person guilty of an offence under this section is liable on conviction on indictment to a fine or imprisonment for a term not exceeding 10 years or both.

11   Suppression, etc., of documents

(1) A person is guilty of an offence if he or she dishonestly, with the intention of making a gain for himself or herself or another, or of causing loss to another, destroys, defaces or conceals any valuable security, any will or other testamentary document or any original document of or belonging to, or filed or deposited in, any court or any government department or office.

(2) (a)   A person who dishonestly, with the intention of making a gain for himself or herself or another, or of causing loss to another, by any deception procures the execution of a valuable security is guilty of an offence.

   (b)   Paragraph (a) shall apply in relation to—

   (i)   the making, acceptance, endorsement, alteration, cancellation or destruction in whole or in part of a valuable security, and

   (ii)   the signing or sealing of any paper or other material in order that it may be made or converted into, or used or dealt with as, a valuable security,

   as if that were the execution of a valuable security.

(3) In this section, "valuable security" means any document—

   (a)   creating, transferring, surrendering or releasing any right to, in or over property,

   (b)   authorising the payment of money or delivery of any property, or

   (c)   evidencing the creation, transfer, surrender or release of any such right, the payment of money or delivery of any property or the satisfaction of any obligation.

(4) A person guilty of an offence under this section is liable on conviction on indictment to a fine or imprisonment for a term not exceeding 10 years or both.

12   Burglary

(1) A person is guilty of burglary if he or she—

   (a)   enters any building or part of a building as a trespasser and with intent to commit an arrestable offence, or

   (b)   having entered any building or part of a building as a trespasser, commits or attempts to commit any such offence therein.

(2) References in subsection (1) to a building shall apply also to an inhabited vehicle or vessel and to any other inhabited temporary or movable structure, and shall apply to any such vehicle, vessel or structure at times when the person having a habitation in it is not there as well as at times when the person is there.

(3) A person guilty of burglary is liable on conviction on indictment to a fine or imprisonment for a term not exceeding 14 years or both.

(4) In this section, "arrestable offence" means an offence for which a person of full age and not previously convicted may be punished by imprisonment for a term of five years or by a more severe penalty.

13   Aggravated burglary

(1) A person is guilty of aggravated burglary if he or she commits any burglary and at the time has with him or her any firearm or imitation firearm, any weapon of offence or any explosive.

(2) In subsection (1)—

"explosive" means any article manufactured for the purpose of producing a practical effect by explosion, or intended by the person having it with him or her for that purpose;

"firearm" means:

(a) a lethal firearm or other lethal weapon of any description from which any shot, bullet or other missile can be discharged,

(b) an air gun (which expression includes an air rifle and an air pistol) or any other weapon incorporating a barrel from which metal or other slugs can be discharged,

(c) a crossbow,

(d) any type of stun gun or other weapon for causing any shock or other disablement to a person by means of electricity or any other kind of energy emission;

"imitation firearm" means anything which is not a firearm but has the appearance of being one;

"weapon of offence" means:

(a) any article which has a blade or sharp point,

(b) any other article made or adapted for use for causing injury to or incapacitating a person, or intended by the person having it with him or her for such use or for threatening such use,

(c) any weapon of whatever description designed for the discharge of any noxious liquid, noxious gas or other noxious thing.

(3) A person guilty of aggravated burglary is liable on conviction on indictment to imprisonment for life.

14   Robbery

(1) A person is guilty of robbery if he or she steals, and immediately before or at the time of doing so, and in order to do so, uses force on any person or puts or seeks to put any person in fear of being then and there subjected to force.

(2) A person guilty of robbery is liable on conviction on indictment to imprisonment for life.

15   Possession of certain articles

(1) A person who is, when not at his or her place of residence, in possession of any article with the intention that it be used in the course of or in connection with—

(a) theft or burglary,

[(aa) robbery,]¹

(b) an offence under section 6 or 7,

(c) an offence under section 17 (blackmail, extortion, demanding money with menaces) of the Criminal Justice (Public Order) Act, 1994, or

(d) an offence under section 112 (taking a vehicle without lawful authority) of the Road Traffic Act, 1961,

is guilty of an offence.

[(1A) A person who, without lawful authority or reasonable excuse, is in possession of any article made or adapted for use in the course of, or in connection with, the commission of an offence referred to in paragraphs (a) to (d) of subsection (1) is guilty of an offence.]²

[(2) It is a defence for a person charged with an offence under subsection (1) to prove that at the time of the alleged offence the article concerned was not in his or her possession for a purpose specified in that subsection.

(2A) It is a defence for a person charged with an offence under subsection (1A) to prove that the article concerned was not made or adapted for use in the course of or in connection with the commission of an offence referred to in paragraphs (a) to (d) of subsection (1).]³

(3) Where a person is convicted of an offence under this section, the court may order that any article for the possession of which he or she was so convicted shall be forfeited and either destroyed or disposed of in such manner as the court may determine.

(4) An order under subsection (3) shall not take effect until the ordinary time for instituting an appeal against the conviction or order concerned has expired or, where such an appeal is instituted, until it or any further appeal is finally decided or abandoned or the ordinary time for instituting any further appeal has expired.

(5) A person guilty of an offence under this section is liable on conviction on indictment to a fine or imprisonment for a term not exceeding 5 years or both.

Amendments

1   Subsection (1)(aa) inserted by Criminal Justice Act 2007, s 47(a)(i).

2   Subsection (1A) inserted by Criminal Justice (Miscellaneous Provisions) Act 2009, s 49(a).

2   Subsection (2) (inserted by Criminal Justice Act 2007, s 47(a)(ii)) substituted and sub-s (2A) inserted by Criminal Justice (Miscellaneous Provisions) Act 2009, s 49(b).

PART 3

HANDLING, ETC. STOLEN PROPERTY AND OTHER PROCEEDS OF CRIME

16   Interpretation (Part 3)

(1) In this Part "principal offender", for the purposes of sections 17 and 18, means the person who has stolen or otherwise unlawfully obtained the property alleged to have been handled or possessed, and cognate words shall be construed accordingly.

(2) For the purposes of this Part, a person is reckless if he or she disregards a substantial risk that the property handled is stolen, and for those purposes "substantial risk" means a risk of such a nature and degree that, having regard to the circumstances in which the person acquired the property and the extent of the information then available to him or her, its disregard involves culpability of a high degree.

(3) This Part is without prejudice to section 31 (as substituted by section 21 of this Act) of the Criminal Justice Act, 1994.

17   Handling stolen property

(1) A person is guilty of handling stolen property if (otherwise than in the course of the stealing) he or she, knowing that the property was stolen or being reckless as to whether it was stolen, dishonestly—

(a) receives or arranges to receive it, or

(b) undertakes, or assists in, its retention, removal, disposal or realisation by or for the benefit of another person, or arranges to do so.

(2) Where a person—

(a) receives or arranges to receive property, or

(b) undertakes, or assists in, its retention, removal, disposal or realisation by or for the benefit of another person, or arranges to do so,

in such circumstances that it is reasonable to conclude that the person either knew that the property was stolen or was reckless as to whether it was stolen, he or she shall be taken for the purposes of this section to have so known or to have been so reckless, unless the court or the jury, as the case may be, is satisfied having regard to all the evidence that there is a reasonable doubt as to whether he or she so knew or was so reckless.

(3) A person to whom this section applies may be tried and convicted whether the principal offender has or has not been previously convicted or is or is not amenable to justice.

(4) A person guilty of handling stolen property is liable on conviction on indictment to a fine or imprisonment for a term not exceeding 10 years or both, but is not liable to a higher fine or longer term of imprisonment than that which applies to the principal offence.

18   Possession of stolen property

(1) A person who, without lawful authority or excuse, possesses stolen property (otherwise than in the course of the stealing), knowing that the property was stolen or being reckless as to whether it was stolen, is guilty of an offence.

(2) Where a person has in his or her possession stolen property in such circumstances (including purchase of the property at a price below its market value) that it is reasonable to conclude that the person either knew that the property was stolen or was reckless as to whether it was stolen, he or she shall be taken for the purposes of this section to have so known or to have been so reckless, unless the court or the jury, as the case may be, is satisfied having regard to all the evidence that there is a reasonable doubt as to whether he or she so knew or was so reckless.

(3) A person to whom this section applies may be tried and convicted whether the principal offender has or has not been previously convicted or is or is not amenable to justice.

(4) A person guilty of an offence under this section is liable on conviction on indictment to a fine or imprisonment for a term not exceeding 5 years or both, but is not liable to a higher fine or longer term of imprisonment than that which applies to the principal offence.

19   Withholding information regarding stolen property

(1) Where a member of the Garda Síochána—

(a) has reasonable grounds for believing that an offence consisting of stealing property or of handling stolen property has been committed,

(b) finds any person in possession of any property,

(c) has reasonable grounds for believing that the property referred to in paragraph (b) includes, or may include, property referred to in paragraph (a) or part of it, or the whole or any part of the proceeds of that property or part, and

(d) informs the person of his or her belief,

the member may require the person to give an account of how he or she came by the property.

(2) If the person fails or refuses, without reasonable excuse, to give such account or gives information that the person knows to be false or misleading, he or she is guilty of an offence and is liable on summary conviction to a fine not exceeding [€5,000]¹ or imprisonment for a term not exceeding 12 months or both.

(3) Subsection (2) shall not have effect unless the person when required to give the account was told in ordinary language by the member of the Garda Síochána what the effect of the failure or refusal might be.

(4) Any information given by a person in compliance with a requirement under subsection (1) shall not be admissible in evidence against that person or his or her spouse in any criminal proceedings, other than proceedings for an offence under subsection (2).

Amendments

1   Amount amended by Criminal Justice Act 2007, s 47(b).

20   Scope of offences relating to stolen property

(1) The provisions of this Part relating to property which has been stolen apply—

(a)   whether the stealing occurred before or after the commencement of this Act, and

(b)   to stealing outside the State if the stealing constituted an offence where and at the time when the property was stolen,

and references to stolen property shall be construed accordingly.

(2) For the purposes of those provisions references to stolen property include, in addition to the property originally stolen and parts of it (whether in their original state or not)—

(a)   any property which directly or indirectly represents, or has at any time represented, the stolen property in the hands of the person who stole the property as being the proceeds of any disposal or realisation of the whole or part of the stolen property or of property so representing the stolen property, and

(b)   any property which directly or indirectly represents, or has at any time represented, the stolen property in the hands of a handler or possessor of the stolen property or any part of it as being the proceeds of any disposal or realisation of the whole or part of the stolen property handled or possessed by him or her or of property so representing it.

(3) However, property shall not be regarded as having continued to be stolen property after it has been restored to the person from whom it was stolen or to other lawful possession or custody, or after that person and any other person claiming through him or her have otherwise ceased, as regards that property, to have any right to restitution in respect of the stealing.

21   Amendment of section 31 of Criminal Justice Act, 1994

The Criminal Justice Act, 1994, is hereby amended by the substitution of the following section for section 31 (money laundering, etc.):¹

Amendments

1   See the amended Act.

22   Amendment of section 56A of Criminal Justice Act, 1994

[...]¹

Amendments

1   Section 22 repealed by Criminal Justice (Mutual Assisstance) Act 2008, s 10(c).

23   Amendment of Criminal Justice Act, 1994

The Criminal Justice Act, 1994, is hereby amended by the insertion of the following section after section 57:¹

Amendments

1   See the amended Act.

PART 4
FORGERY

24   Interpretation (Part 4)

In this Part—

"false" and "making", in relation to an instrument, have the meanings assigned to these words by section 30;

"instrument" means any document, whether of a formal or informal character (other than a currency note within the meaning of Part 5) and includes any—

    (a)   disk, tape, sound track or other device on or in which information is recorded or stored by mechanical, electronic or other means,

    (b)   money order,

    (c)   postal order,

    (d)   postage stamp issued or sold by An Post or any mark denoting payment of postage which is authorised by An Post to be used instead of an adhesive stamp,

    (e)   stamp of the Revenue Commissioners denoting any stamp duty or fee, whether it is an adhesive stamp or a stamp impressed by means of a die,

    (f)   licence or certificate issued by the Revenue Commissioners,

    (g)   cheque, including traveller's cheque, or bank draft,

(h) charge card, cheque card, credit card, debit card or any card combining two or more of the functions performed by such cards,

(i) share certificate,

(j) certified copy, issued by or on behalf of an tArd-Chláraitheoir, of an entry in any register of births, stillbirths, marriages or deaths or in the Adopted Children Register,

(k) certificate relating to such an entry,

(l) a certificate of insurance,

(m) passport or document which can be used instead of a passport,

(n) document issued by or on behalf of a Minister of the Government and permitting or authorising a person to enter or remain (whether temporarily or permanently) in the State or to enter employment therein,

(o) registration certificate issued under Article 11(1)(e)(i) of the Aliens Order, 1946 (S.I. No. 395 of 1946)[or the Immigration Act 2004][1],

(p) public service card,

(q) ticket of admission to an event to which members of the public may be admitted on payment of a fee;

"prejudice" and "induce", in relation to a person, have the meanings assigned to those words by section 31;

"share certificate" means a document entitling or evidencing the title of a person to a share or interest—

(a) in any public stock, annuity, fund or debt of the Government or the State or of any government or state, including a state which forms part of another state, or

(b) in any stock, fund or debt of a body (whether corporate or unincorporated), wherever established.

Amendments

1   Words inserted by Immigration Act 2004, s 16(7).

---

25   Forgery

(1) A person is guilty of forgery if he or she makes a false instrument with the intention that it shall be used to induce another person to accept it as genuine and, by reason of so accepting it, to do some act, or to make some omission, to the prejudice of that person or any other person.

(2) A person guilty of forgery is liable on conviction on indictment to a fine or imprisonment for a term not exceeding 10 years or both.

26   Using false instrument

(1) A person who uses an instrument which is, and which he or she knows or believes to be, a false instrument, with the intention of inducing another person to accept it as genuine and, by reason of so accepting it, to do some act, or to make some omission, or to provide some service, to the prejudice of that person or any other person is guilty of an offence.

(2) A person guilty of an offence under this section is liable on conviction on indictment to a fine or imprisonment for a term not exceeding 10 years or both.

27   Copying false instrument

(1) A person who makes a copy of an instrument which is, and which he or she knows or believes to be, a false instrument with the intention that it shall be used to induce another person to accept it as a copy of a genuine instrument and, by reason of so accepting it, to do some act, or to make some omission, or to provide some service, to the prejudice of that person or any other person is guilty of an offence.

(2) A person guilty of an offence under this section is liable on conviction on indictment to a fine or imprisonment for a term not exceeding 10 years or both.

28   Using copy of false instrument

(1) A person who uses a copy of an instrument which is, and which he or she knows or believes to be, a false instrument with the intention of inducing another person to accept it as a copy of a genuine instrument and, by reason of so accepting it, to do some act, or to make some omission, or to provide some service, to the prejudice of that person or another person is guilty of an offence.

(2) A person guilty of an offence under this section is liable on conviction on indictment to a fine or imprisonment for a term not exceeding 10 years or both.

29   Custody or control of certain false instruments, etc

(1) A person who has in his or her custody or under his or her control an instrument which is, and which he or she knows or believes to be, a false instrument with the intention that it shall be used to induce another person to accept it as genuine and, by reason of so accepting it, to do some act, or to make some omission, or to provide some service, to the prejudice of that person or any other person is guilty of an offence.

(2) A person who, without lawful authority or excuse, has an instrument which is, and which he or she knows or believes to be, a false instrument in his or her custody or under his or her control is guilty of an offence.

(3) A person who makes or has in his or her custody or under his or her control a machine, stamp, implement, paper or any other material, which to his or her knowledge is or has been specially designed or adapted for the making of an instrument with the intention—

    (a)   that it would be used in the making of a false instrument, and

    (b)   that the instrument would be used to induce another person to accept it as genuine and, by reason of so accepting it, to do some act, or to make some omission, or to provide some service, to the prejudice of that person or any other person,

is guilty of an offence.

(4) A person who, without lawful authority or excuse, has in his or her custody or under his or her control any machine, stamp, implement, paper or material which to his or her knowledge is or has been specially designed or adapted for the making of an instrument with the intention that it would be used for the making of a false instrument is guilty of an offence.

(5) In subsections (3) and (4), references to a machine include references to any disk, tape, drive or other device on or in which a program is recorded or stored by mechanical, electronic or other means, being a program designed or adapted to enable an instrument to be made or to assist in its making, and those subsections shall apply and have effect accordingly.

(6) A person guilty of an offence under this section is liable on conviction on indictment to a fine or imprisonment for a term not exceeding—

    (a) in the case of an offence under subsection (2) or (4), 5 years,

    (b) in the case of an offence under subsection (1) or (3), 10 years,

or both.

30   Meaning of "false" and "making"

(1) An instrument is false for the purposes of this Part if it purports—

    (a) to have been made in the form in which it is made by a person who did not in fact make it in that form,

    (b) to have been made in the form in which it is made on the authority of a person who did not in fact authorise its making in that form,

    (c) to have been made in the terms in which it is made by a person who did not in fact make it in those terms,

    (d) to have been made in the terms in which it is made on the authority of a person who did not in fact authorise its making in those terms,

    (e) to have been altered in any respect by a person who did not in fact alter it in that respect,

    (f) to have been altered in any respect on the authority of a person who did not in fact authorise the alteration in that respect,

    (g) to have been made or altered on a date on which, or at a place at which, or otherwise in circumstances in which, it was not in fact made or altered, or

    (h) to have been made or altered by an existing person where that person did not in fact exist.

(2) A person shall be treated for the purposes of this Part as making a false instrument if he or she alters an instrument so as to make it false in any respect (whether or not it is false in some other respect apart from that alteration).

31   Meaning of "prejudice" and "induce"

(1) Subject to subsections (2) and (4), for the purposes of this Part, an act or omission intended to be induced shall be to a person's prejudice if, and only if, it is one which, if it occurs—

    (a) will result, as respects that person—

        (i) in temporary or permanent loss of property,

        (ii) in deprivation of an opportunity to earn remuneration or greater remuneration, or

        (iii) in deprivation of an opportunity to gain a financial advantage otherwise than by way of remuneration,

    or

    (b) will result in another person being given an opportunity—

        (i) to earn remuneration or greater remuneration from him or her, or

        (ii) to gain a financial advantage from him or her otherwise than by way of remuneration,

    or

(c)   will be the result of his or her having accepted any false instrument as genuine, or any copy of it as a copy of a genuine instrument, in connection with his or her performance of any duty.

(2) An act which a person has an enforceable duty to do and an omission to do an act which a person is not entitled to do shall be disregarded for the purposes of this Part.

(3) In this Part references to inducing a person to accept a false instrument as genuine, or a copy of a false instrument as a copy of a genuine one, include references to inducing a machine to respond to the instrument or copy as if it were a genuine instrument or copy of a genuine one.

(4) Where subsection (3) applies, the act or omission intended to be induced by the machine responding to the instrument or copy shall be treated as an act or omission to a person's prejudice.

PART 5
COUNTERFEITING

32   Interpretation (Part 5)

(1) In this Part—

"currency note" and "coin" mean, respectively, a currency note and coin lawfully issued or customarily used as money in the State or in any other state or a territorial unit within it and include a note denominated in euro and a coin denominated in euro or in cent and also any note or coin which has not been lawfully issued but which would, on being so issued, be a currency note or coin within the above meaning; and

"lawfully issued" means issued—

(a)   by or under the authority of the European Central Bank,

(b)   by the Central Bank of Ireland or the Minister for Finance, or

(c)   by a body in a state (other than the State) or a territorial unit within it which is authorised under the law of that state or territorial unit to issue currency notes or coins.

(2) For the purposes of this Part, a thing is a counterfeit of a currency note or coin—

(a)   if it is not a currency note or coin but resembles a currency note or coin (whether on one side only or on both) to such an extent that it is reasonably capable of passing for a currency note or coin of that description, or

(b)   if it is a currency note or coin which has been so altered that it is reasonably capable of passing for a note or coin of some other description.

(3) For the purposes of this Part—

(a)   a thing consisting of or containing a representation of one side only of a currency note, with or without the addition of other material, is capable of being a counterfeit of such a currency note, and

(b)   a thing consisting—

(i)   of parts of two or more currency notes, or

(ii) of parts of a currency note, or of parts of two or more currency notes, with the addition of other material,

is capable of being a counterfeit of a currency note.

33   Counterfeiting currency notes and coins

(1) A person who makes a counterfeit of a currency note or coin, with the intention that he or she or another shall pass or tender it as genuine, is guilty of an offence.

(2) A person guilty of an offence under this section is liable on conviction on indictment to a fine or imprisonment for a term not exceeding 10 years or both.

34   Passing, etc. counterfeit currency notes or coins

(1) A person who—

    (a) passes or tenders as genuine any thing which is, and which he or she knows or believes to be, a counterfeit of a currency note or coin, or

    (b) delivers any such thing to another person with the intention that that person or any other person shall pass or tender it as genuine,

is guilty of an offence.

(2) A person who, without lawful authority or excuse, delivers to another person anything which is, and which he or she knows or believes to be, a counterfeit of a currency note or coin is guilty of an offence.

(3) A person guilty of an offence under this section is liable on conviction on indictment to a fine or imprisonment for a term not exceeding—

    (a) in the case of an offence under subsection (1), 10 years, or

    (b) in the case of an offence under subsection (2), 5 years,

or both.

35   Custody or control of counterfeit currency notes and coins

(1) A person who has in his or her custody or under his or her control any thing which is, and which he or she knows or believes to be, a counterfeit of a currency note or coin, intending either—

    (a) to pass or tender it as genuine, or

    (b) to deliver it to another with the intention that that person or any other person shall pass or tender it as genuine,

is guilty of an offence.

(2) A person who, without lawful authority or excuse, has in his or her custody or under his or her control any thing which is, and which he or she knows or believes to be, a counterfeit of a currency note or coin is guilty of an offence.

(3) A person guilty of an offence under this section is liable on conviction on indictment to a fine or imprisonment for a term not exceeding—

    (a) in the case of an offence under subsection (1), 10 years, or

    (b) in the case of an offence under subsection (2), 5 years,

or both.

36   Materials and implements for counterfeiting

(1) A person who makes, or has in his or her custody or under his or her control, any thing which he or she intends to use, or to permit any other person to use, for the purpose of making a counterfeit of a currency note or coin with the intention that it be passed or tendered as genuine is guilty of an offence.

(2) A person who, without lawful authority or excuse, has in his or her custody or under his or her control any thing which is or has been specially designed or adapted for making a counterfeit of a currency note or coin is guilty of an offence.

(3) A person guilty of an offence under this section is liable on conviction on indictment to a fine or imprisonment for a term not exceeding—

(a)   in the case of an offence under subsection (1), 10 years, or

(b)   in the case of an offence under subsection (2), 5 years,

or both.

37   Import and export of counterfeits

(1) A person who without lawful authority or excuse imports into, or exports from, a member state of the European Union a counterfeit of a currency note or coin is guilty of an offence.

(2) A person guilty of an offence under this section is liable on conviction on indictment to a fine or imprisonment for a term not exceeding 10 years or both.

38   Certain offences committed outside the State

(1) A person who outside the State does any act referred to in section 33, 34, 35, 36 or 37 is guilty of an offence and liable on conviction on indictment to the penalty specified for such an act in the section concerned.

(2) Section 46 shall apply in relation to an offence under subsection (1) as it applies in relation to an offence under section 45.

39   Measures to detect counterfeiting

(1) In this section—

"designated body" means:

(a)   a body licensed to carry on banking business under the Central Bank Act, 1971, or authorised to carry on such business under the ACC Bank Acts, 1978 to 2001, or regulations under the European Communities Acts, 1972 to 1998,

(b)   a building society within the meaning of the Building Societies Act, 1989,

(c)   a trustee savings bank within the meaning of the Trustee Savings Banks Acts, 1989 and 2001,

(d)   An Post,

(e)   a credit union within the meaning of the Credit Union Act, 1997,

(f)   a person or body authorised under the Central Bank Act, 1997, to provide bureau de change business,

(g)   a person who in the course of business provides a service of sorting and redistributing currency notes or coins,

(h)   any other person or body—

(i)   whose business consists of or includes the provision of services involving the acceptance, exchange, transfer or holding of money for or on behalf of other persons or bodies, and

(ii)   who is designated for the purposes of this section by regulations made by the Minister after consultation with the Minister for Finance; and

"recognised code of practice" means a code of practice drawn up for the purposes of this section—

    (a) by a designated body or class of designated bodies and approved by the Central Bank of Ireland, or

    (b) by the Central Bank of Ireland for a designated body or class of such bodies.

(2) A designated body shall—

    (a) withdraw from circulation any notes or coins received by it or tendered to it which it knows or suspects to be counterfeit, and

    (b) transmit them as soon as possible to the Central Bank of Ireland with such information as to the time, location and circumstances of their receipt as may be available.

(3) Counterfeit or suspect currency notes or coins may be transmitted to the Garda Síochána under subsection (2) in accordance with a recognised code of practice.

(4) A recognised code of practice may include provision for—

    (a) procedures to be followed by directors or other officers and employees of a designated body in the conduct of its business,

    (b) instructions to them on the application of this section,

    (c) standards of training in the identification of counterfeit notes and coins,

    (d) procedures to be followed by them on perceiving or suspecting that currency notes or coins are counterfeit,

    (e) different such procedures to be followed in respect of different currencies,

    (f) the retention of documents required for the purposes of criminal proceedings.

(5) Without prejudice to section 58, a designated body which contravenes a provision of subsection (2) of this section or who provides false or misleading information on matters referred to in [that subsection][1] is guilty of an offence under this section and liable—

    (a) on summary conviction, to a fine not exceeding £1,500 or imprisonment for a term not exceeding 12 months or both, or

    (b) on conviction on indictment, to a fine or imprisonment for a term not exceeding 5 years or both.

(6) It shall be a defence in proceedings for an offence under this section—

    (a) for a designated body to show—

        (i) that it had established procedures to enable this section to be complied with, or

        (ii) that it had complied with the relevant provisions of a recognised code of practice,

    and

    (b) for a person employed by a designated body to show that he or she transmitted the currency notes or coins concerned, or gave the relevant information, to another person in accordance with an internal reporting procedure or a recognised code of practice.

(7) Where a designated body, a director, other officer or employee of the body—

    (a) discloses in good faith to a member of the Garda Síochána or any person concerned in the investigation or prosecution of an offence under this Part a suspicion that a currency note or coin is counterfeit or any matter on which such a suspicion is based, or

(b) otherwise complies in good faith with subsection (2) or with a recognised code of practice,

such disclosure or compliance shall not be treated as a breach of any restriction imposed by statute or otherwise on the disclosure of information or involve the person or body making the disclosure in liability in any proceedings.

(8) Every regulation made under this section shall be laid before each House of the Oireachtas as soon as may be after it is made and, if a resolution annulling it is passed by either such House within the next 21 days on which that House has sat after the regulation is laid before it, the regulation shall be annulled accordingly, but without prejudice to the validity of anything previously done under it.

Amendments

1   Words substituted by Criminal Justice (Miscellaneous Provisions) Act 2009, s 50.

PART 6

CONVENTION ON PROTECTION OF EUROPEAN COMMUNITIES' FINANCIAL INTERESTS

40   Interpretation (Part 6)

(1) In this Part—

"active corruption" has the meaning given to it by Article 3.1 of the First Protocol;

"Community official" has the meaning given to it by Article 1.1(b) of the First Protocol;

"Convention" means the Convention drawn up on the basis of Article K.3 of the Treaty on European Union, on the protection of the European Communities' financial interests done at Brussels on 26 July 1995;

"First Protocol" means the Protocol drawn up on the basis of Article K.3 of the Treaty on European Union to the Convention on the protection of the European Communities' financial interests done at Brussels on 27 September 1996;

"fraud affecting the European Communities' financial interests" has the meaning given to it by Article 1.1 of the Convention;

["'money laundering' means an offence under Part 2 of the Criminal Justice (Money Laundering and Terrorist Financing) Act 2010;][1]

"national official", for the purposes of the application in the State of Article 1.1(c) of the First Protocol, means any one of the following persons:

(a)   a Minister of the Government or Minister of State;

(b)   an Attorney General who is not a member of Dáil Éireann or Seanad Éireann;

(c)   the Comptroller and Auditor General;

(d)   a member of Dáil Éireann or Seanad Éireann;

(e)   a judge of a court in the State;

(f)   the Director of Public Prosecutions;

(g)   any other holder of an office who is remunerated wholly or partly out of moneys provided by the Oireachtas;

(h)   any person employed by a person referred to in any of paragraphs (d) to (g) in the performance of that person's official functions; and

(i)   a director of, or an occupier of a position of employment in, a public body as defined in the Ethics in Public Office Act, 1995,

and, for the purposes of the application in the State of Article 4.2 of the First Protocol, any one of the following persons shall be treated as a national official:

(i)   a member of the Commission of the European Communities;

(ii)   a member of the European Parliament;

(iii)   a member of the Court of Justice of the European Communities;

(iv)   a member of the Court of Auditors of the European Communities;

"official" has the meaning given to it by Article 1.1(a) of the First Protocol;

"passive corruption" has the meaning given to it by Article 2.1 of the First Protocol;

"Protocol on Interpretation" means the Protocol drawn up on the basis of Article K.3 of the Treaty on European Union, on the interpretation, by way of preliminary rulings, by the Court of Justice of the European Communities of the Convention on the protection of the European Communities' financial interests done at Brussels on 29 November 1996; and

"Second Protocol" means the Protocol drawn up on the basis of Article K.3 of the Treaty on European Union, to the Convention on the protection of the European Communities' financial interests done at Brussels on 19 June 1997.

(2) For the purposes of sections 42(c) and 45(1)(a)—

(a)   a person benefits from fraud or money laundering if he or she obtains property as a result of or in connection with the commission of an offence under either of those provisions, and

(b)   a person derives a pecuniary advantage from fraud or money laundering if he or she obtains a sum of money as a result of or in connection with the commission of such an offence.

Amendments

1   Definition substituted by Criminal Justice (Money Laundering and Terrorist Financing) Act 2010, s 119.

---

41   Convention and Protocols to have force of law

(1) Subject to the provisions of this Part, the Convention (other than Article 7.2), the First Protocol, the Protocol on Interpretation (other than Article 2(b)) and the Second Protocol (other than Articles 8 and 9) shall have the force of law in the State and judicial notice shall be taken of them.

(2) Judicial notice shall also be taken of any ruling or decision of, or expression of opinion by, the Court of Justice of the European Communities on any question as to the meaning or effect of any provision of the Convention, the First Protocol, the Protocol on Interpretation and the Second Protocol.

(3) For convenience of reference there are set out in Schedules 2 to 9 respectively—

(a)   the text in the English language of the Convention;

(b)   the text in the Irish language of the Convention;

(c)   the text in the English language of the First Protocol;

(d)   the text in the Irish language of the First Protocol;

(e)   the text in the English language of the Protocol on Interpretation;

(f)   the text in the Irish language of the Protocol on Interpretation;

(g)   the text in the English language of the Second Protocol;

(h)   the text in the Irish language of the Second Protocol.

42   Fraud affecting European Communities' financial interests

A person who—

(a)   commits in whole or in part any fraud affecting the European Communities' financial interests,

(b)   participates in, instigates or attempts any such fraud, or

(c)   obtains the benefit of, or derives any pecuniary advantage from, any such fraud,

is guilty of an offence and is liable on conviction on indictment to a fine or imprisonment for a term not exceeding 5 years or both.

43   Active corruption

A person who commits active corruption is guilty of an offence and is liable on conviction on indictment to a fine or imprisonment for a term not exceeding 5 years or both.

44   Passive corruption

An official who commits passive corruption is guilty of an offence and is liable on conviction on indictment to a fine or imprisonment for a term not exceeding 5 years or both.

45   Extra-territorial jurisdiction in case of certain offences

(1) It is an offence for a person to commit fraud affecting the Communities' financial interests or to commit the offence of money laundering, or to participate in, instigate or attempt any such fraud or offence, outside the State if—

(a)   the benefit of the fraud or offence is obtained, or a pecuniary advantage is derived from it, by a person within the State, or

(b)   a person within the State knowingly assists or induces the commission of the fraud or offence, or

(c)   the offender is an Irish citizen, a national official or a Community official working for a European Community institution or a body set up in accordance with the Treaties establishing the European Communities which has its headquarters in the State.

(2) Active or passive corruption committed by a person outside the State is an offence if—

(a)   the offender is an Irish citizen, a national official or a Community official working for a European Community institution or a body set up in accordance with the Treaties establishing the European Communities which has its headquarters within the State, or

   (b)   in the case of active corruption, it is directed against an official, or a member of one of the institutions mentioned in paragraphs (i) to (iv) of the definition of "national official" in section 40, who is an Irish citizen.

(3) A person guilty of an offence under this section is liable on conviction on indictment to a fine or imprisonment for a term not exceeding 5 years or both.

46   Restriction on certain proceedings

(1) Where a person is charged with an offence under section 45, no further proceedings (other than a remand in custody or on bail) shall be taken except by or with the consent of the Director of Public Prosecutions.

(2) Where the Director of Public Prosecutions considers that another member state of the European Union has jurisdiction to try a person charged with an offence under section 45, the Director shall cooperate with the appropriate authorities in the member state concerned with a view to centralising the prosecution of the person in a single member state where possible.

(3) Proceedings for an offence to which this section applies may be taken in any place in the State, and the offence may for all incidental purposes be treated as having been committed in that place.

(4) Proceedings shall not be taken under section 38 of the Extradition Act, 1965, in respect of an act that is an offence under both that section and section 45 of this Act.

47   Extradition for revenue offences

For the purposes of the application in the State of Article 5.3 of the Convention, as applied by Article 12.1 of the Second Protocol, extradition for the offence of fraud against the European Communities' financial interests or money laundering shall not be refused, notwithstanding section 13 of the Extradition Act, 1965, solely on the ground that the offence constitutes a revenue offence as defined in that Act.

PART 7

INVESTIGATION OF OFFENCES

48   Search warrants

(1) This section applies to an offence under any provision of this Act for which a person of full age and capacity and not previously convicted may be punished by imprisonment for a term of five years or by a more severe penalty and to an attempt to commit any such offence.

[(2) If a Judge of the District Court is satisfied by information on oath of a member of the Garda Síochána that there are reasonable grounds for suspecting that evidence of, or relating to the commission of, an offence to which this section applies is to be found in any place, the judge may issue a warrant for the search of that place and any person found there.][1]

(3) A warrant under this section shall be expressed and shall operate to authorise a named member of the Garda Síochána, alone or accompanied by such other persons as may be necessary—

   (a)   to enter, within 7 days from the date of issuing of the warrant (if necessary by the use of reasonable force), the place named in the warrant,

   (b)   to search it and any persons found there,

1032

(c) to examine, seize and retain any thing found there, or in the possession of a person present there at the time of the search, which the member reasonably believes to be evidence of or relating to the commission of an offence to which this section applies, and

(d) to take any other steps which may appear to the member to be necessary for preserving any such thing and preventing interference with it.

(4) The authority conferred by subsection (3)(c) to seize and retain any thing includes, in the case of a document or record, authority—

(a) to make and retain a copy of the document or record, and

(b) where necessary, to seize and, for as long as necessary, retain any computer or other storage medium in which any record is kept.

(5) A member of the Garda Síochána acting under the authority of a warrant under this section may—

(a) operate any computer at the place which is being searched or cause any such computer to be operated by a person accompanying the member for that purpose, and

(b) require any person at that place who appears to the member to have lawful access to the information in any such computer—

　　(i) to give to the member any password necessary to operate it,

　　(ii) otherwise to enable the member to examine the information accessible by the computer in a form in which the information is visible and legible, or

　　(iii) to produce the information in a form in which it can be removed and in which it is, or can be made, visible and legible.

(6) Where a member of the Garda Síochána has entered premises in the execution of a warrant issued under this section, he may seize and retain any material, other than items subject to legal privilege, which is likely to be of substantial value (whether by itself or together with other material) to the investigation for the purpose of which the warrant was issued.

(7) The power to issue a warrant under this section is in addition to and not in substitution for any other power to issue a warrant for the search of any place or person.

(8) In this section, unless the context otherwise requires—

"commission", in relation to an offence, includes an attempt to commit the offence;

"computer at the place which is being searched" includes any other computer, whether at that place or at any other place, which is lawfully accessible by means of that computer;

"place" includes a dwelling;

"thing" includes an instrument (within the meaning of Part 4), a copy of such instrument, a document or a record.

Amendments

1   Subsection (2) substituted by Criminal Justice Act 2006, s 192(1)(a).

49   Obstruction of Garda acting on warrant

(1) A person who—

   (a) obstructs or attempts to obstruct a member of the Garda Síochána acting under the authority of a warrant issued under this Part, or

   (b) is found in or at the place named in the warrant by a member of the Garda Síochána so acting and fails or refuses to give the member his or her name and address when required by the member to do so or gives the member a name and address that is false or misleading, or

   (c) fails without lawful authority or excuse to comply with a requirement under paragraph (b) or section 48(5)(b),

is guilty of an offence and is liable on summary conviction to a fine not exceeding £500 or imprisonment for a term not exceeding 6 months or both.

(2) A member of the Garda Síochána may arrest without warrant any person who is committing an offence under this section or whom the member suspects, with reasonable cause, of having done so.

50   Forfeiture of seized property

(1) This section applies to any thing which has been seized by a member of the Garda Síochána (whether the seizure was effected by virtue of a warrant under section 48 or otherwise) and which the member suspects to be—

   (a) any thing used (whether before or after the commencement of this section), or intended to be used, for the making of any false instrument, or any copy of a false instrument, in contravention of section 25 or 27 respectively,

   (b) any false instrument or any copy of a false instrument used (whether before or after the commencement of this section), or intended to be so used, in contravention of section 26 or 28 respectively,

   (c) any thing the custody or control of which, without lawful authority or excuse, is an offence under section 29,

   (d) any thing which is a counterfeit of a currency note or coin,

   (e) any thing used, whether before or after the commencement of this section, or intended to be used, for the making of any such counterfeit.

(2) A member of the Garda Síochána may, at any time after the seizure of any thing to which this section applies, apply to the judge of the District Court for the time being assigned to the district in which the seizure was effected for an order under this subsection with respect to it; and the judge may, if satisfied both that the thing is one to which this section applies and that it is in the public interest to do so, subject to subsection (4), make such order as the judge thinks fit for its forfeiture and subsequent destruction or disposal.

(3) Subject to subsection (4), the court by or before which a person is convicted of an offence under Part 4 or 5 may order any thing shown to the satisfaction of the court to relate to the offence to be forfeited and either destroyed or dealt with in such other manner as the court may order.

(4) The court shall not order any thing to be forfeited under subsection (3) or (4) where a person claiming to be the owner of or otherwise interested in it applies to be heard by the court, unless an opportunity has been given to the person to show cause why the order should not be made.

51   Concealing facts disclosed by documents

(1) Any person who—

(a) knows or suspects that an investigation by the Garda Síochána into an offence under this Act is being or is likely to be carried out, and

(b) falsifies, conceals, destroys or otherwise disposes of a document or record which he or she knows or suspects is or would be relevant to the investigation or causes or permits its falsification, concealment, destruction or disposal,

is guilty of an offence.

(2) Where a person—

(a) falsifies, conceals, destroys or otherwise disposes of a document, or

(b) causes or permits its falsification, concealment, destruction or disposal,

in such circumstances that it is reasonable to conclude that the person knew or suspected—

(i) that an investigation by the Garda Síochána into an offence under this Act was being or was likely to be carried out, and

(ii) that the document was or would be relevant to the investigation,

he or she shall be taken for the purposes of this section to have so known or suspected, unless the court or the jury, as the case may be, is satisfied having regard to all the evidence that there is a reasonable doubt as to whether he or she so knew or suspected.

(3) A person guilty of an offence under this section is liable on conviction on indictment to a fine or imprisonment for a term not exceeding 5 years or both.

52   Order to produce evidential material

(1) This section applies to any offence under this Act which is punishable by imprisonment for a term of five years or by a more severe penalty.

[(2) If a Judge of the District Court is satisfied by information on oath of a member of the Garda Síochána that—

(a) the Garda Síochána are investigating an offence to which this section applies,

(b) a person has possession or control of particular material or material of a particular description, and

(c) there are reasonable grounds for suspecting that the material constitutes evidence of or relating to the commission of the offence,

the judge may order the person to—

(i) produce the material to a member of the Garda Síochána for the member to take away, or

(ii) give such a member access to it,

either immediately or within such period as the order may specify.]¹

(3) Where the material consists of or includes information contained in a computer, the order shall have effect as an order to produce the information, or to give access to it, in a form in which it is visible and legible and in which it can be taken away.

(4) An order under this section—

(a) in so far as it may empower a member of the Garda Síochána to take away a document, or to be given access to it, shall also have effect as an order empowering the member to take away a copy of the document (and for that purpose the member may, if necessary, make a copy of the document),

(b) shall not confer any right to production of, or access to, any document subject to legal privilege, and

(c) shall have effect notwithstanding any other obligation as to secrecy or other restriction on disclosure of information imposed by statute or otherwise.

(5) Any material taken away by a member of the Garda Síochána, under this section may be retained by the member for use as evidence in any criminal proceedings.

(6) (a) Information contained in a document which was produced to a member of the Garda Síochána, or to which such a member was given access, in accordance with an order under this section shall be admissible in any criminal proceedings as evidence of any fact therein of which direct oral evidence would be admissible unless the information—

    (i) is privileged from disclosure in such proceedings,

    (ii) was supplied by a person who would not be compellable to give evidence at the instance of the prosecution,

    (iii) was compiled for the purposes or in contemplation of any—

        (I) criminal investigation,

        (II) investigation or inquiry carried out pursuant to or under any enactment,

        (III) civil or criminal proceedings, or

        (IV) proceedings of a disciplinary nature,

    or unless the requirements of the provisions mentioned in paragraph (b) are not complied with.

(b) References in sections 7 (notice of documentary evidence to be served on accused), 8 (admission and weight of documentary evidence) and 9 (admissibility of evidence as to credibility of supplier of information) of the Criminal Evidence Act, 1992, to a document or information contained in it shall be construed as including references to a document mentioned in paragraph (a) and the information contained in it, and those provisions shall have effect accordingly with any necessary modifications.

(c) The Criminal Procedure Act, 1967, is amended both in section 6(1)(e) (as amended by section 10 of the Criminal Evidence Act, 1992) and in section 11 (as so amended) by the insertion, after "1992", of "or section 52(6)(b) of the Criminal Justice (Theft and Fraud Offences) Act, 2001,".

(7) A judge of the District Court may, on the application of any person to whom an order under this section relates or a member of the Garda Síochána, vary or discharge the order.

(8) A person who without reasonable excuse fails or refuses to comply with an order under this section is guilty of an offence and liable on summary conviction to a fine not exceeding £1,500 or imprisonment for a term not exceeding 12 months or both.

Amendments

1   Subsection (2) substituted by Criminal Justice Act 2006, s 192(1)(b).

PART 8
TRIAL OF OFFENCES

53   Summary trial of indictable offences

(1) The District Court may try summarily a person charged with an indictable offence under this Act if—

    (a) the Court is of opinion that the facts proved or alleged constitute a minor offence fit to be tried summarily,

    (b) the accused, on being informed by the Court of his or her right to be tried with a jury, does not object to being tried summarily, and

    (c) the Director of Public Prosecutions consents to the accused being tried summarily for the offence.

(2) On conviction by the District Court for an indictable offence tried summarily under subsection (1) the accused shall be liable to a fine not exceeding £1,500 or imprisonment for a term not exceeding 12 months or both such fine and imprisonment.

54   Trial procedure

(1) In any proceedings for an offence or attempted offence under any of sections 6 and 7 and sections 9 to 11 it shall not be necessary to prove an intention dishonestly to cause a loss to, or make a gain at the expense of, a particular person, and it shall be sufficient to prove that the accused did the act charged dishonestly with the intention of causing such a loss or making such a gain.

(2) Any number of persons may be charged in one indictment, with reference to the same theft, with having at different times or at the same time handled or possessed all or any of the stolen property, and the persons so charged may be tried together.

(3) Any person who—

    (a) is a member of a partnership or is one of two or more beneficial owners of any property, and

    (b) steals any property of or belonging to the partnership or such beneficial owners,

is liable to be dealt with, tried and punished as if he or she had not been or was not a member of the partnership or one of such beneficial owners.

(4) If on the trial of a person for stealing any property it appears that the property alleged to have been stolen at one time was taken at different times, the separate takings may, unless the trial judge directs otherwise, be tried together, to a number not exceeding 3, provided that not more than 6 months elapsed between the first and the last of the takings.

(5) Charges of stealing, handling or possessing any property or any part thereof may be included in separate counts of the same indictment and such counts may be tried together.

(6) Any person or persons charged in separate counts of the same indictment with stealing any property or any part thereof may be severally found guilty of stealing, handling or possessing the property or any part thereof.

(7) On the trial of two or more persons indicted for jointly handling or possessing any stolen property the court or jury, as the case may be, may find any of the accused guilty if satisfied that he or she handled or possessed all or any part of such property, whether or not he or she did so jointly with the other accused or any of them.

55 Alternative verdicts

(1) If, on the trial of a person for theft or for unlawfully obtaining property otherwise, it is proved that the person handled or possessed the property in such circumstances as to constitute an offence under section 17 or 18, he or she may be convicted of that offence.

(2) If, on the trial of a person for an offence under section 17 or 18 of handling or possessing stolen or otherwise unlawfully obtained property, it is proved that the person stole or otherwise unlawfully obtained the property, he or she may be convicted of the theft of the property or of the offence consisting of unlawfully obtaining the property.

56 Orders for restitution

(1) Where property has been stolen and either—

(a) a person is convicted of an offence with reference to the theft (whether or not the stealing is the essential ingredient of the offence), or

(b) a person is convicted of any other offence but the first-mentioned offence is taken into consideration in determining his or her sentence,

the court by or before which the person is convicted may on the conviction (whether or not the passing of sentence is in other respects deferred)—

(i) order anyone having possession or control of the property to restore it to any person entitled to recover it from the convicted person,

(ii) on the application of a person entitled to recover from the convicted person any other property directly or indirectly representing the first-mentioned property (as being the proceeds of any disposal or realisation of the whole or part of it or of property so representing it), order that other property to be delivered or transferred to the applicant, or

(iii) order that a sum not exceeding the value of the first-mentioned property shall be paid, out of any money of the convicted person which was taken out of his or her possession when arrested, to any person who, if that property were in the possession of the convicted person, would be entitled to recover it from him or her.

(2) Where the court has power on a person's conviction to make an order against him or her under both paragraph (ii) and paragraph (iii) of subsection (1) with reference to the stealing of the same property, the court may make orders under both paragraphs, if the person in whose favour the orders are made does not thereby recover more than the value of that property.

(3) Where—

(a) the court makes an order under subsection (1)(i) for the restoration of any property, and

(b) it appears to the court that the convicted person has sold the property to a person acting in good faith or has borrowed money on the security of it from a person so acting,

then, on the application of the purchaser or lender the court may order that there shall be paid to the applicant, out of any money of the convicted person which was taken out of his or her possession when arrested, a sum not exceeding the amount paid for the purchase by the applicant or, as the case may be, the amount owed to the applicant in respect of the loan.

(4) (a) The court shall not exercise the powers conferred by this section unless in its opinion the relevant facts sufficiently appear from evidence given at the trial or the available documents, together with admissions made by or on behalf of any person in connection with any proposed exercise of the powers.

    (b) In paragraph (a) "available documents" means—

        (i) any written statements or admissions which were made for use, and would have been admissible in evidence, at the trial,

       (ii) any depositions taken in any proceedings before the trial, and

     (iii) any written statements or admissions used as evidence at the trial or in any such proceedings.

(5) The provisions of section 20 in relation to property which has been stolen shall have effect also in relation to the property referred to in this section.

(6) This section is without prejudice to the Police (Property) Act, 1897 (disposal of property in the possession of the Garda Síochána).

57   Provision of information to juries

(1) In a trial on indictment of an offence under this Act, the trial judge may order that copies of any or all of the following documents shall be given to the jury in any form that the judge considers appropriate:

(a) any document admitted in evidence at the trial,

(b) the transcript of the opening speeches of counsel,

(c) any charts, diagrams, graphics, schedules or agreed summaries of evidence produced at the trial,

(d) the transcript of the whole or any part of the evidence given at the trial,

(e) the transcript of the closing speeches of counsel,

(f) the transcript of the trial judge's charge to the jury,

(g) any other document that in the opinion of the trial judge would be of assistance to the jury in its deliberations including, where appropriate, an affidavit by an accountant summarising, in a form which is likely to be comprehended by the jury, any transactions by the accused or other persons which are relevant to the offence.

(2) If the prosecutor proposes to apply to the trial judge for an order that a document mentioned in subsection (1)(g) shall be given to the jury, the prosecutor shall give a copy of the document to the accused in advance of the trial and, on the hearing of the application, the trial judge shall take into account any representations made by or on behalf of the accused in relation to it.

(3) Where the trial judge has made an order that an affidavit mentioned in subsection (1)(g) shall be given to the jury, the accountant concerned—

(a) shall be summoned by the prosecutor to attend at the trial as an expert witness, and

(b) may be required by the trial judge, in an appropriate case, to give evidence in regard to any relevant accounting procedures or principles.

PART 9

MISCELLANEOUS

58   Liability for offences by bodies corporate and unincorporated

(1) Where—

    (a) an offence under this Act has been committed by a body corporate, and

    (b) the offence is proved to have been committed with the consent or connivance of, or to have been attributable to any neglect on the part of, a person who was either—

        (i) a director, manager, secretary or other officer of the body corporate, or

        (ii) a person purporting to act in any such capacity,

that person, as well as the body corporate, is guilty of an offence and liable to be proceeded against and punished as if he or she were guilty of the first-mentioned offence.

(2) Where the affairs of a body corporate are managed by its members, subsection (1) shall apply in relation to the acts and defaults of a member in connection with the member's functions of management as if he or she were a director or manager of the body corporate.

(3) The foregoing provisions shall apply, with the necessary modifications, in relation to offences under this Act committed by an unincorporated body.

59   Reporting of offences

(1) In this section—

"firm" means a partnership, a corporate or unincorporated body or a self-employed individual;

"relevant person" means a person—

    (a) who audits the accounts of a firm, or

    (b) who otherwise with a view to reward assists or advises a firm in the preparation or delivery of any information, or of any declaration, return, account or other document, which the person knows will be, or is likely to be, used for the purpose of keeping or auditing the accounts of the firm,

but does not include an employee of a firm who—

    (i) in that capacity so assists or advises the firm, and

    (ii) whose income from so doing consists solely of emoluments chargeable to income tax under Schedule E, as defined in section 19 of the Taxes Consolidation Act, 1997.

(2) Where the accounts of a firm, or as the case may be any information or document mentioned in subsection (1)(b), indicate that—

    (a) an offence under this Act (other than sections 8, 12 to 15, 49(1) and 52(8)) may have been committed by the firm concerned, or

    (b) such an offence may have been committed in relation to its affairs by a partner in the firm or, in the case of a corporate or unincorporated body, by a director, manager, secretary or other employee thereof, or by the self-employed individual concerned, the relevant person shall, notwithstanding any professional obligations of privilege or confidentiality, report that fact to a member of the Garda Síochána.

(3) A disclosure in a report made in good faith by a relevant person to a member of the Garda Síochána under subsection (2) shall not be treated as a breach of any restriction imposed by statute or otherwise or involve the person in liability of any kind.

(4) A person who fails, without reasonable excuse, to comply with the duty imposed by subsection (2) is guilty of an offence and is liable on summary conviction to a fine not exceeding £1,500 or imprisonment for a term not exceeding 12 months or both.

60   Evidence in proceedings

(1) For the purposes of any provision of this Act relating to specified conduct outside the State—

    (a) a document purporting to be signed by a lawyer practising in the state or a territorial unit within it where the conduct is alleged to have occurred and stating that the conduct is an offence under the law of that state or territorial unit, and

    (b) a document purporting to be a translation of a document mentioned in paragraph (a) and to be certified as correct by a person appearing to be competent to so certify,

shall be admissible in any proceedings, without further proof, as evidence of the matters mentioned in those documents, unless the contrary is shown.

(2) For the purposes of section 45 a document purporting to be signed by an officer of the Department of Foreign Affairs and stating that a passport was issued by the Department to a specified person on a specified date and that, to the best of the officer's knowledge and belief, the person has not ceased to be an Irish citizen shall be admissible in any proceedings, without further proof, as evidence that the person was an Irish citizen on the date on which the offence under that section with which the person is charged was committed, unless the contrary is shown.

61   Jurisdiction of District Court in certain proceedings

For the purposes of the exercise of jurisdiction by a judge of the District Court in proceedings for an offence under this Act committed on a vessel or hovercraft or on an installation in the territorial seas or in a designated area (within the meaning of the Continental Shelf Act, 1968) the offence may be treated as having been committed in any place in the State.

62   Amendment of section 9 of Married Women's Status Act, 1957

Section 9 of the Married Women's Status Act, 1957, is hereby amended by the substitution for subsection (3) of the following subsection:

    "(3) No criminal proceedings referred to in subsection (1) or (2) shall be taken by a spouse against the other spouse except by or with the consent of the Director of Public Prosecutions.".

63   Amendment of Defence Act, 1954

The Defence Act, 1954, is hereby amended by the substitution for section 156 (as substituted by the Larceny Act, 1990) of the following section:

"156.—(1) Every person subject to military law who—

(a) steals or otherwise unlawfully obtains any property belonging to a person subject to military law or any public service property or service property, or

(b) handles or possesses (within the meaning of section 17 or 18 of the Criminal Justice (Theft and Fraud Offences) Act, 2001) any such property,

is guilty of an offence against military law and shall, on conviction by court-martial, be liable to suffer imprisonment for any term not exceeding two years or any less punishment awardable by a court martial.

(2) The said sections 17 and 18 shall apply to the offences of handling and possessing under subsection (1)(b) of this section as they apply to the offences of handling and possessing stolen or otherwise unlawfully obtained property.".

64   Amendment of Bail Act, 1997

The Schedule to the Bail Act, 1997, is hereby amended by the substitution, for the matter contained in paragraph 17, of "Any offence under the Criminal Justice (Theft and Fraud Offences) Act, 2001." and by the deletion of the section headed "Forgery etc. offences.".

65   Effect of Act and transitional provisions

(1) This Act, save as otherwise provided by it, shall, as regards offences under any of its provisions, have effect only in relation to offences wholly or partly committed on or after the commencement of any such provision.

(2) No repeal or amendment by this Act of any enactment relating to procedure or evidence or to the jurisdiction or powers of any court or to the effect of a conviction shall affect the operation of the enactment in relation to offences committed before the commencement of this Act or to proceedings for any such offence.

(3) If—

(a) a person is charged in the alternative with having committed an offence under a statute or rule of law in force immediately before the commencement of this Act and an offence under this Act, and

(b) it is proved that the person did acts which would constitute either of the offences charged, but it is not proved whether those acts were done before or after such commencement,

the person may be convicted of the first-mentioned offence but shall not be liable to a penalty greater than the lesser of the maximum penalties provided for the two offences with which the person was charged.

(4) Except as regards offences committed before the commencement of this Act and except where the context otherwise requires—

(a) references in any enactment passed before this Act to an offence abolished by this Act shall, subject to any express amendment or repeal made by this Act, have effect as references to the corresponding offence under this Act, and

(b) without prejudice to paragraph (a), references, however expressed, in any enactment, whenever passed, to theft or stealing (including references to stolen goods) or related offences, and references to robbery, burglary, aggravated burglary, receiving or handling stolen property, forgery or counterfeiting shall be construed in accordance with the provisions of this Act, and any such enactment shall have effect accordingly, with any necessary modifications.

(5) (a) The repeal by section 3(1) of sections 23 (robbery), 23A (burglary) and 23B (aggravated burglary) of the Larceny Act, 1916, shall not affect the operation of those sections for the purposes of section 2 of, and paragraph 9 of the Schedule to, the Criminal Law (Jurisdiction) Act, 1976, and accordingly that section and that paragraph shall have effect as if section 3(1) had not been enacted.

(b) References in paragraph (a) to sections 23, 23A and 23B of the Larceny Act, 1916, are to those sections as substituted, or as the case may be inserted, by sections 5 to 7 of the Criminal Law (Jurisdiction) Act, 1976.

(6) On the commencement of this subsection—

(a) subsection (5) shall cease to have effect,

(b) sections 5 to 7 of the Criminal Law (Jurisdiction) Act, 1976, shall be repealed, and

(c) the following paragraph shall be substituted for paragraph 9 of the Schedule to the Criminal Law (Jurisdiction) Act, 1976:[1]

Amendments

1   See the amended Act.

SCHEDULE 1
ENACTMENTS REPEALED

Section 3

Session & Chapter or Number & Year	Short Title	Extent of repeal
(1)	(2)	(3)
24 & 25 Vict., c. 96	Larceny Act, 1861	The whole Act, except sections 12 to 16 and 24 and 25
24 & 25 Vict., c. 98	Forgery Act, 1861	The whole Act
24 & 25 Vict., c. 99	Coinage Offences Act, 1861	The whole Act
24 & 25 Vict., c. 50	Summary Jurisdiction (Ireland) Act, 1862	Sections 4 to 8
35 & 36 Vict., c. 57	Debtors (Ireland) Act, 1872	Section 13
38 & 39 Vict., c. 24	Falsification of Accounts Act, 1875	The whole Act
56 & 57 Vict., c. 71	Sale of Goods Act, 1893	Section 24
3 & 4 Geo. 5, c. 27	Forgery Act, 1913	The whole Act

Session & Chapter or Number & Year	Short Title	Extent of repeal
(1)	(2)	(3)
6 & 7 Geo. 5, c. 50	Larceny Act, 1916	The whole Act
No. 2 of 1951	Criminal Justice Act, 1951	Sections 10 and 13 and ref. nos. 8, 11, 14, 15 and 20 of First Schedule
No. 2 of 1956	Gaming and Lotteries Act, 1956	Section 11
No. 1 of 1963	Official Secrets Act, 1963	Sections 7 and 8
No. 22 of 1984	Criminal Justice Act, 1984	Section 16
No. 9 of 1990	Larceny Act, 1990	The whole Act

SCHEDULE 2

TEXT IN THE ENGLISH LANGUAGE OF THE CONVENTION DRAWN UP ON THE BASIS OF ARTICLE K.3 OF THE TREATY ON EUROPEAN UNION, ON THE PROTECTION OF THE EUROPEAN COMMUNITIES' FINANCIAL INTERESTS DONE AT BRUSSELS ON 26 JULY 1995 CONVENTION

Section 41

DRAWN UP ON THE BASIS OF ARTICLE K.3 OF THE TREATY ON EUROPEAN UNION, ON THE PROTECTION OF THE EUROPEAN COMMUNITIES' FINANCIAL INTERESTS

THE HIGH CONTRACTING PARTIES to this Convention, Member States of the European Union,

REFERRING to the Act of the Council of the European Union of 26 July 1995;

DESIRING to ensure that their criminal laws contribute effectively to the protection of the financial interests of the European Communities;

NOTING that fraud affecting Community revenue and expenditure in many cases is not confined to a single country and is often committed by organized criminal networks;

CONVINCED that protection of the European Communities' financial interests calls for the criminal prosecution of fraudulent conduct injuring those interests and requires, for that purpose, the adoption of a common definition;

CONVINCED of the need to make such conduct punishable with effective, proportionate and dissuasive criminal penalties, without prejudice to the possibility of applying other penalties in appropriate cases, and of the need, at least in serious cases, to make such conduct punishable with deprivation of liberty which can give rise to extradition;

RECOGNIZING that businesses play an important role in the areas financed by the European Communities and that those with decision-making powers in business should not escape criminal responsibility in appropriate circumstances;

DETERMINED to combat together fraud affecting the European Communities' financial interests by undertaking obligations concerning jurisdiction, extradition, and mutual cooperation,

HAVE AGREED ON THE FOLLOWING PROVISIONS:

Article 1
General provisions

1. For the purposes of this Convention, fraud affecting the European Communities' financial interests shall consist of:

   (a) in respect of expenditure, any intentional act or omission relating to:

      — the use or presentation of false, incorrect or incomplete statements or documents, which has as its effect the misappropriation or wrongful retention of funds from the general budget of the European Communities or budgets managed by, or on behalf of, the European Communities,

      — non-disclosure of information in violation of a specific obligation, with the same effect,

      — the misapplication of such funds for purpose other than those for which they were originally granted;

   (b) in respect of revenue, any intentional act or omission relating to:

      — the use or presentation of false, incorrect or incomplete statements or documents, which has as its effect the illegal diminution of the resources of the general budget of the European Communities or budgets managed by, or on behalf of, the European Communities,

      — non-disclosure of information in violation of a specific obligation, with the same effect,

      — misapplication of a legally obtained benefit, with the same effect.

2. Subject to Article 2(2), each Member State shall take the necessary and appropriate measures to transpose paragraph 1 into their national criminal law in such a way that the conduct referred to therein constitutes criminal offences.

3. Subject to Article 2(2), each Member State shall also take the necessary measures to ensure that the intentional preparation or supply of false, incorrect or incomplete statements or documents having the effect described in paragraph 1 constitutes a criminal offence if it is not already punishable as a principal offence or as participation in, instigation of, or attempt to commit, fraud as defined in paragraph 1.

4. The intentional nature of an act or omission as referred to in paragraphs 1 and 3 may be inferred from objective, factual circumstances.

Article 2
Penalties

1. Each Member State shall take the necessary measures to ensure that the conduct referred to in Article 1, and participating in, instigating, or attempting the conduct referred to in Article 1(1), are punishable by effective, proportionate and dissuasive criminal penalties, including, at least in cases of serious fraud, penalties involving deprivation of liberty which can give rise to extradition, it being understood that serious fraud shall be considered to be fraud involving a minimum amount to be set in each Member State. This minimum amount may not be set at a sum exceeding ECU 50 000.

2. However in cases of minor fraud involving a total amount of less than ECU 4 000 and not involving particularly serious circumstances under its laws, a Member State may provide for penalties of a different type from those laid down in paragraph 1.

3. The Council of the European Union, acting unanimously, may alter the amount referred to in paragraph 2.

Article 3
Criminal liability of heads of businesses

Each Member State shall take the necessary measures to allow heads of businesses or any persons having power to take decisions or exercise control within a business to be declared criminally liable in accordance with the principles defined by its national law in cases of fraud affecting the European Community's financial interests, as referred to in Article 1, by a person under their authority acting on behalf of the business.

Article 4
Jurisdiction

1. Each Member State shall take the necessary measures to establish its jurisdiction over the offences it has established in accordance with Article 1 and 2(1) when:

— fraud, participation in fraud or attempted fraud affecting the European Communities' financial interests is committed in whole or in part within its territory, including fraud for which the benefit was obtained in that territory,

— a person within its territory knowingly assists or induces the commission of such fraud within the territory of any other State,

— the offender is a national of the Member State concerned, provided that the law of that Member State may require the conduct to be punishable also in the country where it occurred.

2. Each Member State may declare, when giving the notification referred to in Article 11(2), that it will not apply the rule laid down in the third indent of paragraph 1 of this Article.

Article 5
Extradition and prosecution

1. Any Member State which, under its law, does not extradite its own nationals shall take the necessary measures to establish its jurisdiction over the offences it has established in accordance with Articles 1 and 2(1), when committed by its own nationals outside its territory.

2. Each Member State shall, when one of its nationals is alleged to have committed in another Member State a criminal offence involving the conduct described in Articles 1 and 2(1), and it does not extradite that person to that other Member State solely on the ground of his or her nationality, submit the case to its competent authorities for the purpose of prosecution if appropriate. In order to enable prosecution to take place, the files, information and exhibits relating to the offence shall be transmitted in accordance with the procedures laid down in Article 6 of the European Convention on Extradition. The requesting Member State shall be informed of the prosecution initiated and of its outcome.

3. A Member State may not refuse extradition in the event of fraud affecting the European Communities' financial interests for the sole reason that it concerns a tax or customs duty offence.

4. For the purposes of this Article, a Member State's own nationals shall be construed in accordance with any declaration made by it under Article 6(1)(b) of the European Convention on Extradition and with paragraph 1(c) of the Article.

Article 6
Cooperation

1. If a fraud as defined in Article 1 constitutes a criminal offence and concerns at least two Member States, those States shall cooperate effectively in the investigation, the prosecution and in carrying out the punishment imposed by means, for example, of mutual legal assistance, extradition, transfer of proceedings or enforcement of sentences passed in another Member State.

2. Where more than one Member State has jurisdiction and has the possibility of viable prosecution of an offence based on the same facts, the Member States involved shall cooperate in deciding which shall prosecute the offender or offenders with a view to centralizing the prosecution in a single Member State where possible.

Article 7
Ne bis in idem

1. Member States shall apply in their national criminal laws the 'ne bis in idem' rule, under which a person whose trial has been finally disposed of in a Member State may not be prosecuted in another Member State in respect of the same facts, provided that if a penalty was imposed, it has been enforced, is actually in the process of being enforced or can no longer be enforced under the laws of the sentencing State.

2. A Member State may, when giving the notification referred to in Article 11(2), declare that it shall not be bound by paragraph 1 of this Article in one or more of the following cases:

- (a) if the facts which were the subject of the judgement rendered abroad took place on its own territory either in whole or in part; in the latter case this exception shall not apply if those facts took place partly on the territory of the Member State where the judgement was rendered;
- (b) if the facts which were the subject of the judgment rendered abroad constitute an offence directed against the security or other equally essential interests of that Member State;
- (c) if the facts which were the subject of the judgment rendered abroad were committed by an official of the Member State contrary to the duties of his office.

3. The exceptions which may be the subject of a declaration under paragraph 2 shall not apply if the Member State concerned in respect of the same facts requested the other Member State to bring the prosecution or granted extradition of the person concerned.

4. Relevant bilateral or multilateral agreements concluded between Member States and relevant declarations shall remain unaffected by this Article.

Article 8
Court of Justice

1. Any dispute between Member States on the interpretation or application of this Convention must in an initial stage be examined by the Council in accordance with the procedure set out in Title VI of the Treaty on European Union with a view to reaching a solution.

If no solution is found within six months, the matter may be referred to the Court of Justice of the European Communities by a party to the dispute.

2. Any dispute between one or more Member States and the Commission of the European Communities concerning the application of Article 1 or 10 of this Convention which it has proved impossible to settle through negotiation may be submitted to the Court of Justice.

Article 9
Internal provisions

No provision in this Convention shall prevent Member States from adopting internal legal provisions which go beyond the obligations deriving from this Convention.

Article 10
Transmission

1. Member States shall transmit to the Commission of the European Communities the text of the provisions transposing into their domestic law the obligations imposed on them under the provisions of this Convention.

2. For the purposes of implementing this Convention, the High Contracting Parties shall determine, within the Council of the European Union, the information to be communicated or exchanged between the Member States or between the Member States and the Commission, and also the arrangements for doing so.

Article 11
Entry into force

1. This Convention shall be subject to adoption by the Member States in accordance with their respective constitutional requirements.

2. Member States shall notify the Secretary-General of the Council of the European Union of the completion of their constitutional requirements for adopting this Convention.

3. This Convention shall enter into force 90 days after the notification, referred to in paragraph 2, by the last Member State to fulfil that formality.

Article 12
Accession

1. This Convention shall be open to accession by any State that becomes a member of the European Union.

2. The text of this Convention in the language of the acceding State, drawn up by the Council of the European Union, shall be authentic.

3. Instruments of accession shall be deposited with the depositary.

4. This Convention shall enter into force with respect to any State that accedes to it 90 days after the deposit of its instrument of accession or on the date of entry into force of the Convention if it has not already entered into force at the time of expiry of the said period 90 days.

Article 13
Depositary

1. The Secretary-General of the Council of the European Union shall act as depositary of this Convention.

2. The depositary shall publish in the Official Journal of the European Communities information on the progress of adoptions and accessions, declarations and reservations, and also any other notification concerning this Convention.

SCHEDULE 4
TEXT IN THE ENGLISH LANGUAGE OF THE PROTOCOL DRAWN UP ON THE BASIS OF ARTICLE K.3 OF THE TREATY ON EUROPEAN UNION TO THE CONVENTION ON THE PROTECTION OF THE EUROPEAN COMMUNITIES' FINANCIAL INTERESTS DONE AT BRUSSELS ON 27 SEPTEMBER 1996

Section 41

PROTOCOL

DRAWN UP ON THE BASIS OF ARTICLE K.3 OF THE TREATY ON EUROPEAN UNION TO THE CONVENTION ON THE PROTECTION OF THE EUROPEAN COMMUNITIES' FINANCIAL INTERESTS

THE HIGH CONTRACTING PARTIES to this Protocol, Member States of the European Union,

REFERRING to the Act of the Council of the European Union of 27 September 1996,

DESIRING to ensure that their criminal laws contribute effectively to the protection of the financial interests of the European Communities;

RECOGNIZING the importance of the Convention on the protection of the European Communities' financial interests of 26 July 1995 for combating fraud affecting Community revenue and expenditure;

AWARE that the financial interests of the European Communities may be damaged or threatened by other criminal offences, particularly acts of corruption by or against national and Community officials, responsible for the collection, management or disbursement of Community funds under their control;

CONSIDERING that people of different nationalities, employed by different public agencies or bodies, may be involved in such corruption and that, in the interests of effective action against such corruption with international ramifications, it is important for their reprehensible nature to be perceived in a similar manner under Member States' criminal laws;

NOTING that several Member States' criminal law on crime linked to the exercise of public duties in general and concerning corruption in particular covers only acts committed by or against their national officials and does not cover, or covers only in exceptional cases, conduct involving Community officials or officials of other Member States;

CONVINCED of the need for national law to be adapted where it does not penalize acts of corruption that damage or are likely to damage the financial interests of the European Communities involving Community officials or officials of other Member States;

CONVINCED also that such adaptation of national law should not be confined, in respect of Community officials, to acts of active or passive corruption, but should be extended to other crimes affecting or likely to affect the revenue or expenditure of the European Communities, including crimes committed by or against persons in whom the highest responsibilities are vested;

CONSIDERING that appropriate rules should also be laid down on jurisdiction and mutual cooperation, without prejudice to the legal conditions under which they are to apply in specific cases, including waiver of immunity where appropriate;

CONSIDERING finally that the relevant provisions of the Convention on the protection of the European Communities' financial interests of 26 July 1995 should be made applicable to the criminal acts covered by this Protocol,

HAVE AGREED ON THE FOLLOWING PROVISIONS:

Article 1
Definitions

For the purposes of this Protocol:

1. (a) 'official' shall mean any 'Community' or 'national' official, including any national official of another Member State;

   (b) the term 'Community official' shall mean:

   — any person who is an official or other contracted employee within the meaning of the Staff Regulations of officials of the European Communities or the Conditions of employment of other servants of the European Communities,

   — any person seconded to the European Communities by the Member States or by any public or private body, who carries out functions equivalent to those performed by European Community officials or other servants.

   Members of bodies set up in accordance with the Treaties establishing the European Communities and the staff of such bodies shall be treated as Community officials, inasmuch as the Staff Regulations of the European Communities or the Conditions of employment of other servants of the European Communities do not apply to them;

   (c) the term 'national official' shall be understood by reference to the definition of 'official' or 'public officer' in the national law of the Member State in which the person in question performs that function for the purposes of application of the criminal law of that Member State.

   Nevertheless, in the case of proceedings involving a Member State's official initiated by another Member State the latter shall not be bound to apply the definition of 'national official' except in so far as that definition is compatible with its national law;

2. 'Convention' shall mean the Convention drawn up on the basis of Article K.3 of the Treaty on European Union, on the protection of the European Communities' financial interests, of 26 July 1995[1].

Article 2
Passive corruption

1. For the purposes of this Protocol, the deliberate action of an official, who, directly or through an intermediary, requests or receives advantages of any kind whatsoever, for himself or for a third party, or accepts a promise of such an advantage, to act or refrain from acting in accordance with his duty or in the exercise of his functions in breach of his official duties in a way which damages or is likely to damage the European Communities' financial interests shall constitute passive corruption.

2. Each Member State shall take the necessary measures to ensure that conduct of the type referred to in paragraph 1 is made a criminal offence.

Article 3
Active corruption

1. For the purposes of this Protocol, the deliberate action of whosoever promises or gives, directly or through an intermediary, an advantage of any kind whatsoever to an official for himself or for a third party for him to act or refrain from acting in accordance with his duty or in the exercise of his functions in breach of his official duties in a way which damages or is likely to damage the European Communities' financial interests shall constitute active corruption.

2. Each Member State shall take the necessary measures to ensure that conduct of the type referred to in paragraph 1 is made a criminal offence.

Article 4
Assimilation

1. Each Member State shall take the necessary measures to ensure that in its criminal law the descriptions of the offences constituting conduct of the type referred to in Article 1 of the Convention committed by its national officials in the exercise of their functions apply similarly in cases where such offences are committed by Community officials in the exercise of their duties.

2. Each Member State shall take the necessary measures to ensure that in its criminal law the descriptions of the offences referred to in paragraph 1 of this Article and in Articles 2 and 3 committed by or against its Government Ministers, elected members of its parliamentary chambers, the members of its highest Courts or the members of its Court of Auditors in the exercise of their functions apply similarly in cases where such offences are committed by or against members of the Commission of the European Communities, the European Parliament, the Court of Justice and the Court of Auditors of the European Communities respectively in the exercise of their duties.

3. Where a Member State has enacted special legislation concerning acts or omissions for which Government Ministers are responsible by reason of their special political position in that Member State, paragraph 2 of this Article may not apply to such legislation, provided that the Member State ensures that Members of the Commission of the European

Community are covered by the criminal legislation implementing Articles 2 and 3 and paragraph 1 of this Article.

4. Paragraphs 1, 2 and 3 shall be without prejudice to the provisions applicable in each Member State concerning criminal proceedings and the determination of the competent court.

5. This Protocol shall apply in full accordance with the relevant provisions of the Treaties establishing the European Communities, the Protocol on the Privileges and Immunities of the European Communities, the Statutes of the Court of Justice and the texts adopted for the purpose of their implementation, as regards the withdrawal of immunity.

Article 5
Penalties

1. Each Member State shall take the necessary measures to ensure that the conduct referred to in Articles 2 and 3, and participating in and instigating the conduct in question, are punishable by effective, proportionate and dissuasive criminal penalties, including, at least in serious cases, penalties involving deprivation of liberty which can give rise to extradition.

2. Paragraph 1 shall be without prejudice to the exercise of disciplinary powers by the competent authorities against national officials or Community officials. In determining the penalty to be imposed, the national criminal courts may, in accordance with the principles of their national law, take into account any disciplinary penalty already imposed on the same person for the same conduct.

Article 6
Jurisdiction

1. Each Member State shall take the measures necessary to establish its jurisdiction over the offences it has established in accordance with Articles 2, 3 and 4 where:

    (a) the offence is committed in whole or in part within its territory;

    (b) the offender is one of its nationals or one of its officials;

    (c) the offence is committed against one of the persons referred to in Article 1 or a member of one of the institutions referred to in Article 4(2) who is one of its nationals;

    (d) the offender is a Community official working for a European Community institution or a body set up in accordance with the Treaties establishing the European Communities which has its headquarters in the Member State concerned.

2. Each Member State may declare when giving the notification provided for in Article 9(2) that it will not apply or will apply only in specific cases or conditions one or more of the jurisdiction rules laid down in paragraph 1(b), (c), and (d).

Article 7
Relation to the Convention

1. Articles 3, 5(1), (2) and (4) and Article 6 of the Convention shall apply as if there were a reference to the conduct referred to in Articles 2, 3 and 4 of this Protocol.

2. The following provisions of the Convention shall also apply to this Protocol:

— Article 7, on the understanding that, unless otherwise indicated at the time of the notification provided for in Article 9(2) of this Protocol, any declaration within the meaning of Article 7(2) of the Convention shall also apply to this Protocol,

— Article 9,

— Article 10.

Article 8
Court of Justice

1. Any dispute between Member States on the interpretation or application of this Protocol must in an initial stage be examined by the Council in accordance with the procedure set out in Title VI of the Treaty on European Union with a view to reaching a solution.

If no solution is found within six months, the matter may be referred to the Court of Justice of the European Communities by a party to the dispute.

2. Any dispute between one or more Member States and the Commission of the European Communities concerning Article 1, with the exception of point 1(c), or Articles 2, 3 and 4, or the third indent of Article 7(2) of this Protocol which it has proved impossible to settle through negotiation may be submitted to the Court of Justice of the European Communities.

Article 9
Entry into force

1. This Protocol shall be subject to adoption by the Member States in accordance with their respective constitutional requirements.

2. Member States shall notify the Secretary-General of the Council of the European Union of the completion of the procedures required under their respective constitutional rules for adopting this Protocol.

3. This Protocol shall enter into force 90 days after the notification provided for in paragraph 2 has been given by the State which, being a Member of the European Union at the time of adoption by the Council of the Act drawing up this Protocol, is the last to fulfil that formality. If, however, the Convention has not entered into force on that date, this Protocol shall enter into force on the date on which the Convention enters into force.

Article 10
Accession of new Member States

1. This Protocol shall be open to accession by any State that becomes a member of the European Union.

2. The text of this Protocol in the language of the acceding State, drawn up by the Council of the European Union, shall be authentic.

3. Instruments of accession shall be deposited with the depositary.

4. This Protocol shall enter into force with respect to any State that accedes to it 90 days after the deposit of its instrument of accession or on the date of entry into force of this Protocol if it has not yet entered into force at the time of expiry of the said period of 90 days.

Article 11
Reservations

1. No reservation shall be authorized with the exception of those provided for in Article 6(2).

2. Any Member State which has entered a reservation may withdraw it at any time in whole or in part by notifying the depositary. Withdrawal shall take effect on the date on which the depositary receives the notification.

Article 12
Depositary

1. The Secretary-General of the Council of the European Union shall act as depositary of this Protocol.

2. The depositary shall publish in the Official Journal of the European Communities information on the progress of adoptions and accessions, declarations and reservations and any other notification concerning this Protocol.

SCHEDULE 6
TEXT IN THE ENGLISH LANGUAGE OF THE PROTOCOL DRAWN UP ON THE BASIS OF ARTICLE K.3 OF THE TREATY ON EUROPEAN UNION, ON THE INTERPRETATION, BY WAY OF PRELIMINARY RULINGS, BY THE COURT OF JUSTICE OF THE EUROPEAN COMMUNITIES OF THE CONVENTION ON THE PROTECTION OF THE EUROPEAN COMMUNITIES' FINANCIAL INTERESTS DONE AT BRUSSELS ON 29 NOVEMBER 1996

Section 41

PROTOCOL

DRAWN UP ON THE BASIS OF ARTICLE K.3 OF THE TREATY ON EUROPEAN UNION, ON THE INTERPRETATION, BY WAY OF PRELIMINARY RULINGS, BY THE COURT OF JUSTICE OF THE EUROPEAN COMMUNITIES OF THE CONVENTION ON THE PROTECTION OF THE EUROPEAN COMMUNITIES' FINANCIAL INTERESTS

THE HIGH CONTRACTING PARTIES,

HAVE AGREED on the following provisions, which shall be annexed to the Convention:

Article 1

The Court of Justice of the European Communities shall have jurisdiction, pursuant to the conditions laid down in this Protocol, to give preliminary rulings on the interpretation of the Convention on the protection of the European Communities' financial interests and the Protocol to that Convention drawn up on 27 September 1996, hereinafter referred to as 'the first Protocol'.

Article 2

1. By a declaration made at the time of the signing of this Protocol or at any time thereafter, any Member State shall be able to accept the jurisdiction of the Court of Justice of the European Communities to give preliminary rulings on the interpretation of the Convention on the protection of the European Communities' financial interests and the first Protocol to that Convention pursuant to the conditions specified in either paragraph 2(a) or paragraph 2(b).

2. A Member State making a declaration pursuant to paragraph 1 may specify that either:

(a) any court or tribunal of that State against whose decisions there is no judicial remedy under national law may request the Court of Justice of the European Communities to give a preliminary ruling on a question raised in a case pending before it and concerning the interpretation of the Convention on the protection of the European Communities' financial interests and the first Protocol thereto if that court or tribunal considers that a decision on the question is necessary to enable it to give judgment, or

(b) any court or tribunal of that State may request the Court of Justice of the European Communities to give a preliminary ruling on a question raised in a case pending before it and concerning the interpretation of the Convention on the protection of the European Communities' financial interests and the first Protocol thereto if that court or tribunal considers that a decision on the question is necessary to enable it to give judgment.

Article 3

1. The Protocol on the Statute of the Court of Justice of the European Communities and the Rules of Procedure of that Court of Justice shall apply.

2. In accordance with the Statute of the Court of Justice of the European Communities, any Member State, whether or not it has made a declaration pursuant to Article 2, shall be entitled to submit statements of case or written observations to the Court of Justice of the European Communities in cases which arise pursuant to Article 1.

Article 4

1. This Protocol shall be subject to adoption by the Member States in accordance with their respective constitutional requirements.

2. Member States shall notify the depositary of the completion of their respective constitutional requirements for adopting this Protocol and communicate to him any declaration made pursuant to Article 2.

3. This Protocol shall enter into force 90 days after the notification, referred to in paragraph 2, by the Member State which, being a member of the European Union on the date of adoption by the Council of the Act drawing up this Protocol, is the last to fulfil that formality. However, it shall at the earliest enter into force at the same time as the Convention on the protection of the European Communities' financial interests.

Article 5

1. This Protocol shall be open to accession by any State that becomes a member of the European Union.

2. Instruments of accession shall be deposited with the depositary.

3. The text of this Protocol in the language of the acceding State, drawn up by the Council of the European Union, shall be authentic.

4. This Protocol shall enter into force with respect to any State that accedes to it 90 days after the date of deposit of its instrument of accession, or on the date of the entry into force of this Protocol if the latter has not yet come into force when the said period of 90 days expires.

Article 6

Any State that becomes a member of the European Union and accedes to the Convention on the protection of the European Communities' financial interests in accordance with Article 12 thereof shall accept the provisions of this Protocol.

Article 7

1. Amendments to this Protocol may be proposed by any Member State, being a High Contracting Party. Any proposal for an amendment shall be sent to the depositary, who shall forward it to the Council.

2. Amendments shall be established by the Council, which shall recommend that they be adopted by the Member States in accordance with their respective constitutional requirements.

3. Amendments thus established shall enter into force in accordance with the provisions of Article 4.

Article 8

1. The Secretary-General of the Council of the European Union shall act depositary of this Protocol.

2. The depositary shall publish in the Official Journal of the European Communities the notifications, instruments or communications concerning this Protocol.

SCHEDULE 7
TEXT NOT REPRODUCED HERE

SCHEDULE 9
TEXT IN THE ENGLISH LANGUAGE OF THE PROTOCOL DRAWN UP ON THE BASIS OF ARTICLE K.3 OF THE TREATY ON EUROPEAN UNION, TO THE CONVENTION ON THE PROTECTION OF THE EUROPEAN COMMUNITIES' FINANCIAL INTERESTS DONE AT BRUSSELS ON 19 JUNE 1997

Section 41

SECOND PROTOCOL

DRAWN UP ON THE BASIS OF ARTICLE K.3 OF THE TREATY ON EUROPEAN UNION, TO THE CONVENTION ON THE PROTECTION OF THE EUROPEAN COMMUNITIES' FINANCIAL INTERESTS

THE HIGH CONTRACTING PARTIES to this Protocol, Member States of the European Union,

REFERRING to the Act of the Council of the European Union of 19 June 1997;

DESIRING to ensure that their criminal laws contribute effectively to the protection of the financial interests of the European Communities;

RECOGNIZING the importance of the Convention on the protection of the European Communities' financial interests of 26 July 1995 in combating fraud affecting Community revenue and expenditure;

RECOGNIZING the importance of the Protocol of 27 September 1996 to the said Convention in the fight against corruption damaging or likely to damage the European Communities' financial interests;

AWARE that the financial interests of the European Communities may be damaged or threatened by acts committed on behalf of legal persons and acts involving money laundering;

CONVINCED of the need for national law to be adapted, where necessary, to provide that legal persons can be held liable in cases of fraud or active corruption and money laundering committed for their benefit that damage or are likely to damage the European Communities' financial interests;

CONVINCED of the need for national law to be adapted, where necessary, to penalize acts of laundering of proceeds of fraud or corruption that damage or are likely to damage the European Communities' financial interests and to make it possible to confiscate proceeds of such fraud and corruption;

CONVINCED of the need for national law to be adapted, where necessary, in order to prevent the refusal of mutual assistance solely because offences covered by this Protocol concern or are considered as tax or customs duty offences;

NOTING that cooperation between Member States is already covered by the Convention on the protection of the European Communities' financial interests of 26 July 1995, but that there is a need, without prejudice to obligations under Community law, for appropriate provision also to be made for cooperation between Member States and the Commission to ensure effective action against fraud, active and passive corruption and related money laundering damaging or likely to damage the European Communities' financial interests, including exchange of information between the Member States and the Commission;

CONSIDERING that, in order to encourage and facilitate the exchange of information, it is necessary to ensure adequate protection of personal data;

CONSIDERING that the exchange of information should not hinder ongoing investigations and that it is therefore necessary to provide for the protection of investigation secrecy;

CONSIDERING that appropriate provisions have to be drawn up on the competence of the Court of Justice of the European Communities;

CONSIDERING finally that the relevant provisions of the Convention on the protection of the European Communities' financial interests of 26 July 1995 should be made applicable to certain acts covered by this Protocol,

HAVE AGREED ON THE FOLLOWING PROVISIONS:

Article 1
Definitions

For the purposes of this Protocol:

(a) 'Convention' shall mean the Convention drawn up on the basis of Article K.3 of the Treaty on European Union on the protection of the European Communities' financial interests, of 26 July 1995;

(b) 'fraud' shall mean the conduct referred to in Article 1 of the Convention;

(c) 'passive corruption' shall mean the conduct referred to in Article 2 of the Protocol drawn up on the basis of Article K.3 of the Treaty on European Union to the convention on the protection of the European Communities' financial interests, of 27 September 1996[1],

'active corruption' shall mean the conduct referred to in Article 3 of the same Protocol;

(d) 'legal person' shall mean any entity having such status under the applicable national law, except for States or other public bodies in the exercise of State authority and for public international organizations;

(e) 'money laundering' shall mean the conduct as defined n the third indent of Article 1 of Council Directive 91/308/EEC of 10 June 1991 on the prevention of the use of the financial system for the purpose of money laundering[2], related to the proceeds of fraud, at least in serious cases, and of active and passive corruption.

Article 2
Money laundering

Each Member State shall take the necessary measures to establish moneylaundering as a criminal offence.

Article 3
Liability of legal persons

1. Each Member State shall take the necessary measures to ensure that legal persons can be held liable for fraud, active corruption and money laundering committed for their benefit by any person, acting either individually or as part of an organ of the legal person, who has a leading position within the legal person, based on

— a power of representation of the legal person, or
— an authority to take decisions on behalf of the legal person, or
— an authority to exercise control within the legal person,

as well as for involvement as accessories or instigators in such fraud, active corruption or money laundering or the attempted commission of such fraud.

2. Apart from the cases already provided for in paragraph 1, each Member State shall take the necessary measures to ensure that a legal person can be held liable where the lack of supervision or control by a person referred to in paragraph 1 has made possible the commission of a fraud or an act of active corruption or money laundering for the benefit of that legal person by a person under its authority.

3. Liability of a legal person under paragraphs 1 and 2 shall not exclude criminal proceedings against natural persons who are perpetrators, instigators or accessories in the fraud, active corruption or money laundering.

Article 4
Sanctions for legal persons

1. Each Member State shall take the necessary measures to ensure that a legal person held liable pursuant to Article 3(1) is punishable by effective, proportionate and dissuasive sanctions, which shall include criminal or non-criminal fines and may include other sanctions such as:

(a) exclusion from entitlement to public benefits or aid;
(b) temporary or permanent disqualification from the practice of commercial activities;

    (c)   placing under judicial supervision;

    (d)   a judicial winding-up order.

2. Each Member State shall take the necessary measures to ensure that a legal person held liable pursuant to Article 3(2) is punishable by effective, proportionate and dissuasive sanctions or measures.

Article 5
Confiscation

Each Member State shall take the necessary measures to enable the seizure and, without prejudice to the rights of bona fide third parties, the confiscation or removal of the instruments and proceeds of fraud, active and passive corruption and money laundering, or property the value of which corresponds to such proceeds. Any instruments, proceeds or other property seized or confiscated shall be dealt with by the Member State in accordance with its national law.

Article 6
Cooperation with the Commission of the European Communities

A Member State may not refuse to provide mutual assistance in respect of fraud, active and passive corruption and money laundering for the sole reason that it concerns or is considered as a tax or customs duty offence.

Article 7
Cooperation with the Commission of the European Communities

1. The Member States and the Commission shall cooperate with each other in the fight against fraud, active and passive corruption and money laundering.

To that end, the Commission shall lend such technical and operational assistance as the competent national authorities may need to facilitate coordination of their investigations.

2. The competent authorities in the Member States may exchange information with the Commission so as to make it easier to establish the facts and to ensure effective action against fraud, active and passive corruption and money laundering. The Commission and the competent national authorities shall take account, in each specific case, of the requirements of investigation secrecy and data protection. To that end, a Member State, when supplying information to the Commission, may set specific conditions covering the use of information, whether by the Commission or by another Member State to which that information may be passed.

Article 8
Data protection responsibility for the Commission

The Commission shall ensure that, in the context of the exchange of information under Article 7(2), it shall observe, as regards the processing of personal data, a level of protection equivalent to the level of protection set out in Directive 95/46/EC of the European Parliament and of the Council of 24 October 1995 on the protection of individuals with regard to the processing of personal data and on the free movement of such data.

Article 9
Publication of data protection rules

The rules adopted concerning the obligations under Article 8 shall be published in the Official Journal of the European Communities.

Article 10
Transfer of data to other Member States and third countries

1. Subject to any conditions referred to in Article 7(2), the Commission may transfer personal data obtained from a Member State in the performance of its functions under Article 7 to any other Member State. The Commission shall inform the Member State which supplied the information of its intention to make such as transfer.

2. The Commission may, under the same conditions, transfer personal data obtained from a Member State in the performance of its functions under Article 7 to any third country provided that the Member State which supplied the information has agreed to such transfer.

Article 11
Supervisory authority

Any authority designated or created for the purpose of exercising the function of independent data protection supervision over personal data held by the Commission pursuant to its functions under the Treaty establishing the European Community, shall be competent to exercise the same function with respect to personal data held by the Commission by virtue of this Protocol.

Article 12
Relation to the Convention

1. The provisions of Articles 3, 5 and 6 of the Convention shall also apply to the conduct referred to in Article 2 of this Protocol.

2. The following provisions of the Convention shall also apply to this Protocol:

 — Article 4, on the understanding that, unless otherwise indicated at the time of the notification provided for in Article 16(2) of this Protocol, any declaration within the meaning of Article 4(2) of the Convention, shall also apply to this Protocol,

 — Article 7, on the understanding that the ne bis in idem principle also applies to legal persons, and that, unless otherwise indicated at the time the notification provided for in Article 16(2) of this Protocol is being given, any declaration within the meaning of Article 7(2), of the Convention shall also apply to this Protocol,

 — Article 9,

 — Article 10.

Article 13
Court of Justice

1. Any dispute between Member States on the interpretation or application of this Protocol must in an initial stage be examined by the Council in accordance with the procedure set out in title VI of the Treaty on European Union with a view to reaching a solution.

If no solution is found within six months, the matter may be referred to the Court of Justice by a party to the dispute.

2. Any dispute between one or more Member States and the Commission concerning the application of Article 2 in relation to Article 1(e), and Article 7, 8, 10 and 12(2), fourth indent of this Protocol which it has proved impossible to settle through negotiation may be submitted to the Court of Justice, after the expiry of a period of six months from the date on which one of the parties has notified the other of the existence of a dispute.

3. The Protocol drawn up on the basis of Article K.3 of the Treaty on European Union, on the interpretation, by way of preliminary rulings, by the Court of Justice of the European Communities of the Convention on the protection of the European Communities' financial interests, of 29 November 1996[(1)], shall apply to this Protocol, on the understanding that a declaration made by a Member State pursuant to Article 2 of that Protocol is also valid regarding this Protocol unless the Member State concerned makes a declaration to the contrary when giving the notification provided for in Article 16(2) of this Protocol.

Article 14
Non-contractual liability

For the purposes of this Protocol, the non-contractual liability of the Community shall be governed by the second paragraph of Article 215 of the Treaty establishing the European Community, Article 178 of the same Treaty shall apply.

Article 15
Judicial control

1. The Court of Justice shall have jurisdiction in proceedings instituted by any natural or legal person against a decision of the Commission addressed to that person or which is of direct and individual concern to that person, on ground of infringement of Article 8 or any rule adopted pursuant thereto, or misuse of powers.

2. Articles 168 a (1) and (2), 173, fifth paragraph, 174, first paragraph, 176, first and second paragraphs, 185 and 186 of the Treaty establishing the European Community, as well as the Statute of the Court of Justice of the European Community, shall apply, mutatis mutandis.

Article 16
Entry into force

1. This Protocol shall be subject to adoption by the Member States in accordance with their respective constitutional requirements.

2. Member States shall notify the Secretary-General of the Council of the European Union of the completion of the procedures required under their respective constitutional rules for adopting this Protocol.

3. This Protocol shall enter into force ninety days after the notification provided for in paragraph 2, by the State which, being a member of the European Union on the date of the adoption by the Council of the act drawing up this Protocol, is the last to fulfil that formality. If, however, the Convention has not entered into force on that date, this Protocol shall enter into force on the date on which the Convention enters into force.

4. However, the application of Article 7(2) shall be suspended if, and for so long as, the relevant institution of the European Communities has not complied with its obligation to

publish the data protection rules pursuant to Article 9 or the terms of Article 11 concerning the supervisory authority have not been complied with.

Article 17
Accession of new Member States

1. This Protocol shall be open to accession by any State that becomes a member of the European Union.

2. The text of this Protocol in the language of the acceding State, drawn up by the Council of the European Union, shall be authentic.

3. Instruments of accession shall be deposited with the depositary.

4. This Protocol shall enter into force with respect to any State that accedes to it ninety days after the deposit of its instrument of accession or on the date of entry into force of this Protocol if it has not yet entered into force at the time of expiry of the said period of ninety days.

Article 18
Reservations

1. Each Member State may reserve the right to establish the money laundering related to the proceeds of active and passive corruption as a criminal offence only in serious cases of active and passive corruption. Any Member State making such a reservation shall inform the depositary, giving details of the scope of the reservation, when giving the notification provided for in Article 16(2). Such a reservation shall be valid for a period of five years after the said notification. It may be renewed once for a further period of five years.

2. The Republic of Austria may, when giving its notification referred to in Article 16(2), declare that it will not be bound by Articles 3 and 4. Such a declaration shall cease to have effect five years after the date of the adoption of the act drawing up this Protocol.

3. No other reservations shall be authorized, with the exception of those provided for in Article 12(2), first and second indent.

Article 19
Depositary

1. The Secretary-General of the Council of the European Union shall act as depositary of this Protocol.

2. The depositary shall publish in the Official Journal of the European Communities information on the progress of adoptions and accessions, declarations and reservations and any other notification concerning this Protocol.

European Convention on Human Rights Act 2003

Number 20 of 2003

ARRANGEMENT OF SECTIONS

1.   Interpretation.

2.   Interpretation of laws.

3.   Performance of certain functions in a manner compatible with Convention provisions.

4.   Interpretation of Convention provisions.

5.   Declaration of incompatibility.

6.   Notice of proceedings under Act.

7.   Amendment of Human Rights Commission Act 2000.

8.   Expenses.

9.   Short title and commencement.

SCHEDULE 1

CONVENTION FOR THE PROTECTION OF HUMAN RIGHTS AND FUNDAMENTAL FREEDOMS

SCHEDULE 2

PROTOCOL TO THE CONVENTION FOR THE PROTECTION OF HUMAN RIGHTS AND FUNDAMENTAL FREEDOMS

SCHEDULE 3

PROTOCOL NO. 4 TO THE CONVENTION FOR THE PROTECTION OF HUMAN RIGHTS AND FUNDAMENTAL FREEDOMS SECURING CERTAIN RIGHTS AND FREEDOMS OTHER THAN THOSE ALREADY INCLUDED IN THE CONVENTION AND IN THE FIRST PROTOCOL THERETO

SCHEDULE 4

PROTOCOL NO. 6 TO THE CONVENTION FOR THE PROTECTION OF HUMAN RIGHTS AND FUNDAMENTAL FREEDOMS CONCERNING THE ABOLITION OF THE DEATH PENALTY

SCHEDULE 5

PROTOCOL NO. 7 TO THE CONVENTION FOR THE PROTECTION OF HUMAN RIGHTS AND FUNDAMENTAL FREEDOMS

AN ACT TO ENABLE FURTHER EFFECT TO BE GIVEN, SUBJECT TO THE CONSTITUTION, TO CERTAIN PROVISIONS OF THE CONVENTION FOR THE PROTECTION OF HUMAN RIGHTS AND FUNDAMENTAL FREEDOMS DONE AT ROME ON THE 4th DAY OF NOVEMBER 1950 AND CERTAIN PROTOCOLS THERETO, TO AMEND THE HUMAN RIGHTS COMMISSION ACT 2000 AND TO PROVIDE FOR RELATED MATTERS. [30th June, 2003]

BE IT ENACTED BY THE OIREACHTAS AS FOLLOWS:

1   Interpretation

(1) In this Act unless the context otherwise requires—

"the Convention" means the Convention for the Protection of Human Rights and Fundamental Freedoms done at Rome on the 4th day of November, 1950 (the text of which, in the English language, is, for convenience of reference, set out in Schedule 1 to this Act), as amended by Protocol No. 11 done at Strasbourg on the 11th day of May, 1994;

"Convention provisions" means, subject to any derogation which the State may make pursuant to Article 15 of the Convention, Articles 2 to 14 of the Convention and the following protocols thereto as construed in accordance with Articles 16 to 18 of the Convention:

(a) the Protocol to the Convention done at Paris on the 20th day of March, 1952;

(b) Protocol No. 4 to the Convention securing certain rights and freedoms other than those already included in the Convention and in the First Protocol thereto done at Strasbourg on the 16th day of September, 1963;

(c) Protocol No. 6 to the Convention concerning the abolition of the death penalty done at Strasbourg on the 28th day of April, 1983;

(d) Protocol No. 7 to the Convention done at Strasbourg on the 22nd day of November, 1984;

(the texts of which protocols, in the English language, are, for convenience of reference, set out in Schedules 2, 3, 4 and 5 respectively, to this Act);

"declaration of incompatibility" means a declaration under section 5;

"European Court of Human Rights" shall be construed in accordance with section 4;

"functions" includes powers and duties and references to the performance of functions includes, as respects powers and duties, references to the exercise of the powers and the performance of the duties;

"Minister" means the Minister for Justice, Equality and Law Reform;

"organ of the State" includes a tribunal or any other body (other than the President or the Oireachtas or either House of the Oireachtas or a Committee of either such House or a Joint Committee of both such Houses or a court) which is established by law or through which any of the legislative, executive or judicial powers of the State are exercised;

"rule of law" includes common law;

"statutory provision" means any provision of an Act of the Oireachtas or of any order, regulation, rule, licence, bye-law or other like document made, issued or otherwise created thereunder or any statute, order, regulation, rule, licence, bye-law or other like document made, issued or otherwise created under a statute which continued in force by virtue of Article 50 of the Constitution.

(2) In this Act—

(a) a reference to any enactment shall, unless the context otherwise requires, be construed as a reference to that enactment as amended or extended by or under any subsequent enactment including this Act,

(b) a reference to a section is a reference to a section of this Act unless it is indicated that reference to some other enactment is intended,

(c) a reference to a subsection, paragraph or subparagraph is a reference to a subsection, paragraph or subparagraph of the provision in which the reference occurs unless it is indicated that reference to some other provision is intended.

2 Interpretation of laws

(1) In interpreting and applying any statutory provision or rule of law, a court shall, in so far as is possible, subject to the rules of law relating to such interpretation and application, do so in a manner compatible with the State's obligations under the Convention provisions.

(2) This section applies to any statutory provision or rule of law in force immediately before the passing of this Act or any such provision coming into force thereafter.

3 Performance of certain functions in a manner compatible with Convention provisions

(1) Subject to any statutory provision (other than this Act) or rule of law, every organ of the State shall perform its functions in a manner compatible with the State's obligations under the Convention provisions.

(2) A person who has suffered injury, loss or damage as a result of a contravention of subsection (1), may, if no other remedy in damages is available, institute proceedings to recover damages in respect of the contravention in the High Court (or, subject to subsection (3), in the Circuit Court) and the Court may award to the person such damages (if any) as it considers appropriate.

(3) The damages recoverable under this section in the Circuit Court shall not exceed the amount standing prescribed, for the time being by law, as the limit of that Court's jurisdiction in tort.

(4) Nothing in this section shall be construed as creating a criminal offence.

(5) (a) Proceedings under this section shall not be brought in respect of any contravention of subsection (1) which arose more than 1 year before the commencement of the proceedings.

(b) The period referred to in paragraph (a) may be extended by order made by the Court if it considers it appropriate to do so in the interests of justice.

4 Interpretation of Convention provisions

Judicial notice shall be taken of the Convention provisions and of—

(a) any declaration, decision, advisory opinion or judgment of the European Court of Human Rights established under the Convention on any question in respect of which that Court has jurisdiction,

(b) any decision or opinion of the European Commission of Human Rights so established on any question in respect of which it had jurisdiction,

(c) any decision of the Committee of Ministers established under the Statute of the Council of Europe on any question in respect of which it has jurisdiction,

and a court shall, when interpreting and applying the Convention provisions, take due account of the principles laid down by those declarations, decisions, advisory opinions, opinions and judgments.

5   Declaration of incompatibility

(1) In any proceedings, the High Court, or the Supreme Court when exercising its appellate jurisdiction, may, having regard to the provisions of section 2, on application to it in that behalf by a party, or of its own motion, and where no other legal remedy is adequate and available, make a declaration (referred to in this Act as "a declaration of incompatibility") that a statutory provision or rule of law is incompatible with the State's obligations under the Convention provisions.

(2) A declaration of incompatibility—

  (a) shall not affect the validity, continuing operation or enforcement of the statutory provision or rule of law in respect of which it is made, and

  (b) shall not prevent a party to the proceedings concerned from making submissions or representations in relation to matters to which the declaration relates in any proceedings before the European Court of Human Rights.

(3) The Taoiseach shall cause a copy of any order containing a declaration of incompatibility to be laid before each House of the Oireachtas within the next 21 days on which that House has sat after the making of the order.

(4) Where—

  (a) a declaration of incompatibility is made,

  (b) a party to the proceedings concerned makes an application in writing to the Attorney General for compensation in respect of an injury or loss or damage suffered by him or her as a result of the incompatibility concerned, and

  (c) the Government, in their discretion, consider that it may be appropriate to make an ex gratia payment of compensation to that party ("a payment"),

the Government may request an adviser appointed by them to advise them as to the amount of such compensation (if any) and may, in their discretion, make a payment of the amount aforesaid or of such other amount as they consider appropriate in the circumstances.

(5) In advising the Government on the amount of compensation for the purposes of subsection (4), an adviser shall take appropriate account of the principles and practice applied by the European Court of Human Rights in relation to affording just satisfaction to an injured party under Article 41 of the Convention.

6   Notice of proceedings under Act

(1) Before a court decides whether to make a declaration of incompatibility the Attorney General and the Human Rights Commission shall be given notice of the proceedings in accordance with rules of court.

(2) The Attorney General shall thereupon be entitled to appear in the proceedings and to become a party thereto as regards the issue of the declaration of incompatibility.

7   Amendment of Human Rights Commission Act 2000

The Human Rights Commission Act 2000 is hereby amended in section 11, by the substitution in subsection (3)(b) for "such force;" of:

"such force, and

  (c) the rights, liberties and freedoms conferred on, or guaranteed to, persons by the Convention provisions within the meaning of the European Convention on Human Rights Act 2003;".

8   Expenses

The expenses incurred by the Minister for Finance in the administration of this Act shall be paid out of moneys provided by the Oireachtas and the expenses incurred by any other Minister of the Government in the administration of this Act shall, to such extent as may be sanctioned by the Minister for Finance, be paid out of moneys provided by the Oireachtas.

9   Short title and commencement

(1) This Act may be cited as the European Convention on Human Rights Act 2003.

(2) This Act shall come into operation on such day not later than 6 months after its passing as the Minister may appoint by order.

SCHEDULE 1

CONVENTION FOR THE PROTECTION OF HUMAN RIGHTS AND FUNDAMENTAL FREEDOMS

Section 1

Rome, 4.XI. 1950

THE GOVERNMENTS SIGNATORY HERETO, being members of the Council of Europe,

Considering the Universal Declaration of Human Rights proclaimed by the General Assembly of the United Nations on 10th December 1948;

Considering that this Declaration aims at securing the universal and effective recognition and observance of the Rights therein declared;

Considering that the aim of the Council of Europe is the achievement of greater unity between its members and that one of the methods by which that aim is to be pursued is the maintenance and further realisation of human rights and fundamental freedoms;

Reaffirming their profound belief in those fundamental freedoms which are the foundation of justice and peace in the world and are best maintained on the one hand by an effective political democracy and on the other by a common understanding and observance of the human rights upon which they depend;

Being resolved, as the governments of European countries which are like-minded and have a common heritage of political traditions, ideals, freedom and the rule of law, to take the first steps for the collective enforcement of certain of the rights stated in the Universal Declaration,

Have agreed as follows:

Article 1

Obligation to respect human rights

The High Contracting Parties shall secure to everyone within their jurisdiction the rights and freedoms defined in Section I of this Convention.

Section I
Rights and freedoms

Article 2
Right to life

1 Everyone's right to life shall be protected by law. No one shall be deprived of his life intentionally save in the execution of a sentence of a court following his conviction of a crime for which this penalty is provided by law.

2 Deprivation of life shall not be regarded as inflicted in contravention of this article when it results from the use of force which is no more than absolutely necessary:

a in defence of any person from unlawful violence;

a in order to effect a lawful arrest or to prevent the escape of a person lawfully detained;

c in action lawfully taken for the purpose of quelling a riot or insurrection.

Article 3
Prohibition of torture

No one shall be subjected to torture or to inhuman or degrading treatment or punishment.

Article 4
Prohibition of slavery and forced labour

1 No one shall be held in slavery or servitude.

2 No one shall be required to perform forced or compulsory labour.

3 For the purpose of this article the term "forced or compulsory labour" shall not include:

    a any work required to be done in the ordinary course of detention imposed according to the provisions of Article 5 of this Convention or during conditional release from such detention;

    b any service of a military character or, in case of conscientious objectors in countries where they are recognised, service exacted instead of compulsory military service;

    c any service exacted in case of an emergency or calamity threatening the life or well-being of the community;

    d any work or service which forms part of normal civic obligations.

Article 5
Right to liberty and security

1 Everyone has the right to liberty and security of person. No one shall be deprived of his liberty save in the following cases and in accordance with a procedure prescribed by law:

    a the lawful detention of a person after conviction by a competent court;

    b the lawful arrest or detention of a person for non-compliance with the lawful order of a court or in order to secure the fulfilment of any obligation prescribed by law;

    c the lawful arrest or detention of a person effected for the purpose of bringing him before the competent legal authority on reasonable suspicion of having committed an offence or when it is reasonably considered necessary to prevent his committing an offence or fleeing after having done so;

d the detention of a minor by lawful order for the purpose of educational supervision or his lawful detention for the purpose of bringing him before the competent legal authority;

e the lawful detention of persons for the prevention of the spreading of infectious diseases, of persons of unsound mind, alcoholics or drug addicts or vagrants;

f the lawful arrest or detention of a person to prevent his effecting an unauthorised entry into the country or of a person against whom action is being taken with a view to deportation or extradition.

2 Everyone who is arrested shall be informed promptly, in a language which he understands, of the reasons for his arrest and of any charge against him.

3 Everyone arrested or detained in accordance with the provisions of paragraph 1.c of this article shall be brought promptly before a judge or other officer authorised by law to exercise judicial power and shall be entitled to trial within a reasonable time or to release pending trial. Release may be conditioned by guarantees to appear for trial.

4 Everyone who is deprived of his liberty by arrest or detention shall be entitled to take proceedings by which the lawfulness of his detention shall be decided speedily by a court and his release ordered if the detention is not lawful.

5 Everyone who has been the victim of arrest or detention in contravention of the provisions of this article shall have an enforceable right to compensation.

Article 6
Right to a fair trial

1 In the determination of his civil rights and obligations or of any criminal charge against him, everyone is entitled to a fair and public hearing within a reasonable time by an independent and impartial tribunal established by law. Judgment shall be pronounced publicity but the press and public may be excluded from all or part of the trial in the interests of morals, public order or national security in a democratic society, where the interests of juveniles or the protection of the private life of the parties so require, or to the extent strictly necessary in the opinion of the court in special circumstances where publicity would prejudice the interests of justice.

2 Everyone charged with a criminal offence shall be presumed innocent until proved guilty according to law.

3 Everyone charged with a criminal offence has the following minimum rights:

a to be informed promptly, in a language which he understands and in detail, of the nature and cause of the accusation against him;

b to have adequate time and facilities for the preparation of his defence;

c to defend himself in person or through legal assistance of his own choosing or, if he has not sufficient means to pay for legal assistance, to be given it free when the interests of justice so require;

d to examine or have examined witnesses against him and to obtain the attendance and examination of witnesses on his behalf under the same conditions as witnesses against him;

e to have the free assistance of an interpreter if he cannot understand or speak the language used in court.

Article 7
No punishment without law

1 No one shall be held guilty of any criminal offence on account of any act or omission which did not constitute a criminal offence under national or international law at the time when it was committed. Nor shall a heavier penalty be imposed than the one that was applicable at the time the criminal offence was committed.

2 This article shall not prejudice the trial and punishment of any person for any act or omission which, at the time when it was committed, was criminal according to the general principles of law recognised by civilised nations.

Article 8
Right to respect for private and family life

1 Everyone has the right to respect for his private and family life, his home and his correspondence.

2 There shall be no interference by a public authority with the exercise of this right except such as is in accordance with the law and is necessary in a democratic society in the interests of national security, public safety or the economic well-being of the country, for the prevention of disorder or crime, for the protection of health or morals, or for the protection of the rights and freedoms of others.

Article 9
Freedom of thought, conscience and religion

1 Everyone has the right to freedom of thought, conscience and religion; this right includes freedom to change his religion or belief and freedom, either alone or in community with others and in public or private, to manifest his religion or belief, in worship, teaching, practice and observance.

2 Freedom to manifest one's religion or beliefs shall be subject only to such limitations as are prescribed by law and are necessary in a democratic society in the interests of public safety, for the protection of public order, health or morals, or for the protection of the rights and freedoms of others.

Article 10
Freedom of expression

1 Everyone has the right to freedom of expression. This right shall include freedom to hold opinions and to receive and impart information and ideas without interference by public authority and regardless of frontiers. This article shall not prevent States from requiring the licensing of broadcasting, television or cinema enterprises.

2 The exercise of these freedoms, since it carries with it duties and responsibilities, may be subject to such formalities, conditions, restrictions or penalties as are prescribed by law and are necessary in a democratic society, in the interests of national security, territorial integrity or public safety, for the prevention of disorder or crime, for the protection of health or morals, for the protection of the reputation or rights of others, for preventing the disclosure of information received in confidence, or for maintaining the authority and impartiality of the judiciary.

Article 11
Freedom of assembly and association

1 Everyone has the right to freedom of peaceful assembly and to freedom of association with others, including the right to form and to join trade unions for the protection of his interests.

2 No restrictions shall be placed on the exercise of these rights other than such as are prescribed by law and are necessary in a democratic society in the interests of national security or public safety, for the prevention of disorder or crime, for the protection of health or morals or for the protection of the rights and freedoms of others. This article shall not prevent the imposition of lawful restrictions on the exercise of these rights by members of the armed forces, of the police or of the administration of the State.

Article 12
Right to marry

Men and women of marriageable age have the right to marry and to found a family, according to the national laws governing the exercise of this right.

Article 13
Right to an effective remedy

Everyone whose rights and freedoms as set forth in this Convention are violated shall have an effective remedy before a national authority notwithstanding that the violation has been committed by persons acting in an official capacity.

Article 14
Prohibition of discrimination

The enjoyment of the rights and freedoms set forth in this Convention shall be secured without discrimination on any ground such as sex, race, colour, language, religion, political or other opinion, national or social origin, association with a national minority, property, birth or other status.

Article 15
Derogation in time of emergency

1 In time of war or other public emergency threatening the life of the nation any High Contracting Party may take measures derogating from its obligations under this Convention to the extent strictly required by the exigencies of the situation, provided that such measures are not inconsistent with its other obligations under international law.

2 No derogation from Article 2, except in respect of deaths resulting from lawful acts of war, or from Articles 3, 4 (paragraph 1) and 7 shall be made under this provision.

3 Any High Contracting Party availing itself of this right of derogation shall keep the Secretary General of the Council of Europe fully informed of the measures which it has taken and the reasons therefor. It shall also inform the Secretary General of the Council of Europe when such measures have ceased to operate and the provisions of the Convention are again being fully executed.

Article 16
Restrictions on political activity of aliens

Nothing in Articles 10, 11 and 14 shall be regarded as preventing the High Contracting Parties from imposing restrictions on the political activity of aliens.

Article 17
Prohibition of abuse of rights

Nothing in this Convention may be interpreted as implying for any State, group or person any right to engage in any activity or perform any act aimed at the destruction of any of the rights and freedoms set forth herein or at their limitation to a greater extent than is provided for in the Convention.

Article 18
Limitation on use of restrictions on rights

The restrictions permitted under this Convention to the said rights and freedoms shall not be applied for any purpose other than those for which they have been prescribed.

SECTION II
EUROPEAN COURT OF HUMAN RIGHTS

Article 19
Establishment of the Court

To ensure the observance of the engagements undertaken by the High Contracting Parties in the Convention and the Protocols thereto, there shall be set up a European Court of Human Rights, hereinafter referred to as "the Court". It shall function on a permanent basis.

Article 20
Number of judges

The Court shall consist of a number of judges equal to that of the High Contracting Parties.

Article 21
Criteria for office

1 The judges shall be of high moral character and must either possess the qualifications required for appointment to high judicial office or be jurisconsults of recognised competence.

2 The judges shall sit on the Court in their individual capacity.

3 During their term of office the judges shall not engage in any activity which is incompatible with their independence, impartiality or with the demands of a full-time office; all questions arising from the application of this paragraph shall be decided by the Court.

Article 22
Election of judges

1 The judges shall be elected by the Parliamentary Assembly with respect to each High Contracting Party by a majority of votes cast from a list of three candidates nominated by the High Contracting Party.

1072

2 The same procedure shall be followed to complete the Court in the event of the accession of new High Contracting Parties and in filling casual vacancies.

Article 23
Terms of office

1 The judges shall be elected for a period of six years. They may be re-elected. However, the terms of office of one-half of the judges elected at the first election shall expire at the end of three years.

2 The judges whose terms of office are to expire at the end of the initial period of three years shall be chosen by lot by the Secretary General of the Council of Europe immediately after their election.

3 In order to ensure that, as far as possible, the terms of office of one-half of the judges are renewed every three years, the Parliamentary Assembly may decide, before proceeding to any subsequent election, that the term or terms of office of one or more judges to be elected shall be for a period other than six years but not more than nine and not less than three years.

4 In cases where more than one term of office is involved and where the Parliamentary Assembly applies the preceding paragraph, the allocation of the terms of office shall be effected by a drawing of lots by the Secretary General of the Council of Europe immediately after the election.

5 A judge elected to replace a judge whose term of office has not expired shall hold office for the remainder of his predecessor's term.

6 The terms of office of judges shall expire when they reach the age of 70.

7 The judges shall hold office until replaced. They shall, however, continue to deal with such cases as they already have under consideration.

Article 24
Dismissal

No judge may be dismissed from his office unless the other judges decide by a majority of two-thirds that he has ceased to fulfil the required conditions.

Article 25
Registry and legal secretaries

The Court shall have a registry, the functions and organisation of which shall be laid down in the rules of the Court. The Court shall be assisted by legal secretaries.

Article 26
Plenary Court

The plenary Court shall

    a elect its President and one or two Vice-Presidents for a period of three years; they may be re-elected;

    b set up Chambers, constituted for a fixed period of time;

    c elect the Presidents of the Chambers of the Court; they may be re-elected;

    d adopt the rules of the Court, and

    e elect the Registrar and one or more Deputy Registrars.

Article 27
Committees, Chambers and Grand Chamber

1 To consider cases brought before it, the Court shall sit in committees of three judges, in Chambers of seven judges and in a Grand Chamber of seventeen judges. The Court's Chambers shall set up committees for a fixed period of time.

2 There shall sit as an *ex officio* member of the Chamber and the Grand Chamber the judge elected in respect of the State Party concerned or, if there is none or if he is unable to sit, a person of its choice who shall sit in the capacity of judge.

3 The Grand Chamber shall also include the President of the Court, the Vice-Presidents, the Presidents of the Chambers and other judges chosen in accordance with the rules of the Court. When a case is referred to the Grand Chamber under Article 43, no judge from the Chamber which rendered the judgment shall sit in the Grand Chamber, with the exception of the President of the Chamber and the judge who sat in respect of the State Party concerned.

Article 28
Declarations of inadmissibility by committees

A committee may, by a unanimous vote, declare inadmissible or strike out of its list of cases an application submitted under Article 34 where such a decision can be taken without further examination. The decision shall be final.

Article 29
Decisions by Chambers on admissibility and merits

1 If no decision is taken under Article 28, a Chamber shall decide on the admissibility and merits of individual applications submitted under Article 34.

2 A Chamber shall decide on the admissibility and merits of interState applications submitted under Article 33.

3 The decision on admissibility shall be taken separately unless the Court, in exceptional cases, decides otherwise.

Article 30
Relinquishment of jurisdiction to the Grand Chamber

Where a case pending before a Chamber raises a serious question affecting the interpretation of the Convention or the protocols thereto, or where the resolution of a question before the Chamber might have a result inconsistent with a judgment previously delivered by the Court, the Chamber may, at any time before it has rendered its judgment, relinquish jurisdiction in favour of the Grand Chamber, unless one of the parties to the case objects.

Article 31
Powers of the Grand Chamber

The Grand Chamber shall

    a   determine applications submitted either under Article 33 or Article 34 when a Chamber has relinquished jurisdiction under Article 30 or when the case has been referred to it under Article 43; and

    b   consider requests for advisory opinions submitted under Article 47.

Article 32
Jurisdiction of the Court

1 The jurisdiction of the Court shall extend to all matters concerning the interpretation and application of the Convention and the protocols thereto which are referred to it as provided in Articles 33, 34 and 47.

2 In the event of dispute as to whether the Court has jurisdiction, the Court shall decide.

Article 33
Inter-State cases

Any High Contracting Party may refer to the Court any alleged breach of the provisions of the Convention and the protocols thereto by another High Contracting Party.

Article 34
Individual applications

The Court may receive applications from any person, non-governmental organisation or group of individuals claiming to be the victim of a violation by one of the High Contracting Parties of the rights set forth in the Convention or the protocols thereto. The High Contracting Parties undertake not to hinder in any way the effective exercise of this right.

Article 35
Admissibility criteria

1 The Court may only deal with the matter after all domestic remedies have been exhausted, according to the generally recognised rules of international law, and within a period of six months from the date on which the final decision was taken.

2 The Court shall not deal with any application submitted under Article 34 that

    a is anonymous; or

    b is substantially the same as a matter that has already been examined by the Court or has already been submitted to another procedure of international investigation or settlement and contains no relevant new information.

3 The Court shall declare inadmissible any individual application submitted under Article 34 which it considers incompatible with the provisions of the Convention or the protocols thereto, manifestly ill-founded, or an abuse of the right of application.

4 The Court shall reject any application which it considers inadmissible under this Article. It may do so at any stage of the proceedings.

Article 36
Third party intervention

1 In all cases before a Chamber of the Grand Chamber, a High Contracting Party one of whose nationals is an applicant shall have the right to submit written comments and to take part in hearings.

2 The President of the Court may, in the interest of the proper administration of justice, invite any High Contracting Party which is not a party to the proceedings or any person concerned who is not the applicant to submit written comments or take part in hearings.

Article 37
Striking out applications

1 The Court may at any stage of the proceedings decide to strike an application out of its list of cases where the circumstances lead to the conclusion that

   a   the applicant does not intend to pursue his application; or

   b   the matter has been resolved; or

   c   for any other reason established by the Court, it is no longer justified to continue the examination of the application.

However, the Court shall continue the examination of the application if respect for human rights as defined in the Convention and the protocols thereto so requires.

2 The Court may decide to restore an application to its list of cases if it considers that the circumstances justify such a course.

Article 38
Examination of the case and friendly settlement proceedings

1 If the Court declares the application admissible, it shall

   a   pursue the examination of the case, together with the representatives of the parties, and if need be, undertake an investigation, for the effective conduct of which the States concerned shall furnish all necessary facilities;

   b   place itself at the disposal of the parties concerned with a view to securing a friendly settlement of the matter on the basis of respect for human rights as defined in the Convention and the protocols thereto.

2 Proceedings conducted under paragraph 1.b shall be confidential.

Article 39
Finding of a friendly settlement

If a friendly settlement is effected, the Court shall strike the case out of its list by means of a decision which shall be confined to a brief statement of the facts and of the solution reached.

Article 40
Public hearings and access to documents

1 Hearings shall be in public unless the Court in exceptional circumstances decides otherwise.

2 Documents deposited with the Registrar shall be accessible to the public unless the President of the Court decides otherwise.

Article 41
Just satisfaction

If the Court finds that there has been a violation of the Convention or the protocols thereto, and if the internal law of the High Contracting Party concerned allows only partial reparation to be made, the Court shall, if necessary, afford just satisfaction to the injured party.

Article 42
Judgments of Chambers

Judgments of Chambers shall become final in accordance with the provisions of Article 44, paragraph 2.

Article 43
Referral to the Grand Chamber

1 Within a period of three months from the date of the judgment of the Chamber, any party to the case may, in exceptional cases, request that the case be referred to the Grand Chamber.

2 A panel of five judges of the Grand Chamber shall accept the request if the case raises a serious question affecting the interpretation or application of the Convention or the protocols thereto, or a serious issue of general importance.

3 If the panel accepts the request, the Grand Chamber shall decide the case by means of a judgment.

Article 44
Final judgments

1 The judgment of the Grand Chamber shall be final.

2 The judgment of a Chamber shall become final

a   when the parties declare that they will not request that the case be referred to the Grand Chamber; or

b   three months after the date of the judgment, if reference of the case to the Grand Chamber has not been requested; or

c   when the panel of the Grand Chamber rejects the request to refer under Article 43.

3 The final judgment shall be published.

Article 45
Reasons for judgments and decisions

1 Reasons shall be given for judgments as well as for decisions declaring applications admissible or inadmissible.

2 If a judgment does not represent, in whole or in part, the unanimous opinion of the judges, any judge shall be entitled to deliver a separate opinion.

Article 46
Binding force and execution of judgments

1 The High Contracting Parties undertake to abide by the final judgment of the Court in any case to which they are parties.

2 The final judgment of the Court shall be transmitted to the Committee of Ministers, which shall supervise its execution.

Article 47
Advisory opinions

1 The Court may, at the request of the Committee of Ministers, give advisory opinions on legal questions concerning the interpretation of the Convention and the protocols thereto.

2 Such opinions shall not deal with any question relating to the content or scope of the rights or freedoms defined in Section I of the Convention and the protocols thereto, or with any other question which the Court or the Committee of Minister might have to consider in consequence of any such proceedings as could be instituted in accordance with the Convention.

3 Decisions of the Committee of Ministers to request an advisory opinion of the Court shall require a majority vote of the representatives entitled to sit on the Committee.

Article 48
Advisory jurisdiction of the Court

The Court shall decide whether a request for an advisory opinion submitted by the Committee of Ministers is within its competence as defined in Article 47.

Article 49
Reasons for advisory opinions

1 Reasons shall be given for advisory opinions of the Court.

2 If the advisory opinion does not represent, in whole or in part, the unanimous opinion of the judges, any judge shall be entitled to deliver a separate opinion.

3 Advisory opinions of the Court shall be communicated to the Committee of Ministers.

Article 50
Expenditure on the Court

The expenditure on the Court shall be borne by the Council of Europe.

Article 51
Privileges and immunities of judges

The judges shall be entitled, during the exercise of their functions, to the privileges and immunities provided for in Article 40 of the Statute of the Council of Europe and in the agreements made thereunder.

SECTION III
MISCELLANEOUS PROVISIONS

Article 52
Inquiries by the Secretary General

On receipt of a request from the Secretary General of the Council of Europe any High Contracting Party shall furnish an explanation of the manner in which its internal law ensures the effective implementation of any of the provisions of the Convention.

Article 53
Safeguard for existing human rights

Nothing in this Convention shall be construed as limiting or derogating from any of the human rights and fundamental freedoms which may be ensured under the laws of any High Contracting Party or under any other agreement to which it is a Party.

Article 54
Powers of the Committee of Ministers

Nothing in this Convention shall prejudice the powers conferred on the Committee of Ministers by the Statute of the Council of Europe.

Article 55
Exclusion of other means of dispute settlement

The High Contracting Parties agree that, except by special agreement, they will not avail themselves of treaties, conventions or declarations in force between them for the purpose of submitting, by way of petition, a dispute arising out of the interpretation or application of this Convention to a means of settlement other than those provided for in this Convention.

Article 56
Territorial application

1 Any State may at the time of its ratification or at any time thereafter declare by notification addressed to the Secretary General of the Council of Europe that the present Convention shall, subject to paragraph 4 of this Article, extend to all or any of the territories for whose international relations it is responsible.

2 The Convention shall extend to the territory or territories named in the notification as from the thirtieth day after the receipt of this notification by the Secretary General of the Council of Europe.

3 The provisions of this Convention shall be applied in such territories with due regard, however, to local requirements.

4 Any State which has made a declaration in accordance with paragraph 1 of this article may at any time thereafter declare on behalf of one or more of the territories to which the declaration relates that it accepts the competence of the Court to receive applications from individuals, non-governmental organisations or groups of individuals as provided by Article 34 of the Convention.

Article 57
Reservations

1 Any State may, when signing this Convention or when depositing its instrument of ratification, make a reservation in respect of any particular provision of the Convention to the extent that any law then in force in its territory is not in conformity with the provision. Reservations of a general character shall not be permitted under this article.

2 Any reservation made under this article shall contain a brief statement of the law concerned.

Article 58
Denunciation

1 A High Contracting Party may denounce the present Convention only after the expiry of five years from the date on which it became a party to it and after six months' notice contained in a notification addressed to the Secretary General of the Council of Europe, who shall inform the other High Contracting Parties.

2 Such a denunciation shall not have the effect of releasing the High Contracting Party concerned from its obligations under this Convention in respect of any act which, being capable of constituting a violation of such obligations, may have been performed by it before the date at which the denunciation became effective.

3 Any High Contracting Party which shall cease to be a member of the Council of Europe shall cease to be a Party to this Convention under the same conditions.

4 The Convention may be denounced in accordance with the provisions of the preceding paragraphs in respect of any territory to which it has been declared to extend under the terms of Article 56.

Article 59
Signature and ratification

1 This Convention shall be open to the signature of the members of the Council of Europe. It shall be ratified. Ratifications shall be deposited with the Secretary General of the Council of Europe.

2 The present Convention shall come into force after the deposit of ten instruments of ratification.

3 As regards any signatory ratifying subsequently, the Convention shall come into force at the date of the deposit of its instrument of ratification.

4 The Secretary General of the Council of Europe shall notify all the members of the Council of Europe of the entry into force of the Convention, the names of the High Contracting Parties who have ratified it, and the deposit of all instruments of ratification which may be effected subsequently.

Done at Rome this 4th day of November 1950, in English and French, both texts being equally authentic, in a single copy which shall remain deposited in the archives of the Council of Europe. The Secretary General shall transmit certified copies to each of the signatories.

SCHEDULE 2
PROTOCOL TO THE CONVENTION FOR THE PROTECTION OF HUMAN RIGHTS AND FUNDAMENTAL FREEDOMS

Section 1

Paris, 20.III.1952

THE GOVERNMENTS SIGNATORY HERETO, being members of the Council of Europe,

Being resolved to take steps to ensure the collective enforcement of certain rights and freedoms other than those already included in Section I of the Convention for the Protection of Human Rights and Fundamental Freedoms signed at Rome on 4 November 1950 (hereinafter referred to as "the Convention"),

Have agreed as follows:

Article 1
Protection of property

Every natural or legal person is entitled to the peaceful enjoyment of his possessions. No one shall be deprived of his possessions except in the public interest and subject to the conditions provided for by law and by the general principles of international law.

The preceding provisions shall not, however, in any way impair the right of a State to enforce such laws as it deems necessary to control the use of property in accordance with the general interest or to secure the payment of taxes or other contributions or penalties.

Article 2
Right to education

No person shall be denied the right to education. In the exercise of any functions which it assumes in relation to education and to teaching, the State shall respect the right of parents to ensure such education and teaching in conformity with their own religious and philosophical convictions.

Article 3
Right to free elections

The High Contracting Parties undertake to hold free elections at reasonable intervals by secret ballot, under conditions which will ensure the free expression of the opinion of the people in the choice of the legislature.

Article 4
Territorial application

Any High Contracting Party may at the time of signature or ratification or at any time thereafter communicate to the Secretary General of the Council of Europe a declaration stating the extent to which it undertakes that the provisions of the present Protocol shall apply to such of the territories for the international relations of which it is responsible as are named therein.

Any High Contracting Party which has communicated a declaration in virtue of the preceding paragraph may from time to time communicate a further declaration modifying the terms of any former declaration or terminating the application of the provisions of this Protocol in respect of any territory.

A declaration made in accordance with this article shall be deemed to have been made in accordance with paragraph 1 of Article 56 of the Convention.

Article 5
Relationship to the Convention

As between the High Contracting Parties the provisions of Articles 1, 2, 3 and 4 of this Protocol shall be regarded as additional articles to the Convention and all the provisions of the Convention shall apply accordingly.

Article 6
Signature and ratification

This Protocol shall be open for signature by the members of the Council of Europe, who are the signatories of the Convention; it shall be ratified at the same time as or after the ratification of the Convention. It shall enter into force after the deposit of ten instruments of ratification. As regards any signatory ratifying subsequently, the Protocol shall enter into force at the date of the deposit of its instrument of ratification.

The instruments of ratification shall be deposited with the Secretary General of the Council of Europe, who will notify all members of the names of those who have ratified.

Done at Paris on the 20th day of March 1952, in English and French, both texts being equally authentic, in a single copy which shall remain deposited in the archives of the Council of Europe. The Secretary General shall transmit certified copies to each of the signatory governments.

SCHEDULE 3
PROTOCOL NO. 4 TO THE CONVENTION FOR THE PROTECTION OF HUMAN RIGHTS AND FUNDAMENTAL FREEDOMS SECURING CERTAIN RIGHTS AND FREEDOMS OTHER THAN THOSE ALREADY INCLUDED IN THE CONVENTION AND IN THE FIRST PROTOCOL THERETO

Section 1

Strasbourg, 16.IX.1963

THE GOVERNMENTS SIGNATORY HERETO, being members of the Council of Europe,

Being resolved to take steps to ensure the collective enforcement of certain rights and freedoms other than those already included in Section 1 of the Convention for the Protection of Human Rights and Fundamental Freedoms signed at Rome on 4th November 1950 (hereinafter referred to as the "Convention") and in Articles 1 to 3 of the First Protocol to the Convention signed at Paris on 20th March 1952,

Have agreed as follows:

Article 1
Prohibition of imprisonment for debt

No one shall be deprived of his liberty merely on the ground of inability to fulfil a contractual obligation.

Article 2
Freedom of movement

1 Everyone lawfully within the territory of a State shall, within that territory, have the right to liberty of movement and freedom to choose his residence.

2 Everyone shall be free to leave any country, including his own.

3 No restrictions shall be placed on the exercise of these rights other than such as are in accordance with law and are necessary in a democratic society in the interests of national security or public safety, for the maintenance of *ordre public*, for the prevention of crime, for the protection of health or morals, or for the protection of the rights and freedoms of others.

4 The rights set forth in paragraph 1 may also be subject, in particular areas, to restrictions imposed in accordance with law and justified by the public interest in a democratic society.

Article 3
Prohibition of expulsion of nationals

1 No one shall be expelled, by means either of an individual or of a collective measure, from the territory of the State of which he is a national.

2 No one shall be deprived of the right to enter the territory of the state of which he is a national.

Article 4
Prohibition of collective expulsion of aliens

Collective expulsion of aliens is prohibited.

Article 5
Territorial application

1 Any High Contracting Party may, at the time of signature or ratification of this Protocol, or at any time thereafter, communicate to the Secretary General of the Council of Europe a declaration stating the extent to which it undertakes that the provisions of this Protocol shall apply to such of the territories for the international relations of which it is responsible as are named therein.

2 Any High Contracting Party which has communicated a declaration in virtue of the preceding paragraph may, from time to time, communicate a further declaration modifying the terms of any former declaration or terminating the application of the provisions of this Protocol in respect of any territory.

3 A declaration made in accordance with this article shall be deemed to have been made in accordance with paragraph 1 of Article 56 of the Convention.

4 The territory of any State to which this Protocol applies by virtue of ratification or acceptance by that State, and each territory to which this Protocol is applied by virtue of a declaration by that State under this article, shall be treated as separate territories for the purpose of the references in Articles 2 and 3 to the territory of a State.

5 Any State which has made a declaration in accordance with paragraph 1 or 2 of this Article may at any time thereafter declare on behalf of one or more of the territories to which the declaration relates that it accepts the competence of the Court to receive applications from individuals, non-governmental organisations or groups of individuals as provided in Article 34 of the Convention in respect of all or any of Articles 1 to 4 of this Protocol.

Article 6
Relationship to the Convention

As between the High Contracting Parties the provisions of Articles 1 to 5 of this Protocol shall be regarded as additional articles to the Convention, and all the provisions of the Convention shall apply accordingly.

Article 7
Signature and ratification

1 This Protocol shall be open for signature by the members of the Council of Europe who are the signatories of the Convention; it shall be ratified at the same time as or after the ratification of the Convention. It shall enter into force after the deposit of five instruments of ratification. As regards any signatory ratifying subsequently, the Protocol shall enter into force at the date of the deposit of its instrument of ratification.

2 The instruments of ratification shall be deposited with the Secretary General of the Council of Europe, who will notify all members of the names of those who have ratified.

In witness whereof the undersigned, being duly authorised thereto, have signed this Protocol.

Done at Strasbourg, this 16th day of September 1963, in English and in French, both texts being equally authoritative, in a single copy which shall remain deposited in the archives of the Council of Europe. The Secretary General shall transmit certified copies to each of the signatory states.

SCHEDULE 4
PROTOCOL NO. 6 TO THE CONVENTION FOR THE PROTECTION OF HUMAN RIGHTS AND FUNDAMENTAL FREEDOMS CONCERNING THE ABOLITION OF THE DEATH PENALTY

Section 1

Strasbourg, 28.IV.1983

THE MEMBER STATES OF THE COUNCIL OF EUROPE, signatory to this Protocol to the Convention for the Protection of Human Rights and Fundamental Freedoms, signed at Rome on 4 November 1950 (hereinafter referred to as "the Convention"),

Considering that the evolution that has occurred in several member States of the Council of Europe expresses a general tendency in favour of abolition of the death penalty;

Have agreed as follows:

Article 1
Abolition of the death penalty

The death penalty shall be abolished. No one shall be condemned to such penalty or executed.

Article 2
Death penalty in time of war

A State may make provision in its law for the death penalty in respect of acts committed in time of war or of imminent threat of war; such penalty shall be applied only in the instances laid down in the law and in accordance with its provisions. The State shall communicate to the Secretary General of the Council of Europe the relevant provisions of that law.

Article 3
Prohibition of derogations

No derogation from the provisions of this Protocol shall be made under Article 15 of the Convention.

Article 4
Prohibition of reservations

No reservation may be made under Article 57 of the Convention in respect of the provisions of this Protocol.

Article 5
Territorial application

1 Any State may at the time of signature or when depositing its instrument of ratification, acceptance or approval, specify the territory or territories to which this Protocol shall apply.

2 Any State may at any later date, by a declaration addressed to the Secretary General of the Council of Europe, extend the application of this Protocol to any other territory specified in

the declaration. In respect of such territory the Protocol shall enter into force on the first day of the month following the date of receipt of such declaration by the Secretary General.

3 Any declaration made under the two preceding paragraphs may, in respect of any territory specified in such declaration, be withdrawn by a notification addressed to the Secretary General. The withdrawal shall become effective on the first day of the month following the date of receipt of such notification by the Secretary General.

Article 6
Relationship to the Convention

As between the States Parties the provisions of Articles 1 and 5 of this Protocol shall be regarded as additional articles to the Convention and all the provisions of the Convention shall apply accordingly.

Article 7
Signature and ratification

The Protocol shall be open for signature by the member States of the Council of Europe, signatories to the Convention. It shall be subject to ratification, acceptance or approval. A member State of the Council of Europe may not ratify, accept or approve this Protocol unless it has, simultaneously or previously, ratified the Convention. Instruments of ratification, acceptance or approval shall be deposited with the Secretary General of the Council of Europe.

Article 8
Entry into force

1 This Protocol shall enter into force on the first day of the month following the date on which five member States of the Council of Europe have expressed their consent to be bound by the Protocol in accordance with the provisions of Article 7.

2 In respect of any member State which subsequently expresses its consent to be bound by it, the Protocol shall enter into force on the first day of the month following the date of the deposit of the instrument of ratification, acceptance or approval.

Article 9
Depositary functions

The Secretary General of the Council of Europe shall notify the member States of the Council of:

a any signature;

b the deposit of any instrument of ratification, acceptance or approval;

c any date of entry into force of this Protocol in accordance with Articles 5 and 8;

d any other act, notification or communication relating to this Protocol.

In witness where of the undersigned, being duly authorised thereto, have signed this Protocol.

Done at Strasbourg, this 28th day of April 1983, in English and in French, both texts being equally authentic, in a single copy which shall be deposited in the archives of the Council of Europe. The Secretary General of the Council of Europe shall transmit certified copies to each member State of the Council of Europe.

SCHEDULE 5
PROTOCOL NO. 7 TO THE CONVENTION FOR THE PROTECTION OF HUMAN RIGHTS AND FUNDAMENTAL FREEDOMS

Section 1

Strasbourg, 22.XI.1984

The member States of the Council of Europe signatory hereto,

Being resolved to take further steps to ensure the collective enforcement of certain rights and freedoms by means of the Convention for the Protection of Human Rights and Fundamental Freedoms signed at Rome on 4 November 1950 (hereinafter referred to as "the Convention"),

Have agreed as follows:

Article 1
Procedural safeguards relating to expulsion of aliens

1 An alien lawfully resident in the territory of a State shall not be expelled therefrom except in pursuance of a decision reached in accordance with law and shall be allowed:

    a to submit reasons against his expulsion,

    b to have his case reviewed, and

    c to be represented for these purposes before the competent authority or a person or persons designated by that authority.

2 An alien may be expelled before the exercise of his rights under paragraph 1.a, b and c of this Article, when such expulsion is necessary in the interests of public order or is grounded on reasons of national security.

Article 2
Right of appeal in criminal matters

1 Everyone convicted of a criminal offence by a tribunal shall have the right to have his conviction or sentence reviewed by a higher tribunal. The exercise of this right, including the grounds on which it may be exercised, shall be governed by law.

2 This right may be subject to exceptions in regard to offences of a minor character, as prescribed by law, or in cases in which the person concerned was tried in the first instance by the highest tribunal or was convicted following an appeal against acquittal.

Article 3
Compensation for wrongful conviction

When a person has by a final decision been convicted of a criminal offence and when subsequently his conviction has been reversed, or he has been pardoned, on the ground that a new or newly discovered fact shows conclusively that there has been a miscarriage of justice, the person who has suffered punishment as a result of such conviction shall be compensated according to the law or the practice of the State concerned, unless it is proved that the non-disclosure of the unknown fact in time is wholly or partly attributable to him.

Article 4
Right not to be tried or punished twice

1 No one shall be liable to be tried or punished again in criminal proceedings under the jurisdiction of the same State for an offence for which he has already been finally acquitted or convicted in accordance with the law and penal procedure of that State.

2 The provisions of the preceding paragraph shall not prevent the reopening of the case in accordance with the law and penal procedure of the State concerned, if there is evidence of new or newly discovered facts, or if there has been a fundamental defect in the previous proceedings, which could affect the outcome of the case.

3 No derogation from this Article shall be made under Article 15 of the Convention.

Article 5
Equality between spouses

Spouses shall enjoy equality of rights and responsibilities of a private law character between them, and in their relations with their children, as to marriage, during marriage and in the event of its dissolution. This Article shall not prevent States from taking such measures as are necessary in the interests of the children.

Article 6
Territorial application

1 Any State may at the time of signature or when depositing its instrument of ratification, acceptance or approval, specify the territory or territories to which the Protocol shall apply and state the extent to which it undertakes that the provisions of this Protocol shall apply to such territory or territories.

2 Any State may at any later date, by a declaration addressed to the Secretary General of the Council of Europe, extend the application of this Protocol to any other territory specified in the declaration. In respect of such territory the Protocol shall enter into force on the first day of the month following the expiration of a period of two months after the date of receipt by the Secretary General of such declaration.

3 Any declaration made under the two preceding paragraphs may, in respect of any territory specified in such declaration, be withdrawn or modified by a notification addressed to the Secretary General. The withdrawal or modification shall become effective on the first day of the month following the expiration of a period of two months after the date of receipt of such notification by the Secretary General.

4 A declaration made in accordance with this Article shall be deemed to have been made in accordance with paragraph 1 of Article 56 of the Convention.

5 The territory of any State to which this Protocol applies by virtue of ratification, acceptance or approval by that State, and each territory to which this Protocol is applied by virtue of a declaration by that State under this Article, may be treated as separate territories for the purpose of the reference in Article 1 to the territory of a State.

6 Any State which has made a declaration in accordance with paragraph 1 or 2 of this Article may at any time thereafter declare on behalf of one or more of the territories to which the declaration relates that it accepts the competence of the Court to receive applications from

individuals, non-governmental organisations or groups of individuals as provided in Article 34 of the Convention in respect of Articles 1 to 5 of this Protocol.

Article 7
Relationship to the Convention

As between the States Parties, the provisions of Articles 1 to 6 of this Protocol shall be regarded as additional Articles to the Convention, and all the provisions of the Convention shall apply accordingly.

Article 8
Signature and ratification

This Protocol shall be open for signature by member States of the Council of Europe which have signed the Convention. It is subject to ratification, acceptance or approval. A member State of the Council of Europe may not ratify, accept or approve this Protocol without previously or simultaneously ratifying the Convention. Instruments of ratification, acceptance or approval shall be deposited with the Secretary General of the Council of Europe.

Article 9
Entry into force

1 This Protocol shall enter into force on the first day of the month following the expiration of a period of two months after the date on which seven member States of the Council of Europe have expressed their consent to be bound by the Protocol in accordance with the provisions of Article 8.

2 In respect of any member State which subsequently expresses its consent to be bound by it, the Protocol shall enter into force on the first day of the month following the expiration of a period of two months after the date of the deposit of the instrument of ratification, acceptance or approval.

Article 10
Depositary functions

The Secretary General of the Council of Europe shall notify all the member States of the Council of Europe of:

a any signature;
b the deposit of any instrument of ratification, acceptance or approval;
c any date of entry into force of this Protocol in accordance with Articles 6 and 9;
d any other act, notification or declaration relating to this Protocol.

In witness whereof the undersigned, being duly authorised thereto, have signed this Protocol.

Done at Strasbourg, this 22nd day of November 1984, in English and French, both texts being equally authentic, in a single copy which shall be deposited in the archives of the Council of Europe. The Secretary General of the Council of Europe shall transmit certified copies to each member State of the Council of Europe.

European Arrest Warrant Act 2003

Number 45 of 2003

ARRANGEMENT OF SECTIONS

PART 1
PRELIMINARY AND GENERAL

Section

1. Short title and commencement.

2. Interpretation.

3. Designated States.

4. Application of Act.

4A

5. Corresponding offences.

6. Central Authority in the State.

7. Orders and regulations.

8. Expenses.

PART 2
EUROPEAN ARREST WARRANT

CHAPTER 1
EUROPEAN ARREST WARRANT RECEIVED IN STATE

9. Executing judicial authority in the State.

10. Obligation to surrender.

11. European arrest warrant.

12. Transmission of European arrest warrant.

13. Application to High Court for endorsement to execute European arrest warrant.

14. Arrest without warrant for surrender purposes.

15. Consent to surrender.

16. Committal of person named in European arrest warrant.

17. European arrest warrant relating to more than one offence.

18. Postponement of surrender.

19. Conditional surrender.

20. Additional documentation and information.

21. Movement of persons detained under this Act.

22. Rule of specialty disapplied.

23. Surrender of person by issuing state to other Member State.

24. Surrender of person by issuing state to third state.

25. Searches for purposes of European arrest warrant.

26. Handing over of property.

27. Remand.

28. Transit.

29. Multiple European arrest warrants.

30. European arrest warrants and requests for extradition.

CHAPTER 2
ISSUE OF EUROPEAN ARREST WARRANT BY STATE

31. Definition.

32. Offences to which Article 2.2 of Framework Decision applies.

33. Issue of European arrest warrant by court in State.

34. Transmission of European arrest warrant issued in State.

35. Arrest of person surrendered to State.

36. Deduction of period of detention in executing state from sentence.

PART 3
PROHIBITION ON SURRENDER

37. Fundamental rights.

38. Offence in respect of which a person shall not be surrendered.

39. Pardon or amnesty.

40. Passage of time from commission of offence.

41. Double jeopardy.

42. Proceedings in the State.

43. Age.

44. Commission of offence outside issuing state.

45. Persons convicted in absentia.

45A Identification procedures.

45B Transfer of persons to state from which surrendered.

45C Technical flaws in applications for surrender.

46. Immunity from prosecution.

PART 4
MISCELLANEOUS

47. Amendment of section 3 of Act of 1965.

48. Laying of orders under Act of 1965 before Houses of Oireachtas.

49. Application of Part II of Act of 1965.

50. Repeal of Part III of Act of 1965.

51. Amendment of Extradition (European Convention on the Suppression of Terrorism) Act 1987.

52. Amendment of Act of 2001.

SCHEDULE
PART A
TEXT NOT REPRODUCED HERE

PART B
TEXT IN THE ENGLISH LANGUAGE OF COUNCIL FRAMEWORK DECISION OF 13 JUNE 2002 ON THE EUROPEAN ARREST WARRANT AND THE SURRENDER PROCEDURES BETWEEN MEMBER STATES.

AN ACT TO GIVE EFFECT TO COUNCIL FRAMEWORK DECISION OF 13 JUNE 2002[1] ON THE EUROPEAN ARREST WARRANT AND THE SURRENDER PROCEDURES BETWEEN MEMBER STATES; TO AMEND THE EXTRADITION ACT 1965 AND CERTAIN OTHER ENACTMENTS; AND TO PROVIDE FOR MATTERS CONNECTED THEREWITH. [28th December, 2003]

BE IT ENACTED BY THE OIREACHTAS AS FOLLOWS:

PART 1
PRELIMINARY AND GENERAL

1   Short title and commencement

(1) This Act may be cited as the European Arrest Warrant Act 2003.

(2) This Act comes into operation on 1 January 2004.

2   Interpretation

(1) In this Act, except where the context otherwise requires—

"Act of 1965" means the Extradition Act 1965;

"Act of 2001" means the Extradition (European Union Conventions) Act 2001;

["alert" means an alert entered in the SIS for the arrest and surrender, on foot of a European arrest warrant, of the person named therein;][1]

"Central Authority in the State" shall be read in accordance with section 6;

[Council Decision ' means Council Decision 2007/533/JHA of 12 June 2007 on the establishment, operation and use of the second generation Schengen Information System;][1]

"Eurojust" means the body established by Council Decision of 28 February 2002 setting up Eurojust with a view to reinforcing the fight against serious crime;

"European arrest warrant" means a warrant, order or decision of a judicial authority of a Member State, issued under such laws as give effect to the Framework Decision in that Member State, for the arrest and surrender by the State to that Member State of a person in respect of an offence committed or alleged to have been committed by him or her under the law of that Member State;

"European Communities" has the same meaning as it has in the European Communities Act 1972;

[...][2];

"Framework Decision" means Council Framework Decision of 13 June 2002 on the European arrest warrant and the surrender procedures between Member States, the text of which—

    (a) in the Irish language, is set out in Part A of the Schedule, and

    (b) in the English language, is set out in Part B of the Schedule;

"functions" includes powers and duties, and references to the performance of functions include, as respects powers and duties, references to the exercise of the powers and the carrying out of the duties;

"issuing judicial authority" means, in relation to a European arrest warrant, the judicial authority in the issuing state that issued the European arrest warrant concerned;

"issuing state" means, in relation to a European arrest warrant, a Member State designated under section 3, a judical authority of which has issued that European arrest warrant;

"judicial authority" means the judge, magistrate or other person authorised under the law of the Member State concerned to perform functions the same as or similar to those performed under section 33 by a court in the State;

"Member State" means a Member State of the European Communities (other than the State) or Gibraltar;

"Minister" means the Minister for Justice, Equality and Law Reform;

["Schengen Convention" means the Convention implementing the Schengen Agreement of 14 June 1985 between the Governments of the States of the Benelux Economic Union, the Federal Republic of Germany and the French Republic on the gradual abolition of checks at their common borders done at Schengen on 19 June 1990 and includes any amendment to or modification of that Convention whether before or after the passing of this Act but does not include the Council Decision;

"SIS" means the system referred to in Title IV of the Schengen Convention or, as appropriate, the system established under Chapter 1 of the Council Decision;][1]

"third country" means a country other than the State or a Member State;

"true copy" shall be read in accordance with section 12(7).

(2) In this Act—

    (a) a reference to a section, Part or Schedule is a reference to a section or Part of, or a Schedule to, this Act, unless it is indicated that a reference to some other enactment is intended,

    (b) a reference to a subsection, paragraph or subparagraph is a reference to a subsection, paragraph or subparagraph of the provision in which the reference occurs, unless it is indicated that a reference to some other provision is intended, and

    (c) a reference to any enactment is a reference to that enactment as amended, extended or adapted, whether before or after the passing of this Act, by or under any subsequent enactment.

Amendments

1   Definitions inserted by Criminal Justice (Miscellaneous Provisions) Act 2009, s 4.

2   Definition deleted by Criminal Justice (Miscellaneous Provisions) Act 2009, s 4(c).

---

3   Designated States

(1) For the purposes of this Act, the Minister for Foreign Affairs may,
Member State that has, under its national law, given effect to the Framework ⌐

(2) The Minister for Foreign Affairs may, by order, amend or revoke an order unuⱱ.
section, including an order under this subsection.

4   Application of Act

(1) [...]¹ This Act shall apply in relation to an offence, whether committed or alleged to have
been committed before or after the commencement of this Act.

(2) ...²

(3) ...²

Amendments

1   Words deleted by Criminal Justice (Miscellaneous Provisions) Act 2009, s 5(a).

2   Subsections (2) and (3) deleted by Criminal Justice (Miscellaneous Provisions) Act 2009,
    s 5(b).

[4A   It shall be presumed that an issuing state will comply with the requirements of the
Framework Decision, unless the contrary is shown.]¹

Amendments

1   Section 4A inserted by Criminal Justice (Terrorist Offences) Act 2005, s 69.

5   Corresponding offences

[For the purposes of this Act, an offence specified in a European arrest warrant corresponds
to an offence under the law of the State, where the act or omission that constitutes the offence
so specified would, if committed in the State on the date on which the European arrest
warrant is issued, constitute an offence under the law of the State.]¹

Amendments

1   Section 5 substituted by Criminal Justice (Terrorist Offences) Act 2005, s 70.

6   Central Authority in the State

(1) The Minister shall be the Central Authority in the State for the purposes of this Act.

(2) The Minister may, by order, designate such persons as he or she considers appropriate to
perform such functions of the Central Authority in the State as are specified in the order and

fferent persons may be so designated to perform different functions of the Central Authority in the State.

(3) For so long as an order under subsection (2) remains in force, a reference in this Act to the Central Authority in the State shall, insofar as it relates to the performance of a function specified in the order, be construed as a reference to the person designated by the order to perform the function concerned.

(4) The Minister shall, by notice in writing, inform the General Secretariat of the Council of the European Union of the making of an order under this section and of the names of the persons designated under the order.

(5) The Minister may, by order, amend or revoke an order under this section (including an order under this subsection).

(6) The Central Authority in the State shall, in each year, prepare a report on the operation, in the preceding year, of Part 2, and shall cause copies of each such report to be laid before both Houses of the Oireachtas as soon as may be after it is so prepared.

7   Orders and regulations

Every order and regulation under this Act shall be laid before each House of the Oireachtas as soon as may be after it is made and, if a resolution annulling the order or regulation is passed by either such House within the next 21 days on which that House sits after the order or regulation is laid before it, the order or regulation shall be annulled accordingly, but without prejudice to anything previously done thereunder.

8   Expenses

The expenses incurred by the Minister in the administration of this Act shall, to such extent as may be sanctioned by the Minister for Finance, be paid out of moneys provided by the Oireachtas.

PART 2
EUROPEAN ARREST WARRANT

Chapter 1
European Arrest Warrant Received in State

9   Executing judicial authority in the State

For the purposes of the Framework Decision, the High Court shall be the executing judicial authority in the State.

10   Obligation to surrender

[Where a judicial authority in an issuing state [...]² issues a European arrest warrant in respect of a person—

    (a) against whom that state intends to bring proceedings for an offence to which the European arrest warrant relates,

    (b) who is the subject of proceedings in that state for an offence to which the European arrest warrant relates,

    (c) who has been convicted of, but not yet sentenced in respect of, an offence [in that state]³ to which the European arrest warrant relates, or

    (d)   on whom a sentence of imprisonment or detention has been imposed [in that state][3] in respect of an offence to which the European arrest warrant relates, [...][2]

that person shall, subject to and in accordance with the provisions of this Act and the Framework Decision, be arrested and surrendered to the issuing state.][1]

Amendments

1   Section 10 substituted by Criminal Justice (Terrorist Offences) Act 2005, s 71.

2   Words deleted by Criminal Justice (Miscellaneous Provisions) Act 2009, s 6.

3   Words inserted by Criminal Justice (Miscellaneous Provisions) Act 2009, s 6.

11   European arrest warrant

[(1) A European arrest warrant shall, in so far as is practicable, be in the form set out in the Annex to the Framework Decision.

(1A) Subject to subsection (2A), a European arrest warrant shall specify—

    (a)   the name and the nationality of the person in respect of whom it is issued,

    (b)   the name of the judicial authority that issued the European arrest warrant, and the address of its principal office,

    (c)   the telephone number, fax number and email address (if any) of that judicial authority,

    (d)   the offence to which the European arrest warrant relates, including the nature and classification under the law of the issuing state of the offence concerned,

    (e)   that a conviction, sentence or detention order is immediately enforceable against the person, or that a warrant for his or her arrest, or other order of a judicial authority in the issuing state having the same effect, has been issued in respect of [one of the offences to which the European arrest warrant relates][2],

    (f)   the circumstances in which the offence was committed or is alleged to have been committed, including the time and place of its commission or alleged commission, and the degree of involvement or alleged degree of involvement of the person in the commission of the offence, and

    (g)   (i)   the penalties to which that person would, if convicted of the offence specified in the European arrest warrant, be liable,

         (ii)   where that person has been convicted of the offence specified in the European arrest warrant but has not yet been sentenced, the penalties to which he or she is liable in respect of the offence, or

         (iii)   where that person has been convicted of the offence specified in the European arrest warrant and a sentence has been imposed in respect thereof, the penalties of which that sentence consists.][1]

(2) Where it is not practicable for the European arrest warrant to be in the form referred to in subsection (1), it shall include such information, additional to the information specified in subsection [(1A)],[2] as would be required to be provided were it in that form.

[(2A) If any of the information to which subsection (1A) (inserted by section 72(a) of the Criminal Justice (Terrorist Offences) Act 2005) refers is not specified in the European arrest warrant, it may be specified in a separate document.][3]

(3) [...][4]

(4) For the avoidance of doubt, a European arrest warrant may be issued in respect of one or more than one offence.

Amendments

1   Subsection (1) substituted and subsection (1A) inserted by Criminal Justice (Terrorist Offences) Act 2005, s 72(a).

2   Words substituted by Criminal Justice (Miscellaneous Provisions) Act 2009, s 7.

3   Subsection (2A) (as inserted Criminal Justice (Terrorist Offences) Act 2005, s 72(a)) substituted by Criminal Justice (Miscellaneous Provisions) Act 2009, s 7.

4   Subsection (3) deleted by Criminal Justice (Terrorist Offences) Act 2005, s 72(c).

---

12   Transmission of European arrest warrant

(1) A European arrest warrant shall be transmitted by, or on behalf of, the issuing judicial authority to the Central Authority in the State and, where the European arrest warrant is in a language other than the Irish language, the English language or such other language as the Minister may by order prescribe, a translation of the European arrest warrant into the Irish language or the English language shall be so transmitted with the European arrest warrant.

(2) Such undertakings as are required to be given under this Act shall be transmitted by, or on behalf of, the [issuing judicial authority or the issuing state, as may be appropriate][1] to the Central Authority in the State, and where any such undertaking is in a language other than the Irish language, the English language or such other languages as the Minister may by order prescribe, a translation of that undertaking into the Irish language or the English language shall be so transmitted with the undertaking.

(3) A European arrest warrant, or an undertaking required to be given under this Act [or any other document to be transmitted for the purposes of this Act][2], may be transmitted to the Central Authority in the State by—

     (a)   delivering it to the Central Authority in the State, or

     [(b)   any means capable of producing a written record under conditions allowing the Central Authority in the State to establish its authenticity.][3]

[(3A) An undertaking required under this Act may be set out in the European arrest warrant or in a separate document.][4]

[...][5]

[(7) For the purposes of this Act, a document shall be deemed to be a true copy of an original document if it has been certified as a true copy of the original document by—

     (a)   the issuing judicial authority, or

     (b)   an officer of the central authority of the issuing state.][6]

(8) In proceedings to which this Act applies, a document that purports to be—

(a) a European arrest warrant issued by a judicial authority in the issuing state,

(b) an undertaking required under this Act of [an issuing judicial authority or the issuing state, as may be appropriate,]⁷

[(c) a document referred to in section 11(2A) (inserted by section 72(b) of the Criminal Justice (Terrorist Offences) Act 2005),]⁸

(d) a true copy of such a document,

shall be received in evidence without further proof.

(9) In proceedings to which this Act applies, a document that purports to be a [....]⁹ true copy of a European arrest warrant, undertaking or translation referred to in subsection (8) shall, unless the contrary is shown, be evidence of the European arrest warrant, undertaking or translation concerned, as the case may be.

(10) The Minister may, for the purposes of ensuring the accuracy of documents transmitted in accordance with this section, make regulations prescribing—

(a) the procedures that shall be followed in connection with the transmission of documents in accordance with this section, and

(b) that such features as are specified in the regulations shall be present in any equipment being used in that connection.

[(11) In this section 'European arrest warrant' includes a document referred to in section 11(2A) (inserted by section 72(b) of the Criminal Justice (Terrorist Offences) Act 2005).]¹⁰

Amendments

1 Words substituted by Criminal Justice (Terrorist Offences) Act 2005, s 73(a).

2 Words inserted by Criminal Justice (Miscellaneous Provisions) Act 2009, s 8(a)(i).

3 Subsection (3)(b) substituted by Criminal Justice (Miscellaneous Provisions) Act 2009, s 8(a)(ii).

4 Subsection (3A) inserted by Criminal Justice (Terrorist Offences) Act 2005, s 73(b).

5 Subsections (4), (5) and (6) deleted by Criminal Justice (Miscellaneous Provisions) Act 2009, s 8(b).

6 Subsection (7) substituted by Criminal Justice (Miscellaneous Provisions) Act 2009, s 8(c).

7 Words substituted by Criminal Justice (Terrorist Offences) Act 2005, s 73(f).

8 Subsection (8)(c) inserted by Criminal Justice (Terrorist Offences) Act 2005, s 73(g).

9 Words deleted by Criminal Justice (Miscellaneous Provisions) Act 2009, s 8(d).

10 Subsection (11) substituted by Criminal Justice (Terrorist Offences) Act 2005, s 73(h).

13 Application to High Court for endorsement to execute European arrest warrant

(1) The Central Authority in the State shall, as soon as may be after it receives a European arrest warrant transmitted to it in accordance with section 12, apply, or cause an application to be made, to the High Court for the endorsement by it of the European arrest warrant, or a [...]¹ true copy thereof, for execution of the European arrest warrant concerned.

(2) If, upon an application under subsection (1), the High Court is satisfied that, in relation to a European arrest warrant, there has been compliance with the provisions of this Act, it may endorse—

(a) the European arrest warrant for execution, or

(b) [...]²

(3) A European arrest warrant may, upon there being compliance with subsection (2), be executed by any member of the Garda Síochána in any part of the State and may be so executed notwithstanding that it is not in the possession of the member when he or she executes the European arrest warrant, and the warrant, [...]³ the true copy of the warrant, as the case may be, endorsed in accordance with subsection (2), shall be shown to and a copy thereof given to, the person arrested at the time of his or her arrest or, if the warrant, [...]³ true copy, as the case may be, is not then in the possession of the member, not later than 24 hours after the person's arrest.

(4) A person arrested under a European arrest warrant shall, upon his or her arrest, be informed of his or her right to—

(a) consent to his or her being surrendered to the issuing state under section 15,

(b) obtain, or be provided with, professional legal advice and representation, and

(c) where appropriate, obtain, or be provided with, the services of an interpreter.

(5) A person arrested under a European arrest warrant shall, as soon as may be after his or her arrest, be brought before the High Court, and the High Court shall, if satisfied that that person is the person in respect of whom the European arrest warrant was issued—

(a) remand the person in custody or on bail (and, for that purpose, the High Court shall have the same powers in relation to remand as it would have if the person were brought before it charged with an indictable offence),

(b) fix a date for the purpose of section 16 (being a date that falls not later than 21 days after the date of the person's arrest), and

(c) inform the person that he or she has the right to—

(i) consent to his or her surrender to the issuing state under section 15,

(ii) obtain, or be provided with, professional legal advice and representation, and

(iii) where appropriate, obtain, or be provided with, the services of an interpreter.

Amendments

1 Words deleted by Criminal Justice (Miscellaneous Provisions) Act 2009, s 9(a).

2 Paragraph 2(b) deleted by Criminal Justice (Miscellaneous Provisions) Act 2009, s 9(b).

3 Words deleted by Criminal Justice (Miscellaneous Provisions) Act 2009, s 9(c).

14   [Arrest without warrant for surrender purposes.

(1) A member of the Garda Síochána may arrest any person without a warrant that the member believes, on reasonable grounds, to be a person named in an alert.

(2) A person arrested under this section shall, upon his or her arrest, be informed, in ordinary language, of the reason for the arrest and of his or her right to—

(a) obtain or be provided with professional legal advice and representation, and

(b) where appropriate, obtain or be provided with the services of an interpreter.

(3) A person arrested under this section shall, as soon as may be after his or her arrest—

(a) be furnished with a copy of the alert, and

(b) be brought before the High Court, which court shall, if satisfied that he or she is the person named in the alert—

    (i) inform the person of his or her right to—

        (I) obtain or be provided with professional legal advice and representation, and

        (II) where appropriate, obtain or be provided with the services of an interpreter,

    and

    (ii) remand the person in custody or, at its discretion, on bail for a period not exceeding 14 days (and for that purpose the High Court shall have the same powers in relation to remand as it would have if the person were brought before it charged with an indictable offence) for production to the High Court of the European arrest warrant on foot of which the alert was entered.

(4) Where, in respect of a person remanded in custody or on bail under subsection (3), a European arrest warrant is transmitted to the Central Authority in the State pursuant to section 12—

(a) that person shall be brought before the High Court as soon as may be,

(b) the European arrest warrant shall be produced to the High Court,

(c) a copy shall be given to that person, and

(d) the High Court, if satisfied that the provisions of this Act have been complied with and that the person before it is the person in respect of whom the European arrest warrant was issued, shall—

    (i) inform the person of his or her right to consent to being surrendered to the issuing state under section 15, and

    (ii) if the person does not exercise his or her right to consent under paragraph (i)—

        (I) remand the person in custody or on bail (and for that purpose the High Court shall have the same powers in relation to remand as it would have if the person were brought before it charged with an indictable offence), and

        (II) fix a date for the purposes of section 16 within the period of 21 days next following.

(5) Where, in respect of a person remanded in custody or on bail under subsection (3), the European arrest warrant is not produced on the date fixed by the Court for the purpose under that subsection the person shall be released from custody.][1]

Amendments

2   Section 14 substituted by Criminal Justice (Miscellaneous Provisions) Act 2009, s 10.

15   Consent to surrender

[(1) Where a person is brought before the High Court under section 13, he or she may consent to his or her being surrendered to the issuing state and, if he or she so consents, the High Court shall—

(a) if the European arrest warrant, or a [...]² or true copy thereof, has been endorsed in accordance with section 13 for execution of the warrant,

(b) if it is satisfied that—

(i)   the person voluntarily consents to his or her being surrendered to the issuing state concerned and is aware of the consequences of his or her so consenting, and

(ii)   the person has obtained, or has been afforded the opportunity of obtaining or being provided with professional legal advice before consenting to his or her surrender,

(c) if it is not required, under section 21A, 22, 23 or 24 (inserted by sections 79, 80, 81 and 82 of the Criminal Justice (Terrorist Offences) Act 2005), to refuse to surrender the person under this Act, and

(d) if the surrender of the person is not prohibited by Part 3 or the Framework Decision (including the recitals thereto),

make an order directing that the person be surrendered to such other person as is duly authorised by the issuing state to receive him or her.

(2) Where a person is brought before the High Court under section 14, he or she may consent to his or her being surrendered to the issuing state and, if he or she so consents, the High Court shall—

(a) upon production to the High Court of the European arrest warrant or [a true copy]³ thereof,

(b) if it is satisfied that—

(i)   the person voluntarily consents to his or her being surrendered to the issuing state concerned and is aware of the consequences of his or her so consenting, and

(ii)   the person has obtained, or has been afforded the opportunity of obtaining or being provided with, professional legal advice and representation before consenting to his or her surrender,

(c) if it is not required, under section 21A, 22, 23 or 24 (inserted by sections 79, 80, 81 and 82 of the Criminal Justice (Terrorist Offences) Act 2005), to refuse to surrender the person under this Act, and

(d) if the surrender of the person is not prohibited by Part 3 or the Framework Decision (including the recitals thereto), make an order directing that the person be surrendered to such other person as is duly authorised by the issuing state to receive him or her.]¹

[(3) An order under this section shall take effect upon the expiration of 10 days beginning on the date of the making of the order or such earlier date as the High Court, upon the request of the person to whom the order applies, directs.]⁴

[(3A) An appeal against an order under this section or a decision not to make such an order may be brought in the Supreme Court if, and only if, the High Court certifies that the order or decision involves a point of law of exceptional public importance and that it is desirable in the public interest that an appeal should be taken to the Supreme Court.]⁵

(4) Where the High Court makes an order under this section, it shall—

    (a) inform the person to whom the order relates of his or her right to make a complaint under Article 40.4.2° of the Constitution at any time before his or her surrender to the issuing state,

    (b) record in writing that the person concerned has consented to his or her being surrendered to the issuing state concerned, and

    (c) commit the person to a prison (or, if the person is not more than 21 years of age, to a remand institution) pending the carrying out of the terms of the order.

(5) Subject to subsection (6)[, subsection (7)]⁶ and section 18, a person to whom an order for the time being in force under this section applies shall be surrendered to the issuing state concerned not later than 10 days after—

    [(a) the order takes effect in accordance with subsection (3) (inserted by section 75(b) of the Criminal Justice (Terrorist Offences) Act 2005), or]⁷

    (b) such date (being a date that falls after the expiration of that period) as may be agreed by the Central Authority in the State and the issuing state.

[(6) Where a person—

    (a) appeals an order made under this section, or

    (b) makes a complaint under Article 40.4.2° of the Constitution,

he or she shall not be surrendered to the issuing state while proceedings relating to the appeal or complaint are pending.]⁸

[(7) Where a person (to whom an order for the time being in force under this section applies) is not surrendered to the issuing state within the relevant period specified in subsection (5) and the surrender is not prohibited by reason of subsection (6) the High Court may remand the person in custody or on bail for such further period as is necessary to effect the surrender unless it considers it would be unjust or oppressive to do so.]⁹

(8) Subsection (7) shall not apply if—

    (a) (i) the person has been sentenced to a term of imprisonment for an offence of which he or she was convicted in the State,

        (ii) on the date on which he or she would, but for this subsection, be entitled to be released from custody under subsection (7), all or part of that term of imprisonment remains unexpired, and

        (iii) the person is required to serve all or part of the remainder of that term of imprisonment,

        or

    (b) (i) the person has been charged with or convicted of an offence in the State, and

(ii) on the date on which he or she would, but for this paragraph, be entitled to be released from custody under subsection (7), he or she is required to be in custody by virtue of having been remanded in custody pending his or her being tried, or the imposition of sentence, in respect of that offence.

[(9) Where a person lodges an appeal pursuant to subsection (3A), the High Court may remand the person in custody or on bail pending the hearing of the appeal and, for that purpose, the High Court shall have the same powers in relation to remand as it would have if the person were brought before it charged with an indictable offence.][10]

Amendments

1 Subsections (1) and (2) substituted by Criminal Justice (Terrorist Offences) Act 2005, s 75(a).

2 Words deleted by Criminal Justice (Miscellaneous Provisions) Act 2009, s 11(a).

3 Words inserted by Criminal Justice (Miscellaneous Provisions) Act 2009, s 11(b).

4 Subsection (3) substituted by Criminal Justice (Terrorist Offences) Act 2005, s 75(b).

5 Subsection (3A) inserted by Criminal Justice (Miscellaneous Provisions) Act 2009, s 11(c).

6 Words inserted by Criminal Justice (Miscellaneous Provisions) Act 2009, s 11(d).

7 Subsection (5)(a) substituted by Criminal Justice (Terrorist Offences) Act 2005, s 75(c).

8 Subsection (6) substituted by Criminal Justice (Miscellaneous Provisions) Act 2009, s 11(e).

9 Subsection (7) substituted by Criminal Justice (Miscellaneous Provisions) Act 2009, s 11(f).

10 Subsection (9) substituted by Criminal Justice (Miscellaneous Provisions) Act 2009, s 11(g).

16   Committal of person named in European arrest warrant

[(1) Where a person does not consent to his or her surrender to the issuing state [...][2] the High Court may, upon such date as is fixed under section 13 or such later date as it considers appropriate, make an order directing that the person be surrendered to such other person as is duly authorised by the issuing state to receive him or her, provided that—

(a) the High Court is satisfied that the person before it is the person in respect of whom the European arrest warrant was issued,

(b) the European arrest warrant, or a [...][2] true copy thereof, has been endorsed in accordance with section 13 for execution of the warrant,

(c) where appropriate, an undertaking under section 45 or a [...][2] true copy thereof is provided to the court,

(d) the High Court is not required, under section 21A, 22, 23 or 24 (inserted by sections 79, 80, 81 and 82 of the Criminal Justice (Terrorist Offences) Act 2005), to refuse to surrender the person under this Act, and

(e) the surrender of the person is not prohibited by Part 3 or the Framework Decision (including the recitals thereto).][1]

[(2) Where a person does not consent to his or her surrender to the issuing state [...][4] the High Court may, upon such date as is fixed under section 14 or such later date as it considers appropriate, make an order directing that the person be surrendered to such other person as is duly authorised by the issuing state to receive him or her, provided that—

(a) the European arrest warrant and, where appropriate, an undertaking under section 45, or [...]⁴ true copies thereof are provided to the court,

(b) the High Court is satisfied that the person before it is the person in respect of whom the European arrest warrant was issued,

(c) the High Court is not required, under section 21A, 22, 23 or 24 (inserted by sections 79, 80, 81 and 82 of the Criminal Justice (Terrorist Offences) Act 2005), to refuse to surrender the person under this Act, and

(d) the surrender of the person is not prohibited by Part 3 or the Framework Decision (including the recitals thereto).]³

[(2A) Where the High Court does not—

(a) make an order under subsection (1) on the date fixed under section 13, or

(b) make an order under subsection (2) on the date fixed under section 14,

it may remand the person before it in custody or on bail and, for those purposes, the High Court shall have the same powers in relation to remand as it would have if the person were brought before it charged with an indictable offence.]⁵

[(3) An order under this section shall take effect upon the expiration of 15 days beginning on the date of the making of the order or such earlier date as the High Court, upon the request of the person to whom the order applies, directs.]⁶

(4) When making an order under this section the High Court shall also make an order committing the person to a prison (or if he or she is not more than 21 years of age, to a remand institution) there to remain pending his or her surrender in accordance with the order under this section, and shall inform the person—

(a) that he or she will not, without his or her consent, be surrendered to the issuing state, before the expiration of the period of 15 days specified in subsection (3), and

(b) of his or her right to make a complaint under Article 40.4.2° of the Constitution at any time before his or her surrender to the issuing state.

(5) Subject to subsection (6)[, subsection (7)]⁷ and section 18, a person to whom an order for the time being in force under this section applies shall be surrendered to the issuing state not later than 10 days after—

[(a) the order takes effect in accordance with subsection (3) (inserted by section 76(d) of the Criminal Justice (Terrorist Offences) Act 2005), or]⁸

(b) such date (being a date that falls after the expiration of that period) as may be agreed by the Central Authority in the State and the issuing state.

[(6) Where a person—

(a) appeals an order made under this section, or

(b) makes a complaint under Article 40.4.2 of the Constitution,

he or she shall not be surrendered to the issuing state while proceedings relating to the appeal or complaint are pending.]⁹

[(7) Where a person (to whom an order for the time being in force under this section applies) is not surrendered to the issuing state within the relevant period specified in subsection (5) and the surrender is not prohibited by reason of subsection (6) the High Court may remand the person in custody or on bail for such further period as is necessary to effect the surrender unless it considers it would be unjust or oppressive to do so.]¹⁰

(8) Where the High Court decides not to make an order under this section—

(a) it shall give reasons for its decision, and

(b) the person shall, subject to subsection (9), be released from custody.

(9) [Subsections (7) and (8) shall not apply if]—[11]

(a) (i) the person has been sentenced to a term of imprisonment for an offence of which he or she was convicted in the State,

(ii) on the date on which he or she would, but for this subsection, be entitled to be released under [subsection (7) or (8)][11], all or part of the term of imprisonment remains unexpired, and

(iii) the person is required to serve all or part of the remainder of that term of imprisonment,

or

(b) (i) the person has been charged with or convicted of an offence in the State, and

(ii) on the date on which he or she would, but for this paragraph, be entitled to be released from custody under subsection [(7) or (8)][11], he or she is required to be in custody by virtue of having been remanded in custody pending his or her being tried, or the imposition of sentence, in respect of that offence.

(10) If the High Court has not, after the expiration of 60 days from the arrest of the person concerned under section 13 or 14, made an order under this section or section 15, or has decided not to make an order under this section, it shall direct the Central Authority in the State to inform the issuing judicial authority and, where appropriate, Eurojust in relation thereto and of the reasons therefor specified in the direction, and the Central Authority in the State shall comply with such direction.

(11) If the High Court has not, after the expiration of 90 days from the arrest of the person concerned under section 13 or 14, made an order under this section or section 15, or has decided not to make an order under this section, it shall direct the Central Authority in the State to inform the issuing judicial authority and, where appropriate, Eurojust in relation thereto and of the reason therefor specified in the direction, and the Central Authority in the State shall comply with such direction.

(12) An appeal against an order under this section or a decision not to make such an order may be brought in the Supreme Court [if, and only if, the High Court certifies that the order or decision involves a point of law of exceptional public importance and that it is desirable in the public interest that an appeal should be taken to the Supreme Court.][12]

[(13) Where a person lodges an appeal pursuant to subsection (12), the High Court may remand the person in custody or on bail pending the hearing of the appeal and, for that purpose, the High Court shall have the same powers in relation to remand as it would have if the person were brought before it charged with an indictable offence.][13]

Amendments

1 Subsection (1) substituted by Criminal Justice (Terrorist Offences) Act 2005, s 76(a).

2 Words deleted by Criminal Justice (Miscellaneous Provisions) Act 2009, s 12(a).

2 Subsection (2) substituted by Criminal Justice (Terrorist Offences) Act 2005, s 76(b).

4 Words deleted by Criminal Justice (Miscellaneous Provisions) Act 2009, s 12(b).

5 Subsection (2A) inserted by Criminal Justice (Terrorist Offences) Act 2005, s 76(c).

6   Subsection (3) substituted by Criminal Justice (Terrorist Offences) Act 2005, s 76(d).

7   Words inserted by Criminal Justice (Miscellaneous Provisions) Act 2009, s 12(c).

8   Subsection (5)(a) substituted by Criminal Justice (Terrorist Offences) Act 2005, s 76(e).

9   Subsection (6) substituted by Criminal Justice (Miscellaneous Provisions) Act 2009, s 12(d).

10 Subsection (7) substituted by Criminal Justice (Miscellaneous Provisions) Act 2009, s 12(e).

11 Words substituted by Criminal Justice (Terrorist Offences) Act 2005, s 76(g).

12 Words substituted by Criminal Justice (Miscellaneous Provisions) Act 2009, s 12(f).

13 Subsection (13) inserted by Criminal Justice (Miscellaneous Provisions) Act 2009, s 12(g).

---

17   European arrest warrant relating to more than one offence

Where, in relation to an offence specified in a European arrest warrant, the High Court decides not to make an order under section 15 or 16, it shall not be necessary for the issuing judicial authority to issue another European arrest warrant in respect of such other offences as are specified in that warrant, and, where such other offences are specified in the European arrest warrant, that warrant shall be treated as having been issued in respect of those other offences only.

18   Postponement of surrender

(1) The High Court may, if satisfied that circumstances exist that would warrant the postponement, on humanitarian grounds, of the surrender to the issuing state of a person to whom an order under section 15 or 16 applies, direct that the person's surrender be postponed until such date as the High Court states that, in its opinion, those circumstances no longer exist.

(2) Without prejudice to the generality of subsection (1), circumstances to which that paragraph applies include a manifest danger to the life or health of the person concerned likely to be occasioned by his or her surrender to the issuing state in accordance with section 15(5) or 16(5).

[(2A) Where the High Court decides to postpone a person's surrender under this section, it may remand the person in custody or on bail and, for that purpose, the High Court shall have the same powers in relation to remand as it would have if the person were brought before it charged with an indictable offence.]¹

[(3) Subject to section 19, where a person to whom an order under section 15 or 16 applies—

    (a)   is being proceeded against for an offence in the State, or

    (b)   (i)   has been sentenced to a term of imprisonment for an offence of which he or she was convicted in the State, and

        (ii) is required to serve all or part of that term of imprisonment,

    the High Court may direct the postponement of that person's surrender to the issuing state until—

        (I)   in the case of a person who is being proceeded against for an offence, the date of the final determination of those proceedings (where he or she is not required to serve a term of imprisonment), or s 17

the case of a person who is required to serve all or part of a term of prisonment, the date on which he or she is no longer required to serve any rt of that term of imprisonment.]²

.., ...o subsection (5), a person to whom this section applies shall be surrendered to the issuing state not later than 10 days after such date (being a date that falls after the date specified in subsection (1) or [subsection (3)(b)(I) or (II)]³, as the case may be) as may be agreed by the Central Authority in the State and the issuing state.

(5) Where a person makes a complaint under Article 40.4.2° of the Constitution, he or she shall not be surrendered to the issuing state while proceedings relating to the complaint are pending.

Amendments

1 Subsection (2A) inserted by Criminal Justice (Terrorist Offences) Act 2005, s 77.
2 Subsection (3) substituted by Criminal Justice (Miscellaneous Provisions) Act 2009, s 13(a).
3 Words substituted by Criminal Justice (Miscellaneous Provisions) Act 2009, s 13(b).

19   Conditional surrender

(1) Where a person to whom an order under section 15 or 16 applies—
   (a) has been sentenced to a term of imprisonment for an offence of which he or she was convicted in the State, and
   (b) is, at the time of the making of the order, required to serve all or part of that term of imprisonment,
the High Court may, subject to such conditions as it shall specify, direct that the person be surrendered to the issuing state for the purpose of his or her being tried for the offence to which the European arrest warrant concerned relates.

(2) Where a person is surrendered to the issuing state under this section, then any term of imprisonment or part of a term of imprisonment that the person is required to serve in the State shall be reduced by an amount equal to any period of time spent by that person in custody or detention in the issuing state consequent upon his or her being so surrendered, or pending trial.

20   Additional documentation and information

(1) In proceedings to which this Act applies the High Court may, if of the opinion that the documentation or information provided to it is not sufficient to enable it to perform its functions under this Act, require the [issuing judicial authority or the issuing state, as may be appropriate]¹ to provide it with such additional documentation or information as it may specify, within such period as it may specify,

(2) The Central Authority in the State may, if of the opinion that the documentation or information provided to it under this Act is not sufficient to enable it or the High Court to perform functions under this Act, require the issuing judicial authority or the [issuing state, as may be appropriate]¹ to provide it with such additional documentation or information as it may specify, within such period as it may specify.

(3) In proceedings under this Act, evidence as to any matter to which such proceedings relate may be given by affidavit[, declaration, affirmation, attestation]² or by a statement in writing that purports to have been sworn—

    (a) by the deponent in a place other than the State, and

    (b) in the presence of a person duly authorised under the law of the place concerned to attest to the swearing of such a statement by a deponent,

howsoever such a statement is described under the law of that place.

(4) In proceedings referred to in subsection (3), the High Court may, if it considers that the interests of justice so require, direct that oral evidence of the matters described in the affidavit or statement concerned be given, and the court may, for the purpose of receiving oral evidence, adjourn the proceedings to a later date.

Amendments

1   Words substituted by Criminal Justice (Terrorist Offences) Act 2005, s 78.

2   Words inserted by Criminal Justice (Miscellaneous Provisions) Act 2009, s 14.

21   Movement of persons detained under this Act

(1) The Minister may direct that a person remanded in custody under this Act or committed to a prison or remand institution under section 15 or 16 be removed to a hospital or any other place if the Minister considers that in the interest of the person's health, it is necessary that he or she be so removed, and the person shall, while detained in a hospital or other place pursuant to a direction under this subsection be deemed to be in lawful custody.

(2) Sections 10 and 11 of the Criminal Justice Act 1960 shall apply to a person who is not less than 16, nor more than 21, years of age remanded in custody under this Act or committed to a prison or remand institution under section 15 or 16, subject to the following modifications:

    (a) in section 10(1), the reference to "a person detained under section 9 of this Act or this section" shall be construed as a reference to "a person remanded in custody or committed to a prison or remand institution under the European Arrest Warrant Act 2003";

    (b in section 11(1), the reference to "a person who is detained in a remand institution pursuant to section 9 of this Act" shall be construed as a reference to "a person remanded in custody or committed to a prison or remand institution under the European Arrest Warrant Act 2003"; and

    (c) in section 11(3), the reference to "section 9" shall be construed as a reference to "the European Arrest Warrant Act 2003".

[21A   (1) Where a European arrest warrant is issued in the issuing state in respect of a person who has not been convicted of an offence specified therein, the High Court shall refuse to surrender the person if it is satisfied that a decision has not been made to charge the person with, and try him or her for, that offence in the issuing state.

(2) Where a European arrest warrant is issued in respect of a person who has not been convicted of an offence specified therein, it shall be presumed that a decision has been made to charge the person with, and try him or her for, that offence in the issuing state, unless the contrary is proved.]¹

Amendments

1   Section 21A inserted by Criminal Justice (Terrorist Offences) Act 2005, s 79.

22   Rule of speciality disapplied

[(1) In this section, except where the context otherwise requires, 'offence' means, in relation to a person to whom a European arrest warrant applies, an offence (other than an offence specified in the European arrest warrant in respect of which the person's surrender is ordered under this Act) under the law of the issuing state committed before the person's surrender, but shall not include an offence consisting, in whole, of acts or omissions of which the offence specified in the European arrest warrant consists in whole or in part.

(2) Subject to this section, the High Court shall refuse to surrender a person under this Act if it is satisfied that—

(a)   the law of the issuing state does not provide that a person who is surrendered to it pursuant to a European arrest warrant shall not be proceeded against, sentenced or detained for the purposes of executing a sentence or detention order, or otherwise restricted in his or her personal liberty, in respect of an offence, and

(b)   the person will be proceeded against, sentenced, or detained for the purposes of executing a sentence or detention order, or otherwise restricted in his or her personal liberty, in respect of an offence.

(3) It shall be presumed that, in relation to a person to whom a European arrest warrant applies, the issuing state does not intend to—

(a)   proceed against him or her,

(b)   sentence or detain him or her for a purpose referred to in subsection (2)(a), or

(c)   otherwise restrict him or her in his or her personal liberty,

in respect of an offence, unless the contrary is proved.

(4) The surrender of a person under this Act shall not be refused under subsection (2) if—

(a)   upon conviction in respect of the offence concerned he or she is not liable to a term of imprisonment or detention, or

(b)   the High Court is satisfied that, where upon such conviction he or she is liable to a term of imprisonment or detention and such other penalty as does not involve a restriction of his or her personal liberty, the said other penalty only will be imposed if he or she is convicted of the offence.

(5) The surrender of a person under this Act shall not be refused under subsection (2) if it is intended to impose in the issuing state a penalty (other than a penalty consisting of a restriction of the person's liberty) including a financial penalty in respect of an offence of which the person claimed has been convicted, notwithstanding that where such person fails or refuses to pay the penalty concerned (or, in the case of a penalty that is not a financial

penalty, fails or refuses to submit to any measure or comply with any requirements of which the penalty consists) he or she may, under the law of the issuing state be detained or otherwise deprived of his or her personal liberty.

(6) The surrender of a person under this Act shall not be refused under subsection (2) if the High Court—

    (a) is satisfied that—

        (i) proceedings will not be brought against the person in respect of an offence,

        (ii) a penalty will not be imposed on the person in respect of an offence, and

        (iii) the person will not be detained or otherwise restricted in his or her personal liberty for the purposes of an offence,

    without the issuing judicial authority first obtaining the consent thereto of the High Court,

    (b) is satisfied that—

        (i) the person consents to being surrendered under section 15,

        (ii) at the time of so consenting he or she consented to being so proceeded against, to such a penalty being imposed, or being so detained or restricted in his or her personal liberty, and was aware of the consequences of his or her so consenting, and

        (iii) the person obtained or was afforded the opportunity of obtaining, or being provided with, professional legal advice in relation to the matters to which this section relates,

    (c) is satisfied that—

        (i) such proceedings will not be brought, such penalty will not be imposed and the person will not be so detained or otherwise restricted in his or her personal liberty before the expiration of a period of 45 days from the date of the person's final discharge in respect of the offence for which he or she is surrendered, and

        (ii) during that period he or she will be free to leave the issuing state,

    except where having been so discharged he or she leaves the issuing state and later returns thereto (whether during that period or later), or

    (d) is satisfied that such proceedings will not be brought, such penalty will not be imposed and the person will not be so detained or restricted in his or her personal liberty unless—

        (i) the person voluntarily gives his or her consent to being so proceeded against, such a penalty being imposed, or being so detained or restricted in his or her personal liberty, and is fully aware of the consequences of so doing,

        (ii) that consent is given before the competent judicial authority in the issuing state, and

        (iii) the person obtains or is afforded the opportunity of obtaining, or being provided with, professional legal advice in the issuing state in relation to the matters to which this section relates before he or she gives that consent.

(7) The High Court may, in relation to a person who has been surrendered to an issuing state under this Act, consent to—

- (a) proceedings being brought against the person in the issuing state for an offence,
- (b) the imposition in the issuing state of a penalty, including a penalty consisting of a restriction of the person's liberty, in respect of an offence, or
- (c) proceedings being brought against, or the detention of, the person in the issuing state for the purpose of executing a sentence or order of detention in respect of an offence,

upon receiving a request in writing from the issuing state in that behalf.

(8) The High Court shall not give its consent under subsection (7) if the offence concerned is an offence for which a person could not by virtue of Part 3 or the Framework Decision (including the recitals thereto) be surrendered under this Act.]¹

Amendments

1   Section 22 substituted by Criminal Justice (Terrorist Offences) Act 2005, s 80.

23   Surrender of person by issuing state to other Member State

[(1) In this section, except where the context otherwise requires—

"offence" means, in relation to a person to whom a European arrest warrant applies, an offence under the law of a Member State (other than the issuing state) committed before the person's surrender to the issuing state under this Act; and

"Member State" means a Member State other than the issuing state.

(2) Subject to this section, the High Court shall refuse to surrender a person under this Act if it is satisfied that—

- (a) the law of the issuing state does not provide that a person who is surrendered to it pursuant to a European arrest warrant shall not be surrendered to a Member State pursuant to a European arrest warrant issued by a judicial authority in that Member State in respect of an offence, and
- (b) the person will be surrendered to a Member State pursuant to a European arrest warrant issued by a judicial authority in that Member State in respect of an offence.

(3) It shall be presumed that, in relation to a person to whom a European arrest warrant applies, the issuing state does not intend to surrender him or her to a Member State pursuant to a European arrest warrant issued by a judicial authority in that Member State in respect of an offence, unless the contrary is proved.

(4) The surrender of a person under this Act shall not be refused under subsection (2) if the High Court—

- (a) is satisfied that the issuing judicial authority will not surrender the person to a Member State pursuant to a European arrest warrant issued by a judicial authority in that Member State, without first obtaining the consent thereto of the High Court,
- (b) is satisfied that—
  - (i) the person consents to being surrendered under section 15,
  - (ii) at the time of so consenting he or she consented to being surrendered by the issuing state to a Member State pursuant to a European arrest warrant issued

by a judicial authority in that Member State, and was aware of the consequences of his or her so consenting, and

    (iii) the person obtained or was afforded the opportunity of obtaining, or being provided with, professional legal advice in relation to the matters to which this section relates,

(c) is satisfied that—

    (i) the person will not be surrendered by the issuing state to a Member State pursuant to a European arrest warrant issued by a judicial authority in that Member State, before the expiration of a period of 45 days from the date of the person's final discharge in respect of the offence for which he or she is surrendered under this Act, and

    (ii) during that period he or she will be free to leave the issuing state,

except where having been so discharged he or she leaves the issuing state and later returns thereto (whether during that period or later), or

(d) is satisfied that the person will not be surrendered to a Member State pursuant to a European arrest warrant issued by a judicial authority in that Member State unless—

    (i) the person voluntarily gives his or her consent to being so surrendered and is fully aware of the consequences of his or her so doing,

    (ii) that consent is given before the competent judicial authority in the issuing state, and

    (iii) the person obtains or is afforded the opportunity of obtaining, or being provided with, professional legal advice in the issuing state in relation to the matters to which this section relates before he or she gives that consent.

(5) The High Court may, in relation to a person who has been surrendered to an issuing state under this Act, consent to the person being surrendered by the issuing state to a Member State pursuant to a European arrest warrant issued by a judicial authority in that Member State, upon receiving a request in writing from the issuing state in that behalf.

(6) The High Court shall not give its consent under subsection (5) if the offence concerned is an offence for which a person could not by virtue of Part 3 or the Framework Decision (including the recitals thereto) be surrendered under this Act.]¹

Amendments

1   Section 23 substituted by Criminal Justice (Terrorist Offences) Act 2005, s 81.

---

24   **Surrender of person by issuing state to third state**

[(1) The High Court shall refuse to surrender a person under this Act if it is satisfied that—

(a) the law of the issuing state does not provide that a person who is surrendered to it pursuant to a European arrest warrant shall not be extradited to a third country without the consent of the High Court and the Minister first being obtained, and

(b) the person will be extradited to a third country without such consent first being obtained.

(2) It shall be presumed that, in relation to a person to whom a European arrest warrant applies, the issuing state does not intend to extradite him or her to a third country, unless the contrary is proved.

(3) The issuing state may request, in writing, the High Court to consent to the extradition to a third country by the issuing state of a person surrendered to the issuing state under this Act.

(4) The High Court shall give its consent to a request under subsection (3) if it is satisfied that—

    (a) were the person concerned in the State, and

    (b) were a request for his or her extradition received in the State from the third country concerned,

his or her extradition pursuant to such a request would not be prohibited under the Extradition Acts 1965 to 2001.]¹

Amendments

1   Section 24 substituted by Criminal Justice (Terrorist Offences) Act 2005, s 82.

25   Searches for purposes of European arrest warrant

(1) A member of the Garda Síochána, may, for the purposes of performing functions under section 13 or 14, enter any place (if necessary by the use of reasonable force) and search that place, if he or she has reasonable grounds for believing that a person in respect of whom a European arrest warrant has been issued is to be found at that place.

(2) Where a member of the Garda Síochána enters a place under subsection (1), he or she may search that place and any person found at that place, and may seize anything found at that place or anything found in the possession of a person present at that place at the time of the search that the said member believes to be evidence of, or relating to, an offence specified in a European arrest warrant, or to be property obtained or received at any time (whether before or after the passing of this Act) as a result of or in connection with the commission of that offence.

(3) Subject to subsection (4), a member of the Garda Síochána, who has reasonable grounds for believing that evidence of, or relating to, an offence specified in a European arrest warrant, or property obtained or received at any time (whether before or after the passing of this Act) as a result of, or in connection with, the commission of that offence is to be found at any place, may enter that place (if necessary by the use of reasonable force) and search that place and any person found at that place, and may seize anything found at that place or anything found in the possession of a person present at that place at the time of the search that the member believes to be such evidence or property.

(4) (a) A member of the Garda Síochána shall not enter a dwelling under subsection (3), other than—

      (i) with the consent of the occupier, or

      (ii) in accordance with a warrant issued under paragraph (b).

    (b) On the application of a member of the Garda Síochána, a judge of the District Court may, if satisfied that there are reasonable grounds for believing that—

    (i)   evidence of, or relating to, an offence specified in a European arrest warrant, or

    (ii) property obtained or received at any time (whether before or after the passing of this Act) as a result of or in connection with the commission of that offence,

is to be found in any dwelling, issue a warrant authorising a named member of the Garda Síochána accompanied by such other members of the Garda Síochána as may be necessary, at any time or times, within one month of the date of the issue of the warrant, to enter the dwelling (if necessary by the use of reasonable force) and search the dwelling and any person found at the dwelling, and a member of the Garda Síochána who enters a dwelling pursuant to such a warrant may seize anything found at the dwelling or anything found in the possession of a person present at the dwelling at the time of the search that the member believes to be such evidence or property.

(5) A member of the Garda Síochána who is performing functions under this section may—

    (a) require any person present at the place where the search is carried out to give to the member his or her name and address, and

    (b) arrest otherwise than pursuant to a warrant any person who—

        (i)   obstructs or attempts to obstruct that member in the performance of his or her functions,

        (ii) fails to comply with a requirement under paragraph (a), or

        (iii) gives a name or address which the member has reasonable cause for believing is false or misleading.

(6) A person who—

    (a) obstructs or attempts to obstruct a member of the Garda Síochána in the performance of his or her functions under this section,

    (b) fails to comply with a requirement under paragraph (a) of subsection (5), or

    (c) gives a false name or address to a member of the Garda Síochána,

shall be guilty of an offence and shall be liable on summary conviction to a fine not exceeding €3,000, or to imprisonment for a period not exceeding 6 months, or to both.

(7) In this section "place" includes a ship or other vessel, an aircraft, a railway wagon or other vehicle, and a container used for the transporting of goods.

26   Handing over of property

(1) Subject to the provisions of this section, any property seized under section 25 shall, if a person is surrendered under this Act, be handed over to any person duly authorised by the issuing state to receive it, as soon as may be after the surrender of the person, and the said property shall be so handed over notwithstanding that the surrender of the person cannot be carried out by reason of the death or escape from custody of the person claimed.

(2) Any property seized under section 25 may, if any criminal proceedings to which the property relates are pending in the State, be retained in the State for the purposes of those proceedings or may, if the Central Authority in the State, after consultation with the Director of Public Prosecutions, so directs, be handed over to the issuing state subject to the issuing state agreeing to return the property.

(3) This section shall not operate to abrogate any rights lawfully vested in the State, or any person, in any property to which this section applies and, where any such rights exist, the

property shall not be handed over unless an undertaking is given by the issuing state that it will return the property as soon as may be after the trial of the person surrendered and without charge to the State or person in whom such rights vest.

27 Remand

(1) A person remanded in custody under this Act may be detained in a prison (or, if he or she is not more than 21 years of age, in a remand institution) or, for a period not exceeding 48 hours, in a Garda Síochána station.

(2) A person shall not be remanded on bail or otherwise released from custody under this Act if—

    (a)   (i)   the person has been sentenced to a term of imprisonment for an offence of which he or she was convicted in the State,

            (ii)   on the date of his or her being remanded or on which he or she would, but for this paragraph, be entitled to be released, all or part of the term of imprisonment remains unexpired, and

            (iii)   the person is required to serve all or part of the remainder of that term of imprisonment,

        or

    (b)   (i)   the person has been charged with or convicted of an offence in the State, and

            (ii)   on the date of his or her being remanded or on which he or she would, but for this paragraph, be entitled to be released, he or she is required to be in custody by virtue of having been remanded in custody pending trial for that offence or the imposition of sentence in respect of that offence.

28 Transit

(1) Transit through the State of a person being conveyed from an executing state to an issuing state, upon his or her surrender pursuant to a European arrest warrant, shall be permitted where the Central Authority in the State receives a request in that behalf from the issuing state and where the issuing state provides the Central Authority in the State with the following information:

    (a)   the nationality of the person and such other information as will enable the person to be identified by the Central Authority in the State;

    (b)   information showing that a European arrest warrant has been issued by the issuing state in respect of the person;

    (c)   the nature and classification under the law of the issuing state of the offence to which the European arrest warrant relates;

    (d)   the circumstances in which the offence specified in the European arrest warrant was committed or is alleged to have been committed, including the date and place of its commission.

(2) The transit of a person through the State shall be supervised by members of the Garda Síochána if the Central Authority in the State considers it appropriate, and where a person's transit is so supervised the person shall be deemed to be in the custody of any member of the Garda Síochána who accompanies him or her.

(3)   (a)   This subsection applies to an aircraft that has taken off from a place (other than the State) and that is scheduled to land in a place (other than the State) and on board

which there is a person who is being conveyed to an issuing state upon his or her surrender pursuant to a European arrest warrant.

(b) Where an aircraft to which this subsection applies lands (for whatever reason) in the State, the issuing state shall, upon its landing or as soon as may be after it lands, provide the Central Authority in the State with the information referred to in subsection (1).

(c) While an aircraft to which this subsection applies is in the State, a person referred to in paragraph (a) who is on board that aircraft shall be deemed to be in transit through the State and subsection (2) shall apply accordingly.

(4) Where a person has been extradited by a third country to a Member State this section shall apply subject to the modifications that—

(a) the reference to an executing state shall be construed as a reference to a third state,

(b) references to a European arrest warrant shall be construed as references to an extradition request, and

(c) references to an issuing state shall be construed as references to a Member State.

(5) In this section "executing state" means, in relation to a European arrest warrant, a Member State (a judicial authority of which has ordered the arrest and surrender to the issuing state, pursuant to the European arrest warrant, of a person in respect of whom that warrant was issued).

29 Multiple European arrest warrants

(1) Where the Central Authority in the State receives two or more European arrest warrants in respect of a person, [...]¹ the Central Authority in the State shall, where the High Court has not yet made an order under section 15, or subsection (1) or (2) of section 16, in relation to the person, inform the High Court as soon as may be of the receipt by it of those warrants and the High Court shall, having regard to all the circumstances, decide, in relation to which of those European arrest warrants it shall—

(a) perform functions under section 13, or

(b) where it has already performed such functions in relation to one of those European arrest warrants, perform functions under section 15 or 16, as may be appropriate.

(2) Without prejudice to the generality of subsection (1), the High Court shall in making a decision under subsection (1) have regard to—

(a) the seriousness of the offences specified in the European arrest warrants concerned,

(b) the places where the offences were committed or are alleged to have been committed,

(c) the dates on which the European arrest warrants were issued, and

(d) whether the European arrest warrants concerned were issued for the purposes of bringing proceedings for an offence against the person named in the warrants or for the purposes of executing a sentence or detention order in respect of the person.

Amendments

1 Words deleted by Criminal Justice (Miscellaneous Provisions) Act 2009, s 15.

30   European arrest warrants and requests for extradition

(1) If the Central Authority in the State receives a European arrest warrant in respect of a person and a request from a third country for the extradition of that person, the Central Authority in the State shall, where the High Court has not yet made an order under section 15, or subsection (1) or (2) of section 16, in relation to the person, inform the High Court as soon as may be of the receipt by it of the European arrest warrant and the request for extradition, and the High Court shall, having regard to all the circumstances, decide whether it shall perform functions—

    (a) in relation to the European arrest warrant, under this Act, or

    (b) in relation to the request for extradition, under the Extradition Acts 1965 to 2001.

(2) Without prejudice to the generality of subsection (1), the High Court shall in making a decision under subsection (1) have regard to—

    (a) the seriousness of—

        (i) the offence specified in the European arrest warrant, and

        (ii) the offence to which the request for extradition relates,

    (b) the places where the offences concerned were committed or are alleged to have been committed,

    (c) the date on which the European arrest warrant was issued and the date on which the request for extradition was made,

    (d) whether the European arrest warrant was issued, or the request for extradition was made, for the purposes of bringing proceedings for an offence against the person concerned or for the purposes of executing a sentence or detention order in respect of the person, and

    (e) the relevant extradition provisions.

(3) If the Central Authority in the State receives a European arrest warrant in respect of a person and the State receives a request from the International Criminal Court for the arrest and surrender of the same person, the Central Authority in the State shall, where an order has not yet been made under section 15, or subsection (1) or (2) of section 16, in relation to that person, so inform the High Court, and the High Court shall not perform functions under this Act in relation to the European arrest warrant, unless the arrest and surrender of that person pursuant to such a request is prohibited, or not provided for, under the law of the State.

(4) In this section "extradition provisions" has the same meaning as it has in the Act of 1965.

Chapter 2
Issue of European Arrest Warrant by State

31   Definition

In this Chapter—

"domestic warrant" means a warrant (other than a European arrest warrant) issued, for the arrest of a person, by a court in the State;

"European arrest warrant" means a warrant to which the Framework Decision applies issued by a court, in accordance with this Chapter and for the purposes of—

    (a) the arrest, in a Member State, of that person, and

    (b) the surrender of that person to the State by the Member State concerned.

32　　Offences to which Article 2.2 of Framework Decision applies

(1) For the purposes of paragraph 2 of Article 2 of the Framework Decision, the Minister may, by order, specify the offences under the law of the State to which that paragraph applies.

(2) The Minister may, by order, amend or revoke an order under this section (including an order under this subsection).

(3) This section shall not operate to require that an order under this section be in force before a court may issue a European arrest warrant under section 33.

33　　Issue of European arrest warrant by court in State

[(1) A court may, upon an application made by or on behalf of the Director of Public Prosecutions, issue a European arrest warrant in respect of a person where it is satisfied that—

    (a)　a domestic warrant has been issued for the arrest of that person but has not been executed, and

    (b)　the person may not be in the State, and],¹
      where—

      (i)　the person would, if convicted of the offence concerned, be liable to a term of imprisonment [or detention]² of 12 months or more than 12 months, or

      (ii)　a term of imprisonment [or detention]² of not less than 4 months has been imposed on the person in respect of the offence concerned and the person is required to serve all or part of that term of imprisonment [or detention]².

[(1A) Where a court issues a European arrest warrant in respect of a person under this section, such issue shall be deemed to constitute a request by the court for entry of an alert and of a copy of the European arrest warrant in respect of that person.

(1B) For the purposes of subsection (1), where a member of the Garda Síochána not below the rank of Sergeant states that he or she believes that a person may not be in the State, the statement is admissible as evidence that the person may not be in the State.]³

(2) A European arrest warrant shall, in so far as is practicable, be in the form set out in the Annex to the Framework Decision and shall specify—

    (a)　the name and the nationality of the person to whom it relates,

    (b)　the name, address, fax number and e-mail address of—

      (i)　the District Court Office for the district in which the District Court was sitting when it issued the European arrest warrant,

      (ii)　the Circuit Court Office of the county in which the Circuit Criminal Court was sitting when it issued the European arrest warrant,

      (iii)　the Central Office of the High Court, or

      (iv)　the Registrar of the Special Criminal Court,
      as may be appropriate,

    (c)　the offence to which the European arrest warrant relates including a description thereof,

    (d)　that a conviction, sentence or detention order is immediately enforceable against the person, or that a domestic warrant for his or her arrest has been issued in respect of that offence,

(e) the circumstances in which the offence was committed or is alleged to have been committed, including the time and place of its commission or alleged commission, and the degree of involvement or alleged degree of involvement of the person in the commission of the offence, and

(f) (i) the penalties to which the person named in the European arrest warrant would, if convicted of the offence to which the European arrest warrant relates, be liable,

(ii) where the person named in the European arrest warrant has been convicted of the offence specified therein and a sentence has been imposed in respect thereof, the penalties of which that sentence consists, and

(iii) where the person named in the European arrest warrant has been convicted of the offence specified therein but has not yet been sentenced, the penalties to which he or she is liable in respect of the offence.

(3) Where it is not practicable for the European arrest warrant to be in the form set out in the Annex to the Framework Decision, the European arrest warrant shall, in addition to containing the information specified in subsection (2), include such other information as would be required to be provided were it in that form.

(4) For the avoidance of doubt, a European arrest warrant may be issued in respect of one or more than one offence.

(5) In this section "court" means—

(a) the court that issued the domestic warrant to which subparagraph (i) of section 33(1)(a) applies, or

(b) the High Court.

Amendments

1 Subsection (1)(a) substituted by Criminal Justice (Miscellaneous Provisions) Act 2009, s 16(a).

2 Words inserted by Criminal Justice (Miscellaneous Provisions) Act 2009, s 16(b) and (c).

3 Subsections (1A) and (1B) inserted by Criminal Justice (Miscellaneous Provisions) Act 2009, s 16(d).

34 Transmission of European arrest warrant issued in State

A European arrest warrant issued under section 33 [may]¹ be transmitted to a Member State by the Central Authority in the State.

Amendments

1 Words substituted by Criminal Justice (Miscellaneous Provisions) Act 2009, s 18.

35   Arrest of person surrendered to State

(1) Where a person is surrendered to the State pursuant to a European arrest warrant—

    (a) the domestic warrant issued for his or her arrest and referred to in subparagraph (i) of section 33(1)(a),

    (b) subject to paragraph (c), where more than one such domestic warrant was issued, those domestic warrants, or

    (c) where—

        (i) more than one such domestic warrant was issued, and

        (ii) the executing judicial authority ordered the surrender of the person in respect of one or more but not all of the offences specified in the European arrest warrant,

        the domestic warrants issued in respect of the offences for which the person was surrendered,

may be executed by any member of the Garda Síochána in any part of the State and may be so executed notwithstanding that the domestic warrant concerned is not in the possession of the member when he or she executes the warrant, and the domestic warrant concerned shall be shown to and a copy thereof given to the person arrested at the time of his or her arrest or, if the domestic warrant or copy thereof is not then in the possession of the member, not later than 24 hours after the person's arrest.

(2) Where a person is surrendered to the State pursuant to a European arrest warrant issued by the High Court (whether or not sitting as the Central Criminal Court), the Central Authority in the State shall inform the Central Office of the High Court, in writing, of the person's surrender.

36   Deduction of period of detention in executing state from sentence

(1) Where a person is surrendered to the State pursuant to a European arrest warrant, then any term of imprisonment that the person is required to serve by virtue of the imposition of a sentence by a court in the State (whether before or after the person's surrender) in respect of the offence specified in that European arrest warrant shall be reduced by an amount equal to any period of time spent by that person in custody or detention in the executing state in contemplation, or in consequence, of the execution of the European arrest warrant.

(2) In this section "executing state" means, in relation to a European arrest warrant, a Member State (a judicial authority of which has ordered the arrest and surrender to the State, pursuant to the European arrest warrant, of a person in respect of whom that warrant was issued).

PART 3
PROHIBITION ON SURRENDER

37   Fundamental rights

(1) A person shall not be surrendered under this Act if—

    (a) his or her surrender would be incompatible with the State's obligations under—

        (i) the Convention, or

        (ii) the Protocols to the Convention,

(b) his or her surrender would constitute a contravention of any provision of the Constitution (other than for the reason that the offence specified in the European arrest warrant is an offence to which section 38(1)(b) applies),

(c) there are reasonable grounds for believing that—

    (i) the European arrest warrant was issued in respect of the person for the purposes of facilitating his or her prosecution or punishment in the issuing state for reasons connected with his or her sex, race, religion, ethnic origin, nationality, language, political opinion or sexual orientation, or

    (ii) in the prosecution or punishment of the person in the issuing state, he or she will be treated less favourably than a person who—

        (I) is not his or her sex, race, religion, nationality or ethnic origin,

        (II) does not hold the same political opinions as him or her,

        (III) speaks a different language than he or she does, or

        (IV) does not have the same sexual orientation as he or she does,

        or

    (iii) were the person to be surrendered to the issuing state—

        (I) he or she would be sentenced to death, or a death sentence imposed on him or her would be carried out, or

        (II) he or she would be tortured or subjected to other inhuman or degrading treatment.

(2) In this section—

"Convention" means the Convention for the Protection of Human Rights and Fundamental Freedoms done at Rome on the 4th day of November, 1950, as amended by Protocol No. 11 done at Strasbourg on the 11th day of May, 1994; and

"Protocols to the Convention" means the following protocols to the Convention, construed in accordance with Articles 16 to 18 of the Convention:

(a) the Protocol to the Convention done at Paris on the 20th day of March, 1952;

(b) Protocol No. 4 to the Convention securing certain rights and freedoms other than those already included in the Convention and in the First Protocol thereto done at Strasbourg on the 16th day of September, 1963;

(c) Protocol No. 6 to the Convention concerning the abolition of the death penalty done at Strasbourg on the 28th day of April, 1983;

(d) Protocol No. 7 to the Convention done at Strasbourg on the 22nd day of November, 1984.

38   Offence in respect of which a person shall not be surrendered

(1) Subject to subsection (2), a person shall not be surrendered to an issuing state under this Act in respect of an offence unless—

(a) the offence corresponds to an offence under the law of the State, and—

    (i) under the law of the issuing state the offence is punishable by imprisonment or detention for a maximum period of not less than 12 months, or

    (ii) a term of imprisonment or detention of not less than 4 months has been imposed on the person in respect of the offence in the issuing state, and the person is required under the law of the issuing state to serve all or part of that term of imprisonment,

or

(b) the offence is an offence to which paragraph 2 of Article 2 of the Framework Decision applies [...],[1] and under the law of the issuing state the offence is punishable by imprisonment for a maximum period of not less than 3 years.

(2) The surrender of a person to an issuing state under this Act shall not be refused on the ground that, in relation to a revenue offence—

(a) no tax or duty of the kind to which the offence relates is imposed in the State, or

(b) the rules relating to taxes, duties, customs or exchange control that apply in the issuing state differ in nature from the rules that apply in the State to taxes, duties, customs or exchange control.

(3) In this section "revenue offence" means, in relation to an issuing state, an offence in connection with taxes, duties, customs or exchange control.

Amendments

2   Words deleted by Criminal Justice (Miscellaneous Provisions) Act 2009, s 17.

39   Pardon or amnesty

(1) A person shall not be surrendered under this Act where he or she has been granted a pardon, under Article 13.6 of the Constitution, in respect of an offence consisting of an act or omission that constitutes in whole or in part the offence specified in the European arrest warrant issued in respect of him or her.

(2) A person shall not be surrendered under this Act where he or she has, in accordance with the law of the issuing state, become immune, by virtue of any amnesty or pardon, from prosecution or punishment in the issuing state for the offence specified in the European arrest warrant issued in respect of him or her.

(3) A person shall not be surrendered under this Act where he or she has, by virtue of any Act of the Oireachtas, become immune from prosecution or punishment for an offence consisting of an act or omission that constitutes in whole or in part the offence specified in the European arrest warrant issued in respect of him or her.

40   Passage of time from commission of offence

[...][1]

Amendments

1   Section 40 deleted by Criminal Justice (Miscellaneous Provisions) Act 2009, s 19.

41 Double jeopardy

(1) A person shall not be surrendered under this Act for the purpose of his or her being proceeded against in the issuing state for an offence consisting of an act or omission that constitutes in whole or in part an offence in respect of which final judgment has been given in the State or a Member State.

(2) A person shall not be surrendered under this Act for the purpose of his or her being proceeded against in the issuing state for an offence consisting of the act or omission that constitutes an offence in respect of which final judgment has been given in a third country, provided that where a sentence of imprisonment or detention was imposed on the person in the third country in respect of the second-mentioned offence—

    (a) the person has completed serving the sentence, or

    (b) the person is otherwise no longer liable under the law of the third country to serve any period of imprisonment or detention in respect of the offence.

42 Proceedings in the State

[A person shall not be surrendered under this Act if—

    (a) the Director of Public Prosecutions or the Attorney General is considering, but has not yet decided, whether to bring proceedings against the person for an offence, or

    (b) proceedings have been brought in the State against the person for an offence consisting of an act or omission of which the offence specified in the European arrest warrant issued in respect of him or her consists in whole or in part.][1]

Amendments

1   Section 42 substituted by Criminal Justice (Terrorist Offences) Act 2005, s 83.

43 Age

A person shall not be surrendered under this Act if the offence specified in the European arrest warrant issued in respect of him or her corresponds to an offence under the law of the State in respect of which a person of the same age as the person in respect of whom the European arrest warrant was issued could not be proceeded against by reason of his or her age.

44 Commission of offence outside issuing state

A person shall not be surrendered under this Act if the offence specified in the European arrest warrant issued in respect of him or her was committed or is alleged to have been committed in a place other than the issuing state and the act or omission of which the offence consists does not, by virtue of having been committed in a place other than the State, constitute an offence under the law of the State.

45 Persons convicted in absentia

[A person shall not be surrendered under this Act if—

    (a) he or she was not present when he or she was tried for and convicted of the offence specified in the European arrest warrant, and

(b) (i) he or she was not notified of the time when, and place at which, he or she would be tried for the offence, or

    (ii) he or she was not permitted to attend the trial in respect of the offence concerned,

unless the issuing judicial authority gives an undertaking in writing that the person will, upon being surrendered—

    (I) be retried for that offence or be given the opportunity of a retrial in respect of that offence,

    (II) be notified of the time when, and place at which any retrial in respect of the offence concerned will take place, and

    (III) be permitted to be present when any such retrial takes place.][1]

Amendments

1   Section 45 substituted by Criminal Justice (Miscellaneous Provisions) Act 2009, s 20(a).

[45A   Identification procedures

(1) Where a member of the Garda Síochána arrests a person under any power conferred by this Act, the member of the Garda Síochána may, in order to assist in verifying or ascertaining his or her identity for the purpose of proceedings under this Act and for no other purpose—

    (a) take, or cause to be taken, his or her fingerprint,

    (b) take, or cause to be taken, his or her palm print,

    (c) photograph him or her or cause him or her to be photographed.

(2) Where a fingerprint, palm print or photograph taken pursuant to subsection (1) is lost or damaged, or is otherwise unsuitable for use for the purpose referred to in that subsection, it may be taken on a second or any further occasion.

(3) The powers conferred by subsection (1) shall not be exercised except on the authority of a member of the Garda Síochána not below the rank of inspector.

(4) A member of the Garda Síochána may, where a person fails or refuses to allow his or her fingerprint, palm print or photograph to be taken pursuant to subsection (1), use such force as he or she reasonably considers necessary to take the fingerprint, palm print or photograph or to cause the photograph to be taken.

(5) (a) The powers conferred by subsection (4) shall not be exercised except on the authority of a member of the Garda Síochána not below the rank of superintendent.

    (b) An authorization pursuant to paragraph (a) may be given orally or in writing and if given orally shall be confirmed in writing as soon as practicable.

(6) Where a member of the Garda Síochána intends to exercise a power conferred by subsection (4), he or she shall inform the person—

    (a) of that intention, and

    (b) that an authorization to do so has been given pursuant to subsection (5)(a).

(7) Every fingerprint, palm print or photograph taken pursuant to subsection (4) shall be taken in the presence of a member of the Garda Síochána not below the rank of inspector.

(8) The taking of every fingerprint, palm print or photograph pursuant to subsection (4) shall be video-recorded.

(9) Every fingerprint, palm print or photograph of a person taken in pursuance of a power conferred by this section and every copy and record thereof shall be destroyed within the period of 12 months from the date of the taking of the fingerprint, palm print or photograph, as the case may be, or on the conclusion of proceedings under this Act in relation to the person, whichever occurs later.

(10) A person who obstructs a member of the Garda Síochána in exercise of the powers under this section shall be guilty of an offence and shall, on summary conviction, be liable to a fine not exceeding €5,000 or to imprisonment for a term not exceeding 12 months or to both.

(11) Where a fingerprint, palm print or photograph of a person to whom a European arrest warrant relates is transmitted by or on behalf of an issuing judicial authority, such fingerprint, palm print or photograph shall be received in evidence without further proof.

45B   Transfer of persons to state from which surrendered

(1) Where a national or resident of another state from which he or she is surrendered—

(a) is surrendered to the State pursuant to a European arrest warrant with a view to being prosecuted in the State, and

(b) whose surrender is subject to the condition that he or she, after being so prosecuted, is returned if he or she so consents to that other state in order to serve any custodial sentence or detention order imposed upon him or her in the State,

the Minister shall, following the final determination of the proceedings and if the person consents, issue a warrant for the transfer of the person from the State to that other state in order to serve there any custodial sentence or detention order so imposed.

(2) A warrant issued under subsection (1) shall authorise—

(a) the taking of the person to a place in any part of the State and his or her delivery at a place of departure from the State into the custody of a person authorized by the other state to receive the person, for conveyance to the other state concerned, and the keeping of the person in custody until the delivery is effected, and

(b) the removal of the person concerned, by the person to whom he or she is delivered, from the State.

(3) Where a warrant has been issued in respect of a person under this section, the person shall be deemed to be in legal custody at any time when he or she is being taken under the warrant to or from any place or being kept in custody under the warrant and, if the person escapes or is unlawfully at large, he or she shall be liable to be retaken in the same manner as any person who escapes from lawful custody.

(4) The Minister may designate any person as a person who is for the time being authorised to take the person concerned to or from any place under the warrant or to keep the person in custody under the warrant.

(5) A person authorized pursuant to subsection (4) to take the person concerned to or from any place or to keep the person in custody shall, while so taking or keeping the person, have all the powers, authority, protection and privileges of a member of the Garda Síochána.

(6) The order by virtue of which a person is required to be detained at the time a warrant is issued in respect of him or her under this section shall continue to have effect after his or her

removal from the State so as to apply to him or her if he or she is again in the State at any time when under that order he or she is to be or may be detained.

45C   Technical flaws in applications for surrender

(1) Subject to subsection (2), an application for surrender under section 16 shall not be refused on the grounds of—

    (a) a defect in substance or in form or an omission of non-substantial detail in the European arrest warrant or any accompanying document grounding the application,

    (b) any variance between any such document and the evidence adduced on the part of the applicant at the hearing of the application, or

    (c) failure to comply with any provision of this Act where the Court is satisfied that such failure is of a technical nature and does not impinge on the merits of the application.

(2) Subsection (1) shall not apply where the Court is satisfied that an injustice would thereby be caused to the respondent.][1]

Amendments

2   Section 45A–45C inserted by Criminal Justice (Miscellaneous Provisions) Act 2009, s 20(b).

46   Immunity from prosecution

A person who, by virtue of his or her holding any office or other position, is under the law of the State immune from prosecution for any offence, shall not while he or she holds such office or position be surrendered under this Act.

PART 4

MISCELLANEOUS

47   Amendment of section 3 of Act of 1965

Section 3 of the Act of 1965 is amended by—

    (a) the insertion in subsection (1) of the following definition:[1]

    (b) the substitution of the following subsection for subsection (1A):[1]

    (c) the substitution of the following subsection for subsection (1B) (inserted by section 9 of the Act of 2001):[1]

Amendments

1   See the amended Act.

48 Laying of orders under Act of 1965 before Houses of Oireachtas

The Act of 1965 is amended by the substitution of the following section for section 4 (inserted by section 21 of the Act of 2001):[1]

Amendments

1 See the amended Act.

49 Application of Part II of Act of 1965

Section 8 of the Act of 1965 is amended by—

  (a) the substitution in subsection (1) of—

   (i) "Minister is" for "Government are" where it first occurs, and

   (ii) "Minister for Foreign Affairs may, after consultation with the Minister," for "Government may",

  (b) the substitution in subsection (1A) (inserted by section 23 of the Act of 2001) of "Minister for Foreign Affairs may, after consultation with the Minister," for "Government may",

  (c) the substitution in subsection (2) of "Minister for Foreign Affairs may, after consultation with the Minister", for "Government may",

  (d) the substitution in subsection (6) of "Minister for Foreign Affairs may, after consultation with the Minister," for "Government may", and

  (e) the insertion of the following subsection:

and the said section 8 as so amended is set out in the Table to this section.[1]

Amendments

1 See the amended Act.

50 Repeal of Part III of Act of 1965

(1) Part III of the Act of 1965 is repealed.

(2) Where, before the commencement of this Act, a warrant issued by a judicial authority in a place in relation to which Part III of the Act of 1965 applies was—

  (a) produced to the Commissioner of the Garda Síochána for the purposes of section 43 of the Act of 1965, or

  (b) endorsed for execution under that Part,

then, notwithstanding the repeal of the said Part III effected by subsection (1), that Part shall, on and after the said commencement, continue to apply in relation to that warrant and the person named in that warrant shall be dealt with under and in accordance with that Part.

51   Amendment of Extradition (European Convention on the Suppression of Terrorism) Act 1987

The Extradition (European Convention on the Suppression of Terrorism) Act 1987 is amended by the substitution of the following section for section 10:

"10.—(1) The Minister for Foreign Affairs may, after consultation with the Minister, by order direct that all or any of the provisions of this Act which would, apart from this section, apply only in relation to convention countries shall apply (subject to such exceptions, if any, as may be specified in the order) in relation to any country which is not a convention country and with which there is in force an extradition agreement (within the meaning of the Act of 1965) as they apply in relation to a convention country.

(2) The Minister for Foreign Affairs may, after consultation with the Minister, by order amend or revoke an order under this section including an order under this subsection.

(3) Every order under this section shall be laid before each House of the Oireachtas as soon as may be after it is made and, if a resolution annulling the order is passed by either such House within the next 21 days on which that House sits after the order is laid before it, the order shall be annulled accordingly, but without prejudice to anything previously done thereunder.".

52   Amendment of Act of 2001

The Act of 2001 is amended by—

(a)   the insertion of the following subsection in section 4:

"(1A) The Minister for Foreign Affairs may by order designate a country (other than a Member State of the European Communities) as being deemed to have adopted in whole or in part the Convention of 1995 and any such order shall specify the provisions of this Part that apply to that country.", and

(b)   the insertion of the following subsection in section 10:

"(1A) The Minister for Foreign Affairs may by order designate a country (other than a Member State of the European Communities) as being deemed to have adopted in whole or in part the Convention of 1996 and any such order shall specify the provisions of this Part that apply to that country.".

SCHEDULE

PART A

TEXT IN THE IRISH LANGUAGE OF COUNCIL FRAMEWORK DECISION OF 13 JUNE 2002 ON THE EUROPEAN ARREST WARRANT AND THE SURRENDER PROCEDURES BETWEEN MEMBER STATES.

Text not reproduced here.

PART B

TEXT IN THE ENGLISH LANGUAGE OF COUNCIL FRAMEWORK DECISION OF 13 JUNE 2002
ON THE EUROPEAN ARREST WARRANT AND THE SURRENDER PROCEDURES BETWEEN
MEMBER STATES.

COUNCIL FRAMEWORK DECISION

OF 13 JUNE 2002

ON THE EUROPEAN ARREST WARRANT AND THE SURRENDER PROCEDURES BETWEEN
MEMBER STATES

(2002/584/JHA)

THE COUNCIL OF THE EUROPEAN UNION,

Having regard to the Treaty on European Union, and in particular Article 31(a) and (b) and
Article 34(2)(b) thereof,

Having regard to the proposal from the Commission,

Having regard to the opinion of the European Parliament,

Whereas:

(1) According to the Conclusions of the Tampere European Council of 15 and 16 October
1999, and in particular point 35 thereof, the formal extradition procedure should be
abolished among the Member States in respect of persons who are fleeing from justice after
having been finally sentenced and extradition procedures should be speeded up in respect of
persons suspected of having committed an offence.

(2) The programme of measures to implement the principle of mutual recognition of criminal
decisions envisaged in point 37 of the Tampere European Council Conclusions and adopted
by the Council on 30 November 2000[3], addresses the matter of mutual enforcement of arrest
warrants.

(3) All or some Member States are parties to a number of conventions in the field of
extradition, including the European Convention on extradition of 13 December 1957 and the
European Convention on the suppression of terrorism of 27 January 1977. The Nordic States
have extradition laws with identical wording.

(4) In addition, the following three Conventions dealing in whole or in part with extradition
have been agreed upon among Member States and form part of the Union acquis: the
Convention of 19 June 1990 implementing the Schengen Agreement of 14 June 1985 on the
gradual abolition of checks at their common borders (regarding relations between the
Member States which are parties to that Convention), the Convention of 10 March 1995 on
simplified extradition procedure between the Member States of the European Union and the
Convention of 27 September 1996 relating to extradition between the Member States of the
European Union.

(5) The objective set for the Union to become an area of freedom, security and justice leads
to abolishing extradition between Member States and replacing it by a system of surrender
between judicial authorities. Further, the introduction of a new simplified system of
surrender of sentenced or suspected persons for the purposes of execution or prosecution of
criminal sentences makes it possible to remove the complexity and potential for delay

inherent in the present extradition procedures. Traditional cooperation relations which have prevailed up till now between Member States should be replaced by a system of free movement of judicial decisions in criminal matters, covering both pre-sentence and final decisions, within an area of freedom, security and justice.

(6) The European arrest warrant provided for in this Framework Decision is the first concrete measure in the field of criminal law implementing the principle of mutual recognition which the European Council referred to as the 'cornerstone' of judicial cooperation.

(7) Since the aim of replacing the system of multilateral extradition built upon the European Convention on Extradition of 13 December 1957 cannot be sufficiently achieved by the Member States acting unilaterally and can therefore, by reason of its scale and effects, be better achieved at Union level, the Council may adopt measures in accordance with the principle of subsidiarity as referred to in Article 2 of the Treaty on European Union and Article 5 of the Treaty establishing the European Community. In accordance with the principle of proportionality, as set out in the latter Article, this Framework Decision does not go beyond what is necessary in order to achieve that objective.

(8) Decisions on the execution of the European arrest warrant must be subject to sufficient controls, which means that a judicial authority of the Member State where the requested person has been arrested will have to take the decision on his or her surrender.

(9) The role of central authorities in the execution of a European arrest warrant must be limited to practical and administrative assistance.

(10) The mechanism of the European arrest warrant is based on a high level of confidence between Member States. Its implementation may be suspended only in the event of a serious and persistent breach by one of the Member States of the principle set out in Article 6(1) of the Treaty on European Union, determined by the Council pursuant to Article 7(1) of the said Treaty with the consequences set out in Article 7(2) thereof.

(11) In relations between Member States, the European arrest warrant should replace all the previous instruments concerning extradition, including the provisions of Title III of the Convention implementing the Schengen Agreement which concern extradition.

(12) This Framework Decision respects fundamental rights and observes the principles recognised by Article 6 of the Treaty on European Union and reflected in the Charter of Fundamental Rights of the European Union[(1)], in particular Chapter VI thereof. Nothing in this Framework Decision may be interpreted as prohibiting refusal to surrender a person for whom a European arrest warrant has been issued when there are reasons to believe, on the basis of objective elements, that the said arrest warrant has been issued for the purpose of prosecuting or punishing a person on the grounds of his or her sex, race, religion, ethnic origin, nationality, language, political opinions or sexual orientation, or that that person's position may be prejudiced for any of these reasons.

This Framework Decision does not prevent a Member State from applying its constitutional rules relating to due process, freedom of association, freedom of the press and freedom of expression in other media.

(13) No person should be removed, expelled or extradited to a State where there is a serious risk that he or she would be subjected to the death penalty, torture or other inhuman or degrading treatment or punishment.

(14) Since all Member States have ratified the Council of Europe Convention of 28 January 1981 for the protection of individuals with regard to automatic processing of personal data,

the personal data processed in the context of the implementation of this Framework Decision should be protected in accordance with the principles of the said Convention

HAS ADOPTED THIS FRAMEWORK DECISION:

CHAPTER 1
GENERAL PRINCIPLES

Article 1
Definition of the European arrest warrant and obligation to execute it

1. The European arrest warrant is a judicial decision issued by a Member State with a view to the arrest and surrender by another Member State of a requested person, for the purposes of conducting a criminal prosecution or executing a custodial sentence or detention order.

2. Member States shall execute any European arrest warrant on the basis of the principle of mutual recognition and in accordance with the provisions of this Framework Decision.

3. This Framework Decision shall not have the effect of modifying the obligation to respect fundamental rights and fundamental legal principles as enshrined in Article 6 of the Treaty on European Union.

Article 2
Scope of the European arrest warrant

1. A European arrest warrant may be issued for acts punishable by the law of the issuing Member State by a custodial sentence or a detention order for a maximum period of at least 12 months or, where a sentence has been passed or a detention order has been made, for sentences of at least four months.

2. The following offences, if they are punishable in the issuing Member State by a custodial sentence or a detention order for a maximum period of at least three years and as they are defined by the law of the issuing Member State, shall, under the terms of this Framework Decision and without verification of the double criminality of the act, give rise to surrender pursuant to a European arrest warrant:

— participation in a criminal organisation,
— terrorism,
— trafficking in human beings,
— sexual exploitation of children and child pornography,
— illicit trafficking in narcotic drugs and psychotropic substances,
— illicit trafficking in weapons, munitions and explosives,
— corruption,
— fraud, including that affecting the financial interests of the European Communities within the meaning of the Convention of 26 July 1995 on the protection of the European Communities' financial interests,
— laundering of the proceeds of crime,
— counterfeiting currency, including of the euro,
— computer-related crime,
— environmental crime, including illicit trafficking in endangered animal species and in endangered plant species and varieties,

— facilitation of unauthorised entry and residence,
— murder, grievous bodily injury,
— illicit trade in human organs and tissue,
— kidnapping, illegal restraint and hostage-taking,
— racism and xenophobia,
— organised or armed robbery,
— illicit trafficking in cultural goods, including antiques and works of art,
— swindling,
— racketeering and extortion,
— counterfeiting and piracy of products,
— forgery of administrative documents and trafficking therein,
— forgery of means of payment,
— illicit trafficking in hormonal substances and other growth promoters,
— illicit trafficking in nuclear or radioactive materials,
— trafficking in stolen vehicles,
— rape,
— arson,
— crimes within the jurisdiction of the International Criminal Court,
— unlawful seizure of aircraft/ships,
— sabotage.

3. The Council may decide at any time, acting unanimously after consultation of the European Parliament under the conditions laid down in Article 39(1) of the Treaty on European Union (TEU), to add other categories of offence to the list contained in paragraph 2. The Council shall examine, in the light of the report submitted by the Commission pursuant to Article 34(3), whether the list should be extended or amended.

4. For offences other than those covered by paragraph 2, surrender may be subject to the condition that the acts for which the European arrest warrant has been issued constitute an offence under the law of the executing Member State, whatever the constituent elements or however it is described.

Article 3
Grounds for mandatory non-execution of the European arrest warrant

The judicial authority of the Member State of execution (hereinafter 'executing judicial authority') shall refuse to execute the European arrest warrant in the following cases:

1. if the offence on which the arrest warrant is based is covered by amnesty in the executing Member State, where that State had jurisdiction to prosecute the offence under its own criminal law;

2. if the executing judicial authority is informed that the requested person has been finally judged by a Member State in respect of the same acts provided that, where there has been sentence, the sentence has been served or is currently being served or may no longer be executed under the law of the sentencing Member State;

3. if the person who is the subject of the European arrest warrant may not, owing to his age, be held criminally responsible for the acts on which the arrest warrant is based under the law of the executing State.

Article 4
Grounds for optional non-execution of the European arrest warrant

The executing judicial authority may refuse to execute the European arrest warrant:

1. if, in one of the cases referred to in Article 2(4), the act on which the European arrest warrant is based does not constitute an offence under the law of the executing Member State; however, in relation to taxes or duties, customs and exchange, execution of the European arrest warrant shall not be refused on the ground that the law of the executing Member State does not impose the same kind of tax or duty or does not contain the same type of rules as regards taxes, duties and customs and exchange regulations as the law of the issuing Member State;

2. where the person who is the subject of the European arrest warrant is being prosecuted in the executing Member State for the same act as that on which the European arrest warrant is based;

3. where the judicial authorities of the executing Member State have decided either not to prosecute for the offence on which the European arrest warrant is based or to halt proceedings, or where a final judgment has been passed upon the requested person in a Member State, in respect of the same acts, which prevents further proceedings;

4. where the criminal prosecution or punishment of the requested person is statute-barred according to the law of the executing Member State and the acts fall within the jurisdiction of that Member State under its own criminal law;

5. if the executing judicial authority is informed that the requested person has been finally judged by a third State in respect of the same acts provided that, where there has been sentence, the sentence has been served or is currently being served or may no longer be executed under the law of the sentencing country;

6. if the European arrest warrant has been issued for the purposes of execution of a custodial sentence or detention order, where the requested person is staying in, or is a national or a resident of the executing Member State and that State undertakes to execute the sentence or detention order in accordance with its domestic law;

7. where the European arrest warrant relates to offences which:

    (a) are regarded by the law of the executing Member State as having been committed in whole or in part in the territory of the executing Member State or in a place treated as such; or

    (b) have been committed outside the territory of the issuing Member State and the law of the executing Member State does not allow prosecution for the same offences when committed outside its territory.

Article 5
Guarantees to be given by the issuing Member State in particular cases

The execution of the European arrest warrant by the executing judicial authority may, by the law of the executing Member State, be subject to the following conditions:

1. where the European arrest warrant has been issued for the purposes of executing a sentence or a detention order imposed by a decision rendered and if the person concerned has not been summoned in person or otherwise informed of the date and place of the hearing which led to the decision rendered in absentia, surrender may be subject to the condition that

the issuing judicial authority gives an assurance deemed adequate to g
who is the subject of the European arrest warrant that he or she will ha
apply for a retrial of the case in the issuing Member State and to be pres

2. if the offence on the basis of which the European arrest warrant
punishable by custodial life sentence or life-time detention order, the execution ~~or~~ ~~the said~~
arrest warrant may be subject to the condition that the issuing Member State has provisions
in its legal system for a review of the penalty or measure imposed, on request or at the latest
after 20 years, or for the application of measures of clemency to which the person is entitled
to apply for under the law or practice of the issuing Member State, aiming at a non-execution
of such penalty or measure;

3. where a person who is the subject of a European arrest warrant for the purposes of
prosecution is a national or resident of the executing Member State, surrender may be subject
to the condition that the person, after being heard, is returned to the executing Member State
in order to serve there the custodial sentence or detention order passed against him in the
issuing Member State.

Article 6
Determination of the competent judicial authorities

1. The issuing judicial authority shall be the judicial authority of the issuing Member State
which is competent to issue a European arrest warrant by virtue of the law of that State.

2. The executing judicial authority shall be the judicial authority of the executing Member
State which is competent to execute the European arrest warrant by virtue of the law of that
State.

3. Each Member State shall inform the General Secretariat of the Council of the competent
judicial authority under its law.

Article 7
Recourse to the central authority

1. Each Member State may designate a central authority or, when its legal system so
provides, more than one central authority to assist the competent judicial authorities.

2. A Member State may, if it is necessary as a result of the organisation of its internal judicial
system, make its central authority(ies) responsible for the administrative transmission and
reception of European arrest warrants as well as for all other official correspondence relating
thereto.

Member State wishing to make use of the possibilities referred to in this Article shall
communicate to the General Secretariat of the Council information relating to the designated
central authority or central authorities. These indications shall be binding upon all the
authorities of the issuing Member State.

Article 8
Content and form of the European arrest warrant

1. The European arrest warrant shall contain the following information set out in accordance
with the form contained in the Annex:

   (a) the identity and nationality of the requested person;
   (b) the name, address, telephone and fax numbers and e-mail address of the issuing
   judicial authority;

(c) evidence of an enforceable judgment, an arrest warrant or any other enforceable judicial decision having the same effect, coming within the scope of Articles 1 and 2;

(d) the nature and legal classification of the offence, particularly in respect of Article 2;

(e) a description of the circumstances in which the offence was committed, including the time, place and degree of participation in the offence by the requested person;

(f) the penalty imposed, if there is a final judgment, or the prescribed scale of penalties for the offence under the law of the issuing Member State;

(g) if possible, other consequences of the offence.

2. The European arrest warrant must be translated into the official language or one of the official languages of the executing Member State. Any Member State may, when this Framework Decision is adopted or at a later date, state in a declaration deposited with the General Secretariat of the Council that it will accept a translation in one or more other official languages of the Institutions of the European Communities.

CHAPTER 2
SURRENDER PROCEDURE

Article 9
Transmission of a European arrest warrant

1. When the location of the requested person is known, the issuing judicial authority may transmit the European arrest warrant directly to the executing judicial authority.

2. The issuing judicial authority may, in any event, decide to issue an alert for the requested person in the Schengen Information System (SIS).

3. Such an alert shall be effected in accordance with the provisions of Article 95 of the Convention of 19 June 1990 implementing the Schengen Agreement of 14 June 1985 on the gradual abolition of controls at common borders. An alert in the Schengen Information System shall be equivalent to a European arrest warrant accompanied by the information set out in Article 8(1).

For a transitional period, until the SIS is capable of transmitting all the information described in Article 8, the alert shall be equivalent to a European arrest warrant pending the receipt of the original in due and proper form by the executing judicial authority.

Article 10
Detailed procedures for transmitting a European arrest warrant

1. If the issuing judicial authority does not know the competent executing judicial authority, it shall make the requisite enquiries, including through the contact points of the European Judicial Network[1], in order to obtain that information from the executing Member State.

2. If the issuing judicial authority so wishes, transmission may be effected via the secure telecommunications system of the European Judicial Network.

3. If it is not possible to call on the services of the SIS, the issuing judicial authority may call on Interpol to transmit a European arrest warrant.

4. The issuing judicial authority may forward the European arrest warrant by any secure means capable of producing written records under conditions allowing the executing Member State to establish its authenticity.

5. All difficulties concerning the transmission or the authenticity of any document needed for the execution of the European arrest warrant shall be dealt with by direct contacts between the judicial authorities involved, or, where appropriate, with the involvement of the central authorities of the Member States.

6. If the authority which receives a European arrest warrant is not competent to act upon it, it shall automatically forward the European arrest warrant to the competent authority in its Member State and shall inform the issuing judicial authority accordingly.

Article 11
Rights of a requested person

1. When a requested person is arrested, the executing competent judicial authority shall, in accordance with its national law, inform that person of the European arrest warrant and of its contents, and also of the possibility of consenting to surrender to the issuing judicial authority.

2. A requested person who is arrested for the purpose of the execution of a European arrest warrant shall have a right to be assisted by a legal counsel and by an interpreter in accordance with the national law of the executing Member State.

Article 12
Keeping the person in detention

When a person is arrested on the basis of a European arrest warrant, the executing judicial authority shall take a decision on whether the requested person should remain in detention, in accordance with the law of the executing Member State. The person may be released provisionally at any time in conformity with the domestic law of the executing Member State, provided that the competent authority of the said Member State takes all the measures it deems necessary to prevent the person absconding.

Article 13
Consent to surrender

1. If the arrested person indicates that he or she consents to surrender, that consent and, if appropriate, express renunciation of entitlement to the 'speciality rule', referred to in Article 27(2), shall be given before the executing judicial authority, in accordance with the domestic law of the executing Member State.

2. Each Member State shall adopt the measures necessary to ensure that consent and, where appropriate, renunciation, as referred to in paragraph 1, are established in such a way as to show that the person concerned has expressed them voluntarily and in full awareness of the consequences. To that end, the requested person shall have the right to legal counsel.

3. The consent and, where appropriate, renunciation, as referred to in paragraph 1, shall be formally recorded in accordance with the procedure laid down by the domestic law of the executing Member State.

4. In principle, consent may not be revoked. Each Member State may provide that consent and, if appropriate, renunciation may be revoked, in accordance with the rules applicable under its domestic law. In this case, the period between the date of consent and that of its revocation shall not be taken into consideration in establishing the time limits laid down in Article 17. A Member State which wishes to have recourse to this possibility shall inform the

General Secretariat of the Council accordingly when this Framework Decision is adopted and shall specify the procedures whereby revocation of consent shall be possible and any amendment to them.

Article 14
Hearing of the requested person

Where the arrested person does not consent to his or her surrender as referred to in Article 13, he or she shall be entitled to be heard by the executing judicial authority, in accordance with the law of the executing Member State.

Article 15
Surrender decision

1. The executing judicial authority shall decide, within the timelimits and under the conditions defined in this Framework Decision, whether the person is to be surrendered.

2. If the executing judicial authority finds the information communicated by the issuing Member State to be insufficient to allow it to decide on surrender, it shall request that the necessary supplementary information, in particular with respect to Articles 3 to 5 and Article 8, be furnished as a matter of urgency and may fix a time limit for the receipt thereof, taking into account the need to observe the time limits set in Article 17.

3. The issuing judicial authority may at any time forward any additional useful information to the executing judicial authority.

Article 16
Decision in the event of multiple requests

1. If two or more Member States have issued European arrest warrants for the same person, the decision on which of the European arrest warrants shall be executed shall be taken by the executing judicial authority with due consideration of all the circumstances and especially the relative seriousness and place of the offences, the respective dates of the European arrest warrants and whether the warrant has been issued for the purposes of prosecution or for execution of a custodial sentence or detention order.

2. The executing judicial authority may seek the advice of Eurojust[1] when making the choice referred to in paragraph 1.

3. In the event of a conflict between a European arrest warrant and a request for extradition presented by a third country, the decision on whether the European arrest warrant or the extradition request takes precedence shall be taken by the competent authority of the executing Member State with due consideration of all the circumstances, in particular those referred to in paragraph 1 and those mentioned in the applicable convention.

4. This Article shall be without prejudice to Member States' obligations under the Statute of the International Criminal Court.

Article 17
Time limits and procedures for the decision to execute the European arrest warrant

1. A European arrest warrant shall be dealt with and executed as a matter of urgency.

2. In cases where the requested person consents to his surrender, the final decision on the execution of the European arrest warrant should be taken within a period of 10 days after consent has been given.

3. In other cases, the final decision on the execution of the European arrest warrant should be taken within a period of 60 days after the arrest of the requested person.

4. Where in specific cases the European arrest warrant cannot be executed within the time limits laid down in paragraphs 2 or 3, the executing judicial authority shall immediately inform the issuing judicial authority thereof, giving the reasons for the delay. In such case, the time limits may be extended by a further 30 days.

5. As long as the executing judicial authority has not taken a final decision on the European arrest warrant, it shall ensure that the material conditions necessary for effective surrender of the person remain fulfilled.

6. Reasons must be given for any refusal to execute a European arrest warrant.

7. Where in exceptional circumstances a Member State cannot observe the time limits provided for in this Article, it shall inform Eurojust, giving the reasons for the delay. In addition, a Member State which has experienced repeated delays on the part of another Member State in the execution of European arrest warrants shall inform the Council with a view to evaluating the implementation of this Framework Decision at Member State level.

Article 18
Situation pending the decision

1. Where the European arrest warrant has been issued for the purpose of conducting a criminal prosecution, the executing judicial authority must:

    (a) either agree that the requested person should be heard according to Article 19;

    (b) or agree to the temporary transfer of the requested person.

2. The conditions and the duration of the temporary transfer shall be determined by mutual agreement between the issuing and executing judicial authorities.

3. In the case of temporary transfer, the person must be able to return to the executing Member State to attend hearings concerning him or her as part of the surrender procedure.

Article 19
Hearing the person pending the decision

1. The requested person shall be heard by a judicial authority, assisted by another person designated in accordance with the law of the Member State of the requesting court.

2. The requested person shall be heard in accordance with the law of the executing Member State and with the conditions determined by mutual agreement between the issuing and executing judicial authorities.

3. The competent executing judicial authority may assign another judicial authority of its Member State to take part in the hearing of the requested person in order to ensure the proper application of this Article and of the conditions laid down.

Article 20
Privileges and immunities

1. Where the requested person enjoys a privilege or immunity regarding jurisdiction or execution in the executing Member State, the time limits referred to in Article 17 shall not start running unless, and counting from the day when, the executing judicial authority is informed of the fact that the privilege or immunity has been waived. The executing Member

State shall ensure that the material conditions necessary for effective surrender are fulfilled when the person no longer enjoys such privilege or immunity.

2. Where power to waive the privilege or immunity lies with an authority of the executing Member State, the executing judicial authority shall request it to exercise that power forthwith. Where power to waive the privilege or immunity lies with an authority of another State or international organisation, it shall be for the issuing judicial authority to request it to exercise that power.

Article 21
Competing international obligations

This Framework Decision shall not prejudice the obligations of the executing Member State where the requested person has been extradited to that Member State from a third State and where that person is protected by provisions of the arrangement under which he or she was extradited concerning speciality. The executing Member State shall take all necessary measures for requesting forthwith the consent of the State from which the requested person was extradited so that he or she can be surrendered to the Member State which issued the European arrest warrant. The time limits referred to in Article 17 shall not start running until the day on which these speciality rules cease to apply. Pending the decision of the State from which the requested person was extradited, the executing Member State will ensure that the material conditions necessary for effective surrender remain fulfilled.

Article 22
Notification of the decision

The executing judicial authority shall notify the issuing judicial authority immediately of the decision on the action to be taken on the European arrest warrant.

Article 23
Time limits for surrender of the person

1. The person requested shall be surrendered as soon as possible on a date agreed between the authorities concerned.

2. He or she shall be surrendered no later than 10 days after the final decision on the execution of the European arrest warrant.

3. If the surrender of the requested person within the period laid down in paragraph 2 is prevented by circumstances beyond the control of any of the Member States, the executing and issuing judicial authorities shall immediately contact each other and agree on a new surrender date. In that event, the surrender shall take place within 10 days of the new date thus agreed.

4. The surrender may exceptionally be temporarily postponed for serious humanitarian reasons, for example if there are substantial grounds for believing that it would manifestly endanger the requested person's life or health. The execution of the European arrest warrant shall take place as soon as these grounds have ceased to exist. The executing judicial authority shall immediately inform the issuing judicial authority and agree on a new surrender date. In that event, the surrender shall take place within 10 days of the new date thus agreed.

5. Upon expiry of the time limits referred to in paragraphs 2 to 4, if the person is still being held in custody he shall be released.

Article 24
Postponed or conditional surrender

1. The executing judicial authority may, after deciding to execute the European arrest warrant, postpone the surrender of the requested person so that he or she may be prosecuted in the executing Member State or, if he or she has already been sentenced, so that he or she may serve, in its territory, a sentence passed for an act other than that referred to in the European arrest warrant.

2. Instead of postponing the surrender, the executing judicial authority may temporarily surrender the requested person to the issuing Member State under conditions to be determined by mutual agreement between the executing and the issuing judicial authorities. The agreement shall be made in writing and the conditions shall be binding on all the authorities in the issuing Member State.

Article 25
Transit

1. Each Member State shall, except when it avails itself of the possibility of refusal when the transit of a national or a resident is requested for the purpose of the execution of a custodial sentence or detention order, permit the transit through its territory of a requested person who is being surrendered provided that it has been given information on:

    (a)   the identity and nationality of the person subject to the European arrest warrant;

    (b)   the existence of a European arrest warrant;

    (c)   the nature and legal classification of the offence;

    (d)   the description of the circumstances of the offence, including the date and place.

Where a person who is the subject of a European arrest warrant for the purposes of prosecution is a national or resident of the Member State of transit, transit may be subject to the condition that the person, after being heard, is returned to the transit Member State to serve the custodial sentence or detention order passed against him in the issuing Member State.

2. Each Member State shall designate an authority responsible for receiving transit requests and the necessary documents, as well as any other official correspondence relating to transit requests. Member States shall communicate this designation to the General Secretariat of the Council.

3. The transit request and the information set out in paragraph 1 may be addressed to the authority designated pursuant to paragraph 2 by any means capable of producing a written record. The Member State of transit shall notify its decision by the same procedure.

4. This Framework Decision does not apply in the case of transport by air without a scheduled stopover. However, if an unscheduled landing occurs, the issuing Member State shall provide the authority designated pursuant to paragraph 2 with the information provided for in paragraph 1.

5. Where a transit concerns a person who is to be extradited from a third State to a Member State this Article will apply mutatis mutandis. In particular the expression 'European arrest warrant' shall be deemed to be replaced by 'extradition request'.

CHAPTER 3

EFFECTS OF THE SURRENDER

Article 26

Deduction of the period of detention served in the executing Member State

1. The issuing Member State shall deduct all periods of detention arising from the execution of a European arrest warrant from the total period of detention to be served in the issuing Member State as a result of a custodial sentence or detention order being passed.

2. To that end, all information concerning the duration of the detention of the requested person on the basis of the European arrest warrant shall be transmitted by the executing judicial authority or the central authority designated under Article 7 to the issuing judicial authority at the time of the surrender.

Article 27

Possible prosecution for other offences

1. Each Member State may notify the General Secretariat of the Council that, in its relations with other Member States that have given the same notification, consent is presumed to have been given for the prosecution, sentencing or detention with a view to the carrying out of a custodial sentence or detention order for an offence committed prior to his or her surrender, other than that for which he or she was surrendered, unless in a particular case the executing judicial authority states otherwise in its decision on surrender.

2. Except in the cases referred to in paragraphs 1 and 3, a person surrendered may not be prosecuted, sentenced or otherwise deprived of his or her liberty for an offence committed prior to his or her surrender other than that for which he or she was surrendered.

3. Paragraph 2 does not apply in the following cases:

    (a) when the person having had an opportunity to leave the territory of the Member State to which he or she has been surrendered has not done so within 45 days of his or her final discharge, or has returned to that territory after leaving it;

    (b) the offence is not punishable by a custodial sentence or detention order;

    (c) the criminal proceedings do not give rise to the application of a measure restricting personal liberty;

    (d) when the person could be liable to a penalty or a measure not involving the deprivation of liberty, in particular a financial penalty or a measure in lieu thereof, even if the penalty or measure may give rise to a restriction of his or her personal liberty;

    (e) when the person consented to be surrendered, where appropriate at the same time as he or she renounced the speciality rule, in accordance with Article 13;

    (f) when the person, after his/her surrender, has expressly renounced entitlement to the speciality rule with regard to specific offences preceding his/her surrender. Renunciation shall be given before the competent judicial authorities of the issuing Member State and shall be recorded in accordance with that State's domestic law. The renunciation shall be drawn up in such a way as to make clear that the person has given it voluntarily and in full awareness of the consequences. To that end, the person shall have the right to legal counsel;

1140

(g) where the executing judicial authority which surrendered the person gives its consent in accordance with paragraph 4.

4. A request for consent shall be submitted to the executing judicial authority, accompanied by the information mentioned in Article 8(1) and a translation as referred to in Article 8(2). Consent shall be given when the offence for which it is requested is itself subject to surrender in accordance with the provisions of this Framework Decision. Consent shall be refused on the grounds referred to in Article 3 and otherwise may be refused only on the grounds referred to in Article 4. The decision shall be taken no later than 30 days after receipt of the request.

For the situations mentioned in Article 5 the issuing Member State must give the guarantees provided for therein.

Article 28
Surrender or subsequent extradition

1. Each Member State may notify the General Secretariat of the Council that, in its relations with other Member States which have given the same notification, the consent for the surrender of a person to a Member State other than the executing Member State pursuant to a European arrest warrant issued for an offence committed prior to his or her surrender is presumed to have been given, unless in a particular case the executing judicial authority states otherwise in its decision on surrender.

2. In any case, a person who has been surrendered to the issuing Member State pursuant to a European arrest warrant may, without the consent of the executing Member State, be surrendered to a Member State other than the executing Member State pursuant to a European arrest warrant issued for any offence committed prior to his or her surrender in the following cases:

(a) where the requested person, having had an opportunity to leave the territory of the Member State to which he or she has been surrendered, has not done so within 45 days of his final discharge, or has returned to that territory after leaving it;

(b) where the requested person consents to be surrendered to a Member State other than the executing Member State pursuant to a European arrest warrant. Consent shall be given before the competent judicial authorities of the issuing Member State and shall be recorded in accordance with that State's national law. It shall be drawn up in such a way as to make clear that the person concerned has given it voluntarily and in full awareness of the consequences. To that end, the requested person shall have the right to legal counsel;

(c) where the requested person is not subject to the speciality rule, in accordance with Article 27(3)(a), (e), (f) and (g).

3. The executing judicial authority consents to the surrender to another Member State according to the following rules:

(a) the request for consent shall be submitted in accordance with Article 9, accompanied by the information mentioned in Article 8(1) and a translation as stated in Article 8(2);

(b) consent shall be given when the offence for which it is requested is itself subject to surrender in accordance with the provisions of this Framework Decision;

(c) the decision shall be taken no later than 30 days after receipt of the request;

(d) consent shall be refused on the grounds referred to in Article 3 and otherwise may be refused only on the grounds referred to in Article 4.

For the situations referred to in Article 5, the issuing Member State must give the guarantees provided for therein.

4. Notwithstanding paragraph 1, a person who has been surrendered pursuant to a European arrest warrant shall not be extradited to a third State without the consent of the competent authority of the Member State which surrendered the person. Such consent shall be given in accordance with the Conventions by which that Member State is bound, as well as with its domestic law.

Article 29
Handing over of property

1. At the request of the issuing judicial authority or on its own initiative, the executing judicial authority shall, in accordance with its national law, seize and hand over property which:

(a) may be required as evidence, or

(b) has been acquired by the requested person as a result of the offence.

2. The property referred to in paragraph 1 shall be handed over even if the European arrest warrant cannot be carried out owing to the death or escape of the requested person.

3. If the property referred to in paragraph 1 is liable to seizure or confiscation in the territory of the executing Member State, the latter may, if the property is needed in connection with pending criminal proceedings, temporarily retain it or hand it over to the issuing Member State, on condition that it is returned.

4. Any rights which the executing Member State or third parties may have acquired in the property referred to in paragraph 1 shall be preserved. Where such rights exist, the issuing Member State shall return the property without charge to the executing Member State as soon as the criminal proceedings have been terminated.

Article 30
Expenses

1. Expenses incurred in the territory of the executing Member State for the execution of a European arrest warrant shall be borne by that Member State.

2. All other expenses shall be borne by the issuing Member State.

CHAPTER 4
GENERAL AND FINAL PROVISIONS

Article 31
Relation to other legal instruments

1. Without prejudice to their application in relations between Member States and third States, this Framework Decision shall, from 1 January 2004, replace the corresponding provisions of the following conventions applicable in the field of extradition in relations between the Member States:

(a) the European Convention on Extradition of 13 December 1957, its additional protocol of 15 October 1975, its second additional protocol of 17 March 1978, and the European Convention on the suppression of terrorism of 27 January 1977 as far as extradition is concerned;

(b) the Agreement between the 12 Member States of the European Communities on the simplification and modernisation of methods of transmitting extradition requests of 26 May 1989;

(c) the Convention of 10 March 1995 on simplified extradition procedure between the Member States of the European Union;

(d) the Convention of 27 September 1996 relating to extradition between the Member States of the European Union;

(e) Title III, Chapter 4 of the Convention of 19 June 1990 implementing the Schengen Agreement of 14 June 1985 on the gradual abolition of checks at common borders.

2. Member States may continue to apply bilateral or multilateral agreements or arrangements in force when this Framework Decision is adopted in so far as such agreements or arrangements allow the objectives of this Framework Decision to be extended or enlarged and help to simplify or facilitate further the procedures for surrender of persons who are the subject of European arrest warrants.

Member States may conclude bilateral or multilateral agreements or arrangements after this Framework Decision has come into force in so far as such agreements or arrangements allow the prescriptions of this Framework Decision to be extended or enlarged and help to simplify or facilitate further the procedures for surrender of persons who are the subject of European arrest warrants, in particular by fixing time limits shorter than those fixed in Article 17, by extending the list of offences laid down in Article 2(2), by further limiting the grounds for refusal set out in Articles 3 and 4, or by lowering the threshold provided for in Article 2(1) or (2).

The agreements and arrangements referred to in the second subparagraph may in no case affect relations with Member States which are not parties to them.

Member States shall, within three months from the entry into force of this Framework Decision, notify the Council and the Commission of the existing agreements and arrangements referred to in the first subparagraph which they wish to continue applying.

Member States shall also notify the Council and the Commission of any new agreement or arrangement as referred to in the second subparagraph, within three months of signing it.

3. Where the conventions or agreements referred to in paragraph 1 apply to the territories of Member States or to territories for whose external relations a Member State is responsible to which this Framework Decision does not apply, these instruments shall continue to govern the relations existing between those territories and the other Members States.

Article 32
Transitional provision

1. Extradition requests received before 1 January 2004 will continue to be governed by existing instruments relating to extradition. Requests received after that date will be governed by the rules adopted by Member States pursuant to this Framework Decision. However, any Member State may, at the time of the adoption of this Framework Decision by the Council, make a statement indicating that as executing Member State it will continue to deal with requests relating to acts committed before a date which it specifies in accordance with the extradition system applicable before 1 January 2004. The date in question may not

be later than 7 August 2002. The said statement will be published in the Official Journal of the European Communities. It may be withdrawn at any time.

Article 33
Provisions concerning Austria and Gibraltar

1. As long as Austria has not modified Article 12(1) of the 'Auslieferungs-und Rechtshilfegesetz' and, at the latest, until 31 December 2008, it may allow its executing judicial authorities to refuse the enforcement of a European arrest warrant if the requested person is an Austrian citizen and if the act for which the European arrest warrant has been issued is not punishable under Austrian law.

2. This Framework Decision shall apply to Gibraltar.

Article 34
Implementation

1. Member States shall take the necessary measures to comply with the provisions of this Framework Decision by 31 December 2003.

2. Member States shall transmit to the General Secretariat of the Council and to the Commission the text of the provisions transposing into their national law the obligations imposed on them under this Framework Decision. When doing so, each Member State may indicate that it will apply immediately this Framework Decision in its relations with those Member States which have given the same notification.

The General Secretariat of the Council shall communicate to the Member States and to the Commission the information received pursuant to Article 7(2), Article 8(2), Article 13(4) and Article 25(2). It shall also have the information published in the Official Journal of the European Communities.

3. On the basis of the information communicated by the General Secretariat of the Council, the Commission shall, by 31 December 2004 at the latest, submit a report to the European Parliament and to the Council on the operation of this Framework Decision, accompanied, where necessary, by legislative proposals.

4. The Council shall in the second half of 2003 conduct a review, in particular of the practical application, of the provisions of this Framework Decision by the Member States as well as the functioning of the Schengen Information System.

Article 35
Entry into force

This Framework Decision shall enter into force on the twentieth day following that of its publication in the Official Journal of the European Communities.

Done at Luxembourg, 13 June 2002.

For the Council

The President

M. RAJOY BREY

ANNEX

EUROPEAN ARREST WARRANT

This warrant has been issued by a competent judicial authority. I request that the person mentioned below be arrested and surrendered for the purposes of conducting a criminal prosecution or executing a custodial sentence or detention order.

(a)	Information regarding the identity of the requested person: Name: .... Forename(s): .... Maiden name, where applicable: .... Aliases, where applicable:... Sex:.. Nationality:.. Date of birth: .... Place of birth: .... Residence and/or known address: .... Language(s) which the requested person understands (if known):....................... Distinctive marks/description of the requested person: .... Photo and fingerprints of the requested person, if they are available and can be transmitted, or contact details of the person to be contacted in order to obtain such information or a DNA profile (where this evidence can be supplied but has not been included)

(b)	Decision on which the warrant is based:
1.	Arrest warrant or judicial decision having the same effect:.. Type: ....
2.	Enforceable judgement: .... Reference: ....

(c)	Indications on the length of the sentence:
1.	Maximum length of the custodial sentence or detention order which may be imposed for the offence(s): ....
2.	Length of the custodial sentence or detention order imposed: .... Remaining sentence to be served:... ....

(d) Decision rendered in absentia and:
— the person concerned has been summoned in person or otherwise informed of the date and place of the hearing which led to the decision rendered in absentia,
or
— the person concerned has not been summoned in person or otherwise informed of the date and place of the hearing which led to the decision rendered in absentia but has the following legal guarantees after surrender (such guarantees can be given in advance)
Specify the legal guarantees...
....
....

(e) Offences:
This warrant relates to in total:...offences.
Description of the circumstances in which the offence(s) was (were) committed, including the time, place and degree of participation in the offence(s) by the requested person:
....
....
....
Nature and legal classification of the offence(s) and the applicable statutory provision/code:
....
....
....

1. If applicable, tick one or more of the following offences punishable in the issuing Member State by a custodial sentence or detention order of a maximum of at least 3 years as defined by the laws of the issuing Member State:
❑ participation in a criminal organisation;
❑ terrorism;
❑ trafficking in human beings;
❑ sexual exploitation of children and child pornography;
❑ illicit trafficking in narcotic drugs and psychotropic substances;
❑ illicit trafficking in weapons, munitions and explosives;
❑ corruption;
❑ fraud, including that affecting the financial interests of the European Communities within the meaning of the Convention of 26 July 1995 on the protection of European Communities' financial interests;
❑ laundering of the proceeds of crime;
❑ counterfeiting of currency, including the euro;
❑ computer-related crime;
❑ environmental crime, including illicit trafficking in endangered animal species and in endangered plant species and varieties;
❑ facilitation of unauthorised entry and residence;

❑   murder, grievous bodily injury;
❑   illicit trade in human organs and tissue;
❑   kidnapping, illegal restraint and hostage-taking;
❑   racism and xenophobia;
❑   organised or armed robbery;
❑   illicit trafficking in cultural goods, including antiques and works of art;
❑   swindling;
❑   racketeering and extortion;
❑   counterfeiting and piracy of products;
❑   forgery of administrative documents and trafficking therein;
❑   forgery of means of payment;
❑   illicit trafficking in hormonal substances and other growth promoters;
❑   illicit trafficking in nuclear or radioactive materials;
❑   trafficking in stolen vehicles;
❑   rape;
❑   arson;
❑   crimes within the jurisdiction of the International Criminal Court;
❑   unlawful seizure of aircraft/ships;
❑   sabotage.
II. Full descriptions of offence(s) not covered by section I above:

....
....
....

(f)   Other circumstances relevant to the case (optional information):
(NB: This could cover remarks on extraterritoriality, interruption of periods of time limitation
        and other consequences of the offence)

....
....

(g)   This warrant pertains also to the seizure and handing over of property which may be
        required as evidence:
        This warrant pertains also to the seizure and handing over of property acquired by the
        requested person as a result of the offence:
        Description of the property (and location) (if known):

....
....

(h) The offence(s) on the basis of which this warrant has been issued is(are) punishable by/ has(have) led to a custodial life sentence or lifetime detention order:

— the legal system of the issuing Member State allows for a review of the penalty or measure imposed — on request or at least after 20 years — aiming at a non-execution of such penalty or measure,

and/or

— the legal system of the issuing Member State allow for the application of measures of elemency to which the person is entitled under the law or practice of the issuing Member State, aiming at non-execution of such penalty of measure.

(i) The judicial authority which issued the warrant:

Official name:

Name of its representative:

....

....

Post held (title/grade): ....

....

File reference:...

Address:..

Tel: (country code) (area/city code) (...) ....

Fax: (country code) (area/city code) (...)...

E-mail:..

Contact details of the person to contact to make necessary practical arrangements for the surrender:..

....

Where a central authority has been made responsible for the transmission and administrative reception of European arrest warrants:

Name of the central authority:...

Contact person, if applicable (title/grade and name): ....

Address:..

Tel: (country code) (area/city code) (...) ....

Fax: (country code) (area/city code) (...)...

E-mail:..

Signature of the issuing judicial authority and/or its representative: ....

Name: ....

Post held (title/grade) ....

Date: ....

Official stamp (if available)

Immigration Act 2004

Number 1 of 2004

ARRANGEMENT OF SECTIONS

1. Interpretation.
2. Application of Act.
3. Appointment of officers.
4. Permission to land.
5. Presence in State of non-nationals.
6. Approved port.
7. Examination and detention of non-nationals.
8. Notices to be displayed on ships, railway trains and passenger road vehicles.
9. Obligation of non-nationals to register.
10. Hotel registers.
11. Requirements as to documents of identity and supply of information.
12. Requirement as to production of documents.
13. Offences and power of arrest without warrant.
14. Provision for particular non-nationals.
15. Entry, search and seizure.
16. Amendment of certain enactments.
17. Visa orders.
18. Service of notices.
19. Fees.
20. Regulations and orders.
21. Expenses.
22. Short title.

FIRST SCHEDULE

CONDITIONS REFERRED TO IN SECTION 4(3)(C)

SECOND SCHEDULE

PARTICULARS TO BE FURNISHED ON REGISTRATION

IMMIGRATION ACT 2004

AN ACT TO MAKE PROVISION, IN THE INTERESTS OF THE COMMON GOOD, FOR THE CONTROL OF ENTRY INTO THE STATE, THE DURATION AND CONDITIONS OF STAY IN THE STATE AND OBLIGATIONS WHILE IN THE STATE OF NON-NATIONALS AND TO PROVIDE FOR RELATED MATTERS. [13th February, 2004]

BE IT ENACTED BY THE OIREACHTAS AS FOLLOWS:

1   Interpretation

(1) In this Act, except where the context otherwise requires—

"the Act of 1996" means the Refugee Act 1996;

"the Act of 1999" means the Immigration Act 1999;

"embarking" includes departure by any form of conveyance and departure over a land frontier;

"Great Britain" includes the Channel Islands and the Isle of Man;

"immigration officer" shall be construed in accordance with section 3;

"keeper", in relation to premises where accommodation is provided for reward, includes any person who for reward receives another person to lodge or sleep in the premises, either on his or her own behalf or as manager or otherwise on behalf of another person;

"landing" includes arrival or entry by any form of conveyance and includes entry over a land frontier, and references to landing include references to attempting to land;

"master of a ship" includes the pilot of an aircraft;

"member of a crew" means any person employed in the working or service of a ship;

"the Minister" means the Minister for Justice, Equality and Law Reform;

"non-national" has the meaning assigned to it by the Act of 1999;

"passenger" means any person, other than a member of a crew, travelling or seeking to travel on board a ship, railway train or passenger road vehicle;

"passenger road vehicle" means a vehicle employed on a passenger road service which is licensed under the Road Transport Act 1932;

"permission" shall be construed in accordance with section 4;

"port" includes any place whether on a land or sea frontier where a person lands in or embarks from the State and includes an airport;

"prescribed" means prescribed by regulations made by the Minister and "prescribe" shall be construed accordingly;

"registration district" means the Dublin Metropolitan Area or a Garda Síochána District situated outside that Area;

"registration officer" means the officer in charge of the Garda National Immigration Bureau in the Dublin Metropolitan Area or the Superintendent of the Garda Síochána in a Garda Síochána District outside that Area;

"residence" means a dwelling-place where a non-national ordinarily resides and, where a non-national has more than one dwelling-place, each of such dwelling-places; and "resident" shall be construed accordingly;

"seaman" means an officer or member of a crew;

"ship" includes aircraft.

(2) In this Act—

    (a) a reference to any enactment shall, unless the context otherwise requires, be construed as a reference to that enactment as amended or extended by or under any subsequent enactment including this Act,

    (b) a reference to a section or Schedule is a reference to a section of or a Schedule to this Act unless it is indicated that reference to some other enactment is intended,

(c) a reference to a subsection, paragraph or subparagraph is a reference to the subsection, paragraph or subparagraph of the provision in which the reference occurs unless it is indicated that reference to some other provision is intended.

2   Application of Act

(1) This Act shall not apply to any of the following persons, that is to say:

    (a) a person entitled in the State to privileges and immunities under section 5 of the Diplomatic Relations and Immunities Act 1967;

    (b) a person entitled in the State to privileges and immunities under section 6 of that Act;

    (c) a person entitled in the State to privileges and immunities under any other Act of the Oireachtas or any instrument made thereunder.

(2) Nothing in this Act shall derogate from—

    (a) any of the obligations of the State under the treaties governing the European Communities within the meaning of the European Communities Acts 1972 to 2003,

    (b any act adopted by an institution of those Communities,

    (c) section 9(1) of the Refugee Act 1996,

    (d) the European Communities (Aliens) Regulations 1977 (S.I. No. 393 of 1977), or

    (e) the European Communities (Right of Residence for NonEconomically Active Persons) Regulations 1997 (S.I. No. 57 of 1997).

(3) If, in any proceedings, whether civil or criminal, any question arises under or in relation to a provision of this Act, the Act of 1999 or the Immigration Act 2003 as to whether any person is or is not a non-national, or is or is not a non-national of a particular nationality or otherwise of a particular class, or is or is not a particular non-national specified in an order made under the Act of 1999, the onus of proving (as the case may require) that such person is not a non-national, or is not a non-national of a particular nationality or of a particular class, or is not such a particular non-national, shall lie on such person.

3   Appointment of officers

(1) The Minister may appoint such and so many persons as he or she considers appropriate (referred to in this Act as "immigration officers") to perform the functions conferred on immigration officers by this Act and every person so appointed shall hold office on such terms and conditions as may be determined by the Minister at the time of the appointment.

(2) The Minister may, with the consent of the Minister for Health and Children, appoint such and so many registered medical practitioners (referred to in this Act as "medical inspectors") as he or she considers appropriate to perform the functions conferred on medical inspectors by this Act and every person so appointed shall hold office on such terms and conditions as may be determined by the Minister (with the consent of the Minister for Health and Children) at the time of the appointment.

(3) An immigration officer or a medical inspector appointed under this Act shall have power to enter or board any vessel, and to detain and examine any person arriving at or leaving any port in the State who is reasonably believed by the officer or inspector to be a non-national, and to require the production of a passport or other equivalent identity document by such person, and shall have such other powers and duties as are conferred upon him or her by this Act.

(4) A person appointed by the Minister to be an immigration officer before the commencement of this Act and who was acting as such an officer immediately before such commencement shall upon such commencement be deemed to have been appointed as an immigration officer under this section.

(5) A reference in any Act passed before the commencement of this section or in any instrument made under such an Act to an immigration officer shall be construed as a reference to an immigration officer appointed under this section and, accordingly, a function standing vested in an immigration officer immediately before such commencement under a provision of such an Act or instrument that continues in force after such commencement shall, upon such commencement, stand vested in, and may be performed by, such an officer.

(6) The Minister may revoke an appointment made or deemed to have been made under this section.

4   Permission to land

(1) Subject to the provisions of this Act, an immigration officer may, on behalf of the Minister, give to a non-national a document, or place on his or her passport or other equivalent document an inscription, authorising the non-national to land or be in the State (referred to in this Act as "a permission").

(2) A non-national coming by air or sea from a place outside the State shall, on arrival in the State, present himself or herself to an immigration officer and apply for a permission.

(3) Subject to section 2(2), an immigration officer may, on behalf of the Minister, refuse to give a permission to a person referred to in subsection (2) if the officer is satisfied—

    (a)   that the non-national is not in a position to support himself or herself and any accompanying dependants;

    (b)   that the non-national intends to take up employment in the State, but is not in possession of a valid employment permit (within the meaning of the Employment Permits Act 2003);

    (c)   that the non-national suffers from a condition set out in the First Schedule;

    (d)   that the non-national has been convicted (whether in the State or elsewhere) of an offence that may be punished under the law of the place of conviction by imprisonment for a period of one year or by a more severe penalty;

    (e)   that the non-national, not being exempt, by virtue of an order under section 17, from the requirement to have an Irish visa, is not the holder of a valid Irish visa;

    (f)   that the non-national is the subject of—

        (i)   a deportation order (within the meaning of the Act of 1999),

        (ii)   an exclusion order (within the meaning of that Act), or

        (iii)   a determination by the Minister that it is conducive to the public good that he or she remain outside the State;

    (g)   that the non-national is not in possession of a valid passport or other equivalent document, issued by or on behalf of an authority recognised by the Government, which establishes his or her identity and nationality;

    (h)   that the non-national—

        (i)   intends to travel (whether immediately or not) to Great Britain or Northern Ireland, and

      (ii)   would not qualify for admission to Great Britain or Northern Ireland if he or she arrived there from a place other than the State;

  (i)   that the non-national, having arrived in the State in the course of employment as a seaman, has remained in the State without the leave of an immigration officer after the departure of the ship in which he or she so arrived;

  (j)   that the non-national's entry into, or presence in, the State could pose a threat to national security or be contrary to public policy;

  (k)   that there is reason to believe that the non-national intends to enter the State for purposes other than those expressed by the non-national.

(4) An immigration officer who pursuant to subsection (3) refuses to give a permission to a non-national shall as soon as may be inform the non-national in writing of the grounds for the refusal.

(5) (a) An immigration officer may, on behalf of the Minister, examine a non-national arriving in the State otherwise than by sea or air (referred to subsequently in this subsection as "a non-national to whom this subsection applies") for the purpose of determining whether he or she should be given a permission and the provisions of subsections (3), (4) and (6) shall apply with any necessary modifications in the case of a person so examined as they apply in the case of a person coming by sea or air from a place outside the State.

  (b) A non-national to whom this subsection applies and who is not exempt, by virtue of an order under section 17, from the requirement to have an Irish visa shall have a valid Irish visa.

  (c) A non-national to whom this subsection applies and who is arriving in the State to engage in employment, business or a profession in the State shall within 7 days of entering the State—

     (i)   report in person to the registration officer for the place in which he or she intends to reside,

    (ii)   produce to the officer a valid passport or other equivalent document, issued by or on behalf of an authority recognised by the Government, which establishes his or her identity and nationality, and

   (iii)   furnish such information as the officer may reasonably require regarding the purpose of his or her arrival in the State.

  (d) A non-national to whom this subsection applies shall not remain in the State for longer than one month without the permission of the Minister given in writing by him or her or on his or her behalf by an immigration officer.

(6) An immigration officer may, on behalf of the Minister, by a notice in writing to a non-national, or an inscription placed on his or her passport or other equivalent document, attach to a permission under this section such conditions as to duration of stay and engagement in employment, business or a profession in the State as he or she may think fit, and may by such a notice or inscription at any time amend such conditions as aforesaid in such manner as he or she may think fit, and the non-national shall comply with any such conditions.

(7) A permission under this section may be renewed or varied by the Minister, or by an immigration officer on his or her behalf, on application therefor by the non-national concerned.

(8) A non-national, being a member of a class of persons declared by order under section 17 to require a transit visa to enter the State, shall have a valid transit visa.

(9) A non-national who contravenes subsection (2), paragraph (b), (c) or (d) of subsection (5) or subsection (6) or (8) is guilty of an offence.

(10) In performing his or her functions under subsection (6), an immigration officer shall have regard to all of the circumstances of the non-national concerned known to the officer or represented to the officer by him or her and, in particular, but without prejudice to the generality of the foregoing, to the following matters:

(a)   the stated purpose of the proposed visit to the State,

(b)   the intended duration of the stay in the State,

(c)   any family relationships (whether of blood or through marriage) of him or her with persons in the State,

(d)   his or her income, earning capacity and other financial resources,

(e)   the financial needs, obligations and responsibilities which he or she has or is likely to have in the foreseeable future,

(f)   whether he or she is likely to comply with any proposed conditions as to duration of stay and engagement in employment, business or profession in the State,

(g)   any entitlements of him or her to enter the State under the Act of 1996 or the treaties governing the European Communities within the meaning of the European Communities Acts 1972 to 2003.

5   Presence in State of non-nationals

(1) No non-national may be in the State other than in accordance with the terms of any permission given to him or her before the passing of this Act, or a permission given under this Act after such passing, by or on behalf of the Minister.

(2) A non-national who is in the State in contravention of subsection (1) is for all purposes unlawfully present in the State.

(3) This section does not apply to—

(a)   a person whose application for asylum under the Act of 1996 is under consideration by the Minister,

(b)   a refugee who is the holder of a declaration (within the meaning of that Act) which is in force,

(c)   a member of the family of a refugee to whom section 18(3)(a) of that Act applies, or

(d)   a programme refugee within the meaning of section 24 of that Act.

6   Approved port

(1) A non-national (other than a seaman) coming by sea or air from outside the State shall not, without the consent of the Minister, land elsewhere than at an approved port.

(2) Such ports as may be prescribed shall be approved ports for the purposes of subsection (1).

(3) A non-national who lands in the State in contravention of this section shall be deemed to be a non-national who has been refused a permission.

(4) A non-national who lands in the State in contravention of this section shall be guilty of an offence.

7 Examination and detention of non-nationals

(1) The master of any ship arriving at a port in the State may detain on board any non-national coming in the ship from a place outside the State until the non-national is examined or landed for examination under this section, and shall, on the request of an immigration officer, so detain any such non-national, whether seaman or passenger, whose application for a permission has been refused by an immigration officer, and any such non-national so detained shall be deemed to be in lawful custody.

(2) The master of a ship who fails to comply with a request of an immigration officer under subsection (1) shall be guilty of an offence.

(3) (a) Any non-national landing or embarking at any place in the State shall, on being required so to do by an immigration officer or a member of the Garda Síochána, make a declaration as to whether or not he or she is carrying or conveying any documents and, if so required, shall produce them to the officer or member.

(b) The officer or member may search any such non-national and any luggage belonging to him or her or under his or her control with a view to ascertaining whether the non-national is carrying or conveying any documents and may examine and detain, for such time as he or she may think proper for the purpose of such examination, any documents so produced or found on the search.

(c) In this section, "documents" includes—

(i) any written matter,

(ii) any photograph,

(iii) any currency notes or counterfeit currency notes,

(iv) any information in non-legible form that is capable of being converted into legible form, or

(v) any audio or video recording.

(4) A non-national who contravenes subsection (3) shall be guilty of an offence.

8 Notices to be displayed on ships, railway trains and passenger road vehicles

(1) The master of any ship and the person in charge of any railway train or passenger road vehicle bringing passengers into the State shall display in such ship, railway train or passenger road vehicle in such manner as the Minister may from time to time direct such notice of the provisions of this Act and of any directions given thereunder as the Minister may from time to time direct.

(2) A person who contravenes subsection (1) shall be guilty of an offence.

9 Obligation of non-nationals to register

(1) (a) A register of non-nationals who have permission to be in the State shall be established and maintained by registration officers in such manner as the Minister may direct.

(b) The register may be in a form that is not legible if it is capable of being converted into a legible form.

(c) A registration officer may amend an entry in, or delete an entry from, the register.

(2) Subject to section 2(2), a non-national shall comply with the following requirements as to registration:

- (a) he or she shall, as soon as may be, furnish to the registration officer for the registration district in which he or she is resident, the particulars set out in the Second Schedule, and, unless he or she gives a satisfactory explanation of the circumstances which prevent his or her doing so, produce to the registration officer a valid passport or other equivalent document, issued by or on behalf of an authority recognised by the Government, which establishes his or her identity and nationality;

- (b) he or she shall furnish to the registration officer for the registration district in which he or she is resident particulars of any matter affecting in any manner the accuracy of the particulars previously furnished by him or her for the purpose of registration, within 7 days after the matter has occurred, and generally shall supply to the registration officer all information (including, where required by the registration officer, a recent photograph of him or her) that may be necessary for maintaining the accuracy of the register;

- (c) he or she shall, if about to change his or her residence, furnish to the registration officer for the registration district in which he or she is then resident particulars as to the date on which his or her residence is to be changed and as to his or her intended place of residence;

- (d) on effecting any change of residence from one registration district to another, he or she shall, within 48 hours of his or her arrival in the other registration district, report his or her arrival to the registration officer for that district;

- (e) if at any time he or she is absent from his or her residence for a continuous period exceeding one month, he or she shall report to the registration officer for the district of his or her residence his or her current address and every subsequent change of address, including his or her return to his or her residence;

- (f) he or she shall—
  - (i) subject to section 19(3), on registration obtain from the registration officer a registration certificate;
  - (ii) on every subsequent alteration or addition of any entry in the register relating to his or her registration, produce the certificate to the registration officer in order that, if necessary, a corresponding alteration or addition may be made in the certificate.

(3) If a non-national has no residence in the State, he or she shall attend at the office of a registration officer and, so far as possible, supply the particulars that would be required under this section if he or she were resident in the district of that officer, and shall report to the registration officer for any other district in which he or she stays for more than 24 hours and also give notice of any intended change of address to the registration officer to whom he or she has last reported.

(4) If a non-national who is required under this section to register or report is lodging with, or living as a member of the household of, any other person, it shall be the duty of that person to take reasonable steps (either by giving notice to the registration officer of the presence of the non-national in his or her household or otherwise) to secure compliance with the terms of this Act in respect of the registration of or reporting by the non-national.

(5) A registration certificate shall be in such form and contain such particulars as may be prescribed.

(6) This section shall not apply to—

    (a) a non-national who is under the age of 16 years;

    (b) a non-national who was born in Ireland;

    (c) a non-national not resident in the State who has been in the State for a period of not more than 3 months since the date of his or her last arrival in the State;

    (d) a non-national seaman not resident in the State whose ship remains at a port in the State and who does not land in the State for discharge.

(7) A person who before the commencement of this Act obtained a registration certificate from a registration officer shall be deemed until the date on which the certificate is expressed to expire to have complied with the requirements of this section.

(8) A non-national who contravenes subsection (2), (3) or (4) shall be guilty of an offence.

(9) In this section, "register" means the register maintained under subsection (1) and cognate words shall be construed accordingly.

10   Hotel registers

(1) It shall be the duty of the keeper of every premises to which this section applies to keep in the premises a register in the prescribed form of all non-nationals staying at the premises.

(2) The Minister may make regulations in relation to the following matters:

    (a) the duties of keepers of premises to which this section applies and of persons staying at such premises in relation to the making of entries in a register,

    (b) the maintenance of a register,

    (c) the furnishing and gathering of information required for entry in a register,

    (d) the period for which a register is to be kept.

(3) A register shall be produced by a keeper to a member of the Garda Síochána or an immigration officer if so requested by the member or officer.

(4) A person who contravenes subsection (1) or a provision of regulations under this section that is stated in the regulations to be a penal provision shall be guilty of an offence.

(5) This section applies to a hotel or other place in which lodging or sleeping accommodation is provided on a commercial basis.

11   Requirements as to documents of identity and supply of information

(1) Every person (other than a person under the age of 16 years) landing in the State shall be in possession of a valid passport or other equivalent document, issued by or on behalf of an authority recognised by the Government, which establishes his or her identity and nationality to the satisfaction of an immigration officer.

(2) Every person landing in or embarking from the State shall furnish to an immigration officer such information in such manner as the immigration officer may reasonably require for the purposes of the performance of his or her functions.

(3) A person who contravenes this section shall be guilty of an offence.

(4) This section does not apply to any person (other than a non-national) coming from or embarking for a place in the State, Great Britain or Northern Ireland.

12   Requirement as to production of documents

(1) Every non-national shall produce on demand, unless he or she gives a satisfactory explanation of the circumstances which prevent him or her from so doing—

(a) a valid passport or other equivalent document, issued by or on behalf of an authority recognised by the Government, which establishes his or her identity and nationality, and

(b) in case he or she is registered or deemed to be registered under this Act, his or her registration certificate.

(2) A non-national who contravenes this section shall be guilty of an offence.

(3) In this section "on demand" means on demand made at any time by any immigration officer or a member of the Garda Síochána.

(4) This section does not apply to—

(a) a non-national who is under the age of 16 years, or

(b) a non-national who was born in Ireland.

13   Offences and power of arrest without warrant

(1) A person guilty of an offence under this Act shall be liable on summary conviction to a fine not exceeding €3,000 or to imprisonment for a term not exceeding 12 months or to both.

(2) A member of the Garda Síochána may arrest without warrant a person whom he or she reasonably suspects to have committed an offence under this Act (other than section 10) or section 2(1) of the Employment Permits Act 2003 .

14   Provision for particular non-nationals

(1) The Minister may, by notice in writing, require a non-national who does not have permission to be in the State to comply with either or both of the following conditions:

(a) that he or she reside or remain in a particular district or place in the State,

(b) that he or she report at specified intervals to an immigration officer or member of the Garda Síochána specified in the notice or to the registration officer of the registration district in which he or she is resident,

and the non-national shall comply with the requirement.

(2) A non-national who contravenes this section shall be guilty of an offence.

15   Entry, search and seizure

(1) Where, on the sworn information of a member of the Garda Síochána not below the rank of sergeant, a judge of the District Court is satisfied that—

(a) it is reasonably necessary for the purpose of the enforcement of this Act that a place specified in the information should be searched by members of the Garda Síochána, or

(b) there are reasonable grounds for suspecting that evidence of or relating to an offence under this Act is to be found at a place specified in the information,

the judge may issue a warrant for the search of that place and any persons found at that place.

(2) A warrant issued under this section shall authorise a named member of the Garda Síochána, alone or accompanied by such other members of the Garda Síochána and such other persons as may be necessary—

(a) to enter, within 7 days from the date of the warrant and if necessary by the use of reasonable force, the place named in the warrant,

(b) to search that place and any persons found there, and

(c) to seize anything found there, or anything found in the possession of a person present there at the time of the search, which that member reasonably believes to be evidence of or relating to an offence under this Act.

(3) A member of the Garda Síochána acting in accordance with a warrant issued under this section may require any person found at the place where the search is carried out to give the member his or her name and address.

(4) Any person who—

(a) obstructs or attempts to obstruct any member of the Garda Síochána acting in accordance with a warrant issued under subsection (1),

(b) fails or refuses to comply with a requirement under this section, or

(c) gives a name or address to such a member which is false or misleading,

shall be guilty of an offence.

(5) In this section, "place" includes any dwelling, any building or part of a building and any vehicle, vessel, structure or container used or intended to be used for the carriage of goods by road.

16   Amendment of certain enactments

(1) Section 16A (inserted by section 6 of the Irish Nationality and Citizenship Act 2001) of the Irish Nationality and Citizenship Act 1956 is amended—

(a) by the insertion, in subsection (1)(b)(i), after "the Aliens Act, 1935,", of "or the Immigration Act 2004", and

(b) by the substitution, in subsection (1)(b)(ii), for "that Act" of "those Acts".

(2) Section 7 of the Air Navigation and Transport (Preinspection) Act 1986 is amended, in subsections (1) and (2), by the substitution, for "the Aliens Act, 1935,", of " the Aliens Act 1935, the Immigration Act 2004".

(3) Subsection (4)(a)(ii)(IV) (inserted by section 13 of the Social Welfare (Miscellaneous Provisions) Act 2003) of section 179 of the Social Welfare (Consolidation) Act 1993 is amended by the addition of "or the Immigration Act 2004".

(4) Section 9(3) of the Act of 1996 is amended by the substitution of the following paragraph for paragraph (c):

"(c) A certificate shall be deemed to be a registration certificate for the purposes of section 12 of the Immigration Act 2004 and a person who is the holder of a certificate that is in force shall be deemed to have complied with section 9 of that Act.".

(5) Section 6(1)(b) (as amended by section 10(c)(i) of the Illegal Immigrants (Trafficking) Act 2000) of the Act of 1999 is amended by the insertion before ", or to the Refugee Applications Commissioner" of "or section 9 of the Immigration Act 2004".

(6) Section 5(1) of the Illegal Immigrants (Trafficking) Act 2000 is amended by the insertion of the following paragraph after paragraph (d):

"(dd) a refusal under section 4 of the Immigration Act 2004,".

(7) Section 24 of the Criminal Justice (Theft and Fraud Offences) Act 2001 is amended by the addition to paragraph (o) of the definition of "instrument" of "or the Immigration Act 2004,".

(8) Section 5(1) of the Immigration Act 2003 is amended by the addition of the following paragraphs after paragraph (d):

"(e) a non-national who has failed to comply with section 4(2) of the Immigration Act 2004,

(f) a non-national who has been refused a permission under section 4(3) of that Act,

(g) a non-national who is in the State in contravention of section 5(1) of that Act,

(h) a non-national who has landed in the State in contravention of section 6(1) of that Act,".

17   Visa orders

(1) The Minister may, for the purposes of ensuring the integrity of the immigration system, the maintenance of national security, public order or public health or the orderly regulation of the labour market or for the purposes of reciprocal immigration arrangements with other states or the promotion of tourism, by order declare—

   (a)   that members of specified classes of non-nationals are not required to be in possession of a valid Irish visa within the meaning of the Immigration Act 2003 when landing in the State, or

   (b)   that members of specified classes of non-nationals are required to be in possession of a valid Irish transit visa within the meaning of that Act.

(2) The Minister may by order amend or revoke an order under this section (including an order under this subsection).

18   Service of notices

(1) Where a notice is required or authorised by or under this Act to be served on or given to a person, it shall be addressed to him or her and shall be served on or given to him or her in some one of the following ways:

   (a)   by delivering it to him or her, or

   (b)   by sending it by post in a prepaid registered letter, or by any other form of recorded delivery service prescribed by the Minister, addressed to him or her at the address most recently furnished by him or her to the registration officer pursuant to section 9, or to the Refugee Applications Commissioner pursuant to section 9(4A) of the Act of 1996, as the case may be or, in a case in which an address for service has been furnished, at that address.

(2) Where a notice under this Act has been sent to a person in accordance with subsection (1)(b), the notice shall be deemed to have been duly served on or given to the person on the third day after the day on which it was so sent.

19   Fees

(1) (a) There shall be paid to the Minister by the non-national concerned in respect of the giving of a permission a fee of such amount as may be prescribed with the consent of the Minister for Finance.

(b) There shall be paid to the registration officer concerned by the non-national concerned in respect of the issue of a registration certificate a fee of such amount as may be prescribed with the consent of the Minister for Finance.

(c) There shall be paid to the Minister by the non-national concerned in respect of the issue of a travel document a fee of such amount as may be prescribed with the consent of the Minister for Finance.

(2) The Minister may refuse to give a permission or issue a travel document if the appropriate fee in respect of the issue has not been paid.

(3) The registration officer concerned may refuse to issue a registration certificate if the appropriate fee has not been paid.

(4) A fee payable under this section may be recovered by the person to whom it is payable from the person by whom it is payable as a simple contract debt in any court of competent jurisdiction.

(5) The Public Offices Fees Act 1879 shall not apply in relation to a fee under this section.

(6) Regulations under this section may provide for the waiver in specified circumstances of any prescribed fees, including fees payable by—

(a) adult persons unable without undue hardship to arrange for their payment for themselves and their dependants,

(b) applicants within the meaning of the Act of 1996, and

(c) persons in respect of whom a declaration (within the meaning of that Act) is in force.

(7) In this section, "travel document" means a document (other than a document to which section 4(1) of the Refugee Act 1996 refers) issued solely for the purpose of providing the holder with a document which can serve in lieu of a national passport.

20   Regulations and orders

(1) The Minister may—

(a) by regulations provide, subject to this Act, for any matter referred to in this Act as prescribed or to be prescribed, and

(b) in addition to any other power conferred on him or her by this Act to make regulations, make regulations generally for the purpose of giving full effect to this Act.

(2) Regulations under this Act may contain such incidental, supplementary and consequential provisions as appear to the Minister to be necessary or expedient for the purposes of the regulations.

(3) Every order or regulation made by the Minister under this Act shall be laid before each House of the Oireachtas as soon as may be after it is made, and, if a resolution annulling the order or regulation is passed by either such House within the next subsequent 21 days on which that House has sat after the order or regulation is laid before it, the order or regulation

shall be annulled accordingly but without prejudice to the validity of anything previously done thereunder.

21   Expenses

The expenses incurred by the Minister in the administration of this Act shall, to such extent as may be sanctioned by the Minister for Finance, be paid out of moneys provided by the Oireachtas.

22   Short title

This Act may be cited as the Immigration Act 2004.

FIRST SCHEDULE
CONDITIONS REFERRED TO IN SECTION 4(3)(C)

Section 4

1. Diseases subject to the International Health Regulations for the time being adopted by the World Health Assembly of the World Health Organisation.
2. Tuberculosis of the respiratory system in an active state or showing a tendency to develop.
3. Syphilis.
4. Other infectious or contagious parasitic diseases in respect of which special provisions are in operation to prevent the spread of such diseases from abroad.
5. Drug addiction.
6. Profound mental disturbance, that is to say, manifest conditions of psychotic disturbance with agitation, delirium, hallucinations or confusion.

SECOND SCHEDULE
PARTICULARS TO BE FURNISHED ON REGISTRATION

Section 9

1. Name in full and sex.
2. Present nationality and how and when acquired and previous nationality (if any).
3. Date and place of birth.
4. Profession or occupation.
5. Date, place and mode of arrival in the State.
6. Address of residence in the State.
7. Address of last residence outside the State.
8. Photograph of the non-national (which, if not furnished by the non-national, may be taken by the registration officer).
9. If in government service, the service concerned, nature and duration of service, and rank and appointments held.
10. Particulars of passport or other document establishing nationality and identity.
11. Signature (which, if required, shall be in the characters of the language of the non-national's nationality) and fingerprints if required by the registration officer.
12. Any other matter of which particulars are required by the registration officer.

Criminal Law (Insanity) Act 2006

Number 11 of 2006

ARRANGEMENT OF SECTIONS

1.   Interpretation.

2.   Orders.

3.   Designated centres.

4.   Fitness to be tried.

5.   Verdict of not guilty by reason of insanity.

6.   Diminished responsibility.

7.   Appeals (fitness to be tried).

8.   Appeals (not guilty by reason of insanity).

9.   Appeals (supplemental provisions).

10.   Establishment day.

11.   Mental Health (Criminal Law) Review Board.

12.   Powers of Review Board.

13.   Review of detention.

14.   Temporary release, transfer and other matters.

15.   Transfer of prisoner to designated centre.

16.   Clinical director of designated centre to be notified of date on which prisoner detained in centre ceases to be prisoner, etc.

17.   Review of prisoner's detention in designated centre.

18.   Transfer back to prison.

19.   Notice to be given of intention to adduce evidence as to mental condition, etc.

20.   Application to existing detentions.

21.   Amendment of Defence Act 1954.

22.   Amendment of Infanticide Act 1949.

23   Expenses.

24.   Grants to Review Board.

25.   Repeals and transitional provision.

26.   Short title and commencement.   ´

SCHEDULE 1
MENTAL HEALTH (CRIMINAL LAW) REVIEW BOARD

SCHEDULE 2
ENACTMENTS REPEALED

AN ACT TO AMEND THE LAW RELATING TO THE TRIAL AND DETENTION OF PERSONS SUFFERING FROM MENTAL DISORDERS WHO ARE CHARGED WITH

OFFENCES OR FOUND NOT GUILTY BY REASON OF INSANITY, TO AMEND THE LAW RELATING TO UNFITNESS TO PLEAD AND THE SPECIAL VERDICT, TO PROVIDE FOR THE COMMITTAL OF SUCH PERSONS TO DESIGNATED CENTRES AND FOR THE INDEPENDENT REVIEW OF THE DETENTION OF SUCH PERSONS AND, FOR THOSE PURPOSES, TO PROVIDE FOR THE ESTABLISHMENT OF A BODY TO BE KNOWN AS AN BORD ATHBHREITHNITHE MEABHAIR-SHLÁINTE (AN DLÍ COIRIÚIL), OR, IN THE ENGLISH LANGUAGE, THE MENTAL HEALTH (CRIMINAL LAW) REVIEW BOARD, TO REPEAL THE TRIAL OF LUNATICS ACT 1883, TO AMEND THE INFANTICIDE ACT 1949, AND TO PROVIDE FOR RELATED MATTERS. [12th April, 2006]

BE IT ENACTED BY THE OIREACHTAS AS FOLLOWS:

1 Interpretation

In this Act, save where the context otherwise requires—

"act " includes omission and references to committing an act include references to making an omission;

"the Act of 2001" means the Mental Health Act 2001;

"approved medical officer " means a consultant psychiatrist (within the meaning of the Mental Health Act 2001);

"clinical director " has the meaning assigned to it by the Mental Health Act 2001, and, where an approved medical officer is duly authorised by a clinical director to perform his or her functions under this Act, the officer shall, in relation to those functions, be deemed, for the purposes of this Act, to be a clinical director;

"court " means any court exercising criminal jurisdiction and includes court martial;

"designated centre " shall be construed in accordance with section 3;

"establishment day " means the day appointed under section 10 to be the establishment day;

"intoxication " means being under the intoxicating influence of any alcoholic drink, drug, solvent or any other substance or combination of substances;

"legal representative " means a practising barrister or a practising solicitor;

"mental disorder " includes mental illness, mental disability, dementia or any disease of the mind but does not include intoxication;

"Minister " means the Minister for Justice, Equality and Law Reform;

"patient ", in sections 12, [13, 13A, 13B][1] and 14, means a person detained in a designated centre pursuant to this Act;

"prison " means a place of custody administered by the Minister;

"prisoner " means a person who is in prison on foot of a sentence of imprisonment, on committal awaiting trial, on remand or otherwise;

"Review Board " means the Mental Health (Criminal Law) Review Board established under section 11;

"special court " means a special court established under Article 38.3.1° of the Constitution.

Amendments

1   Words substituted by Criminal Law (Insanity) Act 2010, s 2. The 2010 Act commenced on 8 February 2011 by virtue of SI 50/2011.

2   Orders

Every order made by the Minister or by the Minister for Health and Children under this Act shall be laid before each House of the Oireachtas as soon as may be after it is made.

3   Designated centres

(1) The Central Mental Hospital is hereby designated as a centre (in this Act referred to as a "designated centre") for the reception, detention and care or treatment of persons or classes of persons committed or transferred thereto under the provisions of this Act.

(2) The Minister for Health and Children by order may after consultation with the Mental Health Commission established under section 32 of the Act of 2001, designate a psychiatric centre as a centre (in this Act referred to as a "designated centre") for the reception, detention and, where appropriate, care or treatment of persons or classes of persons committed or transferred thereto under the provisions of this Act.

[(2A) Notwithstanding the generality of subsection (2), the Minister for Health and Children by order may after consultation with the Mental Health Commission, designate a psychiatric centre as a designated centre for the reception and, where appropriate, detention, examination and, where appropriate, care and treatment of persons or classes of persons committed or directed thereto by the District Court under section 4(6)(a) for examination.][1]

(3) Part 4 of the Act of 2001 shall apply to any person who is detained in a designated centre under this Act.

(4) In this section, "psychiatric centre" means a hospital or in-patient facility in which care or treatment is provided for persons suffering from a mental disorder within the meaning of the Act of 2001.

Amendments

1   Subsesction (2A) inserted by Criminal Law (Insanity) Act 2010, s 3. The 2010 Act commenced on 8 February 2011 by virtue of SI 50/2011.

4   Fitness to be tried

(1) Where in the course of criminal proceedings against an accused person the question arises, at the instance of the defence, the prosecution or the court, as to whether or not the person is fit to be tried the following provisions shall have effect.

(2) An accused person shall be deemed unfit to be tried if he or she is unable by reason of mental disorder to understand the nature or course of the proceedings so as to—

    (a)   plead to the charge,

    (b)   instruct a legal representative,

(c)   in the case of an indictable offence which may be tried summarily, elect for a trial by jury,

(d)   make a proper defence,

(e)   in the case of a trial by jury, challenge a juror to whom he or she might wish to object, or

(f)   understand the evidence.

(3) (a)   Where an accused person is before the District Court (in this section referred to as "the Court") charged with a summary offence, or with an indictable offence which is being or is to be tried summarily, any question as to whether or not the accused is fit to be tried shall be determined by the Court.

[(aa)   In a case to which paragraph (a) relates, the Court may request evidence of an approved medical officer to be adduced before it in respect of the accused person for the purposes of—

    (i)   determining whether to adjourn the proceedings until further order to facilitate the accused person in accessing any care or treatment necessary for the welfare of the person,

    (ii)   making a determination as to whether or not the accused person is fit to be tried, or

    (iii)   exercising a power referred to in subsection (6)(a).]¹

(b)   Subject to subsections (7) and (8), in a case to which paragraph (a) relates, the Court determines that an accused person is unfit to be tried, that Court shall adjourn the proceedings until further order, and may—

    (i)   if it is satisfied, having considered the evidence of an approved medical officer adduced pursuant to [subsection (6)(b)]² and any other evidence that may be adduced before it that the accused person is suffering from a mental disorder (within the meaning of the Act of 2001) and is in need of in-patient care or treatment in a designated centre, commit him or her to a specified designated centre until an order is made under section 13 [or 13A]³, or

    (ii)   if it is satisfied, having considered the evidence of an approved medical officer adduced pursuant to [subsection (6)(b)]⁴ and any other evidence that may be adduced before it that the accused person is suffering from a mental disorder or from a mental disorder (within the meaning of the Act of 2001) and is in need of out-patient care or treatment in a designated centre, make such order as it thinks proper in relation to the accused person for out-patient treatment in a designated centre.

(c)   Where in a case to which paragraph (a) relates, the Court determines that the accused person is fit to be tried the proceedings shall continue.

(4) (a)   Where an accused person is before the Court charged with an offence other than an offence to which paragraph (a) of subsection (3) applies, any question as to whether that person is fit to be tried shall be determined by the court of trial to which the person would have been sent forward if he or she were fit to be tried and the Court shall send the person forward to that court for the purpose of determining that issue.

(b) Where an accused person is sent forward to the court of trial under paragraph (a), the question of whether the person is fit to be tried shall be determined by the judge concerned sitting alone.

(c) If the determination under paragraph (b) is that the accused person is fit to be tried, the provisions of the Criminal Procedure Act 1967, shall apply as if an order returning the person for trial had been made by the Court under section 4A of that Act (inserted by section 9 of the Criminal Justice Act 1999) on the date the determination was made but, in any case where section 13 of that Act applies, the person shall be returned for trial.

(d) If the determination under paragraph (b) is that the person is unfit to be tried the provisions of subsection (5) shall apply.

(e) Where the court subsequently determines that the person is fit to be tried the provisions of the Criminal Procedure Act 1967, shall apply as if an order returning the person for trial had been made by the Court on the date the determination was made.

(5) (a) Where an accused person is before a court other than the Court charged with an offence and the question arises as to whether that person is fit to be tried the provisions of this subsection shall apply.

(b) The question of whether the accused person is fit to be tried shall be determined by the judge concerned sitting alone.

[(bb) In a case to which paragraph (a) relates, the court may request evidence of an approved medical officer to be adduced before it in respect of the accused person for the purposes of—

  (i) determining whether to adjourn the proceedings until further order to facilitate the accused person in accessing any care or treatment necessary for the welfare of the person,

  (ii) making a determination as to whether or not the accused person is fit to be tried, or

  (iii) exercising a power referred to in subsection (6)(a).][5]

(c) Subject to subsections (7) and (8), if the judge determines that the accused person is unfit to be tried, he or she shall adjourn the proceedings until further order, and may—

  (i) if he or she is satisfied, having considered the evidence of an approved medical officer adduced pursuant to [subsection (6)(b)][6] and any other evidence that may be adduced before him or her that the accused person is suffering from a mental disorder (within the meaning of the Act of 2001) and is in need of in-patient care or treatment in a designated centre, commit him or her to a specified designated centre until an order is made under section 13 [or 13A],[7] or

  (ii) if he or she is satisfied, having considered the evidence of an approved medical officer adduced pursuant to [subsection (6)(b)][8] and any other evidence that may be adduced before him or her that the accused person is suffering from a mental disorder or from a mental disorder (within the meaning of the Act of 2001) and is in need of out-patient care or treatment in a designated centre, make such order as he or she thinks proper in relation to the accused person for out-patient treatment in a designated centre.

(d) Where the court determines that the accused person is fit to be tried the proceedings shall continue.

[(6) (a) For the purposes of determining whether or not to exercise a power under subsection (3)(b)(i) or (ii) or subsection (5)(c)(i) or (ii), the court, having considered the evidence of an approved medical officer adduced before it in respect of the accused person—

    (i) may for that purpose—

        (I)   commit the accused person to a designated centre for a period of not more than 14 days, or

        (II)   by order direct that the accused person attend a designated centre as an outpatient on such day or days as the court may direct within a period of 14 days from the date of the making of the order,

    and

    (ii) shall direct that the accused person concerned be examined by an approved medical officer at the designated centre.

(b) Within the period authorised by the court under this subsection, the approved medical officer who examined the accused person pursuant to subparagraph (ii) of paragraph (a) shall report to the court on whether or not in his or her opinion the accused person is—

    (i) suffering from a mental disorder (within the meaning of the Act of 2001) and is in need of in-patient care or treatment in a designated centre, or

    (ii) suffering from a mental disorder or a mental disorder (within the meaning of the Act of 2001) and is in need of out-patient care or treatment in a designated centre.]⁹

(7) Where on the trial of an accused person the question arises as to whether or not the person is fit to be tried and the court considers that it is expedient and in the interests of the accused so to do, it may defer consideration of the question until any time before the opening of the case for the defence and if, before the question falls to be determined, the jury by the direction of the court or the court, as the case may be, return a verdict in favour of the accused or find the accused person not guilty, as the case may be, on the count or each of the counts on which the accused is being tried the question shall not be determined and the person shall be acquitted.

(8) Upon a determination having been made by the court that an accused person is unfit to be tried it may on application to it in that behalf allow evidence to be adduced before it as to whether or not the accused person did the act alleged and if the court is satisfied that there is a reasonable doubt as to whether the accused did the act alleged, it shall order the accused to be discharged.

(9) Where evidence is adduced before the court under subsection (8) but the court decides not to order the accused person to be discharged, no person shall publish a report of the evidence or the decision until such time, if any, as—

(a) the trial of the person concludes, or

(b) a decision is made not to proceed with the trial of the person or the trial is otherwise not proceeded with.

(10) A person who contravenes subsection (9) shall be guilty of an offence and shall be liable on summary conviction to a fine not exceeding €3,000 or to imprisonment for a term not exceeding 12 months or to both.

Amendments

1 Subsesction (3)(aa) inserted by Criminal Law (Insanity) Act 2010, s 4(a). The 2010 Act commenced on 8 February 2011 by virtue of SI 50/2011.

2 Words substituted by Criminal Law (Insanity) Act 2010, s 4(b)(i).

3 Words inserted by Criminal Law (Insanity) Act 2010, s 4(b)(ii).

4 Words substituted by Criminal Law (Insanity) Act 2010, s 4(c).

5 Subsection (5)(bb) inserted by Criminal Law (Insanity) Act 2010, s 4(d).

6 Words inserted by Criminal Law (Insanity) Act 2010, s 4(e)(i).

7 Words inserted by Criminal Law (Insanity) Act 2010, s 4(e)(ii).

8 Words substituted by Criminal Law (Insanity) Act 2010, s 4(f).

9 Subsection (6) substituted by Criminal Law (Insanity) Act 2010, s 4(g).

5   Verdict of not guilty by reason of insanity

(1) Where an accused person is tried for an offence and, in the case of the District Court or Special Criminal Court, the court or, in any other case, the jury finds that the accused person committed the act alleged against him or her and, having heard evidence relating to the mental condition of the accused given by a consultant psychiatrist, finds that—

(a) the accused person was suffering at the time from a mental disorder, and

(b) the mental disorder was such that the accused person ought not to be held responsible for the act alleged by reason of the fact that he or she—

(i) did not know the nature and quality of the act, or

(ii) did not know that what he or she was doing was wrong, or

(iii) was unable to refrain from committing the act,

the court or the jury, as the case may be, shall return a special verdict to the effect that the accused person is not guilty by reason of insanity.

(2) If the court, having considered any report submitted to it in accordance with subsection (3) and such other evidence as may be adduced before it, is satisfied that an accused person found not guilty by reason of insanity pursuant to subsection (1) is suffering from a mental disorder (within the meaning of the Act of 2001) and is in need of in-patient care or treatment in a designated centre, the court shall commit that person to a specified designated centre until an order is made under section 13 [or 13A].[1]

(3) (a) For the purposes of subsection (2), if the court considers that an accused person found not guilty by reason of insanity pursuant to subsection (1) is suffering from a mental disorder (within the meaning of the Act of 2001) and may be in need of in-patient care or treatment in a designated centre, the court may commit that person to a specified designated centre for a period of not more than 14 days and direct

that during such period he or she be examined by an approved medical officer at that centre.

(b) The court may, on application to it in that behalf by any party and, if it considers it appropriate to do so, after consultation with an approved medical officer, extend the period of committal under this subsection, but the period or the aggregate of the periods for which an accusedperson may be committed under this subsection shall not exceed 6 months.

(c) Within the period of committal authorised by the court under this subsection the approved medical officer concerned shall report to the court on whether in his or her opinion the accused person committed under paragraph (a) is suffering from a mental disorder (within the meaning of the Act of 2001) and is in need of in-patient care or treatment in a designated centre.

(4) Where on a trial for murder the accused contends—

(a) that at the time of the alleged offence he or she was suffering from a mental disorder such that he or she ought to be found not guilty by reason of insanity, or

(b) that at that time he or she was suffering from a mental disorder specified in section 6(1)(c),

the court shall allow the prosecution to adduce evidence tending to prove the other of those contentions, and may give directions as to the stage of the proceedings at which the prosecution may adduce such evidence.

Amendments

1   Words inserted by Criminal Law (Insanity) Act 2010, s 5. The 2010 Act commenced on 8 February 2011 by virtue of SI 50/2011.

---

6   Diminished responsibility

(1) Where a person is tried for murder and the jury or, as the case may be, the Special Criminal Court finds that the person—

(a) did the act alleged,

(b) was at the time suffering from a mental disorder, and

(c) the mental disorder was not such as to justify finding him or her not guilty by reason of insanity, but was such as to diminish substantially his or her responsibility for the act,

the jury or court, as the case may be, shall find the person not guilty of that offence but guilty of manslaughter on the ground of diminished responsibility.

(2) Subject to section 5(4), where a person is tried for the offence specified in subsection (1), it shall be for the defence to establish that the person is, by virtue of this section, not liable to be convicted of that offence.

(3) A woman found guilty of infanticide may be dealt with in accordance with subsection (1).

7   Appeals (fitness to be tried)

(1) An appeal shall lie to the Circuit Court from a determination by the District Court, pursuant to section 4(3), that an accused person is unfit to be tried.

(2) On an appeal from a determination referred to in subsection (1), the Circuit Court shall, if it allows the appeal, order that the appellant be tried or retried, as the case may be, by the District Court for the offence alleged, but if the District Court, pursuant to section 4(7), postponed consideration of the question as to the accused's fitness to be tried and the Circuit Court is of opinion that the appellant ought to have been found not guilty before the question as to fitness to be tried was considered, the court shall order that the appellant be acquitted.

(3) An appeal shall lie to the Court of Criminal Appeal from a determination by the Central Criminal Court, the Circuit Court or the Special Criminal Court that an accused person is unfit to be tried, and if the Court of Criminal Appeal allows the appeal it shall order that the appellant be tried or retried as the case may be for the offence alleged but if the court concerned, pursuant to section 4(7), postponed consideration of the question as to the accused's fitness to be tried and the Court of Criminal Appeal is of opinion that the appellant ought to have been found not guilty before the question as to fitness to be tried was considered, the court shall order that the appellant be acquitted.

(4) Where an order is made pursuant to subsection (2) or (3) directing the accused be tried or retried, as the case may be, for the offence alleged, the accused may be tried or retried for an offence other than the offence alleged in respect of which he or she was found unfit to be tried being an offence of which he or she might be found guilty on a charge for the offence alleged.

(5) No appeal shall lie to the Supreme Court from a determination by a court that an accused person is unfit to be tried.

8   Appeals (not guilty by reason of insanity)

(1) A person tried for an offence in the District Court and found not guilty by reason of insanity may appeal against the finding to the Circuit Court on any or all of the following grounds:

  (a)   that it was not proved that he or she had committed the act in question;
  (b)   that he or she was not, at the time when the act was committed, suffering from a mental disorder of the nature referred to in section 5(1)(b);
  (c)   that the District Court ought to have made a determination in respect of the person that he or she was unfit to be tried.

(2) If on an appeal to the Circuit Court on the ground referred to in subsection (1)(a), the Court is satisfied that it was not established that the appellant had committed the act in question it shall order that the appellant be acquitted.

(3) If, on an appeal to the Circuit Court on the ground referred to in subsection (1)(b), the court is satisfied that the appellant committed the act alleged but having considered the evidence or any new evidence relating to the mental condition of the appellant given by a consultant psychiatrist is satisfied that he or she was not suffering from a mental disorder of the nature referred to in section 5(1)(b), the court shall substitute a verdict of guilty of the offence charged or of any other offence of which it is satisfied that the person could (by virtue of the charge) and ought to have been convicted, and shall have the like powers of punishing or otherwise dealing with the person as the District Court would have had if the

person had been convicted of the offence in respect of which the verdict of guilty has been so substituted.

(4) If, on appeal to the Circuit Court on the ground set out at subsection (1)(c), the court is satisfied that the appellant ought to have been found unfit to be tried it shall make a finding to that effect and, in that case the provisions of section 4(5)(c) shall apply.

(5) If on appeal to the Circuit Court the court is satisfied, having considered the evidence or any new evidence relating to the mental condition of the appellant, that he or she was at the time that the offence alleged was committed suffering from a mental disorder of the nature referred to in section 5(1)(b) and that but for that disorder the appellant would have been found guilty of the offence charged or of another offence of which the person could have been found guilty by virtue of the charge, the court shall dismiss the appeal.

(6) A person tried on indictment in the Circuit Court, the Central Criminal Court or the Special Criminal Court and found not guilty by reason of insanity may appeal against the finding to the Court of Criminal Appeal on one or more or all of the following grounds:

(a) that it was not proved that he or she had committed the act in question;

(b) that he or she was not, at the time when the act was committed, suffering from any mental disorder of the nature referred to in section 5(1)(b);

(c) that the court ought to have made a determination in respect of this person that he or she was unfit to be tried.

(7) Subject to section 9, if on an appeal to the Court of Criminal Appeal on the grounds referred to in subsection (6)(a) the court is satisfied that it was not proved that the appellant had committed the act in question it shall order that the appellant be acquitted.

(8) Subject to section 9, if on an appeal to the Court of Criminal Appeal on the ground referred to in subsection (6)(b) the court is satisfied that the appellant committed the act alleged but, having considered the evidence or any new evidence relating to the mental condition of the accused given by a consultant psychiatrist, is satisfied that he or she was not suffering from any mental disorder of the nature referred to in section 5(1)(b) the court shall substitute a verdict of guilty of the offence charged or, in the case of murder where section 6(1)(c) applies, guilty of manslaughter on the grounds of diminished responsibility or of any other offence of which it is satisfied that the person could (by virtue of the charge) and ought to have been convicted, and shall have the like powers of punishing or otherwise dealing with the person as the trial court would have had if the person had been convicted of the offence in respect of which the verdict of guilty has been so substituted.

(9) If, on an appeal to the Court of Criminal Appeal, on the ground set out at subsection (6)(c), the court is satisfied that the appellant ought to have been found unfit to be tried it shall make a finding to that effect and, in that case the provisions of section 4(5)(c) shall apply.

(10) If, on an appeal to the Court of Criminal Appeal, the court is satisfied that the appellant was at the time that the offence alleged was committed suffering from a mental disorder of the nature referred to in section 5(1)(b) and that but for that disorder the appellant would have been found guilty of the offence charged or of another offence of which the person could have been found guilty by virtue of the charge, the court shall dismiss the appeal.

9   Appeals (supplemental provisions)

(1) An appeal against a decision by the court of trial (but not a decision by an appellate court), to make or not to make an order of committal under section 4(3)(b), 4(5)(c), 4(6)(a), 5(2) or 5(3) shall lie at the instance of the defence or the prosecution to the Circuit Court or the Court of Criminal Appeal, as may be appropriate, and the court hearing the appeal may, having considered the evidence or any new evidence relating to the mental condition of the accused given by a consultant psychiatrist, make such order, being an order that it was open to the court of trial to make, as it considers appropriate and, without prejudice to the provisions of section 13 relating to the review of orders of committal, no further appeal shall lie from an order made on an appeal under this section.

(2) Where the Circuit Court or the Court of Criminal Appeal allows an appeal against a conviction or against a verdict of not guilty by reason of insanity on the ground that the appellant ought to have been found unfit to be tried, or allows an appeal against a conviction on the ground that the appellant ought to have been found not guilty by reason of insanity, it shall have the same powers to deal with the appellant as the court of trial would have had under section 4 or section 5 if it had come to the same conclusion.

(3) All ancillary and procedural provisions contained in a statute or an instrument made under statute relating to appeals against convictions, including provisions relating to leave to appeal, shall apply with the necessary modifications to appeals under sections 7, 8 and 9(1).

(4) The powers of an appellate court in an appeal under section 7, 8 or 9(1) shall include the power to make any such order as may be necessary for the purpose of doing justice in accordance with the provisions of this Act.

10   Establishment day

The Minister may by order appoint a day to be the establishment day for the purpose of section 11.

Note

The appointed day is 27 September 2006 by virtue of SI 499/2006.

---

11   Mental Health (Criminal Law) Review Board

(1) On the establishment day there shall stand established a board to be known as An Bord Athbhreithnithe Meabhair-Shláinte (An Dlí Coiriúil) or, in the English Language, the Mental Health (Criminal Law) Review Board (in this Act referred to as "the Review Board") to perform the functions conferred on it by or under this Act.

(2) The Review Board shall be independent in the exercise of its functions under this Act and shall have regard to the welfare and safety of the person [whose detention or conditions of discharge it reviews or whose application for unconditional discharge it determines]¹ under this Act and to the public interest.

(3) The provisions of Schedule 1 shall have effect in relation to the Review Board.

Amendments

1   Words substituted by Criminal Law (Insanity) Act 2010, s 6. The 2010 Act commenced on 8 February 2011 by virtue of SI 50/2011.

12   Powers of Review Board

(1) The Review Board shall—

    (a) hold sittings for the purpose of a review by it under this Act and at the sittings may receive submissions and such evidence as it thinks fit,

    (b) take account of the court record (if any) of the proceedings of the court to whose decision the request for review relates and, where such a record exists, the court shall make it available to the Board,

    (c) assign a legal representative to a patient the subject of the review unless he or she proposes to engage one.

(2) The Review Board may, for the purposes of its functions—

    (a) subject to subsection (10), direct in writing the consultant psychiatrist responsible for the care or treatment of a patient the subject of the review concerned to arrange for the patient to attend before the Review Board on a date and at a time and place specified in the direction,

    (b) direct in writing any person whose evidence is required by the Review Board to attend before the Review Board on a date and at a time and place specified in the direction and there to give evidence and to produce any document or thing in his or her possession or power specified in the direction,

    (c) direct any person in attendance before the Review Board to produce to the Review Board any document or thing in his or her possession or power specified in the direction,

    (d) direct in writing any person to send to the Review Board any document or thing in his or her possession or power specified in the direction, and

    (e) give any other directions for the purpose of the proceedings concerned that appear to the Review Board to be reasonable and just.

(3) The reasonable expenses of witnesses directed under subsection (2)(b) to attend before the Review Board shall be paid by the Board out of moneys at the disposal of the Board.

(4) A person who—

    (a) having been directed under subsection (2) to attend before the Review Board and, in the case of a person so directed under paragraph (b) of that subsection, having had tendered to him or her any sum in respect of the expenses of his or her attendance which a witness summoned to attend before the High Court would be entitled to have tendered to him or her, without just cause or excuse disobeys the direction,

    (b) being in attendance before the Review Board pursuant to a direction under paragraph (b) of subsection (2), refuses to take the oath on being required by the Review Board to do so or refuses to answer any question to which the Review Board may legally require an answer or to produce any document or thing in his or her possession or power legally required by the Review Board to be produced by the person,

(c) fails or refuses to send to the Review Board any document or thing legally required by the Review Board under paragraph (d) of subsection (2) to be sent to it by the person or without just cause or excuse disobeys a direction under paragraph (c), (d) or (e) of that subsection, or

(d) does any other thing in relation to the proceedings before the Review Board which, if done in relation to proceedings before a court by a witness in the court, would be contempt of that court,

shall be guilty of an offence and shall be liable on summary conviction to a fine not exceeding €3,000 or to imprisonment for a term not exceeding 12 months or to both.

(5) If a person gives false evidence before a Review Board in such circumstances that, if he or she had given the evidence before a court, he or she would be guilty of perjury, he or she shall be guilty of that offence.

(6) The procedure of the Review Board in relation to a review by it under this Act shall, subject to the provisions of this Act be such as shall be determined by the Review Board with the consent of the Minister and the Review Board shall, without prejudice to the generality of the foregoing, make provision for—

(a) for the purpose of subsection (1)(c), the making, with the consent of the Minister and the Minister for Finance, of a scheme or schemes for the granting by the Review Board of legal aid to patients,

(b) notifying the consultant psychiatrist responsible for the care or treatment of the patient the subject of the review and the patient and his or her legal representative of the date, time and place of the relevant sitting of the Review Board,

(c) giving the patient the subject of the review and his or her legal representative a copy of any document furnished to the Review Board and an indication in writing of the nature and source of any information relating to the matter which has come to notice in the course of the review,

(d) subject to subsection (10), enabling the patient the subject of the review and his or her legal representative to be present at the relevant sitting of the Review Board and enabling the patient the subject of the review to present his or her case to the Review Board in person or through a legal representative,

(e) enabling the Minister, the Director of Public Prosecutions and, where appropriate, the Minister for Defence to be heard or represented at sittings of the Review Board,

(f) enabling written statements to be admissible as evidence by the Review Board with the consent of the patient the subject of the review or his or her legal representative,

(g) enabling any signature appearing on a document produced before the Review Board to be taken, in the absence of evidence to the contrary, to be that of the person whose signature it purports to be,

(h) the examination by or on behalf of the Review Board and the cross-examination by or on behalf of the patient the subject of the review concerned on oath or otherwise as it may determine of witnesses before the Review Board called by it,

(i) the examination by or on behalf of the patient the subject of the review and the cross-examination by or on behalf of the Review Board (on oath or otherwise as the

Review Board may determine), of witnesses before the Review Board called by the patient the subject of the review,

(j) the determination by the Review Board whether evidence at the Review Board should be given on oath or otherwise,

(k) the administration by the Review Board of the oath to witnesses before the Review Board, and

(l) the making of a sufficient record of the proceedings of the Review Board.

(7) A witness whose evidence has been, is being or is to be given before the Review Board in proceedings under this Act shall be entitled to the same privileges and immunities as a witness in a court.

(8) Sittings of a Review Board for the purposes of an investigation by it under this Act shall be held in private.

(9) The following shall be absolutely privileged:

(a) documents of the Review Board and documents of its members connected with the Review Board or its functions, wherever published;

(b) reports of the Review Board, wherever published;

(c) statements made in any form at meetings or sittings of the Review Board by its members or officials and such statements wherever published subsequently.

(10) A patient shall not be required to attend before the Review Board under this section if, in the opinion of the Review Board, such attendance might be prejudicial to his or her mental health, well-being or emotional condition.

13   Review of detention

[...]¹

(1) The Review Board shall ensure that the detention of a patient is reviewed at intervals of such length not being more than 6 months as it considers appropriate and the clinical director of the designated centre where the patient is detained shall comply with any request by the Review Board in connection with the review.

(2) (a) Where the clinical director of a designated centre forms the opinion in relation to a patient detained pursuant to section 4 that the patient is no longer unfit to be tried for an offence he or she shall forthwith notify the court that committed the patient to the designated centre of this opinion and the court shall order that the patient be brought before it, as soon as may be, to be dealt with as the court thinks proper.

[(b) Where the clinical director of a designated centre forms the opinion in relation to a patient detained pursuant to section 202 of the Defence Act 1954, that the patient is no longer unfit to take his or her trial he or she shall forthwith notify the Director of Military Prosecutions (within the meaning of that Act) of this opinion and the Director of Military Prosecutions may direct—

(i) that the matter be referred to the summary court-martial or that the Court-Martial Administrator convene a general court-martial or limited court-martial, as specified in the direction, and

(ii that the person be brought before such court-martial as soon as may be to be dealt with as the court-martial considers proper.]²

(3) Where the clinical director of a designated centre forms the opinion in relation to a patient detained pursuant to section 4 or to section 202 of the Defence Act 1954, that the

patient, although still unfit to be tried, is no longer in need of in-patient care or treatment at a designated centre he or she shall forthwith notify the Review Board of this opinion.

(4) Where the Review Board receives a notification under subsection (3), it shall order that the patient be brought before it as soon as may be, and shall, having heard evidence relating to the mental condition of the patient given by the consultant psychiatrist responsible for his or her care or treatment, determine the question whether or not the treatment referred to in subsection (3) is still required in the same manner as if that question were being determined pursuant to the relevant provision of this Act or the Defence Act 1954, as may be appropriate, and shall make such order as it thinks proper in relation to the patient, [whether for further detention, care or treatment in a designated centre, for his or her conditional discharge under section 13A or for his or her unconditional discharge.][3]

(5) Where the clinical director of a designated centre forms the opinion in relation to a patient detained pursuant to section 5 or section 203 of the Defence Act 1954, that he or she is no longer in need of in-patient care or treatment at a designated centre he or she shall forthwith notify the Review Board of this opinion.

(6) Where the Review Board receives a notification under subsection (5), it shall order that the patient be brought before it, as soon as may be, and shall, having heard evidence relating to the mental condition of the patient given by the consultant psychiatrist responsible for his or her care or treatment, determine the question whether or not the treatment referred to in subsection (5) is still required and shall make such order as it thinks proper in relation to the patient, [whether for further detention, care or treatment in a designated centre, for his or her conditional discharge under section 13A or for his or her unconditional discharge.][4]

(7) A patient detained pursuant to section 4 or to section 202 of the Defence Act 1954, may apply to the Review Board for a review of his or her detention and the Review Board shall, unless satisfied that such a review is not necessary because of any review undertaken in accordance with this section, order that the patient be brought before it, as soon as may be, and—

[(a) if, having heard evidence relating to the mental condition of the patient given by the consultant psychiatrist responsible for his or her care or treatment, the Review Board determines that he or she is no longer unfit to be tried by reason of mental disorder or to participate in proceedings referred to in section 4 it shall order that the patient be brought before the court which committed him or her to the designated centre to be dealt with as that court thinks proper or in the case of a patient detained pursuant to section 202 of the Defence Act 1954, it shall notify the Director of Military Prosecutions (within the meaning of that Act) and the Director of Military Prosecutions may direct—

(i) that the matter be referred to the summary court-martial or that the Court-Martial Administrator convene a general court-martial or limited court-martial, as specified in the direction, and

(ii) that the person be brought before such court-martial as soon as may be to be dealt with as the court-martial considers proper.][5]

(b) if the Review Board determines that the patient, although still unfit to be tried is no longer in need of in-patient care or treatment at a designated centre, the Review Board may make such order as it thinks proper in relation to the patient, [whether for further detention, care or treatment in a designated centre, for his or her conditional discharge under section 13A or for his or her unconditional discharge.]⁶

(8) A patient detained pursuant to section 5 or to section 203 of the Defence Act 1954, may apply to the Review Board for a review of his or her detention and the Review Board shall, unless satisfied that such a review is not necessary because of any review undertaken in accordance with this section, order that the patient be brought before it, as soon as may be, and shall, having heard evidence relating to the mental condition of the patient given by the consultant psychiatrist responsible for his or her care or treatment, determine the question of whether or not the patient is still in need of in-patient treatment in a designated centre and shall make such order as it thinks proper in relation to the patient [whether for further detention, care or treatment in a designated centre, for his or her conditional discharge under section 13A or for his or her unconditional discharge.]⁷

(9) The Review Board may on its own initiative review the detention of a patient detained pursuant to section 4 or 5 or to section 202 or 203 of the Defence Act 1954, and subsection (7) or (8), as appropriate, shall apply to such review as if the patient had applied for the review under the subsection concerned.

Amendments

1   Subsection (1) deleted and following subsections renumbered by Criminal Justice Act, 2006, s 197.

2   Subsection (2)(b) (formerly s (3)(b)) substituted by Defence (Amendment) Act 2007, s 11 and Sch 4.

3   Words substituted by Criminal Law (Insanity) Act 2010, s 7(a). The 2010 Act commenced on 8 February 2011 by virtue of SI 50/2011.

4   Words substituted by Criminal Law (Insanity) Act 2010, s 7(b).

5   Subsection (7)(a) (formerly s (8)(a)) substituted by Defence (Amendment) Act 2007, s 4.

6   Words substituted by Criminal Law (Insanity) Act 2010, s 7(c).

7   Words substituted by Criminal Law (Insanity) Act 2010, s 7(d).

[13A   Persons may be discharged subject to conditions, etc

(1) Subject to subsection (2), the Review Board may, when reviewing the detention of a patient under section 13, make an order for the discharge of the patient subject to such conditions, including conditions relating to out-patient treatment or supervision or both, as it considers appropriate (in this Act referred to as a 'conditional discharge order').

(2) The Review Board shall not make a conditional discharge order in respect of a patient until it is satisfied that such arrangements as appear necessary to the clinical director of the designated centre concerned have been made in respect of the patient, and for that purpose, the clinical director concerned shall make such arrangements as may be necessary for—

(a) facilitating compliance by the patient who is the subject of the proposed order with the conditions of the order,

(b) the supervision of the patient, and

(c)   providing for the return of the patient to the designated centre under section 13B in the event that he or she is in material breach of his or her conditional discharge order.

(3) Where the Review Board makes a conditional discharge order in respect of a person, the Board shall—

(a)   order that the conditions imposed in the order be communicated to the person by notice in writing at the time of his or her discharge, and

(b)   shall explain or cause to have explained to him or her—

   (i)   the effect of the conditional discharge order and the effect of the conditions imposed in the order,

   (ii)   the fact that the person may, under section 13B, be returned to the designated centre if he or she is in material breach of his or her conditional discharge order,

   (iii)   that the Board may in accordance with this section vary or remove any one or more of the conditions or impose further conditions on the application of either the person concerned or the clinical director of the designated centre concerned, and

   (iv)   that the person may in accordance with this section make an application for an unconditional discharge.

(4) A person who is the subject of a conditional discharge order shall comply with the conditions to which his or her discharge is made subject.

(5) The Review Board shall cause a copy of the conditional discharge order to be sent to the Minister and the clinical director of the designated centre concerned.

(6) At any time after the making of a conditional discharge order, the Board on application to it in that behalf by—

(a)   the person who is the subject of the conditional discharge order, or

(b)   the clinical director of the designated centre concerned,

may vary or remove one or more of the conditions of the conditional discharge order, or impose further conditions if it considers it appropriate to do so, and the provisions of this section shall apply to the varied order as if it had been an order made under subsection (1).

(7) An application under subsection (6) shall be on notice to the person concerned and the clinical director of the designated centre concerned, if the applicant is not the clinical director.

(8) (a)   A person who is the subject of a conditional discharge order may make an application in writing to the Review Board for an unconditional discharge (in this Act referred to as an 'application for an unconditional discharge').

(b)   An application for an unconditional discharge may be made at any time after the expiration of 12 months from the date of the person's conditional discharge so long as a period of not less than 12 months elapses between an application and the next subsequent application.

(9) (a)   Where the Review Board receives an application for an unconditional discharge, it shall request that the person (in this subsection referred to as the 'applicant') attend

before it so that it may determine whether or not to discharge the applicant unconditionally.

(b) The Review Board having heard—

    (i) evidence relating to the applicant (including evidence as to the applicant's mental condition and his or her compliance with the conditions of his or her conditional discharge order) given by the clinical director or, at the request of the Board, the consultant psychiatrist responsible for the applicant's treatment and supervision, or by both of them, and

    (ii) any evidence adduced by or on behalf of the applicant, shall, if it thinks proper, make an order for the unconditional discharge of the applicant.

(c) Where the Review Board makes an order for the unconditional discharge of an applicant, the order shall be deemed to be an order for unconditional discharge duly made under section 13.

(d) Where the Review Board does not make an order for unconditional discharge, it shall make such order as it thinks proper for the further conditional discharge of the applicant on the same or different conditions as may be specified in the order, and the provisions of this section shall apply to such further conditional discharge order as if it had been an order made under subsection (1).

13B   **Material breach of conditional discharge order**

(1) A conditional discharge order shall, in respect of a person who is the subject of the conditional discharge order, be deemed to be revoked if the person is in material breach of that order and accordingly the person shall be deemed to be unlawfully at large.

(2) A person is in material breach of his or her conditional discharge order where the clinical director on reasonable grounds believes that the person is in breach of one or more conditions of his or her conditional discharge, and that—

(a) there is a serious likelihood of the person causing serious harm to himself or herself or to other persons, or

(b) the person may be in need of in-patient care or treatment.

(3) Where the clinical director on reasonable grounds believes that a person is in material breach of his or her conditional discharge order, the director shall, unless subsection (4) applies, inform the person in writing of that fact and the reasons for that belief.

(4) Subsection (3) shall not apply where the clinical director on reasonable grounds believes that the material breach is such as to give reasonable grounds for the director to believe that there is a serious likelihood of the person concerned causing immediate and serious harm to himself or herself or to other persons.

(5) The clinical director shall arrange for an officer or servant of the designated centre or an authorised person to effect the person's return to the designated centre and the clinical director may, if necessary, request the Garda Síochána to assist in effecting the return of the person to that centre and the Garda Síochána shall comply with any such request.

(6) Without prejudice to subsection (5) and to any other power conferred by law, a member of the Garda Síochána may arrest without warrant any person whom he or she with reasonable cause suspects to be unlawfully at large pursuant to subsection (1).

(7) A person who is arrested under subsection (6) by a member of the Garda Síochána shall, as soon as practicable, be transferred into the custody of an officer or servant of the designated centre or an authorised person for the purpose of effecting

the return of that person to the designated centre concerned.

(8) A member of the Garda Síochána may for the purposes of this section—

    (a) enter if need be by force any dwelling or other premises where he or she has reasonable cause to believe that the person may be, and

    (b) take all reasonable measures necessary for the return of the person to the designated centre including, where necessary, the detention or restraint of the person.

(9) (a) Notwithstanding the generality of subsection (4), a person who returns or who is returned, as the case may be, to the designated centre concerned pursuant to this section shall as soon as may be upon his or her return be given reasons in writing for his or her return.

    (b) The provisions of this Act shall apply to the person as if the person was being committed for the first time to the designated centre pursuant to section 4 or 5 or to section 202 or 203 of the Defence Act 1954 on the date of his or her return to the centre.

(10) Where a person returns or is returned, as the case may be, to a designated centre pursuant to this section—

    (a) the clinical director of that centre shall forthwith notify the Review Board of that return,

    (b) the Board shall order that the patient be brought before it as soon as may be for the purposes of reviewing the patient's detention, and

    (c) the Board may exercise all the powers available to it under section 13 in relation to that patient.

(11) In this section, 'authorised person', in relation to effecting the return of a person under this section, means a person who is for the time being authorised pursuant to section 13C to provide services relating to such a return.

13C   Arrangements to provide services

(1) The registered proprietor of a designated centre may enter into an arrangement with a person for the purposes of arranging for persons who are members of the staff of that person to provide services relating to effecting the return pursuant to section 13B of persons to that centre.

(2) Where the registered proprietor of a designated centre has entered into an arrangement referred to in subsection (1) with a person, the clinical director of that centre may authorise, in writing and for a period not exceeding 12 months as is specified in the authorisation, such and so many persons who are members of the staff of that person to provide the services referred to in that subsection which are the subject of that arrangement.

(3) In this section—

'register' shall be construed in accordance with section 62 of the Mental Health Act 2001;

'registered proprietor', in relation to a designated centre, means the person whose name is entered in the register as the person carrying on the centre.]¹

Amendments

1   Sections 13A–13C inserted by Criminal Law (Insanity) Act 2010, s 8. The 2010 Act commenced on 8 February 2011 by virtue of SI 50/2011.

14   Temporary release, transfer and other matters

(1) The clinical director of a designated centre may, with the consent of the Minister, direct the temporary release of a patient on such conditions and for such period or periods as the clinical director deems appropriate.

(2) The clinical director of a designated centre may, with the consent of the Minister and the Minister for Health and Children, direct the transfer to another designated centre of a patient on such condition and for such period or periods as the clinical director deems appropriate with the consent of the clinical director of the other centre.

(3) Where the release or transfer of a patient under subsection (1) or (2) is made subject to conditions, the conditions shall be communicated to the patient by notice in writing at the time of his or her release or transfer.

(4) A patient whose temporary release or transfer is directed under this section shall comply with any conditions to which his or her release or transfer is made subject.

(5) A patient who, by reason of having been temporarily released from a designated centre, is at large shall be deemed to be unlawfully at large if—

    (a) the period for which he or she was temporarily released has expired, or

    (b) a condition to which his or her release was made subject has been broken.

(6) Where, by reason of the breach of a condition to which his or her release was made subject, a patient is deemed to be unlawfully at large and is arrested under subsection (7) or otherwise or returns voluntarily, the period for which he or she was temporarily released shall thereupon be deemed to have expired.

(7) Without prejudice to any other power conferred by law, a member of the Garda Síochána shall, or an officer or servant of the designated centre may, arrest without warrant any person whom he or she suspects to be unlawfully at large while subject to an order for his or her detention in a designated centre under this Act and bring him or her back to such centre.

(8) (a) A patient may be removed from a designated centre to a hospital in order to receive medical attention not available in the designated centre and while detained in that hospital he or she shall be in lawful custody.

    (b) Where a patient is removed from a designated centre pursuant to this subsection the clinical director shall within 48 hours of such removal forward a report of the circumstances regarding the removal to the Minister.

(9) The Minister may, where he or she is satisfied that it is in the interests of justice to do so, direct that a patient be removed from a designated centre to a specified place and during such authorised absence the patient shall be deemed to remain in the lawful custody of the designated centre.

15   Transfer of prisoner to designated centre

(1) Where—

   (a) a relevant officer certifies in writing that a prisoner is suffering from a mental disorder for which he or she cannot be afforded appropriate care or treatment within the prison in which the prisoner is detained, and

   (b) the prisoner voluntarily consents to be transferred from the prison to a designated centre for the purpose of receiving care or treatment for the mental disorder,

then the Governor of the prison may direct in writing the transfer of the prisoner to any designated centre for that purpose.

(2) Where 2 or more relevant officers certify in writing that a prisoner is suffering from a mental disorder for which he or she cannot be afforded appropriate care or treatment within the prison in which the prisoner is detained, then the Governor of the prison may direct in writing the transfer of the prisoner to any designated centre for the purpose of the prisoner receiving care or treatment for the mental disorder notwithstanding that the prisoner is unwilling or unable to voluntarily consent to the transfer.

(3) The Governor of a prison who gives a direction under subsection (1) or (2) shall cause—

   (a) the original of the direction to be sent to the clinical director of the designated centre to which the prisoner the subject of the direction is to be transferred,

   (b) a copy of the direction to be given to the prisoner before the prisoner is transferred to the centre,

   (c) a copy of the direction to be sent to the Minister, and

   (d) where subsection (2) is applicable—

      (i) the original of the certification concerned referred to in that subsection to accompany the original referred to in paragraph (a),

      (ii) a copy of that certification to accompany the copy referred to in paragraph (b), and

      (iii) a copy of that certification to accompany the copy referred to in paragraph (c).

(4) A direction under subsection (1) and (2) shall be sufficient authority to transfer the prisoner the subject of the direction from the prison in which the prisoner is detained to the designated centre specified in the direction.

(5) Where a prisoner who has been transferred to a designated centre pursuant to a direction under subsection (1) refuses to receive care or treatment there for a mental disorder, then—

   (a) if 2 or more relevant officers certify in writing that the prisoner is suffering from a mental disorder for which the prisoner should remain in the centre for the purpose of the prisoner receiving care or treatment for the mental disorder, the prisoner shall continue to remain in the centre for that purpose,

   (b) in any other case—

      (i) the prisoner shall be transferred back to the prison from which he or she was transferred to the centre, or

      (ii) the prisoner shall be transferred to such other prison as the Minister considers appropriate in all the circumstances of the case.

(6) Where subsection (5)(a) is applicable to a prisoner transferred to a designated centre, the clinical director of the centre shall cause—

   (a)   a copy of the certification referred to in that subsection to be given to the prisoner as soon as is practicable after the certification has been made, and

   (b)   a copy of that certification to be sent to the Minister as soon as practicable after the certification has been made.

(7) Where a prisoner transferred to a designated centre pursuant to a direction under subsection (1) or (2) is required to appear in court, the prisoner may be transferred to and from court as so required.

(8) A prisoner transferred under this section—

   (a)   from a prison to a designated centre is deemed to be in lawful custody while being so transferred, while at the centre and while being transferred back to prison,

   (b)   from a designated centre to a court is deemed to be in lawful custody while being so transferred, while in court and while being transferred back to the centre,

   (c)   while being so transferred may be escorted by any members of the staff of the prison or centre, and

   (d)   while being so escorted by any such members is deemed to be in their lawful custody.

(9) In this section, "relevant officer " means—

   (a)   an approved medical officer, or

   (b)   a person registered in the General Register of Medical Practitioners established under the Medical Practitioners Acts 1978 to 2002.

16   **Clinical director of designated centre to be notified of date on which prisoner detained in centre ceases to be prisoner, etc**

(1) Where a prisoner is detained in a designated centre pursuant to section 15, the Governor of the prison from which the prisoner was transferred to the centre shall, as soon as it is practicable to do so, give notice in writing to the clinical director of the centre of—

   (a)   the date, if known, on which the prisoner will cease to be a prisoner, and

   (b)   any change to such date.

(2) Nothing in this Act shall be construed as prohibiting or restricting, on and after the date on which a prisoner who is detained in a designated centre pursuant to section 15 ceases to be a prisoner, the voluntary or involuntary admission to or detention in any place of the former prisoner pursuant to the provisions of the Act of 2001 or any other enactment.

(3) Nothing in this Act shall be construed as prohibiting or restricting any steps being taken, before the date on which a prisoner who is detained in a designated centre pursuant to section 15 ceases to be a prisoner, to ascertain whether or not the prisoner should, on or after that date, be admitted or detained as mentioned in subsection (2).

17   **Review of prisoner's detention in designated centre**

(1) Where the Minister is satisfied that it is in the interests of justice to do so, the Minister may direct the Review Board to review the detention of a prisoner in a designated centre in any case where the detention arises pursuant to a certification referred to in section 15(2) or (5)(a).

(2) The Review Board shall ensure that the detention of a prisoner in a designated centre pursuant to section 15 is reviewed at intervals of such length not being more than 6 months as

it considers appropriate and the clinical director of the centre shall comply with any request by the Review Board in connection with the review.

(3) A prisoner detained in a designated centre pursuant to section 15 may apply to the Review Board for a review of his or her detention and the Review Board shall, unless satisfied that the review is, in all the circumstances of the case, not necessary, conduct the review and—

(a) if satisfied that the prisoner is suffering from or continues to suffer from a mental disorder for which he or she cannot be afforded appropriate treatment within the prison from which the prisoner was transferred to the centre, refuse to make an order referred to in paragraph (b),

(b) in any other case, after consultation with the Minister—

(i) order the prisoner to be transferred back to the prison from which he or she was transferred to the centre, or

(ii) order the prisoner to be transferred to such other prison as the Minister considers appropriate in all the circumstances of the case.

(4) Notwithstanding subsection (1), the Review Board may on its own initiative review the detention of a prisoner in a designated centre pursuant to section 15, and subsection (3) shall apply to such review as if the prisoner had applied for the review under that subsection.

(5) This section shall, with all necessary modifications, apply to a prisoner detained in a relevant place before the commencement of this section as it applies to a prisoner detained in a designated centre on or after that commencement.

(6) In subsection (5), "relevant place" means any place which, on or after the commencement of this section, is a designated centre.

18   Transfer back to prison

Where the clinical director of a designated centre forms the opinion in relation to a prisoner detained in the centre pursuant to section 15 that he or she is no longer in need of in-patient care or treatment he or she shall, after consultation with the Minister, direct in writing—

(a) the transfer of the prisoner back to the prison from which he or she was transferred to the centre, or

(b) the transfer of the prisoner to such other prison as the Minister considers appropriate in all the circumstances of the case.

19   Notice to be given of intention to adduce evidence as to mental condition, etc

(1) Where in any proceedings for an offence the defence intends to adduce evidence as to the mental condition of the accused, notice of the intention shall be given to the prosecution within 10 days of the accused being asked how he or she wishes to plead to the charge.

(2) Where the notice referred to in subsection (1) is not given within the period specified in that subsection, then, without prejudice to any other provision of this Act, evidence shall not, without leave of the court, be adduced by the defence during the course of the trial for the offence concerned as to the mental condition of the accused.

(3) A notice referred to in subsection (1) shall be in such form as rules of court provide.

20 Application to existing detentions

(1) This Act shall apply to a person detained under section 17 of the Lunacy (Ireland) Act 1821, as if he or she were a person detained pursuant to an order under section 4 and, accordingly, such a person shall be entitled to the benefit of the provisions of this Act.

(2) This Act shall apply to a person found guilty but insane and detained under section 2 of the Trial of Lunatics Act 1883, as if he or she were a person detained pursuant to an order of the court made under section 5 and, accordingly, such a person shall be entitled to the benefit of the provisions of this Act.

21 Amendment of Defence Act 1954

The Defence Act 1954, is hereby amended by the substitution for sections 202, 203 and 203A thereof of the following sections:

"Mental disorder at time of trial.

202.— (1) Where at the trial by court-martial of a person charged with an offence it appears that such person is by reason of mental disorder unfit to take his trial the following provisions, subject to subsection (4), shall have effect, that is to say:

(a) the court-martial shall find specially that fact,

(b) the court-martial, if it is satisfied having heard evidence relating to the mental condition of the person given by a consultant psychiatrist that such person is suffering from a mental disorder (within the meaning of the Act of 2001) and is in need of in-patient care or treatment in a designated centre, shall commit him to a specified designated centre until an order is made under section 13 of the Criminal Law (Insanity) Act 2006.

(2) A finding under this section shall not require confirmation or be subject to revision.

(3) A person charged with an offence shall not be fit to take his trial if he is unable by reason of mental disorder to understand the nature or course of the proceedings so as to—

(a) plead to the charge,

(b) instruct a legal representative,

(c) make a proper defence, or

(d) understand the evidence.

(4) After the court-martial has found that a person charged with an offence is unfit to take his trial, it may on application to it and without prejudice to any further proceedings allow evidence to be adduced before it as to whether or not that person did the act or made the omission alleged against him and if the court-martial is satisfied that there is a reasonable doubt that the person committed that act or made the omission it shall acquit him.

(5) In this section and in section 203 of this Act 'mental disorder' and 'designated centre' shall have the meanings respectively assigned to them by section 1 of the Criminal Law (Insanity) Act 2006, unless the context otherwise requires.

Mental disorder at time of commission of offence.

> 203.— (1) Where at the trial by court-martial of a person charged with an offence, the court-martial finds that the person did the act or made the omission charged but, having heard evidence relating to his mental condition given by a consultant psychiatrist, finds that he was at the time when he did the act or made the omission suffering from a mental disorder and that the mental disorder was such that he should not be held responsible for the act or omission alleged by reason of the fact that—
>
> (a)   he did not know the nature and quality of the act he was doing, or
>
> (b)   he did not know what he was doing was wrong, or
>
> (c)   he was unable to refrain from committing the act or making the omission,
>
> the court-martial shall specially find that theperson is not guilty by reason of insanity.
>
> (2) If the court-martial having considered any evidence adduced before it is satisfied that the person found not guilty by reason of insanity is suffering from a mental disorder (within the meaning of the Act of 2001) and is in need of in-patient care or treatment in a designated centre the court-martial shall, after consultation with the clinical director of the designated centre concerned, commit him to a specified designated centre until an order is made under section 13 of the Criminal Law (Insanity) Act 2006.
>
> (3) A finding under this section shall not require confirmation or be subject to revision.

Diminished responsibility.

> 203A.— Section 6 of the Criminal Law (Insanity) Act 2006, shall apply with any necessary modifications to a person subject to military law who is tried by court-martial for murder as it applies to a person who is tried for murder.".

22   Amendment of Infanticide Act 1949

Section 1(3) of the Infanticide Act 1949 is hereby amended—

(a)   in subsection (3)(c), by the substitution of "by reason of a mental disorder (within the meaning of the Criminal Law (Insanity) Act 2006)" for "by reason of the effect of lactation", and

(b)   by the substitution of "as for manslaughter and, on conviction may be dealt with under section 6(3) of the Criminal Law (Insanity) Act 2006 as if she had been found guilty of manslaughter on the grounds of diminished responsibility" for "and punished as for manslaughter".

23   Expenses

The expenses incurred by the Minister and the Minister for Health and Children in the administration of this Act shall, to such extent as may be sanctioned by the Minister for Finance, be paid out of moneys provided by the Oireachtas.

24   Grants to Review Board

The Minister may, in each financial year, after consultation with the Review Board in relation to its proposed work programme and expenditure for that year, make grants of such amount

>3

as may be sanctioned by the Minister for Finance out of moneys provided by the Oireachtas towards other expenditure incurred by the Review Board in the performance of its functions.

25 Repeals and transitional provision

(1) The enactments specified in column 3 of Schedule 2 to this Act opposite a reference number specified in column 1 are hereby repealed to the extent specified in column 4 of that Schedule opposite the mention of that reference number.

(2) An instrument made under an enactment repealed by this Act and in force immediately before the commencement of this section shall, notwithstanding the repeal, continue in force after such commencement.

26 Short title and commencement

(1) This Act may be cited as the Criminal Law (Insanity) Act 2006.

(2) This Act shall come into operation on such day or days as, by order or orders made by the Minister under this section, may be fixed therefor either generally or with reference to any particular purpose or provision, and different days may be so fixed for different purposes and different provisions.

SCHEDULE 1

MENTAL HEALTH (CRIMINAL LAW) REVIEW BOARD

Section 11

1. The Review Board shall consist of a chairperson and such number of members as the Minister, after consultation with the Minister for Health and Children, may from time to time as the occasion requires appoint. The Review Board shall have as an ordinary member, at least one approved medical officer.

2. The chairperson shall have had not less than 10 years' experience as a practising barrister or practising solicitor ending immediately before his or her appointment or shall be a judge of or former judge of the Circuit Court, High Court or Supreme Court.

3. The members of the Review Board shall, subject to the provisions of this Schedule, hold office upon such terms and conditions as the Minister may determine.

4. The term of office of a member of the Review Board shall be 5 years and subject to the provisions of this Schedule, he or she shall be eligible for re-appointment as such member.

5. A member of the Review Board may at any time resign his or her office by letter addressed to the Minister and the resignation shall take effect on and from the date of receipt of the letter.

6. A member of the Review Board may be removed from office by the Minister, after consultation with the Minister for Health and Children, for stated reasons.

7. The chairperson other than a chairperson who is a serving judge and each member of the Review Board shall be paid, out of monies provided by the Oireachtas, such remuneration (if any) and such allowances or expenses as the Minister may, with the consent of the Minister for Finance, determine.

8. If a member of the Review Board dies, resigns, becomes disqualified or is removed from office, the Minister may appoint another person to be a member of the Review Board to fill the casual vacancy so occasioned and the person so appointed shall be

appointed in the same manner as the member of the Review Board who occasioned the vacancy and shall hold office for the remainder of the term of office for which his or her predecessor was appointed.

9. The Minister may appoint such and so many persons to be members of the staff of the Review Board as he or she considers necessary to assist the Review Board in the performance of its functions and such members of the staff of the Review Board shall hold their offices or employment on such terms and subject to such conditions and receive such remuneration as the Minister may, with the consent of the Minister for Finance, determine.

10. Members of the staff of the Review Board shall be civil servants within the meaning of the Civil Service Regulation Act 1956.

11. The Review Board shall hold such sittings as may be necessary for the performance of its functions under this Act.

12. Every question at a sitting of the Review Board shall be determined by a majority of the votes of the members voting on the question and, in the case of an equal division of votes, the chairperson shall have a casting vote.

13. Subject to the provisions of this Schedule, the Review Board shall establish its own rules of procedure.

SCHEDULE 2
ENACTMENTS REPEALED

Section 25

Ref No	Session and Chapter or Year and Number	Short Title	Extent of Repeal
(1)	(2)	(3)	(4)
1.	39 & 40 Geo. 3 c.94	Criminal Lunatics Act 1800	The whole Act
2.	1 & 2 Geo. 4 c.33	Lunacy (Ireland) Act 1821	Sections 17 and 18
3.	1 Vict., c.27	Criminal Lunatics (Ireland) Act 1838	Sections 2 and 3
4.	8 & 9 Vict., c. 107	Central Criminal Lunatic Asylum (Ireland) Act 1845	Sections 8 and 12
5.	38 & 39 Vict., c.67	Lunatic Asylums (Ireland) Act 1875	Section 13
6.	46 & 47 Vict., c.38	Trial of Lunatics Act 1883	The whole Act
7.	1924, No. 10	Courts of Justice Act 1924	Section 35
8.	1960, No. 27	Criminal Justice Act 1960	Section 8
9.	1976, No. 4	Juries Act 1976	Section 19(2)
10.[1]	1967, No. 12	Criminal Procedure Act 1967	Section 4A(1)(c)

Amendments

1   Paragraph 10 substituted by Criminal Law (Insanity) Act 2010, s 9. The 2010 Act commenced on 8 February 2011 by virtue of SI 50/2011.

Criminal Law (Sexual Offences) Act 2006

Number 15 of 2006

ARRANGEMENT OF SECTIONS

1.   Definitions.

2.   Defilement of child under 15 years of age.

3.   Defilement of child under the age of 17 years.

4.   Summary trial of offences.

5.   Female child under 17 years of age not guilty of offence.

6.   Application of certain enactments.

7.   Amendment of certain enactments.

8.   Repeals.

9.   Short title.

AN ACT TO PROVIDE FOR OFFENCES IN RELATION TO THE COMMISSION OF SEXUAL ACTS WITH CHILDREN UNDER THE AGE OF 17 YEARS; AND TO PROVIDE FOR MATTERS CONNECTED THEREWITH. [2nd June, 2006]

BE IT ENACTED BY THE OIREACHTAS AS FOLLOWS:

1   Definitions

In this Act—

"Act of 1981" means the Criminal Law (Rape) Act 1981"

"Act of 1990" means the Criminal Law (Rape) (Amendment) Act 1990"

"person in authority" means—

    (a) a parent, step-parent, guardian, grandparent, uncle or aunt of the victim,

    (b) any person who is, for the time being, in loco parentis to the victim, or

    (c) any person who is, for the time being, responsible for the education, supervision or welfare of the victim;

"sexual act" means—

    (a) an act consisting of—

        (i)   sexual intercourse, or

        (ii) buggery,

    between persons who are not married to each other, or

    (b) an act described in section 3(1) or 4(1) of the Act of 1990;

"sexual intercourse" shall be construed in accordance with section 1(2) of the Act of 1981.

2   Defilement of child under 15 years of age

(1) Any person who engages in a sexual act with a child who is under the age of 15 years shall be guilty of an offence and shall be liable on conviction on indictment to imprisonment for life or a lesser term of imprisonment.

(2) Any person who attempts to engage in a sexual act with a child who is under the age of 15 years shall be guilty of an offence and shall be liable on conviction on indictment to imprisonment for life or a lesser term of imprisonment.

(3) It shall be a defence to proceedings for an offence under this section for the defendant to prove that he or she honestly believed that, at the time of the alleged commission of the offence, the child against whom the offence is alleged to have been committed had attained the age of 15 years.

(4) Where, in proceedings for an offence under this section, it falls to the court to consider whether the defendant honestly believed that, at the time of the alleged commission of the offence, the child against whom the offence is alleged to have been committed had attained the age of 15 years, the court shall have regard to the presence or absence of reasonable grounds for the defendant's so believing and all other relevant circumstances.

(5) It shall not be a defence to proceedings for an offence under this section for the defendant to prove that the child against whom the offence is alleged to have been committed consented to the sexual act of which the offence consisted.

3   Defilement of child under the age of 17 years

(1) Any person who engages in a sexual act with a child who is under the age of 17 years shall be guilty of an offence and shall, subject to subsection (3), be liable on conviction on indictment—

(a) to imprisonment for a term not exceeding 5 years, or

(b) if he or she is a person in authority, to imprisonment for a term not exceeding 10 years.

(2) Any person who attempts to engage in a sexual act with a child who is under the age of 17 years shall be guilty of an offence and shall, subject to subsection (4) be liable on conviction on indictment—

(a) to imprisonment for a term not exceeding [5 years,]¹ or

(b) if he or she is a person in authority, to imprisonment for a term not exceeding [10 years.]²

(3) A person who has been convicted of an offence under subsection (1) shall, in respect of any subsequent conviction of an offence under that subsection, be liable on conviction on indictment—

(a) to imprisonment for a term not exceeding 10 years, or

(b) if he or she is a person in authority, to imprisonment for a term not exceeding 15 years.

(4) A person who has been convicted of an offence under subsection (2) shall, in respect of any subsequent conviction of an offence under that subsection be liable on conviction on indictment—

(a) to imprisonment for a term not exceeding [10 years]¹, or

(b) if he or she is a person in authority, to imprisonment for a term not exceeding [15 years.]¹

(5) It shall be a defence to proceedings for an offence under this section for the defendant to prove that he or she honestly believed that, at the time of the alleged commission of the offence, the child against whom the offence is alleged to have been committed had attained the age of 17 years.

(6) Where, in proceedings for an offence under this section, it falls to the court to consider whether the defendant honestly believed that, at the time of the alleged commission of the offence, the child against whom the offence is alleged to have been committed had attained the age of 17 years, the court shall have regard to the presence or absence of reasonable grounds for the defendant's so believing and all other relevant circumstances.

(7) It shall not be a defence to proceedings for an offence under this section for the defendant to prove that the child against whom the offence is alleged to have been committed consented to the sexual act of which the offence consisted.

(8) An offence under subsection (2) shall be an arrestable offence for the purposes of the Criminal Law Act 1997.

(9) No proceedings for an offence under this section against a child under the age of 17 years shall be brought except by, or with the consent of, the Director of Public Prosecutions.

(10) A person who—

    (a)   has been convicted of an offence under this section, and

    (b)   is not more than 24 months older than the child under the age of 17 years with whom he or she engaged or attempted to engage in a sexual act,

shall not be subject to the provisions of the Sex Offenders Act 2001.

Amendments

1   Words substituted by Criminal Law (Sexual Offences) (Amendment) Act 2007, s 5(1)(a).

2   Words substituted by Criminal Law (Sexual Offences) (Amendment) Act 2007, s 5(1)(b).

---

4   Summary trial of offences

(1) The District Court may try summarily a person charged with an offence under section 2(2) or 3(2) if—

    (a)   the court is of opinion that the facts alleged constitute a minor offence fit to be tried summarily,

    (b)   the accused, on being informed by the court of his or her right to be tried with a jury, does not object to being tried summarily for the offence, and

    (c)   the Director of Public Prosecutions consents to the accused being tried summarily for the offence.

(2) Upon conviction of a person by the District Court of an offence under this section, the person shall be liable to a fine not exceeding €5,000 or to imprisonment for a term not exceeding 12 months or to both.

5   Female child under 17 years of age not guilty of offence

A female child under the age of 17 years shall not be guilty of an offence under this Act by reason only of her engaging in an act of sexual intercourse.

6   Application of certain enactments

(1) Sections 3 and 4 of the Act of 1981 shall apply in relation to an offence under this Act subject to the modification that references in those sections to "sexual assault offence" shall be construed as including references to an offence under this Act.

[(1A) References in section 3 of the Act of 1981 to jury shall, in the case of summary proceedings for an offence under this Act, be construed as references to court.]¹

(2) Section 4A of the Act of 1981 is amended, in subsection (6), by the insertion after "rape offence" of ", an offence under the Criminal Law (Sexual Offences) Act 2006".

(3) Sections 6, 7 and 8 of the Act of 1981 shall apply in relation to an offence under this Act subject to the modification that references in those sections to—

    (a)   "sexual assault offence" shall be construed as including references to an offence under this Act, and

    (b)   "rape offence" shall be construed as including references to an offence under this Act.

Amendments

1   Subsection (1A) inserted by Criminal Law (Sexual Offences) (Amendment) Act 2007, s 5(2).

---

7   Amendment of certain enactments

(1) Section 8 of the Act of 1990 is amended—

    (a)   in subsection (2), by the substitution of "section 2 or 3 of the Criminal Law (Sexual Offences) Act 2006" for "section 1 or 2 of the Criminal Law Amendment Act 1935", and

    (b)   in subsection (5), by—

        (i)   the substitution of "section 2 of the Criminal Law (Sexual Offences) Act 2006" for "section 1 of the Criminal Law Amendment Act 1935",

        (ii)   the substitution of "section 3 of the Criminal Law (Sexual Offences) Act 2006" for "section 2 of the Criminal Law Amendment Act 1935", and

        (iii)   the substitution of "the said section 3 or section 3 of the Criminal Law (Sexual Offences) Act 2006," for "the said section 2 or 3".

(2) Section 2 of the Criminal Evidence Act 1992 is amended, in the definition of "sexual offence", by the substitution of the following paragraph for paragraph (iv):¹

(3) The Schedule to the Sexual Offences (Jurisdiction) Act 1996 is amended by—

    (a)   the substitution of the following paragraph for paragraph 1:

         "1. Criminal Law (Sexual Offences) Act 2006.",

         and

    (b)   the deletion of paragraphs 2, 7 and 8.

(4) The Schedule to the Bail Act 1997 is amended by the substitution of the following paragraph for paragraph 10:¹

(5) The Schedule to the Sex Offenders Act 2001 is amended by—

(a) the substitution of the following paragraph for paragraph 7:[1]

(b) the deletion of paragraph 8.

(6) Schedule 1 to the Children Act 2001 is amended by the substitution of the following paragraph for paragraph 4:[1]

Amendments

1   See the amended Act.

---

8   Repeals

The enactments specified in the Schedule are repealed to the extent specified in column (3) thereof.

9   Short title

This Act may be cited as the Criminal Law (Sexual Offences) Act 2006.

SCHEDULE
ENACTMENTS REPEALED

Number and Year	Short title	Extent of Repeal
(1)	(2)	(3)
No. 6 of 1935	Criminal Law Amendment Act 1935	Sections 1(2) and 2
No. 20 of 1993	Criminal Law (Sexual Offences) Act 1993	Sections 3 and 4

Criminal Justice Act 2006

Number 26 of 2006

ARRANGEMENT OF SECTIONS

PART 1

PRELIMINARY AND GENERAL

Section

1. Short title and commencement.

2. Interpretation.

3. Regulations.

4. Expenses.

PART 2

INVESTIGATION OF OFFENCES

5. Designation of place as crime scene.

6. Search warrants in relation to arrestable offences.

7. Power to seize and retain evidence.

8. Arrestable offences.

9. Amendment of section 4 of Act of 1984.

10. Amendment of Criminal Justice (Drug Trafficking) Act 1996.

11. Amendment of section 42 of Criminal Justice Act 1999.

12. Power of Garda Síochána to photograph arrested persons.

13. Amendment of Act of 1984.

14. Amendment of Criminal Justice (Forensic Evidence) Act 1990.

PART 3

ADMISSIBILITY OF CERTAIN WITNESS STATEMENTS

15. Definitions (Part 3).

16. Admissibility of certain witness statements.

17. Witness statements made to members of Garda Síochána.

18. Other witness statements.

19. Regulations concerning certain witness statements which are recorded.

20. Amendment of section 4E of Act of 1967.

PART 4

APPEALS IN CERTAIN CRIMINAL PROCEEDINGS

21. Reference of question of law to Supreme Court.

22. Decision of Court of Criminal Appeal final save on certificate of Court, Attorney General or Director of Public Prosecutions.

23. Amendment of section 2(2) of Criminal Justice Act 1993.

24. Appeal against order for costs.

PART 5
AMENDMENT OF FIREARMS ACTS

25.   Definitions (Part 5).

26.   Amendment of section 1 of Principal Act.

27.   Amendment of section 2 of Principal Act.

28.   New section 2A in Principal Act.

29.   New section 2B in Principal Act.

30.   Substitution of section 3 of Principal Act.

31.   New section 3A in Principal Act.

32.   Substitution of section 4 of Principal Act.

33.   New section 4A in Principal Act.

34.   New section 4B in Principal Act.

35.   Substitution of section 5 of Principal Act.

36.   Amendment of section 6 of Principal Act.

37.   Amendment of section 8 of Principal Act.

38.   Amendment of section 9 of Principal Act.

39.   Amendment of section 10 of Principal Act.

40.   New section 10A in Principal Act.

41.   Amendment of section 11 of Principal Act.

42.   Substitution of section 15 of Principal Act.

43.   New section 15A in Principal Act.

44.   Amendment of section 17 of Principal Act.

45.   Substitution of section 25 of Principal Act.

46.   New section 25A of Principal Act.

47.   New section 25B in Principal Act.

48.   New section 25C in Principal Act.

49.   New section 25D in Principal Act.

50.   Substitution of section 27 of Principal Act.

51.   New section 27A in Principal Act.

AMENDMENT OF FIREARMS ACT 1964

52.   Amendment of section 1 of Firearms Act 1964.

53.   Substitution of section 9 of Firearms Act 1964.

54.   Amendment of section 11 of Firearms Act 1964.

55.   Amendment of section 13 of Firearms Act 1964.

56.   Amendment of section 21 of Firearms Act 1964.

57.   Substitution of section 26 of Firearms Act 1964.

58.   Substitution of section 27 of Firearms Act 1964.

59.   Substitution of section 27A of Firearms Act 1964.

60.   Substitution of section 27B of Firearms Act 1964.

61.   New section 27C in Firearms Act 1964.

AMENDMENT OF CRIMINAL JUSTICE ACT 1984

62.   Amendment of section 15 of Criminal Justice Act 1984.

AMENDMENT OF FIREARMS AND OFFENSIVE WEAPONS ACT 1990

63.   Amendment of Firearms and Offensive Weapons Act 1990.

64.   New section 8A of Firearms and Offensive Weapons Act 1990.

65.   New section 12A in Firearms and Offensive Weapons Act 1990.

66.   Amendment of section 1 of Firearms (Firearm Certificates for Non-Residents) Act 2000.

67.   Amendment of section 2 of Firearms (Firearm Certificates for Non-Residents) Act 2000.

PART 6
AMENDMENT OF EXPLOSIVES ACT 1875

68.   Substitution of section 80 of Explosives Act 1875.

69.   Other amendments of Explosives Act 1875.

PART 7
ORGANISED CRIME

70.   Interpretation (Part 7).

71.   Offence of conspiracy.

71A   Offence of directing a criminal organisation.

71B   Provisions with respect to proof of criminal organisation's existence.

72.   Offence to participate in, or contribute to, certain activities.

72A   Offences under this Part: inferences that may be drawn

73.   Commission of offence for criminal organisation.

74.   Proceedings relating to offences committed outside State.

74A   Aggravating factor: serious offence committed as part of, or in furtherance of, activities of criminal organisation.

74B   Exclusion of evidence in certain circumstances.

75.   Evidence in proceedings under this Part.

76.   Liability for offences by bodies corporate.

77.   Double jeopardy.

78.   Amendment of Act of 1967.

79.   Amendment of Schedule to Bail Act 1997.

PART 8
MISUSE OF DRUGS

section 15A of Act of 1977.

controlled drugs in excess of certain value.

83.   Supply of controlled drugs into prisons and places of detention.

84.   Amendment of section 27 of Act of 1977.

85.   Amendment of section 29 of Act of 1977.

86.   Amendment of section 3(1) of Criminal Justice Act 1994.

PART 9
OBLIGATIONS OF DRUG TRAFFICKING OFFENDERS TO NOTIFY CERTAIN INFORMATION

87.   Definitions (Part 9).

88.   Drug trafficking offences for purposes of this Part.

89.   Persons subject to the requirements of this Part.

90.   Period for which person is subject to requirements of this Part and related matters.

91.   Supply of information to facilitate compliance with this Part.

92.   Notification requirements.

93.   Discharge from obligation to comply with requirements of this Part.

94.   Offences in connection with notification requirements.

95.   Application of this Part to persons convicted outside State.

96.   Certificate as evidence of person's being subject to requirements of this Part.

97.   Proof of foreign conviction in certain cases.

PART 10
SENTENCING

98.   Definitions (Part 10).

99.   Power to suspend sentence.

100.   Imposition of fine and deferral of sentence.

101.   Restriction on movement order.

102.   Electronic monitoring of restriction on movement order.

103.   Variation of restriction on movement order.

104. Provisions regarding more than one restriction on movement order.

105.   Non-compliance with restriction on movement order.

106.   Amendment of section 5 of Criminal Justice Act 1951.

107.   Documentary evidence in relation to offenders.

108.   Temporary release of prisoners.

109.   Documentary evidence in relation to prisoners on temporary release.

110. Amendment of section 2(1) of Criminal Justice Act 1960.

111. Regulations regarding electronic monitoring devices.

112. Electronic monitoring.

PART 11
CIVIL PROCEEDINGS IN RELATION TO ANTI-SOCIAL BEHAVIOUR

113. Interpretation and application of this Part.

114. Behaviour warnings.

115. Civil orders.

116. Appeals against a civil order.

117. Offences.

118. Legal aid.

119. Regulations (legal aid).

PART 12
AMENDMENT OF CHILDREN ACT 2001

120. Interpretation (Part 12).

121. Amendment of section 2 of Act of 2001.

122. Amendment of section 3 of Act of 2001.

123. Substitution of section 18 of Act of 2001.

124. Amendment of section 19 of Act of 2001.

125. Amendment of section 23 of Act of 2001.

126. Substitution of section 48 of Act of 2001.

127. Substitution of section 49 of Act of 2001.

128. Amendment of Title to Part 5 of Act of 2001.

129. Substitution of section 52 of Act of 2001.

130. Amendment of section 53 of Act of 2001.

131. Amendment of section 59 of Act of 2001.

132. New section 76A in Act of 2001.

133. New section 76B in Act of 2001.

134. New section 76C in Act of 2001.

135. Substitution of section 88 of Act of 2001.

136. Amendment of section 96 of Act of 2001.

137. Change in title of principal probation and welfare officer.

138. Amendment of section 91 of Act of 2001.

139. Substitution of section 93 of Act of 2001.

140. Amendment of section 136 of Act of 2001.

141. Substitution of section 149 of Act of 2001.

142. Amendment of section 155 of Act of 2001.

143. New section 156A in Act of 2001.

144. New section 156B in Act of 2001.

145. Amendment of section 157 of Act of 2001.

146. Substitution of section 159 of Act of 2001.

147. New section 159A in Act of 2001.

148. New section 159B in Act of 2001.

149. Amendment of section 161 of Act of 2001.

150. Amendment of section 165 of Act of 2001.

151. Substitution of section 185 of Act of 2001.

152. Substitution of section 186 of Act of 2001.

153. New section 186A in Act of 2001.

154. Substitution of section 198 of Act of 2001.

155. Amendment of section 215 of Act of 2001.

156. Amendment of section 227 of Act of 2001.

157. Amendment of section 230 of Act of 2001.

158. Minor and consequential amendments of Act of 2001.

PART 13
ANTI-SOCIAL BEHAVIOUR BY CHILDREN

159. New section 257A in Act of 2001.

160. New section 257B in Act of 2001.

161. New section 257C in Act of 2001.

162. New section 257D in Act of 2001.

163. New section 257E in Act of 2001.

164. New section 257F in Act of 2001.

165. New section 257G in Act of 2001.

166. New section 257H in Act of 2001.

PART 14
CRIMINAL LAW CODIFICATION ADVISORY COMMITTEE

167. Criminal Law Codification Advisory Committee.

168. Functions of Committee.

169. Membership of Committee.

170. Conditions of office of members of Committee.

171. Vacancies among members of Committee.

172. Meetings and procedure.

173. Programme of Work of Committee.

174. Funding of Committee.

175. Report of Committee.

PART 15
MISCELLANEOUS

176. Reckless endangerment of children.

177. Restriction of section 10(4) of Petty Sessions (Ireland) Act 1851.

178. Amendment of Courts of Justice Act 1924.

179. Amendment of Courts (Supplemental Provisions) Act 1961.

180. Exercise of certain powers by judge of District Court outside district court district.

181. Anonymity of certain witnesses.

182. Information concerning property held in trust.

183. Possession of article intended for use in connection with certain offences.

183A Possession of monies intended for use in connection with certain offences.

184. Amendment of Criminal Justice (Public Order) Act 1994.

185. Amendment of section 19 of Criminal Justice (Public Order) Act 1994.

186. Amendment of section 1 of Criminal Justice (United Nations Convention Against Torture) Act 2000.

187. Amendment of Offences Against the State Act 1939.

188. Amendment of section 5 of Criminal Evidence Act 1992.

189. Amendment of section 16B(7) of Proceeds of Crime Act 1996.

190. Amendment of section 14 of Criminal Assets Bureau Act 1996.

191. Amendment of section 5 of Prevention of Corruption (Amendment) Act 2001.

192. Amendment of Criminal Justice (Theft and Fraud Offences) Act 2001.

193. Amendment of section 25 of Petty Sessions (Ireland) Act 1851.

194. Execution of certain warrants.

195. Imprisonment or distress and sale of goods on conviction on indictment in default of payment of fine.

196. Amendment of section 6(2)(a) of Criminal Law Act 1976.

197. Amendment of section 13 of the Criminal Law (Insanity) Act 2006.

SCHEDULE 1
INCREASE OF CERTAIN PENALTIES UNDER FIREARMS ACTS 1925 TO 2000

SCHEDULE 2
INCREASE IN CERTAIN PENALTIES UNDER EXPLOSIVES ACT 1875

SCHEDULE 3
OFFENCES FOR THE PURPOSES OF RESTRICTION ON MOVEMENT ORDERS

SCHEDULE 4
MINOR AND CONSEQUENTIAL AMENDMENTS OF CHILDREN ACT 2001

AN ACT TO AMEND AND EXTEND THE POWERS OF THE GARDA SÍOCHÁNA IN RELATION TO THE INVESTIGATION OF OFFENCES; TO AMEND CRIMINAL LAW AND

PROCEDURE IN OTHER RESPECTS, INCLUDING PROVISION FOR THE ADMISSIBILITY IN EVIDENCE OF CERTAIN WITNESS STATEMENTS, AN EXTENSION OF THE CIRCUMSTANCES IN WHICH THE ATTORNEY GENERAL IN ANY CASE OR, IF HE OR SHE IS THE PROSECUTING AUTHORITY IN A TRIAL, THE DIRECTOR OF PUBLIC PROSECUTIONS MAY REFER A QUESTION OF LAW TO THE SUPREME COURT FOR DETERMINATION OR TAKE AN APPEAL IN CRIMINAL PROCEEDINGS, PROVISION FOR OFFENCES RELATING TO ORGANISED CRIME, AMENDMENTS TO THE MISUSE OF DRUGS ACT 1977, AN OBLIGATION, IN THE INTERESTS OF THE COMMON GOOD, ON PERSONS CONVICTED ON INDICTMENT OF CERTAIN DRUG TRAFFICKING OFFENCES TO NOTIFY CERTAIN INFORMATION TO THE GARDA SÍOCHÁNA, PROVISIONS IN RELATION TO SENTENCING, A RESTRICTION OF THE OFFENCES TO WHICH SECTION 10(4) OF THE PETTY SESSIONS (IRELAND) ACT 1851 APPLIES, AN AMENDMENT OF THE JURISDICTION OF THE DISTRICT COURT AND THE CIRCUIT COURT IN CRIMINAL MATTERS, THE IMPOSITION OF FIXED CHARGES IN RESPECT OF CERTAIN OFFENCES UNDER THE CRIMINAL JUSTICE (PUBLIC ORDER) ACT 1994 AND AN AMENDMENT OF THE PETTY SESSIONS (IRELAND) ACT 1851 RELATING TO THE ISSUE AND EXECUTION OF CERTAIN WARRANTS; TO AMEND THE FIREARMS ACTS 1925 TO 2000 AND THE EXPLOSIVES ACT 1875; TO MAKE PROVISION IN RELATION TO ANTI-SOCIAL BEHAVIOUR BY ADULTS AND CHILDREN; TO AMEND THE CHILDREN ACT 2001; TO PROVIDE FOR THE ESTABLISHMENT OF A BODY TO BE KNOWN AS AN COISTE COMHAIRLEACH UM CHÓDÚ AN DLÍ CHOIRIÚIL OR, IN THE ENGLISH LANGUAGE AS, THE CRIMINAL LAW CODIFICATION ADVISORY COMMITTEE AND TO PROVIDE FOR RELATED MATTERS. [16th July, 2006]

BE IT ENACTED BY THE OIREACHTAS AS FOLLOWS:

PART 1

PRELIMINARY AND GENERAL

1   Short title and commencement

(1) This Act may be cited as the Criminal Justice Act 2006.

(2) This Act, other than Parts 11 and 13, shall come into operation on such day or days as the Minister may appoint by order or orders either generally or with reference to any particular purpose or provision and different days may be so appointed for different purposes or different provisions.

(3) Parts 11 and 13 come into operation on such day or days as the Minister may, after consulting with the Commissioner of the Garda Síochána, appoint by order or orders either generally or with reference to any particular purpose or provision and different days may be so appointed for different purposes or different provisions.

(4) The Firearms Acts 1925 to 2000, Part 5 and Schedule 1 may be cited together as the Firearms Acts 1925 to 2006 and shall be construed together as one.

(5) The Explosives Act 1875, Part 6 and Schedule 2 may be cited together as the Explosives Acts 1875 and 2006 and shall be construed together as one.

(6) The collective citation "the Misuse of Drugs Acts 1977 to 2006" shall include Part II (other than section 7) of the Criminal Justice Act 1999 and Part 8 (other than section 86) and

those Acts and those Parts (other than the sections specified) shall be construed together as one.

2 Interpretation

(1) In this Act, unless the context otherwise requires—

"Act of 1939" means the Offences Against the State Act 1939;

"Act of 1967" means Criminal Procedure Act 1967;

"Act of 1984" means Criminal Justice Act 1984;

"arrestable offence" has the meaning it has in section 2 (as amended by section 8) of the Criminal Law Act 1997;

"Minister" means Minister for Justice, Equality and Law Reform;

"place" includes a dwelling.

(2) In this Act, where the context so requires—

    (a) a reference to an offence shall be construed as including a reference to a suspected offence, and

    (b) a reference to the commission of an offence shall be construed as including a reference to the attempted commission of an offence.

3 Regulations

(1) The Minister may make regulations prescribing any matter or thing which is referred to in this Act as prescribed or to be prescribed.

(2) Every regulation under this section shall be laid before each House of the Oireachtas as soon as may be after it has been made and, if a resolution annulling the regulation is passed by either such House within the next 21 days on which that House has sat after the regulation is laid before it, the regulation shall be annulled accordingly, but without prejudice to the validity of anything previously done thereunder.

4 Expenses

The expenses incurred by the Minister in the administration of this Act shall, to such extent as may be sanctioned by the Minister for Finance, be paid out of moneys provided by the Oireachtas.

PART 2

INVESTIGATION OF OFFENCES

5 Designation of place as crime scene

(1) Where a member of the Garda Síochána is in—

    (a) a public place, or

    (b) any other place under a power of entry authorised by law or to which or in which he or she was expressly or impliedly invited or permitted to be,

and he or she has reasonable grounds for believing that—

    (i) an arrestable offence was, is being, or may have been committed in the place, or

    (ii) there is, or may be, in the place evidence of, or relating to, the commission of an arrestable offence that was or may have been committed elsewhere, he or she may, pending the giving of a direction under subsection (3) in relation to the place, take such of the steps specified in subsection (4) as he or she reasonably considers necessary to preserve any evidence of, or relating to, the commission of the offence.

(2) A member of the Garda Síochána who exercises powers under subsection (1) shall, as soon as reasonably practicable, request or cause a request to be made to a member of the Garda Síochána not below the rank of superintendent to give a direction under subsection (3) in relation to the place concerned.

(3) A member of the Garda Síochána not below the rank of superintendent may give a direction designating a place as a crime scene if he or she has reasonable grounds for believing that—

   (a) either—

      (i)   an arrestable offence was, is being, or may have been committed in the place, or

      (ii) there is, or may be, in the place evidence of, or relating to, the commission of an arrestable offence that was, or may have been, committed elsewhere,

      and

   (b) it is necessary to designate the place as a crime scene to preserve, search for and collect evidence of, or relating to, the commission of the offence.

(4) A direction under subsection (3) shall authorise such members of the Garda Síochána as a member of the Garda Síochána not below the rank of superintendent considers appropriate to take such steps, including all or any of the following, as they reasonably consider necessary to preserve, search for and collect evidence at the crime scene to which the direction relates:

   (a) delineating and segregating the area of the crime scene by means of notices, markings or barriers;

   (b) directing a person to leave the crime scene;

   (c) removing a person who fails to comply with a direction to leave the crime scene;

   (d) directing a person not to enter the crime scene;

   (e) preventing a person from entering the crime scene;

   (f) permitting a person authorised under subsection (5) to enter the crime scene;

   (g) preventing a person from removing anything which is, or may be, evidence or otherwise interfering with the crime scene or anything at the scene;

   (h) securing the crime scene from any unauthorised intrusion or disturbance;

   (i) searching the crime scene and examining the scene and anything at the scene; and

   (j) photographing or otherwise recording the crime scene or anything at the scene.

(5) A member of the Garda Síochána not below the rank of superintendent may authorise such persons as he or she considers appropriate to enter a crime scene for a specified purpose and for such period as he or she may determine.

(6) The period for which a direction under subsection (3) is in force shall not be longer than is reasonably necessary to preserve, search for and collect the evidence concerned.

(7) A direction under subsection (3) in relation to a place other than a public place shall, subject to subsections (9) to (11), cease to be in force 24 hours after it is given.

(8) (a) A direction under subsection (3) may be given orally or in writing and, if it is given orally, shall be recorded in writing as soon as reasonably practicable but a failure to record the direction shall not by itself render any evidence inadmissible.

(b) A direction under subsection (3) or, if it is given orally, the written record of it shall be signed by the member of the Garda Síochána giving it, shall describe the place thereby designated as a crime scene, shall state the date and time when it is given, the name and rank of the member giving it and that the member has reasonable grounds for believing that the direction is necessary to preserve, search for and collect the evidence concerned.

(9) If a judge of the District Court is satisfied by information on oath of a member of the Garda Síochána not below the rank of superintendent that—

(a) a direction under subsection (3) designating a place as a crime scene is in force,

(b) there are reasonable grounds for believing that there is, or may be, evidence at the crime scene,

(c) the continuance of the direction in force is necessary to preserve, search for and collect any such evidence, and

(d) the investigation of the offence to which any such evidence relates is being conducted diligently and expeditiously,

the judge may make an order continuing the direction in force for such further period, not exceeding 48 hours, as may be specified in the order commencing upon the expiration of the period for which the direction is in force.

(10) A direction under subsection (3) may be continued in force under subsection (9) not more than three times.

(11) If the High Court is satisfied, upon application being made to it in that behalf by a member of the Garda Síochána not below the rank of superintendent, that—

(a) a direction under subsection (3) designating a place as a crime scene is in force,

(b) there are reasonable grounds for believing that there is, or may be, evidence at the crime scene,

(c) exceptional circumstances exist which warrant the continuance of the direction in force to preserve, search for and collect any such evidence, and

(d) the investigation of the offence to which any such evidence relates is being conducted diligently and expeditiously,

the Court may make an order continuing the direction in force for such period as it considers appropriate and that is specified in the order (whether or not the direction has been continued in force under subsection (9)) commencing upon the expiration of the period for which the direction is in force.

(12) A member of the Garda Síochána who intends to make an application under subsection (9) or (11) shall, if it is reasonably practicable to do so before the application is made, give notice of it to—

(a) the occupier of the place the subject of the application, or

(b) if it is not reasonably practicable to ascertain the identity or whereabouts of the occupier or the place is unoccupied, the owner, unless it is not reasonably practicable to ascertain the identity or whereabouts of the owner.

(13) If, on an application under subsection (9) or (11), the occupier or owner of the place concerned applies to be heard by the Court, an order shall not be made under subsection (9) or (11), as may be appropriate, unless an opportunity has been given to the person to be heard.

(14) The High Court or a judge of the District Court, as may be appropriate, may attach such conditions as the Court or the judge considers appropriate to an order under subsection (9) or (11) for the purpose of protecting the interests of the occupier or owner of the place which is the subject of the order.

(15) A direction under subsection (3) shall be deemed to continue in force until the determination of an application under subsection (9) or (11) if—

    (a) the direction is in force when the application is made, and

    (b) the direction would, but for this subsection, expire before the determination of the application by reason of the fact that, pursuant to subsection (13), an opportunity is given to a person to be heard.

(16) A person who obstructs a member of the Garda Síochána in the exercise of his or her powers under this section or who fails to comply with a direction under this section shall be guilty of an offence and shall be liable on summary conviction to a fine not exceeding €3,000 or imprisonment for a term not exceeding 6 months or both.

(17) A member of the Garda Síochána may arrest without warrant any person whom the member reasonably suspects of committing or having committed an offence under subsection (16).

(18) Nothing in this section shall prevent—

    (a) the designation of a place as a crime scene, or

    (b) a member of the Garda Síochána from taking any of the steps referred to in subsection (4) at a place so designated,

if the owner or occupier of the place consents to such designation or the taking of any of those steps.

(19) In this section—

"evidence" means evidence of, or relating to, the commission of an arrestable offence;

"preserve", in relation to evidence, includes any action to prevent the concealment, loss, removal, contamination or destruction of, or damage or alteration to, the evidence.

6   Search warrants in relation to arrestable offences

(1) The Criminal Justice (Miscellaneous Provisions) Act 1997 is amended by—

    (a) the substitution of the following section for section 10:[1]

    (b) the deletion of the First Schedule.

(2) This section shall not affect the validity of a warrant issued under section 10 of the Criminal Justice (Miscellaneous Provisions) Act 1997 before the commencement of this section and such a warrant shall continue in force in accordance with its terms after such commencement.

Amendments

1   See the amended Act.

7   Power to seize and retain evidence

(1) Where a member of the Garda Síochána who is in—

    (a) a public place, or

    (b) any other place under a power of entry authorised by law or to which or in which he or she was expressly or impliedly invited or permitted to be,

finds or comes into possession of any thing, and he or she has reasonable grounds for believing that it is evidence of, or relating to, the commission of an arrestable offence, he or she may seize and retain the thing for use as evidence in any criminal proceedings for such period from the date of seizure as is reasonable or, if proceedings are commenced in which the thing so seized is required for use in evidence, until the conclusion of the proceedings, and thereafter the Police (Property) Act 1897 shall apply to the thing so seized in the same manner as that Act applies to property which has come into the possession of the Garda Síochána in the circumstances mentioned in that Act.

(2) If it is represented or appears to a member of the Garda Síochána proposing to seize or retain a document under this section that the document was, or may have been, made for the purpose of obtaining, giving or communicating legal advice from or by a barrister or solicitor, the member shall not seize or retain the document unless he or she suspects with reasonable cause that the document was not made, or is not intended, solely for any of the purposes aforesaid.

(3) The power under this section to seize and retain evidence is without prejudice to any other power conferred by statute or otherwise exercisable by a member of the Garda Síochána to seize and retain evidence of, or relating to, the commission or attempted commission of an offence.

8   Arrestable offences

Section 2(1) of the Criminal Law Act 1997 is amended in the definition of "arrestable offence" by the substitution of "under or by virtue of any enactment or the common law" for "under or by virtue of any enactment".

9   Amendment of section 4 of Act of 1984

Section 4 of the Act of 1984 is amended—

    (a) in subsection (1), by the substitution of "under or by virtue of any enactment or the common law" for "under or by virtue of any enactment",

    (b) by the substitution of the following subsection for subsection (2):[1]

    (c) in subsection (3)—

        (i) by the insertion of the following paragraph after paragraph (b):[1]

        (ii) in paragraph (c), by the substitution of "paragraph (b) or (bb)" for "paragraph (b)",[1]

    (d) in subsection (9), by the substitution of "for longer than twenty-four hours" for "for longer than twelve hours".

Amendments

1   See the amended Act.

10   Amendment of Criminal Justice (Drug Trafficking) Act 1996

The Criminal Justice (Drug Trafficking) Act 1996 is amended—

   (a)   in section 2—

      (i)   in subsection (1), by the substitution of the following paragraph for paragraph (a):[1]

      (ii)   by the insertion of the following subsection after subsection (7):[1]

   and

   (b)   in section 4(3), by the insertion of the following paragraph as paragraph (a) and the re-lettering of paragraphs (a) and (b) as paragraphs (b) and (c): [1]

Amendments

1   See the amended Act.

11   Amendment of section 42 of Criminal Justice Act 1999

Section 42 of the Criminal Justice Act 1999 is amended—

   (a)   in subsection (2), by the deletion of subsection (2) and substitution with the following: [1]

   and

   (b)   in subsection (5)—

      (i)   in paragraph (a), by the substitution of "the offence or offences in respect of which he or she was arrested" for "the offence in respect of which he or she was arrested", and

      (ii)   in paragraph (b), by the substitution of "the proper investigation of that offence or those offences" for "the proper investigation of that offence".

Amendments

1   See the amended Act.

12   Power of Garda Síochána to photograph arrested persons

(1) Where a person is arrested by a member of the Garda Síochána under any power conferred on him or her by law, the member may photograph the person or cause him or her to be photographed in a Garda Síochána station as soon as may be after his or her arrest for

the purpose of assisting with the identification of him or her in connection with any proceedings that may be instituted against him or her for the offence in respect of which he or she is arrested.

(2) The power conferred by subsection (1) shall not be exercised except on the authority of a member of the Garda Síochána not below the rank of sergeant.

(3) An authority under subsection (2) may be given orally but, if it is given orally, it shall be confirmed in writing as soon as practicable.

(4) The provisions of section 8 of the Act of 1984 shall apply to photographs (including negatives) taken pursuant to this section as they apply to photographs taken pursuant to section 6 of that Act subject to the modification that the reference in section 8(2) of that Act to proceedings for an offence to which section 4 of that Act applies shall be construed as a reference to proceedings for an offence in respect of which the person concerned is arrested, and any other necessary modifications.

(5) A person who refuses to allow himself or herself to be photographed pursuant to this section shall be guilty of an offence and shall be liable on summary conviction to a fine not exceeding €3,000 or imprisonment for a term not exceeding 6 months or both.

(6) The power conferred by this section is without prejudice to any other power exercisable by a member of the Garda Síochána to photograph a person.

13   Amendment of Act of 1984

The Act of 1984 is amended—

    (a)   in section 6(4), by the substitution of "€3,000" for "£1,000",

    (b)   in section 8—

        (i)   in subsection (2), by the substitution of "within the period of twelve months" for "within the period of six months",

       (ii)   by the substitution of the following subsections for subsection (3): and

      (iii)   in subsection (7)—

           (I)   by the substitution of "for a period not exceeding twelve months" for "for a period not exceeding six months", and

          (II)   by the substitution of "for the purpose of proceedings or further proceedings" for "for the purpose of further proceedings",

    and

    (c)   in section 28(4), by the substitution of "€3,000" for "£1,500".

Amendments

1   See the amended Act.

---

14   Amendment of Criminal Justice (Forensic Evidence) Act 1990

The Criminal Justice (Forensic Evidence) Act 1990 is amended—

    (a)   in section 2—

        (i)   in subsection (1)—

        (I)   by the substitution of "the provisions of subsections (4) to (8A)" for "the provisions of subsections (4) to (8)",

        (II) by the substitution of the following paragraph for paragraph (b):
"(b) a swab from any part of the body including the mouth but not from any other body orifice or a genital region,",

        (III) by the substitution of the following paragraph for paragraph (c):
"(c) a swab from a body orifice, other than the mouth, or a genital region,",

        (IV) in paragraph (e), by the deletion of "or mouth",

  (ii) by the insertion of the following subsection after subsection (1):[1]

  (iii) in subsection (2), by the substitution of "the provisions of subsections (3) to (8A)" for "the provisions of subsections (3) to (8)",

  (iv) in subsection (4)(b), by the substitution of "subparagraph (i), (ii) or (iii) of paragraph (a) of subsection (1) of this section" for "subparagraph (i), (ii), (iii) or (iv) of paragraph (a) of subsection (1) of this section",

  (v) in subsection (5), by the insertion in paragraph (a)(ii) after "applies" of "or a drug trafficking offence within the meaning of section 3(1) of the Criminal Justice Act 1994",

  (vi) by the insertion of the following subsection after subsection (8):

  (vii) in subsection (9), by the substitution of "€3,000" for "£1,000",

 (b) in section 4—

  (i) in subsection (2), by the substitution of "within twelve months from the taking of the sample" for "within six months from the taking of the sample", and

  (ii) by the substitution of the following subsections for subsection (3):[1]

 (c) in section 5(2), by the deletion of "and" at the end of paragraph (a) and the insertion of the following paragraph after paragraph (a):[1]

Amendments

1   See the amended Act.

PART 3

ADMISSIBILITY OF CERTAIN WITNESS STATEMENTS

15   **Definitions (Part 3)**

In this Part—

"audiorecording" includes a recording, on any medium, from which sound may by any means be produced, and cognate words shall be construed accordingly;

"proceedings" includes proceedings under section 4E (application by accused for dismissal of charge) of the Act of 1967 where oral evidence (within the meaning of subsection (5) of that section) is given;

"statement" means a statement the making of which is duly proved and includes—

(a)   any representation of fact, whether in words or otherwise,

(b)   a statement which has been videorecorded or audiorecorded, and

(c)   part of a statement;

"statutory declaration" includes a statutory declaration made under section 17 or 18;

"videorecording" includes a recording, on any medium, from which a moving image may by any means be produced, together with the accompanying soundrecording, and cognate words shall be construed accordingly.

16   Admissibility of certain witness statements

(1) Where a person has been sent forward for trial for an arrestable offence, a statement relevant to the proceedings made by a witness (in this section referred to as "the statement") may, with the leave of the court, be admitted in accordance with this section as evidence of any fact mentioned in it if the witness, although available for cross-examination—

(a)   refuses to give evidence,

(b)   denies making the statement, or

(c)   gives evidence which is materially inconsistent with it.

(2) The statement may be so admitted if—

(a)   the witness confirms, or it is proved, that he or she made it,

(b)   the court is satisfied—

　　(i)   that direct oral evidence of the fact concerned would be admissible in the proceedings,

　　(ii) that it was made voluntarily, and

　　(iii) that it is reliable,

and

(c)   either—

　　(i)   the statement was given on oath or affirmation or contains a statutory declaration by the witness to the effect that the statement is true to the best of his or her knowledge or belief, or

　　(ii) the court is otherwise satisfied that when the statement was made the witness understood the requirement to tell the truth.

(3) In deciding whether the statement is reliable the court shall have regard to—

(a)   whether it was given on oath or affirmation or was videorecorded, or

(b)   if paragraph (a)does not apply in relation to the statement, whether by reason of the circumstances in which it was made, there is other sufficient evidence in support of its reliability,

and shall also have regard to—

　　(i)   any explanation by the witness for refusing to give evidence or for giving evidence which is inconsistent with the statement, or

　　(ii) where the witness denies making the statement, any evidence given in relation to the denial.

(4) The statement shall not be admitted in evidence under this section if the court is of opinion—

(a) having had regard to all the circumstances, including any risk that its admission would be unfair to the accused or, if there are more than one accused, to any of them, that in the interests of justice it ought not to be so admitted, or

(b) that its admission is unnecessary, having regard to other evidence given in the proceedings.

(5) In estimating the weight, if any, to be attached to the statement regard shall be had to all the circumstances from which any inference can reasonably be drawn as to its accuracy or otherwise.

(6) This section is without prejudice to sections 3 to 6 of the Criminal Procedure Act 1865 and section 21 (proof by written statement) of the Act of 1984.

17   Witness statements made to members of Garda Síochána

(1) A person who makes a statement to a member of the Garda Síochána during the investigation of an arrestable offence (not being a person who is at that time suspected by any such member of having committed it) may make a statutory declaration that the statement is true to the best of the person's knowledge and belief.

(2) For the purposes of section 1(1)(d) of the Statutory Declarations Act 1938 a member of the Garda Síochána may take and receive a statutory declaration made under subsection (1).

(3) Instead of taking and receiving such a statutory declaration the member may take the person's statement on oath or affirmation and for that purpose may administer the oath or affirmation to him or her.

18   Other witness statements

(1) In this section—

"competent person" means a person employed by a public authority and includes an immigration officer who is deemed to have been appointed as such an officer under section 3 of the Immigration Act 2004;

"public authority" means—

(a) a Minister of the Government,

(b) the Commissioners of Public Works in Ireland,

(c) a local authority within the meaning of the Local Government Act 2001,

(d) the Health Service Executive,

(e) a harbour authority within the meaning of the Harbours Act 1946,

(f) a board or other body (not being a company) established by or under statute,

(g) a company in which all the shares are held by, or on behalf of, or by directors appointed by, a Minister of the Government, or

(h) a company in which all the shares are held by a board or other body referred to in paragraph (f), or by a company referred to in paragraph (g).

(2) A person who makes a statement to a competent person in the course of the performance of the competent person's official duties may make a statutory declaration that the statement is true to the best of the person's knowledge and belief.

(3) For the purposes of section 1(1)(d) of the Statutory Declarations Act 1938 a competent person may take and receive a statutory declaration made under subsection (2).

19   Regulations concerning certain witness statements which are recorded

(1) The Minister may, in relation to any statements of witnesses that may be videorecorded or audiorecorded by members of the Garda Síochána while investigating offences, make provision in regulations for—

(a)   the manner in which any such recordings are to be made and preserved, and

(b)   the period for which they are to be retained.

(2) Any failure by a member of the Garda Síochána to comply with a provision of the regulations shall not of itself—

(a)   render the member liable to civil or criminal proceedings, or

(b)   without prejudice to the power of a court to exclude evidence at its discretion, render inadmissible in evidence anything said during the recording concerned.

20   Amendment of section 4E of Act of 1967

Section 4E (application by accused for dismissal of charge) of the Act of 1967 is amended in subsection (5)(b)—

(a)   by the substitution of "section 4F, or" for "section 4F." in subparagraph (ii), and

(b)   by the addition of the following subparagraph:[1]

Amendments

1   See the amended Act.

PART 4

APPEALS IN CERTAIN CRIMINAL PROCEEDINGS

21   Reference of question of law to Supreme Court

The Act of 1967 is amended by the substitution of the following section for section 34:[1]

Amendments

1   See the amended Act.

---

22   Decision of Court of Criminal Appeal final save on certificate of Court, Attorney General or Director of Public Prosecutions.

The Courts of Justice Act 1924 is amended by the substitution of the following section for section 29:

"Decision of Court of Criminal Appeal final save on certificate of Court, Attorney General or Director of Public Prosecutions.

29.— (1) No appeal shall lie to the Supreme Court from a determination by the Court of Criminal Appeal of any appeal or other matter except in accordance with this section.

(2) A person the subject of an appeal or other matter determined by the Court of Criminal Appeal may appeal the decision of that Court to the Supreme Court if that Court or the Attorney General in any case or, if he or she is the prosecuting authority in the matter, the Director of Public Prosecutions certifies that the decision involves a point of law of exceptional public importance and that it is desirable in the public interest that the person should take an appeal to the Supreme Court.

(3) The Attorney General in any case or, if he or she is the prosecuting authority in the matter, the Director of Public Prosecutions may, in relation to an appeal or other matter determined by the Court of Criminal Appeal and without prejudice to the decision in favour of the accused person, appeal the decision of that Court to the Supreme Court if that Court or the Attorney General in any case or, if he or she is the prosecuting authority in the matter, the Director of Public Prosecutions certifies that the decision involves a point of law of exceptional public importance and that it is desirable in the public interest that the Attorney General or the Director of Public Prosecutions, as may be appropriate, should take an appeal to the Supreme Court.

(4) The Supreme Court shall, in an appeal under subsection (3) of this section, hear argument—

(a) by, or by counsel on behalf of, the Attorney General or the Director of Public Prosecutions, as may be appropriate,

(b) if the accused person so wishes, by counsel on his or her behalf or, with the leave of the Court, by the accused person himself or herself, and

(c) if counsel are assigned under subsection (5) of this section, such counsel.

(5) The Supreme Court shall, in an appeal under subsection (3) of this section, assign counsel to argue in support of the decision if—

(a) the accused person waives his or her right to be represented or heard under subsection (4)(b) of this section, or

(b) notwithstanding the fact that the accused person exercises his or her right to be represented or heard under subsection (4)(b) of this section, the Court considers it desirable in the public interest to do so.

(6) The Supreme Court shall ensure, in so far as it is reasonably practicable to do so, that the identity of the accused person in an appeal under subsection (3) of this section is not disclosed in connection with the appeal unless the person agrees to the use of his or her name in the appeal.

(7) If the accused person wishes to be represented in an appeal under subsection (3) of this section and a legal aid (Supreme Court) certificate is granted under subsection (8) of this section, or is deemed to have been granted under subsection (9) of this section, in respect of him or her, he or she shall be entitled to free legal aid in the preparation and presentation of any argument that he or she wishes to make to the Court and to have a solicitor and counsel assigned to him or her for that purpose in the manner prescribed by regulations under section 10 of the Criminal Justice (Legal Aid) Act 1962.

(8) The accused person may, in relation to an appeal under subsection (3) of this section, apply for a legal aid (Supreme Court) certificate to the Supreme Court either—

(a) by letter addressed to the registrar of the Supreme Court setting out the facts of the case and the grounds of the application, or

(b) to the Supreme Court itself,

and the Court shall grant the certificate if (but only if) it appears to the Court that the means of the person are insufficient to enable him or her to obtain legal aid.

(9) If a legal aid (trial on indictment) certificate was granted in respect of the accused person in relation to the trial on indictment concerned, a legal aid (Supreme Court) certificate shall be deemed to have been granted in respect of him or her in relation to an appeal under subsection (3) of this section.

(10) In this section 'legal aid (Supreme Court) certificate' and 'legal aid (trial on indictment) certificate' have the meanings they have in the Criminal Justice (Legal Aid) Act 1962.".

23   Amendment of section 2(2) of Criminal Justice Act 1993

Section 2(2) of the Criminal Justice Act 1993 is amended by the insertion of ", or such longer period not exceeding 56 days as the Court may, on application to it in that behalf, determine," after "within 28 days".

24   Appeal against order for costs

(1) Where a person tried on indictment is acquitted (whether in respect of the whole or part of the indictment) the Attorney General or the Director of Public Prosecutions, as may be appropriate, may appeal against an order for costs made by the trial court against the Attorney General or the Director of Public Prosecutions in favour of the accused person to the Court of Criminal Appeal.

(2) An appeal under this section shall be made, on notice given to the accused person, within 28 days, or such longer period not exceeding 56 days as the trial court may, on application to it in that behalf, determine, from the day on which the order is made.

PART 5
AMENDMENT OF FIREARMS ACTS

25   Definitions (Part 5)

In this Part "Principal Act" means the Firearms Act 1925.

26   Amendment of section 1 of Principal Act.

Section 1 of the Principal Act is amended by the substitution of the following subsection for subsection (1):[1]

Amendments

1   See the amended Act.

---

27   Amendment of section 2 of Principal Act.

Section 2 of the Principal Act is amended—

(a) by the substitution of the following subsection for subsection (2A):[1]

(b) by the deletion of subsection (2B),

(c) in subsection (4)—

    (i) by the deletion, in paragraph (c), of "this Act" and the insertion of "the Firearms Act 1964",

    (ii) by the substitution of the following paragraph for paragraph (d):[1] and

    (iii) by the substitution of the following paragraphs for paragraph (j):[1]

(d) in subsection (5)(a), by the deletion of "or (h)" and the insertion of ", (h) or (j)",

(e) in subsection (5)(c), by the deletion of "rifle or other gun", and

(f) by the addition of the following subsection:[1]

Amendments

1   See the amended Act.

28   New section 2A in Principal Act

The following section is inserted after section 2 of the Principal Act:[1]

Amendments

1   See the amended Act.

29   New section 2B in Principal Act

The following section is inserted after section 2A of the Principal Act:[1]

Amendments

1   See the amended Act.

30   Substitution of section 3 of Principal Act

The following section is substituted for section 3 of the Principal Act:[1]

Amendments

1   Section 30 substituted by Criminal Justice (Miscellaneous Provisions) Act 2009, s 43.

31   New section 3A in Principal Act

The following section is inserted after section 3 of the Principal Act:[1]

Amendments

1   See the amended Act.

32   Substitution of section 4 of Principal Act.

The following section is substituted for section 4 of the Principal Act:[1]

Amendments

1   See the amended Act.

33   New section 4A in Principal Act.

The following section is inserted after section 4 of the Principal Act:[1]

Amendments

1   See the amended Act.

34   New section 4B in Principal Act

The following section is inserted in the Principal Act after section 4:[1]

Amendments

1   See the amended Act.

35   Substitution of section 5 of Principal Act

The following section is substituted for section 5 of the Principal Act:[1]

Amendments

1   See the amended Act.

36 Amendment of section 6 of Principal Act

Section 6 of the Principal Act is amended—

   (a) by the deletion of "When a Superintendent revokes a firearm certificate" and the insertion of "When a firearm certificate is revoked", and

   (b) in paragraph (a), by the insertion of "of the district in which the person resides" after "Superintendent".

37 Amendment of section 8 of Principal Act

Section 8 of the Principal Act is amended in subsection (1) by the deletion of paragraphs (d), (e), (f) and (g) and the insertion of the following paragraphs:[1]

Amendments

1 See the amended Act.

38 Amendment of section 9 of Principal Act

Section 9 of the Principal Act is amended—

   (a) by the substitution of the following subsection for subsection (4):[1] and

   (b) by the insertion of the following subsections after subsection (9):[1]

Amendments

1 See the amended Act.

39 Amendment of section 10 of Principal Act

Section 10 is amended by the insertion of the following subsections after subsection (4):[1]

Amendments

1 See the amended Act.

40 New section 10A in Principal Act.

[…][1]

Amendments

1 Section 40 repealed by Criminal Justice (Miscellaneous Provisions) Act 2009, s 44.

41   Amendment of section 11 of Principal Act

Section 11 of the Principal Act is amended—

(a) in subsection (2), by the substitution of the following paragraph for paragraph (d):[1] and

(b) by the substitution of the following subsections for subsection (3):[1]

Amendments

1   See the amended Act.

42   Substitution of section 15 of Principal Act

The following section is substituted for section 15 of the Principal Act:[1]

Amendments

1   See the amended Act.

43   New section 15A in Principal Act

The following section is inserted after section 15 of the Principal Act:[1]

Amendments

1   See the amended Act.

44   Amendment of section 17 of Principal Act

Section 17 of the Principal Act is amended by the insertion of the following subsections after subsection (4):[1]

Amendments

1   See the amended Act.

45   Substitution of section 25 of Principal Act

The following section is substituted for section 25 of the Principal Act:[1]

Amendments

1   See the amended Act.

46   New section 25A of Principal Act

The following section is inserted after section 25 of the Principal Act:[1]

Amendments

1   See the amended Act.

47   New section 25B in Principal Act

The following section is inserted in the Principal Act after section 25A: [1]

Amendments

1   See the amended Act.

48

New section 25C in Principal Act

The following section is inserted after section 25B of the Principal Act:[1]

Amendments

1   See the amended Act.

49   New section 25D in Principal Act

The following section is inserted in the Principal Act after section 25C:[1]

Amendments

1   See the amended Act.

50   Substitution of section 27 of Principal Act

The following section is substituted for section 27 of the Principal Act:[1]

Amendments

1   See the amended Act.

51   New section 27A in Principal Act

The following section is inserted after section 27 of the Principal Act:[1]

Amendments

1   See the amended Act.

Amendment of Firearms Act 1964

52   Amendment of section 1 of Firearms Act 1964

Section 1 of the Firearms Act 1964 is amended—

(a) by the substitution of the following definition for the definitions of "the Commissioner" and "the Minister":

(b) by inserting the following definition after that of "the Commissioner":[1]

Amendments

1   See the amended Act.

53   Substitution of section 9 of Firearms Act 1964

The following section is substituted for section 9 of the Firearms Act of 1964:[1]

Amendments

1   See the amended Act.

54   Amendment of section 11 of Firearms Act 1964

Section 11 of the Firearms Act 1964 is amended—

(a) in subsection (1), by the deletion of "Minister may substitute for the description of a firearm in a firearm certificate granted by him" and the insertion of "Minister or the Commissioner may substitute for the description of a firearm in a firearm certificate granted by him or her", and

(b) in subsection (2), by the insertion of—

(i) "(other than a restricted firearm)" after "firearm", where it first occurs, and

(ii) "such" after "another".

55   Amendment of section 13 of Firearms Act 1964.

Section 13 of the Firearms Act 1964 is amended by the insertion of the following subsections after subsection (6):[1]

Amendments

1   See the amended Act.

56   Amendment of section 21 of Firearms Act 1964

Section 21 of the Firearms Act 1964 is amended—

(a) in subsection (1), by the insertion of "or ammunition" after "firearms" and "firearm", where they first occur, and

(b) by the insertion of the following subsection after subsection (2):[1]

Amendments

1   See the amended Act.

57   Substitution of section 26 of Firearms Act 1964

The following section is substituted for section 26 of the Firearms Act 1964:[1]

Amendments

1   See the amended Act.

58   Substitution of section 27 of Firearms Act 1964.

The following section is substituted for section 27 of the Firearms Act 1964:[1]

Amendments

1   See the amended Act.

59   Substitution of section 27A of Firearms Act 1964

The following section is substituted for section 27A of the Firearms Act 1964:[1]

Amendments

1   See the amended Act.

---

60   Substitution of section 27B of Firearms Act 1964.

The following section is substituted for section 27B of the Firearms Act 1964:[1]

Amendments

1   See the amended Act.

---

61   New section 27C in Firearms Act 1964

The following section is inserted in the Firearms Act 1964 after section 27B:[1]

Amendments

1   See the amended Act.

Amendment of Criminal Justice Act 1984

62   Amendment of section 15 of Criminal Justice Act 1984

Section 15 of the Criminal Justice Act 1984 is amended by the substitution of "€2,500" for "£1,000".

Amendment of Firearms and Offensive Weapons Act 1990

63   Amendment of Firearms and Offensive Weapons Act 1990

The Firearms and Offensive Weapons Act 1990 is amended—

    (a) by the repeal of section 4,

    (b) in section 6(1), by the substitution of "paragraph (f) of the definition of "firearm" in section 1(1) of the Principal Act" for "section 4(1)(f)", and

    (c) in section 7(8), by the substitution of "paragraph (g)(ii) of the definition of "firearm" in section 1(1) of the Principal Act" for "section 4(1)(g)".

64   New section 8A of Firearms and Offensive Weapons Act 1990.

The following section is inserted after section 8 of the Firearms and Offensive Weapons Act 1990:[1]

Amendments

1 See the amended Act.

65 New section 12A in Firearms and Offensive Weapons Act 1990.

The following section is inserted after section 12 of the Firearms and Offensive Weapons Act 1990 :[1]

Amendments

1 See the amended Act.

66 Amendment of section 1 of Firearms (Firearm Certificates for Non-Residents) Act 2000

Section 1 of the Firearms (Firearm Certificates for Non-Residents) Act 2000 is amended—

(a) by the insertion of the following definition after the definition of "the Act of 1976"—

""Commissioner" means the Commissioner of the Garda Síochána or a member of the Garda Síochána, or members of a particular rank in the Garda Síochána, not below the rank of superintendent appointed in writing by the Commissioner for the purpose of performing any of the Commissioner's functions under this Act;",

and

(b) by the insertion of the following definition after the definition of "the Principal Act":

""restricted firearm" means a firearm which is declared under section 2B(a) of the Principal Act to be a restricted firearm;".

67 Amendment of section 2 of Firearms (Firearm Certificates for Non-Residents) Act 2000

Section 2 of the Firearms (Firearm Certificates for Non-Residents) Act 2000 is amended—

(a) in subsection (1), by the insertion of ", Commissioner" after "Minister" on both occasions where it occurs,

(b) in subsection (2), by the insertion of the following paragraph after paragraph (a):

"(aa) in case the firearm is a restricted firearm and is intended only for the purposes mentioned in paragraph (a), to the Minister or Commissioner,",

(c) in subsection (4), by the insertion of "or (aa)" after "paragraph (a)", and

(d) in subsection (5), by the insertion of ", Commissioner" after "Minister".

PART 6
AMENDMENT OF EXPLOSIVES ACT 1875

68   Substitution of section 80 of Explosives Act 1875.

The following section is substituted for section 80 of the Explosives Act 1875:[1]

Amendments

1   See the amended Act.

---

69   Other amendments of Explosives Act 1875.

Each provision of the Explosives Act 1875 specified in Schedule 2 to the Criminal Justice Act 2006 is amended in the manner specified in the third and fourth columns opposite the mention of that provision in the first column of that Schedule.

PART 7
ORGANISED CRIME

70   Interpretation (Part 7).

(1) In this Part—

"act" includes omission and a reference to the commission or doing of an act includes a reference to the making of an omission;

["criminal organisation" means a structured group, however organised, that has as its main purpose or activity the commission or facilitation of a serious offence;][1]

"Irish ship" has the meaning it has in section 9 of the Mercantile Marine Act 1955;

"serious offence" means an offence for which a person may be punished by imprisonment for a term of 4 years or more;

["structured group" means a group of 3 or more persons, which is not randomly formed for the immediate commission of a single offence, and the involvement in which by 2 or more of those persons is with a view to their acting in concert; for the avoidance of doubt, a structured group may exist notwithstanding the absence of all or any of the following:

(a)   formal rules or formal membership, or any formal roles for those involved in the group;

(b)   any hierarchical or leadership structure;

(c)   continuity of involvement by persons in the group.][1]

(2) For the purposes of this section facilitation of an offence does not require knowledge of a particular offence the commission of which is facilitated, or that an offence actually be committed.

[(3) For the purposes of the references in sections 71(2)(d) and 74(1)(b)(i) to a person's being ordinarily resident in the State, a person shall be taken to be so resident, on the date of the commission of the offence to which section 71(1) or 74(1), as the case may be, applies, if, for the 12 months immediately preceding that date, the person has his or her principal place of residence in the State.][2]

Amendments

1   Definitions substituted by Criminal Justice (Amendment) Act 2009, s 3(1).

2   Subsection (3) inserted by Criminal Justice (Amendment) Act 2009, s 3(2).

71   Offence of conspiracy

(1) Subject to subsections (2) and (3), a person who conspires, whether in the State or elsewhere, with one or more persons to do an act—

    (a)   in the State that constitutes a serious offence, or

    (b)   in a place outside the State that constitutes a serious offence under the law of that place and which would, if done in the State, constitute a serious offence,

is guilty of an offence irrespective of whether such act actually takes place or not.

(2) Subsection (1) applies to a conspiracy committed outside the State if—

    (a)   the offence, the subject of the conspiracy, was committed, or was intended to be committed, in the State or against a citizen of Ireland,

    (b)   the conspiracy is committed on board an Irish ship,

    (c)   the conspiracy is committed on an aircraft registered in the State, or

    (d)   the conspiracy is committed by an Irish citizen or a [person ordinarily resident in the State.][1]

(3) Subsection (1) shall also apply to a conspiracy committed outside the State in circumstances other than those referred to in subsection (2), but in that case the Director of Public Prosecutions may not take, or consent to the taking of, proceedings for an offence under subsection (1) except in accordance with section 74(3).

(4) A person charged with an offence under this section is liable to be indicted, tried and punished as a principal offender.

(5) [...][2]

Amendments

1   Words substituted by Criminal Justice (Amendment) Act 2009, s 4(a).

2   Subsection (5) deleted by Criminal Justice (Amendment) Act 2009, s 4(b).

[71A   Offence of directing a criminal organisation

(1) In this section—

    (a)   "directs", in relation to activities, means—

        (i)   controls or supervises the activities, or

        (ii)   gives an order, instruction or guidance, or makes a request, with respect to the carrying on of the activities;

    (b)   references to activities include references to—

(i) activities carried on outside the State, and

(ii) activities that do not constitute an offence or offences.

(2) A person who directs, at any level of the organisation's structure, the activities of a criminal organisation is guilty of an offence and shall be liable on conviction on indictment to imprisonment for life or a lesser term of imprisonment.

(3) Any statement made orally, in writing or otherwise, or any conduct, by the defendant implying or leading to a reasonable inference that he or she was at a material time directing the activities of a criminal organisation shall, in proceedings for an offence under this section, be admissible as evidence that the defendant was doing such at that time.

(4) In proceedings under this section, the court or the jury, as the case may be, in determining whether an offence under this section has been committed, may, in addition to any other relevant evidence, also consider—

(a) any evidence of a pattern of behaviour on the part of the defendant consistent with his or her having directed the activities of the organisation concerned at the material time, and

(b) without limiting paragraph (a) or subsection (3)—

(i) whether the defendant has received any benefit from the organisation concerned, and

(ii) evidence as to the possession by the defendant of such articles or documents or other records as would give rise to a reasonable suspicion that such articles, documents or other records were in his or her possession or control for a purpose connected with directing the activities of the organisation concerned.

(5) Any document or other record emanating or purporting to emanate from the organisation concerned from which there can be inferred—

(a) either—

(i) the giving, at the time concerned, of an instruction, order or guidance by the defendant to any person involved in the organisation, or

(ii) the making, at that time, by the defendant of a request of a person so involved,

or

(b) the seeking, at that time, by a person so involved of assistance or guidance from the defendant,

shall, in proceedings for an offence under this section, be admissible as evidence that the defendant was directing the activities of the organisation concerned at the material time.

(6) In this section "document or other record" has the same meaning as it has in section 71B.][1]

Amendments

1 Section 71A inserted by Criminal Justice (Amendment) Act 2009, s 5.

[71B   Provisions with respect to proof of criminal organisation's existence

(1) In proceedings under this Part the opinion of—

   (a) any member of the Garda Síochána, or

   (b) any former member of the Garda Síochána,

who appears to the Court to possess the appropriate expertise (in this section referred to as the ' appropriate expert') shall, subject to section 74B, be admissible in evidence in relation to the issue as to the existence of a particular criminal organisation.

(2) In subsection (1) ' expertise ' means experience, specialised knowledge or qualifications.

(3) Without limiting the matters that can properly be taken into account, in the formation of such opinion, by the appropriate expert, it shall be permissible for that expert, in forming the opinion referred to in subsection (1), to take into account any previous convictions for arrestable offences of persons believed by that expert to be part of the organisation to which the opinion relates.

(4) Without prejudice to subsection (1), in proceedings under this Part the following shall be admissible as evidence that a particular group constitutes a criminal organisation—

   (a) any document or other record emanating or purporting to emanate from the group or created or purporting to be created by the defendant—

      (i)   from which the group's existence as a criminal organisation can be inferred;

      (ii) from which the commission or facilitation by the group of a serious offence or its engaging in any activity in relation thereto can be inferred; or

      (iii) that uses or makes reference to a name, word, symbol or other representation that identifies the group as a criminal organisation or from which name, word, symbol or other representation it can be inferred that it is such an organisation,

   (b) the provision by a group of 3 or more persons of a material benefit to the defendant (or a promise by such a group to provide a material benefit to the defendant), which provision or promise is not made in return for a lawful act performed or to be performed by the defendant.

(5) In subsection (4) ' document or other record ' includes, in addition to a document or other record in writing—

   (a) a disc, tape, sound-track or other device in which information, sounds or signals are embodied so as to be capable (with or without the aid of some other instrument) of being reproduced in legible or audible form,

   (b) a film, tape or other device in which visual images are embodied so as to be capable (with or without the aid of some other instrument) of being reproduced in visual form, and

   (c) a photograph.][1]

Amendments

1   Section 71B inserted by Criminal Justice (Amendment) Act 2009, s 7.

---

72   [Offence to participate in, or contribute to, certain activities

(1) A person is guilty of an offence if, with knowledge of the existence of the organisation referred to in this subsection, the person participates in or contributes to any activity (whether constituting an offence or not)—

    (a)   intending either to—

        (i)   enhance the ability of a criminal organisation or any of its members to commit, or

        (ii)   facilitate the commission by a criminal organisation or any of its members of,

    a serious offence, or

    (b)   being reckless as to whether such participation or contribution could either—

        (i)   enhance the ability of a criminal organisation or any of its members to commit, or

        (ii)   facilitate the commission by a criminal organisation or any of its members of,

    a serious offence.

(2) A person guilty of an offence under this section shall be liable on conviction on indictment to a fine or imprisonment for a term not exceeding 15 years or both.

(3) The reference in subsection (1) to the commission of a serious offence includes a reference to the doing of an act in a place outside the State that constitutes a serious offence under the law of that place and which act would, if done in the State, constitute a serious offence.

(4) In proceedings for an offence under this section it shall not be necessary for the prosecution to prove—

    (a)   that the criminal organisation concerned or any of its members actually committed, as the case may be—

        (i)   a serious offence in the State, or

        (ii)   a serious offence under the law of a place outside the State where the act constituting the offence would, if done in the State, constitute a serious offence,

    (b)   that the participation or contribution of the defendant actually—

        (i)   enhanced the ability of the criminal organisation concerned or any of its members to commit, or

        (ii)   facilitated the commission by it or any of its members of,

    a serious offence, or

    (c)   knowledge on the part of the defendant of the specific nature of any offence referred to in subsection (1)(a) or (b).

(5) In determining whether a person participates in or contributes to an activity referred to in subsection (1), the court may consider, inter alia, whether the person—

    (a)   uses a name, word, symbol or other representation that identifies, or is associated with, the criminal organisation concerned, or

    (b)   receives any benefit from the criminal organisation concerned.

(6) In proceedings for an offence under this section, it shall be presumed, until the contrary is shown, that the participation or contribution (the ' relevant act ') of the defendant referred to

in subsection (1) was engaged in or made with the state of mind on the defendant's part referred to in paragraph (a) or (b) of that subsection if the circumstances under which the relevant act was committed—

    (a)   involved either—

        (i)   the possession by the defendant, whilst in the presence of one or more other persons, of any article or item referred to in the Table to this section, or

       (ii)   there being present in (or, in the case of a false registration plate referred to in paragraph 8 of that Table, present in or affixed to) any vehicle—

          (I)   the use of which appears connected with the relevant act, and

         (II)   of which the defendant and one or more other persons were occupants on or about the date of commission of the relevant act,

         any such article or item,

    and

    (b)   those circumstances are such as give rise to a reasonable suspicion that the defendant's state of mind was as aforesaid at the time of the relevant act's commission.

TABLE

1. Any balaclava, boiler suit or other means of disguise or impersonation, including any article of Garda uniform or any equipment supplied to a member of the Garda Síochána or imitation thereof.

2. Any firearm (within the meaning of section 1 of the Firearms Act 1925), ammunition for a firearm or device that appears to the ordinary observer so realistic as to make it indistinguishable from a firearm.

3. Any knife to which section 9(1) of the Firearms and Offensive Weapons Act 1990 applies, weapon of offence within the meaning of section 10(2) of that Act or weapon to which section 12 of that Act applies.

4. Any implement for burglary or other article or item for gaining access to any premises or other structure without the permission of the owner or occupier thereof, including any key or card that has been stolen or any access code unlawfully procured.

5. Any plan of any premises or other structure unrelated to any lawful activity, trade or purpose being pursued or engaged in by one or more of the persons referred to in subsection (6)(a).

6. Any controlled drug (within the meaning of the Misuse of Drugs Act 1977).

7. Any substantial amounts, in cash, of any currency unrelated to any lawful activity, trade, transaction or purpose being pursued or engaged in by one or more of the persons referred to in subsection (6)(a).

8. Any false vehicle registration plate, that is to say, any plate purporting to be a plate for a mechanically propelled vehicle registered under section 131 of the Finance Act 1992 and displaying an identification mark other than that duly assigned by the Revenue Commissioners under Chapter IV of Part II of that Act and regulations thereunder.

9. Any article or item for making a counterfeit of any currency note or coin or making a counterfeit or otherwise for making a forgery of any credit or debit card.

10. Any article or item for making copies of any work, being an article or item of a design enabling, and held in circumstances indicating that it would likely be used for, the making, on a substantial scale, of infringing copies (within the meaning of Part II of the Copyright and Related Rights Act 2000) of the work without the copyright owner's consent.

11. Any other article or item prescribed for the purposes of subsection (6).][1]

Amendments

1 Section 72 substituted by Criminal Justice (Amendment) Act 2009, s 6.

[72A   Offences under this Part: inferences that may be drawn

(1) Where in any proceedings against a person for an offence under this Part evidence is given that the defendant at any time before he or she was charged with the offence, on being questioned by a member of the Garda Síochána in relation to the offence, failed to answer any question material to the investigation of the offence, then the court in determining whether a charge should be dismissed under Part IA of the Criminal Procedure Act 1967 or whether there is a case to answer and the court (or subject to the judge's directions, the jury) in determining whether the defendant is guilty of the offence may draw such inferences from the failure as appear proper; and the failure may, on the basis of such inferences, be treated as, or as capable of amounting to, corroboration of any evidence in relation to the offence, but a person shall not be convicted of the offence solely or mainly on an inference drawn from such a failure.

(2) Subsection (1) shall not have effect unless—

(a)   the defendant was told in ordinary language when being questioned what the effect of such a failure might be, and

(b)   the defendant was afforded a reasonable opportunity to consult a solicitor before such a failure occurred.

(3) Nothing in this section shall, in any proceedings—

(a)   prejudice the admissibility in evidence of the silence or other reaction of the defendant in the face of anything said in his or her presence relating to the conduct in respect of which he or she is charged, in so far as evidence thereof would be admissible apart from this section, or

(b)   be taken to preclude the drawing of any inference from the silence or other reaction of the defendant which could be properly drawn apart from this section.

(4) The court (or, subject to the judge's directions, the jury) shall, for the purposes of drawing an inference under this section, have regard to whenever, if appropriate, an answer to the question concerned was first given by the defendant.

(5) This section shall not apply in relation to the questioning of a person by a member of the Garda Síochána unless it is recorded by electronic or similar means or the person consents in writing to it not being so recorded.

(6) References in subsection (1) to evidence shall, in relation to the hearing of an application under Part IA of the Criminal Procedure Act 1967 for the dismissal of a charge, be taken to include a statement of the evidence to be given by a witness at the trial.

(7) In this section ' any question material to the investigation of the offence' means:

(a) a question requesting that the defendant give a full account of his or her movements, actions, activities or associations during any specified period relevant to the offence being investigated; and

(b) whichever one, or more than one, of the following is relevant to the offence being investigated—

   (i) a question relating to any statement or conduct of the type referred to in section 71A(3);

   (ii) a question relating to any benefit of the type referred to in section 71A(4)(b)(i) or 71B(4)(b) which the member of the Garda Síochána concerned reasonably believes was received by the defendant or on his or her behalf;

   (iii) a question relating to articles, or documents or other records, of the type referred to in section 71A(4)(b)(ii) or (5)(a);

   (iv) a question relating to any document or other record of the type referred to in section 71B(4)(a)—

      (I) created or purporting to be created by the defendant, or

      (II) found in the possession of the defendant on or about the time of his or her arrest or found on foot of a lawful search of any premises or vehicle occupied by the defendant;

   (v) a question relating to the suspected use by the defendant in a document of, or the suspected reference by him or her in a document to, a name, word, symbol or other representation of the type referred to in section 71B(4)(a)(iii);

   (vi) a question relating to—

      (I) the possession by the defendant, or

      (II) the presence in a vehicle referred to in section 72(6)(a)(ii) and in the circumstances involving the defendant referred to in that provision,

   of any article or item referred to in the Table to section 72:

provided that no question shall be regarded as being material to the investigation of the offence unless the member of the Garda Síochána concerned reasonably believed that the question related to the participation of the defendant in the commission of the offence.

(8) In this section references to a failure to answer include references to the giving of an answer that is false or misleading and references to the silence or other reaction of the defendant shall be construed accordingly.

(9) This section shall not apply in relation to a failure to answer a question if the failure occurred before the commencement of section 9 of the Criminal Justice (Amendment) Act 2009.]¹

Amendments

1   Section 72A inserted by Criminal Justice (Amendment) Act 2009, s 9.

73   Commission of offence for criminal organisation

(1) A person who commits a serious offence for the benefit of, at the direction of, or in association with, a criminal organisation is guilty of an offence.

(2) In proceedings for an offence under subsection (1), it shall not be necessary for the prosecution to prove that the person concerned knew any of the persons who constitute the criminal organisation concerned.

(3) A person guilty of an offence under this section shall be liable on conviction on indictment to a fine or imprisonment for a term not exceeding [15 years][1] or both.

Amendments

1   Words substituted by Criminal Justice (Amendment) Act 2009, s 10.

74   Proceedings relating to offences committed outside State

[(1) A person who does any act in a place outside the State that would, if done in the State, be an offence under section 71A or 72 and either—

    (a)   the act in question is done on board an Irish ship or on an aircraft registered in the State, or

    (b)   the person is—

        (i)   an individual who is an Irish citizen or ordinarily resident in the State, or

        (ii)   a body corporate established under the law of the State or a company within the meaning of the Companies Acts,

then the person is guilty of an offence and shall be liable to be proceeded against and punished as if he or she were guilty of an offence under section 71A or 72, as the case may be.][1]

(2) Where a person is charged with an offence referred to in subsection (1), no further proceedings in the matter (other than any remand in custody or on bail) may be taken except by or with the consent of the Director of Public Prosecutions.

[(2A) Proceedings for—

    (a)   an offence under section 71 in relation to an act committed outside the State, or

    (b)   an offence under subsection (1),

may be taken in any place in the State and the offence may for all incidental purposes be treated as having been committed in that place.][2]

(3) The Director of Public Prosecutions may take, or consent to the taking of, further proceedings against a person for an offence in respect of an act to which subsection (1) of

section 71 applies and that is committed outside the State in the circumstances referred to in subsection (3) of that section if satisfied—

  (a) that—

    (i) a request for a person's surrender for the purpose of trying him or her for an offence in respect of that act has been made under Part II of the Extradition Act 1965 by any country, and

    (ii) the request has been finally refused (whether as a result of a decision of the court or otherwise),

    or

  (b) that—

    (i) a European arrest warrant has been received from an issuing state for the purpose of bringing proceedings against the person for an offence in respect of that act, and

    (ii) a final determination has been made that the European arrest warrant should not be endorsed for execution in the State under the European Arrest Warrant Act 2003 or that the person should not be surrendered to the issuing state concerned,

    or

  (c) that, because of the special circumstances (including, but not limited to, the likelihood of a refusal referred to in paragraph (a)(ii) or a determination referred to in paragraph (b)(ii)), it is expedient that proceedings be taken against the person for an offence under the law of the State in respect of the act.

(4) In this section "European arrest warrant" and "issuing state" have the meanings they have in section 2(1) of the European Arrest Warrant Act 2003.

Amendments

1 Subsection (1) substituted by Criminal Justice (Amendment) Act 2009, s 11(a).

2 Subsection (2A) inserted by Criminal Justice (Amendment) Act 2009, s 11(b).

[74A Aggravating factor: serious offence committed as part of, or in furtherance of, activities of criminal organisation

(1) Where a court is determining the sentence to be imposed on a person for a serious offence, the fact that the offence was committed as part of, or in furtherance of, the activities of a criminal organisation shall be treated for the purpose of determining the sentence as an aggravating factor.

(2) Accordingly, the court shall (except where the sentence for the serious offence is one of imprisonment for life or where the court considers that there are exceptional circumstances justifying its not doing so) impose a sentence that is greater than that which would have been imposed in the absence of such a factor.

(3) The sentence imposed shall not be greater than the maximum sentence permissible for the serious offence.][1]

Amendments

1   Section 74A inserted by Criminal Justice (Amendment) Act 2009, s 12.

[74B   Exclusion of evidence in certain circumstances

Nothing in this Part prevents a court, in proceedings thereunder, from excluding evidence that would otherwise be admissible if, in its opinion, the prejudicial effect of the evidence outweighs its probative value.]¹

Amendments

1   Section 74B inserted by Criminal Justice (Amendment) Act 2009, s 13.

75   Evidence in proceedings under this Part.

(1) In any proceedings for an offence under section 71 —

   (a)   a certificate that is signed by an officer of the Department of Foreign Affairs and states that—

      (i)   a passport was issued by that Department of State to a person on a specified date, and

      (ii)   to the best of the officer's knowledge and belief, the person has not ceased to be an Irish citizen,

   is evidence that the person was an Irish citizen on the date on which the offence concerned is alleged to have been committed, unless the contrary is shown, and

   (b)   a certificate that is signed by the Director of Public Prosecutions or by a person authorised by him or her and that states that any of the matters specified in paragraph (a), (b) or (c) of section 74(3) is evidence of the facts stated in the certificate, unless the contrary is shown.

(2) A document purporting to be a certificate under subsection (1) is deemed, unless the contrary is shown—

   (a)   to be such a certificate,

   (b)   to have been signed by the person purporting to have signed it, and

   (c)   in the case of a certificate signed with the authority of the Minister for Foreign Affairs or the Director of Public Prosecutions, to have been signed in accordance with the authorisation.

76   Liability for offences by bodies corporate.

(1) Where an offence under this Part is committed by a body corporate and is proved to have been committed with the consent, connivance or approval of, or to have been attributable to any wilful neglect on the part of, any person, being a director, manager, secretary or any other officer of the body corporate or a person who was purporting to act in any such capacity, that person, as well as the body corporate, shall be guilty of an offence and shall be

liable to be proceeded against and punished as if he or she were guilty of the first-mentioned offence.

(2) Where the affairs of a body corporate are managed by its members, subsection (1) shall apply in relation to the acts and defaults of a member in connection with his or her functions of management as if he or she were a director or manager of the body corporate.

77   Double jeopardy

A person who is acquitted or convicted of an offence in a place outside the State shall not be proceeded against for an offence under—

(a)   section 71 consisting of the act, or the conspiracy to do an act, that constituted the offence, or

(b)   section 72 consisting of the act that constituted the offence,

of which the person was so acquitted or convicted.

78   Amendment of Act of 1967

The Act of 1967 is amended—

(a)   in section 13(1), by the insertion of "or an offence under section 71, 72 or 73 of the Criminal Justice Act 2006" after "the offence of murder under section 6 or 11 of the Criminal Justice (Terrorist Offences) Act 2005 or an attempt to commit such offence", and

(b)   in section 29(1), by the insertion of the following paragraph after paragraph (k):[1]

Amendments

1   See the amended Act.

---

79   Amendment of Schedule to Bail Act 1997

The Schedule to the Bail Act 1997 is amended by the insertion of the following after paragraph 28:[1]

Amendments

1   See the amended Act.

PART 8

MISUSE OF DRUGS

80   Definition

In this Part "Act of 1977" means Misuse of Drugs Act 1977.

81   Amendment of section 15A of Act of 1977

(1) Section 15A of the Act of 1977 is amended by the insertion of the following subsection after subsection (3):[1]

(2) This section shall not have effect in relation to proceedings for an offence under section 15A of the Act of 1977 instituted before the commencement of this section.

Amendments

1   See the amended Act.

82   Importation of controlled drugs in excess of certain value.

The Act of 1977 is amended by the insertion of the following section after section 15A:[1]

Amendments

1   See the amended Act.

83   Supply of controlled drugs into prisons and places of detention.

The Act of 1977 is amended by the insertion of the following section after section 15B (inserted by section 82 of this Act):[1]

Amendments

1   See the amended Act.

84   Amendment of section 27 of Act of 1977

Section 27 of the Act of 1977 is amended—

   (a) in subsection (3A)—
      (i) by the substitution of "an offence under section 15A or 15B of this Act" for "an offence under section 15A", and
      (ii) by the substitution of the following paragraph for paragraph (a):[1]
            "(a) to imprisonment for life or such shorter period as the court may determine, subject to subsections (3B) to (3CC) of this section or, where subsection (3CCCC) of this section applies, to that subsection, and",
   (b) by the insertion of the following subsection after subsection (3A):[1]
   (c) in subsection (3B), by the substitution of "an offence under section 15A or 15B of this Act" for "an offence under section 15A",
   (d) by the insertion of the following subsections after subsection (3C):[1]

(e) in subsection (3I), by the substitution of "an offence under section 15A or 15B of this Act" for "an offence under section 15A of this Act" and the substitution of "each of those offences" for "that offence", and

(f) by the insertion of the following subsection after subsection (3J):[1]

Amendments

1 See the amended Act.

85 Amendment of section 29 of Act of 1977.

Section 29 of the Act of 1977 is amended by the substitution of the following subsection for subsection (3):[1]

Amendments

1 See the amended Act.

86 Amendment of section 3(1) of Criminal Justice Act 1994.

Section 3(1) of the Criminal Justice Act 1994 is amended in the definition of "drug trafficking offence" by the insertion of the following paragraph after paragraph (bb):[1]

Amendments

1 See the amended Act.

PART 9

OBLIGATIONS OF DRUG TRAFFICKING OFFENDERS TO NOTIFY CERTAIN INFORMATION

87 Definitions (Part 9)

In this Part, unless the context otherwise requires—

"court" means any court exercising criminal jurisdiction and includes a court-martial;

"imprisonment" includes detention in Saint Patrick's Institution and a place of detention provided under section 2 of the Prisons Act 1970, and "prison" shall be construed accordingly;

"prescribed" means prescribed by regulations made by the Minister under this Act;

"relevant date" means the date of conviction for the drug trafficking offence concerned;

"remission from the sentence" means, in relation to the sentence imposed on a person, the remission which the person may earn from the sentence under the rules or practice whereby prisoners generally may earn remission of sentence by industry and good conduct;

"sentence" includes a sentence of imprisonment and an order postponing sentence.

88 Drug trafficking offences for purposes of this Part.

In this Part "drug trafficking offence" has the meaning it has in section 3(1) (as amended by section 86) of the Criminal Justice Act 1994 but does not include such an offence unless the person convicted of it has, in respect thereof, been sentenced to imprisonment for a period of more than one year.

89 Persons subject to the requirements of this Part

(1) Without prejudice to subsections (2) and (3) and section 95, a person is subject to the requirements of this Part if he or she is convicted on indictment of a drug trafficking offence after the commencement of this Part.

(2) A person is also subject to the requirements of this Part if he or she has been convicted on indictment of a drug trafficking offence before the commencement of this Part and, at that commencement, the sentence to be imposed on the person in respect of the offence has yet to be determined.

(3) If a person has been convicted on indictment of a drug trafficking offence before the commencement of this Part and, at that commencement, a sentence has been imposed on the person in respect of the offence and—

   (a) the person is serving the sentence in prison,

   (b) the person is temporarily released under section 2 of the Criminal Justice Act 1960, or

   (c) the sentence is otherwise still in force or current,

the Circuit Court, in the circuit where the person ordinarily resides or has his or her most usual place of abode, may, on application to it in that behalf by a member of the Garda Síochána not below the rank of superintendent, order that the person shall be subject to the requirements of this Part if it considers that the interests of the common good so require and that it is appropriate in all the circumstances of the case.

(4) An application under subsection (3) may be made within a period of 2 months, or such longer period as the Circuit Court may permit, of the commencement of this Part.

90 Period for which person is subject to requirements of this Part and related matters.

(1) A person who, by reason of section 89, is subject to the requirements of this Part shall be so subject for the period referred to in subsection (3) or, in the case of a person referred to in subsection (2) or (3) of section 89, so much (if any) of that period as falls after the commencement of this Part.

(2) Subsection (1) is subject to section 93.

(3) The period mentioned in subsection (1) is the period, beginning with the relevant date, of—

   (a) 12 years if the sentence imposed on the person in respect of the offence concerned is one of imprisonment for life,

   (b) 7 years if the sentence imposed on the person in respect of the offence concerned is one of imprisonment for a term of more than 10 years but not one of imprisonment for life,

   (c) 5 years if the sentence imposed on the person in respect of the offence concerned is one of imprisonment for a term of more than 5 years but not more than 10 years,

(d) 3 years if the sentence imposed on the person in respect of the offence concerned is one of imprisonment for a term of more than one year but not more than 5 years,

(e) one year if the sentence imposed on the person in respect of the offence concerned is one of imprisonment for any term, the operation of the whole of which is suspended (but, if the operation of that term is revived by the court, whichever of the preceding paragraphs is appropriate shall apply instead of this paragraph).

(4) If—

(a) a sentence is imposed on a person in respect of a drug trafficking offence, and

(b) at the time of sentencing the person is aged under 18 years,

subsection (3) shall have effect in relation to that person as if for the references to 12 years, 7 years, 5 years, 3 years and one year in that subsection there were substituted references to 6 years, 3½ years, 2½ years, 1½ years and 6 months, respectively.

(5) If a sentence of imprisonment for any term is imposed on the person referred to in subsection (1) in respect of the offence concerned and the operation of a part of that term is suspended—

(a) the part of that term the operation of which is not suspended shall be regarded as the term of imprisonment imposed on that person for the purposes of subsection (3) (but, if the operation of the first-mentioned part of that term is revived by the court, whichever of paragraphs (a), (b), (c) and (d) of subsection (3) is appropriate shall apply without regard to this paragraph),

(b) paragraph (a) extends to a case in which that suspension is provided for subsequent to the imposition of the sentence.

(6) If a person is or has been sentenced in respect of 2 or more drug trafficking offences and the sentences imposed are consecutive or partly concurrent then subsection (3) shall have effect as if—

(a) in the case of consecutive sentences, the sentence imposed in respect of each of the offences were or had been a sentence equal to the aggregate of those sentences,

(b) in the case of partly concurrent sentences, the sentence imposed in respect of each of the offences were or had been a sentence equal to the aggregate of those sentences after making such deduction as is necessary to ensure that no period of time is counted more than once.

(7) Without prejudice to section 93, a person shall cease to be subject to the requirements of this Part if the conviction in respect of the offence concerned is quashed on appeal or otherwise.

(8) A reference in this section to a sentence imposed on a person shall, if the sentence is varied on appeal, be construed as a reference to the sentence as so varied and, accordingly, the period for which a person is subject to the requirements of this Part, by reason of this section, shall stand reduced or increased, as the case may be, in the event that such a variation is made which results in the sentence falling under a different paragraph of subsection (3) than it did before the variation.

91   Supply of information to facilitate compliance with this Part

The person for the time being in charge of the place where a person subject to the requirements of this Part is ordered to be imprisoned in respect of an offence (whether or not the offence that gave rise to the person's being subject to those requirements) shall notify in writing—

    (a) before the date on which the sentence of imprisonment imposed on the person in respect of the first-mentioned offence expires or, as the case may be, the person's remission from the sentence begins ("the date of release"), the person that he or she is subject to the requirements of this Part, and

    (b) at least 10 days before the date of release, the Commissioner of the Garda Síochána of the fact that that expiry or remission will occur in relation to the person.

92   Notification requirements

(1) A person who is subject to the requirements of this Part shall, before the end of the period of 7 days beginning with—

    (a) the relevant date,

    (b) if an order is made under section 89(3) or 95(3), the date of the order, or

    (c) if the relevant date is prior to the commencement of this Part and no such order is made, that commencement,

notify to the Garda Síochána—

    (i) his or her name and, where he or she also uses one or more other names, each of those names, and

    (ii) his or her home address.

(2) A person who is subject to those requirements shall also, before the end of the period of 7 days beginning with—

    (a) the person's using a name which is not the name, or one of the names, last previously notified by him or her to the Garda Síochána under this section,

    (b) any change of his or her home address,

    (c) the person's having resided or stayed, for a qualifying period, at any place in the State, the address of which has not been notified to the Garda Síochána under this section as being his or her current home address, or

    (d) the person's returning to an address in the State, having, immediately prior to such return, been outside the State for a continuous period of 7 days or more,

notify that name, the effect of that change, the address of that place or, as the case may be, the fact of that return to the Garda Síochána.

(3) If a person who is subject to the requirements of this Part intends to leave the State for a continuous period of 7 days or more he or she shall notify the Garda Síochána of that intention and, if known, the address of the place outside the State he or she intends to reside or stay at.

(4) If a person who is subject to the requirements of this Part is outside the State for a continuous period of 7 days or more and did not intend, on leaving the State, to be outside the State for such a continuous period, the person shall, subject to subsection (5), notify the Garda Síochána, before the expiry of a further period of 7 days, reckoned from the 7th day that he or she is so outside the State, of that fact and the address of the place at which he or she is residing or staying outside the State.

(5) Subsection (4) shall not apply if the person concerned has returned to the State before the expiry of the further period of 7 days mentioned in that subsection.

(6) A notification given to the Garda Síochána by any person shall not be regarded as complying with subsection (1), (2), (3) or (4) unless it also states the person's—

    (a) date of birth,

    (b) name on the relevant date and, where he or she used one or more other names on that date, each of those names, and

    (c) home address on the relevant date.

(7) For the purpose of determining any period for the purposes of subsection (1), (2), (3) or (4), there shall be disregarded any time when the person concerned is—

    (a) remanded in custody,

    (b) serving a sentence in prison, or

    (c) temporarily released under section 2 of the Criminal Justice Act 1960.

(8) A person may give a notification under this section—

    (a) by attending in person at any Garda Síochána station which is a divisional or district headquarters and notifying orally a member of the Garda Síochána at the station of the matters concerned,

    (b) by sending, by post, a written notification of the matters concerned to any Garda Síochána station which is such a headquarters, or

    (c) by such other means as may be prescribed.

(9) The onus of proof of the sending by post of such a notification shall, in any proceedings for an offence under section 94(1)(a), lie on the defendant.

(10) A notification under this section shall be acknowledged in writing and that acknowledgement shall be in such form as may be prescribed.

(11) In this section—

"home address", in relation to any person, means the address of his or her sole or main residence or, if he or she has no such residence, his or her most usual place of abode or, if he or she has no such abode, the place which he or she regularly visits;

"qualifying period" means—

    (a) a period of 7 days, or

    (b) 2 or more periods, in any period of 12 months, which (taken together) amount to 7 days.

93   Discharge from obligation to comply with requirements of this Part

(1) A person who, by reason of sections 89 and 90, is subject to the requirements of this Part for a period of 12 years or 6 years (in the case of a person to whom section 90(4) applies) may apply to the court for an order discharging the person from the obligation to comply with those requirements on the ground that the interests of the common good are no longer served by his or her continuing to be subject to them.

(2) An application under this section shall not be made before the expiration of the period of 8 years, or 4 years in the case of a person to whom section 90(4) applies, from the date of the applicant's release from prison.

(3) The applicant shall, not later than the beginning of such period before the making of the application as may be prescribed, notify the superintendent of the Garda Síochána of the district in which he or she ordinarily resides or has his or her most usual place of abode of his or her intention to make an application under this section.

(4) That superintendent or any other member of the Garda Síochána shall be entitled to appear and be heard at the hearing of that application.

(5) On the hearing of an application under this section, the court shall, if it considers that it is appropriate to do so in all the circumstances of the case, make an order discharging the applicant from the obligation to comply with the requirements of this Part.

(6) In considering an application under this section, the court may have regard to any matter that appears to it to be relevant and may, in particular, have regard to the character of the applicant, his or her conduct after conviction for the offence concerned and the offence concerned.

(7) If the court makes an order discharging the applicant from the obligation to comply with the requirements of this Part, the court shall cause the Garda Síochána to be notified, in writing, of that discharge.

(8) The jurisdiction of the court in respect of an application under this section may be exercised by the judge of the circuit where the applicant ordinarily resides or has his or her most usual place of abode.

(9) Proceedings under this section shall be heard otherwise than in public.

(10) In this section—

"applicant" means the person referred to in subsection (1);

"court" means the Circuit Court;

"date of the applicant's release from prison" means the date on which the applicant's sentence of imprisonment for the purposes of section 90(3) expires or, as the case may be, his or her remission from the sentence begins.

94   Offences in connection with notification requirements

(1) A person who—

   (a)   fails, without reasonable excuse, to comply with subsection (1), (2), (3) or (4) of section 92 or section 95(1), or

   (b)   notifies to the Garda Síochána, in purported compliance with that subsection (1), (2), (3) or (4) or section 95(1), as may be appropriate, any information which he or she knows to be false or misleading in any respect,

shall be guilty of an offence.

(2) A person is guilty of an offence under subsection (1)(a) on the day on which he or she first fails, without reasonable excuse, to comply with subsection (1), (2), (3) or (4), as the case may be, of section 92 or section 95(1) and continues to be guilty of it throughout any period during which the failure continues; but a person shall not be prosecuted under that provision more than once in respect of the same failure.

(3) A person guilty of an offence under this section shall be liable, on summary conviction, to a fine not exceeding €3,000 or imprisonment for a term not exceeding 12 months or both.

(4) In proceedings for an offence under subsection (1)(a) a statement on oath by a member of the Garda Síochána referred to in subsection (5) that no notification of the matters concerned was given by the defendant to the Garda Síochána by any of the means referred to in section 92(8) shall, until the contrary is shown, be evidence that no such notification was given by the defendant.

(5) The member of the Garda Síochána referred to in subsection (4) is a member not below the rank of sergeant who, from his or her evidence to the court, the court is satisfied—

(a) is familiar with the systems operated by the Garda Síochána for recording the fact that particular information has been received by them, and

(b) has made all proper inquiries in ascertaining whether a notification by the defendant of the matters concerned was received by the Garda Síochána.

95   Application of this Part to persons convicted outside State.

(1) If—

(a) a person has been convicted, in a place other than the State, of an offence,

(b) the act constituting the offence concerned would, if done in the State, constitute a drug trafficking offence (within the meaning of this Part) under the law of the State, and either—

(i) the person would, accordingly, be subject to the requirements of this Part by reason of subsection (1) or (2) of section 89, or

(ii) at the commencement of this Part, the person, as a person who has been convicted of an offence mentioned in paragraph (a), is required, under the law of the first-mentioned place in that paragraph (however that requirement is described in that law), to notify to the police in that place information of a similar nature to that required to be notified by a person otherwise subject to the requirements of this Part,

and

(c) the person is, at the time of the conviction, or thereafter becomes, resident in the State,

he or she shall, before the end of the period specified in subsection (2), notify to the Garda Síochána—

(I) his or her name and, where he or she also uses one or more other names, each of those names,

(II) his or her home address, and

(III) the fact of his or her conviction for the offence referred to in paragraph (a).

(2) The period referred to in subsection (1) is the period of 7 days beginning with—

(a) in case the person is already resident in the State upon his or her so first returning and paragraph (c) does not apply, the date on which the person first returns to the State after being convicted of the offence concerned,

(b) in case the person is not so resident and paragraph (c)does not apply, the date on which the person first becomes resident in the State after being convicted of the offence concerned, or

(c) in case the date on which the person so first returns to, or becomes resident in, the State is prior to the commencement of this Part, the commencement of this Part.

(3) The Circuit Court, in the circuit where a person to whom subsection (1) applies ordinarily resides or has his or her most usual place of abode, on application to it in that behalf by a member of the Garda Síochána not below the rank of superintendent, may order that the person shall be subject to the requirements of this Part if it considers that the interests of the common good so require and that it is appropriate in all the circumstances of the case.

(4) An application under subsection (3) may be made within a period of—
- (a) 2 months of the date of the notification under subsection (1), or
- (b) if no such notification is given, 6 months of the date specified in paragraph (a), (b) or (c), as may be appropriate, of subsection (2),

or such longer period as the Circuit Court may permit.

(5) For the purposes of this section, a person shall be deemed to be resident in the State if he or she is ordinarily resident, or has his or her principal residence, in the State, or is in the State for a qualifying period.

(6) Where a person to whom this section applies is charged with an offence under section 94, he or she shall, whether or not he or she would be treated for the purposes of section 94 as having a reasonable excuse apart from this subsection, be treated for those purposes as having a reasonable excuse if he or she believed that the act constituting the offence referred to in subsection (1) would not, if done in the State, constitute any drug trafficking offence (within the meaning of this Part) under the law of the State.

(7) For the purposes of subsection (6), it is immaterial whether a belief is justified or not if it is honestly held.

(8) Subsections (8) to (10) of section 92 shall apply to a notification under subsection (1) as they apply to a notification under that section.

(9) In this section—

"police" means, in relation to the first-mentioned place in subsection (1), any police force in that place, or a member thereof, whether that force is organised at a national, regional or local level;

"home address" and "qualifying period" have the same meanings as they have in section 92.

96   Certificate as evidence of person's being subject to requirements of this Part.

(1) If the conviction, after the commencement of this Part, of a person for an offence gives rise or may give rise to his or her becoming subject to the requirements of this Part, the court before which he or she is convicted of the offence shall forthwith, after the conviction, issue to each of the persons referred to in subsection (6) a certificate stating—
- (a) that the person has been convicted of the offence,
- (b) the sentence, if any, imposed on the person in respect of the offence, and
- (c) that the person has become or, as may be appropriate, may become subject to the requirements of this Part.

(2) If a sentence is imposed on a person in respect of the offence referred to in subsection (1) after a certificate relating to that offence has been issued under that subsection, the court which imposed the sentence shall forthwith, after the imposition of the sentence, issue to each of the persons referred to in subsection (6) a certificate stating the sentence that has been imposed on the person.

(3) A court that makes an order under section 89(3) or 95(3) in respect of a person shall forthwith, after the making of the order, issue to each of the persons referred to in subsection (6) a certificate stating—
- (a) the offence for which the person has been convicted that gave rise to his or her becoming subject to the requirements of this Part,
- (b) the sentence imposed on the person in respect of that offence, and
- (c) that the person has become subject to the requirements of this Part.

(4) If—

    (a) the conviction referred to in subsection (1) or (3)(a) insofar as it relates to an order made under section 89(3) is quashed on appeal or otherwise, or

    (b) the sentence imposed on foot of that conviction is varied on appeal or otherwise,

the court which quashes the conviction or varies the sentence shall forthwith, after the quashing of the conviction or the variation of the sentence, issue to each of the persons referred to in subsection (6) a certificate stating that the conviction has been quashed or stating the variation that has been made in the sentence.

(5) A certificate purporting to be issued under subsection (1), (2), (3) or (4) shall, in any proceedings, be evidence of the matters stated in it without proof of the signature of the officer of the court purporting to sign it or that that person was authorised to sign it.

(6) The persons referred to in subsections (1), (2), (3) and (4) are—

    (a) the Garda Síochána,

    (b) the person convicted of the offence concerned, and

    (c) where appropriate, the person for the time being in charge of the place where the convicted person is ordered to be imprisoned.

(7) The mode of proving a conviction or sentence authorised by subsection (5) shall be in addition to, and not in substitution for, any other authorised mode of proving such conviction or sentence.

(8) Rules of court may make provision in relation to the form of certificates under this section and the manner in which they may be issued.

97   Proof of foreign conviction in certain cases

(1) In proceedings against a person for an offence under section 94 (where the person is a person referred to in section 95(1)), the production to the court of a document that satisfies the condition referred to in subsection (2) and which purports to contain either or both—

    (a) particulars of the conviction in a state, other than the State, of that person for an offence and of the act constituting the offence,

    (b) a statement that, on a specified date, that person was subject to the first-mentioned requirement in section 95(1)(b)(ii),

shall, without further proof, be evidence, until the contrary is shown, of the matters stated therein.

(2) The condition mentioned in subsection (1) is that the document concerned purports to be signed or certified by a judge, magistrate or officer of the state referred to in that subsection and to be authenticated by the oath of some witness or by being sealed with the official seal of a minister of state of that state (judicial notice of which shall be taken by the court).

(3) The condition mentioned in subsection (1) shall be regarded as being satisfied without proof of the signature or certification, and the authentication of it, that appears in or on the document.

PART 10

SENTENCING

98   Definitions (Part 10).

In this Part, unless the context otherwise requires—

"authorised person" means a person who is appointed in writing by the Minister, or a person who is one of a class of persons which is prescribed, to be an authorised person for the purposes of this Part;

"a direction" means a direction given by the Minister under section 2 of the Criminal Justice Act 1960 authorising the release of a person from prison (within the meaning of that section) for a temporary period;

"governor" includes, in relation to a prisoner, a person for the time being performing the functions of governor;

"imprisonment" includes—

(a) detention in Saint Patrick's Institution, and

(b) detention in a place provided under section 2 of the Prisons Act 1970,

and "sentence of imprisonment" shall be construed accordingly;

"mandatory term of imprisonment" includes, in relation to an offence, a term of imprisonment imposed by a court under an enactment that provides that a person who is guilty of the offence concerned shall be liable to a term of imprisonment of not less than such term as is specified in the enactment;

"offender" means a person in respect of whom a restriction on movement order is, or may be, made under section 101;

"probation and welfare officer" means a person appointed by the Minister to be—

(a) a probation officer,

(b) a welfare officer, or

(c) a probation and welfare officer;

"probation and welfare service" means those officers of the Minister assigned to perform functions in the part of the Department of State for which the Minister is responsible commonly known by that name;

"restriction on movement order" means an order made by a court under section 101.

99   Power to suspend sentence

(1) Where a person is sentenced to a term of imprisonment (other than a mandatory term of imprisonment) by a court in respect of an offence, that court may make an order suspending the execution of the sentence in whole or in part, subject to the person entering into a recognisance to comply with the conditions of, or imposed in relation to, the order.

(2) It shall be a condition of an order under subsection (1) that the person in respect of whom the order is made keep the peace and be of good behaviour during—

(a) the period of suspension of the sentence concerned, or

(b) in the case of an order that suspends the sentence in part only, the period of imprisonment and the period of suspension of the sentence concerned,

and that condition shall be specified in the order concerned.

(3) The court may, when making an order under subsection (1), impose such conditions in relation to the order as the court considers—

(a) appropriate having regard to the nature of the offence, and

(b) will reduce the likelihood of the person in respect of whom the order is made committing any other offence,

and any condition imposed in accordance with this subsection shall be specified in that order.

(4) In addition to any condition imposed under subsection (3), the court may, when making an order under subsection (1) consisting of the suspension in part of a sentence of imprisonment or upon an application under subsection (6), impose any one or more of the following conditions in relation to that order or the order referred to in the said subsection (6), as the case may be:

    (a) that the person co-operate with the probation and welfare service to the extent specified by the court for the purpose of his or her rehabilitation and the protection of the public;

    (b) that the person undergo such—

        (i) treatment for drug, alcohol or other substance addiction,

        (ii) course of education, training or therapy,

        (iii) psychological counselling or other treatment,

    as may be approved by the court;

    (c) that the person be subject to the supervision of the probation and welfare service.

(5) A condition (other than a condition imposed, upon an application under subsection (6), after the making of the order concerned) imposed under subsection (4) shall be specified in the order concerned.

(6) A probation and welfare officer may, at any time before the expiration of a sentence of a court to which an order under subsection (1) consisting of the suspension of a sentence in part applies, apply to the court for the imposition of any of the conditions referred to in subsection (4) in relation to the order.

(7) Where a court makes an order under this section, it shall cause a copy of the order to be given to—

    (a) the Garda Síochána, or

    (b) in the case of an order consisting of the suspension of a sentence in part only, the governor of the prison to which the person is committed and the Garda Síochána.

(8) Where a court has made an order under subsection (1) and imposes conditions under subsection (4) upon an application under subsection (6), it shall cause a copy of the order and conditions to be given to—

    (a) the probation and welfare service, and

    (b) (i) the Garda Síochána, or

        (ii) in the case of an order consisting of the suspension of a sentence in part only, the governor of the prison to which the person is committed and the Garda Síochána.

(9) Where a person to whom an order under subsection (1) applies is, during the period of suspension of the sentence concerned, convicted of an offence[, being an offence committed after the making of the order under subsection (1)]¹, [the court before which proceedings for the offence are brought shall, before imposing sentence for that offence]², remand the person in custody or on bail to the next sitting of the court that made the said order.

(10) A court to which a person has been remanded under subsection (9) shall revoke the order under subsection (1) unless it considers that the revocation of that order would be unjust in all the circumstances of the case, and where the court revokes that order, the person shall be required to serve the entire of the sentence of imprisonment originally imposed by the court, or such part of the sentence as the court considers just having regard to all of the

circumstances of the case, less any period of that sentence already served in prison and any period spent in custody ([other than a period spent in custody by the person in respect of an offence referred to in subsection (9)]³) pending the revocation of the said order.

[(10A) The court referred to in subsection (10) shall remand the person concerned in custody or on bail to the next sitting of the court referred to in subsection (9) for the purpose of that court imposing sentence on that person for the offence referred to in that subsection.]⁴

(11)[(a)   Where an order under subsection (1) is revoked under subsection (10), a sentence of imprisonment (other than a sentence consisting of imprisonment for life) imposed on the person concerned under subsection (10A) shall not commence until the expiration of any period of imprisonment required to be served by the person under subsection (10).]⁵

    (b)   This subsection shall not affect the operation of section 5 of the Criminal Justice Act 1951.

(12) Where an order under subsection (1) is revoked in accordance with this section, the person to whom the order applied may appeal against the revocation to such court as would have jurisdiction to hear an appeal against any conviction of, or sentence imposed on, a person for an offence by the court that revoked that order.

(13) Where a member of the Garda Síochána or, as the case may be, the governor of the prison to which a person was committed has reasonable grounds for believing that a person to whom an order under this section applies has contravened the condition referred to in subsection (2) he or she may apply to the court to fix a date for the hearing of an application for an order revoking the order under subsection (1).

(14) A probation and welfare officer may, if he or she has reasonable grounds for believing that a person to whom an order under subsection (1) applies has contravened a condition imposed under subsection (3) or (4), apply to the court to fix a date for the hearing of an application for an order revoking the order under subsection (1).

(15) Where the court fixes a date for the hearing of an application referred to in subsection (13) or (14), it shall, by notice in writing, so inform the person in respect of whom the application will be made, or where that person is in prison, the governor of the prison, and such notice shall require the person to appear before it, or require the said governor to produce the person before it, on the date so fixed and at such time as is specified in the notice.

(16) If a person who is not in prison fails to appear before the court in accordance with a requirement contained in a notice under subsection (15), the court may issue a warrant for the arrest of the person.

(17) A court shall, where it is satisfied that a person to whom an order under subsection (1) applies has contravened a condition of the order, revoke the order unless it considers that in all of the circumstances of the case it would be unjust to so do, and where the court revokes that order, the person shall be required to serve the entire of the sentence originally imposed by the court, or such part of the sentence as the court considers just having regard to all of the circumstances of the case, less any period of that sentence already served in prison and any period spent in custody pending the revocation of the said order.

(18) A notice under subsection (15) shall be addressed to the person concerned by name, and may be given to the person in one of the following ways:

(a) by delivering it to the person;

(b) by leaving it at the address at which the person ordinarily resides or, in a case in which an address for service has been furnished, at that address;

(c) by sending it by post in a prepaid registered letter to the address at which the person ordinarily resides or, in a case in which an address for service has been furnished, to that address.

(19) This section shall not affect the operation of—

(a) section 2 of the Criminal Justice Act 1960 or Rule 38 of the Rules for the Government of Prisons 1947 (S.R. & O. No. 320 of 1947), or

(b) subsections (3G) and (3H) of section 27 of the Misuse of Drugs Act 1977.

[(20) Where a court imposes a sentence of a term of imprisonment that is to run consecutively to a sentence of a term of imprisonment the operation of a part of which is suspended, the first-mentioned sentence shall commence at the expiration of the part of the second-mentioned sentence the operation of which is not suspended.]⁶

Amendments

1   Words inserted by Criminal Justice (Miscellaneous Provisions) Act 2009, s 51.

2   Words substituted by Criminal Justice Act 2007, s 60(a).

3   Words substituted by Criminal Justice Act 2007, s 60(b).

4   Subsection (10A) inserted by Criminal Justice Act 2007, s 60(c).

5   Subsection (11)(a) substituted by Criminal Justice Act 2007, s 60(d).

6   Subsection (20) inserted by Criminal Justice Act 2007, s 60(e).

---

100   Imposition of fine and deferral of sentence.

(1) Where a court makes an order convicting a person of an offence in respect of which the person is liable to both a term of imprisonment and a fine, the court may, subject to subsection (2)—

(a) impose a fine on that person in respect of the offence, and

(b) make an order—

(i) deferring the passing of a sentence of imprisonment for the offence, and

(ii) specifying the term of imprisonment that it would propose to impose on the person in respect of that offence should he or she fail or refuse to comply with the conditions specified in the order.

(2) A court shall not perform functions under subsection (1) unless it is satisfied that—

(a) the person concerned consents to the sentence of imprisonment being deferred,

(b) the person gives an undertaking to comply with any conditions specified in an order made under subsection (1)(b), and

(c) having regard to the nature of the offence concerned and all of the circumstances of the case, it would be in the interests of justice to so do.

(3) An order under subsection (1)(b) shall specify—

> (a) the date (in this section referred to as the "specified date") on which it proposes to pass sentence should the person contravene a condition of the order, being a date that falls not later than 6 months after the making of the order, and
>
> (b) the conditions with which the person concerned is to comply during the period between the making of the order and the specified date, including a condition that the person be of good behaviour and keep the peace.

(4) Where a court makes an order under subsection (1)(b), it shall cause a copy of the order to be given to the person in respect of whom it is made and the Garda Síochána.

(5) A court that has made an order under subsection (1)(b) shall not later than one month before the specified date require the person in respect of whom the order was made, by notice, to attend a sitting of the court on that date and at such time as is specified in the notice.

(6) If a person fails to comply with a requirement in a notice under subsection (5), the court may issue a warrant for the arrest of that person.

(7) Where a member of the Garda Síochána has reasonable grounds for believing that a person to whom an order under subsection (1)(b) applies has contravened a condition of the order, he or she may apply to the court to fix a date for the hearing of an application for an order imposing the term of imprisonment specified in the order in accordance with subsection (1)(b)(ii).

(8) Where the court fixes a date for the hearing of an application referred to in subsection (7), it shall, by notice in writing, so inform the person in respect of whom the application will be made, and such notice shall require the person to appear before it on the date so fixed and at such time as is specified in the notice.

(9) If a person fails to appear before the court in accordance with a requirement contained in a notice under subsection (8), the court may issue a warrant for the arrest of the person.

(10) Upon an application by a member of the Garda Síochána for an order imposing the term of imprisonment specified in accordance with paragraph (b)(ii) of subsection (1), a court may, if it is satisfied that the person in respect of whom the application was made has contravened a condition specified in the order under that subsection, impose the term of imprisonment that it proposed to impose at the time of the making of the order under that subsection (or such lesser term as it considers just in all of the circumstances of the case), unless it considers that it would in all the circumstances be unjust to so do.

(11) On the specified date the court shall, if it is satisfied that the person in respect of whom the order under subsection (1) was made has complied with the conditions specified in the order, not impose the sentence that it proposed to impose when making that order and shall discharge the person forthwith.

(12) On the specified date the court may, if it is satisfied that the person in respect of whom the order under subsection (1) was made has contravened a condition specified in the order, impose the term of imprisonment that it proposed to impose at the time of the making of the order (or such lesser term as it considers just in all of the circumstances of the case) unless it considers that in all of the circumstances of the case it would be unjust to so do, and where it considers that it would be unjust to impose a term of imprisonment it shall discharge the person forthwith.

(13) A notice under subsection (5) or (8) shall be addressed to the person concerned by name, and may be given to the person in one of the following ways:

(a) by delivering it to the person;

(b) by leaving it at the address at which the person ordinarily resides or, in a case in which an address for service has been furnished, at that address;

(c) by sending it by post in a prepaid registered letter to the address at which the person ordinarily resides or, in a case in which an address for service has been furnished, to that address.

(14) Section 18(1) of the Courts of Justice Act 1928 is amended by the insertion of ", including an order under section 100(1) of the Criminal Justice Act 2006" after "the person against whom the order shall have been made".

101   Restriction on movement order

(1) Where a person aged 18 years or more is convicted of an offence specified in Schedule 3 and the court which convicts him or her of the offence considers that it is appropriate to impose a sentence of imprisonment for a term of 3 months or more on the person in respect of the offence, it may, as an alternative to such a sentence, make an order under this section ("a restriction on movement order") in respect of the person.

(2) A restriction on movement order may restrict the offender's movements to such extent as the court thinks fit and, without prejudice to the generality of the foregoing, may include provision—

(a) requiring the offender to be in such place or places as may be specified for such period or periods in each day or week as may be specified, or

(b) requiring the offender not to be in such place or places, or such class or classes of place or places, at such time or during such periods, as may be specified,

or both, but the court may not, under paragraph (a), require the offender to be in any place or places for a period or periods of more than 12 hours in any one day.

(3) A restriction on movement order may be made for any period of not more than 6 months and, during that period, the offender shall keep the peace and be of good behaviour.

(4) A restriction on movement order may specify such conditions as the court considers necessary for the purposes of ensuring that while the order is in force the offender will keep the peace and be of good behaviour and will not commit any further offences.

(5) A restriction on movement order shall specify the restrictions that are to apply to the offender's movements and, in particular, it shall specify—

(a) the period during which it is in force,

(b) the period or periods in each day or week during which the offender shall be in any specified place or places,

(c) the time at which, or the periods during which, the offender shall not be in any specified place or places or any class or classes of place or places.

(6) In determining for the purposes of subsection (2)(a) the period or periods during which the offender shall be in a specified place or places, the court shall have regard to the nature and circumstances of the offence of which the offender has been found guilty and any educational course, training, employment or other activity in which the offender is participating, and it shall ensure, as far as practicable, that that period or those periods do not conflict with the practice by the offender of his or her religion.

(7) In determining for the purpose of subsection (2)(b) the place or places, or class or classes of place or places, the time or the periods to be specified in a restriction on movement order,

the court shall have regard to the nature and circumstances of the offence of which the offender has been found guilty, the time that the offender committed the offence, the place where the offence was committed and the likelihood of the offender committing another offence in the same or similar place or places or class or classes of place or places.

(8) A court shall not make a restriction on movement order in respect of an offender unless it considers, having regard to the offender and his or her circumstances, that he or she is a suitable person in respect of whom such an order may be made and, for that purpose, the court may request a probation and welfare officer to prepare a report in writing in relation to the offender.

(9) A restriction on movement order which restricts the movements of an offender in accordance with subsection (2)(a) shall not be made without the consent of the owner of, or any adult person habitually residing at, the place or places concerned or, as the case may be, the person in charge of the place or places concerned.

(10) A court making a restriction on movement order may include in the order a requirement that the restrictions on the offender's movements be monitored electronically in accordance with section 102, but it shall not include such a requirement unless it considers, having regard to the offender and his or her circumstances, that he or she is a suitable person in respect of whom such a requirement may be made and, for that purpose, the court may request an authorised person to prepare a report in writing in relation to the offender.

(11) Before making a restriction on movement order, the court shall explain to the offender in ordinary language—

(a) the effect of the order, including any requirement which is to be included in the order under section 102,

(b) the consequences which may follow any failure by the offender to comply with the requirements of the order, and

(c) that the court has power under section 103 to vary the order on the application of any person referred to in that section,

and the court shall not make the order unless the offender agrees to comply with its requirements.

(12) The court shall cause certified copies of a restriction on movement order to be sent to—

(a) the offender,

(b) the member in charge of the Garda Síochána station for the area where the offender resides or, where appropriate, the area where he or she is to reside while the order is in force,

(c) where appropriate, an authorised person who is responsible under section 102 for monitoring the offender's compliance with the order.

102   Electronic monitoring of restriction on movement order.

Where the restrictions on an offender's movements in a restriction on movement order are to be monitored electronically, the order shall include—

(a) a provision making an authorised person responsible for monitoring the offender's compliance with it, and

(b) a requirement that the offender shall, either continuously or for such periods as may be specified, have an electronic monitoring device attached to his or her person for the purpose of enabling the monitoring of his or her compliance with the order to be carried out.

103   Variation of restriction on movement order.

(1) Where a restriction on movement order is in force, the court may, if it so thinks proper, on written application by—

    (a) the offender,

    (b) where appropriate, the owner of, or an adult person habitually residing at, the place or places or, as the case may be, the person in charge of the place or places, specified in the order,

    (c) a member of an Garda Síochána, or

    (d) where appropriate, an authorised person who is responsible under section 102 for monitoring the offender's compliance with the order,

vary the order by substituting another period or time or another place for any period, time or place specified in the order.

(2) An application under subsection (1) shall be made on notice to such of the other parties specified in subsection (1) as is appropriate.

(3) Where any party specified in subsection (1) objects to the variation of a restriction on movement order, the court shall not vary the order without hearing from that party.

(4) The court shall cause certified copies of a restriction on movement order varied under this section to be sent to—

    (a) the offender,

    (b) where appropriate, the owner of, or an adult person habitually residing at, the place or places or, as the case may be, the person in charge of the place or places, specified in the order,

    (c) the member in charge of the Garda Síochána station for the area where the offender resides or, where appropriate, the area where he or she is to reside while the order is in force, and

    (d) where appropriate, an authorised person who is responsible under section 102 for monitoring the offender's compliance with the order.

(5) The jurisdiction vested in the court under this section shall be exercised by a judge of the District Court for the time being assigned to the district court district, or, as the case may be, a judge of the Circuit Court for the time being assigned to the circuit, in which the offender resides or is to reside while the restriction on movement order is in force.

104   Provisions regarding more than one restriction on movement order

(1) Where more than one restriction on movement order is in force in respect of an offender at any time, the period during which the offender is required to be in a specified place or places shall, notwithstanding subsections (2) and (3), not be for a period of more than 6 months.

(2) Where a court makes restriction on movement orders in respect of 2 or more offences of which the offender has been found guilty, it may direct that the period for which the offender is required by any of those orders to be in a specified place or places shall be concurrent with or additional to that specified in any other of those orders.

(3) Where a court makes a restriction on movement order and at the time of the making of the order there is in force in respect of the offender another such order (whether made by the same or a different court), the court making the later order may direct in that order that the period for which the offender is required by that order to be in a specified place or places shall be concurrent with or additional to that specified in the earlier order.

105   Non-compliance with restriction on movement order.

(1) Where a restriction on movement order is in force and it appears to a court, on application by a member of an Garda Síochána or, where appropriate, an authorised person who is responsible under section 102 for monitoring the offender's compliance with the order, that the offender has failed, without reasonable cause, to comply with the order or any condition to which it is subject, the court may—

(a)   if the order was made by a court in the district court district, or, as the case may be, the circuit, in which the offender resides or is to reside while the order is in force—

(i)   direct the offender to comply with the order or any such condition in so far as it has not been complied with,

(ii)   revoke the order and make another restriction on movement order in respect of the offender, or

(iii) revoke the order and deal with the case in any other way in which it could have been dealt with before the order was made,

or

(b)   if the order was made by a court in another district court district or, as the case may be, another circuit, remand the offender on bail to a sitting of that court to be dealt with, and for that purpose, paragraph (a) shall apply in relation to that court, with the necessary modifications.

(2) The matters to be taken into account by the court in arriving at a decision pursuant to subsection (1) shall include the extent to which, and the period during which, the offender has complied with the order concerned or any condition to which it is subject.

(3) Where the court proposes to exercise its powers under subsection (1), it shall summon the offender to appear before it and, if the offender does not appear in answer to the summons, it may issue a warrant for his or her arrest.

(4) The jurisdiction vested in the court under this section shall be exercised by a judge of the District Court for the time being assigned to the district court district, or, as the case may be, a judge of the Circuit Court for the time being assigned to the circuit, in which the offender resides or is to reside while the restriction on movement order is in force.

106   Amendment of section 5 of Criminal Justice Act 1951.

Where 2 or more sentences, one of which is a restriction on movement order, are passed on an offender by the District Court and are ordered to run consecutively, the aggregate of the period during which the order in respect of the offender is in force and the period of any term or terms of imprisonment imposed on him or her shall not exceed the maximum period of the aggregate term of imprisonment specified in section 5 of the Criminal Justice Act 1951.

107   Documentary evidence in relation to offenders

(1) Evidence of the presence or absence of the offender in or from a particular place at a particular time may, subject to the provisions of this section, be given by the production of a document or documents being—

(a) a statement produced automatically or otherwise by a device, prescribed by regulations under section 111, by which the offender's whereabouts were electronically monitored, and

(b) a certificate signed by an authorised person who is responsible under section 102 for monitoring the offender's compliance with the order that the statement relates to the whereabouts of the offender at the dates and times shown in the statement.

(2) The statement and certificate mentioned in subsection (1) shall, when produced at a hearing, be evidence, until the contrary is shown, of the facts set out in them.

(3) Neither the statement nor the certificate mentioned in subsection (1) shall be admissible in evidence unless a copy of both has been served on the offender prior to the hearing.

108   Temporary release of prisoners

(1) A direction in respect of a person aged 18 years or more may be subject to a condition restricting the person's movements to such extent as the Minister thinks fit and specifies in the direction and those restrictions may be monitored electronically in accordance with subsection (4).

(2) Without prejudice to the generality of subsection (1), a direction may include provision—

(a) requiring the person to be in such place or places as may be specified for such period or periods in each day or week as may be specified, or

(b) requiring the person not to be in such place or places, or such class or classes of place or places, at such time or during such periods, as may be specified,

or both, but the Minister may not, under paragraph (a), require the person to be in any place or places for a period or periods of more than 12 hours in any one day.

(3) A direction shall not be subject to a condition which restricts the movements of a person in accordance with subsection (2)(a) without the consent of the owner of, or any adult person habitually residing at, the place or places concerned or, as the case may be, the person in charge of the place or places concerned.

(4) Where the restrictions on a person's movements imposed by a condition in a direction are to be monitored electronically, the direction shall include—

(a) a provision making an authorised person responsible for monitoring the person's compliance with the condition and the condition referred to in paragraph (b), and

(b) a condition that the person shall, either continuously or for such periods of not more than 6 months as may be specified have an electronic monitoring device attached to his or her person for the purpose of enabling the monitoring of his or her compliance with the condition restricting his or her movements to be carried out.

(5) A condition shall not be imposed under subsection (1) or (4)(b) unless the person concerned agrees to comply with it, but the absence of such agreement shall not confer an entitlement on that person to be released pursuant to a direction.

109   Documentary evidence in relation to prisoners on temporary release

(1) In any proceedings for an offence under section 6(2) of the Criminal Justice Act 1960 evidence of the presence or absence of the person in or from a particular place at a particular time may, subject to the provisions of this section, be given by the production of a document or documents being—

(a) a statement produced automatically or otherwise by a device, prescribed by regulations made under section 111, by which the person's whereabouts were electronically monitored, and

(b) a certificate signed by an authorised person who is responsible under section 108(4) for monitoring the offender's compliance with the condition in the direction that the statement relates to the whereabouts of the person at the dates and times shown in the statement.

(2) The statement and certificate mentioned in subsection (1) shall, when produced at a hearing, be evidence, until the contrary is shown, of the facts set out in them.

(3) Neither the statement nor the certificate mentioned in subsection (1) shall be admissible in evidence unless a copy of both has been served on the person prior to the hearing.

110   Amendment of section 2(1) of Criminal Justice Act 1960.

Section 2(1) of the Criminal Justice Act 1960 is amended by the insertion of "(including, if appropriate, any condition under section 108 of the Criminal Justice Act 2006)" after "subject to such conditions, as may be specified in the direction".

111   Regulations regarding electronic monitoring devices

The Minister may prescribe by regulations the types of electronic monitoring device that may be used for the purpose of monitoring—

(a) the compliance of offenders with a requirement under section 102, and

(b) the compliance of persons with section 108(4).

112   Electronic monitoring

The Minister may, with the consent of the Minister for Finance, make such arrangements, including contractual arrangements, as he or she considers appropriate with such persons as he or she thinks fit for the monitoring of—

(a) the compliance of offenders with restriction on movement orders, or

(b) the compliance of persons with a condition imposed under section 108(4) in directions in respect of such persons,

or both.

PART 11
CIVIL PROCEEDINGS IN RELATION TO ANTI-SOCIAL BEHAVIOUR

113   Interpretation and application of this Part.

(1) In this Part—

"behaviour warning" has the meaning assigned to it under section 114;

"civil order" means an order described in section 115(1);

"senior member of the Garda Síochána" means a member of the Garda Síochána not below the rank of a superintendent.

(2) For the purposes of this Part, a person behaves in an anti-social manner if the person causes or, in the circumstances, is likely to cause, to one or more persons who are not of the same household as the person—

    (a) harassment,

    (b) significant or persistent alarm, distress, fear or intimidation, or

    (c) significant or persistent impairment of their use or enjoyment of their property.

(3) This Part does not apply—

    (a) in respect of behaviour of a person who is under the age of 18 years at the time the behaviour takes place,

    (b) to any behaviour of a person that takes place before this section comes into force, or

    (c) to any act or omission of a person in respect of which criminal proceedings have been instituted against that person.

114   Behaviour warnings

(1) Subject to subsection (5), a member of the Garda Síochána may issue a behaviour warning to a person who has behaved in an anti-social manner.

(2) The behaviour warning may be issued orally or in writing and, if it is issued orally, it shall be recorded in writing as soon as reasonably practicable and a written record of the behaviour warning shall be served on the person personally or by post.

(3) The behaviour warning or, if it is given orally, the written record of it shall—

    (a) include a statement that the person has behaved in an anti-social manner and indicate what that behaviour is and when and where it took place,

    (b) demand that the person cease the behaviour or otherwise address the behaviour in the manner specified in the warning, and

    (c) include notice that—

        (i) failure to comply with a demand under paragraph (b), or

        (ii) issuance of a subsequent behaviour warning,

may result in an application being made for a civil order.

(4) The member of the Garda Síochána referred to in subsection (1) may require the person to give his or her name and address to the member for purposes of the behaviour warning or the written record of it.

(5) A behaviour warning may not be issued more than one month after the time that—

    (a) the behaviour took place, or

    (b) in the case of persistent behaviour, the most recent known instance of that behaviour took place.

(6) Subject to subsection (7), a behaviour warning remains in force against the person to whom it is issued for 3 months from the date that it is issued.

(7) If an application is made under section 115 in respect of the person, the behaviour warning remains in force against the person until the application is heard or otherwise determined by the District Court.

115   Civil orders

(1) On application made in accordance with this section, the District Court may make an order (a "civil order") prohibiting the respondent from doing anything specified in the order if the court is satisfied that—

(a)   the respondent has behaved in an anti-social manner,

(b)   the order is necessary to prevent the respondent from continuing to behave in that manner, and

(c)   having regard to the effect or likely effect of that behaviour on other persons, the order is reasonable and proportionate in the circumstances.

(2) The court may impose terms or conditions in the civil order that the court considers appropriate.

(3) An application for a civil order may only be made by a senior member of the Garda Síochána and shall be made—

(a)   on notice to the respondent, and

(b)   in the district court district in which the respondent resides at the time.

(4) Before making the application, the senior member of the Garda Síochána must be satisfied that either or both of the following conditions have been met:

(a)   the respondent has been issued a behaviour warning and has not complied with one or more of the demands of that warning;

(b)   the respondent has been issued 3 or more behaviour warnings in less than 6 consecutive months.

(5) The respondent in an application under subsection (1) may not at any time be charged with, prosecuted or punished for an offence if the act or omission that constitutes the offence is the same behaviour that is the subject of the application and is to be determined by the court under subsection (1)(a).

(6) Unless discharged under subsection (7), a civil order remains in force for no more than the lesser of the following:

(a)   two years from the date the order is made;

(b)   the period specified in the order.

(7) The court may vary or discharge a civil order on the application of the person subject to that order or a senior member of the Garda Síochána.

(8) An applicant under subsection (7) shall give notice of the application—

(a)   if the applicant is the person subject to the civil order, to a senior member of the Garda Síochána in the Garda Síochána district in which the applicant resides, or

(b)   if the applicant is a senior member of the Garda Síochána, to the person who is the subject of the civil order.

(9) The standard of proof in proceedings under this section is that applicable to civil proceedings.

(10) The jurisdiction conferred on the District Court by this section may be exercised as follows:

(a)   in respect of subsections (1) and (2), by a judge of the District Court for the time being assigned to the district court district in which the respondent resides at the time the application is made;

(b) in respect of subsection (7), by a judge of the District Court for the time being assigned to the district court district in which the person subject to the civil order resides at the time the application is made.

116   Appeals against a civil order

(1) A person against whom a civil order has been made may, within 21 days from the date that the order is made, appeal the making of the order to the Circuit Court.

(2) An appellant under subsection (1) shall give notice of the appeal to a senior member of the Garda Síochána in the Garda Síochána district in which the appellant resides.

(3) Notwithstanding the appeal, the civil order shall remain in force unless the court that made the order or the appeal court places a stay on it.

(4) An appeal under this section shall be in the nature of a rehearing of the application under section 115 and, for this purpose, subsections (1), (2) and (5) of that section apply in respect of the matter.

(5) If on appeal under this section, the appeal court makes a civil order, the provisions of section 115(6) to (8) apply in respect of the matter.

(6) Notwithstanding the appeal period described in subsection (1), the Circuit Court may, on application by the person subject to the civil order, extend the appeal period if satisfied that exceptional circumstances exist which warrant the extension.

(7) The standard of proof in proceedings under this section is that applicable to civil proceedings.

(8) The jurisdiction conferred on the Circuit Court by this section may be exercised as follows:

(a) in respect of section 115(1) and (2) as those provisions apply to the Circuit Court under subsection (4) of this section, by a judge of the Circuit Court for the time being assigned to the circuit in which the appellant under this section resides at the time the appeal is commenced;

(b) in respect of section 115(7) as it applies to the Circuit Court under subsection (5) of this section, by a judge of the Circuit Court for the time being assigned to the circuit in which the person subject to the civil order resides at the time the application is made;

(c) in respect of subsection (6) of this section, by a judge of the Circuit Court for the time being assigned to the circuit in which the person subject to the civil order resides at the time the application is made.

117   Offences

(1) A person commits an offence who—

(a) fails to give a name and address when required to do so under section 114(4) or gives a name or address that is false or misleading in response to that requirement, or

(b) without reasonable excuse, does not comply with a civil order to which the person is subject.

(2) A member of the Garda Síochána may arrest a person without warrant if the member has reasonable grounds to believe that the person has committed an offence under subsection (1)(b).

(3) A person who commits an offence under subsection (1) is liable, on summary conviction, to the following:

   (a)   for an offence under subsection (1)(a), a fine not exceeding €500;

   (b)   for an offence under subsection (1)(b), a fine not exceeding €3,000 or imprisonment for a term not exceeding 6 months or both.

118   Legal aid

(1) Subject to subsection (2), a person who is the subject of an application for a civil order may be granted a certificate for free legal aid (in this Part referred to as a "legal aid (civil order) certificate") in preparation for and representation at the hearing of—

   (a)   the application,

   (b)   an application by the person to vary or discharge a civil order,

   (c)   any appeal by the person against the making of the civil order, and

   (d)   any proceedings in the High Court or Supreme Court arising out of the making of the application, the appeal or any subsequent proceedings.

(2) A legal aid (civil order) certificate may not be granted under subsection (1) unless it appears to the court hearing the application for the certificate that—

   (a)   the means of the person concerned are insufficient to enable that person to obtain legal aid, and

   (b)   by reason of the gravity of the behaviour alleged to be anti-social or of exceptional circumstances, it is essential in the interests of justice that the person should have legal aid in preparation for and representation at the hearing concerned.

(3) A person who is granted a legal aid (civil order) certificate is entitled—

   (a)   to free legal aid in preparation for and representation at the hearing of the application for a civil order and any proceedings referred to in subsection (1)(b), (c) and (d), and

   (b)   to have, in such manner as may be prescribed,

         (i)   a solicitor assigned to the person in relation to the application for the civil order or any application to vary or discharge it,

         (ii)   a solicitor assigned to the person in relation to any other such proceedings, and

         (iii) if the court granting the certificate considers it appropriate, a counsel assigned to the person in relation to proceedings referred to in subparagraph (ii).

(4) If a legal aid (civil order) certificate is granted, any fees, costs or other expenses properly incurred in preparation for and representation at the proceedings concerned shall, subject to regulations under section 119, be paid out of moneys provided by the Oireachtas.

(5) A person applying for a legal aid (civil order) certificate may be required by the court granting the certificate to furnish a written statement of the person's means.

(6) A person who, for the purpose of obtaining free legal aid under this section, whether for himself or herself or for some other person, knowingly makes a false or misleading statement or representation either orally or in writing, or knowingly conceals any material fact, commits an offence and is liable on summary conviction to a fine not exceeding €2,500 or imprisonment for a term not exceeding 6 months or both.

(7) On conviction of a person for an offence under this section, the court by which the person is convicted may, if in the circumstances of the case it thinks fit, order the person to pay to the Minister the whole or part of any sum paid under subsection (4) in respect of the free legal aid in relation to which the offence was committed, and any sum so paid to the Minister shall be paid into and disposed of for the benefit of the Exchequer in accordance with the directions of the Minister for Finance.

119 Regulations (legal aid)

(1) The Minister may make regulations for carrying section 118 into effect.

(2) The regulations may, in particular, prescribe any of the following:

    (a) the form of certificates granted under that section;

    (b) the rates or scales of payment of any fees, costs or other expenses payable out of moneys provided by the Oireachtas under those certificates;

    (c) the manner in which solicitors and counsel are to be assigned under those certificates.

(3) Regulations under subsection (2)(b) shall not be made without the consent of the Minister for Finance.

(4) Pending the making of regulations under this section, the regulations under section 10 of the Criminal Justice (Legal Aid) Act 1962 apply and have effect, with the necessary modifications, in relation to certificates for free legal aid granted under section 118 of this Act as if they were certificates for free legal aid granted under the Criminal Justice (Legal Aid) Act 1962.

PART 12
AMENDMENT OF CHILDREN ACT 2001

120

Interpretation (Part 12)

In this Part—

"Act of 1908" means the Children Act 1908;

"Act of 1970" means the Prisons Act 1970;

"Act of 1991" means the Child Care Act 1991;

"Act of 2001" means the Children Act 2001.

121 Amendment of section 2 of Act of 2001

Section 2 of the Act of 2001 is amended in subsection (2)—

    (a) by the insertion of the following paragraph after paragraph (a):

    (b) by the deletion of paragraph (c),

    (c) in paragraph (d), by the deletion of "for Education and Science", and

    (d) by the insertion of the following paragraph after paragraph (e):[1]

Amendments

1   See the amended Act.

122   Amendment of section 3 of Act of 2001

Section 3 of the Act of 2001 is amended in subsection (1)—

(a) by the insertion of the following definition:

""anti-social behaviour" is to be construed in accordance with section 257A(2);",

(b) in the definition of "children detention school", by the substitution of "Minister" for "Minister for Education and Science",

(c) in the definition of "detention", by the deletion of "or a children detention centre designated as such by the Minister under section 150",

(d) by the deletion of the definition of "junior remand centre",

(e) in the definition of Minister, by the substitution of "Parts 3 and 11" for "Parts 3, 10 and 11",

(f) in the definition of "prescribed", by the deletion of ", the Minister for Education and Science",

(g) in the definition of "victim" to insert, after "property", "and, in relation to anti-social behaviour by a child, means a person who suffers physical or emotional harm as a consequence of that behaviour".

123

Substitution of section 18 of Act of 2001

The following section is substituted for section 18 of the Act of 2001:[1]

Amendments

1   See the amended Act.

124   Amendment of section 19 of Act of 2001

Section 19 of the Act of 2001 is amended by the substitution of the following subsection for subsection (1):[1]

Amendments

1   See the amended Act.

125   Amendment of section 23 of Act of 2001

Section 23 of the Act of 2001 is amended—

   (a) in subsection (1), by the substitution of "Subject to subsection (6), a child" for "A child",

   (b) in subsections (1)(a), (4) and (5), the insertion of "or anti-social" after "criminal",

   (c) in subsection (1)(c), by the substitution of "is 10 years of age or over that age" for "is of or over the age of criminal responsibility", and

   (d) by the addition of the following subsection: [1]

Amendments

1   See the amended Act.

126   Substitution of section 48 of Act of 2001

The following section is substituted for section 48 of the Act of 2001: [1]

Amendments

1   See the amended Act.

127   Substitution of section 49 of Act of 2001

The following section is substituted for section 49 of the Act of 2001:[1]

Amendments

1   See the amended Act.

128   Amendment of Title to Part 5 of Act of 2001

The title to Part 5 of the Act of 2001 is amended by the substitution of "RESTRICTION ON CRIMINAL PROCEEDINGS AGAINST CERTAIN CHILDREN" for "CRIMINAL RESPONSIBILITY".

129   Substitution of section 52 of Act of 2001

The following section is substituted for section 52 of the Act of 2001:[1]

Amendments

1   See the amended Act.

130   Amendment of section 53 of Act of 2001

Section 53 of the Act of 2001 is amended by the substitution of the following subsection for subsection (1):[1]

Amendments

1   See the amended Act.

131   Amendment of section 59 of Act of 2001

Section 59 of the Act of 2001 is amended by the substitution of the following subsection for subsection (4):[1]

Amendments

1   See the amended Act.

132   New section 76A in Act of 2001

The following section is inserted in the Act of 2001 after section 76, but in Part 8:[1]

Amendments

1   See the amended Act.

133   New section 76B in Act of 2001

The following section is inserted in the Act of 2001 after section 76A:[1]

Amendments

1   See the amended Act.

134   New section 76C in Act of 2001

The following section is inserted in the Act of 2001 after section 76B:[1]

Amendments

1   See the amended Act.

135   Substitution of section 88 of Act of 2001

The following section is substituted for section 88 of the Act of 2001:[1]

Amendments

1   See the amended Act.

136   Amendment of section 96 of Act of 2001

Section 96 of the Act of 2001 is amended by the substitution of the following subsection for subsection (5):[1]

Amendments

1   See the amended Act.

137   Change in title of principal probation and welfare officer

The Act of 2001 is amended by the substitution of "Director of the Probation and Welfare Service" for "principal probation and welfare officer" in sections 79, 87, 106(5), 118(3), 118(4), 124(4), 125(4), 126(4), 126(5), 141(2)(b), 207(1), 207(7), 208(1), 208(4), 209, 230(3)(e), 262(1), 262(2) and 262(3).

138   Amendment of section 91 of Act of 2001

Section 91 of the Act of 2001 is amended—

(a)   in subsection (1)—

(i)   by the deletion of "or" in paragraph (b),

(ii)   by the substitution of "subject, or" for "subject." in paragraph (c), and

(iii) by the insertion of the following paragraph after paragraph (c):

"(d) under section 257D.",

and

(b)   in subsection (4), by the insertion of "or under section 257D" after "charged".

139   Substitution of section 93 of Act of 2001

The following section is substituted for section 93 of the Act of 2001:[1]

Amendments

1   See the amended Act.

140   Amendment of section 136 of Act of 2001

Section 136 of the Act of 2001 is amended—

    (a) by the substitution of the following subsections for subsection (1):[1] and

    (b) by the deletion of subsection (3).

Amendments

1 See the amended Act.

141   Substitution of section 149 of Act of 2001

The following section is substituted for section 149 of the Act of 2001:[1]

Amendments

1 See the amended Act.

142   Amendment of section 155 of Act of 2001

Section 155 of the Act of 2001 is amended—

    (a) by the substitution of the following subsections for subsections (1) to (3):[1]

    (b) by the deletion of subsections (4) and (5), and

    (c) in subsection (6), by the deletion of "in a children detention centre,".

Amendments

1 See the amended Act.

143   New section 156A in Act of 2001

The following section is inserted in the Act of 2001 after section 156, but in Part 9:[1]

Amendments

1 See the amended Act.

144   New section 156B in Act of 2001

The following section is inserted in the Act of 2001 after section 156A:[1]

Amendments

1   See the amended Act.

145   Amendment of section 157 of Act of 2001

Section 157 of the Act of 2001 is amended—

    (a)   by the insertion of the following definitions:

        ""authorised person" means a person authorised by the Minister under section 185;

        "staff" does not include teaching staff;",

    and

    (b)   by the deletion of the definitions of "Inspector" and "Minister".

146   Substitution of section 159 of Act of 2001

The following section is substituted for section 159 of the Act of 2001:[1]

Amendments

1   See the amended Act.

147   New section 159A in Act of 2001

The following section is inserted in the Act of 2001 after section 159:[1]

Amendments

1   See the amended Act.

148   New section 159B in Act of 2001

The following section is inserted in the Act of 2001 after section 159A:[1]

Amendments

1   See the amended Act.

149   Amendment of section 161 of Act of 2001

Section 161 of the Act of 2001 is amended—

   (a) by the substitution of the following subsections for subsection (1):[1]

   (b) by the insertion of the following subsection:[1]

Amendments

1 See the amended Act.

150   Amendment of section 165 of Act of 2001

Section 165 of the Act of 2001 is amended—

   (a) in subsection (1)(b), by the substitution of "risk, and" for "risk,", and

   (b) by the deletion of paragraph (c) of subsection (1).

151   Substitution of section 185 of Act of 2001

The following section is substituted for section 185 of the Act of 2001:[1]

Amendments

1 See the amended Act.

152   Substitution of section 186 of Act of 2001

The following section is substituted for section 186 of the Act of 2001:[1]

Amendments

1 See the amended Act.

153   New section 186A in Act of 2001

The following section is inserted in the Act of 2001 after section 186:[1]

Amendments

1 See the amended Act.

154   Substitution of section 198 of Act of 2001

The following section is substituted for section 198 of the Act of 2001:[1]

Amendments

1   See the amended Act.

155   Amendment of section 215 of Act of 2001

Section 215 of the Act of 2001 is amended—

(a) by the substitution of the following subsection for subsection (2):[1] and

(b) by the deletion of subsection (3).

Amendments

1   See the amended Act.

156   Amendment of section 227 of Act of 2001

Section 227(1) of the Act of 2001 is amended—

(a) by the substitution of "and to" for "and ensure",

(b) in paragraph (a), by the substitution of "advise on the coordination of" for "coordinate",

(c) in paragraph (b), by the substitution of "advise on" for "ensure",

(d) by the substitution of the following paragraph for paragraph (c):[1] and

(e) by the deletion of paragraph (d).

Amendments

1   See the amended Act.

157   Amendment of section 230 of Act of 2001

Section 230 of the Act of 2001 is amended—

(a) in subsection (1), by the substitution of "11" for "12", and

(b) by the substitution of the following subsection for subsection (3):[1]

Amendments

1   See the amended Act.

158   Minor and consequential amendments of Act of 2001

Each provision of the Act of 2001 specified in Schedule 4 to the Criminal Justice Act 2006 is amended in the manner specified in the third column opposite the mention of that provision in the second column of that Schedule.

PART 13
ANTI-SOCIAL BEHAVIOUR BY CHILDREN

159

New section 257A in Act of 2001

The following title and section is inserted in the Act of 2001 after section 257:[1]

Amendments

1   See the amended Act.

---

160   New section 257B in Act of 2001

The following section is inserted in the Act of 2001 after section 257A:[1]

Amendments

1   See the amended Act.

---

161   New section 257C in Act of 2001

The following section is inserted in the Act of 2001 after section 257B:[1]

Amendments

1   See the amended Act.

---

162   New section 257D in Act of 2001

The following section is inserted in the Act of 2001 after section 257C:[1]

Amendments

1   See the amended Act.

163

New section 257E in Act of 2001

The following section is inserted in the Act of 2001 after section 257D:[1]

Amendments

1   See the amended Act.

164   New section 257F in Act of 2001

The following section is inserted in the Act of 2001 after section 257E:[1]

Amendments

1   See the amended Act.

165   New section 257G in Act of 2001

The following section is inserted in the Act of 2001 after section 257F:[1]

Amendments

1   See the amended Act.

166   New section 257H in Act of 2001

The following section is inserted in the Act of 2001 after section 257G:[1]

Amendments

1   See the amended Act.

PART 14
CRIMINAL LAW CODIFICATION ADVISORY COMMITTEE

167   Criminal Law Codification Advisory Committee

There stands established a body, which shall be known as An Coiste Comhairleach um Chódú an Dlí Choiriúil or, in the English language as, the Criminal Law Codification Advisory Committee and is in this Part referred to as the "Committee", to perform the functions assigned to it by this Act.

168 Functions of Committee

(1) The function of the Committee shall be to oversee the development of a programme for the codification of the criminal law.

(2) Without prejudice to the generality of subsection (1), the Committee shall—

(a) plan, monitor and review the implementation of a programme for the development of a criminal code ("the code"),

(b) advise and assist the Minister on consolidation of areas of criminal law for inclusion in the code,

(c) advise and assist the Minister in relation to the amendment and future maintenance of the code,

(d) undertake or commission, or collaborate or assist in, research projects relating to the codification of criminal law,

(e) consult, on any particular matter which the Committee considers relevant, persons qualified to give opinions thereon,

(f) monitor, review and advise and assist the Minister on international developments in the codification of criminal law in so far as they may be relevant to the development of the code,

(g) advise and assist the Minister on any other related issues, including issues submitted by the Minister to the Committee for consideration.

169 Membership of Committee

(1) The Committee shall consist of the following members, that is to say, a chairperson and such and so many ordinary members as may be appointed from time to time as occasion requires by the Minister.

(2) The members of the Committee shall be appointed by the Minister from among persons who in the opinion of the Minister have experience of, and expertise including Human Rights expertise in relation to, matters connected with the functions of the Committee.

170 Conditions of office of members of Committee

(1) The Minister may at any time, for stated reasons, terminate a person's membership of the Committee.

(2) A member of the Committee may resign his or her membership of the Committee by notice in writing given to the Minister, and the resignation shall take effect on the day on which the Minister receives the notice.

(3) A member of the Committee shall, subject to the provisions of this Part, hold office upon such terms and conditions (including terms and conditions relating to remuneration and allowances for expenses) as the Minister, with the consent of the Minister for Finance, may from time to time determine.

171 Vacancies among members of Committee

If a member of the Committee dies, resigns, or ceases to be a member of the Committee, the Minister may appoint a person to be a member of the Committee to fill the vacancy so occasioned in the same manner as the member of the Committee who occasioned the vacancy was appointed.

172   Meetings and procedure

(1) The Committee shall hold such and so many meetings as may be necessary for the performance of its functions and the achievement of its programme of work and may make such arrangements for the conduct of its meetings and business (including the establishment of subcommittees and the fixing of a quorum for a meeting) as it considers appropriate.

(2) The Committee may act notwithstanding one or more vacan-cies among its members.

(3) Subject to the provisions of this Part, the Committee shall regulate its own procedure by rules or otherwise.

(4) At a meeting of the Committee—

    (a) the chairperson of the Committee shall, if present, be the chairperson of the meeting, or

    (b) if and so long as the chairperson of the Committee is not present, or if that office is vacant, the members of the Committee who are present shall choose one of their number to be chairperson of the meeting.

(5) A member of the Committee, other than the chairperson, who is unable to attend a meeting of the Committee, may nominate a deputy to attend in his or her place.

173   Programme of Work of Committee

(1) The Minister shall, as soon as may be after the commencement of this Part and thereafter, at least once in every 2 years, after consultation with the Committee, determine a programme of work to be undertaken by the Committee over the ensuing specified period.

(2) Notwithstanding subsection (1), the Minister may, from time to time, amend the programme of work, including the period to which the programme relates.

174   Funding of Committee

For the purposes of expenditure by the Committee in the performance of its functions, the Minister may in each financial year, with the consent of the Minister for Finance, advance to the Committee out of moneys provided by the Oireachtas such sum or sums as the Minister, after consultation with the Committee, may determine.

175   Report of Committee

(1) The Committee shall, not later than 3 months after the end of each calendar year, prepare and submit to the Minister a report on the performance of its functions and activities during the preceding year and the Minister shall cause copies of the report to be laid before each House of the Oireachtas within a period of 2 months from the receipt of the report.

(2) A report under subsection (1) shall be in such form as the Minister may approve and shall include information in such form and regarding such matters as the Minister may from time to time direct.

(3) The Committee shall supply to the Minister such information regarding the performance of its functions as the Minister may from time to time require.

PART 15
MISCELLANEOUS

176   Reckless endangerment of children

(1) In this section—

"abuser" means an individual believed by a person who has authority or control over that individual to have seriously harmed or sexually abused a child or more than one child;

"child" means a person under 18 years of age, except where the context otherwise requires;

"serious harm" means injury which creates a substantial risk of death or which causes permanent disfigurement or loss or impairment of the mobility of the body as a whole or of the function of any particular member or organ;

"sexual abuse" means an offence under paragraphs 1 to 13 and 16(a) and (b) of the Schedule to the Sex Offenders Act 2001.

(2) A person, having authority or control over a child or abuser, who intentionally or recklessly endangers a child by—

(a)   causing or permitting any child to be placed or left in a situation which creates a substantial risk to the child of being a victim of serious harm or sexual abuse, or

(b)   failing to take reasonable steps to protect a child from such a risk while knowing that the child is in such a situation,

is guilty of an offence.

(3) Where a person is charged with an offence under subsection (2), no further proceedings in the matter (other than any remand in custody or on bail) shall be taken except by or with the consent of the Director of Public Prosecutions.

(4) A person guilty of an offence under this section is liable on conviction on indictment, to a fine or to imprisonment for a term not exceeding 10 years or both.

177

Restriction of section 10(4) of Petty Sessions (Ireland) Act 1851

(1) The Criminal Justice Act 1951 is amended by the substitution of the following section for section 7:[1]

(2) This section shall not have effect in relation to an offence committed before the commencement of this section.

Amendments

1   See the amended Act.

---

178   Amendment of Courts of Justice Act 1924

The Courts of Justice Act 1924 is amended by the insertion of the following section after section 79:

> **"Exercise of jurisdiction by District Court judges in criminal cases.**
>
> 79A.— (1) Where, in respect of a crime committed in the State—

(a) the accused does not reside in the State,

(b) he or she was not arrested for and charged with the crime in the State, and

(c) either—

    (i) the crime was committed in more than one district court district, or

    (ii) it is known that it was committed in one of not more than five district court districts, but the particular district concerned is not known,

then, for the purposes of section 79 of this Act, the crime shall be deemed to have been committed in each of the districts concerned and a judge assigned to any of the districts concerned may deal with the case.

(2) Where the circumstances of a crime committed in the State fall within paragraphs (a) and (b), but not (c), of subsection (1) of this section and the district court district in which the crime was committed is not known, then, for the purposes of section 79 of this Act, the crime shall be deemed to have been committed in the Dublin Metropolitan District.

(3) A case does not fall within this section unless it is shown that reasonable efforts have been made to ascertain the whereabouts of the accused for the purposes of arresting him or her for and charging him or her with the crime concerned.

(4) Where a judge for the time being assigned to a district court district exercises jurisdiction in a criminal case by virtue of this section, the judge or any other judge assigned to the district shall have jurisdiction in the case until its conclusion in the District Court notwithstanding that it is later established that, but for this subsection, he or she would not have had jurisdiction in the case.

(5) A judge for the time being assigned to a district court district who exercises jurisdiction in a criminal case by virtue of this section may deal with the case in any court area within his or her district.".

179 Amendment of Courts (Supplemental Provisions) Act 1961

The Courts (Supplemental Provisions) Act 1961 is amended—

(a) in section 25(4), by the insertion of "and section 25A of this Act" after "subsection (3) of this section", and

(b) by the insertion of the following section after section 25:[1]

Amendments

1 See the amended Act.

---

180 Exercise of certain powers by judge of District Court outside district court district

The Courts (Supplemental Provisions) Act 1961 is amended by the insertion of the following section after section 32:[1]

Amendments

1   See the amended Act.

181   Anonymity of certain witnesses

(1) Where in any criminal proceedings—

    (a)   it is proposed to call a person to give evidence, and

    (b)   the person has a medical condition,

an application may be made for an order under this section prohibiting the publication of any matter relating to the proceedings which would identify the person as a person having that condition.

(2) An application for such an order may be made at any stage of the proceedings and shall be made—

    (a)   in case the accused person has been sent forward for trial, to the trial judge,

    (b)   in case the proceedings are proceedings on appeal, to the judge, or a judge, of the appeal court,

    (c)   in any other case, to a judge of the District Court.

(3) An order under this section may be made only where the judge concerned is satisfied that—

    (a)   the person concerned has a medical condition,

    (b)   his or her identification as a person with that condition would be likely to cause undue distress to him or her, and

    (c)   the order would not be prejudicial to the interests of justice.

(4) An appeal from a refusal or grant of an application for an order under this section shall lie—

    (a)   in relation to proceedings before the District Court, to a judge of the Circuit Court,

    (b)   in relation to proceedings before the Circuit Criminal Court or a Special Criminal Court, to a judge of the High Court, and

    (c)   in relation to proceedings before the Central Criminal Court or the Court of Criminal Appeal, to a judge of the Supreme Court,

at the instance of the prosecution or the defence.

(5) Where—

    (a)   an accused person is sent forward for trial, and

    (b)   an order has been made by a judge of the District Court under this section,

the trial judge may, on application made in that behalf, vary or revoke the order.

(6) Where—

    (a)   an appeal is being taken against a decision of a court in criminal proceedings, and

    (b)   the trial judge has made an order under this section,

the judge, or a judge, of the appeal court may, on application made in that behalf, vary or revoke the order.

(7) An application under this section, or an appeal under subsection (4), may be made by the prosecution or the defence on notice to the other party to the proceedings and shall be made to the judge concerned in chambers.

(8) Each of the following persons who publishes or broadcasts any matter in contravention of an order under this section is guilty of an offence and is liable on conviction on indictment to a fine not exceeding €25,000 or imprisonment for a term not exceeding 3 years or both:

    (a) if the matter is published in a newspaper or periodical, any proprietor, editor or publisher of the newspaper or periodical;

    (b) if the matter is published otherwise, the person who publishes it; or

    (c) if the matter is broadcast, any person transmitting or providing the programme in which the broadcast is made and any person having functions in relation to the programme corresponding to those of an editor of a newspaper.

(9) Where a person is charged with an offence under subsection (8), it is a defence to prove that at the time of the alleged offence the person was not aware, and neither suspected nor had any reason to suspect, that the publication or broadcast concerned was of any such matter as is mentioned in subsection (1).

(10) (a) Where an offence under subsection (8) has been committed by a body corporate and it is proved to have been so committed with the consent or connivance of or to be attributable to any neglect on the part of any person who, when the offence was committed, was a director, manager, secretary or other officer of the body corporate, or a person purporting to act in any such capacity, that person, as well as the body corporate, shall be guilty of an offence and shall be liable to be proceeded against and punished as if he or she were guilty of the first-mentioned offence.

    (b) Where the affairs of a body corporate are managed by its members, paragraph (a) shall apply in relation to the acts and defaults of a member in connection with the functions of management as if he or she were a director or manager of the body corporate.

(11) In this section—

"broadcast" means the transmission, relaying or distribution by wireless telegraphy of communications, sounds, visual images or signals, intended for reception by the public generally or a section of it, whether the broadcast is so received or not, and cognate words shall be construed accordingly;

"publish" means publish, other than by way of broadcast, to the public generally or a section of it;

"trial judge" and "judge", in relation to proceedings before a Special Criminal Court, means a member of that Court, and the references in subsections (2)(a) and (5)(a) to an accused person being sent forward for trial include, where appropriate, references to such a person being charged before that Court.

182   Information concerning property held in trust

(1) For the purposes of an investigation into whether a person has committed an arrestable offence a member of the Garda Síochána not below the rank of superintendent may apply to a judge of the High Court for an order for the disclosure of information regarding any trust in which the person may have an interest or with which the person may be otherwise connected.

(2) On such an application the judge, if satisfied—

(a) that there are reasonable grounds for suspecting that a person—
  (i) has committed an arrestable offence, and
  (ii) has some interest in or other connection with the trust,
(b) that information regarding the trust is required for the purposes of such an investigation, and
(c) that there are reasonable grounds for believing that it is in the public interest that the information should be disclosed for the purposes of the investigation, having regard to the benefit likely to accrue to the investigation and any other relevant circumstances,

may order the trustees of the trust and any other persons (including the suspected person) to disclose to the applicant or other member of the Garda Síochána designated by the applicant such information as he or she may require for those purposes in relation to the trust, including the identity of the settlor and any or all of the trustees and beneficiaries.

(3) An order under this section—

(a) shall not confer any right to production of, or access to, any information subject to legal privilege, and
(b) shall have effect notwithstanding any other obligation as to secrecy or other restriction on disclosure of information imposed by statute or otherwise.

(4) A judge of the High Court may vary or discharge an order under this section on the application of any person to whom it relates or a member of the Garda Síochána.

(5) A trustee or other person who without reasonable excuse—

(a) fails or refuses to comply with an order under this section, or
(b) discloses information which is false or misleading,

is guilty of an offence and liable—

(i) on summary conviction, to a fine not exceeding €3,000 or imprisonment for a term not exceeding 12 months or both, or
(ii) on conviction on indictment, to a fine or imprisonment for a term not exceeding 5 years or both.

(6) Any information disclosed by a person in accordance with this section is not admissible in evidence in any criminal proceedings against the person or his or her spouse, except in any proceedings for an offence under subsection (5)(b).

(7) In this section "information" includes—

(a) a document or record, and
(b) information in non-legible form.

183   Possession of article intended for use in connection with certain offences

[(1) A person is guilty of an offence if he or she possesses or controls any article in circumstances giving rise to a reasonable inference that he or she possesses or controls it for a purpose connected with the commission, preparation, facilitation or instigation of—

(a) an offence under section 15 of the Non-Fatal Offences against the Person Act 1997,
(b) a drug trafficking offence within the meaning of section 3(1) of the Criminal Justice Act 1994,
(c) murder,
(d) murder to which section 3 of the Criminal Justice Act 1990 applies, or

(e) the common law offence of kidnapping to which section 2 of, and paragraph 4 of the Schedule to, the Criminal Law (Jurisdiction) Act 1976 applies.

(2) It is a defence for a person charged with an offence under this section to prove that at the time of the alleged offence he or she did not possess or control the article concerned for a purpose specified in subsection (1).

(3) Where a person is charged with an offence under this section, no further proceedings in the matter (other than any remand in custody or on bail) may be taken except by or with the consent of the Director of Public Prosecutions.

(4) A person guilty of an offence under this section is liable on conviction on indictment to a fine or to imprisonment for a term not exceeding 5 years or both.

(5) In this section—

"article" means a substance, document or thing;

"document" includes—

(a) a map, plan, graph, drawing, photograph or record, or

(b) a reproduction in permanent legible form, by a computer or other means (including enlarging), of information in non-legible form;

"information in non-legible form" includes information on microfilm, magnetic tape or disk.][1]

Amendments

1   Section 183 substituted by Criminal Justice Act 2007, s 46.

[183A   Possession of monies intended for use in connection with certain offences

(1) A person is guilty of an offence if he or she possesses or controls monies of a value of not less than €5,000 in circumstances giving rise to a reasonable inference that he or she possesses or controls the assets concerned for a purpose connected with the commission, preparation, facilitation or instigation of—

(a) an offence under section 14 of the Criminal Justice (Theft and Fraud Offences) Act 2001,

(b) an offence under section 15 of the Non-Fatal Offences against the Person Act 1997,

(c) a drug trafficking offence within the meaning of section 3(1) of the Criminal Justice Act 1994,

(d) an offence under section 17 of the Criminal Justice (Public Order) Act 1994,

(e) murder,

(f) murder to which section 3 of the Criminal Justice Act 1990 applies, or

(g) the common law offence of kidnapping to which section 2 of, and paragraph 4 of the Schedule to, the Criminal Law (Jurisdiction) Act 1976 applies.

(2) It is a defence for a person charged with an offence under this section to prove that at the time of the alleged offence he or she did not possess or control the assets concerned for a purpose specified in subsection (1).

(3) Where a person is charged with an offence under this section, no further proceedings in the matter (other than any remand in custody or on bail) may be taken except by or with the consent of the Director of Public Prosecutions.

(4) A person guilty of an offence under this section is liable on conviction on indictment to a fine or to imprisonment for a term not exceeding 5 years or both.

(5) In this section—

"monies" means coins and notes in any currency, bank drafts, postal orders, certificates of deposit and any other similar instruments easily convertible into money.]¹

Amendments

1   Section 183A inserted by Criminal Justice Act 2007, s 46.

184   Amendment of Criminal Justice (Public Order) Act 1994

The Criminal Justice (Public Order) Act 1994 is amended by the insertion of the following sections after section 23:¹

Amendments

1   See the amended Act.

185   Amendment of section 19 of Criminal Justice (Public Order) Act 1994

Section 19 of the Criminal Justice (Public Order) Act 1994 is amended—

(a)   by the substitution of the following subsection for subsection (1):¹
(b)   in subsection (2), by the substitution of "€5,000" for "£1,000" and by the substitution of "7 years" for "5 years",
(c)   by the substitution of the following subsection for subsection (3):¹
(d)   in subsection (4), by the substitution of "€2,500" for "£500", and
(e)   in subsection (6)—

   (i)   by the insertion of the following definitions:¹
         and
   (ii) in the definition of "peace officer", by the insertion of ", a member of the fire brigade, ambulance personnel" after "a prison officer".

Amendments

1   See the amended Act.

186 Amendment of section 1 of Criminal Justice (United Nations Convention Against Torture) Act 2000

The definition of "torture" in section 1(1) of the Criminal Justice (United Nations Convention Against Torture) Act 2000 is amended by the insertion after "omission" of "done or made, or at the instigation of, or with the consent or acquiescence of a public official".

187 Amendment of Offences Against the State Act 1939

The Offences Against the State Act 1939 is amended—

a) in section 30, by the insertion of the following subsection after subsection (4C):[1] and

(b) in section 30A—

    (i) in subsection (2)(b), by the substitution of "subsections (4), (4A), (4B) and (4D)" for "subsections (4), (4A) and (4B)", and

    (ii) in subsection (3), by the substitution of "for the purpose of charging him or her with that offence forthwith or bringing him or her before a Special Criminal Court as soon as practicable so that he or she may be charged with that offence before that Court" for "for the purpose of charging him with that offence forthwith".

Amendments

1 See the amended Act.

---

188 Amendment of section 5 of Criminal Evidence Act 1992

(1) Section 5 of the Criminal Evidence Act 1992 is amended in subsection (4)(b) by the insertion of the following subparagraph after subparagraph (ii):[1]

(2) This section shall be deemed to have come into operation on 1 January 2003.

Amendments

1 See the amended Act.

---

189 Amendment of section 16B(7) of Proceeds of Crime Act 1996

Section 16B(7) of the Proceeds of Crime Act 1996 is amended by the insertion of "of the Criminal Assets Bureau Act 1996" after "Sections 14 to 14C".

190 Amendment of section 14 of Criminal Assets Bureau Act 1996

(1) Section 14 of the Criminal Assets Bureau Act 1996 is amended by the substitution of the following subsection for subsection (1):[1]

(2) This section shall not affect the validity of a warrant issued under section 14 of the Criminal Assets Bureau Act 1996 before the commencement of this section and such a warrant shall continue in force in accordance with its terms after such commencement.

Amendments

1   See the amended Act.

191   Amendment of section 5 of Prevention of Corruption (Amendment) Act 2001

(1) Section 5 of the Prevention of Corruption (Amendment) Act 2001 is amended by the substitution of the following subsection for subsection (1):

> "(1) If a judge of the District Court is satisfied by information on oath of a member of the Garda Síochána, or if a member of the Garda Síochána not below the rank of superintendent is satisfied, that there are reasonable grounds for suspecting that evidence of or relating to the commission of an offence or suspected offence under the Prevention of Corruption Acts 1889 to 2001 punishable by imprisonment for a term of 5 years or by a more severe penalty ('an offence') is to be found in any place, he or she may issue a warrant for the search of that place and any persons found at that place.".

(2) This section shall not affect the validity of a warrant issued under section 5 of the Prevention of Corruption (Amendment) Act 2001 before the commencement of this section and such a warrant shall continue in force in accordance with its terms after such commencement.

192   Amendment of Criminal Justice (Theft and Fraud Offences) Act 2001

(1) The Criminal Justice (Theft and Fraud Offences) Act 2001 is amended—

(a)   in section 48, by the substitution of the following subsection for subsection (2):[1] and

(b)   in section 52, by the substitution of the following subsection for subsection (2):[1]

(2) This section shall not affect the validity of a warrant issued under section 48, or an order made under section 52, of the Criminal Justice (Theft and Fraud Offences) Act 2001 before the commencement of this section and such a warrant or order shall continue in force in accordance with its terms after such commencement.

Amendments

1   See the amended Act.

193   Amendment of section 25 of Petty Sessions (Ireland) Act 1851

Section 25 of the Petty Sessions (Ireland) Act 1851 is amended by the substitution of the following paragraph for paragraph 1:[1]

Amendments

1   See the amended Act.

194   Execution of certain warrants

A warrant for the arrest of a person or an order of committal of a person may, notwithstanding section 26 of the Petty Sessions (Ireland) Act 1851, be executed by a member of the Garda Síochána in any part of the State.

195   Imprisonment or distress and sale of goods on conviction on indictment in default of payment of fine

(1) Where on conviction on indictment a fine is imposed a court may order that, in default of due payment of the fine, the person liable to pay the fine shall be imprisoned for a term not exceeding 12 months.

(2) Where on conviction on indictment a fine is imposed on a body corporate, the fine may, in default of due payment, be levied by distress and sale of the goods of the body corporate.

(3) In this section "fine" includes any compensation, costs or expenses in addition to a fine ordered to be paid.[1]

Amendments

1   Section 195 repealed by Fines Act 2010, s 22 which has not yet come into operation (February 2011)..

196   Amendment of section 6(2)(a) of Criminal Law Act 1976

196.— Section 6(2)(a) of the Criminal Law Act 1976 is amended by the substitution of "€3,000" for "£500".

197   Amendment of section 13 of the Criminal Law (Insanity) Act 2006

(1) Section 13 of the Criminal Law (Insanity) Act 2006 is amended by the deletion of subsection (1).

(2) Accordingly the following consequential amendments to that section have effect:

   (a)   subsections (2) to (10) are renumbered as subsections (1) to (9);

   (b)   in the renumbered subsection (4), "subsection (3)" is substituted for "subsection (4)" where it occurs;

   (c)   in the renumbered subsection (6), "subsection (5)" is substituted for "subsection (6)" where it occurs; and

   (d)   in the renumbered subsection (9), "subsection (7) or (8)" is substituted for "subsection (8) or (9)".

SCHEDULE 1
INCREASE OF CERTAIN PENALTIES UNDER FIREARMS ACTS 1925 TO 2000

Section 64

Section of Act	Subject matter	Word(s) deleted	Words substituted
(1)	(2)	(3)	(4)
Amendment of Firearms Act 1925			
12(4)	Register to be kept by firearms dealer	fifty pounds	€3,000
12(5)		twenty-five pounds	€1,500
13(2)	Inspections of stock of firearms dealer	ten pounds	€1,000 or imprisonment for a term not exceeding 6 months or both
21(4)	Search for and seizure of certain firearms, etc.	liable on summary conviction thereof in the case of a first offence to a penalty not exceeding ten pounds, and in the case of a second or any subsequent offence to a penalty not exceeding twenty pounds	liable on summary conviction to a fine not exceeding €1,000 or imprisonment for a term not exceeding 6 months or both
22(2)	Powers of members of Garda Síochána	ten pounds	€1,000
Amendment of Firearms and Offensive Weapons Act 1990			
7(6)(a)	Possession, sale, etc. of silencers	£1,000	€5,000
7(6)(b)		five years	7 years
8(a)	Reckless discharge of firearm	£1,000	€5,000
8(b)		five years	7 years
9(7)(a)	Possession of knives, etc.	£1,000	€5,000
9(7)(b)		£1,000	€5,000
10(3)(a)	Trespassing with knife, etc.	£1,000	€5,000
11(a)	Production of article capable of inflicting serious injury	£1,000	€5,000
12(3)(a)	Power to prohibit manufacture, etc. of offensive weapons	£1,000	€5,000

Section of Act	Subject matter	Word(s) deleted	Words substituted
(1)	(2)	(3)	(4)
12(3)(b)		five years	7 years

Amendment of Firearms (Firearm Certificates for Non-Residents) Act 2000

Section of Act	Subject matter	Word(s) deleted	Words substituted
3(4)(a)	Prohibition of false information and alteration of firearm certificates	£1,000	€2,500
3(4)(b)		£10,000	€20,000

SCHEDULE 2
INCREASE IN CERTAIN PENALTIES UNDER EXPLOSIVES ACT 1875

Section 69

Section of Act	Subject Matter	Words deleted	Words substituted
(1)	(2)	(3)	(4)
4	Making explosives in unauthorised place	to a penalty not exceeding one hundred pounds a day for every day during which he so manufactures	, on summary conviction, to a fine not exceeding €5,000 or, on conviction on indictment, to a fine not exceeding €10,000
5	Keeping explosives	to a penalty not exceeding two shillings for every pound of gunpowder so kept	, on summary conviction, to a fine not exceeding €5,000 or, on conviction on indictment, to a fine not exceeding €10,000
9	Regulation of explosives factories and magazines	to a penalty not exceeding in the case of the first offence fifty pounds, and in the case of a second or any subsequent offence one hundred pounds, and in addition fifty pounds for every day during which such breach continues	, on summary conviction, to a fine not exceeding €5,000 or, on conviction on indictment, to a fine not exceeding €10,000

Section of Act	Subject Matter	Words deleted	Words substituted
(1)	**(2)**	**(3)**	**(4)**
10	General rules for factories and magazines	to a penalty not exceeding ten pounds, and in addition (in the case of a second offence) ten pounds for every day during which such breach continues	, on summary conviction, to a fine not exceeding €5,000 or, on conviction on indictment, to a fine not exceeding €10,000
11	Special rules for regulation of workmen in factories or magazines	forty shillings	€100
13	Devolution and determination of licence	twenty shillings	€50
17	General rules for stores	to a penalty not exceeding ten pounds, and in addition (in the case of a second offence) ten pounds for every day during which such breach continues	, on summary conviction, to a fine not exceeding €5,000 or, on conviction on indictment, to a fine not exceeding €10,000
19	Special rules for regulation of workmen in stores	forty shillings	€100
22	General rules for registered premises	to a penalty not exceeding two shillings for every pound of gunpowder in respect of which, or being on the premises in which, the offence was committed	, on summary conviction, to a fine not exceeding €5,000 or, on conviction on indictment, to a fine not exceeding €10,000
30	Restriction on sale of explosives in highways, etc.	to a penalty not exceeding forty shillings	, on summary conviction, to a fine not exceeding €2,500 or, on conviction on indictment, to a fine not exceeding €5,000
31	Sale of explosives to children	thirteen years	18 years

1289

Section of Act	Subject Matter	Words deleted	Words substituted
(1)	(2)	(3)	(4)
		to a penalty not exceeding five pounds	, on summary conviction, to a fine not exceeding €2,500 or, on conviction on indictment, to a fine not exceeding €5,000
32	Explosives to be sold in closed packages labelled	to a penalty not exceeding forty shillings	, on summary conviction, to a fine not exceeding €2,500 or, on conviction on indictment, to a fine not exceeding €5,000
33	General rules as to packing of explosives for conveyance	to a penalty not exceeding twenty pounds	on summary conviction, to a fine not exceeding €2,500 or, on conviction on indictment, to a fine not exceeding €5,000
34	Bye-laws by harbour authority	pecuniary penalties not exceeding twenty pounds for each offence, and ten pounds for each day during which the offence continues	on summary conviction, a fine not exceeding €5,000 or, on conviction on indictment, a fine not exceeding €10,000
35	Bye-laws by railway and canal company	pecuniary penalties not exceeding twenty pounds of each offence, and ten pounds for each day during which the offence continues	on summary conviction, a fine not exceeding €5,000 or, on conviction on indictment, a fine not exceeding €10,000
36	Bye-laws as to wharves in which explosives loaded or unloaded	pecuniary penalties not exceeding twenty pounds for each offence, and ten pounds for each day during which the offence continues	on summary conviction, a fine not exceeding €5,000 or, on conviction on indictment, a fine not exceeding €10,000
37	Byelaws as to conveyance by road or otherwise	pecuniary penalties not exceeding twenty pounds for each offence, and ten pounds for each day during which the breach continues	on summary conviction, a fine not exceeding €5,000 or, on conviction on indictment, a fine not exceeding €10,000

Section of Act	Subject Matter	Words deleted	Words substituted
(1)	(2)	(3)	(4)
40	Application of Part I to explosives other than gunpowder	to a penalty not exceeding one hundred pounds, and to a further penalty not exceeding two shillings for every pound of such explosive	on summary conviction, to a fine not exceeding €5,000 or, on conviction on indictment, to a fine not exceeding €10,000
43	Manufacture, etc. of specially dangerous explosives	to a penalty not exceeding ten shillings for every pound of such explosive brought in the ship	on summary conviction, to a fine not exceeding €5,000 or, on conviction on indictment, to a fine not exceeding €10,000
		to a penalty not exceeding ten shillings for every pound of such explosive delivered or sold or found in his possession	, on summary conviction, to a fine not exceeding €5,000 or, on conviction on indictment, to a fine not exceeding €10,000
55	Powers of Government inspectors	liable to a penalty not exceeding one hundred pounds for each offence	guilty of an offence and liable, on summary conviction, to a fine not exceeding €1,000
56	Notice to remedy dangerous practices, etc.	to a penalty not exceeding twenty pounds for every day during which he so fails to comply	, on summary conviction, to a fine not exceeding €1,000
63	Notice of accidents	to a penalty not exceeding twenty pounds	, on summary conviction, to a fine not exceeding €5,000 or, on conviction on indictment, to a fine not exceeding €10,000
66	Inquiry into accidents	shall for every such offence incur a penalty not exceeding ten pounds and in the case of a failure to comply with a requisition for making any return or producing any document, not exceeding ten pounds during every day that such failure continues	is guilty of an offence and liable on summary conviction, to a fine not exceeding €5,000 or, on conviction on indictment, to a fine not exceeding €10,000

Section of Act	Subject Matter	Words deleted	Words substituted
(1)	(2)	(3)	(4)
69	Duty and power of local authority	to a penalty not exceeding twenty pounds	, on summary conviction, to a fine not exceeding €1,000
73	Search for explosives	to a penalty not exceeding fifty pounds	, on summary conviction, to a fine not exceeding €1,000
74	Seizure and detention of explosives	to a penalty not exceeding fifty pounds	, on summary conviction, to a fine not exceeding €5,000 or, on conviction on indictment, to a fine not exceeding €10,000
77	Penalty on and removal of trespassers	to a penalty not exceeding five pounds	, on summary conviction, to a fine not exceeding €3,000 or, on conviction on indictment, to a fine not exceeding €5,000
		to a penalty not exceeding fifty pounds	, on summary conviction, to a fine not exceeding €5,000 or, on conviction on indictment, to a fine not exceeding €10,000
79	Imprisonment for wilful act or neglect endangering life or limb	of the case, to imprisonment, with or without hard labour, for a period not exceeding six months	of the case— (a) on summary conviction, to imprisonment for a term not exceeding 12 months or both the pecuniary penalty and such imprisonment, or (b) on conviction on indictment, to imprisonment for a term not exceeding 5 years or both the pecuniary penalty and such imprisonment

Section of Act	Subject Matter	Words deleted	Words substituted
(1)	(2)	(3)	(4)
81	Forgery and falsification of documents	to imprisonment, with or without hard labour, for a term not exceeding two years	on summary conviction, to a fine not exceeding €5,000 or imprisonment for a term not exceeding 12 months or both or, on conviction on indictment, to a fine not exceeding €10,000 or imprisonment for a term not exceeding five years or both
82	Defacing notices	two pounds	€100

SCHEDULE 3
OFFENCES FOR THE PURPOSES OF RESTRICTION ON MOVEMENT ORDERS
Section 101

1 Criminal Justice (Public Order) Act 1994

section 6 (threatening, abusive or insulting behaviour in public place)

section 8 (failure to comply with direction of member of Garda Síochána)

section 11 (entering building, etc., with intent to commit an offence)

section 13 (trespass on building, etc.)

section 16 (affray)

section 19 (assault or obstruction of peace officer)

2 Non-Fatal Offences Against the Person Act 1997

section 2 (assault)

section 3 (assault causing harm)

section 9 (coercion)

section 10 (harassment)

SCHEDULE 4
MINOR AND CONSEQUENTIAL AMENDMENTS OF CHILDREN ACT 2001
Section 158

Amendment No.	Section of Act	Amendment
1.	4, 5(2), 6	", the Minister for Education and Science" deleted.
2.	22, 24(2), 25, 26(1) and (2), 28(2)(a), 30(3)(a), 32, 38(f), 39(3)(i)	"or anti-social" inserted after "criminal".
3.	28(2)(c)	"or engaging in further anti-social behaviour" inserted after "offences".
4.	31(2)(b), 39(3)(h)	"or further criminal or anti-social behaviour by the child" after "offences".

Amendment No.	Section of Act	Amendment
5.	54	Section deleted.
6.	71(1)(a)	"Parts 8 and 12A" substituted for "Part 8".
7.	95	Definition of "children detention centre" deleted.
8.	98(h)	"or children detention centre" deleted.
9.	103(1)	Paragraph (c) deleted.
10.	103(1)(e)	"or children detention centre" and "or person for the time being in charge of the centre, as appropriate" deleted.
11.	142	"or children detention centre" deleted.
12.	143	", in the case of a child under 16 years of age," deleted.
13.	145	"under 16 years of age" deleted.
14.	147	Section deleted.
15.	150	Section deleted.
16.	151(1)	"who is between 16 and 18 years of age" deleted.
17.	151(2) and 151(3)	"children detention school" substituted for "children detention centre".
18.	152	Section deleted.
19.	153	Section deleted.
20.	154	", in any children detention centre designated under section 150 of the Children Act, 2001," deleted.
21.	158	"appropriate educational, training and other programmes and facilities" substituted for "educational and training programmes and facilities".
22.	167(4)(c)	"Minister for Education and Science" substituted for "Minister for Justice, Equality and Law Reform".
23.	179	"with the consent of the Minister" inserted after "time".
24.	187	Section deleted.
25.	188	Section deleted.
26.	189	Section deleted.
27.	203(3)	"Minister and" inserted before "board of management" and "the board's" deleted.

Amendment No.	Section of Act	Amendment
28.	204(9)	"Minister and" inserted before "board of management" and "board's" deleted.
29.	214	Subsection (2) deleted.
30.	225(2)	"Minister for Justice, Equality and Law Reform" substituted for "Minister for Education and Science".
31.	263	"(a) while in transit to a court from a remand centre or children detention school," substituted for paragraph (a). "(c) while awaiting removal pursuant to this Act to a remand centre or children detention school." substituted for paragraph (c).
32.	265	"or a place of detention designated under section 150" deleted.

Criminal Law (Sexual Offences) (Amendment) Act 2007

Number 6 of 2007

ARRANGEMENT OF SECTIONS
1. Definitions.
2. Soliciting or importuning for purposes of commission of sexual offence.
3. Application of certain enactments.
4. Amendment of certain enactments.
5. Amendment of Act of 2006.
6. Meeting child for purpose of sexual exploitation.
7. Short title.

AN ACT TO AMEND THE CRIMINAL LAW (SEXUAL OFFENCES) ACT 1993, THE CHILD TRAFFICKING AND PORNOGRAPHY ACT 1998 AND THE CRIMINAL LAW (SEXUAL OFFENCES) ACT 2006; AND TO PROVIDE FOR MATTERS CONNECTED THEREWITH.

[7th March, 2007]

BE IT ENACTED BY THE OIREACHTAS AS FOLLOWS:

1   Definitions

In this Act—

"Act of 1981" means Criminal Law (Rape) Act 1981;

"Act of 1990" means the Criminal Law (Rape) (Amendment) Act 1990;

"Act of 1993" means the Criminal Law (Sexual Offences) Act 1993;

"Act of 2006" means the Criminal Law (Sexual Offences) Act 2006.

2   Soliciting or importuning for purposes of commission of sexual offence

The Act of 1993 is amended by the substitution of the following section for section 6 (inserted by section 250 of the Children Act 2001):

Amendments

1   See the amended Act.

---

3   Application of certain enactments

(1) Section 4A of the Act of 1981 is amended, in subsection (6), by the insertion after "an offence under the Criminal Law (Sexual Offences) Act 2006 " (inserted by section 6(2) of the Act of 2006) of "an offence under section 6 of the Criminal Law (Sexual Offences) Act 1993".

(2) References in section 3 of the Act of 1981 to jury shall, in the case of summary proceedings for an offence under section 6 (inserted by section 2), be construed as references to court.

(3) Sections 3, 4, 6, 7 and 8 of the Act of 1981 shall apply to an offence under section 6 of the Act of 1993 subject to the modification that references in any of those sections to—

  (a) sexual assault offence shall be construed as including references to an offence under section 6 of the Act of 1993, and

  (b) rape offence shall be construed as including references to an offence under section 6 of the Act of 1993.

(4) Section 26 of the Civil Legal Aid Act 1995 is amended, in subsection (3)(b), by the substitution of "an offence under section 6 (inserted by section 2 of the Criminal Law (Sexual Offences)(Amendment) Act 2007) of the Criminal Law (Sexual Offences) Act 1993, or of an offence under the Criminal Law (Sexual Offences) Act 2006 " for "unlawful carnal knowledge under section 1 or 2 of the Criminal Law Amendment Act, 1935 ".

4   Amendment of certain enactments

(1) Section 2 of the Criminal Evidence Act 1992 is amended, in the definition of "sexual offence", by the insertion of the following paragraph: [1]

(2) The Schedule to the Sexual Offences (Jurisdiction) Act 1996 is amended by the insertion of the following paragraph: [1]

(3) The Schedule to the Bail Act 1997 is amended by the insertion of the following paragraph: [1]

(4) The Schedule to the Sex Offenders Act 2001 is amended by the insertion of the following paragraph: [1]

Amendments

1   See the amended Act.

5   Amendment of Act of 2006

(1) Section 3 of the Act of 2006 is amended—

  (a) in paragraph (a) of subsection (2), by the substitution of "5 years" for "2 years",

  (b) in paragraph (b) of subsection (2), by the substitution of "10 years" for "4 years",

  (c) in paragraph (a) of subsection (4), by the substitution of "10 years" for "4 years", and

  (d) in paragraph (b) of subsection (4), by the substitution of "15 years" for "7 years".

(2) Section 6 of the Act of 2006 is amended by the insertion of the following subsection: [1]

Amendments

1   See the amended Act.

6   Meeting child for purpose of sexual exploitation

Section 3 of the Child Trafficking and Pornography Act 1998 is amended by—

    (a)   the insertion of the following subsections:[1]
        and

    (b)   the substitution of the following subsection for subsection (3):[1]

Amendments

1   See the amended Act.

7   Short title

This Act may be cited as the Criminal Law (Sexual Offences) (Amendment) Act 2007.

Prisons Act 2007

Number 10 of 2007

ARRANGEMENT OF SECTIONS
Only Parts 1 and 6 are reproduced here

PART 1
PRELIMINARY AND GENERAL

Section

1. Short title, commencement and collective citation.

2. Interpretation (general).

3. Expenses.

....

PART 6
MISCELLANEOUS

33. Certain applications to court to be heard using videolink.

34. Application of section 33 to children in remand centres or children detention schools and other detained persons.

35. Prison rules.

36. Prohibition of unauthorised possession or use of mobile telecommunications device by prisoner.

37. Amendment of National Minimum Wage Act 2000.

38. Payment by prisoners for requested services.

39. Absence from prison on compassionate, etc., grounds.

40. Lawful custody of prisoners while absent from prison.

41. Minor and consequential amendments.

42. Repeals.

43. Regulations.

AN ACT TO ENABLE THE MINISTER FOR JUSTICE, EQUALITY AND LAW REFORM TO ENTER INTO AGREEMENTS FOR THE PROVISION OF SERVICES RELATING TO THE ESCORT OF PRISONERS BY PERSONS OTHER THAN PRISON OFFICERS; TO PROVIDE FOR THE CONDUCT OF INQUIRIES BY GOVERNORS OF PRISONS INTO ALLEGED BREACHES OF DISCIPLINE BY PRISONERS, FOR THE SANCTIONS THAT MAY BE IMPOSED AFTER SUCH INQUIRIES AND FOR THE ESTABLISHMENT OF APPEAL TRIBUNALS TO HEAR APPEALS AGAINST FORFEITURES SO IMPOSED OF REMISSION OF PORTION OF SENTENCES; TO ENABLE SPECIAL REQUIREMENTS TO BE PROVIDED FOR IN RELATION TO THE CONSTRUCTION OR EXTENSION OF PRISONS AND OTHER PLACES OF DETENTION, INCLUDING APPROVAL THEREOF BY A RESOLUTION OF EACH HOUSE OF THE OIREACHTAS AND CONFIRMATION BY ACT OF THE OIREACHTAS OF THE RESOLUTION; TO PROVIDE FOR THE

APPOINTMENT OF AN INSPECTOR OF PRISONS; TO PROVIDE FOR THE GIVING OF EVIDENCE BY PRISONERS IN CERTAIN TYPES OF PROCEEDINGS BEFORE THE COURTS BY LIVE TELEVISION LINK; TO AMEND AND REPEAL CERTAIN ENACTMENTS IN RELATION TO PRISONS AND PRISONERS AND TO PROVIDE FOR MATTERS CONNECTED THEREWITH. [31st March, 2007]

BE IT ENACTED BY THE OIREACHTAS AS FOLLOWS:

PART 1
PRELIMINARY AND GENERAL

1   Short title, commencement and collective citation

(1) This Act may be cited as the Prisons Act 2007.

(2) This Act shall come into operation on such day or days as the Minister may appoint by order or orders either generally or with reference to any particular purpose or provision, and different days may be so appointed for different purposes or provisions.

(3) This Act and the Prisons Acts 1826 to 1980 may be cited together as the Prisons Acts 1826 to 2007.

2   Interpretation (general)

In this Act—

" governor " means the governor of a prison or an officer of the prison acting on his or her behalf;

" Minister " means the Minister for Justice, Equality and Law Reform;

" prison " means a place of custody administered by or on behalf of the Minister (other than a Garda Síochána station) and includes—

(a)   St. Patrick's Institution,

(b)   a place provided under section 2 of the Prisons Act 1970,

(c)   a place specified under section 3 of the Prisons Act 1972;

" prisoner " means a person who is ordered by a court to be detained in a prison and includes a prisoner who is in lawful custody outside a prison;

" prison rules " means any rules for the government of prisons made under section 35 or other enactment and in force at a material time.

3   Expenses

The expenses incurred by the Minister in the administration of this Act shall, to such extent as may be sanctioned by the Minister for Finance, be paid out of moneys provided by the Oireachtas.

....

PART 6
MISCELLANEOUS

33   Certain applications to court to be heard using videolink

(1) This section applies to an application to a court in criminal proceedings where—

(a) the application is one of those specified in subsection (11),

(b) the accused or person convicted of the offence concerned ("the prisoner") is in a prison,

(c) the application is made or to be made by the Director of Public Prosecutions or by the prisoner, and

(d) the prisoner is legally represented or has obtained legal advice or been given the opportunity of obtaining or being provided with such advice.

(2) An application to which this section applies may be heard without the prisoner being present in court if the court so directs on being satisfied that—

(a) to do so would not be prejudicial to the prisoner,

(b) the interests of justice do not require his or her presence at the hearing,

(c) the facilities provided by a live television link between the court and the prison concerned are such as to enable—

    (i) the prisoner to participate in, and to view and hear, the proceedings before the court,

    (ii) those present in the court to see and hear the prisoner, and

    (iii) the prisoner and his or her legal representative to communicate in confidence during the hearing,

(d) to do so is otherwise appropriate having regard to—

    (i) the nature of the application,

    (ii) the complexity of the hearing,

    (iii) the age of the prisoner, and

    (iv) his or her mental and physical capacity,

and

(e) no other circumstances exist that warrant the prisoner's presence in court for the hearing.

(3) An application for such a direction may be made ex parte to the judge, or a judge, of the court concerned by or on behalf of the Director of Public Prosecutions or the prisoner.

(4) On such an application the judge, if he or she considers it desirable in the interests of justice to do so, may require notice of the application to be given to the prisoner or his or her legal representative or, as the case may be, to the Director of Public Prosecutions.

(5) Where the court decides not to give a direction under this section, it shall state its reasons for not doing so.

(6) At any time after a direction under this section is given, an application may be made to the court by or on behalf of the prisoner to revoke the direction on the ground that one or more than one of the considerations mentioned in paragraphs (a) to (e) of subsection (2) do not apply in the prisoner's case.

(7) The court may at any time revoke a direction, whether on an application under subsection (6) or not.

(8) If, on an application under subsection (6), the court refuses to revoke a direction, it shall state its reasons for the refusal.

(9) Where the provisions of this section are complied with in relation to the hearing of an application to which this section applies, the prisoner is deemed to be present in court for the

purposes of any enactment or rule of law or order of any court requiring the presence in court of an accused or convicted person during criminal proceedings against him or her.

(10) Nothing in this section affects the right of the prisoner to be present during any criminal proceedings other than the hearing of an application to which this section applies.

(11) The following applications (other than applications under subsections (3) and (6)) are specified for the purposes of subsection (1):

    (a) an application for bail or free legal aid;

    (b) in relation to proceedings on indictment, any other application except—

        (i) an application made at the commencement of the trial,

        (ii) an application relating to the arraignment or sentence of the prisoner, or

        (iii) any other application that appears to the court to require the presence of the prisoner at the hearing, including—

            (I) an application relating to the capacity of the prisoner to stand trial, or

            (II) an application to dismiss the charges against the prisoner on the ground that there is not sufficient evidence to put him or her on trial;

    (c) in relation to proceedings in the District Court, any other application to the Court before the date on which—

        (i) a trial before it begins or the court accepts a plea of guilty, or

        (ii) the accused is sent forward for trial or sentence;

    (d) any application in appeal proceedings or any subsequent proceedings.

(12) In this section "criminal proceedings" means proceedings for an offence and includes any appeal proceedings or subsequent proceedings.

34   Application of section 33 to children in remand centres or children detention schools and other detained persons

Section 33 also applies to an application to a court in criminal proceedings where the accused or person convicted of the offence concerned is in a remand centre, or a children detention school, within the meaning of the Children Act 2001 or, where the Minister for Health and Children, after consultation with the Minister, by order so directs, a designated centre within the meaning of the Criminal Law (Insanity) Act 2006 and has effect accordingly, with the necessary modifications.

35   Prison rules

(1) The Minister may make rules for the regulation and good government of prisons.

(2) Without prejudice to the generality of subsection (1) and to Part 3, such rules may provide for—

    (a) the duties and conduct of the governor and officers of a prison,

    (b) the classification of prisoners,

    (c) the treatment of prisoners, including their diets, clothing, maintenance, employment, instruction, discipline and correction,

    (d) the provision of facilities and services to prisoners, including educational facilities, medical services and services relating to their general moral and physical welfare,

    (e) the acts which constitute breaches of prison discipline committed by prisoners while inside a prison or outside it in the custody of a prison officer or prisoner custody officer,

(f)   the remission of portion of a prisoner's sentence,

(g)   the manner of publication of decisions of an Appeal Tribunal,

(h)   the entry to a prison of a member of the Garda Síochána in the performance of his or her functions,

(i)   photographing and measuring prisoners and taking fingerprints and palmprints from them, and

(j)   testing prisoners for intoxicants, including alcohol and other drugs.

(3) The governor of a prison or an officer of the prison acting on his or her behalf may give to a member of the Garda Síochána copies of—

(a)   photographs, measurements, fingerprints or palmprints obtained in accordance with rules under this section, and

(b)   documents relating to the testing of prisoners under subsection (2)(j).

(4) Rules under this section shall be laid before each House of the Oireachtas as soon as may be after they are made and, if a resolution annulling the rules is passed by either such House within the next 21 days on which the House has sat after they are laid before it, the rules shall be annulled accordingly, but without prejudice to the validity of anything previously done thereunder.

(5) Rules under section 12 of the General Prisons (Ireland) Act 1877 and the Prisons (Ireland) Act 1907, and regulations made under section 8 of the Penal Servitude Act 1891, that were in force immediately before the commencement of this section by virtue of section 19(8) of the Criminal Justice (Miscellaneous Provisions) Act 1997 shall continue in force as if made under this section and may be amended or revoked accordingly.

36   Prohibition of unauthorised possession or use of mobile telecommunications device by prisoner

(1) A prisoner who, without the permission of the governor of the prison, possesses or uses a mobile telecommunications device, or a person who supplies such a device to a prisoner without such permission, is guilty of an offence and liable—

(a)   on summary conviction, to a fine not exceeding €5,000 or imprisonment for a term not exceeding 12 months or both, or

(b)   on conviction on indictment, to a fine not exceeding €10,000 or imprisonment for a term not exceeding 5 years or both.

(2) Subsection (1) applies also to a prisoner while in custody outside the prison.

(3) In this section "mobile telecommunications device" includes a component of such a device.

37   Amendment of National Minimum Wage Act 2000

Section 5 of the National Minimum Wage Act 2000 is amended by the numbering of the section as subsection (1) and the insertion of the following subsection:

"(2) This Act does not apply to any non-commercial activity or work engaged in by prisoners under the supervision of the governor or person in charge of the prison concerned, including—

(a)   any cleaning or kitchen work or other work relating to the operation of the prison;

(b) activity of an educational, training or work experience nature which is intended to prepare prisoners for their re-integration into society;

(c) the production of goods or services which are—

(i) sold or provided for the purpose of raising funds for charitable purposes or providing facilities for prisoners, or

(ii) disposed of or provided without charge or for a nominal charge.

38 Payment by prisoners for requested services

The Minister may provide, by prison rules or otherwise, that prisoners shall pay (whether directly or by way of credit deduction) for specified goods or services requested by them that are not available without charge to prisoners generally, including—

(a) telephone calls,

(b) access to electronic devices,

(c) private medical treatment, or

(d) escorts provided outside the prison for matters not related to the imprisonment of those prisoners,

but the payments or deductions shall not exceed the full cost of providing the goods or services.

39 Absence from prison on compassionate, etc., grounds

(1) The Minister may—

(a) on compassionate grounds, or

(b) for the purpose of assessing a prisoner's suitability for early release or facilitating his or her re-integration into society, or

(c) to enable a prisoner to assist in the investigation of an offence,

order that he or she be taken to a specified person or place within the State for a specified purpose during a specified period and return at the end of that period.

(2) The order may provide that the prisoner shall be returned to the prison forthwith if, during the period so specified—

(a) the prisoner is not of good behaviour,

(b) a breach of the peace involving the prisoner occurs, or

(c) he or she attempts to escape from lawful custody or is helped by another person in so attempting.

40 Lawful custody of prisoners while absent from prison

(1) A prisoner who—

(a) is absent from a prison pursuant to an order under section 39 or another enactment or an order of a court, or

(b) is being brought to or from a prison or court,

may be placed in the custody of a prison officer, a prisoner custody officer or a member of the Garda Síochána.

(2) A prisoner in such custody is deemed to be in lawful custody.

41   Minor and consequential amendments

(1) Section 13(3) of the Criminal Justice Act 1960 is amended by—

  (a)   the substitution of the following paragraph for paragraph (a):
        and

  (b)   the insertion of the following paragraph:

 (2) Section 22(3) of the Criminal Procedure Act 1967 is amended by the insertion of ", by the governor of the prison to which the person has been committed or a prison officer designated by the governor" after "justice of the Court".

(3) Section 3(3) of the Criminal Justice Act 1990 is amended by the substitution of the following definition for the definition of "prison officer":

(4) Section 19(6) of the Criminal Justice (Public Order) Act 1994 is amended by the substitution of the following definition for the definition of "prison officer":

42   Repeals

The following enactments are repealed:

  (a)   section 3(3) of the Prisons (Visiting Committees) Act 1925;

  (b)   section 1(2) of the Prisons Act 1933;

  (c)   section 19 of the Criminal Justice (Miscellaneous Provisions) Act 1997.

43   Regulations

(1) The Minister may make regulations for the purpose of giving full effect to this Act.

(2) The regulations may contain such consequential, supplementary or incidental provisions as may be necessary or expedient for that purpose.

Criminal Justice Act 2007

Number 29 of 2007

ARRANGEMENT OF SECTIONS

PART 1
PRELIMINARY AND GENERAL

1. Short title, collective citations, construction and commencement.
2. Definitions.
3. Repeals.
4. Expenses.

PART 2
AMENDMENT OF ENACTMENTS RELATING TO BAIL

5. Amendment of section 1 of Act of 1997.
6. Statement by applicants for bail charged with serious offences.
7. Evidence in applications for bail under section 2.
8. Amendment of section 5 of Act of 1997.
9. Amendment of section 6 of Act of 1997.
10. Application of section 6 in relation to certain appellants.
11. Electronic monitoring of certain persons admitted to bail.
12. Evidence of electronic monitoring.
13. Arrangements for electronic monitoring.
14. Amendment of section 8 of Act of 1997.
15. Estreatment of recognisance and forfeiture of moneys paid into court.
16. Regulations.
17. Amendment of Schedule to Act of 1997.
18. Amendment of section 22 of Act of 1967.
19. Amendment of section 28 of Act of 1967.
20. Amendment of section 31 of Act of 1967.
21. Amendment of section 68 of Children Act 2001.
22. Amendment of section 11 of Act of 1984.
23. Amendment of section 13 of Act of 1984.

PART 3
SENTENCING

24. Interpretation (Part 3).
25. Commission of another offence within specified period.
26. Monitoring orders and protection of persons orders.
26A Post-release orders in cases of certain offences.
27. Amendment of Criminal Justice (Legal Aid) Act 1962.

Part 4
Inferences to be Drawn in Certain Circumstances

28.   Inferences from failure or refusal to account for objects, marks, etc.

29.   Inferences from failure or refusal to account for accused's presence at a particular place.

30.   Inferences from failure of accused to mention particular facts.

31.   Amendment of section 2 of Offences Against the State (Amendment) Act 1998.

32.   Regulations.

Part 5
Misuse of Drugs

33.   Amendment of section 27 of Misuse of Drugs Act 1977.

Part 6
Amendment of Firearms Acts 1925 to 2006

34.   Amendment of section 2 of Act of 1925.

35.   Amendment of section 15 of Act of 1925.

36.   Amendment of section 26 of Act of 1964.

37.   Amendment of section 27 of Act of 1964.

38.   Amendment of section 27A of Act of 1964.

39.   Amendment of section 27B of Act of 1964.

40.   Amendment of section 12A of Act of 1990.

Part 7
Amendment of Garda Síochána Act 2005

41.   Establishment and functions of Garda Síochána Executive Management Board.

42.   Special inquiries relating to Garda Síochána.

43.   Other amendments to Act of 2005.

Part 8
Amendments to the Sea-Fisheries Acts 2003 and 2006

44.   Amendments to Sea-Fisheries Acts 2003 and 2006.

Part 9
Miscellaneous

45.   Amendment of Garda Síochána (Complaints) Act 1986.

46.   Amendment of Act of 2006.

47.   Amendment of section 15 of Criminal Justice (Theft and Fraud Offences) Act 2001.

48.   Amendment of Act of 1984.

49.   Destruction of records.

50.   Powers of detention for specified offences.

51.   Rearrest.

52.   Application of certain provisions of Act of 1984.

53.   Amendment of Criminal Justice (Forensic Evidence) Act 1990.

54.   Amendment of section 5 of Criminal Justice (Drug Trafficking) Act 1996.

55.   Amendment of section 9 of Act of 1984.

56.   Copy of recording of questioning by Garda Síochána to be given to accused.

57.   Admission in evidence of recording of questioning of accused by Garda Síochána.

58.   Amendment of section 8 of Criminal Assets Bureau Act 1996.

59.   Amendment of section 29 of Courts of Justice Act 1924.

60.   Amendment of section 99 of Act of 2006.

SCHEDULE 1

ENACTMENTS REPEALED

SCHEDULE 2

OFFENCES FOR THE PURPOSES OF PART 3

AN ACT TO AMEND CERTAIN ENACTMENTS, INCLUDING THE BAIL ACT 1997, THE CRIMINAL JUSTICE ACT 1984, THE CRIMINAL JUSTICE (LEGAL AID) ACT 1962, THE OFFENCES AGAINST THE STATE (AMENDMENT) ACT 1998, THE MISUSE OF DRUGS ACT 1977, THE FIREARMS ACTS 1925 TO 2006, THE GARDA SÍOCHÁNA ACT 2005, THE CRIMINAL JUSTICE ACT 2006, THE CRIMINAL ASSETS BUREAU ACT 1996 AND THE SEA-FISHERIES ACTS 2003 AND 2006, TO AMEND THE LAW IN RELATION TO SENTENCING IN CERTAIN RESPECTS, TO MAKE PROVISION IN RELATION TO THE ADMINISTRATION OF CAUTIONS BY MEMBERS OF THE GARDA SÍOCHÁNA TO PERSONS IN RELATION TO OFFENCES, TO PROVIDE FOR ADDITIONAL POWERS OF DETENTION BY THE GARDA SÍOCHÁNA OF PERSONS SUSPECTED OF CERTAIN OFFENCES FOLLOWING ARREST OR REARREST OF SUCH PERSONS IN CONNECTION WITH THE INVESTIGATION OF SUCH OFFENCES, AND TO PROVIDE FOR RELATED MATTERS. [9th May, 2007]

BE IT ENACTED BY THE OIREACHTAS AS FOLLOWS:

PART 1

PRELIMINARY AND GENERAL

1   Short title, collective citations, construction and commencement

(1) This Act may be cited as the Criminal Justice Act 2007.

(2) This Act (other than Part 8) comes into operation on such day or days as the Minister may appoint by order or orders either generally or with reference to any particular purpose or provision, and different days may be so appointed for different purposes or different provisions.

(3) The Bail Act 1997 and Part 2 may be cited together as the Bail Acts 1997 and 2007.

(4) The Misuse of Drugs Acts 1977 to 2006 and Part 5 may be cited together as the Misuse of Drugs Acts 1977 to 2007 and shall be construed together as one.

(5) The Firearms Acts 1925 to 2006 and Part 6 may be cited together as the Firearms Acts 1925 to 2007 and shall be construed together as one.

(6) The Garda Síochána Act 2005 and Part 7 may be cited together as the Garda Síochána Acts 2005 to 2007.

(7) The Sea-Fisheries Acts 2003 and 2006 and Part 8 may be cited together as the Sea-Fisheries Acts 2003 to 2007.

2   Definitions

In this Act—

"Act of 1925" means Firearms Act 1925;

"Act of 1964" means Firearms Act 1964;

"Act of 1967" means Criminal Procedure Act 1967;

"Act of 1984" means Criminal Justice Act 1984;

"Act of 1990" means Firearms and Offensive Weapons Act 1990;

"Act of 1997" means Bail Act 1997;

"Act of 2005" means Garda Síochána Act 2005;

"Act of 2006" means Criminal Justice Act 2006;

"explosive" means an explosive within the meaning of the Explosives Act 1875 and any other substance or thing that is an explosive substance within the meaning of the Explosive Substances Act 1883;

"firearm" has the meaning it has in section 1 of the Act of 1925;

"Minister" means Minister for Justice, Equality and Law Reform.

3   Repeals

(1) Subject to subsection (2), the enactments specified in Schedule 1 are repealed to the extent specified in column 3 of that Schedule.

(2) The repeal by subsection (1) of the enactments specified in Schedule 1 does not affect the application of those enactments to a failure to mention a fact to which those enactments relate if the failure occurred before the repeal comes into operation, and those enactments apply to such a failure as if they had not been repealed.

4   Expenses

The expenses incurred by the Minister in the administration of this Act shall, to such extent as may be sanctioned by the Minister for Finance, be paid out of moneys provided by the Oireachtas.

PART 2
AMENDMENT OF ENACTMENTS RELATING TO BAIL

5   Amendment of section 1 of Act of 1997

Section 1 of the Act of 1997 is amended in subsection (1) by the insertion of the following definitions:

"'authorised person' means a person who is appointed in writing by the Minister, or a person who is one of a prescribed class of persons, to be an authorised person for the purposes of sections 6B and 6C;

'Minister' means Minister for Justice, Equality and Law Reform;

'prescribed' means prescribed by regulations made by the Minister;".

6   Statement by applicants for bail charged with serious offences

The Act of 1997 is amended by the insertion of the following section after section 1:[1]

Amendments

1   See the amended Act.

7   Evidence in applications for bail under section 2

The Act of 1997 is amended by the insertion of the following section after section 2:[1]

Amendments

1   See the amended Act.

8   Amendment of section 5 of Act of 1997

Section 5 of the Act of 1997 is amended—

(a)   in subsection (1), by the substitution of "any moneys to be paid into court under a recognisance" for "any recognisance",

(b)   in subsection (2), by the substitution of the following paragraph for paragraph (a):[1] and

(c)   in subsection (3), by the substitution of "moneys paid" for "recognisance paid".

Amendments

1   See the amended Act.

9   Amendment of section 6 of Act of 1997

Section 6 of the Act of 1997 is amended—

(a)   in subsection (1), by the substitution of the following paragraph for paragraph (a):[1] and

(b)   by the insertion of the following subsection after subsection (3):[1]

Amendments

1   See the amended Act.

10   Application of section 6 in relation to certain appellants

The Act of 1997 is amended by the insertion of the following section after section 6:[1]

Amendments

1   See the amended Act.

11   Electronic monitoring of certain persons admitted to bail

The Act of 1997 is amended by the insertion of the following section after section 6A:[1]

Amendments

1   See the amended Act.

12   Evidence of electronic monitoring

The Act of 1997 is amended by the insertion of the following section after section 6B:[1]

Amendments

1   See the amended Act.

13   Arrangements for electronic monitoring

The Act of 1997 is amended by the insertion of the following section after section 6C:[1]

Amendments

1   See the amended Act.

14   Amendment of section 8 of Act of 1997

Section 8 of the Act of 1997 is amended—

    (a)   in subsection (1), by the insertion of "(if any)" after "amounts",

(b) in subsection (2), by the substitution of "any moneys conditioned to be paid under a recognisance" for "any recognisance", and

(c) in subsection (3), by the substitution of "where the courthouse at which the arrested person is conditioned to appear is situate" for "in which the Garda Síochána station is situate".

15   Estreatment of recognisance and forfeiture of moneys paid into court

The Act of 1997 is amended by the substitution of the following section for section 9:[1]

Amendments

1   See the amended Act.

16   Regulations

The Act of 1997 is amended by the insertion of the following section after section 11:[1]

Amendments

1   See the amended Act.

17   Amendment of Schedule to Act of 1997

The Schedule to the Act of 1997 is amended—

(a) by the substitution of the following paragraph for paragraph 14:[1]

(b) by the substitution of the following paragraph for paragraph 16: [1]

(c) by the insertion of the following paragraph after paragraph 16:[1]
    and

(d) by the substitution of the following paragraph for paragraph 30:[1]

Amendments

1   See the amended Act.

18   Amendment of section 22 of Act of 1967

Section 22 of the Act of 1967 is amended—

(a) by the insertion of the following subsection after subsection (1): [1]

(b) by the substitution of the following subsections for subsections (2) and (3): [1]

Amendments

1 See the amended Act.

19 Amendment of section 28 of Act of 1967

Section 28 of the Act of 1967 is amended by the substitution of the following subsection for subsection (3):[1]

Amendments

1 See the amended Act.

20 Amendment of section 31 of Act of 1967

Section 31 of the Act of 1967 is amended by the substitution of the following subsection for subsection (3):[1]

Amendments

1 See the amended Act.

21 Amendment of section 68 of Children Act 2001

Section 68 of the Children Act 2001 is amended by the substitution of the following subsection for subsection (4):[1]

Amendments

1 See the amended Act.

22 Amendment of section 11 of Act of 1984

Section 11 of the Act of 1984 is amended by the substitution of the following subsection for subsection (1): [1]

Amendments

1 See the amended Act.

Amendment of section 13 of Act of 1984

Section 13 of the Act of 1984 is amended—

  (a) in subsection (1), by the substitution of "€5,000" for "£1,000", and

  (b) by the addition of the following subsection:[1]

Amendments

1 See the amended Act.

PART 3
SENTENCING

24   Interpretation (Part 3)

(1) In this Part—

"imprisonment" includes—

  (a) detention in Saint Patrick's Institution,

  (b) detention in a place provided under section 2 of the Prisons Act 1970, and

  (c) detention in a place specified under section 3 of the Prisons Act 1972,

and "prison" and "sentence of imprisonment" shall be construed accordingly;

"remission from the sentence" means, in relation to the sentence imposed on a person, the remission which he or she may earn from that sentence under the rules or practice whereby prisoners generally may earn remission of sentence by industry and good conduct.

(2) In this Part, references to an offence specified in Schedule 2 shall include—

  (a) references to participation as an accomplice of a person who commits such an offence, and

  (b) references to an offence of attempting or conspiring to commit, or inciting the commission of, such an offence.

25   Commission of another offence within specified period

(1) Subject to subsections (2) and (3), where a person (other than a person under the age of 18 years)—

  (a) has been convicted on indictment of an offence specified in Schedule 2 (in this section referred to as "the first offence"),

  (b) has been sentenced to imprisonment for a term of not less than 5 years in respect of that offence, and

  (c) who is convicted on indictment of an offence specified in Schedule 2 (in this section referred to as "the subsequent offence") that is committed—

     (i) during the period of 7 years from the date of conviction of the first offence and, for the purpose of determining that period, there shall be disregarded any period of imprisonment in respect of the first offence or the subsequent offence, or

     (ii) during any such period of imprisonment,

(in this section the total period comprising the periods referred to in subparagraphs (i) and (ii) is referred to as "the specified period"),

the court shall, in imposing sentence on the person in respect of the subsequent offence, specify as the minimum term of imprisonment to be served by the person, a term of not less than three quarters of the maximum term of imprisonment prescribed by law in respect of such an offence and, if the maximum term so prescribed is life imprisonment, the court shall specify a term of imprisonment of not less than 10 years.

(2) Subsection (1) shall not apply if any of the following provisions apply in respect of the subsequent offence:

    (a)   section 2 of the Criminal Justice Act 1990;

    (b)   section 15(8) of the Act of 1925;

    (c)   section 26(8), 27(8), 27A(8) or 27B(8) of the Act of 1964;

    (d)   section 12A(13) of the Act of 1990; or

    (e)   section 27(3F) of the Misuse of Drugs Act 1977.

(3) Subsection (1) shall not apply where the court is satisfied that it would be disproportionate in all the circumstances of the case to specify as the minimum term of imprisonment to be served by the person concerned the term of imprisonment referred to in that subsection in respect of the subsequent offence.

(4) Subsection (1) shall apply to a person in respect of the subsequent offence only if that offence is committed after the commencement of this section and that subsection shall apply to a person whether the first offence is committed before or after such commencement.

(5) If, in relation to a sentence of a term of imprisonment imposed on a person in respect of the first offence—

    (a)   the operation of the whole term is suspended, then subsection (1) shall not apply to that offence, or

    (b)   the operation of a part of the term is suspended, the part of that term the operation of which is not suspended shall be regarded as the term of imprisonment imposed on the person in respect of the first offence for the purposes of subsection (1).

(6) Subsection (1) shall not apply to a person if the conviction in respect of the first offence is quashed on appeal or otherwise.

(7) A reference in this section to a sentence imposed on a person in respect of the first offence shall—

    (a)   if the sentence is varied on appeal, be construed as a reference to the sentence as so varied, or

    (b)   if, on the application of the Director of Public Prosecutions under section 2 of the Criminal Justice Act 1993, the sentence is quashed by the Court of Criminal Appeal and another sentence is imposed in place of it by that Court on the person, be construed as a reference to that other sentence.

(8) For the purposes of subsections (1)(c) and (10), a period of imprisonment means any time when the person concerned is—

    (a)   remanded in custody,

    (b)   serving a sentence in prison, or

    (c)   temporarily released under section 2 of the Criminal Justice Act 1960.

(9) References in this section to the subsequent offence shall include references to a second or subsequent offence specified in Schedule 2 of which a person (other than a person under the age of 18 years) is convicted on indictment during the specified period.

(10) The specified period in relation to a person to whom subsection (1) applies shall expire only when the person has not been convicted of an offence specified in Schedule 2 —

    (a) during the period of 7 years from the date of conviction of the subsequent offence and, for the purpose of determining that period, there shall be disregarded any period of imprisonment in respect of the first offence or the subsequent offence, or

    (b) during any such period of imprisonment.

(11) If, following the application of subsection (1) to a person in respect of a conviction on indictment of an offence specified in Schedule 2 —

    (a) his or her conviction in respect of the first offence is quashed on appeal or otherwise, or

    (b) the sentence imposed on the person in respect of the first offence is varied on appeal so that it no longer falls under subsection (1)(b,

the person may apply to the court that imposed the sentence on him or her in respect of the subsequent offence to review it and the court may, if it considers it appropriate to do so, vary that sentence.

(12) (a) If a sentence imposed on a person in respect of a conviction on indictment of an offence specified in Schedule 2 does not fall under subsection (1)(b) but the sentence is—

        (i) varied on appeal, or

        (ii) on the application of the Director of Public Prosecutions under section 2 of the Criminal Justice Act 1993, quashed by the Court of Criminal Appeal and another sentence is imposed in place of it by that Court on the person,

    so that the sentence then falls under subsection (1)(b), subsection (1) shall apply in respect of an offence specified in Schedule 2 ("the subsequent offence") committed by the person within the specified period.

    (b) If, in the circumstances referred to in paragraph (a), a sentence has, at the time of the appeal referred to in subparagraph (i) of that paragraph concerned or, as the case may be, the application referred to in subparagraph (ii) of that paragraph concerned, been imposed on the person concerned in respect of the subsequent offence, the Director of Public Prosecutions may apply to the court that imposed the sentence to review it and the court shall apply subsection (1) to that person in respect of the subsequent offence and, if appropriate, vary the sentence accordingly.

(13) The power conferred by section 23 of the Criminal Justice Act 1951 to commute or remit a punishment shall not, in the case of a person serving a sentence of imprisonment imposed in accordance with subsection (1) in respect of the subsequent offence, be exercised before the expiry of the minimum term of imprisonment specified by the court in accordance with that subsection less any reduction of that term arising under subsection (14).

(14) The rules or practice whereby prisoners generally may earn remission of sentence by industry and good conduct shall apply in the case of a person serving a sentence imposed in accordance with subsection (1) in respect of the subsequent offence and the minimum term of imprisonment specified by the court in accordance with that subsection shall be reduced by the amount of any remission so earned by the person.

(15) Any powers conferred by rules made under section 2 of the Criminal Justice Act 1960 to release temporarily a person serving a sentence of imprisonment shall not, in the case of a person serving a sentence imposed in accordance with subsection (1) in respect of the subsequent offence, be exercised during the period for which the commutation or remission of his or her punishment is prohibited by subsection (13) unless for grave reason of a humanitarian nature, and any release so granted shall be only of such limited duration as is justified by that reason.

(16) The reference in subsection (15) to section 2 of the Criminal Justice Act 1960 shall be construed to include that section as applied by section 4 of the Prisons Act 1970.

26   **Monitoring orders and protection of persons orders**

(1) Where a person (other than a person under the age of 18 years) (in this section referred to as "the offender") is convicted on indictment of an offence specified in Schedule 2, the court shall consider whether it is appropriate to make an order or orders under this section in relation to the offender for the purpose of monitoring the offender after release from prison or for the purpose of protecting any person.

(2) The court may make an order (in this section referred to as a "monitoring order") in relation to the offender requiring the offender, as soon as practicable after the order comes into force, to notify in writing an inspector of the Garda Síochána of the district in which his or her home is located of the address of it and to notify in writing such an inspector of any change of address of his or her home or any proposed absence for a period of more than 7 days from his or her home before any such change of address or any such absence, as the case may be, occurs.

(3) A monitoring order may be made for such period, not exceeding 7 years, as the court considers appropriate.

(4) The court may make an order (in this section referred to as a "protection of persons order") in relation to the offender for the purpose of protecting the victim of the offence concerned or any other person named in the order from harassment by the offender while the order is in force.

(5) The court may provide in a protection of persons order that the offender is prohibited from engaging in any behaviour that, in the opinion of the court, would be likely to cause the victim of the offence concerned or any other person named in the order fear, distress or alarm or would be likely to amount to intimidation of any such person.

(6) A protection of persons order may be made for such period, not exceeding 7 years, as the court considers appropriate.

(7) A monitoring order or a protection of persons order in relation to the offender shall come into force on the date on which—

    (a) the sentence of imprisonment imposed on him or her in respect of the offence concerned expires or, as the case may be, his or her remission from the sentence begins, or

    (b) if the offender is imprisoned in respect of another offence, the date on which that sentence of imprisonment expires or, as the case may be, his or her remission from that sentence begins,

whichever is the later.

(8) Where a monitoring order or a protection of persons order is made (whether or not it is in force), the court that made the order may, if it so thinks proper, on the application of the offender vary or revoke the order if it is satisfied that by reason of such matters or circumstances specified in the application that have arisen or occurred since the making of the order that it should be varied or revoked.

(9) An application under subsection (8) shall be made on notice to an inspector of the Garda Síochána of the district in which the offender ordinarily resided at the time that the order was made or, if appropriate, an inspector of the Garda Síochána of the district in which the home of the offender is located at the time of the application.

(10) A person who fails, without reasonable cause, to comply with a monitoring order or a protection of persons order shall be guilty of an offence and shall be liable on summary conviction to a fine not exceeding €2,000 or imprisonment for a term not exceeding 6 months or both.

(11) Nothing in this section shall affect any other order, restriction or obligation, or any condition attaching thereto, to which the offender is subject whether made or imposed under statute or otherwise apart from this section while a monitoring order or a protection of persons order is in force.

(12) In this section "home", in relation to the offender, means his or her sole or main residence or, if he or she has no such residence, his or her most usual place of abode or, if he or she has no such abode, the place which he or she regularly visits.

[26A   Post-release orders in cases of certain offences

(1) Where, on or after the commencement of a scheme under subsection (10), a person (other than a person under the age of 18 years), in this section referred to as ' the offender ', is convicted on indictment of—

(a)   an offence under Part 7 of the Act of 2006, or

(b)   an offence (other than an offence referred to in paragraph (a)) specified in Schedule 2 that has been committed as part of, or in furtherance of, the activities of a criminal organisation,

the court shall, in determining the sentence to be imposed on the offender in respect of that offence, consider whether it is appropriate to make an order under this section (in this section referred to as a ' post-release (restrictions on certain activities) order ') in relation to him or her for the purpose of the offender's being subject, after his or her release from prison, to the restrictions and conditions subsequently mentioned in this section.

(2) A post-release (restrictions on certain activities) order shall not be made in relation to the offender unless the court considers that, having regard to—

(a)   the evidence given in the trial of the offender for the offence concerned, and

(b)   evidence that is given to the court in relation to the sentence to be imposed for that offence,

it is in the public interest to make such an order, and in determining whether to make such order the court shall take account of such matters as the court considers appropriate, including the offender's previous criminal record and the other circumstances relating to him or her.

(3) There is, by virtue of this subsection, conferred on the court power to make, as part of the offender's sentence, a post-release (restrictions on certain activities) order in relation to him

or her, that is to say, an order imposing one or more (and no other) of the following restrictions and conditions:

    (a) restrictions on the offender's movements, actions or activities;

    (b) conditions subject to which the offender may engage in any activity;

    (c) restrictions on the offender's association with others or conditions subject to which the offender may associate with others,

being restrictions and conditions, as to both their nature and extent, that—

    (i) are determined by the court to be no more than is reasonably necessary to be imposed in the public interest, and

    (ii) fall into a category of restrictions and conditions specified in a scheme made under subsection (10).

(4) A post-release (restrictions on certain activities) order may be made for such period, not exceeding 7 years, as the court considers appropriate.

(5) A post-release (restriction of certain activities) order in relation to the offender shall come into force on the date on which—

    (a) the sentence of imprisonment imposed on him or her in respect of the offence concerned expires or, as the case may be, his or her remission from the sentence begins, or

    (b) if the offender is imprisoned in respect of another offence, the date on which that sentence of imprisonment expires or, as the case may be, his or her remission from that sentence begins,

whichever is the later.

(6) Where a post-release (restriction of certain activities) order is made (whether or not it is in force), the court that made the order may, if it so thinks proper, on the application of the offender vary or revoke the order if it is satisfied that by reason of such matters or circumstances specified in the application that have arisen or occurred since the making of the order that it should be varied or revoked.

(7) An application under subsection (6) shall be made on notice to an inspector of the Garda Síochána of the district in which the offender ordinarily resided at the time that the order was made or, if appropriate, an inspector of the Garda Síochána of the district in which the home of the offender is located at the time of the application.

(8) A person who fails, without reasonable cause, to comply with a post-release (restriction of certain activities) order shall be guilty of an offence and shall be liable on summary conviction to a fine not exceeding €5,000 or imprisonment for a term not exceeding 12 months or both.

(9) Nothing in this section shall affect any other order, restriction or obligation, or any condition attaching thereto, to which the offender is subject whether made or imposed under statute (including section 26) or otherwise apart from this section while a post-release (restrictions of certain activities) order is in force.

(10) (a) As soon as practicable, but not later than 6 months, after the commencement of section 14 of the Criminal Justice (Amendment) Act 2009, the Minister shall prepare a scheme specifying 2 or more categories of restrictions and conditions that may be imposed by post-release (restrictions on certain activities) orders and lay a draft of the scheme before each House of the Oireachtas.

(b)   If the draft of the scheme, so laid, is approved by a resolution passed by each such House, the Minister shall make the scheme as soon as practicable thereafter.

(11) In this section "home", in relation to the offender, means his or her sole or main residence or, if he or she has no such residence, his or her most usual place of abode or, if he or she has no such abode, the place which he or she regularly visits.]¹

Amendments

1   Section 26A inserted by Criminal Justice (Amendment) Act 2009, s 14(1).

27   Amendment of Criminal Justice (Legal Aid) Act 1962

The Criminal Justice (Legal Aid) Act 1962 is amended—

(a)   by the insertion of the following sections after section 6:
(b)   in section 7, by the addition of the following subsection:
      and
(c)   in section 9(2), by the substitution of ", a legal aid (Supreme Court) certificate, a legal aid (monitoring order) certificate or a legal aid (protection of persons order) certificate" for "or a legal aid (Supreme Court) certificate".

PART 4
INFERENCES TO BE DRAWN IN CERTAIN CIRCUMSTANCES

28   Inferences from failure or refusal to account for objects, marks, etc

(1) The Act of 1984 is amended by the substitution of the following section for section 18:¹

(2) This section shall not apply to a failure or refusal to account for the presence of an object, substance or mark or for the condition of clothing or footwear if the failure or refusal occurred before the commencement of this section.

(3) Subsection (1) shall not affect the application of section 18 of the Act of 1984 to a failure or refusal to account for the presence of an object, substance or mark or for the condition of clothing or footwear if the failure or refusal occurred before the commencement of this section, and that section shall apply to such a failure or refusal as if subsection (1) had not been enacted.

Amendments

1   See the amended Act.

29   Inferences from failure or refusal to account for accused's presence at a particular place

(1) The Act of 1984 is amended by the substitution of the following section for section 19:¹

(2) This section shall not apply to a failure or refusal of a person to account for his or her presence if the failure or refusal occurred before the commencement of this section.

(3) Subsection (1) shall not affect the application of section 19 of the Act of 1984 to a failure or refusal of a person to account for his or her presence if the failure or refusal occurred before the commencement of this section, and that section shall apply to such a failure or refusal as if subsection (1) had not been enacted.

Amendments

1   See the amended Act.

30   Inferences from failure of accused to mention particular facts

The Act of 1984 is amended by the insertion of the following section after section 19:[1]

Amendments

1   See the amended Act.

31   Amendment of section 2 of Offences Against the State (Amendment) Act 1998

(1) Section 2 of the Offences Against the State (Amendment) Act 1998 is amended—

    (a)   in subsection (1), by—

        (i)   the substitution of "in determining whether a charge should be dismissed under Part IA of the Criminal Procedure Act 1967" for "in determining whether to send forward the accused for trial", and

        (ii)   the substitution of "a person shall not be convicted of the offence solely or mainly on an inference drawn from such a failure" for "a person shall not be convicted of the offence solely on an inference drawn from such a failure",

    (b)   by the substitution of the following subsection for subsection (2):

        "(2) Subsection (1) shall not have effect unless—

        (a)   the accused was told in ordinary language when being questioned what the effect of such a failure might be, and

        (b)   the accused was afforded a reasonable opportunity to consult a solicitor before such a failure occurred.",

    and

    (c)   by the insertion of the following subsections after subsection (3):

        "(3A) The court (or, subject to the judge's directions, the jury) shall, for the purposes of drawing an inference under this section, have regard to whenever, if appropriate, an answer to the question concerned was first given by the accused.

(3B) This section shall not apply in relation to the questioning of a person by a member of the Garda Síochána unless it is recorded by electronic or similar means or the person consents in writing to it not being so recorded.

(3C) References in subsection (1) to evidence shall, in relation to the hearing of an application under Part IA of the Criminal Procedure Act 1967 for the dismissal of a charge, be taken to include a statement of the evidence to be given by a witness at the trial.".

(2) This section shall not apply to a failure to answer a question to which section 2 of the Offences Against the State (Amendment) Act 1998 relates if the failure occurred before the commencement of this section.

32   Regulations

(1) The Minister may make regulations providing for the administration of cautions by members of the Garda Síochána to persons in relation to offences.

(2) The regulations may include provision for—

  (a) the form of caution to be administered to a person—

    (i)   at any time before the person is charged with an offence, on being questioned by a member of the Garda Síochána in relation to the offence,

    (ii) when the person is being charged with an offence or informed by a member of the Garda Síochána that he or she might be prosecuted for it, or

    (iii) in any other circumstances in which a caution is required, and

  (b) the procedures that are to apply in circumstances where a person to whom a caution has been administered is to have the caution withdrawn and a different caution administered to him or her.

(3) Regulations under this section may provide for different forms of caution to be administered to a person in different circumstances and in different classes of cases.

(4) A failure on the part of any member of the Garda Síochána to observe any provision of the regulations shall not of itself render that member liable to any criminal or civil proceedings or of itself affect the admissibility in evidence of anything said by, or the silence of, a person to whom subsection (2)(a) applies.

(5) Regulations under this section may contain such incidental, supplementary and consequential provisions as appear to the Minister to be necessary or expedient for the purposes of the regulations.

(6) Every regulation made under this section shall be laid before each House of the Oireachtas as soon as may be after it is made and, if a resolution annulling the regulation is passed by either such House within the next 21 days on which that House has sat after the regulation is laid before it, the regulation shall be annulled accordingly, but without prejudice to the validity of anything previously done thereunder.

PART 5
MISUSE OF DRUGS

33   Amendment of section 27 of Misuse of Drugs Act 1977

Section 27 of the Misuse of Drugs Act 1977 is amended by the substitution of the following subsections for subsections (3A) to (3K):[1]

Amendments

1   See the amended Act.

PART 6

AMENDMENT OF FIREARMS ACTS 1925 TO 2006

34   Amendment of section 2 of Act of 1925

Section 2 of the Act of 1925 is amended—

  (a) in subsection (5)(a), by the substitution of ", (j) or (k)" for "or (j)", and

  (b) by the insertion of the following subsection after subsection (6):[1]

Amendments

1   See the amended Act.

35   Amendment of section 15 of Act of 1925

Section 15 of the Act of 1925 is amended—

  (a) by the insertion of the following subsection after subsection (4):[1]
       and

  (b) in subsection (5), by the insertion of ", subject to subsection (6)," after "and for this purpose the court may".

Amendments

1   See the amended Act.

36   Amendment of section 26 of Act of 1964

Section 26 of the Act of 1964 is amended—

  (a) by the insertion of the following subsection after subsection (4):[1]
       and

  (b) in subsection (5), by the insertion of ", subject to subsection (6)," after "and for this purpose the court may".

Amendments

1   See the amended Act.

37   Amendment of section 27 of Act of 1964

Section 27 of the Act of 1964 is amended—

(a) by the insertion of the following subsection after subsection (4):

"(4A) The purpose of subsections (5) and (6) of this section is to provide that in view of the harm caused to society by the unlawful possession and use of firearms, a court, in imposing sentence on a person (other than a person under the age of 18 years) for an offence under this section, shall specify as the minimum term of imprisonment to be served by the person a term of not less than 10 years, unless the court determines that by reason of exceptional and specific circumstances relating to the offence, or the person convicted of it, it would be unjust in all the circumstances to do so.",

and

(b) in subsection (5), by the insertion of ", subject to subsection (6)," after "and for this purpose the court may".

38   Amendment of section 27A of Act of 1964

Section 27A of the Act of 1964 is amended—

(a) in subsection (1), by the insertion of "or ammunition" after "firearm",

(b) by the insertion of the following subsection after subsection (4):[1] and

(c) in subsection (5), by the insertion of ", subject to subsection (6)," after "and for this purpose the court may".

Amendments

1   See the amended Act.

---

39   Amendment of section 27B of Act of 1964

Section 27B of the Act of 1964 is amended—

(a) by the insertion of the following subsection after subsection (4):[1] and

(b) in subsection (5), by the insertion of ", subject to subsection (6)," after "and for this purpose the court may".

Amendments

1   See the amended Act.

---

40   Amendment of section 12A of Act of 1990

Section 12A of the Act of 1990 is amended—

(a) by the insertion of the following subsection after subsection (9):[1]

(b) in subsection (10), by the insertion of ", subject to subsection (11)," after "and for this purpose the court may", and

(c) in subsection (13)(b), by the insertion of "27" after "section 26,".

Amendments

1 See the amended Act.

PART 7

AMENDMENT OF GARDA SÍOCHÁNA ACT 2005

41   Establishment and functions of Garda Síochána Executive Management Board

The Act of 2005 is amended by the insertion of the following Chapter after section 33:

"CHAPTER 3A

Establishment and functions of Garda Síochána Executive Management Board

Establishment day.

33A.— The Minister shall, by order, appoint a day to be the establishment day for the purposes of this Chapter.

Establishment of Garda Síochána Executive Management Board.

33B.— On the establishment day, a body to be known as An Bord Bainistíochta Feidhmiúcháin an Gharda Síochána or, in the English language, the Garda Síochána Executive Management Board (in this Chapter referred to as "the Board") stands established to perform the function assigned to it by this Chapter.

Membership of Board.

33C.— (1) The Board consists of—

(a) executive members who are responsible for performing the Board's function, and

(b) 3 non-executive members, who participate in an advisory capacity in relation to the performance of that function.

(2) The executive members of the Board are—

(a) the Garda Commissioner, who is its chairperson,

(b) the Deputy Garda Commissioners, and

(c) a member of the civilian staff of the Garda Síochána of a grade equivalent to that of Deputy Garda Commissioner.

(3) The non-executive members of the Board are persons who are not serving or former members of the Garda Síochána or its civilian staff.

(4) At least one of the non-executive members of the Board shall be a woman and at least one of them shall be a man.

Appointment, etc., of non-executive members.

33D.— (1) The non-executive members of the Board shall—

(a) be appointed by the Government on the nomination of the Minister,

(b) be persons who have expertise in the strategic and financial management of organisations, the management of their human resources or the planning and review functions relating to them or have other relevant experience, and

(c) serve on the Board in a non-executive capacity to provide advice in relation to annual policing plans, budgetary matters, allocation of resources, technology, equipment, setting of targets, training, development and leadership and other related matters.

(2) Subject to subsection (5), a non-executive member holds office for a period of 4 years and is eligible for re-appointment for a second term.

(3) The terms and conditions of appointment of non-executive members, including those relating to remuneration, shall be determined by the Minister in consultation with the Minister for Finance.

(4) A non-executive member may at any time resign his or her office by letter addressed to the Minister, and the resignation takes effect on the date of receipt of the letter.

(5) A non-executive member may be removed from office by the Government for stated reasons or if in the opinion of the Government the member has become incapable through ill health or incapacity of effectively performing the duties of the office.

(6) Whenever the number of non-executive members falls below 3, the vacancy or vacancies shall be filled by appointment in accordance with subsection (1).

(7) A non-executive member who is appointed to fill a vacancy holds office for the remainder of the term of office of the replaced member.

(8) The Board may act notwithstanding any such vacancy or any resulting non-compliance with section 33C(4).

(9) A person ceases to be a non-executive member as soon as he or she—

(a) is nominated as a member of Seanad Éireann,

(b) is elected as a member of either House of the Oireachtas or of the European Parliament,

(c) is regarded pursuant to Part XIII of the Second Schedule to the European Parliament Elections Act 1997 as having been elected to the European Parliament to fill a vacancy, or

(d) becomes a member of a local authority.

Function of Board

33E.— (1) The function of the Board is to keep under review the performance by the Garda Síochána of its functions and the arrangements and strategies in place to support and enhance the performance of those functions.

(2) In particular, the Board shall keep under review the adequacy of—

(a) the performance by the Garda Síochána of its functions,

(b) the arrangements and strategies in place to support and enhance that performance,

(c) the corporate governance arrangements and structures within the Garda Síochána,

(d) the arrangements for the recruitment, training and development of the members and civilian staff of the Garda Síochána, and

(e)   the mechanisms in place within the Garda Síochána for the measurement of performance and accountability of such members and staff.

Provision of information to non-executive members by Garda Commissioner.

33F.— The Garda Commissioner shall make available to the non-executive members of the Board any information which is relevant to the performance of their functions.

Reports to Minister.

33G.— (1) The Board shall furnish to the Minister, at six-monthly intervals, a report on the performance of its function.

(2) The Minister shall cause a copy of the report to be laid before each House of the Oireachtas as soon as may be after its receipt.

Saving.

33H.— The performance by the Board of its function is without prejudice to, and in no way limits, the performance by the Garda Commissioner of his or her functions under section 26 or his or her accountability for the direction, control, management and operational efficiency of the Garda Síochána.".

42   Special inquiries relating to Garda Síochána

The Act of 2005 is amended by the substitution of the following section for section 42:

"Special inquiries relating to Garda Síochána.

42.— (1) The Minister, with respect to any matter considered by him or her to be of public concern, may by order appoint a person to—

(a)   inquire into any aspect of administration, operation, practice or procedure of the Garda Síochána, or the conduct of its members, and

(b)   make a report to the Minister on the conclusion of the inquiry.

(2) A person who, in the Minister's opinion, has the experience, qualifications, training or expertise appropriate for the inquiry may be appointed to conduct the inquiry.

(3) The Minister shall specify the terms of reference of the inquiry in the order under subsection (1) and may, by order, made at any time before the submission of the final report, amend those terms for the purpose of clarifying, limiting or extending the scope of the inquiry.

(4) For the purpose of the inquiry, the appointed person—

(a)   may require a member of the Garda Síochána, or any other person, who possesses information or possesses or controls a document or thing that is relevant to the inquiry to provide the information, document or thing to the appointed person, and

(b)   where appropriate, may require the member or other person to attend before the appointed person for that purpose.

(5) The member or other person shall co-operate with the inquiry and answer fully and truthfully any question put to him or her by the appointed person.

(6) Where the member or other person fails to comply with a requirement under subsection (4), the High Court may, on application by the appointed person and on notice to the member or other person—

(a)   order the member or person to comply with the requirement, and

(b)   include in the order any other provision it considers necessary to enable the order to have full effect.

(7) If the member or other person fails to comply with such an order, the Court may treat the failure for all purposes as if it were a contempt of the Court.

(8) A failure by the member to comply with a requirement under subsection (4) may be the subject of disciplinary action in accordance with the Disciplinary Regulations.

(9) Any information, document or thing provided by a person in accordance with a requirement under subsection (4) is not admissible in any criminal proceedings against the person, and this shall be explained to the person in ordinary language by the appointed person.

(10) The Minister may publish all or part of any report received under this section.

(11) This section applies even if the matter considered by the Minister to be of public concern arose before the passing of this Act.

(12) The power to order an inquiry under this Act is additional to any power conferred by this or another Act relating to inquiries or investigations.

(13) In this section—

"appointed person" means a person appointed under this section to conduct an inquiry;

"criminal proceedings" does not include disciplinary proceedings.".

43   Other amendments to Act of 2005

The Act of 2005 is amended—

(a)   in section 11(2), by the substitution of ", Deputy Garda Commissioner or Assistant Garda Commissioner" for "Deputy Garda Commissioner",

(b)   in section 15, by the addition of the following subsection:

> "(6) A reserve member is a volunteer and does not perform his or her functions as such a member under a contract of employment.",

(c)   in section 39—

> (i)   in subsection (1), by the insertion of "or a designated officer of the Ombudsman Commission" after "rank", and
>
> (ii)   in subsections (3) and (4), by the insertion of "or designated officer" after "rank",

(d)   in section 44—

> (i)   in subsection (2)(a), by the insertion of "or a member of the civilian staff of the Garda Commissioner of a grade equivalent to that of Deputy Garda Commissioner" after "Deputy Garda Commissioner", and
>
> (ii)   by the addition of the following subsection:
>
> > "(7) The audit committee may act notwithstanding one or more than one vacancy in its membership, including a vacancy that results in subsection (2) not being complied with.",

(e)   in section 47(3), by the substitution of the following paragraph for paragraph (a):

> "(a) the period beginning on 1 July 2007 and ending 3 months after that date, and",

(f)   in section 75(3)(c), by the insertion of "chairperson of the" after "the",

(g) in section 79(10), by the insertion of "Commission" after "Ombudsman",

(h) in section 82(2), by the substitution of "under the provisions" for "under the provision",

(i) in section 94(7), by the substitution of "may have been committed" for "has been committed",

(j) in section 98(1), by the deletion of ", in relation to the member of the Garda Síochána under investigation,",

(k) in section 99(1), by the deletion of "in the prescribed form",

(l) in section 117(6)(b), by the substitution of "with such police service or" for "with any", and

(m) in section 122(1)(h), by the insertion of ", including the retirement ages of reserve members and other ranks in the Garda Síochána" after "members".

PART 8

AMENDMENTS TO THE SEA-FISHERIES ACTS 2003 AND 2006

44   **Amendments to Sea-Fisheries Acts 2003 and 2006**

The Sea-Fisheries and Maritime Jurisdiction Act 2006 is amended—

(a) by inserting after section 17 the following new section:

"Search warrants.

17A.— (1) This section applies to an offence under the Sea-Fisheries Acts 2003 to 2007.

(2) A judge of the District Court, by information on oath of a sea-fisheries protection officer, may, if he or she is satisfied that there are reasonable grounds for suspecting that evidence of, or relating to the commission of, an offence to which this section applies is to be found in any place, issue a warrant for the search of that place and any persons found there.

(3) A warrant under this section shall be expressed and shall operate to authorise a named sea-fisheries protection officer, alone or accompanied by such other persons as may be necessary—

    (a) to enter (if necessary by the use of reasonable force) and on production of the warrant (if so requested), within 7 days from the date of issuing of the warrant, the place named in the warrant,

    (b) to search it and any persons found there,

    (c) while there, to exercise any of the functions of a sea-fisheries protection officer—

        (i) under section 17, and

        (ii) under section 18, if the place is a sea-fishing boat,

    (d) to otherwise examine, take, remove and detain any thing found there, or in the possession of a person present there at the time of the search, which the sea-fisheries protection officer reasonably believes to be evidence of or relating to the commission of an offence to which this section applies, and

1332

(e)   to take any other steps which may appear to the sea-fisheries protection officer to be necessary for preserving any such thing and preventing interference with it.

(4) The authority conferred by subsection (3)(d) to take, remove and detain any thing includes, in the case of records, authority—

(a)   to make and retain a copy of the records, and

(b)   where necessary, to seize and, for as long as necessary, retain any computer or other storage medium in which any record is kept.

(5) A sea-fisheries protection officer acting under the authority of a warrant under this section may—

(a)   operate any computer at the place which is being searched or cause any such computer to be operated by a person accompanying the officer for that purpose, and

(b)   require any person at that place who appears to the officer to have lawful access to the information in any such computer—

   (i)   to give to the officer any password necessary to operate it,

   (ii)   otherwise to enable the officer to examine the information accessible by the computer in a form in which the information is visible and legible, or

   (iii)   to produce the information in a form in which it can be removed and in which it is, or can be made, visible and legible.

(6) Where any sea-fisheries protection officer has entered a place in the execution of a warrant issued under this section, he or she may seize and detain any material, other than items subject to legal privilege, which is likely to be of substantial value (whether by itself or together with other material) to the investigation for the purpose of which the warrant was issued.

(7) The power to issue a warrant under this section—

(a)   is without prejudice to the exercise of a function by a sea-fisheries protection officer under any other provision of the Sea-Fisheries Acts 2003 to 2007, and

(b)   is in addition to and not in substitution for any other power to issue a warrant for the search of any place or person.

(8) A sea-fisheries protection officer to whom a warrant under this section has been issued shall, if not in uniform and if requested by a person affected, produce evidence of his or her authority as such an officer.

(9) In this section—

'commission', in relation to an offence, includes an attempt to commit the offence;

'computer at the place which is being searched' includes any other computer, whether at that place or at any other place, which is lawfully accessible by means of that computer;

'place' includes a dwelling, a building or other structure or part of a building or other structure, a vehicle, a sea-fishing boat or other vessel, an aircraft, an installation in the territorial seas or in a designated area (within the meaning of the Continental Shelf Act 1968) and a tent, caravan or other temporary or movable structure;

'thing' includes any thing that may be inspected by a sea-fisheries protection officer pursuant to section 17 or 18.",

(b) in section 28—

(i) by substituting for subsection (1) the following:

"(1) A person guilty of an offence committed on board a sea-fishing boat under a provision of—

(a) Chapter 2 specified in column (2) of Table 1, or

(b) the Act of 2003 specified in column (2) of Table 2,

is liable, on conviction on indictment, to the fine specified in column (3) of that Table at the reference number at which that provision is specified in respect of the category of sea-fishing boat mentioned in that column and to the forfeiture specified in subsection (5).

(1A) A person guilty of an offence under section 11, 12, 13, 14 or 15, which is not committed on board a sea-fishing boat, in respect of the buying, handling, weighing, trans-shipping, transporting, landing, processing, storing, documenting or selling of fish is liable, on conviction on indictment, to a fine not exceeding €100,000. Any fish found to which the offence relates used in the commission of the offence are, as a statutory consequence of the conviction, forfeited.",

and

(ii) in subsection (2), by substituting "subsection (1) or (1A)" for "subsection (1)",

and

(c) in section 29, by inserting "or under section 28(1A)" after "Table".

PART 9

MISCELLANEOUS

45   Amendment of Garda Síochána (Complaints) Act 1986

(1) Paragraph 2 of the First Schedule to the Garda Síochána (Complaints) Act 1986 is amended by the insertion of the following subparagraph after subparagraph (3):

"(3A) Notwithstanding subparagraphs (2) and (3), the term of office of a member of the Board ceases on the commencement of Schedule 1 to the Garda Síochána Act 2005 in so far as that Schedule relates to the repeal of this Act.".

(2) Paragraph 1 of the Third Schedule to that Act is amended by the insertion of the following subparagraph after subparagraph (3):

"(3A) Notwithstanding subparagraphs (2) and (3), the term of office of a member of the Board ceases on the commencement of Schedule 1 to the Garda Síochána Act 2005 in so far as that Schedule relates to the repeal of this Act.".

46   Amendment of Act of 2006

The Act of 2006 is amended by the substitution of the following sections for section 183:[1]

Amendments

1   See the amended Act.

---

47   Amendment of section 15 of Criminal Justice (Theft and Fraud Offences) Act 2001

The Criminal Justice (Theft and Fraud Offences) Act 2001 is amended—

   (a)   in section 15—

      (i)   in subsection (1), by the insertion of the following paragraph after paragraph (a):

      "(aa) robbery,",

      and

      (ii)   by the substitution of the following subsection for subsection (2):[1]

      and

   (b)   in section 19(2), by the substitution of "€5,000" for "£1,500".

Amendments

1   See the amended Act.

---

48   Amendment of Act of 1984

The Act of 1984 is amended—

   (a)   in section 6—

      (i)   by the insertion of the following subsection after subsection (1):[1]

      and

      (ii)   by the substitution of the following subsection for subsection (2):[1]

      and

   (b)   by the insertion of the following section after section 6:[1]

      and

   (c)   in section 15(2), by the substitution of "€5,000" for "€2,500".

Amendments

1   See the amended Act.

---

49   Destruction of records

The Act of 1984 is amended by the substitution of the following section for section 8:[1]

Amendments

1   See the amended Act.

---

50   Powers of detention for specified offences

(1) This section applies to—

    (a)   murder involving the use of a firearm or an explosive,

    (b)   murder to which section 3 of the Criminal Justice Act 1990 applies,

    (c)   an offence under section 15 of the [Act of 1925,]¹

    (d)   an offence under section 15 of the Non-Fatal Offences against the Person Act 1997 involving the use of a [firearm, or]¹

    [(e)   an offence under Part 7 of the Criminal Justice Act 2006.]²

(2) Where a member of the Garda Síochána arrests without warrant, whether in a Garda Síochána station or elsewhere, a person (in this section referred to as "the arrested person") whom he or she, with reasonable cause, suspects of having committed an offence to which this section applies, the arrested person—

    (a)   if not already in a Garda Síochána station, may be taken to and detained in a Garda Síochána station, or

    (b)   if he or she is arrested in a Garda Síochána station, may be detained in the station,

for such a period or periods authorised by subsection (3) if the member of the Garda Síochána in charge of the station concerned has at the time of the arrested person's arrival at the station or his or her arrest in the station, as may be appropriate, reasonable grounds for believing that his or her detention is necessary for the proper investigation of the offence.

(3)   (a)   The period for which a person may be detained pursuant to subsection (2) shall, subject to the provisions of this subsection, not exceed 6 hours from the time of his or her arrest.

    (b)   A member of the Garda Síochána not below the rank of superintendent may direct that a person detained pursuant to subsection (2) be detained for a further period not exceeding 18 hours if he or she has reasonable grounds for believing that such further detention is necessary for the proper investigation of the offence concerned.

    (c)   A member of the Garda Síochána not below the rank of chief superintendent may direct that a person detained pursuant to a direction under paragraph (b) be detained for a further period not exceeding 24 hours if he or she has reasonable grounds for believing that such further detention is necessary for the proper investigation of the offence concerned.

    (d)   A direction pursuant to paragraph (b) or (c) may be given orally or in writing and, if given orally, shall be recorded in writing as soon as practicable.

    (e)   Where a direction has been given pursuant to paragraph (b) or (c), the fact that the direction was given, the date and time when it was given and the name and rank of the member of the Garda Síochána who gave it shall be recorded.

    (f)   The direction or, if it was given orally, the written record of it shall be signed by the member of the Garda Síochána giving it and—

      (i)   shall state the date and time when it was given, the member's name and rank and that he or she had reasonable grounds for believing that such further detention was necessary for the proper investigation of the offence concerned, and

     (ii) shall be attached to and form part of the custody record (within the meaning of the Criminal Justice Act 1984 (Treatment of Persons in Custody in Garda Síochána Stations) Regulations 1987 (S.I. No. 119 of 1987)) in respect of the person concerned.

(g)   (i)   A member of the Garda Síochána not below the rank of chief superintendent may apply to a judge of the Circuit Court or District Court for a warrant authorising the detention of a person detained pursuant to a direction under paragraph (c) for a further period not exceeding 72 hours if he or she has reasonable grounds for believing that such further detention is necessary for the proper investigation of the offence concerned.

     (ii) On an application pursuant to subparagraph (i) the judge concerned shall issue a warrant authorising the detention of the person to whom the application relates for a further period not exceeding 72 hours if, but only if, the judge is satisfied that such further detention is necessary for the proper investigation of the offence concerned and that the investigation is being conducted diligently and expeditiously.

(h)   (i)   A member of the Garda Síochána not below the rank of chief superintendent may apply to a judge of the Circuit Court or District Court for a warrant authorising the detention of a person detained under a warrant issued pursuant to paragraph (g)(ii) for a further period not exceeding 48 hours, if he or she has reasonable grounds for believing that such further detention is necessary for the proper investigation of the offence concerned.

     (ii) On an application pursuant to subparagraph (i) the judge concerned shall issue a warrant authorising the detention of the person to whom the application relates for a further period not exceeding 48 hours if, but only if, the judge is satisfied that such further detention is necessary for the proper investigation of the offence concerned and that the investigation is being conducted diligently and expeditiously.

(4) On an application pursuant to subsection (3) the person to whom the application relates shall be produced before the judge concerned and the judge shall hear any submissions made and consider any evidence adduced by or on behalf of the person and the member of the Garda Síochána making the application.

[(4A) (a) Without prejudice to paragraph (b), where a judge hearing an application under subsection (3) is satisfied, in order to avoid a risk of prejudice to the investigation concerned, that it is desirable to do so, he or she may—

     (i)   direct that the application be heard otherwise than in public, or

    (ii) exclude from the Court during the hearing all persons except officers of the Court, persons directly concerned in the proceedings, bona fide representatives of the Press and such other persons as the Court may permit to remain.

(b) On the hearing of an application under subsection (3), the judge may, of his or her own motion or on application by the member of the Garda Síochána making the application under subsection (3), where it appears that—

    (i) particular evidence to be given by any member of the Garda Síochána during the hearing (including evidence by way of answer to a question asked of the member in cross-examination) concerns steps that have been, or may be, taken in the course of any inquiry or investigation being conducted by the Garda Síochána with respect to the suspected involvement of the person to whom the application relates, or any other person, in the commission of the offence to which the detention relates or any other offence, and

    (ii) the nature of those steps is such that the giving of that evidence concerning them could prejudice, in a material respect, the proper conducting of any foregoing inquiry or investigation,

direct that, in the public interest, the particular evidence shall be given in the absence of every person, including the person to whom the application relates and any legal representative (whether of that person or the applicant), other than—

    (I) the member or members whose attendance is necessary for the purpose of giving the evidence to the judge; and

    (II) if the judge deems it appropriate, such one or more of the clerks or registrars of the Court as the judge determines.

(c) If, having heard such evidence given in that manner, the judge considers the disclosure of the matters to which that evidence relates would not have the effect referred to in paragraph (b)(ii), the judge shall direct the evidence to be re-given in the presence of all the other persons (or, as the case may be, those of them not otherwise excluded from the Court under paragraph (a)).

(d) No person shall publish or broadcast or cause to be published or broadcast any information about an application under this section other than a statement of—

    (i) the fact that the application has been brought by a named person in relation to a particular investigation, and

    (ii) any decision resulting from the application.

(e) If any matter is published or broadcast in contravention of paragraph (d), the following persons, namely—

    (i) in the case of a publication in a newspaper or periodical, any proprietor, any editor and any publisher of the newspaper or periodical,

    (ii) in the case of any other publication, the person who publishes it, and

    (iii) in the case of a broadcast, any person who transmits or provides the programme in which the broadcast is made and any person having functions in relation to the programme corresponding to those of the editor of a newspaper,

shall be guilty of an offence and shall be liable—

    (I) on summary conviction to a fine not exceeding €5,000 or imprisonment for a term not exceeding 12 months or both, or

    (II) on conviction on indictment, to a fine not exceeding €50,000 or imprisonment for a term not exceeding 3 years or both.

(f)   Where an offence under this subsection has been committed by a body corporate and is proved to have been committed with the consent or connivance of or to be attributable to any neglect on the part of a person being a director, manager, secretary or other officer of the body corporate, or a person who was purporting to act in any such capacity, that person as well as the body corporate shall be guilty of an offence and be liable to be proceeded against and punished as if he or she were guilty of the first-mentioned offence.

(g)   Where the affairs of a body corporate are managed by its members, paragraph (f) shall apply in relation to the acts and defaults of a member in connection with his or her functions of management as if he or she were a director or manager of the body corporate.

(h)   In this subsection—

"broadcast" means the transmission, relaying or distribution by wireless telegraphy, cable or the internet of communications, sounds, signs, visual images or signals, intended for direct reception by the general public whether such communications, sounds, signs, visual images or signals are actually received or not;

"publish" means publish, other than by way of broadcast, to the public or a portion of the public.

(4B) Save where any rule of law requires such an issue to be determined by the Court, in an application under subsection (3) no issue as to the lawfulness of the arrest or detention of the person to whom the application relates may be raised.

(4C) (a)   In an application under subsection (3) it shall not be necessary for a member of the Garda Síochána, other than the member making the application, to give oral evidence for the purposes of the application and the latter member may testify in relation to any matter within the knowledge of another member of the Garda Síochána that is relevant to the application notwithstanding that it is not within the personal knowledge of the member.

(b)   However, the Court hearing such an application may, if it considers it to be in the interests of justice to do so, direct that another member of the Garda Síochána give oral evidence and the Court may adjourn the hearing of the application for the purpose of receiving such evidence.]³

(5) When issuing a warrant pursuant to subsection (3) the judge concerned may order that the person concerned be brought before a judge of the Circuit Court or District Court at a specified time or times during the period of detention specified in the warrant and if, upon the person's being so brought before such a judge, he or she is not satisfied that the person's detention is justified, the judge shall revoke the warrant and order the immediate release from custody of the person.

(6) If at any time during the detention of a person pursuant to this section there are no longer reasonable grounds for believing that his or her detention is necessary for the proper investigation of the offence to which the detention relates, he or she shall, subject to subsection (7), be released from custody forthwith unless he or she is charged or caused to be charged with an offence and is brought before a court as soon as may be in connection with such charge or his or her detention is authorised apart from this Act.

(7) If at any time during the detention of a person pursuant to this section a member of the Garda Síochána, with reasonable cause, suspects that person of having committed an offence

to which this section applies, other than the offence to which the detention relates and the member of the Garda Síochána then in charge of the Garda Síochána station has reasonable grounds for believing that the continued detention of the person is necessary for the proper investigation of that other offence, the person may continue to be detained in relation to the other offence as if that offence was the offence for which the person was originally detained.

(8) A person shall not be detained pursuant to this section for more than 168 hours from the time of his or her arrest, not including any period which is to be excluded under subsection (8) or (8A) of section 4 of the Act of 1984 (as applied by section 52) in reckoning a period of detention.

[(9) Notwithstanding subsections (3) and (8), if—

(a) an application is to be made, or is made, under subsection (3) for a warrant authorising the detention for a further period of a person detained under that subsection, and

(b) the period of detention under that subsection has not expired at the time of the arrival of the person concerned at the court house for the purposes of the hearing of the application but would, but for this subsection, expire before, or during the hearing (including, if such should occur, any adjournment of the hearing),

it shall be deemed not to expire until the final determination of the application; and, for purposes of this subsection—

(i) a certificate signed by the court clerk or registrar in attendance at the court house concerned stating the time of the arrival of the person concerned at that court house shall be evidence, until the contrary is shown, of the time of that person's arrival there;

(ii) "court house" includes any venue at which the hearing of the application takes place.]⁴

(10) Nothing in this section shall affect the operation of section 30 of the Offences Against the State Act 1939, section 4 of the Act of 1984 or section 2 of the Criminal Justice (Drug Trafficking) Act 1996.

Amendments

1   Subsection (1)(c) and (d) amended by Criminal Justice (Amendment) Act 2009, s 23(1).

2   Subsection (1)(e) inserted by Criminal Justice (Amendment) Act 2009, s 23(1).

3   Subsections (4A)–(4C) inserted by Criminal Justice (Amendment) Act 2009, s 23(2)(a).

4   Subsections (9) substituted by Criminal Justice (Amendment) Act 2009, s 23(2)(b).

---

51   Rearrest

[(1) Where a person arrested on suspicion of having committed an offence is detained pursuant to section 50 and is released without any charge having been made against him or her, he or she shall not—

(a) be arrested again in connection with the offence to which the detention related, or

(b) be arrested for any other offence of which, at the time of the first arrest, the member of the Garda Síochána by whom he or she was arrested suspected, or ought reasonably to have suspected him or her, of having committed,

except on the authority of a warrant issued by a judge of the Circuit Court or the District Court who is satisfied on information supplied on oath by a member of the Garda Síochána not below the rank of superintendent that either of the following cases apply, namely:

(i) further information has come to the knowledge of the Garda Síochána since the person's release as to his or her suspected participation in the offence for which his or her arrest is sought,

(ii) notwithstanding that the Garda Síochána had knowledge, prior to the person's release, of the person's suspected participation in the offence for which his or her arrest is sought, the questioning of the person in relation to that offence, prior to his or her release would not have been in the interests of the proper investigation of the offence.

(1A) An application for a warrant under this section shall be heard otherwise than in public.][1]

(2) When issuing a warrant under subsection (1), the judge concerned may order that the person concerned be brought before a judge of the Circuit Court or District Court on arrest or at any specified time or times during the period of detention authorised by section 50 as applied by subsection (3) and if, upon the person's being so brought before such a judge, he or she is not satisfied that the person's detention is justified, the judge shall revoke the warrant and order the immediate release from custody of the person.

(3) Section 50 shall apply to a person arrested in connection with an offence to which that section relates under a warrant issued pursuant to subsection (1), as it applies to a person to whom that section applies, with the following and any other necessary modifications:

(a) in subsection (3), the substitution for paragraphs (c) and (d) of the following paragraphs:

"(c) A member of the Garda Síochána not below the rank of chief superintendent may apply to a judge of the Circuit Court or District Court for a warrant authorising the detention of a person detained pursuant to a direction under paragraph (b) for a further period not exceeding 24 hours if he or she has reasonable grounds for believing that such further detention is necessary for the proper investigation of the offence concerned.

(d) On an application under paragraph (c) the judge concerned shall issue a warrant authorising the detention of the person to whom the application relates for a further period not exceeding 24 hours if, but only if, the judge is satisfied that such further detention is necessary for the proper investigation of the offence concerned and that the investigation is being conducted diligently and expeditiously.";

and

(b) in paragraph (g)(i) of subsection (3), the substitution of "under a warrant issued pursuant to paragraph (d)" for "pursuant to a direction under paragraph (c)".

(4) A person arrested in connection with an offence other than one to which section 50 relates, under a warrant issued pursuant to subsection (1), shall, subject to subsection (2), be dealt with under section 4 of the Act of 1984 in like manner as a person arrested without warrant to whom the said section 4 applies.

(5) Notwithstanding subsection (1), a person to whom that subsection relates may be arrested for any offence for the purpose of charging him or her with that offence forthwith.

(6) Where a person who has been arrested under section 30 of the Offences Against the State Act 1939 or detained under section 4 of the Act of 1984 or section 2 of the Criminal Justice (Drug Trafficking) Act 1996 in connection with an offence is released without any charge having been made against him or her, he or she shall not be detained pursuant to section 50 —

(a) in connection with the first-mentioned offence, or

(b) in connection with an offence to which section 50 relates and which, at the time of the first arrest, the member of the Garda Síochána by whom he or she was arrested, suspected, or ought reasonably to have suspected, him or her of having committed.

Amendments

1   Subsection (1) and (1A) substituted for sub-s (1) by Criminal Justice (Amendment) Act 2009, s 23(3).

52   Application of certain provisions of Act of 1984

Sections 4(4), 4(7), 4(8), 4(8A), [4(8B)], 4(11), 5, 6(1) to (4), 6A, 8, 18, 19 and 19A of the Act of 1984 shall apply with any necessary modifications in relation to persons detained under section 50 as they apply to persons detained under section 4 of that Act.

Amendments

1   Words inserted by Criminal Justice (Amendment) Act 2009, s 23(4).

53   Amendment of Criminal Justice (Forensic Evidence) Act 1990

The Criminal Justice (Forensic Evidence) Act 1990 is amended—

(a) in section 2—

(i) in subsection (1), by the substitution of "section 2 of the Criminal Justice (Drug Trafficking) Act 1996 or section 50 of the Criminal Justice Act 2007," for "or section 2 of the Criminal Justice (Drug Trafficking) Act, 1996,",

(ii) in subsection (3), by the insertion in paragraph (b) after "section 3(1) of the Criminal Justice Act, 1994" of "or an offence to which section 50 of the Criminal Justice Act 2007 applies", and

(iii) in subsection (5), by the insertion in paragraph (a)(ii) after "within the meaning of 3(1) of the Criminal Justice Act 1994" of "or an offence to which section 50 of the Criminal Justice Act 2007 applies", and

(b) in section 4(2), by the substitution of "section 2 of the Criminal Justice (Drug Trafficking) Act 1996 or section 50 of the Criminal Justice Act 2007," for "or section 2 of the Criminal Justice (Drug Trafficking) Act, 1996,".

54   Amendment of section 5 of Criminal Justice (Drug Trafficking) Act 1996

Section 5 of the Criminal Justice (Drug Trafficking) Act 1996 is amended by—

    (a) the insertion of "4(8A)," after "4(8),", and

    (b) the substitution of ", 6A, 8, 18, 19 and 19A" for "and 8".

55   Amendment of section 9 of Act of 1984

Section 9 of the Act of 1984 is amended by—

    (a) the insertion of "4(8A)," after "4(8),", and

    (b) the substitution of ", 6(3), 6A, 18, 19 and 19A" for "and 6(3)".

56   Copy of recording of questioning by Garda Síochána to be given to accused

(1) Where a person is before a court charged with an offence, a copy of any recording of the questioning of the person by a member of the Garda Síochána while he or she was detained in a Garda Síochána station, or such questioning elsewhere, in connection with the investigation of the offence shall be given to the person or his or her legal representative only if the court so directs and subject to such conditions (if any) as the court may specify.

(2) A recording referred to in subsection (1) of the questioning of a person shall not be given to the person by the Garda Síochána except in accordance with a direction or order of a court made under that subsection or otherwise and Regulation 16 of the Criminal Justice Act 1984 (Electronic Recording of Interviews) Regulations 1997 (S.I. No. 74 of 1997) is hereby revoked.

(3) In this section—

"recording" means a recording on tape of—

    (a) an oral communication, statement or utterance, or

    (b) a series of visual images which, when reproduced on tape, appear as a moving picture,

or both;

"tape" includes—

    (a) a disc, magnetic tape, soundtrack or other device in which sounds or signals may be embodied for the purpose of being reproduced (with or without the aid of some other instrument) in audible form, and

    (b) a film, disc, magnetic tape or other device in which visual images may be embodied for the purpose of being reproduced (with or without the aid of some other instrument) in visual form.

57   Admission in evidence of recording of questioning of accused by Garda Síochána

(1) A court may admit in evidence at the trial of a person in respect of an offence—

    (a) a recording by electronic or similar means, or

    (b) a transcript of such a recording,

or both of the questioning of the person by a member of the Garda Síochána at a Garda Síochána station or elsewhere in connection with the investigation of the offence.

(2) Any statement made by the person concerned that is recorded in a recording which is admitted in evidence under subsection (1) may be admissible in evidence at the trial concerned notwithstanding the fact that—

(a) it was not taken down in writing at the time it was made, or

(b) that statement is not in writing and signed by the person who made it,

or both.

(3) This section shall not affect the admissibility in evidence at the trial of a person in respect of an offence of any statement that is recorded in writing made by the person during questioning by a member of the Garda Síochána at a Garda Síochána station or elsewhere in connection with the investigation of the offence (whether or not that statement is signed by the person) and irrespective of whether the making of that statement is recorded by electronic or similar means.

58   Amendment of section 8 of Criminal Assets Bureau Act 1996

Section 8 of the Criminal Assets Bureau Act 1996 is amended—

(a) in subsection (2), by the substitution of "subject to subsections (5), (6), (6A), (6B), (6C) and (7)" for "subject to subsections (5), (6) and (7)", and

(b) by the insertion of the following subsections after subsection (6):[1]

Amendments

1   See the amended Act.

---

59   Amendment of section 29 of Courts of Justice Act 1924

Section 29 of the Courts of Justice Act 1924 is amended—

(a) in subsection (1), by the substitution of "Subject to subsection (9A) of this section, no appeal shall lie" for "No appeal shall lie",

(b) by the insertion of the following subsection after subsection (5):

"(5A) The Supreme Court, in an appeal under subsection (2) or (3) of this section, may, if it considers it appropriate to do so, hear argument and make a determination in relation to any part (not only the point of law of exceptional public importance which is the subject of the certificate concerned issued under whichever of those subsections is appropriate) of the decision of the Court of Criminal Appeal concerned.",

and

(c) by the insertion of the following subsection after subsection (9):

"(9A) This section shall not affect the operation of section 3 of the Criminal Justice Act 1993 .".

60   Amendment of section 99 of Act of 2006

Section 99 of the Act of 2006 is amended—

(a) in subsection (9), by the substitution of "the court before which proceedings for the offence are brought shall, before imposing sentence for that offence" for "the court before which proceedings for the offence were brought shall, after imposing sentence for that offence",

(b) in subsection (10), by the substitution of "other than a period spent in custody by the person in respect of an offence referred to in subsection (9)" for "other than a period during which the person was serving a sentence of imprisonment in respect of an offence referred to in subsection (9)",

(c) by the insertion of the following subsection after subsection (10):

(d) in subsection (11), by the substitution of the following paragraph for paragraph (a): and

(e) by the addition of the following subsection:

SCHEDULE 1
ENACTMENTS REPEALED

Section 3

Number and Year	Short Title	Extent of Repeal
(1)	(2)	(3)
No. 29 of 1996	Criminal Justice (Drug Trafficking) Act 1996	Section 7.
No. 39 of 1998	Offences Against the State (Amendment) Act 1998	Section 5.

SCHEDULE 2
OFFENCES FOR THE PURPOSES OF PART 3

Sections 25 and 26.

COMMON LAW OFFENCES

1. Murder.

NON-FATAL OFFENCES AGAINST THE PERSON

2. An offence under any of the following provisions of the Non-Fatal Offences Against the Person Act 1997:

    (a) section 4 (causing serious harm);

    (b) section 5 (threats to kill or cause serious harm);

    (c) section 15 (false imprisonment).

EXPLOSIVES OFFENCES

3. An offence under any of the following provisions of the Explosive Substances Act 1883:

    (a) section 2 (causing explosion likely to endanger life or damage property);

    (b) section 3 (possession, etc., of explosive substances);

    (c) section 4 (making or possessing explosives in suspicious circumstances).

FIREARMS OFFENCES

4.   An offence under section 15 (possession of firearm with intent to endanger life) of the Act of 1925.

5.   An offence under any of the following provisions of the Act of 1964:

   (a)   section 26 (possession of firearms while taking vehicle without authority);

   (b)   section 27 (prohibition of use of firearms to assist or aid escape);

   (c)   section 27A (possession of firearm or ammunition in suspicious circumstances);

   (d)   section 27B (carrying firearm with criminal intent).

6.   An offence under section 12A (shortening barrel of shotgun or rifle) of the Act of 1990.

AGGRAVATED BURGLARY

7.   An offence under section 13 (aggravated burglary) of the Criminal Justice (Theft and Fraud Offences) Act 2001.

DRUG TRAFFICKING OFFENCES

8.   A drug trafficking offence within the meaning of section 3(1) of the Criminal Justice Act 1994.

ORGANISED CRIME

9.   An offence under any of the following provisions of the Act of 2006:

   (a)   section 71 (offence of conspiracy);

   [(b) section 71A (directing activities of a criminal organisation);

   (ba) section 72 (offence to participate in, or contribute to, certain activities);][1]

BLACKMAIL, EXTORTION AND DEMANDING MONEY WITH MENACES

10.   An offence under section 17 (blackmail, extortion and demanding money with menaces) of the Criminal Justice (Public Order) Act 1994.

Amendments

1   Paragraph 9(b) substituted and (ba) inserted by Criminal Justice (Amendment) Act 2009, s 14(2).

Criminal Law (Human Trafficking) Act 2008

Number 8 of 2008

ARRANGEMENT OF SECTIONS

1. Interpretation.

2. Trafficking, etc., of children.

3. Trafficking, taking, etc., of child for purpose of sexual exploitation.

4. Trafficking of persons other than children.

5. Soliciting or importuning for purposes of prostitution of trafficked person.

6. Offences by bodies corporate.

7. Jurisdiction.

8. Proceedings relating to offences committed outside State.

9. Double jeopardy.

10. Exclusion of members of public from proceedings.

11. Anonymity of victims of trafficking.

12. Amendment of Criminal Evidence Act 1992.

13. Amendment of Act of 2001.

14. Amendment of Bail Act 1997.

15. Short title and commencement.

AN ACT TO GIVE EFFECT TO COUNCIL FRAMEWORK DECISION OF 19 JULY 2002 ON COMBATING TRAFFICKING IN HUMAN BEINGS; TO GIVE EFFECT, IN PART, TO THE UNITED NATIONS PROTOCOL TO PREVENT, SUPPRESS AND PUNISH TRAFFICKING IN PERSONS, ESPECIALLY WOMEN AND CHILDREN, SUPPLEMENTING THE UNITED NATIONS CONVENTION AGAINST TRANSNATIONAL ORGANISED CRIME, DONE AT NEW YORK ON 15 NOVEMBER 2000, AND THE COUNCIL OF EUROPE CONVENTION ON ACTION AGAINST TRAFFICKING IN HUMAN BEINGS DONE AT WARSAW ON 16 MAY 2005; FOR THOSE PURPOSES TO AMEND CERTAIN ENACTMENTS; TO AMEND SECTION 3 OF THE SEX OFFENDERS ACT 2001; AND TO PROVIDE FOR MATTERS CONNECTED THEREWITH. [7th May, 2008]

BE IT ENACTED BY THE OIREACHTAS AS FOLLOWS:

1   Interpretation

In this Act—

" Act of 1998 " means the Child Trafficking and Pornography Act 1998;

"Act of 2001" means the Sex Offenders Act 2001;

"child" means a person under the age of 18 years;

"exploitation" means—

    (a) labour exploitation,

    (b) sexual exploitation, or

    (c) exploitation consisting of the removal of one or more of the organs of a person;

"labour exploitation" means, in relation to a person (including a child)—

    (a) subjecting the person to forced labour,

    (b) forcing him or her to render services to another, or

    (c) enslavement of the person or subjecting him or her to servitude or a similar condition or state;

" sexual exploitation " means, in relation to a person—

    (a) the production of pornography depicting the person either alone or with others,

    (b) causing the person to engage in sexual activity for the purpose of the production of pornography,

    (c) the prostitution of the person,

    (d) the commission of an offence specified in the Schedule to the Act of 2001 against the person; causing another person to commit such an offence against the person; or causing the person to commit such an offence against another person, or

    (e) otherwise causing the person to engage or participate in any sexual, indecent or obscene act;

"trafficks" means, in relation to a person (including a child)—

    (a) procures, recruits, transports or harbours the person, or

        (i) transfers the person to,

        (ii) places the person in the custody, care or charge, or under the control, of, or

        (iii) otherwise delivers the person to,

        another person,

    (b) causes a person to enter or leave the State or to travel within the State,

    (c) takes custody of a person or takes a person—

        (i) into one's care or charge, or

        (ii) under one's control,

        or

    (d) provides the person with accommodation or employment.

2   Trafficking, etc., of children

(1) A person who trafficks a child for the purposes of the exploitation of the child shall be guilty of an offence.

(2) A person who—

    (a) sells a child, offers or exposes a child for sale or invites the making of an offer to purchase a child, or

    (b) purchases or makes an offer to purchase a child,

shall be guilty of an offence.

(3) A person who causes an offence under subsection (1) or (2) to be committed shall be guilty of an offence.

(4) A person who attempts to commit an offence under subsection (1), (2) or (3) shall be guilty of an offence.

(5) A person guilty of an offence under this section shall be liable upon conviction on indictment—

   (a) to imprisonment for life or a lesser term, and

   (b) at the discretion of the court, to a fine.

(6) In this section "exploitation" does not include sexual exploitation.

3   Trafficking, taking, etc., of child for purpose of sexual exploitation

Section 3 (amended by section 6 of the Criminal Law (Sexual Offences) (Amendment) Act 2007) of the Act of 1998 is amended by—

   (a) the substitution of the following subsections for subsections (1) and (2):[1] and

   (b) the substitution of the following subsections for subsection (3):[1]

Amendments

1   See the amended Act.

---

4   Trafficking of persons other than children

(1) A person (in this section referred to as the "trafficker") who traffics another person (in this section referred to as the "trafficked person"), other than a child or a person to whom subsection (3) applies, for the purposes of the exploitation of the trafficked person shall be guilty of an offence if, in or for the purpose of trafficking the trafficked person, the trafficker—

   (a) coerced, threatened, abducted or otherwise used force against the trafficked person,

   (b) deceived or committed a fraud against the trafficked person,

   (c) abused his or her authority or took advantage of the vulnerability of the trafficked person to such extent as to cause the trafficked person to have had no real and acceptable alternative but to submit to being trafficked,

   (d) coerced, threatened or otherwise used force against any person in whose care or charge, or under whose control, the trafficked person was for the time being, in order to compel that person to permit the trafficker to traffick the trafficked person, or

   (e) made any payment to, or conferred any right, interest or other benefit on, any person in whose care or charge, or under whose control, the trafficked person was for the time being, in exchange for that person permitting the trafficker to traffick the trafficked person.

(2) In proceedings for an offence under this section it shall not be a defence for the defendant to show that the person in respect of whom the offence was committed consented to the commission of any of the acts of which the offence consists.

(3) A person who traffics a person who is mentally impaired for the purposes of the exploitation of the person shall be guilty of an offence.

(4) A person who—

   (a) sells another person, offers or exposes another person for sale or invites the making of an offer to purchase another person, or

   (b) purchases or makes an offer to purchase another person,

shall be guilty of an offence.

(5) A person who causes an offence under subsection (1), (3) or (4) to be committed shall be guilty of an offence.

(6) A person who attempts to commit an offence under subsection (1), (3), (4) or (5) shall be guilty of an offence.

(7) A person guilty of an offence under this section shall be liable upon conviction on indictment—

   (a) to imprisonment for life or a lesser term, and

   (b) at the discretion of the court, to a fine.

(8) In this section "mentally impaired" has the same meaning as it has in the Criminal Law (Sexual Offences) Act 1993 .

5   Soliciting or importuning for purposes of prostitution of trafficked person

(1) Where, for the purposes of the prostitution of a trafficked person, a person (other than that trafficked person) solicits or importunes another person, including that trafficked person, in any place, he or she shall be guilty of an offence.

(2) A person (other than the trafficked person in respect of whom the offence under subsection (1) is committed) who accepts, or agrees to accept a payment, right, interest or other benefit from a person for a purpose mentioned in subsection (1) shall be guilty of an offence.

(3) A person guilty of an offence under this section shall be liable—

   (a) on summary conviction to a fine not exceeding €5,000 or a term of imprisonment not exceeding 12 months, or both, or

   (b) on conviction on indictment to a fine or a term of imprisonment not exceeding 5 years, or both.

(4) In proceedings for an offence under this section it shall be a defence for the defendant to prove that he or she did not know and had no reasonable grounds for believing, that the person in respect of whom the offence was committed was a trafficked person.

(5) This section is in addition to, and not in substitution for, section 7 of the Act of 1993 in so far as an offence under that section is committed by, or in respect of, a trafficked person.

(6) In this section—

"Act of 1993" means the Criminal Law (Sexual Offences) Act 1993;

"solicits or importunes" has the same meaning as it has in the Act of 1993;

"trafficked person" means—

   (a) a person in respect of whom an offence under subsection (1) or (3) of section 4 has been committed, or

   (b) a child who has been trafficked for the purpose of his or her exploitation.

6   Offences by bodies corporate

Where an offence under this Act is committed by a body corporate and is proved to have been so committed with the consent or connivance of or to be attributable to any neglect on the part of any person, being a director, manager, secretary or other officer of the body corporate, or a person who was purporting to act in such capacity, that person shall, as well as the body corporate, be guilty of an offence and shall be liable to be proceeded against and punished as if he or she were guilty of the first-mentioned offence.

7   Jurisdiction

(1) Where a person who is an Irish citizen or ordinarily resident in the State does an act in a place other than the State that, if done in the State, would constitute an offence under section 2 or 4, or section 3 (other than subsections (2A) and (2B)) of the Act of 1998, he or she shall be guilty of an offence and shall be liable on conviction on indictment to a fine, or imprisonment for life, or both.

(2) Where a person does an act in relation to an Irish citizen in a place other than the State that, if done in the State, would constitute an offence under section 2 or 4, or section 3 (other than subsections (2A) and (2B)) of the Act of 1998, he or she shall be guilty of an offence and shall be liable on conviction on indictment to a fine, or imprisonment for life, or both.

(3) Where a person conspires with, or incites, in the State, another person to do an act in a place other than the State that, if done in the State, would constitute an offence under section 2 or 4, or section 3 (other than subsections (2A) and (2B)) of the Act of 1998, he or she shall be guilty of an offence and shall be liable on conviction on indictment to a fine, or imprisonment for life, or both.

(4) Where a person who is an Irish citizen or ordinarily resident in the State conspires with, or incites, in a place other than the State, another person to do an act in a place other than the State that, if done in the State, would constitute an offence under section 2 or 4, or section 3 (other than subsections (2A) and (2B)) of the Act of 1998, he or she shall be guilty of an offence and shall be liable on conviction on indictment to a fine, or imprisonment for life, or both.

(5) Where a person conspires with, or incites, in the State or in a place other than the State, another person to do an act in relation to an Irish citizen in a place other than the State that, if done in the State, would constitute an offence under section 2 or 4, or section 3 (other than subsections (2A) and (2B)) of the Act of 1998, he or she shall be guilty of an offence and shall be liable on conviction on indictment to a fine, or imprisonment for life, or both.

(6) Where a person conspires with, or incites, in a place other than the State, a person who is an Irish citizen or ordinarily resident in the State to do an act in a place other than the State that, if done in the State, would constitute an offence under section 2 or 4, or section 3 (other than subsections (2A) and (2B)) of the Act of 1998, he or she shall be guilty of an offence and shall be liable on conviction on indictment to a fine, or imprisonment for life, or both.

(7) Where a person attempts to commit an offence under subsection (1), (2), (3), (4), (5) or (6), he or she shall be guilty of an offence and shall be liable on conviction on indictment to a fine, or imprisonment for life, or both.

(8) For the purposes of this section a person shall be deemed to be ordinarily resident in the State if—

    (a) he or she has had his or her principal residence in the State for the period of 12 months immediately preceding the alleged commission of the offence,

    (b) it is a company registered under the Companies Acts, or

    (c) in the case of any other body corporate, it is established under the law of the State.

8   Proceedings relating to offences committed outside State

Proceedings for an offence under section 7 may be taken in any place in the State and the offence may for all incidental purposes be treated as having been committed in that place.

9   Double jeopardy

(1) Where a person has been acquitted of an offence in a place other than the State, he or she shall not be proceeded against for an offence under this Act consisting of the alleged act or acts constituting the first-mentioned offence.

(2) Where a person has been convicted of an offence in a place other than the State, he or she shall not be proceeded against for an offence under this Act consisting of the act or acts constituting the first-mentioned offence.

10   Exclusion of members of public from proceedings

(1) In proceedings for an offence under section 2 or 4, or section 3 (other than subsections (2A) and (2B)) of the Act of 1998, or incitement or conspiracy to commit any such offence, all persons, other than officers of the court, persons directly concerned in the proceedings and such other persons (if any) as the judge of the court may determine, shall be excluded from the court during the proceedings.

(2) In proceedings to which this section applies the verdict or decision and the sentence (if any) shall be pronounced in public.

11   Anonymity of victims of trafficking

(1) Where a person is charged with an offence under section 2 or 4, or section 3 (other than subsections (2A) and (2B)) of the Act of 1998, any person who publishes or broadcasts any information, including—

(a)   any photograph of, or that includes a depiction of, the alleged victim of the offence, or

(b)   any other representation of the physical likeness, or any representation that includes a depiction of the physical likeness, of the alleged victim of the offence,

that is likely to enable the identification of the alleged victim of the offence, shall, subject to any direction under subsection (2), be guilty of an offence and shall be liable upon conviction on indictment to a fine, or imprisonment for a term not exceeding 10 years, or both.

(2) The judge of the court in which proceedings for an offence under section 2 or 4, or section 3 (other than subsections (2A) and (2B)) of the Act of 1998, are brought may, where he or she considers that the interests of justice so require, direct that such information to which subsection (1) applies as he or she shall specify in the direction may be published or broadcast in such manner and subject to such conditions as he or she may specify in the direction.

(3) A direction under this section shall be in writing.

(4) A person who contravenes a direction under this section, including a condition in such a direction, shall be guilty of an offence and shall be liable upon conviction on indictment to a fine, or imprisonment for a term not exceeding 10 years, or both.

(5) In this section—

"broadcasts" means transmits, relays or distributes by wireless telegraphy or by any other means, or by wireless telegraphy in conjunction with any other means, of communications, sounds, signs, visual images or signals intended for reception by any person whether such communications, sounds, signs, visual images or signals are received by that person or not;

"publishes" means publishes to any person, and includes publishes on the internet.

12   Amendment of Criminal Evidence Act 1992

The Criminal Evidence Act 1992 is amended—

    (a)   in the definition of "sexual offence" (inserted by section 16 of the Criminal Justice (Miscellaneous Provisions) Act 1997) in section 2, by—

        (i)   the deletion of paragraph (iv) (inserted by section 7(2) of the Criminal Law (Sexual Offences) Act 2006), and

        (ii)   the substitution of the following paragraph for paragraph (e):

    and

    (b)   by the substitution of the following section for section 12 (amended by section 10 of the Act of 1998):[1]

Amendments

1   See the amended Act.

---

13   Amendment of Act of 2001

The Act of 2001 is amended—

    (a)   in section 3, by—

        (i)   the substitution of the following paragraph for paragraph (a) of subsection (2):[1]

        (ii)   the substitution of the following paragraph for paragraph (ii) of subsection (2):[1]

        (iii)   the insertion of the following subsection:[1]

    (b)   in section 12, by the substitution of the following subsection for subsection (3):[1]

    (c)   in section 33, by the insertion of the following subsection:[1]

    (d)   in the Schedule, by the insertion of the following paragraph:[1]

Amendments

1   See the amended Act.

---

14   Amendment of Bail Act 1997

The Schedule to the Bail Act 1997 is amended by the insertion of the following paragraph:[1]

Amendments

1   See the amended Act.

15   Short title and commencement

(1) This Act may be cited as the Criminal Law (Human Trafficking) Act 2008.

(2) This Act shall come into operation one month after its passing.

Criminal Justice (Surveillance) Act 2009

Number 19 of 2009

1. Interpretation.
2. Application of Act.
3. Surveillance.
4. Application for authorisation.
5. Authorisation.
6. Variation or renewal of authorisation.
7. Approval for surveillance in cases of urgency.
8. Tracking devices.
9. Retention of materials relating to applications and reports.
10. Restriction of disclosure of existence of authorisations and other documents.
11. Complaints procedure.
12. Review of operation of this Act by designated judge.
13. Confidentiality of information.
14. Admissibility of evidence.
15. Disclosure of information.
16. Regulations.
17. Amendment of Garda Síochána Act 2005.
18. Amendment of Courts (Supplemental Provisions) Act 1961.
19. Short title.

AN ACT TO PROVIDE FOR SURVEILLANCE IN CONNECTION WITH THE INVESTIGATION OF ARRESTABLE OFFENCES, THE PREVENTION OF SUSPECTED ARRESTABLE OFFENCES AND THE SAFEGUARDING OF THE STATE AGAINST SUBVERSIVE AND TERRORIST THREATS, TO AMEND THE GARDA SÍOCHÁNA ACT 2005 AND THE COURTS (SUPPLEMENTAL PROVISIONS) ACT 1961 AND TO PROVIDE FOR MATTERS CONNECTED THEREWITH. [12th July, 2009]

BE IT ENACTED BY THE OIREACHTAS AS FOLLOWS:

1 Interpretation

In this Act—

"Act of 1993" means the Interception of Postal Packets and Telecommunications Messages (Regulation) Act 1993;

"arrestable offence" has the meaning it has in section 2 (as amended by section 8 of the Criminal Justice Act 2006) of the Criminal Law Act 1997;

"authorisation" means an authorisation for the carrying out of surveillance issued under section 5 or varied or renewed under section 6;

"document" includes—

(a) any book, record or other written or printed material in any form, and

(b) any recording, including any data or information stored, maintained or preserved electronically or otherwise than in legible form;

"judge" means a judge of the District Court;

"member of the Defence Forces" means a member of the Defence Forces within the meaning of section 1 of the Defence (Amendment) Act 1990, other than a member of the Reserve Defence Force within the meaning of the Defence Act 1954;

"member of the Garda Síochána" means a member of the Garda Síochána within the meaning of section 3 of the Garda Síochána Act 2005, other than a person referred to in paragraph (b) of that definition;

"Minister" means the Minister for Justice, Equality and Law Reform;

"place" includes—

(a) a dwelling or other building,

(b) a vehicle, whether mechanically propelled or not,

(c) a vessel, whether sea-going or not,

(d) an aircraft, whether capable of operation or not, and

(e) a hovercraft;

"relevant Minister" means—

(a) the Minister, in relation to approvals granted by a superior officer of, and documents and information in the custody of, the Garda Síochána,

(b) the Minister for Defence, in relation to approvals granted by a superior officer of, and documents and information in the custody of, the Defence Forces, and

(c) the Minister for Finance, in relation to approvals granted by a superior officer of, and documents and information in the custody of, the Revenue Commissioners;

"revenue offence" means an offence under any of the following provisions that is an arrestable offence:

(a) section 186 of the Customs Consolidation Act 1876;

(b) section 1078 of the Taxes Consolidation Act 1997;

(c) section 102 of the Finance Act 1999;

(d) section 119 of the Finance Act 2001;

(e) section 79 (inserted by section 62 of the Finance Act 2005) of the Finance Act 2003;

(f) section 78 of the Finance Act 2005;

"superior officer" means—

(a) in the case of the Garda Síochána, a member of the Garda Síochána not below the rank of superintendent;

(b) in the case of the Defence Forces, a member of the Defence Forces not below the rank of colonel; and

(c) in the case of the Revenue Commissioners, an officer of the Revenue Commissioners not below the rank of principal officer;

"surveillance" means—

    (a) monitoring, observing, listening to or making a recording of a particular person or group of persons or their movements, activities and communications, or

    (b) monitoring or making a recording of places or things,

by or with the assistance of surveillance devices;

"surveillance device" means an apparatus designed or adapted for use in surveillance, but does not include—

    (a) an apparatus designed to enhance visual acuity or night vision, to the extent to which it is not used to make a recording of any person who, or any place or thing that, is being monitored or observed,

    (b) a CCTV within the meaning of section 38 of the Garda Síochána Act 2005, or

    (c) a camera, to the extent to which it is used to take photographs of any person who, or any thing that, is in a place to which the public have access;

"tracking device" means a surveillance device that is used only for the purpose of providing information regarding the location of a person, vehicle or thing;

"written record of approval" means a written record of approval prepared by a superior officer under section 7(6) or 8 6).

2   Application of Act

(1) This Act applies to surveillance carried out by members of the Garda Síochána, members of the Defence Forces and officers of the Revenue Commissioners.

(2) Nothing in this Act shall render unlawful any activity that would otherwise be lawful.

(3) An authorisation or approval under this Act may not be issued or granted in respect of an activity that would constitute an interception within the meaning of the Act of 1993.

(4) For the avoidance of doubt, it is hereby declared that this Act does not apply to the following:

    (a) the use of a closed circuit television system in a Garda Síochána station;

    (b) the recording by electronic or other similar means under section 27 of the Criminal Justice Act 1984 of the questioning of a person by members of the Garda Síochána at Garda Síochána stations or elsewhere in connection with the investigation of offences;

    (c) the recording by electronic or other similar means of any evidence given, or statement made, by a person for the purposes of any court proceedings.

3   Surveillance

A member of the Garda Síochána, a member of the Defence Forces or an officer of the Revenue Commissioners shall carry out surveillance only in accordance with a valid authorisation or an approval granted in accordance with section 7 or 8.

4   Application for authorisation

(1) A superior officer of the Garda Síochána may apply to a judge for an authorisation where he or she has reasonable grounds for believing that—

    (a) as part of an operation or investigation being conducted by the Garda Síochána concerning an arrestable offence, the surveillance being sought to be authorised is necessary for the purposes of obtaining information as to whether the offence has been committed or as to the circumstances relating to the commission of the offence, or obtaining evidence for the purposes of proceedings in relation to the offence,

(b) the surveillance being sought to be authorised is necessary for the purpose of preventing the commission of arrestable offences, or

(c) the surveillance being sought to be authorised is necessary for the purpose of maintaining the security of the State.

(2) A superior officer of the Defence Forces may apply to a judge for an authorisation where he or she has reasonable grounds for believing that the surveillance being sought to be authorised is necessary for the purpose of maintaining the security of the State.

(3) A superior officer of the Revenue Commissioners may apply to a judge for an authorisation where he or she has reasonable grounds for believing that—

(a) as part of an operation or investigation being conducted by the Revenue Commissioners concerning a revenue offence, the surveillance being sought to be authorised is necessary for the purpose of obtaining information as to whether the offence has been committed or as to the circumstances relating to the commission of the offence, or obtaining evidence for the purpose of proceedings in relation to the offence, or

(b) the surveillance being sought to be authorised is necessary for the purpose of preventing the commission of revenue offences.

(4) In a case in which surveillance carried out under section 7 is sought under subsection (10) of that section to be continued by application under this section, the information on oath supporting the application shall include a copy of the written record of approval concerned, a summary of the results of the surveillance carried out and the reasons why continued surveillance is required.

(5) A superior officer who makes an application under subsection (1), (2), (3) or (4) shall also have reasonable grounds for believing that the surveillance being sought to be authorised is—

(a) the least intrusive means available, having regard to its objectives and other relevant considerations,

(b) proportionate to its objectives, having regard to all the circumstances including its likely impact on the rights of any person, and

(c) of a duration that is reasonably required to achieve its objectives.

5   Authorisation

(1) An application under section 4 for an authorisation and under section 6 for a variation or renewal of an authorisation—

(a) shall be made ex parte and shall be heard otherwise than in public, and

(b) may be made to a judge assigned to any district court district.

(2) Subject to subsection (4), the judge shall issue such authorisation as he or she considers reasonable, if satisfied by information on oath of the superior officer concerned that—

(a) the requirements specified in subsection (1), (2) or (3), as the case may be, of section 4 are fulfilled, and

(b) to do so is justified, having regard to the matters referred to in section 4(5) and all other relevant circumstances.

(3) An information on oath of a superior officer specifying the grounds for his or her belief that the surveillance is necessary for the purpose of preventing the commission of arrestable offences referred to in section 4(1)(b), or the commission of revenue offences referred to in section 4(3)(b), need not specify a particular arrestable offence or a particular revenue offence, as the case may be, in respect of which the authorisation is being sought.

(4) The judge shall not issue an authorisation if he or she is satisfied that the surveillance being sought to be authorised is likely to relate primarily to communications protected by privilege.

(5) An authorisation may impose such conditions in respect of the surveillance authorised as the judge considers appropriate.

(6) An authorisation shall be in writing and shall specify—

    (a) particulars of the surveillance device that is authorised to be used,

    (b) the person who, or the place or thing that, is to be the subject of the surveillance,

    (c) the name of the superior officer to whom it is issued,

    (d) the conditions (if any) subject to which the authorisation is issued, and

    (e) the date of expiry of the authorisation.

(7) An authorisation may authorise the superior officer named in it, or any member of the Garda Síochána, any member of the Defence Forces or any officer of the Revenue Commissioners designated by that superior officer, accompanied by any other person whom he or she considers necessary, to enter, if necessary by the use of reasonable force, any place for the purposes of initiating or carrying out the authorised surveillance, and withdrawing the authorised surveillance device, without the consent of a person who owns or is in charge of the place.

(8) An authorisation shall expire on the day fixed by the judge that he or she considers reasonable in the circumstances and that is not later than 3 months from the day on which it is issued.

(9) Subject to any conditions imposed by the judge under subsection (5), an authorisation shall have effect both within the district court district to which the judge is assigned and in any other part of the State.

6   Variation or renewal of authorisation

(1) A judge may, on application in that behalf by the superior officer to whom an authorisation was issued, if satisfied by information on oath of that superior officer justifying the variation or renewal of the authorisation—

    (a) vary the authorisation, or

    (b) renew the authorisation, on the same or different conditions, for such further period, not exceeding 3 months, as the judge considers appropriate.

(2) An application for a renewal under this section shall be made before the authorisation concerned, or any previous renewal of that authorisation, as the case may be, has expired.

(3) Where an application for a renewal under this section has been made and the authorisation concerned would, but for this subsection, expire during the hearing of the application, it shall be deemed not to expire until the determination of the application.

7   Approval for surveillance in cases of urgency

(1) A member of the Garda Síochána, a member of the Defence Forces or an officer of the Revenue Commissioners may carry out surveillance without an authorisation if the surveillance has been approved by a superior officer in accordance with this section.

(2) A member or officer referred to in subsection (1) may apply to a superior officer for the grant of an approval to carry out surveillance if he or she believes on reasonable grounds that the requirements of subsection (1), (2) or (3), as the case may be, of section 4 are fulfilled and that the surveillance is justified having regard to the matters referred to in section 4(5), but that, before an authorisation could be issued—

   (a) it is likely that a person would abscond for the purpose of avoiding justice, obstruct the course of justice or commit an arrestable offence or a revenue offence, as the case may be,

   (b) information or evidence in relation to the commission of an arrestable offence or a revenue offence, as the case may be, is likely to be destroyed, lost or otherwise become unavailable, or

   (c) the security of the State would be likely to be compromised.

(3) A superior officer to whom an application under subsection (2) is made shall approve the carrying out of such surveillance as he or she considers appropriate, having regard to the information in the application, if he or she is satisfied that there are reasonable grounds for believing that an authorisation would be issued under section 5 but that one or more of the conditions of urgency specified in subsection (2) apply.

(4) An approval may be granted subject to conditions, including as to the duration of the surveillance.

(5) An approval under this section permits the member or officer concerned, accompanied by any other person whom he or she considers necessary, to enter, if necessary by the use of reasonable force, any place for the purposes of initiating or carrying out the approved surveillance, and withdrawing the approved surveillance device, without the consent of a person who owns or is in charge of the place.

(6) A superior officer who approves the carrying out of surveillance under this section shall, as soon as practicable and, in any case, not later than 8 hours after the surveillance has been approved, prepare a written record of approval of that surveillance.

(7) A written record of approval shall be in such form as the relevant Minister may prescribe by regulations and shall include—

   (a) particulars of the surveillance device that is approved to be used,

   (b) the person who, or the place or thing that, is to be the subject of the surveillance,

   (c) the name of the member of the Garda Síochána, member of the Defence Forces or officer of the Revenue Commissioners to whom the approval is granted,

   (d) the conditions (if any) subject to which the approval is granted,

   (e) the time at which the approval is granted, and

   (f) the duration of the approved surveillance.

(8) The member or officer shall not carry out surveillance under this section for a period of more than 72 hours from the time at which the approval is granted.

(9) The superior officer who approved the carrying out of surveillance may vary that approval, or any condition attached to it, at any time before the expiry of the period of 72 hours.

(10) (a) If the superior officer who approved the carrying out of surveillance believes on reasonable grounds that surveillance beyond the period of 72 hours is warranted, he or she shall, as soon as possible but in any case before the expiry of that period, make an application under section 4(4) for an authorisation to continue the surveillance.

(b) Where an application under section 4(4) has been made and the period referred to in paragraph (a) would, but for this paragraph, expire during the hearing of the application, it shall be deemed not to expire until the determination of the application.

(11) A superior officer who approves the carrying out of surveillance under this section shall make a report as soon as possible and, in any case, not later than 7 days after the surveillance concerned has been completed, specifying the grounds on which the approval was granted, and including a copy of the written record of approval and a summary of the results of the surveillance.

(12) A report under subsection (11) shall be made to—

(a) in the case of a member of the Garda Síochána, a member of the Garda Síochána of the rank of Assistant Commissioner,

(b) in the case of an officer of the Defence Forces, a general officer within the meaning of section 2 (as amended by section 2(b) of the Defence (Amendment) Act 1979) of the Defence Act 1954, and

(c) in the case of an officer of the Revenue Commissioners, an officer of the Revenue Commissioners of the rank of Assistant Secretary.

8   Tracking devices

(1) Notwithstanding sections 4 to 7, a member of the Garda Síochána, a member of the Defence Forces or an officer of the Revenue Commissioners may, for a period of not more than 4 months or such shorter period as the Minister may prescribe by regulations, monitor the movements of persons, vehicles or things using a tracking device if that use has been approved by a superior officer in accordance with this section.

(2) A member or officer referred to in subsection (1) may apply to a superior officer for the grant of an approval to use a tracking device if he or she believes on reasonable grounds that—

(a) the requirements of subsection (1), (2) or (3), as the case may be, of section 4 are fulfilled and that surveillance is justified having regard to the matters referred to in paragraphs (b) and (c) of section 4(5), but that the use of a tracking device would be sufficient for obtaining the information or evidence in the circumstances concerned, and

(b) the information or evidence sought could reasonably be obtained by the use of a tracking device for a specified period that is as short as is practicable to allow the information or evidence to be obtained.

(3) A superior officer to whom an application under subsection (2) is made shall approve such use of a tracking device as he or she considers appropriate, having regard to the

information in the application, if he or she is satisfied that there are reasonable grounds for believing that an authorisation would be issued under section 5 and that the conditions specified in subsection (2) apply.

(4) An approval may be granted subject to conditions, including as to the duration of the use of the tracking device.

(5) An approval under this section permits the member or officer concerned, accompanied by any other person whom he or she considers necessary, to place the tracking device and remove it at the end of its use, without the consent of a person who owns or is in charge of the vehicle or thing on which it is placed.

(6) A superior officer who approves the use of a tracking device under this section shall, as soon as practicable and, in any case, not later than 8 hours after the use has been approved, prepare a written record of approval of the use of the tracking device.

(7) A written record of approval shall be in such form as the relevant Minister may prescribe by regulations and shall include—

    (a) particulars of the tracking device that is approved to be used,

    (b) the person who, or the vehicle or thing that, is to be monitored,

    (c) the name of the member of the Garda Síochána, member of the Defence Forces or officer of the Revenue Commissioners to whom the approval is granted,

    (d) the conditions (if any) subject to which the approval is granted,

    (e) the time at which the approval is granted, and

    (f) the duration of the use approved.

(8) Without prejudice to the maximum period for which an approval granted under this section may have effect, the superior officer who approves the use of a tracking device under this section may vary that approval, or any condition attached to it, at any time before the expiry of that approval.

(9) A superior officer who approves the use of a tracking device under this section shall make a report as soon as possible and, in any case, not later than 7 days after its use has ended, specifying the grounds on which the approval was granted, and including a copy of the written record of approval and a summary of the results of the monitoring.

(10) A report under subsection (9) shall be made to—

    (a) in the case of a member of the Garda Síochána, a member of the Garda Síochána of the rank of Assistant Commissioner,

    (b) in the case of an officer of the Defence Forces, a general officer within the meaning of section 2 (as amended by section 2 (b) of the Defence (Amendment) Act 1979) of the Defence Act 1954, and

    (c) in the case of an officer of the Revenue Commissioners, an officer of the Revenue Commissioners of the rank of Assistant Secretary.

(11) The Minister may, in the interests of the protection of the privacy and other rights of persons, the security of the State, and the aims of preventing the commission of, and detecting, arrestable offences, make regulations prescribing a period of less than 4 months as the maximum period for which approvals granted under this section may have effect, and such regulations may prescribe different periods in respect of different purposes or circumstances.

9   Retention of materials relating to applications and reports

(1) An application for an authorisation under section 4 or 6, and any documents supporting the application, shall be retained until—

(a)   the day that is 3 years after the day on which the authorisation concerned ceases to be in force, or

(b)   the day on which they are no longer required for any prosecution or appeal to which they are relevant,

whichever is later.

(2) A written record of approval prepared under section 7(6) or 8(6), and a report made under section 7(11) or 8(9), shall be retained until—

(a)   the day that is 3 years after the day on which the written record of approval is prepared or the report concerned is made, or

(b)   the day on which they are no longer required for any prosecution or appeal to which they are relevant,

whichever is later.

(3) The documents obtained as a result of surveillance carried out or tracking devices used under this Act, other than those referred to in subsections (1) and (2), shall be retained until—

(a)   the day that is 3 years after the end of the surveillance or monitoring concerned, or

(b)   the day on which they are no longer required for any prosecution or appeal to which they are relevant,

whichever is later.

(4) Subject to subsection (5), the documents referred to in subsections (1) to (3) shall be destroyed as soon as practicable after they are no longer required to be retained under those subsections.

(5) The relevant Minister may authorise in writing the retention of any of the documents referred to in this section where he or she considers it necessary to do so having regard to—

(a)   the interests of the protection of the privacy and other rights of persons,

(b)   the security of the State,

(c)   the aims of preventing the commission of, and detecting, arrestable offences, and

(d)   the interests of justice.

10   Restriction of disclosure of existence of authorisations and other documents

(1) The relevant Minister shall ensure that information and documents to which this Act applies are stored securely and that only persons who he or she authorises for that purpose have access to them.

(2) In the interests of the protection of the privacy and other rights of persons, the security of the State, and the aims of preventing the commission of, and detecting, arrestable offences, the relevant Minister may make regulations prescribing—

(a)   the persons or categories of persons who are to have access for the purposes of this section to information with respect to the existence of authorisations, approvals granted under sections 7 and 8 and documents referred to in section 9,

(b)   the procedures and arrangements for the secure storage, and the maintenance of the security, of that information and those documents, and

(c) the number of copies that may be made of those documents and the destruction of those copies as soon as possible after they are no longer required under section 9.

(3) Notwithstanding section 13, the Minister may make regulations respecting the disclosure or non-disclosure, to the person who was its subject or other persons whose interests are materially affected by it, of the existence of an authorisation or an approval under section 7 or 8, provided that any disclosure authorised by such regulations is—

(a) consistent with the purposes for which the authorisation or approval concerned was issued or granted,

(b) consistent with the security of the State, the protection of persons' privacy and other rights and the aims of preventing and detecting the commission of arrestable offences, and

(c) unlikely to hinder the investigation in the future of such offences.

(4) Any regulation made under subsection (3) may—

(a) require consultation by the Minister, in any particular case of disclosure, with such classes of persons as may be prescribed,

(b) prescribe categories of persons (other than the subjects of the authorisations or approvals) whose interests are materially affected by authorisations or approvals, to whom disclosure is to be made, and

(c) permit the imposition of terms and conditions limiting the extent or detail of disclosure as necessary, having regard to the matters referred to in subsection (3).

11   Complaints procedure

(1) A person who believes that he or she might be the subject of an authorisation or an approval under section 7 or 8 may apply to the Referee for an investigation into the matter.

(2) A superior officer who makes a report under section 7(11) or 8(9), or receives a report under section 7(12) or 8(10), may apply to the Referee for an investigation into a matter if he or she believes that such an investigation would be in the interests of justice.

(3) If an application is made under this section (other than one that the Referee considers to be frivolous or vexatious), the Referee shall investigate—

(a) whether an authorisation was issued or an approval was granted as alleged in the application, and

(b) if so, whether there has been a relevant contravention.

(4) If, after investigating the matter, the Referee concludes that there has been a relevant contravention, the Referee shall—

(a) notify the applicant, and any other person whose interests are materially affected by the relevant contravention, in writing of that conclusion, and

(b) make a report of his or her findings to the Taoiseach.

(5) In the circumstances referred to in subsection (4), the Referee may also, if he or she is of opinion that the relevant contravention was material and that to do so would be justified in the circumstances, by order do one or more of the following things:

(a) direct—

(i) the quashing of the authorisation or the reversal of the approval, and

      (ii) the destruction of the written record of approval concerned, the report under section 7(11) or 8(9) concerned, and any information or documents obtained as a result of the authorisation or approval;

  (b) make a recommendation for the payment of such sum, not exceeding €5,000, specified in the order by way of compensation to the person who was the subject of the authorisation or approval;

  (c) report the matter and any recommendation under paragraph (b) to—

      (i) the Garda Síochána Ombudsman Commission, in the case of a contravention by the Garda Síochána,

      (ii) the Minister for Defence, in the case of a contravention by the Defence Forces,

      (iii) the Minister for Finance, in the case of a contravention by the Revenue Commissioners;

  (d) report the matter and any recommendation under paragraph (b) to the judge designated under section 12.

(6) If the Referee is of opinion that, in all the circumstances, it would not be in the public interest to—

  (a) notify, under subsection (4)(a), the applicant or the other person, if any, of a conclusion that there has been a relevant contravention,

  (b) direct the quashing, reversal or destruction under subsection (5)(a), or

  (c) make a recommendation for the payment of a sum by way of compensation under subsection (5)(b),

he or she shall decline to do so.

(7) If, after investigating the matter, the Referee concludes that there has not been a relevant contravention, the Referee shall give notice in writing to the applicant stating only that there has been no such contravention.

(8) A decision of the Referee under this section is final.

(9) A relevant contravention that is not material does not of itself constitute a cause of action at the suit of a person who was the subject of the authorisation or approval concerned.

(10) A person in charge of a Garda Síochána station within the meaning of section 99(10) of the Garda Síochána Act 2005, a place under the control of the Defence Forces or the Revenue Commissioners or any other place in which documents relevant to an investigation under this section are kept shall ensure that the Referee has access to those places, and to the authorisations, written records of approval, reports and other relevant documents that the Referee may request.

(11) The Referee—

  (a) may, on his or her own initiative, and

  (b) shall, where a case has been referred to him or her by the designated judge under section 12(8),

investigate whether there has been a relevant contravention and this section (other than subsection (7)) shall apply to such an investigation as if the references to " the applicant " in subsections (4) and (6) were to "the person who was the subject of the authorisation or approval".

(12) In this section—

"Referee" means the holder of the office of Complaints Referee under the Act of 1993;

"relevant contravention" means a contravention of a provision of sections 4 to 8.

12   Review of operation of this Act by designated judge

(1) After consulting with the Minister, the President of the High Court shall invite a judge of the High Court to undertake (while serving as such a judge) the duties specified in this section and, if the invitation is accepted, the Government shall designate the judge for the purposes of performing those functions.

(2) The designated judge holds office in accordance with the terms of the designation.

(3) The functions of the designated judge are to—

    (a) keep under review the operation of sections 4 to 8, and

    (b) report to the Taoiseach from time to time and at least once every 12 months concerning any matters relating to the operation of those sections that the designated judge considers should be reported.

(4) For the purpose of performing his or her functions the designated judge may investigate any case in which an authorisation is issued under section 5 or renewed or varied under section 6 or an approval is granted under section 7 or 8.

(5) A person in charge of a Garda Síochána station within the meaning of section 99(10) of the Garda Síochána Act 2005, a place under the control of the Defence Forces or the Revenue Commissioners or any other place in which documents relevant to the performance of the functions of the designated judge are kept shall ensure that the designated judge has access to those places, and to the authorisations, written records of approval, reports and other relevant documents that the designated judge may request.

(6) The Taoiseach shall ensure that a copy of a report under subsection (3)(b) is laid before each House of the Oireachtas not later than 6 months after it is made, together with a statement of whether any matter has been excluded under subsection (7).

(7) If the Taoiseach considers, after consultation with the designated judge, that the publication of any matter in a report, copies of which are to be laid before the Houses under subsection (6), would be prejudicial to the security of the State, the Taoiseach may exclude that matter from those copies.

(8) Where the designated judge investigates a case under subsection (4) and is of the opinion that it is in the interests of justice to do so, he or she may refer that case to the Referee for an investigation under section 11(11).

13   Confidentiality of information

(1) A person shall not disclose, inside or outside the State, any information in connection with the operation of this Act in relation to surveillance carried out under an authorisation or under an approval granted in accordance with section 7 or 8, including any information or documents obtained as a result of such surveillance, or reveal the existence of an application for the issue of an authorisation, the variation or renewal of an authorisation under section 6 or the grant of an approval under section 7 or 8, unless the disclosure is to an authorised person and is—

    (a) for the purposes of the prevention, investigation or detection of crime,

    (b) for the prosecution of offences,

(c) in the interests of the security of the State, or

(d) required under any other enactment.

(2) A relevant person who contravenes subsection (1) shall be guilty of an offence and shall be liable—

(a) on summary conviction, to a fine not exceeding €3,000 or imprisonment for a term not exceeding 12 months or both, or

(b) on conviction on indictment, to a fine not exceeding €50,000 or imprisonment for a term not exceeding 5 years or both.

(3) A person other than a relevant person who contravenes subsection (1) shall be guilty of an offence and shall be liable—

(a) on summary conviction, to a fine not exceeding €1,000 or imprisonment for a term not exceeding 6 months or both, or

(b) on conviction on indictment, to a fine not exceeding €10,000 or imprisonment for a term not exceeding 2 years or both.

(4) In this section—

"authorised person" means—

(a) a person referred to in section 62(4)(a) of the Garda Síochána Act 2005,

(b) the Minister for Defence,

(c) the Minister for Finance, and

(d) a person the disclosure to whom is—

(i) authorised by the Commissioner of the Garda Síochána, the Chief of Staff of the Defence Forces or a Revenue Commissioner, or

(ii) otherwise authorised by law;

"relevant person" means a person who is or was—

(a) a member of the Garda Síochána, a member of the Defence Forces or an officer of the Revenue Commissioners,

(b) a reserve member of the Garda Síochána within the meaning of the Garda Síochána Act 2005,

(c) a member of the Reserve Defence Force within the meaning of the Defence Act 1954,

(d) a member of the civilian staff of the Garda Síochána or of the Defence Forces, or

(e) engaged under a contract or other arrangement to work with or for the Garda Síochána, the Defence Forces or the Revenue Commissioners.

14   Admissibility of evidence

(1) Evidence obtained as a result of surveillance carried out under an authorisation or under an approval granted in accordance with section 7 or 8 may be admitted as evidence in criminal proceedings.

(2) Nothing in this Act is to be construed as prejudicing the admissibility of information or material obtained otherwise than as a result of surveillance carried out under an authorisation or under an approval granted in accordance with section 7 or 8.

(3) (a) Information or documents obtained as a result of surveillance carried out under an authorisation or under an approval granted in accordance with section 7 or 8 may be admitted as evidence in criminal proceedings notwithstanding any error or

omission on the face of the authorisation or written record of approval concerned, if the court, having regard in particular to the matters specified in paragraph (b), decides that—

    (i) the error or omission concerned was inadvertent, and

    (ii) the information or document ought to be admitted in the interests of justice.

(b) The matters referred to in paragraph (a) are the following:

    (i) whether the error or omission concerned was serious or merely technical in nature;

    (ii) the nature of any right infringed by the obtaining of the information or document concerned;

    (iii) whether there were circumstances of urgency;

    (iv) the possible prejudicial effect of the information or document concerned;

    (v) the probative value of the information or document concerned.

(4) (a) Information or documents obtained as a result of surveillance carried out under an authorisation or under an approval granted in accordance with section 7 or 8 may be admitted as evidence in criminal proceedings notwithstanding any failure by any member of the Garda Síochána, member of the Defence Forces or officer of the Revenue Commissioners concerned to comply with a requirement of the authorisation or approval concerned, if the court, having regard in particular to the matters specified in paragraph (b), decides that—

    (i) the member or officer concerned acted in good faith and that the failure was inadvertent, and

    (ii) the information or document ought to be admitted in the interests of justice.

(b) The matters referred to in paragraph (a) are the following:

    (i) whether the failure concerned was serious or merely technical in nature;

    (ii) the nature of any right infringed by the obtaining of the information or document concerned;

    (iii) whether there were circumstances of urgency;

    (iv) the possible prejudicial effect of the information or document concerned;

    (v) the probative value of the information or document concerned.

(5) It shall be presumed, until the contrary is shown, that a surveillance device or tracking device used by a member of the Garda Síochána, a member of the Defence Forces or an officer of the Revenue Commissioners for the purposes referred to in this Act is a device capable of producing accurate information or material without the necessity of proving that the surveillance device or tracking device was in good working order.

15   Disclosure of information

(1) Unless authorised by the court, the existence or non-existence of the following shall not be disclosed by way of discovery or otherwise in the course of any proceedings:

(a) an application under section 4 or 6;

(b) an authorisation;

(c) an approval granted under section 7 or 8;

(d) surveillance carried out under an authorisation or under an approval granted under section 7;

(e) the use of a tracking device under section 8; and

    (f) documentary or other information or evidence in relation to—

        (i) the decision to apply for an authorisation or an approval under section 7 or 8, or

        (ii) anything referred to in paragraphs (a) to (e).

(2) The court shall not authorise the disclosure if it is satisfied that to do so is likely to create a material risk to—

    (a) the security of the State,

    (b) the ability of the State to protect persons from terrorist activity, terrorist-linked activity, organised crime and other serious crime,

    (c) the maintenance of the integrity, effectiveness and security of the operations of the Garda Síochána, the Defence Forces or the Revenue Commissioners, or

    (d) the ability of the State to protect witnesses, including their identities.

(3) Notwithstanding subsection (2), the court may authorise the disclosure, subject to such conditions as it considers justified, if in all of the circumstances it is in the interests of justice to do so.

(4) In this section—

"organised crime" has the meaning it has in Part 7 of the Criminal Justice Act 2006;

"terrorist activity" and "terrorist-linked activity" have the meanings they have in section 4 of, and Schedule 2 to, the Criminal Justice (Terrorist Offences) Act 2005.

16   Regulations

(1) The Minister, the Minister for Defence and the Minister for Finance may make regulations prescribing any matter or thing which is referred to in this Act as prescribed or to be prescribed by him or her.

(2) Regulations made under this section may contain such incidental, supplementary and consequential provisions as appear to the Minister of the Government making them to be necessary or expedient for the purposes of the regulations.

(3) Every regulation under this section shall be laid before each House of the Oireachtas as soon as may be after it has been made and, if a resolution annulling the regulation is passed by either such House within the next 21 days on which that House has sat after the regulation is laid before it, the regulation shall be annulled accordingly, but without prejudice to the validity of anything previously done thereunder.

17   Amendment of Garda Síochána Act 2005

The definition of "enactment" in section 98(5) of the Garda Síochána Act 2005 is amended by—

    (a) deleting "and" at the end of paragraph (a),

    (b) in paragraph (b), substituting " Postal and Telecommunications Services Act 1983, and" for " Postal and Telecommunications Services Act 1983;", and

    (c) inserting the following after paragraph (b):

        "(c) any provision of the Criminal Justice (Surveillance) Act 2009;".

18   Amendment of Courts (Supplemental Provisions) Act 1961

Section 32A(1) (inserted by section 180 of the Criminal Justice Act 2006) of the Courts (Supplemental Provisions) Act 1961 is amended—

(a) in paragraph (c), by substituting "such assets or proceeds;" for "such assets or proceeds.", and

(b) by inserting the following after paragraph (c):[1]

Amendments

1   See the amended Act.

---

19   Short title

This Act may be cited as the Criminal Justice (Surveillance) Act 2009.

Criminal Justice (Miscellaneous Provisions) Act 2009

Number 28 of 2009

ARRANGEMENT OF SECTIONS

PART 1
PRELIMINARY AND GENERAL

1. Short title and commencement.
2. Interpretation.
3. Expenses.

PART 2
AMENDMENTS TO EUROPEAN ARREST WARRANT ACT 2003

4. Amendments to section 2 of Act of 2003.
5. Amendments to section 4 of Act of 2003.
6. Amendments to section 10 of Act of 2003.
7. Amendments to section 11 of Act of 2003.
8. Amendments to section 12 of Act of 2003.
9. Amendments to section 13 of Act of 2003.
10. Amendment to section 14 of Act of 2003.
11. Amendments to section 15 of Act of 2003.
12. Amendments to section 16 of Act of 2003.
13. Amendments to section 18 of Act of 2003.
14. Amendment to section 20 of Act of 2003.
15. Amendment to section 29 of Act of 2003.
16. Amendments to section 33 of Act of 2003.
17. Amendment to section 38 of Act of 2003.
18. Amendment to section 34 of Act of 2003.
19. Deletion of section 40 of Act of 2003.
20. New sections 45 to 45C of Act of 2003.

PART 3
SCHENGEN INFORMATION SYSTEM

21. Interpretation.
22. Exchange of Information for purposes of Council Decision and Schengen Convention.
23. Data Protection.
24. Amendments to section 27 of Extradition Act 1965.

PART 4
AMENDMENT OF FIREARMS ACTS

25. Amendments to section 1 of Principal Act.

26. Amendment to section 2 of Principal Act.

27. New section 2C of Principal Act.

28. Amendment to section 3 of Principal Act.

29. Amendment to section 3A of Principal Act.

30. New sections 3B, 3C and 3D of Principal Act.

31. Commissioner to conduct annual review.

32. Amendment to section 4B of Principal Act.

33. New section 4C of Principal Act.

34. Reporting of loss of firearm or ammunition.

35. New section 9A of Principal Act.

36. New section 17 of Principal Act.

37. Amendment to section 9 of Act of 1964.

38. Repeal of section 21 of Act of 1964.

39. Amendment to section 9 of Act of 1990.

40. New sections 9A to 9I of Act of 1990.

41. Amendment to section 16 of Act of 1990.

42. Amendment to section 2 of Act of 2000.

43. Amendment to section 30 of Act of 2006.

44. Repeal of section 40 of Act of 2006.

PART 5
MISCELLANEOUS

45. Amendment to section 2 of Act of 1857.

46. New section 2A of Act of 1857.

47. Amendment to section 4 of Criminal Justice Act 1984.

48. Amendment of Bail Act 1997.

49. Amendment to section 15 of Act of 2001.

50. Amendment to section 39 of Act of 2001.

51. Amendment to section 99 of Criminal Justice Act 2006.

52. Amendment to Regulation 12 of Criminal Justice Act 1984 (Treatment of Persons in Custody in Garda Síochána Stations) Regulations 1987.

AN ACT TO GIVE FURTHER EFFECT TO THE COUNCIL FRAMEWORK DECISION OF 13 JUNE 2002 ON THE EUROPEAN ARREST WARRANT AND THE SURRENDER PROCEDURES BETWEEN MEMBER STATES, AND TO GIVE EFFECT TO THE COUNCIL DECISION 2007/533/JHA OF 12 JUNE 2007 ON THE ESTABLISHMENT, OPERATION AND USE OF THE SECOND GENERATION SCHENGEN INFORMATION SYSTEM, AND FOR THOSE AND OTHER PURPOSES TO AMEND THE EUROPEAN ARREST WARRANT ACT 2003, EXTEND THE APPLICATION OF THE DATA PROTECTION ACTS 1988 AND 2003 AND AMEND THE EXTRADITION ACT 1965, TO

AMEND THE LAW RELATING TO THE REGULATION AND CONTROL OF FIREARMS AND AMMUNITION AND FOR THAT AND OTHER PURPOSES TO AMEND THE FIREARMS ACTS 1925 TO 2007, TO AMEND CERTAIN OTHER ENACTMENTS AND TO PROVIDE FOR RELATED MATTERS. [21st July, 2009]

BE IT ENACTED BY THE OIREACHTAS AS FOLLOWS:

Note

Part 3 (ss 21–24) and s 52 have not yet come into operation (February 2011).

PART 1
PRELIMINARY AND GENERAL

1   Short title and commencement

(1) This Act may be cited as the Criminal Justice (Miscellaneous Provisions) Act 2009.

(2) The Firearms Acts 1925 to 2007 and Part 4 may be cited together as the Firearms Acts 1925 to 2009 and shall be construed together as one.

(3) This Act shall come into operation on such day or days as the Minister may, by order or orders either generally or with reference to any particular purpose or provision, appoint and different days may be so appointed for different purposes or different provisions.

2   Interpretation

In this Act—

"Act of 1857" means the Summary Jurisdiction Act 1857;

"Act of 1964" means the Firearms Act 1964;

"Act of 1990" means the Firearms and Offensive Weapons Act 1990;

"Act of 2000" means the Firearms (Firearm Certificates for Non- Residents) Act 2000;

"Act of 2001" means the Criminal Justice (Theft and Fraud Offences) Act 2001;

"Act of 2003" means the European Arrest Warrant Act 2003;

"Act of 2006" means the Criminal Justice Act 2006;

"Firearms Acts" means the Firearms Acts 1925 to 2007;

"the Minister" means the Minister for Justice, Equality and Law Reform;

"Principal Act" means the Firearms Act 1925.

3   Expenses

The expenses incurred by the Minister in the administration of this Act shall, to such extent as may be sanctioned by the Minister for Finance, be paid out of moneys provided by the Oireachtas.

PART 2
AMENDMENTS TO EUROPEAN ARREST WARRANT ACT 2003

4   Amendments to section 2 of Act of 2003

Section 2 of the Act of 2003 is hereby amended in subsection (1)—

- (a) by the insertion of the following definitions after the definition of "Act of 2001":[1]
- (b) by the insertion of the following definition after the definition of "Central Authority in the State":[1]
- (c) by the deletion of the definition of "facsimile copy", and
- (d) by the insertion of the following definitions after the definition of 'Minister': [1]

Amendments

1   See the amended Act.

---

5   Amendments to section 4 of Act of 2003

Section 4 of the Act of 2003 is hereby amended—

- (a) in subsection (1) by the substitution for "(1) Subject to subsections (2) and (3), this" of "This", and
- (b) by the deletion of subsections (2) and (3).

6   Amendments to section 10 of Act of 2003

Section 10 (as inserted by section 71 of the Criminal Justice (Terrorist Offences) Act 2005) of the Act of 2003 is hereby amended—

- (a) by the deletion of the word "duly",
- (b) in paragraph (c) by the insertion after "offence" of "in that state",
- (c) in paragraph (d)—
  - (i)   by the insertion after "imposed" of "in that state", and
  - (ii) by the deletion of the following words:

  "and who fled from the issuing state before he or she—
  - (i)   commenced serving that sentence, or
  - (ii) completed serving that sentence".

7   Amendments to section 11 of Act of 2003

Section 11 (as amended by section 72 of the Criminal Justice (Terrorist Offences) Act 2005) of the Act of 2003 is hereby amended—

- (a) in subsection (1A) by the substitution in paragraph (e) for "the offence" of "one of the offences to which the European arrest warrant relates",
- (b) in subsection (2) by the substitution of "(1A)" for "(1)" in the second place that it occurs, and
- (c) by the substitution for subsection (2A) of the following:[1]

1374

Amendments

1 See the amended Act.

8 Amendments to section 12 of Act of 2003

Section 12 (as amended by section 73 of the Criminal Justice (Terrorist Offences) Act 2005) of the Act of 2003 is hereby amended—

  (a) in subsection (3)—

    (i) by the insertion after "this Act" of "or any other document to be transmitted for the purposes of this Act", and

    (ii) by the substitution for paragraph (b) of the following paragraph:[1]

  (b) by the deletion of subsections (4), (5) and (6),

  (c) by the substitution for subsection (7) of the following:[1] and

  (d) in subsection (9) by the deletion of the words "facsimile copy or".

Amendments

1 See the amended Act.

9 Amendments to section 13 of Act of 2003

Section 13 of the Act of 2003 is hereby amended—

  (a) in subsection (1) by the deletion of the words "facsimile copy or",

  (b) in subsection (2) by the deletion of paragraph (b), and

  (c) in subsection (3) by the deletion of the words "the facsimile copy of the warrant or" and ", facsimile copy".

10 Amendment to section 14 of Act of 2003

Section 14 of the Act of 2003 is amended by the substitution for that section of the following:[1]

Amendments

1 See the amended Act.

11 Amendments to section 15 of Act of 2003

Section 15 (as amended by section 75 of the Criminal Justice (Terrorist Offences) Act 2005) is hereby amended—

(a) in subsection (1)(a) by the deletion of the words "facsimile or",

(b) in subsection (2)(a) by the substitution for "facsimile or true copies" of "a true copy",

(c) by the insertion after subsection (3) of the following new subsection:[1]

(d) in subsection (5) by the insertion after "subsection (6)" of ", subsection (7)",

(e) by the substitution for subsection (6) of the following: [1]

(f) by the substitution for subsection (7) of the following: [1]
and

(g) by the substitution for subsection (9) of the following: [1]

Amendments

1   See the amended Act.

12   Amendments to section 16 of Act of 2003

Section 16 (as amended by section 76 of the Criminal Justice (Terrorist Offences) Act 2005) of the Act of 2003 is hereby amended—

(a) in subsection (1)—

(i) by the deletion of the words "or has withdrawn his or her consent under section 15(9)", and

(ii) by the deletion from paragraphs (b) and (c) of the words "facsimile or",

(b) in subsection (2)—

(i) by the deletion of "or has withdrawn his or her consent under section 15(9)", and

(ii) in paragraph (a) thereof by the deletion of "or facsimile",

(c) in subsection (5) by the insertion after "subsection (6)" of ", subsection (7)",

(d) by the substitution for subsection (6) of the following: [1]

(e) by the substitution for subsection (7) of the following: [1]

(f) in subsection (12) by the substitution for "on a point of law only." of "if, and only if, the High Court certifies that the order or decision involves a point of law of exceptional public importance and that it is desirable in the public interest that an appeal should be taken to the Supreme Court.", and

(g) by the insertion of the following new subsection after subsection (12):[1]

Amendments

1   See the amended Act.

13   Amendments to section 18 of Act of 2003

Section 18 (as amended by section 77 of the Criminal Justice (Terrorist Offences) Act 2005) of the Act of 2003 is hereby amended—

(a) by the substitution for subsection (3) of the following subsection:[1]
    and

(b) in subsection (4) by the substitution for "subsection (3)(i) or (ii)" of "subsection (3)(b)(I) or (II)".

Amendments

1 See the amended Act.

14   Amendment to section 20 of Act of 2003

Section 20 of the Act of 2003 is hereby amended in subsection (3) by the insertion after "affidavit" of ", declaration, affirmation, attestation".

15   Amendment to section 29 of Act of 2003

Section 29 of the Act of 2003 is hereby amended by the deletion of "neither of which or not all of which, as the case may be, have been issued by the same issuing state,".

16   Amendments to section 33 of Act of 2003

Section 33 of the Act of 2003 is hereby amended—

(a) by the substitution for subsection (1)(a) of the following subsection:[1]

(b) in subsection (1)(b)(i) by the insertion of "or detention" after "imprisonment",

(c) in subsection (1)(b)(ii) by the insertion of "or detention" after "imprisonment" in each place where it occurs, and

(d) by the insertion of the following subsections after subsection (1):[1]

Amendments

1 See the amended Act.

17   Amendment to section 38 of Act of 2003

Section 38 of the Act of 2003 is hereby amended in subsection (1)(b) by the deletion of "or is an offence that consists of conduct specified in the paragraph,".

18   Amendment to section 34 of Act of 2003

The Act of 2003 is hereby amended in section 34 by the substitution for "shall" of "may".

19   Deletion of section 40 of Act of 2003

The Act of 2003 is hereby amended by the deletion of section 40.

20   New sections 45 to 45C of Act of 2003

The Act of 2003 is hereby amended—

   (a) by the substitution for section 45 of the following section:[1]
        and

   (b) by the insertion of the following new sections after section 45:[1]

Amendments

1   See the amended Act.

PART 3
SCHENGEN INFORMATION SYSTEM

Note

Part 3 has not yet come into operation (February 2011).

---

21   Interpretation

(1) In this Part—

"Council Decision" means Council Decision 2007/533/JHA of 12 June 2007 on the establishment, operation and use of the second generation Schengen Information System;

"Schengen Convention" means the Convention implementing the Schengen Agreement of 14 June 1985 between the Governments of the States of the Benelux Economic Union, the Federal Republic of Germany and the French Republic on the gradual abolition of checks at their common borders done at Schengen on 19 June 1990 and includes any amendment to or modification of that Convention whether before or after the passing of this Act but does not include the Council Decision.

(2) A word or expression that is used in this Part and also in the Council Decision or the Schengen Convention shall, unless the contrary intention appears, have the same meaning in this Part as it has in the Council Decision or, as the case may be, Schengen Convention.

22   Exchange of Information for purposes of Council Decision and Schengen Convention

(1) A member of the Garda Síochána, an officer of customs and excise or any other person or category of persons of a description specified in an order made by the Minister under this section may provide and receive information for the purposes of the operation of the Council Decision or Schengen Convention.

(2) The Minister may make an order designating any person or category of persons of a description specified in the order as a person who may provide and receive information for the purposes of the operation of the Council Decision or Schengen Convention.

(3) An order under this section shall, as soon as may be after it is made, be laid before each of the Houses of the Oireachtas and if a resolution annulling the order or regulation is passed by either such House within the next 21 days on which that House has sat after the order is laid before it, the order shall be annulled accordingly, but without prejudice to the validity of anything previously done thereunder.

23   Data Protection

(1) The Data Protection Commissioner is hereby designated as the national supervisory authority for the purposes of Article 60 of the Council Decision and Article 114 of the Schengen Convention.

(2) The Data Protection Acts 1988 and 2003 shall apply and have effect with any necessary modification to the collection, processing, keeping, use and disclosure of personal data for the purposes of the operation of the Council Decision and the Schengen Convention.

24   Amendments to section 27 of Extradition Act 1965

Section 27 (as amended by sections 6(b) and 8 of the Extradition (Amendment) Act 1994 and sections 5 and 20(d) of the Extradition (European Conventions) Act 2001) is amended—

    (a) by the insertion after subsection (3) of the following new subsections:[1]

        and

    (b) by the insertion of the following subsection after subsection (11):[1]

Amendments

1   See the amended Act.

PART 4
AMENDMENT OF FIREARMS ACTS

25   Amendments to section 1 of Principal Act

Section 1 of the Principal Act is amended—

    (a) in the definition of "firearm" in subsection (1) (as substituted by section 26 of the Act of 2006) by the insertion in paragraph (f) of "or paragraph (h)" after "foregoing paragraphs", and

    (b) by the addition of the following definitions after the definition of "muzzle energy":[1]

Amendments

1   See the amended Act.

---

26   Amendment to section 2 of Principal Act

Section 2 (as amended by the Act of 1964, the Firearms (Proofing) Act 1968, the Firearms Act 1971, the Act of 2006 and the Criminal Justice Act 2007) of the Principal Act is amended—

(a) in subsection (4) by the substitution of the following paragraph for paragraph (g):[1] and

(b) in subsection (6) by the deletion of "(d),".

Amendments

1   See the amended Act.

27   New section 2C of Principal Act

The following section is inserted after section 2B (inserted by section 29 of the Criminal Justice Act 2006) of the Principal Act:[1]

Amendments

1   See the amended Act.

28   Amendment to section 3 of Principal Act

Section 3 of the Principal Act is amended by the substitution for subsection (3) of the following subsection:[1]

Amendments

1   See the amended Act.

29   Amendment to section 3A of Principal Act

Section 3A (inserted by section 31 of the Act of 2006) of the Principal Act is amended by the substitution for that section of the following:[1]

Amendments

1   See the amended Act.

30   New sections 3B, 3C and 3D of Principal Act

The Principal Act is hereby amended by the insertion of the following new sections after section 3A (as substituted by section 29 of this Act):¹

Amendments

1   See the amended Act.

31   Commissioner to conduct annual review

The Principal Act is amended by the insertion of the following section after section 3D (inserted by section 30):¹

Amendments

1   See the amended Act.

32   Amendment to section 4B of Principal Act

Section 4B (inserted by section 34 of the Act of 2006) of the Principal Act is amended in subsection (2)(a) by the substitution for "authorisation" of "certification".

33   New section 4C of Principal Act

The Principal Act is amended by the insertion of the following new section after section 4B (inserted by section 34 of Act of 2006):¹

Amendments

1   See the amended Act.

34   Reporting of loss of firearm or ammunition

The Principal Act is amended by the insertion of the following section after section 5:¹

"5A.— (1) Where a firearm or ammunition is lost (whether by theft or otherwise) after the commencement of this section, the certificate holder to whom the firearm or ammunition relates, shall within three days of becoming aware of the loss, report the loss to the issuing person who granted the certificate.

(2) A person who fails, without reasonable excuse, to report the loss of a firearm or ammunition in accordance with this section shall be guilty of an offence.

(3) A person guilty of an offence under this section shall be liable—

(a)   in case the firearm is a restricted firearm or the ammunition is restricted ammunition—

> (i)   on summary conviction, to a fine not exceeding €5,000 or imprisonment for a term not exceeding 12 months or both, or
>
> (ii)   on conviction on indictment, to a fine not exceeding €20,000 or imprisonment not exceeding 5 years or both,
>
> or
>
> (b)   in any other case—
>
> (i)   on summary conviction, to a fine not exceeding €2,500 or imprisonment for a term not exceeding 6 months or both, or
>
> (ii)   on conviction on indictment, to a fine not exceeding €10,000 or imprisonment not exceeding 3 years or both.".[1]

Amendments

1   Section 34 is not yet in operation (February 2011).

35   New section 9A of Principal Act

The Principal Act is amended by the insertion of the following section after section 9:[1]

Amendments

1   See the amended Act.

36   New section 17 of Principal Act

The following section is substituted for section 17 of the Principal Act:

> **"Restrictions on the import of firearms, prohibited weapons and ammunition.**
>
> 17.— (1) Without prejudice to the provisions of the Firearms (Firearms Certificates for Non-Residents) Act 2000, no person, other than a registered firearm dealer, shall import into the State any firearm, ammunition, or prohibited weapon.
>
> (2) A continuing licence to import firearms or ammunition may on application in the prescribed manner be granted by the Minister if he or she thinks fit so to do to any registered firearms dealer, and every such continuing licence shall operate and be expressed to authorise the importation into the State of firearms and ammunition generally or of any specified class or classes of firearms and ammunition through the port, by the registered dealer, during the period and subject to the conditions named in such licence.
>
> (3) An occasional licence to import into the State a firearm or prohibited weapon, with or without ammunition therefor, may, on application in the prescribed manner, be granted by the Minister if he or she thinks fit so to do to any registered firearms dealer and every such occasional licence shall operate and be expressed to authorise the importation into the State of the firearm and the quantity of ammunition (if any)

specified in such licence through the port, by the registered firearms dealer, within the time and subject to the conditions named in such licence.

(4) Notwithstanding subsections (1) to (3) of this section, a licence for importing a firearm, ammunition or prohibited weapon may not be granted unless—

(a) the applicant has a good reason for importing it,

(b) granting the licence would not prejudice public safety or security, and

(c) if the application relates to a restricted firearm or restricted ammunition, the applicant possesses an authorisation under section 10 of this Act.

(5) An applicant for a licence under this section shall supply in writing any further information that the Minister may require in the performance of his or her functions under this section.

(6) The reason for refusing an application for a licence under this section or for its renewal shall be communicated in writing to the applicant.

(7) Every continuing licence granted by the Minister under this section may be varied or revoked by the Minister at any time before its expiration. The reason for varying or revoking the licence shall be communicated in writing to the licensee or former licensee.

(8) If any person imports into the State a firearm or prohibited weapon or any ammunition without or otherwise than in accordance with a licence under this section authorising such importation or, in the case of ammunition, in quantities in excess of those so authorised, or fails to comply with any condition named in a licence granted to him or her under this section, he or she shall be guilty of an offence under this Act and shall be punishable accordingly.

(9) The possession of a licence granted under this section shall not relieve any person from the obligation to obtain or hold any certificate, permit, or authority required by any other provision of this Act.

(10) This section shall not apply to the importation into the State of any firearms, ammunition or prohibited weapon which is so imported under the authority of the Minister for Defence for the use of the Defence Forces of the State or under the authority of the Minister for the use of any lawful police force in the State.".

Amendments

1 Section 36 is not yet in operation (February 2011).

37   Amendment to section 9 of Act of 1964

Section 9 (as substituted by section 53 of the Act of 2006) of the Act of 1964 is amended by the substitution for subsection (6) of the following:[1]

Amendments

1   See the amended Act.

38   Repeal of section 21 of Act of 1964

Section 21 of the Act of 1964 is hereby repealed.

39   Amendment to section 9 of Act of 1990

Section 9 of the Act of 1990 is amended in subsection (7) by the substitution for paragraph (a) of the following paragraph:[1]

Amendments

1   See the amended Act.

40   New sections 9A to 9I of Act of 1990

The Act of 1990 is amended by the insertion of the following sections after section 9 (as amended by section 39 of this Act):[1]

Amendments

1   See the amended Act.

41   Amendment to section 16 of Act of 1990

Section 16 of the Act of 1990 is amended by the substitution for that section of the following:[1]

Amendments

1   See the amended Act.

42   Amendment to section 2 of Act of 2000

Section 2 of the Act of 2000 is amended by the substitution of the following for subsection (6):

"(6) A firearm certificate granted to a person under this section after the date of commencement of section 42 of the Criminal Justice (Miscellaneous Provisions) Act 2009 shall continue in force for a period of 1 year from the date on which it is granted, unless previously revoked.".

43   Amendment to section 30 of Act of 2006

The following section is substituted for section 30 of the Act of 2006:[1]

Amendments

1   See the amended Act.

44   Repeal of section 40 of Act of 2006

Section 40 of the Act of 2006 is hereby repealed.

PART 5
MISCELLANEOUS

45   Amendment to section 2 of Act of 1857

Section 2 (as extended by section 51 of the Courts (Supplemental Provisions) Act 1961) of the Summary Jurisdiction Act 1857 is hereby amended by the insertion after "such Case" of "or such longer period as may be provided for by Rules of Court".

46   New section 2A of Act of 1857

The Act of 1857 is hereby amended by the insertion after section 2 of the following new section:[1]

Amendments

1   See the amended Act.

47   Amendment to section 4 of Criminal Justice Act 1984

Section 4 (as amended by section 2 of the Criminal Justice (Miscellaneous Provisions) Act 1997 and section 34 of the Criminal Justice Act 1999) of the Criminal Justice Act 1984 is hereby amended—

(a) by the deletion of subsection (6), and

(b) in subsection (9), by the deletion of "(6) or".

Note

Section 47 is not yet in operation (February 2011).

48   Amendment of Bail Act 1997

The Bail Act 1997 is hereby amended—

(a) in section 5, by the insertion of the following subsection after subsection (4)—

(b) in section 9 (as substituted by section 15 of the Criminal Justice Act 2007), by the substitution for that section of the following:[1]

and

(c) in the Schedule to the Act by—

    (i) the insertion after paragraph 7 of the following paragraph:[1]

    (ii) the substitution in paragraph 28 of the following subparagraphs for subparagraph (c): [1]

    (iii) the substitution of the following paragraph for paragraph 28A (inserted by section 79 of the Criminal Justice Act 2006):

"Offences under the Criminal Justice Act 2006.

28A. Any offence under the following provisions of the Criminal Justice Act 2006 —

    (a) section 71, 72 or 73 (organised crime);

    (b) section 176 (reckless endangerment of children);

    (c) section 183 (possession of article intended for use in connection with certain offences);

    (d) section 183A (possession of monies intended for use in connection with certain offences).", [1]

and

    (iv) the insertion after paragraph 33 of the following paragraph: [2]

Amendments

1   Section 48(c)(ii) is not yet in operation (February 2011).

2   See the amended Act.

---

49   **Amendment to section 15 of Act of 2001**

Section 15 of the Act of 2001, as amended by section 47 of the Criminal Justice Act 2007, is hereby amended—

(a) by the insertion after subsection (1) of the following:[1]

and

(b) in subsection (2) (as substituted by section 47 of the Criminal Justice Act 2007) by the substitution for that subsection of the following subsections:[1]

Amendments

1   See the amended Act.

---

50   Amendment to section 39 of Act of 2001

Section 39 of the Act of 2001 is hereby amended in subsection (5) by the substitution for "those subsections" of "that subsection".

51   Amendment to section 99 of Criminal Justice Act 2006

Section 99 (as amended by section 60 of the Criminal Justice Act 2007) of the Criminal Justice Act 2006 is hereby amended in subsection (9) by the insertion after "convicted of an offence" of ", being an offence committed after the making of the order under subsection (1)".

52   Amendment to Regulation 12 of Criminal Justice Act 1984 (Treatment of Persons in Custody in Garda Síochána Stations) Regulations 1987

Regulation 12 of the Criminal Justice Act 1984 (Treatment of Persons in Custody in Garda Síochána Stations) Regulations 1987 (S.I. No. 119 of 1987) is hereby amended by the deletion of paragraphs (7)(a)(ii), (12)(c) and (12)(d)."

Note

Section 52 has not yet come into operation (February 2011).

Criminal Justice (Amendment) Act 2009

Number 32 of 2009

ARRANGEMENT OF SECTIONS

PART 1
PRELIMINARY AND GENERAL

1.   Short title.

2.   Definitions.

PART 2
ORGANISED CRIME

3.   Amendment of section 70 of Act of 2006 – definition of "criminal organisation", etc.

4.   Amendment of section 71 of Act of 2006.

5.   Directing activities of a criminal organisation.

6.   Organised crime: offence to participate in, or contribute to, certain activities.

7.   Evidential provisions as to proof of criminal organisation's existence.

8.   Certain offences under Part 7 of Act of 2006 to be scheduled offences.

9.   New section 72A of Act of 2006.

10.   Amendment of section 73 of Act of 2006.

11.   Amendment of section 74 of Act of 2006.

12.   New section 74A of Act of 2006.

13.   New section 74B of Act of 2006.

14.   New section 26A of Act of 2007 and amendment of Schedule 2 to that Act.

15.   Amendment of Bail Act 1997.

16.   Increase of penalty for intimidation of witnesses, jurors, etc.

17.   Amendment of Criminal Procedure Act 1967.

PART 3
OFFENCES UNDER CERTAIN ENACTMENTS: PROVISION FOR EXTRA-TERRITORIAL EFFECT

18.   Amendment of section 7 of Act of 1939.

19.   Amendment of sections 7 and 8 of Act of 1997.

20.   Amendment of section 41 (substantive elements of offence) of Act of 1999.

PART 4
AMENDMENTS CONCERNING DETENTION AND RE-ARREST POWERS

21.   Amendment of sections 30 and 30A of Act of 1939.

22.   Amendment of sections 2, 4, 5 and 11 of Act of 1996.

23.   Amendment of sections 50, 51 and 52 of Act of 2007.

24.   Amendment of sections 4, 9 and 10 of Act of 1984.

PART 5

MISCELLANEOUS

25.   Directing activities of an unlawful organisation.

26.   Search warrant applications to be heard otherwise than in public.

SCHEDULE

AN ACT—

TO PROVIDE FOR ADDITIONAL MEASURES WITH RESPECT TO COMBATING ORGANISED CRIME AND, IN PARTICULAR, WITH RESPECT TO COUNTERING THE INCREASED LEVELS OF VIOLENCE TOWARDS, AND INTIMIDATION OF, MEMBERS OF THE PUBLIC PERPETRATED BY CRIMINAL ORGANISATIONS AND SECURING CONDITIONS IN WHICH OFFENCES COMMITTED BY THOSE ASSOCIATED WITH SUCH ORGANISATIONS CAN, IN DUE COURSE OF LAW, BE INVESTIGATED AND PROSECUTED AND, FOR THAT PURPOSE, TO AMEND PART 7 OF THE CRIMINAL JUSTICE ACT 2006 AND CERTAIN OTHER ENACTMENTS;

TO AMEND THE LAW IN RELATION TO THE INVESTIGATION OF OFFENCES, INCLUDING IN RELATION TO THE DETENTION OF SUSPECTS AND THEIR RE-ARREST IN CERTAIN CIRCUMSTANCES, AND TO OTHERWISE AMEND CRIMINAL LAW AND PROCEDURE; AND

TO PROVIDE FOR RELATED MATTERS. [23rd July, 2009]

BE IT ENACTED BY THE OIREACHTAS AS FOLLOWS:

PART 1

PRELIMINARY AND GENERAL

1   Short title

This Act may be cited as the Criminal Justice (Amendment) Act 2009.

2   Definitions

In this Act—

"Act of 1939" means the Offences against the State Act 1939;

"Act of 1984" means the Criminal Justice Act 1984;

"Act of 1996" means the Criminal Justice (Drug Trafficking) Act 1996;

"Act of 1997" means the Criminal Law Act 1997;

"Act of 1999" means the Criminal Justice Act 1999;

"Act of 2006" means the Criminal Justice Act 2006;

"Act of 2007" means the Criminal Justice Act 2007.

PART 2

ORGANISED CRIME

3   Amendment of section 70 of Act of 2006 – definition of "criminal organisation", etc

(1) Section 70(1) of the Act of 2006 is amended—

    (a) by substituting the following for the definition of "criminal organisation":[1] and

    (b) by substituting the following for the definition of "structured group":[1]

(2) Section 70 of the Act of 2006 is further amended by adding the following subsection: [1]

Amendments

1   See the amended Act.

---

4   Amendment of section 71 of Act of 2006

Section 71 of the Act of 2006 is amended—

    (a) in subsection (2)(d), by substituting "person ordinarily resident in the State" for "stateless person habitually resident in the State", and

    (b) by deleting subsection (5).

5   Directing activities of a criminal organisation

The Act of 2006 is amended by inserting the following section after section 71:[1]

Amendments

1   See the amended Act.

---

6   Organised crime: offence to participate in, or contribute to, certain activities

The Act of 2006 is amended by substituting the following section for section 72:[1]

Amendments

1   See the amended Act.

---

7   Evidential provisions as to proof of criminal organisation's existence

The Act of 2006 is amended by inserting the following section after section 71A (inserted by section 5):[1]

Amendments

1   See the amended Act.

8   Certain offences under Part 7 of Act of 2006 to be scheduled offences

(1) It is hereby declared that the ordinary courts are inadequate to secure the effective administration of justice and the preservation of public peace and order in relation to an offence under each of the following provisions of Part 7 of the Act of 2006, namely, sections 71A, 72, 73 and 76.

(2) An offence specified in subsection (1) shall be deemed to be a scheduled offence for the purposes of Part V of the Act of 1939 as if an order had been made under section 36 of the Act of 1939 in relation to it and subsection (3) of that section and section 37 of the Act of 1939 shall apply to such an offence accordingly.

(3) Nothing in subsection (1) or (2) shall be construed as affecting, or limiting in any particular case, the exercise—

(a) by the Government of any of their powers under any provision of section 35 or 36 of the Act of 1939,

(b) by the Director of Public Prosecutions of his or her power under section 45(2) of the Act of 1939 to direct that a person not be sent forward for trial by the Special Criminal Court on a particular charge, or

(c) by the Government or the Director of Public Prosecutions of any other of their powers under Part V of the Act of 1939 or by any other person of his or her powers under that Part.

(4) This section shall, subject to subsection (5), cease to be in operation on and from the date that is 12 months from the passing of this Act unless a resolution has been passed by each House of the Oireachtas resolving that this section should continue in operation.

(5) This section may be continued in operation from time to time by a resolution passed by each House of the Oireachtas before its expiry for such period as may be specified in the resolutions.

(6) Before a resolution is passed by either House of the Oireachtas under this section, the Minister for Justice, Equality and Law Reform shall prepare a report, and shall cause a copy of it to be laid before that House, of the operation of this section during the period beginning on the passing of this Act, or as may be appropriate, the date of the latest previous report under this subsection in relation to this section and ending not later than 21 days before the date of the moving of the resolution in that House.

9   New section 72A of Act of 2006

The Act of 2006 is amended by inserting the following section after section 72:[1]

Amendments

1   See the amended Act.

10   Amendment of section 73 of Act of 2006

Section 73 of the Act of 2006 is amended by substituting, in subsection (3), "15 years" for "10 years".

11   Amendment of section 74 of Act of 2006

Section 74 of the Act of 2006 is amended—

    (a) by substituting the following subsection for subsection (1): [1]
        and

    (b) by inserting the following subsection after subsection (2):[1]

Amendments

1   See the amended Act.

12   New section 74A of Act of 2006

The Act of 2006 is amended by inserting the following section after section 74:[1]

Amendments

1   See the amended Act.

13   New section 74B of Act of 2006

The Act of 2006 is amended by inserting the following section after section 74A (inserted by section 12):[1]

Amendments

1   See the amended Act.

14   New section 26A of Act of 2007 and amendment of Schedule 2 to that Act

(1) The Act of 2007 is amended by inserting the following section after section 26:[1]

(2) Schedule 2 to the Act of 2007 is amended, in paragraph 9, by substituting the following subparagraphs for subparagraph (b):[1]

Amendments

1   See the amended Act.

15   Amendment of Bail Act 1997

The Schedule to the Bail Act 1997 is amended, in paragraph 28A, by inserting "71A," after "71,".

16   Increase of penalty for intimidation of witnesses, jurors, etc

Section 41 of the Act of 1999 is amended by substituting, in subsection (5)(b), "15 years" for "10 years".

17   Amendment of Criminal Procedure Act 1967

The Criminal Procedure Act 1967 is amended—

   (a)   in section 13(1), by inserting "71A," after "or an offence under section 71,", and
   (b)   in section 29(1), by inserting, in paragraph (l), "71A," after "an offence under section 71,".

PART 3
OFFENCES UNDER CERTAIN ENACTMENTS: PROVISION FOR EXTRA-TERRITORIAL EFFECT

18   Amendment of section 7 of Act of 1939

(1) Section 7 of the Act of 1939 is amended—

   (a)   in subsection (1), by inserting "(whether in or outside the State)" after "Every person who", and
   (b)   in subsection (2), by inserting "(whether in or outside the State)" after "Every person who".

(2) Section 7 of the Act of 1939 is further amended by inserting the following after subsection (2):[1]

Amendments

1   See the amended Act.

19   Amendment of sections 7 and 8 of Act of 1997

(1) Section 7 of the Act of 1997 is amended by inserting the following subsection after subsection (1):

(2) Section 7 of the Act of 1997 is further amended—

   (a)   in subsection (2), by inserting ", whether in or outside the State," after "any act",

(b) by inserting the following subsection after subsection (2):[1]
and

(c) by inserting the following subsections after subsection (7): [1]

(3) Section 8 of the Act of 1997 is amended, in subsection (1), by substituting "accepts (or agrees to accept), whether in or outside the State, for not disclosing that information any consideration" for "accepts or agrees to accept for not disclosing that information any consideration".

(4) Section 8 of the Act of 1997 is further amended—

(a) by inserting the following after subsection (1): [1]
and

(b) by inserting the following subsections after subsection (4): [1]

Amendments

1   See the amended Act.

20   Amendment of section 41 (substantive elements of offence) of Act of 1999

Section 41 of the Act of 1999 is amended—

(a) in subsection (1)(a), by substituting "who (whether in or outside the State) harms" for "who harms", and

(b) by inserting the following subsections after subsection (3):[1]

Amendments

1   See the amended Act.

PART 4
AMENDMENTS CONCERNING DETENTION AND RE-ARREST POWERS

21   Amendment of sections 30 and 30A of Act of 1939

(1) Section 30 of the Act of 1939 is amended—

(a) by inserting the following subsection after subsection (3):[1]

(b) by inserting the following subsection after subsection (4B): [1]

Amendments

1   See the amended Act.

22   Amendment of sections 2, 4, 5 and 11 of Act of 1996

(1) Section 2 of the Act of 1996 is amended—

    (a) in subsection (2)(b), by substituting ' superintendent' for ' chief superintendent',

    (b) by inserting the following subsections after subsection (3):[1]

    (c) by substituting the following subsection for subsection (7A): [1]

(2) Section 4 of the Act of 1996 is amended by substituting the following subsection for subsection (1):[1]

(3) Section 5 of the Act of 1996 is amended by inserting "4(8B)," after "4(8A),".

(4) Section 11 of the Act of 1996 is repealed and, accordingly, sections 2, 3, 4, 5 and 6 of that Act (being the sections to which that section 11 related) shall continue in operation indefinitely.

Amendments

1   See the amended Act.

23   Amendment of sections 50, 51 and 52 of Act of 2007

(1) Section 50 of the Act of 2007 is amended in subsection (1)—

    (a) by substituting, in paragraph (c), "Act of 1925," for "Act of 1925, or",

    (b) by substituting, in paragraph (d), "firearm, or" for "firearm.", and

    (c) by inserting the following paragraph after paragraph (d):

(2) Section 50 of the Act of 2007 is further amended—

    (a) by inserting the following subsection after subsection (4):[1]

    (b) by substituting the following subsection for subsection (9): [1]

(3) Section 51 of the Act of 2007 is amended by substituting the following subsections for subsection (1):[1]

(4) Section 52 of the Act of 2007 is amended by inserting "4(8B)," after "4(8A),".

Amendments

1   See the amended Act.

24   Amendment of sections 4, 9 and 10 of Act of 1984

(1) Section 4 of the Act of 1984 is amended—

    (a) by inserting the following subsection after subsection (8A): [1]
        and

    (b) in subsection (9) by substituting ", (8A) or (8B)" for "or (8A)".

(2) Section 9 of the Act of 1984 is amended by inserting "4(8B)," after "4(8A),".

(3) Section 10 of the Act of 1984 is amended by substituting the following subsection for subsection (1):¹

Amendments

1   See the amended Act.

PART 5

MISCELLANEOUS

25   Directing activities of an unlawful organisation

The Offences against the State (Amendment) Act 1998 is amended by substituting the following section for section 6:

"Directing an unlawful organisation.

6.— (1) In this section—

    (a)   ' directs ', in relation to activities, means—

        (i)   controls or supervises the activities, or

        (ii)   gives an order, instruction or guidance, or makes a request, with respect to the carrying on of the activities;

    (b)   ' serious offence ' means an offence for which a person may be punished by imprisonment for a term of 4 years or more;

    (c)   ' unlawful organisation ' means an organisation in respect of which a suppression order has been made under section 19 of the Act of 1939;

    (d)   references to activities include references to—

        (i)   activities carried on outside the State, and

        (ii)   activities that do not constitute an offence or offences.

(2) A person who directs, at any level of the organisation's structure, the activities of an unlawful organisation shall be guilty of an offence and shall be liable on conviction on indictment to imprisonment for life or a lesser term of imprisonment.

(3) Any statement made orally, in writing or otherwise, or any conduct, by the defendant implying or leading to a reasonable inference that he or she was at a material time directing the activities of an unlawful organisation shall, in proceedings for an offence under this section, be admissible as evidence that the defendant was doing such at that time.

(4) In proceedings under this section, the court or the jury, as the case may be, in determining whether an offence under this section has been committed, may, in addition to any other relevant evidence, also consider—

    (a)   any evidence of a pattern of behaviour on the part of the defendant consistent with his or her having directed the activities of the organisation concerned at the material time, and

    (b)   without limiting paragraph (a) or subsection (3)—

        (i)   whether the defendant has received any benefit from the organisation concerned, and

1397

(ii)   evidence as to the possession by the defendant of such articles or documents or other records as would give rise to a reasonable suspicion that such articles, documents or other records were in his or her possession or control for a purpose connected with directing the activities of the organisation concerned.

(5) Any document or other record emanating or purporting to emanate from the organisation concerned from which there can be inferred—

  (a) either—

      (i)   the giving, at the time concerned, of an instruction, order or guidance by the defendant to any person involved in the organisation, or

      (ii)   the making, at that time, by the defendant of a request of a person so involved,

      or

  (b) the seeking, at that time, by a person so involved of assistance or guidance from the defendant,

shall, in proceedings for an offence under this section, be admissible as evidence that the defendant was directing the activities of the organisation concerned at the material time.

(6) The expression ' other record ' in this section shall receive a like construction to that which is provided for by section 2 of the Act of 1939 with respect to the expression ' document '.".

26   Search warrant applications to be heard otherwise than in public

An application under any enactment to a court, or a judge of a court, for a search warrant shall be heard otherwise than in public.

Courts and Court Officers Act 2009

Number 36 of 2009

ARRANGEMENT OF SECTIONS

PART 1
PRELIMINARY AND GENERAL

1. Short title and commencement.

2. Definition.

3. Regulations.

4. Expenses.

PART 2
TEMPORARY CUSTODY

5. Definitions (Part 2).

6. Persons held for section 7 purposes.

7. Purposes of temporary custody.

8. Beginning and end of temporary custody.

9. Consequences of placement in temporary custody.

10. Handing over of medications, etc., when person in temporary custody.

11. Functions of holding area officer.

12. Regulations relating to temporary custody.

PART 3
COMBINED COURT OFFICE

13. Definitions (Part 3).

14. Establishment of combined court offices.

15. Variation of functions or dissolution of combined court office.

16. Consultations.

17. Special Criminal Court.

18. Combined court office: deemed powers and functions.

19. Combined court office manager.

20. Management and control of combined court office.

21. Staff of combined court office.

22. Functions of staff.

23. Continuity of administration of justice not to be affected.

24. Amendment of Courts Service Act 1998.

PART 4
MISCELLANEOUS PROVISIONS

25. Amendment of section 22 of Criminal Procedure Act 1967.

26. Amendment of section 24 of Petty Sessions (Ireland) Act 1851.

SCHEDULE

COURTS AND COURT OFFICERS ACT 2009

AN ACT TO PROVIDE FOR THE PLACEMENT IN TEMPORARY CUSTODY OF CERTAIN DETAINED PERSONS IN ORDER TO FACILITATE THEIR APPEARANCE BEFORE A COURT; TO PROVIDE FOR THE ESTABLISHMENT OF COMBINED COURT OFFICES; TO AMEND THE COURTS SERVICE ACT 1998, THE CRIMINAL PROCEDURE ACT 1967 AND THE PETTY SESSIONS (IRELAND) ACT 1851, AND TO PROVIDE FOR RELATED MATTERS. [24th November, 2009]

BE IT ENACTED BY THE OIREACHTAS AS FOLLOWS:

PART 1
PRELIMINARY AND GENERAL

1 Short title and commencement

(1) This Act may be cited as the Courts and Court Officers Act 2009.

(2) This Act shall come into operation on such day or days as the Minister may appoint by order or orders either generally or with reference to any particular purpose or provisions and different days may be so appointed for different purposes or different provisions.

2 Definition

In this Act "Minister" means the Minister for Justice, Equality and Law Reform.

3 Regulations

(1) The Minister may make regulations prescribing any matter or thing which is referred to in this Act as prescribed or to be prescribed.

(2) Regulations under this Act may contain such incidental, supplementary and consequential provisions as appear to the Minister to be necessary or expedient for the purpose of the regulations.

(3) Every regulation under this section shall be laid before each House of the Oireachtas as soon as may be after it has been made and, if a resolution annulling the regulation is passed by either such House within the next 21 days on which that House has sat after the regulation is laid before it, the regulation shall be annulled accordingly, but without prejudice to the validity of anything previously done thereunder.

4 Expenses

The expenses incurred by the Minister in the administration of this Act shall, to such extent as may be sanctioned by the Minister for Finance, be paid out of moneys provided by the Oireachtas.

PART 2
TEMPORARY CUSTODY

5   Definitions (Part 2)

In this Part—

"Act of 2007" means the Prisons Act 2007;

"governor" has the same meaning as it has in the Act of 2007;

"holding area officer" means—

(a)   a governor, or a member of the Garda Síochána, in whose temporary custody a person is placed under section 6,

(b)   a person who assumes the duties of a holding area officer under section 11(6),

(c)   a member in charge who assumes the powers and functions of a holding area officer under paragraph (a) of section 11(7),or

(d)   a member of the Garda Síochána to whom the powers and functions referred to in paragraph (c) are transferred under paragraph (b) of section 11(7);

"member in charge" means a member of the Garda Síochána who is in charge of a Garda Síochána station referred to in section 11(7);

"Prison Rules" means the Prison Rules 2007 (S.I. No. 252 of 2007);

"prisoner" has the same meaning as it has in the Act of 2007;

"prison officer" has the same meaning as it has in section 19(6) (as inserted by section 41(4) of the Act of 2007) of the Criminal Justice (Public Order) Act 1994;

"temporary custody" shall be construed in accordance with subsections (1) and (2) of section 6.

6   Persons held for section 7 purposes

(1) A prisoner may be placed in the temporary custody of a member of the Garda Síochána where the placement is for a purpose referred to in section 7.

(2) A person who is lawfully in the custody of the Garda Síochána may be placed in the temporary custody of a governor where the placement is for a purpose referred to in section 7.

(3) Without prejudice to the generality of subsections (1) and (2), a person who is placed in temporary custody under either of those subsections may be placed in a place in or adjacent to a court building in which the appearance or hearing referred to in section 7 concerned is to be held.

(4) A prisoner or a person who is lawfully in the custody of the Garda Síochána who is not placed in temporary custody under subsection (1) or (2) may be placed in a place referred to in subsection (3) for a purpose referred to in section 7.

7   Purposes of temporary custody

A prisoner or other person may be placed in temporary custody under section 6 for the purposes of facilitating—

(a)   a court appearance by that person, or

(b)   his or her participation, as a witness or in another capacity, in a court hearing involving him or her.

8 **Beginning and end of temporary custody**

(1) Without prejudice to any other enactment, the temporary custody of a prisoner under section 6(1)—

    (a) shall commence from the moment the prisoner is placed in the custody of the holding area officer, and

    (b) shall cease from—

        (i) such time as the prisoner is returned to the governor in whose custody he or she was before the temporary custody commenced, or

        (ii) such time as the prisoner is released by order of the court,

as the case may be.

(2) Without prejudice to any other enactment, the temporary custody of a person under section 6(2)—

    (a) shall commence from the moment the person is placed in the custody of the holding area officer, and

    (b) shall cease from—

        (i) such time as the person is returned to the person in whose custody he or she was before the temporary custody commenced or another member of the Garda Síochána, or

        (ii) such time as the person is released by order of the court,

as the case may be.

9 **Consequences of placement in temporary custody**

(1) A prisoner who is placed in temporary custody under section 6(1) shall be deemed, for the duration of the placement, to remain in the custody of the governor in whose custody he or she was before being so placed.

(2) A person who is placed in temporary custody under section 6(2) shall be deemed, for the duration of the placement, to remain in the custody of the Garda Síochána.

10 **Handing over of medications, etc., when person in temporary custody**

(1) On placing a person in temporary custody under section 6, the governor or member of the Garda Síochána in whose custody that person was shall hand to the holding area officer concerned—

    (a) any medication or prescription for medication that he or she possesses in respect of the person,

    (b) any information relating to the person's health that he or she is aware of, and

    (c) any additional articles, documents or information that the Minister may prescribe.

(2) When a holding area officer returns a person placed in temporary custody under section 6 to a person mentioned in subsection (1)(b)(i) or subsection (2)(b)(i) of section 8, the holding area officer shall hand to that person—

    (a) any medication or prescription for medication that he or she possesses in respect of the person who was in temporary custody,

    (b) any information relating to the person's health that he or she is aware of, and

    (c) any additional articles, documents or information that the Minister may prescribe.

11   Functions of holding area officer

(1) Notwithstanding section 9, a holding area officer shall, as regards a person who has been placed in his or her temporary custody under section 6—

    (a)   prevent his or her escape from lawful custody,

    (b)   prevent the commission of an offence by him or her,

    (c)   ensure that he or she behaves in an orderly and disciplined fashion,

    (d)   bring him or her to a court or court office, as required,

    (e)   ensure his or her appearance before a court, and

    (f)   comply with any order of a court relating to his or her custody, treatment or transfer.

(2) A holding area officer may search, in accordance with the Prison Rules, the person of any person who has been placed in his or her temporary custody under section 6 if he or she is of the opinion that it is necessary to do so to perform his or her functions under this Part.

(3) A holding area officer may, where necessary, use all reasonable force in the performance of his or her functions under this Part.

(4) Where section 6(4) applies to a person who is lawfully in the custody of the Garda Síochána, a member of the Garda Síochána in whose custody that person is shall, without prejudice to any other enactment, have the powers and functions of a holding area officer under subsections (1) to (3).

(5) Nothing in this section shall be construed as limiting the powers under the Prison Rules of a holding area officer who is a prison officer.

(6) Where section 6(1) applies, a member of the Garda Síochána who is of a higher rank than the holding area officer may authorise the transfer of the powers and functions of that holding area officer under this Part to another member of the Garda Síochána, and that other member shall assume those powers and functions.

(7) Where section 6(1) applies, and the prisoner placed in temporary custody is or has been placed in a Garda Síochána station, then notwithstanding that any other member of the Garda Síochána is also a holding area officer under this Part, the member in charge of that Garda Síochána station—

    (a)   shall assume the powers and functions of a holding area officer under this Part, and

    (b)   where he or she considers it necessary for the performance of any of his or her functions, and for such period or periods as he or she considers necessary, may authorise the transfer of any or all of the powers and functions assumed under paragraph (a) to another member of the Garda Síochána.

(8) Where subsection (7)(b) applies, the transfer of the powers and functions concerned to a member of the Garda Síochána shall be construed as reserving to the member in charge the right to exercise those powers and to perform those functions concurrently with that member.

12   Regulations relating to temporary custody

The Minister may prescribe—

    (a)   the standards to be employed in the safekeeping of a person who has been placed in temporary custody under section 6,

    (b)   standards and procedures relating to the orderly management of any place in which such a person is to be held,

    (c)   the records on the temporary custody of such a person to be kept, and

    (d) the—

         (i) articles, documents or information which are to be handed over, and

        (ii) procedures, including record keeping, that are to be followed,

where subsection (1) or (2) of section 10 applies.

PART 3
COMBINED COURT OFFICE

13   Definitions (Part 3)

In this Part—

"Act of 1939" means the Offences Against the State Act 1939;

"constituent court office" means—

    (a) a court office, the business or some of the business of which shall be transacted in a combined court office under section 14 or 15,or

    (b) a registrar or other person deemed to be a constituent court office under section 17(2),

and "constituent court" shall be construed accordingly;

"combined court office" means an office established under section 14;

"combined court office manager", in relation to a combined court office, means a person appointed under section 19 to be the manager of that office;

"court office" means any office of, or attached to, any of the following:

    (a) the Supreme Court;

    (b) the High Court;

    (c) the President of the High Court;

    (d) the Circuit Court;

    (e) the District Court;

and, for the purposes of this definition, a district probate registry shall be deemed to be an office attached to the High Court;

"enactment" means an Act or a statutory instrument or any portion of an Act or statutory instrument;

"Special Criminal Court" means a court established under Part V of the Act of 1939.

14   Establishment of combined court offices

(1) Notwithstanding any other enactment, the Courts Service may establish a combined court office in accordance with this section and section 16.

(2) In establishing a combined court office under subsection (1), the Courts Service shall—

    (a) designate two or more court offices to be constituent court offices of that combined court office, and

    (b) specify the business of the constituent court offices that shall be transacted in the combined court office.

(3) The Courts Service shall, as soon as may be after a combined court office is established, publish notice of that fact and of the matters referred to in subsection (2) relating to that office in Iris Oifigiúil, but failure to so publish shall not affect the validity of the establishment of the combined court office concerned.

15   Variation of functions or dissolution of combined court office

(1) The Courts Service may vary the functions of a combined court office, including by—

    (a) varying the business of the constituent court offices which is to be transacted there, other than any business that is the subject of an order under section 17(1),

    (b) designating another court office to be a constituent court office of that combined court office, and

    (c) removing from the business of the combined court office any business of a constituent court office, other than any business that is the subject of an order under section 17(1).

(2) The power to establish a combined court office conferred by section 14(1) includes the power to dissolve such an office, except where to dissolve the office would affect an order made under section 17(1).

(3) Sections 14(3) and 16 apply, with any necessary modifications, when the Courts Service exercises its powers under subsection (1) or (2).

16   Consultations

Before establishing a combined court office under section 14, the Courts Service shall consult with—

    (a) the Chief Justice, where a proposed constituent court office is an office attached to the Supreme Court,

    (b) the President of the High Court, where a proposed constituent court office is an office attached to the High Court or the President of the High Court,

    (c) the President of the Circuit Court, where a proposed constituent court office is an office of, or attached to, the Circuit Court,

    (d) the President of the District Court, where a proposed constituent court office is an office of, or attached to, the District Court.

17   Special Criminal Court

(1) Notwithstanding any other enactment, the Government may, by order, provide that specified business of a Special Criminal Court, other than business that is required to be transacted by or before a judge or judges of such a Court, shall be transacted in a combined court office.

(2) A registrar appointed for the purposes of a Special Criminal Court under section 39 of the Act of 1939, or any person acting under the direction of such a registrar, in the transaction of the business that is the subject of an order under subsection (1), is deemed to be a constituent court office for the purposes of this Part.

18   Combined court office: deemed powers and functions

Where, under section 14, 15 or 17, the business of a constituent court office shall be transacted in a combined court office, for the purpose of the transaction the following shall apply:

    (a) the combined court office is deemed to be an office of or attached to the constituent court concerned;

(b) the combined court office manager of that combined court office and the members of staff of the Courts Service employed in that office under section 21 are deemed to be officers attached to, or attached to an office of, that constituent court;

(c) any reference in an enactment to an office of or attached to that constituent court or to an officer or member of staff of that court is, save where the context otherwise requires, deemed to include that combined court office or an officer or member of staff of that combined court office, as the case may be.

19   Combined court office manager

Notwithstanding any provision of any other enactment, where a combined court office is established under section 14, the Courts Service shall appoint—

(a) a member of its staff, or

(b) a county registrar,

to be the manager of that combined court office.

20   Management and control of combined court office

(1) Notwithstanding any provision of any other enactment, including any enactment conferring such powers on an officer of a constituent court, a combined court office manager shall, subject to subsection (2), have the management and control of the combined court office.

(2) In performing the function referred to in subsection (1), the combined court office manager shall in regard to all matters of general administration, be subject to the general directions of the Courts Service.

21   Staff of combined court office

There shall be employed in a combined court office such and so many members of the staff of the Courts Service as the Courts Service shall from time to time determine.

22   Functions of staff

(1) The Courts Service may, notwithstanding any other provision of any enactment, appoint any member of staff of the Courts Service employed in a combined court office under section 21 as one or more of the following:

(a) a District Court clerk;

(b) a principal officer, within the meaning of Part I of the Court Officers Act 1926, of any office attached to the High Court or the President of the High Court.

(2) A combined court office manager may, notwithstanding any other provision of any enactment, direct any member of staff of the Courts Service employed in a combined court office under section 21 to act as registrar to any of the following constituent courts:

(a) the Central Criminal Court;

(b) the Court of Criminal Appeal;

(c) the Courts-Martial Appeal Court;

(d) the Circuit Court.

(3) Where, under subsection (2), a person is directed to act as registrar to a court mentioned in paragraphs (a) to (d) of that subsection, any reference in an enactment to a registrar of the court concerned is deemed to include such a person.

23   Continuity of administration of justice not to be affected

(1) The continuity of the administration of justice shall not be interrupted by the—

(a) establishment of a combined court office under section 14,

(b) variation of the functions, or the dissolution, of a combined courts office under section 15,or

(c) making of an order under section 17.

(2) Without prejudice to the generality of subsection (1)—

(a) on the establishment of a combined court office under section 14, the variation of the functions of a combined court office under section 15, or the making of an order under section 17(1), the business of a constituent court office shall be continued in the combined court office,

(b) where business has begun to be transacted in a combined court office which, by virtue of the variation of the functions, or dissolution, of that office under section 15,is subsequently required to be transacted in another court office, that business shall be continued in that other court office, and

(c) where the Government make an order under section 17(1), the business concerned that was transacted in a combined court office shall be continued by or before the registrar, or any person acting under the direction of such a registrar, of the Special Criminal Court concerned.

24   Amendment of Courts Service Act 1998

Section 6(2) of the Courts Service Act 1998 is amended—

(a) in paragraph (i), by deleting "and",

(b) in paragraph (j), by substituting "designate court venues, and" for "designate court venues.", and

(c) by inserting the following after paragraph (j):

"(k) establish, vary the functions of, or dissolve, a combined court office under sections 14 and 15 of the Courts and Court Officers Act 2009.".

PART 4

MISCELLANEOUS PROVISIONS

25   Amendment of section 22 of Criminal Procedure Act 1967

Section 22 of the Criminal Procedure Act 1967 is amended by inserting the following subsection after subsection (1A) (inserted by section 18(a) of the Criminal Justice Act 2007):[1]

Amendments

1   See the amended Act.

---

26 Amendment of section 24 of Petty Sessions (Ireland) Act 1851

Section 24 of the Petty Sessions (Ireland) Act 1851 is amended by the insertion of the following paragraph after paragraph 2:[1]

Amendments

1 See the amended Act.

Criminal Justice (Money Laundering and Terrorist Financing) Act 2010

Number 6 of 2010

ARRANGEMENT OF SECTIONS

PART 1
PRELIMINARY

1.   Short title and commencement.

2.   Interpretation.

3.   Regulations.

4.   Repeals and revocations.

5.   Expenses.

PART 2
MONEY LAUNDERING OFFENCES

6.   Interpretation (Part 2).

7.   Money laundering occurring in State.

8.   Money laundering outside State in certain circumstances.

9.   Attempts, outside State, to commit offence in State.

10.   Aiding, abetting, counselling or procuring outside State commission of offence in State.

11.   Presumptions and other matters.

12.   Location of proceedings relating to offences committed outside State.

13.   Consent of DPP required for proceedings for offences committed outside State.

14.   Certificate may be evidence in proceedings under this Part.

15.   Double jeopardy.

16.   Revenue offence committed outside State.

PARTS 3 AND 4 NOT REPRODUCED HERE

PART 5
MISCELLANEOUS

110. Service of documents.

111. Offences — directors and others of bodies corporate and unincorporated bodies.

112. Disclosure of information in good faith.

113. Amendment of Bail Act 1997.

114. Amendment of Central Bank Act 1942.

115. Amendment of Courts (Supplemental Provisions) Act 1961.

116. Consequential amendment of Central Bank Act 1997.

117. Consequential amendment of Criminal Justice Act 1994.

118. Consequential amendment of Criminal Justice (Mutual Assistance) Act 2008.

119. Consequential amendment of Criminal Justice (Theft and Fraud Offences) Act 2001.

120. Consequential amendment of Investor Compensation Act 1998.

121. Consequential amendment of Taxes Consolidation Act 1997.

122. Consequential amendment of Taxi Regulation Act 2003.

AN ACT TO PROVIDE FOR OFFENCES OF, AND RELATED TO, MONEY LAUNDERING IN AND OUTSIDE THE STATE; TO GIVE EFFECT TO DIRECTIVE 2005/60/EC OF THE EUROPEAN PARLIAMENT AND OF THE COUNCIL OF 26 OCTOBER 2005 ON THE PREVENTION OF THE USE OF THE FINANCIAL SYSTEM FOR THE PURPOSE OF MONEY LAUNDERING AND TERRORIST FINANCING; TO PROVIDE FOR THE REGISTRATION OF PERSONS DIRECTING PRIVATE MEMBERS' CLUBS; TO PROVIDE FOR THE AMENDMENT OF THE CENTRAL BANK ACT 1942 AND THE COURTS (SUPPLEMENTAL PROVISIONS) ACT 1961; TO PROVIDE FOR THE CONSEQUENTIAL REPEAL OF CERTAIN PROVISIONS OF THE CRIMINAL JUSTICE ACT 1994; THE CONSEQUENTIAL AMENDMENT OF CERTAIN ENACTMENTS AND THE REVOCATION OF CERTAIN STATUTORY INSTRUMENTS; AND TO PROVIDE FOR RELATED MATTERS. [5th May, 2010]

BE IT ENACTED BY THE OIREACHTAS AS FOLLOWS:

PART 1
PRELIMINARY

1   Short title and commencement

(1) This Act may be cited as the Criminal Justice (Money Laundering and Terrorist Financing) Act 2010.

(2) This Act shall come into operation on such day or days as may be appointed by order or orders made by the Minister, either generally or with reference to a particular purpose or provision, and different days may be so appointed for different purposes and different provisions.[1]

(3) An order under subsection (2) may, in respect of the repeal of the provisions of the Criminal Justice Act 1994 specified in section 4, and the revocation of the statutory instruments specified in Schedule 1 effected by section 4(2), appoint different days for the repeal of different provisions of the Criminal Justice Act 1994 and the revocation of different statutory instruments or different provisions of them.

Note

[1] This Act come into operation on 15 July 2010 by virtue of the Criminal Justice (Money Laundering and Terrorist Financing) Commencement Order 2010 (SI 342/2010).

---

2   Interpretation

(1) In this Act—

"Implementing Directive" means Commission Directive 2006/70/EC of 1 August 2006 laying down implementing measures for Directive 2005/60/EC of the European Parliament and of the Council as regards the definition of "politically exposed person" and the technical criteria for simplified customer due diligence procedures and for exemption on grounds of a financial activity conducted on an occasional or very limited basis;

"Minister" means the Minister for Justice, Equality and Law Reform;

"money laundering" means an offence under Part 2;

"prescribed" means prescribed by the Minister by regulations made under this Act;

"property" means all real or personal property, whether or not heritable or moveable, and includes money and choses in action and any other intangible or incorporeal property;

"terrorist financing" means an offence under section 13 of the Criminal Justice (Terrorist Offences) Act 2005;

"Third Money Laundering Directive" means Directive 2005/60/EC of the European Parliament and of the Council of 26 October 2005 on the prevention of the use of the financial system for the purpose of money laundering and terrorist financing2, as amended by the following:

(a) Directive 2007/64/EC of the European Parliament and of the Council of 13 November 2007 on payment services in the internal market amending Directives 97/7/EC, 2002/65/EC, 2005/60/EC and 2006/48/EC and repealing Directive 97/5/EC3;

(b) Directive 2009/110/EC of the European Parliament and of the Council of 16 September 2009 on the taking up, pursuit and prudential supervision of the business of electronic money institutions amending Directives 2005/60/EC and 2006/48/EC and repealing Directive 2000/46/EC4.

(2) A word or expression used in this Act and also in the Third Money Laundering Directive or the Implementing Directive has, unless the contrary intention appears, the same meaning in this Act as in that Directive.

3   Regulations

(1) The Minister may, after consulting with the Minister for Finance, by regulations provide for any matter referred to in this Act as prescribed or to be prescribed.

(2) Regulations under this Act may contain such incidental, supplementary and consequential provisions as appear to the Minister to be necessary or expedient for the purposes of the regulations.

(3) Every regulation made under this Act shall be laid before each House of the Oireachtas as soon as may be after it is made and, if a resolution annulling the regulation is passed by either such House within the next 21 days on which that House has sat after the regulation is laid before it, the regulation shall be annulled accordingly, but without prejudice to the validity of anything previously done under the regulation.

4   Repeals and revocations

(1) Sections 31, 32, 32A, 57(1) to (6) and (7)(a), 57A and 58(2) of the Criminal Justice Act 1994 are repealed.

(2) The statutory instruments specified in column (1) of Schedule 1 are revoked to the extent specified in column (3) of that Schedule.

5   Expenses

The expenses incurred by the Minister in the administration of this Act shall, to such extent as may be sanctioned by the Minister for Finance, be paid out of moneys provided by the Oireachtas and the expenses incurred by the Minister for Finance in the administration of this Act shall be paid out of moneys provided by the Oireachtas.

PART 2

MONEY LAUNDERING OFFENCES

6   Interpretation (Part 2)

In this Part—

"criminal conduct" means—

    (a)   conduct that constitutes an offence, or

    (b)   conduct occurring in a place outside the State that constitutes an offence under the law of the place and would constitute an offence if it were to occur in the State;

"proceeds of criminal conduct" means any property that is derived from or obtained through criminal conduct, whether directly or indirectly, or in whole or in part, and whether that criminal conduct occurs before, on or after the commencement of this Part.

7   Money laundering occurring in State

(1) A person commits an offence if—

    (a)   the person engages in any of the following acts in relation to property that is the proceeds of criminal conduct:

        (i)   concealing or disguising the true nature, source, location, disposition, movement or ownership of the property, or any rights relating to the property;

        (ii)   converting, transferring, handling, acquiring, possessing or using the property;

        (iii)   removing the property from, or bringing the property into, the State,

        and

    (b)   the person knows or believes (or is reckless as to whether or not) the property is the proceeds of criminal conduct.

(2) A person who attempts to commit an offence under subsection (1) commits an offence.

(3) A person who commits an offence under this section is liable—

    (a)   on summary conviction, to a fine not exceeding €5,000 or imprisonment for a term not exceeding 12 months (or both), or

    (b)   on conviction on indictment, to a fine or imprisonment for a term not exceeding 14 years (or both).

(4) A reference in this section to knowing or believing that property is the proceeds of criminal conduct includes a reference to knowing or believing that the property probably comprises the proceeds of criminal conduct.

(5) For the purposes of subsections (1) and (2), a person is reckless as to whether or not property is the proceeds of criminal conduct if the person disregards, in relation to property, a risk of such a nature and degree that, considering the circumstances in which the person carries out any act referred to in subsection (1) or (2), the disregard of that risk involves culpability of a high degree.

(6) For the purposes of subsections (1) and (2), a person handles property if the person—

    (a)   receives, or arranges to receive, the property, or

    (b)   retains, removes, disposes of or realises the property, or arranges to do any of those things, for the benefit of another person.

(7) A person does not commit an offence under this section in relation to the doing of any thing in relation to property that is the proceeds of criminal conduct so long as—

    (a)   the person does the thing in accordance with a direction, order or authorisation given under Part 3, or

    (b)   without prejudice to the generality of paragraph (a), the person is a designated person, within the meaning of Part 4, who makes a report in relation to the property, and does the thing, in accordance with section 42.

8   **Money laundering outside State in certain circumstances**

(1) A person who, in a place outside the State, engages in conduct that would, if the conduct occurred in the State, constitute an offence under section 7 commits an offence if any of the following circumstances apply:

    (a)   the conduct takes place on board an Irish ship, within the meaning of section 9 of the Mercantile Marine Act 1955,

    (b)   the conduct takes place on an aircraft registered in the State,

    (c)   the conduct constitutes an offence under the law of that place and the person is—

        (i)   an individual who is a citizen of Ireland or ordinarily resident in the State, or

        (ii) a body corporate established under the law of the State or a company registered under the Companies Acts,

    (d)   a request for the person's surrender, for the purpose of trying him or her for an offence in respect of the conduct, has been made under Part II of the Extradition Act 1965 by any country and the request has been finally refused (whether or not as a result of a decision of a court), or

    (e)   a European arrest warrant has been received from an issuing state for the purpose of bringing proceedings against the person for an offence in respect of the conduct, and a final determination has been made that—

        (i)   the European arrest warrant should not be endorsed for execution in the State under the European Arrest Warrant Act 2003, or

        (ii) the person should not be surrendered to the issuing state.

(2) A person who commits an offence under this section is liable—

    (a)   on summary conviction, to a fine not exceeding €5,000 or imprisonment for a term not exceeding 12 months (or both), or

(b)   on conviction on indictment, to a fine or imprisonment for a term not exceeding 14 years (or both).

(3) A person who has his or her principal residence in the State for the 12 months immediately preceding the commission of an offence under this section is, in a case where subsection (1)(c) applies, taken to be ordinarily resident in the State on the date of the commission of the offence.

(4) In this section, "European arrest warrant" and "issuing state" have the same meanings as they have in the European Arrest Warrant Act 2003.

9   Attempts, outside State, to commit offence in State

(1) A person who attempts, in a place outside the State, to commit an offence under section 7(1) is guilty of an offence.

(2) A person who commits an offence under this section is liable—

(a)   on summary conviction, to a fine not exceeding €5,000 or imprisonment for a term not exceeding 12 months (or both), or

(b)   on conviction on indictment, to a fine or imprisonment for a term not exceeding 14 years (or both).

10   Aiding, abetting, counselling or procuring outside State commission of offence in State

(1) A person who, in a place outside the State, aids, abets, counsels or procures the commission of an offence under section 7 is guilty of an offence.

(2) A person who commits an offence under this section is liable—

(a)   on summary conviction, to a fine not exceeding €5,000 or imprisonment for a term not exceeding 12 months (or both), or

(b)   on conviction on indictment, to a fine or imprisonment for a term not exceeding 14 years (or both).

(3) This section is without prejudice to section 7(1) of the Criminal Law Act 1997.

11   Presumptions and other matters

(1) In this section "specified conduct" means any of the following acts referred to in section 7(1) (including section 7(1) as applied by section 8 or 9):

(a)   concealing or disguising the true nature, source, location, disposition, movement or ownership of property, or any rights relating to property;

(b)   converting, transferring, handling, acquiring, possessing or using property;

(c)   removing property from, or bringing property into, the State or a place outside the State.

(2) In proceedings for an offence under section 7, 8 or 9, where an accused has engaged, or attempted to engage, in specified conduct in relation to property that is the proceeds of criminal conduct, in circumstances in which it is reasonable to conclude that the accused—

(a)   knew or believed the property was the proceeds of criminal conduct, or

(b)   was reckless as to whether or not the property was the proceeds of criminal conduct, the accused is presumed to have so known or believed, or been so reckless, unless the court or jury, as the case may be, is satisfied, having regard to the whole of the evidence, that there is a reasonable doubt that the accused so knew or believed or was so reckless.

(3) In proceedings for an offence under section 7, 8 or 9, where an accused has engaged in, or attempted to engage in, specified conduct in relation to property in circumstances in which it is reasonable to conclude that the property is the proceeds of criminal conduct, those circumstances are evidence that the property is the proceeds of criminal conduct.

(4) For the purposes of subsection (3), circumstances in which it is reasonable to conclude that property is the proceeds of criminal conduct include any of the following:

    (a) the value of the property concerned is, it is reasonable to conclude, out of proportion to the income and expenditure of the accused or another person in a case where the accused engaged in the specified conduct concerned on behalf of, or at the request of, the other person;

    (b) the specified conduct concerned involves the actual or purported purchase or sale of goods or services for an amount that is, it is reasonable to conclude, out of proportion to the market value of the goods or services (whether the amount represents an overvaluation or an undervaluation);

    (c) the specified conduct concerned involves one or more transactions using false names;

    (d) the accused has stated that he or she engaged in the specified conduct concerned on behalf of, or at the request of, another person and has not provided information to the Garda Síochána enabling the other person to be identified and located;

    (e) where an accused has concealed or disguised the true nature, source, location, disposition, movement or ownership of the property, or any rights relating to the property, the accused has no reasonable explanation for that concealment or disguise.

(5) Nothing in subsection (4) limits the circumstances in which it is reasonable to conclude, for the purposes of subsection (3), that property is the proceeds of criminal conduct.

(6) Nothing in this section prevents subsections (2) and (3) being applied in the same proceedings.

(7) Subsections (2) to (6) extend to proceedings for an offence under—

    (a) section 10, or

    (b) section 7(1) of the Criminal Law Act 1997 of aiding, abetting, counselling or procuring the commission of an offence under section 7, 8 or 9,

and for that purpose any reference to an accused in subsections (2) to (6) is to be construed as a reference to a person who committed, or is alleged to have committed, the offence concerned.

(8) In proceedings for an offence under this Part, or an offence under section 7(1) of the Criminal Law Act 1997 referred to in subsection (7)(b), it is not necessary, in order to prove that property is the proceeds of criminal conduct, to establish that—

    (a) a particular offence or a particular class of offence comprising criminal conduct was committed in relation to the property, or

    (b) a particular person committed an offence comprising criminal conduct in relation to the property.

(9) In proceedings for an offence under this Part, or an offence under section 7(1) of the Criminal Law Act 1997 referred to in subsection (7)(b), it is not a defence for the accused to show that the accused believed the property concerned to be the proceeds of a particular offence comprising criminal conduct when in fact the property was the proceeds of another offence.

12   Location of proceedings relating to offences committed outside State

Proceedings for an offence under section 8, 9 or 10 may be taken in any place in the State and the offence may for all incidental purposes be treated as having been committed in that place.

13   Consent of DPP required for proceedings for offences committed outside State

If a person is charged with an offence under section 8, 9 or 10, no further proceedings in the matter (other than any remand in custody or on bail) may be taken except by, or with the consent of, the Director of Public Prosecutions.

14   Certificate may be evidence in proceedings under this Part

(1) In any proceedings for an offence under this Part in which it is alleged that property the subject of the offence is the proceeds of criminal conduct occurring in a place outside the State, a certificate—

    (a) purporting to be signed by a lawyer practising in the place, and

    (b) stating that such conduct is an offence in that place,

is evidence of the matters referred to in that certificate, unless the contrary is shown.

(2) A certificate referred to in subsection (1) is taken to have been signed by the person purporting to have signed it, unless the contrary is shown.

(3) In a case where a certificate referred to in subsection (1) is written in a language other than the Irish language or the English language, unless the contrary is shown—

    (a) a document purporting to be a translation of that certificate into the Irish language or the English language, as the case may be, and that is certified as correct by a person appearing to be competent to so certify, is taken—

        (i) to be a correct translation of the certificate, and

        (ii) to have been certified by the person purporting to have certified it,

    and

    (b) the person is taken to be competent to so certify.

(4) In any proceedings for an offence under section 8 committed in the circumstances referred to in section 8(1)(c), a certificate purporting to be signed by an officer of the Department of Foreign Affairs and stating that—

    (a) a passport was issued by that Department to a person on a specified date, and

    (b) to the best of the officer's knowledge and belief, the person has not ceased to be an Irish citizen,

is evidence that the person was an Irish citizen on the date on which the offence is alleged to have been committed, and is taken to have been signed by the person purporting to have signed it, unless the contrary is shown.

(5) In any proceedings for an offence under section 8 committed in the circumstances referred to in section 8(1)(d) or (e), a certificate purporting to be signed by the Minister and

stating any of the matters referred to in that paragraph is evidence of those matters, and is taken to have been signed by the Minister, unless the contrary is shown.

15   Double jeopardy

A person who has been acquitted or convicted of an offence in a place outside the State shall not be proceeded against for an offence under section 8, 9 or 10 consisting of the conduct, or substantially the same conduct, that constituted the offence of which the person has been acquitted or convicted.

16   Revenue offence committed outside State

For the avoidance of doubt, a reference in this Part to an offence under the law of a place outside the State includes a reference to an offence in connection with taxes, duties, customs or exchange regulation.

PARTS 3 AND 4 NOT REPRODUCED HERE

PART 5
MISCELLANEOUS

110   Service of documents

(1) A notice or other document that is required or permitted, under this Act, to be served on or given to a person shall be addressed to the person by name and may be served or given to the person in one of the following ways:

(a)   by delivering it to the person;

(b)   by leaving it at the address at which the person ordinarily resides or carries on business;

(c)   by sending it by post in a pre-paid registered letter to the address at which the person ordinarily resides or carries on business;

(d)   if an address for service has been furnished, by leaving it at, or sending it by post in a pre-paid registered letter to, that address;

(e)   in the case of a direction to an individual or body (whether incorporated or unincorporated) under Part 3 not to carry out any specified service or transaction at a branch or place of business of the body or individual, by leaving it at, or by sending it by post in a pre-paid registered letter to, the address of the branch or place of business (as the case may be);

(f)   if the person giving notice considers that notice should be given immediately and a fax machine is located at an address referred to in paragraph (b), (c), (d) or (e),by sending it by fax to that machine, but only if the sender's fax machine generates a message confirming successful transmission of the total number of pages of the notice.

(2) For the purposes of this section—

(a)   a company registered under the Companies Acts is taken to be ordinarily resident at its registered office, and

(b)   any body corporate other than a company registered under the Companies Acts or any unincorporated body is taken to be ordinarily resident at its principal office or place of business in the State.

(3) Nothing in subsection (1)(e) prevents the serving or giving of a direction or other document for the purposes of Part 3 under any other provision of this section.

(4) This section is without prejudice to any mode of service or of giving a notice or any other document provided for under any other enactment or rule of law.

(5) This section does not apply in relation to the service of a notice on the Minister referred to in section 100(2).

111   Offences — directors and others of bodies corporate and unincorporated bodies

Where an offence under this Act is committed by a body corporate or by a person purporting to act on behalf of a body corporate or on behalf of an unincorporated body of persons, and is proved to have been committed with the consent or connivance, or to be attributable to any wilful neglect, of a person who, when the offence is committed, is—

   (a) a director, manager, secretary or other officer of the body, or a person purporting to act in that capacity, or
   (b) a member of the committee of management or other controlling authority of the body, or a person purporting to act in that capacity,

that person is taken to have also committed the offence and may be proceeded against and punished accordingly.

112   Disclosure of information in good faith

(1) This section applies to the disclosure in good faith, to a member of the Garda Síochána or to any person who is concerned in the investigation or prosecution of an offence of money laundering or terrorist financing, of—

   (a) a suspicion that any property has been obtained in connection with any such offence, or derives from property so obtained, or
   (b) any matter on which such a suspicion is based.

(2) A disclosure to which this section applies shall not be treated, for any purpose, as a breach of any restriction on the disclosure of information imposed by any other enactment or rule of law.

113   Amendment of Bail Act 1997

The Schedule to the Bail Act 1997 is amended by inserting the following paragraph after paragraph 34 (inserted by section 48 of the Criminal Justice (Miscellaneous Provisions) Act 2009):[1]

Amendments

1   See the amended Act.

---

114   Amendment of Central Bank Act 1942

(1) In this section, "Act of 1942" means the Central Bank Act 1942.

(2) Section 33AK(5) (inserted by section 26 of the Central Bank and Financial Services Authority of Ireland Act 2003) of the Act of 1942 is amended by deleting paragraph (n).

(3) The Act of 1942 is amended by inserting the following after section 33AN (inserted by section 10 of the Central Bank and Financial Services Authority of Ireland Act 2004):

"Application of Part to credit unions

33ANA.—(1) This Part applies in relation to—

(a) the commission or suspected commission by a credit union of a contravention of—

    (i) a provision of Part 4 of the Criminal Justice (Money Laundering and Terrorist Financing) Act 2010,

    (ii) any direction given to the credit union under a provision of Part 4 of that Act,

    (iii) any condition or requirement imposed on the credit union under a provision of Part 4 of that Act or under any direction given to the credit union under a provision of that Part, or

    (iv) any obligation imposed on the credit union by this Part or imposed by the Regulatory Authority pursuant to a power exercised under this Part, and

(b) participation, by a person concerned in the management of a credit union, in the commission by the credit union of such a contravention.

(2) For those purposes—

(a) a reference in this Part to a regulated financial service provider includes a reference to a credit union,

(b) a reference in this Part to a prescribed contravention includes a reference to a contravention, by a credit union, of a provision, direction, condition, requirement or obligation referred to in subsection (1), and

(c) a reference in this Part to a person concerned in the management of a regulated financial service provider includes a reference to a person concerned in the management of a credit union.

(3) Nothing in this section limits the application of this Part in relation to matters other than those referred to in subsection (1).

(4) This section has effect notwithstanding anything to the contrary in section 184 of the Credit Union Act 1997.".

(4) Schedule 2 (substituted by section 31 of the Central Bank and Financial Services Authority of Ireland Act 2003) to the Act of 1942 is amended in Part 1 by inserting the following at the end of the Part:

No. —— of 2010	Criminal Justice (Money Laundering and Terrorist Financing) Act 2010	Part 4

115   Amendment of Courts (Supplemental Provisions) Act 1961

Section 32A(1) of the Courts (Supplemental Provisions) Act 1961 (inserted by section 180 of the Criminal Justice Act 2006) is amended as follows:

(a) in paragraph (d) (inserted by section 18 of the Criminal Justice (Surveillance) Act 2009) by substituting "Criminal Justice (Surveillance) Act 2009;" for "Criminal Justice (Surveillance) Act 2009.";

(b) by inserting the following paragraph after paragraph (d):[1]

Amendments

1   See the amended Act.

116   Consequential amendment of Central Bank Act 1997

Section 28 (substituted by section 27 of the Central Bank and Financial Services Authority of Ireland Act 2004) of the Central Bank Act 1997 is amended, in the definitions of "bureau de change business" and "money transmission service", by substituting the following for paragraphs (a) and (b) of those definitions:

> "(a) by a person or body that is required to be licensed, registered or otherwise authorised by the Bank under a designated enactment (other than under this Part) or designated statutory instrument, or".

117   Consequential amendment of Criminal Justice Act 1994

(1) In this section, "Act of 1994" means the Criminal Justice Act 1994.

(2) Section 3(1) of the Act of 1994 is amended in the definition of "drug trafficking" by substituting the following for paragraph (d):

> "(d) engaging in any conduct (whether or not in the State) in relation to property obtained, whether directly or indirectly, from anything done in relation to a controlled drug, being conduct that—
>
> (i)   is an offence under Part 2 of the Criminal Justice (Money Laundering and Terrorist Financing) Act 2010 ("Part 2 of the Act of 2010") or would have been an offence under that Part if the Part had been in operation at the time when the conduct was engaged in, or
>
> (ii) in the case of conduct in a place outside of the State, other than conduct referred to in subparagraph (i)—
>
> > (I)   would be an offence under Part 2 of the Act of 2010 if done in corresponding circumstances in the State, or
> >
> > (II) would have been an offence under that Part if done in corresponding circumstances in the State and if the Part had been in operation at the time when the conduct was engaged in, or".

(3) Section 3(1) of the Act of 1994 is amended in the definition of "drug trafficking offence"by substituting the following for paragraph (e):

> "(e) an offence under Part 2 of the Criminal Justice (Money Laundering and Terrorist Financing) Act 2010, or under section 31 of this Act (as in force before the commencement of that Part), in relation to the proceeds of drug trafficking,".

118   Consequential amendment of Criminal Justice (Mutual Assistance) Act 2008

Section 94(3) of the Criminal Justice (Mutual Assistance) Act 2008 is amended by substituting "Part 2 of the Criminal Justice (Money Laundering and Terrorist Financing) Act 2010"for "section 31 of the Criminal Justice Act 1994, as substituted by section 21 of the Criminal Justice (Theft and Fraud Offences) Act 2001".

119   Consequential amendment of Criminal Justice (Theft and Fraud Offences) Act 2001

Section 40(1) of the Criminal Justice (Theft and Fraud Offences) Act 2001 is amended by substituting the following for the definition of "money laundering":[1]

Amendments

1   See the amended Act.

120   Consequential amendment of Investor Compensation Act 1998

(1) In this section, "Act of 1998"means the Investor Compensation Act 1998.

(2) Section 30(1) of the Act of 1998 is amended in the definition of "net loss"by substituting the following for subparagraph (iii):

"(iii)   money or investment instruments arising out of transactions in respect of which an offence has been committed under the Criminal Justice (Money Laundering and Terrorist Financing) Act 2010 ("Act of 2010"),

   (iv)   money or investment instruments arising out of transactions in respect of which an offence has been committed under a provision of Part IV of the Criminal Justice Act 1994 prior to the repeal of that provision by the Act of 2010,

   (v)   money or investment instruments arising out of transactions in respect of which an offence has been committed under a provision of section 57 or 58 of the Criminal Justice Act 1994 prior to the repeal of that provision by the Act of 2010, or

   (vi)   money or investment instruments arising out of transactions in respect of which there has been a criminal conviction, at any time, for money laundering, within the meaning of Directive 2005/60/EC of the European Parliament and of the Council of 26 October 2005 on the prevention of the use of the financial system for the purpose of money laundering and terrorist financing12.".

(3) Section 35 of the Act of 1998 is amended by substituting the following for subsection (3):

   "(3) Notwithstanding the time limits provided for in subsections (1) and (2), the competent authority may direct the Company or a compensation scheme approved under section 25, as appropriate, to suspend any payment to an eligible investor, where the investor has been charged with any of the following offences, pending the judgment of a court in respect of the charge:

   (a)   an offence under the Criminal Justice (Money Laundering and Terrorist Financing) Act 2010 ("Act of 2010");

   (b)   an offence committed, prior to the repeal by the Act of 2010 of any of the following provisions of the Criminal Justice Act 1994, under that provision:

      (i)   a provision of Part IV;

      (ii)   section 57;

      (iii)   section 58;

   (c)   an offence otherwise arising out of, or relating to, money laundering, within the meaning of Directive 2005/60/EC of the European Parliament and of the

Council of 26 October 2005 on the prevention of the use of the financial system for the purpose of money laundering and terrorist financing13.".

121   Consequential amendment of Taxes Consolidation Act 1997

(1) In this section, "Act of 1997" means the Taxes Consolidation Act 1997.

(2) Section 898F (substituted by section 90 of, and Schedule 4 to, the Finance Act 2004) of the Act of 1997 is amended as follows:

(a)   in subsection (3) by substituting "which is acceptable for the purposes of Chapter 3 of Part 4 of the Criminal Justice (Money Laundering and Terrorist Financing) Act 2010" for "it acquires by virtue of section 32 of the Criminal Justice Act 1994";

(b)   in subsection (4) by substituting "which is acceptable for the purposes of Chapter 3 of Part 4 of the Criminal Justice (Money Laundering and Terrorist Financing) Act 2010" for "it acquires by virtue of section 32 of the Criminal Justice Act 1994";

(c)   in subsection (5)(a) (substituted by section 124(1)(a) of the Finance Act 2006) by inserting "(or has done so, before the relevant commencement date, in accordance with this section as in force before that date)" after "in accordance with this section";

(d)   by inserting the following paragraph after subsection (6)(a):

"(aa)   A paying agent who—

(i)   before the relevant commencement date, established the identity and residence of an individual under this section as in force before that date, and

(ii)   was required, immediately before the relevant commencement date and as a result of paragraph (a), to continue to treat that individual as so identified and so resident,

shall continue to treat that individual as so identified and so resident until such time as the paying agent is in possession, or aware, of information which can reasonably be taken to indicate that the individual has been incorrectly identified or is not so resident or has changed his or her residence.";

(e)   in subsection (6)(b) by inserting "or (aa)" after "paragraph (a)";

(f)   in subsection (7) by inserting "(or as established, before the relevant commencement date, in accordance with this section as in force before that date)" after "this section";

(g)   by inserting the following subsection after subsection (7):

"(8) In this section, 'relevant commencement date' means the date on which section 121(2) of the Criminal Justice (Money Laundering and Terrorist Financing) Act 2010 comes into operation.".

(3) Section 898G (substituted by section 90 of, and Schedule 4 to, the Finance Act 2004) of the Act of 1997 is amended as follows:

(a)   in subsection (2) by substituting "Chapter 3 of Part 4 of the Criminal Justice (Money Laundering and Terrorist Financing) Act 2010" for "section 32 of the Criminal Justice Act 1994";

(b)   in subsection (4)(b) by substituting "Chapter 3 of Part 4 of the Criminal Justice (Money Laundering and Terrorist Financing) Act 2010" for "section 32 of the Criminal Justice Act 1994";

(c) in subsection (5)(b)(iii) by substituting "Chapter 3 of Part 4 of the Criminal Justice (Money Laundering and Terrorist Financing) Act 2010" for "section 32 of the Criminal Justice Act 1994";

(d) in subsection (6)(a) (substituted by section 124(1)(b)of the Finance Act 2006) by inserting "(or has done so, before the relevant commencement date, in accordance with this section as in force before that date)" after "in accordance with this section";

(e) by inserting the following paragraph after subsection (8)(a):

"(aa) A paying agent who—

(i)   before the relevant commencement date, established the identity and residence of an individual under this section as in force before that date, and

(ii) was required, immediately before the relevant commencement date and as a result of paragraph (a), to continue to treat that individual as so identified and so resident,

shall continue to treat that individual as so identified and so resident until such time as the paying agent is in possession, or aware, of information which can reasonably be taken to indicate that the individual has been incorrectly identified or is not so resident or has changed his or her residence.";

(f) in subsection (8)(b) by inserting "or (aa)" after "paragraph (a)";

(g) in subsection (9) by inserting "(or as established, before the relevant commencement date, in accordance with this section as in force before that date)" after "this section";

(h) by inserting the following subsection after subsection (9):

"(10) In this section, 'relevant commencement date' means the date on which section 121(3) of the Criminal Justice (Money Laundering and Terrorist Financing) Act 2010 comes into operation.".

122   Consequential amendment of Taxi Regulation Act 2003

Section 36(1)(f) of the Taxi Regulation Act 2003 is amended by substituting "Part 2 of the Criminal Justice (Money Laundering and Terrorist Financing) Act 2010" for "Part IV of the Criminal Justice Act 1994".

Fines Act 2010

Number 8 of 2010

ARRANGEMENT OF SECTIONS

PART 1
PRELIMINARY AND GENERAL

Section

1. Short title and commencement.
2. Definition.

PART 2
INCREASE OF FINES

3. Definitions.
4. Class A fines.
5. Class B fines.
6. Class C fines.
7. Class D fines.
8. Class E fines.
9. Increase in amount of certain fines upon conviction on indictment.
10. Summary trial of indictable offences.
11. Regulations to remove difficulties.

PART 3
PAYMENT AND RECOVERY OF FINES

12. Definitions.
13. Service of documents.
14. Capacity of person to pay fine.
15. Payment of fines by instalments.
16. Appointment of receiver in default of payment of fine.
17. Monies recovered by receiver under section 16.
18. Community service order in default of payment of fine.
19. Imprisonment in default of payment of fine.
20. Approval by Government of persons for purposes of section 16.
21. Publication of list of names of persons who fail to pay fines on time.
22. Repeal.

AN ACT TO MAKE PROVISION IN RELATION TO THE MAXIMUM FINES THAT A COURT MAY IMPOSE IN RESPECT OF OFFENCES TRIED SUMMARILY AND CERTAIN OFFENCES TRIED ON INDICTMENT; TO PROVIDE THAT A COURT IN IMPOSING A FINE UPON CONVICTION OF A PERSON OF AN OFFENCE SHALL TAKE ACCOUNT

OF A PERSON'S FINANCIAL CIRCUMSTANCES; TO PROVIDE FOR THE PAYMENT OF SUCH FINES BY INSTALMENT IN CERTAIN CIRCUMSTANCES; TO MAKE PROVISION IN RELATION TO THE POWERS OF THE COURT WHERE THERE HAS BEEN A FAILURE ON THE PART OF A CONVICTED PERSON TO PAY A FINE; FOR THOSE PURPOSES TO AMEND THE CRIMINAL JUSTICE (COMMUNITY SERVICE) ACT 1983 AND THE COURTS (NO. 2) ACT 1986; AND TO PROVIDE FOR MATTERS CONNECTED THEREWITH. [31st May, 2010]

BE IT ENACTED BY THE OIREACHTAS AS FOLLOWS:

PART 1
PRELIMINARY AND GENERAL

Note

Part 1 came into operation on 4 January 2011 by virtue of SI 662/2010.

---

1   Short title and commencement

(1) This Act may be cited as the Fines Act 2010.

(2) This Act shall come into operation on such day or days as the Minister may appoint by order or orders either generally or with reference to any particular purpose or provision and different days may be so appointed for different purposes or provisions.

2   Definition

In this Act "Minister" means the Minister for Justice, Equality and Law Reform.

PART 2
INCREASE OF FINES

Note

Part 2 came into operation on 4 January 2011 by virtue of SI 662/2010.

---

3   Definitions

In this Part—

"class A fine" means a fine not exceeding €5,000;

"class B fine" means a fine not exceeding €4,000;

"class C fine" means a fine not exceeding €2,500;

"class D fine" means a fine not exceeding €1,000;

"class E fine" means a fine not exceeding €500;

"commencement date" means the date of the coming into operation of this Part;

"enactment" means—

    (a) an Act of the Oireachtas,

    (b) a statute that was in force in Saorstát Éireann immediately before the date of the coming into operation of the Constitution and that continues in force by virtue of Article 50 of the Constitution, or

    (c) an instrument made under—

        (i) an Act of the Oireachtas, or

        (ii) such a statute.

4   Class A fines

(1) Where an enactment enacted on or after the commencement date provides that a person who commits an offence under that or any other enactment shall be liable, upon summary conviction, to a class A fine, the reference to class A fine shall be construed as a reference to class A fine within the meaning of this Part.

(2) Subject to subsection (3), where an enactment enacted during a period specified in column (2) of the Table opposite a particular reference number specified in column (1) of the Table provides that a person who commits an offence under the enactment shall be liable, upon summary conviction, to a fine not exceeding an amount that falls within the range of amounts specified in column (3) of the Table opposite the same reference number, a person who commits that offence after the commencement date shall, upon summary conviction, not be liable to that fine, but shall instead be liable to a class A fine.

(3) Where an enactment enacted before the commencement date provides that a person who commits an offence under the enactment shall be liable, upon summary conviction, to a fine not exceeding an amount that—

    (a) was provided for by virtue of a subsequent enactment enacted during a period specified in column (2) of the Table opposite a particular reference number specified in column (1) of the Table, and

    (b) falls within the range of amounts specified in column (3) of the Table opposite the same reference number,

a person who commits that offence after the commencement date shall, upon summary conviction, not be liable to that fine but shall instead be liable to a class A fine.

TABLE

Ref No (1)	Period (2)	Range of amounts (3)
1.	1 January 1997 to day immediately before commencement date	Not greater than €5,000 but greater than €4,000
2.	1 January 1990 to 31 December 1996	Not greater than €5,000 but greater than €2,769
3.	1 January 1980 to 31 December 1989	Not greater than €5,000 but greater than €2,328
4.	1 January 1975 to 31 December 1979	Not greater than €5,000 but greater than €970

Ref No (1)	Period (2)	Range of amounts (3)
5.	1 January 1965 to 31 December 1974	Not greater than €5,000 but greater than €491
6.	1 January 1945 to 31 December 1964	Not greater than €5,000 but greater than €234
7.	1 January 1915 to 31 December 1944	Not greater than €5,000 but greater than €127
8.	Period ending on 31 December 1914	Not greater than €5,000 but greater than €100

5 Class B fines

(1) Where an enactment enacted on or after the commencement date provides that a person who commits an offence under that or any other enactment shall be liable, upon summary conviction, to a class B fine, the reference to class B fine shall be construed as a reference to class B fine within the meaning of this Part.

(2) Subject to subsection (3), where an enactment enacted during a period specified in column (2) of the Table opposite a particular reference number specified in column (1) of the Table provides that a person who commits an offence under the enactment shall be liable, upon summary conviction, to a fine not exceeding an amount that falls within the range of amounts specified in column (3) of the Table opposite the same reference number, a person who commits that offence after the commencement date shall, upon summary conviction, not be liable to that fine, but shall instead be liable to a class B fine.

(3) Where an enactment enacted before the commencement date provides that a person who commits an offence under the enactment shall be liable, upon summary conviction, to a fine not exceeding an amount that—

    (a) was provided for by virtue of a subsequent enactment enacted during a period specified in column (2) of the Table opposite a particular reference number specified in column (1) of the Table, and

    (b) falls within the range of amounts specified in column (3) of the Table opposite the same reference number,

a person who commits that offence after the commencement date shall, upon summary conviction, not be liable to that fine but shall instead be liable to a class B fine.

TABLE

Ref No (1)	Period (2)	Range of amounts (3)
1.	1 January 1997 to day immediately before commencement date	Not greater than €4,000 but greater than €2,500
2.	1 January 1990 to 31 December 1996	Not greater than €2,769 but greater than €1,731
3.	1 January 1980 to 31 December 1989	Not greater than €2,328 but greater than €1,455

Ref No (1)	Period (2)	Range of amounts (3)
4.	1 January 1975 to 31 December 1979	Not greater than €970 but greater than €606
5.	1 January 1965 to 31 December 1974	Not greater than €491 but greater than €307
6.	1 January 1945 to 31 December 1964	Not greater than €234 but greater than €147
7.	1 January 1915 to 31 December 1944	Not greater than €127 but greater than €79
8.	Period ending on 31 December 1914	Not greater than €100 but greater than €50

6   Class C fines.

(1) Where an enactment enacted on or after the commencement date provides that a person who commits an offence under that or any other enactment shall be liable, upon summary conviction, to a class C fine, the reference to class C fine shall be construed as a reference to class C fine within the meaning of this Part.

(2) Subject to subsection (3), where an enactment enacted during a period specified in column (2) of the Table opposite a particular reference number specified in column (1) of the Table provides that a person who commits an offence under the enactment shall be liable, upon summary conviction, to a fine not exceeding an amount that falls within the range of amounts specified in column (3) of the Table opposite the same reference number, a person who commits that offence after the commencement date shall, upon summary conviction, not be liable to that fine, but shall instead be liable to a class C fine.

(3) Where an enactment enacted before the commencement date provides that a person who commits an offence under the enactment shall be liable, upon summary conviction, to a fine not exceeding an amount that—

    (a) was provided for by virtue of a subsequent enactment enacted during a period specified in column (2) of the Table opposite a particular reference number specified in column (1) of the Table, and

    (b) falls within the range of amounts specified in column (3) of the Table opposite the same reference number,

a person who commits that offence after the commencement date shall, upon summary conviction, not be liable to that fine but shall instead be liable to a class C fine.

TABLE

Ref No (1)	Period (2)	Range of amounts (3)
1.	1 January 1997 to day immediately before commencement date	Not greater than €2,500 but greater than €1,000
2.	1 January 1990 to 31 December 1996	Not greater than €1,731 but greater than €692

Ref No (1)	Period (2)	Range of amounts (3)
3.	1 January 1980 to 31 December 1989	Not greater than €1,455 but greater than €582
4.	1 January 1975 to 31 December 1979	Not greater than €606 but greater than €242
5.	1 January 1965 to 31 December 1974	Not greater than €307 but greater than €123
6.	1 January 1945 to 31 December 1964	Not greater than €147 but greater than €59
7.	1 January 1915 to 31 December 1944	Not greater than €79 but greater than €32
8.	Period ending on 31 December 1914	Not greater than €50 but greater than €25

7   Class D fines

(1) Where an enactment enacted on or after the commencement date provides that a person who commits an offence under that or any other enactment shall be liable, upon summary conviction, to a class D fine, the reference to class D fine shall be construed as a reference to class D fine within the meaning of this Part.

(2) Subject to subsection (3), where an enactment enacted during a period specified in column (2) of the Table opposite a particular reference number specified in column (1) of the Table provides that a person who commits an offence under the enactment shall be liable, upon summary conviction, to a fine not exceeding an amount that falls within the range of amounts specified in column (3) of the Table opposite the same reference number, a person who commits that offence after the commencement date shall, upon summary conviction, not be liable to that fine, but shall instead be liable to a class D fine.

(3) Where an enactment enacted before the commencement date provides that a person who commits an offence under the enactment shall be liable, upon summary conviction, to a fine not exceeding an amount that—

  (a) was provided for by virtue of a subsequent enactment enacted during a period specified in column (2) of the Table opposite a particular reference number specified in column (1) of the Table, and

  (b) falls within the range of amounts specified in column (3) of the Table opposite the same reference number,

a person who commits that offence after the commencement date shall, upon summary conviction, not be liable to that fine but shall instead be liable to a class D fine.

TABLE

Ref No (1)	Period (2)	Range of amounts (3)
1.	1 January 1997 to day immediately before commencement date	Not greater than €1,000 but greater than €500
2.	1 January 1990 to 31 December 1996	Not greater than €692 but greater than €346
3.	1 January 1980 to 31 December 1989	Not greater than €582 but greater than €291
4.	1 January 1975 to 31 December 1979	Not greater than €242 but greater than €121
5.	1 January 1965 to 31 December 1974	Not greater than €123 but greater than €61
6.	1 January 1945 to 31 December 1964	Not greater than €59 but greater than €29
7.	1 January 1915 to 31 December 1944	Not greater than €32 but greater than €16
8.	Period ending on 31 December 1914	Not greater than €25 but greater than €6

8   Class E fines

(1) Where an enactment enacted on or after the commencement date provides that a person who commits an offence under that or any other enactment shall be liable, upon summary conviction, to a class E fine, the reference to class E fine shall be construed as a reference to class E fine within the meaning of this Part.

(2) Subject to subsection (3), where an enactment enacted during a period specified in column (2) of the Table opposite a particular reference number specified in column (1) of the Table provides that a person who commits an offence under the enactment shall be liable, upon summary conviction, to a fine not exceeding an amount that falls within the range of amounts specified in column (3) of the Table opposite the same reference number, a person who commits that offence after the commencement date shall, upon summary conviction, not be liable to that fine, but shall instead be liable to a class E fine.

(3) Where an enactment enacted before the commencement date provides that a person who commits an offence under the enactment shall be liable, upon summary conviction, to a fine not exceeding an amount that—

(a) was provided for by virtue of a subsequent enactment enacted during a period specified in column (2) of the Table opposite a particular reference number specified in column (1) of the Table, and

(b) falls within the range of amounts specified in column (3) of the Table opposite the same reference number,

a person who commits that offence after the commencement date shall, upon summary conviction, not be liable to that fine but shall instead be liable to a class E fine.

TABLE

Ref No (1)	Period (2)	Range of amounts (3)
1.	1 January 1997 to day immediately before commencement date	Not greater than €500
2.	1 January 1990 to 31 December 1996	Not greater than €346
3.	1 January 1980 to 31 December 1989	Not greater than €291
4.	1 January 1975 to 31 December 1979	Not greater than €121
5.	1 January 1965 to 31 December 1974	Not greater than €61
6.	1 January 1945 to 31 December 1964	Not greater than €29
7.	1 January 1915 to 31 December 1944	Not greater than €16
8.	Period ending on 31 December 1914	Not greater than €6

9   Increase in amount of certain fines upon conviction on indictment

(1) Subject to subsection (2), where the maximum fine upon conviction on indictment of an offence is specified in an enactment that was enacted during a period specified in column (2) of the Table opposite a particular reference number specified in column (1) of the Table, a person who commits that offence after the commencement date shall not be liable to that fine, but shall, instead, be liable, upon conviction on indictment, to a fine not exceeding an amount calculated by multiplying the said maximum fine by the multiplier specified in column (3) of the Table opposite the same reference number.

(2) Where the maximum fine upon conviction on indictment of an offence specified in an enactment was provided for by virtue of a subsequent enactment that was enacted during a period specified in column (2) of the Table opposite a particular reference number specified in column (1) of the Table, a person who commits that offence after the commencement date shall not be liable to that fine, but shall, instead, be liable, upon conviction on indictment, to a fine not exceeding an amount calculated by multiplying the said maximum fine by the multiplier specified in column (3) of the Table opposite the same reference number.

TABLE

Ref No (1)	Period (2)	Multiplier (3)
1.	1 January 1990 to 31 December 1996	1.75
2.	1 January 1980 to 31 December 1989	2
3.	1 January 1975 to 31 December 1979	5
4.	1 January 1965 to 31 December 1974	10
5.	1 January 1945 to 31 December 1964	21
6.	1 January 1915 to 31 December 1944	39
7.	Period ending on 31 December 1914	50

10   Summary trial of indictable offences

(1) Section 4(1) (amended by section 17 of the Act of 1984) of the Criminal Justice Act 1951 is amended by the substitution of "class A fine within the meaning of Part 2 of the Fines Act 2010" for "fine not exceeding £1,000".

(2) Section 13(3)(a) (amended by section 17 of the Act of 1984) of the Criminal Procedure Act 1967 is amended by the substitution of "class A fine within the meaning of Part 2 of the Fines Act 2010" for "fine not exceeding £1,000".

(3) Section 53(2) of the Criminal Justice (Theft and Fraud Offences) Act 2001 is amended by the substitution of "class A fine within the meaning of Part 2 of the Fines Act 2010" for "fine not exceeding £1,500".

(4) In this section "Act of 1984" means the Criminal Justice Act 1984.

11   Regulations to remove difficulties

(1) If, in any respect, any difficulty arises in bringing any provision of this Part into operation or in relation to the operation of any such provision, the Minister may, by regulations, do anything which appears to him or her to be necessary or expedient for removing that difficulty, for bringing that provision into operation or for securing or facilitating its operation, and any such regulations may modify any provision of this Part so far as may be necessary or expedient for carrying such provision into effect for the purposes aforesaid, but no regulations shall be made under this section in relation to any provision of this Part after the expiration of 3 years commencing on the day on which the provision came into operation.

(2) Where regulations are proposed to be made under this section, a draft of the regulations shall be laid before each House of the Oireachtas and the regulations shall not be made until a resolution approving the draft has been passed by each such House.

PART 3
PAYMENT AND RECOVERY OF FINES

12   Definitions

In this Part—

"Act of 1983" means the Criminal Justice (Community Service) Act 1983;

"Act of 1986" means the Courts (No. 2) Act 1986;

"approved person" has the meaning assigned to it by section 20;

"class A fine" has the same meaning as it has in Part 2;

"class B fine" has the same meaning as it has in Part 2;

"fine" means a fine imposed by a court on a person consequent upon his or her being convicted of an offence by that court;

"financial circumstances" means, in relation to a person who has been convicted of an offence—

(a) the amount of the person's annual income,

(b) the aggregate value of all property (real and personal) belonging to the person,

(c) the aggregate amount of all liabilities of the person including any duty (moral or legal) to provide financially for members of his or her family or other persons,

(d) the aggregate of all monies owing to the person, the dates upon which they fall due to be paid and the likelihood of their being paid, and

(e) such other circumstances as the court considers appropriate.

Note

Section 12 came into operation on 4 January 2011 by virtue of SI 662/2010.

13   Service of documents

(1) A notification under subsection (2) of section 16 shall be addressed to the person concerned by name, and may be so served on or given to the person in one of the following ways:

(a) by delivering it to the person;

(b) by leaving it at the address at which the person ordinarily resides or, in a case in which an address for service has been furnished, at that address; or

(c) by sending it by post in a prepaid registered letter to the address at which the person ordinarily resides or, in a case in which an address for service has been furnished, to that address.

(2) For the purpose of this section, a company within the meaning of the Companies Acts shall be deemed to be ordinarily resident at its registered office, and every other body corporate and every unincorporated body of persons shall be deemed to be ordinarily resident at its principal office or place of business.

Note

Section 13 has not yet come into operation (February 2011).

14   Capacity of person to pay fine

(1) The purpose of this section is to ensure as far as practicable that, where a court imposes a fine on a person, the effect of the fine on that person or his or her dependants is not significantly abated or made more severe by reason of his or her financial circumstances.

(2) Where a person of full age is convicted of an offence, the court shall, in determining the amount of the fine (if any) to impose in respect of the offence, take into account the person's financial circumstances.

(3) For the purpose of this section, a court may, in making a determination under subsection (2), impose a fine that is greater than, less than or equal to the otherwise appropriate fine, but in any case a court shall not impose a fine that is—

(a) greater than the maximum fine (if any), or

(b) less than the minimum fine (if any),

to which a person would be liable upon conviction of the offence concerned.

(4) Where a court has convicted a person in his or her absence or if a person who has been convicted of an offence fails or refuses to provide the court with information as to his or her financial circumstances, the court shall impose such fine as it considers appropriate in respect of the offence concerned taking into account such information (if any) as is known to the court concerning those circumstances.

(5) For the purposes of subsection (2), the court may, by direction in writing, require the person convicted to attend before the court and provide the court with all such information as the court may require in relation to his or her financial circumstances.

(6) A person who knowingly or recklessly makes a statement (orally or in writing) that is false or misleading in any material respect to a court discharging its function under subsection (2) concerning a person's financial circumstances shall be guilty of an offence and shall be liable—

    (a) upon summary conviction to a class B fine or imprisonment for a term not exceeding 6 months or both, or

    (b) upon conviction on indictment to a fine not exceeding €25,000 or imprisonment for a term not exceeding 5 years or both.

(7) A person who fails or refuses to comply with a direction under subsection (5) shall be guilty of an offence and shall be liable—

    (a) upon summary conviction to a class B fine or imprisonment for a term not exceeding 6 months or both, or

    (b) upon conviction on indictment to a fine not exceeding €25,000 or imprisonment for a term not exceeding 5 years or both.

(8) This section does not apply in relation to the imposition of a fine where the court has no discretion in the determination of the amount of the fine.

(9) In this section "otherwise appropriate fine" means the fine that the court would impose on the person in respect of the offence concerned if, in determining the amount of the fine, it were not required to take into account the person's financial circumstances.

Note

Section 14 came into operation on 4 January 2011 by virtue of SI 662/2010.

---

15   Payment of fines by instalments

(1) If, upon the application of a person on whom a court has imposed a fine, the court is satisfied that to require the person to pay the fine in full by the due date for payment would cause undue financial hardship to the person or his or her dependants, the court may direct that the fine be paid by instalments.

(2) Where a court gives a direction under subsection (1)—

    (a) the amounts of the instalments and the intervals at which they are to be paid shall, without prejudice to paragraph (b), be specified in the direction, and

    (b) the person to whom the direction applies shall, subject to subsection (3), pay the final instalment of the fine concerned not later than one year, or such shorter period as the court may specify, after the due date for payment.

(3) Upon the application of a person to whom a direction under subsection (1) applies, the court that gave the direction may, by further direction—

    (a) extend the period for payment of the fine for such period as it considers appropriate provided that such period shall expire not later than 2 years after the due date for payment, and

    (b) in consequence of that extension (but without prejudice to paragraph (a)), vary the amounts of the instalments concerned and the intervals at which they are to be paid.

(4) A court shall not extend a period for payment of a fine under subsection (3) unless it is satisfied that—

    (a) the financial circumstances of the person in respect of whom the extension concerned is granted have changed to the extent that requiring him or her to comply with subsection (2) would cause undue financial hardship to the person or his or her dependants, and

    (b) the change in the person's financial circumstances is not due to his or her culpable neglect.

(5) An application referred to in subsection (3) shall—

    (a) be made as soon as may be after the change in the person's financial circumstances has occurred and—

       (i) before the expiration of the period of one year referred to in subsection (2), or

       (ii) where the court specifies a shorter period in accordance with the said subsection (2), before the expiration of the period so specified,

    and

    (b) be notified in writing by the person to the Courts Service not later than 7 days before the making of the application.

(6) A court shall, when imposing a fine on a person, inform the person of his or her entitlement to make an application referred to in subsection (1).

(7) An application referred to in subsection (1) may be made at any time before the notification of the receiver under subsection (2) of section 16.

(8) This section shall only apply to fines that are greater than €100.

(9) In this section "due date for payment" means, in relation to a fine, the date by which the fine would, but for a direction under this section, be required to be paid in accordance with the order of the court that imposed the fine.

Note

Section 15 has not yet come into operation (February 2011).

---

16   **Appointment of receiver in default of payment of fine**

(1) A court shall, when imposing a fine on a person consequent upon his or her being convicted of an offence, make an order (in this section referred to as a "recovery order") appointing an approved person (in this section referred to as a "receiver") to—

(a) recover—

    (i) the fine, or, as may be appropriate, that part of the fine that, upon the notification of the receiver under subsection (2), remains unpaid, and

    (ii) the fees of the receiver and the expenses reasonably incurred by the receiver in the performance of his or her functions, or

(b) seize and sell property belonging to the first-mentioned person and recover from the proceeds of the sale of that property a sum equal to the amount of—

    (i) the fine, or, as may be appropriate, that part of the fine that, upon the notification of the receiver under subsection (2), remains unpaid, and

    (ii) the fees of the receiver and the expenses reasonably incurred by the receiver in the performance of his or her functions.

(2) A recovery order shall not enter into force unless the person in respect of whom the order is made fails to pay the fine by the due date for payment and, where the person so fails, the order shall have effect from the day immediately following the day on which the Courts Service notifies the receiver concerned in writing that the person has failed to pay the fine by that date.

(3) A recovery order may authorise the receiver appointed thereunder (alone or accompanied by such and so many members of the Garda Síochána as he or she considers necessary) to—

(a) enter (if necessary by the use of reasonable force) any premises, including a dwelling, at which he or she has reasonable grounds for believing property belonging to the person is located,

(b) demand, and take possession of (if necessary by the use of reasonable force), any property specified in the order or that belongs to the person,

(c) issue receipts in respect of any property of which the receiver has taken possession,

(d) manage, dispose of, retain or otherwise deal with the property,

(e) insure the property, and

(f) inspect, at all reasonable times, any books, documents or other records that contain information relating to property belonging to the person.

(4) A receiver shall perform his or her functions subject to any directions or conditions specified in the recovery order by which he or she is appointed, including any directions or conditions with regard to the receiver's paying amounts received by him or her into court.

(5) A receiver may, at any time after receiving a notification under subsection (2), apply to the court that made the recovery order under which he or she was appointed for directions in relation to the performance of his or her functions under this Act.

(6) Any person who is in possession of property belonging to the person in relation to whose property a receiver has been appointed shall deliver that property to the receiver upon the receiver making a demand of him or her in that behalf.

(7) (a) Where the receiver sells property belonging to the person in relation to whose property the receiver has been appointed and the proceeds of the sale exceed the amount of the fine or the amount of the fine remaining unpaid, as the case may be, the receiver shall pay to the person so much of those proceeds as exceeds that amount.

(b) In this subsection "fine" includes the fees of the receiver and any expenses reasonably incurred by the receiver in the performance of his or her functions.

(8) A person who—

(a) fails to comply with subsection (6), or

(b) obstructs or interferes with a receiver in the course of the performance by him or her of his or her functions or impedes the performance by the receiver of those functions,

shall be guilty of an offence and shall be liable upon summary conviction to a class A fine or imprisonment for a term not exceeding 12 months or both.

(9) (a) The Minister may, by order, specify—

(i) the fees that a receiver may deduct from any sum or sums recovered by him or her, or obtained from the proceeds of the sale of any property by him or her, in accordance with this section, or

(ii) the rates at which fees that may be so deducted shall be calculated.

(b) The Minister shall not make an order under this subsection without the consent of the Minister for Finance.

(10) The receiver shall make and maintain a record in writing of—

(a) the fees deducted, and

(b) the expenses incurred and deducted,

by him or her from the sum or sums recovered, or the proceeds of the sale of any property sold, by him or her pursuant to a recovery order.

(11) The receiver shall, not later than 6 months after the performance by him or her of his or her functions pursuant to a recovery order, give to the Courts Service the record required to be made and maintained under subsection (10) relating to that recovery order.

(12) If a receiver makes, or causes to be made, an entry in a record required to be made and maintained under subsection (10) that—

(a) is false or misleading in any material respect, and

(b) he or she knows to be false or misleading,

he or she shall be guilty of an offence and shall be liable—

(i) upon summary conviction to a class A fine or imprisonment for a term not exceeding 12 months or both, or

(ii) upon conviction on indictment to a fine not exceeding €50,000 or imprisonment for a term not exceeding 5 years or both.

(13) A record required to be made and maintained under subsection (10) shall be in such form as the Courts Service shall determine.

(14) In this section—

"due date for payment" means, in relation to a fine—

(a) the date specified by the court that imposed the fine as being the date by which the fine is required to be paid, or

(b) where a direction is given under section 15, the date by which the final instalment of the fine is required to be paid in accordance with that direction;

"property" means land or personal property.

Note

Section 16 has not yet come into operation (February 2011).

17   Monies recovered by receiver under section 16.

Monies paid into the court or otherwise received by it as a result of the appointment of a receiver under section 16 shall be paid to the Minister for Finance and such monies shall be paid to, or disposed of for the benefit of, the Exchequer in such manner as the Minister for Finance may direct.

Note

Section 17 has not yet come into operation (February 2011).

18   Community service order in default of payment of fine

(1) The Act of 1983 is amended—

  (a) by the insertion of the following definitions in subsection (1) of section 1:[1]

  (b) by the insertion of the following subsections in section 2:[1]

  (c) in section 3, by—

      (i)   the insertion of the following subsection: [1]

      and

      (ii) the substitution of the following subsection for subsection (2): [1]

          "(2) A community service order shall require the offender to perform, in accordance with this Act, unpaid work for such number of hours as are specified in the order, being—

          (a)   in the case of an offender to whom subsection (1) of section 2 applies, not less than 40 hours and not greater than 240 hours,

          (b)   in the case of an offender to whom subsection (2) of section 2 applies who was convicted on indictment of the offence concerned, not less than 40 hours and not greater than 240 hours, and

          (c)   in the case of an offender to whom subsection (2) of section 2 applies who was convicted summarily of the offence concerned, not less than 30 hours and not greater than 100 hours.",

  (d) by the insertion, in section 5, of the following subsections: [1]

  (e) by the insertion, in section 7, of the following subsection: [1]

(2) Section 2 of the Act of 1983 as it stood immediately before the commencement of this section shall, immediately after such commencement, be subsection (1) of the said section 2.

Amendments

1   See the amended Act.

Note

Section 18 has not yet come into operation (February 2011).

19   Imprisonment in default of payment of fine.

The Act of 1986 is amended—

(a)   in section 2, by—

    (i)   the substitution of the following subsection for subsection (1):

      "(1) Where a court is satisfied that—

      (a)   a receiver appointed under section 16 of the Fines Act 2010 has been unable to recover—

        (i)   a fine imposed on a person consequent upon his or her summary conviction of an offence, or

        (ii) a sum or sums from the proceeds of the sale of property belonging to that person sufficient to pay that fine,

        and

      (b)   that, in relation to the person, the provisions of section 4 of the Criminal Justice (Community Service) Act 1983 have not been complied with,

      it may make an order committing the person to prison for a term not exceeding the appropriate period of imprisonment specified in the Table.",

    (ii) the insertion of the following subsections:

      "(1A) Where a court has made a community service order within the meaning of subsection (1A) (inserted by section 18(1)(c) of the Fines Act 2010)of section 3 of the Criminal Justice (Community Service) Act 1983 consequent upon the summary conviction of a person of an offence, it shall, if satisfied that the person in respect of whom it made the order fails to comply with a requirement specified in subsection (1)(b) of section 7 of that Act, make an order committing the person to prison for a term not exceeding the appropriate period specified in the Table.

      (1B) For the purposes of determining the appropriate period of imprisonment specified in the Table,

    the amount of the fine shall be the fine less—

      (a)   any sum or sums paid by the person on whom the fine was imposed in satisfaction of part of the fine, and

      (b)   any sum or sums recovered (whether from the proceeds of the sale of property belonging to the person or otherwise) by the receiver appointed under section 16 of the Fines Act 2010.",

(iii) the insertion, after the words "ordered to be paid", in the definition of "fine" in subsection (4), of the following ", but does not include the fees of, or expenses incurred by, a receiver appointed under section 16 of the Fines Act 2010",

and

(iv) the insertion of the following Table:

TABLE

Amount of Fine	Period of Imprisonment
Not greater than €500	5 days
Greater than €500 but not greater than €1,500	10 days
Greater than €1,500 but not greater than €3,000	20 days
Greater than €3,000	30 days

(b) by the insertion of the following section:

"Imprisonment on conviction on indictment in default of payment of fine.

2A.—(1) Where a court is satisfied that—

(a) a receiver appointed under section 16 of the Fines Act 2010 has been unable to recover—

(i) a fine imposed on a person consequent upon his or her conviction on indictment of an offence, or

(ii) a sum or sums from the proceeds of the sale of property belonging to that person sufficient to pay that fine,

and

(b) that, in relation to the person, the provisions of section 4 of the Criminal Justice (Community Service) Act 1983 have not been complied with,

it may make an order committing the person to prison for a term not exceeding 12 months.

(2) Where a court has made a community service order within the meaning of subsection (1A) of section 3 of the Criminal Justice (Community Service) Act 1983 consequent upon the conviction of a person on indictment of an offence, it shall, if satisfied that the person in respect of whom it made the order fails to comply with a requirement specified in subsection (1)(b) of section 7 of that Act, make an order committing the person to prison for a term not exceeding 12 months.

(3) A court shall, for the purpose of determining the term for which a person shall be committed to prison under this section, take account of—

(a) any sum or sums paid by the person in satisfaction of part of the fine, and

(b) any sum or sums recovered (whether from the proceeds of the sale of property belonging to the person or otherwise) by the receiver appointed under section 16 of the Fines Act 2010.

(4) In this section 'fine' has the same meaning as it has in section 2 (amended by subparagraph (iii) of section 19(a) of the Fines Act 2010) of this Act.".

20   Approval by Government of persons for purposes of section 16.

(1) The Government may, upon the nomination of the Minister, approve such person or persons for the purposes of section 16, and a person so approved is in this Part referred to as an "approved person".

(2) The Minister shall not make a nomination under this section without the consent of the Minister for Finance.

(3) The Government may attach such conditions to an approval under this section as it considers appropriate.

21   Publication of names of persons who fail to pay fines on time.

(1) The Courts Service may, from time to time, publish in such manner as it considers appropriate (including on the internet) a list of the names and addresses of persons who have failed to pay fines imposed on them by the due date for payment.

(2) In any particular case—

  (a) the Courts Service shall not publish a person's name and address pursuant to this section before the notification of the receiver under subsection (2) of section 16 of the person's failure to pay the fine by the due date for payment, and

  (b) the Courts Service shall not publish a person's name and address in accordance with this section if, after the due date for payment but before the person's name and address are so published, the person pays the fine concerned.

(3) The Courts Service shall remove the name and address of a person published in a list referred to in subsection (1) on the internet—

  (a) not later than 8 weeks after they were so published, or

  (b) if the person pays the fine concerned before the expiration of that period, upon the payment by the person of the fine,

whichever occurs earlier.

(4) In this section "due date for payment" means, in relation to a fine—

  (a) the date specified by the court that imposed the fine as being the date by which the fine is required to be paid, or

  (b) where a direction is given under section 15, the date by which the final instalment of the fine is required to be paid in accordance with that direction.

Note

Section 21 has not yet come into operation (February 2011).

22   Repeal

The following enactments are repealed:

    (a)   section 43(2) of the Criminal Justice Administration Act 1914; and

    (b)   section 195 of the Criminal Justice Act 2006.

Note

Section 22 has not yet come into operation (February 2011).

Criminal Justice (Psychoactive Substances) Act 2010

Number 22 of 2010

ARRANGEMENT OF SECTIONS

1. Interpretation.
2. Exclusions from application of Act.
3. Prohibition of sale, etc. of psychoactive substances.
4. Prohibition of sale of certain objects.
5. Prohibition of advertising of psychoactive substances, etc.
6. Sale, etc. of psychoactive substances permitted in certain circumstances.
7. Prohibition notice.
8. Prohibition order.
9. Variation of prohibition orders.
10. Closure order.
11. Variation or discharge of closure orders.
12. Powers of Garda Síochána to enter and search, etc.
13. Power of Garda Síochána to search persons, vehicles, etc.
14. Powers of officers of Customs and Excise.
15. Obstruction.
16. Taking of samples.
17. Laboratories.
18. Provisions relating to evidence in proceedings under Act.
19. Disposal of things seized.
20. Offences.
21. Jurisdiction.
22. Amendment of Customs and Excise (Miscellaneous Provisions) Act 1988.
23. Amendment of Bail Act 1997.
24. Expenses.
25. Regulations and orders.
26. Short title and commencement.

AN ACT TO PREVENT THE MISUSE OF DANGEROUS OR OTHERWISE HARMFUL PSYCHOACTIVE SUBSTANCES; TO PROVIDE FOR OFFENCES RELATING TO THE SALE, IMPORTATION, EXPORTATION OR ADVERTISEMENT OF THOSE SUBSTANCES; TO PROVIDE FOR OFFENCES RELATING TO THE SALE AND ADVERTISEMENT OF CERTAIN OBJECTS FOR USE IN THE CULTIVATION OF CERTAIN PLANTS IN CONTRAVENTION OF THE MISUSE OF DRUGS ACT 1977; TO PROVIDE FOR POWERS OF THE GARDA SÍOCHÁNA IN RELATION TO THE INVESTIGATION OF THOSE OFFENCES; TO MAKE PROVISION IN RELATION TO THE ISSUING OF PROHIBITION

NOTICES BY CERTAIN MEMBERS OF THE GARDA SÍOCHÁNA TO CERTAIN PERSONS IN RELATION TO ACTIVITIES THAT ARE PROHIBITED; TO PROVIDE FOR THE MAKING BY THE DISTRICT COURT OF PROHIBITION ORDERS AND CLOSURE ORDERS IN CERTAIN CIRCUMSTANCES; TO AMEND THE CUSTOMS AND EXCISE (MISCELLANOUS PROVISIONS) ACT 1988; AND TO PROVIDE FOR RELATED MATTERS. [14th July, 2010]

BE IT ENACTED BY THE OIREACHTAS AS FOLLOWS:

Note

This Act came into operation on 23 August 2010 by virtue of the Criminal Justice (Psychoactive Substances) Act 2010 (Commencement) Order 2010 (SI 401/2010).

---

1   Interpretation

(1) In this Act—

"Act of 1977" means the Misuse of Drugs Act 1977;

"advertisement" includes every form of advertisement, whether or not to the public, in a newspaper or other publication, on television or radio, by display of a notice, by electronic communication, including by means of the internet, or by any other means;

"certificate of analysis" shall be construed in accordance with section 17;

"consumption", in relation to a psychoactive substance, means to consume the substance (whether or not the substance concerned has been dissolved or dispersed in or diluted or mixed with any other substance)—

    (a) orally,

    (b) by smoking, insufflating or inhaling it,

    (c) by injecting it,

    (d) by applying it externally to the body of the person, or

    (e) by otherwise introducing it into the body of a person;

"controlled drug" has the same meaning as it has in section 2 of the Act of 1977;

"electronic" includes electrical, digital, magnetic, optical, electromagnetic, biometric, photonic and any other form of related technology;

"electronic communication" includes a communication of information in the form of data, text, images or sound (or any combination of them) by means of guided or unguided electromagnetic energy, or both;

"hydroponic", in relation to cultivation, means the cultivation of plants in liquid containing nutrients under controlled conditions of light, temperature and humidity, without the use of soil;

"Minister" means the Minister for Justice and Law Reform;

"place" includes—

(a)   a dwelling or other building,

(b)   a structure or stall of any kind,

(c)   a vehicle;

"psychoactive substance" means a substance, product, preparation, plant, fungus or natural organism which has, when consumed by a person, the capacity to—

(a)   produce stimulation or depression of the central nervous system of the person, resulting in hallucinations or a significant disturbance in, or significant change to, motor function, thinking, behaviour, perception, awareness or mood, or

(b)   cause a state of dependence, including physical or psychological addiction;

"sell", in relation to a substance or object, means to sell or supply or cause to be sold or supplied, whether for profit or otherwise, either directly or through another person and includes—

(a)   to offer for sale, to invite to buy, to distribute or to expose or keep for sale, supply or distribution, and

(b)   to possess for any of the purposes referred to in paragraph (a);

"supply" includes giving without payment;

"vehicle" means any conveyance in or by which any person or thing, or both, is or are, as the case may be, transported which is designed for use on land, in water or in the air, or in more than one of those ways, and includes—

(a)   a part of a vehicle,

(b)   an article designed as a vehicle but not capable of functioning as a vehicle,

(c)   any container, trailer, tank or any other thing which is or may be used for the storage of goods in the course of carriage and is designed or constructed to be placed on, in, or attached to, any vehicle.

(2) In this Act, a reference to the commission of an offence includes a reference to an attempt to commit the offence.

2   Exclusions from application of Act

(1) This Act shall not apply to—

(a)   a medicinal product within the meaning of section 1(1) of the Irish Medicines Board Act 1995,

(b)   an animal remedy within the meaning of section 1 of the Animal Remedies Act 1993 authorised in accordance with—

(i)   the European Communities (Animal Remedies) (No. 2) Regulations 2007 (S.I. No. 786 of 2007), or

(ii)   Regulation (EC) No. 726/2004 of the European Parliament and of the Council of 31 March 2004 as amended,

prescribed or sold for administration to an animal in accordance with those provisions,

(c)   intoxicating liquor within the meaning of section 77 of the Licensing Act 1872,

(d)   a tobacco product within the meaning of section 2 of the Public Health (Tobacco) Act 2002,

   (e)   food within the meaning of section 2 of the Food Safety Authority of Ireland Act 1998 which has been placed on the market in compliance with food legislation within the meaning of that section,

   (f)   unless otherwise expressly provided for in this Act, a controlled drug, or

   (g)   such other substance, product, preparation, plant, fungus or natural organism as may be specified by order under subsection (2).

(2) The Minister may, after consultation with the Minister for Health and Children and such other Minister of the Government as he or she considers appropriate, by order declare that this Act shall not apply in relation to a substance, product, preparation, plant, fungus or natural organism specified in the order and so long as an order under this subsection is in force, this Act shall not apply in relation to the substance, product, preparation, plant, fungus or natural organism so specified in the order.

3   Prohibition of sale, etc. of psychoactive substances

(1) A person who sells a psychoactive substance knowing or being reckless as to whether that substance is being acquired or supplied for human consumption shall be guilty of an offence.

(2) A person who imports or exports a psychoactive substance knowing or being reckless as to whether that substance is being acquired or supplied for human consumption shall be guilty of an offence.

(3) Where in any proceedings for an offence under subsection (1) or (2), it is proved that a person sold, or imported or exported, as the case may be, a psychoactive substance, and the court is satisfied having had regard to—

   (a)   any indication given by the person concerned orally or in writing, by means of the internet or by electronic communication or any indication otherwise given by means of any packaging, leaflets, notices or by any other object or thing that the substance concerned may have psychoactive effects or that it may be consumed in a way similar to a controlled drug,

   (b)   any indication in or at any place to which the proceedings for the offence relate that suggests the consumption of controlled drugs, including the presence of any apparatus, equipment or thing which may reasonably be associated with the consumption of controlled drugs, and

   (c)   whether it is reasonable to find that the substance concerned is being sold or imported or exported, as the case may be, for an alternative lawful purpose, taking into account the cost and quantity of the substance being sold or being imported or exported, as the case may be,

that it is reasonable to assume that the person knew or was reckless as to whether the substance was being acquired or supplied for human consumption, it shall be presumed, until the court is satisfied to the contrary, that the person had such knowledge or was so reckless.

(4) A court may be satisfied under subsection (3) notwithstanding any oral or written statement made, any indication given on any packaging, label or leaflet or any indication given by means of the internet or by any electronic communication, that the substance to which the proceedings relate is not a psychoactive substance or is not intended or fit for human consumption.

(5) Without prejudice to any other defence that may be available, it shall be a defence for a person against whom proceedings for an offence under subsection (1) or (2) are brought to

prove that he or she was, at the time of the alleged offence, a person referred to in section 6(2).

4   Prohibition of sale of certain objects

A person who sells any object knowing that it will be used to cultivate by hydroponic means any plant in contravention of section 17 of the Act of 1977 shall be guilty of an offence.

5   Prohibition of advertising of psychoactive substances, etc

(1) A person who publishes or displays or causes to be published or displayed any advertisement knowing or being reckless as to whether the advertisement—

   (a)   indicates an intention—

      (i)   to sell or import or export a psychoactive substance for human consumption, or

      (ii) to sell any object for use in cultivating by hydroponic means any plant in contravention of section 17 of the Act of 1977,

   (b)   promotes the consumption of a substance or a combination of substances for its or their, as the case may be, psychoactive effects and provides information on how or where a psychoactive substance may be obtained, or

   (c)   provides information on how an object may be used to cultivate by hydroponic means any plant in contravention of section 17 of the Act of 1977,

shall be guilty of an offence.

(2) Without prejudice to any other defence that may be available, it shall be a defence for a person against whom proceedings for an offence under subsection (1) are brought to prove that he or she was, at the time of the alleged offence, a person referred to in section 6(2).

6   Sale, etc. of psychoactive substances permitted in certain circumstances

(1) This section applies where a person is—

   (a)   a registered medical practitioner within the meaning of section 2 of the Medical Practitioners Act 2007,

   (b)   a registered dentist, being a person whose name is entered for the time being in the Register of Dentists established under section 26 of the Dentists Act 1985,

   (c)   a registered nurse, being a person whose name is entered for the time being in the register of nurses established under section 27 of the Nurses Act 1985,

   (d)   a registered pharmacist, druggist or pharmaceutical assistant, being a person registered in a register set up under section 13 of the Pharmacy Act 2007, or

   (e)   a member of such class of persons as the Minister may, after consultation with the Minister for Health and Children and such other Minister of the Government as he or she thinks appropriate, by order designate.

(2) It shall not be an offence for a person referred to in subsection (1) to sell, import or export a psychoactive substance or to publish or display or cause to be published or displayed any advertisement relating to a psychoactive substance if—

   (a)   the sale, importation or exportation or advertisement of the substance concerned was for the purpose of his or her profession, and

   (b)   the sale, importation or exportation or advertisement of the substance by that person in the course of his or her profession was otherwise lawful.

7   Prohibition notice

(1) A member of the Garda Síochána not below the rank of superintendent may serve personally or by registered post a written notice (in this Act referred to as a "prohibition notice") on a person if he or she is of opinion that the person is, at any place, engaged in the activity of—

    (a) selling—

        (i) a psychoactive substance for human consumption,

        (ii) any object for use in cultivating by hydroponic means any plant in contravention of section 17 of the Act of 1977,

    (b) importing or exporting a psychoactive substance for human consumption,

    (c) publishing or displaying or causing to be published or displayed any advertisement which—

        (i) indicates an intention to sell or import or export a psychoactive substance for human consumption or to sell any object for use in cultivating by hydroponic means any plant in contravention of section 17 of the Act of 1977,

        (ii) promotes the consumption of a substance or a combination of substances for its or their, as the case may be, psychoactive effects and provides information on how or where a psychoactive substance may be obtained, or

        (iii) provides information on how an object may be used to cultivate by hydroponic means any plant in contravention of section 17 of the Act of 1977.

(2) A prohibition notice shall be signed and dated by the member of the Garda Síochána concerned and shall—

    (a) state that he or she is of the opinion that the person is engaged in an activity referred to in subsection (1) and the reasons for that opinion,

    (b) specify the psychoactive substance, object or advertisement to which the activity relates and in respect of which the opinion is held and may, where appropriate, specify any place where, in his or her opinion, the activity concerned is taking place,

    (c) direct the person to cease forthwith selling or advertising, as the case may be, the substance or object specified in the notice or, as may be appropriate, importing or exporting the substance specified in the notice,

    (d) specify the possible consequences of failure to comply with the directions specified in the notice.

(3) A direction specified in a prohibition notice shall have effect immediately upon service of the notice.

(4) The service of a prohibition notice under this section in respect of a person shall not prevent the service of a further prohibition notice under this section in respect of the person.

(5) A member of the Garda Síochána not below the rank of superintendent may at any time withdraw a prohibition notice if he or she is satisfied that the notice was served in error or is incorrect in some material respect.

8   Prohibition order

(1) Where a prohibition notice has been served on a person and a member of the Garda Síochána not below the rank of superintendent is of opinion that the person is not in compliance with a direction contained in the notice, he or she may apply to the District Court for an order (in this Act referred to as a "prohibition order") prohibiting that person from engaging in or continuing to engage in the activity of selling or advertising, as the case may be, such substance or object as may be specified in the order or, as may be appropriate, importing or exporting such substance as may be specified in the order.

(2) An application for a prohibition order shall be made on notice to the person who is the subject of the prohibition notice concerned and to any other person in relation to whom the court directs that notice of the application be given.

(3) The court may make a prohibition order in respect of a person if—

    (a)   having considered the evidence before it which shall, in the case of an application in respect of the activity referred to in paragraph (a)(i) or (b) of section 7(1), include a certificate of analysis in respect of the substance concerned, and

    (b)   having had regard to all the circumstances of the case, including, in the case of an application in respect of the activity referred to in paragraph (a)(i) or (b) of section 7(1), the matters referred to in subsection (4), it is satisfied that—

        (i)   the person concerned has, after the service of the prohibition notice, sold or advertised, as the case may be, a psychoactive substance or an object specified in the notice served on him or her or, as may be appropriate, imported or exported a substance specified in the notice served on him or her, and

        (ii) it is necessary to prevent the person from engaging in or continuing to engage in the activity concerned,

unless the court considers that making the order would be unjust in all the circumstances of the case.

(4) When considering an application for a prohibition order which relates to the activity referred to in paragraph (a)(i) or (b) of section 7(1), the court shall, notwithstanding any oral or written statement made, any indication given on any packaging, label or leaflet or any indication given by means of the internet or by any electronic communication, that the substance to which the application relates is not a psychoactive substance or is not intended or fit for human consumption, have regard to—

    (a)   any indication given by the respondent orally or in writing, by means of the internet or by electronic communication or any indication otherwise given by means of any packaging, leaflets, notices or by any other object or thing that the substance concerned may have psychoactive effects or that it may be consumed in a way similar to a controlled drug,

    (b)   any indication in or at any place specified in the application that suggests the consumption of controlled drugs, including the presence of any apparatus, equipment or thing which may reasonably be associated with the consumption of controlled drugs, and

    (c)   whether it is reasonable to find that the substance concerned is being sold or imported or exported, as the case may be, for an alternative lawful purpose, taking into account the cost and quantity of the substance being sold or being imported or exported, as the case may be.

(5) A prohibition order—

(a) shall specify the psychoactive substance, object or advertisement to which the order relates and, where the court considers it appropriate to do so, may specify any place to which the order relates,

(b) shall specify the grounds upon which the order is made,

(c) shall provide for notice of it to be given to any person who appears to be or is affected by it, unless the court is satisfied that it is not reasonably possible to ascertain his, her or their whereabouts,

(d) shall state that it shall come into effect immediately upon service of the order, and

(e) may contain such terms, conditions and restrictions as the court considers necessary or expedient in the circumstances.

(6) A person who fails or refuses to comply with a prohibition order shall be guilty of an offence.

(7) A prohibition order shall remain in force unless—

(a) it is varied or discharged on appeal under this section, or

(b) it is varied under section 9.

(8) An appeal shall lie to the Circuit Court from the making of a prohibition order but the bringing of such an appeal shall not affect the operation of the prohibition order, unless the court or the Circuit Court, on application to it in that behalf within 7 days from the date of the making of the order, makes an order staying its operation pending the determination of the appeal.

(9) A prohibition order shall not operate to affect any lawful obligations of any person under any lawful contract or agreement and those obligations shall continue to be determined in accordance with the contract or agreement, as the case may be.

(10) The making of a prohibition order under this section shall not in respect of a person prevent the making of a further prohibition order under this section in respect of the person.

(11) Notwithstanding the generality of any other enactment or rule of law concerning the regulation of the sittings and the vacations of the District Court, such special sittings of the District Court as may be necessary for the purposes of this section shall take place during court vacation periods for the determination of an application under this section.

9   Variation of prohibition orders

(1) Where the District Court makes a prohibition order under section 8—

(a) prohibiting a person from engaging in or continuing to engage in specified activities at a specified place, and

(b) the place specified in the order is not owned by the person who is the subject of the prohibition order,

the court, on application to it in that behalf by the owner of the place concerned, at any time after the making of a prohibition order may, if it considers it appropriate to do so, vary the order.

(2) In determining whether to vary a prohibition order, the court shall have regard to whether there would be a serious risk of injustice if the order were not so varied.

(3) An application under subsection (1) shall be made on notice to—

    (a) the person who is the subject of the prohibition order, unless it is not reasonably practicable to ascertain the whereabouts of the person, and

    (b) a member of the Garda Síochána not below the rank of superintendent in the Garda Síochána district in which the person who is subject to the prohibition order resides.

(4) An appeal shall lie to the Circuit Court from a refusal to vary a prohibition order.

10   Closure order

(1) Where a person is convicted of an offence under section 3, 4, 5 or 8(6), the court may, in addition to, or as an alternative to, any other penalty, make an order (in this Act referred to as a "closure order") prohibiting the person, at the place concerned or at any other place as may be specified in the order, from operating any business or engaging in any specified activities, which may reasonably be considered to be connected with the sale, importation or exportation or advertisement of psychoactive substances for human consumption or, as may be appropriate, the sale or advertisement of an object for use in cultivating by hydroponic means any plant in contravention of section 17 of the Act of 1977.

(2) Without prejudice to the power of the court to have regard to all of the matters that appear to it to be relevant, the court may, in particular, have regard to whether any prohibition order is in force in respect of the person concerned, whether the prohibition order has been complied with and any conduct of the person, or other person employed by that person, in relation to the operation of the place concerned.

(3) A closure order—

    (a) shall specify the business, activities, the place and, where appropriate, the psychoactive substance or object to which it relates,

    (b) shall specify the grounds upon which the order is made,

    (c) shall provide for notice of it to be given to the owner of the place and any other person who appears to be or is affected by it, unless the court is satisfied that it is not reasonably possible to ascertain his, her or their whereabouts,

    (d) shall state that it shall come into effect immediately upon service of the order or on such later date as may be specified in the order, and

    (e) may contain such terms, conditions and restrictions as the court considers necessary or expedient in the circumstances.

(4) A closure order may be made for such period not exceeding 5 years as the court thinks appropriate and shall remain in force for that period unless—

    (a) it is varied or discharged under section 11,or

    (b) it is varied or discharged on appeal.

(5) A closure order shall come into effect immediately upon service of the order, or on such later date as may be specified in the order, and the bringing of an appeal against the conviction or closure order shall not affect the operation of the order, unless the court or the Circuit Court, on application to it in that behalf within 7 days from the date of the making of the order, makes an order staying its operation pending the determination of the appeal.

(6) A closure order shall not operate to affect any lawful obligations of any person under any lawful contract or agreement and those obligations shall continue to be determined in accordance with the contract or agreement, as the case may be.

(7) Subject to subsection (1), a closure order shall not operate to prevent a person from carrying out any lawful activities in the place concerned.

(8) A person who fails or refuses to comply with a closure order shall be guilty of an offence.

11   Variation or discharge of closure orders

(1) The District Court, on application to it in that behalf, by—

    (a) the person who is subject to a closure order,

    (b) the owner of the place which is specified in the order, or

    (c) a member of the Garda Síochána not below the rank of superintendent,

at any time after the making of a closure order and before the date on which the order ceases to be in force may, if it considers it appropriate to do so, vary or discharge the order.

(2) In determining whether to vary or discharge a closure order, the court shall have regard to whether there would be a serious risk of injustice if the order were not so varied or discharged, as the case may be.

(3) An application under subsection (1) shall be made on notice to—

    (a) where the occupier of the place is not the applicant, the occupier of the place, unless it is not reasonably practicable to ascertain the identity or whereabouts of the occupier, and

    (b) where the owner of the place is not the applicant, the owner of the place, unless it is not reasonably practicable to ascertain the identity or whereabouts of the owner, and

    (c) where the applicant is not a member of the Garda Síochána, a member of the Garda Síochána not below the rank of superintendent in the Garda Síochána district in which the person to whom the closure order applies resides.

(4) An appeal shall lie to the Circuit Court from a refusal to vary or discharge a closure order.

12   Powers of Garda Síochána to enter and search, etc

(1) Where a member of the Garda Síochána has reasonable grounds for believing that a person is, at any place—

    (a) selling a psychoactive substance for human consumption or any object for use in cultivating by hydroponic means any plant in contravention of section 17 of the Act of 1977,

    (b) importing or exporting a psychoactive substance for human consumption,

    (c) publishing or displaying or causing to be published or displayed any advertisement which—

        (i)   indicates an intention to sell or import or export a psychoactive substance for human consumption or to sell any object for use in cultivating by hydroponic means any plant in contravention of section 17 of the Act of 1977,

        (ii) promotes the consumption of a substance or a combination of substances for its or their, as the case may be, psychoactive effects and provides information on how or where a psychoactive substance may be obtained, or

        (iii) provides information on how an object may be used to cultivate by hydroponic means any plant in contravention of section 17 of the Act of 1977, he or she may, subject to subsection (3), enter (if necessary by the use of reasonable force) or, where the place concerned is a vehicle, stop and enter (if necessary by the use of reasonable force) any such place, and, at such place—

(i) carry out or have carried out such examinations, tests, inspections and checks of anything reasonably believed to be a psychoactive substance or any machinery, instrument or other thing used in the preparation, handling, storage, transport or sale of psychoactive substances, as he or she reasonably considers to be necessary for the purposes of this Act,

(ii) take such reasonable samples of, or from, any substances or of, or from, anything for the purposes of analysis and examination which he or she reasonably considers to be necessary for the purposes of this Act,

(iii) seize and detain any machinery, instrument or other thing used in the preparation, handling, storage, transport or sale of psychoactive substances or anything which is reasonably believed to be or to contain a psychoactive substance in relation to which a contravention of this Act is being or has been committed,

(iv) inspect and take copies of any books, records, other documents (including documents stored in non-legible form) or extracts therefrom, which he or she finds in the course of his or her inspection, and remove any such books, records or documents from such place and detain them for such period as he or she reasonably considers to be necessary for the purposes of this Act,

(v) require any person present in the place or, where the place is a vehicle, require the person who is for the time being in charge or control of the vehicle to give his or her name and address to the member,

(vi) search or cause to be searched any person present in the place,

(vii) require any person at the place or the owner or person in charge of the place and any person employed there to give to him or her such assistance and information and to produce to him or her such books, records or other documents (and in the case of records or documents stored in non-legible form, produce to him or her a legible reproduction thereof) that are in that person's power or procurement, as he or she may reasonably require for the purposes of his or her functions under this Act,

(viii) direct that such products, substances or objects found at the place as he or she, upon reasonable grounds, believes contravene a provision of this Act not be sold or moved from the place, without his or her consent, and

(ix) secure for later inspection any place or part of any place in which a product, substance or object is found or ordinarily kept, or books, records or documents are found or ordinarily kept, for such period as may reasonably be necessary for the purposes of his or her functions under this Act.

(2) When performing a function under this Act, a member of the Garda Síochána may, subject to subsection (4), be accompanied by such other members of the Garda Síochána or such other persons as he or she considers appropriate.

(3) A member of the Garda Síochána shall not enter a dwelling, other than with the consent of the occupier or in accordance with a warrant issued under subsection (4).

(4) If a judge of the District Court is satisfied by information on oath of a member of the Garda Síochána not below the rank of sergeant that there are reasonable grounds for believing that—

(a) any evidence of, or relating to, the commission of an offence under this Act is to be found in any dwelling,

(b) any books, records or other documents (including documents stored in non-legible form) relating to the commission of an offence under this Act are being stored or kept in any dwelling, or

(c) a dwelling is occupied in whole or in part by a person engaged in any trade, business or activity referred to in paragraph (a), (b) or (c) of subsection (1),

the judge may issue a warrant authorising a named member of the Garda Síochána accompanied by such other members of the Garda Síochána or such other named persons as the member thinks necessary, at any time or times, within one month from the date of issue of the warrant, to enter (if necessary by the use of reasonable force) the dwelling and perform the functions under subsection (1).

(5) This section is without prejudice to any other power conferred by statute or otherwise exercisable by a member of the Garda Síochána to enter a place, to search a person or to seize and retain evidence of, or relating to, the commission or attempted commission of an offence.

(6) The power to issue a warrant under this section is without prejudice to any other power conferred by statute to issue a warrant for the search of any place or person.

(7) In this section—

"record" includes, in addition to a record in writing—

(a) a disc, tape, sound-track or other device in which information, sounds or signals are embodied so as to be capable (with or without the aid of some other instrument) of being reproduced in legible or audible form,

(b) a film, tape or other device in which visual images are embodied so as to be capable (with or without the aid of some other instrument) of being reproduced in visual form, and

(c) a photograph,

and any reference to a copy of a record includes—

(i) in the case of a record to which paragraph (a) applies, a transcript of the sounds or signals embodied therein,

(ii) in the case of a record to which paragraph (b) applies, a still reproduction of the images embodied therein, and

(iii) in the case of a record to which paragraphs (a) and (b) apply, such a transcript together with such a still reproduction.

13   Power of Garda Síochána to search persons, vehicles, etc

(1) Without prejudice to the generality of section 12, where a member of the Garda Síochána who is in—

(a) a public place, or

(b) any other place under a power of entry authorised by law or to which or in which he or she was expressly or impliedly invited or permitted to be, with reasonable cause suspects a person of committing or having committed an offence under this Act, he or she may without warrant—

(i) search the person and, if he or she considers it necessary for that purpose, detain the person for such time as is reasonably necessary for making the search,

(ii) search any vehicle in which he or she suspects that any evidence of, or relating to, the commission of an offence under this Act may be found and for the purpose of carrying out the search may, if he or she thinks fit, require the person who for the time being is in control of such vehicle to bring it to a stop and when stopped to refrain from moving it, or in case such vehicle is already stationary, to refrain from moving it, or

(iii) examine (by opening or otherwise) and seize and retain anything found in the course of a search under this section which with such cause appears to him or her to be something which might be required as evidence in proceedings for an offence under this Act.

(2) A member of the Garda Síochána may, for the purpose of conducting a search of a person under this section, require the person to accompany him or her to a Garda Síochána station for that purpose.

(3) A member of the Garda Síochána may, for the purpose of conducting a search of a vehicle under this section, make any one or more or all of the following requirements of the person who appears to him or her to be the owner or in control or charge for time being of the vehicle:

(a) require such person, pending the commencement of the search, not to remove from the vehicle any substance, object or other thing;

(b) where the search relates to a vehicle and the place at which he or she finds the vehicle is in the member's reasonable opinion unsuitable for such search, require such person forthwith to take the vehicle or cause it to be taken to a place which he or she considers suitable for such search and which is specified by him or her;

(c) require the person to be in or on or to accompany the vehicle for so long as the requirement under this subsection remains in force or until the search is completed, as the case may be.

(4) Where there is a failure or refusal to comply with a requirement under—

(a) subsection (2), the member of the Garda Síochána concerned may arrest without warrant the person of whom the requirement was made for the purposes of conducting the search, or

(b) subsection (3)(b), such member of the Garda Síochána concerned may take the vehicle concerned, or cause it to be taken, to a place which he or she considers suitable for a search under this section.

(5) Where a requirement described in subsection (3)(a) is made of a person, the search in relation to which the requirement is made shall be carried out as soon as is practicable.

(6) This section is without prejudice to any other power conferred by statute or otherwise exercisable by a member of the Garda Síochána to search a person or to seize and retain evidence of, or relating to, the commission of an offence.

14   **Powers of officers of Customs and Excise**

(1) Where an officer of Customs and Excise has reasonable grounds for believing that a person is at any place importing or exporting a psychoactive substance for human consumption, he or she may exercise all the powers available to a member of the Garda Síochána under section 12.

(2)   (a)   Without prejudice to the generality of subsection (1), where an officer of Customs and Excise who is in—

        (i)   a public place, or

        (ii)   any other place under a power of entry authorised by law or to which or in which he or she was expressly or impliedly invited or permitted to be,

      with reasonable cause suspects a person of committing or having committed an offence under section 3(2), he or she may exercise all the powers available to a member of the Garda Síochána under section 13.

  (b)   An officer of Customs and Excise may, for the purpose of conducting a search of a person under section 13, require the person to accompany him or her to a customs office

or to such other place as may be specified by the officer for that purpose.

(3) Without prejudice to the generality of subsections (1) and (2), an officer of Customs and Excise may seize and detain any thing which he or she with reasonable cause suspects is being imported or exported in contravention of section 3(2) and may for that purpose open any packet (including any postal packet) or container containing, or which he or she suspects of containing, a psychoactive substance.

15   **Obstruction**

(1) Any person who—

  (a)   obstructs or interferes with a member of the Garda Síochána or an officer of Customs and Excise in the course of exercising a power conferred on him or her by this Act or a warrant under section 12(4),

  (b)   fails or refuses to comply with a request or requirement of the member or officer, as the case may be, pursuant to section 12 or 13,

  (c)   fails or refuses to answer a question asked by the member or officer, as the case may be, pursuant to section 12,or

  (d)   in purported compliance with such request or requirement under section 12 or 13 or in answer to such question under section 12, gives information to the member or officer, as the case may be, that he or she has reasonable cause for believing is false or misleading in any material respect,

shall be guilty of an offence and shall be liable on summary conviction to a fine not exceeding €5,000 or imprisonment for a term not exceeding 12 months or both.

(2) A member of the Garda Síochána or an officer of Customs and Excise, as the case may be, may arrest without warrant any person whom he or she with reasonable cause suspects is committing or has committed an offence under this section.

16   **Taking of samples**

(1) A member of the Garda Síochána or an officer of Customs and Excise who takes a sample of a product or a sample of any substance or article, pursuant to section 12, shall divide the sample into 3 approximately equal parts, and place each part into separate

containers each of which he or she shall forthwith seal and mark in such a manner as to identify it as part of the sample taken by him or her.

(2) Where a member or an officer, as the case may be, has complied with subsection (1) he or she shall—

    (a) offer one of the sealed containers to the owner or person for the time being in charge or possession of the product, substance or article from which the sample concerned was taken,

    (b) retain one of the said sealed containers, and

    (c) forward, or cause to be forwarded, one of the sealed containers to a designated laboratory for the purposes of analysis.

(3) Where a product, substance or article is contained in a container and its division into parts is (for whatever reason) not practicable, a member of the Garda Síochána or officer of Customs and Excise, as the case may be, who wishes to take samples of such a product, substance or article for the purposes of analysis, shall take possession of 3 such containers belonging to the same batch, and each such container shall be deemed to be part of a sample for the purposes of subsection (1), and the provisions of subsections (1) and (2) shall apply thereto accordingly.

17   Laboratories

(1) The Forensic Science Laboratory of the Department of Justice and Law Reform is hereby designated as a laboratory (in this Act referred to as a "designated laboratory") for the examination, inspection, testing or analysis of substances for the purposes of this Act and each person who is engaged in the analysis of samples at that laboratory is hereby designated as an analyst (in this Act referred to as a "designated analyst").

(2) The Minister may, after consultation with the Minister for Health and Children, for the purposes of this Act designate, by notice in writing published in Iris Oifigiúil—

    (a) a laboratory as a designated laboratory at which samples taken for the purposes of this Act may be analysed, and

    (b) as a designated analyst a person as being a person who, or a class of persons the members of which, may, at a designated laboratory, analyse samples taken under this Act.

(3) As soon as practicable after a sample taken by a member of the Garda Síochána or an officer of Customs and Excise, as the case may be, under this Act has been received at a designated laboratory it shall be analysed by a designated analyst at the laboratory.

(4) As soon as practicable after compliance with subsection (3),a designated analyst engaged in the analysis of samples at the designated laboratory concerned shall forward the results of the analysis (in this Act referred to as a "certificate of analysis") carried out on the sample concerned to the Garda Síochána station or customs office, as the case may be, from which the sample was forwarded.

(5) A certificate of analysis shall be in such form as may be specified by the Minister.

18   Provisions relating to evidence in proceedings under Act

(1) Any application under section 8 (other than proceedings under subsection (6) of that section) shall be an application in civil proceedings and shall be determined accordingly.

(2) Any statement or admission made by a person in proceedings under section 8 or any finding by a court in those proceedings shall not be admissible as evidence in proceedings brought against the person for an offence under this Act, other than proceedings in relation to an offence under subsection (6) of that section.

(3) It shall be presumed until the contrary is proved in any proceedings under this Act that section 16 has been complied with.

(4) In any proceedings under this Act, a certificate purporting to be signed by a person employed or engaged at a designated laboratory stating the capacity in which that person is so employed or engaged and stating any one or more of the following, namely—

(a) that the person received a sample submitted to the designated laboratory,

(b) that, for such period as is specified in the certificate, the person had in his or her custody a sample so submitted, or

(c) that the person gave to such other person as is specified in the certificate a sample so submitted,

shall, unless the contrary is proved, be evidence of the matters stated in the certificate.

(5) In any proceedings under this Act, a certificate of analysis purporting to be signed by a designated analyst stating any one or more of the following, namely—

(a) that he or she carried out any procedure for the purpose of detecting the presence of any substance in the sample so submitted, or

(b) that the sample concerned contained such substance or such amount thereof as is specified in the certificate,

shall, unless the contrary is proved, be evidence of the matters stated in the certificate.

(6) In any proceedings under this Act a court may, if it considers that the interests of justice so require, direct that oral evidence of the matters stated in a certificate under this section be given and the court may, for the purpose of receiving oral evidence, adjourn the proceedings to a later date.

(7) A certificate under this section shall be in such form as may be specified by the Minister.

19   Disposal of things seized

(1) Where in the course of exercising any powers under this Act a member of the Garda Síochána or an officer of Customs and Excise finds or comes into possession of any substance, product, object, machinery, instrument, book, record (within the meaning of section 12), any other document or other thing and he or she has reasonable grounds for believing that it is evidence of any offence or suspected offence under this Act, he or she may seize and retain it for use in evidence in any criminal or civil proceedings for such period from the date of seizure as is reasonable or, if proceedings are commenced in which the thing so seized is required for use in evidence, until the conclusion of the proceedings, and thereafter the Police (Property) Act 1897 and, where appropriate, section 25 of the Criminal Justice Act 1951 shall apply to the thing so seized in the same manner as that Act and the said section 25 apply to property which has come into the possession of the Garda Síochána in the circumstances mentioned in that Act.

(2) If it is represented or appears to a member of the Garda Síochána or an officer of Customs and Excise proposing to seize or retain a document under this Act that the document was, or may have been, made for the purpose of obtaining, giving or communicating legal advice from or by a barrister or solicitor, the member or officer, as the

case may be, shall not seize or retain the document unless he or she suspects with reasonable cause that the document was not made, or is not intended, solely for any of those purposes.

(3) Where any substance, product, object, machinery, instrument, book, record (within the meaning of section 12), any document or other thing which is seized from or forfeited by a person under this Act is duly disposed of by or on behalf of the State the costs of such disposal, less any moneys arising from such disposal, shall (except where such costs have been waived in writing) be recoverable from such person as a simple contract debt in any court of competent jurisdiction.

(4) The power under this section to seize and retain evidence is without prejudice to any other power conferred by statute or otherwise exercisable by a member of the Garda Síochána or an officer of Customs and Excise to seize and retain evidence of, or relating to, the commission or attempted commission of an offence.

20   Offences

(1) A person who is guilty of an offence under this Act (other than an offence under section 15) shall be liable—

(a) on summary conviction, to a fine not exceeding €5,000 or imprisonment for a term not exceeding 12 months or both, or

(b) on conviction on indictment, to a fine or imprisonment for a term not exceeding 5 years or both.

(2) Where an offence under this Act is committed by a body corporate and is proved to have been committed with the consent or connivance of, or to be attributable to wilful neglect on the part of, any director, manager, secretary or other officer of such body corporate or a person who was purporting to act in any such capacity, that officer or person shall be guilty of an offence and shall be liable to be proceeded against and punished as if he or she were guilty of the first-mentioned offence.

(3) On conviction for an offence under this Act the court may, in addition to any other penalty, order any substance, product, object or any apparatus, equipment or thing to which the offence relates to be forfeited and either destroyed or dealt with in such manner as the court thinks fit; however a court shall not order anything to be forfeited under this subsection if a person claiming to be the owner of or otherwise interested in it applies to be heard by the court, unless an opportunity has been given to him or her to show cause why the order should not be made.

21   Jurisdiction

The jurisdiction of the District Court under this Act shall, in relation to a place that is a structure, stall or vehicle, be exercised by a judge for the time being assigned to the district court district in which—

(a) the structure, stall or vehicle concerned was alleged to have been used for the sale or advertisement of a psychoactive substance for human consumption or an object for use in cultivating by hydroponic means any plant in contravention of section 17 of the Act of 1977, or as may be appropriate, the importation or exportation of a psychoactive substance, or

(b) the structure, stall or vehicle is kept when not in use.

22   Amendment of Customs and Excise (Miscellaneous Provisions) Act 1988

Section 2 of the Customs and Excise (Miscellaneous Provisions) Act 1988 is amended in subsection (1)—

    (a)   by the insertion of "or a psychoactive substance within the meaning of section 1 of the Criminal Justice (Psychoactive Substances) Act 2010" after "a controlled drug" in each place that it occurs, and

    (b)   by the substitution of ", under the Misuse of Drugs Acts 1977 to 2007 or under the Criminal Justice (Psychoactive Substances) Act 2010" for "or under the Misuse of Drugs Acts 1977 and 1984".

23   Amendment of Bail Act 1997

The Schedule to the Bail Act 1997 is amended by the insertion of the following paragraph after paragraph 35:[1]

Amendments

1   See the amended Act.

---

24   Expenses

The expenses incurred by the Minister in the administration of this Act shall, to such extent as may be sanctioned by the Minister for Finance, be paid out of moneys provided by the Oireachtas.

25   Regulations and orders

(1) The Minister may make regulations to do anything that appears necessary or expedient for bringing this Act into operation.

(2) Where a provision of this Act requires or authorises the Minister to make regulations, such regulations—

    (a)   may make different provision for different circumstances or cases, classes or types, and

    (b)   may contain such incidental, consequential or supplemental provisions as the Minister considers necessary or expedient for the purposes of this Act.

(3) Every order (other than an order made under section 26(2)) and regulation made by the Minister under this Act shall be laid before each House of the Oireachtas as soon as may be after it is made and, if a resolution annulling the order or regulation, as the case may be, is passed by either such House within the next 21 days on which the House has sat after the order or regulation is laid before it, the order or regulation shall be annulled accordingly, but without prejudice to the validity of anything previously done thereunder.

26   Short title and commencement

(1) This Act may be cited as the Criminal Justice (Psychoactive Substances) Act 2010.

(2) This Act shall come into operation on such day or days as the Minister may appoint, by order or orders, either generally or with reference to any particular purpose or provision and different days may be so appointed for different purposes and different provisions.

Criminal Procedure Act 2010

Number 27 of 2010

ARRANGEMENT OF SECTIONS

PART 1
PRELIMINARY AND GENERAL

1. Short title and commencement.

2. Interpretation.

3. Expenses.

PART 2
IMPACT OF CRIME ON VICTIM

4. Amendment of section 5 of Act of 1993.

5. Evidence through television link.

6. Evidence through intermediary.

PART 3
EXCEPTIONS TO RULE AGAINST DOUBLE JEOPARDY

CHAPTER 1
INTERPRETATION

7. Interpretation (Part 3).

CHAPTER 2 APPLICATION FOR RE-TRIAL ORDERS UNDER PART 3

8. Application by Director seeking re-trial order where new and compelling evidence becomes available.

9. Application by Director for re-trial order where previous acquittal tainted.

10. Re-trial orders.

11. Amendment of Act of 1962.

12. Orders to safeguard fairness of re-trial.

13. Effect of re-trial order.

14. Appeals on point of law to Supreme Court.

CHAPTER 3 APPROVAL OF DISTRICT COURT FOR EXERCISE OF CERTAIN POWERS RELATING TO PERSONS ACQUITTED OF RELEVANT OFFENCES

15. Certain powers may be used only in accordance with Act.

16. Arrest of person in respect of whom section 15 applies may be authorised by District Court in certain circumstances.

17. Arrest in certain circumstances of person in respect of whom section 15 applies where person is in prison etc.

18. Search warrant in aid of investigation relating to relevant offences may be authorised by District Court in certain circumstances.

CHAPTER 4 MISCELLANEOUS

19. Admissibility of evidence in proceedings under Part.

20. Other appeals or review rights not affected.

21. Application of section 6 of Prosecution of Offences Act 1974.

22. Rules of court and expeditious hearings.

PART 4
APPEALS AND MATTERS RELATING TO APPEALS

CHAPTER 1
WITH PREJUDICE PROSECUTION APPEALS

23. Appeals by Director etc., in certain criminal proceedings.

24. No appeal in certain circumstances.

25. Orders to safeguard fairness of re-trial.

26. Order for re-trial following appeal under section 23.

27. Amendment of section 3 of Criminal Justice Act 1994.

28. Other appeals or review rights not affected.

29. Application of section 6 of Prosecution of Offences Act 1974.

30. Rules of court and expeditious hearings.

CHAPTER 2 MISCELLANEOUS MATTERS RELATING TO APPEALS

31. Amendment of Courts of Justice Act 1924.

32. Amendment of section 44 of Offences Against the State Act 1939.

PART 5
MISCELLANEOUS PROVISIONS

CHAPTER 1
GIVING OF EVIDENCE

33. Amendment of Criminal Justice (Evidence) Act 1924.

34. Expert evidence adduced by defence.

35. Return or disposal of property to be used as evidence. Chapter 2 Miscellaneous amendments

36. Amendment of section 22 of Courts Act 1991.

37. Amendment of Act of 1967.

38. Amendment to First Schedule to Criminal Justice Act 1951.

AN ACT TO AMEND AND EXTEND THE CRIMINAL JUSTICE ACT 1993; TO AMEND CRIMINAL LAW AND PROCEDURE IN OTHER RESPECTS, INCLUDING MAKING PROVISION FOR EXCEPTIONS TO THE RULE AGAINST DOUBLE JEOPARDY SO AS TO ENABLE THE COURT OF CRIMINAL APPEAL TO HEAR AND DETERMINE APPLICATIONS BROUGHT IN CERTAIN CIRCUMSTANCES BY THE DIRECTOR OF PUBLIC PROSECUTIONS TO QUASH CERTAIN ACQUITTALS AND TO HAVE PERSONS WHO ARE THE SUBJECT OF THOSE APPLICATIONS RE-TRIED, AND TO PROVIDE

FOR AN APPEAL TO THE SUPREME COURT ON A POINT OF LAW FROM A DETERMINATION OF THE COURT OF CRIMINAL APPEAL IN RESPECT OF SUCH APPLICATIONS; TO EXTEND THE POWERS OF THE GARDA SÍOCHÁNA IN RELATION TO THE INVESTIGATION OF CERTAIN OFFENCES; TO EXTEND THE CIRCUMSTANCES IN WHICH THE DIRECTOR OF PUBLIC PROSECUTIONS OR THE ATTORNEY GENERAL, AS MAY BE APPROPRIATE, MAY TAKE AN APPEAL IN CRIMINAL PROCEEDINGS; TO AMEND THE CRIMINAL JUSTICE (EVIDENCE) ACT 1924 AND TO AMEND AND EXTEND THE LAW RELATING TO EVIDENCE IN OTHER RESPECTS; TO AMEND THE CRIMINAL JUSTICE ACT 1994, THE COURTS ACT 1991, THE CRIMINAL PROCEDURE ACT 1967, THE CRIMINAL JUSTICE (LEGAL AID) ACT 1962, THE CRIMINAL JUSTICE ACT 1951, THE OFFENCES AGAINST THE STATE ACT 1939 AND THE COURTS OF JUSTICE ACT 1924; AND TO PROVIDE FOR RELATED MATTERS. [20th July, 2010]

BE IT ENACTED BY THE OIREACHTAS AS FOLLOWS:

PART 1
PRELIMINARY AND GENERAL

1   Short title and commencement

(1) This Act may be cited as the Criminal Procedure Act 2010.

(2) This Act shall come into operation on such day or days as the Minister may appoint by order or orders either generally or with reference to any particular purpose or provision and different days may be so appointed for different purposes or different provisions.

Note

This Act came into operation on 1 September 2010 by virtue of the Criminal Procedure Act 2010 (Commencement) Order 2010 (SI 414/2010).

---

2   Interpretation

(1) In this Act unless the context otherwise requires—

"Act of 1962" means the Criminal Justice (Legal Aid) Act 1962;

"Act of 1967" means the Criminal Procedure Act 1967;

"Act of 1993" means the Criminal Justice Act 1993;

"broadcast" has the meaning it has in section 2 of the Broadcasting Act 2009;

"children detention school" has the meaning it has in section 3(1) of the Children Act 2001;

"Director" means the Director of Public Prosecutions;

"legal aid (Supreme Court) certificate" has the meaning it has in the Act of 1962;

"legal aid (trial on indictment) certificate" has the meaning it has in the Act of 1962;

"Minister" means the Minister for Justice and Law Reform;

"prison" has the meaning it has in section 2 of the Prisons Act 2007;

"publication" means publication, other than by way of broadcast, to the public or a portion of the public.

(2) In this Act, unless the context otherwise requires, references to—

(a) a jury shall, in relation to proceedings conducted before a court sitting without a jury, be construed as references to that court, and

(b) a person being sent forward for trial include, where appropriate, references to such a person being sent or being sent forward for trial to, or charged before, a Special Criminal Court.

3   Expenses

The expenses incurred by the Minister in the administration of this Act shall, to such extent as may be sanctioned by the Minister for Finance, be paid out of moneys provided by the Oireachtas.

PART 2

IMPACT OF CRIME ON VICTIM

4   Amendment of section 5 of Act of 1993

The Act of 1993 is amended by the substitution of the following section for section 5:[1]

Amendments

1   See the amended Act.

---

5   Evidence through television link

The Act of 1993 is amended by the insertion of the following section after section 5:[1]

Amendments

1   See the amended Act.

---

6   Evidence through intermediary

6.—The Act of 1993 is amended by the insertion of the following section after section 5A:[1]

Amendments

1   See the amended Act.

PART 3

EXCEPTIONS TO RULE AGAINST DOUBLE JEOPARDY

Chapter 1

Interpretation

7   Interpretation (Part 3)

In this Part, unless the context otherwise requires—

"Act of 1984" means the Criminal Justice Act 1984;

"acquittal" includes a verdict of not guilty returned by a jury and a verdict of not guilty returned by a jury by direction of a court;

"application for a re-trial order" means an application under section 8 or 9;

"compelling evidence", in relation to a person, means evidence which—

(a)   is reliable,

(b)   is of significant probative value, and

(c)   is such that a jury might reasonably be satisfied beyond a reasonable doubt of the person's guilt in respect of the offence concerned;

"Court" means the Court of Criminal Appeal;

"legal aid (re-trial order) certificate" has the meaning it has in the Act of 1962;

"new and compelling evidence", in relation to a person, means evidence—

(a)   which was not adduced by the prosecution in the proceedings in respect of which the person was acquitted (nor in any appeal proceedings to which the original proceedings related), and

(b)   which could not, with the exercise of due diligence, have been adduced during those proceedings, and

(c)   is evidence which—

(i)   is reliable,

(ii)   is of significant probative value, and

(iii) is such that when taken together with all the other evidence adduced in the proceedings concerned, a jury might reasonably be satisfied beyond a reasonable doubt of the person's guilt in respect of the offence concerned;

"offence against the administration of justice" means—

(a)   an offence under section 1 of the Prevention of Corruption Act 1906 in so far as the offence concerned relates to criminal proceedings,

(b)   an offence under section 41 of the Criminal Justice Act 1999,

(c)   attempting to pervert the course of justice,

(d)   perjury, or

(e)   conspiring or inciting another person to commit any of the offences referred to in paragraphs (a) to (d);

"place" includes—

(a)   a dwelling or other building,

(b)   a vehicle, whether mechanically propelled or not,

(c)   a vessel, whether sea-going or not,

(d) an aircraft, whether capable of operation or not,

(e) a hovercraft; "relevant offence" means an offence specified in the Schedule; "retrial order" means an order of the Court under subsection (1) or

(2) of section 10.

Chapter 2
Application for re-trial orders under Part 3

8   **Application by Director seeking retrial order where new and compelling evidence becomes available**

(1) Subject to subsection (7), this section applies where a person—

(a) is, on or after the commencement of this section, sent forward for trial in respect of a relevant offence and is, or

(b) has, before the commencement of this section, been sent forward for trial but has not yet been tried in respect of a relevant offence and is, on or after such commencement,

tried on indictment in respect of the offence, and acquitted of that offence (whether at the trial, on appeal against conviction or on appeal from such a decision on appeal).

(2) For the purposes of this section, a person who has been acquitted of a relevant offence in proceedings referred to in subsection (1) shall be deemed to also have been acquitted of any relevant offence in respect of which he or she could have been convicted in the proceedings concerned by virtue of the first-mentioned offence charged in the indictment, other than an offence for which he or she has been convicted.

(3) The Director may apply to the Court for a re-trial order where it appears to him or her—

(a) that there is new and compelling evidence against a person referred to in subsection (1) in relation to the relevant offence concerned, and

(b) that it is in the public interest to do so.

(4) Only one application for a re-trial order may be made by the Director in respect of a person in relation to a relevant offence that was the subject of the application and no further application may be made irrespective of whether the person concerned is subsequently acquitted of the offence concerned in a re-trial ordered pursuant to an application under this section.

(5) An application for a re-trial order under subsection (3) shall be on notice to the person concerned.

(6) If a person fails to appear before the Court in respect of the hearing of the application, the Court, if it is satisfied that it is, in all the circumstances, in the interests of justice to do so, may proceed to hear and determine the application in the absence of the person.

(7) This section shall not apply to a relevant offence in respect of which a person was the subject of a special verdict under section 5 of the Criminal Law (Insanity) Act 2006.

9   **Application by Director for re-trial order where previous acquittal tainted**

(1) This section applies where—

(a) a person—

(i) is, on or after the commencement of this section, sent forward for trial in respect of an offence (irrespective of whether or not the offence is a relevant offence) and is, or

1470

      (ii)   has, before the commencement of this section, been sent forward for trial but has not yet been tried in respect of an offence (irrespective of whether or not the offence is a relevant offence) and is, on or after such commencement,

tried on indictment in respect of the offence, and acquitted of that offence (whether at the trial, on appeal against conviction or on appeal from such a decision on appeal), and

    (b)   the person, or another person, has been convicted of an offence against the administration of justice relating to the proceedings which resulted in the acquittal referred to in paragraph (a).

(2) For the purposes of this section, a person who has been acquitted of an offence in proceedings referred to in subsection (1)(a), shall be deemed to also have been acquitted of any offence in respect of which he or she could have been convicted in the proceedings concerned by virtue of the first-mentioned offence charged in the indictment, other than an offence for which he or she has been convicted.

(3) The Director may apply to the Court for a re-trial order where it appears to him or her—

    (a)   there is compelling evidence against a person referred to in subsection (1)(a), and

    (b)   that it is in the public interest to do so.

(4) No application for a re-trial order in respect of a person may be made by the Director under this section where proceedings relating to an offence against the administration of justice referred to in subsection (1)(b) are pending before any court.

(5) Only one application for a re-trial order may be made by the Director in respect of a person in relation to an offence that was the subject of the application and no further application may be made irrespective of whether the person concerned is subsequently acquitted of the offence concerned in a re-trial ordered pursuant to an application under this section.

(6) An application for a re-trial order under subsection (3) shall be on notice to the person concerned.

(7) If a person fails to appear before the Court in respect of the hearing of the application, the Court, if it is satisfied that it is, in all the circumstances, in the interests of justice to do so, may proceed to hear and determine the application in the absence of the person.

(8) For the purposes of subsection (1)(b), the reference to "convicted of an offence", in relation to a person, includes a reference to the conviction of a person after signing a plea of guilty and being sent forward for sentence under section 13(2)(b) of the Criminal Procedure Act 1967.

10   Re-trial orders

(1) If on hearing an application under section 8, the Court is satisfied—

    (a)   that there is new and compelling evidence against a person referred to in section 8(1), and

    (b)   that, having had regard to the matters referred to in subsection (3), it is, in all the circumstances, in the interests of justice to do so,

the Court shall make a re-trial order quashing the person's acquittal and directing that the person be re-tried for the relevant offence, subject to such conditions and directions (including conditions and directions as to placing a stay on the re-trial) as the Court considers necessary or expedient to ensure the fairness of the re-trial ordered under this subsection.

(2) If on hearing an application under section 9, the Court is satisfied—

    (a)   there is compelling evidence against a person referred to in section 9(1)(a), and

    (b)   hat, having had regard to the matters referred to in subsection (3), it is, in all the circumstances, in the interests of justice to do so,

the Court shall make a re-trial order quashing the person's acquittal and directing that the person be re-tried for the offence concerned, subject to such conditions and directions (including conditions and directions as to placing a stay on the re-trial) as the Court considers necessary or expedient to ensure the fairness of the re-trial ordered under this subsection.

(3) In determining whether to make an order under subsection (1) or (2), the Court shall have regard to—

    (a)   whether or not it is likely that any re-trial could be conducted fairly,

    (b)   the amount of time that has passed since the act or omission that gave rise to the indictment,

    (c)   the interests of any victim of the offence concerned, and

    (d)   any other matter which the Court considers relevant to the application.

(4) For the purposes of determining whether to make an order under subsection (1) or (2), the Court may—

    (a)   order the production of any document, exhibit or other thing connected with the proceedings to which the application relates,

    (b)   order any person who would have been a compellable witness in the proceedings to which the application relates to attend for examination and be examined before the Court, whether or not the person was called in those proceedings,

    (c)   receive the evidence, if tendered, of any witness, or

    (d)   generally make such order as may be necessary for doing justice in the application before the Court.

(5) Evidence may be admitted in a hearing under this section, whether or not it would have been admissible in earlier proceedings against the person who is the subject of the application under section 8 or 9.

(6) Subject to subsection (1) or (2), where the Court makes a re-trial order, the re-trial shall take place as soon as practicable.

(7) In this section "document", in relation to an application by the Director under section 9, includes a transcript of the trial of any person referred to in section 9(1)(b).

11   Amendment of Act of 1962

The Act of 1962 is amended—

    (a)   by the insertion of the following section after section 6B:[1]

    (b)   in section 7, by the addition of the following subsection:[1]
        and

    (c)   in section 9(2), by the substitution of ", a legal aid (protection of persons order) certificate or a legal aid (re-trial order) certificate" for "or a legal aid (protection of persons order) certificate".

Amendments

1   See the amended Act.

12   Orders to safeguard fairness of re-trial

(1) Subject to this section, an application for a re-trial order shall be conducted in open court.

(2) Where the Court is hearing an application for a re-trial order under section 8 or 9 and is satisfied that it is in the interests of justice to do so, it may exclude from the Court during the proceeding—

    (a) the public or any portion of the public, or

    (b) any particular person or persons,

other than bona fide representatives of the Press.

(3) The Court may, if it considers that it is in the interests of justice to do so, make an order prohibiting the publication or broadcast of—

    (a) any evidence given or referred to at a hearing of an application for a re-trial order, or

    (b) any matter identifying or having the effect of identifying any person who is the subject of an application for a re-trial order, or any other person connected with the re-trial for which an order is sought under section 8 or 9.

(4) An order under subsection (3) ceases to have effect (unless it specifies an earlier date)—

    (a) when there is no longer any step that could be taken which would lead to the person concerned being re-tried pursuant to a re-trial order, or

    (b) where the person concerned is re-tried pursuant to a re-trial order, at the conclusion of the trial.

(5) (a) If any matter is published or broadcast in contravention of subsection (3), the following persons, namely—

        (i)   in the case of a publication in a newspaper or periodical, any proprietor, any editor and any publisher of the newspaper or periodical,

        (ii) in the case of any other publication, the person who publishes it, and

        (iii) in the case of a broadcast, any person who transmits or provides the programme in which the broadcast is made and any person having functions in relation to the programme corresponding to those of the editor of a newspaper,

    shall be guilty of an offence.

    (b) A person guilty of an offence under paragraph (a) shall be liable—

        (i)   on summary conviction, to a fine not exceeding €5,000 or to imprisonment for a term not exceeding 12 months or to both, or

        (ii) on conviction on indictment, to a fine not exceeding €50,000 or to imprisonment for a term not exceeding 3 years or to both.

    (c) Where an offence under paragraph (a) is committed by a body corporate and is proved to have been so committed with the consent, connivance or approval of, or to be attributable to, any neglect on the part of a person being a director, manager, secretary or other officer of the body corporate or any other person who was acting or purporting to act in any such capacity, that person as well as the body corporate shall be guilty of an offence and be liable to be proceeded against and punished as if he or she were guilty of the first-mentioned offence.

(d) Where the affairs of a body corporate are managed by its members, paragraph (c) shall apply in relation to the acts and defaults of a member in connection with his or her functions of management as if he or she were a director or manager of the body corporate.

(6) Nothing in this section shall affect the operation of any other enactment that imposes restrictions on the extent to which information relating to court proceedings may be published or broadcast.

13 Effect of re-trial order

(1) Where a person is ordered under subsection (1) or (2) of section 10 to be re-tried for an offence, he or she may, notwithstanding any rule of law, be again indicted and tried and, if found guilty, sentenced for that offence.

(2) In a case to which subsection (1) relates, the Court may—

(a) order that the person concerned be detained in custody or admitted to bail pending the re-trial on such terms as the Court thinks proper,

(b) where the person concerned does not appear before the Court for the hearing and determination of the application, issue a warrant for his or her arrest.

(3) A legal aid (re-trial order) certificate which was granted in relation to the proceedings under section 8 or 9 shall have effect as if it had been granted also in relation to the re-trial ordered in respect of that person.

(4) A person who was not granted a legal aid (re-trial order) certificate and who is the subject of a re-trial order may apply for a legal aid (trial on indictment) certificate and section 3 of the Act of 1962 shall, with any necessary modifications, apply to that application.

14 Appeals on point of law to Supreme Court

(1) An appeal shall lie to the Supreme Court by the acquitted person or the Director from a determination of the Court under subsection (1) or (2) of section 10 if that Court, the Attorney General or the Director certifies that the determination involves a point of law of exceptional public importance and that it is desirable in the public interest that an appeal should be taken to the Supreme Court.

(2) The Supreme Court may, for the purposes of its decision on such an appeal, either—

(a) remit the case to the Court to deal with, or

(b) deal with it itself and for that purpose exercise any powers of that Court under this Part.

(3) Where an appeal has been made to the Supreme Court under subsection (1) and a legal aid (Supreme Court) certificate is granted under subsection (4), or is deemed to have been granted under subsection (5) in respect of the person who is the subject of the appeal, he or she shall be entitled to free legal aid in the preparation and conduct of any argument that he or she wishes to make to that Court and to have a solicitor and counsel assigned to him or her for that purpose in the manner prescribed by regulations under section 10 of the Act of 1962.

(4) The acquitted person may, in relation to proceedings under this section apply for a legal aid (Supreme Court) certificate to the Supreme Court either—

    (a) by letter to the registrar of the Supreme Court setting out the facts of the case and the grounds of the application, or

    (b) to the Supreme Court itself,

and the Court shall grant the certificate if (but only if) it appears to the Court that the means of the person are insufficient to enable him or her to obtain legal aid.

(5) If a legal aid (re-trial order) certificate was granted under the Act of 1962 in respect of the person in relation to an application for a re-trial order, a legal aid (Supreme Court) certificate shall be deemed to have been granted in respect of him or her in relation to the proceedings under this section.

(6) Section 12 of this Act shall, with any necessary modifications, apply to an appeal under this section as it applies to an application for a re-trial order.

Chapter 3

Approval of District Court for exercise of certain powers relating to persons acquitted of relevant offences

15   Certain powers may be used only in accordance with Act

(1) This section applies where a person—

    (a) is, on or after the commencement of this section, sent forward for trial in respect of a relevant offence and is, or

    (b) has, before the commencement of this section, been sent forward for trial but has not yet been tried in respect of a relevant offence and is, on or after such commencement,

tried on indictment in respect of the offence, and acquitted of that offence (whether at the trial, on appeal against conviction or on appeal from such a decision on appeal).

(2) For the purposes of this section, a person who has been acquitted of a relevant offence in proceedings referred to in subsection (1) shall be deemed to also have been acquitted of any relevant offence in respect of which he or she could have been convicted in the proceedings concerned by virtue of the first-mentioned offence charged in the indictment, other than an offence for which he or she has been convicted.

(3) A member of the Garda Síochána shall not, either with or without the consent of a person referred to in subsection (1), do any of the following in connection with the person's suspected participation in a relevant offence in respect of which that person was acquitted, except in so far as it is authorised in accordance with the provisions of this Act:

    (a) arrest and detain the person;

    (b) interview the person;

    (c) search the person or cause him or her to be searched;

    (d) photograph the person or cause him or her to be photographed;

    (e) take or cause to be taken, the person's fingerprints or palm prints;

    (f) take or cause to be taken from the person, a sample for the purposes of forensic testing;

    (g) seize and retain for testing or for use as evidence anything in the person's possession;

    (h) search a place owned or occupied, or partly owned or occupied by the person.

16 Arrest of person in respect of whom section 15 applies may be authorised by District Court in certain circumstances

(1) A person in respect of whom section 15 applies may be arrested again for a relevant offence in respect of which he or she has been acquitted in accordance with, and only in accordance with, this section.

(2) Subject to subsection (3), a judge of the District Court who is satisfied—

(a) by information on oath by a member of the Garda Síochána not below the rank of superintendent that the member concerned has information regarding a relevant offence in respect of which the person was acquitted which has come to the knowledge of the Garda Síochána only since the person's acquittal, and

(b) that the information referred to in paragraph (a) is likely to reveal or confirm the existence of new and compelling evidence in relation to the person's suspected participation in the relevant offence for which his or her arrest is sought,

may authorise the arrest of that person.

(3) A judge of the District Court may authorise the arrest of the person concerned in respect of, and only of, the relevant offence in respect of which the person was acquitted.

(4) A person arrested pursuant to this section—

(a) shall be taken forthwith to a Garda Station and may be detained there for such period or periods as is authorised under section 4 of the Act of 1984, and

(b) subject to this section, shall be dealt with as though he or she had been detained under that section.

(5) If—

(a) at any time during the detention of a person under this section there are no longer reasonable grounds for—

(i) suspecting that the person has committed the relevant offence in respect of which he or she was arrested under this section, or

(ii) believing that his or her detention is necessary for the proper investigation of the relevant offence,

or

(b) by reason of the expiry of the period or periods referred to in subsection (4)(a), the detention shall be terminated forthwith, and he or she shall without delay be released, unless his or her detention is authorised apart from this section.

(6) Subsections (5) and (5A) of section 4 and section 10 of the Act of 1984 shall not apply to a person arrested and detained under this section.

(7) Proceedings under this section shall be heard otherwise than in public.

(8) This section shall not apply to a relevant offence in respect of which a person was the subject of a special verdict under section 5 of the Criminal Law (Insanity) Act 2006.

(9) This section is without prejudice to the power of the Court to issue a warrant for the arrest of a person in respect of whom a retrial order has been made under subsection (1) of section 10.

17   **Arrest in certain circumstances of person in respect of whom section 15 applies where person is in prison etc**

(1) A person in respect of whom section 15 applies who is detained in a prison or a children detention school may be arrested again for a relevant offence in respect of which he or she has been acquitted in accordance with, and only in accordance with, this section.

(2) Subject to subsection (3), a judge of the District Court who is satisfied—

(a) by information on oath by a member of the Garda Síochána not below the rank of superintendent that the member concerned has information regarding a relevant offence in respect of which the person was acquitted which has come to the knowledge of the Garda Síochána only since the person's acquittal, and

(b) that the information referred to in paragraph (a) is likely to reveal or confirm the existence of new and compelling evidence in relation to the person's suspected participation in the relevant offence for which his or her arrest is sought,

may authorise the arrest of that person.

(3) A judge of the District Court may authorise the arrest of the person concerned in respect of, and only of, the relevant offence for which the person was acquitted.

(4) A person arrested pursuant to this section—

(a) shall be taken forthwith to a Garda Station and may, subject to subsection (6), be detained there for such period or periods as is authorised under section 4 of the Act of 1984, and

(b) subject to this section, shall be dealt with as though he or she had been detained under that section.

(5) Subsections (4), (5) and (5A) of section 4 and section 10 of the Act of 1984 shall not apply to a person arrested and detained under this section.

(6) If at any time during the detention of a person under this section there are no longer reasonable grounds for—

(a) suspecting that the person has committed the relevant offence in respect of which he or she was arrested under this section, or

(b) believing that his or her detention is necessary for the proper investigation of the relevant offence,

the detention shall be terminated.

(7) On termination of the detention in accordance with subsection (6) or by reason of the expiry of the period or periods referred to in subsection (4)(a), the member of the Garda Síochána in charge of the Garda Station where the person is detained shall transfer him or her, or cause him or her to be transferred back to the governor of the prison or, as the case may be, the Director of the children detention school where the person was detained at the time of the arrest under this section.

(8) Proceedings under this section shall be heard otherwise than in public.

(9) This section shall not apply to a relevant offence in respect of which a person was the subject of a special verdict under section 5 of the Criminal Law (Insanity) Act 2006.

(10) Nothing in this section shall affect the power of the Court to issue a warrant for the arrest of a person in respect of whom an order has been made under subsection (1) of section 10.

18   Search warrant in aid of investigation relating to relevant offences may be authorised by District Court in certain circumstances

(1) A place that is owned or occupied, or partly owned or occupied by a person in respect of whom section 15 applies may be searched in connection with a relevant offence in respect of which he or she has been acquitted in accordance with, and only in accordance with, this section.

(2) A judge of the District Court who is satisfied—

   (a)   by information on oath by a member of the Garda Síochána not below the rank of superintendent that the member concerned has information regarding a relevant offence in respect of which the person was acquitted which has come to the knowledge of the Garda Síochána since the person's acquittal,

   (b)   that there are reasonable grounds for suspecting that evidence of, or relating to, the matters referred to in paragraph (a) is to be found in a place owned or occupied or partly owned or occupied by the person concerned,

   (c)   that the information referred to in paragraph (a) is likely to reveal or confirm the existence of new and compelling evidence in relation to the person's suspected participation in the relevant offence concerned,

may issue a warrant for the search of that place and any persons found at that place.

(3) A search warrant under this section shall be expressed, and shall operate, to authorise a named member, accompanied by such other members or persons or both as the member thinks necessary—

   (a)   to enter, at any time or times within one week of the date of issue of the warrant, on production if so requested of the warrant, and if necessary by the use of reasonable force, the place named in the warrant,

   (b)   to search it and any persons found at that place, and

   (c)   to seize anything found at that place, or anything found in the possession of a person present at that place at the time of the search, that the member reasonably believes to be evidence of, or relating to, the commission of the relevant offence.

(4) A member acting under the authority of a search warrant under this section may—

   (a)   require any person present at the place where the search is being carried out to give to the member his or her name and address,

   (b)   arrest without warrant any person who—

      (i)   obstructs or attempts to obstruct the member in the carrying out of his or her duties,

      (ii)   fails to comply with a requirement under paragraph (a),or

      (iii)   gives a name or address which the member has reasonable cause for believing is false or misleading.

(5) A person who obstructs or attempts to obstruct a member acting under the authority of a search warrant under this section, who fails to comply with a requirement under subsection (4)(a), or who gives a false or misleading name or address to a member shall be guilty of an offence and shall be liable on summary conviction to a fine not exceeding €3,000 or imprisonment for a term not exceeding 6 months or both.

(6) Proceedings under this section shall be heard otherwise than in public.

(7) This section shall not apply to a relevant offence in respect of which a person was the subject of a special verdict under section 5 of the Criminal Law (Insanity) Act 2006.

(8) Nothing in this section shall affect the operation of section 7 of the Criminal Justice Act 2006.

Chapter 4
Miscellaneous

19   Admissibility of evidence in proceedings under Part

(1) A failure on the part of a member of the Garda Síochána to observe any provision of this Part shall not of itself render that member liable to any criminal or civil proceedings or (without prejudice to the power of the court to exclude evidence at its discretion) shall not of itself affect the admissibility of any evidence obtained otherwise than in accordance with this Part.

(2) A failure on the part of any member of the Garda Síochána to observe any provision of this Part shall render that member liable to disciplinary proceedings.

20   Other appeals or review rights not affected

Nothing in this Part shall affect any right of appeal or review provided by this Act or any other enactment or rule of law.

21   Application of section 6 of Prosecution of Offences Act 1974

Section 6 of the Prosecution of Offences Act 1974 shall, with any necessary modifications, apply to communications made to the persons mentioned in that section for the purpose of influencing the making of a decision in relation to an application under this Part as it applies to such communications made for the purposes of making a decision to withdraw or not to initiate criminal proceedings or any particular charge in criminal proceedings.

22   Rules of court and expeditious hearings

Rules of court may make provision for the expeditious hearing of—

(a) proceedings under this Part, and

(b) re-trials ordered under section 10.

PART 4
APPEALS AND MATTERS RELATING TO APPEALS

Chapter 1
With prejudice prosecution appeals

23   Appeals by Director etc., in certain criminal proceedings

(1) Where on or after the commencement of this section, a person is tried on indictment and acquitted of an offence, the Director, if he or she is the prosecuting authority in the trial, or the Attorney General as may be appropriate, may, subject to subsection (3) and section 24, appeal the acquittal in respect of the offence concerned on a question of law to the Supreme Court.

(2) Where on or after the commencement of this section, a person's conviction of an offence on indictment is quashed on appeal by the Court of Criminal Appeal and that Court makes no order for the re-trial of the person in respect of the offence, the Director, if he or she is the

prosecuting authority in the trial, or the Attorney General as may be appropriate, may, subject to subsection (3) and section 24, appeal the decision of the Court of Criminal Appeal not to order a re-trial of the offence concerned on a question of law to the Supreme Court.

(3) An appeal under this section shall lie only where—

(a) a ruling was made by a court during the course of a trial referred to in subsection (1) or the hearing of an appeal referred to in subsection (2), as the case may be, which erroneously excluded compelling evidence, or

(b) a direction was given by a court during the course of a trial referred to in subsection (1), directing the jury in the trial to find the person not guilty where—

(i) the direction was wrong in law, and

(ii) the evidence adduced in the proceedings was evidence upon which a jury might reasonably be satisfied beyond a reasonable doubt of the person's guilt in respect of the offence concerned.

(4) An appeal under this section shall be made on notice to the person who is the subject of the appeal within 28 days, or such longer period not exceeding 56 days as the Supreme Court may, on application to it in that behalf, determine, from the day on which the person was acquitted or the conviction was quashed, as the case may be.

(5) Where a person fails to appear before the Supreme Court in respect of the appeal, the Court, if it is satisfied that it is, in all the circumstances, in the interests of justice to do so, may proceed to hear and determine the appeal in the absence of the person concerned.

(6) For the purposes of considering an appeal under this section the Supreme Court shall hear argument—

(a) by, or by counsel on behalf of, the Director, or as the case may be, the Attorney General,

(b) by the person who is the subject of the appeal or by counsel on his or her behalf, and

(c) if counsel are assigned under subsection (7), by such counsel.

(7) The Supreme Court shall assign counsel to argue in support of the acquittal referred to in subsection (1) or the decision of the Court of Criminal Appeal not to order a re-trial referred to in subsection (2), as the case may be if—

(a) the person who is the subject of the appeal does not wish to be represented or heard under subsection (6)(b),or

(b) notwithstanding the fact that the person concerned exercises his or her right to be represented or heard under subsection (6)(b), the Court considers it desirable in the public interest to do so.

(8) Where an appeal has been made to the Supreme Court under this section and a legal aid (Supreme Court) certificate is granted under subsection (9), or is deemed to have been granted under subsection (10), in respect of the person who is the subject of the appeal he or she shall be entitled to free legal aid in the preparation and conduct of any argument that he or she wishes to make to the Supreme Court and to have a solicitor and counsel assigned to him or her for that purpose in the manner prescribed by regulations under section 10 of the Act of 1962.

(9) The person may, in relation to proceedings under this section apply for a legal aid (Supreme Court) certificate to the Supreme Court either—

(a) by letter to the registrar of the Supreme Court setting out the facts of the case and the grounds of the application, or

(b) to the Supreme Court itself,

and the Court shall grant the certificate if (but only if) it appears to the Court that the means of the person are insufficient to enable him or her to obtain legal aid.

(10) If a legal aid (trial on indictment) certificate was granted under the Act of 1962 in respect of the person concerned in relation to the earlier proceedings in respect of the offence concerned, a legal aid (Supreme Court) certificate shall be deemed to have been granted in respect of him or her in relation to the proceedings under this section.

(11) On hearing an appeal under this section the Supreme Court may—

(a) quash the acquittal or reverse the decision of the Court of Criminal Appeal, as the case may be, and order the person to be re-tried for the offence concerned if it is satisfied—

    (i) that the requirements of subsection (3)(a) or (3)(b), as the case may be, are met, and

    (ii) that, having regard to the matters referred to in subsection (12), it is, in all the circumstances, in the interests of justice to do so,

or

(b) if it is not so satisfied, affirm the acquittal or the decision of the Court of Criminal Appeal, as the case may be.

(12) In determining whether to make an order under subsection (11)(a), the Supreme Court shall have regard to—

(a) whether or not it is likely that any re-trial could be conducted fairly,

(b) the amount of time that has passed since the act or omission that gave rise to the indictment,

(c) the interest of any victim of the offence concerned, and

(d) any other matter which it considers relevant to the appeal.

(13) (a) The Supreme Court may make an order for a re-trial under this section subject to such conditions and directions as it considers necessary or expedient (including conditions and directions in relation to the staying of the re-trial) to ensure the fairness of the re-trial.

(b) Subject to paragraph (a), where the Supreme Court makes an order for a re-trial under this section, the re-trial shall take place as soon as practicable.

(14) In this section "compelling evidence", in relation to a person, means evidence which—

(a) is reliable,

(b) is of significant probative value, and

(c) is such that when taken together with all the other evidence adduced in the proceedings concerned, a jury might reasonably be satisfied beyond a reasonable doubt of the person's guilt in respect of the offence concerned.

24   No appeal in certain circumstances

No appeal shall lie under section 23 from an acquittal following a re-trial ordered under subsection (1) or (2) of section 10.

25   Orders to safeguard fairness of re-trial

(1) Subject to this section, a proceeding under section 23 shall be conducted in open court.

(2) Where the Supreme Court is conducting a proceeding under section 23 and is satisfied that it is in the interests of justice to do so, it may exclude from the court during the proceeding—

   (a)   the public or any portion of the public, or

   (b)   any particular person or persons,

other than bona fide representatives of the Press.

(3) The Supreme Court may, if it considers that it is in the interests of justice to do so, make an order prohibiting the publication or broadcast of—

   (a)   any evidence given or referred to during the proceeding, or

   (b)   any matter identifying or having the effect of identifying any person who is the subject of an appeal under section 23, or any other person connected with the re-trial for which an order is sought.

(4) An order under subsection (3) ceases to have effect (unless it specifies an earlier date)—

   (a)   when there is no longer any step that could be taken which would lead to the person concerned being re-tried pursuant to an order under section 23,or

   (b)   where the person concerned is re-tried pursuant to an order under section 23, at the conclusion of the trial.

(5) (a)   If any matter is published or broadcast in contravention of subsection (3), the following persons, namely—

      (i)   in the case of a publication in a newspaper or periodical, any proprietor, any editor and any publisher of the newspaper or periodical,

      (ii)   in the case of any other publication, the person who publishes it, and

      (iii) in the case of a broadcast, any person who transmits or provides the programme in which the broadcast is made and any person having functions in relation to the programme corresponding to those of the editor of a newspaper,

   shall be guilty of an offence.

   (b)   A person guilty of an offence under paragraph (a) shall be liable—

      (i)   on summary conviction, to a fine not exceeding €5,000 or to imprisonment for a term not exceeding 12 months or to both, or

      (ii)   on conviction on indictment, to a fine not exceeding €50,000 or to imprisonment for a term not exceeding 3 years or to both.

   (c)   Where an offence under paragraph (a) is committed by a body corporate and is proved to have been so committed with the consent, connivance or approval of, or to be attributable to, any neglect on the part of a person being a director, manager, secretary or other officer of the body corporate or any other person who was acting or purporting to act in any such capacity, that person as well as the body corporate shall be guilty of an offence and be liable to be proceeded against and punished as if he or she were guilty of the first-mentioned offence.

   (d)   Where the affairs of a body corporate are managed by its members, paragraph (c) shall apply in relation to the acts and defaults of a member in connection with his or her functions of management as if he or she were a director or manager of the body corporate.

(6) Nothing in this section shall affect the operation of any other enactment that imposes restrictions on the extent to which information relating to court proceedings may be published or broadcast.

26   Order for re-trial following appeal under section 23

(1) Where a person is ordered under section 23 to be re-tried for an offence he or she may, notwithstanding any rule of law, be again indicted and tried and, if found guilty, sentenced for that offence.

(2) In a case to which subsection (1) relates, the Supreme Court may—

    (a) order that the person concerned be detained in custody or admitted to bail pending the re-trial on such terms as that Court thinks proper,

    (b) where the person does not appear before the Court for the hearing and determination of the appeal, issue a warrant for his or her arrest.

(3) A legal aid (Supreme Court) certificate which was granted in relation to the proceedings under section 23, or in the case of a person who waived his or her right to be represented in respect of those proceedings and a legal aid (trial on indictment) certificate was granted to him or her in respect of the original proceedings, the legal aid (trial on indictment) certificate, shall have effect as if it had been granted also in relation to a re-trial ordered under section 23.

27   Amendment of section 3 of Criminal Justice Act 1994

Subsection 16 of section 3 of the Criminal Justice Act 1994 is amended, in paragraph (f), by the substitution of the following subparagraph for subparagraph (i):[1]

Amendments

1   See the amended Act.

---

28   Other appeals or review rights not affected

Nothing in this Chapter shall affect any right of appeal or review provided by this Act or any other enactment or rule of law.

29   Application of section 6 of Prosecution of Offences Act 1974

Section 6 of the Prosecution of Offences Act 1974 shall, with any necessary modifications, apply to communications made to the persons mentioned in that section for the purpose of influencing the making of a decision in relation to a proceeding under this Chapter as it applies to such communications made for the purposes of making a decision to withdraw or not to initiate criminal proceedings or any particular charge in criminal proceedings.

30   Rules of court and expeditious hearings

Rules of court may make provision for the expeditious hearing of proceedings under section 23 or re-trials ordered under that section.

Chapter 2
Miscellaneous matters relating to appeals

31   Amendment of Courts of Justice Act 1924

The Courts of Justice Act 1924 is amended—

(a) in section 29—

    (i) by the insertion of the following subsections after subsection (2):

        "(2A) Subject to subsection (2B), a person who has appealed his or her conviction to the Court of Criminal Appeal and who has been granted a re-trial by that Court, may, without prejudice to the determination by the Court to grant a re-trial, appeal to the Supreme Court in respect of a matter raised by him or her in the Court of Criminal Appeal in relation to which that Court—

        (a) did not make a determination, or

        (b) made a determination against him or her.

        (2B) A person may only appeal to the Supreme Court where—

        (a) the matter which is the subject of the appeal is one that is relevant to the conduct of his or her defence in the re-trial, and

        (b) the Court of Criminal Appeal or the Attorney General in any case or, if he or she is the prosecuting authority in the matter, the Director of Public Prosecutions, certifies that the matter involves a point of law of exceptional public importance and that it is desirable in the public interest that the person should take an appeal to the Supreme Court.",

and

    (ii) by the substitution, in subsection (5A) of "(2), (2A), (2B) or (3)" for "(2) or (3)",

(b) by the substitution of the following section for section 31:

"Appeal from Central Criminal Court

31.—A person convicted on indictment before the Central Criminal Court may appeal under this Act to the Court of Criminal Appeal.",

(c) by the substitution of the following section for section 32:

"Court of Criminal Appeal may make certain orders pending determination of appeal

32.—The Court of Criminal Appeal shall have power to make any order it may think fit, including an order admitting the appellant to bail, pending the determination of determination his appeal.",

and

(d) in section 33, by the substitution of the following subsection for subsection (1):

"(1) The appeal shall be heard and determined by the Court of Criminal Appeal ('the court')on—

    (a) a record of the proceedings at the trial and on a transcript thereof verified by the judge before whom the case was tried, and

    (b) where the trial judge is of opinion that the record or transcript referred to in paragraph (a) of this subsection does not reflect what took place during the trial, a report by him as to the defects which he considers such record or transcript, as the case may be, contains,

with power to the court to hear new or additional evidence, and to refer any matter for report by the said judge.".

32   Amendment of section 44 of Offences Against the State Act 1939

The Offences Against the State Act 1939 is amended, in section 44, by the substitution of the following subsection for subsection (1):¹

Amendments

1   See the amended Act.

PART 5
MISCELLANEOUS PROVISIONS
Chapter 1
Giving of Evidence

33   Amendment of Criminal Justice (Evidence) Act 1924

The Criminal Justice (Evidence) Act 1924 is amended—

(a)   in section (1)(f)—
  (i)   in subparagraph (ii)—
    (I)   by the substitution of "questions of any witness" for "questions for the witnesses for the prosecution", and
    (II)   by the substitution of "person in respect of whom the offence was alleged to have been committed" for "prosecutor",
  and
  (ii)   by the insertion of the following subparagraph after subparagraph (iii):
    "(iiia) the person has personally or by the person's advocate asked questions of any witness for the purpose of making, or the conduct of the defence is such as to involve, imputations on the character of a person in respect of whom the offence was alleged to have been committed and who is deceased or is so incapacitated as to be unable to give evidence; or",
  and
(b)   by the insertion of the following section after section 1:
    "Evidence of character
    1A.—Where a person charged with an offence intends to adduce evidence, personally or by the person's advocate, of a witness, including the person, that would involve imputations on the character of a prosecution witness or a person in respect of whom the offence is alleged to have been committed and who is either deceased or so incapacitated as to be unable to give evidence, or evidence of the good character of the person—

    (a)   the person may do so only if he or she—

        (i)   has given, either personally or by his or her advocate, at least 7 days' notice to the prosecution of that intention, or

        (ii)   has applied to the court, citing the reasons why it is not possible to give the notice, and been granted leave to do so,

        and

    (b)   notwithstanding section 1(f), the person may be called as a witness and be asked, and the prosecution may ask any other witness, questions that—

        (i)   would show that the person has been convicted of any offence other than the one wherewith he or she is then charged, or is of bad character, or

        (ii)   would show that the person in respect of whom the offence was alleged to have been committed is of good character.".

34   Expert evidence adduced by defence

(1) An accused shall not call an expert witness or adduce expert evidence unless leave to do so has been granted under this section.

(2) Where the defence intends to call an expert witness or adduce expert evidence, whether or not in response to such evidence presented by the prosecution, notice of the intention shall be given to the prosecution at least 10 days prior to the scheduled date of the start of the trial.

(3) A notice under subsection (2) shall be in writing and shall include—

    (a)   the name and address of the expert witness, and

    (b)   any report prepared by the expert witness concerning a matter relevant to the case, including details of any analysis carried out by or on behalf of, or relied upon by, the expert witness, or a summary of the findings of the expert witness.

(4) The court may grant leave to call an expert witness or adduce expert evidence even if no report or summary of the findings are included as required by subsection (3)(b), if the court is satisfied that the accused took all reasonable steps to secure the report or summary before giving the notice.

(5) The court shall grant leave under this section to call an expert witness or adduce expert evidence, on application by the defence, if it is satisfied that the expert evidence to be adduced satisfies the requirements of any enactment or rule of law relating to evidence and that—

    (a)   subsections (2) and (3) have been complied with,

    (b)   where notice was not given at least 10 days prior to the scheduled date of the start of the trial, it would not, in all the circumstances of the case, have been reasonably possible for the defence to have done so, or

    (c)   where the prosecution has adduced expert evidence, a matter arose from that expert's testimony that was not reasonably possible for the defence to have anticipated and it would be in the interests of justice for that matter to be further examined in order to establish its relevance to the case.

(6) The prosecution shall be heard in an application under subsection (4) or (5).

(7) A notice required by this section to be given to the prosecution may be given by delivering it to the prosecutor, or by leaving it at his or her office or by sending it by registered post to his or her office.

(8) Where the court grants leave under this section, the prosecution shall be given a reasonable opportunity to consider the report or summary before the expert witness gives the evidence or the evidence is otherwise adduced.

(9) In this section—

"expert evidence" means evidence of fact or opinion given by an expert witness, and

"expert witness" means a person who appears to the court to possess the appropriate qualifications or experience about the matter to which the witness's evidence relates.

35   Return or disposal of property to be used as evidence

(1) This section applies where property that is to be entered in evidence in a criminal trial is to be—

    (a)   returned to its owner, or

    (b)   disposed of,

before the trial begins.

(2) Where the prosecution proposes to dispose of property that is to be entered in evidence or return it to its owner before the scheduled date of the start of the trial, the prosecution shall serve a notice under this section (the "prosecution notice") on the accused at any time that is at least 23 days prior to that date.

(3) The prosecution notice shall contain a description of the property in sufficient detail to identify it and a statement as to the relevance of the property to the proceedings, together with—

    (a)   one or more photographs of the property, and

    (b)   any report that the prosecution proposes to enter in evidence arising from the analysis of the property, including analysis of any materials found in or on the property (the "prosecution report of evidence").

(4) Not later than 7 days after service of the prosecution notice under subsection (2), the defence shall serve on the prosecution a notice in writing (the "defence notice") that indicates one of the following:

    (a)   that the defence accepts the prosecution notice and agrees to the return or disposal of the property;

    (b)   that the defence wishes to provide to the prosecution a report that conforms with subsection (3) (the "defence report of evidence");

    (c)   that the defence requires the property to be available as an exhibit at the trial.

(5) Where the defence notice served under subsection (4) is a notice mentioned in paragraph (b) of that subsection, then, notwithstanding section 34, the defence shall, not later than 7 days after service of that notice, serve the defence report of evidence on the prosecution.

(6) Where a defence report of evidence is served on the prosecution under subsection (5), the prosecution shall, not later than 3 days prior to the scheduled date of the start of the trial, provide to the defence and the court a notice stating whether it accepts or rejects that notice (the "prosecution notice of reply").

(7) If the defence notice under subsection (4) is made under paragraph (a) of that subsection or is made under paragraph (b) of that subsection and a defence report of evidence is served under subsection (5) and accepted under subsection (6), then—

  (a) a member of the Garda Síochána not below the rank of inspector shall, on receipt by him or her of a copy of the notice referred to in subsection (4) or (6), cause the property to be returned or disposed of, as the case may be,

  (b) the member referred to in paragraph (a) shall keep a written record of the return or disposal of the property, and

  (c) where the property is returned to its owner, the owner shall acknowledge in writing the receipt of the property.

(8) The following rules apply to admissibility of evidence:

  (a) where subsection (4)(a) applies, the prosecution report of evidence is proof of the facts stated therein, unless the contrary is shown;

  (b) where subsection (4)(b) applies and a defence report of evidence is served on the prosecution under subsection (5) and accepted under subsection (6), the defence report of evidence is proof of the facts stated therein, unless the contrary is shown;

  (c) where subsection (4)(c) applies, the property may be admitted as evidence in any trial in which the property is otherwise admissible;

  (d) in any other case, a report prepared under subsection (3) or (5) may be admitted as evidence in any trial in which the property is otherwise admissible.

(9) Any person who prepares information contained in a report under subsection (3) or (5) may be called to give evidence in relation to all or any part of the report, and may be cross-examined on that evidence.

Chapter 2
Miscellaneous amendments

36   Amendment of section 22 of Courts Act 1991

Section 22 of the Courts Act 1991 is amended, in subsection (5), by the deletion of "if the complaint or accusation has been substantiated on oath and".

37   Amendment of Act of 1967

The Act of 1967 is amended—

  (a) in section 4, by the substitution in subsection (2), of "instituted or continued except by the Attorney General" for "instituted or continued except by, or on behalf or with the consent of, the Attorney General",

  (b) in section 4B, by the substitution of the following subsection for subsection (1):[1] and

  (c) in section 24(5), by the substitution of the following paragraph for paragraph (a):[1]

Amendments

1   See the amended Act.

---

38   Amendment to First Schedule to Criminal Justice Act 1951

The First Schedule to the Criminal Justice Act 1951 is amended by the insertion of the following reference:[1]

Amendments

1   See the amended Act.

SCHEDULE
RELEVANT OFFENCES

COMMON LAW OFFENCES

1. Murder (including murder to which section 3 of the Criminal Justice Act 1990 applies).
2. Manslaughter.
3. Treason.
4. Rape.

GENOCIDE, CRIMES AGAINST HUMANITY, WAR CRIMES AND ANCILLARY OFFENCES

5. An offence under sections 7 and 8 of the International Criminal Court Act 2006.

TORTURE

6. An offence under any of the following provisions of the Criminal Justice (United Nations Convention against Torture) Act 2000:
   (a) section 2(1) (offence of torture by a public official);
   (b) section 2(2) (offence of torture instigated by a public official);
   (c) section 3(a) (attempt or conspiracy to commit torture);
   (d) section 3(b) (obstructing prosecution of another). Sexual offences
7. Any offence under section 3 (aggravated sexual assault) and section 4 (rape) of the Criminal Law (Rape) (Amendment) Act 1990.
8. Any offence under section 2 of the Criminal Law (Sexual Offences) Act 2006 (defilement of child under 15 years of age).
9. An offence under section 1 of the Punishment of Incest Act 1908 (incest by males).

OFFENCES AGAINST THE PERSON

10. An offence under any of the following provisions of the Non-Fatal Offences Against the Person Act 1997:
    (a) section 4 (causing serious harm);
    (b) section 6(5) (syringe offences);
    (c) section 8(2) (placing or abandoning syringe);
    (d) section 15(1) (false imprisonment).

TRAFFICKING

11. An offence under section 3(1) of the Child Trafficking and Pornography Act 1998 (trafficking, taking etc., for the purposes of sexual exploitation).

12. Any offence under section 2 (trafficking etc., of children) and section 4 (trafficking of persons other than children) of the Criminal Law (Human Trafficking) Act 2008.

OFFENCES AGAINST THE STATE

13. An offence under section 6 of the Offences Against the State (Amendment) Act 1998 (directing an unlawful organisation).

14. An offence under any of the following provisions of the Criminal Justice (Terrorist Offences) Act 2005:

  (a) section 9(1) (hostage taking);
  (b) section 9(2) (attempted hostage taking);
  (c) section 10(1) (terrorist bombing);
  (d) section 10(2) (terrorist bombing causing major economic loss);
  (e) section 10(3) (attempted bombing).

ORGANISED CRIME

15. An offence under section 71A of the Criminal Justice Act 2006 (directing a criminal organisation).

DRUGS OFFENCES

16. Any offence under sections 15(1) (possession of controlled drugs for unlawful sale or supply), 15A (offence relating to possession of drugs with value of £10,000 or more) and 15B (importation of controlled drugs in excess of certain value) of the Misuse of Drugs Act 1977.

FIREARMS OFFENCES

17. An offence under section 15 of the Firearms Act 1925 (possession of firearms with intent to endanger life).

18. An offence under section 27 of the Firearms Act 1964 (prohibition of use of firearms to resist arrest or aid escape).

EXPLOSIVES OFFENCES

19. An offence under section 2 of the Explosive Substances Act 1883 (causing explosion likely to endanger life or damage property).

DAMAGING PROPERTY

20. An offence of arson under section 2(1) or (3) or an offence under section 2(2) (whether arson or not) of the Criminal Damage Act 1991 (damaging of property).

ROBBERY AND BURGLARY

21. Any offence under section 13(1) (aggravated burglary) and section 14(1) (robbery) of the Criminal Justice (Theft and Fraud Offences) Act 2001.

AIR NAVIGATION OFFENCES

22. An offence under section 11 of the Air Navigation and Transport Act 1973 (unlawful seizure of aircraft).

23.   An offence under section 3(1) of the Air Navigation and Transport Act 1975 (unlawful acts against the safety of navigation).

MARITIME SECURITY OFFENCES

24.   An offence under section 2(1) of the Maritime Security Act 2004.

ACCOMPLICES

25.   References in this Schedule to an offence include references to participation as an accomplice of a person who commits the offence.

ATTEMPTS AND CONSPIRACY

26.   An offence of attempting or conspiring to commit any offence mentioned in a preceding paragraph of this Schedule.

Criminal Justice Act 1984 (Treatment of Persons in Custody in Garda Síochána Stations) Regulations 1987

SI 119 of 1987

ARRANGEMENT OF SECTIONS

PRELIMINARY AND GENERAL

1. Title and commencement.
2. Interpretation.
3. General.
4. Member in charge.
5. Duties of member in charge.
6. Custody record.

ARRESTED PERSONS

7. Record of arrest and detention.
8. Information to be given to an arrested person.
9. Notification to solicitor or other persons.
10. Enquiries.
11. Visits and communications.
12. Interviews (general).
13. Interviews (persons under seventeen years).
14. Foreign nationals.
15. Charge sheets.

PERSONS OTHER THAN ARRESTED PERSONS

16. Provisions relating to persons other than arrested persons.

PROVISIONS APPLICABLE GENERALLY

17. Searches.
18. Fingerprints, etc.
19. Conditions of custody.
20. Persons in custody not to be ill-treated.
21. Medical treatment.
22. Mentally handicapped persons.
23. Other matters to be recorded.
24. Preservation of custody records.

PRELIMINARY AND GENERAL

I, GERARD COLLINS, Minister for Justice, in exercise of the powers conferred on me by section 7 of the Criminal Justice Act, 1984 (No. 22 of 1984), hereby make the following

Regulations with respect to which, pursuant to that section, a draft has been laid before each House of the Oireachtas and a resolution approving of the draft has been passed by each such House:

1   Title and commencement

(1) These Regulations may be cited as the Criminal Justice Act, 1984 (Treatment of Persons in Custody in Garda Síochána Stations) Regulations, 1987.

(2) These Regulations shall come into operation one month after the date on which they are made.

2   Interpretation

(1) In these Regulations:—

"the Act" means the Criminal Justice Act, 1984 (No. 22 of 1984);

"adult" means a person not below the age of eighteen years and

"adult relative" shall be construed accordingly;

"arrested person" means a person who is taken on arrest to, or arrested in, a station;

"custody" means custody in a Garda Síochána station;

"custody record" means a record kept under Regulation 6;

"district" means a Garda Síochána district;

"doctor" means a registered medical practitioner;

"member" means a member of the Garda Síochána;

"member in charge" has the meaning assigned to it by Regulation 4(1);

"station" means a Garda Síochána station;

"superintendent" means a superintendent of the Garda Síochána and, in relation to a district, means a superintendent who is in charge of the district and includes an inspector of the Garda Síochána who is in charge of the district in the superintendent's absence.

(2) In these Regulations a reference to a person signing a document shall include, in the case of a person unable to write, a reference to the person making his mark.

(3) In Regulations 12(8) and 18(1) "appropriate adult", in relation to a person in custody, means—

(a) in case the person is married and his spouse is an adult and is readily available, his spouse, and

(b) in any other case, his parent or guardian or, where a parent or guardian is not readily available, an adult relative or some other responsible adult, as may be appropriate, in attendance at the station pursuant to subparagraph (b) or (c) of Regulation 13(2).

(4) If and for so long as the member in charge of a station in which a person is in custody has reasonable grounds for believing that the person is not below the age of seventeen years, the provisions of these Regulations shall apply as if he had attained that age.

(5) In these Regulations a reference to a Regulation is a reference to a regulation of these Regulations and a reference to a paragraph or subparagraph is a reference to the paragraph or subparagraph of the provision in which the reference occurs, unless it is indicated that reference to some other Regulation or provision, as may be appropriate, is intended.

3   General

(1) In carrying out their functions under these Regulations members shall act with due respect for the personal rights of persons in custody and their dignity as human persons, and shall have regard for the special needs of any of them who may be under a physical or mental disability, while complying with the obligation to prevent escapes from custody and continuing to act with diligence and determination in the investigation of crime and the protection and vindication of the personal rights of other persons.

(2) There shall be no unnecessary delay in dealing with persons in custody.

4   Member in charge

(1) In these Regulations "member in charge" means the member who is in charge of a station at a time when the member in charge of a station is required to do anything or cause anything to be done pursuant to these Regulations.

(2) The superintendent in charge of a district shall issue instructions in writing from time to time, either generally or by reference to particular members or members of particular ranks or to particular circumstances, as to who is to be the member in charge of each station in the district.

(3) As far as practicable, the member in charge shall not be a member who was involved in the arrest of a person for the offence in respect of which he is in custody in the station or in the investigation of that offence.

(4) The superintendent in charge of a district shall ensure that a written record is maintained in each station in his district containing the name and rank of the member in charge at any given time.

5   Duties of member in charge

(1) The member in charge shall be responsible for overseeing the application of these Regulations in relation to persons in custody in the station and for that purpose shall visit them from time to time and make any necessary enquiries.

(2) Paragraph (1) is without prejudice to the responsibilities and duties of any other member in relation to persons in custody.

(3) Where it appears to the member in charge that a direction given or action taken by a member of higher rank is inconsistent with the proper application of these Regulations, he shall inform that member accordingly and, unless the matter is resolved, report it without delay to another member of or above the rank of superintendent.

(4) (a) Where, by reason of the number of persons in custody or other circumstances, the member in charge is unable to carry out adequately the duty imposed on him by paragraph (1) in relation to visiting persons in custody and making any necessary enquiries, he may authorise in writing another member to carry out that duty.

     (b) The authorisation shall specify the reasons for giving it and shall terminate when these reasons no longer apply.

     (c) In the case of the Bridewell Station, Dublin, the member with particular responsibility for the cell area shall be deemed to have been authorised under subparagraph (a) by the member in charge and subparagraph (b) shall not apply.

6   Custody record

(1) A record (in these Regulations referred to as the custody record) shall be kept in respect of each person in custody.

(2) The member in charge shall record or cause to be recorded in the custody record as soon as practicable such information as is required to be recorded by these Regulations. Each entry in the record shall be signed or initialled by the member making it.

(3) Where a person in custody is transferred to another station, the member in charge of the station from which he is transferred shall send with him the custody record relating to him, or a copy of it, to the member in charge of that other station.

(4) Without prejudice to the responsibility of any other member for the accuracy and completeness of any entry which he has made in a custody record, the member in charge shall be responsible for the accuracy and completeness of all entries made in the custody record while he is the member in charge.

(5) Paragraph (2) does not apply to a record referred to in Regulation 10(5) or paragraph (10) or (11) of Regulation 12.

ARRESTED PERSONS

7   Record of arrest and detention

(1) in relation to an arrested person, a record shall be made of—

   (a)   the date, time and place of arrest and the identity of the arresting member (or other person effecting the arrest),

   (b)   the time of arrival at the station,

   (c)   the nature of the offence or other matter in respect of which he was arrested, and

   (d)   any relevant particulars relating to his physical or mental condition.

(2) In the case of a person who is being detained in a station pursuant to section 4 of the Act the member in charge at the time of the person's arrival at the station shall, when authorising the detention, enter in the custody record and sign the following statement:

> "I have reasonable grounds for believing that the detention of (insert here the name of the person detained) is necessary for the proper investigation of the offence(s) in respect of which he/she has been arrested."

(3) (a)   Where a direction has been given by an officer of the Garda Síochána under section 4(3)(b) of the Act that a person be detained for a further period not exceeding six hours, the fact that the direction was given, the date and time when it was given and the name and rank of the officer who gave it shall be recorded.

   (b)   The direction or (if it was given orally) the written record of it shall be signed by the officer giving it and—

      (i)   shall state the date and time when it was given and the officer's name and rank and that the officer had reasonable grounds for believing that such further detention was necessary for the proper investigation of the offence concerned, and

      (ii)   shall be attached to and form part of the custody record.

(4) Where a direction has been given under section 30 of the Offences against the State Act, 1939 (No. 13 of 1939), that a person be detained for a further period not exceeding twenty-

four hours, the fact that the direction was given, the date and time when it was given and the name and rank of the officer who gave it shall be recorded.

8   Information to be given to an arrested person

(1) The member in charge shall without delay inform an arrested person or cause him to be informed—

(a)   in ordinary language of the offence or other matter in respect of which he has been arrested,

(b)   that he is entitled to consult a solicitor, and

(c)   (i)   in the case of a person not below the age of seventeen years, that he is entitled to have notification of his being in custody in the station concerned sent to another person reasonably named by him, or

   (ii)   in the case of a person under the age of seventeen years, that a parent or guardian (or, if he is married, his spouse) is being given the information required by Regulation 9(1)(a)(i) and is being requested to attend at the station without delay.

The information shall be given orally. The member in charge shall also explain or cause to be explained to the arrested person that, if he does not wish to exercise a right specified in subparagraph (b) or (c)(i) immediately, he will not be precluded thereby from doing so later.

(2) The member in charge shall without delay give the arrested person or cause him to be given a notice containing the information specified in subparagraphs (b) and (c) of paragraph (1) and such other information as the Commissioner of the Garda Síochána, with the approval of the Minister for Justice, may from time to time direct.

(3) Paragraphs (1) and (2) apply only in relation to the member in charge of the station to which an arrested person is taken on arrest or in which he is arrested.

(4) The time of the giving of the information specified in paragraph (1) and the notice specified in paragraph (2) shall be recorded. The member in charge shall ask the arrested person or cause him to be asked to sign the custody record in acknowledgement of receipt of the notice. If he refuses to sign, the refusal shall be recorded.

9   Notification to solicitor or other persons

(1)   (a)   Where an arrested person is under the age of seventeen years, the member in charge of the station concerned shall as soon as practicable—

   (i)   inform or cause to be informed a parent or guardian of the person—

      (I)   of his being in custody in the station,

      (II)   in ordinary language of the offence or other matter in respect of which he has been arrested, and

      (III)   of his entitlement to consult a solicitor, and

   (ii)   request the parent or guardian to attend at the station without delay.

   (b)   If the member in charge is unable to communicate with a parent or guardian, he shall inform the arrested person or cause him to be informed without delay of that fact and of his entitlement to have notification of his being in custody in the station concerned sent to another person reasonably named by him.

(c) If the arrested person is married, this paragraph shall have effect with the substitution of references to his spouse for the references to a parent or guardian.

(2) (a) Where an arrested person has asked for a solicitor or has asked that a person reasonably named by him should be notified of his being in custody in the station concerned—

    (i) the member in charge shall notify or cause to be notified the solicitor or that person accordingly as soon as practicable, and

    (ii) if the solicitor or the named person cannot be contacted within a reasonable time or if the solicitor is unable or unwilling to attend at the station, the person shall be given an opportunity to ask for another solicitor or that another person reasonably named by him should be notified as aforesaid and, if the person asks for another solicitor or asks that another person reasonably named by him should be notified as aforesaid, the member in charge shall notify or cause to be notified that other solicitor or person accordingly as soon as practicable.

(b) If the arrested person is under the age of seventeen years, subparagraph (a) shall also apply in relation to a request for a solicitor by a parent of his or his guardian or spouse or by an adult who is present during the questioning of the arrested person in accordance with subparagraph (b) or (c) of Regulation 13(2) with the substitution of references to a parent of his, his guardian or spouse or such an adult for the references to an arrested person.

(3) Where an arrested person is being transferred to another station, the member in charge of the station from which he is being transferred shall inform any person who has been notified or informed under this Regulation, or cause him to be informed, of the transfer as soon as practicable.

(4) Any request made by a person under this Regulation and the time at which it was made and complied with and any action taken by a member under this Regulation and the time at which it was taken shall be recorded.

10 Enquiries

(1) Information as to the station where an arrested person is in custody shall be given—

(a) if the arrested person consents, in response to an enquiry by a solicitor whose presence has not been requested by him;

(b) if the arrested person consents and the member in charge is satisfied that giving the information will not hinder or delay the investigation of crime, in response to an enquiry by any other person.

(2) As soon as practicable after a person is taken on arrest to, or arrested in, a station other than a district headquarters, the member in charge of the station shall notify the district headquarters for the district or cause it to be notified accordingly and shall also, as soon as practicable, notify the district headquarters for the district or cause it to be notified if the person is transferred to another station or ceases to be in the custody of the Garda Síochána.

(3) Where a person is in custody in a district other than that in which he resides, the member in charge shall also, as soon as practicable, notify or cause to be notified the district headquarters for the district in which the person resides.

(4) A notification to a district headquarters under this Regulation and the time of the notification shall be recorded.

(5) A record shall be kept in each district headquarters of persons whose whereabouts have been notified to it under this Regulation and of the times of the notifications.

(6) The Commissioner of the Garda Síochána may from time to time designate a station or stations in the Dublin Metropolitan Area for the purpose of receiving notifications under this Regulation and, if and for so long as a station or stations is or are so designated, then notwithstanding anything in this Regulation, as respects a district in that Area—

    (a)   the said notifications shall be made to the station, or one of the stations, so designated and, in case the person in custody resides in a district outside that Area, to the district headquarters for that district, and

    (b)   paragraphs (4) and (5) shall have effect as if the reference in paragraph (4) to a district headquarters were a reference to a station so designated and as if the reference in paragraph (5) to each district headquarters were a reference to the station or, as the case may be, each of the stations so designated.

(7) In this Regulation "district headquarters" means the Garda Síochána headquarters for a district.

11   Visits and communications

(1) An arrested person shall have reasonable access to a solicitor of his choice and be enabled to communicate with him privately.

(2) Where an arrested person has not had access to a solicitor in accordance with paragraph (1) and a solicitor whose presence has not been requested by the arrested person presents himself at the station and informs the member in charge that he wishes to visit that person, the person shall be asked if he wishes to consult the solicitor and, if he does so wish, the said paragraph (1) shall apply accordingly.

(3) A consultation with a solicitor may take place in the sight but out of hearing of a member.

(4) An arrested person may receive a visit from a relative, friend or other person with an interest in his welfare provided that he so wishes and the member in charge is satisfied that the visit can be adequately supervised and that it will not hinder or delay the investigation of crime.

    (5)   (a)   An arrested person may make a telephone call of reasonable duration free of charge to a person reasonably named by him or send a letter (for which purpose writing materials and, where necessary, postage stamps shall be supplied on request) provided that the member in charge is satisfied that it will not hinder or delay the investigation of crime. A member may listen to any such telephone call and may terminate it if he is not so satisfied and may read any such letter and decline to send it if he is not so satisfied.

         (b)   Subparagraph (a) is without prejudice to the provision of paragraph (1).

(6) Before an arrested person has a supervised visit or communicates with a person other than his solicitor, he shall be informed that anything he says during the visit or in the communication may be given in evidence.

12   Interviews (general)

(1) Before an arrested person is interviewed, the member conducting the interview shall identify himself and any other member present by name and rank to the arrested person.

(2) The interview shall be conducted in a fair and humane manner.

(3) Not more than two members shall question the arrested person at any one time and not more than four members shall be present at any one time during the interview.

(4) If an interview has lasted for four hours, it shall be either terminated or adjourned for a reasonable time.

(5) As far as practicable interviews shall take place in rooms set aside for that purpose.

(6) Where an arrested person asks for a solicitor, he shall not be asked to make a written statement in relation to an offence until a reasonable time for the attendance of the solicitor has elapsed.

(7) (a) Except with the authority of the member in charge, an arrested person shall not be questioned between midnight and 8 a.m. in relation to an offence, which authority shall not be given unless—

   (i) he has been taken to the station during that period,

   (ii) in the case of a person detained under section 4 of the Act, he has not consented in writing to the suspension of questioning in accordance with subsection (6) of that section, or[1]

   (iii) the member in charge has reasonable grounds for believing that to delay questioning the person would involve a risk of injury to persons, serious loss of or damage to property, destruction of or interference with evidence or escape of accomplices.

   (b) Subparagraph (a)(i) is subject to the provisions of Regulation 19(2).

(8) (a) Where an arrested person is deaf or there is doubt about his hearing ability, he shall not be questioned in relation to an offence in the absence of an interpreter, if one is reasonably available, without his written consent (and, where he is under the age of seventeen years, the written consent of an appropriate adult) or in the circumstances specified in paragraph (7)(a)(iii).

   (b) A consent shall be signed by the arrested person and be recorded in the custody record or a separate document.

   (c) Where an arrested person has requested the presence of an interpreter under subparagraph (a) and one is not reasonably available, any questions shall be put to him in writing.

(9) An arrested person who is under the influence of intoxicating liquor or drugs to the extent that he is unable to appreciate the significance of questions put to him or his answers shall not be questioned in relation to an offence while he is in that condition except with the authority of the member in charge, which authority shall not be given except in the circumstances specified in paragraph (7)(a)(iii).

(10) If, while being interviewed, an arrested person makes a complaint to a member in relation to his treatment while in custody, the member shall bring it to the attention of the member in charge, if he is not present at the interview, and record it or cause it to be recorded in the record of the interview.

(11) (a) A record shall be made of each interview either by the member conducting it or by another member who is present. It shall include particulars of the time the interview began and ended, any breaks in it, the place of the interview and the names and ranks of the members present.

(b) Where an interview is not recorded by electronic or other similar means, the record shall—

  (i) be made in the notebook of the member concerned or in a separate document and shall be as complete as practicable,

  (ii) if it is practicable to do so and the member concerned is of opinion that it will not interfere with the conduct of the interview, be made while the interview is in progress or otherwise as soon as practicable afterwards, and

  (iii) be signed by the member making it and include the date and time of signature.

(12) (a) A record shall be made of the times during which an arrested person is interviewed and the members present at each interview.

(b) Where an authority is given pursuant to this Regulation, the fact that it was given, the name and rank of the member giving the authority and the reasons for doing so shall be recorded.

(c) The fact that an arrested person has consented in writing under section 4(6) of the Act to the suspension of questioning between midnight and 8 a.m. shall be recorded and the consent shall be attached to and form part of the custody record.

(d) The particulars specified in section 4(6)(d) of the Act shall be recorded.[1]

Amendments

1 Subparas (7)(a)(ii), (12)(c) and (12)(d) deleted by Criminal Justice (Miscellaneous Provisions) Act 2009, s 52 which is not yet in operation (February 2011).

---

13 **Interviews (persons under seventeen years)**

(1) Except with the authority of the member in charge, an arrested person who is under the age of seventeen years shall not be questioned in relation to an offence or asked to make a written statement unless a parent or guardian is present, which authority shall not be given unless—

(a) it has not been possible to communicate with a parent or guardian in accordance with Regulation 9(1)(a),

(b) no parent or guardian has attended at the station concerned within a reasonable time of being informed that the person was in custody and of being requested so to attend,

(c) it is not practicable for a parent or guardian to attend within a reasonable time, or

(d) the member in charge has reasonable grounds for believing that to delay questioning the person would involve a risk of injury to persons or serious loss of or damage to property, destruction of or interference with evidence or escape of accomplices:

Provided that a parent or guardian may be excluded from the questioning with the authority of the member in charge which authority shall not be given unless—

    (i)   the parent or guardian concerned is the victim of, or has been arrested in respect of, the offence being investigated,

   (ii)   the member in charge has reasonable grounds—

        (I)   for suspecting him of complicity in the offence, or

       (II)   for believing that he would, if present during the questioning, be likely to obstruct the course of justice, or

      (III)   while so present, his conduct has been such as to amount to an obstruction of the course of justice.

(2) Where an arrested person who is under the age of seventeen years is to be questioned in relation to an offence in the absence of a parent or guardian, the member in charge shall, unless it is not practicable to do so, arrange for the presence during the questioning of—

    (a)   the other parent or another guardian,

    (b)   if the other parent or another guardian is not readily available or his presence, having regard to the proviso to paragraph (1), is not appropriate, an adult relative, or

    (c)   if the other parent or another guardian or an adult relative is not readily available or the presence of the other parent or another guardian is, having regard to the said proviso, not appropriate, some other responsible adult other than a member.

(3) Where a request for the attendance of a solicitor is made during the questioning by the parent or guardian, spouse, adult relative or other adult present, Regulation 12(6) shall apply as if the request had been made by the arrested person.

(4) Where an authority is given to a member to question an arrested person in the absence of a parent or guardian, or to exclude a parent, guardian or other person from the questioning pursuant to paragraph (1) or (2), the fact that the authority was given, the name and rank of the member giving it, the reasons for doing so and the act ion taken in compliance with the said paragraph (2) shall be recorded.

(5)   (a)   This Regulation is without prejudice to the provisions of Regulation 12.

      (b)   This Regulation (other than paragraph (3)), in its application to a person under the age of seventeen years who is married to an adult, shall have effect with the substitution of references to the person's spouse for the references (other than those in subparagraphs (a), (b) and (c) of paragraph (2)) to a parent or guardian and as if "a parent or guardian" were substituted for "the other parent or another guardian" in each place where it occurs in those subparagraphs.

14   Foreign nationals

(1) The member in charge shall without delay inform or cause to be informed any arrested person who is a foreign national that he may communicate with his consul and that, if he so wishes, the consul will be notified of his arrest. The member in charge shall, on request, cause the consul to be notified as soon as practicable. Any communication addressed to him shall be forwarded as soon as practicable.

(2) Consular officers shall be entitled to visit one of their nationals, or a national of another State for whom, by formal or informal arrangement, they offer consular assistance, who is an

arrested person and to converse and correspond with him and to arrange for his legal representation.

(3) This Regulation is without prejudice to the application to a national of a foreign country of the provisions of a consular convention or arrangement between the State and that country.

(4) If the member in charge has reasonable grounds for believing that an arrested person who is a foreign national is a political refugee or is seeking political asylum, a consular officer shall not be notified of his arrest or given access to or information about him except at the express request of the foreign national.

(5) A record shall be made of the time when a foreign national was informed or notified in accordance with this Regulation, when any request was made, when the request was complied with and when any communication was forwarded to a consul.

(6) In this Regulation "consul" means, in relation to a foreign national, the diplomatic or consular representative of that person's own country either in the State or accredited to the State on a non- residential basis, or a diplomatic or consular representative of a third country which may formally or informally offer consular assistance to a national of a country which has no resident representative in the State.

15   Charge sheets

(1) Where a person in custody is charged with an offence, a copy of the charge sheet containing particulars of the offence shall be given to him as soon as practicable. Where the person charged is under the age of seventeen years, a copy of the charge sheet shall also be given to the person's parent or guardian or (where the person is married to an adult) to the spouse if present when the person is charged or, if not present, shall be forwarded as soon as practicable.

(2) A record shall be made of the time when the person was charged with an offence. The charge sheet number (or numbers) shall also be recorded. Where a copy of a charge sheet is given to a person in the station, he shall be asked to sign the custody record in acknowledgement of its receipt. If he refuses to sign it, the refusal shall be recorded.

PERSONS OTHER THAN ARRESTED PERSONS

16   Provisions relating to persons other than arrested persons

(1) This Regulation applies to a person in custody other than an arrested person.

(2) Information as to the station where a person to whom this Regulation applies is in custody shall be given in response to an enquiry by—

   (a) his solicitor,

   (b) if the person consents, another solicitor,

   (c) if the person consents and the member in charge is satisfied that giving the information will not prejudice the person's safe custody, any other person.

(3) Regulation 10, except paragraph (1), shall have effect in relation to a person to whom this Regulation applies and who is expected to remain in custody overnight.

   (4) (a) Where a person to whom this Regulation applies has asked for a solicitor, the member in charge shall notify the solicitor or cause him to be notified accordingly.

    (b) If the solicitor cannot be contacted within a reasonable time or if he is unable or unwilling to attend at the station, the person shall be given an opportunity to ask for another solicitor.

(5) (a) Paragraphs (1) and (2) of Regulation 11 shall have effect in relation to a person to whom this Regulation applies.

    (b) Such a person may receive a visit from a relative, friend or other person with an interest in his welfare provided that he so wishes and the member in charge is satisfied that the visit can be adequately supervised and that it will not be prejudicial to the interests of justice.

(6) Regulation 14, except paragraph (1), shall have effect in relation to a foreign national to whom this Regulation applies.

PROVISIONS APPLICABLE GENERALLY

17   Searches

(1) A member conducting a search of a person in custody shall ensure, so far as practicable, that the person understands the reason for the search and that it is conducted with due respect for the person being searched.

(2) A person in custody shall not be searched by a person (other than a doctor) of the opposite sex.

(3) Where a search of a person in custody involves removal of clothing, other than headgear or a coat, jacket, glove or similar article of clothing, no person of the opposite sex shall be present unless either that person is a doctor or the member in charge considers that the presence of that person is necessary by reason of the violent conduct of the person to be searched.

(4) A search of a person in custody involving removal of underclothing shall, where practicable, be carried out by a doctor.

(5) Where clothing or footwear of a person is retained, replacements of a reasonable standard shall be provided.

(6) A record shall be made of a search of a person in custody including the name of the person conducting the search and the names of those present.

(7) Particulars of any property taken from or handed over by a person in custody shall be recorded. The person shall be asked to sign the record of such property as being correct. If he refuses to do so, the refusal shall be recorded at the time of refusal.

18   Fingerprints, etc

(1) (a) Fingerprints, palm prints or photographs shall not be taken of, or swabs or samples taken from, a person in custody (otherwise than pursuant to a power conferred on a member by law) except with his written consent and, where he is under the age of seventeen years, the written consent of an appropriate adult.

    (b) A consent shall be signed and be recorded in the custody record or a separate document.

(2) The fact that fingerprints, palm prints, photographs, swabs or samples have been taken of or from a person in custody shall be recorded.

(3) Where the authority of a member of the Garda Síochána of a specified rank is required for the taking of fingerprints, palm prints or photographs of a person in custody, the name and rank of the member giving the authority shall be recorded.

19   Conditions of custody

(1) A person shall be kept in custody only in a station which has facilities to enable him to be treated in accordance with these Regulations for the period during which he is expected to be in custody in that station.

(2) A person in custody shall be allowed such reasonable time for rest as is nencessary.

(3) A person in custody shall be provided with such meals as are nencessary and, in any case, at least two light meals and one main meal in any twenty-four hour period. He may have meals supplied at his own expense where it is practicable for the member in charge to arrange this.

(4) Access to toilet facilities shall be provided for a person in custody.

(5) Where it is necessary to place persons in custody in cells, as far as practicable not more than one person shall be kept in each cell. Persons of the opposite sex shall not be placed in a cell together. A violent person shall not be placed in a cell with other persons if this can be avoided.

(6) Where a person is kept in a cell, a member shall visit him at intervals of approximately half an hour. A drunken person or a person under the influence of drugs shall be visited and spoken to and if necessary roused for this purpose at intervals of approximately a quarter of an hour for a period of two hours or longer if his condition warrants it.

(7) A member shall be accompanied when visiting a person in custody of the opposite sex who is alone in a cell.

(8) A person in custody under the age of seventeen years shall not be kept in a cell unless there is no other secure accommodation available and where practicable shall not be placed in a cell with an adult other than an adult relative.

20   Persons in custody not to be ill-treated

(1) No member shall subject a person in custody to ill-treatment of any kind or the threat of ill-treatment(whether against the person himself, his family or any other person connected with him) or permit any other person to do so.

(2) No member shall use force against a person in custody except such reasonable force as is necessary—

    (a)   in self-defence,

    (b)   to secure compliance with lawful directions,

    (c)   to prevent his escape, or

    (d)   to restrain him from injuring himself or others, damaging property or destroying or interfering with evidence.

(3) If a member uses force which causes injury to a person in custody, he shall, if he is not the member in charge, report the circumstances to that member, who shall report the matter to the superintendent in charge of the district. If the force is used by the member in charge, he shall report the circumstances to that superintendent.

(4) If it comes to the notice of a member that there has been a contravention of paragraph (1), (2) or (3) by another member—

(a) he shall report the matter to the member in charge or (in case the contravention is by the member in charge) to the superintendent in charge of the district, and

(b) unless the matter has already been reported to that superintendent, the member in charge shall report it to him.

(5) The action taken in accordance with paragraph (3) or (4) shall be recorded.

(6) On receiptof a report under paragraph (3) or (4) by a superintendent, he shall investigate the matter without delay or cause it to be so investigated.

(7) If a person in custody makes a complaint concerning the conduct of a member (whether before or after his arrest) or, if such a complaint is made on his behalf, the fact that a complaint was made shall be recorded. Particulars of the complaint shall be recorded in a separate document, a copy of which shall be attached to and form part of the custody record. If the complaint alleges physical ill-treatment, the member in charge shall arrange for the person to be medically examined as soon as practicable unless, in a case where the allegation relates to another member, he considers the complaint to be frivolous or vexatious.

21   Medical treatment

(1) If a person in custody—

(a) is injured,

(b) is under the influence of intoxicating liquor or drugs and cannot be roused,

(c) fails to respond normally to questions or conversation (otherwise than owing to the influence of intoxicating liquor alone),

(d) appears to the member in charge to be suffering from a mental illness, or

(e) otherwise appears to the member in charge to need medical attention,

The member in charge shall summon a doctor or cause him to be summoned, unless the person's condition appears to the member in charge to be such as to necessitate immediate removal to a hospital or other suitable place. The member in charge shall ensure that any instructions given by a doctor in relation to the medical care of a person in custody are complied with.

(2) Notwithstanding that paragraph (1) may not apply, medical advice shall be sought if the person in custody claims to need medication relating to a heart condition, diabetes, epilepsy or other potentially serious condition or the member in charge considers it necessary because the person has in his possession any such medication.

(3) The removal of a person in custody to a hospital or other suitable place and the time of removal shall be recorded. Any instructions given by a doctor regarding the medical care of a person in custody and the steps taken to comply with them shall also be recorded.

(4) If a person in custody asks to be examined by a doctor of his choice at his own expense, the member in charge shall, if and as soon as practicable, make arrangements accordingly. This shall not preclude his examination by another doctor summoned by the member in charge provided that the person in custody consents to the examination.

(5) A record shall be made of any medical examination sought by the member in charge or person in custody, the time the examination was sought and the time it was carried out. If it is not practicable to accede to a request by a person in custody for medical examination by the doctor of his choice at his own expense, the relevant circumstances shall also be recorded.

(6) Where a person in custody has been removed to a hospital or other suitable place, an immediate relative and any other person required to be notified under Regulation 9 of the

person's detention shall be so informed as soon as practicable. The time at which the relative and other person were informed shall be recorded.

22   Mentally handicapped persons

(1) The provisions of these Regulations relating to persons under the age of seventeen years shall apply, in addition to any other applicable provisions, in relation to a person in custody not below that age whom the member in charge suspects or knows to be mentally handicapped.

(2) In the application of Regulation 13(2)(c) to such a person, the responsible adult referred to in that provision shall, where practicable, be a person who has experience in dealing with the mentally handicapped.

23   Other matters to be recorded

Particulars relating to any of the following matters (including the relevant time and the act ion, if any, taken by a member in relation thereto) shall also be recorded:

(a) visits to persons in custody by the member in charge or other members,

(b) any other visits to them,

(c) telephone and other enquiries concerning them,

(d) telephone calls made or letters sent by them,

(e) any requests made by them or by persons attending at the station and seeking to visit them,

(f) meals supplied to them,

(g) the ending of their custody (release, station bail, etc.).

24   Preservation of custody records

(1) Custody records shall be preserved for at least twelve months or, if any proceedings to which a custody record would be relevant are instituted or any complaint is made in respect of the conduct of a member while a person was in custody, until the final determination of the proceedings or complaint, whichever is the later.

(2) When a person ceases to be in custody, he or his legal representative shall, on request made within twelve months thereafter, be supplied as soon as practicable with a copy of the custody record relating to him or of such entries in it as he may specify.

Rules of the Superior Courts (Criminal Justice Act 1999) 2005

SI 295 of 2005

We, the Superior Courts Rules Committee, constituted pursuant to the provisions of the Courts of Justice Act, 1936, section 67, and reconstituted pursuant to the provisions of the Courts of Justice Act, 1953, section 15, by virtue of the powers conferred upon us by the Courts of Justice Act, 1924, section 36, and the Courts of Justice Act, 1936, section 68 (as applied by the Courts (Supplemental Provisions) Act, 1961, section 48), and the Courts (Supplemental Provisions) Act, 1961, section 14, and of all other powers enabling us in this behalf, do hereby make the following Rules of Court.

1   Order 85 of the Rules of the Superior Courts is amended by the insertion of the following rule as rule 10 of Order 85 immediately after the existing rule 9 thereof.

"10.(1) In this rule, save where the context otherwise requires, "the Act" means the Criminal Procedure Act 1967 as amended by the Criminal Justice Act 1999 .

(2) The following applications shall be brought by notice of motion (and without any affidavit), bearing the title of the proceedings to which they relate:

(i)   An application pursuant to section 4E(1) of the Act to dismiss one or more of the charges against an accused;

(ii) An application pursuant to section 4F(1) of the Act for an order for the taking of evidence by way of sworn deposition or through a live television link pursuant to Part III of the Criminal Evidence Act 1992 or section 39 of the Criminal Justice Act 1999 through such a link:

(iii) An application in relation to a certificate concerning a publication or broadcast in contravention of section 4J(1) of the Act.

(3) Where any application pursuant to sub-rule (2) above is brought by an accused, notice of such application shall be given to the Director of Public Prosecutions not less than fourteen days before the date on which the application is due to be heard and in a case where there is more than one accused, such notice shall also be given to the other accused.

(4) In the case of an application brought by the Director of Public Prosecutions, notice of the said application shall be served on the accused or all of them, if more than one, not less than fourteen days before the date upon which the application is due to be heard.

(5) In any case concerning an application or inquiry relating to a certificate issued pursuant to section 4J(2) of the Act or relating to an order sought under section 4K(3) of the Act, such application shall be on notice to the person, body or party concerned, and the moving party shall give fourteen days' notice of the date of hearing for such application to every other party to the proceedings.

(6) In any case where, on an ex parte application made to it for that purpose, the Court is satisfied that the interests of justice so require, it may direct that any application pursuant to Part IA of the Act be made on such shorter period of notice than that provided for in section 4E(2) of the Act or as required pursuant to sub-rule (4) or (5) above.

(7) The Court may give directions for the filing of affidavits or oral evidence as it thinks proper in the circumstances or such other directions as to service as appear appropriate."

2. This rule shall come into operation on the 8th day of July 2005 and shall apply to any proceedings in being after the commencement of Part III of the Criminal Justice Act 1999 other than those already returned for trial before that commencement date.

3. This rule shall be construed together with the Rules of the Superior Courts 1986 to 2005 and may be cited as the Rules of the Superior Courts (Criminal Justice Act 1999) 2005.